DICTIONARY OF
HISTORIC DOCUMENTS

Revised Edition

DICTIONARY OF HISTORIC DOCUMENTS

Revised Edition

GEORGE CHILDS KOHN, *Editor*

Foreword by **LEONARD LATKOVSKI, PH.D.**

Facts On File, Inc.

Dictionary of Historic Documents, Revised Edition

Copyright © 2003, 1991 by George Childs Kohn

Facts On File, Inc.
132 West 31st Street
New York NY 10001

Library of Congress Cataloging-in-Publication Data

Dictionary of historic documents, revised edition / George Childs Kohn ;
foreword by Leonard Latkovski.
p.   cm.
Includes bibliographical references and index.
ISBN 0-8160-4772-3 (acid-free paper)
1. History—Sources—Dictionaries.
D9 .D525 2003
016.90908—dc21   2002073856

Facts On File books are available at special discounts when purchased in bulk quantities for businesses, associations, institutions, or sales promotions. Please call our Special Sales Department in New York at 212/967-8800 or 800/322-8755.

You can find Facts On File on the World Wide Web at
http://www.factsonfile.com.

Text and cover design by Cathy Rincon

Printed in the United States of America.

VB BVC 10 9 8 7 6 5 4 3 2

This book is printed on acid-free paper.

CONTENTS

Editor
George Childs Kohn

❧

Contributors
Joan R. Bothell
Charles W. Carey, Jr.
Kathleen G. Colket
Beverly R. Dorsey
Jutta K. Kohn
Ceila A. Robbins
Ashwinee Sadanand
Elizabeth A. Schick
Genevieve Slomski
Thomas Wiloch

FOREWORD

The beginning of the 21st century seems a fitting and appropriate time to reflect on what documents, past and present, are the most important. That difficult question was addressed in preparing the revised edition of the *Dictionary of Historic Documents*, which includes major international agreements during the last decade of the 20th century, such as the Charter of Paris for a New Europe; Maastricht Treaty; North American Free Trade Agreement (NAFTA); Rio Declaration; Kyoto Protocol; Treaties of the World Intellectual Property Organization (WIPO); Convention on the Prohibition of the Use, Stockpiling, Production and Transfer of Antipersonnel Mines and Their Destruction; and the United Nations Declaration of Commitment on HIV/AIDS.

Important social and religious documents of the 1990s have also been added, such as the Soviet Law on Freedom of Conscience, the Church of England's Priests Measure (Ordination of Women), New Catechism of the Catholic Church, France's Declaration of Repentance, Megan's Law, Oregon's Death with Dignity Act, and Americans with Disabilities Act. This period has also seen the emergence of a new type of terrorism, which has resulted in documents like the U.S. Aviation Security and Antiterrorism Act, Britain's Terrorism Act of 2000, Canada's Anti-Terrorism Act of 2001, United Nations Resolution 1373 (Declaration on Terrorism), and the USA-PATRIOT Act.

In addition to new entries covering 1990 to 2002, the revised volume contains various, significant prior documents not in the original edition. These "new" entries range from women's rights documents, such as the Marquis de Condorcet's *On the Admission of Women to Citizenship,* Olympe de Gouges's Declaration of the Rights of Woman and the Female Citizen, and Mary Wollstonecraft's *Vindication of the Rights of Women,* to Frederick Douglass's "What to the Slave Is the Fourth of July?" Speech, the Wannsee Protocol, and Adolf Hitler's Last Will and Political Testament. Others are the United Nations Resolution 3236, Vatican II's *Nostra Aetate,* Baruch's Proposals for the Control of Atomic Energy, Japan's Constitution of 1946, the, Solidarity Charter, Iran's Constitution of 1981, the HAMAS Covenant, and the Reykjavík Agreement of 1986.

In this work a "historic" document is defined as a significant written item of public record. This definition maintains the traditional, and somewhat narrow but suitable, interpretation that a document be written and recorded and of a public nature. A written record of "historic" importance should have sufficient force to influence people and events either in its immediate time-period or in subsequent periods. Furthermore, a historic document need not be an official one initially; it may be the product of an individual or of a small private or public group, but ultimately it must become a key, or distinct, part of public events.

Assembling a comprehensive collection of significant and major documents is indeed a challenge. Making such a listing balanced and useful certainly adds another degree of difficulty. Because of the vast number of available public documents—political, legal, economic, scientific, religious, philosophical, and literary, among others—the selection process becomes critical. Historic documents have to be of major consequence in a particular period or afterward. Historians and other experts help determine this. Yet special problems arise. For instance, sometimes the impact or "weight" of a particular document is not universally recognized. Also some time-periods have produced massive numbers of documents of all descriptions. Determination for inclusion in a book such as this must then be based upon the documents that are the most conspicuous or far-reaching or extraordinary—a difficult process, which has been handled commendably in this singular reference work.

Although documents may vary greatly by type and form, most of those listed here are traditional ones: treaties, charters, laws, constitutions, judicial decisions, decrees, proclamations, bulls, concordats, protocols, and so forth. They range from ancient to modern, from the Hammurabi Code and the Edict of Worms to the Atlantic Charter and the Wye

River Memorandum. Also included are distinct speeches, letters, tracts, pamphlets, reports, essays, and doctrines that deserve the designation "historic." In this latter group are such examples as Emile Zola's "J'accuse," Franklin Roosevelt's "Four Freedoms" Speech, and John Locke's *Essay Concerning Human Understanding.* Although a wider range of items of written public record can assuredly be defined as documents, almost no items from the following categories are included in the book: diaries, biographies, poems, novels, musical compositions, plays, and stone inscriptions. Some books, fiction and nonfiction, are notable exceptions that properly qualify as landmark historical documents. Thus included are certain political and economic works, such as Adolf Hitler's *Mein Kampf,* Karl Marx's *Das Kapital,* and Adam Smith's *The Wealth of Nations.* In addition, several literary works with a political and social message have entries in the dictionary; examples are Harriet Beecher Stowe's *Uncle Tom's Cabin,* Edmund Morel's *The Black Man's Burden,* and Leo Tolstoy's *War and Peace.* Also included are a few scientific works of major impact; Galileo's *Dialogue on the Two Chief Systems of the World,* Charles Darwin's *Origin of Species,* and Albert Einstein's Special Relativity Theory are examples.

Documents from all periods of Western civilization are covered, but those from the past three centuries predominate. To choose key written records from antiquity to the Middle Ages is far less difficult than from the Renaissance to the modern period. The closer we come chronologically to the present, the more demanding and complicated becomes the task of selecting landmark documents. Understandably so. The explosion of intellectual, social, and political activity with the Enlightenment and the Industrial Revolution (and later the scientific age and the present information age) generated a greater variety of "historic" writings. This has clearly presented a challenge in identifying the most formative and outstanding documents. In this proliferation of diverse writings are François Babeuf's "Manifesto of the Equals," the Ems Telegram, the Balfour Declaration, the *Dominus Iesus* Declaration, and many notable U.S. Supreme Court decisions.

The focus of the dictionary is chiefly Western. While non-Western ideas and events have shaped history, the modern era, which has produced a greater proportion of historic documents, has been one in which Western civilization has been dominant. In particular, the development of political liberalism and democracy in France, England, and the United States is reflected in the documents listed in this book. However, the documents of the 20th century, while still Western-oriented, are much more internationally focused. They indicate the rapid progress of events, the movements, issues, crises, and diplomatic problems of the modern era, including nationalism, imperialism, anticolonialism, the two world wars, the cold war, human and civil rights, and conflicts in the Middle East, Asia, and Africa.

The dictionary also contains some well-known documents whose authenticity is disputed. Among these controversial or spurious "historic" writings are the Donation of Constantine, the Mecklenburg Resolves (Mecklenburg "Declaration of Independence"), and the Tanaka Memorial. Their inclusion in the book does not authenticate them in any way but merely notes them as influential.

The *Dictionary of Historic Documents* is an authoritative, convenient reference guide to significant documents of the world from ancient times to the present. Intended for use by both the general public and the scholarly community, the revised edition contains nearly 2,400 entries—documents that have influenced and helped steer the course of human history. Because this book is clearly a dictionary, not an encyclopedia, the information is essentially limited to definitions, names of persons and places, dates, events, and cross-references. Using the "Further reading" reference at the end of each entry and selective bibliography at the book's end, readers have sources from which to draw much information for deciphering and interpreting particular documents. It is hoped that readers will use the book readily to identify and penetrate many of the foremost and controlling documents of history.

—Leonard Latkovski, Ph.D.
Professor of History
Hood College

PREFACE

The first edition of this book appeared about a dozen years ago and received considerable praise. This revised, updated, and enlarged edition represents my strong conviction that much of Western history or civilization has been influenced and distinguished by many famous (and not so famous) public documents or written records. Among the most important are the Magna Carta, Abraham Lincoln's Gettysburg Address, the Communist Manifesto, the Universal Declaration of Human Rights, United Nations Resolution 212, Joseph Stalin's "Cold War" Speech, and the Camp David Accords, to name a few that have been included in this reference book.

Presently, a large part of world history has been shaped by many famous Western documents as well as by many less familiar (and some fairly unknown) public documents, such as the Clementine Vulgate, British North America Act, Government of Ireland Act, Rio Branco Law, Treaty of Tordesillas, Polish Constitution of 1791, Danton's "Audacity" Speech, Pillersdorf Constitution, Syllabus of Errors, *Plessy* v. *Ferguson*, Horace Greeley's "Prayer," Thomson-Urrutia Treaty, and Family Compacts. Some readers may question why I included some documents that they consider fairly insignificant and left out others that they deem important. That is their opinion and privilege. Guided by many objective historical sources and comments, I was forced to make many choices among thousands of amazingly diverse documents. In the end, what was selected for inclusion became principally my decision. I am, however, immeasurably indebted to numerous historians and other experts, past and present. A book such as this one unavoidably relies heavily on the work of others in their specific fields. Any concise dictionary of this scope and with certain space limitations is bound to have some noteworthy, inadvertent omissions. Obviously no reference work can contain everything about anything. I welcome any suggestions from readers.

Throughout, the entries are alphabetically listed under the documents' commonly known or familiar names. If they have variant or alternative names (as many do), a "see" reference directs the reader from these names to the main one used in the book. In addition, "see also" and cross-references are used, referring the reader to related entries. A wide-ranging, single-volume dictionary demands brief treatment in format; accordingly priority has been given to identification and explication of when, where, why, and how the documents came into being and their significance. Included at the end of each entry are bibliographic primary and/or secondary sources for each particular document in a "Further reading" reference. Readers will thus be able to delve deeper into the material, if they wish. However, readers should be aware that addresses of websites change frequently; those listed in the dictionary were current as of press time. The dictionary also has a timetable of documents with entries in this book, a select bibliography, listing of documents by category, and a general index.

Many thanks are extended to the book contributors, who helped me immensely in the research and writing and who are listed separately on a preceding page. In the preparation of the book's revised edition, I would like to thank the Facts On File staff, particularly my editor, Claudia Schaab, whose interest and support were indispensable. I am also grateful for the valuable advice of Dr. Leonard Latkovski, a friend and consultant, who wrote the foreword. Thanks also go to the numerous other persons who helped in the revision of the dictionary.

—George Childs Kohn

A

Aarau, Treaty of Swiss peace treaty concluded at Aarau (Aargau) on August 11, 1712, terminating the Second Villmergen War (1712) between the Protestant (Bern and Zurich) and Roman Catholic cantons. It marked the beginning of the Protestant ascendancy in Switzerland. The agreement provided equal religious rights in the common lordships for both factions and revoked the 1531 Peace of Kappel. The battle of Villmergen (July 25), representing the last armed conflict between the rival cantons, had been won by Protestant Bern, and the ensuing treaty greatly undermined the authority of the Catholic cantons over their dependent states. It also increased the importance of Bern and Zurich.

Further reading: Charles Gilliard and J. C. Biaudet, *A History of Switzerland*, trans. D. L. B. Hartley (Westport, Conn.: Greenwood Press, 1978); William Martin, *Switzerland, from Roman Times to the Present* (New York: Praeger, 1971).

ABC Treaty Agreement signed in Buenos Aires on May 25, 1915, by the foreign ministers of Argentina, Brazil, and Chile (the ABC powers), declaring that the signatories' disputes, which could not be settled diplomatically or submitted for arbitration, would be placed before a mediation commission (of neutral powers) for inquiry and report. The document further provided that the commission would respond to any single government's request for inquiry; it bound each signatory not to begin hostilities or war before the commission concluded its report, or before the passage of one year. The treaty was concluded in order to improve relations among the ABC powers, agreeing also to a five-year period of peace among the three nations. Later in 1915 Uruguay, Bolivia, and Guatemala associated with the ABC powers to help Mexico, which had been torn apart by the Mexican Revolt of 1914–15.

Further reading: Salvatore Bizzarro, *Historical Dictionary of Chile* (Metuchen, N.J.: Scarecrow Press, 1972); Robert M. Levine, *Historical Dictionary of Brazil* (Metuchen, N.J.: Scarecrow Press, 1979); J. Fred Rippy, Percy A. Martin, and Isaac J. Cox, *Argentina, Brazil and Chile Since Independence* (New York: Russell and Russell, 1963).

Aberdeen Act Act introduced in the British Parliament by British Foreign Secretary Lord Aberdeen (George Hamilton Gordon) and passed by Parliament in 1845, stipulating stricter measures to be taken against the Brazilian slave trade. Brazil's decision not to renew the BRAZILIAN-BRITISH TREATY OF 1826, which made the slave trade illegal, precipitated the legislation. Specifically, the bill provided that the involvement of Brazilian vessels in the slave trade would be considered piracy and that the British would exercise the right to try such vessels in admiralty and vice-admiralty courts. Brazil, where slavery had become an integral part of the economy, considered the act to be an infringement of Brazilian sovereignty. In the years following the bill's adoption, the slave trade actually increased.

See also: BRAZILIAN SLAVE EMANCIPATION ACT.

1

Further reading: Emilia Viotti de Costa, *The Brazilian Empire* (Chicago: University of Chicago Press, 1985); G. M. Young and W. D. Handcock, eds., *English Historical Documents* (New York: Routledge, 1996).

Abjuration, Act of   By the states-general (parliament) of the Netherlands, declaration of Dutch independence on January 26, 1581, from the rule of King Philip II of Spain. It stated that Philip II's tyranny over the provinces of the Netherlands had caused him to lose his sovereignty. The overthrow of the Spanish supremacy had been a long-term goal (since 1568), resulting in the 1576 Pacification of GHENT and the 1579 Union of Arras and 1579 Union of UTRECHT. The Calvinist-dominated northern provinces wanted to elect a prince who would help them succeed against Spain. They did not seek a reconciliation with the Catholic King Philip since it would affect their supremacy. The Spanish ban on Dutch rebel leader William I of Orange in 1580 hastened the passage of this act. Intended as an act of independence for the Low Countries, its ultimate effect was restricted to the northern provinces participating in the Union of Utrecht.

See also: ARRAS, TREATY OF (1579).

Further reading: Bartholomew Landheer, ed., *The Netherlands* (Berkeley, Calif.: University of California Press, 1943); Sir Charles Petrie, *Philip II of Spain* (London: Eyre and Spottiswoode, 1963).

Ableman v. Booth   Case decided by the U.S. Supreme Court on March 7, 1859, on the broad issue of state and federal powers. In 1854 the Wisconsin Supreme Court freed an abolitionist editor, Sherman Booth, who had been convicted in federal court of aiding a runaway slave, in violation of the FUGITIVE SLAVE LAW OF 1850. The Supreme Court reversed the state court's decision. The majority opinion, written by Chief Justice Roger Taney, denied the right of the state judiciary to interfere in federal cases; it also upheld the constitutionality of the Fugitive Slave Law. The Wisconsin legislature responded by passing a resolution attempting to nullify the Supreme Court ruling.

Further reading: Stanley Campbell, *The Slave Catchers: Enforcement of the Fugitive Slave Law, 1850–1860* (Chapel Hill: University of North Carolina Press, 1970); Henry Steele Commager, ed., *Documents of American History*, 8th ed. (New York: Appleton-Century-Crofts, 1968); Robert F. Cushman, *Leading Constitutional Decisions*, 15th ed. (Englewood Cliffs, N.J.: Prentice-Hall, 1977); Mark Mikula and L. Mpho Mabunda, eds., *Great American Court Cases*, 4 vols. (Farmington Hills, Mich.: Gale Group, 1999).

ABM Treaty   See ANTI-BALLISTIC MISSILE TREATY.

Åbo, Treaty of (1743)   Peace accord signed at Åbo (Turku, Finland) on August 7, 1743, ending the Russo-Swedish War of 1741–43. Effected through British mediation,

the treaty provided for Russia's retention of a part of southeast Finland, her restoration of the Grand Duchy of Finland to Sweden, and the granting of some trade privileges to Sweden. In exchange, the Swedes agreed to elect to their throne the Russian-sponsored candidate, Duke Adolphus Frederick of Holstein-Gottorp-Eutin, who was a cousin of Czarina Elizabeth of Russia. The settlement reflected a rise in Russian political influence in Sweden, where 12,000 Russian troops were allowed to be stationed for protection against foreign countries unhappy with the election to the Swedish Crown.

See also: VÄRÄLA, TREATY OF.

Further reading: Ingmar Andersson, *A History of Sweden* (New York: Praeger, 1968); Nicholas V. Riasanovsky, *A History of Russia*, 3d ed. (New York: Oxford University Press, 1977).

Åbo, Treaty of (1812)   Treaty concluded between Czar Alexander I of Russia and Crown Prince Charles XIV John (also known as French Marshal Jean Baptiste Bernadotte) of Sweden in Åbo (Turku, Finland) in August 1812, through which the two reaffirmed an agreement made several months earlier (see ST. PETERSBURG, TREATY OF [1812]). By the treaty Alexander re-extended his offer to aid Charles John militarily in his plans to seize Norway from Denmark; in return Charles John promised to supply forces against the French army in northern Germany. After Great Britain too had lent support for Sweden's plans of annexation in 1813, Sweden entered the war against France; the allies, however, did not come through with the promised aid.

See also: KIEL, TREATY OF; UNION, ACT OF [UNION OF SWEDEN AND NORWAY].

Further reading: George Maude, *Historical Dictionary of Finland* (Lanham, Md.: Scarecrow Press, 1995); Pavel N. Miliukov, et al., *History of Russia*, trans. C. L. Markmann (New York: Funk & Wagnalls, 1968).

Abominations, Tariff of   See TARIFF ACT OF 1828, U.S.

Aboriginal Land Rights Act of 1976   Important federal legislation by Australia's Parliament granting traditional aboriginal communities the right to have freehold titles to former reserve lands in the Northern Territory, announced on May 27, 1976, by Aboriginal Affairs Minister Ian Viner. Enacted following the recommendations of the Woodward Royal Commission (1972–74), the act also explained how aborigines could claim other crown lands by proving strong traditional bonds. These lands, managed by the Aboriginal Land Councils, would be held by the Aboriginal Land Trusts. Mining rights on aboriginal lands would remain with the federal government, which would, however, pay royalties to the community. Within the next decade, the aboriginal groups owned more than 139,000 square miles in the Northern Territory. Subsequently, similar legislation was passed in South Australia (1976 and 1980) and in New South Wales (1983).

Further reading: Ruth S. Kerr, *Aboriginal Land Rights: A Comparative Assessment* (Brisbane, Australia: Queensland Parliamentary Library, Resources and Publications Section, 1991); Nicolas Peterson, ed., *Aboriginal Land Rights: A Handbook* (Canberra, Australia: Australian Institute of Aboriginal Studies, 1981).

Abrams v. United States U.S. Supreme Court decision issued on November 10, 1919, upholding the U.S. SEDITION ACT OF 1918. The court's majority ruled that pamphlets criticizing the U.S. expeditionary force to Siberia (Russia) were prohibited under the act and that the FIRST AMENDMENT did not protect a right to promote disaffection in wartime (the court upheld the conviction of some Russian emigrants for distributing the pamphlets). In his notable dissent, Justice Oliver Wendell Holmes argued for the protection of free speech, even of unpopular opinions, unless such ideas pose an imminent threat to national safety: "the ultimate good desired is better reached by free trade in ideas . . . the best test of truth is the power of the thought to get itself accepted in the competition of the market." Justice Louis Brandeis agreed with Holmes.

Further reading: Zechariah Chafee, *Free Speech in the United States* (Cambridge, Mass.: Harvard University Press, 1941); John W. Johnson, *Historic U.S. Court Cases, 1690–1990: An Encyclopedia* (New York: Garland Publishing, 1992); Mark Mikula and L. Mpho Mabunda, eds., *Great American Court Cases,* 4 vols. (Farmington Hills, Mich.: Gale Group, 1999); Richard Polenberg, *Fighting Faiths: The Abrams Case, the Supreme Court, and Free Speech* (New York: Viking, 1987).

Abydos, Tablet of Carved inscription or glyptic narrative on the walls of the great temple built by King Seti I (reigned 1318–1304 B.C.) at Abydos, ancient city on the Nile River in central Egypt. Written in hieroglyphics, this bas-relief engraving consists of a series of cartouches (name rings), each of which contains the name of an ancient Egyptian king (pharaoh). This list of kings has helped scholars determine the succession of Egyptian rulers beginning with Menes (fl. c. 3100 B.C.) and ending with Seti I. The names often correspond to those given by Manetho, an Egyptian historian of about 300 B.C. whose arrangement of ancient Egyptian rulers into 30 dynasties is still in use.

Further reading: Omm Sety and Hanny El Zeini, *Abydos: Holy City of Ancient Egypt* (Los Angeles, Calif.: L.L. Co., 1981).

Acheson-Lilienthal Report U.S. proposal issued on February 28, 1946, by a committee headed by Undersecretary of State Dean Acheson and Tennessee Valley Authority chairman David Lilienthal, on the international control of nuclear energy. The plan suggested an international atomic development authority that would have complete power worldwide over nuclear research and development. This plan, with the addition of a requirement for international inspection of nuclear facilities, was submitted to the United Nations on June 14 by U.S. delegate Bernard Baruch. It was rejected by the Soviet Union on the grounds that it infringed on national sovereignty.

Further reading: Bernard M. Baruch, *The International Control of Atomic Energy, Speech by Bernard M. Baruch* (New York: Freedom House, 1946); James Roy Newman and Byron S. Miller, *The Control of Atomic Energy: A Study of Its Social, Economic, and Political Implications* (New York: Whittlesey House, 1948); *A Report on the International Control of Atomic Energy. Prepared for the Secretary of State's Committee on Atomic Energy by a Board of Consultants* (Washington, D.C.: U.S. Government Printing Office, 1946).

Acilian Law (Lex Acilia de Repetundarum) Major Roman legislation reforming membership in the court on extortion; proposed by Tribune Marcus Acilius Glabrio at the instigation of Tribune Caius Sempronius Gracchus, who was successfully sponsoring judicial, social, and economic reforms in 123 and 122 B.C. The Acilian Law of 123 B.C. remodeled the court for the trial of suits for the recovery of damages from Roman officials guilty of extortion from citizens. Senators and their relatives (brothers, sons, and fathers) and magistrates in office were barred from selection for the court, whose 50 jurors were to include landholders and prosperous businessmen (the equestrian order or equites). Control of the court now became a standing dispute between the senatorial and equestrian orders in the Roman Republic.

Further reading: Ernest G. Hardy, *Roman Laws and Charters* (Oxford, England: Clarendon Press, 1912).

"Acres of Diamonds" Speech, Conwell's Inspirational speech or lecture given by American Baptist minister Russell H. Conwell more than 6,000 times between 1876 and 1925. Heard first by Conwell's Civil War regiment, the speech quickly gained fame because of its dominant theme: "It is your duty to be rich." Everyone has the "opportunity to be rich"—to have "acres of diamonds"—because "you must look around and see what people need and then invest yourself, or your money, in that which they need most." Conwell believed that the rich are rich because God made them so, and his lecture (some 13 million people heard it) was a rationalization of the robber-baron mentality of the Gilded Age (c. 1870–95) in America.

Further reading: Russell Herman Conwell, *Acres of Diamonds: All Good Things Are Possible. Right Where You Are and Now!* (Joshua Tree, Calif.: Tree of Life Publications, 1993).

Acte Additionel See ADDITIONAL ACT, FRENCH.

Act of Explanation See EXPLANATION, ACT OF.

Act of Mediation   See NAPOLÉON'S MEDIATION CONSTITUTION.

Act of Seclusion   See SECLUSION, ACT OF.

Act of Settlement (1662)   See SETTLEMENT, ACT OF (1662).

Act of Settlement (1701)   See SETTLEMENT, ACT OF (SUCCESSION ACT).

Act of Settlement and Explanation   See EXPLANATION, ACT OF.

Act of Six Articles   See SIX ARTICLES, ACT OF.

Act of Succession   See SUCCESSION, ACT OF (1534).

Acts of Supremacy   See SUPREMACY, ACT OF (1534); SUPREMACY, ACT OF (1559).

Acts of Uniformity   See UNIFORMITY, ACTS OF.

Acts of Union   See UNION, ACTS OF.

Adair* v. *United States   U.S. Supreme Court ruling of January 27, 1908, that declared unconstitutional the Erdman Act of 1898, which prohibited railroads engaged in interstate commerce from requiring workers, as a condition of employment, to agree not to join a labor union. William Adair, an agent of the Louisville & Nashville Railroad, who had fired a worker because of his union membership, was convicted of violation of the Erdman Act. In a six-to-two decision, the Supreme Court overruled this conviction, declaring the act an unreasonable violation of the Fifth Amendment protections of liberty and property. The Court stated that union membership did not fall under congressional authority to regulate interstate commerce.

Further reading: Leonard W. Levy and Kenneth L. Karst, eds., *Encyclopedia of the American Constitution* 2d ed. (New York: Macmillan Reference, 2000); Elias Lieberman, *Unions Before the Bar* (New York: Harper & Row, 1950); Mark Mikula and L. Mpho Mabunda, eds., *Great American Court Cases,* 4 vols. (Farmington Hills, Mich.: Gale Group, 1999).

Adalbero's Plea to Elect Hugh Capet   Address given by Archbishop Adalbero of Rheims in A.D. 987 before the assembly of nobles gathered at Senlis to elect a new French king; apparently influenced the eventual decision in favor of Hugh Capet, the count of Paris. Archbishop Adalbero began by asking the nobles "in all prudence and rectitude, not to sacrifice reason and truth to our personal likes and dislikes." He dismissed the claim of Charles, duke of lower Lorraine and uncle of the late king, saying that "the throne cannot be acquired by hereditary right." Besides, he argued, Charles was "feeble and without honor, faith or character," served a foreign king, and had married below him. To ensure the welfare and prosperity of the state, he urged them to elect Hugh Capet—"the most illustrious among us all by reason of his exploits, his nobility, and his military following." Adalbero's speech was greatly applauded, and Capet was unanimously elected king.

Further reading: Georges Duby, *France in the Middle Ages, 987–1460: From Hugh Capet to Joan of Arc* (Cambridge, Mass.: Blackwell, 1991).

Adamson Act   Legislation enacted by the U.S. Congress on September 3, 1916, that established an eight-hour day for railroad workers operating on interstate lines, without a reduction in their wages. It replaced the 10-hour day and provided time-and-a-half for overtime. The act was passed as an emergency measure to avoid a threatened strike by railway workers that might have hindered U.S. preparations for World War I (1914–18). The railroads claimed that the act was unconstitutional, effectively raising wages rather than limiting hours, because normal operation required more than eight hours of work. In *Wilson* v. *New* (1917) the Supreme Court upheld the act under the federal government's right to regulate interstate commerce.

Further reading: Frank Warren Hackett, *The Adamson Act Decision* (St. Louis: n.p., 1918).

Adams-Onís Treaty (Transcontinental Treaty)   Agreement signed at Washington, D.C., on February 22, 1819, and ratified on February 22, 1821, whereby Spain abandoned all claims to West Florida (which had been seized by U.S. troops under Andrew Jackson the previous year), ceded East Florida to the United States, and gave up its claims to the Pacific Northwest. In exchange the United States renounced its rights to Texas and agreed to pay up to $5,000,000 in claims of American citizens against Spain. The treaty was negotiated by U.S. secretary of state John Quincy Adams and Spanish minister Luis de Onís.

Further reading: Flagg Bemis, *John Quincy Adams and the Foundations of American Foreign Policy* (New York: Knopf, 1950); Thomas Carson, ed., *Gale Encyclopedia of U.S. Economic History* (Farmington Hills, Mich.: Gale Group, 1999); Charles L. Phillips and Alan Axelrod, eds., *Encyclopedia of Historical Treaties and Alliances,* 2 vols. (New York: Facts On File, 2001).

Adams's First Annual Message   Address delivered by U.S. president John Quincy Adams to Congress on December 6, 1825, near the end of his first year in office. In this message Adams introduced a crucial issue for his administration when he referred to the Panama Congress, a meeting of Latin American nations to which he later urged the U.S. Congress to send representatives. The message also discussed Adams's policies of government support for internal improvements—not only of roads and canals, but also of educational and scientific institutions. He also urged further exploration of the American continent.

Further reading: Worthington Chauncey Ford, ed., *Writings of John Quincy Adams* (Westport, Conn.: Greenwood Press, 1968).

Addis Ababa, Treaty of (1896) Peace treaty concluded at the Ethiopian capital of Addis Ababa on October 26, 1896, between Italy, under the premiership of the imperialistic Antonio di Rudini, and Ethiopia, under Emperor Menelik II; brought to an end the Italo-Ethiopian War of 1895–96. The war was a continuation of Italy's determination to secure a foothold in northern Africa, which she had failed to do during the 1887–89 hostilities (see UCCIALLI, TREATY OF). Through the 1896 treaty Italy, defeated in the war, agreed to recognize the independence of Ethiopia and to renounce all her claims to a protectorate over that country; and the Mareb River was accepted as the border between Ethiopia and Eritrea, Italy's coastal colony in northeast Africa. Italy's defeat was the first defeat of a European power by an African power.

Further reading: Lapiso G. Dilebo, *The Italo-Ethiopian War of 1887–1896: From Dogali to Adwa* (Addis Ababa, Ethiopia: Artistic Print, Enterprise, 1996); Charles L. Phillips and Alan Axelrod, eds., *Encyclopedia of Historical Treaties and Alliances,* 2 vols. (New York: Facts On File, 2001).

Additional Act, French (Acte Additionel) Decree supplementary to the FRENCH CONSTITUTION OF 1814 enacted on June 1, 1815, by Napoléon Bonaparte at the insistence of the council of state, constitutional bodies, and the press. Intended to appease the liberal middle classes, it was a compromise that pleased no one. The decree withdrew the property qualification required for suffrage, reintroduced electoral colleges and universal suffrage, and conferred hereditary peerage on the senate—the last, a concession Napoléon had refused in the FRENCH CONSTITUTION OF 1804. Seeking to create a parliamentary monarchy, Napoléon promised to establish a bicameral legislature. Soon after its proclamation at an impressive ceremony (*Champ de mai*), the French deputies organized themselves into constituent assemblies and initiated steps for its revision.

Further reading: Frank M. Anderson, *The Constitutions and Other Select Documents Illustrative of the History of France, 1789–1901* (Minneapolis: H. W. Wilson, 1908).

Address to the Christian Nobility of the German Nation, Luther's Formal letter written by reformer Martin Luther in August 1520, addressed to the princes and other rulers of Germany under Holy Roman Emperor Charles V. As a manifesto written in German (to ensure its availability to the general populace), it called for secular intervention to bring about reforms in the nation's religious, social, and economic life, and to amend grievances against the papacy that church leaders had rejected. Luther refuted the pope's exclusive right to interpret the scriptures, the pope's claim that spiritual authority was superior to temporal authority, and the tradition that only the pope had the right to convene church councils.

See also: EXSURGE DOMINE.

Further reading: Martin Luther, "Address to the Christian Nobility of the German National." Excerpts selected by J. H. Robinson. Hanover Historical Text Project website. Available online at http://history.hanover.edu/texts/luthad.html.

"Address to the People of South Carolina," Calhoun's Manifesto written by U.S. vice president John C. Calhoun and dated July 26, 1831, promoting the doctrine that the individual states have the power to nullify, or veto, federal laws. Restating publicly the views earlier expressed anonymously in Calhoun's EXPOSITION AND PROTEST, the vice president argued that the foundation of the union rested upon the principle of state sovereignty, which protects the minority against abuses by the majority. He described the federal government as merely an "agent" of the sovereign states. His discussion of this issue continued in Calhoun's "FORT HILL LETTER."

Further reading: Terea Celsi, *John C. Calhoun and the Roots of War* (Morristown, N.J.: Silver Burdett Press, 1991); John Niven, *John C. Calhoun and the Price of Union* (Baton Rouge: Louisiana State University Press, 1988); Clyde N. Wilson, ed., *The Essential Calhoun: Selections from Writings, Speeches, and Letters* (New Brunswick, N.J.: Transaction Publishers, 2000).

Addyston Pipe and Steel Company v. United States Ruling of the U.S. Supreme Court on December 4, 1899, based on the SHERMAN ANTI-TRUST ACT, that enjoined six producers of cast-iron pipe from maintaining an agreement to eliminate competition among themselves. In its unanimous decision, the Supreme Court ruled that the companies, in establishing a market-allocation scheme, had conspired to interfere with the flow of interstate commerce, to limit competition, and to fix prices. The decision strengthened the effectiveness of the Sherman Anti-Trust Act, which had been weakened in the 1895 case of UNITED STATES v. E.C. KNIGHT.

Further reading: Supreme Court of the United States, *Addyston Pipe and Steel Company v. United States.* Antitrustcases.com website. Available online at http://laws.findlaw.com/US/175/211.html.

Adkins v. Children's Hospital U.S. Supreme Court decision issued on April 9, 1923, that invalidated a 1918 congressional act establishing a wage board in Washington, D.C., to fix minimum wages for women adequate to maintain a decent standard of living. In its five-to-three decision, the Court ruled that the act infringed on the due process clause of the FIFTH AMENDMENT by interfering with the freedom of an employer and an employee to make a contract. Justice Oliver Wendell Holmes, in dissent, argued that Congress had a right "to remove conditions leading to ill health, immorality, and the deterioration of the race." The decision was overturned in WEST COAST HOTEL COMPANY V. PARRISH in 1937.

Further reading: Supreme Court of the United States, "Adkins v. Children's Hospital." Legal Information Institute website, "Historic Supreme Court Decisions by Party Name." Available online at http://supct.law.cornell.edu./supct/cases/name.htm.

Adler v. Board of Education

U.S. Supreme Court decision issued on March 3, 1952, that upheld a New York law requiring the New York Board of Regents to deny employment in the public schools to members of organizations that advocated or taught the doctrine of overthrowing the United States government by force, violence, or any unlawful means. The Board of Regents was instructed to prepare a list of such subversive organizations. Membership in them constituted "prima facie evidence" for disqualification from employment. The 6-2 decision was overturned in *Keyishian v. Board of Regents* in 1967.

Further reading: Supreme Court of the United States, "Adler v. Board of Education." Legal Information Institute website, "Historic Supreme Court Decisions by Party Name." Available online at http://supct.law.cornell.edu/supct./cases/name.htm.

Administration of Justice Act

Statute passed by the British Parliament on May 21, 1774, and one of the series of laws known as the COERCIVE ACTS. To quell the fears of royal or crown officials in Massachusetts, the law provided that judges, soldiers, and revenue officers indicted for murder or other serious crimes committed in the execution of their official duties could be tried in England or another colony, thus avoiding hostile juries in Massachusetts. The act was viewed by the colonists as an attempt by Britain to impose a military despotism on Massachusetts.

Further reading: David Ammerman, *In the Common Cause: American Response to the Coercive Acts of 1774* (Charlottesville: University Press of Virginia, 1974); Henry Steele Commager, ed., *Documents of American History*, 8th ed. (New York: Appleton-Century-Crofts, 1968).

Adrianople, Treaty of (1444)

Truce between the Ottoman sultan Murad II and John Hunyadi, Hungarian leader victoriously crusading against the Ottoman Turks; signed at Adrianople (Edirne, Turkey) on June 12, 1444, and later ratified by the Treaty of SZEGEDIN. Mediated by George Branković, whose Serbian forces had also been crusading against the Ottomans, the truce agreement insisted on the return of Murad and his army to Anatolia (Turkey) and restored to Branković all Serbian territory taken since 1427. Ottoman rule was acknowledged in Bulgaria in return for Murad's recognition of the autonomous state of Serbia and Hungarian control over Wallachia. A 10-year truce was also concluded but broken.

Further reading: Camil Muresanu, *John Hunyadi: Defender of Christendom* (Iasi, Romania: Center for Romanian Studies, 2001).

Adrianople, Treaty of (1829)

Peace treaty concluded at Adrianople or Edirne on September 16, 1829, between Russia and the Ottoman Empire, ending their war (1828–29) over disputed territorial possessions in the Caucasus, the Balkans, and the Danubian river basin. Russian forces were victorious in the war, and by the treaty, Russia gained control over the Danubian principalities of Wallachia and Moldavia (although in theory these territories had gained autonomy), the Caucasian province of Georgia, the eastern (Caucasian) coast of the Black Sea, including the fortresses of Poti and Anapa, and over the mouth of the Danube River. The treaty also provided for free navigation of Russian vessels in Turkish waters and for Serbian and Greek independence; it required the Turks to pay Russia a large indemnity. Several of these treaty provisions had already been included in the Convention of Akkerman (1826) and the Treaty of BUCHAREST (1812).

Further reading: Charles L. Phillips and Alan Axelrod, eds., *Encyclopedia of Historical Treaties and Alliances*, 2 vols. (New York: Facts On File, 2001).

Adulteration (Sale) of Food and Drugs Act

In Britain, major legislation of August 11, 1875, to combat the manufacture and sale of adulterated food and drugs. It was part of a series of public health reforms (see PUBLIC HEALTH ACT OF 1875, BRITISH) initiated by Prime Minister Benjamin Disraeli. According to the act, a maximum fine of £50 would be levied on first-time offenders caught adulterating food and drugs intended for sale. For a second offense, punishment was imprisonment. The selling of any food or drug that did not meet with the buyer's specific requirement was punishable with a maximum fine of £20. The provisions of the act, however, were not effectively enforced.

Further reading: *Knight's Public Health Acts and Other Statutes Relating to Housing, Food, and Allied Subjects, 1875–1950* (London: C. Knight, 1951); *The Public Health Acts, Annotated, Together with the Various Incorporated Statutes and Orders of the Minister of Health*, 12th ed. (London: Butterworth, 1950–).

Advances to Settlers Act

First major reform legislation passed by the Liberal government of New Zealand in 1894, allowing farmers to borrow money (against security) from the government at affordable rates of interest. The government's funding came from overseas borrowing. Sir Joseph G. Ward (colonial treasurer), who initiated the scheme, successfully negotiated with bankers and loan companies overseas in 1895 and secured a 3 percent loan. Established farmers took advantage of this policy to refinance their old debts and improve their farms. To facilitate these transactions, an Advances to Settlers Office was set up. State loans became a permanent part of the system in New Zealand.

Further reading: Tom Brooking, *Lands for the People? The Highland Clearances and the Colonisation of New Zealand: A Biography of John McKenzie* (Dunedin, New Zealand: University of Otago Press, 1996); Geoffrey W. Rice, ed., *The Oxford History of New Zealand*, 2d ed. (New York: Oxford University Press, 1992).

Affirmation Bill, British

Bill introduced into the British Parliament in 1881 and again in 1883, seeking to legalize affirmation in the House of Commons and thereby remove the last religious barrier for membership to the House. The issue came up when Charles Bradlaugh (newly elected member of Parliament from Northampton) refused, as a free-thinker, to take the oath of office, which included the words "so help me, God." He claimed the right to make an affirmation of his loyalty instead—an opportunity that the opposition seized to stir up a controversy. Bradlaugh relented and offered to take the oath but was refused the right. He was involved in eight lawsuits, was unseated and reelected four times, and finally, in January 1886, allowed to take the oath. The Affirmation Bill was eventually passed in 1888.

Further reading: Hypatia Bradlaugh Bonner, *Charles Bradlaugh: A Record of His Life and Work by His Daughter, Hypatia Bradlaugh V. Bonner* (London: T. F. Unwin, 1895).

Afghan Constitution of 1923 (Afghan Fundamental Law)

Afghanistan's first constitution, promulgated on April 9, 1923, by Emir Amanullah Khan, providing for an absolute and hereditary monarchy aided by various advisory bodies. Based on Turkish administrative laws and the PERSIAN CONSTITUTION OF 1906, it declared Islam the official religion and the emir the "Defender of the Faith." Hindus and Jews were guaranteed religious liberties, but they had to pay a special tax and wear identifying emblems. Slavery was prohibited, elementary education made compulsory and universal, foreigners excluded from teaching, and journalists and missionaries denied entry. Advisory bodies besides the council of state were (1) the *durbar shahi* (mainly noblemen, with membership hereditary); (2) the *khawanin mulki* (people's representatives, half elected, half appointed by the emir); (3) the *loy jirgah* or the great national council (assembly of tribal leaders and clergy); and (4) a cabinet of ministers. Executive power was vested in the emir, with all the above bodies answerable directly to him. Repealed by Nadir Shah in 1929, it was replaced by the AFGHAN CONSTITUTION OF 1931.

Further reading: Yu V. Gankovsky, *A History of Afghanistan* (Moscow: Progress, 1985); Percy M. Sykes, *A History of Afghanistan*, 2 vols. (New York: AMS Press, 1975).

Afghan Constitution of 1931

New constitution for Afghanistan promulgated on October 13, 1931, by the king, Nadir Shah, confirming his rule and declaring the Afghan throne hereditary on fulfillment of certain conditions. Its 16 sections and 110 articles defined the rights, duties, and privileges of the bicameral legislature (a 116-member national consultative assembly, elected by Afghan males over the age of 20, and a house of peers appointed by the king). The king had complete control over cabinet and civil service appointments, foreign policies, and war and peace decisions, and veto powers over legislative proposals; he also functioned as the final court of appeal. The Hanafite rite of the "sacred religion of Islam" was declared the official religion of the nation and the monarch, and the discriminatory provisions against non-Muslims were dropped (see AFGHAN CONSTITUTION OF 1923). Schools were brought under government control, primary education made compulsory, torture declared illegal, and minor restrictions placed on the press. Personal liberties and property rights were guaranteed and tribal claims to territorial or regional sovereignty abolished.

Further reading: Yu V. Gankovsky, *A History of Afghanistan* (Moscow: Progress, 1985); Percy M. Sykes, *A History of Afghanistan*, 2 vols. (New York: AMS Press, 1975).

Afghan Fundamental Law

See AFGHAN CONSTITUTION OF 1923.

AFL-CIO, Constitution of the

Document setting out the goals and organization of the giant federation of autonomous U.S. labor unions formed by the merger of the American Federation of Labor and the Congress of Industrial Organizations (AFL-CIO) on December 2, 1955. The constitution gave craft and industrial unions equal rank and granted the new federation substantial power over national union affairs. The primary governing body is a biennial convention, in which national unions are represented in proportion to their membership. An executive council governs between conventions. The AFL-CIO goals include improved wages and working conditions, collective bargaining, passage of legislation favorable to labor, strengthening of the labor movement, and encouraging the use of union-made goods.

Further reading: *Constitution of the AFL-CIO, and Other Official Documents Relating to the Achievement of Labor Unity* (Washington, D.C.: American Federation of Labor and Congress of Industrial Organizations, 1956).

Afonsine Ordinances (Ordenações Affonsinas)

First great codification of Portuguese laws, initiated by King Edward about 1435 and completed in 1446 during the reign of his son, King Afonso V. The code, inspired no doubt by Spain's Code of the SEVEN PARTS, was a composite of customary, Visigothic, and Roman law. It defined the limits of royal authority and covered subjects such as succession, inheritance, rights and privileges of nobles, and criminality (with an amended penal code). Also included were strict regulations governing the Jews of Portugal. In 1521 the code, revised, was replaced by the Manueline Ordinances (*Ordenações Manuelinas*), a fundamental legal code made during the reign of Portugal's King Manuel I and used by administrators at home and in overseas colonies, like Brazil.

Further reading: Carl O. Penny, *A Critical Edition of Chapters 1–46 of the Leal Conselheiro by Duarte, King of Portugal* (Ann Arbor, Mich.: Xerox University Microfilms, 1975).

Age of Consent Act

Law by the British government in India in 1891, forbidding consummation of marriage unless the bride was at least 12 years old (10 being the previous limit). The act was initiated by Behramji Malabari after a Hindu child-wife died under mysterious circumstances in Calcutta. Its passage angered the orthodox Hindus, particularly in Calcutta. In Poona, the militant Bal Gangadhar Tilak violently attacked the bill in his vernacular newspaper, the *Kesari*. He denounced its Hindu supporters as traitors and carried his anti-British crusade into schools and colleges. The act was abolished more than six decades later.

Further reading: Ainslie T. Embree, ed., *Encyclopedia of Asian History*, 4 vols. (New York: Charles Scribner's Sons, 1988).

Agreement of the People

Paper presented by the Levellers (a radical faction of the Army Agitators, part of the parliamentarian army during the Great English Civil War) to the army council at the Putney debates on October 28, 1647. They proposed the dissolution of the present Parliament on September 30, 1648, and the setting up of biennial parliaments with six-month sessions, the other 18 months being controlled by the executive council. The Levellers also called for equality for all citizens before the law, for the sovereignty of the House of Commons, for religious freedom, for equal electoral areas, and for relief from pressure to enter military service. The agreement was presented by the army council, in an amended form, to the Rump Parliament in January 1649.

See also: NEWPORT, TREATY OF.

Further reading: William Haller and Godfrey Davies, eds., *The Leveller Tracts, 1647–1653* (Gloucester, Mass.: P. Smith, 1964); Andrew Sharp, ed., *The English Levellers* (New York: Cambridge University Press, 1998); Don Marion Wolfe, ed., *Leveller Manifestoes of the Puritan Revolution* (New York: Humanities Press, 1967).

Agricultural Act of 1947, British

Legislation of August 6, 1947, assuring British farmers of guaranteed prices and markets for their produce. Introduced by the Labour government of Prime Minister Clement Attlee following the worst year (1946) for British agriculture, the act was to create a "stable and efficient agricultural industry," producing an expanding share of the nation's requirements at minimum prices and ensuring adequate returns and decent living conditions for the farmers. The act sought to remove all hindrances to production by speeding up the construction of houses and hostels and the supply of agricultural machinery and by providing incentives to encourage more people to take to farming. County and district agricultural committees were charged with the initiation and administration of these plans.

Further reading: John F. Phillips, *The Agriculture Act, 1947* (London: E. & F. N. Spon & Eyre & Spottiswoods, 1948); George Winder, *Modern Rural Rides: . . . with Some Reference to the Agricultural Act of 1947* (London: Hutchinson, 1964).

Agricultural Adjustment Act of 1933, U.S.

New Deal legislation enacted by the U.S. Congress on May 12, 1933, to raise farm income and commodity prices, and to reduce surpluses of basic commodities, by curtailing production. Farmers who voluntarily reduced their production of staple products were to receive payments derived from taxes levied on the processors of certain farm products. Restricted commodities included hogs, corn, wheat, cotton, rice, dairy items, and tobacco. In 1934 the list was enlarged to include cattle, sugar, flax, grain sorghums, peanuts, barley, and rye. The act established the Agricultural Adjustment Administration to oversee the program. In 1936, in *UNITED STATES* v. *BUTLER*, the Supreme Court declared parts of the act invalid.

Further reading: Murray R. Benedict, *Farm Policies of the United States, 1790–1950: A Study of Their Origins and Development* (Millwood, N.Y.: Kraus Reprint Co., 1975); David E. Hamilton, *From New Day to New Deal: American Farm Policy from Hoover to Roosevelt, 1928–1933* (Chapel Hill: University of North Carolina Press, 1991); Richard S. Kirkendall, *Social Scientists and Farm Politics in the Age of Roosevelt* (Ames: Iowa State University Press, 1982).

Agricultural Adjustment Act of 1938, U.S.

Federal legislation enacted on February 16, 1938, that authorized the Agricultural Adjustment Administration to fix national acreage allotments for staple crops in order to reduce farm surpluses and stabilize farm prices. It established an "ever-normal granary" plan to store surpluses for use in bad years. The U.S. government encouraged farmers to operate within the allotments by offering them loans based on the "parity" price (a figure based on the 1909–14 farm purchasing power) of the stored surpluses; these surpluses would be sold in lean years and the loans repaid. If two-thirds of participating farmers agreed, the secretary of agriculture was authorized to fix marketing quotas when a surplus of an export commodity threatened price levels. The act also established a permanent soil conservation program. It was a modification of the U.S. AGRICULTURAL ADJUSTMENT ACT OF 1933.

Further reading: Melvyn Dubofsky and Stephen Burwood, eds., *Agriculture During the Great Depression* (New York: Garland Press, 1990); John Mark Hansen, *Gaining Access: Congress and the Farm Lobby, 1919–1981* (Chicago: University of

Chicago Press, 1991); Richard S. Kirkendall, *Social Scientists and Farm Politics in the Age of Roosevelt* (Ames: Iowa State University Press, 1982).

Agricultural Marketing Act of 1929, U.S.

Federal legislation enacted on June 15, 1929, that established the Federal Farm Board, consisting of eight members and the U.S. secretary of agriculture, to promote the marketing of agricultural products through cooperatives and stabilization corporations. Implementing the farm relief policy of President Herbert Hoover's administration, the act replaced the subsidy and price-fixing proposals of the MCNARY-HAUGEN BILL. The act authorized a revolving fund of $500 million in low-interest loans for the purchase, handling, and sale of certain agricultural surpluses by cooperatives and stabilization corporations, to stabilize prices. Its efforts proved unsuccessful, and the Farm Board was terminated in 1933.

Further reading: Murray R. Benedict, *Farm Policies of the United States, 1790–1950* (Millwood, N.Y. Kraus Reprint Co., 1975); David E. Hamilton, *From New Day to New Deal: American Farm Policy from Hoover to Roosevelt, 1928–1933* (Chapel Hill: University of North Carolina Press, 1991).

Aigun, Treaty of   See PEKING, TREATY OF (1860).

Air Quality Act of 1967, U.S.

Federal U.S. legislation, enacted in 1967, that established a regional system for the enactment and enforcement of federal and state air-quality standards. It directed the Department of Health, Education, and Welfare to designate air-quality control regions, based on climatic, meteorological, and topographical factors that affect the interchange and diffusion of atmospheric pollutants, and also based on jurisdictional boundaries and urban-industrial concentrations. The states were given the responsibility for setting standards for air quality, based on federal criteria. The act was strengthened by the CLEAN AIR ACT OF 1970.

Further reading: *Air Quality Control Act of 1967* (Washington, D.C.: U.S. Government Printing Office, 1967).

Aix-la-Chapelle, Convention of

Decisions taken at the Congress of Aix-la-Chapelle (September–November 1818), the first of the post–Napoleonic War conferences, convened to discuss normalization of relations with France, which had completed its obligations under the 1814 Paris Treaty. The convention agreed to withdraw troops from French territory, settle the payment of reparations, and dissolve the ambassadors' conference in Paris. The signatories of the Quadruple Alliance (Great Britain, Russia, Prussia, and Austria) included France in a newly formed Quintuple Alliance. The convention also reviewed and approved the security systems guarding Napoléon at St. Helena, confirmed the rights of the Jews, and ordered Sweden to pay Denmark the compensation promised in the 1814 Treaty of KIEL. The conference highlighted major differences of opinion, notably between the British and Russian camps, and foreshadowed the end of the European coalition.

Further reading: Pamela M. Pilbeam, *The Constitutional Monarchy in France, 1814–1848: Revolution and Stability* (Harlow, England: Longman, 1999).

Aix-la-Chapelle, Treaty of (1668)

French agreement made at Aix-la-Chapelle (Aachen) on May 2, 1668, with members of the 1668 Triple Alliance (the English, Swedes, and Dutch), ending the War of Devolution (1667–68) without addressing the central issue that had led to it (French king Louis XIV's claims to the Spanish Netherlands). By the treaty, France returned to Spain the places of Cambrai, Aire, and Saint-Omer in Flanders, and the region of Franche-Comté (Free County of Burgundy); France retained 12 fortified frontier towns in Flanders and in the Spanish Netherlands (including Charleroi, Douai, Lille, Tournai, Oudenaarde, Armentières, and Courtrai [Kortrijk]), many of which had been conquered in the war. Since the main issue was deferred, the treaty proved to be merely a temporary truce, with Louis XIV having postponed his ambitious plans for expansion.

See also: NIJMEGEN, TREATIES OF; TRIPLE ALLIANCE OF 1668.

Further reading: Charles L. Phillips and Alan Axelrod, eds., *Encyclopedia of Historical Treaties and Alliances*, 2 vols. (New York: Facts On File, 2001).

Aix-la-Chapelle, Treaty of (1748)

Treaty negotiated and signed initially by Britain, France, and the Netherlands on October 18, 1748—and later accepted by Austria, Spain, Sardinia, Genoa, and Modena—concluding the War of the Austrian Succession (1740–48); the succession of Maria Theresa of Austria to the Hapsburg territories by virtue of the PRAGMATIC SANCTION OF 1713 had been the precipitating issue in this war, mainly between France, Prussia, Spain, and Sardinia on one side and Austria and Britain on the other. Based on the mutual restoration of conquests, the treaty returned Louisbourg and Cape Breton (both in Nova Scotia) to France; returned Madras in India to Britain; the barrier towns to the Netherlands; Parma, Piacenza, and Guastalla to Spain; and Silesia and Glatz to Prussia (though not a signatory to the treaty). The Pragmatic Sanction was recognized, as was the Protestant Hanoverian royal succession to the British throne and to the German electorate of Hanover.

Further reading: Charles L. Phillips and Alan Axelrod, eds., *Encyclopedia of Historical Treaties and Alliances*, 2 vols. (New York: Facts On File, 2001).

Akkerman, Convention of

Agreement concluded on October 7, 1826, in the Moldavian town of Akkerman (Belgorod-Dnestrovsky) between Russia and the Ottoman Empire, through which the Ottoman Turks agreed to demands presented to them by Russia regarding territories in the Caucasus, Balkans, and Danubian river basin. The Turks complied upon threat of war. Through the convention the terms of the Treaty of BUCHAREST of 1812, which included Ottoman recognition of Serbia's autonomy and Russia's possession of certain Caucasus territories, were reaffirmed. The Ottomans also agreed to withdraw their forces from the Danubian principalities of Moldavia and Wallachia (formerly Turkish possessions); agreed to the free navigation of Russian commercial vessels through the Dardanelles and Bosporus; and granted free trading privileges to Russian merchants in the Ottoman Empire.

See also: ADRIANOPLE, TREATY OF (1829).

Further reading: Marian Kent, *The Great Powers and the End of the Ottoman Empire* (Boston: G. Allen & Unwin, 1984).

Alabama Letters   Letters written by U.S. Whig presidential candidate Henry Clay in July 1844, concerning the annexation of Texas. Following the furor raised by his opposition to annexation in his RALEIGH LETTER, Clay moderated his position in the Alabama letters. In an effort to please both the South, which favored annexation and slavery, and the North, which opposed both, Clay stated that he did not object to annexation if it could be accomplished without destroying the integrity of the Union and without a war against Mexico. The letters, by failing to show a firm stand on the issue, cost Clay support from both sides, and he lost the election.

Further reading: Calvin Colton, ed., *The Works of Henry Clay: Comprising His Life, Correspondence and Speeches, 10 vols.* (New York: G. P. Putnam's Sons, 1978); Robert V. Remini, *Henry Clay: Statesman for the Union* (New York: W. W. Norton, 1991); Kimberly C. Shankman, *Compromise and the Constitution: The Political Thought of Henry Clay* (Lanham, Md.: Lexington Books, 1999).

Alais, Peace of (Edict, or Peace, of Grace)   Settlement signed at Alais (Alès), France, on June 28, 1629; negotiated by Cardinal de Richelieu (chief minister of King Louis XIII of France) with the defeated Huguenot (French Protestant) forces after their defeat at Alais, one of the main Huguenot strongholds. Louis XIII pardoned "by grace" the rebels and confirmed the basic text of the Edict of NANTES of 1598 and revoked its supplementary articles. Thus, while the Huguenots were assured freedom of worship and granted civil liberties, they were stripped of their military power and political privileges. They lost their troops, all their fortresses were ordered demolished, and they agreed not to establish "any separate body, independent of the will of their sovereign." Roman Catholic worship was reintroduced in former Huguenot strongholds. This effectively diffused any major threat from them and was a significant diplomatic and political triumph for Richelieu and the French king, Louis XIII.

See also: LOUIS XIII'S EDICT OF 1626; NANTES, REVOCATION OF THE EDICT OF.

Further reading: Mack P. Holt, *The French Wars of Religion, 1562–1629* (New York: Cambridge University Press, 1999).

Alaska Purchase Treaty   Treaty concluded on March 30, 1867, by which the United States purchased Alaska from Russia for $7.2 million. The treaty was negotiated by Baron Edoard de Stoeckl, Russian minister to the United States, and U.S. secretary of state William Seward. The Russians considered Alaska a financial liability, which they were reluctant to administer and defend. Seward, an expansionist, was the prime promoter of the purchase, which was for many years considered foolish, hence the names "Seward's Folly" and "Seward's Icebox" for the territory. There were rumors that Senate ratification (April 9) was accomplished through Russian bribery of key senators.

Further reading: Thomas Carson, ed., *Gale Encyclopedia of U.S. Economic History* (Farmington Hills, Mich.: Gale Group, 1999); Charles L. Phillips and Alan Axelrod, eds., *Encyclopedia of Historical Treaties and Alliances,* 2 vols. (New York: Facts On File, 2001).

Albany Plan of Union   Proposal for a federation or union of the British colonies in America, drafted principally by Benjamin Franklin and approved by the Albany Congress in June 1754. Delegates from the colonial assemblies of New Hampshire, Massachusetts, Connecticut, Rhode Island, New York, Pennsylvania, and Maryland were summoned to Albany, New York, to work out a common plan of defense as war against the French and hostile Iroquois Indians threatened; they sought a treaty with the Indians and a permanent union of the colonies. Franklin's plan provided for a union with a representative council elected by the colonial assemblies triennially, which would have the power to impose taxes, nominate civil officials, regulate Indian affairs, and control the military. A president-general, appointed by the British Crown, would preside over the council and would hold veto power. The individual colonies, unwilling to give up so much power, rejected the Albany Plan, as did the British, thinking it would decrease the power of Parliament and the king.

Further reading: "The Albany Plan of Union 1754." A Hypertext on American History website. Available online at http://odur.let.rug.nl/~usa/D/1751-1775/7yearswar/albany.htm.

Alcáçovas, Treaty of   Peace pact made at Alcáçovas, in Estremadura, Portugal, on September 4, 1479, resolving a war of succession (Castilian Civil War of 1474–79) between Portuguese king Afonso V and Spanish king Ferdinand V and queen Isabella I of Castile and León. Ratified at Toledo, Spain, on March 6, 1480, the treaty provided that Afonso (defeated in the war) renounce his claims to the Castilian throne (through marriage to his niece Juana la Beltraneja of Castile) and to the Canary Islands. In return, the Spanish recognized

Portuguese rights to the islands of the Azores, Cape Verde, and Madeira. Ferdinand and Isabella, who pardoned the Spaniards who had supported Portugal in the war and restored their property, were to give their eldest daughter in marriage to Afonso's young grandson; Juana (whose marriage to Afonso had not been solemnized) retired to a convent.

Further reading: William H. Prescott, *History of the Reign of Ferdinand and Isabella, the Catholic* (New York: AMS Press, 1968); Paul Stevens, *Ferdinand and Isabella* (New York: Chelsea House, 1988).

Aldrich-Vreeland Act

Legislation enacted by the U.S. Congress on May 30, 1908, as an emergency currency law, designed to defend the dollar and maintain high interest and tariff rates. In order to give some elasticity to the currency, the act authorized national banks to issue circulating notes (based on commercial paper) and state and local government bonds and established a graduated tax up to 10 percent on such notes. It also established the National Monetary Commission, headed by Rhode Island's senator Nelson W. Aldrich (chief architect of the act, cosponsored by Representative Edward B. Vreeland of New York), to investigate the banking and currency systems of the United States and Europe and to recommend to Congress changes in the American banking system.

Further reading: Victor Morawetz, *The Banking and Currency Problem in the United States,* 2d ed. (New York: North American Review Pub., 1909).

Alessandria, Armistice of

Armistice concluded on June 15, 1800, between French general Napoléon Bonaparte and Austrian general Baron von Melas following the Austrian defeat in the Battle of Marengo (June 14, 1800) in northwestern Italy. The document (signed at Alessandria, near Marengo) required the Austrians to evacuate Piedmont and Lombardy west of the Mincio and Mantua Rivers and to grant France control over all fortresses in that region. Austria, still allied with Great Britain, continued to fight France until February 1801, when she signed a separate peace with France (see LUNÉVILLE, TREATY OF). Napoléon had already gained control of much of Italy through the 1797 Treaties of TOLENTINO and CAMPO FORMIO and the earlier Armistice of CHERASCO.

Further reading: Robert B. Asprey, *The Rise of Napoleon Bonaparte* (New York: Basic Books, 2000).

Alexandropol, Treaty of

Treaty concluded at Alexandropol (Leninakan, Armenian Russia) on December 2, 1920, by Armenia and Turkey, bringing an end to the most recent Turkish offensive in Transcaucasia against Armenia, the object of which had been to gain control of territory that the Turks had failed to gain possession of during World War I (1914–18). The treaty provided for Turkey's recognition of Armenian independence; for Armenia's cession to Turkey of the cities of Kars and Ardahan, as well as all territory that had been part of Turkey before 1914; for a new Turko-Armenian border along the Akhourian River; and for the autonomy of the territories of Nakhichevan and Sharour under Turkish protection. The Turks had concluded the treaty under pressure from Soviet Russia, the forces of which had entered Armenia from the north, and which, the following day, effected the annexation of Armenia.

See also: BATUM, TREATY OF; KARS, TREATY OF; MOSCOW, TREATY OF (1921).

Further reading: Azmi Suslu, *Armenians in the History of the Turks: Basic Text Book* (Kars, Turkey: Rectorate of the Kafkas University, 1995).

Algeciras, Act of

Concluding act of the Conference of Algeciras (January 16–April 7, 1906), convened by Morocco's sultan Abd al-Aziz IV to resolve the Franco-German dispute over Morocco. It affirmed Morocco's independence while increasing French control in key areas. The act, signed by 11 European countries, Russia, and the United States, was accepted by the sultan on June 18, 1906. Its main provisions were (1) recognition of the sultan's sovereignty; (2) policing rights for France and Spain in Morocco and for France along the Algerian border; (3) formation of an international body, French-dominated and authorized to intervene in Moroccan affairs, if necessary; (4) European supervision over 60 percent of custom's levies' collections; (5) special port police force to protect European interests; (6) Morocco's state bank, its sole financial agent, to be dominated by the French consortium (Banque de Paris et des Pays-Bas); and (6) earlier treaties on Morocco upheld, unless contradictory to the above act. In seeking to satisfy European interests, the Algeciras Conference entirely ignored Moroccan demands.

See also: TANGIER, CONVENTION AND STATUTE OF.

Further reading: E. N. Anderson, *First Moroccan Crisis, 1904–1906* (Hamden, Conn.: Archon Books, 1930, repr., 1966); Charles L. Phillips and Alan Axelrod, eds., *Encyclopedia of Historical Treaties and Alliances,* 2 vols. (New York: Facts On File, 2001); Reeva S. Simon, Philip Mattar, and Richard W. Bulliet, eds., *Encyclopedia of the Modern Middle East* (New York: Simon & Schuster, 1996).

Alhambra Decree (Edict of Expulsion)

Law promulgated on March 31, 1492, by Ferdinand V and Isabella I (the "Catholic kings") from the captured Alhambra, majestic Moorish palace, near Granada, Spain. It ordered the expulsion of Jews from Castile, Aragón, Sicily, and Sardinia unless they agreed to be baptized Christians before July 31 of that year. Seigneurs (feudal lords) were promised the land of the expelled Jews as a reward for enforcing the decree, in justification of which the monarchs cited "the great harm suffered by Christians from the contact, intercourse, and communication . . . with the Jews, who always attempt in various ways to seduce faithful Christians from our Holy Catholic Faith." A Jewish delegation appealed in vain to the monarchs to withdraw the edict, which displaced over 200,000 Spanish Jews and augmented the expulsions of the Inquisition. The decree was later imitated in Portugal (1496) and Navarre (1498). In 1992 Spain's king Juan Carlos issued a royal decree of atonement, formally canceling the 500-year-old Alhambra Decree.

Further reading: Ovid Jacob's website, available online at http://www.sirius.com/~ovid/alhambra.decree.html; David Raphael, *The Expulsion 1492 Chronicles: An Anthology of Medieval Chronicles Relating to the Expulsion of the Jews from Spain and Portugal* (North Hollywood, Calif.: Carmi House Press, 1992).

Alien Act of 1798, U.S.   Federal legislation enacted on June 25, 1798, that authorized the president to order the deportation from the United States of all aliens deemed dangerous to the public peace and safety or reasonably suspected of "treasonable or secret machinations against the government." Failure to obey such an order was punishable by imprisonment and loss of the possibility of U.S. citizenship. As one of the ALIEN AND SEDITION ACTS OF 1798, the act frightened many foreigners into leaving the country, although it was not enforced. The law expired in two years and was not renewed.

Further reading: Leonard W. Levy, *Legacy of Suppression* (Cambridge, Mass.: Belknap Press, 1960); James Roger Sharp, *American Politics in the Early Republic: The New Nation in Crisis* (New Haven, Conn.: Yale University Press, 1993); James Morton Smith, *Freedom's Fetters: The Alien and Sedition Laws and American Civil Liberties* (Ithaca, N.Y.: Cornell University Press, 1956).

Alien and Sedition Acts of 1798, U.S.   Set of four laws enacted in 1798 by the U.S. Congress, then controlled by the Federalist Party, and directed against European refugees who supported the opposing Republican Party. The laws, which reflected hostility toward France arising from publication of the "XYZ" REPORT and a fear of an imminent war with that nation, were the U.S. NATURALIZATION ACT OF 1798, the U.S. ALIEN ACT OF 1798, the U.S. ALIEN ENEMIES ACT OF 1798, and the U.S. SEDITION ACT OF 1798. All four acts were controversial and of questionable constitutionality.

Further reading: Edward W. Knappman, ed., *Great American Trials* (Detroit: Gale Research, 1994); John C. Miller, *Crisis in Freedom: The Alien and Sedition Acts* (Boston: Little, Brown, 1951); James Roger Sharp, *American Politics in the Early Republic: The New Nation in Crisis* (New Haven, Conn.: Yale University Press, 1993); James Morton Smith, *Freedom's Fetters: The Alien and Sedition Laws and American Civil Liberties* (Ithaca, N.Y.: Cornell University Press, 1956).

Alien Enemies Act of 1798, U.S.   Federal legislation enacted on July 6, 1798, that authorized the U.S. president, in times of declared war, to arrest, imprison, and remove all male citizens or subjects of the hostile nation who were aged 14 years or older. This act was one of the U.S. ALIEN AND SEDITION ACTS OF 1798.

Further reading: James Roger Sharp, *American Politics in the Early Republic: The New Nation in Crisis* (New Haven, Conn.: Yale University Press, 1993); James Morton Smith, *Freedom's Fetters: The Alien and Sedition Laws and American Civil Liberties* (Ithaca, N.Y.: Cornell University Press, 1956).

Alien Registration Act, U.S. (Smith Act)   U.S. legislation enacted on June 28, 1940, that strengthened existing laws concerning the admission and deportation of aliens and required the registration and fingerprinting of all aliens living in the United States. Its primary purpose, however, as the United States was being drawn into World War II, was to reduce subversive activities, particularly communist-led strikes that might injure the American defense industry. The act, sponsored by U.S. representative Howard W. Smith of Virginia, declared it illegal to advocate or teach the forceful overthrow of the U.S. government or knowingly to join a group that did so. In 1951 the Supreme Court upheld the constitutionality of the act in *DENNIS ET AL. V. UNITED STATES.*

Further reading: Michael R. Belknap, *Cold War Political Justice: The Smith Act, the Communist Party, and American Civil Liberties* (Westport, Conn.: Greenwood press, 1977); Zechariah Chafee, Jr., *Free Speech in the United States* (Union, N.J.: Lawbook Exchange, 1967, repr., 2000); Leonard W. Levy and Kenneth L. Karst, eds., *Encyclopedia of the American Constitution*, 2d ed. (New York: Macmillan Reference, 2000).

Aliens Immigration Restriction Act   Legislation by the Volksraad (Transvaal's legislature) on November 26, 1896, that enabled it to arbitrarily control the immigration of "Uitlanders"—Europeans and Americans who had come to the Transvaal in South Africa after the gold rush there (1886). When Britain's colonial secretary Joseph Chamberlain pleaded for its cancellation, the Pretoria government replied that it would not "tolerate any interference or meddling however . . . well meant, in [the Transvaal's] internal affairs." Chamberlain then bolstered the British forces in the region, which forced the Transvaal government to repeal the law in 1897. The enactment of this legislation brought into sharp focus the issue of Britain's supremacy in the region.

Further reading: Christopher Saunders, *Historical Dictionary of South Africa* (Metuchen, N.J.: Scarecrow Press, 1983).

Alinagar, Treaty of   Agreement of February 9, 1757, between Robert Clive (the British representative in India) and Siraj-ud-Daulah (nawab of Bengal) to mark the formal surrender of the city of Calcutta to the British East India Company. The treaty permitted the fortification of the city and the coinage of money. The nawab, who had captured Calcutta (and briefly renamed it "Alinagar") in June 1756, feared an attack from the Afghans who had already invaded Delhi, and decided to take the easy way out by making peace with the British. For Clive, who had recovered Calcutta from the nawab on January 2, the treaty was merely the first step in Britain's seizure of Bengal, which continued with the defeat of Siraj-ud-Daulah later the same year.

Further reading: Kalikinkar Datta, *Siraj-ud-Daulah* (Bombay, India: Orient Longman, 1971); Robert Harvey, *Clive: The Life and Death of a British Emperor* (New York: St. Martin's press, 2000).

All-African People's Conference Resolutions of 1958
Resolutions endorsed at a nongovernmental conference attended by some 300 delegates from 28 African countries at Accra, Ghana, on December 5–13, 1958. The delegates, agreeing to matters of common concern, established a permanent All-African People's Conference and made resolves about racism, discrimination, tribalism, religious separatism, boundaries, and federations, among other subjects. Extremely important were the following: "That the All-African People's Conference vehemently condemns colonialism and imperialism in whatever shape or form these evils are perpetuated; That the political and economic exploitation of Africa by Imperialist Europeans should cease forthwith; . . . That fundamental human rights be extended to all men and women in Africa."

Further reading: Kwame Nkrumah, *All-African People's Conference* (Accra, Ghana: Government Printer, c. 1959).

Alliance of 1815, Holy   See HOLY ALLIANCE OF 1815.

Alma-Ata Declaration   Protocol to the MINSK AGREEMENT signed on December 21, 1991, in Alma-Ata, Kazakhstan, by 11 of the 12 former Soviet republics (Armenia, Azerbaijan, Belarus, Kazakhstan, Kyrgyzstan, Moldova, Tajikistan, Turkmenistan, Uzbekistan, Ukraine, and the Russian Federation), it formally established the Commonwealth of Independent States (CIS). Within days, President Mikhail S. Gorbachev resigned and the Soviet Union was dissolved. Georgia joined the CIS in late 1993. Described as "an alliance of fully independent states," CIS's policy decisions would be coordinated by the Council of Heads of State (state presidents) and the Council of Heads of Government (state prime ministers). Russia would assume the former Soviet seat on the Security Council of the United Nations, while Ukraine and Belarus would retain their U.N. membership. The military and nuclear arsenal would remain under a central command.

Further reading: *The Europa World Yearbook, 1999* (London: Europa Publications, 1999).

Altmark, Treaty of   Truce of six years concluded at Altmark in Sweden on September 25, 1629, by Sweden and Poland, bringing a temporary end to the Polish-Swedish struggle for hegemony in the Baltic, a struggle that had by then become part of the Thirty Years' War (1618–48). By the document

Sweden gained control of Livonia (a northern Baltic province on the Gulf of Riga) and a part of the coast of Prussia, thus establishing Sweden's control over the Baltic coast from the Gulf of Finland to Danzig (Gdansk, Poland). The elector of Brandenburg, allied with Sweden, received Marienburg (Malbork, Poland), as well as other strategically important cities in west Prussia. Despite Polish King Sigismund III's refusal to renounce his claim to the Swedish throne, his country had clearly lost the war.

Further reading: Ingmar Andersson, *A History of Sweden* (New York: Praeger, 1968); Norman Davies, *God's Playground: A History of Poland,* 2 vols. (New York: Columbia University Press, 1982); Michael Roberts, ed., *Sweden as a Great Power, 1611–1697: Government, Society, Foreign Policy* (New York: St. Martin's, 1968).

Altranstädt, Treaty of   Agreement concluded on September 24, 1706, between Sweden's king Charles XII and associates of Poland's king Augustus II (without his consent), following a series of victorious battles waged by Charles against Poland during the Great Northern War (1700–1721). Augustus was to renounce his Polish crown in favor of Stanislaus I, whom Charles supported, and to break his alliance with the Russian czar. The majority of Poles remained loyal to Augustus, who did not abide by any of the treaty's terms and who, as elector of Saxony, attacked the Swedish-held Baltic province of Livonia as an ally of Russia.

Further reading: Ingmar Andersson, *A History of Sweden* (New York: Praeger, 1968); Norman Davies, *God's Playground: A History of Poland,* 2 vols. (New York: Columbia University Press, 1982).

Amalfitan Code (Amalfian Code, Tables of Amalfi, Tavole Amalfitane, Tabula Amalphitana, Capitula et Ordinationes Curiae Maritimae Nobilis Civitatis Amalphae)   Code of law relating to commerce and navigation on the high seas, supposedly compiled at Amalfi, near Naples, Italy, in the late 11th century or early 12th century. Based on the eighth-century maritime code of Byzantine emperor Leo III, it was observed by all Italy and accepted as the standard maritime law throughout the Mediterranean until about 1570. Widely influential until the 1700s, it was instrumental in the development of similar nautical regulations in other early Italian maritime republics.

Further reading: John H. Pryor, *Commerce, Shipping, and Naval Warfare in the Medieval Mediterranean* (London: Variorum Reprints, 1987).

Amboise, Edict of (Peace of Amboise, Edict of Pacification)   Royal proclamation issued on March 19, 1563, by France's queen mother Catherine de Médicis, from the château of Amboise in the Loire valley, ending the first French War of Religion (1562–63). It set free the Huguenot (French Protestant) leader, the prince of Condé, and granted liberty

of conscience to the Protestants (Calvinists) (see JANUARY, EDICT OF). However, Protestant services were restricted to the houses of the Huguenot nobility—a clause that angered reformers John Calvin (see INSTITUTES OF THE CHRISTIAN RELIGION) and Admiral Gaspard de Coligny because it ignored the Protestant masses who were prevented from hosting local congregations. The Huguenots were to restore to the Roman Catholics the churches they had occupied. They were still barred from holding public office. Neither the Catholics nor the Huguenots were satisfied with the terms of the edict, which was no more than a temporary and uneasy truce.

See also: CHÂTEAUBRIANT, EDICT OF; ROMORANTIN, EDICT OF.

Further reading: Mack P. Holt, *The French Wars of Religion, 1562–1629* (New York: Cambridge University Press, 1999).

American Anti-Imperialist League, Platform of the

Set of principles condemning U.S. colonialism in the Philippines, issued on October 18, 1899, by a coalition of local and regional anti-imperialist organizations meeting in Chicago. The platform declared that U.S. efforts to control the Philippines after that nation had declared its independence from Spain constituted "criminal aggression" and violated the fundamental principles of American government. The league condemned the use of American military force to suppress the Filipino rebellion against U.S. control, calling the slaughter of Filipinos a "needless horror" in an unjust war, and urged Congress to cease the war immediately. Though the league attracted many influential supporters, the rebellion collapsed and the Philippines remained a U.S. possession until 1946.

Further reading: Erving Winslow, *The Anti-Imperialist League: Apologia pro vita sua* (Boston: Anti-Imperialist League, c. 1908).

American Anti-Slavery Society, Constitution of the (Declaration of Sentiments of the American Anti-Slavery Convention)

Basic principles and rules, prepared by William Lloyd Garrison and issued in Philadelphia on December 4, 1833, by the founding convention of the militant, abolitionist American Anti-Slavery Society. The constitution condemned the institution of slavery as a danger to prosperity, peace, and union, as well as contrary to "natural justice," republican government, and Christian belief; called for immediate emancipation of all slaves and abolition of the domestic slave trade; and opposed expatriation of the freed slaves. The society also declared as goals the elimination of prejudice and the "intellectual, moral, and religious improvement" of people of color in order to secure their civil and religious equality with whites.

Further reading: John G. Whittier, *The Anti-Slavery Convention of 1833* (Boston: Directors of the Old South, 1897).

American Federation of Labor, Constitution of the

Document defining the basic principles and organization of this federation of trade and labor unions, adopted in 1932 at its 52nd annual convention. The objectives of the federation included the formation of local, national, and international unions, cooperation among unions at all levels, aid for the sale of union-label goods, passage of legislation in the interest of working people, influencing public opinion on behalf of organized labor, and encouragement of the labor press in America. Revenue was to be derived from member unions, and a defense fund was established to support unions engaged in protracted strikes or lockouts. While maintaining "the right of each trade to manage its own affairs," the constitution set up an executive council "to secure the unification of all labor organizations."

Further reading: *American Federation of Labor*, 5 vols. (Westport, Conn.: Greenwood Press, 1977); Stuart B. Kaufman, ed., *The Samuel Gompers Papers: The Early Years of the American Federation of Labor, 1887–90* (Urbana: University of Illinois Press, 1987).

American Presidents, Declaration of
See DECLARATION OF AMERICAN PRESIDENTS.

American Prohibitory Act
See RESTRAINING ACT OF 1775, BRITISH.

American Scholar, The
Famous address delivered by American poet and essayist Ralph Waldo Emerson before the Harvard Phi Beta Kappa Society's annual gathering at Cambridge, Massachusetts, on August 31, 1837. Describing the scholar as the "delegated intellect" in the "divided or social state," Emerson observed that when victimized by society, "he tends to become a mere thinker, or still worse, the parrot of other men's thinking." Emerson then examined in great detail the main influences on the scholar: (1) nature, which "becomes to him the measure of his attainments"; (2) "the mind of the Past—in whatever form, whether of literature, of art, of institutions that mind is inscribed"; and (3) action—"Without it, he is not yet man. Without it, thought can never ripen into truth." His duties are: "to guide men by showing them facts amidst appearances," to "relinquish display and immediate fame," to "resist vulgar prosperity," and to be brave and free. Finally, Emerson challenged the scholar: "It is for you to know all, it is for you to dare all!"

Further reading: C. David Mead, comp., *"The American Scholar" Today: Emerson's Essay and Some Critical Views* (New York: Dodd, Mead, 1970).

Americans with Disabilities Act
World's first and most comprehensive civil rights legislation (enacted July 26, 1990) aimed at protecting the more than 43 million U.S. citizens with disabilities from discrimination in the areas of employment, public accommodations, transportation, state and local

government services, and telecommunications. Title I, regulated by the Equal Employment Opportunity Commission (EEOC), prohibits discrimination in employment policies and practices. The U.S. Department of Transportation oversees implementation of Title II, which requires state and local governments to guarantee the disabled full and equal access to services and transportation. Title III, administered by the U.S. Department of Justice, prohibits discrimination against the disabled by public businesses. Title IV, regulated by the Federal Communications Commission (FCC), requires telephone companies and government-funded public service television to provide services accessible by the disabled.

Further reading: *Americans with Disabilities Act Handbook.* (Washington, D.C.: Equal Employment Opportunity Commission & Department of Justice, 1991); Deborah S. Kearney, *The New ADA—Compliance and Costs* (Kingston, Mass.: R. S. Means Company, 1992).

American Taxation Speech, Burke's

Impassioned speech, entitled "On American Taxation," made by Edmund Burke, Whig member of the British Parliament, in the House of Commons in April 1774, advocating a more liberal policy toward the American colonies. He said "leave America, if she has taxable matter in her, to tax herself." The speech was delivered during the debates that followed Britain's imposition of duties on the colonies. Burke said Britain should "be content to bind America by laws of trade" rather than burden her by taxes and cause her to call Britain's sovereignty into question. Viewing Parliament's power of taxing as an "instrument of empire, and not as a means of supply," he felt that Britain had already benefited from her American trade and would continue to, even if she never taxed the colonies. His views found little support in Parliament.

See also: THOUGHTS ON THE CAUSE OF THE PRESENT DISCONTENTS.

Further reading: David Bromwich, ed., *On Empire, Liberty, and Reform: Speeches and Letter of Edmund Burke* (New Haven, Conn.: Yale University Press, 2000); *Speech of E. Burke, Esq.; on American Taxation, April 19, 1774,* 3d ed. (New York: Readex Microprint, 1985).

American Tobacco Company v. *United States*

U.S. Supreme Court decision issued on May 29, 1911, ordering the reorganization of the American Tobacco Company, a giant tobacco trust. As in the ruling in STANDARD OIL COMPANY OF NEW JERSEY ET AL. V. UNITED STATES, the Supreme Court declared that the company had tried to restrain trade and monopolize the tobacco industry, in violation of the SHERMAN ANTI-TRUST ACT. The Court declared that while the act did not prohibit "normal and usual contracts essential to individual freedom" and free trade, it did not permit unreasonable restraint of trade and could not be circumvented by "disguise or subterfuge."

Further reading: United States Supreme Court, Antitrustcases.com web site, Available online at http://www.antitrustcases.com/summaries/221us106.htm.

Amiens, Mise of

Mediation decision or award of French king Louis IX at Amiens, France, on January 23, 1264, in the dispute between English king Henry III and his barons, confirming the pope's annulment of the PROVISIONS OF OXFORD and reasserting the rights of the monarchy in England. The mise restored absolute power to Henry, providing he did not "derogate in any way from the royal privileges, charters, liberties, statutes, and laudable customs" of England. Also, he was allowed to appoint his own advisers and could dismiss officials at will. The restrictions on aliens were lifted and their security guaranteed. Both parties (the barons and Henry) were to pardon each other, "renounce all rancor," and promise not to "harm nor offend the other" on any issue submitted to arbitration. Though both parties had agreed to Louis's mediation, the barons were unhappy with his award, and the Barons' War (1263–65) broke out again.

See also: KENILWORTH, DICTUM OF; LEWES, MISE OF.

Further reading: David Carpenter, *The Reign of Henry III* (Rio Grande, Ohio: Hambleden Press, 1996).

Amiens, Treaty of (1802)

Agreement signed at Amiens, France, on March 27, 1802, by Britain on the one side and France, Spain, and the Batavian Republic (Holland) on the other, establishing 14 months of peace in Europe between the French Revolutionary Wars (1792–1802) and the Napoleonic Wars (1803–15). Britain surrendered almost all conquests: The Dutch got Cochin in India and the Cape and Spice Islands but ceded Ceylon (Sri Lanka) to the British; the Spanish received Minorca but ceded Trinidad to the British; and the French recovered territories in India and Africa and the islands of St. Lucia, Martinique, Tobago, and St. Pierre and Miquelon. The signatories acknowledged the independence of Malta and the rights and boundaries of the Ottoman Empire and Portugal. France agreed to evacuate Naples and the papal states but retained Portuguese Guinea (Guinea-Bissau). Several thorny issues between Britain and France (the Belgian provinces, Savoy, Switzerland, and Britain's continental trade) remained unresolved, however.

Further reading: Henry Adams, *History of the United States During the Administrations of Jefferson and Madison,* 2 vols., (Englewood Cliffs, N.J.: Prentice-Hall, 1963); Paddy Griffith, *The Art of War of Revolutionary France, 1789–1802* (Mechanicsburg, Pa.: Stackpole Books, 1998); Charles L. Phillips and Alan Axelrod, eds., *Encyclopedia of Historical Treaties and Alliances,* 2 vols. (New York: Facts On File, 2001); Ernst L. Presseisen, *Amiens and Munich: Comparisons in Appeasement* (The Hague: Martinus Nijhoff, 1978).

Amnesty Act of 1872, U.S.

General amnesty passed by Congress on May 22, 1872, reenfranchising most supporters of the Confederacy. The FOURTEENTH AMENDMENT (1868) had barred more than 150,000 rebels from holding civil or military office unless Congress, by a two-thirds vote, removed their disabilities. Congress proceeded to pass individual amnesty acts, especially for those willing to join the radical Republicans, but public demand grew for broader action, and general amnesty became an issue in the presidential campaign of 1872. Only some 500 to 750 high Confederate officials were excepted from the 1872 act. All disabilities were removed by 1898.

Further reading: Jean Edward Smith, *Grant* (New York: Simon & Schuster, 2001).

Amparo, Writ of

Writ originating in the Mexican state constitution of Yucatán in 1842. The *amparo* (meaning "protection"), a concept that incorporates the characteristics of English injunctions such as habeas corpus, mandamus, and certiorari, is a federal order that can be issued by a federal judge on behalf of any citizen. Its purpose is to provide judicial protection against damage to individual interests or violations of public rights guaranteed by the constitution; federal actions that infringe on the sovereignty of the states; or state actions that invade the federal sphere of action. The *amparo* is usually regarded as Mexico's most valuable and useful contribution to jurisprudence.

Further reading: Richard D. Baker, *Judicial Review in Mexico: A Study of the Amparo Suit* (Austin: University of Texas Press, 1971); Barbara A. Tenenbaum, ed., *Encyclopedia of Latin American History and Culture* (New York: Charles Scribner's Sons, 1996).

Amritsar, Treaty of

Agreement made between Sir Charles Metcalfe on behalf of the British East India Company and Ranjit Singh, ruler of the Sikhs (a religious sect), on April 15, 1809, at Amritsar (sacred Sikh city in India's Punjab region). It eliminated a major source of conflict between the British and Sikhs by establishing the Sutlej River as the northwestern boundary of the company's territories; the British recognized Ranjit Singh as the king of Punjab to the west of the river and brought the cis-Sutlej states under their control. The treaty checked Ranjit Singh's westward expansion, as the British hoped, and brought peace to the region until the outbreak of the First Anglo-Sikh War in 1845.

Further reading: Ainslie T. Embree, ed., *Encyclopedia of Asian History,* 4 vols. (New York: Charles Scribner's Sons, 1988).

Anaconda Plan

Strategic military plan devised by Winfield Scott, commanding general of the Union army; proposed in May 1861 to defeat the Confederacy. Scott's plan was to occupy a line along the Mississippi River as far as the Gulf of Mexico with an army of 60,000 soldiers under General George B. McClellan and to blockade Confederate ports, thus enveloping the insurgent states. It also called for the seizure of Richmond, the Confederate capital, and for the Union army in the East to merge with the Union army in the West after the latter had cut up the Confederacy. The Union would then wait for pro-Union Southerners to persuade the Confederate government to seek peace. Scott thought this strategy would bring an end to the Civil War (1861–65) with less bloodshed than any other plan. Although the plan was at first ridiculed as "Scott's Anaconda," some of its features were eventually incorporated into the war strategy. The plan's name derived from the anaconda snake, which crushes its prey to death.

Further reading: Mark M. Boatner, *The Civil War Dictionary* (New York: David McKay, 1988).

Ancón, Treaty of

Treaty between Chile and Peru signed on October 20, 1883, at Ancón, Peru. After losing the War of the Pacific (1879–84), Peru ceded the coastal teritory of Tarapacá to Chile and agreed to the Chilean occupation of Tacna and Arica, after which, in 1929, the former was returned to Peru and the latter annexed by Chile. Not until 20 years later did Bolivia and Chile negotiate a mutually satisfactory settlement, in which the Chileans promised Bolivia free access to the ports of Antofagasta and Arica in exchange for Atacama.

Further reading: Salvatore Bizzarro, *Historical Dictionary of Chile* (Metuchen, N.J.: Scarecrow Press, 1972).

Andrássy Note

Memorandum written in late 1875 by Count Gyula Andrássy, Austro-Hungarian foreign minister, and sent to the signatories of the 1856 Treaty of PARIS. Andrássy wanted to prevent Russia from profiting from insurrections against Ottoman rule in the Balkans; he called for religious freedom in Herzegovina and Bosnia, local tax and revenue-use reforms, and joint Christian-Muslim supervision of reforms. The proposals were accepted by the major European powers and the Ottoman sultan, but were rejected by the insurgents in Bosnia and Herzegovina.

See also: BERLIN MEMORANDUM.

Further reading: L. S. Stavrianos, *The Balkans since 1453* (New York: Rinehart, 1958).

Andrusovo, Treaty of

Peace treaty between Czar Alexis of Russia and King John II Casimir of Poland, concluding the Russo-Polish War of 1658–67; signed on January 20, 1667, at the town of Andrusovo, Russia. Both parties agreed to a truce of 13 years, owing to their common fear of the Ottoman Turks, who had agreed to aid the Zaporozhye Cossacks (inhabitants of the Ukraine, unhappy with both Russian and Polish rule) and who had enlisted the Crimean Tartars to help in their conquest of the entire Ukraine. By the treaty, Poland ceded the Smolensk, Seversk, and Chernigov provinces to Russia, which also received the eastern Ukraine and Kiev (for two years, but Poland never recovered Kiev). Poland retained the western Ukraine and was given control over Belorussia. The district of Zaporozhye was to be under mutual Russo-Polish rule.

Further reading: Norman Davies, *God's Playground: A History of Poland,* 2 vols. (New York: Columbia University Press, 1982); Joseph L. Wieczynski, ed., *The Modern Encyclopedia of Russian and Soviet History,* 47 vols. (Gulf Breeze, Fla.: Academic International Press, 1976–88).

Anglo-Brazilian Treaty of 1826 See BRAZILIAN-BRITISH TREATY OF 1826.

Anglo-Chinese Treaty of 1984
Agreement concerning sovereignty over Hong Kong, signed by Britain's prime minister Margaret Thatcher and China's premier Zhao Ziyang in Beijing on December 19, 1984. Negotiated earlier in 1984 and approved by the British Parliament and Hong Kong's legislative council, the treaty stated that the British Crown colony of Hong Kong and other nearby lands would revert to China in 1997, when Britain's 99-year lease on the territory was to expire. China agreed to allow Hong Kong to keep her capitalist system for 50 years after the formal transfer to Chinese sovereignty in 1997. In addition, China agreed to keep Hong Kong as a free port and to preserve the present rights and freedoms of her citizens after 1997, when Hong Kong would become a special administrative zone of China.

Further reading: Douglas W. Lee, "Hong Kong 1982–1984: Irredentism in the Chinese Practice of International Law," *International Legal Perspectives* 2 (Fall 1987): 3–29; Yao-chi Chin, *The Hong Kong Talks and Hong Kong Politics* (Hong Kong: Hong Kong Institute of Asia-Pacific Studies, 1991).

Anglo-Chinese Treaty of 1928
British agreement with China on August 8, 1928, formally recognizing the new Chinese Nationalist government in Nanking (Nanjing). In return, Britain demanded, and was promised, compensation for the losses sustained by her nationals at Nanking during civil unrest. This was followed, on December 20, 1928, by the signing of a new tariff treaty to replace the existing tariff provisions. By this, China was granted complete national autonomy in tariffs (see NINE POWER PACTS), with the right to impose any tonnage duties she thought reasonable. The Nanking government agreed to use the tariff structure approved at the Tariff Conference of 1926 and to take steps to abolish "likin" (customs and coast-trade duties and other taxes on imported goods). Negotiated by Sir Miles Lampson and Dr. C. T. Wang, the treaty abolished the preferential tariffs and was similar to the agreements signed by other European powers and by the United States.

Further reading: Richard Stremski, *Britain's China Policy, 1920–1928* (Ann Arbor, Mich.: University Microfilms, 1968).

Anglo-Egyptian Sudan Treaty of 1953
Agreement between Egypt's new military government and Britain on February 12, 1953, ending the CONDOMINIUM AGREEMENTS OF 1899 and promising independence for Sudan after a three-year transition period. Meanwhile, an elected parliament (advised by two international commissions) would restrict the authority of the governor general of Sudan. Two other commissions would help the cabinet and the governor general's office. In November–December 1953, elections were held in Sudan and the new constituent assembly was asked, at the end of the transition period, to choose between total independence or some form of connection with Egypt. It opted for total independence. On January 1, 1956, the independent republic of Sudan was proclaimed.

Further reading: M. W. Daly, *Imperial Sudan: The Anglo-Egyptian Condominium, 1934–1956* (New York: Cambridge University Press, 1991).

Anglo-Egyptian Treaty of 1936
Treaty concluded between Great Britain and Egypt on August 26, 1936; declared Egypt a sovereign independent state, without actually terminating Britain's military occupation, even though Britain's protectorate had officially ended in 1922. The two countries pledged to maintain close ties, particularly in wartime, but Britain had to gradually evacuate her forces, stationing a maximum of 10,000 troops and 400 Royal Air Force pilots in the Suez Canal area until Egypt could protect it herself. Britain's lease over the Alexandria naval base was extended for eight years, while the 20-year military alliance allowed her to impose censorship and martial law during emergency. The British high commissioner's post was upgraded to ambassadorial rank. Britain's support gained Egypt entry (May 1937) into the League of Nations and participation at the Montreaux Convention, which abolished the Western powers' capitulatory rights in Egypt. The treaty ended the mixed courts, making foreigners subject to Egyptian law. Egypt abrogated the treaty in 1951.

Further reading: Margaret George, *The Warped Vision: British Foreign Policy, 1933–39* (Pittsburgh, Pa.: University of Pittsburgh Press, 1965).

Anglo-French Agreement on Oil in the Near and Middle East
Memorandum signed by representatives of the governments of Great Britain and France on April 24, 1920, agreeing to cooperate "in those countries where the oil interests of the two nations can be usefully united." Of special importance was joint participation in the exploitation of Mesopotamian oil fields and in the transportation (by pipelines and railways) of oil from Mesopotamia (Iraq) and Persia (Iran) to ports on the eastern Mediterranean. France allowed the British to use facilities at these ports for oil exportation, exempting them from certain fees and duties. The French government allowed Franco-British groups (complying with French laws) to acquire oil in French-held areas of North Africa, while the British government granted similar advantages to the French in its crown colonies.

See also: U.S. POLICY ON "OPEN DOOR" FOR OIL IN THE NEAR AND MIDDLE EAST.

Further reading: Marian Kent, *Oil and Empire: British Policy and Mesopotamian Oil, 1900–1920* (London: Macmillan, 1976).

Anglo-French Channel Agreement   Agreement announced on February 6, 1964, between the British and French governments for the construction of a railroad tunnel under the English Channel. The 31-mile tunnel—23 miles under the sea—would connect Sangatté (near Calais) in France with Westenhanger (near Folkestone) in England. The agreement did not indicate when construction would commence, only that it would take five to six years to complete and cost approximately $400 million. The first digging on site began in late 1987 (giant American-built boring machines in England and France drilling toward each other); British and French workers finally linked up and shook hands on December 1, 1990. The $15 billion channel tunnel (or "chunnel") made it possible to travel from Paris to London by high-speed train in three hours when it opened in May 1994.

Further reading: Drew Fetherston, *The Chunnel: The Amazing Story of the Undersea Crossing of the English Channel* (New York: Times Books, 1997).

Anglo-French Entente   See ENTENTE CORDIALE.

Anglo-French-Russian Agreement about Asiatic Turkey (Sykes-Picot Agreement)   Agreement of May 16, 1916, between Great Britain and France, which, with Russia's approval, outlined the terms of the partition of Asia Minor and the Arab territories of the Ottoman Empire. Negotiated by Sir Mark Sykes (British member of Parliament) and George Picot (French diplomat) in an effort to reconcile conflicting French and Arab interests in the region, it allotted Mesopotamia and the ports of Haifa and Acre to Britain, Syria to France, and Armenia and Kurdistan to Russia. The Arabs received the small region sandwiched between the French and British territories, over which the two countries were to retain control. Britain received permission for her proposed railway line from Haifa to Baghdad and the use of it to transport troops, if necessary. Syria's subsequent protests over French control created an embarrassing controversy in which Britain and France were to be embroiled for many years.

See also: MUDROS, ARMISTICE OF; SÈVRES, TREATY OF.

Further reading: Efraim Karsh and Inari Karsh, *Empires of the Sand: The Struggle for Mastery in the Middle East, 1789–1923* (Cambridge, Mass.: Harvard University Press, 1999); Rashid Khalidi, *British Policy towards Syria and Palestine, 1906–1914: A Study of the Antecedents of the Hussein-McMahon Correspondence, the Sykes-Picot Agreement, and the Balfour Declaration* (London: Ithaca Press, 1980).

Anglo-German Agreement of 1898   Defensive alliance concluded on August 30, 1898, whereby Britain and Germany agreed to collaborate on a loan to Portugal. Britain was inter- ested in securing the lease or cession of Delagoa Bay (key route to the Transvaal), and Germany threatened to negotiate with France if she was excluded from the deal. The secret clauses provided that if Portugal defaulted on payment, Germany would receive the northern half of Mozambique and part of Angola whereas Britain would get the southern section of Mozambique and the rest of Angola. Regarding the deal as blackmail, Britain was keen on maintaining it on "paper" only, whereas Germany expected to reap the dividends immediately. Learning of the secret clauses, Portugal refused the loan and, in 1899, forced Britain to sign an agreement reaffirming the integrity of her African colonies.

Further reading: Kenneth Bourne, *The Foreign Policy of Victorian England, 1830–1902* (Oxford, England: Clarendon Press, 1970); A. W. Ward et al., eds., *The Cambridge History of British Foreign Policy, 1783–1919* (New York: Octagon Books, 1970).

Anglo-German Naval Agreement of 1935   Pact concluded between Great Britain and Germany on June 18, 1935, altering the naval provisions of the 1919 Treaty of VERSAILLES and establishing a "permanent relationship" between the British and German navies. Germany's total fleet tonnage was restricted so as not to exceed 35 percent of the aggregate tonnage of the fleet of the British Commonwealth; her submarine strength, however, was permitted to equal that of the Commonwealth. Adolf Hitler's intention in negotiating this agreement was to win Britain's confidence and vitiate the Anglo-French alliance. France remained unconvinced of Hitler's sincerity and was proved correct when Hitler denounced the agreement on April 28, 1939.

Further reading: Charles L. Phillips and Alan Axelrod, eds., *Encyclopedia of Historical Treaties and Alliances*, 2 vols. (New York: Facts On File, 2001).

Anglo-German Treaty of 1899 (Samoan Treaty)   Agreement of November 14, 1899, as to the disposition of Samoa, which was partitioned between Germany and the United States, with Great Britain receiving compensation elsewhere. Claims of the three countries to the strategically located South Pacific islands, which were important coaling stations, had been disputed for 20 years, since all three had negotiated treaty rights there in 1878–79. A three-way protectorate since 1888 had resulted in strained relations among the three powers during the previous decade. In November 1899, faced with the Boer War in South Africa and hoping to improve Anglo-German relations, Britain agreed to relinquish her portion of Samoa in return for the Tonga Islands, the Savage Islands, lesser islands of the Solomon archipelago, and a slice of Togoland. Germany received the two larger Samoan islands, Upolu and Savaii. The United States acquired the remainder of the Samoan group, including Tutuila, with the harbor of Pago Pago.

Further reading: Kenneth Bourne, *The Foreign Policy of Victorian England, 1830–1902* (Oxford, England: Clarendon Press, 1970); A. W. Ward et al., eds., *The Cambridge History of British Foreign Policy, 1783–1919* (New York: Octagon Books, 1970).

Anglo-Iraqi Treaty of 1930

Treaty made on June 30, 1930, acknowledging Iraq's independence, thus ending Britain's mandate but assuring her of a preferential status in Iraq. Ratified by the Iraqi Parliament on November 16, 1930, the 25-year treaty came into effect with Iraq's entry (which Britain had promised to sponsor) into the League of Nations on October 3, 1932. The two countries were to maintain a "close alliance" with "full and frank consultation" on foreign policy issues and assurances of mutual aid in wartime. Iraq leased Britain two airbase sites and granted British troops access to all Iraqi facilities during war. In return, Britain agreed to provide the Iraqi forces with military aid, training, and equipment. Iraq agreed to recruit only British experts, when foreign assistance was required. The British high commissioner (for Iraq) would be replaced by an ambassador with precedence over all other diplomatic agents. The treaty met with a mixed response in Iraq but proved crucial for Britain in the Middle East campaigns of World War II (1939–45).

Further reading: Reeva S. Simon, Philip Mattar, and Richard W. Bulliet, eds., *Encyclopedia of the Modern Middle East* (New York: Simon & Schuster, 1996).

Anglo-Irish Accord of 1985 (Hillsborough Agreement)

Agreement signed by the prime ministers of Britain and Ireland, Margaret Thatcher and Garret FitzGerald, respectively, at Hillsborough Castle, County Down, Northern Ireland, on November 15, 1985. Ireland was given a formal consultative role in the governing of Northern Ireland (a British province) in exchange for, in effect, recognizing Northern Ireland's union with Britain. British and Irish cabinet ministers would work together on matters affecting Northern Ireland and border cooperation between the two Irelands. The Irish Dail (legislature) and British House of Commons both approved the agreement, which aimed to reconcile Northern Ireland's Roman Catholic and Protestant communities at the expense of the Irish Republican Army (IRA, seeking the complete integration of Ireland, north and south). Protestant loyalists denounced the accord as a first step toward integration, and sullen resistance and some violence occurred.

Further reading: *Anglo-Irish Agreement 1985* (Dublin: Stationery Office, 1985); *Hillsborough: The Balance Sheet, 1985–88: A Failure* (Dublin: Sinn Fein Publicity Department, 1989); Anthony J. P. Kenny, *The Road to Hillsborough: The Shaping of the Anglo-Irish Agreement* (New York: Pergamon Press, 1986).

Anglo-Irish Treaty of 1921

Pact concluded on December 6, 1921, resulting in the birth of the Irish Free State. The agreement, between the British government of Prime Minister David Lloyd George and Irish representatives granted Ireland equal constitutional status within the British Empire, on a par with Canada, Australia, New Zealand, and South Africa. Ireland's executive was answerable to Parliament, which was invested with the authority "to make laws for the peace, order, and good government of Ireland." It covered only 26 of the 32 counties, the six Ulster counties (Northern Ireland) retaining their separation (see GOVERNMENT OF IRELAND ACT). The Dail Eireann (Irish Assembly) ratified the treaty in January 1922, but it was rejected by the Irish Republicans, whose leader, Eamon De Valera, resigned in protest. Ireland's new provisional government reached an understanding with De Valera but it was not enough to avert defeat for the Republicans in the June elections. This led to civil war. The Dail met in September to draft and approve its new constitution, which was duly ratified by the British Parliament.

Further reading: Frank Gallagher, *The Anglo-Irish Treaty*, ed. Thomas P. O'Neill (London: Hutchinson, 1965).

Anglo-Italian Agreement of 1925 (Milner-Scialoja Agreement, Egyptian-Italian Treaty)

Treaty of December 6, 1925, redefining Egypt's western frontiers with Libya, based on an exchange of notes (April 10–13, 1920) between Italian foreign minister Vittorio Scialoja and British colonial secretary Viscount Alfred Milner. Britain formally withdrew from the negotiations after her protectorate over Egypt ended in 1922, leaving Italy (whose Fascist regime had conquered Libya) and Egypt to continue the dialogue. Accordingly, Libya obtained the oasis of Jaghbub while Egypt retained al-Sallum; a mixed commission was appointed to consider the administrative details involved in the demarcation of the new frontier. Italy declared that she would not press for the extradition of Libyans who had sought political asylum in Egypt. Formal ratifications were exchanged in Rome on April 25, 1933.

Further reading: Martin Clark, *Modern Italy, 1871–1982* (New York: Longman, 1984); Frank J. Coppa, ed., *Dictionary of Modern Italian History* (Westport, Conn.: Greenwood Press, 1985).

Anglo-Italian Agreements of 1891

Two agreements between the British and Italian governments (March 24 and April 15, 1891) regarding the demarcation of their respective colonies surrounding the Red Sea. The agreements became necessary when Italy's expansion plans (northward along the Red Sea and westward toward the Nile River) became known. Anxious to protect the Nile and its tributaries from other European countries, Britain agreed to make some concessions to Italy. It acknowledged Italy's authority over all of Ethiopia, to within 100 miles of the Nile. Italy promised to leave the question of the Atbara River water supply entirely to Britain. On March 24, 1891, both countries accepted the Juba River as the border between British East Africa and Italian Somaliland.

Further reading: Martin Clark, *Modern Italy, 1871–1982* (New York: Longman, 1984); Frank J. Coppa, ed., *Dictionary of Modern Italian History* (Westport, Conn.: Greenwood Press, 1985).

Anglo-Italian Agreements of 1937 and 1938

Between Great Britain and Italy, two agreements defining their respective roles in the Mediterranean and the Near East. The first (January 2, 1937), popularly known as the "Gentleman's Agreement," was merely a promise to guarantee the independence of Spain and to respect each other's interests in the region. Its violation led to the NYON AGREEMENT. The second (April 16, 1938), a sequel to the Nyon Agreement, contained specific proposals for ending the hostilities between them. Britain acknowledged Italy's supremacy over Ethiopia and agreed to support her claim at the League of Nations Council. Italy was to remove her "volunteers" (troops) from Spain at the end of the Spanish Civil War of 1936–39 and stop her hostile anti-British propaganda in the eastern Mediterranean. They agreed to maintain the status quo in the Red Sea. The agreement, implemented November 16, 1938, was perhaps precipitated by the Nazi German occupation of Austria in mid-March, by Britain's desire to break up the Adolf Hitler–Benito Mussolini friendship, and by Mussolini's search for a powerful ally to counteract Hitler's influence.

Further reading: Martin Clark, *Modern Italy, 1871–1982* (New York: Longman, 1984); Frank J. Coppa, ed., *Dictionary of Modern Italian History* (Westport, Conn.: Greenwood Press, 1985).

Anglo-Japanese Commercial Treaty of 1894

See AOKI-KIMBERLEY TREATY.

Anglo-Japanese Treaty of 1902

Defensive military alliance between Britain and Japan, signed in London on January 30, 1902; the basis of their policies in the Far East until after the World War I (1914–18). Valid for five years, it provided for the protection of their respective interests in China and Korea, while reaffirming the independence of both those countries. If either party became involved in a war with a third party, the ally was to maintain a neutral position, but, if a fourth power joined the war, the allies agreed to combine forces to repel the attack. Neither party could enter into a separate agreement with another power (mainly Russia) without the other's consent. Published on February 11, the alliance was renewed in 1905 and in 1911 (this time for 10 years) before being abandoned in favor of the Four-Power Treaty, which became operative in 1923, with France and the United States of America.

Further reading: *Anglo-Japanese Treaties* (Washington, D.C.: U.S. Government Printing Office, 1922); Ainslie T. Embree, ed., *Encyclopedia of Asian History*, 4 vols. (New York: Charles Scribner's Sons, 1988); *Japan: An Illustrated Encyclopedia*. 2 vols. (New York: Kodansha, 1993); Ian H. Nish,

The Anglo-Japanese Alliance: The Diplomacy of Two Island Empires, 1894–1907 (Westport, Conn.: Greenwood Press, 1966, repr., 1976).

Anglo-Persian Agreement of 1919

Postwar agreement made on August 9, 1919, at Tehran, whereby Britain recognized Persia's (Iran's) independence and promised to help her in rebuilding the Persian economy. The Persian administrative and military systems would be reorganized and modernized with the help of British experts and equipment. The British government would also procure the substantial funds necessary for these reforms (the initial loan was £2 million, payable at 7 percent over 20 years). Joint enterprises were to be encouraged to improve trade, communications, and the famine situation in Persia. The two countries agreed to redraft the existing customs tariff in Persia's favor and to review and revise previous treaties between them. Britain promised to support Persia's claims for damages sustained in World War I and for any warranted border rectifications. George N. Curzon, British viceroy in India, directed the negotiations, which were conducted primarily by Sir Percy Cox and Vusuq al-Dawlah.

Further reading: Reeva S. Simon, Philip Mattar, and Richard W. Bulliet, eds., *Encyclopedia of the Modern Middle East* (New York: Simon & Schuster, 1996).

Anglo-Persian Agreement of 1933

Agreement concluded with Persia (Iran) on May 28, 1933, by the Anglo-Persian Oil Company, making more equitable Persia's financial compensation for the company's exploitation of oil in Persia. The agreement, which was to be valid for 60 years, stipulated that the company pay Persia a variety of fixed sums for every ton of oil sold or exported up to and over a certain number of tons, which sums were to be increased after 15 years. The agreement permitted the company to extract oil from 250,000 square miles of land, or about half as much as had previously been allocated to it, and after 1938 permitted it to use only 100,000 square miles. The agreement also stipulated that the company gradually bring Persians into its workforce. The agreement represented a significant improvement over an earlier Anglo-Persian Agreement (of 1901), by which the Persian government had granted William K. d'Arcy a 60-year oil-drilling concession (which had been assumed by the Anglo-Persian Oil Company in 1909).

Further reading: Margaret George, *The Warped Vision: British Foreign Policy, 1933–39* (Pittsburgh, Pa.: University of Pittsburgh Press, 1965).

Anglo-Russian Convention of 1755

Defense subsidy treaty made between Great Britain and Russia (under the influence of Austria) on September 19, 1755. Russia agreed to maintain on her western borders an armed force of 55,000 troops. In exchange for this Russian "threat" to Prussia and France (by which Britain hoped to discourage any aggression against her ally of Hanover), Britain agreed to provide Russia with an annual subsidy payment of £100,000. Further, Russia also agreed, for an additional subsidy payment, to go to war on Britain's behalf if she was attacked. Relations deteriorated in January 1756, when the British concluded the Treaty of WESTMINSTER with Prussia.

Further reading: Walter L. Dorn, *Competition for Empire, 1740–1763* (New York: Harper & Brothers, 1940).

Anglo-Russian Entente of 1907
Convention between the two inveterate adversaries (Britain and Russia), signed on August 31, 1907. The agreement, made possible largely because of Russia's willingness to compromise following her defeat by Japan in 1905, was a major step toward the evolution of the Triple Entente (Britain, France, and Russia) in the years preceding World War I. Because Anglo-Russian rivalry in the Far East had been virtually eliminated by the Russo-Japanese War of 1904–5, the agreement focused on disputed areas in the Near East. Persia (Iran) was divided into three spheres: the northern one, adjacent to the Caucasus, was given to Russia; the southeastern section, bordering India, was to be the British sphere; and the central sphere, including the Persian Gulf, was to remain neutral. The Russians relinquished Afghanistan as a sphere of influence, promising that any future contact with it would be through British channels. In return, Britain pledged to maintain the status quo in Afghanistan. Tibet was recognized as belonging to China.

See also: ENTENTE CORDIALE.

Further reading: Rogers Platt Churchill, *The Anglo-Russian Convention of 1907* (Freeport, N.Y.: Books for Libraries, 1939, repr., 1972); John Arthur Marriott, *Anglo-Russian Relations, 1689–1953*, 2d ed. (London: Methuen, 1944); Reeva S. Simon, Philip Mattar, and Richard W. Bulliet, eds., *Encyclopedia of the Modern Middle East* (New York: Simon & Schuster, 1996).

Anglo-Soviet Agreement of 1941
Anglo-Soviet pact signed in Moscow on July 12, 1941, following Germany's attack on the Soviet Union. The Soviet Union immediately accepted British prime minister Winston Churchill's offer of technical and economic aid to "any man or State who fights against Nazism." This led to the conclusion of a mutual-aid agreement, whereby the two governments promised each other support and all kinds of assistance during the war against Hitler's Nazi Germany (World War II [1939–45]). They also agreed not to "negotiate nor conclude an armistice or treaty of peace except by mutual agreement." In another agreement, on August 16, 1941, Britain advanced £10 million worth of arms and other war materials to the Soviet Union on credit. On May 26, 1942, the mutual-aid pact was converted into a 20-year treaty.

Further reading: J. C. Hurewitz, *The Middle East and North Africa in World Politics: A Documentary Record*, 2 vols., 2d ed. (New Haven, Conn.: Yale University Press, 1975–79);

Reeva S. Simon, Philip Mattar, and Richard W. Bulliet, eds. *Encyclopedia of the Modern Middle East* (New York: Simon & Schuster, 1996).

Angostura, Congress of
Congress called at Angostura (Ciudad Bolívar, Venezuela) on February 15, 1819, by Simón Bolívar for the purpose of establishing a constitutional regime. At the congress a constitution was adopted and Bolívar was elected commander in chief of the patriot army and proclaimed president of the republic of Venezuela. He then left on his expedition to wrest New Granada from the Spaniards (with the goal of uniting New Granada and Venezuela into a single independent state). In December of 1819, when the Congress of Angostura created the republic of Colombia (to be comprised of Venezuela, New Granada, and Quito, Ecuador, after these territories had been liberated from Spanish rule), Bolívar was elected president of the new republic, often referred to as Gran Colombia (Great Colombia).

See also: BOLÍVAR'S ADDRESS AT ANGOSTURA.

Further reading: Donna K. Rudolph and G. A. Rudolph, *Historical Dictionary of Venezuela* (Metuchen, N.J.: Scarecrow Press, 1971).

Ankara, Pact of
Tripartite agreement concluded on October 19, 1939, among Britain, France, and Turkey, pledging "mutual assistance in resistance to aggression should the necessity arise." Turkey, however, was exempted from entering into any conflict with the Soviet Union. Valid for a 15-year period, its terms were considered equally binding as bilateral commitments between Turkey and each of the two powers. Britain and France jointly agreed to loan Turkey £25 million to purchase military supplies from them and £18.5 million to release their frozen balances with her. The agreement provided for repayment of both loans, at 4 percent and 3 percent, respectively, over a 20-year period. Precipitated by Italy's invasion of Albania (April 1939), the treaty's military clauses were complex; they provided for a coordination of efforts in maintaining the status quo in the region and for an exchange of all vital information in this regard.

Further reading: Reeva S. Simon, Philip Mattar, and Richard W. Bulliet, eds., *Encyclopedia of the Modern Middle East*, 4 vols. (New York: Macmillan, 1996).

Ankara, Treaty of (Franklin-Bouillon Agreement)
Treaty concluded in Ankara, Turkey, on October 20, 1921, by French diplomat Henry Franklin-Bouillon and Foreign Minister Yusuf Kemal Bey of the Turkish nationalist (Ankara) government (to be distinguished from the sultan's government at Constantinople), bringing an end to the hostilities between France and Turkey, which were part of the more general hostilities between the Turkish nationalists and the Allies (see SÈVRES, TREATY OF). The treaty provided for the withdrawal of France's forces from southeastern Anatolia (Cilicia); for France's recognition of the nationalists' government

at Ankara; for Turkey's possession of the Baghdad railway, from the Jaihan River to Rasul-Ain in Mesopotamia (Iraq); for the establishment of Turkey's border with Syria, a country in which France had special interests. The treaty had the effect of freeing nationalist forces to fight the allies on other fronts; and of establishing France as a major influence in Turkey independent of Great Britain, which had been the dominant Western influence there since the 19th century.

Further reading: George Lenczowski, *The Middle East in World Affairs* (Ithaca, N.Y.: Cornell University Press, 1982); Reeva S. Simon, Philip Mattar and Richard W. Bulliet, eds., *Encyclopedia of the Modern Middle East* (New York: Simon & Schuster, 1996).

Annapolis Convention, Report of the

Convention on interstate commerce held at Annapolis, Maryland, in September 1786, and attended by 12 commissioners from New York, New Jersey, Pennsylvania, Delaware, and Virginia. Dissatisfaction with the ARTICLES OF CONFEDERATION and financial difficulties had led Virginia to call for the convention, but the scanty attendance precluded solutions to the problems. Instead, the convention report, drafted by Alexander Hamilton, called for a new convention (the Constitutional Convention), to be held at Philadelphia in May 1787, to discuss not just problems of interstate commerce but all matters "necessary to render the constitution of the Federal Government adequate to the exigencies of the Union."

See also: U.S. CONSTITUTION.

Further reading: Andrew Cunningham McLaughlin, *The Confederation and the Constitution, 1783–1789* (New York: Collier Books, 1905, repr., 1962); Gordon S. Wood, comp., *The Confederation and the Constitution: The Critical Issues* (Boston, Mass.: Little, Brown, 1973).

Annates' Statutes

Two English laws by which the king, Henry VIII, secured for himself control over the payment of annates (first year's revenue of an ecclesiastical benefice) from the Church of England to the Church of Rome. By the statute of 1532, Henry reserved the right to cancel the annates paid by all newly installed bishops to the pope. The statute of 1534 was more drastic. Thereby, Henry broke off the Church of England's financial arrangement with the Church in Rome by channeling all annates' payments into the royal treasury. The first statute (mainly a pressure tactic) was intended to intimidate Rome into issuing a favorable verdict regarding Henry's divorce from Catherine of Aragon and marriage to Anne Boleyn. The second statute was enacted when the pope, Clement VII, failed to oblige; it hastened the final break with Rome by England.

Further reading: G. R. Elton, *Reform and Reformation: England, 1509–1558* (Cambridge, Mass.: Harvard University Press, 1977); Jasper Ridley, *Henry VIII: The Politics of Tyranny* (New York: Viking Penguin, 1985).

Annexation Manifesto, Canadian

Manifesto signed by 325 prominent, English-speaking Montreal businessmen and politicians and printed in the Montreal *Gazette* on October 11, 1849, containing the signatories' arguments in support of Canada's annexation to the United States. The document's authors denounced Great Britain's abandonment of a system of trade that had provided the British North American colonies with trade advantages; they blamed Great Britain for the Canadian provinces' subsequent economic hardship and argued that the situation would be greatly improved through annexation to the United States, as Canada would thereby gain access not only to the world's largest market but also to increased trade with foreign countries. This call for annexation was short-lived, finding little support, for most Canadians disliked the political consequences of the manifesto (government in the hands of the French Canadians was preferable by many).

Further reading: Samuel E. Moffett, *The Americanization of Canada* (Toronto: University of Toronto Press, 1972); Donald F. Warner, *The Idea of Continental Union; Agitation for the Annexation of Canada to the United States, 1849–1893* (Lexington: University of Kentucky Press, 1960).

Antarctic Treaty of 1959

Treaty signed in Washington, D.C., on December 1, 1959, by representatives of Argentina, Australia, Belgium, Chile, France, Japan, New Zealand, Norway, South Africa, the Soviet Union, the United Kingdom, and the United States, establishing their agreement to maintain the Antarctic as a demilitarized territory. The 14-article document provided that the Antarctic was to be used for peaceful purposes only; that military activities there would be prohibited; that scientific investigation would be permitted to all; that scientific personnel and any discoveries of a scientific nature were to be exchanged; and that nuclear explosions and the disposal of nuclear waste would be prohibited. Other countries eventually became signatories of the treaty, which also provided inspection rights to assure that its terms were not violated.

Further reading: *Antarctic Treaty Between the United States of America and Other Governments, Signed at Washington, December 1, 1959* (Washington, D.C.: U.S. Government Printing Office, 1961); Richard Dean Burns, ed., *Encyclopedia of Arms Control and Disarmament*, 3 vols. (New York: Charles Scribner's Sons, 1993); Gillian D. Triggs, ed., *The Antarctic Treaty Regime: Law, Environment and Resources* (New York: Cambridge University Press, 1987).

Anti-Ballistic Missile Treaty (ABM Treaty)

One of two arms limitation agreements (see STRATEGIC ARMS LIMITATION TREATY OF 1972) signed in Moscow on May 26, 1972, by Soviet general secretary Leonid I. Brezhnev and the United States president Richard M. Nixon. It restricted each country to two antiballistic missile (ABM) systems (one focused on the enemy's capital, the other on its offensive missile force) and no more than 100 ABM interceptor missiles and launchers at any site. The radar complexes at each site would be reduced, too. The treaty, however, allowed the "modernization and replacement of ABM systems and their components" and also the technical verification of violations, the process of which each party agreed not to interfere with or deliberately impede. A standing consultative commission was established to discuss ongoing issues pertinent to the treaty. Valid for an "unlimited duration," the treaty was subject to review every five years. On December 13, 2001, President George W. Bush announced the unilateral withdrawal of the United States from the ABM Treaty (which would take effect in six months).

See also: INTERMEDIATE NUCLEAR FORCES TREATY; NUCLEAR NON-PROLIFERATION TREATY OF 1968; STRATEGIC ARMS LIMITATION TREATY OF 1979.

Further reading: Richard Dean Burns, ed., *Encyclopedia of Arms Control and Disarmament,* 3 vols. (New York: Charles Scribner's Sons, 1993); Antonia Handler Chayes and Paul Doty, eds., *Defending Deterrence: Managing the ABM Treaty Regime into the 21st Century* (Washington, D.C.: Pergamon-Brassey's International Defense Publishers, 1989); Ernest J. Yanarella, *The Missile Defense Controversy* (Lexington: University Press of Kentucky, 1977).

Anti-Comintern Pact (German-Japanese Pact of 1936)

Pact signed on November 25, 1936, by Foreign Minister Joachim von Ribbentrop of Germany and Foreign Minister Shiratori Toshio of Japan, ostensibly formalizing the two powers' opposition to the spread of communism and the Communist International, but in reality establishing a third arm to the Rome-Berlin Axis (see GERMAN-ITALIAN PACT OF 1936). The document contained the two powers' agreement to work together against communism and their secret pledge to mutually assist one another both economically and diplomatically in the event that either party were at war with the Soviet Union. Italy became a signatory to the pact on November 6, 1937.

See also: AXIS POWERS, PACT OF THE; STEEL, PACT OF.

Further reading: *Japan: An Illustrated Encyclopedia,* 2 vols. (New York: Kodansha, 1993); Charles L. Phillips and Alan Axelrod, eds., *Encyclopedia of Historical Treaties and Alliances,* 2 vols. (New York: Facts On File, 2001).

Antigua, Treaty of

Treaty signed on April 30, 1968, establishing the Caribbean Free Trade Association (CARIFTA) among Antigua, Barbados, Guyana, and Trinidad and Tobago. Jamaica joined on June 27, and other Caribbean countries followed. Customs duties on most goods traded between members were immediately withdrawn. Some goods were transferred to a reserve list; duties on these were gradually eliminated over five years (in the more developed countries) and 10 years (in the less developed Caribbean states). Since the bulk (94 percent) of the trade of the British Common-

wealth's Caribbean states was conducted outside the region, CARIFTA's role in the regional economy was considerably limited. It was superseded in 1973 by the Caribbean Community and Common Market, established then by the Treaty of Chaguaramas.

See also: CARIBBEAN COMMUNITY AND COMMON MARKET AGREEMENT; LOMÉ CONVENTION.

Further reading: Cambridge University Press eds., *Cambridge Encyclopedia of Latin America and the Caribbean* (Cambridge, England: Cambridge University Press, 1985); Claudio Véliz, *Latin America and the Caribbean* (New York: Praeger, 1968).

Anti-Socialist Law, German

Repressive measure directed against organizations and activities of Germany's Social Democratic Workers' Party, approved by the Reichstag on October 19, 1878. German chancellor Otto von Bismarck, who greatly feared socialism, used two failed assassination attempts against Emperor William I as a pretext for the anti-socialist legislation, although neither assassin was a socialist. The law prohibited all social democratic, socialist, and communist associations, meetings, or publications. In certain districts, the government was empowered to abrogate the freedom of speech and assembly, and to expel socialist agitators. These repressive measures resulted in a temporary reduction in the Social Democratic representation in the Reichstag; but by 1884, the Social Democratic vote was larger than it had been before the law was passed.

Further reading: Erich Eyck, *Bismarck and the German Empire* (New York: W. W. Norton, 1968).

Anti-Terrorism Act, Canadian

Legislation (Bill C-36) introduced in the Canadian House of Commons on October 15, 2001, in response to the terrorist attacks of September 11, 2001, on the United States. In addition to safeguarding the lives and property of Canadians, the bill's purpose was to prevent Canada from being used as a base for further attacks on the United States. Modeled after the USA-PATRIOT ACT, the bill amended several existing laws to make it easier for government officials to identify and shut down terrorist organizations operating in Canada. It toughened the penalties for committing acts of terrorism and increased the number of federal court judgeships to expedite the prosecution of suspected terrorists. It gave the Canadian government the power to seize the assets of terrorist groups, to refrain from disclosing evidence in criminal proceedings that might "be injurious to international relations or national defense or security," to use electronic surveillance against terrorist organizations, and to detain suspected terrorists indefinitely. The bill included provisions for removing hate propaganda from Internet sites and created a new crime: "mischief motivated by bias, prejudice or hate." The original bill was attacked by civil liberties advocates on the grounds that it infringed on the rights of nonterrorists; despite being amended on November 20, 2001, to correct such abuses, debate over the bill continued for several months.

Further reading: Department of Justice, Canada, "Highlights of Anti-Terrorism Act." available online at http://canada.justice.gc.ca/en/news/nr/2001/doc_27787.html.

Anti-War Pact, Argentine   Treaty sponsored by Argentine president Carlos Saavedra Lamas and concluded in Rio de Janeiro on October 10, 1933, by the governments of Argentina, Brazil, Chile, Mexico, Paraguay, and Uruguay, condemning war and requiring its signatories to abide by terms designed to prevent war. Most significant, the document required that any signatory power involved in an international dispute must submit that dispute to arbitration and conciliation commissions, the establishment of which was also stipulated by the treaty; it also required signatories to recognize only those territorial settlements reached through pacific means and obliged signatories to use any and all means permissible under international law against any state involved in violent conflict.

See also: GONDRA TREATY.

Further reading: J. Fred Rippy, Percy A. Martin, and Isaac J. Cox, *Argentina, Brazil and Chile since Independence* (New York: Russell & Russell, 1963).

Antoninian Constitution   See CARACALLA, EDICT OF.

Antwerp, Truce of   See TWELVE YEARS' TRUCE.

Anzac Pact (Canberra Pact)   Bilateral treaty concluded in Canberra, Australia, on January 21, 1944, wherein Australia and New Zealand ("Anzac," for Australian and New Zealand Army Corps) resolved to cooperate and work together in addressing matters of mutual concern, such as security, defense, civil aviation, postwar settlements, and the welfare of the Pacific nations. They declared their right to be actively associated with postwar peace treaties and with the planning of the proposed international peace and security organization. Within this framework, they proposed a regional zone of defense in the Southwest Pacific and South Pacific areas, for which they would share the responsibility of policing. They supported the formation of a South Seas Regional Commission to promote the development of the Pacific countries and urged the convening of an international conference to discuss regional issues. A permanent secretariat would be set up to implement and coordinate their bilateral schemes.

Further reading: *The Anzac Pact* (New York: 1950).

ANZUS Pact   Mutual security treaty signed in San Francisco on September 1, 1951, among Australia, New Zealand, and the United States "for the preservation of peace and security" in the Pacific region. Reaffirming their commitment to the UNITED NATIONS CHARTER, the three nations (ANZUS as an acronym) agreed to consult and help each other if their "territorial integrity, political independence or security" was threatened in the Pacific. An ANZUS council (consisting of the foreign ministers or their deputies) would be established to facilitate implementation of the treaty and coordinate efforts with other regional authorities in contributing to the security of the region. Ratified by the Australian Parliament in 1952, it was held to be indefinitely valid; ANZUS was headquartered in the Australian capital of Canberra.

Further reading: Alan Burnett, Thomas Durell-Young, and Christine Wilson, eds. *The ANZUS Documents* (Canberra, Australia: Department of International Relations, Research School of Pacific Studies, Australian National University, 1991); Charles L. Phillips and Alan Axelrod, eds., *Encyclopedia of Historical Treaties and Alliances,* 2 vols. (New York: Facts On File, 2001); J. G. Starke, *The Anzus Treaty Alliance* (New York: Cambridge University Press, 1965).

Aoki-Kimberley Treaty (Anglo-Japanese Commercial Treaty of 1894)   On July 16, 1894, in London, by Aoki Shuzo (Japan's ambassador to Great Britain) and John W. Kimberley (British foreign secretary); agreement that greatly enhanced Japan's emergent international position. Operative July 17, 1899, the treaty ended Britain's extraterritorial rights, while partially restoring Japan's tariff autonomy, which had been denied in the previous commercial treaty of 1858. After August 4, 1899, all westerners were to be subject to Japanese courts. Following Britain's lead, other Western powers soon signed similar treaties with Japan. A new treaty in 1911 gave Japan full control over her tariffs.

Further reading: Ainslie T. Embree, ed., *Encyclopedia of Asian History,* 4 vols. (New York: Charles Scribner's Sons, 1988); *Japan: An Illustrated Encyclopedia* 2 vols. (New York: Kodansha, 1993).

Apatzingán, Constitution of   Provisional constitution issued on October 22, 1814, by the Mexican Congress of Chilpancingo at its headquarters in Apatzingán, Michoacán. Consisting of 242 articles, the constitution established a republican form of government with three separate branches (executive, legislative, and judicial). The congress was to oversee the government and choose the three members of the plural executive and the five members of the judicial branch's review tribunal. Also mandated was the abolition of slavery and the equality of all citizens before the law. Although the constitution never become operative (the independence movement was crushed and its leader executed), it was important in raising the morale of the insurgents by giving their cause dignity and legality.

Further reading: Donald C. Briggs and Narvin Alisky, *Historical Dictionary of Mexico* (Metuchen, N.J.: Scarecrow Press, 1981).

Apostles' Creed (Apostolicum)   Traditional confession of faith, widely accepted in the Christian Church, dating back in its present form to about A.D. 600. Each of the creed's 12 clauses was originally ascribed to Jesus Christ's 12 apostles, but actually they were formulated in the Roman Church about A.D. 200. The Roman baptismal confession expanded into what is now the Apostles' Creed, originally written in Latin. Its familiar opening words are "I believe in God the Father Almighty, creator of heaven and earth; and in Jesus Christ, his only son, our Lord. . . ." Roman Catholics and many Protestants regularly use the creed, but it is not formally accepted by the Eastern Orthodox Church.

Further reading: Inos Biffi, *The Apostles' Creed* (Grand Rapids, Mich.: W. B. Eerdmans, 1994); H. Ray Dunning, *A Layman's Guide to the Apostles' Creed* (Kansas City, Mo.: Beacon Hill Press of Kansas City, 1995).

Apostolicae Curae Papal bull issued by Pope Leo XIII on September 13, 1896, reconfirming the Roman Catholic Church's position that Anglican orders were invalid. In the document, the pope reminded his readers of the authority of past decisions regarding the question of the ordination of Anglican priests, beginning in the 16th century during the reign of England's queen Mary and continuing down to the present day. He further argued that Anglican ordination was theologically invalid due to its failure to signify outwardly, in its ritualistic forms, what it was meant to effect inwardly. The decision was a disappointment for those who had hoped for a gradual reconciliation of differences between the Roman Catholic and Anglican Churches.

Further reading: Friedrich Nippold, *The Papacy in the XIXth Century* (New York: Putnam, 1900).

Apostolic Constitutions (Ordinances of the Holy Apostles through Clement) Large collection (eight books) of ecclesiastical laws of the early Christian Church, legendarily ascribed to Saint Clement I of Rome (pope, A.D. 88–97) but generally accepted as the work of an unknown Syrian compiler about A.D. 380. The first six books contain instructions about Christian duties of the clergy and laity, dealing with ethics, liturgy, and rites. The seventh book restates greatly the Twelve Apostles' teachings and contains some Jewish and liturgical prayers. More liturgical material is covered in the eighth book, which also holds the so-called Apostolic Canons, a collection of 85 religious rules and principles.

Further reading: David A. Fiensy, *Prayers Alleged to Be Jewish: An Examination of the Constitutions Apostolorum* (Chico, Calif.: Scholars Press, 1985); W. Jardine Grisbrooke, *The Liturgical Portions of the Apostolic Constitution: A Text for Students* (Bramcote, England: Grove Books, 1990).

Apostolicum See APOSTLES' CREED.

April Constitution of 1848 See PILLERSDORF CONSTITUTION.

April Laws See MARCH LAWS.

April Theses Proposal written by the famous Russian revolutionary Vladimir Ilyich Lenin and issued on April 17 (April 4, Old Style), 1917, consisting of propositions to be carried out immediately in order to bring about a successful conclusion to the Bolshevik Revolution (1917) in Russia. In the document, Lenin proposed that the provisional government be overthrown and that all power be transferred to the soviets, or workers' committees; that Russia withdraw from World War I (1914–18), even if that should require the conclusion of a separate peace with the Central Powers; that land be transferred to the peasants; that private ownership be abolished; and that control over all land, farming, banking, and industry be transferred to the soviets. Although there was widespread opposition to the theses when first presented, Lenin refused to compromise, and by the end of April the Bolshevik Party Conference agreed to endorse them.

See also: OCTOBER REVOLUTION, PROCLAMATION OF THE.

Further reading: Lenin Works Archive website, available online at http://www.marxists.org/archive/lenin/works/1917/apr/04.htm.

Arab League Charter Charter signed in Cairo, Egypt, on March 22, 1945, forming the League of Arab States (or Arab League). Egypt, Syria, Iraq, Lebanon, Transjordan (Jordan), Saudi Arabia, and Yemen were the league's founding members; they were later joined by 14 other Arab countries and admitted the Palestine Liberation Organization in 1976. The charter stated that the members would strengthen, promote, and coordinate their economic, political, and cultural affairs and that disputes among them should be settled through peaceful mediation, not by force. The league has a permanent secretariat (headquartered first in Cairo and then in Tunis), special committees, and a council (in which each state has one vote, with decisions obligating only the states that vote for them). The league has loosely cooperated militarily in actions against Israel but has been hindered by differences among the Arab states; it suspended Egypt as a member after she signed a peace treaty with Israel in 1979.

Further reading: Anita L. P. Burdett, ed., *The Arab League: British Documentary Sources, 1943–1963*, 10 vols. (London: Archive Editions, 1995); *Pact of the Arab League* (Washington, D.C.: Arab Office, c. 1945); Charles L. Phillips and Alan Axelrod, eds., *Encyclopedia of Historical Treaties and Alliances*, 2 vols. (New York: Facts On File, 2001).

Arafat's Geneva Speech of 1988 Speech delivered by Palestine Liberation Organization (PLO) Chairman Yasir Arafat to the United Nations General Assembly in Geneva, Switzerland, on December 13, 1988, containing his proposals to bring an end to hostilities between Israel and the PLO. The PLO chairman called for an international peace conference to be held under the auspices of the United Nations;

recommended that a U.N. peacekeeping force assume control of the occupied territories, the Gaza Strip, and the West Bank, in order to protect the inhabitants and to oversee the withdrawal of Israeli forces from those areas; and promised that the PLO would work toward the conclusion of a settlement based upon UNITED NATIONS RESOLUTIONS 242 and 338. The speech also contained the PLO's implicit recognition of Israel's right to exist, and a condemnation of Israel's occupation of the territories and her treatment of the Palestinians. Although Israel's Prime Minister Yitzhak Shamir denounced the speech, the United States, Israel's closest and most powerful ally, accepted it as a positive move and the following day agreed to resume official contact with the PLO.

Further reading: Janet Wallach and John Wallach, *Arafat: In the Eyes of the Beholder* (New York: Birch Lane Press, 1997).

Aragonese Privileges of Union (Magna Carta of Aragón)

Series of privileges forced (December 28, 1287) from King Alfonso III by a union of Aragonese nobles. Thereby, Alfonso agreed to convene "a general court of the Aragonese" in Zaragoza every November. Those assembled were entitled to elect and dismiss councillors. Also, he promised (at the risk of being deposed) not to capture, torture, or execute any noble pending sentence pronounced by Aragón's Justicia (court of justice) "with the counsel and consent of the court of Aragón, or the greater part of it." As surety for his promises, he agreed to transfer 16 fortresses (including Daroca, Huesca, Morella, and Xativa) to the nobles and to free them from their oaths of allegiance should he or his successors renege on his word. He also yielded custody of his prisoner, King Charles II of Naples, and produced six loyal nobles as hostages. Thus, considerable power was vested in the Cortes (legislature) and the Justicia, forcing the king into dependence on them.

Further reading: Kenneth B. Wolf, trans., *Conquerors and Chroniclers of Early Modern Spain* (Liverpool, England: Liverpool University Press, 1990).

Aranjuez, Convention of (1779)

Franco-Spanish alliance formed on April 12, 1779, at Aranjuez, Spain, and directed toward the recovery of Gibraltar from Britain. It was concluded after King George III of England refused Spain's offer of mediation (in return for Gibraltar) in his war against France. Thereby, the allies bound themselves to continue the war until Gibraltar was won and agreed not to make separate peace with Britain. Both countries also hoped to further independent political ends through the alliance. Spain, intent on expanding her territories (see SAN ILDEFONSO, TREATY OF [1762]) in the New World, refused to participate in the Franco-American alliance (see PARIS, TREATIES OF [1778]), or to recognize American independence even though she secretly subsidized American efforts. In June 1779, Spain declared war against Britain.

Further reading: Samual Flagg Bemis, *The Diplomacy of the American Revolution* (Westport, Conn.: Greenwood Press, 1957, repr., 1983).

Argentine Anti-War Pact
See ANTI-WAR PACT, ARGENTINE.

Argentine Constitution of 1853

Constitution that emerged after delegates from Argentine provinces met at a constituent convention in Santa Fe between November 1852 and May 1853. Striking a balance between federalist and centralist notions of political organization, Argentina's form of government was defined as "representative, federal, republican." The federal government, however, was given considerable powers of intervention in provincial affairs involving threats to public order or national security. The constitution established a bicameral legislature loosely based on the United States model, with a chamber of deputies and senate. Also, the president of the Argentine Confederation was given a six-year term of office. The Constitution of 1853, one of the key documents of Argentine history, endured (with several interruptions) for more than 75 years.

Further reading: Santoa Primo Amadeo, *Argentine Constitutional Law* (New York: Columbia University Press, 1943); *Princeton University Latin American Pamphlet Collection: Constitutions, Laws and Codes from Argentine* (microform) (Princeton, N.J.: Princeton University Library, 1989); Barbara A. Tenenbaum, ed., *Encyclopedia of Latin American History and Culture* (New York: Charles Scribner's Sons, 1996).

Argentine Constitution of 1949

Constitution adopted on March 11, 1949, by the Argentine Constituent Assembly, effectively instituting the dictatorship of President Juan D. Perón. In addition to increasing the presidential term from four to six years, the constitution provided that the president could succeed himself and included provisions making the president dominant over the legislative and judicial branches of the government. The document also authorized the state's ownership of the country's sources of minerals and energy; implied the state's ultimate control over private property; and affirmed the state's control over foreign trade—policies that, incidentally, were Perón's. This constitution remained in force until Perón's fall from power in Argentina on September 19, 1955, when a four-man military junta took control.

Further reading: *La Constitución de 1949: Comentado por sus autores* (Buenos Aires: Editorial El Coloquio, 1975); Barbara A. Tenenbaum, ed., *Encyclopedia of Latin American History and Culture* (New York: Charles Scribner's Sons, 1996).

Arias Peace Plan
See CENTRAL AMERICAN PEACE PLAN.

Ariel, Rodó's

Essay published in 1900 by José Enrique Rodó (aristocratic ascetic) of Uruguay, analyzing the nature of democracy and the pitfalls in the path of its development.

Famous for its efforts to define the true character of Latin America, as Latin American youth of his generation envisioned it, Rodó described this character as idealistic or spiritual. Contrasting with it were the materialism and pragmatism that he envisioned as being the obsessions of the United States, causes of bad taste, mediocrity, and brutality. Thus the Yankee was Calibán (a brutish slave in Shakespeare's *Tempest*) and the southern (Latin) American was Ariel. Calibán was successful but not sensitive, democratic but common; Ariel represented higher, more subtantial values. Since its publication, "Ariel" has had a lasting and profound, if somewhat distorted, effect on Latin American thinking about the United States.

Further reading: Margaret Sayers Peden, trans., *Ariel* (Austin: University of Texas Press, 1988); Barbara A. Tenenbaum, ed., *Encyclopedia of Latin American History and Culture* (New York: Charles Scribner's Sons, 1996).

Arita's "Greater East Asia Co-Prosperity Sphere" Speech

Public address delivered on radio by Japan's foreign minister Hachiro Arita on June 29, 1940, revealing Japanese imperialist plans for control of all Eastern Asia. He stated that the "closely related" peoples of the region should naturally "first form a sphere of their own for co-existence and co-prosperity," that Japan hoped to establish a "new order in East Asia," that the Chinese Nationalists under Chiang Kai-shek were obstructing peace, and that Japan's war in China for the past three years was to destroy evil and bring justice. Under Japan, the countries of East Asia and the South Seas would be united in a single sphere of stability, well-being, and prosperity, Arita asserted.

Further reading: Kodansha, eds., *Kodansha Encyclopedia of Japan*, 9 vols. (Tokyo: Kodansha, 1983).

Arms, Assize of

English king Henry II's ordinance of 1181 requiring all knights and freemen to maintain a supply of weapons (arms) proportionate to their income, in readiness to defend their king and country. All freemen and burgesses were to be equipped with a quilted doublet (gambeson), an iron cap, and a lance, while those rating 10 or 16 marks in chattels or rent were to be slightly better equipped. All knights were ordered to have a hauberk, helmet, shield, and lance. Export of military supplies and ships was prohibited. Local juries of knights and freemen were to supervise implementation of the assize under the direction of traveling justices. Those found not bearing arms risked capture. Everyone to whom the law applied had to swear loyalty to the king and promise to fight for his cause. Henry also extended his assize to his continental possessions.

See also: CLARENDON, CONSTITUTIONS OF.

Further reading: Carl Stephenson and Frederick George Marcham, eds., *Sources of English Constitutional History: A Selection of Documents from A.D. 600 to the Present* (New York: Harper & Row, 1937).

Army Regulation Act of 1871, British

Act initiated by Secretary of War Edward Cardwell for the complete reorganization of the British army. An earlier (June 1870) order-in-council had subordinated the commander in chief to the secretary of war, who reorganized the army into three departments, bringing them under one roof for the first time. The act abolished the age-old practice of buying and selling commissions and promotions, enabling Cardwell to recruit and train a professional team. He set up a small general staff and a training course for officers. Short service was introduced (six years in the Colors [regular armed forces] and six in the reserves), and the men were taught a trade, thus creating better-trained reserves. The infantry regiments were divided into 69 military districts, each identified by a local name. This replaced the earlier system of numbered identification and created a rapport between soldiers and civilians. The artillery was similarly revamped, but Cardwell was not successful in his reforms with the cavalry. His reforms strengthened the British army to 150,000 men, of whom 135,000 were regulars.

Further reading: I. F. W. Beckett and John Gooch, *Politicians and Defence: Studies in the Formulation of British Defence Policy, 1845–1970* (Manchester, England: Manchester University Press, 1981); Robert Biddulph, *Lord Cardwell at the War Office: A History of His Administration, 1868–1874* (London: J. Murray, 1904).

Arras, Treaty of (1414)

Pact negotiated at Arras in southern Flanders in September 1414, and ratified in February 1415, ending the civil war between the Burgundians and Armagnacs for control of France. Achieved largely through the mediation of the young dauphin, Louis of Guienne, it repealed the sentence banishing Burgundy's duke John the Fearless and denied amnesty to 500 of his faithful followers. Ousted from power and living in exile in Flanders, John tacitly approved England's 1415 invasion of France during the Hundred Years' War (1337–1457). Later, in 1419, he was assassinated during a conference with Charles (later King Charles VII), the dauphin since the death of Louis in 1417, who now led the Armagnacs.

See also: CABOCHIEN ORDINANCE.

Further reading: Christopher Allmand, *The Hundred Years War: England and France at War, c. 1300–c. 1450* (Cambridge, England: Cambridge University Press, 1988).

Arras, Treaty of (1435)

Peace treaty between France's king Charles VII and Burgundy's duke Philip the Good, concluded at Arras, France, on September 21, 1435, during the Hundred Years' War (1337–1457). Philip was recognized as sovereign of Burgundy for life, while Charles was acknowledged as the supreme king of France. Also, Philip was granted possession of the Somme towns, subject to payment, and received Charles's disavowal of the murder of Philip's father, Duke John the Fearless, in 1419. (The Burgundians under

John and later Philip opposed the Armagnacs under Charles VI and later Charles VII for control of France.) The Arras treaty ended the Armagnac-Burgundian fighting and upset the English-Burgundian alliance, formed by the 1420 Treaty of TROYES, when Philip recognized King Henry V of England as heir to the throne of France. In 1436, when English support collapsed in Paris, Charles and his army took control.

Further reading: Christopher Allmand, *The Hundred Years War: England and France at War, c. 1300–c. 1450* (Cambridge, England: Cambridge University Press, 1988); Edouard Perroy, *The Hundred Years War* (New York: Capricorn, 1965).

Arras, Treaty of (1482)   Treaty determining the future of the Burgundian estates, signed by Maximilian (archduke of Austria) and Louis XI (king of France) on December 23, 1482, at Arras, France. The issue arose when Mary of Burgundy (Maximilian's wife) died in March 1482, and the estates subsequently rejected Maximilian's claim for regency on behalf of his infant son, Philip. Separately, they negotiated and finalized an agreement with Louis XI, forcing Maximilian to merely append his signature. Margaret, his daughter, was to marry Louis's son, the dauphin (later King Charles VIII), bringing as dowry Artois, Franche-Comté, and Burgundy provinces. France reasserted her sovereignty over Flanders, through the Parlement of Paris, and Philip was to acknowledge this fact on maturity. Louis also recovered Picardy and the Somme towns (see CONFLANS, TREATY OF), received Boulogne, and reconfirmed the earlier charters granted to Flanders. By excluding England and Brittany, Louis sought to break the traditional Burgundian alliance and establish a stable relationship with Maximilian. This treaty reversed the 1435 Treaty of ARRAS.

See also: SENLIS, TREATY OF.

Further reading: *Miscellaneous Documents, 1483* [including terms of the Treaty of Arras, 23 December 1482, between Louis XI and Maximilian of Austria] (Ann Arbor, Mich.: University Microfilms International, 1938).

Arras, Treaty of (1579)   Peace pact concluded on May 17–19, 1579, at Arras (in Artois) between Spain and the Netherlands' Roman Catholic southern provinces (united allies since the Union of Arras in January 1579), consequently rupturing the union of the neighboring Low Countries achieved by the Pacification of GHENT. Signed by representatives of the provinces of Artois and Hainaut and the Wallon (French-speaking) towns of Douai, Lille, and Orchies, with the Spanish governor of the Netherlands, Alessandro Farnese, the treaty called for the withdrawal of all Spanish and foreign troops and for the strengthening of Roman Catholicism in the provinces. Spain was to respect the autonomy of the provinces and to debar foreigners from assuming government posts. The northern, Protestant Calvinist-dominated provinces of the Netherlands had earlier organized themselves into the Union

of UTRECHT. These two pacts or unions led to the eventual partition of the Low Countries.

See also: ABJURATION, ACT OF; VERVINS, TREATY OF.

Further reading: Robin Briggs, *Early Modern France, 1560–1715* (Oxford, England: Oxford University Press, 1977).

Articles of Confederation, U.S.   Plan of union for the newly independent United States that was framed by a committee appointed by the Second Continental Congress and presented on July 12, 1776. A draft approved on November 15, 1777, was sent to the 13 states (colonies) for ratification, which had to be unanimous, and did not become law until March 1, 1781. The Articles established a congress made up of two to seven delegates from each state, with every state possessing one vote. Congress would have the power to manage Indian and foreign affairs, establish a postal system, regulate coinage, borrow money, and settle disputes between states. All rights not specifically granted to the federal government were retained by the states. Each state was obliged to contribute to a common treasury in proportion to the value of surveyed lands and improvements, and to supply its quota of troops, based on the number of white inhabitants. The Articles proved to be ineffective, largely because the federal government lacked the means to enforce its measures. By 1786, they were widely viewed as deficient and were replaced by the U.S. CONSTITUTION in 1789.

Further reading: Merrill Jensen, ed., *The Articles of Confederation: An Interpretation of the Social-Constitutional History of the American Revolution, 1774–1781* (Madison: University of Wisconsin Press, 1940, repr., 1970); Merrill Jensen, ed., *The Documentary History of the Ratification of the Constitution*, vol. 1: *Constitutional Documents and Records. 1776–1787* (Madison: State Historical Society of Wisconsin, 1976); Merrill Jensen, *The New Nation: A History of the United States During the Confederation, 1781–1789* (Boston, Mass.: Northeastern University Press, 1950, repr., 1981); Forrest McDonald, *E Pluribus Unum: The Formation of the American Republic. 1776–1790* (Indianapolis, Ind.: Liberty Press, 1965, repr., 1979).

Articles of New England Confederation   See NEW ENGLAND CONFEDERATION, ARTICLES OF.

Artisans' Dwellings Act (Artizans' and Labourers' Dwellings Improvement Act)   Legislation in 1875 by British prime minister Benjamin Disraeli's government to provide better housing for the working classes. It was drafted by Richard Cross of the Home Office, on the basis of proposals from earlier housing laws, and gave the local boards permission to acquire and clear slum areas and rehouse the inhabitants. Owners whose homes were demolished were to be compensated at market rates. The boards were also ordered to appoint sanitary inspectors and medical officers to carry out these tasks. Slum clearance was not an accepted idea then, and was rarely enforced. The act was the forerunner of subsequent housing acts in Britain.

Further reading: Eyre Lloyd, *The Law of Compensation under the Lands Clauses and Railways Clauses Consolidation Acts, the Artizans and Labourers Dwellings Improvement Act, 1875, . . . ,* 4th ed. (Woodbridge, Conn.: Research Publications, 1990).

Art of War English translation of Chinese treatise, *Ping-fa,* on the subject of war and strategy, written about 400 B.C. by the Chinese general Sun-tzu (Sunzi). It reveals a profound understanding of the practical and philosophical bases of war, emphasizing politics, tactics, and intelligence (secret agents). "All warfare is based on deception," said Sun-tzu, who instructed his followers: "Hold out baits to entice the enemy. Feign disorder, and crush him." Modern strategists (notably the Chinese Communists) have been clearly influenced by his tactics concerning guerrilla warfare: "Know the enemy, know yourself . . . Know the ground, know the weather; your victory will then be total." Sun-tzu said that success comes from avoiding an enemy's strength and striking his weakness.

Further reading: Sun-tzu, *The Art of War* (New York: Delacorte, 1989).

Ashbourne Act (Irish Land Act of 1885) In August 1885, during the caretaker prime ministry of Britain's Lord Salisbury, legislation establishing the first state-aided scheme of land purchase in Ireland. Named after the first Baron Ashbourne, who introduced it, the act allowed Irish tenants to borrow the full purchase price of their land, repayable at 4 percent over 49 years; a sum of £5 million was distributed on an immediate basis to tenants wishing to buy their lands or farms from their landlords, with additional funding in 1888. In Ulster, nearly 25,400 tenants purchased their land holdings. A total of 942,600 acres were bought, giving an average of 37 acres at 17½ years rental. Based on Gladstone's IRISH LAND ACT OF 1881, this was the first of many land purchase acts (in 1887, 1891, 1896, and 1903) and, in its modest way, led to the ultimate solution of the Irish land problem.

Further reading: Christopher Haigh, ed., *The Cambridge Historical Encyclopedia of Great Britain and Ireland* (Cambridge, England: Cambridge University Press, 1985); D. J. Hickey and J. E. Doherty, *A Dictionary of Irish History Since 1800* (Dublin: Gill & Macmillan, 1980).

Ashburton Treaty See WEBSTER-ASHBURTON TREATY.

Ashcroft v. Free Speech Coalition U.S. Supreme Court ruling in 2002 that invalidated the CHILD PORNOGRAPHY PREVENTION ACT OF 1996. CPPA had outlawed the use of modern computer, photographic, and photocopy technology in manipulating images to make adults look like children, thus getting around existing laws prohibiting child pornography.

Since the act made illegal the process by which virtual child pornography is made, even in instances when children are not used in its production, the law was attacked for violating FIRST AMENDMENT rights of freedom of expression as well as existing standards regarding pornography in general. Shortly after CPPA's enactment, a lawsuit was filed by the Free Speech Coalition, a trade association of businesses involved in the production and distribution of pornography, against John Ashcroft, the U.S. attorney general. Although the act was upheld in federal district court, in 1999 the ninth U.S. circuit court struck down CPPA on the grounds that its provisions concerning the creation of virtual child pornography were unconstitutionally vague and too broad. Specifically, it held that some of the material prohibited by CPPA was not considered obscene under MILLER V. CALIFORNIA, an earlier Supreme Court decision that established guidelines for determining what is pornographic. On April 16, 2002, the Supreme Court upheld that latter decision, with a 6-3 ruling.

Further reading: "*Ashcroft, Attorney General, et al. v. Free Speech Coalition, et al.,*" Legal Information Institute, available online at http://supct.law.cornell.edu/supct/html/00-795.ZS .html; Bill Bickel, "Virtual Child Pornography: Should It Be Illegal?" About.com, available online at http://crime.about. com/library/weekly/aavirtualchildpornography.htm.

Asiatic Registration Bill of 1907, South African (Asiatic Law Amendment Act) Reenactment by the government of the Transvaal (a British Crown colony in South Africa) of its Ordinance of 1906, to control the immigration of Asians, mainly Indians. Passed on March 22, 1907, because of public demand, it required all Asians to register their names and carry certificates marked with their fingerprints. The Indian lawyer Mohandas Karamchand Gandhi organized a passive resistance against the act, protesting against the compulsion rather than the fingerprinting. A temporary compromise was reached in January 1908, allowing the Asians to register voluntarily and suspending prosecutions against them. Gandhi wanted the act to be repealed, the government refused to do so, and the hostilities continued.

Further reading: Christopher Saunders, *Historical Dictionary of South Africa* (Metuchen, N.J.: Scarecrow Press, 1983).

Aśoka's Pillar Edicts See PILLAR EDICTS, AŚOKA'S.

Assize of Arms See ARMS, ASSIZE OF.

Assize of Clarendon See CLARENDON, ASSIZE OF.

Assize of Darrien Presentment See DARRIEN PRESENTMENT, ASSIZE OF.

Assize of Northampton See NORTHAMPTON, ASSIZE OF.

Assize of Woodstock   See WOODSTOCK, ASSIZE OF.

Assizes of Jerusalem   See JERUSALEM, ASSIZES OF.

Association, the (Continental Association)   Plan adopted by the First Continental Congress on October 20, 1774, in an attempt to use economic coercion to force Britain to redress American colonial grievances. The plan's provisions included pledges that, in the absence of a resolution of differences, the colonies would cease importing goods from Britain as of December 1; the slave trade in the colonies would also be discontinued on December 1; consumption of British goods would stop by March 1, 1775; and exports to Britain, Ireland, and the West Indies would end by September 1, 1775. The Association was to be enforced by committees elected in each county, town, and city, and the principal means of enforcement would be publicity and the boycotting of goods from any province that failed to follow its provisions. The Association was widely adopted and was operating in 12 colonies by April 1775.

Further reading: Leonard W. Levy and Kenneth L. Karst, eds., *Encyclopedia of the American Constitution* 2d ed. (New York: Macmillan Reference, 2000).

Association of Southeast Asian Nations, Pact of the   Nonmilitary alliance established on August 8, 1967, by Malaysia, Indonesia, Singapore, Thailand, and the Philippines "to promote active collaboration and mutual assistance in matters of common interest in the economic, social, cultural, technical, scientific, and administrative fields." ASEAN (acronym for the association) consists of a ministerial conference (foreign ministers, meeting annually), a standing committee (meets between ministerial conferences if necessary), and a secretariat (set up in 1976). It was joined by Brunei in January 1984. Regionally, ASEAN was active in attempting to establish a zone of peace, freedom, and neutrality through a "Treaty of Amity and Cooperation in Southeast Asia" and a "Declaration of Concord" signed in February 1976. Agreements of cooperation were also reached with Australia, New Zealand, and the European Economic Community.

Further reading: Ainslie T. Embree, editor, *Encyclopedia of Asian History*, 4 vols. (New York: Charles Scribner's Sons, 1988).

Associations Law, French   Statute in France governing right of association, introduced by conservative Republican premier Pierre-Marie-René Waldeck-Rousseau, and passed by parliament on July 1, 1901. The new law removed previous restrictions on the right of association, and legalized association for all legitimate purposes. Religious associations, however, were required to obtain specific authorization from the state, which was permitted to limit their scope and activity. No member of an unauthorized congregation was allowed to teach, and all congregations without official sanction were to

be dissolved. The bill was popular with the anticlerical lower class, and was used by Waldeck-Rousseau's successor, Emile Combes, as a weapon in his anticlerical campaign.

See also: COMBES'S BILL.

Further reading: Boris A. Blick, *Waldeck-Rousseau (1894–1904)* (Ann Arbor, Mich.: University Microfilms, 1961).

Assumption Act, U.S.   Federal legislation enacted in 1790 by which the national government of the United States assumed the debts incurred by individual states during the American Revolution (1775–83). This measure, proposed by Alexander Hamilton, was generally favored by northern states, which had the largest unpaid debts, but was opposed by southern states, most of which had arranged to discharge their debts and feared that the act would increase the tax burden on their citizens. The issue was settled by compromise: Hamilton agreed to support a southern plan to locate the nation's capital along the Potomac in exchange for southern support of the assumption act.

Further reading: Henry Steele Commager, ed., *Documents of American History*, 8th ed. (New York: Appleton-Century-Crofts, 1968).

Athanasian Creed (Quicumque Vult)   Formal statement (in some 40 verses) of Roman Catholic doctrine concerning the Trinity and the Incarnation, probably written in Arles, France, in the fifth century A.D. It sets forth the views of Saint Athanasius (hence its name), who wrote angry polemics against supporters of Arianism in the fourth century (see NICENE CREED). The creed, a firm, orthodox stand, opens with the words "quicumque vult" ("whoever wishes" [to be saved]), declaring that obedience to Catholicism is essential for one's salvation. It stated that "as the reasonable soul and flesh is one man, so God and Man is one Christ." The creed was not used in the liturgy of the Church of Rome until the 10th century, though it had been received earlier in the churches of France, Spain, and Germany.

Further reading: "Athanasian Creed," Christian Classics Ethereal Library website, available online at http://www.ccel.org/creeds/athanasian.creed.html.

Athis-sur-Orge, Treaty of   Treaty concluded at Athis-sur-Orge, France, on June 23, 1305, imposed on the Flemish by Philip IV, king of France, after his troops had registered a partial victory at Mons-en-Pévèle. The count of Flanders, Robert of Béthune, on succeeding to his father's fief, was to do homage to the French monarch. The people of Flanders who had fought against France were ordered to pay a considerable war indemnity over four years. Philip assumed control of the castellanies of Lille, Douai, Béthune, Cassel, and Courtrai, and razed the city walls of Ghent, Burges, Ypres, Lille, and Douai. Once every five years, all inhabitants had to swear loyalty to the king. Three thousand citizens of Burges were to go on a pilgrimage to atone for sins. Further, Count Robert could not enter into any pact without the king's permission. The Flanders towns delayed ratification until 1309, after certain changes had been introduced in their favor. Subsequently, recovery of the indemnity posed problems and tensions redeveloped.

Further reading: Joseph R. Strayer, *The Reign of Philip the Fair* (Princeton, N.J.: Princeton University Press, 1980).

Atkins v. *Virginia*

U.S. Supreme Court ruling in 2002 that the execution of mentally retarded criminals is unconstitutional. In 1996 Daryl R. Atkins shot and killed a man while robbing him. Two years later, he was convicted in a Virginia court of capital murder and sentenced to death. The decision was appealed to the Supreme Court on the grounds that Atkins, who had an IQ of only 59, was mentally retarded; therefore, the death sentence represented cruel and unusual punishment, which is prohibited by the EIGHTH AMENDMENT. The Court overturned the Virginia court's decision, 6–3. In so doing, it also went against the precedent the Court itself had set in *Penry* v. *Lynaugh* (1989), which allowed the execution of a mentally retarded criminal on the grounds that a national consensus against such executions did not exist. At the time, only the federal government and two states disallowed such executions. By 2002, however, an additional 28 states had passed legislation prohibiting the execution of the mentally retarded. To the Court's mind, this new development constituted a national consensus against such executions, thus invalidating the rationale behind its 1989 ruling.

Further reading: *"Atkins v. Virginia,"* Legal Information Institute, available online at http://supct.law.cornell.edu/supct/html/00-8452.ZS.html; Richard W. Garnett, "Personal Problems: The Supremes Ignore the Constitution in *Atkins*," National Review Online, available online at http://www.nationalreview.com/comment/comment-garnett062002.asp.

Atlantic Charter

Anglo-American statement of principles for world peace issued on August 14, 1941, by British prime minister Winston Churchill and U.S. president Franklin D. Roosevelt at the conclusion of their meeting at sea, off the coast of Newfoundland, during World War II (1939–45). It expressed their hopes for peace "after the final destruction of the Nazi tyranny" so that people could travel freely and live "in freedom from fear and want." Their countries, it clarified, were not interested in territorial gains nor in seeing any gains made against the wishes of the people. They affirmed their respect for the sovereign rights of all nationalities and promised help in restoring self-government where it had been denied. Additional provisions were equal access to trade and raw materials for all nations and better collaboration between them to improve economic and labor conditions and social security. Finally, they reiterated their commitment to disarmament "pending the establishment of a wider and permanent system of general security," an idea that led to the formation of the United Nations (see UNITED NATIONS CHARTER). Ten Allied nations endorsed the Atlantic Charter.

Further reading: *The Atlantic Charter* (London: Chatto & Windus, 1942); Douglas Brinkley and David Facey-Crowther, *The Atlantic Charter* (New York: St. Martin's Press, 1994); Charles L. Phillips and Alan Axelrod, eds., *Encyclopedia of Historical Treaties and Alliances,* 2 vols. (New York: Facts On File, 2001); Julius Stone, *The Atlantic Charter: New Worlds for Old* (London: Angus & Robertson, 1943).

Atomic Energy Act of 1954, U.S.

Federal U.S. legislation enacted on August 30, 1954, that allowed private companies to participate in atomic energy research, development, and production. A revision of the Atomic Energy Act of 1946, the new act permitted private power companies, licensed and regulated by the Atomic Energy Commission, to own nuclear power plants and nuclear materials, and to obtain patents on atomic inventions. The act allowed some information on atomic weapons to be shared with European allies and information on the peaceful uses of atomic energy to be shared with friendly nations.

Further reading: Leonard W. Levy and Kenneth L. Karst, eds., *Encyclopedia of the American Constitution,* 2d ed. (New York: Macmillan Reference, 2000); Elizabeth S. Rolph, *Nuclear Power and the Public Safety* (Lexington, Mass.: Lexington Books, 1979).

Augsburg, Peace of

Religious peace treaty promulgated on September 25, 1555; concluded by Roman Catholic and Lutheran princes at a diet of the Holy Roman Empire held earlier that year in Augsburg, Germany. The document stated that all hostility due to religious differences was forbidden; that only Lutheranism and Roman Catholicism were acceptable forms of faith (on this point the peace was not nearly as inclusive as the Compact of WARSAW, which allowed the practice of any faith); that each ruling prince was allowed to determine for himself the faith of his subjects; that church property confiscated by Protestants before 1552 was to remain in their hands; that all Catholic lands were to remain under Catholic jurisdiction; and that Lutherans and Catholics were equally eligible for all offices of state and for seats in the imperial diet. Highly significant of the treaty's terms was the subordination of religion to state control.

See also: PASSAU, TREATY OF.

Further reading: "The Religious Peace of Augsburg, 1555," excerpted by E. Reich, ed., Crown and the Cross website, available online at http://www.geocities.com/Athens/Sparta/5414/PeaceofAugsburg.htm.

Augsburg, Treaty of the League of

Defensive alliance signed on July 9, 1686, establishing the League of Augsburg, a coalition consisting of the Holy Roman emperor (Leopold I), the king of Sweden (Charles XI), the king of Spain (Charles II), and the electors of Bavaria, Saxony, and the Palatinate, as well as the Dutch Republic—all directed against the king of France (Louis XIV). The primary intention of the treaty's signatories was to curb Louis XIV's eastward territorial expansions; disregarding the 1684 Truce of REGENSBURG, Louis's army had occupied the Palatinate. The league did not formulate any plans for a unified military command, and some of its smaller princes were afraid of attacking France—factors that undermined the league's effectiveness. The league became known as the GRAND ALLIANCE OF 1689 after the new King William III of England (Prince William of Orange) had joined it. Peace was eventually restored with the 1697 Treaty of RYSWICK.

Further reading: John A. Lynn, *The Wars of Louis XIV, 1667–1714* (New York: Longman, 1999).

Augsburg Confession (Confessio Augustana) Protestant Lutheran statement of faith and doctrine written by Philip Melanchthon (follower of the outlawed German religious reformer Martin Luther) and presented to the Holy Roman Emperor Charles V at the Diet of Augsburg on June 25, 1530. It contained 21 articles on the fundamental beliefs of Lutheranism and seven articles on matters of dispute concerning the Roman Catholic Church (such as mandatory celibacy for priests, the practice of only one kind of Holy Communion, and the sale of indulgences), which Lutherans wished to see reformed. Although the orthodoxy of the Lutherans had been emphasized by Melanchthon, the diet turned down all innovations and said all Protestants must return to their allegiance to the Roman Catholic Church. The confession became the basic creed of the Lutheran Church.

See also: CONFESSIO AUGUSTANA VARIATA.

Further reading: "The Augsburg Confession (1530)," Project Wittenberg website, available online at http://www.iclnet.org/pub/resources/text/wittenberg/wittenberg-boc.html#ac.

Augsburg Interim Provisional agreement drawn up in 1548 at a diet in Augsburg, Germany, ostensibly by a Protestant prince but actually by order of the Holy Roman Emperor Charles V. It attempted to bring about an interim accord between Roman Catholics and Lutherans until religious issues in dispute could be put before a general council. Its compromising terms were intentionally imprecise, such that both Catholic and Protestant views appeared to be theoretically supported. The document specifically endorsed the Christian doctrine of justification by faith alone and the practice of Holy Communion by Catholics and Protestants. Marriage of priests was also permitted.

See also: RATISBON INTERIM.

Further reading: Roland H. Bainton, *Age of the Reformation* (Melbourne, Fla.: Krieger, 1983)

Augusta, Treaty of (1763) Pact of friendship signed on November 10, 1763, at the Congress of Augusta by representatives of the Creek, Cherokee, Choctaw, Chickasaw, and Catawba tribes; fixed the boundaries of the colony of Georgia. The congress was convened on orders of the British government for the purpose of informing the southern tribes of the conclusion of the French and Indian War (1754–63) and resolving various trade and boundary issues. Also involved were officials from Virginia, North Carolina, South Carolina, and Georgia, as well as John Stuart, superintendent of Indian Affairs in the Southern District. The treaty established Georgia's southern boundary from the St. Marys River to the Chattahoochee and then along the 31st parallel to the Mississippi River.

Further reading: Charles Colcock Jones, Jr., *The History of Georgia,* vol. 2 (Boston: Houghton Mifflin, 1883, repr., 1965).

Augusta, Treaty of (1773) Treaty negotiated in 1773 by the chiefs of the Cherokee and Creek nations with Governor James Wright of Georgia and John Stuart, superintendent of Indian Affairs in the Southern District, to settle the Indians' debts to various white traders. By this agreement, signed on June 1, 1773, the tribes granted to Georgia two land parcels, one bounded by the Altamaha and Ogeechee Rivers and the other between the upper stretches of the Ogeechee and Savannah Rivers. The Indians' debts were to be paid from the sale of these land parcels, which included over 2 million acres.

Further reading: Charles Colcock Jones, Jr., *The History of Georgia,* vol. 2 (Boston: Houghton Mifflin, 1883, repr., 1965).

Augustinus Long treatise by Cornelis Jansen on the teachings of St. Augustine, published posthumously in Louvain (Belgium) in August 1640. Intended as a rebuttal against the neoscholastic theologians of the Catholic Counter-Reformation, *Augustinus* sparked the movement known as Jansenism and a religious controversy lasting several decades. Jansen, a Dutch Roman Catholic theologian who began writing the treatise in 1628, showed that the teachings of St. Augustine were in direct opposition to those of the Jesuits, whom he faulted. A three-part work, *Augustinus* was published without the Holy See's consent (see IN EMINENTI). The first part traces the continuity between pelagian, semi-pelagian, and Jesuit doctrines. The second discusses the two extreme states of man—an angel before his fall, a demon after it. In the third, Jansen presents his sobering conclusions on human nature and divine grace, stressing the sovereign will of God. *Augustinus* and five propositions extracted from it (see CUM OCCASIONE IMPRESSIONIS LIBRI) were widely condemned by those in authority, particularly by the popes and France's king Louis XIV.

See also: CLEMENT IX, PEACE OF.

Further reading: Saint Augustine, *The Confessions of St. Augustine* (New York: Prentice-Hall, 1931); Saint Augustine,

St. Augustine's City of God (New York: Oxford University Press, 1963).

Au Milieu des Sollicitudes   See INTER INNUMERAS.

Aurelian Laws (Leges Aureliae)

Roman legislation undoing some of the CORNELIAN LAWS, initiated by the praetor Lucius Aurelius Cotta in 75 B.C. The first Aurelian Law allowed the tribunes to seek higher office once again; they also reclaimed their former right to initiate legislation, with the power of veto. The censors then regained the right of ousting unfit senators (72 B.C.). The power of the Senate was weakened by the Aurelian Law of 70 B.C., which altered the makeup of juries in public courts; henceforth each jury was to be filled by senators, equestrians (or *equites*), and tribunes of the treasury (*tribuni aerarii*—a class of well-to-do property owners slightly below the equestrians, whose business interests they shared), each of these groups with one-third of a jury's membership.

Further reading: Michael Crawford, *Roman Statutes* (London: Institute of Classical Studies, School of Advanced Study, University of London, 1996).

Ausgleich (Compromise of 1867)

Agreement prepared primarily under the influence of Hungarian statesmen Francis Déak and Gyula Andrássy and approved by the Austrian Parliament on May 29, 1867, providing for the autonomy of Hungary (which thenceforth included Hungary proper, Transylvania, and Croatia) and Hungary's union with Austria through the union of their crowns. Thus it was established that the Austrian emperor would serve as the Hungarian king; that Hungary would rule herself according to her constitution (see MARCH LAWS) and through her own parliament; that, in what remained of the Austrian Empire, the German Austrians would rule according to their own constitution, using the FEBRUARY PATENT as a basis (see AUSTRIAN CONSTITUTION OF 1867); and that matters common to both Hungary and the remaining Hapsburg lands, such as foreign affairs, finance, and war, would be the responsibility of joining ministries and would be discussed at annual meetings by representatives from both parliaments (Austria and Hungary).

See also: OCTOBER DIPLOMA.

Further reading: Frank N. Magill, ed., *Great Events from History, Modern European Series*, 3 vols. (Englewood Cliffs, N.J.: Salem Press, 1973).

Australian Colonies Government Act

British legislation of August 5, 1850, promoting the district of Port Philip (in the colony of New South Wales in Australia) to the status of a new colony known as Victoria, with its capital at Melbourne. Initiated following a petition from Port Philip residents, who complained of being underrepresented in the self-governing New South Wales Legislative Council, the act provided for a 30-member legislative council (two-thirds elected, one-third appointed by the British Crown). The governor and his council could pass any laws provided they did not conflict with English laws and involve crown lands or revenues. Similar legislation was enacted in the colonies of Tasmania, South Australia, and Western Australia—the idea being to establish a system of government based on the British model and to give the Australian people the right to determine their own affairs.

Further reading: Pauline Jones, *Beginnings of Permanent Government* (Melbourne, Australia: Victorian Government Printing Office, 1981); Davis McCaughey et al., *Victoria's Colonial Governors, 1839–1900* (Carlton, Australia: Melbourne University Press, 1993).

Australian Public Schools Act of 1866   See PUBLIC SCHOOLS ACT OF 1866, AUSTRALIAN.

Austrian Constitution of 1848   See PILLERSDORF CONSTITUTION.

Austrian Constitution of 1861   See FEBRUARY PATENT.

Austrian Constitution of 1867 (December Constitution, Fundamental Laws)

Constitution adopted on December 21, 1867, by the German-dominated Austrian parliament, reforming the FEBRUARY PATENT. The constitution provided that Austria's citizens would possess freedom of speech, press, and assembly, and equality before the law; and that all nationalities within the ethnically diverse state would be equal with respect to their cultures and use of their languages. Despite these democratic provisions, representation in parliament was restricted, and the emperor had the right to issue laws through his cabinet should the parliament not be in session. Although the nationalists had been demanding greater autonomy, the government was opposed to further federalization of Austria, having only months earlier granted autonomy to Hungary (see AUSGLEICH).

Further reading: Lothar Hobelt, *Parliamentary Politics in a Multinational Setting: Late Imperial Austria* (Minneapolis: Center for Austrian Studies, University of Minnesota, 1992).

Austrian Ultimatum to Serbia

Ultimatum made by the Austrian government on July 23, 1914, to the Serbian government in Belgrade; it provided Serbia with 48 hours to comply with Austrian demands. The ultimatum was provoked by the June 28 assassination of Austrian archduke Francis Ferdinand by a Bosnian revolutionary, with Serbia's knowledge and tacit consent. Through the document the Austrians demanded that all anti-Austrian propaganda in schools and nationalist organizations come to an end; that all officials involved in anti-Austrian propaganda be dismissed; that Austrian and Serbian officials begin an investigation into the assassination of the archduke; and that those suspected of involvement in the assassination be arrested. Serbia's failure to comply fully with the demands led to Austria's declaration of war on Serbia on July 28, 1914, and the start of World War I (1914–18).

Further reading: Harold Temperley, *The History of Serbia* (New York: Howard Fertig, 1969).

Austro-German Agreement of 1936

Agreement concluded on July 11, 1936, by Austria and Germany, bringing an end to many years of mutual hostility, which had been characterized by Austria's anti-Nazi stance and Germany's hostile measures in return. The terms of the agreement included Germany's recognition of Austria's sovereignty; each party's agreement not to interfere in the other's internal affairs; and Austria's pledge to see that her policies with regard to Germany were consistent with Austria's self-proclaimed status as a German state. The agreement was preceded by the ROME PROTOCOLS OF 1934, which established closer relations between Austria and Italy, and which had been a source of tension between Italy and Germany. The present treaty thus removed that source of tension, and put Italy and Germany, both revisionist powers, in a much stronger diplomatic position with regard to France and Great Britain.

See also: GERMAN-ITALIAN PACT OF 1936.

Further reading: Wilfred Fest, *Dictionary of German History, 1806–1945* (New York: St. Martin's, 1978); Hajo Holborn, *A History of Modern Germany, 1840–1945* (New York: Knopf, 1969).

Austro-German Treaty of Alliance (Dual Alliance)

Defensive alliance between Germany and Austria, signed October 5, 1879. The formal alliance committed the signatories to provide mutual assistance should either be attacked by Russia. In case of an attack by any other power, the two allies pledged benevolent neutrality. The defensive nature of the alliance was intended to free Germany from supporting Austrian activities in the Balkans, while allowing Austria to preserve neutrality in any French war of revenge against Germany. The agreement was the first formal alliance of its kind since the 1814 Congress of Vienna and began a new era of formal alliances that were not specifically for the purpose of conducting war. Originally signed for a period of five years, the alliance was regularly renewed, and, until its dissolution in 1918, formed the cornerstone of German and Austrian foreign policy.

Further reading: Arthur Rosenberg, *Imperial Germany: The Birth of the German Republic, 1871–1918* (New York: Oxford University Press, 1931); Sir Adolphus William Ward, *Germany, 1815–1890* (Cambridge, England: Cambridge University Press, 1916).

Austro-Polish Alliance of 1683

Treaty of alliance concluded on April 1, 1683, between King John III Sobieski of Poland and Holy Roman Emperor Leopold I. Poland (in union then with Lithuania) agreed to raise an army of 40,000 soldiers and pledged to help in the defense of the imperial city of Vienna (the emperor's residence) should it be attacked by the Ottoman Turks. The Holy Roman Empire agreed to raise a 60,000-man army, to give Poland-Lithuania 1.2 million ducats (gold coins) to help pay for its army, and to aid in the defense of the Polish city of Kraków in case of Turkish attack. The alliance was made in time for their combined forces to defeat the Turks at the famous battle at Vienna on September 12, 1683. The Ottoman Empire was less of a menace to Western Europe afterward.

Further reading: Norman Davies, *God's Playground: A History of Poland*, 2 vols. (New York: Columbia University Press, 1982); W. F. Reddaway, ed., *The Cambridge History of Poland to 1696* (Cambridge, England: Cambridge University Press, 1950).

Austro-Russian and Russo-Prussian Treaties of 1795 (Third Treaty of Partition of Poland)

Treaties concluded between Austria and Russia and between Prussia and Russia on January 3, 1795, and October 24, 1795, respectively, in which the three powers came to terms on the distribution of Polish lands following the 1794 Polish national uprising against these three partitioning powers. Through the former treaty Austria and Russia made territorial arrangements without regard to Prussia, with Austria receiving territory in Galicia and part of Mazovia as far north as the Bug and Narew rivers; Russia received the Ukraine and the remainder of Lithuania. Through the latter, and final, treaty, which formalized the third and final partition of Poland, Prussia received all of Mazovia, including Warsaw, and Russia received the Ukraine and the remainder of Lithuania, as in the settlement with Austria. Austria later agreed to these terms, thus acquiring the Galician province up to the new Prussian border. These treaties completely erased an independent Poland from the map in this third partition of the country.

See also: DELIMITATION, ACT OF; RUSSO-PRUSSIAN TREATY OF 1793; ST. PETERSBURG, TREATY OF (1772).

Further reading: Charles L. Phillips and Alan Axelrod, eds., *Encyclopedia of Historical Treaties and Alliances*, 2 vols. (New York: Facts On File, 2001).

Autonomy Bills, Canadian

See CANADIAN AUTONOMY BILLS OF 1905.

Aviation Security and Antiterrorism Act of 1996, U.S.

Legislation enacted by the U.S. Congress on August 2, 1996, to combat international terrorism. The act was introduced after a terrorist bomb exploded aboard Pan Am flight 103; the airplane crashed in Lockerbie, Scotland, killing all crew members and passengers, most of whom were U.S. citizens. The aviation security portion of the act directed the Federal Aviation Administration to deploy explosive detection devices at all commercial airports and to implement other detection measures, such as the use of specially trained dogs.

It also required airports to conduct criminal history record checks and employment investigations of all personnel who screened passengers or handled baggage, and put the Federal Bureau of Investigation in charge of assessing the adequacy of security measures at high-risk airports. The antiterrorism portion of the act made certain terrorist acts punishable under the Racketeer Influenced and Corrupt Organizations Act (see RICO LAW), which gives the federal government special powers to use in combatting organized crime. It also required the president to develop an action plan for dealing with those nations known to support international terrorism.

Further reading: Library of Congress, "Aviation Security and Antiterrorism Act of 1996," Bill Summary & Status for the 104th Congress, available online at http://thomas.loc.gov/cgi-bin/bdquery/z?d104:HR03953:@@@D&summ2=m&.

Axis Powers, Pact of the (German-Italian-Japanese Pact, Tripartite Pact)

Pact concluded in Berlin on September 27, 1940, by Germany, Italy, and Japan, establishing a tripartite alliance among them as World War II (1939–45) got under way. The treaty provided that the three signatory powers would mutually recognize the creation of a new world order in which Germany and Italy would predominate in the West, and Japan would predominate in Asia; that the present document would not affect any signatory party's political relationship with the Soviet Union (see MOLOTOV-RIBBENTROP PACT); and that, in the event of an attack upon any of the signatory powers by a power not yet at war, in either Europe or Asia (such a power was understood to refer to the United States, although not specifically mentioned), the other powers would provide that party with military, economic, and political aid against that power.

See also: STEEL, PACT OF.

Further reading: Charles L. Phillips and Alan Axelrod, eds., *Encyclopedia of Historical Treaties and Alliances*, 2 vols. (New York: Facts On File, 2001).

Ayala, Plan of

Revolutionary program issued by Emiliano Zapata on November 28, 1911, renouncing Francisco I. Madero as president of Mexico for not fulfilling the promises of the Mexican Revolution begun in 1910 in imposing José María Pino Suárez as vice president. The plan recognized Pascual Orozco as chief of the Liberating Revolution; if he did not accept, Zapata himself was to be the chief. The plan also demanded the immediate restitution to towns and poor farmers of fields, waters, and timber. Also, one-third of monopolist holdings would be expropriated with prior indemnification; those who opposed the plan would lose all their property. Although Zapata's plan failed, his tenacity later forced President Venustiano Carranza to issue the law of January 6, 1915, the starting point of Mexico's agrarian legislation, and a more precise juridicial formulation than the one contained in the Plan of Ayala.

Further reading: Donald C. Briggs and Narvin Alisky, *Historical Dictionary of Mexico* (Metuchen, N.J.: Scarecrow Press, 1981).

Ayutla, Plan of

Liberal proclamation of March 1854, issued by the town of Ayutla, Guerrero, Mexico (under the leadership of the guerrilla leader Juan Álvarez) stating that a constituent assembly be convened. The assembly's task was to devise a new basic charter for the republic so that Mexico would not immediately revert to her customary militarism after the impending revolution (1855). The plan's objective was to break the power of the army and the church, thereby making possible the erection of a liberal, federal republic where civil rights were respected and where economic freedom would facilitate the redistribution of national wealth.

Further reading: Helen Delpar, ed., *Encyclopedia of Latin America* (New York: McGraw-Hill, 1974); Michael C. Meyer and William L. Sherman, *The Course of Mexican History* (Oxford, England: Oxford University Press, 1983).

B

Bacon's *Novum Organum* See *NOVUM ORGANUM.*

Baden, Articles of Articles endorsed by seven liberal Swiss cantons (Bern, Lucerne, rural Basel, Solothurn, St. Gall, Aargau, and Thurgau) on January 20, 1834, in Baden, declaring the supremacy of the rights of the state over those of the Christian Church (particularly those of the Roman Catholic Church). Specifically, the signatories petitioned for the right to freedom of worship, secular education, mixed marriages, fewer religious holidays, and the inspection of monasteries, among other issues. The articles were greeted with condemnation from the conservative camp. Although the articles had no lasting effect, the religious conflict eventually led to war, and to the revision of the SWISS FEDERAL PACT OF 1815.

See also: SWISS CONSTITUTION OF 1848.

Further reading: Charles Gilliard and J. C. Biaudet, *A History of Switzerland*, trans. D. L. B. Hartley (Westport, Conn.: Greenwood Press, 1978); William Martin, *Switzerland from Roman Times to the Present* (New York: Praeger, 1971).

Baden, Third Land Peace of Peace treaty signed on March 7, 1656, at Baden, Switzerland, by the 13 cantons of the Swiss Confederation. It temporarily concluded a religious conflict (the First Villmergen War [1656]) that had pitted the Protestant cantons of Bern and Zürich against the Roman Catholic cantons of Schwyz, Uri, Luzern, Unterwalden, and Zug; Catholic forces had won. Essentially a reassertion of the 1531 Peace of KAPPEL, the treaty upheld the Catholic position that each canton in the confederation could determine its own form of religion. Each maintained its own autonomy and had to pay its own war costs. Zurich had wanted each canton to be represented in the confederation according to its power and wealth (of which Zurich had the most), while the Catholic cantons wanted their individual autonomy.

Further reading: Charles Gilliard and J. C. Biaudet, *A History of Switzerland*, trans. D. L. B. Hartley (Westport, Conn.: Greenwood Press, 1978); William Martin, *Switzerland from Roman Times to the Present* (New York: Praeger, 1971).

Baden, Treaty of Agreement between the Holy Roman Empire and France, made at Baden, Switzerland, on September 7, 1714. It helped end the War of the Spanish Succession (1701–14), along with the Treaties of UTRECHT and RASTATT. By the terms of the Baden treaty, the empire received ratification of the Treaty of RYSWICK, and the electors of Bavaria and Köln were reinstated in their lands and offices. The free town of Landau was left in French hands.

Further reading: Linda Frey and Marsha Frey, eds., *The Treaties of the War of the Spanish Succession* (Westport, Conn.: Greenwood Press, 1995).

Badeni Language Ordinances Laws of April 5, 1897, which established parity in the Austro-Hungarian Empire between German and local languages, and elevated Czech to an administrative language in Bohemia and Moravia. Formulated by Austrian prime minister Count Kasimir Felix Badeni, the ordinances required officials to reply to public inquiries in the same language in which they were addressed. In addition, all officials were also required to prove current knowledge of both German and Czech. The new laws were a result of active agitation by the nationalist Young Czech Party, but they angered the German nationalists and failed to satisfy the Czechs. Violent public demonstrations against the ordinances, as well as parliamentary opposition, forced Badeni to resign and precipitated a grave constitutional crisis.

Further reading: Bruce M. Garver, *The Young Czech Party, 1874–1901, and the Emergence of a Multi-Party System* (New Haven, Conn.: Yale University Press, 1978).

Baghdad Pact (Middle East Treaty Organization)

Mutual defense agreement concluded by Turkey and Iraq on February 18, 1955, in Baghdad and joined later that year by Britain, Pakistan, and Iran, to guard against possible advances by the Soviet Union into the Middle East. Britain transferred two bases in Iraq to local management, securing in return refueling and air passage rights. She promised to help Iraq, if attacked, and to continue military support (see ANGLO-IRAQI TREATY OF 1930). Though not a signatory, the United States had suggested and encouraged the formation of the pact as a defense for small nations and a warning to aggressors in the region. The names Baghdad Pact and Middle East Treaty Organization (METO) were dropped in 1959 after Iraq withdrew from the pact following a coup d'état that ousted the pro-Western government of the country in 1958. The other signatories then reorganized themselves to form the Central Treaty Organization (CENTO). Britain and Iraq were both criticized for their involvement in the Baghdad Pact, which divided the Arabs into two camps and helped heighten the Middle East crisis.

Further reading: *The Baghdad Pact: Origins and Political Setting* (London: Royal Institute of International Affairs, 1956); J. A. S. Grenville and Bernard Wasserstein, eds., *Major International Treaties of the Twentieth Century*, 2d ed. (New York: Routledge, 2001); Magnus Persson, *Great Britain, the United States, and the Security of the Middle East: The Formation of the Baghdad Pact* (Stockholm: Almquist & Wiksell, 1998); Elie Podeh, *The Quest for Hegemony in the Arab World: The Struggle Over the Baghdad Pact* (Boston: E. J. Brill, 1995).

Bailey v. Drexel Furniture Company (Child Labor Tax Case)

U.S. Supreme Court ruling issued on May 15, 1922, that invalidated the U.S. CHILD LABOR ACT OF 1919, which had levied prohibitive taxes on the products of child labor sold in interstate commerce. Chief Justice William Howard Taft, writing for the majority, argued that the tax was intended not to raise revenue but to regulate the employment of children, a right that was reserved to the states by the TENTH AMENDMENT. He stated that the act imposed a penalty, not a true excise tax, and therefore violated constitutional limitations on congressional power.

Further reading: Mark Mikula and L. Mpho Mabunda, eds., *Great American Court Cases*, 4 vols. (Farmington Hills, Mich.: Gale Group, 1999); Eva R. Rubin, *The Supreme Court and the American Family: Ideology and Issues* (Westport, Conn.: Greenwood Press, 1986); Carl B. Swisher, *History of the Supreme Court of the United States*, vol. 10: *The Judiciary and Responsible Government, 1921–30* (New York: Macmillan, 1974); Stephen B. Wood, *Constitutional Politics in the Progressive Era: Child Labor and the Law* (Chicago: University of Chicago Press, 1968).

Baker v. Carr

U.S. Supreme Court decision issued on March 26, 1962, ruling that state legislative apportionment practices were subject to judicial review and control. In 1959 some Tennessee citizens sued state election officials for depriving them of federal constitutional rights because no legislative reapportionment had been made in the state since 1901, despite a state constitutional requirement that the legislature allocate, at least every 10 years, senators and representatives according to the number of qualified voters in each county or district. The lack of reapportionment had produced inequities in representation. The Supreme Court reversed *Colegrove v. Green* (1946) in deciding that legislative districting controversies could be heard by federal courts.

Further reading: Archibald Cox, *The Warren Court: Constitutional Decision as an Instrument of Reform* (Cambridge, Mass.: Harvard University Press, 1967); Bernard Grofman, *Voting Rights, Voting Wrongs: The Legacy of Baker v. Carr* (New York: Twentieth Century Fund, 1990); John W. Johnson, *Historic U.S. Court Cases, 1690–1990: An Encyclopedia* (New York: Garland Publishing, 1992); Mark Mikula and L. Mpho Mabunda, eds., *Great American Court Cases*, 4 vols. (Farmington Hills, Mich.: Gale Group, 1999).

Bakhchisarai, Treaty of

Agreement concluded at Bakhchisarai, Crimea, on January 13, 1681, between Russia and the Ottoman Empire, following several attempts to reach a settlement concerning the Russo-Turkish frontier. The treaty provided that the Dnieper River would serve as the Russo-Turkish border; that Russia would retain Kiev, Vasilkov, and several smaller towns; that a neutral area would be established between the Bug River and Dnieper River; that the Cossacks were to be recognized as Russian subjects; that the Crimean Tatars (Tartars) were to be allowed to continue to live a nomadic way of life near the Russian border, and that peace was to last 20 years.

Further reading: Hugh Ragsdale, ed., *Imperial Russian Foreign Policy* (Washington, D.C./New York: Woodrow Wilson Center Press/Cambridge University Press, 1993).

Bald, Book of (Leech Book of Bald)

Anglo-Saxon medical treatise believed to have been dictated by Bald, an early physician, to Cild; contains detailed magical and herbal prescriptions for a variety of ailments and prescribes the medicinal use of leeches to draw the blood of patients. It is one of a series of Leechbooks, vernacular manuals of basic medical practice, which appeared during the A.D. 900s and may actually be a compilation from Latin medical writers. Eighty-eight remedies are described in Part I, 67 in Part II, and 76 in Part III. The book is a splendid example of the exalted status accorded to medical knowledge in England's Anglo-Saxon period (c. 500–1066).

Balfour Act (Education Act of 1902)   Parliamentary legislation of December 21, 1902, reorganizing Britain's educational system; established by the EDUCATION ACT OF 1870. The most salient legislation of Lord Balfour's government, it abolished the school boards and entrusted elementary and secondary education to the statutory committees of the borough and county councils. It was based on the recommendations of the Bryce Commission and included the denominational schools too. The provision of secondary education was recognized as a state responsibility and the education budget was increased. This resulted in rapid expansion of state education; within five years, the number of secondary schools almost doubled. Drafted mainly by Permanent Secretary Robert Morant, the act succeeded in fulfilling its objectives of unifying and improving primary and secondary education.

Further reading: Geoffrey Alderman, *Modern Britain (1700–1983)* (London: Croom Helm, 1986); Joel H. Wiener, ed. *Great Britain—The Lion at Home: A Documentary History of Domestic Policy (1689–1973)*, 4 vols. (New York: Chelsea House, 1974).

Balfour Declaration   Statement made by Britain's foreign secretary, Arthur J. Balfour, in a letter of November 2, 1917, to British Zionist leader Lionel Walter Rothschild (second Baron Rothschild), indicating British support for "the establishment in Palestine of a national home for the Jewish people." Britain hoped thereby to win Jewish backing for the Allied cause in World War I (1914–18) and to protect her own interests in Egypt's sensitive Suez Canal area. Prompted also by rumors that Germany was thinking of a similar declaration, it promised to protect the "civil and religious rights of the existing non-Jewish communities in Palestine." It did not fully satisfy the Zionist hope for an eventual Jewish state. Two of Britain's leading cabinet ministers, Edwin S. Montagu and George N. Curzon, opposed the declaration. It was endorsed by the major Allied powers and approved (July 24, 1922) by the League of Nations in Britain's mandate over Palestine.

Further reading: Ronald Sanders, *The High Walls of Jerusalem: A History of the Balfour Declaration and the Birth of the British Mandate for Palestine* (New York: Holt Rinehart & Winston, 1984).

Balkan Pact (Balkan Entente)   Pact concluded in Athens on February 9, 1934, by Greece, Romania, Yugoslavia, and Turkey, reflecting the four signatory powers' desire to maintain peace in the Balkan Peninsula. The terms of the pact (which was primarily the work of Romania's foreign minister Nicholas Titulescu) included the signatory powers' pledge to ensure the security of their frontiers and their agreement not to enter into political agreements with any Balkan state that was not a party to the pact without prior consultation with the pact's signatories. Through a protocol annexed to the pact on the same day, the signatories pledged to recognize all existing treaties to which any signatory was a party, to come to the defense of any party to the pact, which was attacked by another Balkan state or the combination of a Balkan state and another power, and declared that an act of aggression committed by a signatory would be grounds to exclude that party from the privileges of the pact. Despite the lengthy provisions, the treaty provided for nothing more than a guarantee of the signatories' frontiers in the event of a Bulgarian attack.

Further reading: Robert Joseph Kerner, *The Balkan Conferences and the Balkan Entente, 1930–1935: A Study in Recent History of the Balkans and Near Eastern Peoples* (Westport, Conn.: Greenwood Press, 1970); *Nicholas Titulesca: The European Statesman of the League of Nations* (Paris: Editions Nagard, 1982); I. M. Oprea, *Nicolae Titulescu's Diplomatic Activity* (Bucharest: Socialist Republic of Romania, 1968).

Balkan Treaties of 1866–68   Series of treaties concluded between Serbia under the leadership of Prince Michael Obrenovich and Romania under Prince Carol I (May 26, 1867, and January 1868) and between Serbia and Montenegro (September 23, 1866), providing for alliances between the signatory powers against the Ottoman Empire, of which they were a part. The treaties were generally treaties of friendship, although the Serbian-Montenegrin Treaty went so far as to provide terms for the possible union of the two provinces. The primary objective of the treaties was to coordinate the efforts of these Balkan provinces against the Ottoman Turks, and to bring about the formation of an independent Balkan state under Serbian leadership.

See also: VOESLAU, TREATY OF.

Further reading: L. S. Stavrianos, *The Balkans since 1453* (New York: Rinehart, 1958); Harold Temperley, *The History of Serbia* (New York: Howard Fertig, 1969).

Balta Liman, Convention of   Agreement concluded on May 1, 1849, between representatives of Russia and the Ottoman Empire in the Turkish town of Balta Liman, through which both powers took measures to control the internal politics of the Danubian principalities of Wallachia and Moldavia, following revolutionary activity there in 1848. The document provided that both powers would continue to occupy the principalities, which they had occupied since they crushed the revolutionary rising in 1848; that the hospodars (the political leaders of the principalities) would be nominated by the Ottoman sultan and their nomination approved by Russia, thus replacing the former system by which the noblemen appointed their own leaders; and that the assemblies of noblemen would be replaced by assemblies consisting of individuals appointed by the hospodars. The convention was to remain in effect for seven years.

Further reading: Barbara Jelavich, *Russia's Balkan Entanglements, 1806–1914* (New York: Cambridge University Press, 1991); Hugh Ragsdale, ed., *Imperial Russian Foreign Policy* (Washington, D.C., New York: Woodrow Wilson Center Press/Cambridge University Press, 1993).

Baltic Pact (Baltic Entente)

Treaties endorsed in Geneva, Switzerland, on September 12, 1934, and ratified in Riga, Latvia, on November 3, 1934, by representatives of the Baltic states of Lithuania, Latvia, and Estonia, providing for "cooperation and good understanding" among them. The pact, which was to remain in effect for 10 years, provided that the three countries would mutually support one another in defense of independence and their diplomatic affairs, and consult with one another on foreign policy matters of common concern; that representatives of each country would meet together at least twice a year; that all conflicts between any of the parties were to be concluded through pacific means; and that treaties to be concluded by any signatory of the pact with a foreign power were to be made known to all signatories prior to their conclusion.

Baltic States Declaration of Independence of 1991

Joint declaration of Estonia, Latvia, and Lithuania issued as part of their plan to achieve full independence from the Soviet Union. The three Soviet republics had already declared their individual sovereignty (see ESTONIAN DECLARATION OF SOVEREIGNTY OF 1988, LATVIAN DECLARATION OF INDEPENDENCE OF 1990, and LITHUANIAN DECLARATION OF INDEPENDENCE OF 1990). The Soviet Union's leader, Mikhail S. Gorbachev, supported the autonomy of the republics in all areas except defense and foreign affairs, but he insisted that they remain part of the Soviet Union. On December 1, 1990, representatives of the supreme councils of the three republics met in Vilnius, Lithuania; one result of the meeting was their joint declaration of sovereign independence on January 11, 1991. In it, the republics called on the Soviet Union to abandon its policy of economic and military threats to keep them in the union, called for talks with the Soviets concerning full independence, petitioned other European nations and international organizations to offer to serve as third parties in such talks, and asked that the question of Baltic independence be placed on the agendas of the various European multinational organizations.

Further reading: Baltic Assembly, "Pre-History," available online at http://www.baltasam.org/organization/history.html.

Balzac v. Porto Rico

U.S. Supreme Court decision, issued on April 10, 1922, that declared Porto Rico (now Puerto Rico) to be a territory of the United States that was not incorporated into the Union; its residents, though they had been made U.S. citizens by the JONES ACT OF 1917, therefore did not automatically enjoy all of the rights protected by the U.S. CONSTITUTION. An editor named Balzac appealed a Puerto Rican criminal libel conviction on the ground that he had been denied a jury trial, a right guaranteed by the SIXTH AMENDMENT. The Supreme Court ruled that the right to a jury trial does not apply in unincorporated territories because it is not a "fundamental right which goes wherever the jurisdiction of the United States extends."

Further reading: Carl B. Swisher, *History of the Supreme Court of the United States*, vol. 10: *The Judiciary and Responsible Government, 1921–30* (New York: Macmillan, 1974).

Bandung Resolutions

Ten-point declaration for the promotion of international peace and cooperation, unanimously adopted by 29 African and Asian nations at the conclusion of the Bandung Conference (April 18–24, 1955) convened by Indonesia, India, Burma, Ceylon (now Sri Lanka), and Pakistan. It incorporated resolutions drawn from the UNITED NATIONS CHARTER and from Indian prime minister Jawaharlal Nehru's own five principles: (1) respect for basic human rights, as in the United Nations Charter; (2) respect for the sovereignty and territorial integrity of all countries; (3) acceptance of the equality of races and nations; (4) nonintervention in the internal affairs of another country; (5) respect each nation's right to self-defense; (6) avoid exerting pressure on other countries and entering into collective defense agreements serving the interests of the big powers; (7) maintain nonaggression against another's political or territorial integrity; (8) settle international disputes by peaceful means; (9) promotion of mutual interest and cooperation; and (10) respect for international obligations and justice.

Further reading: George McTurnan Kahin, *The Asian-African Conference, Bandung, Indonesia, April 1955* (Ithaca, N.Y.: Cornell University Press, 1956); Richard Wright and Gunnar Myrdal, *The Color Curtain: A Report on the Bandung Conference* (Jackson: University Press of Mississippi, 1995).

Bank Charter Act of 1844, British

Important banking legislation of July 19, 1844, which stabilized the British economy by linking the issuance of banknotes to a fixed currency reserve and by separating the Bank of England's note-issuing department from its banking department. As a protection against financial crises, the bank was allowed to issue notes only up to £14 million (amount covered by government securities); notes issued in excess of that amount were required to be backed (pound for pound) by gold reserves. Directed against the proliferating joint-stock banks, which issued banknotes without adequate gold reserves, the law forbade new banks from issuing notes—in an attempt to gradually eliminate all notes except those of the Bank of England. Scottish banks, however, could continue to issue notes.

Further reading: John E. Cairnes, *An Examination into the Principles of Currency Involved in the Bank Charter Act of 1844* (Fairfield, N.J.: Augustus M. Kelley, 1989).

Bankhead-Jones Farm Tenant Act U.S. legislation sponsored by Senator John Hollis Bankhead II of Alabama and Representative John M. Jones of Texas and enacted on July 22, 1937, to stop the decline in farm ownership and to check the growth of tenant farming and sharecropping. The federal act established the Farm Security Administration (FSA) and authorized it to grant low-interest, long-term loans to farm tenants, sharecroppers, and farm workers who wished to purchase their own farms. It encouraged the retirement of worn-out land and provided rehabilitation loans, educational assistance, and technical aid. The FSA also regulated the wages and hours of migrant workers and provided them with sanitary and medical facilities.

Further reading: Arthur M. Schlesinger, Jr., *The Age of Roosevelt,* vol. 2: *The Coming of the New Deal* (Boston: Houghton Mifflin, 1958).

Bank Holiday Declaration, Roosevelt's Edict issued by U.S. President Franklin D. Roosevelt on March 5, 1933, and effective the following day, declaring a four-day national banking holiday, halting all transactions in banks (including Federal Reserve banks), trust companies, credit unions, and other financial institutions. It also placed an embargo on the export of silver, gold, and currency. Roosevelt, claiming authority under the Trading with the Enemy Act of 1917, intended the emergency measure to allow time to prepare legislation to handle the national crisis of bank failures and to protect the nation's diminishing gold reserves. The edict allowed the use of scrip so that businesses might continue.

Further reading: Charles Cary Colt, *28 Days: A History of the Banking Crises* (New York: Greenberg, 1933); Marcus Nadler and Jules I. Bogen, *The Banking Crisis: The End of an Epoch* (New York: Arno Press, 1980); James Francis Thaddeus O'Connor, *The Banking Crisis and Recovery under the Roosevelt Administration* (New York: Da Capo Press, 1971); Lawrence Sullivan, *Prelude to Panic: The Story of the Bank Holiday* (Washington, D.C.: Statesman Press, 1936).

Banking Act of 1947, Australian Controversial Australian legislation of November 27, 1947, authorizing the Commonwealth Bank to take over the business hitherto conducted by private banks. Introduced into the Australian parliament by Prime Minister Joseph Chifley on October 15, 1947, it was viewed by the opposition as an extension of the Banking Act of 1945 and a further tightening of the government's control over the private banking system. The process of nationalization was to be effected either by voluntary or compulsory acquisition of assets (applicable to all banks,

whether incorporated in Australia or not) or by compulsory acquisition of shares (only banks incorporated in the country). The legislation did not affect state or savings banks. It was denounced by the opposition as dictatorial and unconstitutional and is believed to have led to the downfall of Australia's Labour government in 1949.

Further reading: F. K. Crowley, ed., *Modern Australia in Documents* (Melbourne, Australia: Wren Publishing, 1973).

Banking Act of 1933, U.S. (Glass-Steagall Banking Act) New Deal legislation sponsored by Senator Carter Glass of Virginia and Representative Henry B. Steagall of Alabama and enacted on June 16, 1933, that reformed the national banking system and created the Federal Deposit Insurance Corporation (FDIC) to guarantee individual bank deposits under $5,000, in order to restore public confidence in banks. The act increased the power of the Federal Reserve Board to control credit, especially to prevent speculation, and separated commercial and investment banking. Commercial banks belonging to the Federal Reserve system were prohibited from selling stocks and bonds and engaging in securities speculation, while investment banks were forbidden to carry on deposit banking. The act also allowed branch banking and opened membership in the Federal Reserve system to savings and industrial banks.

Further reading: John Edson Brady, ed., *Banking Act of 1933 and the Emergency Bank Act of 1933* (Cambridge, Mass.: Banking Law Journal, 1933); James Francis Thaddeus O'Connor, *The Banking Crisis and Recovery under the Roosevelt Administration* (New York: Da Capo Press, 1971); Susan Estabrook Kennedy, *The Banking Crisis of 1933* (Lexington: University Press of Kentucky, 1973); Marcus Nadler and Jules I. Bogen, *The Banking Crisis: The End of an Epoch* (New York: Arno Press, 1980).

Banking Act of 1935, U.S. New Deal legislation enacted on August 23, 1935, that increased centralization of the American banking system and federal control of the system, continuing banking reforms begun under the U.S. BANKING ACT OF 1933. The 1935 act reorganized the Federal Reserve Board, changing its name to the Board of Governors of the Federal Reserve System and increasing its power in credit management. The new seven-member board had more authority over rediscount rates, reserve requirements of member banks, and open-market operations. The Federal Deposit Insurance Corporation (FDIC) was given new supervisory powers and made a permanent organization; state banks were required to join the Federal Reserve System by 1942 if they wished to benefit from FDIC.

Further reading: *Banking Act of 1935* (New York: American Institute of Banking, 1935); Marcus Nadler and Jules I. Bogen, *The Banking Crisis: The End of an Epoch* (New York: Arno Press, 1980); James Francis Thaddeus O'Connor, *The Banking Crisis and Recovery under the Roosevelt Administration*

(New York: Da Capo Press, 1971); Lawrence Sullivan, *Prelude to Panic: The Story of the Bank Holiday* (Washington, D.C.: Statesman Press, 1936).

Bank of Augusta v. Earle   U.S. Supreme Court decision issued in 1839, establishing that in the absence of specific state action to the contrary, a corporation chartered by one state was presumed to have the right to do business, under interstate comity, in other states; a state did have the right to exclude a corporation by positive action. The case arose when an Alabama citizen refused to honor bills of exchange from a Georgia bank, arguing that a "foreign" corporation had no right to make a contract in another sovereign state. Chief Justice Roger Taney also ruled that a corporation did not possess all the U.S. constitutional rights of a natural person.

Further reading: Carl B. Swisher, *History of the Supreme Court of the United States,* vol. 5: *The Taney Period, 1836–64* (New York: Macmillan, 1974).

Bantustan Program   South African policy, enacted through the Promotion of Bantu Self-Government Act (1959), intended to transform the black African tribal areas (the great majority being Bantu) into self-governing states (Bantustans, or homelands). Formulated by South Africa's prime minister H.F. Verwoerd and W.M. Eiselen (secretary of native administration), the act recognized eight ethnically grouped, national Bantu territorial units and outlined the procedures leading to each's eventual self-government. It abolished the representation of Bantus by whites in the parliament and appointed five commissioners-general to facilitate direct consultation between Bantustans and the South African government. The system of authorities, as established by the Bantu Authorities Act of 1951, was maintained. Transkei, the largest of the Bantustans, secured limited self-government in 1963 and became the first independent black African homeland in South Africa in 1976. The creation of these segregated and highly fragmented homelands was merely another step in the government's policy of apartheid (racial segregation).

Further reading: Jeffrey Butler, *The Black Homelands of South Africa: The Political and Economic Development of Bophuthatswana and KwaZulu* (Berkeley: University of California Press, 1977); Christopher R. Hill, *Bantustans: The Fragmentation of South Africa* (New York: Oxford University Press, 1964); Patrick Laurence, *The Transkei: South Africa's Politics of Partition* (Johannesburg, South Africa: Ravan Press, 1976); Barbara Rogers, *Divide and Rule: South Africa's Bantustans* (London: International Defence & Aid Fund, 1980).

Barcelona, Treaty of (1493)   Pact of alliance between French king Charles VIII and Spanish king Ferdinand V and queen Isabella I; concluded at Barcelona, Spain, on January 19, 1493. The Spanish monarchs promised to help if Charles was invaded by any of his enemies—England's king Henry VII, Holy Roman Emperor Maximilian I, or Archduke Philip of Austria (later, Spain's king Philip I)—and promised that none of their children would be married into any of those royal families without Charles's consent. Charles, in need of goodwill and support for his forthcoming Italian campaign, unconditionally restored the disputed regions of Roussillon and Cerdagne (Cerdaña) to Spanish rule.

See also: ÉTAPLES, TREATY OF; SENLIS, TREATY OF.

Further reading: J. N. Hillgarth, *The Spanish Kingdoms, 1250–1516,* 2 vols. (Oxford, England: Clarendon Press, 1976–78); Henry Kamen, *Inquisition and Society in Spain: In the Sixteenth and Seventeenth Centuries* (Bloomington: Indiana University Press, 1985).

Barcelona, Treaty of (1529)   Pact of alliance between Holy Roman Emperor Charles V (Charles I of Spain) and Pope Clement VII; signed in Barcelona, Spain, on June 29, 1529. They agreed to work together to bring peace to Italy and to repel the Turkish advance. The pope restored to Charles the investiture of Naples, receiving Ravenna, Modena, Reggio, Rubiera, and Cervisa in return, and also a promise to restore the Medici in Florence. Charles and his troops were pardoned for sacking Rome in 1527. Clement, having recovered most of his temporal powers albeit in subservience to the emperor, recognized Ferdinand as king of Bohemia and Hungary. Charles and the pope also agreed to take a united stand against heresy. The new alliance culminated in Charles's coronation (February 24, 1530) at Bologna, the last imperial coronation performed by a pope. It was followed by Charles's reconciliation with the French king (see CAMBRAI, PEACE OF) and strengthened the Hapsburg domination of Italy.

See also: CATEAU-CAMBRÉSIS, TREATY OF.

Further reading: Geoffrey Barraclough, *The Medieval Papacy* (New York: Harcourt, Brace & World, 1968); Fernand Mourret and Newton Thompson, eds., *History of the Catholic Church* (St. Louis, Mo.: B. Herder, 1945).

Barmen Declaration (Theological Declaration of Barmen)   Declaration issued in May 1934, under the influence of Swiss Protestant theologian Karl Barth (then a professor at the University of Bonn), by representatives of Lutheran, Reformed, and United Protestant churches during a meeting attended by German Protestant leaders in the German city of Barmen, declaring their opposition to National Socialism, or Nazism. The document, consisting of six articles, reaffirmed the major tenets of the Christian faith and condemned the practices and ideology of the National Socialists. The declaration was written in the form of a confession of faith and is still used as such in some Protestant denominations. Barth's refusal to take an oath of allegiance to Adolf Hitler, Nazi chancellor of Germany, caused him to lose his professorship at Bonn and to be deported to Switzerland in 1935.

Further reading: Eberhard Jungel, *Christ, Justice, and Peace: Toward a Theology of the State in Dialogue with the*

Barmen Declaration (Edinburgh, Scotland: T & T Clark, 1992); Robert T. Osborn, *The Barmen Declaration as a Paradigm for a Theology* (Lewiston, N.Y.: Edwin Mellen, 1991).

Barrier Treaties   Three agreements granting the Dutch republic (the Netherlands) rights to certain fortresses and towns (as a barrier) along the southern Spanish (subsequently Austrian) Netherlands as a protection against French incursions. The first treaty (October 29, 1709) restored to the Dutch a dozen forts and towns taken by the French in 1701. Britain agreed to it, and in return the Dutch supported the Hanoverian succession in Britain, where later the Tories rejected the treaty in 1712 as harmful to British trade. The second treaty (January 29, 1713), signed just before the Treaty of UTRECHT, secured for the Dutch from the French garrison rights at various forts in the Spanish Netherlands. The third treaty (November 15, 1715) was signed at Antwerp by Britain, the Dutch republic, and Holy Roman Emperor Charles VI, who now ruled the Austrian Netherlands. The Dutch gained control of seven fortresses on the French border of the Austrian Netherlands. The treaty was eventually repealed by the 1785 Treaty of FONTAINEBLEAU.

See also: GRAND ALLIANCE OF 1701; RYSWICK, TREATY OF.

Further reading: Bartholomew Landheer, ed., *The Netherlands* (Berkeley: University of California Press, 1943); Alan Palmer, *An Encyclopedia of Napoleon's Europe* (New York: St. Martin's Press, 1984); Hubert N. B. Richardson, *Dictionary of Napoleon and His Times* (London: Cassell, 1920).

Barron v. Baltimore   U.S. Supreme Court decision issued on February 16, 1833, holding that the first 10 amendments to the U.S. Constitution (the Bill of Rights) were binding upon the federal government but not upon the state governments. John Barron, a wharf owner, sued the city of Baltimore for diverting water from his pier and destroying its use as a dock, claiming protection under the FIFTH AMENDMENT guarantee against government seizure of private property without compensation. Chief Justice John Marshall, in denying Barron's claim, limited the protections of the U.S. BILL OF RIGHTS.

Further reading: David Currie, *The Constitution in the Supreme Court: The First Hundred Years, 1789–1888* (Chicago: University of Chicago Press, 1985); John W. Johnson, *Historic U.S. Court Cases, 1690–1990: An Encyclopedia* (New York: Garland Publishing, 1992); Mark Mikula and L. Mpho Mabunda, eds., *Great American Court Cases,* 4 vols. (Farmington Hills, Mich.: Gale Group, 1999); George White, *History of the Supreme Court of the United States,* vol. 4: *The Challenge of Jacksonian Democracy: The Marshall Court, 1826–35* (New York: Macmillan, 1974).

Baruch's Proposals for the Control of Atomic Energy
Delivered to the United Nations Atomic Energy Commission in June 1946; proposed plans concerning the international control of atomic energy and weapons presented by American financier Bernard M. Baruch, who had been appointed by President Harry S. Truman to represent the United States at the commission. The Baruch plan called for universal nuclear disarmament, strict regulation on the production of fissionable materials, and an enforcement mechanism not subject to U.N. Security Council veto. When the Soviet Union objected to the idea and the U.S. Senate seemed set against any such arrangement, Baruch's proposals were dropped.

Further reading: Bernard Baruch, *The International Control of Atomic Energy: Scientific Information Transmitted to the United Nations* (Washington, D.C.: Department of State, 1946).

Bärwalde, Treaty of   Subsidy treaty signed at Bärwalde (Barwice, Poland) on January 23, 1631, securing continued Swedish military cooperation with France in the Thirty Years' War (1618–48) against Spain. King Louis XIII of France (advised by Cardinal de Richelieu) contracted to pay King Gustavus II of Sweden an annual subsidy of 1 million livres (coins) for six years, in return for maintaining an army of 30,000 infantry and 6,000 cavalry in Germany. Gustavus promised to protect the religious liberties of the Catholics in Germany and agreed not to end the war without consulting the French king. In a separate agreement, he promised to avoid confrontation with any pro-French prince or power (referring to the duke of Bavaria and the Catholic League) in Europe. He also accepted the demolition of the Spanish fortresses in the Grisons (Swiss canton). The five-year alliance was almost entirely to Sweden's advantage, and Richelieu was compelled to renew the subsidy treaty on April 19, 1633.

See also: WESTPHALIA, PEACE OF.

Further reading: W. F. Reddaway, ed., *The Cambridge History of Poland to 1696* (Cambridge, England: Cambridge University Press, 1950); Michael Roberts, ed., *Sweden as a Great Power 1611–1697: Government, Society, Foreign Policy* (New York: St. Martin's Press, 1968).

Basel, Treaties of (1795)   Two peace treaties concluded by France in 1795 at Basel, Switzerland—the first with Prussia on April 5 and the second with Spain on July 22. Prussia, financially drained during the French revolutionary wars (1792–1802), withdrew from the First Coalition of European states against France and agreed to France's temporary control of the left bank of the Rhine (while the French agreed to evacuate the right bank) until peace could be made with Austria; in secret provisions, Prussia approved permanent annexation of the left bank of the Rhine by France, which in return agreed to compensate Prussia by secularizing ecclesiastical lands on the right bank. Through France's treaty with Spain, the latter ceded Santo Domingo (the eastern two-thirds of the island of Hispaniola) to France, while regaining other territories taken by the French in the wars.

Further reading: Georges Lefebvre, *The French Revolution: From Its Origins to 1793* and *From 1793 to 1799,* 2 vols. (New

York: Columbia University Press, 1962); Alan Palmer, *An Encyclopedia of Napoleon's France* (New York: St. Martin's Press, 1984).

Basel, Treaty of (1499)

Peace treaty concluded at Basel on September 22, 1499, ending the Austro-Swiss War of 1499 or Swiss-Swabian War, which had pitted Holy Roman Emperor Maximilian I (supported by the Swabian cities of south Germany) against the Swiss Confederation (backed by the French). The victorious Swiss forced the emperor to make peace and to grant de facto recognition of Swiss independence. The war had ensued after the Swiss refused to accept recently enacted imperial legislation, including payment of an imperial tax.

Further reading: E. Bonjour, H. S. Offler, and G. R. Potter, *A Short History of Switzerland* (Oxford, England: Clarendon Press, 1952); William Martin, *Switzerland: From Roman Times to the Present* (London: Elek Books, 1971).

Basel Compacta

See PRAGUE, COMPACTS OF.

Basel Declaration of 1897 (Basel Program)

Official declaration of the World Zionist Organization, drawn up by a special commission (including writer Max Simon Nordau) in August 1897, stating that "Zionism strives to create for the Jewish people a home in Palestine secured by public law." Several days later the first World Zionist Congress, organized by Theodor Herzl in Basel, Switzerland, agreed to the declaration, or so-called Basel Program, which included the Zionist organization's resolve to obtain the necessary support from foreign governments for its goal, to make Jews aware of the importance of establishing a national homeland in Palestine, and to promote the settlement there of Jewish farmers and industrial workers and others.

Further reading: Macmillan, eds., *Encyclopedia of Judaica*, 16 vols. (New York: Macmillan, 1972).

Basic Law of 1949, West German

Provisional constitution of the Federal Republic of Germany passed by the West German Parliamentary Council in Bonn on May 8, 1949, providing a basis upon which a new democratic government could be formed in West Germany. The constitution provided for a parliament with two houses, of which the Bundesrat (upper house) would be elected by the republic's individual states and the Bundestag (lower house) would be elected by direct universal suffrage. The president was to be elected for a five-year term by a federal assembly composed of delegates from both houses of the parliament. The president was to nominate the chancellor, who would in turn state his choice for cabinet ministers. The states had the right to pass their own laws, although the federal government had the exclusive right to pass laws on foreign policy, currency, citizenship, and others. The constitution also guaranteed fundamental human rights (including equality of all, without prejudice on the basis of sex, race, language, religion, or political orientation) and freedom of the press and of expression. The constitution was confirmed by the Western allied military authorities several days later.

Further reading: Walter Stahl, ed., *The Politics of Postwar Germany* (New York: Praeger, 1963).

Bassein, Treaty of

Alliance between Baji Rao II, the Maratha peshwa of Poona in India, and the British East India Company on December 31, 1802, which split the Maratha league and led eventually to the British control of the Deccan region. Following the death of Nana Fadnavis (the peshwa's minister) in 1800, both Sindhia and Holkar (the other Maratha chiefs) sought to have the peshwa under their control. However, the peshwa put his adopted brother on the throne and escaped to Bassein, where he asked for British help. In return, he agreed to maintain a military force of at least six battalions stationed within his territories, to bar from service all Europeans hostile to the British, to renounce his claims to Surat and Baroda, and to consult the British on foreign policy issues. His powers undermined, the British restored him to the throne in May 1803. This treaty led to the Second Maratha War (1803–5), where the British defeated the other Maratha powers.

Further reading: H. H. Dodwell, *The Cambridge History of India* (Delhi, India: S. Chand, 1964); Brian Gardner, *The East India Company: A History* (New York: McCall, 1972).

Batum, Treaty of

Treaty concluded in the Transcaucasian town of Batum (Batumi or Batoum) on June 4, 1918, by representatives of Turkey (the Ottoman Empire) and Armenia, temporarily ending the hostilities between the two that had commenced upon the Soviet evacuation from Transcaucasia (see BREST-LITOVSK, TREATY OF). The terms of the treaty provided for peace and eternal friendship between the two countries; for the establishment of a new Turko-Armenian boundary, the Turks thus acquiring a significant part of Armenian territory; for Armenia's obligation to inform the Turkish government of any Armenian-Azerbaijani border agreements; for Armenia's agreement to disband her army and to rely solely on Turkish forces to maintain peace domestically; and for Armenia's agreement to guarantee the religious and cultural freedom of Muslims (the majority of Armenians were Christian). Armenia's obligation to adhere to these humiliating terms, which would have reduced her to a Turkish protectorate, ended upon Turkey's defeat by the Allies in World War I (1914–18).

See also: ALEXANDROPOL, TREATY OF; KARS, TREATY OF.

Further reading: Vahan M. Kurkjian, *A History of Armenia* (New York: Armenian General Benevolent Union, 1958).

Bautzen, Treaty of

Peace treaty concluded at Bautzen in southeastern Germany in 1018, ending the prolonged warring between Boleslav I, the Polish crowned duke who was the first to call himself king, and Henry II, the Holy Roman emperor. Boleslav retained control of the imperial lands of Lusatia and Meissen (Misnia), which he had seized as part of his expansionist policy, but he was forced to relinquish to Henry the principality of Bohemia.

Further reading: Norman Davies, *God's Playground: A History of Poland,* 2 vols. (New York: Columbia University Press, 1982).

Bayard-Chamberlain Treaty   Compact drafted in 1888 by a joint British-American commission concerning American fishing rights in Canadian waters. After the United States abrogated the Treaty of WASHINGTON in 1885, Canadian seizures of U.S. fishing vessels led to retaliatory threats. The 1888 draft treaty provided for a commission to define American rights in Canadian waters, recognized exclusive Canadian rights in certain bays, and promised further concessions if the United States removed tariff duties on Canadian fish. The U.S. Senate rejected the treaty on August 21, 1888. Nonetheless a modus vivendi worked out by the joint commission, granting the United States privileges in Canadian ports, remained in effect until 1923.

Further reading: Joseph Ingersoll Doran, *Our Fishery Rights in the North Atlantic* (Philadelphia: Allen, Lane & Smith, 1888); Allan Nevins, *Grover Cleveland: A Study in Courage* (Norwalk, Conn.: Easton Press, 1932, repr., 1989).

Bayonne, Treaty of   King Charles IV's ignominious abdication of the Spanish throne in favor of the French emperor Napoléon Bonaparte, "the only person who could restore order in Spain," by a treaty signed at Bayonne, France, on May 6, 1808. Charles IV insisted only that the new ruler (Napoléon later nominated his brother, Joseph) preserve the Roman Catholic faith and the territorial integrity of Spain and her empire. He received estates in France, a pension of 8,000,000 francs, and the crown diamonds. His eldest son, Ferdinand VII, to whom he had renounced the throne (March 18) was forced to sign a formal abdication restoring it to Charles IV, who would then surrender it to Napoléon. Ferdinand VII received 1 million francs and Navarre, and his siblings 400,000 francs each. Manuel de Godoy, who had drawn up the document with Napoléon and Marshal Géraud Duroc, recovered his confiscated property. When news of the abdication became public, the Spanish people rose up in revolt against Napoléon's treachery; thus began the Peninsular War (1808–14).

Further reading: John Palmer and Brian Powell, eds., *The Treaty of Bayonne (1388), with Preliminary Treaties of Trancoso (1387)* (Exeter, England: University of Exeter, 1988).

Bayonne Decree   French emperor Napoléon Bonaparte's response on April 17, 1808, to the United States's EMBARGO ACT OF 1807; ordered the seizure of any vessel claiming allegiance to the United States. Napoléon claimed that in doing so he was actually facilitating the enforcement of the Embargo

Act overseas. Denying, in principle, the existence of American shipping, the decree was based on the assumption that all American ships in French harbors were in reality British ships operating with false documents (see FONTAINEBLEAU DECREES, MILAN DECREES, ORDERS IN COUNCIL OF 1807). The implementation of the decree resulted in the seizure of almost $10 million worth of U.S. ships and cargo, and was widely criticized. Two years later, Napoléon introduced the RAMBOUILLET DECREE.

Further reading: Geoffrey J. Ellis, *The Napoleonic Empire* (Atlantic Highlands, N.J.: Humanities Press International, 1991); James H. Robinson, ed., *The Napoleonic Period* (Philadelphia: Department of History of the University of Pennsylvania, 1895).

Beaulieu, Edict of   Edict of pacification reluctantly issued by France's king Henry III at Beaulieu after he signed the Peace of MONSIEUR in May 1576. It gave the Huguenots (French Protestants) freedom of worship everywhere except in Paris and allowed them eight centers (cities) of refuge and dominance. The Huguenots were also granted admission to all public offices, equal representation with the Roman Catholics in all *parlements,* and the right to have their own schools and synods. Estates and appanages (property given by the king) were returned to Huguenot leaders, notably to Henry III's eldest brother, Francis, duke of Alençon, who had the title "Monsieur" and now obtained the appanages of Anjou, Touraine, and Berry.

Further reading: Mack P. Holt, *The French Wars of Religion, 1562–1629* (New York: Cambridge University Press, 1999).

Bec, Compromise of   See COMPROMISE OF 1107, ENGLISH.

Belfast (Ulster) Covenant of 1912   Covenant signed at a mass rally in Belfast on September 28, 1912, its half-million signatories pledging to "use all means which may be necessary to defeat the present conspiracy to set up a Home Rule Parliament in Ireland." The meeting was convened to express opposition to the HOME RULE BILL OF 1913, introduced by Britain's prime minister Herbert Asquith in April. Sir Edward Carson, former British attorney general for Ireland, was chosen to lead the covenanters. Their initial plans were to reject home rule for Ireland entirely. Later, they modified their stand and demanded that Ulster province be left out of the bill's coverage.

See also: GOVERNMENT OF IRELAND ACT.

Further reading: Christopher Haigh, ed., *The Cambridge Historical Encyclopedia of Great Britain and Ireland* (Cambridge, England: Cambridge University Press 1985); D. J. Hickey and J. E. Doherty, *A Dictionary of Irish History since 1800* (Dublin: Gill & Macmillan, 1980).

Belgian Constitution of 1831

Liberal monarchical constitution promulgated by Belgium's new national congress in Brussels in February 1831. The Belgians had successfully risen against Dutch domination to win independence in 1830. The new constitution said that "all powers have their source in the nation" and contained a declaration of the rights of citizens. Belgium's monarch, who was to be chosen by representatives of the people and had to swear a constitutional oath, received authority to veto legislation and dissolve parliament, which was to have upper and lower legislative houses elected regularly, by secret ballot, by an electorate of qualified property taxpayers (not by universal suffrage). Written into this constitution were various checks and balances of monarchic and democratic power; the judiciary was kept independent of the state; constitutional revisions were anticipated. In June 1831, Prince Leopold of Saxe-Coburg was chosen as Leopold I, king of the Belgians.

Further reading: Louis de Lichtervelde, *Le Congrès national: L'ouvre et les hommes* (Brussels: Renaissance du livre, 1945).

Belgian Neutrality Treaty (Treaty of London)

Pact first made on January 20, 1831, by which Britain, France, Russia, Austria, and Prussia guaranteed the independence and neutrality of Belgium, which had broken away from its union with Holland. Meeting in London, the powers gave up all territorial claims upon Belgian territory and "exclusive influence on her policy." The preliminary agreement was that Holland would retain the boundaries of 1790 while Belgium received everything else except Luxembourg. Britain and France were divided over the fate of the border fortresses, Luxembourg, and the selection of a new sovereign, issues that led to bitter and prolonged negotiations. On November 15, 1831, Belgium accepted a revised version of the treaty, but Austria, Prussia, and Russia delayed their ratification until April–May 1832, pending Holland's acceptance. Continued opposition from Holland delayed full and final settlement of the Belgian question until 1839.

See also: LONDON, TREATY OF (1839).

Further reading: Emile Cammaerts, *A History of Belgium from the Roman Invasion to the Present Day* (New York: Appleton, 1921); E. H. Kossman, *The Low Countries, 1780–1940* (Oxford, England: Clarendon Press, 1978).

Belgic Confession (Confessio Belgica)

Profession of faith of the Reformed (Calvinistic) Church in the southern Low Countries (now Belgium) and in northern France, drafted by reformer Guido de Brès and published in Rouen, France, in 1561. Revised by a synod in Antwerp in 1566 and sanctioned by various other synods in the next 15 years, the Belgic Confession won full approval at the Synod of Dort in 1619 (see DORT, CANONS OF). Its statements were very similar to the Gallican Confession (1559), which the Reformed Church of France accepted and which claimed salvation came to those chosen by God and declared the Bible as the sole rule of faith. The Belgic formulary gave a simpler expression of the sacraments and other church doctrines.

See also: HEIDELBERG CATECHISM.

Further reading: Lepusculus Vallensis, *The Belgic Confession and Its Biblical Basis* (Caledonia, Mich.: Inheritance Publications, 1993); G. Van Rongen, *The Church: Its Unity in Confession and History* (Pella, La.: Inheritance Publications, 1998).

Belgrade, Treaty of

Peace agreement made between the Ottoman Empire (Turkey) and Austria in the Serbian capital of Belgrade on September 18, 1739, concluding the Austro-Turkish War of 1737–39. By the treaty, Austria gave up control of northern Serbia, including Belgrade, and territory in Wallachia and Bosnia. As a result, Austria lost gains acquired by the 1718 Treaty of PASSAROWITZ and strength in the Balkan region. For two more weeks the Russians carried on their war with the Ottoman Turks until the Treaty of NISSA.

Further reading: Justin McCarthy, *The Ottoman Turks: An Introductory History to 1923* (New York: Longman, 1997); Donald Quataert, *The Ottoman Empire, 1700–1922* (New York: Cambridge University Press, 2000).

Bell Trade Act (Philippine Trade Act of 1946)

U.S. legislation sponsored by Representative Charles Jasper Bell of Missouri and enacted on April 30, 1946, that continued free trade with the Philippine Islands after their independence (July 4, 1946) and until 1954, with a gradual imposition of tariff duties in the following 20 years. The act also established quotas on Philippine exports to the United States and set the value of the Philippine currency in relation to the U.S. dollar at two-to-one. It granted U.S. businesses rights to exploit natural resources and operate public utilities in the Philippines. The act aroused strong opposition in the islands, and the United States agreed to pay $800 million in war damage claims if the Philippines agreed to ratify it.

Further reading: Ainslie T. Embree, ed., *Encyclopedia of Asian History*, 4 vols. (New York: Charles Scribner's Sons, 1988).

Benedict XIV's Encyclical of 1740 (Ubi Primum)

First encyclical of modern times, sent on December 3, 1740, by Pope Benedict XIV (reigned 1740–58) to all the Roman Catholic bishops "in peace and communion." (An encyclical is commonly a pastoral letter written by the pope—usually in Latin—to instruct his bishops in matters of discipline, doctrine, and morals; it is not considered infallible and is subject to change.) In *Ubi Primum*, the first of his many encyclicals, Benedict XIV outlined the episcopal duties. Able administrator that he was, he frequently used this form to remind his bishops of their duties: of residence, training of the clergy, and pastoral visitation.

Further reading: Claudia Carlen, comp., *The Papal Encyclicals* (Wilmington N.C.: McGrath Publishing Co., 1981); Catholic University of America Editorial Staff, *New Catholic Encyclopedia* (New York: McGraw-Hill, 1967); Anne Fremantle, *The Papal Encyclicals in Their Historical Context* (New York: Mentor-Omega Books, 1963).

Benedictine Rule (Regula Monachorum)

Monastic regulations for cenobitic life written in Latin by St. Benedict of Nursia about A.D. 535–540. Devised for the monastery he had founded at Monte Cassino, Italy, the Benedictine Rule consisted of a prologue and 73 chapters setting forth strict guidelines for monasticism. It required monks to be under the control of an abbot; to accept a religious life of poverty, chastity, and obedience in one community (house); and to lead a daily, balanced routine involving worship, study, and manual labor (in the open air if possible). Also emphasized were moderation, cooperation, and tolerance of human differences and faults. The rule, later adopted by each autonomous Benedictine monastery, became a major guide for monastic discipline in the West.

Further reading: *Benedictine Monachism; Studies in Benedictine Life and Rule* (New York: Barnes & Noble, 1962); Cardinal Gasquet, trans., *The Rule of Saint Benedict* (London: Chatto & Windus, 1925).

Benelux Economic Union Agreement

Treaty signed on February 3, 1958, binding Belgium, the Netherlands, and Luxembourg (the Benelux countries) into a 50-year economic union, intended to pursue coordinated economic, financial, and foreign trade policies and to facilitate free movement of people, goods, capital, and services within their borders. The treaty, which took effect in 1960, established a free labor market, uniform postage and transport rates, and eventually (1970) abolished border controls. The union is headquartered in Brussels, Belgium, and its daily operations are managed by a secretariat-general, based on policy decisions formulated during the quarterly sessions of a committee of ministers. The Benelux countries are part of the larger European Economic Community.

See also: ROME, TREATIES OF (1957).

Further reading: G. J. Ashworth and Raymond Charles Riley, *Benelux: An Economic Geography of Belgium, the Netherlands, and Luxembourg* (New York: Holmes & Meier, 1975); *Documentation* (Brussels, Belgium: Secrétariat général de l'Union économique Benelux, c. 1968).

Bergerac, Treaty of (Peace, or Edict, of Poitiers)

Treaty announced on September 17, 1577, at the Peace of Bergerac or Poitiers in France, following the defeat of the Huguenots (French Protestants) by King Henry III's forces in the Sixth War of Religion (1576–77). Based on Queen Mother Catherine de Médicis's negotiations with Henry of Navarre (then leader of the Huguenot rebels), the treaty essentially reiterated the 1576 Peace of MONSIEUR, without provisions affecting national unity and state sovereignty. It reintroduced the Roman Catholic religion all over the country and, in a major concession to the Catholic majority, restricted Protestant services to certain specified areas only. All leagues (notably the Holy League, backed by Catholic duke Henry of Guise) were ordered dissolved and, in a spirit of compassion, the rights of Protestants and Catholics were affirmed. Sometimes called the King's Peace (for Henry III boasted about it as an edict), the treaty's uneasy terms lasted until 1584.

See also: NEMOURS, TREATY OF.

Further reading: Mack P. Holt, *The French Wars of Religion, 1562–1629* (New York: Cambridge University Press, 1999).

Bering Sea Treaty

Treaty signed by the United States and Great Britain on February 29, 1892, to resolve a dispute over pelagic (deep-sea) sealing rights in the Bering Sea. With the purchase of Alaska in 1867, the United States had acquired the Pribilof Islands, the site of seal breeding grounds. To prevent other nations (especially Canada) from overhunting the herds at sea, the United States in 1890 declared dominion over the Bering Sea, calling it a *mare clausum* (closed sea). The Anglo-American arbitration treaty of 1892 referred the matter to an international tribunal, which ruled in 1893 against the U.S. claim to exclusive rights in the Bering Sea but did prohibit pelagic sealing around the Pribilof Islands at specified times each year.

Further reading: Bering Sea Tribunal of Arbitration, *Fur Seal Arbitration . . . Concerning the Jurisdictional Rights of the United States in the Waters of Bering Sea* (Washington, D.C.: Government Printing Office, 1895); James T. Gay, *American Fur Seal Diplomacy: The Alaskan Fur Seal Controversy* (New York: P. Lang, 1987); Gerald O. Williams, *The Bering Sea Fur Seal Dispute: A Monograph on the Maritime History of Alaska* (Eugene, Oreg.: Alaska Maritime Publications, 1984).

Berkeley's *Treatise Concerning the Principles of Human Knowledge*

Philosophical work written by Irish philosopher and Anglican bishop George Berkeley and published in 1710, containing an exposition of the author's doctrine of immaterialism. According to Berkeley, material substances did not exist themselves, but rather existed as the ideas and perceptions of minds or spirits; consequently, spirits were the only true substances. Based on this Berkeley concluded that, ultimately, all that man perceived as reality consisted of perceptions or ideas in the mind of the supreme spirit, or God. Through the work Berkeley attained relative prominence among his contemporaries and lasting fame for evincing divine or spiritual intelligence within conscious knowledge.

Further reading: Steven M. Cahn, ed., *Classics of Western Philosophy* (Indianapolis, Ind.: Hackett Pub., 1985); Robert J. Fogelin, *Routledge Philosophy Guidebook to Berkeley and the Principles of Human Knowledge* (New York: Routledge, 2001);

T. E. Jessop, ed., *Philosophical Writings of George Berkeley* (New York: Greenwood Press, 1969); Charles J. McCracken and I. C. Tipton, *Berkeley's Principles and Dialogues: Background Source Materials* (New York: Cambridge University Press, 2000).

Berlin, Convention of (1833)

Agreement, signed in Berlin by representatives of Russia, Austria, and Prussia on October 15, 1833, through which these three eastern powers sought to maintain the status quo in Europe. Through the document the signatory powers declared their intention and right to intervene on behalf of any power that requested their aid in dealing with internal unrest; and their intention to support militarily any member of the alliance, should that party, upon its attempt to carry out the former provision, experience opposition from a third party. They further agreed that no power had the right to intervene under any circumstances if a request for intervention had not been made. At this time incidents of revolutionary unrest had been occurring throughout Europe.

See also: MÜNCHENGRÄTZ AGREEMENT.

Further reading: Alan W. Palmer, *Metternich* (New York: Harper & Row, 1972).

Berlin, Peace of

Peace treaty closing the First Silesian War (1740–42), made between Prussia and Austria at Berlin on July 28, 1742 (see BRESLAU, TREATY OF [1742]). The war had originated with Prussian king Frederick II's attempt to annex the Austrian province of Silesia, at a time when Austrian archduchess Maria Theresa's claim to the imperial throne was contested by the leading European powers. By the treaty, Austria confirmed Prussia's control over Upper and Lower Silesia, was permitted to retain the principality of Teschen (part of Silesia), and obtained Prussia's promise to withdraw from the alliance against her.

Further reading: M. S. Anderson, *The War of the Austrian Succession, 1740–1748* (New York: Longman, 1995); Edward Crankshaw, *Maria Theresa* (London: Constable, 1996); David Fraser, *Frederick the Great: King of Prussia* (London: Penguin Books, 2000).

Berlin, Treaty of (1878)

Result of the Congress of Berlin, June 13–July 13, 1878, which met to revise the Treaty of SAN STEFANO. The concept of a large Bulgarian state was rejected, and Bulgaria was partitioned into three sections: an autonomous Bulgaria proper; Eastern Rumelia, under partial Turkish rule; and Macedonia, which remained fully under Turkish control. Austria-Hungary received Bosnia and Herzegovina. Russia kept the Bessarabian territory acquired in the Treaty of San Stefano, and also acquired the Black Sea port of Batum. Great Britain responded to the Russian acquisition of Batum by announcing, in effect, that she would abide by the sultan's decision to close the straits only if convenient. Although the Treaty of Berlin ushered in 34 years of peace in Europe, it failed to satisfy the smoldering nationalism in the Balkans, which later ignited World War I.

Further reading: Barbara Jelavich, *The Habsburg Empire in European Affairs, 1814–1918* (Hamden, Conn.: Archon Books, 1969, repr., 1975); W. N. Medlicott, *The Congress of Berlin and After: A Diplomatic History of the Near Eastern Settlement, 1878–1880* (Hamden, Conn.: Archon Books, 1938, repr., 1963); Charles L. Phillips and Alan Axelrod, eds., *Encyclopedia of Historical Treaties and Alliances*, 2 vols. (New York: Facts On File, 2001); Reeva S. Simon, Philip Mattar, and Richard W. Bulliet, eds., *Encyclopedia of the Modern Middle East* (New York: Simon & Schuster, 1996).

Berlin, Treaty of (1921)

See U.S.-GERMAN PEACE TREATY OF 1921.

Berlin Act of 1885

General act passed on February 26, 1885, in Berlin, Germany, at the West Africa Conference (November 15, 1884–February 26, 1885), which had been proposed by Portugal to discuss the status of the Congo basin. Fifteen countries, including the United States and the major European powers, participated in the conference, which was chaired by German Chancellor Otto von Bismarck (joint convener with French Premier Jules Ferry). The act's main provisions were (1) acceptance of neutrality of the Congo basin (including German colonies); (2) creation of a free-trade zone, with guaranteed freedom of trade and navigation in the Niger and Congo river basins; (3) ban on slave trade, with all powers "to strive for the suppression of slavery and especially of the slave trade"; (4) denial of Portugal's claims to the Congo estuary, with the Congo Free State established under the personal control of Belgium's king Leopold II; (5) formulation of guidelines to settle colonial claims, with "effective occupation" being the key; and (6) ban on the use of colored troops in inter-European wars.

Further reading: Stig Forster et al., eds., *Bismarck, Europe, and Africa: The Berlin Africa Conference 1884–1885 and the Onset of Partition* (New York: Oxford University Press, 1988); Arthur B. Keith, *The Belgian Congo and the Berlin Act* (New York: Negro Universities Press, 1970).

Berlin Act of 1889 (Samoa Act)

Agreement signed in Berlin on June 14, 1889, by the United States, Great Britain, and Germany concerning the status of the Samoan Islands. Treaties with Samoan chiefs granting commercial and naval rights, signed by the three Western powers from 1878 on, had led to increasing international friction. After a naval clash was averted when a hurricane destroyed foreign ships in the Samoan harbor of Apia, the United States, Britain, and Germany agreed to guarantee the neutrality and independence of the Samoan Islands under a tripartite protectorate. The agreement provided for government under a chief justice and the president of the Apia municipal council.

Further reading: Great Britain Foreign Office, Historical Section, *Former German Possessions in Oceania* (London: H.M. Stationery Office, 1920); Hermann Hiery and John M. MacKenzie, *European Impact and Pacific Influence: British and German Colonial Policy in the Pacific Islands and the Indigenous Response* (London: German Historical Institute, 1997); George H. Ryden, *The Foreign Policy of the United States in Relation to Samoa* (New York: Octagon Books, 1975).

Berlin Declaration of 1957   Declaration signed in Berlin on July 28, 1957, by Foreign Minister Heinrich von Brentano of West Germany, David K. Bruce of the United States, Sir Christopher Steel of Britain, and Maurice Couve de Murville of France, the three latter of whom were ambassadors to West Germany; reaffirmed that the reunification of Germany was both the responsibility of these four grand alliance powers and a prerequisite to any European security settlement. The declaration's main points included the signatory powers' agreement that Germany be permitted to rearm; that the reunification of Germany was the joint responsibility of the four great powers; that any all-German government must be freely elected; that neither neutrality nor demilitarization should be required of a united Germany; that the reunified Germany must be free to join the North Atlantic Alliance; that assurances would be given to Germany's neighbors, plus the Soviet Union and all her satellites, of Germany's peaceful intentions; and that any European security arrangement would be subject to Germany's reunification.

See also: TREATY ON THE FINAL SETTLEMENT WITH RESPECT TO GERMANY.

Further reading: Peter Alter, *The German Question and Europe: A History* (London: Arnold, 2000); Jurgen Thomaneck and William J. Niven, *Dividing and Uniting Germany* (New York: Routledge, 2001).

Berlin Decree   Decree issued in the German city of Berlin by Emperor Napoléon Bonaparte of France on November 21, 1806, in which he proclaimed a blockade of all trade with Great Britain. In the document Napoléon declared that no British vessel, nor any vessel from Britain's colonial possessions, would thenceforth be admitted to any port in the French Empire; he forbade any Briton to enter territory within or allied with the French Empire; and he forbade all commerce and correspondence between Great Britain and any of these territories. Adherence to the blockade (or "Continental System") was stipulated in many of the peace settlements that Napoléon concluded with defeated powers during the Napoleonic Wars (1803–15).

Further reading: Henry Steele Commager, ed., *Documents of American History*, 8th ed. (New York: Appleton-Century-Crofts, 1968); Geoffrey J. Ellis, *The Napoleonic Empire* (Atlantic Highlands, N.J.: Humanities Press International, 1991); James H. Robinson, ed., *The Napoleonic Period* (Philadel-

phia: Department of History of the University of Pennsylvania, 1895).

Berlin Memorandum   Joint statement from Russia, Germany, and Austria-Hungary concerning the serious anti-Turkish rebellions in the Balkans; sent from Berlin on May 13, 1876, to London, Paris, and Rome. The memorandum, drafted by the Austro-Hungarian foreign minister, Count Gyula Andrássy, called for the Turks to institute stringent reforms in their Balkan provinces, and hinted at possible sanctions if the reforms were not effected. Italy and France accepted the memorandum; but Great Britain rejected it, and, as a warning against interference in the Balkans, sent her fleet to Besika Bay, just outside the Dardanelles. Nothing came of the memorandum, as it was ignored by the Turks, and not enforced by the six Great Powers. Less than a year later, on April 24, 1877, Russia declared war on Turkey.

See also: ANDRÁSSY NOTE.

Further reading: Charles K. Burns, *The Balkan Policy of Count Gyula Andrassy* (Ann Arbor, Mich.: University Microfilms International, 1985); David Harris, *A Diplomatic History of the Balkan Crisis of 1875–1878; the First Year* (Hamden, Conn.: Archon Books, 1969).

Berne Bill, U.S.   Legislation implementing U.S. membership in the BERNE CONVENTION OF 1886, passed by Congress and signed into law by President Ronald W. Reagan on October 31, 1988. It conformed U.S. copyright laws to Berne international rules (this was needed before the United States could ratify the Berne Convention). U.S. registration of copyright was required for American literary and artistic works but foreign works were exempted from the requirement; statutory protections were increased against infringement of U.S. works outside the United States. The technical changes made in U.S. laws increased international copyright protection for American authors, artists, and copyright holders.

Further reading: Margaret C. Jasper and Mavis Fowler, *The Law of Copyright*, 2d ed. (Dobbs Ferry, N.Y.: Oceana Publications, 2000).

Berne Convention of 1886   International copyright convention protecting literary and artistic works, signed at Berne, Switzerland, September 9, 1886. The convention, which has been regularly revised since its inception, protects the rights of authors and artists when their work is reproduced in any form, whether printed or performed. Included in this category is "any production in the literary, scientific, or artistic domain." In addition to protecting original works, the convention also applies to translations, adaptations, and musical arrangements, which are "protected as original works, without prejudice to the rights of the author of the original works."

Further reading: Sam Ricketson, *The Berne Convention for the Protection of Literary and Artistic Works: 1886–1986* (London: Centre for Commercial Law Studies, Queen Mary College, 1987).

Berwick, Pacification of   See DUNSE, PACIFICATION OF.

Beyond Good and Evil (Jenseits von Gut und Böse)
Major work written and published in 1886 by German philosopher Friedrich Nietzsche, advancing ideas seeking to establish the primacy of will power and the preservation of life. Encompassing Nietzsche's wide-ranging interests, it dealt with the origin and nature of moral value, the history and psychology of religion and human motivation, and the link between man and historical processes. Nietzsche's interest lay in motivations in philosophy rather than in the truth of statements. Asserting that the will to power was fundamental, he argued that it expressed itself in expansive, assimilating, and positive values in all life forms. Critical of early philosophical formulations that considered, to different degrees, human prejudices and fears, Nietzsche sought to examine human passions in the study of the origins of morals. His thought had matured under the impact of the theory of evolution (see ORIGIN OF SPECIES), and this work came after a long period of literary accomplishments but prior to a tragic illness that ravaged his mind.

Further reading: Friedrich Wilhelm Nietzsche, *Beyond Good and Evil: Prelude to a Philosophy of the Future* (New York: Cambridge University Press, 2001).

Bible, Authorized (King James) Version of the
English translation of the Bible prepared by 54 scholars commissioned by King James I of England; published for the Church of England after seven years of work in 1611. In their work the scholars, led by the Anglican theologian Lancelot Andrewes, relied heavily on the Bishops' Bible, a 1568 English translation that was largely a recasting of William Tyndale's translation of 1525–26. They also continued the use of the older ecclesiastical words, such as "charity" instead of "love," and used a style that was alternately richly ornate and very simple. This collection of sacred writings of the Christian religion, containing notably the scriptures of the Old and New Testaments, has had enormous influence on writers and others; much of the beautiful English phraseology derived from Tyndale's version. The King James Version has also been important in keeping the English language relatively unchanged since that time. Today the Modern Authorized Version, a rendering of the original with updated punctuation and orthography, is still much in use.

See also: VULGATE.

Further reading: Frederick F. Bruce, *The English Bible: A History of Translations* (New York: Oxford University Press, 1970); Gerald Hammond, *The Making of the English Bible* (New York: Philosophical Library, 1983).

Bible, Gutenberg (Mazarin Bible)
Landmark edition of the VULGATE printed by Johann Gutenberg in Mainz, Germany, about 1455. Considered the first complete book printed from movable metal type, its first known copy was discovered in the library of French statesman and Cardinal Jules Mazarin about 1670. The work's Latin text, however, is not divided into chapters and verses as in modern bibles. Only 21 complete copies remain of about 200 copies originally printed of Gutenberg's masterpiece, which is sometimes called the 42-line Bible because of the number of lines in each column. A Latin *Psalterium,* issued in 1457, was ascribed also to Gutenberg, who had then lost his printing firm in a ruinous lawsuit won by his rich partner, Johann Fust.

Further reading: James Thorpe, *The Gutenberg Bible: Landmark in Learning,* 2d ed. (San Marino, Calif.: Huntington Library, 1999); William B. Todd, *The Gutenberg Bible: New Evidence of the Original Printing: A Paper* (Chapel Hill, N.C.: Hanes Foundation, Rare Book Collection/University Library, University of North Carolina at Chapel Hill, 1982).

Bidlack Treaty (New Granada Treaty)
Treaty named after the U.S. chargé d'affaires in New Granada, Benjamin Alden Bidlack; concluded between the United States and New Granada (Colombia and Panama) on December 12, 1846, granting the United States right of transit across the Isthmus of Panama by any means of transport. In exchange, the United States guaranteed the neutrality of the isthmus and New Granada's sovereignty over it. However, after a U.S. company built a railroad across the isthmus in 1855, the Colombian government often appealed to the United States to intervene in order to keep the isthmus open during times of civil war. Consequently, American influence in the area was considerably increased.

Further reading: Basil C. Hedrick and Anne K. Hedrick, *Historical Dictionary of Panama* (Metuchen, N.J.: Scarecrow Press, 1970).

Bigelow Papers
Series of political satirical verses written by Massachusetts poet and critic James Russell Lowell, collected from periodicals and published in book form in 1848 and 1867. The first volume, purporting to be the collected verse of a Yankee farmer and the prose commentary of an upper-class New England minister, focused on antislavery issues and opposed the Mexican War (1846–47) as an attempt to extend slavery. The second volume supported unionism and the Northern cause in the U.S. Civil War (1861–65). The *Bigelow Papers* proved an important moral influence against slavery and helped establish Lowell's reputation as a satirist.

Further reading: Marjorie R. Kaufman, ed., *The Poetical Works of James Russell Lowell* (Boston: Houghton Mifflin, 1978).

Bill of Rights, Canadian
Parliamentary statute passed by Canadian prime minister John G. Diefenbaker's government and, on August 10, 1960, granted royal assent by Great

Britain. The bill declared that all Canadian citizens have a right to life, liberty, and enjoyment of property. They are also guaranteed freedom of speech, religion, assembly, language, education, and the press, as well as the right of equality before and protection of the law (with the right to a fair trial, habeas corpus, and legal counsel) without discrimination on the basis of race, religion, or sex. Because of a fear of provincial dissent, the Diefenbaker government chose not to seek to make the bill a constitutional amendment; it pertained only to Canadian federal legislation but would not be obtained during wartime.

See also: CHARTER OF RIGHTS AND FREEDOMS, CANADIAN.

Further reading: Prentice-Hall of Canada, eds., *Canadian Historical Document Series,* 3 vols. (Scarborough, Ontario: Prentice-Hall of Canada, 1965–66).

Bill of Rights, English   See DECLARATION OF RIGHTS, ENGLISH.

Bill of Rights, Hawaiian

Petition addressed to the U.S. Congress by the legislature of Hawaii in 1923; attempted to define Hawaii's rights as a U.S. territory. Protesting congressional discrimination against the islands, the bill asserted Hawaii's rights to the privileges and benefits of a state in matters where its responsibilities and functions were the same as a state's, including the right to share in financial legislation and appropriations that applied to the states as a whole, among them "all acts in aid of good roads, education, farm loans, maternity, home economics, training in agriculture, trade and industry, and other acts of a like nature." President Calvin Coolidge and Congress formally recognized this bill of rights.

Further reading: Roger Bell, *Last Among Equals: Hawaiian Statehood and American Politics* (Honolulu: University of Hawaii Press, 1984).

Bill of Rights, International

Comprehensive document endorsed by the UNESCO-sponsored Commission on Human Rights in 1966; consisted of the UNIVERSAL DECLARATION OF HUMAN RIGHTS, two covenants, and an optional protocol. The Universal Declaration had been presented by the United Nations General Assembly in December 1948, and is often used as a yardstick by which to judge the human rights records of various countries. The International Covenant on Civil and Political Rights lists the rights guaranteed under it (not all of them overlapping with those mentioned in the declaration) and established an international Human Rights Committee. Signatories of the covenant's optional protocol recognized the Human Rights Committee's right to examine complaints of violation received from victims and to submit its report. The International Covenant on Economic, Social, and Cultural Rights is committed to helping member countries realize the full potential of their rights under the covenant; discrimination (on any grounds) in the enjoyment of these rights was expressly forbidden. Periodic progress re-

ports were to be made to UNESCO (the United Nations Educational, Scientific, and Cultural Organization).

Further reading: Conor Gearty and Adam Tomkins, eds., *Understanding Human Rights* (London: Mansell, 1996); *The International Bill of Human Rights* (New York: U.N. Centre for Human Rights, 1996).

Bill of Rights, U.S.

First 10 amendments to the U.S. CONSTITUTION, which enumerate the fundamental rights of citizens. Introduced in the First Continental Congress to overcome fears that the new federal system would not protect individual liberties, they went into effect in 1791. The FIRST AMENDMENT deals with freedom of religion, speech, assembly, and the press. The Second and Third protect the civilian population against military excesses by granting citizens the right to keep and bear arms and by prohibiting the quartering of troops in private homes in peacetime. The FOURTH, FIFTH, SIXTH, and EIGHTH AMENDMENTS safeguard rights in criminal cases, and the SEVENTH AMENDMENT preserves the right to jury trial in civil cases. The NINTH AMENDMENT says that no rights are abridged merely because they are not enumerated in the Constitution, and the TENTH AMENDMENT reserves to the states or the people all powers not delegated to the United States by the Constitution. Initially the Bill of Rights was considered binding only on the national government; the FOURTEENTH AMENDMENT applied these guarantees to state governments as well.

Further reading: Milton R. Konvitz, *Bill of Rights Reader: Leading Constitutional Cases,* 5th ed. (Ithaca, N.Y.: Cornell University Press, 1973); R. A. Rutland, *The Birth of the Bill of Rights,* (Boston: Northeastern University Press, 1991).

Biltmore Resolution

Policy worked out at a Zionist conference at the Biltmore Hotel in New York City in May 1942; demanded unrestricted Jewish immigration to Palestine, a Jewish army, and the establishment of Palestine as a Jewish commonwealth. The program was promoted by David Ben-Gurion, representing the international Jewish Agency, who later became the first prime minister of the newly created state of Israel (1948).

Further reading: Walter Lacqueur and Barry Rubin, eds., *The Israel-Arab Reader: A Documentary History of the Middle East Conflict,* 5th ed. (New York: Penguin Books, 1995); Reeva S. Simon, Philip Mattar, and Richard W. Bulliet, eds., *Encyclopedia of the Modern Middle East* (New York: Simon & Schuster, 1996).

Bipartisan Campaign Reform Act of 2002, U.S. (McCain-Feingold Bill, Shays-Meehan Bill)

Legislation signed into law on March 27, 2002, that overhauled the financing of political campaigns for federal office in the United States. Sponsored by Senator John S. McCain of Arizona, Senator Russell D. Feingold of Wisconsin, Representative Christopher Shays of Connecticut, and Representative

Martin T. Meehan of Massachusetts, the act's primary aim is to restrict the contribution of "soft" money to the national political parties. Unlike "hard" money, which is contributed to a specific candidate, soft money is used by the parties for generic campaign activities such as getting out the vote. Under the old campaign finance laws, soft money could be contributed in unlimited amounts by individuals and organizations alike, resulting in a small number of wealthy people and well-funded special interest groups threatening to take over the electoral process. The act also raises the limits on hard money contributions from $1,000 to $2,000 to a single candidate, and from $25,000 per year to $95,000 every two years for multiple political contributions. In addition, it increases the requirements for reporting political contributions and expenditures, requires more complete identification of an advertisement's sponsors and authorizers within the advertisement itself, and curtails so-called issue advertising, which pretends to address a particular issue but in fact advocates the election or defeat of a particular candidate. The act was slated to take effect on November 6, the day after the 2002 congressional elections.

Further reading: "Bipartisan Campaign Reform Act of 2002," Alliance for Justice, available online at http://www.afi.org/news/bcrabriefingfinal.html; "President Signs Campaign Finance Reform Act," The White House, Office of the Press Secretary, available online at http://www.whitehouse.gov/news/releases/2002/03/print/20020327.html.

Bismarck's Army Bill of 1887

Law increasing the strength of the German army for a period of seven years (septennium). Since the founding of the German Empire in 1871, army bills had been voted for a seven-year period, with the size based on the previous census. Although the term of the previous septennium was not due to expire until March 1888, German chancellor Otto von Bismarck proposed the new bill in September 1886, to begin in April 1887, with an increase based on the census of 1885. When the Reichstag (legislative assembly) voted the requested increase for a three-year period only, Bismarck dissolved it, waging a successful electoral campaign on the threat of war with France. In reality, Bismarck was more likely concerned with obtaining a conservative parliamentary majority against the time when the liberal crown prince, the future Frederick III, would become emperor of Germany. Ironically, the seven-year army bill was passed by the new Reichstag, shortly before the crown prince was diagnosed as having terminal cancer.

Further reading: Erich Eyck, *Bismarck and the German Empire* (New York: W. W. Norton, 1968); Hajo Holborn, *A History of Modern Germany, 1840–1945* (New York: Knopf, 1969).

Bituminous Coal Conservation Act, U.S.

See GUFFEY-SNYDER BITUMINOUS COAL STABILIZATION ACT.

Björkö, Treaty of

Abortive Russo-German treaty of alliance, signed by Kaiser William II of Germany and Czar Nicholas II of Russia, at Björkö, Finland, on July 24, 1905. The treaty called for each side to aid the other in Europe, if either were attacked by another European power. The document was prepared impulsively by William II during a brief vacation with his cousin Nicholas II, but was opposed by officials in both Russia and Germany, and never went into effect. The German chancellor, Prince Bernhard von Bülow, objected to the agreement on the grounds that it was limited to Europe; and Russian foreign minister Count Vladimir Lasmsdorff rejected it because it excluded Russia's principal ally, France.

Further reading: Katharine A. Lerman, *The Chancellor as Courtier: Bernhard von Bulow and the Governance of Germany, 1900–1909* (New York: Cambridge University Press, 1990).

Black Act (Waltham Black Act)

English statute urged by King George I; passed in 1722 to punish the Waltham deerstalkers and stealers who came to Epping Forest (a royal hunting ground) disguised with blackened faces. A person caught entering any forest, park, or warren for the purpose of hunting or taking deer or other wildlife and appearing with a blackened or otherwise concealed face could be charged with a felony. The act, which was chiefly to suppress lawless persons (the so-called blacks) in the Waltham area, was eventually repealed in 1827.

Further reading: Alfred Leutscher, *Epping Forest: Its History and Wildlife* (Newton Abbot, England: David & Charles, 1974).

Black Code of Louis XIV (Code Noir)

Compilation of laws intended to improve the treatment and working conditions of black slaves in the West Indies; published by King Louis XIV in France in 1685. Slave owners were ordered not to force the slaves to work on Sundays and holidays; they were allowed to be baptized and to marry. Minimum standards of food, clothing, and care (during sickness) were established for slave owners; any owner found abusing his authority risked punishment. It ruled that a slave family—husband, wife, and minor child—could no longer be sold separately. The Code Noir also eased the emancipation process by allowing any owner above 20 years of age to free a slave without bureaucratic hassles. While most of these French laws were generally ignored, their codification itself must be considered a major humanitarian achievement of its time.

Further reading: Alcée Fortier, ed., *Louisiana*, 2 vols. (Madison, Wisc.: Century Historical Association, 1914).

Black Codes, U.S.

Statutes passed by the former Confederate states in 1865–66 regulating the status of some 4 million newly freed black slaves. Though the codes differed from state to state, all were intended to control and suppress freedom, ensure a supply of cheap labor, and continue white supremacy. While blacks were granted rights to marry, to own personal property, and to sue other blacks in court, they were denied the rights to testify against whites in court, to vote, to serve on juries. Employment, freedom of speech and movement, and ownership of real estate were restricted. To override these codes Congress passed the CIVIL RIGHTS ACT OF 1866 and the FOURTEENTH AMENDMENT.

Further reading: Thomas Carson, ed., *Gale Encyclopedia of U.S. Economic History* (Farmington Hills, Mich.: Gale Group, 1999); Theodore B. Wilson, *The Black Codes of the South* (Tuscaloosa: University of Alabama Press, 1965).

Black Man's Burden, The   Polemical book written and published in London (1920) by British social reformer Edmund D. Morel, criticizing the European white man's enslavement, exploitation, and destruction of the African peoples (the "black man's burden"). Although the Africans had not been crushed by the white man's occupation, importation of diseases, and slave trade, they were now seriously threatened by industrial capitalism's demands, economic bondage, and the wage slavery of the modern world. Morel contended that the African was "really helpless against the material god of the white man, as embodied in the trinity of imperialism, capitalistic-exploitation, and militarism." His words caused much hot debate and indignation.

Further reading: William Henry Holtzclaw, *The Black Man's Burden* (New York: Haskell House, 1971).

Bland-Allison Act   Legislation coauthored by Representatives Richard P. Bland of Missouri and William B. Allison of Iowa and passed by the U.S. Congress on February 28, 1878, to provide for freer coinage of silver. After the COINAGE ACT OF 1873 eliminated the silver dollar from U.S. currency, a free-silver movement developed, supported especially by Western farmers and silver miners, who demanded a return to bimetallism. The Bland-Allison Act was an attempt to compromise between the call for free, unlimited silver coinage and the demands of Eastern financiers for a gold standard. The act required the Treasury Department to purchase between $2 million and $4 million worth of silver each month for coinage. It was passed over the veto of President Rutherford B. Hayes and remained in effect until replaced by the SHERMAN SILVER PURCHASE ACT of 1890.

Further reading: Thomas Carson, ed., *Gale Encyclopedia of U.S. Economic History* (Farmington Hills, Mich.: Gale Group, 1999); Henry Benajah Russell, *International Monetary Conferences* (New York: Arno Press, 1898, repr., 1974).

Blanqui's *La Patrie en Danger,* No. 50   French socialist Louis A. Blanqui's scathing exposition (issue number 50 of his newspaper *La Patrie en Danger* ["Our Country in Danger"], on October 30, 1870) of the true character of France's Government of National Defense, formed after Louis Bonaparte's surrender to the Prussian forces in September 1870. Referring to the period between 1792 and 1870, witness

to "the passage of ten ordinary centuries," he contrasted the enthusiastic mood of 1792 with the speculative one of 1870. Blanqui praised the heroism of the people and the revolutionary government of 1792, criticizing the present "counter-revolutionary power which proscribes Republicans, courts Royalists and is the humble servant of the invader." The government, he said, was not like a parcel to be dragged along on one's journey, because "it is the luggage that chooses the way and rules the traveller," the government that controls the people. Condemning the present government for pandering to the monarchists, the aristocracy, and the clergy, Blanqui concluded: "It is digging the grave of France."

Further reading: Patrick H. Hutton, *The Cult of the Revolutionary Tradition: The Blanquists in French Politics, 1864–1893* (Berkeley: University of California Press, 1981); Alan B. Spitzer, *The Revolutionary Theories of Louis Auguste Blanqui* (New York: Columbia University Press, 1957).

"Blood and Iron" Speech, Bismarck's   Speech delivered on September 30, 1862, by Prussia's president Otto von Bismarck to the finance committee of the Prussian Parliament. Attempting to persuade the committee to vote for an increase in the army budget (desired by Prussia's king William I), it contained a glimpse of Bismarck's plan to make Prussia the leading force in the movement for the unification of Germany. In the speech Bismarck expressed Prussia's dissatisfaction with her present boundaries (thereby implying the need to expand them) and expressed his intention to build up Prussia's armed forces. He concluded with the words: "Not by speeches and majorities will the great questions of the day be decided—that was the mistake of 1848 and 1849—but by iron and blood." The rhythm of the final phrase soon turned to "blood and iron," seemingly more in step with Bismarck's expectations and beliefs that, through this means alone, Prussia would solve the problems of German unification.

Further reading: Erich Eyck, *Bismarck and the German Empire* (New York: W. W. Norton, 1968).

"Blood, Toil, Tears, and Sweat" Speech, Churchill's   British prime minister Winston Churchill's first speech before the House of Commons (May 13, 1940), inviting its confidence in the new administration and outlining the government's immediate priorities. With the continuing uncertainties of the war (World War II [1939–45]) and now a new government, Britain was at a crucial juncture—needing a clear definition of goals and a renewed fighting spirit. Churchill, with his eloquence, provided just that in his speech. The country, he said, was facing a grim ordeal, being "in the preliminary stage of one of the greatest battles in history," and he had "nothing to offer but blood, toil, tears, and sweat." The government's policy was to continue to "wage war against a monstrous tyranny," the ultimate goal being "victory at all costs, victory in spite of all terror, victory, however long and hard the road may be; for without victory, there is no survival." He said that he was beginning his tasks with hope and invited the support of all: "Come then, let us go forward together with our united strength."

Further reading: David Cannadine, ed., *Blood, Toil, Tears and Sweat: The Speeches of Winston Churchill* (Boston: Houghton Mifflin, 1989).

Blue Law of 1624, Virginia

Colonial law, regulating conduct, which made church attendance on Sunday mandatory. Penalty for absence was one pound of tobacco. The law also required that each plantation must have a house or a room for worship. The Anglicans (members of the Church of England) in Virginia advocated the measure, often considered the first "blue law" in colonial America (though the term came to be attached afterward much more to certain statutes passed by the Puritans in New England in the 1600s).

Further reading: David N. Laband and Deborah Hendry Heinbuch, *Blue Laws: The History, Economics, and Politics of Sunday-Closing Laws* (Lexington, Mass.: Lexington Books, 1987).

Blue Law of 1634, Massachusetts

Law passed by the Massachusetts General Court prohibiting the purchase of linen, woolen, or silk, as well as clothes with silver, gold, silk, or thread lace on them. Clothing with slashing (underlayer of contrasting color) was limited to a slash in the back and in each sleeve. In addition, the Puritans in the Massachusetts Bay colony mandated Sunday church attendance in 1634. The term "blue law" probably derives from the fact that the Puritans in the various New England colonies printed their laws on blue paper.

Further reading: Silas Andrus, comp., *The Blue Laws: The Earliest Laws of Connecticut and New Haven Colonies* (Storrs, Conn.: Bibliopola Press, 1999); David N. Laband and Deborah Hendry Heinbuch, *Blue Laws: The History, Economics, and Politics of Sunday-Closing Laws* (Lexington, Mass.: Lexington Books, 1987).

Blue Law of 1639, Massachusetts

Law enacted on September 4, 1639, by the General Court of Massachusetts, against the drinking of toasts. It stated, "the common custom of drinking to one another is a mere useless ceremony, and draweth on the abominable practice of drinking healths." The impossibility of forcibly quelling this old custom forced the law's repeal in the Massachusetts Bay colony in 1645.

Further reading: Silas Andrus, comp., *The Blue Laws: The Earliest Laws of Connecticut and New Haven Colonies* (Storrs, Conn.: Bibliopola Press, 1999); David N. Laband and Deborah Hendry Heinbuch, *Blue Laws: The History, Economics, and Politics of Sunday-Closing Laws* (Lexington, Mass.: Lexington Books, 1987).

Blue Law of 1640, Connecticut

Law passed by the Connecticut General Court of New Haven colony; made church attendance compulsory and prohibited "worldly work." It also imposed immobility, stating "nor shall any person go from his or her place of abode on the Lord's Day, unless to or from public worship of God . . . unless it be on some work or business of necessity or mercy." The colonial statute was an attempt to control religious and personal behavior and provided punishment for offenders.

Further reading: *The Blue Laws of Connecticut* (New York: Truth Seeker Company, 1899); David N. Laband and Deborah Hendry Heinbuch, *Blue Laws: The History, Economics, and Politics of Sunday-Closing Laws* (Lexington, Mass.: Lexington Books, 1987).

Blue Law of 1660, Connecticut

Law passed by the Connecticut General Court of New Haven colony; ordered all married men to live with their wives. Any man who remained separated from his wife for more than three years was ordered removed from the colony. The 1660 law was an update of earlier puritanical "blue laws" in colonial Connecticut, which regulated personal and sexual conduct.

Further reading: Silas Andrus, comp., *The Blue Laws: The Earliest Laws of Connecticut and New Haven Colonies* (Storrs, Conn.: Bibliopola Press, 1999); *The Blue Laws of Connecticut* (New York: Truth Seeker Company, 1899); David N. Laband and Deborah Hendry Heinbuch, *Blue Laws: The History, Economics, and Politics of Sunday-Closing Laws* (Lexington, Mass.: Lexington Books, 1987).

Bogotá, Declaration of

Declaration signed in Bogotá, Colombia, on August 16, 1966, by representatives of Chile, Venezuela, Colombia, Peru, and Ecuador, consisting of statements of the signatories' collective support for the economic development of Latin America. Specifically, the document expressed the signatories' support for Latin American economic integration, leading ultimately to a Latin American common market, and for an increase in the role played by the Alliance for Progress, to which the United States had been providing substantial assistance, in the economic development of the hemisphere. In addition, the declaration called for an end to the Vietnam War; for an end to the arms race; and for the commitment of the funds thus saved to the economic development of poorer countries.

See also: DECLARATION OF AMERICAN PRESIDENTS.

Further reading: Leslie Bethell, ed., *The Cambridge History of Latin America* (Cambridge, England: Cambridge University Press, 1985); Helen Delpar, ed., *Encyclopedia of Latin America* (New York: McGraw-Hill, 1974); George Pendle, *A History of Latin America*, rev. ed. (Baltimore: Penguin, 1969).

Bogotá, Pact of (Inter-American Treaty on Pacific Settlement)

Pact negotiated at an Inter-American conference in Bogotá, Colombia, in April 1948; established the obligation for all signatory states to settle their disputes peaceably. The pact called for the use of traditional settlement procedures, including diplomacy, conciliation, arbitration, mediation, ajudication, and use of the World Court. However, the pact applied only to states that ratified it; also, all existing peaceful settlement agreements in effect for those states were superseded by the pact when ratified. The pact, encouraged by the United States, has been ratified and put into force by only 13 Latin American states; many states prefer not to be bound by stipulated settlement procedures.

Further reading: Leslie Bethell, ed., *The Cambridge History of Latin America* (Cambridge, England: Cambridge University Press, 1985); Helen Delpar, ed., *Encyclopedia of Latin America* (New York: McGraw-Hill, 1974); George Pendle, *A History of Latin America*, rev. ed. (Baltimore: Penguin, 1969).

Bogotá, Treaty of (1914)   See THOMSON-URRUTIA TREATY.

Boland Amendment   U.S. legislation introduced by Senator Edward P. Boland of Massachusetts, passed by Congress on December 20, 1982, and signed the next day by President Ronald W. Reagan; prohibited the U.S. government from using defense funds to support the military and paramilitary forces (the Contras) fighting against Nicaragua's Sandinista government. The law, part of an emergency spending bill, barred the Central Intelligence Agency (CIA) and U.S. Defense Department from furnishing equipment, training, advice, or support "for military activities for the purpose of overthrowing the government of Nicaragua or provoking a military exchange between Nicaragua and Honduras." The amendment expired on August 8, 1985, and afterward any U.S. agency apart from the CIA and the Defense Department could legally aid the Nicaraguan contras. In late 1986 Boland was named to the House committee probing the Iran-Contra arms scandal (profits from arms sales to Iran [to influence the release of Americans held hostage in Lebanon] were allegedly channeled to the Contras).

Further reading: Cynthia J. Arnson, *Crossroads: Congress, the Reagan Administration, and Central America*, 2d ed. (University Park: Pennsylvania State University Press, 1993); U.S. Congress, House Select Committee to Investigate Covert Arms Transactions with Iran and Senate Select Committee on Secret Military Assistance to Iran and the Nicaraguan Opposition, *Report of the Congressional Committees Investigating the Iran-Contra Affair* (100th Cong., 1st sess., 1987. H. Rept. 433, S. Rept. 216); Leonard W. Levy and Kenneth L. Karst, eds., *Encyclopedia of the American Constitution*, 2d ed. (New York: Macmillan Reference, 2000); Thomas W. Walker, ed., *Reagan Versus the Sandinistas: The Undeclared War on Nicaragua* (Boulder, Colo.: Westview Press, 1987).

Bolívar's Address at Angostura   Address given by Simón Bolívar at a congress called by him in Angostura (now Ciudad Bolívar, Venezuela) in 1819 for the purpose of providing a temporary basis of political organization for the newly created state of Gran Colombia (comprising Venezuela, New Granada, and Quito—now Ecuador). Believing that only democracy was capable of providing absolute liberty, in his famous address Bolívar proposed a type of constitution and political organization that he maintained would ensure that liberty: a strong centralized representative republic with full administrative authority, one that guaranteed "the sovereignty of the people, the division of powers, civil liberty, the prohibition of slavery, [and] the abolition of monarchy and special privileges." In its combination of realism and vision, Bolívar's address is considered one of his two most outstanding social and political documents.

See also: BOLÍVAR'S "LETTER FROM JAMAICA."

Further reading: *Modern History Sourcebook: Simon de Bolivar: Message to the Congress of Angostura, 1819*, available online at http://www.fordham.edu/halsall/mod/1819bolivar.html.

Bolívar's "Letter from Jamaica"   Letter written in Spanish (La Carta de Jamaica) by Simón Bolívar in 1814 while living in self-exile in Jamaica. Rather than withdrawing from the struggle for South American independence during his exile, Bolívar planned the military reconquest of northern South America and contemplated a political system that would be viable in the post-independence period. In his famous letter, Bolívar argues against monarchy and for a constitutional republicanism modeled after the government of Great Britain. Republics would have a hereditary upper house, an elected lower house, and a president elected for life. The "Letter from Jamaica" is considered to be the most outstanding political document of Bolívar's career.

Further reading: Simon D. Dawidowicz, *Simon Bolivar: The Man and His Message: Letter from Jamaica* (Miami: Florida International University, 1989); Mark A. Kishlansky, ed., *Sources of World History: Readings for World Civilization*, vol. 2, 2d ed. (Belmont, Calif.: West/Wadsworth, 1999).

Bolling v. Sharpe   U.S. Supreme Court decision issued on May 17, 1954, that overturned segregation in the public schools of the District of Columbia. Spottswood T. Bolling, Jr., and other black students in the district had asserted that the segregated school system violated their constitutional rights to due process under the FIFTH AMENDMENT. The Court ruled that although the FOURTEENTH AMENDMENT protections, which ended segregation in the states under BROWN V. BOARD OF EDUCATION OF TOPEKA, KANSAS, did not apply in the district, the due process protections on the Fifth Amendment did apply and made racial discrimination an unconstitutional, arbitrary deprivation of liberty for black children.

Further reading: David P. Currie, *The Constitution in the Supreme Court: The Second Century, 1888–1986* (Chicago: University of Chicago Press, 1990); L. A. Graglia, *Disaster by Degree: The Supreme Court Decisions on Race and the Schools* (Ithaca, N.Y.: Cornell University Press, 1976); Leonard W.

Levy and Kenneth L. Karst, eds., *Encyclopedia of the American Constitution*, 2d ed. (New York: Macmillan Reference, 2000); Mark Mikula and L. Mpho Mabunda, eds., *Great American Court Cases*, 4 vols. (Farmington Hills, Mich.: Gale Group, 1999).

Bologna, Concordat of (Concordat of Francis I)

Agreement between King Francis I of France and Pope Leo X at Bologna, Italy, in 1516, rescinding the PRAGMATIC SANCTION OF BOURGES. Negotiations were initiated following the French conquest of the duchy of Milan (supported by the pope) at the Battle of Marignano (1515). Francis cleverly manipulated the talks, with the resulting "compromise" strengthening French royal power while making some concessions to the pope. Francis renounced the principle of the Council of Basel (1431–49) that had made the papacy subordinate to the national church councils; he received in return the right to appoint French bishops, abbots, and priors (these would normally be confirmed by the pope). Francis also resumed the payment of annates (first year's revenues of ecclesiastics, paid to the pope).

Further reading: William H. Jervis, *The Gallican Church; a History of the Church of France, from the Concordat of Bologna, A.D. 1516, to the Revolution* (London: J. Murray, 1872); Frank N. Magill, ed., *Great Events from History, Modern European Series*, 3 vols. (Englewood Cliffs, N.J.: Salem Press, 1973).

Bolting Act

Statute enacted by Sir Edmund Andros in 1678, granting New York City a monopoly on the bolting (sifting and refining) and packing of flour for export. Andros was acting both as the British governor of the New York colony and as the deputy of the duke of York (later King James II), proprietor of New York. The act also reaffirmed the city's status as the sole port of entry for the colony. It remained in force until 1694 and is commemorated on the official seal of New York by flour barrels and windmill sails.

Further reading: Peter R. Christoph and Florence A. Christoph, eds., *The Andros Papers: Files of the Provincial Secretary of New York During the Administration of Governor Sir Edmund Andros, 1674–1680* (Syracuse, N.Y.: Syracuse University Press, 1989).

Bonus Bill of 1817, U.S.

Federal legislation passed by Congress on March 3, 1817, to create a permanent fund for internal transportation improvements, such as roads and canals, by using profits from the second Bank of the United States, established in 1816. Introduced by Congressman John C. Calhoun, the bill set aside for the fund the bonus of $1.5 million, paid by the bank as a price of its charter, and all future dividends from $7 million in bank stock held by the U.S. government. The bill was vetoed by James Madison as the last official act of his presidency. Madison argued that the U.S. CONSTITUTION did not authorize Congress to construct roads or canals or to improve waterways and suggested a constitutional amendment.

Further reading: Henry Steele Commager, ed., *Documents of American History*, 8th ed. (New York: Appleton-Century-Crofts, 1968).

Bonus Bill of 1924, U.S.

Federal legislation passed by the U.S. Congress on May 19, 1924, over the veto of President Calvin Coolidge, providing "adjusted compensation" for veterans of World War I (1914–18), with payment to be deferred until 1945. Each veteran was to receive $1 a day for service within the United States and $1.25 a day for service abroad, payable in endowment insurance policy certificates. Certificates valued at $3.5 billion were issued, averaging about $1,000 per veteran. During the Great Depression veterans pressed for early redemption of the certificates. In 1936, over the veto of President Franklin Roosevelt, Congress approved immediate payment.

Further reading: Jennifer D. Keene, *Doughboys, the Great War, and the Remaking of America* (Baltimore: Johns Hopkins University Press, 2001).

Bossuet's Four Articles

See FOUR ARTICLES, BOSSUET'S.

Boston Port Act

First of the COERCIVE ACTS, enacted by the British Parliament on March 31, 1774, as punishment for the Boston Tea Party (December 16, 1773), when colonists threw tea from ships of the British East India Company into Boston harbor. The act, which became effective on June 1, 1774, closed the customhouse and port of Boston, Massachusetts, until the company was paid for the destroyed tea and until Britain's King George III was assured of the Boston colonists' loyalty. In the interim, Marblehead became the port of entry.

Further reading: David Ammerman, *In the Common Cause: American Response to the Coercive Acts of 1774* (Charlottesville: University Press of Virginia, 1974); Henry Steele Commager, ed., *Documents of American History*, 8th ed. (New York: Appleton-Century-Crofts, 1968); William MacDonald, *Select Charters and Other Documents Illustrative of American History, 1606–1775* (New York: Macmillan, 1899).

Boulogne, Edict of (Treaty of La Rochelle, First Edict of Poitiers)

Treaty of La Rochelle confirmed and proclaimed by the Edict of Boulogne (First Edict of Poitiers) on July 8, 1573, ending the Fourth War of Religion (1572–73) in France by promising the Huguenots (Protestants) restoration of the favorable terms of the 1570 Truce of St. Germain (which ended the Third War of Religion [1568–70]). It recognized Huguenot christenings and marriages as valid and granted freedom of religious practice for all nobility subservient to the higher judiciary. The royal French garrisons at La Rochelle, Nîmes, and Montauban were lifted and Huguenot assemblies permitted in the last two cities. The settlement fostered the creation of a nationwide Protestant League, aggravating the religious rift between Catholics and Protestants in France and threatening the unity of the state.

See also: BERGERAC, TREATY OF; MONSIEUR, PEACE OF; NEMOURS, TREATY OF.

Further reading: Mack P. Holt, *The French Wars of Religion, 1562–1629* (New York: Cambridge University Press, 1999).

Bowers v. Hardwick   U.S. Supreme Court decision issued on June 30, 1986, ruling that an 1816 Georgia State law, which made sodomy a crime even if committed in the privacy of one's home, did not violate an individual's constitutional right to privacy. The case involved Michael Hardwick, a homosexual who had been arrested in his home in Georgia for engaging in homosexual activity, thus violating the Georgia law; although Hardwick was not prosecuted, he subsequently challenged the law's constitutionality. The decision was made despite the fact that married couples had gained the right of sexual privacy in a 1965 Supreme Court ruling. The court based its decision primarily on the fact that a precedent had been set by a number of state laws against sodomy, dating from the 17th century to the present day.

Further reading: Ellen Alderman, *The Right to Privacy* (New York: Alfred A. Knopf, 1995); Leonard W. Levy and Kenneth L. Karst, eds., *Encyclopedia of the American Constitution,* 2d ed. (New York: Macmillan Reference, 2000); Mark Mikula and L. Mpho Mabunda, eds., *Great American Court Cases,* 4 vols. (Farmington Hills, Mich.: Gale Group, 1999).

Boxer Protocol   Treaty of September 7, 1901, between China and 11 world powers (Austria-Hungary, Belgium, France, Germany, Great Britain, Italy, Japan, the Netherlands, Russia, Spain, and the United States), concluding the Boxer Rebellion of 1899–1900. The rebellion against imperialist interference in China, led by a secret, xenophobic society, was supressed by the combined efforts of American, British, French, German, and Japanese forces. The settlement provided for punishment of the rebellion's ringleaders by either execution or exile. In addition, China was forced to relinquish control of the route from Peking (Beijing) to the sea; to adopt a 5 percent import tariff; to pay a large indemnity; and to apologize both for the assassination of the German and Japanese ministers and for the desecration of Christian cemeteries.

Further reading: Charles L. Phillips and Alan Axelrod, eds., *Encyclopedia of Historical Treaties and Alliances,* 2 vols. (New York: Facts On File, 2001).

Boy Scouts of America v. Dale   Assistant scoutmaster James Dale's case against the Boy Scouts of America (BSA) for expelling him when it learned from a newspaper article that he was gay. The case resulted on June 28, 2000, in the U.S. Supreme Court's narrowly upholding (5-4) the ban, thus reversing a 1999 decision by the New Jersey Supreme Court. Dale's suit was based on a New Jersey statute banning discrimination in public places on account of sexual orientation; however, the U.S. Supreme Court held that this law was superseded by the right to freedom of association protected by the FIRST AMENDMENT and that Dale's presence in the BSA sent a message that the organization "accepts homosexual conduct as a legitimate form of behavior." BSA had argued that as a private institution it had the right to exclude anyone from its membership. Dale's attorney countered that the BSA should not be treated as a private institution and that it had not shown how its message or mission had been adversely affected by Dale's homosexuality.

Further reading: John C. O'Quinn, " 'How Solemn Is the Duty of the Mighty Chief': Mediating the Conflict of Rights in *Boy Scouts of America* v. *Dale*," *Harvard Journal of Law and Public Policy*, 24 (Fall 2000): 319–68.

Brabant Constitution (Joyeuse Entrée of Brabant)   Charter of liberties issued at Louvain on January 3, 1356, by Duke Wenceslas and Duchess Johanna upon acceding to the duchy of Brabant (now divided between the Netherlands and Belgium). The rights of the duchy's towns and assemblies were affirmed, as was the duchy's indivisibility and union with Limburg. The duke was required to seek the consent of the towns before declaring war, concluding alliances, and coining money; his officers could be chosen from his own people. Citizens were entitled to renounce allegiance to the duke if he violated the charter. Its articles confirmed the maintenance of free trade and public roads and the adherence to due process of law in all matters. The charter became an important weapon in the Netherlanders' later fight against invading forces of absolutism; it was abolished in 1789 by Holy Roman Emperor Joseph II.

Further reading: Bartholomew Landheer, ed., *The Netherlands* (Berkeley: University of California Press, 1943); Edouard Perroy, *The Hundred Years War* (New York: Capricorn Books, 1965).

Brady Handgun Violence Prevention Act (Brady Bill)   U.S. legislation signed on November 30, 1993, by President Bill Clinton and implemented on February 28, 1994, establishing a five-day waiting period for prospective handgun buyers. During this period, law enforcement officials are required to perform background checks to prevent convicted felons, minors, illegal immigrants, and substance abusers from attempting to purchase handguns. States receive $200 million annually to set up a nationwide computerized registry for handgun buyers. The law also raises federal license fees for firearms. It was named after former White House press secretary James S. Brady, who was seriously wounded during an attempt on President Ronald Reagan's life and has since dedicated his life to gun control issues.

Further reading: "Brady Handgun Violence Prevention Act," available online at http://www-2.cs.cmu.edu/afs/cs/usv/wbardwel/public/nfalist/brady_act.txt.

Brandenburg v. Ohio U.S. Supreme Court decision issued on June 9, 1969, protecting free speech unless such speech represents a clear threat of violence. It overturned an Ohio criminal syndicalism act under which the defendant had been convicted of leading a gathering of 12 hooded, armed figures who burned a cross and denounced blacks and Jews. The Supreme Court ruled that constitutional guarantees of free speech and free press prevent a state from forbidding the advocacy of the use of force or of law violation "except where such advocacy is directed to inciting or producing imminent lawless action and is likely to incite or produce such action."

Further reading: Lee Epstein and Thomas G. Walker, *Constitutional Law for a Changing America: Rights, Liberties, and Justice,* 2d ed. (Washington, D.C.: Congressional Quarterly Press, 1995); Leonard W. Levy and Kenneth L. Karst, eds., *Encyclopedia of the American Constitution,* 2d ed. (New York: Macmillan Reference, 2000); Mark Mikula and L. Mpho Mabunda, eds., *Great American Court Cases,* 4 vols. (Farmington Hills, Mich.: Gale Group, 1999).

Brazilian-British Treaty of 1826
Treaty concluded on November 23, 1826, by Brazil and Great Britain, stipulating that Brazil terminate all involvement in the slave trade. The treaty specifically provided that any Brazilian involvement in the slave trade would, after 1830, be illegal. Great Britain had argued that Brazil was obliged to acquiesce on this issue as a result of her newly gained independence from Portugal; previous British-Portuguese agreements had stipulated that Portuguese colonial possessions, such as Portuguese West Africa (Angola), cease exporting slaves to non-Portuguese territories across the Atlantic. Nevertheless, Brazil viewed the treaty as a sacrifice of her own interests.

See also: ABERDEEN ACT; BRAZILIAN SLAVE EMANCIPATION ACT.

Further reading: E. Bradford Burns, *A History of Brazil* (New York: Columbia University Press, 1970); Robert M. Levine, *Historical Dictionary of Brazil* (Metuchen, N.J.: Scarecrow Press, 1979); Emilia Viotti de Costa, *The Brazilian Empire* (Chicago: University of Chicago Press, 1985).

Brazilian Constitutional Amendment of 1834 (Acto Adicional of 1834)
Amendment to the BRAZILIAN CONSTITUTION OF 1824, issued in 1834; provided for the right of the Brazilian provinces to elect their own legislative assemblies, for the abolition of the entailing of estates, and for the suppression of the council of states, a reactionary assembly under Dom Pedro I (Brazil's emperor). Also, the number of regents was reduced from three to one, and the provincial governments were given control over primary and secondary education. The amendment, adopted as a concession to the provinces' demand for more self-government, introduced a form of federalism in an attempt to preserve Brazil's threatened unity.

Further reading: E. Bradford Burns, *A History of Brazil* (New York: Columbia University Press, 1970); Robert M. Levine, *Historical Dictionary of Brazil* (Metuchen, N.J.: Scarecrow Press, 1979); Emilia Viotti de Costa, *The Brazilian Empire* (Chicago: University of Chicago Press, 1985).

Brazilian Constitution of 1824
Constitution written by Brazil's emperor Pedro I with the aid of 10 appointed counselors and promulgated on March 25, 1824. A moderate document, it called for a centralized monarchist state, weak provincial and local governments, and a restricted electorate; yet it also contained many guarantees, such as freedom of the press and of worship, protection from arbitrary arrest, the right of bail, and the right to primary education and property. It did not, however, address the issue of slavery. *Poder moderator* ("moderating power") and executive powers resided with the emperor; legislative power was delegated to an appointed senate. Largely respected by Pedro II, the constitution remained the basic law of Brazil until the formation of the republic in 1889.

See also: BRAZILIAN CONSTITUTIONAL AMENDMENT OF 1834.

Further reading: Barbara A. Tenenbaum, ed., *Encyclopedia of Latin American History and Culture* (New York: Charles Scribner's Sons, 1996).

Brazilian Constitution of 1891
Constitution promulgated on February 24, 1891, by the provisional government of Manuel Deodoro da Fonseca, after the overthrow of Emperor Pedro II of Brazil in 1889. The new constitution, which was presidential, federal, and republican in nature, provided the framework for Brazilian government during the First Republic. The 20 recognized Brazilian states were granted such political and economic powers as levying import and export taxes; owning mineral rights within their boundaries; and maintaining their own militias. However, the president could proclaim a state of siege, intervene in states' internal affairs, and replace elected governors. Suspended by President Getulio Vargas at the end of the First Republic, the constitution was replaced by a new one in 1934.

See also: GOLDEN LAW, BRAZILIAN.

Further reading: Barbara A. Tenenbaum, ed., *Encyclopedia of Latin American History and Culture* (New York: Charles Scribner's Sons, 1996).

Brazilian Constitution of 1934
New constitution promulgated in Brazil on July 16, 1934, ending a dictatorship under President Getulio Vargas. A mixture of liberal and conservative elements, it provided for a president elected by congress and ineligible for reelection after serving a four-year term, a chamber of deputies of 250 members elected by popular vote, and universal suffrage of men and women reaching

age 18 and literate (criminals, beggars, and enlisted soldiers could not vote). Other provisions strengthened the power of the government over states' rights and the economy; separated church and state (with some privileges to the Roman Catholic Church); and established an eight-hour work day, a six-day work week, no child labor, a minimum wage, a paid vacation, and collective bargaining. There were also regulations restricting immigration, giving church and civil marriages the same status, and prohibiting divorce. In 1934 Vargas was elected president under the new constitution, which was replaced by his own new constitution in 1937 (November 10), granting him dictatorial powers for the alleged purpose of fighting communist and fascist rivals in Brazil.

Further reading: Barbara A. Tenenbaum, ed., *Encyclopedia of Latin American History and Culture* (New York: Charles Scribner's Sons, 1996).

Brazilian Constitution of 1946

Constitution drafted by a panel selected by the Brazilian Institute of Lawyers and approved by the newly elected congress, which met as a constituent assembly. The constitution declared Brazil to be a republic, providing for the separation of powers, but weighted the federal government at the expense of the states, whose constitutions were to be written to comply with the federal document. The presidential term was limited to five years, however, and the president could not succeed himself. In an effort to create a national political focus, the constitution declared that candidates for federal office must be nominated by parties with a national rather than regional base. The franchise excluded illiterates and men enlisted in the armed forces. The constitution remained in effect until 1966.

Further reading: Barbara A. Tenenbaum, ed., *Encyclopedia of Latin American History and Culture* (New York: Charles Scribner's Sons, 1996).

Brazilian Constitution of 1967

Fifth constitution of Brazil promulgated on January 24, 1967, by the administration of President Humberto Castello Branco and approved by congress. Incorporating the reform program of the new regime and providing for its legal continuity, the 1967 constitution altered the balance of power among executive, legislature, and judiciary to strengthen the authority of the president, and between national and state government to reinforce federal supremacy. One controversial provision required the indirect election of the president, governors, and mayors of state capitals. As in the 1946 constitution, the president could not succeed himself, yet the powers granted to him in a state of emergency, which he could declare, were extensive. In 1969 the fifth constitution was so drastically amended that it was virtually abrogated.

See also: BRAZILIAN CONSTITUTION OF 1946.

Further reading: Barbara A. Tenenbaum, ed., *Encyclopedia of Latin American History and Culture* (New York: Charles Scribner's Sons, 1996).

Brazilian Constitution of 1988

New constitution completed by the 559-member congress in Brasilia and promulgated on October 5, 1988, introducing new democratic reforms into the authoritarian state of Brazil. The document included articles providing for a presidential election, by popular vote, to be held in 1989 (this would be the first such election in nearly 30 years); for the workers' right to strike; for the abolition of torture and censorship; for the reduction of the work week from 48 hours to 40 hours; for an increase in congressional powers; and for an increase in the authority of state and municipal governments. The constitution, Brazil's eighth, was criticized for not being democratic enough, because its wording intimated a dominant military role in government again (the armed forces had the right "to defend the constitutional powers"). New controls were put on foreign capital and a ban put on expropriation of land under cultivation (unless marijuana was being grown on it).

Further reading: Albert Blaustein and Gilbert Flanz, eds., *Constitutions of the Countries of the World* (Dobbs Ferry, N.Y.: Oceana Publications, 1993); Barbara A. Tenenbaum, ed., *Encyclopedia of Latin American History and Culture* (New York: Charles Scribner's Sons, 1996).

Brazilian Slave Emancipation Act

Act proposed by members of a liberal Brazilian ministry, headed by Prime Minister João Alfredo Correia de Oliveira, and passed by congress; on May 13, 1888, signed by Brazilian emperor Pedro II's daughter Princess Isabella, acting as regent. It ordered the complete abolition of slavery in Brazil. Although antislavery sentiment had been mounting for years, the act caused an uproar among plantation owners because it specified that slaves would be emancipated without compensation to slave owners. Some 700,000 slaves were freed, causing their owners to lose $200 million, reportedly, in "property." The unpopular act contributed to the Brazilian monarchy's downfall the following year.

See also: ABERDEEN ACT; BRAZILIAN-BRITISH TREATY OF 1826; RIO BRANCO LAW.

Further reading: David Baronov, *The Abolition of Slavery in Brazil: The "Liberation" of Africans Through the Emancipation of Capital* (Westport, Conn.: Greenwood Press, 2000); Leslie Bethell, *The Abolition of the Brazilian Slave Trade* (New York: Cambridge University Press, 1970); Robert Brent Toplin, *The Abolition of Slavery in Brazil* (New York: Atheneum, 1972).

Bread-Basket Bill

Prussian law prohibiting public funding of the Roman Catholic Church until previous anticlerical legislation of the Kulturkampf (struggle between the church and government over control of educational and ecclesiastical appointments) was obeyed by Prussian bishops. The measure, passed in April 1875, was in response to a papal encyclical of February 5, 1875, which threatened excommunication to those who obeyed the Prussian anticlerical laws. The following month, two years after the beginning of the Kulturkampf, another law dissolved all Catholic religious orders in Prussia, except those devoted exclusively to nursing the sick. Like the other anticlerical measures of the Kulturkampf, the new laws failed to have the desired effect of eradicating Catholicism in Prussia, and most were repealed by 1887.

See also: MAY LAWS.

Further reading: Richard J. Helmstadter, *Freedom and Religion in the Nineteenth Century* (Stanford, Calif.: Stanford University Press, 1997); Ronald J. Ross, *The Failure of Bismarck's Kulturkampf: Catholicism and State Power in Imperial Germany, 1871–1887* (Washington, D.C.: Catholic University of America Press, 1998); Helmut W. Smith, *German Nationalism and Religious Conflict: Culture, Ideology, Politics, 1870–1914* (Princeton, N.J.: Princeton University Press, 1995).

Breda, Declaration of

English proclamation issued by the exiled King Charles II from Breda (Holland) on April 4, 1660, promising a general amnesty to all former enemies of the royal house of Stuart of Scotland and England (except regicides and others specified by Parliament). It assured religious freedom and payment of arrears in salary to, and future employment of, the army, and it authorized Parliament to determine land settlements. Drafted by Edward Hyde on the advice of George Monck, each clause in the declaration was to be ratified by Parliament and, in return for these concessions, the king was to be restored to the throne.

See also: INDEMNITY AND OBLIVION, ACT OF.

Further reading: Carl Stephenson and Frederick George Marcham, eds., *Sources of English Constitutional History: A Selection of Documents from A.D. 600 to the Present* (New York: Harper & Row, 1937).

Breda, Treaty of (Peace of Breda)

Peace treaty at Breda on July 21, 1667, among England, the Dutch republic (Holland), France, and Denmark, ending the Second Anglo-Dutch War (1665–67), in which the Dutch were supported by France and Denmark. The Dutch had the upper hand in the primarily naval war but hurried to make peace in order to cope with French king Louis XIV's invasion of the Spanish Netherlands in the War of Devolution. By the treaty, England received the New Netherlands (New York and New Jersey) and some colonies in Africa from the Dutch, and recovered the islands of Antigua, Montserrat, and St. Kitts in the West Indies from France. The Dutch kept Pulo Run, in the East Indies, and Surinam. France received Acadia from England and retained French Guiana. The altered English Navigation Acts allowed Dutch ships to transport English goods that had been shipped down the Rhine, and restricted the word "contraband" to mean "implements of war." Thus, the Dutch maintained their supremacy in world trade whereas England was unable to make any headway in the spice trade.

Further reading: Milos Safranek, ed., *The Angel of Peace* (New York: Pantheon Books, 1944).

Brehon Laws

Ancient legal rules of Ireland in archaic Gaelic, probably first written down in the fifth century A.D. The existing oral, traditional laws were recorded and administered by the brehons (ancient Irish jurists) to members of Ireland's clans or tribes. To hold land or a post depended on kinship with a clan, whose strength lay in all its occupied territory and solidarity. Landholding nobles could contract with clansmen who wanted the right to graze livestock on their lands. The conditions of land tenure between nobles and clansmen were set by law, as was the liability or lack of it imposed on the clansmen's families. The penalty for committing a crime, major or minor, was usually payment of damages to the victim's family. The laws lasted among the native Irish until about 1650.

See also: KILKENNY, STATUTES OF.

Further reading: Christopher Haigh, ed., *The Cambridge Historical Encyclopedia of Great Britain and Ireland* (Cambridge, England: Cambridge University Press, 1985).

Breslau, Treaty of (1741)

Agreement concluded on June 5, 1741, by France and Prussia during the First Silesian War (1741–42). Prussia's king Frederick II the Great had fought determinedly to annex the Austrian territory of Silesia. By the treaty, France recognized Prussia's control over Lower Silesia (which Frederick had invaded in 1740); in return, Frederick pledged his support for Bavarian elector Charles Albert's claim to the imperial throne (see NYMPHENBURG, TREATY OF).

Further reading: M. S. Anderson, *The War of the Austrian Succession, 1740–1748* (New York: Longman, 1995); Edward Crankshaw, *Maria Theresa* (London: Constable, 1996); David Fraser, *Frederick the Great: King of Prussia* (London: Penguin Books, 2000).

Breslau, Treaty of (1742)

Peace agreement mediated by Britain and made at Breslau (Wroclaw, Silesia, Poland) on June 11, 1742, between Prussia under King Frederick II the Great and Austria under Archduchess Maria Theresa; ended the First Silesian War (1740–42), which was part of the general War of the Austrian Succession (1740–48). Austria had decided to make peace with Prussia, whose annexation of Lower and Upper Silesia and the county of Glatz (Klodzko) was accepted. Prussia also assumed the 1.7 million-rix-dollar debt upon Silesia, owed to Dutch and British creditors, and Frederick agreed to withdraw from the coalition against Maria Theresa. The terms were reconfirmed in the 1742 Peace of BERLIN, although Maria Theresa became reconciled to the loss of Silesia only in 1763 with the Treaty of HUBERTUSBURG.

Further reading: M. S. Anderson, *The War of the Austrian Succession, 1740–1748* (New York: Longman, 1995); Edward Cranshaw, *Maria Theresa* (London: Constable, 1996); David Fraser, *Frederick the Great: King of Prussia* (London: Penguin Books, 2000).

Brest, Act of Union of   Religious agreement between the Roman Catholic Church and the Ruthenian Church of the Greek Orthodox faith in western Ukraine; made in the city of Brest (or Brest-Litovsk) in October 1596. Ruthenian Orthodox believers were accepted into the Roman Catholic Church provided they recognized the supremacy of the pope and the church's doctrine of the Eucharist. By the act, Ruthenian priests were allowed to marry as before and permitted to keep their separate hierarchy and their Slavonic rites. Many of the Orthodox faith opposed the union and regarded the Uniates (those accepted by the Roman Church) as schismatics. By the Union of Uzhgorod in 1649, a similar accord was affected between the Ruthenian and Roman Churches in Hungary.

Further reading: Iurii Fedoriv, *History of the Church in Ukraine* (St. Catherines, Ontario: St. Sophia Religious Association of Ukraininan Catholics in Canada, 1983); Borys A. Gudziak, *Crisis and Reform: The Kievan Metropolitanate, the Patriarchate of Constantinople, and the Genesis of the Union of Brest* (Ann Arbor, Mich.: University Microfilms International, 1993).

Brest-Litovsk, Treaty of   Agreement ending World War I (1914–18) between Soviet Russia and the Central Powers (Germany, Austria-Hungary, and Turkey); signed at Brest-Litovsk (Brest, Belorussia) on March 3, 1918. Soviet Russia, exhausted by the war and by her own revolution, had pleaded for a peace without "annexations or indemnities," but reluctantly agreed to the German-demanded, harsh terms of the treaty, which called for Russia's renunciation of Russian Poland; the Baltic provinces of Estonia, Latvia, and Lithuania; the Transcaucasian provinces of Georgia, Armenia, and Azerbaijan; the Ukraine; and Finland—all of which had been part of the Russian Empire. Germany, which later added a large indemnity to her demands, failed to win Allied approval for the treaty, but the Soviets did ratify it on March 15; Allied premiers and foreign ministers, meeting at London, called the treaty "a political crime against the Russian people" (March 18). Under the conditions of the WORLD WAR I ARMISTICE the Central Powers were forced to annul the treaty on November 11, 1918, and two days later the Soviet government did likewise.

See also: BATUM, TREATY OF; MOSCOW, TREATY OF (1920); RIGA, TREATY OF (1920); VERSAILLES, TREATY OF (1919).

Further reading: G. Gratz and R. Schüller, *The Economic Policy of Austria-Hungary During the War in Its External Relations* (New Haven, Conn.: Yale University Press, 1928); Charles L. Phillips and Alan Axelrod, eds., *Encyclopedia of Historical Treaties and Alliances*, 2 vols. (New York: Facts On File, 2001); John W. Wheeler-Bennett, *The Treaty of Brest-Litovsk and Germany's Eastern Policy* (Oxford, England: Clarendon Press, 1940).

Brétigny, Treaty of   Provisional settlement made between France and England at Brétigny, Normandy, on May 8, 1360, ending the first phase of the Hundred Years' War (1337–1457). The ransom for France's captive king John II was reduced from 4 million ecus (gold or silver coins) to 3 million; he would be freed on payment of the first 600,000 ecus, and after six annual payments of 400,000 ecus each, all the other hostages would be released by the English, whose king Edward III promised to renounce his claim to the French throne and who was promised sovereignty over Aquitaine, Calais, Ponthieu, and Guînes one year after John's release.

See also: CALAIS, TREATY OF.

Further reading: Charles L. Phillips and Alan Axelrod, eds., *Encyclopedia of Historical Treaties and Alliances*, 2 vols. (New York: Facts On File, 2001).

Bretton Woods Agreement   Agreement concluded on July 22, 1944, in Bretton Woods, New Hampshire, by representatives of the 44 nations attending the conference there; contained their recommendations for the establishment of the International Monetary Fund (IMF) and the International Bank for Reconstruction and Development (IBRD). The agreement required that free trade—which would prohibit tariffs, devaluation of currencies to gain trade advantages, limitations on the convertibility of currencies, etc.—prevail among member nations. It established that the IMF's function would be to provide short-term loans to countries needing to pay for goods and services, the objective of which was to maintain stability in exchange rates; and that the IBRD's function would be to provide backward and war-torn nations with capital necessary for long-term development. The funds were to be provided by member countries. The loans were intended to provide an impetus for growth in post–World War II international trade.

Further reading: Thomas Carson, ed., *Gale Encyclopedia of U.S. Economic History* (Farmington Hills, Mich.: Gale Group, 1999); Armand von Dormael, *Bretton Woods: Birth of a Monetary System* (New York: Holmes & Meier, 1978); Alfred E. Eckes, Jr., *A Search for Solvency: Bretton Woods and the International Monetary System, 1944–71* (Austin: University of Texas Press, 1975); Richard N. Gardner, *Sterling-Dollar Diplomacy in Current Perspective*, rev. ed. (New York: Columbia University Press, 1980).

Breviary of Alaric (Breviarium Alaricianum, Lex Romana Visigothorum)   Summary of Roman laws and imperial decrees issued in A.D. 506 at Toulouse by Visigothic king Alaric II of Spain and southwestern Gaul (France). Written in Latin for his kingdom's Roman subjects, and for Visigothic use, the breviary was based heavily on the THEODOSIAN CODE and contained practical legal commentaries. Roman common law (*jus*) and statute law (*leges*) were clearly stated and arranged for use in Visigothic courts, which settled disputes between the conquered Gallo-Roman population and the Visigoths (who were quickly Romanized by the Breviary of Alaric, which survived as a major stimulus of Roman law for more than 500 years in countries north and west of the Alps).

Further reading: Frank N. Magill, ed., *Great Events from History, Ancient and Medieval Series,* 3 vols. (Englewood Cliffs, N.J.: Salem Press, 1972).

Bricker Amendment

Bricker Amendment Amendment to the U.S. CONSTITUTION, introduced in the Senate on January 7, 1953, by Senator John W. Bricker of Ohio, to limit the U.S. president's right to make treaties and executive agreements and to limit the scope of international treaties to which the United States could be a party. The amendment would have required both houses of Congress, not just the Senate, to ratify treaties, and declared that a treaty would become "effective as internal law . . . only through legislation which would be valid in the absence of a treaty." The opposition of Republican president Dwight Eisenhower to this Republican-sponsored measure was instrumental in defeating the amendment, which was rejected by the Senate on February 26, 1954, by a one-vote margin.

Further reading: Louis Henkin, *Foreign Affairs and the Constitution,* 2d ed. (New York: Oxford University Press, 1996); Leonard W. Levy and Kenneth L. Karst, eds., *Encyclopedia of the American Constitution,* 2d ed. (New York: Macmillan Reference, 2000); Duane Tannenbaum, *The Bricker Amendment Controversy: A Test of Eisenhower's Political Leadership* (Ithaca, N.Y.: Cornell University Press, 1988).

Bright Clause

Bright Clause Important clause in the IRISH LAND ACT OF 1870, inserted by John Bright (British politician, reformer, orator, and cofounder of the Anti-Corn Law League), by which the British government agreed to provide loans to tenants desirous of purchasing their holdings from their landlords. The tenant could borrow not more than two-thirds of the price, repayable at 5 percent over 35 years. With the average price equivalent to 23½ years rental, 877 tenants took advantage of the offer and purchased their holdings, thus creating a small class of peasant proprietors. The situation of those tenants who were unable to afford the high terms of the loan only worsened with the agricultural depression of the 1870s. Bright's clause was important in that peasant ownership proved to be the ultimate answer to the land problem.

Further reading: Donald Read, *Cobden and Bright: A Victorian Political Partnership* (London: Edward Arnold, 1967); Keith Robbins, *John Bright* (London: Routledge & K. Paul, 1979).

British Army Regulation Act of 1871

British Army Regulation Act of 1871 See ARMY REGULATION ACT OF 1871.

British Catholic Emancipation Act

British Catholic Emancipation Act See CATHOLIC EMANCIPATION ACT, BRITISH.

British Declaration of War in 1939

British Declaration of War in 1939 Announcement by Britain's prime minister Neville Chamberlain to the House of Commons on September 3, 1939, in a broadcast to the nation, of Britain's decision to enter into war against Germany in retaliation for the German invasion of Poland (September 1, 1939). Britain was thereby honoring her commitment, made earlier in the year, to defend Poland against aggression. Chamberlain, realizing that the Western democracies' policy of appeasement with Nazi Germany's Adolf Hitler had utterly failed, concluded with the words: "This is a sad day for all of us, and to none is it sadder than to me. Everything that I have worked for . . . has crashed into ruins . . . I trust I may live to see the day when Hitlerism has been destroyed and a liberated Europe has been re-established." Within a few hours, France also declared war on Germany, and thus began World War II (1939–45).

Further reading: David Dutton, *Neville Chamberlain* (London: Arnold, 2001); Nelson Thomson Learning, *1939 Britain's Response to Germany's Invasion of Poland,* available online at http://www.nelson.com/nelson/school/discovery/cantext/wwii/1939brit.htm.

British-Greek-Turkish Agreements of 1959

British-Greek-Turkish Agreements of 1959 Agreements signed in London on February 19, 1959, by Prime Minister Harold Macmillan of Britain, Premier Constantine Karamanlis of Greece, Premier Adnan Menderes of Turkey, the Greek Cypriot leader Archbishop Makarios III, and the Turkish Cypriot leader Fazil Kutchuk, affirming the independence of the Republic of Cyprus. One agreement included both the collective guarantee of Greece, Turkey, and Britain, and the separate guarantee of the new republic, to ensure the maintenance of the republic's independence, territorial integrity, and security, without, under any circumstance, allowing for its union with another power or its partition. Other agreements provided that the republic's president would be a Greek Cypriot elected by the island's Greek population, while the vice president would be a Turkish Cypriot elected by the island's Turkish population; that 30 percent of the parliament's members would be Turkish Cypriot, while the remainder would be Greek Cypriot; and that the island's military bases would remain under British control. The compromise ended years of discord among Cyprus's Greek population, who desired union with Greece, the Turkish population who opposed it, and the British, who were reluctant to grant full independence to territory over which they had had control for many years.

Further reading: R. F. Holland, *Britain and the Revolt in Cyprus, 1954–1959* (New York: Oxford University Press, 1998); E. Kartakes, ed., *Constantine Karamanlis in Thought and Action* (Athens: Roes Publications, 1999); Stanley Mayes, *Makarios: A Biography* (London: Macmillan, 1981).

British Labour Party's Charter of Freedom for Colonial Peoples

British Labour Party's Charter of Freedom for Colonial Peoples Pronouncement of principle made by members of the 41st Annual Conference of the Labour Party in Britain in 1942, calling for "a charter of freedom for colonial peoples abolishing all forms of imperialist exploitation." Its main proposals were that all citizens of the colonies be given the same political, economic, and social rights as citizens in Britain, that colonies be replaced by states (named for their particular country) having equal status with other British Commonwealth nations, that democratic governments be formed and systems of communal land tenure be retained in all colonial areas (notably in Africa), and that a Commonwealth council of colonial peoples be formed, with representatives determined by the population of each former colonial state and taken, partly, from indigenous national groups.

Further reading: *The Old World and the New Society; a Report on the Problems of War and Peace Reconstruction* (London: Labour Party, 1942).

British-Malayan Agreements of 1956 and 1957

Two agreements between Britain and Malaya, signed prior to and immediately following the granting of Malayan independence (August 31, 1957). The first (February 8, 1956) summarized the decisions of the London Conference (January 18–February 6, 1956), declaring that "every effort" would be made to achieve independence by August 1957. Meanwhile, Britain would transfer control of internal defense and security, finance, commerce, and industry to Malayan officials; give the chief minister greater control; withdraw her advisers to the Malay rulers; and appoint a commission to draft a constitution for the new state. The Defense and Mutual Assistance Treaty (October 12, 1957) provided for British aid in expanding Malayan forces, the stationing of British troops, and the retention of her bases in Malaya. Both countries were to consult each other and take joint action in the event of an armed attack or threat. However, Britain could not use her forces in Malaya without the Malay government's permission.

Further reading: Kim Hoong Khong, *Merdeka! British Rule and the Struggle for Independence in Malaya, 1945–1957* (Petaling Jaya, Malaysia: Institute for Social Analysis, 1984); Simon C. Smith, *British Relations with the Malay Rulers from Decentralization to Malayan Independence, 1930–1957* (New York: Oxford University Press, 1995).

British Metropolitan Police Act

Major reform act creating the first disciplined civilian police force in the Greater London area; formulated by Sir Robert Peel, home secretary and leader of the House of Commons, and passed by a Tory-dominated British Parliament in 1829. Until then Britain had had no efficient police system for keeping public order and preventing crime. Peel, who had created the Irish constabulary while serving as chief secretary for Ireland (1812–18), signalized himself by this 1829 act, which reorganized and centralized the London metropolitan police force, whose members came to be called "Peelers" or "Bobbies." The London police force, which replaced the uncoordinated parish constables and watchmen, was put under the control of the home secretary, who was in turn answerable to Parliament

for the force. The act was the basis of Britain's modern metropolitan police system.

Further reading: Wilbur R. Miller, *Cops and Bobbies: Police Authority in New York and London, 1830–1870*, 2d ed. (Columbus: Ohio State University Press, 1999); Elaine A. Reynolds, *Before the Bobbies: The Night Watch and Police Reform in Metropolitan London, 1720–1830* (Stanford, Calif.: Stanford University Press, 1998); Haia Shpayer-Makov, *The Making of a Policeman: The Social History of a Labour Force in Metropolitan London, 1829–1914* (Burlington, Vt.: Ashgate, 2001).

British Nationality Act of 1948

Legislation passed on July 30, 1948, allowing each member of the British Commonwealth of Nations to define its own citizens (see BRITISH NATIONALITY AND NEW ZEALAND CITIZENSHIP ACT; SOUTH AFRICAN CITIZENSHIP ACT) while conferring the status of British subject on all of them. Prompted by the Canadian Citizenship Act of 1946, the act created a "citizenship of the United Kingdom and Colonies," replacing the old classification of British subjects as all persons born within "the King's dominions." The new citizenship was also deemed applicable in the case of British subjects abroad, who had not acquired the citizenship of a Commonwealth country. This was to create severe immigration hassles for Britain when her former colonies in East Africa refused to grant citizenship to thousands of Asians. Citizens of the Republic of Ireland (see IRELAND ACT, REPUBLIC OF) would continue being treated as if they were still members of the Commonwealth.

Further reading: Clive Parry, *British Nationality, Including Citizenship of the United Kingdom and Colonies and the Status of Aliens* (London: Stevens, 1951).

British Nationality and New Zealand Citizenship Act

Bill passed on August 18, 1948, introducing an independent citizenship for New Zealanders while maintaining their status as British subjects (see BRITISH NATIONALITY ACT OF 1948). The new citizenship could be obtained by birth, descent, registration, naturalization, or by New Zealand's annexation of territory. Thereby, British subjects born, naturalized, or ordinarily resident in New Zealand in 1948 or British subjects born in Western Samoa automatically became New Zealand citizens, as did British subjects born outside New Zealand to native-born or naturalized fathers, or female British subjects married to New Zealand citizens. A year's residence could qualify an adult British subject, Commonwealth, or Irish citizen to register for citizenship. British subjects could be called for military service. Amended in 1959, 1961, and 1962, this act is the present law of nationality.

Further reading: A. H. McLintock, *Encyclopedia of New Zealand* (Wellington, New Zealand: R. E. Owen 1966); W. H. Oliver and B. R. Williams, eds., *The Oxford History of New Zealand* (Wellington, New Zealand: Oxford University Press, 1981).

British North America Act

Act passed by the British Parliament on March 29, 1867, providing for the union of the provinces of Canada, New Brunswick, and Nova Scotia to form the Dominion of Canada. The act provided that the Dominion be divided into four provinces (Quebec, Ontario, Nova Scotia, and New Brunswick), each with its own government controlling its internal affairs; that the federal government would consist of an executive government (under the jurisdiction of Great Britain), an appointed Senate, and an elected House of Commons; that the federal government would have control over such matters as taxation, trade, and transportation and communications among the provinces; and that the other British North American colonies could be admitted into the union. Later, the act became part of the CANADIAN CONSTITUTION ACT OF 1982.

See also: QUEBEC RESOLUTIONS; UNION, ACT OF (UNION OF UPPER AND LOWER CANADA).

Further reading: Carl Stephenson and Frederick George Marcham, eds., *Sources of English Constitutional History: A Selection of Documents from A.D. 600 to the Present* (New York: Harper & Row, 1937).

British Protective Tariff Acts of 1932 (Import Duties Act)

British legislation (February 29, 1932) levying a general tariff of 10 percent on all goods (except foodstuffs and industrial raw materials), a striking reversal of Britain's century-old commitment to free trade. Goods from the Commonwealth countries were exempt. An Import Duties Advisory Committee, headed by Sir George May, was immediately established to suggest changes; it recommended increasing the general tariff to 20 percent and up to 30 percent on some luxury goods. Simultaneously, a new corn law (see CORN LAW OF 1815, CORN LAW OF 1828) assured British farmers $1 per bushel of wheat. These protectionist measures were endorsed by the Conservative majority in the national government and opposed by the Labour Party. Implemented March 1, 1932, the legislation was introduced by Neville Chamberlain to deal with the economic crisis of 1931, to serve as a bargaining point for British goods abroad, and to revitalize British industries.

Further reading: Great Britain Board of Trade, *Report on the Import Duties Act Inquiry (1934) Presented to Parliament in Pursuance of the Import Duties Act, 1932*, 2 vols. (London: H.M. Stationery Office, 1937).

Brown v. Board of Education of Topeka, Kansas

Landmark U.S. Supreme Court decision issued on May 17, 1954, declaring that racial segregation in public schools was unconstitutional. Reversing *PLESSY V. FERGUSON*, which allowed for "separate but equal" facilities, the Court now unanimously ruled that "separate educational facilities are inherently unequal" and violate the equal protection guarantees of the FOURTEENTH AMENDMENT. The case was brought before the Court by the National Association for the Advancement of Colored People (NAACP) on behalf of Linda Brown, a Topeka student who attended an all-black elementary school. The decision led to nationwide desegregation in educational and other institutions and gave impetus to the civil rights movement in America.

Further reading: Leon Friedman, ed., *Argument: The Oral Argument Before the Supreme Court in Brown v. Board of Education of Topeka, 1952–1955* (New York: Chelsea House, 1983); John W. Johnson, *Historical U.S. Court Cases, 1690–1990: An Encyclopedia* (New York: Garland Press, 1992); Richard Kluger, *Simple Justice: The History of Brown v. Board of Education and Black America's Struggle for Equality,* (New York: Alfred A. Knopf, 1976); Mark Mikula and L. Mpho Mabunda, eds., *Great American Court Cases,* 4 vols. (Farmington Hills, Mich.: Gale Group, 1999).

Brundisium, Treaty of

Ancient Roman pact of peace concluded by Marc Antony and Octavian (Augustus) at Brundisium (Brindisi, Italy) in 40 B.C., temporarily ending hostilities between them over imperial power during the Roman Civil War of 43–31 B.C. Octavian was to hold all the western provinces (Spain, Gaul, Sicily, Sardinia, Dalmatia) except Africa (which was to be retained by the triumvir Marcus Aemilius Lepidus). The Roman provinces east of the Ionian Sea were to be held by Antony, who was to marry Octavian's sister Octavia to bind the pact. Italy was to be held in common, but was really controlled by Octavian.

See also: MISENUM, TREATY OF; TITIAN LAW.

Further reading: Charles L. Phillips and Alan Axelrod, eds., *Encyclopedia of Historical Treaties and Alliances,* 2 vols. (New York: Facts On File, 2001).

Brussels Act of 1890 (General Act of Brussels)

Resolution passed on July 2, 1890, concluding an international conference held in Brussels, Belgium, and signed by all major European countries, the United States, Turkey, Persia, and Zanzibar; it provided measures for the cessation of slave trading, which had grown to alarming levels during the latter half of the 19th century (especially in Africa's Congo region). The act proposed that each individual country's armed services become involved in the drive against slave trading: at points of origin, where the people were captured, at points of destination, and along routes of transit; and that any such involvement with slave trading be treated as a criminal offense. The sale of firearms was also prohibited by the act.

Further reading: Brussels Conference, *General Act, Declaration and Protocols of the Brussels Slave Trade Conference with Annexes to the Protocols, 1890* (Shannon: Irish University Press, 1971).

Brussels Treaty of 1948

Fifty-year mutual assistance pact entered into (March 17, 1948) by Britain, France, the Netherlands, Belgium, and Luxembourg, pledging military support in the event of an armed attack, and closer economic ties. It established a Permanent Military Committee to coordinate policies and forces, and several economic and social subcommittees, which led the way toward eventual Western European integration (see ROME, TREATIES OF [1957]; SCHUMAN PLAN). Signed after the Communists seized power in Czechoslovakia (February 25, 1948), the treaty was also intended as a united front against possible German or Soviet aggression. Discussions were conducted to broaden the pact by including Iceland, Italy, Denmark, Canada, and the United States. The Vandenberg Resolution (May 19, 1948) allowed the United States to begin formal negotiations for a NORTH ATLANTIC TREATY linking Western Europe and North America. The Brussels powers merged to form the North Atlantic Treaty Organization (NATO) in April 1949.

Further reading: Charles L. Phillips and Alan Axelrod, eds., *Encyclopedia of Historical Treaties and Alliances,* 2 vols. (New York: Facts On File, 2001).

Bryan-Chamorro Treaty

Treaty between Nicaragua and the United States, negotiated by U.S. secretary of state William Jennings Bryan with Nicaragua's foreign minister Emiliano Chamorro and signed on August 5, 1914; it provided a payment to Nicaragua of $3 million for the exclusive right of the United States to construct an interoceanic canal through the country. The United States was also granted a 99-year lease of the Great and Little Corn Islands and the right to a naval base on the Gulf of Fonseca. While the Central American Court of Justice condemned Nicaragua for signing the treaty, and declared that Nicaragua had infringed upon the rights of Costa Rica and El Salvador, it did not invalidate the treaty; neither the United States nor Nicaragua recognized the decision, but the treaty was never enforced because of the territorial objections of neighboring countries. And after completion of the Panama Canal in 1914, interest in an additional canal also subsided.

Further reading: Dana G. Munro, *Intervention and Dollar Diplomacy in the Caribbean, 1900–1921* (Westport, Conn.: Greenwood Press, 1964, repr., 1980); Barbara A. Tenenbaum, ed., *Encyclopedia of Latin American History and Culture* (New York: Charles Scribner's Sons, 1996).

Bubble Act (South Sea Bubble Act)

English company law passed by the Parliament of King George I in 1720, to end the wild speculation in shares following the dramatic developments at the South Sea Company (which was founded in 1711 to capitalize on the anticipated trade monopolies with Spain's American colonies). The act prohibited new companies (post-1718) from issuing transferable shares or misusing old charters. In 1719, Parliament approved the South Sea Company's scheme of assuming the national debt. Inspired by the Mississippi Scheme of France, speculators rushed to invest and stock prices soared. To deter competition, the company tried using the Bubble Act against them, but public confidence was rapidly eroding and the company collapsed in September 1720. The Bubble Act was repealed on July 5, 1825.

Further reading: Armand B. DuBois, *The English Business Company after the Bubble Act, 1720–1800* (New York: Octagon Books, 1971).

Bucharest, Treaty of (1812)

Treaty concluded at Bucharest on May 28, 1812, between Russia and the Ottoman Empire (Turkey), ending a six-year war in which Russia had been fighting for control over Turkish territory in the Caucasus and Danubian river basin. Through the treaty Russia gained the province of Bessarabia (part of the Danubian principality of Moldavia); the Russo-Turkish border was set along the Pruth River; Serbia was granted automony; Russia returned to Turkey certain territories in the western Caucasus captured in the war (including Poti and Anapa), while retaining others, thus providing Russia with naval bases on the eastern (Caucasus) coast of the Black Sea. The peace was welcomed by both parties, for the Turks had become exhausted by war, and the Russians were having to cope with the invading Grand Army of Napoléon and its imminent assault on Moscow.

See also: AKKERMAN, CONVENTION OF.

Further reading: Stanford Shaw and Ezel Kural Shaw, *History of the Ottoman Empire and Modern Turkey,* 2 vols. (New York: Cambridge University Press, 1977); Reeva S. Simon, Philip Mattar, and Richard W. Bulliet, eds., *Encyclopedia of the Modern Middle East* (New York: Simon & Schuster, 1996).

Bucharest, Treaty of (1886)

Succinct peace treaty signed at Bucharest on March 3, 1886, concluding the Serbo-Bulgarian war of 1885–86. The Serbs had declared war on Bulgaria, November 13, 1885, in order to prevent the union of Bulgaria and Eastern Rumelia, or to gain territorial compensation for such a union. The Bulgars defeated the Serbs at Slivnitza, on November 17, but were prevented from invading Serbia by Austrian intervention. The treaty restored the status quo antebellum, terms that were quite favorable to the defeated Serbs, who also paid no indemnity.

Further reading: Arthur E. Huhn, *The Struggle of the Bulgarians for National Independence under Prince Alexander: A Military and Political History of the War Between Bulgaria and Servia in 1885* (Ann Arbor, Mich.: University Microfilms International, 1994).

Bucharest, Treaty of (1913)

Treaty concluded at Bucharest, Romania, on August 10, 1913, between Bulgaria and a coalition consisting of Serbia, Greece, Montenegro, and Romania, bringing an end, together with the Treaty of CONSTANTINOPLE (1913), to the Second Balkan War (1913). Through the treaty Serbia gained control over northern and central Macedonia (including Kosovo, Skopje, and Bitola); Greece gained a large part of coastal Macedonia, plus Thessaloniki (Salonica); Romania received northern Dobruja, located along the Black Sea; and Bulgaria was left with a part of eastern Macedonia. The war originated over Serbia and Greece's discontent with the earlier settlement ending the First Balkan War (1912–13) (see LONDON, TREATY OF [1913]); both Serbia and Greece, together with Bulgaria, had claims on Macedonia; Romania and the Ottoman Empire (Turkey) joined the fighting in order to acquire territory for themselves.

Further reading: Charles L. Phillips and Alan Axelrod, eds., *Encyclopedia of Historical Treaties and Alliances,* 2 vols. (New York: Facts On File, 2001); Stanford Shaw and Ezel Kural Shaw, *History of the Ottoman Empire and Modern Turkey,* 2 vols. (New York: Cambridge University Press, 1977); Reeva S. Simon, Philip Mattar, and Richard W. Bulliet, eds., *Encyclopedia of the Modern Middle East* (New York: Simon & Schuster, 1996).

Bucharest, Treaty of (1918)

Treaty concluded on May 7, 1918, among Romania and Germany, Austria-Hungary, and Bulgaria, providing terms for peace between the two sides during World War I (1914–18). Romania had been defeated by the Central Powers. The treaty (signed in Bucharest) provided that Romania would cede her coastal province of Dobruja to Bulgaria; cede the Carpathian passes in the north to Austria-Hungary; and grant Germany a lease of 90 years on her oil wells. The Romanians, through the petition of Premier Alexandru Marghiloman, gained the Central Powers' approval for her annexation of Bessarabia, which was then under Russian control. Owing to the Central Powers' defeat later in 1918, the terms of the treaty never went into effect.

Further reading: Gusztav Gratz and Richard Schuller, *The Economic Policy of Austria-Hungary During the War in Its External Relations* (New Haven, Conn.: Yale University Press, 1928); *Texts of the Roumanian "Peace": With Map* (Wilmington, Del.: Scholarly Resources, 1974).

Bucharest, Treaty of (1921)

Treaty concluded at Bucharest on March 3, 1921, by Romania and Poland, expanding upon the French-directed foreign policy in the region, which had already been established in the LITTLE ENTENTE TREATIES, the goal of which was to maintain the status quo in post–World War I Europe. The treaty provided that, in the event of an unprovoked attack on either party's eastern frontier, the other party would come to the former's defense; it obligated each party, in the event of war, not to conclude a separate peace with any other power; and it required that neither party conclude an alliance with any other power without making the agreement known first to the other party. In addition, the treaty contained an article providing for the conclusion of a military convention, which was to guarantee the present treaty. The treaty was to remain in effect for five years.

Further reading: Eliza Campus, *The Little Entente and the Balkan Alliance* (Bucharest: Editura Academiei Republicii Socialiste Romania, 1978); Robert Machray, *The Little Entente* (New York: H. Fertig, 1970).

Buczacz, Treaty of

Short-lived Polish-Turkish peace concluded on October 18, 1672, at Buczacz (Buchach, Ukraine); reluctantly accepted by Poland's King Michael Wisniowiecki with the Ottoman Turks, after the latter had occupied the Polish Ukrainian province of Podolia in the Polish-Turkish War of 1671–77. By the treaty, Poland ceded Podolia to the Turks, recognized Cossack hetman (leader) Pyotr Doroshenko as ruler of the western Ukraine and a vassal of the Ottoman sultan, and agreed to pay an annual tribute of 220,000 ducats (gold coins) to the sultan. The Polish diet refused to ratify the treaty, and the war resumed under John III Sobieski, elected Poland's new king in 1674 following Michael's death.

See also: ANDRUSOVO, TREATY OF; KARLOWITZ, PEACE OF; ZURAVNO, TREATY OF.

Further reading: Dariusz Kolodziejczyk, *Ottoman-Polish Diplomatic Relations (15th–18th Century): An Annotated Edition of 'Ahdnames and Other Documents* (Boston: Brill, 2000).

Budapest Conventions of 1877

Military and political conventions between Russia and Austria, signed in Budapest on January 15, 1877. (The political convention was actually signed on March 17, 1877, but was antedated to January 15.) The conventions bound Austria to a benevolent neutrality in any Russo-Turkish conflict. In the event of a dissolution of the Ottoman Empire, Russia might invade Bulgaria, while Bosnia and Herzegovina would go to Austria. Serbia and Montenegro would comprise a neutral zone. It was agreed, moreover, that no large, compact, Slavic state would be created in the Balkans, although the establishment of several smaller ones would be allowed.

See also: SAN STEFANO, TREATY OF.

Further reading: Stanford Shaw and Ezel Kural Shaw, *History of the Ottoman Empire and Modern Turkey,* 2 vols. (New York: Cambridge University Press, 1977); Reeva S. Simon, Philip Mattar, and Richard W. Bulliet, eds., *Encyclopedia of the Modern Middle East* (New York: Simon & Schuster, 1996).

Bulgarian Horrors and the Question of the East

Pamphlet written and published in Great Britain in 1876 by British statesman William Ewart Gladstone, condemning both the Turkish actions taken against the Bulgarians that year as well as the British government, whose policies supported the perpetrators. In the pamphlet Gladstone attacked the Ottoman Turks' massacre of approximately 15,000 Bulgarians during the uprising there in 1876; the uprising had been part of the more general uprising against Ottoman rule in the Balkans, which lasted from 1875 to 1878. He further urged his government to adopt policies that would bring about the expulsion of the Turks from Bulgaria. The pamphlet aroused anti-Turkish sentiment in Great Britain and put pressure on Prime Minister Benjamin Disraeli's government to modify its foreign policy. Great Britain had, at that time, been in support of the Ottoman Empire (Turkey) in opposition to Russia.

Further reading: David Harris, *Britain and the Bulgarian Horrors of 1876* (Chicago: University of Chicago Press, 1939); Reeva S. Simon, Philip Mattar, and Richard W. Bulliet, eds., *Encyclopedia of the Modern Middle East* (New York: Simon & Schuster, 1996).

Bundestag Election Law   Law passed by the Bundestag, or lower house of the West German parliament, in Bonn on March 15, 1956, outlining the rules to be followed in the 1957 Bundestag elections. The law provided that two votes were to be cast by each voter in the election, one being cast directly for a candidate and the other for a party or coalition of parties. Those votes cast for the parties or coalition of parties were to be counted on a national basis, rather than separately in each state. In addition, the law required that, in order for a party to hold a seat in the Bundestag, it must have won at least 5 percent of the total vote or three seats by direct election. This last measure was intended to discourage small parties allied with one another from participating in the election. The upper house, or Bundesrat, passed the law on March 23, 1956.

Further reading: Uwe W. Kitzinger, *German Electoral Politics, a Study of the 1957 Campaign* (Oxford, England: Clarendon Press, 1960).

Bunker Hill Speech, Webster's   Speech delivered by Massachusetts congressman Daniel Webster at the laying of the cornerstone for the Bunker Hill Monument on June 17, 1825, the 50th anniversary of the American Revolutionary War battle of Bunker Hill. In this patriotic address, Webster eloquently and dramatically celebrated the men who fought there. His comments to the surviving soldiers, praising them for their contributions to their country and to freedom, were particularly stirring to his audience. Webster also discussed representative government in the United States. The speech contributed to his growing reputation as a brilliant orator.

Further reading: Wayland M. Parrish and Marie H. Nichols, eds., *American Speeches* (New York: Longman, Green, 1954); Edwin P. Whipple, ed., *The Great Speeches and Orations of Daniel Webster: With an Essay on Daniel Webster as a Master of English Style* (New York: Gryphon Editions, 1994).

Burgos, Concordat of   Agreement signed by Ferdinand II of Spain in 1512, between the crown and the bishops of the Indies, outlining the manner in which the royal prerogatives were to be exercised with regard to ecclesiastical government. The most significant item of the concordat was the redonation of tithes. The crown delegated to the bishops in the Indies the collection and distribution in perpetuity of tithes on all products except precious metals. The settlement, while generous, was also politically advantageous to the crown, since it ensured that the money would be spent by men whom it appointed, and according to the rules it approved.

Further reading: William H. Prescott et al., *History of the Reign of Ferdinand and Isabella* (New York: Heritage Press, 1967); Xavier Rubert de Ventos, *The Hispanic Labyrinth: Tradition and Modernity in the Colonization of the Americas* (New Brunswick, N.J.: Transaction Publishers, 1991).

Burgos, Laws of   Body or system of 32 Spanish laws enacted by King Ferdinand II in Burgos, Spain, on December 27, 1512. They sought to alleviate the cruelties perpetrated against West Indian natives under the *encomienda* (feudal) labor system. While one-third of the Indians would work in the settlers' mines for nine months of the year, pregnant women would not be sent to the mines after their fourth month. Sons of chiefs would be taught to read and write. Those natives found competent to govern themselves would be allowed to live as free men. Although never adequately enforced, these laws constituted the first systematic code governing the conduct of settlers in America, particularly in their relation with the native Indians.

Further reading: Lewis Hanke, *The Spanish Struggle for Justice in the Conquest of America* (Philadelphia: University of Pennsylvania Press, 1949); Barbara A. Tenenbaum, ed., *Encyclopedia of Latin American History and Culture* (New York: Charles Scribner's Sons, 1996).

Burgundian Code (Lex Gundobada)   Written code of laws promulgated by the Burgundian king Gundobad in Lyons about A.D. 502. The Burgundian kingdom (a part of the Roman Empire) covered what is now southeast France and western Switzerland and reached as far south as the Mediterranean. Based on the THEODOSIAN CODE, Gundobad's law applied to the Burgundians; he also issued a separate code, the Burgundian Roman Law (Lex Romana Burgundionum), for his Gallo-Roman subjects; this law was used to settle Roman-Burgundian disputes. By the Burgundian Code, one-third of Gundobad's conquered territory was granted to his conquered Gallo-Roman subjects. Gundobad's son and successor, Sigismund, added to the law code in A.D. 519.

Further reading: Katherine F. Drew, trans., *The Burgundian Code: Book of Constitutions or Law of Gundobad* (Philadelphia: University of Pennsylvania Press, 1976); Mark A. Kishlansky, ed., *Sources of the West: Readings in Western Civilization*, vol. 1, 4th ed. (New York: Addison Wesley Longman, 2001).

Burke Act   Federal U.S. legislation enacted on May 8, 1906, and intended to modify the DAWES SEVERALTY ACT to protect Indian landholdings from whites. Like the earlier law, the Burke Act granted to Native Americans who renounced their tribal allegiance full title to the homestead after a 25-year probationary period, but unlike the Dawes act, it granted citizenship only after the probationary period ended. Indian agents could, however, grant citizenship earlier to Indians they deemed trustworthy. The act also prohibited the sale of liquor to Indians who were not citizens. Many Indians resented the act as patronizing, and it was amended in 1924, when all Native Americans were made citizens.

Further reading: Ian Westbury and Susan Westbury, *Indians in the American System: Past and Present* (Chicago: University of Chicago Graduate School of Education, 1975).

Burke's American Taxation Speech   See AMERICAN TAXATION SPEECH, BURKE'S.

Burke-Wadsworth Act (Selective Training and Service Act)   Federal legislation sponsored by Senator Edward R. Burke of Nebraska and Representative James W. Wadsworth, Jr., of New York and enacted on September 16, 1940; established the first peacetime program of compulsory military service in the United States. Passed as the threat of U.S. involvement in World War II increased, the act required the registration of all men between 21 and 35 years old. It prohibited the use of bounties and substitutes and limited service to a 12-month period. The order of call-up was to be based on the drawing of lots. The draft was to be administered by a network of local boards under the national Selective Service System.

Further reading: Leonard W. Levy and Kenneth L. Karst, eds., *Encyclopedia of the American Constitution* 2d ed. (New York: Macmillan Reference, 2000).

Burlingame Treaty   Treaty between the United States and China, negotiated by "envoy extraordinary" of the emperor of China, Anson Burlingame, and signed on July 28, 1868; recognized China's basic sovereign rights in international law. The treaty, a supplement to the U.S.-CHINESE TREATY OF 1858, acknowledged Chinese territorial jurisdiction within China, guaranteed that the United States would not intervene in China's domestic affairs, confirmed the Chinese government's discretion in granting trade privileges in China, and provided for free Chinese immigration to the United States. It gave citizens of the two countries mutual "most favored nation" privileges within each other's borders. Anti-Chinese agitation led to revision of the treaty in 1880, allowing the United States to limit entry of Chinese laborers.

See also: CHINESE EXCLUSION ACT OF 1882; CHINESE EXCLUSION ACT OF 1892; CHINESE EXCLUSION ACT OF 1902.

Further reading: Frederick Wells Williams, *Anson Burlingame and the First Chinese Mission to Foreign Powers* (New York: Russell & Russell, 1912, repr., 1972).

Bush's "Freedom and Fear Are at War" Speech, George W.   Address delivered by U.S. president George W. Bush before a joint session of Congress on September 20, 2001, in response to the suicide bomber attacks on the World Trade Center in New York City and the Pentagon in Washington, D.C., nine days earlier. Bush identified the attackers as members of al-Qaeda, an Islamic extremist organization that earlier had attacked U.S. embassies in Tanzania and Kenya and the USS *Cole* while on patrol off the coast of Yemen. Al-Qaeda and its leader, Osama bin Laden, had established bases and training camps in Afghanistan, and Bush demanded that the Taliban, the Islamic ruling faction in Afghanistan, surrender bin Laden and his lieutenants and expel al-Qaeda. To prevent further terrorist attacks from taking place, Bush announced the creation of the Office of Homeland Security, which henceforth would be responsible for coordinating the antiterrorist efforts of dozens of federal agencies. He called on the leaders of other nations, particularly those belonging to the North Atlantic Treaty Organization, to join the United States in the "war" against terrorism. He announced that the U.S. military had been put on full alert in preparation for an attack against al-Qaeda should the Taliban fail to cooperate fully with the U.S. demands put forth. He pledged federal aid for New York City, and he pledged his untiring efforts to end international terrorism and preserve "freedom and security for the American people."

Further reading: Jeanne Cummings and David Rogers, "Bush Says 'Freedom and Fear Are at War,' " *Wall Street Journal*, September 21, 2001, pp. A3, A6; "President Declares 'Freedom at War with Fear': Address to a Joint Session of Congress and the American People," the White House, available online at http://www.whitehouse.gov/news/releases/2001/09/20010920-8.html.

Bush's Inaugural Address, George H. W.   Speech delivered by George Herbert Walker Bush on January 20, 1989, at his inauguration as 41st president of the United States. Outlining his vision of a time of peace and prosperity, of a "world refreshed by freedom," Bush called on Americans "to make kinder the face of the nation and gentler the face of the world." He urged people to rise above materialism, partisanship, and intolerance. He called for a new activism to attack problems of drug abuse, street crime, poverty, and homelessness through private-sector and voluntary initiatives, not federal action alone. He also urged renewed cooperation between the executive and legislative branches and announced continued closeness with the Soviet Union.

Further reading: George Bush, "Inaugural Address," available online at http://www.bartleby.com/124/pres63.html.

Bush's Inaugural Address, George W.   Address on January 20, 2001, to the nation by George W. Bush, newly sworn in as the 43rd president of the United States, stressing national unity and "civility, courage, compassion and character." He began his 14-minute speech by thanking President Bill Clinton for his service to the country and praising Vice President Albert Gore for a "contest conducted with spirit and ended with grace." Bush pledged to "reclaim America's schools," reform Social Security and Medicare, lower taxes, and "build our defenses beyond challenge." Compassion, "the work of a

nation, not just a government," was needed to eradicate poverty, which "is unworthy of our nation's promise," he stated. Referring to the interdependence of "public interest" and "private character," he urged Americans "to seek a common good beyond your comfort" and promised to "bring the values of our history to the care of our times."

Further reading: George W. Bush, "Inaugural Address," available online at http://www.whitehouse.gov/news/inaugural-address.html.

Bush v. *Gore (George W. Bush* v. *Albert A. Gore)*

Republican presidential candidate George W. Bush's appeal (December 9, 2000) to the U.S. Supreme Court to block the statewide manual recount of all "undervotes" in Florida as ordered (December 8, 2000) by the Florida Supreme Court at the request of rival candidate Albert A. Gore. The outcome of this case determined the U.S. presidency. In a highly controversial and narrow 5-4 ruling issued on December 12, 2000, the Supreme Court reversed the Florida court's decision, bringing an abrupt end to the manual recounting and, ultimately, to the very close and bitterly contested election. The majority argued that the recount would not be fair unless the statewide process was standardized first, and that could not be completed before the December 12, 2000, deadline established for the state's electoral college vote. Seven of the nine judges agreed that "the use of standardless manual recounts violates the equal protection and the due process clauses" of the U.S. CONSTITUTION.

Further reading: Supreme Court of the United States, *"George W. Bush, et al., petitioners* v. *Albert Gore, Jr. et al,"* FindLaw, available online at http://laws.findlaw.com/us/000/00-949.html.

Butler's Act   See EDUCATION ACT OF 1944, BRITISH.

Butler's General Order No. 28   Order issued by General Benjamin Franklin Butler, military governor of Union-occupied New Orleans, on May 15, 1862. Because of the hostility and insults directed toward Union troops by New Orleans residents, particularly women, Butler ordered that any female insulting or showing contempt for any U.S. officer or soldier should be treated as a prostitute. This order and other dictatorial actions earned Butler the title the "beast of New Orleans" and raised a storm of public protest. He was removed from command of New Orleans on December 16, 1862.

Further reading: James Ford Rhodes, *History of the United States from the Compromise of 1850 to the McKinley-Bryan Campaign of 1896* (Port Washington, N.Y.: Kennikat Press, 1919, repr., 1967).

Byzantine Agrarian Code (Farmer's Law, Leges Rusticae)   Law code designed to protect the rural property of free peasants, farmers, and small landowners, drawn up evidently for the agricultural Byzantine society during the reign of Emperor Leo III the Isaurian (A.D. 717–741). Property owners in farming communes and villages were responsible for paying taxes, and they gained legal protection from property damage, thievery, and other offenses. Punishments were enacted for lawbreakers of collective agricultural practices and taxation (landowners failing to pay taxes forfeited their holdings to persons who paid them for them). The code especially influenced the growing Slavic peasantry in the Balkan region.

Further reading: John J. Norwich, *Byzantium: The Early Centuries* (New York: Alfred A. Knopf, 1999).

Cable Act U.S. legislation drafted by Ohio congressman John Levi Cable and enacted on September 2, 1922, establishing that women neither gain nor lose American citizenship through marriage. An alien woman married to an American remains an alien, unless she decides to become a naturalized U.S. citizen after three years of residence in the country. Previously, an alien woman who married an American automatically became a citizen herself. Also under the Cable Act, a female U.S. citizen does not lose her citizenship if she marries an alien. This replaced a 1907 law that provided that a woman who married an alien would take her husband's citizenship. The Cable Act was amended in 1930 and 1931. Later legislation continued to maintain that a woman's citizenship was independent of marriage.

Further reading: John L. Cable, *Decisive Decisions of United States Citizenship* (Charlottesville, Va.: Michie Co., 1967).

Cabochien Ordinance (Ordonnance Cabochienne) Law promulgated on May 26–27, 1413, by King Charles VI of France, detailing, in 258 articles, a series of administrative reforms intended to appease rebels led by French skinner Simon Caboche. Compiled from previous ordinances, it vested power in the council (in charge of political administration), the Parlement (looking after judicial affairs), and the Chambre des Comptes (controlling finance). Officers were to be elected by one of these three bodies. Locally, too, all important decisions were to be taken by councils of officials and notables. These councils were also entrusted with the election of local officials. Aiming at efficiency, the ordinance sought to create a monarchy acting in concert with royal officials. The day after its promulgation, riots occurred again and brutal scenes were witnessed all round. The Armagnac leaders initiated steps to quell the violence (see ARRAS, TREATY OF [1414]). Eventually, the king was forced to withdraw the ordinance.

Further reading: R. C. Famiglietti, *Royal Intrigue: Crisis at the Court of Charles VI, 1392–1420* (New York: AMS Press, 1986).

Cade's Complaint Petition with 15 grievances, drafted in May 1450 by Jack Cade, complaining about corruption in government, high taxes and prices, and England's military failures in Normandy (in the Hundred Years' War [1337–1457]). Cade assumed the name John Mortimer, proclaiming himself the cousin of Duke Richard of York (whose recall from exile he demanded). Cade also demanded administrative and economic reforms and the inclusion of the dukes of York, Norfolk, and Exeter in the councils of King Henry VI (Richard's rival), instead of the duke of Suffolk and his group. Led by Cade, some 30,000 protesters, mainly from Kent and Sussex, vowed to "find a remedy" and "if not, we shall die in the attempt." They were eventually routed, and Cade and others were killed.

Further reading: I. W. M. Harvey, *Jack Cade's Rebellion of 1450* (New York: Oxford University Press, 1991).

Calais, Treaty of   Agreement made at Calais, France, on October 24, 1360, revising the Treaty of BRÉTIGNY and ending the first phase of the Hundred Years' War (1337–1457) between England and France. King John II the Good of France agreed to cede all of Aquitaine to his English adversary, King Edward III, by November 30, 1361, at the latest. His renunciation of sovereignty to this key territory (which would have reduced his kingdom by one-third), to be reciprocated by Edward's surrender of his far-fetched claim to the French Crown was, however, astutely deferred to a special agreement to be exchanged after the transfer of territory was complete. The two kings promised to maintain "a firm alliance and friendship" and to abrogate all alliances made by one side against the other. After John II's death in 1364, his son Charles (Charles V) did not honor and fulfill the treaty's terms, and war soon erupted again.

Further reading: Richard Barber, *Edward, Prince of Wales and Aquitaine: A Biography of the Black Prince* (Woodbridge, England: Boydell Press, 1978); Alfred H. Burne, *The Hundred Years' War: A Military History* (London: Penguin, 2002); Robin Neillands, *The Hundred Years War*, rev. ed. (New York: Routledge, 2001).

Calhoun's *Disquisition on Government*   See DISQUISITION ON GOVERNMENT, CALHOUN'S.

Calhoun's "Fort Hill Letter"   See "FORT HILL LETTER," CALHOUN'S.

Calhoun's Last Speech on the Slavery Question (Calhoun's Speech on the Compromise of 1850)   Speech given to the U.S. Congress on March 4, 1850, written by South Carolina senator John C. Calhoun, opposing the COMPROMISE OF 1850 and denouncing Northern aggression; because Calhoun was gravely ill, the speech was read for him by his friend Senator James M. Mason. Calhoun argued that, if the union were to be preserved, the South had to be given equal rights in the newly acquired U.S. territories and antislavery agitation must end. He also proposed a constitutional amendment restoring to the South the power it held "before the equilibrium between the sections was destroyed by the action of this government." The weak Calhoun sat and watched as his words were read; he died four weeks later, at age 68.

Further reading: Teresa Celsi et al., eds., *John C. Calhoun and the Roots of War*, (Morristown, N.J.: Silver Burdett Press, 1991); John Niven, *John C. Calhoun and the Price of Union* (Baton Rouge: Louisiana State University Press, 1988); Clyde N. Wilson, ed., *The Essential Calhoun: Selections from Writings, Speeches, and Letters* (New Brunswick, N.J.: Transaction Publishers, 2000); Charles M. Wiltse, *John C. Calhoun: Sectionalist, 1840–1850* (Indianapolis, Ind.: Bobbs-Merrill, 1951).

Calmar, Union of   See KALMAR, UNION OF.

Calpurnian Law (Lex Calpurnia)   First Roman law against extortion, sponsored by Lucius Calpurnius Piso, tribune of the plebeians, and enacted in 149 B.C. It instituted a special, permanent court for the trial of suits brought by provincials (inhabitants of a Roman province) seeking to recover money unjustly collected (extorted) by abusive provincial governors. At the time, the provincial communities suffered increasingly the oppression of their military governors. The court consisted of 50 jurors drawn from the Roman Senate, with a praetor (magistrate) as the presiding officer. No appeal was allowed following the court's decision in a case.

Further reading: H. F. Jolowicz and Barry Nicholas, *Historical Introduction to the Study of Roman Law,* 3d ed. (Holmes Beach, Fla.: Gaunt, 1996); Joseph Anthony Charles Thomas, *Textbook of Roman Law* (New York: North-Holland, 1976); Alan Watson, *The Law of the Ancient Romans* (Dallas: Southern Methodist University Press, 1970).

Caltabelotta, Peace of   Settlement concluded on August 31, 1302, at Caltabelotta (near Sciacca on Italy's south coast) between Charles II (the Angevin king of Naples) and Frederick II (the Aragonese king of Sicily), ending the War of the Sicilian Vespers (1282–1302). Sicily remained under Aragonese rule but Frederick was denied the title of king, and after his death the throne was to revert to Angevin rule. To ensure this, he was to marry Charles's youngest daughter, Eleanora. His heirs were promised Sardinia or Cyprus or 100,000 ounces of gold in compensation. The settlement also called for the mutual withdrawal of troops and for the exchange of prisoners. Pope Boniface VIII suggested that Frederick assume the title of "King of Trinacria" instead, and that his reign begin from the signing of the treaty. He also received Frederick and the Sicilians back into the Roman Catholic Church. The Sicilian question continued to resurface and was not decisively resolved until many decades later.

See also: UNAM SANCTUM.

Further reading: Steven Runciman, *The Sicilian Vespers: A History of the Mediterranean World in the Later Thirteenth Century* (New York: Cambridge University Press, 1992).

Calvo Clause   Clause (originating in the CALVO DOCTRINE of 1868) often inserted in public contracts between a government and a foreign national or corporation; stipulated that the latter renounces any claim to diplomatic assistance from his or its own government in the event that litigation arises from the contract. The Calvo Clause challenged the doctrine espoused by European states that their citizens had a right to just treatment with regard to claims resulting from, for example, wars or revolutions, regardless of the treatment accorded by Latin states to their own citizens. Several countries, including Mexico, have incorporated the Calvo Clause into their constitutions.

Further reading: Harold Eugene Davis, John J. Finan, and F. Taylor Peck, *Latin American Diplomatic History: An Intro-*

duction (Baton Rouge: Louisiana State Press, 1977); Donald Richard Shea, *The Calvo Clause: A Problem of Inter-American and International Law and Diplomacy* (Minneapolis: University of Minnesota Press, 1955); Ann Van Wynen Thomas and A. J. Thomas, Jr., *No-Intervention: The Law and Its Import in the Americas* (Dallas: Southern Methodist University Press, 1956).

Calvo Doctrine   Doctrine proposed by the Argentine jurist Carlos Calvo in a treatise on international law published in 1868. It maintained that no nation has the right to exert diplomatic pressure or use armed force against another nation for the purpose of pursuing private claims or collecting debts owed to its citizens. The doctrine was significant in its attempt to force foreign property owners to seek judicial review of their claims against Latin American countries within each country itself, rather than to rely on diplomatic intervention.

See also: CALVO CLAUSE.

Further reading: Harold Eugene Davis, John J. Finan, and F. Taylor Peck, *Latin American Diplomatic History: An Introduction* (Baton Rouge: Louisiana State Press, 1977); Donald Richard Shea, *The Calvo Clause: A Problem of Inter-American and International Law and Diplomacy* (Minneapolis: University of Minnesota Press, 1955); Ann Van Wynen Thomas and A. J. Thomas, Jr., *No-Intervention: The Law and Its Import in the Americas* (Dallas: Southern Methodist University Press, 1956).

Cambrai, Peace of (Paix des Dames, Ladies' Peace)
Peace treaty negotiated and signed in Cambrai, France, on August 3, 1529, by Louise of Savoy on behalf of her son King Francis I of France and Margaret of Austria on behalf of her nephew Holy Roman Emperor Charles V. After Charles's troops had sacked Rome in 1526 (see COGNAC, TREATY OF), Francis retaliated by invading Milan and Naples. These two ambitious rulers soon found themselves in a deadlock situation, which the two ladies (Louise and Margaret) cunningly helped to break (during the Second Italian War [1526–30] between Charles V and Francis I). By the treaty, Francis agreed to give up his claims to Naples, Flanders, and Artois, took over the possessions of Duke Charles of Bourbon (prince of Orange), and abandoned Venice and his other allies. Charles relinquished his claims to Burgundy, provided he was paid a large ransom for the release of two French princes (Francis's sons) whom he held hostage pending French ratification of the 1526 Treaty of MADRID. Francis soon reneged on the treaty and thrice unsuccessfully attacked Italy. The 1559 Treaty of CATEAU-CAMBRÉSIS ultimately resolved the issues.

Further reading: Dorothy M. Mayer, *The Great Regent: Louise of Savoy, 1476–1531* (New York: Funk & Wagnalls, 1966).

Cambridge Agreement   Decision signed into agreement by 12 Puritan members of the Massachusetts Bay Company, under the leadership of John Winthrop, at a meeting in Cambridge (England) on August 26, 1629; they agreed to emigrate from England to America with their families, provided the company's charter and government were also transferred abroad. Transfer of the charter (see MASSACHUSETTS BAY COLONY, CHARTER OF) meant that a business company would be changed into a plantation; by ratifying the agreement, the company repositioned its emphasis from commerce to religion. The purpose of the action was to guard against interference in the enterprise by non-Puritans in England. The agreement was authorized, and the Puritans set up a self-governing colony in New England soon afterward.

Further reading: Charles McLean Andrews, *The Colonial Period of American History*, vol. 1 (New Haven, Conn.: Yale University Press, 1964, repr., 1974).

Cambridge Platform   Principles drawn up by the Cambridge Synod of Congregational churches upon urging by the General Court of Massachusetts in 1648. The synod consisted of ministers from Massachusetts and Connecticut who desired a formal statement of policy and a confession of faith due to the current Presbyterian ascendancy in England and the actions of local Presbyterians. Written by Richard Mather, the platform endorsed the WESTMINSTER CONFESSION OF FAITH as its creed and formulated the relations of church and state as well as the duties of the clergy. The platform was formed from partly Congregational and partly Presbyterian practices.

Further reading: Henry Wilder Foote, *The Cambridge Platform of 1648* (Boston: Beacon Press, 1949).

Camp David Accords   Two agreements (a so-called framework for peace) signed by President Anwar el-Sadat of Egypt and Prime Minister Menachem Begin of Israel on September 17, 1978, after a 13-day conference at Camp David, Maryland (the U.S. presidential retreat). U.S. president Jimmy Carter engineered and led the long, intense negotiations between Sadat and Begin, who agreed to work for a full peace treaty within three months to end 30 years' hostility between their two countries. Israel would return to Egypt the Sinai Peninsula taken in the Arab-Israeli War of 1967 (Six-Day War) and would halt, temporarily, building new settlements in the West Bank (area west of the Jordan River, occupied by Israel after the war). The Palestine Liberation Organization (PLO), hard-line Arab states, and the Soviet Union denounced the accords, which initiated talks aimed at a full peace (see ISRAELI-EGYPTIAN PEACE TREATY).

Further reading: Reeva S. Simon, Philip Mattar, and Richard W. Bulliet, eds., *Encyclopedia of the Modern Middle East* (New York: Simon & Schuster, 1996); Shibley Telhami, *Power and Leadership in International Bargaining: The Path to the Camp David Accords* (New York: Columbia University Press, 1990).

Campo Formio, Treaty of   Peace treaty signed by Napoléon Bonaparte (for France) and Count Ludwig Cobenzl (for Austria) in the town of Campo Formio, Italy, on October 17, 1797, bringing an end to Austria's participation in the War of the First Coalition (1792–98) against France (part of the French Revolutionary Wars [1792–1802]). The settlement provided for Austria's annexation of most of the Venetian territories, including the city of Venice, Istria, and Dalmatia; Austria's recognition of the newly formed Cisalpine Republic (see LEOBEN, PEACE OF) and the republic of Genoa; and Austria's cession of the Austrian Netherlands (Belgium) to France. France retained the Ionian Islands. Secret provisions obliged Austria to support French annexation of the left bank of the Rhine River from Basel to Andernach. France promised to help Austria secure Salzburg and nearby Bavarian territory. The treaty turned out to be merely a truce, as the Second Coalition of powers was formed against France in 1798.

See also: RASTATT, TREATY OF; TOLENTINO, TREATY OF.

Further reading: Charles L. Phillips and Alan Axelrod, eds., *Encyclopedia of Historical Treaties and Alliances*, 2 vols. (New York: Facts On File, 2001).

Canada Act (Constitution Act of 1791)   Act of the British Parliament on June 10, 1791, dividing the Canadian province of Quebec into Upper Canada (now Ontario), which was largely British and Protestant, and Lower Canada (now Quebec), which was largely French and Catholic. As a result of the QUEBEC ACT of 1774, Quebec's government and laws were generally French in character; but British loyalists, who had fled the United States and resettled in Canada after the American Revolution (1775–83), wished to live under English law. To reduce the antagonism between the two populations, the Canada Act gave each new province its own legislature and institutions, although both were given a form of the British constitution.

Further reading: Carl Stephenson and Frederick George Marcham, eds., *Sources of English Constitutional History: A Selection of Documents from A.D. 600 to the Present* (New York: Harper & Row, 1937).

Canadian Annexation Manifesto   See ANNEXATION MANIFESTO, CANADIAN.

Canadian Anti-Terrorism Act   See ANTI-TERRORISM ACT, CANADIAN.

Canadian Autonomy Bills of 1905   Federal legislation passed on July 5, 1905, creating the provinces of Alberta and Saskatchewan out of territory in the northwestern region of Canada that had been acquired by the Dominion of Canada in the 19th century (see NORTHWEST TERRITORIES ACT OF 1875). Through the bills, the two new provinces gained representation in Canada's federal parliament and obtained the right to receive federal grants, as well as guarantees for the continued operation of both English-speaking Protestant and French-speaking Catholic schools. This last provision aroused the opposition of a majority in both provinces, which wished to form their own education policy. Alberta and Saskatchewan were admitted to the Canadian confederation on September 1, 1905.

See also: BRITISH NORTH AMERICA ACT; MANITOBA ACT OF 1870.

Further reading: Robert Bothell, Ian Drummond, and John English, *Canada, 1900–1945* (Toronto: University of Toronto Press, 1987); Prentice-Hall of Canada, eds., *Canadian Historical Document Series*, 3 vols. (Scarborough, Ontario: Prentice-Hall of Canada, 1965–66).

Canadian Bill of Rights   See BILL OF RIGHTS, CANADIAN.

Canadian Charter of Rights and Freedoms   See CHARTER OF RIGHTS AND FREEDOMS, CANADIAN.

Canadian Combines Investigation Act of 1910   Legislation introduced by Canadian liberal politician W. L. Mackenzie King and enacted on May 4, 1910, containing earlier legislation (the Combines Investigation Act of 1889) with additional provisions intended to prevent a decrease in competition in Canadian business. The act prohibited agreements, dealing with the manufacture of products, that would lead to a decrease in competition; prohibited mergers and monopolies that would decrease competition; prohibited agreements designed to increase prices; provided for public investigation of alleged monopolies; and provided that transgressors of the law would be penalized in certain instances.

Further reading: *Amendments to the Combines Investigation Act: A Schematic Presentation of the Act and the Bill* (Ottawa: Consumer & Corporate Affairs Canada, 1984); *Combines Investigation Act* (Ottawa, Canada: J. O. Patenaude, 1939).

Canadian Constitution Act of 1982   Act drafted in Ottawa and passed by all Canadian provinces, except Quebec, and by the British Parliament and granted royal assent on March 29, 1982, in London by Queen Elizabeth II of Great Britain; gave Canada control over her own constitution. (Until the act's passage the BRITISH NORTH AMERICA ACT, while serving as Canada's effective constitution, was a British document, and amendments to it required British approval.) In addition to providing Canada with a procedure by which the constitution could be amended, the act provided for the addition of a Canadian CHARTER OF RIGHTS AND FREEDOMS to the constitution, and it renamed the British North America Act the Constitution Act of 1867. The act became formally effective when Queen Elizabeth proclaimed the document in Ottawa on April 17, 1982.

Further reading: Bayard William Reesor, *The Canadian Constitution in Historical Perspective: With a Clause-by-Clause*

Analysis of the Constitution Acts and the Canada Act (Scarborough, Ontario: Prentice-Hall Canada, 1992).

Canadian Criminal Code Amendment Act

Legislation proposed by Canadian prime minister Pierre Elliott Trudeau and enacted into law on May 14, 1969 (took effect on August 26, 1969), introducing changes into Canada's criminal code. Among the bill's more controversial changes were its provision permitting a woman to have an abortion if her pregnancy was threatening her health, and its provision permitting individuals to engage in homosexual acts in private. Other sections legalized games of chance, which were administered by licensed organizations; made drivers of cars and trucks suspected of driving while intoxicated subject to breath tests; and prohibited possession of firearms in certain instances. The bill was vehemently opposed by conservatives.

Further reading: Desmond H. Brown, *The Genesis of the Canadian Criminal Code of 1892* (Toronto: University of Toronto Press, 1989).

Canadian Family Allowances Act of 1944

Act passed in 1944 by Canadian prime minister Mackenzie King's liberal government, providing for the payment of monthly allowances to families with children. This social legislation provided that monthly payments of between $5 and $7 per child be made to mothers with children aged 16 or younger. The first payments were made in July 1945 and continued until 1973, when the legislation was revised. Approximately three and a half million children were said to have benefited from the measure during the first year of its implementation.

Further reading: Robert Bothell, Ian Drummond, and John English, *Canada, 1900–1945* (Toronto: University of Toronto Press, 1987); Prentice-Hall of Canada, *Canadian Historical Document Series*, 3 vols. (Scarborough, Ontario: Prentice-Hall of Canada, 1965–66).

Canadian Federal Income Tax Law (Income War Tax Act)

Legislation enacted in 1917 by the Canadian government, establishing Canada's first federal income tax on both personal and corporate income, and providing a means to cover new federal expenditures associated with World War I (1914–18). The bill provided for a tax of 4 percent on corporate income and a tax of 1 percent on the personal income of unmarried persons up to $2,000, with "supertaxes" of 2 percent being levied on incremental increases in income in excess of that amount. In addition, married persons were exempt from paying a tax on the first $2,000, and provision was made for lower tax rates on incomes in excess of that amount. Until 1917 Canada's government had raised money through such measures as customs duties and postal rates.

Further reading: Prentice-Hall of Canada, eds., *Canadian Historical Document Series*, 3 vols. (Scarborough, Ontario: Prentice-Hall of Canada, 1965–66).

Canadian Naval Bill of 1910 (Naval Service Act of 1910)

Bill proposed by Canadian prime minister Wilfrid Laurier and passed by the Canadian Parliament on May 4, 1910, providing for the creation of a small Canadian navy. In addition, the bill provided that the navy could be placed under British control in an emergency situation. The bill was a compromise reached by Laurier in response to the demands of Great Britain and Canadian imperialists that Canada contribute forces to the British Royal Navy, and the vehement opposition of French Canadians, who resisted greater involvement in British affairs. Neither group supported the bill. By 1914 Canada's navy consisted of two warships.

Further reading: Robert Bothell, Ian Drummound, and John English, *Canada, 1900–1945* (Toronto: University of Toronto Press, 1987); Prentice-Hall of Canada, eds., *Canadian Historical Document Series*, 3 vols. (Scarborough, Ontario: Prentice-Hall of Canada, 1965–66).

Canadian Official Languages Act

Act passed by the Canadian Parliament and, on July 9, 1969, granted royal assent by Great Britain, making both English and French the official languages of Canada. While the BRITISH NORTH AMERICA ACT had guaranteed the right to use both languages in parliament and in federal courts, the act of 1969 went a step further by guaranteeing the right to use both languages in all federal institutions and by stipulating that bilingual federal facilities be established in any district in which 10 percent of the population was either French or English. The bill also stipulated that a commissioner be appointed to ensure its implementation.

Further reading: Richard J. Joy, *Canada's Official Languages: The Progress of Bilingualism* (Toronto: University of Toronto Press, 1992).

Canadian Old Age Security Act of 1951

Landmark social legislation passed by the Canadian parliament in 1951, providing for financial assistance to the nation's elderly. The act provided that the federal government would pay $40 a month to all Canadians over 70 years of age and the same sum to all Canadians between the ages of 65 and 69 who were in need, and that the cost of the program (estimated to be approximately $365 million a year) would be met by a tax of 2 percent on sales, personal income, and corporate profits. It was estimated that approximately 860,000 old persons would benefit from the legislation.

Further reading: Prentice-Hall of Canada, eds., *Canadian Historical Document Series*, 3 vols. (Scarborough, Ontario: Prentice-Hall of Canada, 1965–66).

Canadian Preferential Tariff of 1897

See FIELDING TARIFF ACT.

Canadian Public Order (Temporary Measures) Act of 1970   See PUBLIC ORDER (TEMPORARY MEASURES) ACT OF 1970, CANADIAN.

Canadian Rebellion Losses Bill   See REBELLION LOSSES BILL, CANADIAN.

Canadian Seventy-two Resolutions   See QUEBEC RESOLUTIONS.

Canadian Tariff Act of 1930 (Dunning Tariff)   High protective tariff proposed by Canadian minister of finance Charles A. Dunning and made effective on May 2, 1930, stipulating increases and changes in Canada's tariff policy. Most significantly, the act provided that, in the event that another country were to impose higher tariff rates on Canadian products, Canada would reciprocate by raising her rates correspondingly. In addition, preferential treatment was given to trade with Great Britain. The new law was enacted in retaliation to increases in tariff rates imposed by the United States on Canadian goods (see SMOOT-HAWLEY TARIFF ACT).

Further reading: Robert Bothell, Ian Drummond, and John English, *Canada, 1900–1945* (Toronto: University of Toronto Press, 1987); Prentice-Hall of Canada, eds., *Canadian Historical Document Series,* 3 vols. (Scarborough, Ontario: Prentice-Hall of Canada, 1965–66).

Canadian Unemployment Insurance Act of 1940   Legislation enacted into law on August 7, 1940, by Canadian prime minister Mackenzie King's liberal government, establishing that the federal government would assume responsibility for providing unemployment insurance to unemployed Canadians. The administration of unemployment insurance had previously been the provincial governments' responsibility. The bill made unemployment insurance mandatory for all employed persons, except for those employed in specified professions, which included fishing, hunting, agriculture, teaching, and the armed forces; required that the employer and employee would contribute specified sums to the Unemployment Insurance Fund; required that the federal government would contribute a sum equal to one-fifth of the combined employer-employee contribution; and provided that payments would be made to unemployed persons who were covered by the insurance, able to work, but unable to find work. Approximately 3 million workers benefited in 1940–41 from the legislation.

Further reading: Robert Bothell, Ian Drummond, and John English, *Canada, 1900–1945* (Toronto: University of Toronto Press, 1987); Prentice-Hall of Canada, eds., *Canadian Historical Document Series,* 3 vols. (Scarborough, Ontario: Prentice-Hall of Canada, 1965–66).

Canadian War Measures Act   See WAR MEASURES ACT, CANADIAN.

Canak, Treaty of (Treaty of the Dardanelles)   Agreement signed by Great Britain and the Ottoman Empire on January 5, 1809, at Canak or Chanak (Canakkale in modern Turkey); declared that no warships of any country should pass through the Straits of the Dardanelles and the Bosporus. It hinted at the STRAITS CONVENTION of 1841, by which other major powers agreed to the same prohibition. The treaty was meant to deter Russian ships in the Black Sea from using the straits to enter the Mediterranean, thus giving more security to the British against any possible Russian threat. The treaty also reaffirmed Britain's commercial and consular privileges in the Ottoman Empire, as well as secretly securing British aid for the Ottoman Turks should France declare war against them.

Further reading: Reeva S. Simon, Philip Mattar, and Richard W. Bulliet, eds., *Encyclopedia of the Modern Middle East,* 4 vols. (New York: Macmillan, 1996).

Canberra Pact   See ANZAC PACT.

Canon Law, Code of (Codex Juris Canonici)   Code of canon law promulgated "to the whole world" by Roman Catholic pope Benedict XV on Pentecost Sunday, May 27, 1917, consisting of over 2,000 laws developed by the Roman Catholic Church since the beginning of the history of the church. Most significant among the laws included were those developed at the great ecumenical councils and the general synods; those promulgated by the papacy; and those developed by Pope Pius X, Benedict's predecessor, concerning the reform of the administrative body of the Roman Catholic Church. It was during the reign of Pope Pius X that the codification of canon law was undertaken.

Further reading: *New Catholic Encyclopedia,* 17 vols. (Palatine, Ill.: Jack Heraty & Associates, 1967, repr., 1981).

Canons of 1640   Seventeen liturgical canons published by convocation of the clergy in 1640, as a supplement to the canons of the Church of England of 1604. The canons supported the divine-right theory of kings and declared resistance to be unlawful. All ordained members of the clergy had to take the controversial "et cetera oath" by which they swore not to alter the present government of the church, which contained everything needed to attain salvation. The canons also contained Archbishop William Laud's innovations (e.g., use of the communion table as an altar surrounded by rails). King Charles I of England had given his assent under the Great Seal, but Parliament had not confirmed them, and it declared, on December 15, that they were not binding on clergy or laymen. On December 16, the canons were declared illegal. The House of Commons impeached Archbishop Laud and he was imprisoned in the Tower of London on December 18, 1640.

Further reading: *Constitutions and Canons Ecclesiasticall: Treated upon by the Archbishops of Canterbury and York, . . . in*

Their Severall Synods Begun at London and York, 1640: . . . (Ann Arbor, Mich.: University Microfilms, 1967).

Canopus, Decree of (Table of Tanis)
Ancient Egyptian decree issued at Canopus (near Alexandria, Egypt) in 238 B.C. in honor of King Ptolemy III (Ptolemy Euergetes) and his wife Berenice II, daughter of the king of Cyrene. Promulgated by priests, the decree is a stele (slab of limestone) inscribed in demotics, hieroglyphics, and Greek, which was discovered at Tanis (Sanal-Hajar al-Qibliyah, in the eastern Nile River delta) by archaeological excavators in 1866. This ancient record has provided scholars with valuable information about deciphering hieroglyphic and demotic picture-character writing.

Further reading: E. A. Wallis Budge, *The Decrees of Memphis and Canopus*, 3 vols. (New York: AMS Press, 1976).

Cantwell v. Connecticut
U.S. Supreme Court decision issued on May 20, 1940, upholding the FIRST AMENDMENT right to the free exercise of religion. Newton Cantwell, a Jehovah's Witness, was convicted of a breach of the peace for publically playing a recording that attacked organized religion and, in violation of a Connecticut statute, for soliciting funds without a state certificate. In its unanimous decision, the Supreme Court ruled that Cantwell had a constitutional right "peacefully to impart his views to others," even when such views were offensive to some citizens. The Court also ruled that the First Amendment "embraces two concepts—freedom to believe and freedom to act. The first is absolute but . . . the second cannot be." While the state has the right to regulate conduct to preserve public peace and safety, it may not use that right to censor a religion.

Further reading: Robert F. Cushman, *Leading Constitutional Decisions*, 15th ed. (Englewood Cliffs, N.J.: Prentice-Hall, 1977); Sheldon Goldman, *Constitutional Law: Cases and Essays* (New York: Harper & Row, 1987); Paul L. Murphy, *The Constitution in Crisis Times, 1918–1969* (New York: Harper & Row, 1972).

Canuleian Law (Lex Canuleia)
Marriage law enacted in ancient Rome in 445 B.C., sponsored by and named for Cneius Canuleius, a Roman tribune and politician. It legalized marriages between patricians and plebeians and legitimized their children, who inherited their father's social status or rank. The law discontinued the old caste system, which had disallowed and pronounced as illegitimate marriages between the orders (plebeians and patricians) and thus sustained social inequality between them (strongly resented by the plebes, who felt socially inferior without the right of intermarriage).

Further reading: H. F. Jolowicz and Barry Nicholas, *Historical Introduction to the Study of Roman Law,* 3d ed. (Holmes Beach, Fla.: Gaunt, 1996); Joseph Anthony Charles Thomas, *Textbook of Roman Law* (New York: North-Holland, 1976); Alan Watson, *The Law of the Ancient Romans* (Dallas: Southern Methodist University Press, 1970).

Capper-Volstead Act (U.S. Cooperative Marketing Act)
Federal U.S. legislation enacted on February 18, 1922, that exempted various agricultural associations, producers, and cooperatives from antitrust laws. It permitted farmers to buy and sell cooperatively in interstate commerce and established a system of agricultural credit for periods from six months to three years. The U.S. secretary of agriculture was empowered to administer the act and to prevent these agricultural associations from developing into monopolies. The act was sponsored by Senator Arthur Capper of Kansas and Representative Andrew Joseph Volstead of Minnesota to provide relief to distressed farmers following World War I (1914–18).

Further reading: Edward V. Jesse, *Antitrust Treatment of Agricultural Marketing Cooperatives* (Madison: Research Division, College of Agricultural and Life Sciences, University of Wisconsin–Madison, 1983).

Caracalla, Edict of (Constitutio Antoniniana de Civitate, Antoninian Constitution of Citizenship)
Famous edict issued in A.D. 212 by the Roman emperor Caracalla (Marcus Aurelius Antoninus), granting Roman citizenship to all freeborn, adult male inhabitants of the empire. Those affected were primarily the provincials (residents of the provinces), who were considered aliens under the Roman law. Caracalla's motives for the citizenship extension are unclear; he may have wanted to raise revenue through the citizen's inheritance tax (which he doubled to 10 percent), to show vaingloriously his power (he had had his rival brother, Geta, assassinated in A.D. 212), or to end distinctions among peoples of the empire for better financial and judicial administration.

Further reading: H. F. Jolowicz and Barry Nicholas, *Historical Introduction to the Study of Roman Law,* 3d ed. (Holmes Beach, Fla.: Gaunt, 1996); Joseph Anthony Charles Thomas, *Textbook of Roman Law* (New York: North-Holland, 1976); Alan Watson, *The Law of the Ancient Romans* (Dallas: Southern Methodist University Press, 1970).

Carbonari, Proclamation of the
Revolutionary proclamation issued on June 24, 1817, by the Italian Carbonari (members of a secret political society seeking to free Italy from foreign domination [French and Austrian rule] and to establish a republic). Organized supposedly in 1808, the Carbonari ("charcoal burners") derived their name from the independent charcoal burners of the mountains, with whom they first met to form their movement. The proclamation exhorted the people to shake off "the government of idiots" and "the yoke of oppression" and to arm themselves, for "the scythe of Pestilence and Famine will complete your destruction and that of our children, if you delay any longer to protect yourselves." The Carbonari took a leading role in subsequent Italian uprisings and were gradually absorbed by the Risorgimento movement (see MAZZINI'S INSTRUCTIONS TO YOUNG ITALY).

Further reading: Silvio Pellico, *My Prisons*, trans. I. G. Capaldi (Westport, Conn.: Greenwood Press, 1978).

Carey Desert Land Grant Act   Federal U.S. legislation, passed on August 18, 1894, that made federally owned arid lands available to settlers for agricultural purposes. The act authorized the president to turn over to each of the public-land states (those created out of the public domain) up to 1 million acres of public desert land to sell to settlers for irrigation, reclamation, cultivation, and occupancy. The states could charge no more than 50¢ per acre (though additional fees could be levied for water rights), and tract size could range up to 160 acres. At least 20 acres of the tract had to be cultivated or the land would revert to public domain. But large-scale irrigation was prohibitively expensive until the NEWLANDS RECLAMATION ACT authorized federal funds for irrigation.

Further reading: United States Code, Title 43, Section 641, "Grant of Desert Land to States Authorized," FindLaw website, available online at http://caselaw.lp.findlaw.com/casecode/uscodes/43/chapters/14/sections/section_641.html.

Caribbean Community and Common Market Agreement (Treaty of Chaguaramas)   Agreement on July 4, 1973, by which Trinidad and Tobago, Guyana, Barbados, and Jamaica created the Caribbean Common Market (CARICOM), replacing the Caribbean Free Trade Association (see ANTIGUA, TREATY OF). CARICOM's aim was to develop regional cooperation and unity through economic integration (such as common external tariffs) and thereby overcome North American pressures and Caribbean handicaps related to small size and slow development. Belize and the East Caribbean Common Market (Antigua, Dominica, Grenada, Montserrat, St. Kitts–Nevis–Anguilla, St. Lucia, and St. Vincent) joined CARICOM in 1974; the Bahamas joined in 1983. CARICOM's existence, though, has been a troubled one—political differences among members, strongly similar economies leading to competition for the same markets, and balance-of-payments deficits being among the many causes of dissension.

See also: LOMÉ CONVENTION.

Further reading: Barbara A. Tenenbaum, ed., *Encyclopedia of Latin American History and Culture* (New York: Charles Scribner's Sons, 1996.

Carlsbad Decrees   Decrees drawn up by statesman Prince Clemens von Metternich, representing Austria, endorsed by King Frederick William III of Prussia, and on September 20, 1819, ratified by the diet of the German Confederation, the loose union of German states created at the Congress of Vienna (1814–15). Through the document it was agreed that any decision made by the federal diet (at Frankfurt) would be superior to that of any sovereign of an individual German state, when the latter endorsed liberal views; that all pub-

lications reflecting liberal views were to be banned; that no liberal was to hold a university post; that all secret societies were to be investigated; and that all revolutionaries were to be reported to the federal diet. The decrees reflected the reactionary views held by the monarchs during this period when revolutionary movements in Spain and Naples seemed to threaten the status quo in Germany.

See also: GERMAN CONFEDERATION, ACT OF.

Further reading: Enno E. Kraehe, ed., *The Metternich Controversy* (Huntington, N.Y.: R. E. Krieger Pub., 1977).

Carnegie's "Wealth" Article   Essay, sometimes called "The Gospel of Wealth," written by American industrialist and philanthropist Andrew Carnegie and published in the *North American Review* in June 1889; he defended laissez-faire capitalism and also argued that rich men must use their surplus wealth to benefit the community. After claiming that competition and inequality of wealth are the inevitable costs of material development, Carnegie enunciated the duties of the rich man: to live modestly, to provide moderately for his dependents, and to administer all surplus revenues as trust funds, which he must administer to advance the general welfare of the community. The millionaire should be the "trustee for the poor." Carnegie followed this philosophy in his own life, donating some $350 million to various social, educational, and cultural causes.

Further reading: Joseph Frazier Wall, ed., *The Andrew Carnegie Reader* (Pittsburgh, Pa.: University of Pittsburgh Press, 1992); Thomas Carson, ed., *Gale Encyclopedia of U.S. Economic History* (Farmington Hills, Mich.: Gale Group, 1999).

Cartagena, Pact of   Agreement signed on May 16, 1907, at Cartagena, Spain, by Great Britain, France, and Spain, concerning the maintenance of the status quo in the Mediterranean. The three powers agreed to "enter into communication . . . should new circumstances arise tending to alter the territorial status quo," either in the Mediterranean or on the Atlantic coasts of Europe or Africa. The signatories further agreed to consult each other before taking any action should such new circumstances occur. The pact was intended, in part, as a check on suspected German designs on the Balearic Islands and the Canary Islands. The pact was confirmed again at Cartagena in 1913, and was still in effect at the outbreak of World War I; however, Spain chose not to become an ally of Britain and France, and remained neutral during the war.

Further reading: Raanan Rein, *Spain and the Mediterranean since 1898* (Portland, Ore.: F. Cass, 1999).

Carter's Inaugural Address   Address delivered by Jimmy Carter on January 20, 1977, at his inauguration as 39th president of the United States. Calling for renewed faith in the American system after the upheavals of the 1960s, Carter focused on the issues of human rights, environmental quality, nuclear arms control, and the goals of peace and justice. Arguing that the nation must be strong domestically if it was to be strong abroad, that it must set a model of a democratic system worthy of emulation, he urged a "quiet strength based not merely on the size of an arsenal but on the nobility of ideas" and promised to fight wars on poverty, ignorance, and injustice. After noting that " 'more' is not necessarily 'better,' " he argued that the United States must recognize limits, not only in material possessions and natural resources but in its ability to solve all problems.

Further reading: Jimmy Carter, "Inaugural Address," Bartleby.com web site available online at http://www.bartleby.com/124/pres60.html.

Castro's "I Am a Marxist-Leninist" Speech

Speech delivered by Fidel Castro Ruz, prime minister of Cuba, in which he explained how he had made the transition from a "political illiterate" and "ignoramus" to a full-fledged communist. The speech, which was broadcast to the Cuban people via television and radio, began on the night of December 1, 1961, and concluded three hours later in the wee hours of the morning. From the beginning of the Cuban Revolution in 1959, he said, he had been a Marxist but had not understood Marxism very well. The events of 1961, however, which included a trade embargo of Cuba by the United States and a failed U.S.-sponsored invasion of the island at the Bay of Pigs, convinced him all the more of the need to join the struggle against capitalist imperialism. After declaring Marxism to be the one true revolutionary theory, he declared, "I say here, with complete satisfaction and confidence, that I am a Marxist-Leninist, and shall remain so till the last days of my life." The speech served to cement Cuba's relations with the Soviet Union and to further sour, if possible, its relations with the United States.

Further reading: Robert E. Quirk, *Fidel Castro: The Full Story of His Rise to Power, His Regime, His Allies, and His Adversaries* (New York: W. W. Norton, 1993).

Cateau-Cambrésis, Treaty of (Paix Malheureuse)

Treaty of peace concluded at Le Cateau, France, on April 3, 1559, among envoys of King Henry II of France, King Philip II of Spain, and Queen Elizabeth I of England, finally resolving the 65-year-long Franco-Spanish struggle over control of Italy and, in particular, ending the Hapsburg-Valois War of 1547–49. France and Spain were financially exhausted when Henry II (a Valois) and Philip II (a Hapsburg) negotiated the treaty, by which France surrendered all claims to Genoa, Naples, Milan, and Corsica and acknowledged Spanish control of Franche-Comté and Italy, except for Turin, Saluzzo, and Pignerol. Savoy and Piedmont went to Spain's ally Emmanuel Philibert, who was to marry Henry's sister Margaret of Valois. France was allowed to retain the three bishoprics of Toul, Metz, and Verdun (captured from the Hapsburgs in 1552) and the port city of Calais (seized from England, Spain's ally, in 1558). Henry sealed the treaty by promising his daughter (Elizabeth of Valois) in marriage to Philip II.

See also: CAMBRAI, PEACE OF.

Further reading: Frank N. Magill, ed., *Great Events from History, Modern European Series*, 3 vols. (Englewood Cliffs, N.J.: Salem Press, 1973); Maurice Mullard and Paul Spicker, *Social Policy in a Changing Society* (New York: Routledge, 1998); Jervis Wegg, *Antwerp, 1477–1559, from the Battle of Nancy to the Treaty of Cateau Cambresis* (London: Methuen, 1916).

Catechism of the Catholic Church, New

First major catechism issued by the Roman Catholic Church in more than 400 years, initially drafted in Latin, then in French, and approved by Pope John Paul II in 1992, with the English translation published in 1994. The massive 800-page volume, compiled by a team of bishops and cardinals under the leadership of Joseph Cardinal Ratzinger and chief editor Christoph Schonborn, was described as a "compendium of all Catholic doctrine regarding both faith and morals." Its central theme was Christian unity—it even suggested reconciliation with the Eastern Orthodox Church. The text is divided into four parts—creed, sacraments, commandments, and prayer—and each of its 2,865 paragraphs is numbered and cross-referenced throughout the tome.

Further reading: Richard John Neuhaus, "The new catechism and Christian unity," *Theology Today* 53 (July 1996): 171–76; United States Catholic Conference, Inc.—Libreria Editrice Vaticana, *Catechism of the Catholic Church* (New York: Catholic Book Publishing, 1994).

Catherine the Great's Charter to the Nobility

See CHARTER TO THE NOBILITY, CATHERINE II'S.

Catherine the Great's Declaration of Armed Neutrality

Statement issued by Russia's czarina Catherine II the Great on February 28, 1780, and endorsed by Denmark and Sweden in 1780, Prussia and Austria in 1782, and Portugal in 1783. Seeking to protect Russian commercial interests, Catherine proclaimed in the document the right of all neutral ships to pass freely between ports of belligerent nations and the right to carry goods of belligerents, except contraband. Also, Catherine suggested (successfully) that these nations form a confederation or league. The declaration was especially directed against Great Britain, which at the time engaged in acts hostile to neutral vessels. Though the declaration had little effect against Britain, it represented an important contribution to the development of maritime law.

Further reading: William S. Carpenter, "The United States and the League of Neutral of 1780," *American Journal of International Law* 15 (1921): 511–22; Piers Mackesy, *The War for America, 1775–1783* (Lincoln: University of Nebraska Press, 1993).

Catherine the Great's Decree Annexing the Crimea

Proclamation issued on April 8, 1783, by Russia's czarina Catherine II the Great, announcing her country's annexation of the Crimea (a peninsula on the northern Black Sea coast). Crimea ceased to be an independent khanate or state and became subject to Russian rule. Although the annexation was opposed by the Ottoman Empire (Turkey), the Turks were not prepared to challenge the Russians, and thus Catherine the Great secured more coastline on the Black Sea and ports for her growing naval squadron in the region.

See also: JASSY, TREATY OF.

Further reading: Alan W. Fisher, *The Russian Annexation of the Crimea, 1772–1783* (Cambridge, England: Cambridge University Press, 1970).

Catholic Emancipation Act, British (Catholic Reform or Relief Bill)

Parliament-approved bill, framed by Sir Robert Peel in the prime ministry of the duke of Wellington and signed by Britain's king George IV on April 13, 1829; ended legal discrimination against Roman Catholics by emancipating them from religious and political disabilities in the United Kingdom of Great Britain and Ireland. The act gave Catholics the right to vote, to sit in the British Parliament, and to hold any public office (except those of regent, lord chancellor of England, and lord lieutenant of Ireland). Catholics had to take an oath recognizing the Protestant royal succession, vowing not to upset the Church of England, and declaring that the pope had no authority in British domestic matters. Full Catholic emancipation was achieved in 1871 when the UNIVERSITIES TESTS ACT declared the nation's universities open to Roman Catholics.

Further reading: Tom Bartlett, *The Fall and Rise of the Irish Nation: The Catholic Question 1690–1830* (Dublin: Gill and Macmillan, 1992); Wendy Hinde, *Catholic Emancipation: A Shake to Men's Mind* (Cambridge, Mass.: Blackwell, 1992); Brian Jenkins, *Era of Emancipation: British Government of Ireland, 1812–1830* (Kingston, Ontario: McGill-Queen's University Press, 1988); Robert C. Shipkey, *Robert Peel's Irish Policy, 1812–1846* (New York: Garland, 1987).

Cave Commission Report

In South Africa, findings of the Cave Commission appointed by the British government in July 1919 to fix the compensation payable to the British South Africa Company (chartered company) for surrendering its powers and assets to the new Rhodesian government. The commission, chaired by Viscount George Cave, published its report in January 1921 and determined the sum at £4,435,225. The value of lands previously used by the company for commercial gain and the benefits it had derived from distributing land for terms other than cash were to be subtracted from this amount. The company's claim for interest was rejected, but the value of public works handed over to the Rhodesians (estimated at £830,000) was to be added on.

Further reading: Hugh M. Hole, *The Making of Rhodesia* (London: Cass, 1967); Dougal O. Malcolm, *The British South Africa Company: Incorporated by Royal Charter, 1889–1939* (London: Fitch, 1939).

Central African Customs and Economic Union

Association (whose French acronym is UDEAC) formed by Cameroon, Central African Republic, Republic of the Congo, Gabon (all formerly French colonies in Central Africa), and Equatorial Guinea on December 8, 1964, under the Brazzaville Convention (operative on January 1, 1966), to encourage customs and economic cooperation among members. As a first step, customs duties were abolished on all trade among member countries. In 1972, travel restrictions were lifted to enable citizens of member states to travel freely within the UDEAC region. Subsequently, the UDEAC proposed joint undertakings (in road transport, for instance), industrial integration, and a coordination of regional tax policies and investment codes. Its secretariat is located in Bangui, Central African Republic. Chad (a later member) and the Central African Republic withdrew from the UDEAC to form a rival organization, only to rejoin the UDEAC later.

See also: WEST AFRICAN ECONOMIC COMMUNITY TREATY.

Further reading: Wilfred A. Ndongko, *Central African Customs and Economic Union: Evolution, Performance and Prospects*, bilingual ed. (Yaoundé, Cameroon: CEPER, 1988).

Central American Peace Plan (Guatemala Accord, Arias Peace Plan)

Agreement signed in Guatemala City on August 7, 1987, by the presidents of Costa Rica, El Salvador, Guatemala, Honduras, and Nicaragua, containing a plan for peace in the region. The document's main points included a call for an end to armed conflict in Central America; for governments and enemy opposition groups in the region to open peace discussions with one another; for political amnesty; and for the governments' endorsement of democratic reforms, including freedom of the press and political organization. A special international commission of 13 Central and South American foreign ministers and other officials was to monitor progress toward peace. The agreement was the collective response of the five above-mentioned Central American nations to the protracted, ongoing wars in El Salvador and Nicaragua and to the antidemocratic practices of the ruling Nicaraguan Sandinistas. The agreement was largely based on a 1987 peace proposal made by Costa Rican president Oscar Arias Sánchez.

Further reading: *Negotiations in Central America: 1981–1987*, rev. ed. (Washington, D.C.: Department of State, 1987); *Nicaragua, Civil Liberties, and the Central American Peace Plan* (Washington, D.C.: Puebla Institute, 1988); *Procedure to Establish Steady and Long-Standing Peace in Central America*, English and Spanish ed. (San José, Costa Rica: Oficina de Apoyo de la Presidencia de la República, 1987).

Central American Treaty of Union   Treaty of union signed at a meeting in Ampala, Honduras, on June 20, 1895, by Honduran president Policarpo Bonilla (who convened the meeting) and the presidents of Nicaragua and El Salvador, providing for a union of the three nations and thus forming the Greater Republic of Central America. The Honduran president's initiative had been motivated by the recent intervention of Great Britain and the United States in the region's affairs, a situation that, he was convinced, could be avoided only by a union of Central American states. The union survived long enough to frame a constitution (1898), which provided for an elected president and congress, but soon after the union was dissolved because of Salvadoran opposition.

See also: UNITED PROVINCES OF CENTRAL AMERICA, DECLARATION OF INDEPENDENCE OF THE.

Further reading: Gustavo Niederlein, *The State of Nicaragua of the Greater Republic of Central America* (Philadelphia: Philadelphia Commercial Museum, 1898).

Ceprano, Concordat of   Pact resolving the church-state conflict over ecclesiastical investitures; concluded on June 29, 1080, at Ceprano, Italy, between Robert Guiscard, duke of Apulia, and Pope Gregory VII. By this agreement, Guiscard swore loyalty to the pope and, while indicating his reservation regarding the March of Fermo, Salerno, and Amalfi, promised his support in the defense of the papacy. The pope lifted his ban against Guiscard and granted him investiture of the lands given to him by Popes Nicholas II and Alexander II and of his conquered territories. In lieu of the latter, Guiscard contracted to pay the pope an annual compensation. The pope recognized the conquests of the count of Loritello, but stipulated that henceforth Vatican territory was to be considered inviolable. Mediated by Abbot Desiderus of Monte Cassino (later Pope Victor III), the alliance was a triumph for Guiscard, who received more than he had surrendered.

Further reading: G. A. Loud, *The Age of Robert Guiscard: Southern Italy and the Norman Conquest* (New York: Longman, 2000); John J. Norwich, *The Normans in Sicily* (New York: Penguin Books, 1992).

Chaguaramas, Treaty of   See CARIBBEAN COMMUNITY AND COMMON MARKET AGREEMENT.

Champagne Speech, Townshend's   Speech delivered by Charles Townshend, Britain's chancellor of the exchequer, on the night of May 8, 1767, in which the eccentricities of his character came to the fore. That morning, after attending to the business of the British East India Company, he informed the House of Commons that, by doing so, he had atoned for the failings of his past life. In the evening, during a dinner party at his house, he gave his infamous speech, in which he praised and satirized himself and heaped ridicule on William Pitt's (Lord Chatham's) "wild incapacity." He mocked the government, likening it to a "weathercock"—an epithet that had often been attached to him. For a statesman of his stature, it was a damaging and an immature performance.

Further reading: Francis E. Townsend, *New Horizons* (Chicago: J. L. Stewart Publishing, 1943).

Chapelier Law   See LAW ON ASSOCIATIONS, FRENCH.

Chapultepec, Act of   Agreement signed by 21 American republics on March 3, 1945, during the Inter-American Conference on Problems of War and Peace held at Chapultepec Castle in Mexico City; it provided for common action against an aggressor from without or within the Western Hemisphere (World War II [1939–45] was still in progress). The act proclaimed that an attack against any American state would be considered an act of aggression against all, thus calling for collective action against the aggressor. A turning point in the development of inter-American relations, the Act of Chapultepec expanded the Monroe Doctrine's unilateral guarantee against intervention in the hemisphere into a mutual security system; and for the first time it included provisions that would ban aggression by one American state against another.

See also: BOGOTÁ, PACT OF; RIO TREATY.

Further reading: Charles L. Phillips and Alan Axelrod, eds., *Encyclopedia of Historical Treaties and Alliances*, 2 vols. (New York: Facts On File, 2001).

Charles, Death Warrant of   Signed by 59 commissioners, the death warrant of King Charles I of England sentenced him on January 27, 1649, "as a tyrant, traitor, murderer and public enemy." Following Pride's Purge (when Parliament was purged of all members, mostly Presbyterians, sympathetic to the king), he had been brought to trial by the Rump Parliament on the charge that he had "traitorously and maliciously levied war against the present Parliament, and the people therein represented." A court of 135 commissioners (with John Bradshaw as president and John Cook as prosecutor) considered the evidence and declared the king guilty. Charles refused to plead because he did not believe that any court had the authority to try the king. Shortly before his execution on January 30, he proclaimed himself to be a martyr for the people whose "liberty and freedom consists in having of government" not in "having a share in government. A subject and a sovereign are clean different things."

See also: NEWPORT, TREATY OF.

Further reading: Graham Edwards, *The Last Days of Charles I* (Stroud, England: Sutton, 1999); A. W. McIntosh, *The Death Warrant of King Charles I: "The Mystery of the Death Warrant of Charles I: Some Further Historic Doubts"* (London: House of Lords Record Office, 1981); Jason Peacey, ed., *The Regicides and the Execution of Charles I* (New York: Palgrave, 2001).

Charles IV's Golden Bull   See GOLDEN BULL OF 1356.

Charles River Bridge v. *Warren Bridge*

U.S. Supreme Court decision issued on February 14, 1837, establishing the principle that legislative grants are to be interpreted narrowly and that any ambiguity must be resolved in favor of the public, not the corporation. The decision modified the ruling in *DARTMOUTH COLLEGE* V. *WOODWARD*, which protected private contracts against legislative interference. Here the Charles River Bridge Company, which held a state charter for a toll bridge and claimed monopoly rights, sued to prevent the Warren Bridge Company from constructing a competing free bridge. Chief Justice Roger Taney rejected the monopolistic claim because it was not specified in the original charter and would injure the public welfare.

Further reading: Carl Brent Swisher, *Roger B. Taney* (New York: Macmillan, 1936); Charles Warren, *The Supreme Court in United States History* (Littleton, Colo.: F. B. Rothman, 1922, repr., 1987).

Charter of Liberties (Charter of Franchises and Liberties)

Document enacted in 1683 by the New York colony's first general (representative) assembly under English rule (under Governor Thomas Dongan). The charter placed legislative power in the assembly, a council, and the governor. Written chiefly by the assembly speaker, Matthias Nicolls, it stipulated that the consent of the assembly, which was to meet no less than once every three years, was required for the imposition of taxes. The right to vote was given all freemen; freedom of worship and trial by jury were guaranteed; and bases of landowning, inheritance, and court law were stated in the charter. Never fully confirmed, the charter became inoperative soon after the duke of York acceded to the British throne as King James II in 1685.

See also: DONGAN CHARTER.

Further reading: John Romeyn Brodhead, *History of the State of New York* (New York: Harper Brothers, 1853–71); New York State Historical Association, *History of the State of New York*, 5 vols. (Port Washington, N.Y.: I. J. Friedman, 1962).

Charter of Liberties (Charter of Privileges)

Constitution granted to Pennsylvania by William Penn, the colony's proprietor, in 1701. The charter reframed Pennsylvania's previous bicameral legislative structure (under which the colonial assembly could only approve or reject laws initiated by the provincial council). Under the new charter, the legislature became unicameral, with the council eliminated and the assembly cast as the chief lawmaking body. The proprietor's control was limited to the appointment of the governor. The Charter of Liberties served as the basis for Pennsylvania's government up until the American Revolution (1775–83).

See also: FRAME OF GOVERNMENT, PENN'S.

Further reading: J. Paul Selsam, *The Pennsylvania Constitution of 1776* (New York: Octagon Books, 1936, repr., 1971);

W. R. Shepherd, *History of Proprietary Government in Pennsylvania* (New York: AMS Press, 1896, repr., 1967).

Charter of Paris for a New Europe

Document welcoming a "New Era of Democracy, Peace and Unity" signed on November 21, 1990, at the conclusion of the Paris summit of the Conference on Security and Cooperation in Europe (CSCE). The member states affirmed that democracy and respect for human rights were critical for peace and security in the region. To promote these, the charter created several institutions: the Conflict Prevention Centre, the Office for Democratic Institutions, and the High Commissioner for National Minorities. It also established three consultative groups: the Council of Ministers, the Committee of Senior Officials, and regular summit meetings of heads of state or government. The charter pledged support for the Ten Principles of Helsinki Final Act and welcomed the Treaty of CONVENTIONAL FORCES IN EUROPE. It redefined the role of the CSCE (soon succeeded by the Organization for Security and Cooperation in Europe) in a rapidly changing Europe.

Further reading: R. Apple, "34 Leaders Adopt Pact Proclaiming a United Europe," *New York Times,* January 22, 1990, p. A1; Conference for Security and Cooperation in Europe, "Charter of Paris for a New Europe," Organization for Security and Cooperation in Europe website, available online at http://www.osce.org/docs/english/1990-1999/summits/paris90e.htm;

Charter of Rights and Freedoms, Canadian

Bill of Rights sponsored by Canadian prime minister Pierre Elliott Trudeau and incorporated into the Canadian constitution (see BRITISH NORTH AMERICA ACT; CANADIAN CONSTITUTION ACT OF 1982). Effective on April 17, 1982, it provided Canada with her only Bill of Rights, as an actual part of the constitution. The charter was comprehensive, affirming democratic rights, equality between men and women, language rights, legal rights, and fundamental rights. The prospective inclusion of the charter in the constitution was a subject of debate during the period prior to the patriation of the constitution, arousing the opposition of those who wished to see issues involving individual rights remain a legislative concern. The charter replaced Canada's 1960 BILL OF RIGHTS.

Further reading: Jonathan L. Black-Branch, *Rights and Realities: The Judicial Impact of the Canadian Charter of Rights and Freedoms on Education, Case Law, and Political Jurisprudence* (Brookfield, Vt.: Ashgate, 1997); Paul Howe and Peter H. Russell, eds., *Judicial Power and Canadian Democracy* (Montreal: McGill-Queen's University Press, 2001); Christopher P. Manfredi, *Judicial Power and the Charter: Canada and the Paradox of Liberal Constitutionalism* (New York: Oxford University Press, 2001); F. L. Morton and Rainer Knopff, *The Charter Revolution and the Court Party* (Peterborough, Ontario: Broadview Press, 2000).

Charter 77, Czech   Manifesto signed by 242 Czech citizens (dated January 1, 1977) and published in Western newspapers on January 6 and 7, 1977, after being smuggled out of Czechoslovakia. It condemned the communist Prague government's failure to observe the 1975 HELSINKI ACCORD on human rights, which had been in force in Czechoslovakia since early 1976. The document charged the government with denying the right of higher education to individuals whose parents held views contrary to its own and with stifling freedom of expression, opinion, and conscience by prohibiting any view not in conformity with its own. It also accused the government of usurping the citizens' right to partake in public affairs and of obstructing the citizens' right to privacy by exercising its self-proclaimed right to tap telephones, conduct searches of homes, and censor mail. The document declared the formation of "Charter 77," an organization aiming to promote human and civil rights in Czechoslovakia and abroad. Publication of the charter, which was the first major act of dissent since the "Prague Spring" (see TWO THOUSAND WORDS), led to the detention of four of the charter's signatories and a threat published in the paper *Rude Pravo* against all dissenters.

Further reading: Harold Gordon Skilling, *Charter 77 and Human Rights in Czechoslovakia* (Boston: Allen & Unwin, 1981).

Charter to the Nobility, Catherine II's   Charter issued by Czarina Catherine II the Great of Russia on April 21, 1785, to the Russian nobility, in which the collective rights of the nobility were recognized. The charter was essentially a codification of privileges already in existence. In the document Catherine declared the Russian nobles' freedom from corporal punishment; their exemption from paying certain taxes and from compulsory state service; and their right to be tried in court by peers. In addition she declared their right, on a local level, to participate directly in such concerns as the care for orphans and widows, the raising of the funds for educational institutions, and, to a certain extent, the administration of governmental services, such as the local police and court system.

Further reading: David M. Griffiths and George E. Munro, *Catherine II's Charters of 1785 to the Nobility and the Towns* (Salt Lake City, Utah: C. Schlacks, 1991).

Chartist Petition of 1838.   See PEOPLE'S CHARTER.

Chartist Petition of 1848 (Monster Petition)   Lengthy petition signed, supposedly, by several million Chartists (political reformers), calling for the British government's acceptance of the PEOPLE'S CHARTER of 1838. In London (Kennington Common), a mass demonstration was held by the Chartists on April 10, 1848, to support the presentation of their national petition to the House of Commons. It was prompted by poor harvests in Britain and the revolutionary climate on the Continent. Police quietly dispersed the three-mile-long procession, and the petition was eventually conveyed by Feargus O'Connor and other leaders to the Commons in three cabs. It was rejected by Parliament and ridiculed for its many thousands of fictitious signatures. The Chartist movement never recovered from this blow.

Further reading: Mark A. Kishlansky, *Sources of the West: Readings in Western Civilization*, vol. 2, 4th ed. (New York: Addison Wesley Longman, 2001).

Chastenoy, Peace of   See MONSIEUR, PEACE OF.

Châteaubriant, Edict of   Repressive decree issued at Châteaubriant on June 27, 1551, by King Henry II of France in an attempt to check the growing influence of Calvinist Protestantism in the country. The edict's 46 articles codified all the previous sanctions against the Huguenots (French Protestants). It forbade the printing, sale, or even possession of reformist and unorthodox literature and rewarded informants against heretics with one-third of their goods. Inferior tribunals called the presidial courts (*juges des presidaux*) were established to try heretical crimes, and a close watch was maintained on civil and ecclesiastical judges reported to be lenient on heretics. If convicted, most heretics received the death sentence. One of the many persecutory measures introduced by Henry II during his reign, the edict also required anyone wanting to be a judge to produce a certificate confirming that he was a good Roman Catholic.

Further reading: Frederic J. Baumgartner, *Henry II, King of France 1547–1559* (Durham, N.C.: Duke University Press, 1988).

Chaumont, Treaties of   Alliance signed at Chaumont, France, on March 1, 1814, by representatives of the allied powers (Great Britain, Russia, Prussia, and Austria) near the close of the Napoleonic Wars (1803–15). By the treaties, which were arranged primarily under the influence of British foreign minister Lord Castlereagh, the allies separately pledged themselves in favor of the continued struggle against Napoleonic France, until the latter was reduced to (or consented to accept) her 1792 borders; the number of troops and monetary funds to be provided by each ally for the common defense was also stipulated. The allies also agreed to convene periodically to maintain good understanding among themselves, and subscribed that the alliance should continue in effect for 20 years. Furthermore, they agreed secretly that the German states should become a federated, independent entity.

See also: PARIS, TREATY OF (1814), VIENNA, FINAL ACT OF THE CONGRESS OF.

Further reading: Léo Lamarre, *La diplomatie et la guerre, 1814: Le Traité de Chaumont-en-Bassigny* (Colombey-les-Deux-Eglises, France: N. Mourot, 1988).

Chechnyan (Chechen) Declaration of Independence

Proclamation on November 2, 1991, of independence from the Russian Federation by the parliament of the autonomous republic of Chechnya, that prompted Soviet president Boris Yeltsin to declare a state of emergency on November 8 and threaten the use of force. The declaration came within days of General Dzhokhar Dudayev's election as Chechen president and his assumption of emergency powers. Even as the Supreme Soviet met on November 10 to discuss Yeltsin's decree, he sent 600 soldiers to Chechnya. The next day, the Supreme Soviet denounced both the decisions, thus forcing Yeltsin to withdraw his decree. Chechnya stayed away from the Russian general elections in December 1993 and rejected Russia's new 1993 constitution (see RUSSIAN CONSTITUTION OF 1993). Eventually though, opposition to Dudayev's policies led to a devastating civil war in 1994.

Further reading: Stasys Knezys and Romanas Sedlickas, *The War in Chechnya* (College Station: Texas A&M University Press, 1999); Anatol Lieven, *Chechnya—Tombstone of Russian Power* (New Haven, Conn.: Yale University Press, 1998).

Chefoo (Yantai) Convention

At Chefoo (Yantai, a seaside resort in Shandong province, China) on September 13, 1876, a meeting convened by Britain to claim redress for the murder of the official interpreter, Augustus Margary, on the Burmese border and the exclusion of his authorized expedition. These were two of the six demands presented by Sir Thomas Wade (negotiator for Britain) to his Chinese counterpart, Li Hungchang. In addition, Wade asked for 150,000 taels of silver as compensation, for a reinterpretation of the clauses concerning diplomatic audiences with the Chinese emperor, for a lifting of all but the tariff duty on British trade, and for an immediate settlement of all these claims. The first three demands were easily met but the remaining three created much dissension, since the other European nations demanded to be consulted in the matter of treaty amendments. Ten additional ports were opened to foreign trade. China ratified the convention on September 17, 1876, but Britain's ratification was delayed until 1885.

Further reading: Kenneth Bourne et al., *British Documents on Foreign Affairs . . . Volume 22, Chefoo Convention and Its Aftermath, 1876–1885* (Frederick, Md.: University Publications of America, 1994); James C. Cooley, *The Censor at the Yamen: The Diplomatic Career of Sir Thomas Francis Wade* (Ann Arbor, Mich.: University Microfilms International, 1971); Robert K. Douglas, *Li Hungchang* (Washington, D.C.: University Publications of America, 1977).

Cherasco, Armistice of

Armistice concluded at Cherasco, Italy, on April 28, 1796, between the Italian province of Sardinia and revolutionary France during General Napoléon Bonaparte's first Italian campaign in the French Revolutionary Wars (1792–1802). In return for peace with France, Sardinia under King Victor Amadeus III agreed to cede her mainland possessions of Savoy and Nice to France and to abandon her alliance with Austria. Sardinia had entered the war in 1792 allied with Austria, whose dominions included much of Italy. Napoléon's Italian campaign began with this conquest and was followed by further territorial acquisitions through the 1797 Treaties of CAMPO FORMIO and TOLENTINO as well as others.

See also: ALESSANDRIA, ARMISTICE OF; PARIS, TREATY OF (1796).

Further reading: Robert B. Asprey, *The Rise of Napoleon Bonaparte* (New York: Basic Books, 2000).

Cherasco, Treaties of

Series of treaties concluded (April–June 1631) among France, Spain, Savoy, and the Holy Roman Emperor, ending the War of the Mantuan Succession (1628–31). The main issue was resolved at Cherasco, Italy, by the treaty of June 19, 1631—when Spain renounced her claim to the Mantuan crown, allowing France to crown the duke of Nevers as ruler of Mantua (a northern Italian city). Nevers also obtained the city of Casale. France and the Holy Roman Empire renounced their respective territorial gains in Italy. However, France had previously finalized a secret agreement with Victor Amadeus of Savoy, whereby he had conceded Pignerol to France. Chief negotiators for the Cherasco treaties were Cardinal de Richelieu of France, Victor Amadeus of Savoy, and Jules Mazarin, papal emissary. The treaties secured for France one of the strategic gateways to Italy.

Further reading: Anthony Levi, *Cardinal Richelieu and the Making of France* (New York: Carroll & Graf, 2000); G. R. R. Treasure, *Richelieu and Mazarin* (New York: Routledge, 1998).

Cheribon Agreement (Linggadjati Agreement)

Agreement concluded by the Netherlands and the Republic of Indonesia at Linggadjati Hill near Cheribon (Tjirebon) on November 15, 1946, and signed in Batavia (Jakarta) on March 25, 1947; it brought a temporary end to the conflict between the two, which had originated over the Netherlands' determination to restore Dutch authority over Indonesia following World War II (1939–45) and the Indonesian nationalists' determination to gain full independence from their former colonial masters. Through the document the Netherlands recognized the Republic of Indonesia, which consisted of Java, Madura, and Sumatra; both agreed to the formation, before January 1, 1949, of a United States of Indonesia, which would include the Republic of Indonesia, Kalimantan (Borneo), and the Great East, and which, together with the Netherlands, would be united under the Dutch crown; and finally, both agreed that all disputes were to be settled through pacific means. Little more than a year passed before rebels once again ignited the Indonesian War of Independence (1945–49).

See also: HAGUE AGREEMENT OF 1949; RENVILLE AGREEMENT.

Further reading: Benedict R. O'G. Anderson, *Java in a Time of Revolution; Occupation and Resistance, 1944–1946* (Ithaca, N.Y.: Cornell University Press, 1972); Indonesia Departemen Penerangan, *The Indonesian Revolution, Basic Documents and the Idea of Guided Democracy* (Jakarta, Indonesia: Department of Information, 1960); Robert J. McMahon, *Colonialism and Cold War: The United States and the Struggle for Indonesian Independence, 1945–49* (Ithaca, N.Y.: Cornell University Press, 1981).

Cherokee Nation v. Georgia

U.S. Supreme Court decision, issued on March 18, 1831, that defined the legal status of American Indians as "domestic dependent nations," not foreign nations, and eventually led to the Cherokee removal from Georgia to Oklahoma. In the early 19th century the rich Cherokee lands in Georgia were coveted by white settlers. When the Georgia legislature in 1828 passed statutes claiming ownership of all Cherokee territory and annulling all Cherokee laws and customs, the Indians sought a U.S. Supreme Court injunction to prevent the execution of these laws. Writing for the majority, Chief Justice John Marshall ruled that the Court had no jurisdiction over the case because the Cherokees did not constitute a foreign nation, with sovereignty rights over their own lands.

See also: *WORCESTER* V. *GEORGIA*.

Further reading: Allen Guttmann, *States' Rights and Indian Removal: The Cherokee Nation v. the State of Georgia,* (Boston: D. C. Heath, 1965); Edward W. Knappman, *Great American Trials,* (Detroit: Gale Research, 1994); Ulrich Bonnell Phillips, *Georgia and State Rights* (Macon, Ga.: Mercer University Press, 1902, repr., 1984); Thurman Wilkins, *Cherokee Tragedy,* (Norman: University of Oklahoma Press, 1986).

Child Labor Act of 1919, U.S.

Section of a general federal U.S. taxation bill enacted on February 24, 1919, and designed to control child labor by assessing a tax on the products of that labor. The act levied an excise tax of 10 percent upon the net profits of mines that employed children under the age of 16, or factories that employed children under the age of 14, or that allowed children between 14 and 16 to work more than eight hours a day, or six days a week, or after 7 P.M., or before 6 A.M. In 1922 the U.S. Supreme Court overturned the act as unconstitutional, ruling in *BAILEY* V. *DREXEL FURNITURE COMPANY* that it attempted to assert federal control over state matters.

Further reading: Leonard W. Levy and Kenneth L. Karst, eds., *Encyclopedia of the American Constitution,* 2d ed. (New York: Macmillan Reference, 2000); Stephen B. Wood, *Constitutional Politics in the Progressive Era: Child Labor and the Law* (Chicago: University of Chicago Press, 1968).

Child Pornography Prevention Act of 1996, U.S. (Child Pornography Protection Act)

Legislation enacted by the U.S. Congress to further prevent the creation, distribution, and possession of child pornography. It passed the U.S. Senate on September 30, 1996, and was signed into law by President Bill Clinton in 1997. Earlier acts, notably the Sexual Exploitation of Children Act of 1977, the Child Protection Act of 1984, the Child Sexual Abuse and Pornography Act of 1986, and the Child Protection and Obscenity Enforcement Act of 1988, had outlawed actual depictions of sexual activity involving children, defined by law as anyone under the age of 18. However, these laws did not address virtual pornographic images created via modern computer or photographic and photocopy technology that make adults look like children. The Child Pornography Prevention Act closed this legal loophole by making the creation of virtual child pornography a federal offense. Because the act outlaws the very process by which virtual child pornography is made, even though actual children are not involved, it was accused of creating a "thought crime," a concept unprecedented in American jurisprudence. In 1999 the ninth U.S. circuit court struck down the act on the grounds that its provisions concerning the creation of virtual child pornography were unconstitutionally vague and too broad. In 2001 the U.S. Supreme Court upheld that decision, 6-3, in *ASHCROFT* V. *FREE SPEECH COALITION*.

Further reading: Bill Bickel, "Virtual Child Pornography: Should It Be Illegal?" About.com, available online at http://crime.about.com/library/weekly/aavirtualchildpornography. htm; "Child Pornography Laws," Cyber Tipline, available online at http://www.missingkids.com/html/ncmec_default_ec_childporn_laws.html; "Child Pornography Prevention Act," Declan McCullagh's politechbot.com, available online at http://www.politechbot.com/docs/cppa.text.html.

Chilean Constitution of 1833

Constitution formally advanced by Chile's president Joaquín Prieto on May 25, 1833. In 1831 Chilean conservatives set up a Grand Constituent Convention to amend the short-lived liberal constitution of 1828; however, several months later a radically different document emerged. It contained a strong emphasis on presidential authority, established a bicameral legislature consisting of an indirectly elected senate and a chamber of deputies, and gave all Chilean males over 25 (and with appropriate property) the right to vote. Also, the Roman Catholic Church was established as the official state religion. The constitution of 1833, one of the key political documents of the national period of Chilean history, remained in effect until 1925.

Further reading: Charles W. Tooke, trans., *Political Constitution of the Republic of Chile: Promulgated May 25, 1833, with the Amendments Down to May 1, 1899* (Urbana, Ill.: Press of the Herald, 1899).

Chilean Constitution of 1925

Constitution adopted in Chile on August 30, 1925, by a constituent assembly convened by President Arturo Alessandri. This constitution provided for separation of church and state; guaranteed complete religious freedom; declared property rights to be subject to the maintenance and progress of social order; made primary education mandatory; and proclaimed that a member of the congress could not simultaneously be a member of the president's cabinet. The term of the president, who would be elected by direct popular vote, was increased to six years. Also, the president was to appoint cabinet members in a manner similar to that provided by the U.S. CONSTITUTION. The Constitution of 1925 was significant in abolishing the parliamentary system until then in effect in Chile.

Further reading: *Constitution of the Republic of Chile, 1925* (Washington, D.C.: General Secretariat, Organization of American States, 1972).

Chilean Constitution of 1980   New constitution approved by plebiscite in Chile in September 1980, instituting a formidable presidential system of government under the revised CHILEAN CONSTITUTION OF 1925. The voters approved an eight-year term as president for General Augusto Pinochet Ugarte, who had seized power on September 11, 1973 (the popularly elected Marxist president, Salvador Allende Gossens, had been overthrown and mysteriously killed); Pinochet had ruled repressively since then as head of a five-man military junta. The 1980 constitution, which went into effect on March 11, 1981 (President Pinochet was inaugurated the same day), granted Pinochet an option to serve a subsequent eight-year presidential term; also, political parties were permitted to organize in time for Chile's congressional elections in 1990. In 1988 Pinochet lost in a plebiscite over extension of his term and then lost to Patricio Aylwin in popular elections; the constitution allowed Pinochet to stay in office until March 1990, when the new president (Aylwin) was sworn in.

Further reading: Paul W. Garber and Philip C. Garber, trans., *The Political Constitution of Chile: An English Translation* (Boston: P. W. Garber, 1981).

Chilpancingo, Congress of   Congress convened at Chilpancingo, Guerrero, New Spain, in 1813 by José María Morelos y Pavón, priest and leader of the Mexican rebels in the struggle for independence; its purpose was to set up a government of the insurgent movement. At the congress, where he was appointed generalissimo of the insurgent government, Morelos propounded his views on the proper social, economic, and political organization of a free and independent Mexico. His program of land reform and ideas on the dispossession of the church's nonreligious properties became a part of Mexican revolutionary and liberal doctrine for a century. Moreover, under his guidance the first Mexican constitution was drawn up in 1814.

See also: APATZINGÁN, CONSTITUTION OF.

Further reading: John A. Caruso, *The Liberators of Mexico* (New York: Pageant Press, 1954); Wilbert H. Timmons, *Morelos; Priest, Soldier, Statesman of Mexico* (El Paso: Texas Western College Press, 1963).

Chinese-British Treaty of 1928   See ANGLO-CHINESE TREATY OF 1928.

Chinese Engagement   Agreement in January 1874 ending the fighting between two Chinese secret societies (the Ghee Hin and Hai San) over control of tin mining in the Larut region of Perak, on the Malay Peninsula. British colonial authorities arranged the signing of the agreement by the two Chinese adversaries, who promised to disarm, take down their fortifications, exchange prisoners, and pay a large fine if they broke the peace. About the same time, the British reached an accord with Malay chiefs (see PANGKOR ENGAGEMENT), thus beginning to take control over some Malay states.

Further reading: Richard O. Winstedt and Richard J. Wilkinson, *A History of Perak* (Singapore: Printers Ltd., 1934).

Chinese Exclusion Act of 1882   Legislation passed by the U.S. Congress suspending the immigration of Chinese laborers to the United States for 10 years. Though the BURLINGAME TREATY of 1868 had permitted immigration, by the 1870s the large influx of Chinese laborers, especially to California, was producing increasing resentment among competing white laborers. In 1879 Congress passed a bill prohibiting further Chinese immigration, but it was vetoed by U.S. president Rutherford B. Hayes. The following year a new treaty with China gave the United States the right to limit or suspend the entry of Chinese labor, but not to prohibit it absolutely. The 1882 suspension of immigration was renewed in 1892 and was followed by other exclusionary legislation. These acts were repealed in 1943.

Further reading: Sucheng Chan, ed., *Entry Denied: Exclusion and the Chinese Community in America, 1882–1943* (Philadelphia: Temple University Press, 1991); Andrew Gyory, *Closing the Gate: Race, Politics, and the Chinese Exclusion Act* (Chapel Hill: University of North Carolina Press, 1998); Roderick Duncan McKenzie, *Oriental Exclusion: The Effect of American Immigration Laws, Regulations, and Judicial Decisions upon the Chinese and Japanese on the American Pacific Coast* (New York: J. S. Ozer, 1971); Elmer C. Sandmeyer, *The Anti-Chinese Movement in California* (Urbana: University of Illinois Press, 1991).

Chinese Exclusion Act of 1892   Renewal by the U.S. Congress of the CHINESE EXCLUSION ACT OF 1882, suspending the immigration of Chinese laborers to the United States for 10 years. It was a violation of an 1880 treaty with China, which allowed the United States to "regulate, limit or suspend" immigration but not to prohibit it entirely. A new treaty of 1894 permitted this absolute ban on immigration for 10 years. The exclusionary acts were repealed in 1943 and were replaced by a quota system.

Further reading: Sucheng Chan, ed., *Entry Denied: Exclusion and the Chinese Community in America, 1882–1943* (Philadelphia: Temple University Press, 1991); Andrew Gyory,

Closing the Gate: Race, Politics, and the Chinese Exclusion Act (Chapel Hill: University of North Carolina Press, 1998); Roderick Duncan McKenzie, *Oriental Exclusion: The Effect of American Immigration Laws, Regulations, and Judicial Decisions upon the Chinese and Japanese on the American Pacific Coast* (New York: J. S. Ozer, 1971); Elmer C. Sandmeyer, *The Anti-Chinese Movement in California* (Urbana: University of Illinois Press, 1991).

Chinese Exclusion Act of 1902

Legislation enacted by the U.S. Congress on April 29, 1902, that suspended Chinese immigration to the United States indefinitely. Favored by organized labor, especially within California, it succeeded the CHINESE EXCLUSION ACTS OF 1882 and 1892, which had prohibited Chinese immigration for 10-year periods. The act, more restrictive than previous measures, extended the law to the Philippines and Hawaii and prevented Chinese migration from these islands to the mainland. The 1902 prohibition remained in effect until 1943, when immigration was permitted under a strict quota system.

Further reading: Sucheng Chan, ed., *Entry Denied: Exclusion and the Chinese Community in America, 1882–1943* (Philadelphia: Temple University Press, 1991); Delber L. McKee, *Chinese Exclusion Versus the Open Door Policy, 1900–1906: Clashes over Chinese Policy in the Roosevelt Era* (Detroit: Wayne State University Press, 1977); Roderick Duncan McKenzie, *Oriental Exclusion: The Effect of American Immigration Laws, Regulations, and Judicial Decisions upon the Chinese and Japanese on the American Pacific Coast* (New York: J. S. Ozer, 1971); Elmer C. Sandmeyer, *The Anti-Chinese Movement in California* (Urbana: University of Illinois Press, 1991).

Chisholm v. Georgia

U.S. Supreme Court decision of February 18, 1793, that upheld the right of citizens of one state to sue another state in federal courts. Citizens of South Carolina who were the heirs of Alexander Chisholm, a loyalist whose property had been confiscated by the state of Georgia during the American Revolution (1775–83), sued that state for compensation. Georgia denied the Supreme Court's jurisdiction and refused to appear. The Court ruled in favor of Chisholm. State protests against the decision led to passage of the ELEVENTH AMENDMENT (ratified in 1798), denying federal jurisdiction in suits by a citizen of one state against another state.

Further reading: Leonard W. Levy and Kenneth L. Karst, eds., *Encyclopedia of the American Constitution,* 2d ed. (New York: Macmillan Reference, 2000); Ulrich Bonnell Phillips, *Georgia and State Rights* (Macon, Ga.: Mercer University Press, 1902, repr., 1984).

Christianae Religionis Institutio

See INSTITUTES OF THE CHRISTIAN RELIGION.

Churchill's "Blood, Toil, Tears, and Sweat" Speech.

See "BLOOD, TOIL, TEARS, AND SWEAT" SPEECH, CHURCHILL'S.

Churchill's "Iron Curtain" Speech

See "IRON CURTAIN" SPEECH, CHURCHILL'S.

Churchill's "So Much Owed" Speech.

See "SO MUCH OWED" SPEECH, CHURCHILL'S.

Churchill's "Their Finest Hour" Speech.

See "THEIR FINEST HOUR" SPEECH, CHURCHILL'S.

Churchill's "We Shall Never Surrender" Speech

See "WE SHALL NEVER SURRENDER" SPEECH, CHURCHILL'S.

Churchill White Paper of 1922

Official statement of British policy issued as a white paper through the authority of British colonial secretary Winston Churchill in June 1922; it interpreted the earlier BALFOUR DECLARATION, which confirmed Britain's support of the establishment of a Jewish national home in Palestine. The statement made it plain that although Britain's policy was to support the establishment of a Jewish national home in Palestine, her policy in no way included any support for a completely Jewish Palestine or a subordination of Arabic culture and language to that of the Jews. The statement also determined that the immigration of the Jews could continue only as long as the Palestinian economy had the capacity to accommodate it. Neither the Palestinians nor the Jews welcomed the statement.

See also: PASSFIELD REPORT.

Further reading: J. C. Hurewitz, *The Middle East and North Africa in World Politics: A Documentary Record,* 2d ed., vol. 2: *British and French Supremacy, 1914–1945* (New Haven, Conn.: Yale University Press, 1979); Reeva S. Simon, Philip Mattar, and Richard W. Bulliet, eds., *Encyclopedia of the Modern Middle East* (New York: Simon & Schuster, 1996).

Cicero's Orations Against Catiline

Four famous speeches delivered by the Roman Consul Marcus Tullius Cicero against conspiratorial rival Catiline (Lucius Sergius Catilina) in the Senate in 63 B.C. The first oration (November 8) was an excoriation, in which Cicero saw the Roman Republic as a common father and Catiline as intending to commit parricide. With evidence gained from Catiline's mistress, Cicero implied that he was conspiring against the state and that he was a thief and adulterer. Cicero called on Jupiter to safeguard Rome and to punish Catiline. At the end, Catiline left the Senate and fled to Etruria, where he organized a 20,000-man army. The next day (November 9) Cicero gave his second speech, saying Catiline had surrounded himself with perverts and asking again for Jupiter's help. Incriminating evidence against Catiline was soon obtained by the Senate, which heard (December 3) Cicero announce that the Conspiracy of Catiline had been foiled with the arrest and imprisonment of seven guilty abettors. Cicero's fourth speech (December 5) secured the death sentence for the imprisoned conspirators, who were immediately put to death as *hostes* (enemies) without appeal. Catiline was shortly killed on the battlefield.

See also: SENATUS CONSULTUM ULTIMUM OF 63 B.C.

Further reading: William Underwood and Thomas Clark, eds., *Select Orations of Cicero* (New York: D. McKay, 1966); Augustus S. Wilkins, ed., *The Orations of Cicero Against Catiline* (New York: St. Martins Press, 1972).

Cider Act, British   Bill proposed by Sir Francis Dashwood, Britain's chancellor of the exchequer, in 1763 to raise revenue to meet Britain's war debts. He suggested an excise of four shillings on every hogshead (large cask) of cider and every bin of wine. The tax fell equally on all varieties of cider and affected farmers in certain counties only. The proposal led to strong opposition in the cider-making counties and elsewhere, and also in parliament, where William Pitt spoke out strongly against it. The bill passed both Houses of Parliament by a fair margin, backed by Prime Minister Bute (John Stuart), who resigned, supposedly over this issue, shortly thereafter (April 1763).

Further reading: Thomas Alcock, *Observations on That Part of a Late Act of Parliament Which Lays an Additional Duty on Cyder and Perry* (New Haven, Conn.: Research Publications, 1975).

Cigarette Labeling and Advertising Act, U.S.   See SMOKING AND HEALTH.

City of God (De Civitate Dei)   Saint Augustine's reasoned philosophical defense of Christianity, a compendium of 22 books written between 413 and 426 to counteract pagan criticism that Alaric's Visigothic sack of Rome (410) was a direct consequence of Christianity's neglect of the gods. Saint Augustine divided his work into two unequal parts. In part one, books one to five explain that calamities are not caused by the neglect of gods, while books six to 10 argue that one cannot accrue any advantages for now or the future by worshipping gods. In part two, the allegory of the two cities—the City of God and the Terrestrial City—is developed. Books 11 to 14 deal with their origin, books 15 to 18 with their growth, and books 19 to 22 define their ultimate goals. A classic view of the Christian philosophy of history, the *City of God* is one of the masterpieces of Latin literature and of medieval thought.

See also: CONFESSIONS.

Further reading: St. Augustine, *The City of God*, trans. Marcus Dods (New York: Modern Library, 1993).

Civil Aeronautics Act, U.S. (Lea-McCarran Act)
Federal legislation sponsored by Representative Clarence F. Lea of California and Senator Patrick A. McCarran of Nevada and enacted on June 23, 1938, that established the Civil Aeronautics Authority (CAA) to regulate the civil aviation industry. The agency, consisting of five members appointed by the U.S. president, was empowered to regulate rates and schedules for commercial passenger, freight, and mail flights; to promulgate safety rules; to oversee financial matters; and to approve or disapprove mergers and agreements between airline companies. The CAA was also given the authority to establish new air routes. The Civil Aeronautics Board (CAB) was set up under the CAA.

Further reading: I. R. Barnes et al., *Aviation Transport . . .* (Durham, N.C.: Duke University School of Law, 1946); Henry G. Hotchkiss, *A Treatise on Aviation Law . . . Including . . . the Civil Aeronautics Act of 1938 . . .*, 2d ed. (New York: Baker, Voorhis, 1938).

Civil Constitution of the Clergy   Major French revolutionary document (see DECLARATION OF THE RIGHTS OF MAN AND OF THE CITIZEN; FRENCH DECREE ABOLISHING FEUDALISM), establishing a civil constitution for the French church and making it a subsidiary of the state (July 12, 1790). The ecclesiastical structure was completely revamped: old dioceses were abolished, each new diocese constituting a department. Bishops and parish priests were to be elected and the pope was denied the rights of institution. Papal prerogative was further undermined by the suppression of annates (payments made to the Vatican) and by requiring every papal document to be approved by the French government. The pope, still the spiritual head of the French church, was deprived of all temporal control. Clergy were required to swear an oath of loyalty to the king (Louis XVI) and the new constitution of the state. This caused a major schism, leading to the pope's condemnation of the document and contributing, eventually, to Louis XVI's antirevolutionary stance.

Further reading: *New Catholic Encyclopedia*, 17 vols. (Palatine, Ill.: Jack Heraty & Associates, 1967, repr., 1981).

"Civil Disobedience," Thoreau's   Influential essay written by American author and naturalist Henry David Thoreau, who advocated civil disobedience as a means for an individual to protest governmental actions that he considers unjust. The essay was originally given in 1849 as a lecture called "Resistance to Civil Disobedience" and then published that year in his friend Elizabeth Peabody's volume, *Aesthetic Papers*. It was written after Thoreau had spent a night in prison for refusing to pay a poll tax used to finance the Mexican War, which Thoreau opposed as imperialistic and an attempt to extend slavery. Thoreau argued that there is a higher law than the civil law, and that the higher law must be followed, regardless of the penalty: "Under a government which imprisons any unjustly, the true place for a just man is also a prison." The essay, titled "Civil Disobedience" in 1866, influenced many social and political reformers, including Mohandas Gandhi and Martin Luther King, Jr.

Further reading: Henry David Thoreau, *Walden and Civil Disobedience: Complete Texts with Introductions, Historical Contexts, Critical Essays* (Boston: Houghton Mifflin, 2000).

Civil Marriage Act of 1836, British   See MELBOURNE'S SIX ACTS.

Civil Rights Act of 1866, U.S.

First federal U.S. legislation enacted to ensure equal rights for blacks. Passed by Congress on March 13, 1866, it was vetoed by President Andrew Johnson, who charged that it was an unwarranted invasion of states' rights; Congress overrode the veto on April 9. The act, designed to overcome the restrictive BLACK CODES, conferred citizenship upon black people and granted the same civil rights to all persons born in the United States, except Native Americans. Because there was some doubt about the constitutionality of the act, Congress incorporated most of its provisions into the FOURTEENTH AMENDMENT.

Further reading: Charles S. Bullock III and Charles M. Lamb, *Implementation of Civil Rights Policy* (Monterey, Calif.: Brooks/Cole Publishing, 1984); Theodore Eisenberg, *Civil Rights Legislation* (Charlottesville, Va.: Michie Co., 1981); Harold M. Hyman and William M. Wiecek, *Equal Justice under Law: Constitutional Development, 1835–1875* (New York: Harper & Row, 1982); Leonard W. Levy and Kenneth L. Karst, eds., *Encyclopedia of the American Constitution,* 2d ed. (New York: Macmillan Reference, 2000).

Civil Rights Act of 1875, U.S.

Federal act designed to promote social equality for blacks, passed by Congress on March 1, 1875. The act sought to guarantee to all citizens—regardless of race, color, or previous condition of servitude—equal rights in public places, such as inns, theaters, restaurants, and public conveyances. Denial of these rights was punishable by payment to the aggrieved person and fine or imprisonment. Many whites refused to obey the act, and in the CIVIL RIGHTS CASE OF 1883 the Supreme Court declared the act to be unconstitutional. The 1875 act was the last federal civil rights legislation until the CIVIL RIGHTS ACT OF 1957.

Further reading: Charles S. Bullock III and Charles M. Lamb, *Implementation of Civil Rights Policy* (Monterey, Calif.: Brooks/Cole Publishing, 1984); Milton R. Konvitz, *A Century of Civil Rights* (New York: Columbia University Press, 1961); Leonard W. Levy and Kenneth L. Karst, eds., *Encyclopedia of the American Constitution,* 2d ed. (New York: Macmillan Reference, 2000).

Civil Rights Act of 1957, U.S.

Federal legislation enacted on September 9, 1957, to protect the voting and other civil rights of all American citizens, especially blacks. It established the federal Civil Rights Commission, created a civil rights division in the U.S. Department of Justice to prosecute civil rights violators, and permitted the federal government to seek injunctions to protect civil rights. The commission was authorized to investigate violations of voting and equal-protection rights under the law and to recommend new legislation to Congress. The first civil rights legislation since Reconstruction (1867–77), the act was generally considered weak; it was strengthened by the CIVIL RIGHTS ACT OF 1960.

Further reading: Carl M. Brauer, *John F. Kennedy and the Second Reconstruction* (New York: Columbia University Press, 1977); Charles S. Bullock III and Charles M. Lamb, *Implementation of Civil Rights Policy* (Monterey, Calif.: Brooks/Cole Publishing, 1984); Leonard W. Levy and Kenneth L. Karst, eds., *Encyclopedia of the American Constitution,* 2d ed. (New York: Macmillan Reference, 2000).

Civil Rights Act of 1960, U.S.

Federal legislation enacted on May 6, 1960, seeking to strengthen the U.S. CIVIL RIGHTS ACT OF 1957. The act provided criminal penalties for obstruction of court orders for school desegregation, required that election records be kept for two years and be available to the U.S. Department of Justice, provided for education of children of military personnel where schools were closed to avoid desegregation, and established a system of court-appointed voting referees to register black voters who had been denied registration in areas where there was a pattern of racial discrimination.

Further reading: Carl M. Brauer, *John F. Kennedy and the Second Reconstruction* (New York: Columbia University Press, 1977); Charles S. Bullock III and Charles M. Lamb, *Implementation of Civil Rights Policy* (Monterey, Calif.: Brooks/Cole Publishing, 1984); Leonard W. Levy and Kenneth L. Karst, eds., *Encyclopedia of the American Constitution,* 2d ed. (New York: Macmillan Reference, 2000).

Civil Rights Act of 1964, U.S.

Federal legislation enacted on July 2, 1964, providing the strongest American civil rights legislation since Reconstruction (1867–77). It prohibited discrimination in all public accommodations (including hotels, gas stations, restaurants, and theaters), if their operations affect commerce, and in any program receiving federal funds. Recipients of federal funds found to discriminate would lose that funding. The act prohibited employers from refusing to hire, from firing, or from discriminating against any individual because of race, religion, or sex, and established the Equal Employment Opportunity Commission to enforce these provisions. It also required state voting registrars to apply qualification standards equally.

Further reading: Charles S. Bullock III and Charles M. Lamb, *Implementation of Civil Rights Policy* (Monterey, Calif.: Brooks/Cole Publishing, 1984); Arthur Lawson and Lex K. Larson, *Employment Discrimination* (New York: Matthew Bender, 1981); Leonard W. Levy and Kenneth L. Karst, eds., *Encyclopedia of the American Constitution,* 2d ed. (New York: Macmillan Reference, 2000).

Civil Rights Act of 1968, U.S.   Federal legislation enacted on April 11, 1968, intended to end discrimination based on race, color, religion, or national origin in housing in the United States. The fair-housing act implemented, in three stages, prohibitions on discrimination in the sale or rental of federally owned housing and multi-unit dwellings with federally insured or underwritten mortgages, in multi-unit housing except for owner-occupied dwellings of four or fewer units, and in single-family houses sold or rented through brokers. It prohibited discrimination in the financing of housing and in brokerage services. The act was passed in the wake of the assassination of American civil rights leader Reverend Dr. Martin Luther King, Jr., on April 4, 1968.

Further reading: Charles S. Bullock III and Charles M. Lamb, *Implementation of Civil Rights Policy* (Monterey, Calif.: Brooks/Cole Publishing, 1984); James C. Harvey, *Black Civil Rights During the Johnson Administration* (Jackson: University and College Press of Mississippi, 1973); Leonard W. Levy and Kenneth L. Karst, eds., *Encyclopedia of the American Constitution*, 2d ed. (New York: Macmillan Reference, 2000).

Civil Rights Cases of 1883, U.S.   Decision of the U.S. Supreme Court that struck down the U.S. CIVIL RIGHTS ACT OF 1875 as unconstitutional. The Court, ruling on five separate cases in which blacks had been denied equal accommodations or privileges on account of color, held that the 1875 civil rights act attempted to protect social, rather than civil, rights, and that the federal government had no jurisdiction over such matters. The Court denied a claim of protection under the Thirteenth Amendment on the grounds that the discrimination had nothing to do with slavery. It also ruled that the FOURTEENTH AMENDMENT prohibited the states, not individuals, from depriving people of their civil rights. Protection against private acts of discrimination had to derive from state, not federal, statutes.

Further reading: Leonard W. Levy and Kenneth L. Karst, eds., *Encyclopedia of the American Constitution*, 2d ed. (New York: Macmillan Reference, 2000).

Civil Rights Restoration Act, U.S.   New federal legislation designed to restore civil rights protections disclaimed by the U.S. Supreme Court's 1984 opinion in *GROVE CITY COLLEGE* V. *BELL*; enacted on March 22, 1988, when both houses of Congress overrode a presidential veto. The act stated, in effect, that federal law violations (discrimination on the basis of race, sex, age, or physical handicap) by institutions receiving federal funds affected all parts of the institutions, not just those parts or programs receiving federal money. The law applied specifically to all departments and agencies of state and local governments, and universities, colleges, and public school systems, if any part, program, or activity was federally funded. Corporations and private organizations were subject to almost the same regulations. Individuals with contagious diseases, including AIDS (acquired immune deficiency syndrome), gained civil rights protection as handicapped, provided they posed no danger to others' health and safety or could not do their jobs.

Further reading: Leonard W. Levy and Kenneth L. Karst, eds., *Encyclopedia of the American Constitution*, 2d ed. (New York: Macmillan Reference, 2000).

Civil Service Law of 1933, German   Law concluded on April 7, 1933, by the Nazi (National Socialist) government of Germany, headed by Chancellor Adolf Hitler, legalizing the dismissal of all "non-Aryan" officials (those not Caucasian Gentiles). Specifically, an individual of non-Aryan descent could be legally dismissed if he or she were an official of the Reich (government) or any of the German states, communities, or districts. Also included in this group were retired officials; individuals who, as social insurance employees, had the same rights that officials possessed; unskilled officials who had commenced service during the period since the end of World War I (1914–18); and individuals with a political orientation not in harmony with that of the state. Excluded from this group were officials who had been employed since the beginning of World War I, or those who had fought during that war.

See also: ENABLING ACT OF 1933, GERMAN.

Further reading: Bronwyn R. McFarland-Icke, *Nurses in Nazi Germany: Moral Choice in History* (Princeton, N.J.: Princeton University Press, 1999).

Civil Works Emergency Relief Act, U.S.   Federal legislation enacted on February 15, 1934, that authorized $950 million for the Federal Emergency Relief Administration (FERA) to operate its civil works and direct relief program through fiscal 1935. The act authorized a federal emergency work relief program that employed 2.5 million workers by January 1935. In 1935 state and local governments resumed direct relief efforts, and the work relief program was incorporated into the Works Progress Administration.

Further reading: William E. Leuchtenburg, *Franklin D. Roosevelt and the New Deal, 1932–1940* (New York: Harper & Row, 1963).

Clarendon, Assize of   King Henry II's comprehensive assize or enactment at Clarendon in February 1166, revamping England's judicial system by instituting elaborate procedures for the detection and punishment of crime. The first of his many legislative reforms, it set up a grand (or presenting) jury, consisting of 12 "lawful" men of every hundred, with four of every village, to inform the royal circuit judges of the severe crimes committed in each district and to identify by name any accused or suspect robbers, murderers, or thieves. If found guilty by the king's justices, they were stripped of their goods and chattels and, in extreme cases, their limbs were amputated. Even if cleared, they still risked expulsion from the country if judged as men of ill repute. Feudal courts could levy fines instead of conducting trials. There were three groups of judges: circuit, "on the bench" at Westminster, and one that accompanied the king's court when it moved out of London. In 1176, many of its clauses were amended in the Assize of NORTHAMPTON.

Further reading: Carl Stephenson and Frederick George Marcham, eds., *Sources of English Constitutional History: A Selection of Documents from A.D. 600 to the Present* (New York: Harper & Row, 1937).

Clarendon, Constitutions of

King Henry II's promulgation at Clarendon in January 1164 of a series of 16 articles regulating church-state relations in England—actually, a reiteration of the customs established during the earlier reign of King Henry I. The articles, which the English bishops were forced to swear to in the presence of the barons, clamped down severely on spiritual courts and privileges. For instance, clerics could not leave the country or appeal to Rome without royal consent. Nor could the election of bishops and abbots (who had to do homage to the king) or the excommunication of laymen take place without Henry's approval. Vacant sees and abbeys and their revenues were appropriated by the king. The most controversial clause was the one stipulating that the king's officers would determine whether clergymen accused of crime should be tried in lay or spiritual courts. Those found guilty by the latter were denied church protection. The archbishop of Canterbury, Thomas à Becket, protested against these provisions and was exiled. The king, however, did not alter any of the articles.

See also: ARMS, ASSIZE OF; CLARENDON, ASSIZE OF; DARRIEN PRESENTMENT, ASSIZE OF; NORTHAMPTON, ASSIZE OF; WOODSTOCK, ASSIZE OF.

Further reading: David D. Douglas, ed., *English Historical Documents* (London: Eyre & Spottiswoode, 1950–77); *New Catholic Encyclopedia,* 17 vols. (Palatine, Ill.: Jack Heraty & Associates, 1967, repr., 1981).

Clarendon Code

Series of four acts passed by the Anglican-dominated Cavalier Parliament of King Charles II of England (during the ministry of Lord Chancellor Edward Hyde, first earl of Clarendon) to destroy the power of the Nonconformists (those who failed to conform to the Church of England). The code's name is inaccurate because Clarendon did not draft it nor did he even entirely approve of it, being, like the new king, more tolerant. Following the English Civil War and the unsuccessful 1657 revolt of the Fifth Monarchy Men (religious group expecting the imminent second coming of Christ and conspiring to murder Lord Protector Cromwell), the Anglicans became more convinced that dissenters were social revolutionaries and initiated the code's acts out of both fear and revenge. The CORPORATION ACT OF 1661 barred dissenters from municipal office, the Act of UNIFORMITY passed in 1662 barred them from church office, and the 1664 CONVENTICLE ACT and the 1665 FIVE MILE ACT se-

verely curtailed their freedom of worship. Charles tried, unsuccessfully, to mitigate the harsh effects of the code by introducing his Declarations of INDULGENCE. Despite the persecution of dissenters, the newly created world of Nonconformity gained in strength and continued to coexist with Anglicanism (the faith of the Church of England).

Further reading: George Miller, *Edward Hyde, Earl of Clarendon* (Boston: Twayne Publishers, 1983); Paul Seaward, *The Cavalier Parliament and the Reconstruction of the Old Regime, 1661–1667* (New York: Cambridge University Press, 1989).

Clark Memorandum on the Monroe Doctrine

Memorandum dated December 17, 1928, but published in 1930, written by U.S. undersecretary of state J. Reuben Clark, limiting the U.S. right to intervene in Latin American affairs. The memorandum effectively repudiated the ROOSEVELT COROLLARY to the MONROE DOCTRINE, stating that the doctrine does not concern purely inter-American relations except when the security of the United States is threatened. The Monroe Doctrine, he said, "states a case of the United States vs. Europe, and not . . . the United States vs. Latin America." For Latin American nations, the doctrine was "not an instrument of violence and oppression, but an . . . effective guaranty of their freedom, independence, and territorial integrity against the imperialistic designs of Europe."

Further reading: Carl N. Flanders and Stephen A. Flanders, *Dictionary of American Foreign Affairs* (New York: Macmillan, 1993).

Clay's Compromise Speech

Speech delivered in the U.S. Senate by Kentucky senator Henry Clay on February 5–6, 1850, outlining the main features of the COMPROMISE OF 1850 and urging its passage. In this speech Clay appealed to both the North and the South for concessions in settling differences over slavery and the newly acquired U.S. territories, and warned against Southern secession. Dissolution of the union, he argued, would fail to achieve the Southern goals of establishing slavery in the territories, restoring slavery in the District of Columbia, expediting recovery of fugitive slaves, and discouraging slaves from escaping. He claimed that states had no constitutional right to secede, and that any attempt to dissolve the union would inevitably lead to a disastrous war.

Further reading: Henry Clay, *The Papers of Henry Clay* (Lexington: University Press of Kentucky, 1959–88).

Clayton Anti-Trust Act

Federal U.S. legislation enacted on October 15, 1914, that supplemented the SHERMAN ANTI-TRUST ACT, outlawing specific practices that would "substantially lessen competition or tend to create a monopoly in any line of commerce." It prohibited exclusive sales contracts, discrimination in prices among different producers, interlocking directorates in large corporations engaged in the same business, rebates, and the acquisition of stock by one company in another. Labor unions and agricultural cooperatives were exempted from the act, on the grounds that "the labor of a human being is not a commodity or article of commerce."

Further reading: Thomas Carson, ed., *Gale Encyclopedia of U.S. Economic History* (Farmington Hills, Mich.: Gale Group, 1999); Carl Kayson and Donald F. Turner, *Antitrust Policy: An Economic and Legal Analysis* (Cambridge, Mass.: Harvard University Press, 1959); A. D. Neale and D. G. Goyder, *The Antitrust Laws of the United States of America,* 3d ed. (Cambridge, England: Cambridge University Press, 1980); Myron W. Watkins, *Public Regulation of Competitive Practices* (New York: National Industrial Conference Board, 1940).

Clayton-Bulwer Treaty   Treaty between the United States and Great Britain signed on April 19, 1850, by the American secretary of state John M. Clayton and the English ambassador Sir Henry Lytton Bulwer. The treaty between the two countries guaranteed the strict neutrality of any interoceanic canal opened across Nicaragua or elsewhere in Central America. Britain and the United States agreed that neither would seek to control any canal that might be built, nor to occupy or establish colonies in, or exercise control over, any part of Central America. Although it stabilized matters between the United States and Britain for control of the Isthmus of Panama, the treaty was later superseded by the Hay-Pauncefote Treaty of 1901.

See also: HAY-PAUNCEFOTE TREATIES.

Further reading: *Clayton-Bulwer Treaty* (Washington, D.C.: U.S. Government Printing Office, 1900); Charles L. Phillips and Alan Axelrod, eds., *Encyclopedia of Historical Treaties and Alliances,* 2 vols. (New York: Facts On File, 2001); Ira Dudley Travis, *The History of the Clayton-Bulwer Treaty* (Ann Arbor, Mich.: The Association, 1900); Mary W. Williams, *Anglo-American Isthmian Diplomacy, 1815–1915* (Baltimore, Md.: Lord Baltimore Press, 1916).

Clean Air Act of 1963, U.S.   Federal legislation, enacted in 1963, that for the first time explicitly authorized federal regulatory action to abate interstate air pollution problems in the United States. It provided federal grants to develop state and local regulatory control programs and to study motor-vehicle emissions of hydrocarbons, sulfur dioxide, and oxides of nitrogen. The act was amended in 1965 to increase federal aid to localities and federal authority to abate interstate air pollution. The amendments authorized the U.S. Department of Health, Education, and Welfare (now the departments of Health and Human Services and of Education) to establish national standards for exhaust emissions of automobiles and light trucks, and provided for international conferences on air pollution problems.

Further reading: *Clean Air Act* (Washington, D.C.: U.S. Government Printing Office, 1963).

Clean Air Act of 1970, U.S.   Federal U.S. legislation enacted on December 31, 1970, that provided for national ambient air quality standards, and set deadlines for the abatement of most mobile and stationary sources of air pollution that adversely affect public health and welfare. It established the principle that clean air must be maintained and placed authority to administer the program under the new Environmental Protection Agency (EPA). The act requires that states submit for EPA approval air quality plans to achieve federally mandated goals. The plans must assure the achievement of primary standards, to protect public health, and secondary standards, to avoid any adverse environmental effects; limit emissions; set compliance schedules; and include land-use and transportation control. The EPA can establish its own emission standards for pollutants deemed hazardous to health and for motor vehicle emissions. The act provided for vehicle testing, maintenance requirements, and recalls.

Further reading: Donald C. Bacon, Roger H. Davidson, and Morton Keller, eds., *The Encyclopedia of the United States Congress* (New York: Simon & Schuster, 1995); Environment and Natural Resources Policy Division of the Congressional Research Service of the Library of Congress for the Committee on Environment and Public Works, U.S. Senate, *A Legislative History of the Clean Air Act Amendments of 1990: Together with a Section-by-Section Index* (Buffalo, N.Y.: W. S. Hein, 1998); R. Shep Melnick, *Regulation and the Courts: The Case of the Clean Air Act* (Washington, D.C.: Brookings Institution, 1983).

Clean Air Act of 1990, U.S.   Extensive legislation signed into law by U.S. president George H. W. Bush on November 15, 1990, updating and tightening federal air pollution standards in order to curb acid rain, urban smog, and toxic chemicals. The goal of the new law, passed by Congress earlier that November, was to cut acid rain pollutants by half and eliminate most of the toxic chemical emissions from industrial plants by the end of the century, as well as reduce dirty air through more controls on pollution emitted by automobiles. Environmental groups praised the regulations, the implementation of which was expected to cost as much as $25 billion a year; industry representatives expressed much less approval.

Further reading: Donald C. Bacon, Roger H. Davidson, and Morton Keller, eds., *The Encyclopedia of the United States Congress* (New York: Simon & Schuster, 1995); Gary C. Bryner, *Blue Skies, Green Politics: The Clean Air Act of 1990* (Washington, D.C.: CQ Press, 1993).

Clean Water Restoration Act of 1966, U.S.   See WATER QUALITY ACT, U.S.

Clement, First Letter of   Official letter almost certainly written by Saint Clement I of Rome (pope and first of the apostolic fathers) and sent to the Christian Church in Corinth about A.D. 96. It reflects the Roman Church's emerging authority to intervene in the affairs of other churches, to resolve differences, and to maintain order in the church. Clement's letter argued against the ouster of elders from the Corinthian church by younger members. It declared that the Apostles and the will of God had established the church's ministerial hierarchy and structure of ecclesiastical authority. It influenced the idea of the episcopacy and the theory of the apostolic succession (the Apostles' transmission of spiritual authority through the regular ordination and uninterrupted succession of bishops in the church).

Further reading: *New Catholic Encyclopedia,* 17 vols. (Palatine, Ill.: Jack Heraty & Associates, 1967, repr., 1981).

Clement IX, Peace of (Clementine Peace, Peace of the Church)

Pope Clement IX's peace initiative, ending on January 19, 1669, the persecution of the Jansenists by the government of King Louis XIV of France (see AUGUSTINUS). Chief negotiator for the French government was the foreign minister, Hugues de Lionne. The pope skillfully broke the impasse between the two sides by coaxing the four Jansenist bishops to finally sign a formulary accepting the supremacy of the Roman Catholic Church in matters of doctrine (see CUM OCCASIONE IMPRESSIONIS LIBRI). A few months earlier, he had persuaded Jansenist leader Antoine Arnauld (see PROVINCIAL LETTERS) to use his talents in the defense of the church. Louis XIV, entangled in the War of Devolution (1667–68), readily issued a decree forbidding the persecution of the Jansenists. It was a brief reprieve, even though the Jansenists continued to be discriminated against.

Further reading: *New Catholic Encyclopedia,* 17 vols. (Palatine, Ill.: Jack Heraty & Associates, 1967, repr., 1981).

Clement XIV's Bull Suppressing the Jesuits (Dominus ac Redemptor)

Bull ordering the suppression of the Society of Jesus (the Jesuit order) issued on July 21, 1773, by Pope Clement XIV. He sought thereby to avert a possible rift (threatened by France and Spain) in the Roman Catholic Church, to prevent the mushrooming of regional churches, and to "secure the advantage of the Church and the tranquillity of the nations." In effect, he was responding to pressure from the Catholic states, particularly France and Spain. He decreed the abolition of all existing Jesuit "offices, ministries, administrations, houses, schools, and habitation in all provinces, kingdoms, and states whatsoever." Further, "we suppress all its statutes, customs, decrees, and constitutions, even when fortified by oath, apostolic confirmation, or otherwise." All Catholic states were required to accept and promulgate the bull. Only Czarina Catherine II of Russia and, until 1780, King Frederick II of Prussia, refused. Its promulgation failed to improve the Vatican's image in Europe.

Further reading: *New Catholic Encyclopedia,* 17 vols. (Palatine, Ill.: Jack Heraty & Associates, 1967, repr., 1981).

Clementine Vulgate   See VULGATE.

Clericis Laicos

Famous bull issued in February 1296 by Pope Boniface VIII, which forbade lay rulers to levy taxes on the clergy without papal consent. Both King Philip IV of France and King Edward I of England had decided to tax church property and personnel to raise revenues to wage the ongoing Anglo-French War of 1294–98. French Cistercian clergy appealed to Boniface. "Antiquity reports that laymen are exceedingly hostile to the clergy; and our experience certainly shows this to be true at present . . ." began the papal bull, which went on to state that clergy who pay taxes and secular rulers who demand or receive such taxes shall both incur excommunication. Philip responded by forbidding the export of precious metals (a major source of papal revenues), and Edward outlawed the clergy. In a papal bull of September 1296, Boniface relented, decreeing that voluntary church payments could be made to the state for defense purposes, and an apparent reconciliation occurred with Philip and Edward.

Further reading: *New Catholic Encyclopedia,* 17 vols. (Palatine, Ill.: Jack Heraty & Associates, 1967, repr., 1981).

Clermont, Proclamation of the Council of

Pope Urban II's impassioned speech at the conclusion of the Council of Clermont (November 18–27, 1095) urging those present to join forces and liberate Jerusalem from "the enemies of Christ" (the Turks)—the signal launching the First Crusade (1095–99). Speaking eloquently in his native French, Urban reminded his audience of the glory and greatness of France and her brave leaders and counseled them to bury their differences and "undertake this journey eagerly for the remission of your sins, with the assurance of the reward of imperishable glory in the kingdom of heaven." So moved were his listeners that they cried out in unison: "It is the will of God! It is the will of God!" Thanking God for this tumultous response, the Pope cautioned the old, the infirm, and unaccompanied women against joining the expedition; he advised laymen and clergy to seek the blessings of their religious superiors before setting out. August 15, 1096, was set as the departure date for the Crusade.

Further reading: Frank N. Magill, ed., *Great Events from History, Ancient and Medieval Series,* 3 vols. (Englewood Cliffs, N.J.: Salem Press, 1972); Jonathan Phillips, ed., *The First Crusade: Origins and Impact* (New York: St. Martin's Press, 1997).

Clinton's First Inaugural Address

Bill Clinton's address on January 20, 1993, to the nation as incoming U.S. president, setting an optimistic tone by using the metaphors of "spring" and celebrating the "mystery of American renewal." Citing the urgent need to invest in the future of the American people by providing health care and reducing crime, poverty, and the national debt, he said, "There is nothing wrong with America that cannot be cured by what is right with America."

Positioning himself in the tradition of former presidents George Washington, Thomas Jefferson, and Franklin Roosevelt, Clinton said, "We must bring to our task today the vision and will of those who came before us." "America must continue to lead the world," while meeting the challenges at home and abroad, he added. Finally, he urged all Americans to "answer the call."

Further reading: "Inaugural Address of United States President William J. Clinton," University of Oklahoma College of law website, available online at http://www.law.ou.edu/hist/clinton.html.

Clinton's Second Inaugural Address Inaugural address on January 20, 1997, marking the beginning of President Bill Clinton's second term in office. It recalled the successes of the past century and urged Americans to "lift our eyes towards the challenges that await us in the next century." His new government's mission was "to give all Americans a real opportunity to build better lives." However, he cautioned that there is "work that government alone cannot do," so we have to take "time from our own lives to serve others." He pledged to improve public education and its access to technology and ensure that "new miracles of medicine" reach "families too long denied." Also, he committed himself to ending "the divide of race." Closing on a conciliatory note, he urged building bridges "for every American to cross over to a blessed land of new promises."

Further reading: "The Second Inaugural Address of President William J. Clinton," University of Oklahoma Law Center website, available online at http://www.law.ou.edu/hist/clinton2.html; Transcript of "Newshour Special: Reaction to President Clinton's Inaugural Address," PBS website, available online at http://www.pbs.org/newshour/inaugural97/reaction_1-20.html.

Cobden-Chevalier Treaty Anglo-French commercial treaty signed on January 23, 1860, introducing a free-trade policy between Great Britain and France and easing tensions. British economist Richard Cobden, a member of Parliament and leader of the national movement to repeal the corn laws, proposed and negotiated the treaty with French economist Michel Chevalier. A mutual reduction of tariffs was agreed to: France reduced duties on coal and English manufactures, and Britain reciprocated by lowering duties on French wines, brandy, and other items. As a result, British exports to France doubled in value during the next decade.

Further reading: J. A. Hobson, *Richard Cobden: The International Man* (New York: Barnes & Noble, 1968); Donald Read, *Cobden and Bright: A Victorian Political Partnership* (London: Edward Arnold, 1967).

Code Frédéric Codification of legal reforms undertaken by Justice Minister (later Chancellor) Baron Samuel von Cocceji, on the orders (January 12, 1746) of King Frederick II the Great of Prussia. The laws laid the foundation of a uniform judicial system in the country. Instructed to replace "the corrupt administration of the law" with justice "swift and solid, fair, reasonable and cheap," Cocceji introduced many reforms, including fixed salaries for judges, quick resolution of pending lawsuits, verbal instead of written pleadings, and no fees until the conclusion of a case. The king renounced his right to interfere in civil cases, though all sentences required his approval; he asked that the offender's social status be considered in determining the death penalty. Cocceji died (1755) before completing the formulation of a national code or the implementation of his legal reforms. His successor, Johann von Carmer, was commissioned to continue the work. Frederick II died in 1786; the code, which he is credited with drafting, was not promulgated until 1794.

Further reading: David Fraser, *Frederick the Great: King of Prussia* (New York: Fromm International, 2001).

Code Napoléon See NAPOLEONIC CODE.

Code Noir See BLACK CODE OF LOUIS XIV.

Code of Dušan See ZABONNIK.

Code of 1650 See LUDLOW'S CODE.

Code of the Seven Parts See SEVEN PARTS, CODE OF THE.

Codex Juris Canonici See CANON LAW, CODE OF.

Coercion Acts, British See PEACE PRESERVATION ACT OF 1870, BRITISH.

Coercion Acts of 1817, British Measures passed by the British Parliament in March 1817 to cope with violent public challenges to authority by radicals and others discontented over severe unemployment, high food prices, bad harvests, and no parliamentary representation for the working class. The acts suspended habeas corpus temporarily, prohibited seditious gatherings, and punished those found guilty of undermining the allegiance of soldiers and sailors. They also extended protection to the prince regent against attempts of treason. These and other repressive measures fueled the activities of the radicals and culminated, on August 16, 1819, in the Peterloo Massacre, where several were killed and hundreds injured in a clash between workers and local militia in Manchester, during a public forum on parliamentary reform and repeal of the corn laws. The government retaliated by passing the SIX ACTS OF 1819.

Further reading: Donald Read, *Peterloo: The "Massacre" and Its Background* (Clifton, N.J.: A. M. Kelley, 1973).

Coercive Acts (Intolerable Acts, Restraining Acts) Series of laws passed by the British Parliament in 1774 at the personal wish of the king, George III. Designed largely to punish Massachusetts for the Boston Tea Party (1773) and other expressions of rebellion, they also asserted a more vigorous British colonial policy. The Coercive Acts included the BOSTON PORT ACT, the MASSACHUSETTS GOVERNMENT ACT, the ADMINISTRATION OF JUSTICE ACT, and the QUARTERING ACT OF 1774. The colonists tended to view the QUEBEC ACT as one in this series as well. Colonial reaction to the Coercive Acts was sympathetic to Massachusetts and led to the assembly of the First Continental Congress.

Further reading: George Elliott Howard, *The Preliminaries of the Revolution* (New York: AMS Press, 1970); Claude Halstead Van Tyne, *The Causes of the War of Independence* (Boston: Houghton Mifflin, 1922).

Cognac, Treaty of

Agreement of May 22, 1526, establishing the Holy League of Cognac, an alliance among France's king Francis I, Pope Clement VII, Duke Francesco II Sforza of Milan, and the dukes of Venice and Florence; it was intended to prevent Holy Roman Emperor Charles V from assuming control of Italy. England's king Henry VIII, though not a member, was sympathetic to the league. Francis saw this as an opportunity to avenge the humiliating terms of the 1526 Treaty of MADRID, forced on him by Charles after the Battle of Pavia (1525). However, the imperial army proved too strong; it expelled Sforza from Milan on July 24, 1526, and on September 21 sacked Rome. The pope's resulting peace with Charles temporarily forced him into near dependency on the emperor.

See also: CAMBRAI, PEACE OF.

Further reading: *New Catholic Encyclopedia,* 17 vols. (Palatine, Ill.: Jack Heraty & Associates, 1967, repr., 1981).

Cohens v. Virginia

U.S. Supreme Court decision issued on March 3, 1821, asserting the right of the Supreme Court to review decisions of state courts. The unanimous ruling, written by Chief Justice John Marshall, emerged from the Court's review of the conviction of P. J. and M. J. Cohen for selling federal lottery tickets in Virginia in violation of state law. When the Cohens appealed their conviction in federal court, Virginia claimed that the Supreme Court had no jurisdiction, under the ELEVENTH AMENDMENT. By hearing the case, the Supreme Court, using the principle of national supremacy, firmly established the right of federal courts to review state court decisions concerning constitutional issues. The Cohens' conviction, however, was upheld.

Further reading: Albert J. Beveridge, *The Life of John Marshall* (Holmes Beach, Fla.: Gaunt, 1916, repr., 1997); Charles Grove Hains, *The Role of the Supreme Court in American Government and Politics, 1789–1835* (Berkeley: University of California Press, 1994); Robert J. Janusik, ed., *Encyclopedia of the American Judicial System,* vol. 1 (New York: Charles Scribner's Sons, 1987); Leonard W. Levy and Kenneth L. Karst, eds.,

Encyclopedia of the American Constitution, 2d ed. (New York: Macmillan Reference, 2000).

Coinage Act of 1792, U.S. (Mint Act)

Federal U.S. legislation enacted on April 2, 1792, that provided for a new national currency, established both gold and silver as national monetary standards, and created a national mint. The act established a decimal system of coinage, with the dollar as the basic monetary unit. The value of gold was set at 15 times the value of silver; the gold dollar was valued at 24.75 grains of gold and the silver dollar at 371.25 grains of silver. The act followed the recommendations of U.S. secretary of the treasury Alexander Hamilton's report to Congress of 1791.

Further reading: Alonzo Barton Hepburn, *History of Coinage and Currency in the United States and the Perennial Contest for Sound Money* (New York: Greenwood Press, 1968); Arthur Nussbaum, *A History of the Dollar* (New York: Columbia University Press, 1957).

Coinage Act of 1873, U.S. (Demonetization Act)

Act passed by Congress on February 12, 1873, that demonetized silver, omitting from the coinage the standard silver dollar of 412.5 grains. This demonetization made gold the sole standard for U.S. currency, thus ending legal bimetallism. The act came at a time when silver supplies were increasing as a result of new discoveries in the West. Silver interests, calling the act the "crime of '73," charged that dropping silver dollars from the coinage was part of a gold conspiracy, but most historians discount that charge.

Further reading: Alonzo Barton Hepburn, *History of Coinage and Currency in the United States and the Perennial Contest for Sound Money* (New York: Greenwood Press, 1968); Arthur Nussbaum, *A History of the Dollar* (New York: Columbia University Press, 1957).

Colbert's Letter on Mercantilism

French finance minister Jean-Baptiste Colbert's letter of 1664 to the town and people of Marseilles, France, explaining his mercantilist policies. Writing on behalf of King Louis XIV, Colbert announced the establishment of a council, which, meeting fortnightly, would consider "all the interest of merchants and the means conducive to the revival of commerce." An annual fund of 1 million livres (old French coins) would be reserved "for the encouragement of manufactures and the increase of navigation," and assistance given to those seeking to start or revitalize industries. Public highways would be repaired and maintained, river tolls gradually phased out, commercial freedom granted to French traders overseas, and maritime traders substantially subsidized. Finally, he urged that the contents of his letter be publicized throughout Marseilles so that traders and merchants "may be the more desirous of applying themselves to commerce." Colbert hoped that these policies would help reenergize France's sagging industries and finances.

Further reading: Glenn J. Ames, *Colbert, Mercantilism, and the French Quest for Asian Trade* (DeKalb: Northern Illinois University Press, 1996); Charles W. Cole, *Colbert and a Century of French Mercantilism* (New York: Colombia University Press, 1939).

Coleman v. Miller U.S. Supreme Court decision issued on June 5, 1939, limiting judicial authority over the process of ratifying constitutional amendments. The case concerned the validity of the Kansas senate's ratification in 1937 of a child labor amendment passed by Congress in 1924 (the state had rejected the amendment in 1925). The ratification was challenged on the grounds that the earlier rejection was final and that the approval had not occurred within a "reasonable" period. The Supreme Court disallowed both arguments, declaring that Congress, not the Court, should decide both issues. The amendment process, the Court declared, was political, "not subject to judicial guidance, control or interference at any point."

Further reading: Leonard W. Levy and Kenneth L. Karst, eds., *Encyclopedia of the American Constitution*, 2d ed. (New York: Macmillan Reference, 2000).

Collector v. Day U.S. Supreme Court decision of April 3, 1871, that held invalid a federal income tax on the salary of a state official. Massachusetts probate judge Day, who had paid the Civil War income tax upon his salary under protest, sued to recover it and won in the U.S. circuit court for Massachusetts. The tax collector then sued out a writ of error. By an 8-1 decision the Supreme Court ruled that Congress could not levy a tax upon the salary of a state judicial officer. A large area of intergovernmental tax immunities grew from this decision until 1939, when the Court ruling in *GRAVES* V. *NEW YORK EX REL. O'KEEFE* ended such immunities.

Further reading: Lawrence Boyd Evans, *Cases on American Constitutional Law*, 7th ed. (Chicago: Callaghan, 1957); Leonard W. Levy and Kenneth L. Karst, eds., *Encyclopedia of the American Constitution*, 2d ed. (New York: Macmillan Reference, 2000).

Cologne Declaration Statement issued on January 26, 1989, by 167 prominent Roman Catholic theologians from West Germany, Switzerland, Austria, and the Netherlands, criticizing Pope John Paul II's teachings, recent conservative bishop appointments, attempts to control scholars, and opposition to artificial birth control. The seven-page tract in German, whose eminent signatories included Fathers Hans Küng and Edward Schillebeeckx, complained of some "antagonism from above, which heightens the conflicts in the church by means of rigid discipline." The Catholic priests and professors particularly upbraided the pontiff's belief that criticism of the church's birth-control ban meant an attack on the "fundamental pillars of Christian teaching." They maintained that the 1968 papal encyclical *HUMANAE VITAE* did not absolutely forbid artificial forms of contraception.

See also: INSTRUCTION ON THE ECCLESIAL VOCATION OF THE THEOLOGIAN.

Further reading: Hermann Haring, *Hans Kung: Breaking Through* (London: SCM Press, 1998); William A. Herr, *Catholic Thinkers in the Clear: Giants of Catholic Thought from Augustus to Rahner* (Allen, Tex.: Thomas More Press, 1985); Philip Kennedy, *Schillebeeckx* (Collegeville, Minn.: Liturgical Press, 1993).

Colombian Act of 1811 See FEDERATION OF THE UNITED PROVINCES OF NEW GRANADA, ACT OF.

Colombian Agrarian Reform Law of 1973 Legislation passed by the Colombian Congress in 1973, calling for measures to be taken in order to increase the productivity of land in Colombia. The legislation provided that the Agrarian Reform Institute would be bailed out of bankruptcy; that the amount of land possessed by any one individual would be reduced; that the individual would have three years to return the land to productivity; and that badly operated estates would be expropriated. The legislation became a controversial issue among liberals, who supported the reforms, and conservatives, who supported the landowners.

Further reading: Robert H. Davis, *Historical Dictionary of Colombia* (Metuchen, N.J.: Scarecrow Press, 1977).

Colombian Constitution of 1821 Constitution drafted at the Congress of Cúcuta in 1821 for the newly established state of Gran, or Great, Colombia (which eventually incorporated Venezuela, New Granada, and Quito, after their liberation from Spanish control). The government was reorganized as a centralized representative republic (with Simón Bolívar as president); power was divided into legislative, executive, and judicial branches. The constitution called for a bicameral legislature elected from the three major regions of the republic. While the constitution was bold and visionary, it also was sufficently realistic in its compromise of divergent points of view.

See also: ANGOSTURA, CONGRESS OF.

Further reading: Robert H. Davis, *Historical Dictionary of Colombia* (Metuchen, N.J.: Scarecrow Press, 1977).

Colombian Constitution of 1886 Constitution drafted (during the rule of President Rafael Núñez) by a national council (assuming the powers of a constituent convention) meeting at Bogotá in 1885, and promulgated in 1886. Under the constitution, a centralized republic was established; the states were abolished and replaced by administrative departments; the Roman Catholic Church was declared to be the official church, thereby restoring to it most of the powers and privileges it had possessed in colonial times; and the president of the republic was to be elected for a term of six years, directly by the people. The Colombian Constitution, a great victory for clerics and conservatives, remained in effect until 1936.

Further reading: Robert H. Davis, *Historical Dictionary of Columbia* (Metuchen, N.J.: Scarecrow Press, 1977).

Colombo Plan for Cooperative Development

Report prepared by the British Commonwealth Consultative Committee and published as a White Paper on November 28, 1950, containing proposals designed to facilitate the economic development of the south and southeast Asian nations of India, Pakistan, Ceylon (Sri Lanka), Malaya, Singapore, and North Borneo (including Brunei and Sarawak). The goals, as projected by the reports' authors (experts from seven Eastern and Western countries of the Commonwealth), were to increase food production in these nations by 10 percent, or by 6 million tons; electricity generating capacity by 67 percent, or 1.1 million kilowatts; the amount of land under cultivation by 33 percent, or 13 million acres; and the amount of land under irrigation by 17 percent, or 13 million acres. The cost of the plan was estimated to be £1.868 billion ($5.04 billion), which the countries hoped to obtain from their sterling balances in London in addition to private investment and international bank loans. The plan was to take effect July 1, 1951. Its object was to lessen the appeal of communism in the region. The plan's organization was launched from and headquartered in Ceylon's capital of Colombo.

Further reading: Ademola Adeleke, *Ties Without Strings?: The Colombo Plan and the Geopolitics of International Aid, 1950–1980* (Ottawa: National Library of Canada, 1999); Colombo Plan Consultative Committee, *The Colombo Plan for Cooperative Economic and Social Development in Asia and the Pacific* (Colombo, Sri Lanka: Colombo Plan Bureau, 1979).

Columbus's First Voyage Journal

Methodical record or log kept by Christopher Columbus during his first voyage to the New World (America), from August 3, 1492, to March 15, 1493, and turned over to King Ferdinand II and Queen Isabella I upon his return to Palos, Spain. Columbus wrote that he carried a letter of introduction for the ruler of China (whom he later believed he had come upon), that he had been given a noble title, that he had been granted the right to rule any conquests he made, and that he had seized several natives to take back to Spain. He also spoke of acquiring great territories and riches for Spain, as well as converting the heathen natives to Christianity, among other commentaries. The journal survives as an abstract made by the Spanish missionary and historian Bartolomé de Las Casas, a contemporary of Columbus. Several copies were made of the journal, but none are known to exist today; Las Casas had consulted a copy belonging to Columbus's eldest son, Diego. Similar records of Columbus's subsequent voyages have not been found.

Further reading: Christopher Columbus, *Journal of the First Voyage* (Warminster, England: Aris & Phillips, 1989).

Combes's Bill (French Law of Separation)

Parliamentary statute passed on December 9, 1905, proclaiming separation of church and state, and guaranteeing freedom of conscience. The new law nullified the close relationship between the state and the Catholic Church established by the CONCORDAT OF 1801. All religious groups were required to form private holding corporations to own and manage church property. The measure accomplished its purpose of curtailing the political authority of the church, but also resulted in a concomitant increase in the church's spiritual authority. The bill was framed by premier Emile Combes, but was not passed until almost a year after his resignation in January 1905.

See also: ASSOCIATIONS LAW, FRENCH.

Further reading: Paul Sabatier and Robert E. Dell, *Disestablishment in France* (New York: C. Scribner's Sons, 1906).

Combines Investigation Act of 1910, Canadian

See CANADIAN COMBINES INVESTIGATION ACT OF 1910.

Common Man's Charter, Ugandan

"Charter for the Common Man" announced on October 8, 1969, by Uganda's President Milton Obote, outlining his plans for the country's future development. In an attempt to stabilize the economy after a year of political unrest, Obote declared his government's commitment to closing the ranks between rich and poor. He pledged stringent government controls and nationalization of the means of production and distribution, thereby vesting control in the people. According to his socialist charter, cooperative banks would be established and local and foreign investments used for priority projects. Shortly afterwards, the Banking Act was enacted and required foreign banks to be incorporated in Uganda and to have a paid-up capital of $2.76 million, before obtaining a license to operate.

Further reading: Tertit Aasland, *On the Move to the Left in Uganda, 1969–1971: The Common Man's Charter. Dissemination and Attitude* (Uppsala, Sweden: Nordiska Afrikainstitutet, 1974).

Common Order, Book of (Knox's Liturgy, Order of Geneva)

Scottish theologian John Knox's handbook of worship originally drafted for the reformed English congregations in exile in Geneva, Switzerland, in 1556. It was prescribed by the Scottish General Assembly in 1562, revised in 1564, and used in this form until 1645, when it was replaced by the Westminister Assembly's *Directory of Public Worship*. In the liturgy, Knox attempted to establish a general system of public worship with the minister himself saying most of the prayers (in the Calvinist tradition). Unlike England's *Book of COMMON PRAYER*, the liturgy did not impose specific prayers on the people; it contained procedures for the sacraments and for Sunday and weekday services, among others. Overall, it laid down broad guidelines for public worship in the reformed faith used in the Protestant Church of Scotland.

See also: DISCIPLINE, FIRST BOOK OF.

Further reading: Church of Scotland, *Book of Common Order* (Richmond, Va.: Outlook Publishing, 1979).

Common Prayer, Book of   Anglican Church's official service book for priests and worshipers, presenting, in one compact volume, the morning and evening prayers, the rules for administering sacraments and other rites, the Psalter, and the Ordinal (added in 1552). Compiled by Thomas Cranmer (the archbishop of Canterbury) and others from a host of Latin manuals, it was introduced in 1549 as the First Prayer Book of King Edward VI and imposed nationwide via his Act of Uniformity in 1549. Conservatives and radicals opposed it as being too vague, so it was reissued in 1552 with major revisions. Following a brief interlude of Roman Catholicism (1553–58), the same prayer book was restored by Queen Elizabeth I in 1559 by another Act of Uniformity. Puritan protests against this prayer book led to another revision by a church convocation, issued via the 1662 Act of Uniformity. A later attempt (1927–28) at revising the test ended in failure. However, the Anglican Church and the Protestant Episcopal Church in the United States developed and adopted a modern liturgical version of the book in the late 1970s.

See also: *DISCIPLINE, FIRST BOOK OF*; UNIFORMITY, ACTS OF.

Further reading: Church of England, *The Book of Common Prayer and Administration of the Sacraments and Other Rites and Ceremonies of the Church According to the Use of the Church of England* (New York: Holt, 1992); G. J. Cuming, *The Godly Order: Texts and Studies Relating to the Book of Common Prayer* (London: Alcuin Club, 1983).

Common Sense   Pamphlet written by Thomas Paine and published in Philadelphia in January 1776; it strongly urged Americans to claim independence from Britain. Paine argued that reconciliation was impossible and described some of the disadvantages suffered by the American colonies through their connection with Britain. He asserted that the colonies tended to get entangled in foreign wars because they acquired Britain's enemies and had also recently become the target of Britain's hostilities. He argued that it was impossible for Britain to govern effectively from such a distance and that the colonies were capable of governing themselves. He described a possible plan of representative government and urged formation of a constitutional convention. *Common Sense,* with 120,000 copies circulated in its first three months, was highly influential in advancing the idea of American independence.

Further reading: Henry Steele Commager and Richard B. Morris, eds., *The Spirit of 'Seventy-Six: The Story of the American Revolution as Told by Participants* (New York: Bonanza Books, 1958, rep., 1983); Moncure Daniel Conway, ed., *The Writings of Thomas Paine*, 4 vols. (New York: B. Franklin, 1969).

***Common Sense about the War,* Shaw's**   Controversial pamphlet by the noted British playwright George Bernard Shaw, written in 1914, criticizing Britain and her Allies' role in World War I, which had just begun. It first appeared as a supplement to the *New Statesman* on November 14, 1914, and earned him instant notoriety. In it, he charged that the Allies, along with Germany, were equally to blame for the war. In the early days of the war, it was a courageous statement to make; soon, his antiwar speeches began to be censored and he was stripped of his membership in the Dramatists' Club. The war proved to be the turning point of his prolific career, for afterward his writing turned pessimistic and tragic comic in general, a reaction to his disillusionment with democracies.

Further reading: Harold Owen, *Common Sense about the Shaw: Being a Candid Criticism of "Common Sense about the War" by Bernard Shaw* (London: G. Allen & Unwin, 1915); Bernard Shaw, *Common Sense about the War* (London: Statesman Pub., 1915).

Commonwealth v. Hunt   Decision of the Supreme Judicial Court of Massachusetts issued in 1842, marking the first legal recognition of American labor unions as lawful institutions, so long as the methods of achieving their ends were "honorable and peaceful." Massachusetts Chief Justice Lemuel Shaw also ruled that strikes for a closed shop were legal. The case involved the conviction for criminal conspiracy of members of the Boston Journeymen Bootmakers Society who called a strike against a manufacturer for employing a nonmember. The decision reversed previous rulings declaring unions to be unlawful conspiracies and improved the legal standing of unions in other states as well.

Further reading: Duke Nordlinger Stern, *Cases in Labor Law* (Columbus, Ohio: Grid, 1977).

Communications Decency Act, U.S.   Legislation enacted by the U.S. Congress on February 1, 1996, to prevent the sending of obscene or harassing messages via the Internet. Part of the Telecommunications Act of 1996, the act amended the Communications Act of 1934, which outlawed obscene and harassing telephone calls, by also outlawing indecent or unwelcome messages sent by electronic mail. The act was introduced by Senators James Exon of Nebraska and Slade Gorton of Washington and provided for fines and jail terms for the originators of such messages, as well as for the Internet service providers, commercial online services, bulletin board systems, and electronic mail providers that transmitted or handled the messages. In essence, the act required Internet companies to police and censor the untold billions of messages being sent by their customers. The companies decried the act because it imposed a Herculean task upon them, while civil liberties groups attacked the act on the grounds that it violated First Amendment rights to freedom of speech and Fifth Amendment rights to avoid self-incrimination. The American Civil Liberties Union and 19 other libertarian organizations challenged the act in federal court in a case known as *ACLU* v. *Reno I,* or the CDA Case. On June 26,

1997, the Supreme Court voted 7-2 to invalidate the act because it violated the First Amendment's guarantee of freedom of speech.

Further reading: Yaman Akdeniz, *Sex on the Net: The Dilemma of Policing Cyberspace* (London: South Street, 1999); Solveig Bernstein, *Beyond the Communications Decency Act: Constitutional Lessons of the Internet* (Washington, D.C.: Cato Institute, 1996); Lilian Edwards and Charlotte Waelde, eds., *Law and the Internet: Regulating Cyberspace* (Evanston, Ill.: Hart Pub., 1997); Bernard D. Reams and William H. Manz, *Federal Communications Law: A Legislative History of the Telecommunications Act of 1996 . . . Including the Communications Decency Act* (Buffalo, N.Y.: W. S. Hein, 1997).

Communist Control Act of 1954, U.S.

Federal legislation, enacted on August 24, 1954, that outlawed the Communist Party. It declared the party an "instrumentality of conspiracy" to overthrow the U.S. government and a clear and present danger to the nation's security. It strengthened the MCCARRAN ACT by providing severe penalties for communists who did not register, refused collective-bargaining powers to communist-controlled unions, and removed the legal "rights, privileges, and immunities" of the party. Though criticized by some commentators as repressive, the act was widely supported by U.S. congressional liberals and conservatives alike.

Further reading: M. J. Heale, *American Anticommunism: Combating the Enemy Within, 1830–1970* (Baltimore: Johns Hopkins University Press, 1990); Robert Justin Goldstein, *Political Repression in Modern America: From 1870 to the Present* (Urbana: University of Illinois Press, 1978); Leonard W. Levy and Kenneth L. Karst, eds., *Encyclopedia of the American Constitution*, 2d ed. (New York: Macmillan Reference, 2000).

Communist Information Bureau (Cominform), Manifesto Establishing the

Declaration made by the communist parties of nine European countries on October 4, 1947, following a conference at Wilcza Gora, Poland, and forming the Communist Information Bureau (Cominform), whose purpose was to coordinate the policies and activities of the communist parties of the Soviet Union, Yugoslavia, Bulgaria, Romania, Czechoslovakia, Hungary, Poland, France, and Italy. The manifesto declared that two opposing political camps had arisen in the world since World War II (1939–45): the American-British imperialistic, capitalistic forces, with plans to unleash a new war, dominate the world, and crush democratic movements, versus the anti-imperialistic, democratic forces. It further stated that the United States aimed to subjugate Europe, China, Indonesia, and South America economically and politically. The communist parties must "refuse to be intimidated and black-mailed" and must fight subjugation of their countries; they must also beware of traitorous rightist socialists, "who aim at hiding the true face of imperialism behind the mask of democracy and socialist

phraseology." In 1956 the Cominform was dissolved by Soviet initiative.

Further reading: Giuliano Procacci, ed., *The Cominform: Minutes of the Three Conferences, 1947/1948/1949* (Milan, Italy: Fondazione Giangiacomo Feltrinelli, 1994).

Communist International (Comintern), Constitution and Rules of the

Formal principles and laws adopted by the Sixth World Congress in Moscow in 1928, governing the affairs of the Communist International (Comintern) or Third International, an organization of national communist parties formed in Moscow in March 1919. The constitution manifested the Comintern's goals of the internationalization of communism and the institutionalization of the idea of world revolution, developing outward from Moscow. It outlined the Comintern's structure, methods, membership, and operations. The World Congress was identified as the "supreme body of the Communist International," and the congress, consisting of representatives of all parties and organizations allied with the Comintern, was to convene once every two years. An executive committee, elected by the congress, was to rule when the congress was not in session. At the Second World Congress, which met in Moscow in 1920, the conditions for joining the Comintern had been adopted by delegates from 37 countries. Minor policies were initiated in the Third, Fourth, and Fifth World Congresses (in 1921, 1922, and 1924, respectively). Only one World Congress (the Seventh and last) was held between 1928 and 1943, when Soviet dictator Joseph V. Stalin officially dissolved the Comintern (whose goals at the time were tertiary to the defeat of Fascism and Nazism).

Further reading: Jane Degras, *Communist International Documents, 1919–1943* (London: Frank Cass, 1971); John Riddell, ed., *Founding the Communist International: Proceedings and Documents of the First Congress, March 1919* (New York: Pathfinder Press, 1988).

Communist Manifesto (Manifesto of the Communist Party, Manifest der Kommunistischen Partei)

Tract or pamphlet written in 1847 for a meeting of the Communist League (in London) by the German social philosopher Karl Marx and his associate and compatriot Friedrich Engels; the authors attempted to explain scientifically how society had developed to a point when a classless society would begin to emerge. According to the authors, the workers of their day, who had been exposed to the vicissitudes of the capitalist market and who had been exploited by it, had grown to such numbers as to be able to unite and together abolish all ownership of property by the bourgeoisie, and to place, forcibly if necessary, the machinery that controlled the economy in the hands of the workers. Ultimately, the authors claimed, the state would be ruled by the workers, and a socialist, classless society would emerge. Written in German and published as a pamphlet in 1848, the *Communist Manifesto* was eventually translated into almost every language, to stir social change in many parts of the world. Its famous final line is usually rendered as "Workers of the world, unite!"

Further reading: Karl Marx and Friedrich Engels, *The Communist Manifesto: A Modern Edition* (New York: Verso Books, 1998).

Compiègne Armistice   Armistice concluded in the forest of Compiègne in France (the site of the signing of the armistice formalizing Germany's defeat in World War I) on June 22, 1940, by General Charles Huntziger of France and Colonel General Wilhelm Keitel, Hitler's plenipotentiary, of Germany; it formalized France's capitulation to German forces during World War II (1939–45). The peace terms, which were not negotiable, called for an immediate cessation of hostilities; for the demobilization and disarmament of French forces; the release of all German prisoners of war; France's cession to Germany of northern, northeastern, and western France, including Paris; and for Germany's occupation of this territory at France's expense. The French government was permitted to choose whether it preferred to rule in the unoccupied territory or in Paris and was permitted to maintain a small force in the unoccupied territory. The armistice was to take effect upon the conclusion of a similar agreement between France and Italy and was to remain in effect until a formal peace was signed.

See also: FRANCO-GERMAN PACT OF 1938.

Further reading: Avalon Project, Yale University Law School, *Franco-German Armistice: June 25, 1940*, available online at http://www.yale.edu/lawweb/avalon/wwi/frgearm.htm; Brenton H. Smith, *The Collapse of France in World War II and the Armistice Conventions of June 1940* (Ann Arbor, Mich.: University Microfilms International, 1959).

Compromise of 1850   Set of bills passed by the U.S. Congress in September 1850 to settle several slavery issues and preserve the Union. By 1850 the United States was divided over the question of slavery in new U.S. territories and California, the slave trade, and fugitive slave laws. The "great compromiser," Senator Henry Clay of Kentucky, proposed a plan that would admit California as a free state, admit New Mexico and Utah without determining their slavery status (leaving the matter to popular sovereignty), prohibit the slave trade in the District of Columbia, and provide the stricter FUGITIVE SLAVE LAW OF 1850. The compromise merely postponed final settlement of the slavery issue.

Further reading: Holman Hamilton, *Prologue to Conflict: The Crisis and Compromise of 1850* (Lexington: University of Kentucky Press, 1964); John Niven, *John C. Calhoun and the Price of Union* (Baton Rouge: Louisiana State University Press, 1988); David M. Potter, *The Impending Crisis, 1848–1861* (New York: Harper & Row, 1976); James Ford Rhodes, *History of the United States from the Compromise of 1850 to the*

McKinley-Bryan Campaign of 1896 (Port Washington, N.Y.: Kennikat Press, 1919, repr., 1967).

Compromise of 1867   See AUSGLEICH.

Compromise of 1107, English (Compromise of London, Compromise of Bec)   Compromise agreement between England's king Henry I and Archbishop Anselm of Canterbury, ratified in London on August 1, 1107, after the compromise over the investiture controversy had been reached on August 15, 1106, at the abbey of Bec in Normandy, France. Under threat of excommunication and preoccupied with his Norman campaign, Henry I formally surrendered the royal right of investiture—hitherto, a symbolic gesture of the fiefs granted. The Catholic Church conceded in leaving the choice of prelates to the king. He was also entitled to receive homage and secular duties for the temporalities he had conferred on the prelacies. Intended as a temporary measure, the compromise permanently resolved the controversy and healed a 12-year rift with the church. On August 11, the archbishop responded by consecrating prelates to fill vacancies in the English Church. The compromise set a precedent and was to have important repercussions on church-state relations in other countries.

See also: CORONATION CHARTER OF HENRY I.

Further reading: Paschal Baumstein, *Anselm's Intellect and the Embrace of Bec* (Belmont, N.C.: Belmont Abbey, 1988); Norman F. Cantor, *Church, Kingship, and Lay Investiture in England, 1089–1135* (New York: Octagon Books, 1969).

Comstock Law   Statute passed by Congress in 1873 prohibiting the sending of obscene materials through the U.S. mails. The act derived its popular name from Anthony Comstock, an anti-obscenity crusader who lobbied for the bill. Comstock, a founder of the New York Society for the Suppression of Vice, also served as a special agent of the U.S. Post Office department, helping to enforce the act. The bill essentially allowed law enforcement agencies themselves to determine what constituted obscenity. Comstock's crusade, called "licensed bigotry" by some critics, caused thousands of arrests and the destruction of 160 tons of printed materials.

Further reading: Anna L. Bates, *Weeder in the Garden of the Lord: Anthony Comstock's Life and Career* (Lanham, Md.: University Press of America, 1995); Marjorie Heins, *Not in Front of the Children: "Indecency," Censorship and the Innocence of Youth* (New York: Hill & Wang, 2001).

Concord, Formula of   See TORGAU, BOOK OF.

Concordat of 1482   Pope Sixtus IV's agreement in 1482 with King Ferdinand V and Queen Isabella I of Castile and León, establishing royal control over appointments to vacant benefices. The issue surfaced in 1479 when the pope appointed his nephew, Cardinal San Giorgio, to the benefice of

Cuenca, overriding the wishes of Isabella, who wanted to bestow it on her chaplain, Alfonso de Burgos, in exchange for the bishopric of Córdoba. Following a bitter debate and the king's threat to summon an ecclesiastical council, Sixtus IV reluctantly agreed to appoint to the higher echelons of the Castilian Church only those who had been nominated by the Spanish monarchs. As such, the agreement was quite limited in scope, but it represented another successful attempt to assert royal control over ecclesiastical affairs.

Further reading: Gregorio Leti, *Il Nipotismo di Roma, or, The History of the Popes Nephews from the Time of Sixtus IV, Anno 1471, to the Death of the Late Pope Alexander VII, Anno 1667: . . .*, trans. William Aglionby (Ann Arbor Mich.: University Microfilms International, 1980).

Concordat of 1741

Papal agreement with Naples concluded on June 2, 1741, by Pope Benedict XIV with King Charles of Naples (later Charles III of Spain), granting major concessions to Naples. Guided by the reformist lawyer Bernardo Tanucci, Charles was able to eradicate some of the worst ecclesiastical abuses. He secured the setting-up of mixed (half lay, half clerical) law courts (thus allowing laymen to judge ecclesiastical issues and persons), levied taxes on the clergy (though at half the rate), and reduced their numbers from 100,000 to 81,000. The pope also granted the *placet*, by which the king could prevent the Vatican's decrees from taking automatic effect in his kingdom. These concessions, inspired no doubt by the antipapal writings of the prominent Neapolitan lawyer Pietro Giannone, did not bring the desired peace and the excesses of the wealthy and privileged Neapolitan clergy continued.

Further reading: Renee Haynes, *Philosopher King: The Humanist Pope Benedict XIV* (London: Weidenfeld & Nicolson, 1970).

Concordat of 1753

Papal agreement with Spain concluded on January 11, 1753, between Pope Benedict XIV and King Ferdinand VI of Spain, ending a rift of several decades by securing major concessions for Spain. These were achieved largely through the astute diplomacy of the Spanish minister, the marquis of Ensenada. Pope Benedict (reigned 1740–58) transferred to the king complete control over the temporal affairs of the Spanish church, including appointments and income. He also gave up his authority of declaring exemption for church lands in Spain. While this move enhanced royal absolutism in Spain, it did not please the Spanish clergy; some bishops openly expressed their resistance, risking censure and perhaps dismissal. The complete subordination of the Spanish church to the state was not realized until the reign of Charles III, who succeeded Ferdinand VI.

Further reading: Renee Haynes, *Philosopher King: The Humanist Pope Benedict XIV* (London: Weidenfeld & Nicolson, 1970).

Concordat of 1801

Concordat concluded between Pope Pius VII and First Consul Napoléon Bonaparte of France on July 16, 1801, through which the Roman Catholic Church and the revolutionary French government became reconciled. Through the document Napoléon recognized the Catholic faith as the religion of the majority of the French people, at the same time, however, proclaiming freedom of conscience; Napoléon secured the right to appoint bishops, with his appointments to be confirmed by the pope; the church abandoned its claims to confiscated ecclesiastical lands; the clergy were to be paid by the government; and the pope was given control of the Papal States, but without Bologna, Ferrara, and Romagna. The document thus restored prestige to the church in France and gave the French state a degree of control over the papacy.

See also: ORGANIC ARTICLES OF APRIL 8, FRENCH.

Further reading: Friedrich Nippold, *The Papacy in the XIXth Century* (New York: Putnam, 1900); Margaret M. O'Dwyer, *The Papacy in the Age of Napoleon and the Restoration: Pius VII, 1800–23* (Lanham, Md.: University Press of America, 1985).

Concordat of 1851

Papal-Spanish agreement concluded on March 16, 1851, resolving, without reference to the Spanish Cortes (parliament), the long-standing grievances between Spain and the Vatican (Pope Pius IX). Spain adopted Catholicism as her official religion "to the exclusion of all others" and promised to contribute toward the maintenance of the clergy, who recovered control over education and censorship and could settle marital disputes without civil mediation. In return, the Spanish crown secured the right to appoint bishops. The Vatican accepted the secularization of church lands confiscated in the 1830s. Three religious orders were reestablished. Spanish public opinion regarding the concordat was divided; the radicals felt too many concessions were granted, the Carlists felt there were not enough.

Further reading: Friedrich Nippold, *The Papacy in the XIXth Century* (New York: Putnam, 1900).

Concordat of 1855

Concordat concluded in August 1855 between Austria's emperor Francis Joseph (under the influence of Roman Catholic cardinal Joseph Othmar von Rauscher) and Pope Pius IX, providing for a significant increase of power and influence of the Roman Catholic Church in certain secular matters over which it had had no control for about a century. Through the agreement the church was granted control over censorship; jurisdiction in marriage; protection of the state; and a tremendous amount of power in education, in that its clergy had the right to ensure that nothing would be taught that was in conflict with the teachings of the Catholic Church. The conclusion of the concordat occurred at a time when reactionary policies were flourishing in response to revolutionary and nationalistic unrest throughout the ethnically diverse Austrian Empire. Austria annulled the concordat following the issue of the DOGMA OF PAPAL IN-FALLIBILITY in 1870.

Further reading: Friedrich Nippold, *The Papacy in the XIXth Century* (New York: Putnam, 1900).

Concordat of 1862 Papal-Ecuadoran agreement concluded in Rome on September 26, 1862, by President Gabriel García Moreno of Ecuador and Pope Pius IX, providing (in its 25 articles) for the Roman Catholic Church's enjoyment of certain privileges in the republic of Ecuador. The document's more significant terms included the state's recognition of the Roman Catholic religion as the state religion; the church's right to oversee all schools, both public and private; and the state's renunciation of the right of patronage (by which it had exercised ultimate control over all ecclesiastical decisions and actions). The law, which was sponsored by pro-clerical president Moreno, aroused intense opposition among liberals. The concordat remained in force until 1906.

Further reading: Albert William Bork and George Maier, *Historical Dictionary of Ecuador* (Metuchen, N.J.: Scarecrow Press, 1973); Friedrich Nippold, *The Papacy in the XIXth Century* (New York: Putnam, 1900).

Concordat of 1887 Papal-Colombian agreement (consisting of 33 articles) concluded in Rome on December 31, 1887, by Pope Leo XIII and President Rafael Núñez of the republic of Colombia, providing for the Roman Catholic Church's enjoyment of special privileges in the republic. The document's more significant terms included Colombia's recognition of the Roman Catholic religion as the state religion; the church's right to supervise education; the exemption of the clergy from military service; the church's right to own property; and the Vatican's right to nominate candidates, subject to governmental approval, to vacant ecclesiastical sees. Because many Latin American governments had laws that limited the power of the church, the papacy considered the concordat to be a model document.

Further reading: Robert H. David, *Historical Dictionary of Columbia* (Metuchen, N.J.: Scarecrow Press, 1977); Friedrich Nippold, *The Papacy in the XIXth Century* (New York: Putnam, 1900).

Concordat of 1933 German-papal agreement concluded on July 20, 1933, between Vice Chancellor Franz von Papen of Germany and Secretary of State Eugenio Pacelli (later Pope Pius XII) of the Vatican, providing for an alliance that was to last until 1945. Through the concordat the Roman Catholic Church had the right to administer her own schools; the Holy See (the pope's office or court) had the right to publish freely and to communicate freely with all believers in Germany; priests were required to have German citizenship and to have received their training in either Germany or Rome; bishops were required to swear allegiance to the German state before assuming their offices; and the Holy See was to submit to the state for its approval the names of all candidates to the church's bishoprics and archbishoprics.

See also: LATERAN TREATIES OF 1929.

Further reading: Carlo Falconi, *The Popes in the Twentieth Century: From Pius X to John XXIII* (Boston: Little, Brown, 1967).

Concordat of 1964 Papal-Hungarian agreement signed in Budapest on September 15, 1964, by papal envoy Agostino Casaroli and Hungarian church leader Joseph Prantner, initiating the normalization of relations between the Vatican and communist Hungary. Since 1945, church affairs in Hungary had been checked by communist governmental restrictions. By the concordat, Hungary's government acknowledged the Roman Catholic Church's right to conduct free diocesan elections, to communicate freely with all members of the church hierarchy, and to conduct freely religious education in churches and schools; the government also accepted the freedom of the religious orders. The church, in return, agreed that its priests and bishops would fulfill their obligation of pledging their fidelity to the Hungarian state and constitution.

Further reading: Carlo Falconi, *The Popes in the Twentieth Century: From Pius X to John XXIII* (Boston: Little, Brown, 1967); Paul Ignatus, *Hungary* (London: Ernest Benn, 1972).

Concordat of Ceprano See CEPRANO, CONCORDAT OF.

Concordat of Francis I See BOLOGNA, CONCORDAT OF.

Condominium Agreements of 1899 Between Britain and Egypt, agreements of January 19 and July 10, 1899, leading to the establishment of the Anglo-Egyptian Condominium that ruled jointly over Sudan from 1899 to the formation of the Republic of Sudan (January 1, 1956). With Britain's approval, the khedive of Egypt could appoint a governor general with sole charge of civil and military affairs in the Sudan. The flags of both countries were to be flown, and Egyptian law could be enforced at the governor's discretion. Egypt's role in the condominium was largely nominal, since Britain governed Sudan as if it were one of her own colonies, with British officers in key civil and military posts. The condominium, which had a troubled reign, was repealed by the ANGLO-EGYPTIAN SUDAN TREATY OF 1953.

Further reading: Robert O. Collins and Francis M. Deng, eds., *The British in the Sudan, 1898–1956: The Sweetness and the Sorrow* (Stanford, Calif.: Hoover Institution Press, Stanford University, 1984); M. W. Daly, *Empire on the Nile: The Anglo-Egyptian Sudan, 1898–1934* (New York: Cambridge University Press, 1986).

Conduct of the Allies, The English author Jonathan Swift's scathing political pamphlet in support of the Tory drive for peace, published on November 27, 1711. It attacked the Whig policies favoring the War of the Spanish Succession

(1701–14) and defended a "Peace without Spain." Swift wrote that England's role should have been only marginal since she had not been threatened by Louis XIV of France, except perhaps in his recognition of the Pretender. He suggested that British interests may have been better served by a naval war in the West Indies against French and Spanish territories. The war was creating a massive national debt, which would soon overpower the country. England, according to Swift, had become a puppet in the hands of the allies—bearing the brunt of the human and material losses while the Dutch cut down on their responsibilities, and the Holy Roman emperor deprived England of Toulon, France, by sending troops to crush a rebellion in Hungary instead. Directed primarily against the English general Marlborough and the House of Lords, the pamphlet is widely considered the best party pamphlet ever written.

Further reading: Jonathan Swift, *The Conduct of the Allies* (Oxford, England: Clarendon Press, 1916).

Confederate Constitution

Compact adopted at Montgomery, Alabama, on March 11, 1861, by the Confederate Congress, as the law of the Confederate States of America. Modeled on the U.S. Constitution, the document provided for a central government with three branches and a division of power between the central institution and state governments, while stressing the "sovereign and independent character" of each state. The president was elected for a single six-year term. The constitution protected the rights of slaveholders, especially in interstate traffic in slaves, and established slavery in the territories. The international slave trade, however, was banned. Protective tariffs were also forbidden.

Further reading: Richard N. Current, ed., *Encyclopedia of the Confederacy* (New York: Simon & Schuster, 1993); Leonard W. Levy and Kenneth L. Karst, eds., *Encyclopedia of the American Constitution,* 2d ed. (New York: Macmillan Reference, 2000).

Confessio Augustana See AUGSBURG CONFESSION.

Confessio Augustana Variata

Modified edition of the AUGSBURG CONFESSION, written in 1540 by the German humanist Philip Melanchthon to satisfy the proponents of the Protestant Eucharistic doctrine of Swiss reformer Huldreich Zwingli and French reformer John Calvin. The change was in article 10 describing the understanding of the Eucharistic sacrament, the Lord's Supper. Instead of affirming the actual presence of Christ in the bread and wine during the Eucharist (unacceptable to the Zwinglians and Calvinists), the presence of Christ was described in far less precise terms, thus allowing for the belief that Christ's presence was to be understood symbolically, as the Zwinglians and Calvinists believed.

Further reading: Hubert Cunliffe-Jones, *A History of Christian Doctrine* (Edinburgh, Scotland: T&T Clark, 1997); Bjarne W. Teigen, *I Believe; a Study of the Augsburg Confession*

and the Apology of the Augsburg Confession (Mankato, Minn.: Lutheran Synod Book Co., 1980).

Confessio Belgica See BELGIC CONFESSION.

Confessions (Confessiones)

Record of Saint Augustine's great spiritual and emotional journey from the cradle to his Christian conversion (c. A.D. 400). A long prayer thanking the Creator for transforming his soul from one of anger to one of election by God, its central theme can be expressed thus: "Thou hast made us for Thyself and our heart is restless until it rest in Thee." Saint Augustine, bishop of Hippo (in Algeria), divided his work into 13 books. Books 1 to 9 recount his search for the ultimate truth, from his academic life at Carthage to his disillusionment with Manicheism (a dualistic religion), to his initiation into the works of Plato (see REPUBLIC, THE) and the ecstatic moment of his final conversion near Milan. Book 10 is concerned with memory, book 11 presents a theory of time, and the last two books contain an allegorical interpretation of the opening biblical verses of Genesis. Highly original in form, content, and style, it is considered one of the classics of Christian antiquity.

See also: CITY OF GOD.

Further reading: Augustine, *Confessions and Enchiridion* trans. and ed. Albert C. Outler (Philadelphia: Westminster Press, 1955); also available online, Christian Classics Ethereal Library, at http://ccel.org/a/augustine/confessions/confessions-bod.html.

Confirmation of Charters (Confirmatio Cartarum)

English document confirming former charters of liberties, wrung from King Edward I at Ghent, Flanders, by the barons in 1297. Many English barons, angered by heavy taxation, had disobeyed the king's orders to invade Gascony, France, during the Anglo-French War of 1294–98. They were supported by Archbishop Robert de Winchelsea and the middle class (also angered by increasing taxes). While Edward was campaigning in Flanders, they secured the Confirmation of Charters, which upheld the MAGNA CARTA and documents signed by King Henry III (see OXFORD, PROVISIONS OF). It also forbade nonfeudal tax levies by the crown without parliamentary consent. Edward's autocratic temper led to more baronial opposition and more concessions by him in 1301.

Further reading: Richard L. Perry, ed., *Sources of Our Liberties* (New York: American Bar Foundation, 1959).

Confiscation Act of 1861, U.S.

Law passed by Congress on August 6, 1861, authorizing the seizure, through federal courts, of property, including slaves, used to aid the Confederacy. The bill, an attempt to weaken the South through slave emancipation, passed over the objectives of President Abraham Lincoln, who, though he opposed slavery, feared this act would alienate those border states still loyal to the Union. The following year Lincoln requested, and

Congress issued, a resolution providing compensation to states undertaking a program of gradual emancipation. When that program failed, Congress passed the U.S. CONFISCATION ACT OF 1862.

Further reading: Richard N. Current, ed., *Encyclopedia of the Confederacy* (New York: Simon & Schuster, 1993); Leonard W. Levy and Kenneth L. Karst, eds., *Encyclopedia of the American Constitution,* 2d ed. (New York: Macmillan Reference, 2000); James G. Randall, *Constitutional Problems under Lincoln* (Urbana: University of Illinois Press, 1951).

Confiscation Act of 1862, U.S.   Law passed by Congress on July 17, 1862, providing for the seizure of property of disloyal slaveowners and the emancipation of their slaves. The property of local, state, and Confederate civil and military officials was specifically noted as subject to confiscation. Like the U.S. CONFISCATION ACT OF 1861, the 1862 act treated slave emancipation as a punishment for insurrection, not a moral goal in its own right. Signed by President Abraham Lincoln, the act was unenforceable until Union armies occupied the South. Again Lincoln's proposal for gradual, compensated emancipation failed, and in September 1862 the president issued his preliminary EMANCIPATION PROCLAMATION.

Further reading: Richard N. Current, ed., *Encyclopedia of the Confederacy* (New York: Simon & Schuster, 1993); Leonard W. Levy and Kenneth L. Karst, eds., *Encyclopedia of the American Constitution,* 2d ed. (New York: Macmillan Reference, 2000); James G. Randall, *Constitutional Problems under Lincoln* (Urbana: University of Illinois Press, 1951).

Conflans, Treaty of   Peace treaty in October 1465, ending the War of the Public Weal waged by a coalition of French dukes (League for the Public Weal) against King Louis XI of France. It was negotiated following the king's defeat at the battle of Montlhéry. Concluded at Conflans and at Saint-Maur-les-Fossés, the treaty actually consisted of separate agreements with each of the dukes. Charles the Bold, duke of Burgundy, regained the Somme towns and was also given the counties of Guines, Péronne, Montdidier, and Roye. The king's brother, the duke of Berri, received in exchange for his duchy the strategically located duchy of Normandy. The count of Saint-Pol was mollified by receiving the sword of Constable of France, while the duke of Nemours returned empty-handed. Having made these commitments, which he had no intention of fulfilling, Louis began breaking up the league by using subtle diplomatic tactics.

Further reading: Paul M. Kendall, *Louis XI* (London: Phoenix, 2001).

Confucian *Analects*   Ethical precepts and sayings attributed to the Chinese philosopher and teacher Confucius (c. 551–479 B.C.); taken from notes made by disciples and later collected together by the scholar Dsong Hüan (A.D. 127–200). Considered the basic "scripture" of Confucianism, this com-

pilation consists of 20 sections and 496 chapters, relating aphorisms, conversations, discourse, and travels of the Master (Confucius). Correct conduct in society is stressed, along with the obligation to be virtuous and with social relationships to be honored faithfully. The *Analects* or *Lun Yü* ("Dialogues") state that sound judgment and self-discipline direct the noble to act properly in all relationships. A leader or ruler must be an exemplar of virtue if society is to function smoothly.

Further reading: Confucius, *The Analects*, trans. Arthur Waley (New York: Alfred A. Knopf, 2000).

Congo Report, Casement's   Shocking report alleging slave labor conditions in the Congo Free State, written by Irish-born British consul Roger Casement in 1903 following his investigatory journey for the British government into the region. Casement's complaints of cruel exploitation of the wild-rubber cutters and gatherers in the Upper Congo brought strong condemnation of Leopold II, king of the Belgians, who had established the Congo Free State under his personal rule. Casement reported evidence of the white man's inhumanity to the natives, who suffered beatings, imprisonment, food shortages, starvation, and killings while laboring in the rubber trade. Although Leopold denied the accusations, he was forced to send a three-man commission to check out the Congo situation; the commission corroborated Casement's findings in 1904.

Further reading: Brian Inglis, *Roger Casement* (Belfast, Ireland: Blackstaff Press, 1974, repr., 1993); John de Courcy MacDonnell, *King Leopold II: His Rule in Belgium and the Congo* New York: Argosy-Antiquarian, 1905, repr., 1970).

Congo Treaty of 1894   Agreement made on May 12, 1894, between Britain and the Congo Free State for a mutual exchange of territory, intended to be advantageous to Britain. Britain secured the strategic 25-kilometer corridor between Lakes Tanganyika and Albert Edward, to facilitate construction of its proposed Cape-to-Cairo telegraph and railway system. In return, Britain leased to Belgium's king Leopold II (under whose personal rule the Congo Free State was set up in 1885) the entire area west of the Upper Nile from Lake Albert to Fashoda and west to 30°E. Also, he and his successors were leased a substantially larger region west of the above (to 25°E) and north of the Congo-Nile watershed. The deal was hastily struck amidst fears of a French attack, and contradicted earlier agreements with France and Germany. Both countries protested and Britain and the Congo Free State were forced to abort the deal (August 1894). The treaty was a part of Britain's efforts to control the Nile, and its failure only confirmed the strength of the Franco-German alliance.

Further reading: Lois A. C. Raphael, *The Cape-to-Cairo Dream; a Study in British Imperialism* (New York: Octagon Books, 1973); Henry W. Wack, *The Story of the Congo Free State; Social, Political, and Economic Aspects of the Belgian*

System of Government in Central Africa (New York: Argosy-Antiquarian, 1970).

Connally-Fulbright Resolutions

Congressional resolutions passed in 1943, expressing U.S. intentions to help establish and to join an international peacekeeping organization, the first step toward the United Nations. On September 21, the U.S. House of Representatives approved a resolution, introduced by Representative J. William Fulbright of Arkansas, calling for "the creation of appropriate international machinery with power adequate to establish and maintain a just and lasting peace." On November 5 the Senate adopted a similar measure, introduced by Senator Thomas T. Connally of Texas, which stipulated that any treaty made to effect this resolution would require a two-thirds vote of the U.S. Senate.

Further reading: Carl N. Flanders and Stephen A. Flanders, *Dictionary of American Foreign Affairs* (New York: Macmillan, 1993).

Connecticut, Charter of

Legal charter for Connecticut secured by Governor John Winthrop by petition to King Charles II of England, granted on April 23, 1662. It superseded the Fundamental Orders of Connecticut yet retained and incorporated essential characteristics of those orders into the new charter. In 1687, in an attempt by England's king James II to annul the charter, England requested its surrender to Sir Edmund Andros, governor of the Dominion of New England. However, during an oration by Governor Robert Treat of Connecticut against its surrender, the lights were extinguished and the charter was whisked away by Joseph Wadsworth and placed in a hollow tree, later known as the Charter Oak. The charter remained as basic law of Connecticut until 1818.

See also: FUNDAMENTAL ORDERS OF CONNECTICUT.

Further reading: Albert Carlos Bates, *The Charter of Connecticut: A Study* (Hartford, Conn.: Connecticut Historical Society, 1932); *The Charter of Connecticut, 1662* (New Haven, Conn.: Tercentenary Commission/Yale University Press, 1933).

Connecticut Compromise   See GREAT COMPROMISE.

Consolidación, Law of

Royal Spanish decree enforced in Mexico between 1805 and 1809 that provided for the conversion of the landholdings of religious institutions into cash, then for the transfer of this capital to the Spanish treasury. The *consolidación*, essentially a financial operation aimed at the nationalization of the land held by religious communities in Mexico, netted approximately 10 million pesos during the term of its enforcement. This measure dealt a severe blow both to Mexican religious institutions, which held much of the country's real estate and mortgages, as well as to wealthy conservatives, who were deeply involved in loans and debts on realty.

Further reading: Donald C. Briggs and Marvin Alisky, *Historical Dictionary of Mexico* (Metuchen, N.J.: Scarecrow Press, 1981).

Constance, Decrees of the Council of

Declarations made by the Roman Catholic Council of Constance, meeting at the city of Constance in southern Germany from November 1414 to April 1418; they dealt with the religious heresy of Jan Hus and the Great Schism (political division in the Roman Catholic Church). The decrees established that Pope John XXIII was to be deposed, that Pope Benedict XIII was to be deposed, and that Pope Martin V was to be the new pope. Also issued were the decree known as *Sacrosancta* (1415), which affirmed that the general council was superior to a pope, and the decree called *Frequens* (1417), which established the church requirement for frequent meetings of general councils. Lastly, the religious writings of John Wyclif (Wycliffe), an English reformer, were condemned, and Hus (a Bohemian reformer) was ordered to be burned at the stake as a heretic.

Further reading: John Hine Mundy and Kennerly M. Woody, eds., *The Council of Constance: The Unification of the Church* (New York: Columbia University Press, 1961); James Hamilton Wylie, *The Council of Constance to the Death of John Hus: Being the Ford Lectures Delivered in the University of Oxford in Lent Term, 1900* (New York: Longmans, Green, 1900).

Constance, Peace of

Treaty concluded on June 12, 1446, between Zurich and the Swiss Confederation of towns. Zurich, which had had ambitious territorial claims, and which had allied itself with the Hapsburg emperor Frederick III (who also had hopes of regaining territories once in his possession), was vehemently opposed by the confederation. Throughout the long war (1436–46) the alliance's (Zurich and Austria) large army had not been able to defeat the small confederate army. Finally in 1446, the Austrians (Hapsburgs) were defeated by the Swiss Confederation. In the peace that followed, Zurich agreed to renounce its alliance with Austria; Zurich was accepted into the confederation; and there was a return to prewar frontiers.

Constance, Treaty of

Treaty concluded by Frederick I (Frederick Barbarossa), king of Germany and Holy Roman emperor, and the Lombard towns on January 25, 1183, in which Frederick sacrificed control over the towns for peace with them. Throughout the preceding period these northern Italian towns had been militarily winning for themselves many of the rights and privileges once claimed by the emperor. Frederick sought to reclaim these for himself, but succeeded in obtaining only the towns' promise to do homage to the emperor and to let him alone invest the consuls. Frederick renounced all royal rights and privileges in the towns and recognized their right to declare war and to manage their own local affairs.

Further reading: Medieval Sourcebook, "Barbarossa and the Lombards," Medieval Source Book website, available online at http://www.fordham.edu/halsall/source/barbarossa-lombards.html; Peter Munz, *Frederick Barbarossa: A Study in Medieval Politics* (Ithaca, N.Y.: Cornell University Press, 1969).

Constantine, Donation of (Constitutum Donatio Constantini)

Spurious imperial edict-deed, supposedly issued by Roman emperor Constantine I the Great in A.D. 324, granting to Pope (Saint) Sylvester I and his papal successors imperial sovereignty and spiritual authority over Rome, Italy, and the entire Western Empire. According to legend, the donation was Constantine's reward to Sylvester for miraculously healing him of leprosy and converting him to Christianity. Constantine withdrew from Rome to move to Byzantium, which became the Eastern Roman Empire's center of power as the capital city of Constantinople (Istanbul). Papal powers and territorial claims were deduced from the donation throughout the Middle Ages, until Italian humanist Lorenzo Valla proved (1440) the document to be fraudulent. It is generally thought to have been written during the papacy of Stephen II (A.D. 752–57), by someone in his chancery, when church power faced erosion by the state.

Further reading: Horst Fuhrmann, ed. "Constitutum Constantini." Bibliotheca Augustana website, available online in Latin at http://www.fh-agusburg.de/~harsch/Chonologia/Lspost08/DonatioConstantini/don_text.html.

Constantine I the Great, Edicts of

See THEODOSIAN CODE.

Constantinople, Peace of (1562)

Peace agreement concluded in 1562 by Holy Roman Emperor Ferdinand I and Ottoman Sultan Sulayman I, formalizing or confirming a truce made in 1547 between the Holy Roman and Ottoman Empires. It reaffirmed that western and northern Hungary were to remain under the control of Ferdinand (i.e., Hapsburg rule); that central Hungary was to stay under Ottoman control; and that Transylvania was to retain a degree of independence, such that it would have its own national ruler but under Turkish authority.

Further reading: L. Carl Brown, *The Imperial Legacy: The Ottoman Imprint on the Balkans and the Middle East* (New York: Columbia University Press, 1996); Halil Inalcik, *The Ottoman Empire: The Classical Age, 1300–1600* (London: Phoenix Press, 2000); Halil Inalcik and Cemal Kafadar, eds., *Suleyman the Second and His Time,* (Istanbul: Isis Press, 1993).

Constantinople, Treaty of (1700)

Treaty signed at Constantinople (Istanbul, Turkey) on July 3, 1700, between Russia and the Ottoman Empire, confirming the provisions of the 1699 Peace of KARLOWITZ. Russian control of the strategic fortress-cities of Azov, Taganrog, Pavlovsk, and Mius (all near the Ottoman Turkish border) was officially confirmed. Both parties agreed to maintain a military-free zone in their border regions. In addition, the Turks agreed to accept a Russian government representative at Constantinople and to free all Russian prisoners of war.

Further reading: Pál Fodor and Géza Dávid, eds., *Ottomans, Hungarians, and Habsburgs in Central Europe: The Military Confines in the Era of Ottoman Conquest* (Boston: Brill, 2000); Vladimir Matveyev, *The Karlowitz Congress and the Debut of Russia's Multilateral Diplomacy* (London: Centre for the Study of Diplomacy, University of Leicester, 2000).

Constantinople, Treaty of (1913)

Treaty concluded in Constantinople (Istanbul) on September 29, 1913, between Bulgaria and the Ottoman Empire (Turkey), bringing an end, together with the 1913 Treaty of BUCHAREST, to the Second Balkan War (1913). The terms of the treaty provided that defeated Bulgaria would agree to Turkey's repossession of Adrianople (Edirne), plus territory up to the Maritsa River. In addition, the two countries agreed to resume diplomatic relations, exchange prisoners, and establish a general amnesty. The war had arisen over Serbia and Greece's dissatisfaction over the settlement ending the First Balkan War (1912–13) (see LONDON, TREATY OF [1913]), and their decision to compensate themselves territorially at Bulgaria's expense. Turkey and Romania then joined the coalition against Bulgaria, with the former regaining Adrianople.

Further reading: Charles L. Phillips and Alan Axelrod, eds., *Encyclopedia of Historical Treaties and Alliances,* 2 vols. (New York: Facts On File, 2001).

Constantinople Convention

See SUEZ CANAL CONVENTION.

Constitución Vitalicia ("lasting for life")

Name given to the constitution framed by Simón Bolívar in 1826 and intended for adoption in Peru and Colombia. It provided for a lifelong presidency and the right of the president to name his own successor; declared that the vice president was the responsible head of the administration, subject to impeachment by congress and the supreme court; and called for an independent judiciary. While there was no provision for real local self-government, there was a complicated procedure advanced for appointing local officials. There was to be freedom of worship for non-Catholics, and the exercise of the right of ecclesiastical patronage by the government was provided for. Although never accepted in Colombia, the *constitución* was adopted in Bolivia; a similar system was adopted, but later rejected, in Peru.

Further reading: Albert P. Blaustein and Jay A. Sigler, *Constitutions That Made History* (New York: Paragon House, 1988).

Constitution, U.S. See U.S. CONSTITUTION.

Constitution Act of 1791, British See CANADA ACT.

Constitutions of Clarendon See CLARENDON, CONSTITUTIONS OF.

Continental Association See ASSOCIATION, THE.

Conventicle Act, Swedish Law enacted in 1726, enforcing the orthodox Lutheran faith and banning other religious denominations in Sweden. Introduced specifically to counteract the growing popularity of Pietism (movement for a revival of piety in Lutheranism), the act prohibited the holding of prayer meetings in private homes and attended by outsiders. This was intended to clamp down on dissenting congregations and prevent radical and divisive religious behavior from escalating into a movement. The act, not repeated until 1860, ensured that the Swedish Church developed along traditional paths during the next century.

Further reading: Ingmar Andersson, *A History of Sweden* (New York: Praeger, 1968); Andrew A. Stomberg, *A History of Sweden* (New York: Macmillan, 1931).

Conventicle Act of 1664 Third English law or act of the CLARENDON CODE, banning conventicles (religious gatherings) of five or more persons (excluding families) who were not in conformity with the Church of England (Anglican Church). It was promoted to prevent the deposed clergy from starting their own congregations (see UNIFORMITY, ACT OF). Anyone participating or preaching in a dissenting (nonconformist) congregation, or permitting a building to be used for such a gathering, was to be punished. The act lapsed in 1668, was reenacted in a milder form in 1670, and was finally repealed by the TOLERATION ACT OF 1689.

Further reading: Carl Stephenson and Frederick George Marcham, eds., *Sources of English Constitutional History: A Selection of Documents from* A.D. *600 to the Present* (New York: Harper & Row, 1937).

Conventional Armed Forces in Europe, Treaty on Treaty prescribing limits on nonnuclear weapons deployed between the Atlantic Ocean and the Ural Mountains by the NATO and (former) Warsaw Pact countries, signed on November 19, 1990, during the Paris summit of the Conference on Security and Co-operation in Europe (see CHARTER OF PARIS FOR A NEW EUROPE). It restricted both groups to 20,000 battle tanks, 30,000 armored combat vehicles, 20,000 pieces of artillery, 6,800 combat aircraft, and 2,000 attack helicopters. All excess weapons would be destroyed or adapted for nonmilitary use and all inactive weapons stored in designated areas. Nearly 40 percent of the cuts were borne by the Soviet Union and other Warsaw Pact countries. No single member nation could deploy more than a specified number of weapons in Europe. The reductions would be implemented in three phases over a 40-month period. The treaty allowed for "declared site inspections" and some "challenge inspections." At the request of Russia and Ukraine, the treaty was amended on July 23, 1997, by assigning weapons limits to individual countries rather than to "groups of states parties." (The Warsaw Pact was dissolved in 1991.)

Further reading: Organization for Security and Co-operations in Europe, "Treaty on Conventional Armed Forces in Europe," OSCE website, available online at "http://www.osce.org/docs/english/cfee.htm.

Convention for the Amelioration of the Wounded in Time of War See GENEVA CONVENTION OF 1864.

Convention for the Suppression of Slavery, International Report of the League of Nations' Temporary Slavery Commission (established in 1924), adopted by the league's assembly on September 25, 1926. The report was almost exhaustive in its coverage of various types of slavery prevalent in the world, except for the issue of "forced labor," which it referred to the International Labor Organization. However, in terms of actual proposals, the report was quite vague. The League of Nations's greatest success in suppressing slavery came in countries where it had a mandate—the German colonies and the ex-holdings of the Ottoman Empire (Turkey). For instance, Ethiopia was denied admission into the league unless it made efforts to eradicate slavery, while Liberia was promised financial aid on the condition that it take steps to abolish its intertribal slavery system.

Further reading: Office of the High Commissioner of Human Rights, "Slavery Convention." Office of the United Nations High Commissioner for Human Rights website, available online at http://www.unhchr.ch/html/menu3/b/f2sc.htm.

Convention on the Prevention and Punishment of the Crime of Genocide Agreement adopted by the United Nations General Assembly on December 9, 1948, classifying genocide, whether during time of war or peace, as a crime under international law and pledging measures to prevent and punish it. The convention defined genocide as an act intended to destroy, fully or in part, any national, ethnic, racial, or religious group. It declared the crime itself, or any conspiracy, incitement, or involvement in it, as a punishable offense. The signatories promised to take measures for extradition, if needed, and resolved to consider setting up an international judicial body (perhaps a department of the International Court of Justice), to try those charged with genocide. The convention was prompted by the gruesome crimes perpetrated in the Nazi camps during World War II (1939–45).

See also: UNIVERSAL DECLARATION OF HUMAN RIGHTS.

Further reading: Office of the High Commissioner of Human Rights, "Convention on the Prevention and Punishment of the Crime of Genocide." Office of the United Nations High Commissioner for Human Rights website, available online at http://www.unhchr.ch/html/menu3/b/p_genoci.htm.

Convention on the Prohibition of the Use, Stockpiling, Production, and Transfer of Antipersonnel Mines and on Their Destruction

Treaty adopted on September 18, 1997, in Oslo, Norway, and signed on December 3–4, 1997, in Ottawa, Canada, banning the use, manufacture, transfer, and stockpiling of antipersonnel land mines. According to the International Campaign to Ban Landmines (its coordinator won the Nobel Peace Prize later in 1997), the more than 100 million land mines deployed worldwide annually killed or mained about 25,000 people. The treaty would come into force six months after 40 countries had ratified it. Members then had four years to destroy all their existing land mines and 10 years to clear the mined areas in their countries. They were also required to give six months' notice before withdrawing from the treaty and to wait until any ongoing armed conflicts had ended. China, Russia, and the United States sent observers to Ottawa but had not approved it as of May 10, 2002, by which time 142 countries had signed or acceded to it and 122 had ratified it.

Further reading: International Campaign to Ban Landmines, "The Latest News from the Campaign," ICBL website, available online at http://www.icbl.org.

Convention on the Settlement of Investment Disputes

Agreement advocating peaceful settlement of investment disputes; drafted under World Bank supervision and signed on March 18, 1965, in Washington, D.C., by 67 countries and later ratified by 63 (Ethiopia, Ireland, New Zealand, and Sudan failed to endorse it). Recognizing a need for international arbitration facilities to settle investment disputes between countries, the convention established the International Center for Settlement of Investment Disputes (ICSID) as a subsidiary of the International Bank for Reconstruction and Development (IBRD). The ICSID would consist of an administrative council, a secretariat, a panel of conciliators, and a panel of arbitrators. Having agreed to submit their dispute to conciliation or arbitration, both parties were bound to consider the recommendation or award made by the panels.

Further reading: The World Bank Group ICSID, *International Centre for Settlement of Investment Disputes,* International Centre for Settlement of Investment Disputes, available online at http://www.worldbank.org/icsid/basicdoc/9.htm.

Conwell's "Acres of Diamonds" Speech

See "ACRES OF DIAMONDS" SPEECH, CONWELL'S.

Cooperative Marketing Act, U.S.

See CAPPER-VOLSTEAD ACT.

Cooper Union Speech, Lincoln's

Successful speech delivered by Abraham Lincoln on February 27, 1860, at Cooper Union in New York City; helped make Lincoln, an Illinois politician until then little known on the East Coast, a formidable candidate for the Republican presidential nomination. A distinguished but skeptical audience was won over by Lincoln's careful discussion of Stephen A. Douglas's doctrine of popular sovereignty and of Southern attitudes toward the North and the Republican Party. He appealed for sectional understanding while condemning Northern extremism and Southern threats of disunion. Lincoln argued that compromise with the issue of extending slavery was impossible.

Further reading: Roy P. Basler, *Abraham Lincoln: His Speeches and Writings* (New York: Da Capo Press, 1990).

Cooper v. *Aaron*

U.S. Supreme Court decision issued on September 29, 1958, declaring that the states were required to obey the Court's mandate to end segregation in the public schools, following BROWN V. BOARD OF EDUCATION OF TOPEKA, KANSAS. The unanimous decision stated that the attempts of the legislature and governor of Arkansas to resist court-ordered desegregation were unconstitutional. State regulation of education must be consistent with federal constitutional requirements of equal justice under law. State officials cannot nullify, either directly or indirectly, through "evasive schemes for segregation," the constitutional rights of children to be protected against discrimination.

See also: EISENHOWER'S SPEECH CONCERNING LITTLE ROCK.

Further reading: Leonard W. Levy and Kenneth L. Karst, eds., *Encyclopedia of the American Constitution,* 2d ed. (New York:Macmillan Reference, 2000).

Copenhagen, Treaty of

Peace treaty signed on June 6, 1660, by Sweden and Denmark, bringing fighting between the countries to an end and relative peace to the Baltic region for the next 15 years. Denmark formally surrendered Scania, or Skane, (southernmost Sweden) but retained the Baltic island of Bornholm and Norway's Trondheim district. Both Sweden and Denmark pledged to keep the Öresund (Danish Sound) open to foreign vessels. Although Sweden's military campaign against Denmark and her hope to become master of the Baltic had failed, she remained an important power in European politics.

See also: OLIVA, TREATY OF; ROSKILDE, TREATY OF.

Further reading: Ingmar Andersson, *A History of Sweden* (New York: Praeger, 1968); T. K. Derry, *A History of Scandinavia* (Minneapolis: University of Minnesota Press, 1979); Stewart Oakley, *A Short History of Denmark* (New York: Praeger, 1972); Andrew A. Stomberg, *A History of Sweden* (New York: Macmillan, 1931).

Coppage v. *Kansas*

U.S. Supreme Court decision of January 25, 1915, declaring unconstitutional state laws forbidding "yellow dog" contracts—that is, contracts in which employers required their workers not to join labor unions. The case arose when a Kansas railway worker was fired for refusing to sign a contract that would have compelled him to resign from his union. A state court upheld the Kansas statute prohibiting yellow dog contracts, but the U.S. Supreme Court ruled that the law violated the due-process clause of the FOUR-TEENTH AMENDMENT, by denying an employer the right to contract freely with workers. Yellow dog contracts were later outlawed by the NORRIS–LA GUARDIA ACT.

Further reading: Leonard W. Levy and Kenneth L. Karst, eds., *Encyclopedia of the American Constitution,* 2d ed. (New York: Macmillan Reference, 2000).

Coppino Act Act passed by the Italian parliament on July 15, 1877, under the influence of Michelle Coppino, minister of education, providing measures for the reform of elementary education. Through the act the education of children between the ages of six and nine became both free and required (elementary school attendance was compulsory for four years), and religious education was no longer a required part of the elementary school curriculum. The act was passed during the prime ministry of Agostino Depretis, which was responsible for many other social and economic reforms. Because of widespread failure to enforce the law, its positive effects were negligible, although it helped drop the level of illiteracy in Italy.

See also: CREDARO ACT.

Further reading: Martin Clark, *Modern Italy, 1871–1982* (New York: Longman, 1984); Denis Mack Smith, *Italy: A Modern History* (Ann Arbor: University of Michigan Press, 1959).

Corbeil, Treaty of Pact made at Corbeil, France, on May 11, 1258, between King Louis IX of France and King James I of Aragón, severing Catalonia's remaining ties with France. Realizing the futility of reviving his feudal claims in Languedoc against France, James I renounced his claims in Carcassonne, Nîmes, Béziers, Foix, Agde, Albi, Narbonne, Toulouse, Gévaudan, Rouerque, and later also in Provence. Louis IX surrendered France's interests in Roussillon, Conflent, Cerdagne, Barcelona, Urgel, Ampurias, Besalú, Gerona, and Vich —all frontline territories of the Spanish March. The border was fixed along the Pas-de-Salces in the Pyrenees. The pact was cemented by the marriage (solemnized in 1262) of James's daughter Isabella to Louis's son, Philip (later King Philip III). In 1283, Philip III obtained the pope's support in annulling the treaty and reasserted French claims in those areas.

See also: AMIENS, MISE OF; LEWES, MISE OF; LOUIS IX'S LAWS; PARIS, TREATY OF (1259); PRAGMATIC SANCTION OF ST. LOUIS.

Further reading: Elizabeth M. Hallam, *Capetian France, 987–1328* (New York: Longman, 1980); Sir Maurice Powicke, *The Thirteenth Century, 1216–1307* (London: Oxford University Press, 1962).

Córdoba, Treaty of (Convention of Córdoba) Formal agreement between Mexico and Spain, signed at Córdoba, Mexico, on August 24, 1821, providing that the Mexican nation, thereafter to be called the Mexican Empire, was to be recognized as independent. Under the treaty, the new empire's congress was to elect an emperor if no suitable European member of royalty could be found. The recently appointed Spanish viceroy in Mexico, Juan O'Donojú, who was without money and soldiers to battle Mexican revolutionaries, was forced to sign the treaty, by which he also agreed to the newly written Plan of IGUALA.

Further reading: Wallace L. McKeehan, *Plan of Iguala and the Treaty of Cordova,* Mexican Independence, available online at http://www.tamu.edu/ccbn/dewitt/iguala.htm.

Corfu Declaration (Pact of Corfu) Declaration endorsed on July 20, 1917, by Serbian Premier Nikola Pašić, leader of the Serbian government-in-exile, which was located in Corfu (Kérkira, Greece), and by Serbian, Croatian, and Slovenian representatives of the Yugoslav Committee, which was based in London; it called for the creation of an independent Yugoslav nation. The document included the proposals that the new nation be governed by a constitutional monarchy led by the Serbian Karageorgević (Karadjordjević) dynasty; that all religions of the new state, which were to include Roman Catholicism, Eastern Orthodoxy, and Islam, and all three nationalities, would enjoy equal rights. The authors of the pact failed, however, to agree on such critical issues as the frontiers of the new state and the nature of its future constitution. The movement to form an independent state in the Balkan Peninsula had originated during the 19th century. Its object had been to overcome the oppressive rule of the Hapsburgs and the Ottoman Empire, both of which were dissolved by the end of World War I (1914–18).

Further reading: Alex N. Dragnich, *Serbia, Nikola Pasic, and Yugoslavia* (New Brunswick, N.J.: Rutgers University Press, 1974); Nikola Pasic and Ante Trumbic, *The Declaration of Corfu* (Washington, D.C.: Jugoslav National Council, 1917).

Cornelian Laws (Leges Cornelia) Body of Roman reform laws secured by dictator Lucius Cornelius Sulla in 81–80 B.C. The reorganization measures restored much authority to the Roman senate, whose membership was increased from 300 to 600 by enrolling many equestrians who had backed Sulla; made senators once again eligible for all juries; deprived the tribunes of the right to initiate legislation in the Tribal Assembly; abolished the censors' control over admissions to the senate; regulated the process of appointing provincial governors; and increased the number of quaestors (public prosecutors) to 20 and the number of praetors (city magistrates) from six to eight. Most important was Sulla's introduction of a more expeditious judicial system, including the establishment of standing jury-trial courts for criminal cases of bribery, fraud, embezzlement, treason, assassination, and assault with violence. Sulla laid the foundation of Roman criminal law. He relinquished his dictatorial power in 79 B.C., retired to his country estate, and died in 78 B.C.

See also: DOMITIAN LAW.

Further reading: H. F. Jolowicz and Barry Nicholas, *Historical Introduction to the Study of Roman Law*, 3d ed. (Holmes Beach, Fla.: Gaunt, 1996); Joseph Anthony Charles Thomas, *Textbook of Roman Law* (New York: North-Holland, 1976); Alan Watson, *The Law of the Ancient Romans* (Dallas: Southern Methodist University Press, 1970).

Cornerstone Speech, Stephens's   Speech delivered by Alexander Hamilton Stephens, vice president of the Confederate States of America, in which Hamilton described slavery as the basic foundation of the Confederate government. The speech was given on March 21, 1861, at Savannah, Georgia. In it, Stephens declared that the "cornerstone" of the Confederacy stands "upon the great truth that the Negro is not equal to the white man; that slavery . . . is his natural and moral condition." During the U.S. Civil War Stephens, an ardent supporter of states' rights and civil liberties for whites, was often in conflict with Jefferson Davis, president of the Confederacy, over Davis's attempts to strengthen his government's war powers.

Further reading: Richard N. Current, ed., *Encyclopedia of the Confederacy* (New York: Simon & Schuster, 1993).

Corn Law of 1815, British   Law passed by the British Parliament in 1815 to regulate the importation of corn (in England, chiefly wheat). It forbade the import of foreign corn or grain until the price of homegrown had reached 80 shillings a quarter, after which it was to be imported duty-free. The act was designed to protect the interests of landlords following the Napoleonic Wars (1803–15), when Britain was in the midst of an agricultural and industrial depression. It created, however, class conflicts and was too rigid to be really effective. Besides, the domestic price went down. The act was replaced by the CORN LAW OF 1828, which had a sliding scale of duties.

Further reading: Alon Kadish, *The Corn Laws: The Formation of Popular Economics in Britain* (London: Pickering & Chatto, 1996); J. R. Wordie, *Agriculture and Politics in England, 1815–1939* (New York: St. Martin's Press, 2000).

Corn Law of 1828, British   Law proposed by the duke of Wellington, Britain's prime minister, and William Huskisson, leader of the House of Commons, to alleviate hardships to the consumer caused by the CORN LAW OF 1815; passed by Parliament on July 15, 1828. It allowed corn (grain, mainly wheat) to be imported and established import duties on a sliding scale; this meant higher duties on foreign grain when domestic prices were low, and lower duties when English prices increased. Wellington's support for the law angered both landlords and liberals, who recalled that he had earlier resisted it when George Canning, Wellington's predecessor as prime minister, had proposed it. Poor harvests in the late 1830s led to formation of the Anti–Corn Law League, and eventually abolition of the corn laws in June 1846.

Further reading: Alon Kadish, *The Corn Laws: The Formation of Popular Economics in Britain* (London: Pickering & Chatto, 1996); Frank N. Magill, ed., *Great Events from History, Modern European Series*, 3 vols. (Englewood Cliffs, N.J.: Salem Press, 1973); Paul A. Pickering, *The People's Bread: A History of the Anti-Corn Law League* (New York: Leicester University Press, 2000); J. R. Wordie, *Agriculture and Politics in England, 1815–1939* (New York: St. Martin's Press, 2000).

Cornwallis Code   Series of administrative reforms inaugurated by Charles Cornwallis, British governor general of India, in 1793; permanently fixed and stabilized land revenues in the Indian provinces of Bengal, Bihar, Orissa, and (in 1795) Benares (Varanasi), authorizing zamindars (native revenue collectors) to make the land tax collections. The Cornwallis System (also called the Bengal System) contained no provision to check the zamindars' exploitation of the peasantry. In Madras and (later) Bombay, revenues were collected directly from the peasants, while in India's northwest and central provinces collection was through villages or estates. The system divided the British East India Company into three branches—revenue, judicial, and commercial—with members of the first two barred from private trading. District collectors were put in charge of local administration. The judicial branch was revamped according to the British model. And native Indians were excluded from senior posts.

Further reading: Arthur Aspinall, *Cornwallis in Bengal* (New Delhi, India: Uppal Pub. House, 1987); Franklin B. Wickwire and Mary Wickwire, *Cornwallis, the Imperial Years* (Chapel Hill: University of North Carolina Press, 1980).

Coronation Charter of Henry I   Earliest of England's constitutional charters of liberties; announced by Henry I during his coronation as king on August 5, 1100. Seeking public confidence, Henry I promised far-reaching reforms including the renunciation of the "evil customs" of his predecessor (William II) and a return of the laws of King Edward the Confessor, with emendations. He declared the church free from "unjust exactions" and promised not to sell or lease its property or to interfere in its demesne during a vacancy (see CLARENDON, CONSTITUTIONS OF). Among other measures to remedy abuses of feudal custom were (1) baronial lands redeemed by "a just and lawful *relief*"; (2) free royal consent in marriage of a daughter or female relative; (3) widow remarriage only by her consent; (4) common mintage (forced levy) abolished; (5) disposition of personal property according to will; (6) remittance of murder-fines incurred before coronation, and of all arrears owed to Henry's brother, Rufus; (7) demesne of knights declared "quit of all gelds and all work";

and (8) seized property restored. Forests were retained under royal control.

See also: MAGNA CARTA.

Further reading: Carl Stephenson and Frederick George Marcham, eds., *Sources of English Constitutional History: A Selection of Documents from A.D. 600 to the Present* (New York: Harper & Row, 1937).

Corporation Act

First law of the CLARENDON CODE, passed by the Cavalier Parliament of King Charles II of England on November 20, 1661. It declared Presbyterians, Roman Catholics, and other dissenters ineligible to hold membership (office) in any corporations. The intention was to break up the power of the dissenters and help the return of the Anglicans (members of the Church of England) to Parliament. The act required all officeholders (in boroughs) to receive the sacrament according to the Church of England, disavow the SOLEMN LEAGUE AND COVENANT OF 1643, and swear oaths of allegiance, nonresistance, and supremacy. Indemnity acts were passed annually from 1727, and the act was repealed in 1828.

Further reading: Carl Stephenson and Frederick George Marcham, eds., *Sources of English Constitutional History: A Selection of Documents from A.D. 600 to the Present* (New York: Harper & Row, 1937).

Corpus Juris Civilis

See JUSTINIAN CODE.

Corrupt and Illegal Practices Prevention Act, British

Legislation of August 25, 1883, aimed at checking corruption in Britain; later used as a model for modern procedures and the first to be effectively enforced. The act clearly defined corrupt practices and severely increased the penalties for offenders. It stipulated that all the political parties together should not spend more than £800,000 during a general election; the 1880 election costs had amounted to £2.5 million. Government control was tightened to ensure that no single candidate spent more than a certain sum for election purposes. The act was specifically directed against the smaller boroughs in England, where corruption was rampant.

See also: CORRUPT PRACTICES PREVENTION ACT OF 1854, BRITISH.

Further reading: Ernest A. Jelf, *The Corrupt and Illegal Practices Preventions Acts, 1883 and 1895* (Woodbridge, Conn.: Primary Source Media, 1996).

Corrupt Practices Prevention Act of 1854, British

Act of August 10, 1854, initiated by the British home secretary, Lord John Russell, which levied a fine on anyone caught bribing, cheating, intimidating, or exerting undue influence on voters during parliamentary elections. It ordered candidates to produce itemized accounts of their election expenses, which would then be scrutinized by specially appointed auditors. This act was amended and revised by the act of 1883, which is still considered the foundation for modern procedures in Great Britain.

Further reading: John Clerk, *A Practical Treatise on the Law of Elections of the United Kingdom and the Corrupt Practices Prevention Act, 1854* (Woodbridge, Conn.: Research Publications, 1994).

Council of Europe, Statute of the

Statute signed in London on May 5, 1949, by which 10 European nations formed an association to further European integration, encourage social and economic progress, and protect human rights. Great Britain, France, Belgium, the Netherlands, Luxembourg, Denmark, Norway, Sweden, Ireland, and Italy were the 10 original members (21 countries are now involved). The statute provided for a committee of ministers (one seat per member) and a consultative assembly (18 members each for Britain, France, and Italy; six each for Sweden and the Netherlands; four each for Belgium, Denmark, Ireland, and Norway; and three for Luxembourg). New members would be admitted depending on their human rights records. The Council of Europe appointed several expert and special committees to conduct its activities. Among its finest achievements was the adoption of the EUROPEAN CONVENTION FOR THE PROTECTION OF HUMAN RIGHTS AND FUNDAMENTAL FREEDOMS. The council's headquarters are in Strasbourg, France.

See also: BRUSSELS TREATY OF 1948; WESTERN EUROPEAN UNION ACCORD.

Further reading: A. H. Robertson, *The Council of Europe*, 2d ed. (London: Stevens, 1961); *Statute of the Council of Europe, with Amendments* (Strasbourg, France: Council of Europe, 1966).

Course of Positive Philosophy (Cours de Philosophie Positive)

Major six-volume work written by French philosopher Auguste Comte in 1830–42, establishing the discipline of sociology and the philosophy of positivism. He postulated three stages in history: theological (where society is dominated by priests), metaphysical (characterized by challenges to the existing order), and positive (seeing the reemergence of order and social responsibility). Comte's goal was twofold: to base the discipline of sociology on a positive foundation, like the natural sciences, and to demonstrate that different fields in the natural sciences (not including mathematics) were interdependent. He divided the study of society ("social physics" in his words) into two parts: social statics and social dynamics. Social statics, deducible from human physiology and dealing with the framework of society, demanded the subservice of woman to man and the superiority of some races over others. Social dynamics, the transition of society from one condition to another, interested him more in his attempt to obtain laws of history like the laws of science.

Further reading: Gertrud Lenzer, ed., *Auguste Comte and Positivism: The Essential Writings* (New York: Harper, 1975).

Covode Resolution   Resolution passed by the U.S. House of Representatives on February 24, 1868, impeaching President Andrew Johnson for "high crimes and misdemeanors." The resolution cited 11 charges, including alleged violations of the TENURE OF OFFICE ACT and the Command of the Army Act (which largely deprived the president of command of the army by requiring that he issue all military orders through the general of the army, Ulysses S. Grant). The resolution also claimed that Johnson had attempted to bring disgrace and ridicule upon Congress. The Senate failed by one vote to achieve the two-thirds majority necessary to convict the president.

Further reading: Roy F. Nichols, *The Disruption of American Democracy* (New York: Macmillan, 1948); Mark Summers, *The Plundering Generation: Corruption and Crisis of the Union, 1849–1861* (New York: Oxford University Press, 1988).

Coxey's Program   Plan proposed by businessman and reformer Jacob S. Coxey, during America's depression following the Panic of 1893, to create employment and increase the supply of money in circulation by having Congress authorize the issue of $500 million in legal tender notes, not backed by specie, to be used for road construction. In March 1894, Coxey, a Populist, led a band of several hundred unemployed workers out of Massillon, Ohio, to march on Washington, D.C. In an anticlimactic ending, "Coxey's army" dissolved after its leader, while trying to read a petition at the Capitol, was arrested on May 1 for carrying banners and walking on the Capitol lawn.

Further reading: Donald Le Crone McMurry, *Coxey's Army: A Study of the Industrial Army Movement of 1984* (Seattle: University of Washington Press, 1929, repr., 1968); Carlos A. Schwantes, *Coxey's Army: An American Odyssey* (Moscow: University of Idaho Press, 1985); Henry I. Tragle, comp., *Coxey's Army* (New York: Grossman Publishers, 1974).

Coyle v. Smith   U.S. Supreme Court decision issued on May 29, 1911, which ruled that Congress may not impose certain restrictive conditions upon territories seeking admission to statehood. The Court declared that restrictions related to domestic matters, to matters that fall within state jurisdiction under the federal Constitution—such as a congressional requirement that Utah ban polygamy—were not binding. If such restrictions were permitted, Congress would be able to extend its powers beyond those mandated by the U.S. CONSTITUTION and states would have varying degrees of autonomy.

Further reading: Leonard W. Levy and Kenneth L. Karst, eds., *Encyclopedia of the American Constitution* 2d ed. (New York: Macmillan Reference, 2000).

Cranmer's Forty-two Articles   See FORTY-TWO ARTICLES.

Creative Evolution (L'Évolution Créatrice)   Celebrated work written by French philosopher Henri Bergson and published in 1907, expounding his "process" philosophy popularized through his writings. Accepting evolution as a scientific fact, Bergson rejected the mechanistic view of the evolutionary process expressed in many philosophic writings. To him, evolution signified the endurance of a vital impulse (*élan vital*), creative and constantly changing. This surging spirit could only be realized through "bathing in the full stream of experience." Bergson differentiated between evolution through instinct (as in insects) and evolution through intelligence (as in man). The book's concluding chapter provides a brilliant summary of the history of philosophical thought, showing how it ignored the wonder and importance of becoming by masking the true nature of reality with static concepts. Bergson's work, imbued with a poetic quality, helped him win the Nobel Prize in literature in 1927.

Further reading: Henri Bergson, *Creative Evolution* (Mineola, N.Y.: Dover, 1998).

Credaro Act   Act drafted by Italy's minister of education Luigi Credaro and passed by the Italian parliament in 1911, providing for a major reform of education in the country. Specifically, the act transferred the responsibility of administrating elementary schooling from small communities to the province; and the financial burden, which could not be met by these small communities, passed to the ministry in Rome. The Italian government, which had been at pains to raise the quality of education since the unification of Italy, had little time to put the reform into effect before the outbreak of World War I, which Italy entered in 1915.

See also: COPPINO ACT.

Further reading: Elmiro Argento, *Italian Education from 1859 to 1923: A Study in Educational Expectations and Performance* (Ann Arbor, Mich.: University Microfilms International, 1986).

Crépy, Treaty of   Peace treaty concluded between the French king Francis I and Holy Roman Emperor Charles V at Crépy (Créspy), in northern France, on September 18, 1544. Hastily and reluctantly concluded by Francis when the emperor's armies began moving into France, the treaty brought to an end the last or Fourth Italian War (1542–44) between Charles V and Francis I. Francis renounced his claims to Naples, Flanders, and Artois, while Charles gave up his claim to Burgundy. Piedmont and Savoy would be returned to their rightful rulers. The two sovereigns' families were to be united through the marriage of Francis's second son, the duke of Orleans, to either Charles's daughter (giving the Netherlands or Franche-Comté as dowry) or his niece (with Milan as her dowry); the duke's death in 1545 prevented this part of the treaty from being implemented. Francis also promised to root out heresy in France and to help defend Christendom against the Turks.

See also: CAMBRAI, PEACE OF.

Further reading: Martin Clark, *Modern Italy, 1871–1982* (New York: Longman, 1984); Denis Mack Smith, *Italy: A Modern History* (Ann Arbor: University of Michigan Press, 1959).

"Crime Against Kansas" Speech, Sumner's

Long antislavery speech delivered before Congress by Senator Charles Sumner of Massachusetts on May 19–20, 1856, vehemently denouncing the KANSAS-NEBRASKA ACT as a "crime against Kansas" and a "swindle." Sumner, a leading abolitionist, attacked the "slave oligarchy" for its "rape" of Kansas and insulted the authors of the act, calling Senator Stephen A. Douglas of Illinois a "nameless animal" and Senator Andrew Butler of South Carolina a lover of the "harlot" of slavery. Infuriated by the speech, Butler's nephew, Representative Preston Brooks of South Carolina, beat Sumner so severely with a cane on May 22, 1856, that Sumner could not return to the Senate for more than three years.

Further reading: Nineteenth Century Documents Project, Furman University, *Speech of Charles Sumner of Massachusetts, in the Senate of the United States, May 18, 1856, The Crime Against Kansas: The Apologies for the Crime: The True Remedy,* available online at http://www.furman.edu/~benson/docs/sumnerksh2.htm.

Crime Control Acts, U.S.

See OMNIBUS CRIME CONTROL AND SAFE STREETS ACT OF 1968, U.S.; ORGANIZED CRIME CONTROL ACT OF 1970, U.S.

Crimes Bill of 1887, British

Legislation of April 18, 1887, introduced by Arthur J. Balfour (chief secretary for Ireland in Lord Salisbury's second prime ministry), to curb the wave of unrest in Ireland. Previous legislation (see PEACE PRESERVATION ACT OF 1870) had been unable to quell the agitation, resulting partly from the "Plan of Campaign" scheme whereby the Irish tenants, acting in consortium, would offer their landlords a fair rent and, if they refused, pay it into a "war" chest. This led to mass-scale evictions (since the landlords had organized themselves too) and even more turmoil. The act enabled Balfour to authorize trial without jury and to treat certain offenses as crimes in "declared" areas. In the British Parliament, it received a stormy reception, with the Irish and the Liberal members staging a walkout and dissociating themselves from such a measure.

See also: LAND PURCHASE ACT OF 1891, IRISH.

Further reading: Catherine Shannon, *Arthur J. Balfour and Ireland, 1874–1922* (Washington, D.C.: Catholic University of America Press, 1988).

Critique of Pure Reason (Kritik der Reinen Vernunft)

German philosopher Immanuel Kant's epistemological classic, first published in 1781 and revised in 1787. Kant, a central figure of the Enlightenment, sought in this "critique" to reconcile British empiricism (Locke, Berkeley, and Hume) with the rationalism of the Continent (Descartes, Leibniz, and Wolff). The introduction is followed by a 400-page section "Transcendental Doctrine of Elements" (three subsections deal with transcendental aesthetic, analytic, and dialectic, respectively) exploring the sources of human knowledge. The second section, "Transcendental Doctrine of Method," is a draft methodology of "pure reason" and its a priori ideas. Metaphysics, Kant reasoned, could be established on a scientific footing, if he could prove the existence and conditions of synthetic a priori truths, derived from human sensibility (cast in space and time) and understanding. Kant believed that with the publication of this "critique," he had accomplished a Copernican revolution in philosophy.

Further reading: Immanuel Kant, *Critique of Pure Reason,* trans. and ed. Paul Guyer (New York: Cambridge University Press, 1998).

Crittenden Compromise (Crittenden Plan or Amendments)

Proposed amendments to the U.S. CONSTITUTION presented to the Senate by Senator John J. Crittenden of Kentucky on December 18, 1860, in a last-minute attempt to stave off secession and civil war. The compromise accepted the boundary between free and slave territories established by the MISSOURI COMPROMISE and extended the line westward to the Pacific Coast, for all territory then held or thereafter acquired. It prohibited Congress from abolishing slavery in the South, upheld the FUGITIVE SLAVE LAW OF 1850, and preserved slavery in the District of Columbia, but also called for suppression of the African slave trade. The compromise was defeated, largely because the president-elect, Abraham Lincoln, opposed acceptance of slavery in the territories.

Further reading: James Ford Rhodes, *History of the United States from the Compromise of 1850 to the McKinley-Bryan Campaign of 1896* (Port Washington, N.Y.: Kennikat Press, 1919, repr., 1967).

Croatian-Hungarian Compromise of 1868 (Nagoda, Law XXX of 1868)

Agreement concluded by the Croatian and Hungarian parliaments in September 1868, providing for a degree of Croatian autonomy within the kingdom of Hungary. Through the document Croatia was to be responsible for her own internal affairs; use of the Croatian language was unrestricted; and issues common to both Croatia and Hungary, such as commerce and transportation, were to be their joint responsibility. Restricting Croatian autonomy was the provision that the leading Croatian official, the *ban,* was to be nominated by the Hungarian prime minister and appointed by the king.

See also: AUSGLEICH.

Further reading: Ivo Goldstein, *Croatia: A History* (Montreal: McGill-Queens University Press, 2000).

"Cross of Gold" Speech   Attack upon America's gold standard delivered by William Jennings Bryan on July 8, 1896, at the Democratic National Convention in Chicago. In this dramatic speech, the former congressman from Nebraska called for the free and unlimited coinage of silver to relieve the economic distress of farmers and industrial workers, attacking his opponents for their hard-money views: "You shall not press down upon the brow of labor this crown of thorns, you shall not crucify mankind upon a cross of gold." The speech helped gain Bryan the Democratic nomination for the presidency. He lost the election to Republican William McKinley.

Further reading: William Jennings Bryan, *Cross of Gold: Speech Delivered Before the National Democratic Convention at Chicago, July 9, 1896* (Lincoln: University of Nebraska Press, 1996); William Jennings Bryan, *The First Battle: A Story of the Campaign of 1896* (Poughkeepsie, N.Y.: Vivisphere, 2000); Thomas Carson, ed., *Gale Encyclopedia of U.S. Economic History* (Farmington Hills, Mich.: Gale Group, 1999).

Crown Lands Ordinance of 1902   Legislation by the British Foreign Office in 1902 to settle the distribution of crown (public) lands in its East Africa protectorate. It ruled that no applicant could buy more than 1,000 acres at one time except with the British foreign secretary's permission. Further, if he did not occupy the land or develop it satisfactorily, it could be forfeited. The maximum duration of the lease was 99 years, and it could not be transferred without the commissioner's approval. Temporary occupation licenses, valid for a year on a property not exceeding five acres, could be issued to natives and Indians ("such other persons, not being Europeans or Americans, as the Commissioner may think fit"). Thus, the administration could, and did, discriminate against Indians by issuing them temporary licenses only. Unhappy over its provisions, the European settlers called for its revision.

Further reading: Holly E. Hanson, *When the Miles Came: Land and Social Order in Buganda, 1850–1928* (Ann Arbor, Mich.: UMI Dissertation Services, 1999).

Crown Proceedings Act, British   Major legislation passed by the British Parliament in 1947, which introduced some measure of control over administrative acts, thus modifying the prevalent British common-law system. It authorized judicial reviews of executive action and decision, enabling the crown itself to be sued for torts committed by its ministers or their departments. Before passage of the Crown Proceedings Act, ministers and their departments could not be sued in tort because of the old English legal principle that "the king can do no wrong."

Further reading: Clanville L. Williams, *Crown Proceedings, an Account of Civil Proceedings by and Against the Crown as Affected by the Crown Proceedings Act, 1947* (London: Stevens, 1948).

Crow's Nest Pass Agreement   Agreement concluded between the Canadian government and the Canadian Pacific Railway in 1897, providing for the government's grant of financial assistance to the Canadian Pacific Railway in return for the company's reduction of freight rates on grain and other products. According to the agreement, the company would use the grant to build a westward extension of its railway through Crow's Nest Pass into the British Columbian interior. Its purpose in building the extension was to maintain control over (and keep American competitors out of) southwestern Canada in the wake of the discovery of substantial mineral deposits there. While the government supported the venture, it would have suffered politically had it not also addressed the farmers' complaints regarding high freight rates. The rates ("Crow Rates") remained in effect until 1984.

Further reading: National Archives of Canada, *The Crow's Nest Pass Agreement*, The Canadian West, available online at http://www.archives.ca/05/0529/052920/05292083_e.html.

Cuban Constitution of 1901   Constitution adopted on February 21, 1901, by a constituent assembly called in Havana by U.S. general Leonard Wood, military governor of Cuba from late 1899 to 1902. The constitution called for the establishment of a republican government and for a duly elected president and a bicameral congress. Inserted into the Cuban Constitution was the PLATT AMENDMENT, which allowed the United States to control Cuba's economic, domestic, and international affairs and set up a naval base at Guantánamo Bay in southeast Cuba.

Further reading: Charles E. Chapman, "The Cuban Constitution and Congress," *California Law Review* 14, no. 1 (1925): 22–35; Louis A. Perez, *Cuba under the Platt Amendment, 1902–1934* (Pittsburgh, Pa.: University of Pittsburgh Press, 1986); *Translation of the Proposed Constitution for Cuba, the Official Acceptance of the Platt Amendment, and the Electoral Law* (Washington, D.C.: Division of Insular Affairs, U.S. War Department, 1901).

Cuban Constitution of 1940   Constitution drafted at a constituent assembly convened in 1939 in Cuba by Fulgencio Batista, and put into effect on September 15, 1940, replacing the original law of 1901. The new constitution, inspired by reform-oriented groups as well as the newly legalized Communist Party, consisted of 286 articles, many of which were devoted to social and economic improvements in an effort to curb foreign economic domination of Cuba. Political measures included a semi-parliamentary governmental structure designed to limit the executive power. An advanced labor code and a provision for restricting large landholdings were also introduced. Although the constitution was suspended in 1952 following Batista's coup and subsequent dictatorship, the reinstatement and implementation of the 1940 constitution became a major goal of Fidel Castro's revolutionary movement against Batista.

See also: CUBAN CONSTITUTION OF 1901.

Further reading: Latin American Studies Program, Rose-Hulman Institute of Technology, *Cuban Constitution of 1940*, Cuban History, available online at http://www.rose-hulman. edu/~delacova/constitution-1940.htm.

Cuban Constitution of 1976 Constitution approved by the First Congress of the Cuban Communist Party in Havana in December 1975, and endorsed by the Cuban citizenry in a national referendum on February 15, 1976, effectively institutionalizing Cuban leader Fidel Castro's revolution and confirming the establishment of a Cuban socialist state. Like the SOVIET CONSTITUTION OF 1918, after which it was modeled, the Cuban document declared that Cuba was a socialist state; that Cuba's economy was based on socialist principles; and that freedom of speech, press, and religion were guaranteed, provided that the exercise of those freedoms was not in opposition to the goals of the state. And while the document provided for an indirectly elected national assembly, which would elect a council of state, the chairman of which would be the head of the government, it also, like its Soviet counterpart, declared that the Cuban Communist Party possessed the leading role in governing the state. The constitution was the country's first after 16 years of dictatorial rule under Fidel Castro.

Further reading: *Constitution of the Republic of Cuba* (New York: Center for Cuban Studies, 1976).

Cullom Act See INTERSTATE COMMERCE ACT, U.S.

Cum Occasione Impressionis Libri Papal bull issued by Pope Innocent X on May 31, 1653, condemning five propositions on the relationship of grace and freedom derived from Cornelis Jansen's *AUGUSTINUS* and thought to express the central principles of Jansenism. Published on June 9,

1653, the bull was more specific than *IN EMINENTI* in its rejection of Jansenism's subordination of the human free will and its gloomy view of man's role in the universe. Jansen's followers, led by the French priest Antoine Arnauld (see PROVINCIAL LETTERS), accepted the papal condemnation but protested that the propositions were not derived from *Augustinus*; the Jansenists drew attention to the distinction between matters of doctrine (*droit*), which were the church's domain, and matters of fact (*fait*), which were not. On October 16, 1656, Pope Alexander VII reconfirmed his predecessor Innocent's bull.

See also: CLEMENT IX, PEACE OF.

Further reading: Norman D. Kurland, *Antoine Arnauld: Theological and Philosophical Controversies in the Seventeenth Century* (Ann Arbor, Mich.: University Microfilms, 1974); Alexander Sedgwick, *Jansenism in Seventeenth-Century France: Voices from the Wilderness* (Charlottesville: University Press of Virginia, 1977).

Currency Act of 1764, British (Colonial Currency Act) Measure forbidding the issue of paper (unsound) money in any of the American colonies; passed by the British Parliament on April 19, 1764. At the time British traders (especially in Virginia) complained about being paid in depreciated currency (because the colonies had printed vast amounts of money during the French and Indian War [1756–63]). The act also banned the use of colonial currency for payment of imported English goods. It resulted in a severe money shortage and caused much colonial unrest.

Further reading: Joseph A. Ernst, *Money and Politics in America, 1755–1775; a Study in the Currency Act of 1764 and the Political Economy of Revolution* (Chapel Hill: University of North Carolina Press, 1973); Jack P. Greene, *Negotiated Authorities: Essays in Colonial Political and Constitutional History* (Charlottesville: University Press of Virginia, 1994).

Czech Charter of 77 See CHARTER 77, CZECH.

Czechoslovakia's Two Thousand Words See TWO THOUSAND WORDS.

D

Danbury Hatters' Case   See *LOEWE* v. *LAWLOR*.

Danish Great Charter (Handfaestning, Magna Carta of Denmark)   Charter considered the first written Danish constitution; promulgated by King Eric V (Eric Klipping) of Denmark in July 1282, in response to pressure from the Danish nobility. The document, similar to England's MAGNA CARTA, defined the rights of the nobles while introducing restrictions on the power of the monarch. It bound the king to convene a general assembly (*Parlamentum*) every year; this judicial and legislative body (the *Danehof*) consisted mainly of representatives from the aristocracy. The king was to rule through the Council of the Realm (a select group of nobles). In addition, Eric agreed not to imprison or fine anyone except in accordance with the law and until legal judgment had been pronounced; he accepted the principle of habeas corpus. Precursor to the present constitution, the charter ended one phase of the continuing struggle between the crown and the nobility.

Further reading: Byron J. Nordstrom, ed., *Dictionary of Scandinavian History* (Westport, Conn.: Greenwood Press, 1986); Stewart Oakley, *A Short History of Denmark* (New York: Praeger, 1972).

Danton's "Audacity" Speech   Fiery speech made on September 2, 1792, by Georges-Jacques Danton, French revolutionary leader and politician, before France's Legislative (National) Assembly. Informed of Verdun's imminent col-lapse before an invading allied army, and seeking to rouse the nation to action, Danton ardently declared: "In order to conquer these enemies, gentlemen, we need audacity, again audacity, forever audacity—and France will be saved." He demanded that commissars be appointed to direct the war efforts of the people, that couriers be dispatched to publicize decrees, and that the death penalty be served "for anyone refusing either to serve in person or to surrender his arms." This pithy speech, which took hardly three minutes to deliver, is considered among the finest of his career.

See also: LAW OF THE 40 SOUS.

Further reading: Norman Hampson, *Danton* (London: Duckworth, 1978).

Dardanelles, Treaty of the   See CANAK, TREATY OF.

Darnel's Case   See FIVE KNIGHTS' CASE.

Darrien Presentment, Assize of   English possessory assize or writ introduced in 1179 by King Henry II to determine which patron had last presented (*de ultima presentatione*) a clerk to the particular benefice under dispute. The writ authorized the sheriff to summon an assize to decide the issue. Once determined, the person was given the advowson and entitled to present again. Thus, the king ensured that cases of advowson would be judged in the royal court. The assize was promulgated to circumvent the third Lateran Council's declaration (1179) stipulating that if the presentation to a benefice was delayed by more than three months, it would automatically lapse to the bishop. The Darrien Presentment (last presentation), which shared its summary procedure and interest in possession with two other possessory assizes (Novel Disseisin and Mort d'Ancestor), was not abolished until 1833.

Further reading: Carl Stephenson and Frederick George Marcham, eds., *Sources of English Constitutional History: A Selection of Documents from A.D. 600 to the Present* (New York: Harper & Row, 1937).

Darrow's "Against Capital Punishment" Speech

Speech delivered by attorney Clarence Darrow during a debate with Judge Alfred J. Talley in New York on October 26, 1924. Sponsored by the League for Public Discussion, the debate grew out of Talley's attack on Darrow's controversial defense of two wealthy young men, Nathan F. Leopold, Jr., and Richard A. Loeb, who were convicted of murder but saved from execution by Darrow's eloquence. In the debate Darrow argued that, while capital punishment had never prevented murder, the main question was one of feeling: "If you love the thought of somebody being killed, why, you are for it. If you hate the thought of somebody being killed, you are against it."

Further reading: University of Missouri–Kansas City Law School, *Illinois v. Nathan Leopold and Richard Loeb*, Famous American Trials, available online at http://www.law.umkc.edu/faculty/projects/ftrials/leopleob/leopold.htm.

Dartmouth College v. Woodward

U.S. Supreme Court decision of February 2, 1819, that upheld the sanctity of the college charter as a contract under the U.S. CONSTITUTION protecting it from state legislative action. In 1816 the New Hampshire legislature altered Dartmouth College's 1769 charter, bringing the private institution under public control. The old board of trustees refused to accept the change and sued. The Supreme Court's opinion, written by Chief Justice John Marshall, stated that the legislative revision of the charter was an unconstitutional impairment of contractual obligations. This landmark decision encourages business growth by limiting state control over charters of private corporations. It was modified later by the decision in *CHARLES RIVER BRIDGE v. WARREN BRIDGE*.

Further reading: Albert J. Beveridge, *The Life of John Marshall* (Holmes Beach, Fla.: Gaunt, 1916, repr., 1997).

Das Kapital (Capital)

Monumental work written by German social philosopher Karl Marx, urging an end to private ownership and means of production; the first volume was published in Berlin, Germany, in 1867. The second and third volumes, edited by Marx's colleague Friedrich Engels, were published after Marx's death (1883), in 1885 and 1894; the fourth volume, edited by Karl Kautsky, was printed in 1905–10. Marx argued that capitalists necessarily exploited workers in an inequitable distribution of the products of labor; owners of industrial enterprises, with their primary interest in profits, had to keep wages as low as possible. As rich owners became richer, Marx predicted, they would be motivated to buy out less successful owners, who would be forced to become workers. This would force workers to join together and eventually to take over the means of production, at which time the proletariat (wageworkers) would become the ruling class. Marx laid the foundation for socialism as a political philosophy.

Further reading: Karl Marx, *Capital: A Critique of Political Economy,* trans. Ben Fowkes, 2 vols. (New York: Penguin, 1992); Karl Marx, *Das Kapital: A Critique of Political Economy,* ab. ed. (Washington, D.C.: Regnery 1996).

Dawes Plan

Proposal to stabilize Germany's currency and establish a schedule for the payment of Germany's World War I reparations to the Allies; prepared by an international commission headed by U.S. budget director Charles G. Dawes and adopted by the Allies in August 1924. By 1923 Germany had defaulted on the reparations specified by the 1919 Treaty of VERSAILLES and was in danger of collapse. The plan proposed to reorganize Germany's currency system and set a graduated schedule of reparations payments (rising from 1 billion gold marks in 1924–25 to 2.5 billion in 1928–29, and continuing at that rate until the allied debt was paid). The plan was replaced by the YOUNG PLAN in 1930.

Further reading: Roy Lawrence Garis, *Principles of Money, Credit, and Banking* (New York: Macmillan, 1934).

Dawes Severalty Act

Federal U.S. legislation enacted on February 8, 1887, that provided for the dissolution of the American Indian tribes as legal entities and the distribution of tribal lands among individual members. The act granted citizenship to Indians who renounced tribal allegiance and "adopted the habits of civilized life." It allotted to heads of families 160 acres of reservation land and to adult single people 80 acres; the land was initially awarded in trust, with full title to be transferred after 25 years. Many Indians, unprepared for homesteading and farming, lost their lands to whites. In 1906 Congress passed the BURKE ACT, amending the Dawes Act, in an effort to protect Indian landholdings.

Further reading: Native American Documents Project, *An Act to Provide for the Allotment of lands in Severalty to Indians on the Various Reservations (General Allotment Act or Dawes Act), Statutes at large 24, 388–91, NADP Document A1887,* Native American Documents Project, California State University, San Marcos, available online at http://www.csum.edu/nadp/adawes.htm.

Dawson Agreement

Accord among the leaders of the Nicaraguan Revolution of 1910, signed in Managua, Nicaragua, on November 5, 1910, and arranged by the United States representative Thomas C. Dawson. By the terms of the agreement, General Juan J. Estrada was recognized as chief executive of Nicaragua (early the following year he was legally elected by a constituent convention), and Adolfo Díaz was named vice president for a two-year term. The agreement also called for the adoption of a constitution guaranteeing free elections and the rights of foreigners and for the creation of a commission, which included United States representatives, for the purpose of assessing the problem of foreign claims. Dawson had been sent to disentangle and settle Nicaragua's domestic and foreign financial affairs; Estrada had come to power following the downfall of José Santos Zelaya's dictatorial regime in late 1909.

Further reading: John E. Finding, *The United States and Zelaya: A Study in the Diplomacy of Expediency* (Ann Arbor, Mich.: University Microfilms, 1972).

"Day of Infamy" Speech, Roosevelt's   See ROOSEVELT'S WAR MESSAGE.

Dayton Peace Accord

Agreement establishing the basis for peace in Bosnia and Herzegovina, reached on November 21, 1995, at Wright-Patterson Air Force Base in Dayton, Ohio, between the Republic of Bosnia and Herzegovina, the Republic of Croatia, and the Federal Republic of Yugoslavia. It was formally signed in Paris on December 14, 1995, when the General Framework Agreement (11 Articles) came into effect. All parties agreed to respect one another's sovereignty, human rights, and the rights of refugees and displaced persons. They also promised cooperation with all agencies in implementation of the accord and in bringing war criminals to justice under international law. The main agreement was accompanied by 11 annexes, each dealing with a different aspect, ranging from the military to the preservation of national monuments.

Further reading: James M. B. Lyon, "Will Bosnia Survive Dayton?" *Current History* 99 (March 2000): 110–17; United States of America Department of State, "Summary of the Dayton Peace Agreement," United States of America Department of State, available online at http://www.state.gov/www/regions/eur/bosnia/dayton.html.

Dead Sea Scrolls

Ancient papyrus and leather manuscripts dating from the mid-third century B.C. to A.D. 68; discovered in 1947 by a goatherd boy in a cave at Khirbet Qumran on the northwest shore of the Dead Sea in present-day Jordan (in territory now occupied by Israel). Discoveries of similar documents occurred at Wadi al-Murabba'ah, Nahal Hever and Ze'elim, Wadi Daliyeh, and Masada in the 1950s to mid-1960s. In all of these sites near the Dead Sea, archaeologists and Bedouins found hundreds of scrolls and fragments written in Hebrew, Aramaic, and Greek. In 11 caves at Qumran were well-preserved writings from the Hebrew Old Testament, including laws, rules, hymns, psalms, and commentaries. At the four other sites, biblical fragments, letters, legal documents, listings, and records of Jewish revolts

against Roman rule helped historians further to re-create the history of the Jews and early Christians in the area. It is now certain that Qumran was the center of the Essene sect, an ascetic order of Jews founded in the second century B.C. that existed until A.D. 68.

Further reading: Robert H. Eisenman and James M. Robinson, *A Facsimile Edition of the Dead Sea Scrolls* (Washington, D.C.: Biblical Archaeology Society, 1991); Peter W. Flint and James C. VanderKam, eds., *The Dead Sea Scrolls after Fifty Years: A Comprehensive Assessment* (Boston: Brill, 1998); Menahem Mansoor, *The Dead Sea Scrolls: A Textbook and Study Guide,* 2d ed. (Grand Rapids, Mich.: Baker Book House, 1983); Stephen A. Reed, comp., *The Dead Sea Scrolls Catalogue: Documents, Photographs, and Museum Inventory Numbers* (Atlanta, Ga.: Scholars Press, 1994).

Deasy's Act   See IRISH LAND ACT OF 1860.

Death with Dignity Act, Oregon's

Legislation passed by the Oregon state legislature granting terminally-ill patients the right to die via physician-assisted suicide. The act permitted patients to obtain prescriptions for lethal medications from their doctors, which the patients could then administer to themselves. It expressly forbade euthanasia, whereby the doctor or some third party could administer the medications. The act was first passed as a citizens' initiative in November 1994, but because of complicated legal proceedings it did not become law until October 27, 1997. Fewer than 30 persons per year took advantage of the law to end their lives, most of whom were dying from cancer. In 2001, the U.S. Department of Justice filed suit in federal court to have the law overturned on the grounds that the medications being prescribed fell under the purview of the Federal Controlled Substances Act and therefore could not be prescribed legally anywhere in the United States.

Further reading: Oregon Public Health Services, Center for Health Statistics (and Vital Records), "Oregon's Death with Dignity Act," Oregon Department of Human Services, available online at http://www.ohd.hr.state.or.us/chs/pas/pas.htm.

Debré Law

Legislation passed on December 30, 1959, lifting the ban on governmental aid to Roman Catholic schools in France. Introduced by Premier Michel Debré, with the backing of President Charles de Gaulle, the bill passed the National Assembly by a vote of 427-71 and the Senate by 173-99. It announced a grant of 30 billion francs ($60 million) to be distributed to private (mainly Catholic) schools during 1960. Private schools desirous of obtaining financial help from the state were required to enter into a contract, which, in return, allowed the state to exert limited control over such schools. Ironically, Education Minister André Boulloche had resigned on December 23 in protest over the state's lack of control over the curriculum in Catholic schools. Former

French premier Guy Mollet and a group of radicals, socialists, and anticlerical communists, vainly opposed the bill in parliament.

Further reading: Aline Coutrot, *The Fight over the 1959 Private Education Law in France* (Indianapolis, Ind.: Bobbs-Merill Co., 1966).

December Constitution See AUSTRIAN CONSTITUTION OF 1867.

Decembrist Manifesto
Manifesto prepared by a group of Russian revolutionaries (a group that included some of the best-educated Russian citizens) and issued on December 26, 1825; it aimed at the reformation of Russia's political and social life. In the document, the authors called for the abolition of the present government and the installation of a provisional government, which would be responsible for the restructuring of Russia's political, judicial, and military organizations, and for ensuring the equality of all classes; they also called for freedom of the press, for the individual's right to public trial, and for the emancipation of the serfs. The issue of the manifesto precipitated a revolt. The new czar, Nicholas I, was able to crush the opposition, and the manifesto came to no effect.

Further reading: Anatole Gregory Mazour, *The First Russian Revolution, 1825: The Decembrist Movement, Its Origins, Development, and Significance* (Stanford, Calif.: Stanford University Press, 1937, repr., 1961); Marc Raeff, *The Decembrist Movement* (Englewood Cliffs, N.J.: Prentice-Hall, 1966).

Declaration and Resolves of the First Continental Congress (Declaration of Rights and Grievances)
Opinions and complaints of the First Continental Congress and adopted by the congress on October 14, 1774. The document argued that the American colonists were being deprived of their rights as Englishmen and included 10 resolutions describing those rights (such as "life, liberty, and property," the benefits of the common law of England, and peaceable assembly and petition) and protesting the colonists' lack of representation in the British Parliament. It declared that their rights were violated specifically by 13 acts passed by Parliament since 1763, including the STAMP ACT OF 1765, the Townshend Revenue Act of 1767, the COERCIVE ACTS, and the QUEBEC ACT. In reaction to these violations of rights, it pledged economic sanctions against Britain until the protested laws were repealed.

Further reading: The Avalon Project "the Avalon Project at the Yale Law School Declaration and Resolves of the first Continental Congress," Avalon Project available online at http://www.yale.edu/lawweb/avalon/resolves.htm.

Declaration Concerning Religion, Ethics, and the Crisis in the Clinton Presidency
Declaration signed in September 1998 by 138 nationally renowned theologians, protesting "the manipulation of religion and the debasing of moral affairs." Fearing that the U.S. religious community might be asked to vouch for Clinton's "politically motivated and incomplete repentance," they expressed concern about its impact on the younger generation and urged society "to seek the integrity of both public and private morality." Further, they proposed a scholarly, nonpartisan setting where the constitutional, ethical, and religious implications of this issue may be extensively discussed.

Further reading: *Wall Street Journal*, "Declaration Concerning Religion, Ethic, and the Crisis in the Clinton Presidency November 30, 1998, A22.

Declaration of American Presidents
Document signed in Punta del Este, Uruguay, at the close of a conference on inter-American cooperation on April 14, 1967, by 17 American presidents attending the meeting, including U.S. president Lyndon Johnson; it declared the signatories' plan for Latin American economic development. The plan called for the establishment of a Latin American common market by 1970 and for the implementation of programs to raise the standard of living of inhabitants of rural regions, to promote education and to improve health care in Latin America; it proposed measures designed to increase Latin American trade with foreign countries and, in order to fund these initiatives, called for a reduction in military spending by Latin American countries. Of those attending the conference, only Ecuadoran president Otto Arosemena Gómez refused to sign the document, declaring that the United States had not committed enough aid to Latin America.

See also: BOGOTÁ, DECLARATION OF.

Further reading: Organization of American States, *Declaration of the Presidents of the American Republic in Panama*, Summit of the Americas Information Network, available online at http://www.summit-americas.org/declarat%20presidents-panama%201956-eng.htm.

Declaration of Human Rights See UNIVERSAL DECLARATION OF HUMAN RIGHTS.

Declaration of Independence, American
Document written by Thomas Jefferson and made public on July 4, 1776. It opened with the theoretical explanation for America's separation from Great Britain, justifying the decision through appeal to the doctrine of natural rights. Arguing that governments derive "their just powers from the consent of the governed," Jefferson went on to assert the right to revolt against an unjust government. The abuses of King George III against the colonists were then listed to provide justification for the renunciation of all ties with Great Britain. Though edited by members of Congress (notably Benjamin Franklin and John Adams), Jefferson's ideas remained basically intact. Revisions were completed on July 4 and sent immediately to a printer in Philadelphia, who printed it under that date. The official

signing of the document by all the delegates to the Second Continental Congress was on August 2, 1776; most of the 56 names on the document were signed before August 6, but at least six signatures were attached later.

See also: LEE'S RESOLUTIONS; OLIVE BRANCH PETITION; VIRGINIA BILL OF RIGHTS.

Further reading: Carl Lotus Becker, *The Declaration of Independence: A Study in the History of Political Ideas* (New York: Random House, 1958); Indiana University School of Law–Bloomington, *The Declaration of Independence of the Thirteen Colonies*, School of Law–Bloomington, available online at http://www.law.indiana.edu/uslawdocs/declaration.html. Pauline Maier, *American Scripture: Making the Declaration of Independence* (New York: Knopf, 1997); Charles L. Phillips and Alan Axelrod, eds., *Encyclopedia of Historical Treaties and Alliances,* 2 vols. (New York: Facts On File, 2001).

Declaration of Independence, Texas   See TEXAS DECLARATION OF INDEPENDENCE.

Declaration of Independence for Women   See WOMEN'S RIGHTS, DECLARATION OF.

Declaration of Reciprocal Assistance and Cooperation for the Defense of the Nations of the Americas   See HAVANA, ACT OF.

Declaration of Repentance   Formal apology to Jews issued on September 30, 1997, at Drancy (outside Paris) by France's Roman Catholic Church, for its tacit acceptance of the French government's role in the persecution of Jews during World War II. The government had passed a series of anti-Semitic laws and deported thousands of French Jews to death camps in Poland and Germany. Amid several hundred people including Catholic clergy and Jewish leaders gathered at a memorial (the site of an internment camp), Archbishop Olivier de Beranger confessed "that silence was a mistake" and asked for forgiveness. He also apologized for the "anti-Jewish stereotypes" regularly fostered by the church. This apology, the French church's most straightforward admission of guilt, followed President Jacques Chirac's official admission of complicity in 1995.

Further reading: Martin S. Alexander, ed., *French History since Napoleon* (London: Arnold, 1999); Roger Cohen, "French Church Issues Apology to Jews on War," *New York Times*, October 1, 1997, pp. A1–2; R. N. S., "French Catholics Repent Holocaust Silence," *Christian Century* 114 (October 22, 1997): 939–45.

Declaration of Rights, English (Bill of Rights)   Statement issued by England's Convention Parliament on February 13, 1689, and later enacted as a Bill of Rights on December 16, 1689, affirming the ancient constitutional rights of the English realm. It declared that England's king James II had forfeited his crown by certain illegal acts, that the English people had special inviolable and civil rights, that William III and Mary II were now the country's lawful sovereigns jointly, and that succession of the crown passed to Mary's heirs and subsequently to Princess Anne (later queen) and her heirs. It also asserted that a Roman Catholic could not be England's sovereign. By its provisions and implications, the political power was handed to Parliament, whose consent was needed to make or suspend laws and to levy money.

See also: SETTLEMENT, ACT OF.

Further reading: Carl Stephenson and Frederick George Marcham, eds., *Sources of English Constitutional History: A Selection of Documents from* A.D. *600 to the Present* (New York: Harper & Row, 1937).

Declaration of Rights, Shelley's   See SHELLEY'S DECLARATION OF RIGHTS.

Declaration of Rights, Virginia   See VIRGINIA BILL OF RIGHTS.

Declaration of Rights and Grievances   Petition issued on October 19, 1765, by the Stamp Act Congress in New York City, condemning the STAMP ACT OF 1765 and assuring the American colonies that "no taxes ever have been or can be constitutionally imposed on them, except by their respective legislatures." At the congress or meeting, which had been initiated by the Massachusetts legislature, were 28 delegates from nine colonies. The petition, which contained 14 resolutions and which was probably drafted by John Dickinson (a Pennsylvania delegate), protested that the colonists' individual rights and liberties as recognized subjects of the British crown were being violated. It also denounced the increased powers of the nonjury vice admiralty courts, which were trying violators of recent British trade regulations.

Further reading: *Authentick Account of the Proceedings of the Congress Held at New York,* A.D. *1765, on the Subject of the American Stamp Act* (New York: Readex Microprint, 1983); Henry Steele Commager, ed., *Documents of American History,* 8th ed. (New York: Appleton-Century-Crofts, 1968); Edmund S. Morgan, *Prologue to Revolution: Sources and Documents on the Stamp Act Crisis, 1764–1766* (Chapel Hill: University of North Carolina Press, 1959); Peter D. G. Thomas, *British Politics and the Stamp Act Crisis: The First Phase of the American Revolution 1763–1767* (New York: Clarendon Press, 1975).

Declaration of Rights of Negro Peoples of the World
Statement drawn up in 1920 in New York City by delegates at an international convention of the Universal Negro Improvement Association (founded by U.S. black leader Marcus Garvey in 1914). It declared that blacks have suffered injustices, discrimination, and "inhuman, unchristian, and unciv-

ilized treatment" in most every part of the world and that European nations had taken control of nearly all of Africa, "the Motherland of all Negroes." All blacks were "free citizens of Africa," it stated, and they had the right "to reclaim the treasures and possession of the vast continent of [their] fore-fathers."

Further reading: Universal Negro Improvement Association and African Communities League, *Declaration of Rights of the Negro Peoples of the World*, Universal Negro Improvement Association and African Communities League, available online at http://www.unia-acl.org/azchive/declare.htm.

Declaration of Sports (Book of Sports)

Statement by King James I of England in 1618, who tried to counteract the growing influence of Sabbatarianism by publishing a list of traditional games and festivities that were permissible after the Sunday religious service. Sports such as dancing, archery, leaping, vaulting, May games, Morris dances, Whitsun-ales, and the stacking of the Maypole were permitted; bear and bull baiting, bowling, and interludes were banned. Nonconformists and those not attending the services could not take part. Initially, the king ordered the book to be read aloud in the parishes but, noticing the opposition to it, he did not insist. The book was reissued by King Charles I in 1633, when it again aroused the anger of many Puritans.

Further reading: Department of History, Hanover College, *Charles I the Declaration of Sports*, Department of History, Hanover College, available online at http://history.hanover.edu/early/charlesI.htm.

Declaration of the Four States on the Question of General Security

See MOSCOW CONFERENCE DECLARATIONS OF 1943.

Declaration of the French Clergy

See FOUR ARTICLES, BOSSUET'S.

Declaration of the Rights of Man and of the Citizen (La Déclaraton des Droits de l'Homme et du Citoyen)

French document drafted by Emmanuel J. Sieyès (Abbé Sieyès), approved by the National Assembly in Paris on August 27, 1789, and signed by France's king Louis XVI on October 5, 1789. Its 17 articles affirmed human liberties and served as a preface to the FRENCH CONSTITUTION OF 1791. The first article stated its basic principle: "Men are born and remain free and equal in rights . . ."; the second defined these rights as "liberty, property, security, and resistance to oppression." Another article declared all citizens "equally admissible to all public offices, positions, and employment" (see FRENCH DECREE ABOLISHING FEUDALISM). Other articles affirmed "free communication of ideas and opinions" ("one of the most precious rights of man"), the rights of citizens to vote on taxes, and the accountability of public servants. And public confiscation of property (property "being sacred and

inviolable") had to be justly compensated. Like the American DECLARATION OF INDEPENDENCE, this declaration reflected the general disillusionment with the monarchical system and heralded the birth of a new era.

Further reading: Georg Jellinek, *The Declaration of the Rights of Man and of Citizens: A Contribution to Modern Constitutional History* (Westport, Conn.: Hyperion Press, 1979).

Declaration of the Rights of Woman and the Female Citizen (Déclaration des Droits de la Femme et de la Citoyenne)

Powerful feminist manifesto by the revolutionary Parisian playwright Olympe de Gouges in 1791 challenging male supremacy as reflected in France's National Assembly's DECLARATION OF THE RIGHTS OF MAN AND OF THE CITIZEN. Defined in the preamble as "a solemn declaration of the natural, inalienable and sacred rights of woman," it consisted of 17 articles, a postscript, and a "Form of Social Contract Between Man and Woman," and urged men to emulate the "harmonious togetherness" of the sexes in nature. It stressed equal rights for men and women, including total equality in the "eyes of the law," arguing that if "woman has the right to mount the scaffold, she must equally have the right to mount the rostrum." Marriage should be a social contract with everything being equally divided between the two partners. Gouges was scorned and ridiculed for these bold and provocative statements and for her monarchist views. She was charged with treason and executed in November 1793.

See also: EQUALITY OF MEN AND WOMEN, THE; *VINDICATION OF THE RIGHTS OF WOMAN*.

Further reading: Darline Gay Levy et al., *Women in Revolutionary Paris, 1789–1795: Selected Documents Translated with Notes and Commentary* (Urbana: University of Illinois Press, 1979).

Declarations of Liberty of Conscience

See INDULGENCE, DECLARATIONS OF.

Declaratory Act of 1766

Declaration made by the British Parliament on March 18, 1766, when it repealed the STAMP ACT OF 1765. It reaffirmed the right of the king and parliament to make laws "to bind the [American] colonies in all cases whatsoever," despite the lack of colonial representation in Parliament. The act attempted to explain Parliament's constitutional supremacy in the relationship between Britain and her colonies. Many colonists, however, saw the act as an intimidation to self-government.

Further reading: *Dictionary of American History*, rev. ed. (New York: Charles Scribner's Sons, 1976); Carl Stephenson and Frederick George Marcham, eds., *Sources of English Constitutional History: A Selection of Documents from A.D. 600 to the Present* (New York: Harper & Row, 1937); William MacDonald, *Select Charters and Other Documents Illustrative of American History, 1606–1775* (Littleton, Colo.: F. B. Rothman, 1993).

Decretal of Gratian (*Concordantia Discordantium Canonum*)

Italian scholar Gratian's compilation (1140) of approximately 4,000 texts of canon law. It quickly became the standard text for the study of medieval canon law, which it established as a separate discipline. Gratian, a Camaldolite monk in Bologna, drew upon previous collections, using the Lateran Council of 1139 as the cutoff date; he tried to reconcile the differences (errors and contradictions) among earlier, apparently contrary, texts of canon law. This and the fact that Gratian's collection is systematically organized, on the lines of Roman law, enhanced its reputation. Part one deals with law in general and with ecclesiastics, part two explores ecclesiastical causes, and part three is concerned with rites. The decretal had no canonical authority as a collection, but its influence (see DECRETALS OF 1234) on the development of every aspect of church government was tremendous. It was to canon law what the *Four Books of SENTENCES* were to theology.

See also: FALSE DECRETALS.

Further reading: Brian Tierney, *Foundations of the Conciliar Theory: The Contribution of the Medieval Canonists from Gratian to the Great Schism,* (New York: Brill, 1998); Anders Winroth, *The Making of Gratian's Decretum* (New York: Cambridge University Press, 2000).

Decretals of 1234 (*Liber Decretalium Gregorii IX*)

Collection of decretals (papal letters responding to a specific question) and conciliar decisions commissioned in 1230 by Pope Gregory IX and, on September 5, 1234, promulgated through his bull *Rex Pacificus* as the only official text of canon law after the DECRETAL OF GRATIAN. The compilation was entrusted to Raymond of Penafort, a Spanish canonist and Gregory's chaplain and confessor, and derived added juridicial authority from the pope, whose bull also ensured that another similar collection could not be compiled without special permission from the Holy See. In the manner of previous collections, it is divided into five books: judges (*judex*), trial (*judicium*), clergy (*clerus*), marriage (*connubium*), and crime (*crimen*). The material, however, is systematically reorganized to create an authentic, exclusive collection of decretals and constitutions, the first such with a papal seal of approval.

See also: FALSE DECRETALS.

Further reading: Joseph R. Strayer, ed., *Dictionary of the Middle Ages,* 13 vols. (New York: Charles Scribner's Sons, 1989).

De Ecclesia (Of the Church)

Dogmatic constitution of the Roman Catholic Church promulgated by Pope Paul VI in Rome at the Second Vatican Council on November 21, 1964. It completed the work of the First Vatican Council (1869–70), which had planned to augment the DOGMA OF PAPAL INFALLIBILITY with a teaching on the bishops' authority, but failed owing to the Italian nationalists' takeover of Rome during the Italian unification movement. *De Ecclesia* stated that collectively the bishops, together with the pope, were to share equally in governing the church (though a special place would still be reserved for the pope, the "rock" upon which the church was built). The document also redefined the role of the deacon as that of assisting in pastoral duties in areas where priests were few; it also reaffirmed the role of the church as the way to salvation and described the laity's obligation to integrate work for the salvation of others with daily activities.

Further reading: Peter Hebblethwaite, *Paul VI: The First Modern Pope* (London: Fount, 1994); Vatican Council, *Dogmatic Constitution on the Church: Lumen Gentium, Solemnly Promulgated by His Holiness, Pope Paul VI, on November 21, 1964* (Boston: Pauline Books & Media, 1998).

Defense of India Act, British

Wartime legislation (1915) in India (then a British colony), authorizing the government to arrest, detain, or restrict the freedom of persons suspected of involvement in revolutionary crimes. Passed following the outbreak of World War I in 1914, it was to end six months after the war did. It provided for the appointment of a special legal tribunal to try those suspects who were denied recourse to appeal. Under this act, nearly 800 persons were interned by 1918. India's populace thought these measures severely repressive, but did not unleash the full fury of its anger until after the passage of the ROWLATT ACTS in 1919. The Rowlatt or the "black acts" further extended these repressive policies.

Further reading: *Rowlatt Sedition Committee Report* (Calcutta: New Age Publishers, 1973); Stanley Wolpert, *A New History of India*, 6th ed. (New York: Oxford University Press, 2000).

Defense of Marriage Act, U.S.

President Bill Clinton's enactment on September 21, 1996, of the Defense of Marriage Act (DOMA) recognized marriage as a legal union "between one man and one woman as husband and wife," thereby denying federal recognition to same-sex marriages. It also ruled that partners in such marriages were not eligible for federal benefits such as the right to file joint tax returns. Further, states could opt not to recognize such marriages performed legally in another state. The bill had been shepherded through the 104th Congress as a preemptive response against an expected ruling by the Hawaiian supreme court that would legalize same-sex marriages.

Further reading: The Human Rights Campaign, "What the Defense of Marriage Act Does," The Human Rights Campaign Working for lesbian, gay, bisexual, and transgender equal rights, available online at http://www.hrc.org/issues/marriage/background/domadoes.asp.

Defense of the Realm Acts, British

Series of parliamentary acts (acronym DORA) passed during 1914–15 to enable Britain's government to make regulations "for public safety and defense" during World War I (1914–18). The first of these acts was passed in August 1914; successive acts merely broadened the scope of the regulations. These generally authorized a greater control of armament plants, production and distribution in factories, and the use of factories for defense purposes. Advisory commissions were set up to implement these regulations, which usually were not strictly enforced. Wages and prices were tightly controlled. Britain's war office obtained the right to censor all cables and foreign correspondence, and newspapers could be prosecuted for printing unauthorized news or speculating about future policies. Parliamentary affairs could be reported uncensored.

Further reading: Carl Stephenson and Frederick George Marcham, eds., *Sources of English Constitutional History: A Selection of Documents from A.D. 600 to the Present* (New York: Harper & Row, 1937).

de Gaulle's Speech of June 18, 1940

Speech delivered by General Charles de Gaulle of France and broadcast from London to the French people on June 18, 1940 (the day after French generals acknowledged their defeat and requested an armistice from Germany during World War II); it contained his statements of faith in France's ultimate victory over Germany. The speech was essentially an emotional call to the French people to maintain faith that their defeat was not final, and that the war, which was a world war, could be won by uniting with Britain against Germany. De Gaulle also personally invited all Frenchmen, officers, engineers, and skilled workmen in the armaments industry to come to England to meet with him. Although de Gaulle did not announce the establishment of any movement in his speech, the Free French Movement traced its origin back to the speech.

Further reading: Simon Berthon, *Allies at War: The Bitter Rivalry among Churchill, Roosevelt, and de Gaulle* (New York: Carroll & Graf, 2001); Charles de Gaulle, *The Complete War Memoirs of Charles de Gualle*, trans. Jonathan Griffin and Richard Howard (New York: Carroll & Graf, 1998).

De Jure Belli ac Pacis

See *ON THE LAW OF WAR AND PEACE*.

de Klerk's "Season of Violence Is Over" Speech

Dramatic, courageous speech delivered by South Africa's president F. W. de Klerk before parliament in Cape Town on February 2, 1990, legalizing more than 60 opposition groups, including the exiled African National Congress (ANC), the United Democratic Front, and the South African Communist Party. He also announced that well-known ANC leader Nelson Mandela would soon be unconditionally released from prison after more than 27 years there, for attempting to overthrow the government; he was freed on February 11. De Klerk also declared a moratorium on all executions and lifted most restrictions imposed during a 43-month-old state of emergency. These were the chief steps demanded by Mandela and

the ANC as conditions for negotiations on a new constitution that would end the black majority's exclusion from national politics. Said de Klerk: "The season of violence is over. The time for reconstruction and reconciliation has arrived." Though he did not end the country's apartheid system, de Klerk was praised at home and abroad, but met strong, right-wing Afrikaner opposition.

See also: FREEDOM CHARTER.

Further reading: F. W. de Klerk, *Speech by the State President of South Africa, Mr. F. W. De Klerk, on the Occasion of the Independence of Namibia, Windhoek, 20 March 1990,* F. W. de Klerk Foundation, available online at http://www.fwdklerk.org.za/archives/900321.nam.htm.

Delhi Pact of 1950

See NEHRU-LIAQUAT PACT.

Delhi Pact of 1931, Gandhi's (Gandhi-Irwin Pact)

Pact (March 5, 1931) wherein Mohandas Gandhi, leader of the Indian National Congress, and Lord Irwin, British viceroy in India (1926–31), resolved some of their differences; it led to the congress's participation at the Second Round Table Conference in London (1931). Gandhi agreed to suspend his civil disobedience campaign (see GANDHI'S ANNOUNCEMENT OF A *SATYAGRAHA* [CIVIL DISOBEDIENCE] STRUGGLE); the British viceroy promised to release political detainees, restore property seized in lieu of tax arrears, and withdraw the extra police security from disturbed areas and the repressive ordinances passed since 1930. The congress's boycott of British goods was to be discontinued, but peaceful picketing to discourage the use of foreign goods was allowed. At the Round Table Conference, the congress was to help draft a federal constitution for a self-governing India, with safeguards "in the interests of India." Though Gandhi conceded more than he secured, the pact was important in India's independence movement, being the first time that Britain and India had negotiated as equals.

Further reading: Jack C. Winslow and Verrier Elwin, *The Dawn of Indian Freedom* (London: G. Allen & Unwin, 1931); Stanley Wolpert, *Gandhi's Passion: The Life and Legacy of Mahatma Gandhi* (New York: Oxford University Press, 2001); Stanley Wolpert, *A New History of India*, 6th ed. (New York: Oxford University Press, 2000).

De Lima v. Bidwell

U.S. Supreme Court decision made on May 27, 1901, on the claim of Elias S. A. De Lima, an importer of goods from Puerto Rico to the United States, that duties amounting to $13,000 had been wrongfully collected from him by George R. Bidwell, collector of the Port of New York. It decided that the duties had been wrongfully collected and had to be returned. The court's judgment was based on its understanding that, at the time the duties had been collected, Puerto Rico was a United States possession, and that, consequently, tariff laws regulating trade between the United States and foreign countries were not applicable. Puerto Rico had become a U.S. possession in 1898, when Spain ceded the island to the United States (see PARIS, TREATY OF [1898]).

Further reading: John Holladay Latané, *America as a World Power* (St. Clair Shores, Mich.: Scholarly Press, 1907, repr., 1970).

Delimitation, Act of   Act concluded in St. Petersburg on January 26, 1797, by Russia, Prussia, and Austria, two years after the conclusion of the AUSTRO-RUSSIAN AND RUSSO-PRUSSIAN TREATIES OF 1795, which formalized the third partition of Poland. The document confirmed the final partition of Poland, through which Russia added Lithuania and the Ukraine to her empire; Prussia gained Mazovia; and Austria gained the remainder of Galicia, including Kraków. In addition, the three contracting parties declared that the partition was permanent and irrevocable, and that the name of the former power (Poland) was to be suppressed.

Further reading: Jerzy Lukowski, *The Partitions of Poland: 1772, 1793, 1795* (London: Longman, 1999).

de Lôme Letter   Private letter to a Cuban friend written in December 1897 by Enrique Depuy de Lôme, Spanish minister to the United States; stolen from a Havana post office and published in the *New York Journal* on February 9, 1898, the letter helped to fuel the U.S. movement, already aroused because of Spanish policies in Cuba, toward war with Spain. In the letter de Lôme called U.S. president William McKinley "weak and a bidder for the admiration of the crowd." Cuban revolutionaries released the document to a U.S. newspaper owned and published by William Randolph Hearst, who favored a war with Spain. Although de Lôme resigned immediately, sentiment for war grew and hostilities erupted in April 1898.

Further reading: Henry Steele Commager, ed., *Documents of American History*, 8th ed. (New York: Appleton-Century-Crofts, 1968).

Demarcation, Bull of (Inter Caetera)   Bull issued in May 1493 by Pope Alexander VI (a Spaniard) at the behest of Ferdinand II and Isabella I of Spain; it defined the pagan areas that Spain and Portugal might claim after the discoveries of Columbus's first voyage. The Catholic sovereigns (Ferdinand and Isabella) wished to get Columbus's newly found islands formally recognized as a Spanish possession, and to open the way for the acquisition of further territory to the west. The papal bull proclaimed that all lands west of a line passing through the Azores belonged to Spain, while all new discoveries to the east were to become the property of Portugal. For 300 years the bull remained the basic formal title of the Spanish Crown to the lands of the New World.

See also: TORDESILLAS, TREATY OF.

Further reading: Roger Bigelow Merriman, *The Rise of the Spanish Empire* (New York: Cooper Square Publishers, 1918, repr., 1962).

Demonetization Act, U.S.   See COINAGE ACT OF 1873, U.S.

De Motu Cordis et Sanguinis in Animalibus   See ON THE MOTION OF THE HEART AND BLOOD IN ANIMALS.

Dennis et al. v. United States   U.S. Supreme Court decision, issued on June 4, 1951, that upheld the provisions of the SMITH ALIEN REGISTRATION ACT of 1940 that prohibited advocating the forceful overthrow of the U.S. government. Eleven high-ranking Communist Party leaders had been convicted in New York of conspiring to teach and advocate the violent destruction of the government and conspiring to organize the Communist Party in the United States in order to advance that purpose. No overtly violent acts were charged. In its six-to-two decision, the Supreme Court confirmed the convictions, modifying its previous requirement that the law could prohibit only speech that represented a "clear and present danger." Dissenting opinions argued that the act violated FIRST AMENDMENT guarantees of free speech.

Further reading: Leonard W. Levy and Kenneth L. Karst, eds., *Encyclopedia of the American Constitution*, 2d ed. (New York: Macmillan Reference, 2000).

Dentists' Act, British   Great Britain's first Dentists' Act, passed in 1878, to upgrade the education and practice of dentistry. The General Medical Council set up a register wherein it published the names of those qualified to practice as "dental surgeons." It also developed a curriculum for training in dentistry. This was to include three years in a medical school and dental hospital and two years' apprenticeship in dental mechanics. The act, however, did not prevent unqualified individuals from posing as dentists.

Further reading: Kingsley Wood, *Dental Registration: Being a Practical Guide to the New Dentists Act* (London: Balliere, Tindall & Cox, 1921).

Deogaon, Treaty of   Treaty between the Maratha raja of Berar, Raghuji Bhonsle II, and the British East India Company on December 17, 1803; it reduced the raja to vassal status at the end of the first phase of the Second Maratha War (1803–5). The negotiations were conducted by Sir Arthur Wellesley (later first duke of Wellington), whose decisive victory over the raja at Argaon in November 1802 had put him in a commanding position. The raja surrendered Cuttack and Balasore in Orissa to the company (making British territory continuous between Calcutta and Madras) and all of Berar west of the Wardha River to the nizam of Hyderabad, and agreed to accept the presence of a British resident and a small military force in his capital.

Further reading: Jac Weller, *Wellington in India* (London: Greenhill Books 2000).

De Rerum Natura   See ON THE NATURE OF THINGS.

De Revolutionibus Orbium Coelestium. See ON THE REVOLUTIONS OF THE HEAVENLY BODIES.

Descartes's Discourse on Method See DISCOURSE ON METHOD.

Desert Land Act, U.S. Legislation passed by Congress on March 3, 1877, allowing settlers to acquire large tracts of federally owned dry land on condition that they irrigate the property. The act permitted settlers to purchase up to 640 acres, with a down payment of 25¢ per acre and a payment of $1 an acre more after three years if the tract had been irrigated. Thousands of homesteaders attempted to establish small farms, but few succeeded in obtaining enough water to grow crops. Instead, the act benefited cattle barons, who collected vast holdings by registering lands in the names of their cowhands. By 1890 3.5 million acres had been distributed.

Further reading: *Dictionary of American History,* rev. ed. (New York: Charles Scribner's Sons, 1976); Paul Wallace Gates, *History of Public Land Law Development* (Washington, D.C.: Zenger Publishing, 1978); Clyde E. Stewart, *Homesteading in the Middle Twentieth Century: The Desert Land Act of 1877: Review Draft* (Logan, Utah: Farm Economics Division, Economic Research Service, U.S. Department of Agriculture, 1961).

Destroyers-for-Bases Agreement Mutual defense agreement announced by U.S. president Franklin D. Roosevelt on September 2, 1940, by which the United States transferred 50 World War I destroyers to Great Britain (then struggling to resist the German Blitzkrieg) in exchange for 99-year leases on British naval and air bases in the Western Hemisphere. The destroyers, used to escort convoys, helped Britain to protect her sea lanes. Linking British survival with American security, Roosevelt called the exchange the "most important action in the reinforcement of our national defense . . . since the Louisiana Purchase."

Further reading: Philip Goodhart, *Fifty Ships That Saved the World* (Garden City, N.Y.: Doubleday, 1965); Waldo Heinrichs, *Threshold of War: Franklin D. Roosevelt and American Entry into World War II* (New York: Oxford University Press, 1988).

Deulino, Truce of Armistice of 14½ years concluded on December 11, 1618, by the Russian state and the Polish-Lithuanian republic in the town of Deulino. Through the document it was agreed that Russia would hand over to the republic the territories of Smolensk, Seversk, and Chernigov, as well as other cities. These were territories that had been captured by the Poles during their leader Ladislas IV's military campaign against Russia, notably against Moscow. Ladislas failed to take Moscow, however, and agreed in the treaty to renounce his claim to the Muscovite throne, which he had secured through a 1610 agreement with Muscovite boyars

(aristocrats), who had at that time sought his intervention in order to protect them from political instability during the "Time of Troubles" (1604–13) in Russian dynastic history.

Further reading: Richard Butterwick, *The Polish-Lithuanian Monarchy in European Context c. 1500–1795* (New York: Palgrave, 2001).

de Valera's Letter on Irish Grievances Letter written and sent by Irish leader Eamon de Valera on February 12, 1921, to every member of the House of Commons in London, protesting Britain's "unjust war" against the people of Ireland. The British Black and Tans (the Royal Irish Constabulary's popular name, from the color of the uniform) had been recruited and engaged (since 1919) in bloody fighting against the Sinn Fein rebels in Ireland. De Valera said that torturing of prisoners, assassinations, outrages against women and girls, floggings, lootings, and other uncivilized and barbaric acts had been committed by the troops employed by the British government, which was primarily responsible and should end the violence. Later that year an Anglo-Irish treaty was signed, forming northern (Ulster) and southern Ireland (recognized as the Irish Free State in 1922).

Further reading: Christopher Haigh, ed., *The Cambridge Historical Encyclopedia of Great Britain and Ireland* (Cambridge, England: Cambridge University Press, 1985); D. J. Hickey and J. E. Doherty, *A Dictionary of Irish History since 1800* (Dublin: Gill & Macmillan, 1980).

Dewey's *Human Nature and Conduct* See HUMAN NATURE AND CONDUCT.

Dialogue Concerning the Two Chief Systems of the World (Dialogo Sopra i due Massimi Sistemi del Mondo)
Scientific treatise written by Italian astronomer Galileo Galilei from 1624 to 1630 and published in Florence in 1632, disclaiming the work of Alexandrian astronomer Ptolemy and Greek philosopher Aristotle, and demonstrating the truth of Polish astronomer Copernicus's theories (see ON THE REVOLUTIONS OF THE HEAVENLY BODIES). Written in the form of a dialogue among figures representing Copernicus, Ptolemy, Aristotle, and an educated layman, whom the others attempt to persuade to adopt their views, the treatise contained a thinly veiled affirmation of the Copernican view that the Earth rotated around its own axis and that the planets rotated around the Sun. This earned Galileo the ire of the Roman Catholic Church, which held that the Earth was the center of the universe around which all other bodies rotated, and which had granted Galileo permission to write the work on the condition that he not favor one view over the other. Ultimately Galileo faced the Inquisition, was sentenced to life imprisonment, and the *Dialogue* was placed on the Index of Prohibited Books by the Roman Catholic Church.

Further reading: Galileo Galilei, *Dialogue Concerning the Two Chief Systems, Ptolemaic and Copernican,* trans. Stillman

Drake (New York: Modern Library, 2001); Frank N. Magill, ed., *Great Events from History, Modern European Series*, 3 vols. (Englewood Cliffs, N.J.: Salem Press, 1973); Milton K. Munitz, *Theories of the Universe: From Babylonian Myth to Modern Science* (Glencoe, Ill.: Free Press, 1957).

Dickerson v. United States

Case in which the U.S. Supreme Court reaffirmed on June 26, 2000, its 1966 ruling in MIRANDA V. ARIZONA thereby superseding a 1968 federal law (Section 3501). In 1997, Charles Dickerson was charged with robbing a bank in Alexandria, Virginia. He was not read his Miranda rights and incriminated himself in statements made to the Federal Bureau of Investigation (FBI). Prosecutors petitioned a federal court to admit these facts as evidence against him, since they were voluntarily made (as required under Section 3501). That request was denied and the Justice Department refused to appeal it. Instead, the Washington Legal Foundation petitioned the U.S. Fourth Circuit Court of Appeals in Richmond, which ruled that Dickerson's statement was admissible since Miranda was not a constitutional requirement. Stating that Miranda warnings "have become part of our national culture" and that the 1966 ruling was a "constitutional decision," the Supreme Court voted 7-2 to reaffirm it. The decision, which strengthened the civil rights of defendants, was welcomed by civil liberties groups and criticized by many law-enforcement groups.

Further reading: Erwin Chemerinsky, "The Court Should Have Remained Silent: Why the Court Erred in Deciding *Dickerson v. United States*," *University of Pennsylvania Law Review* 149 (November 2000): 287–309.

Dickinson's Farmer's Letters

See FARMER'S LETTERS, DICKINSON'S.

Dillingham Immigration Act

See EMERGENCY QUOTA ACT, U.S.

Dingley Tariff Act

Highly protective U.S. tariff legislation passed on July 24, 1897, and named for Congressman Nelson Dingley. It replaced the WILSON-GORMAN TARIFF ACT of 1894. In response to America's depression following the Panic of 1893 and treasury deficits, this act raised tariff rates to the highest level (on average, 57 percent) in U.S. history. It imposed high tariffs on raw and manufactured wool, restored the tariff on hides, and increased the rates on silks and linens. Rates on metals and cottons, however, changed little. The act was replaced by the PAYNE-ALDRICH TARIFF ACT of 1909.

Further reading: Thomas Carson, ed., *Gale Encyclopedia of U.S. Economic History* (Farmington Hills, Mich.: Gale Group, 1999); Tom E. Terrill, *The Tariff, Politics, and American Foreign Policy, 1874–1901* (Westport, Conn.: Greenwood Press, 1973).

Diocletian's Edict of A.D. 301

See EDICT OF MAXIMUM PRICES.

Diploma Leopoldinum (Leopoldina)

Edict issued by the Holy Roman Emperor Leopold I on December 4, 1691, to the Transylvanian Estates, through which the emperor hoped to placate the Transylvanian extremists who had enlisted the support of the Ottoman sultan in order to gain freedom from the Hapsburgs. Through the document Leopold granted Transylvania her own constitution, guaranteed religious toleration and the annual convocation of her diet, and pledged that only Transylvanians would be appointed to state posts (except to the post of commander in chief, which was to be occupied by a German). Transylvania, legally part of the Hungarian holy crown, resented her being governed separately from her motherland; Hungary and Transylvania were not reunited until 1848.

Further reading: John P. Spielman, *Leopold I of Austria* (New Brunswick, N.J.: Rutgers University Press, 1977).

Discipline, First Book of

Proposals by theologian John Knox for the reorganization of the new Scottish Church (Presbyterianism), published in 1560 at the request of the Scottish government. Written in Edinburgh in collaboration with five reformed ministers, they actually derived from the Genevian "Ordonnances" (ecclesiastical laws drafted by Protestant theologian John Calvin in Geneva, Switzerland). In the book's nine chapters, Knox discussed the constitutional framework of the church, its finances, and its policies. He visualized the church as being actively involved in social programs—particularly in initiating poverty relief measures and in establishing nationally a system of compulsory education up to the university level. The book was hailed by Knox's supporters but, in Parliament, the nobility objected to his schemes as being a drain on the church's ecclesiastical revenues. The book did not receive parliamentary confirmation and was, therefore, never enforced.

See also: COMMON ORDER, BOOK OF.

Further reading: *The First Book of Discipline*, with introduction and commentary by James K. Cameron (Edinburgh, Scotland: St. Andrew Press, 1972).

Discourse on Method (Discours de la Méthode)

Metaphysical essay written by French philosopher René Descartes and published anonymously in 1637, containing his "method" through which, Descartes held, one could attain certainty with regard to the truth of ideas. His method stipulated that one could not accept anything as true unless all doubt as to its truth could be dispelled; and that all opinions that were not understood with perfect clarity had to be analyzed systematically and in detail. Descartes also acknowledged the possibility that *all* man's beliefs could be false and, consequently, that truth might never be known definitively by man. This possibility Descartes dismissed with his dictum

"Cogito, ergo sum" ("I think, therefore I am"), a dictum that, according to Descartes, was indubitable and therefore proof that absolute certainty could be attained. The famous essay served as a preface to a book containing his works, *Geometry, Dioptrics and Meteors*.

Further reading: René Descartes, *Discourse on Method, and Related Writings* (New York: Penguin Books, 1999); Georges Dicker, *Descartes: An Analytical and Historical Introduction* (New York: Oxford University Press, 1993); Leon Roth, *Descartes's Discourse on Method* (Philadelphia: R. West, 1937, repr., 1976)

Discourse on the Origin of Inequality (Discours sur l'Origine et les Fondements de l'Inégalité parmi les Hommes)

Philosophical essay (1755) written by Jean-Jacques Rousseau, French author born in Geneva, Switzerland; it discussed the cause of inequality among men, the subject of the Dijon Academy's annual contest. Dedicated to his fellow Genevans, the essay distinguishes between two kinds of inequality—the natural or physical and the moral or political—and pleads eloquently for a return to the state of nature, which he visualized as a state of peace and of natural goodness. Men, Rousseau argued, brought their miseries upon themselves by abandoning their natural state in favor of a society built on principles of inequality. He did not, however, advocate the abolition of society and property, as his critics later alleged. Rather, he suggested that those seeking peace of mind should retire and find solace in nature, while those wanting to actively participate in society should try to improve it from within.

See also: NARCISSE.

Further reading: Jean-Jacques Rousseau, *Discourse on the Origin of Inequality* (New York: Oxford University Press, 1994).

Discourse on Style (Discours sur le Style)

Address delivered on August 21, 1753, by the famous French naturalist Georges-Louis Leclerc, count de Buffon, on his induction into the French Academy (Académie Française). It contains the oft-quoted line "The style is the man himself" ("Le style c'est l'homme même"), by which Buffon meant that style represented man's achievement at its best, not something artificial or ornamental or individually cultivated as a characteristic. Buffon spoke in favor of a simple, straightforward style of literary expression and criticized the affectations and infatuations of his time.

Further reading: Lane Cooper, ed., *Theories of Style, with Special Reference to Prose Composition: Essays, Excerpts, and Translations* (New York: Macmillan, 1922).

Disestablishment Act of 1869

British parliamentary act of July 26, 1869, for the dissolution of the Church of Ireland, making it a voluntary body as of January 1, 1871. A fulfillment of Prime Minister William Gladstone's electoral policy, the act simultaneously divested the church of its substantial property and bequests (valued at £600,000 per annum in 1867), which were placed with a Commission of Irish Church Temporalities. The compensation paid (£16 million) constituted half the value of the confiscated properties; the balance was to be used in poverty relief, support of higher education, and to encourage agriculture and fisheries. Some of the church land was offered to, and purchased by, tenants. The act abolished all formal religion in Ireland and was passed despite considerable opposition in England and Ireland.

Further reading: Desmond Bowen, *The Protestant Crusade in Ireland, 1800–70: A Study of Protestant-Catholic Relations Between the Act of Union and Disestablishment* (Dublin: Gill & Macmillan, 1978); R. W. Fowell and L. George Dibdin, *The Welsh Disestablishment Bill, 1912, with Explanatory Notes, and Compared with the Previous Bills and with the Irish Disestablishment Act of 1869* (London: Central Church Committee for Defence and Instruction, 1912); Hugh Shearman, *Privatising a Church: The Disestablishment and Disendowment of the Church of Ireland* (Armagh, Northern Ireland: Ulster Society, 1995).

Disestablishment Bill of 1914, Welsh

See WELSH DISESTABLISHMENT BILL OF 1914.

Dispatch of 1854

Detailed memorandum from Sir Charles Wood (president, Board of Control, British East India Company) forwarded through the Court of Directors (via Dispatch 49 of July 19, 1854), wherein he urged the government of India to create "a properly articulated scheme of education from the primary school to the university," citing, as a guideline, the English-directed methods used to promote rural education in India's Northwest Provinces. Wood advocated the setting up of private and state-awarded scholarships and the establishing of universities at Calcutta, Bombay, and Madras, modeled on London University. Education of women was to receive top priority. Study of the vernacular languages and of Sanskrit, Arabic, and Persian was to be encouraged and faculties in law and civil engineering set up. The dispatch recognized that no immediate results could be expected from these measures and that their success would depend more on the people than on the government.

Further reading: *Christian Missions and Government Education in India: Review of a Letter Addressed to the Court of Directors of the East-India Company by the Earl of Ellenborough, (while President of the Board of Control;) . . .* (Cambridge, England: Chadwyck-Healey, 1987); Elmer H. Cutts, *British Educational Policy in India under the East India Company* (Cambridge, Mass.: Harvard University Library Microreproduction Service, 1977).

Displaced Persons Act of 1948, U.S.

Emergency federal legislation enacted on June 25, 1948, that authorized the admission of World War II European refugees into the United

States. The act permitted the entry of 205,000 displaced persons, including 3,000 nonquota orphans, over the following two years. It relaxed national origins provisions of the JOHNSON-REED ACT to allow more refugees from Eastern Europe but required that refugees pass security investigations and have an assured home and job in the United States. U.S. president Harry S Truman signed the bill reluctantly, calling it inhumane and discriminatory against Jews and Catholics. The act was renewed several times. By the time it expired in 1952, more than 415,000 persons had entered the United States under its provisions.

Further reading: Howard Alexander Smith, *Displaced Persons Problem* (Washington, D.C.: U.S. Government Printing Office, 1948).

Disquisition on Government, Calhoun's

Treatise on the nature of democratic government written by South Carolina statesman John C. Calhoun and published after his death in 1850. Calhoun argued that men, though social beings, acted in their own self-interest unless restrained by government. The people are protected from unrestrained government by constitutions, but minority views require protection from the conflicting interests of the majority. Calhoun then advanced his theory of the "concurrent" or constitutional majority, which would give each interest group "either a concurrent voice in making and executing laws, or a veto on their execution." He described society as an organic body in which the whole can act only with the agreement of the parts.

Further reading: Clyde N. Wilson, ed., *The Essential Calhoun: Selections from Writings, Speeches, and Letters* (New Brunswick, N.J.: Transaction Publishers, 2000).

Dix's Memorial to the Legislature of Massachusetts

Report on the facilities for the retarded and mentally ill in Massachusetts; written by humanitarian Dorothea Dix and delivered to the state's legislature in January 1843. The result of two years of investigation, the account documented serious abuse and neglect of "the miserable, the desolate, the outcast" in state prisons, almshouses, hospitals, and insane asylums. Dix reported that the mentally ill were often confined—sometimes chained, unwashed, and naked—in cages, closets, and cellars, and beaten or lashed to compel obedience. Few efforts were made to treat even those illnesses deemed remediable. The report and Dix's efforts led to reform in Massachusetts and throughout the United States.

Further reading: infoUSA "Memorial to the Massachusetts Legislature (1843) Dorthed Dix," International Information Programs, available online at http://usinfo.state.gov/usa/infousa/facts/democrac/15.htm.

Doctrine of Justification, Joint Declaration on the

Historic declaration signed on October 31, 1999, in Augsburg, Germany, by representatives of the Roman Catholic Church and the Churches of the Lutheran World Federation, seeking to bridge the 500-year-old rift between these two religious bodies. Drafted over several decades, the declaration's final version was publicly opposed by theologians on both sides and did not get official approval until mid-1998. Along with its "Official Common Statement" and "Annex," it affirmed "a consensus in basic truths on the doctrine of justification," which is based on "the incarnation, death and resurrection of Christ." Further, any differences in interpretation would no longer be reason for condemnation of the doctrine by either side.

Further reading: Justification organization, *Joint Declaration on the Doctrine of Justification*, Justification organization, available online at http://www.justification.org/Joint_eng.htm; Margaret O'Gara, "Lutherans and Catholics," *Commonweal* 127 (January 14, 2000): 8–9; Douglas A. Sweeney, "Taming the Reformation," *Christianity Today* 44 (January 10, 2000): 63–65.

Dogma of Papal Infallibility

Dogma decreed by the First Vatican Council (a general council of the Roman Catholic Church) through the influence of Pope Pius IX on July 18, 1870, proclaiming the infallibility of the pope when speaking *ex cathedra,* that is, while speaking as pastor and teacher of the Christians, on matters of faith and morals. It was held that, at those times when speaking ex cathedra, the pope was inspired by God himself. The Vatican council declared it "a dogma divinely revealed," while proclaiming the universality of the pope's episcopate. The dogma caused numerous secular governments to take an antagonistic stand against the Roman Catholic Church.

See also: CONCORDAT OF 1855; GUARANTEES, LAW OF.

Further reading: Margaret O'Gara, *Triumph in Defeat: Infallibility, Vatican I, and the French Minority Bishops* (Washington, D.C.: Catholic University of America Press, 1988); John R. Page, *What Will Dr. Newman Do?: John Henry Newman and Papal Infallibility, 1865–1875* (Collegeville, Minn.: Liturgical Press, 1994).

Domesday Book (Doomsday Book)

Outstanding administrative record, made in 1086–87 of title deeds in the Middle Ages; it was a two-volume summary of an extensive land survey of England that had been ordered by William I the Conqueror. The name "Domesday," or "Doomsday," refers to the book's utmost authority in judgment (or doom) on all matters contained in it. It was based on detailed surveys of all the counties (except Northumberland, Durham, Westmorland, Cumberland, and northern Lancashire) conducted by panels of royal commissioners. Volume one or "Great Domesday" contains the final summary of all the counties surveyed except Essex, Norfolk, and Suffolk. The comprehensive, unedited record for these counties is presented in volume two or "Little Domesday." Under each county is enumerated, in descending hierarchical order, a list of all the landowners with minute details of their holdings (the extent, value, past and present ownership, livestock, resources, liabilities, and so forth of the properties). The historical record of many English towns and villages begins with this unique document, which, despite arguments over its intended purpose, is also a fertile source book for scholars researching the Anglo-Norman period in England. The *Domesday Book* is preserved in London's Public Record Office.

Further reading: R. Welldon Finn, *Domesday Book: A Guide* (London: Phillimore, 1973); Vivian H. Galbraith, *The Making of Domesday Book* (Oxford: Clarendon Press, 1961, repr., 1981); John Morris, ed., *Domesday Book: Text and Translation,* 38 vols. (Chichester, Phillimore, 1975–92); Peter Sawyer, ed., *Domesday Book: A Reassessment* (Baltimore: E. Arnold, 1985).

Dominus ac Redemptor   See CLEMENT XIV'S BULL SUPPRESSING THE JESUITS.

Dominus Iesus Declaration

Paper issued on September 5, 2000, by the Vatican's Congregation for the Doctrine of Faith (CDF) with the endorsement of Pope John Paul II, seeking (in the words of its chief author Joseph Cardinal Ratzinger) to "clarify certain truths of the faith" amid "doctrinal errors and ambiguities that have become widespread in modern theological and ecclesial circles." Written in a dense style suitable for theologians, it drew criticism for forcefully asserting that the true Church of Christ could only "subsist" in the Roman Catholic Church and for defining churches not directly descended from the apostles as "ecclesial communities." True salvation, the declaration maintained, was thus possible only through the Catholic Church and all Christians were urged to seek it there. The 36-page document lamented the dilution of essential Catholic beliefs and claimed that interdenominational and interfaith dialogues were part of the church's evangelical mission.

Further reading: Roman Curia, *Declaration "Dominus Iesus" on the Unicity and Salvific Universality of Jesus Christ and the Church,* Congregation for the Doctrine of the Faith, available online at http://www.vatican.va/roman_curia/congregations/cfaith/index.htm.

Domitian Law (Lex Domitia)

Ancient Roman law sponsored by the plebeian tribune Gnaeus Domitius Ahenobarbus and enacted in 104 B.C.; it assigned election to the priestly colleges of pontifices and augures to an assembly of 17 tribes (that is, by a minority of the 35 tribes or political divisions of the Roman people). Cooptations to vacancies in the priestly colleges, the law stated, were restricted to persons previously chosen in a 17-tribe assembly picked by lot (so the gods could wield their influence!); this was how the pontifex maximus (chief priest) was elected. The Domitian Law (which had lessened patrician control over priestly appointments) was revoked by Lucius Cornelius Sulla when he was dictator of Rome in 81 B.C.; the habit of coopting the college members was restored. In 63 B.C. the law was again revived by Gaius Julius Caesar, who consequently won election that year as pontifex maximus.

See also: OGULNIAN LAW.

Further reading: Brian W. Jones, *The Emperor Domitian* (New York: Routledge, 1992).

Donation of Constantine   See CONSTANTINE, DONATION OF.

Donation of Pepin   See PEPIN, DONATION OF.

Dongan Charter

Charter of government granted and signed by Colonel Thomas Dongan, British colonial governor of New York, to the people of the city of New York in 1686. It supplanted a 1683 CHARTER OF LIBERTIES and established a municipal government consisting of six aldermen and various other officials—all to be elected by freemen (citizens) of the town; the governor, however, was to appoint the mayor, recorder, clerk, and sheriff. The merchant class won a larger measure of home rule through the Dongan Charter, which was rather liberal at times in furthering civil rights. Dongan granted similar charters to some Long Island towns, Schenectady, and Albany (whose similarly named Dongan Charter confirmed upon it a monopoly of the fur trade). New York's Dongan Charter was in force until 1731 (see MONTGOMERIE CHARTER).

Further reading: Albert Edward McKinley, "The Transition from Dutch to English Rule in New York," *American Historical Review* 6 (July 1901): 693–725.

Doomsday Book   See DOMESDAY BOOK.

Dort, Canons of

Canons drawn up at the conclusion of the Synod of Dort (November 13, 1618–May 9, 1619) at Dordrecht (Dort or Dordt), a port city in the province of South Holland. Convened mainly to discuss the controversy created by the Arminians' (Remonstrants') rejection of the Calvinist doctrine of predestination (see LAMBETH ARTICLES, REMONSTRANCE OF 1610), the synod's strong anti-Arminian bias was reflected in the 93 canons agreed upon during the concluding session. The five preliminary articles (April 23, 1619) affirmed: unconditional election; restricted atonement; man's depravity; the irresistibility of grace; and the ultimate perseverance of saints. Arminianism was condemned (nearly 200 Arminian clergy lost their livings) and Calvinist principles and the other two theological pillars of the Dutch Reformed (Calvinistic) Church (the BELGIC CONFESSION and the HEIDELBERG CATECHISM) were reaffirmed.

Further reading: P. G. Feenstra, *Unspeakable Comfort: A Commentary on the Canons of Dort* (Winnipeg: Premier Printing, 1997); Norman L. Geisler, *Chosen but Free,* 2d ed. (Minneapolis: Bethany House, 2001); Laurence M. Vance, *The*

Other Side of Calvinism, rev. ed. (Pensacola, Fla.: Vance Publications, 1999).

Douglass's "What to the Slave Is the Fourth of July?" Speech

Eloquent speech delivered on July 5, 1852, before the Rochester Ladies' Anti-Slavery Society in Rochester, New York, by Frederick Douglass. Douglass, a former slave who had moved to the strongly abolitionist community in 1847, contrasted the freedoms celebrated on America's Fourth of July with the ongoing slavery of millions of black Americans at the time. Answering the speech's title question, Douglass stated that to a slave the Fourth of July is "a day that reveals to him more than all the other days of the year, the gross injustice and cruelty to which he is the constant victim." In the speech, Douglass praised the American Revolution and its ideals, argued that the liberties championed by the Founding Fathers apply to all men, including blacks, called for an end to slavery, and criticized the role played by American churches in supporting and excusing the slave trade.

Further reading: Douglass Archives, *What to the Slave Is the Fourth of July?* Douglass Archives of American Public Address, available online at http://douglass.speech.nwu.edu/doug_alo.htm; *Frederick Douglass: Selected Speeches and Writings* (Chicago: Lawrence Hill, 1999).

Dover, Treaty of

Agreement of May 22, 1670, between King Charles II of England and King Louis XIV of France (mediated by Charles's sister, Henrietta Anne), which ended the TRIPLE ALLIANCE OF 1668 and set the scene for the Third Anglo-Dutch War (1672–78). In one of the treaty's many secret clauses, Charles pledged to declare war on Holland and to extend toleration to Roman Catholics. He also promised that he and his brother (James II) would soon convert to Catholicism. Louis agreed to pay Charles £200,000 a year and the support of 6,000 French troops as long as the war lasted. Charles accepted the offer because he thought it would relieve him from financial dependence on Parliament. In 1672, he issued his second DECLARATION OF INDULGENCE only to have it withdrawn by Parliament.

Further reading: Cyril H. Hartmann, ed., *Charles II and Madame* (London: W. Heinemann, 1934).

Downing Street Declaration of 1993

Historic declaration of December 15, 1993, wherein the British and Irish governments announced the attainment of peace in Northern Ireland as their top priority and laid the framework for future peace negotiations (see GOOD FRIDAY AGREEMENT OF 1998). Disavowing any "selfish strategic or economic interest" in Northern Ireland, Britain acknowledged the "right of self-determination" of all the people of Ireland, and also that it could lead to a united Ireland. The Irish government accepted that a united Ireland would only be realized through the "agreement and consent of a majority of people of Northern Ireland." It agreed to propose constitutional changes in that event. All "democratically-mandated" parties committed to peace would be allowed at the negotiating table. The declaration was warmly received except by the Democratic Union Party (DUP) and Sinn Fein (the political wing of the Irish Republican Army).

Further reading: Tim Pat Coogan, *The Troubles—Ireland's Ordeal 1966–1996 and the Search for Peace* (Boulder, Colo.: Roberts Rinehart, 1996); Thomas Hennessey, *A History of Northern Ireland 1920–1996* (New York: St. Martin's Press, 1997).

Draco, Laws of (Draconian Code)

Legendary Greek constitution, alleged to be the first written Athenian laws for the people (previously, the unwritten laws had been known only to the nobles). Publicized about 621 B.C., they were apparently written by an Athenian named Draco, an archon (chief magistrate) and noble elected to codify the unwritten laws of state for the benefit of the citizenry, which had become angered over unjust judicial decisions by the ruling nobles and demanded a written code of laws. Draco's laws enfranchised the hoplites (lower-class foot soldiers), secured more legal justice for the people, and decreed most criminal offenses punishable by death. This harshness led to the saying that the laws were written in blood, not ink, and made the word "draconian" synonymous with unmerciful. The laws were later mitigated (see SOLON, LAWS OF).

Further reading: Edwin Carawan, *Rhetoric and the Law of Draco* (New York: Clarendon Press, 1998); Michael Gagarin, *Drakon and Early Athenian Homicide Law* (New Haven, Conn.: Yale University Press, 1981).

Drago Doctrine

Policy enunciated on December 29, 1902, by Argentina's minister of foreign relations, Luis M. Drago, stating that European powers must not use armed force or territorial occupation to collect public debts that American nations owed to foreign powers. Drago's protest note to Washington was written after Great Britain, Germany, and Italy sent a joint naval force to Venezuela to seek repayment of certain loans. Drago argued that a sovereign state had the right to choose the manner and time for payment of its debts. Intended as a corollary of the MONROE DOCTRINE, the Drago Doctrine was adopted in a modified form by the Hague Peace Conference of 1907.

Further reading: John Holladay Latané, *A History of American Foreign Policy*, rev. ed. (Garden City, N.Y.: Doubleday, Doran & Co., 1934); Dexter Perkins, *A History of the Monroe Doctrine* (Boston: Little, Brown 1955).

Drapier's Letters

Four letters by Irish-born English satirist Jonathan Swift, who published them under the pseudonym M. B. Drapier in 1724, protesting against the British government's granting of a patent to William Wood to mint copper coins for Ireland. The Irish government had petitioned Parliament in 1720 for the legal issuance of copper coinage, but had not been consulted in the Wood matter, which evidently was decided on the basis of bribes paid by Wood to the duchess of Kendal, who was King George I's mistress. In the letters, the Irish were told of these iniquities, as well as alleged debasement of the Irish coinage. Swift's words induced the Irish to refuse to accept Wood's coins, which the British government then withdrew with displeasure. Swift became a national hero in Ireland consequently.

Further reading: Jonathan Swift, *The Drapier's Letters*, ed. Herbert Davis (Oxford: Clarendon Press, 1935); Jonathan Swift, *The Drapier's Letters and Other Works, 1724–1725* (Roslyn, N.Y.: Black's Readers Service Company, 1932).

Dred Scott v. Sandford Landmark lawsuit decided by the U.S. Supreme Court on March 6, 1857, on the status of slavery in federal territories. In 1834 Dred Scott, a black slave, was taken by his owner from Missouri, a slave state, to Illinois, a free state, and then to Wisconsin Territory, where slavery was prohibited by the MISSOURI COMPROMISE; he later returned to Missouri. In 1846 Scott sued his owner for freedom on the grounds that he had become free through residence in a free state and a free territory. The Supreme Court ruled that residence in a free state did not confer freedom on a slave, that blacks were not citizens and could not sue in federal courts, and that Congress had no power to prohibit slavery in the territories, making the Missouri Compromise unconstitutional. At the time of the ruling, Scott's nominal owner was John F. A. Sanford, whose name was officially misspelled in the court records as "Sandford." The verdict fueled the sectional controversy over slavery.

Further reading: Walter Ehrlich, *They Have No Rights: Dred Scott's Struggle for Freedom* (Westport, Conn.: Greenwood Press, 1979); Don Edward Fehrenbacher, *The Dred Scott Case: Its Significance in American Law and Politics* (New York: Oxford University Press, 1978); Don Edward Fehrenbacher, *Slavery, Law and Politics: The Dred Scott Case in Historical Perspective* (New York: Oxford University Press, 1981); Vincent C. Hopkins, *Dred Scott's Case* (New York: Russell & Russell, 1967).

Dresden, Treaty of Peace treaty signed in Dresden on December 25, 1745, bringing an end to the Second Silesian War (1744–45) between Archduchess Maria Theresa of Austria and King Frederick II the Great of Prussia. A series of Prussian victories had compelled Maria Theresa to seek peace and accept Frederick's conquest of Silesia. The 1742 Treaties of BRESLAU and BERLIN were ratified, and Frederick recognized the recent election of Maria Theresa's husband, Francis I, as Holy Roman emperor.

Further reading: M. S. Anderson, *The War of the Austrian Succession, 1740–1748* (New York: Longman, 1995); Edward Crankshaw, *Maria Theresa* (London: Constable, 1996); David Fraser, *Frederick the Great: King of Prussia* (London: Penguin Books, 2000).

Dreyfus Contract Contract signed in Paris on July 5, 1869, by Nicolás de Piérola, Peru's minister of finance, and the French commercial house of Auguste Dreyfus, in order to avert national bankrupcy in Peru. According to its terms, Dreyfus was to receive 2 million tons of guano (fertilizer) and become Peru's exclusive guano consignee in Europe and other parts of the world. In return, the firm was to advance the Peruvian government 2 million soles (monetary units) and agreed to pay the government 700,000 soles per month until March 1871. Also, Dreyfus was to assume the obligation of servicing Peru's foreign debt, which amounted to 5 million soles per year. The Dreyfus agreement was to become one of the most controversial documents in the economic history of Peru.

Further reading: John P. Olinger, *Dreyfus Freres, Guano and Peruvian Government Finance, 1869–1880: A Chapter in Economic Imperialism* (Binghamton: State University of New York at Binghamton, 1973).

Drogheda, Statute of (Poynings's Act) Legislation (December 1494) granting the English king and his council control over the Irish parliament. Ninth of 49 acts (see POYNINGS'S LAWS) passed during the Drogheda session (December 1, 1494–March–April 1495), it is associated with the name of Sir Edward Poynings, King Henry the VII's lord deputy of Ireland (September 1494–December 1495). It required legislative drafts and notice of meetings of the Irish Parliament to be submitted to the king and his council (the English Parliament was not involved) for approval. Thus, the Irish parliament could not legally convene in Ireland except by permission of the lord chancellor of England, nor could it propose amendments to any government legislation. Stripped of its independent legislative authority, the Irish Parliament was thereby reduced to dummy status. The statute was part of a wider policy of subjugation, intended to destroy the Yorkist conspirators in Ireland and protect the English Crown. It was repealed in 1782.

Further reading: W. N. Osborough, ed., *The Irish Statutes: Edward II to the Union, AD 1310–1800* (Portland, Ore.: Round Hall Press, 1995).

Dual Alliance of 1892 See FRANCO-RUSSIAN ALLIANCE OF 1892.

Dual Alliance of 1879 See AUSTRO-GERMAN TREATY OF ALLIANCE.

Dufferin Proposals (Dufferin Report) Proposals for the reorganization of the Egyptian government, drafted by Lord Dufferin (Britain's ambassador to the Ottoman Porte), and presented on February 6, 1883. Dufferin was in Egypt to suggest ways of ending Britain's role there; instead, his proposals envisaged a stronger British presence. He proposed a 30-member legislative council and an 82-member legislative assembly (half its members appointed) with powers to examine bills and approve taxes. The khedive would continue as head of the country, advised by a group of ministers (many of them European). Consultative councils would assist local governors. The British resident would maintain and strengthen British interests in Egypt. British military expenses in the region would be partly (£4 million) borne by Egypt. Sir Evelyn Baring (Lord Cromer) was appointed Britain's agent and consul general in Egypt. Later that year, the Dufferin Report was incorporated into the ORGANIC ACT OF 1883.

Further reading: Lawrence J. L. Dundas, *Lord Cromer; Being the Authorized Life of Evelyn Baring, First Earl of Cromer* (London: Hodder & Stoughton, 1932); Reeva S. Simon, Philip Mattar, and Richard W. Bulliet, eds., *Encyclopedia of the Modern Middle East*, 4 vols. (New York: Macmillan, 1996).

Dulles's Speech Opposing the Spread of Communism "by Any Means"

Speech delivered by U.S. secretary of state John Foster Dulles before the Overseas Press Club in New York City on March 29, 1954. He affirmed America's sympathy for the French in their "gallant struggle" in Indochina (French Indochina War of 1946–54) and U.S. resolve to take the "serious risks" involved to deter further communist aggression, which "might lead to action at places and by means of free-world choosing, so that aggression would cost more than it could gain." Dulles asserted that "the imposition on Southeast Asia of the political system of Communist Russia and its Communist China ally, by whatever means, must be a grave threat to the whole free community."

See also: EISENHOWER'S "DOMINO THEORY" STATEMENT.

Further reading: John Foster Dulles, *War or Peace* (New York: Macmillan, 1957).

Duncan v. Kahanomoku

U.S. Supreme Court decision, issued on February 25, 1946, stating that the imposition of martial law was not a basis for suspending constitutional guarantees of fair trial that existed elsewhere in the United States. Under the authority of the Hawaii Organic Act, the governor of Hawaii had declared martial law immediately after the Japanese attack on Pearl Harbor (1941). In its 7-2 decision, the Supreme Court ruled that although the governor, to maintain an orderly civil government and defend the island, had the power to declare martial law, this authority did not allow the supplanting of civilian courts by military tribunals.

Further reading: Leonard W. Levy and Kenneth L. Karst, eds., *Encyclopedia of the American Constitution*, 2 ed. (New York: Macmillan Reference, 2000).

Dunning Tariff   See CANADIAN TARIFF ACT OF 1930.

Dunse, Pacification of (Pacification of Berwick)

Agreement of June 18, 1639, between King Charles I and the Scottish Covenanters (Presbyterians); it ended the First Bishops' War in 1639 (Charles's English army invaded Scotland with a view to force the Presbyterian Church into accord with the Church of England). The Covenanters were camping on Dunse Law hill (near the towns of Dunse and Berwick) in protest against the imposition of episcopacy and the English prayer book, and the king, who wanted to avoid a war, proposed discussions for peace. It was agreed that church matters would henceforth be determined by a new convocation (generally assembly). When the convocation met, it decided to abolish episcopacy and restore Presbyterianism in Scotland and to divest bishops of their titles and sees.

Further reading: *His Majesties Declaration, Concerning His Subjects in Scotland* (New York: Da Capo Press, 1971); Magnus Magnusson, *Scotland: The Story of a Nation* (New York: Atlantic Monthly Press, 2000); Raymond C. Paterson, *A Land Afflicted: Scotland and the Coventanter Wars, 1638–1690* (Edinburgh, Scotland: J. Donald Publishers, 1998).

Durham's Report

Report written in England by Lord Durham (John B. Lambton), governor in chief of the British North American provinces, and presented to the British Colonial Office on February 4, 1839; it contained a discussion of the causes of Canada's 1837 rebellions by both French- and English-speaking Canadians against the colonial governments in Lower and Upper Canada (Quebec and Ontario, respectively) and his recommendations on bringing peace to the crisis. While Durham found seeds of conflict in the racial tensions in Lower Canada, his primary concern was with the nature of colonial rule. His recommendations thus included the legislative union of Upper and Lower Canada, in order to reduce racial tensions by facilitating the assimilation of French Canadians into English-speaking culture, and the responsibility of the executive (British-appointed) government to an elected assembly in all matters except foreign affairs, trade, and constitutional changes. The report was welcomed by reformers and condemned by colonialists and French Canadians.

See also: NINETY-TWO RESOLUTIONS, PAPINEAU'S; TEN RESOLUTIONS, RUSSELL'S.

Further reading: Carl Stephenson and Frederick George Marcham, eds., *Sources of English Constitutional History: A Selection of Documents from A.D. 600 to the Present* (New York: Harper & Row, 1937).

Dušan, Code of   See ZABONNIK.

E

Earl Spencer's Eulogy to Princess Diana Moving tribute to Princess Diana by her younger brother, Earl (Charles) Spencer, during her funeral ceremony held on September 6, 1997, at Westminster Abbey in London, drawing loud applause from mourners inside and outside the abbey. Diana, he said, had "a natural nobility," was "classless," and "needed no royal title to continue to generate her particular brand of magic." Saying that his sister had considered leaving Britain because of the media frenzy surrounding her, Lord Spencer criticized the newspapers for sneering at "her genuinely good intentions." Finally, he pledged to Diana to help raise her sons (his nephews) so that besides observing duty and tradition, they "can sing openly as you planned."

Further reading: Earl Spencer, "Eulogy to Princess Diana," *New York Times*, September 6, 1997; UK Law Online, "Princess Diana, Privacy laws and Press freedom in the United Kingdom," UK law online centre for criminal justice studies University of Leeds, available online at http://www.leeds.ac.uk/law/hamlyn/diana.htm.

East African Cooperation Treaty See KAMPALA, TREATY OF.

Ecclesiastical Titles Assumption Act Effective August 1, 1851, controversial British legislation forbidding the Roman Catholic Church from assuming titles that had already been adopted by the United Church of England and Ireland. An expression of the anti-Catholic feeling still prevalent in the country, the immediate provocation for the act was Rome's aggressive division (September 30, 1850) of Britain into bishoprics, supervised by the Catholic archbishop of Westminster. Violators of the law were to be fined £100. The law was introduced into Parliament by Lord John Russell and did not apply to the titles assumed from the Church of Scotland. It was repealed in 1871.

Further reading: Edward R. Norman, *Anti-Catholicism in Victorian England* (New York: Barnes & Noble, 1968); Frank H. Wallis, *Popular Anti-Catholicism in Mid-Victorian Britain* (Lewiston, Maine: E. Mellen Press, 1993); John Wolfe, *The Protestant Crusade in Great Britain, 1829–1860* (New York: Oxford University Press, 1991).

Ecloga Code of Roman civil law promulgated in A.D. 726 by Leo III the Isaurian, the able Byzantine (Eastern Roman) emperor who revitalized the empire. It represented a simplified revision or edition of the JUSTINIAN CODE of the sixth century A.D. Written in Greek first, this practical manual was noted for its benevolent Christian-oriented provisions and its enactments concerning marriage and property rights. Capital punishment was also modified to either dismemberment or mutilation in many crime instances. In 726 Leo also issued an edict forbidding the use and worship of icons (holy images) in an effort to check superstition and miracle-mongering; it was mildly enforced and many people protested against iconoclasm (the destroying of icons), which was finally refuted by the Second Council of Nicaea in A.D. 787.

Further reading: Edwin Hanson Freshfield, *Roman Law in the Later Roman Empire: The Isaurian Period, Eighth Century, the Ecloga* (Cambridge, England: Bowes & Bowes, 1932); H. F. Jolowicz and Barry Nicholas, *Historical Introduction to the Study of Roman Law* 3d ed. (Holmes Beach, Fla.: Gaunt, 1996); Joseph Anthony Charles Thomas, *Textbook of Roman Law* (New York: North-Holland, 1976); Alan Watson, *The Law of the Ancient Romans* (Dallas: Southern Methodist University Press, 1970).

Economic Consequences of the Peace

Brilliant polemical essay written by English economist John Maynard Keynes and published in late 1919, criticizing the 1919 Treaty of VERSAILLES. Keynes had gone to the Paris Peace Conference as the chief British treasury official but had resigned his post in protest against what he considered financially excessive and unworkable war reparations from defeated Germany. In the essay, he sharply challenged the treaty's terms from the classic, laissez-faire economic viewpoint (later he turned to active government intervention in a free economy). He correctly predicted that the inequitable reparations would cease to be paid after a few years and that nationalism and German economic instability would bring momentous European problems. Keynes also gave biting portraits of British prime minister David Lloyd George, French Premier Georges Clemenceau, and U.S. president Woodrow Wilson at the 1919 Paris Peace Conference.

Further reading: Donald Maggridge, ed., *Collected Writings of John Maynard Keynes* (New York: Cambridge University Press, 1995).

Economic Opportunity Act, U.S.

Federal legislation enacted on August 20, 1964, that established the Office of Economic Opportunity and authorized funding for a variety of programs designed to implement U.S. president Lyndon B. Johnson's announced "war on poverty." Among the programs established were the Job Corps, to provide training for youths aged 16 to 21; a work-study program to aid low-income students; on-the-job training for youths; urban and rural community-action programs designed to ensure "maximum feasible participation" by the poor; adult education programs; the VISTA (Volunteers in Service to America) program of volunteer social service workers and teachers for the disadvantaged; Head Start, to aid poor preschool children; and assistance for migrant workers and their families.

Further reading: Thomas Carson, ed., *Gale Encyclopedia of U.S. Economic History* (Farmington Hills, Mich.: Gale Group, 1999); Sar A. Levitan, *The Great Society's Poor Law: A New Approach to Poverty* (Baltimore: Johns Hopkins Press, 1969); Leonard W. Levy and Kenneth L. Karst, eds., *Encyclopedia of the American Constitution*, 2d ed. (New York: Macmillan Reference, 2000); Daniel P. Moynihan, *Maximum Feasible Misunderstanding: Community Action in the War on Poverty* (New York: Free Press, 1969).

Ecthesis (Ekthesis)

Doctrinal formula or edict issued in A.D. 638 by the Byzantine (Eastern Roman) emperor Heraclius, proposing monothelitism (Christ has but one will though two natures) as the imperial doctrine of Christianity. It was an attempt to reconcile monophysitism (Christ has but one nature) in the East with the orthodox West (He has two natures). Though Pope Honorius I agreed, his successor, Pope Severinus, refused to acknowledge the Ecthesis, which Heraclius eventually repudiated and accredited to Sergius, the late patriarch of Constantinople, before he died (A.D. 641). The monothelite heresy flared up again in A.D. 648, when Byzantine emperor Constans II issued a decree, TYPE, prohibiting mention of monothelitism.

Further reading: John F. Haldon, *Byzantium in the Seventh Century: The Transformation of a Culture* (New York: Cambridge University Press, 1990); Andreas N. Stratos, *Byzantium in the Seventh Century* (Amsterdam: Adolf M. Hakkert, 1968).

Edict of 1724, French

Royal declaration issued by France's king Louis XV on May 14, 1724, intensifying anti-Huguenot (anti-Protestant) measures in the country. It introduced severe penalties for those found participating in illegal Huguenot assemblies: a life sentence at the galleys for a man, life imprisonment for a woman, and certain death for presiding clergy. The edict declared only Roman Catholic marriages as legal and forced the children of converted Catholics to baptize their children within 24 hours of birth. The refusal of new converts to take the sacraments during illness was punished by confiscation of their property and permanent exile. Protestants were still barred from all official posts. Its passage and the resulting persecution of the Huguenots led to another exodus from France.

See also: EDICT OF TOLERATION OF 1787, FRENCH; NANTES, REVOCATION OF THE EDICT OF.

Further reading: George Peabody Gooch, *Louis XV* (Westport, Conn.: Greenwood Press, 1976).

Edict of Amboise   See AMBOISE, EDICT OF.

Edict of Grace   See ALAIS, PEACE OF.

Edict of January   See JANUARY, EDICT OF.

Edict of Maximum Prices (Edictum de Maximis Pretiis)

Reform measure promulgated by the Roman emperor Diocletian in A.D. 301, establishing a maximum legal price for every important commodity (notably foodstuffs and clothing) and every form of labor and professional service in the whole Roman Empire. General economic decline and currency collapse had led to Diocletian's attempt to check inflationary prices and wages by government control. Death was the penalty for all who broke the edict of prices, which soon made worse an "economy of scarcity" and caused riots. The government finally ceased enforcing it to restore production and distribution; it was eventually voided by Emperor Constantine I the Great.

Further reading: H. F. Jolowicz and Barry Nicholas, *Historical Introduction to the Study of Roman Law,* 3d ed. (Holmes Beach Fla.: Gaunt, 1996); Joseph Anthony Charles Thomas, *Textbook of Roman Law* (New York: North-Holland, 1976); Alan Watson, *The Law of the Ancient Romans* (Dallas: Southern Methodist University Press, 1970).

Edict of Milan See MILAN, EDICT OF.

Edict of Nantes See NANTES, EDICT OF.

Edict of Pacification See AMBOISE, EDICT OF.

Edict of Poitiers See BERGERAC, TREATY OF.

Edict of Restitution See RESTITUTION, EDICT OF.

Edict of Revocation See NANTES, REVOCATION OF THE EDICT OF.

Edict of Romorantin See ROMORANATIN, EDICT OF.

Edict of Theodoric (Edictum Theodorici) Compilation of 154 Roman laws and regulations issued in A.D. 506 by Theodoric the Great, king of the Ostrogoths (East Goths) and beneficent ruler of Italy for 33 years (until his death in A.D. 526). The "edict" was a manual systematizing the already existing laws, along with a few new ones, and covering important court cases. This collection of briefly and simply stated decisions was for the administrative use of judges and lawyers; both Romans and Ostrogoths adhered to the Roman law, but the latter were not subject to Roman judges. Theodoric ruled peacefully with justice, preserving Roman laws while keeping an Ostrogothic army.

Further reading: H. F. Jolowicz and Barry Nicholas, *Historical Introduction to the Study of Roman Law,* 3d ed. (Holmes Beach, Fla.: Gaunt, 1996); Joseph Anthony Charles Thomas, *Textbook of Roman Law* (New York: North-Holland, 1976); Alan Watson, *The Law of the Ancient Romans* (Dallas: Southern Methodist University Press, 1970).

Edict of Toleration, Galerius's First edict of toleration of Christianity, reluctantly issued by the Roman emperor Galerius on April 30, A.D. 311, a few days before he died of disease. The ruthless Galerius, who had rigorously persecuted the Christians, may have sought mercy from their God for his long illness. By the edict, he extended clemency and a pardon to the suffering Christians, legally permitting them to practice their religion and to reestablish their churches, provided "they shall in no way offend against public order." Galerius also called upon them to pray for his, the empire's, and their

own welfare. Christianity had made a major advance, for now one could be both a loyal Roman and a good Christian.

See also: MILAN, EDICT OF.

Further reading: H. F. Jolowicz and Barry Nicholas, *Historical Introduction to the Study of Roman Law,* 3d ed. (Holmes Beach, Fla.: Gaunt, 1996); Joseph Anthony Charles Thomas, *Textbook of Roman Law* (New York: North-Holland, 1976); Alan Watson, *The Law of the Ancient Romans* (Dallas: Southern Methodist University Press, 1970).

Edict of Toleration of 1781 (Edict of Tolerance, Toleranzpatent) Decree issued by Holy Roman Emperor Joseph II of Austria on October 19, 1781, in the spirit of the enlightened European monarchs of that period. In the document, while clearly upholding the supremacy of the Roman Catholic Church and faith, the emperor granted limited religious freedom to Christians of the Protestant and Greek Orthodox faiths in the Hapsburg (Austrian) dominions. Specifically, he declared that Protestants and Greek Orthodox had the right of public worship (provided they covered all religious expenses incurred by such believers in a given area) and the right to become citizens, hold public office, and earn academic degrees. The provisions, however, did not apply to Jews, who were freed from numerous disabilities through another edict issued by Joseph II on January 2, 1782.

Further reading: Derek Edward Dawson Beales, *Joseph II* (New York: Cambridge University Press, 2001).

Edict of Toleration of 1782 (Toleranzpatent) Edict issued by Holy Roman Emperor Joseph II on January 2, 1782, through which the emperor, influenced by the ideas of the Enlightenment, pledged to the Jews of Vienna and lower Austria certain fundamental rights. Specifically he declared the Jews' right to attend state educational institutions and to engage in economic activity (with the exception, however, of owning property); he promised the Jews his protection against abuses inflicted upon them and prohibited the forced conversion of Jews.

See also: EDICT OF TOLERATION OF 1781.

Further reading: Derek Edward Dawson Beales, *Joseph II* (New York: Cambridge University Press, 2001).

Edict of Toleration of 1787, French (Edict of Versailles) French king Louis XVI's promulgation at Versailles in November 1787, easing some of the restrictions placed on Huguenots (Protestants) (see EDICT OF 1724, FRENCH; NANTES, REVOCATION OF THE EDICT OF). It restored most of their civil rights; for instance, their property was protected and provisons made for the registration of their births, deaths, and marriages. While some measure of religious toleration was reestablished, the Huguenots were still declared ineligible for official posts and did not enjoy complete freedom of worship. Compared with the religious persecution of the previous decades, this edict represented a marked improvement in the

French government's treatment of Huguenots, who are spoken of as "non-Catholics" in the edict.

Further reading: John Hardman, *Louis XVI: The Silent King* (London: Edward Arnold, 1993, rep., 2000).

Edictum Perpetuum   See PERPETUAL EDICT.

Edinburgh, Treaty of (Treaty of Leith)

Accord signed on July 6, 1560, by England, Scotland, and France in Edinburgh, freeing Scotland from French domination and fostering a new Anglo-Scottish amity. The French troops (except the 120 guarding Dunbar and Inchkeith) were to vacate Scotland immediately, leaving the Scots to determine their own religious affairs. Francis II and Mary (France's king and queen) were acknowledged as sovereigns of Scotland, but they were prevented from assuming the English coat-of-arms or from declaring war or peace on behalf of Scotland. Aliens were barred from administering civil or criminal justice or from holding high office in Scotland. A parliament was to be convened in August to settle the religious question. England temporarily postponed her claim for the return of Calais (see CATEAU-CAMBRÉSIS, TREATY OF) and invalidated Elizabeth I's alliance with the Lords of the Congregation (Scotland's leading Protestants). Despite these minor concessions, the treaty was a major victory for England and the Protestant cause in Scotland (see DISCIPLINE, FIRST BOOK OF).

Further reading: Norman Macdougall, *An Antidote to the English: The Auld Alliance, 1295–1560* (East Linton, Scotland: Tuckwell Press, 2001); John Mcleod, *Dynasty: The Stuarts, 1560–1807* (New York: St. Martin's Press, 2001); Jenny Wormald, *Mary, Queen of Scots: Politics, Passion and Kingdom Lost* (New York: St. Martin's Press, 2001).

Education Act of 1870, British (Forster Elementary Education Act)

Parliamentary bill passed on August 9, 1870, introducing universal elementary education in England and Wales, drafted by William Edward Forster, vice president of Prime Minister William Gladstone's Committee of Privy Council on Education. It charged locally elected school boards with setting up board (or public) schools in areas where no voluntary schools existed, to be funded by government grants, local rates, and school fees. Denominational religious instruction was forbidden in these schools. Good voluntary (church or private) schools were to be maintained with increased government assistance, but no help from the local rates, and they could impart religious instruction. Attendance was not compulsory and left to the school boards to enforce. Forster's aim was to "cover the country with good schools." In this, his act was eminently successful, though the dual system of education it set up is often seen to have hampered the growth of English education.

See also: BALFOUR ACT.

Further reading: H. C. G. Matthew, *Gladstone 1809–1898* (Cambridge, England: Clarendon Press, 1997).

Education Act of 1902, British   See BALFOUR ACT.

Education Act of 1944, British (Butler's Act)

Britain's most notable wartime legislation (August 3, 1944), requiring the local authorities in England and Wales to provide free secondary education for all. The first major educational reform since the BALFOUR ACT of 1902, it created the Ministry of Education and revamped the financial structure of the voluntary schools. Promoted by Richard A. Butler, president of the Board of Education, the act raised the school-leaving age to 15 and revived (but did not implement) a part-time education scheme for those under 18. The local authorities were also entrusted with providing school meals, free milk, and periodic medical checkups. Religious instruction was to be included in the daily curriculum. The act went into effect on April 1, 1945, shortly before the end of World War II (1939–45).

Further reading: Michael Barber, *The Making of the 1944 Education Act* (New York: Cassell, 1994); Gary McCulloch, *Education Reconstruction: The 1944 Education Act and the Twenty-First Century* (Portland, Ore.: Woburn Press, 1994); F. B. Sullivan, *Lord Butler: The 1944 Act in Retrospect* (Milton Keynes, England: Open University Press, 1980).

Education Reform Act of 1988, British

Major law enacted by the British Parliament on July 29, 1988, radically changing the traditional English educational system. Supported by the conservative government (notably Prime Minister Margaret Thatcher and Education Secretary Kenneth W. Baker) and opposed by the Labour Party, the act (passed with 5,000 amendments) established a uniform "national core curriculum," required students to take formal tests at the ages of seven, 11, 14, and 16, and permitted parents to vote to "opt out" of control by local education authority in favor of a "Grant-Maintained Schools Trust" to be administered centrally. Other provisions included the abolition of tenure for university professors appointed or promoted after November 1987 and, effective in 1990, cessation of the Inner London Education Authority (England's major local authority), whose powers would be distributed among 13 London boroughs. The reforms were to improve poor teaching and achievement, but opponents saw them as a "recipe for disaster" in the future.

Further reading: Clyde Chitty, *The Educational System Transformed*, 2d ed. (Tisbury, England: Baseline, 1999).

Education Reform Act of 2002, U.S.   See NO CHILD LEFT BEHIND ACT.

Edward VIII's Abdication Message

King Edward VIII's announcement on December 10, 1936, before the British House of Commons of his immediate renunciation of the British throne; his decision to marry Mrs. Wallis Simpson, a two-time American divorcee, had threatened to spark a major constitutional crisis. A king's burden, he reminded the House, "is so heavy that it can only be borne in circumstances different from those in which I now find myself." Conscious of his inability to "discharge this heavy task with efficiency or with satisfaction to Myself," he felt he had made the right decision "for the stability of the Throne and Empire and the happiness of My peoples." He thanked everyone for the consideration shown to him, confident that his successor could rely on it too. Finally, he urged the House to immediately implement his Instrument of Abdication and to approve the succession of his brother, the duke of York, who became King George V on December 11, 1936, when a bill of abdication was passed by the British Parliament.

Further reading: Carl Stephenson and Frederick George Marcham, eds., *Sources of English Constitutional History: A Selection of Documents from A.D. 600 to the Present* (New York: Harper & Row, 1937).

Edwards v. California   U.S. Supreme Court decision, issued on November 24, 1941, that invalidated a California law designed to exclude poor immigrants from the state. The "anti-Okie" statute, which made it a misdemeanor for anyone knowingly to bring or assist in bringing into the state a non-resident indigent person, was an effort to reduce the huge influx of impoverished migrants and resultant financial burden on the state. In its unanimous opinion the Supreme Court declared the statute an unconstitutional barrier to interstate commerce and an invalid exercise of the state's police powers. The case involved a California resident, Fred F. Edwards, who had transported his unemployed brother-in-law to California from Texas in 1940.

Further reading: Leonard W. Levy and Kenneth L. Karst, eds. *Encyclopedia of the American Constitution* 2d ed. (New York: Macmillan Reference, 2000).

Egyptian-British Treaty of 1936   See ANGLO-EGYPTIAN TREATY OF 1936.

Egyptian-Italian Treaty   See ANGLO-ITALIAN AGREEMENT OF 1925.

Eight Articles, Protocol of the   See PROTOCOL OF THE EIGHT ARTICLES.

Eighteenth Amendment, U.S.   Amendment to the U.S. CONSTITUTION, ratified in 1919, that prohibited the manufacture, sale, and transportation of intoxicating beverages in the United States, as well as the importation and exportation of such beverages. The bipartisan amendment was the result of political pressure by the prohibition movement, led by the Anti-Saloon League. The VOLSTEAD ACT, passed in 1919 to enforce the amendment, was widely violated by bootleggers and illicit manufacturers, and in 1933 the Eighteenth Amendment was repealed by the TWENTY-FIRST AMENDMENT.

Further reading: Jack S. Blocker, Jr., *American Temperance Movements: Cycles of Reform* (Boston: Twayne, 1989); Thomas Carson, ed., *Gale Encyclopedia of U.S. Economic History* (Farmington Hills, Mich.: Gale Group, 1999); Leonard W. Levy and Kenneth L. Karst, eds., *Encyclopedia of the American Constitution* 2d ed. (New York: Macmillan Reference, 2000).

Eighth Amendment, U.S.   Amendment to the U.S. CONSTITUTION, adopted in 1791, that prohibits "excessive bail," "excessive fines," and "cruel and unusual punishment." The indefiniteness of these phrases led to considerable debate when Congress was deliberating the BILL OF RIGHTS. The U.S. Supreme Court has ruled that bail is excessive if it is larger than necessary to assure the presence of the accused at the trial. Capital punishment has been challenged in the courts as "cruel and unusual punishment" under the Eighth Amendment.

Further reading: Eugene W. Hickok, Jr., ed., *The Bill of Rights: Original Meaning and Current Understanding* (Charlottesville: University Press of Virginia, 1991); Leonard W. Levy and Kenneth L. Karst, eds., *Encyclopedia of the American Constitution,* 2d ed. (New York: Macmillan Reference, 2000).

Einstein's Letter of 1939   Letter from German-born refugee physicist Albert Einstein to U.S. president Franklin D. Roosevelt on August 2, 1939, informing him of the possibility of constructing a new type of extremely powerful bomb derived from nuclear chain reactions in a large mass of uranium. Such a bomb, Einstein wrote, could destroy an entire port and surrounding territory. He urged the United States to speed up experimental work and warned that Germany was also engaged in atomic research. The letter, probably drafted by Hungarian-born refugee physicist Leo Szilard, stimulated the development of the nuclear bomb. Einstein, a pacifist, later considered his recommendation to build an atomic bomb to be "the great mistake" in his life.

Further reading: Albert Einstein, *Ideas and Opinions* (New York: Bonanza Books, 1988).

Einstein's Special Relativity Theory   Physical theory formulated by Albert Einstein, German-Swiss-American physicist, in four separately published scientific writings in 1905. Written in German while he was a Swiss citizen working in Bern, his papers introduced an entirely new perspective on the motion and speed of light, along with his famous equation $E=mc^2$ (energy [E] of a quantity of matter, with mass [m], equals the product of the mass and the square of the velocity of light [c^2]). Einstein further proposed that simultaneously appearing events in one frame of reference or system may not appear so in another, and yet both frames of reference may be correct because absolute motion and time are immeasurable (thus removed from physical analysis). Also, space and time together were viewed by him in a four-dimensional continuum called space-time. In 1916 Einstein published his general theory of relativity, an amplification of his special (so-called restricted) theory. His complicated ideas changed our understanding of the laws of gravitation and electromagnetism and made possible the splitting of the atom.

Further reading: Albert Einstein, *Relativity: The Special and the General Theory* (New York: Crown, 1995).

Eisenhower Doctrine   Doctrine proposed by U.S. President Dwight D. Eisenhower, on January 5, 1957, and adopted by Congress on March 9, authorizing military aid for any Middle Eastern nation requesting such assistance in order to resist communist aggression. Eisenhower warned Congress that "if power-hungry Communists should . . . estimate that the Middle East is inadequately defended, they might be tempted to use open measures of armed attack." The doctrine, promulgated after the withdrawal of British, French, and Israeli troops from Egypt during the 1956 Suez Canal crisis, was an effort to forestall Soviet attempts to fill a power vacuum. Eisenhower used the doctrine to send U.S. forces to protect a pro-Western government in Lebanon in July 1958.

Further reading: Leonard W. Levy and Louis Fisher, eds., *Encyclopedia of the American Presidency*, 2 vols. (New York: Simon & Schuster, 1994); Robert I. Vexler, ed., *Dwight D. Eisenhower, 1890–1969: Chronology, Documents, Bibliographical Aids* (Dobbs Ferry, N.Y.: Oceana Publications, 1970).

Eisenhower's "Atoms for Peace" Speech   Speech delivered by U.S. president Dwight D. Eisenhower at the United Nations on December 8, 1953, proposing that the major atomic powers—particularly the United States and the Soviet Union—pool their atomic energy resources for socially useful purposes. Denouncing the folly of an international arms race and the possible destruction of all civilization, he suggested instead the establishment of an international atomic energy agency, under the aegis of the United Nations, to study the peaceful uses of atomic power. "It is not enough," he said, "to take this weapon out of the hands of the soldiers. It must be put into the hands of those who will know how . . . to adapt it to the arts of peace." He also announced the willingness of the United States to meet with other nations to discuss disarmament.

Further reading: *Atoms for Peace: Dwight D. Eisenhower's Address to the United Nations* (Washington, D.C.: National Archives and Records Administration, 1989); Robert I. Vexler, ed., *Dwight D. Eisenhower, 1890–1969: Chronology. Documents. Bibliographical Aids* (Dobbs Ferry, N.Y.: Oceana Publications, 1970).

Eisenhower's "Domino Theory" Statement   Tenet outlined by U.S. president Dwight D. Eisenhower before the press in Washington, D.C., in early 1954, holding that as one Asian country falls to communism its neighbor follows until all are lost. Voiced earlier by newspaper columnist Joseph W. Alsop, Jr., the theory applied particularly to the possible loss

of Vietnam in the French Indochina War of 1946–54 (an inferred communist effort to overrun southeast Asia). If France lost, Eisenhower said, "many human beings [would] pass under a dictatorship . . . Finally you have . . . what you would call the 'falling domino' principle. You have a row of dominoes set up, you knock over the first one, and what will happen to the last one is the certainty that it will go over very quickly. So you could have a beginning of a disintegration that would have the most profound influences."

See also: DULLES'S SPEECH OPPOSING THE SPREAD OF COMMUNISM "BY ANY MEANS."

Further reading: Robert I. Vexler, ed., *Dwight D. Eisenhower, 1890–1969: Chronology, Documents, Bibliographical Aids* (Dobbs Ferry, N.Y.: Oceana Publications, 1970).

Eisenhower's Farewell Address   Address to the American public delivered by U.S. president Dwight D. Eisenhower on January 17, 1961, as he prepared to leave office. Eisenhower pointed out the dangers not only of the ruthless, hostile communist ideology but also of the military establishment and arms industry built to combat the global ambitions of that ideology. He warned against "the acquisition of unwarranted influence, whether sought or unsought, by the military-industrial complex," whose enormous power, if not properly meshed with peaceful methods and goals, could threaten American liberties and the democratic process. He also warned that centralized research could inhibit intellectual curiosity and that public policy could become "the captive of the scientific-technological elite." He urged the nation not to plunder tomorrow's resources for today's comforts and argued that disarmament must be a continuing imperative.

Further reading: Robert I. Vexler, ed., *Dwight D. Eisenhower, 1890–1969: Chronology, Documents, Bibliographical Aids* (Dobbs Ferry, N.Y.: Oceana Publications, 1970).

Eisenhower's "Open Skies" Proposal   Address on disarmament delivered by U.S. president Dwight D. Eisenhower on July 21, 1955, at a summit conference in Geneva, Switzerland. Declaring that the United States was prepared to enter a "sound and reliable agreement" for arms reduction, with provisions for inspection, Eisenhower proposed that the United States and the Soviet Union give each other "a complete blueprint of our military establishments" and allow mutual aerial photography ("open skies") for reconnaissance purposes. The French and British approved the proposals but the Russians rejected them.

Further reading: Richard Dean Burns, *Encyclopedia of Arms Control and Disarmament*, 3 vols. (New York: Charles Scribner's Sons, 1993).

Eisenhower's Speech Concerning Little Rock   Speech delivered by U.S. president Dwight D. Eisenhower on September 24, 1957, announcing that he had sent federal troops to preserve order in Little Rock, Arkansas, where white mobs were violently resisting efforts to desegregate the public schools—efforts mandated by the U.S. Supreme Court (see BROWN V. BOARD OF EDUCATION OF TOPEKA, KANSAS). Declaring that "mob rule cannot be allowed to override the decisions of our courts," Eisenhower justified the dispatch of U.S. army troops as necessary to preserve peace and order (not to enforce integration) when state and local authorities failed to do so. Though the speech was conciliatory, many Southerners were enraged by Eisenhower's action.

See also: COOPER V. AARON.

Further reading: Robert I. Vexler, ed., *Dwight D. Eisenhower, 1890–1969: Chronology, Documents, Bibliographical Aids* (Dobbs Ferry N.Y.: Oceana Publications, 1970).

Eisenhower's "Spirit of Geneva" Speech

Address given by U.S. president Dwight D. Eisenhower before the American Bar Association in Philadelphia on August 24, 1955, following his propitious meeting at the 1955 Geneva Summit Conference with European heads of state. Despite the competing Soviet and American philosophies of government, he saw improved, peaceful relations between these two great powers. Americans' responsibility was to present "freedom's case to the world" in a "crusade for peace"—as U.S. chief justice John Marshall had "presented the case for the [U.S.] Constitution to the American public more than a hundred years ago." The opportunity to foster a just peace, provided by "the spirit of Geneva," confronted America now, Eisenhower said. U.S.-Soviet relations grew better until the unsuccessful Paris Summit conference of 1960.

Further reading: Dwight D. Eisenhower, *Peace with Justice: Selected Addresses* (New York: Columbia University Press, 1961); Robert I. Vexler, ed., *Dwight D. Eisenhower, 1890–1969: Chronology, Documents, Bibliographical Aids* (Dobbs Ferry, N.Y.: Oceana Publications, 1970).

Eisenhower's Statement about the U-2 Affair

Statement released by U.S. president Dwight D. Eisenhower on May 25, 1960, after the Soviet Union shot down (on May 1) an American U-2 reconnaissance plane 1,200 miles inside Soviet territory. Initial U.S. claims that the U-2 was doing weather research were followed by an admission that it was engaged in aerial reconnaissance. As a result of the incident, Soviet premier Nikita Khrushchev scuttled a planned summit conference. On May 25 Eisenhower defended the reconnaissance program for national security but announced that such flights had now ceased. He refused to accede to Khrushchev's demands for a condemnation of the flights as espionage, a public apology, and punishment of those responsible. The statement reiterated EISENHOWER'S "OPEN SKIES" PROPOSAL, but U.S.-Soviet relations were severely damaged by the incident.

Further reading: Robert I. Vexler, ed., *Dwight D. Eisenhower, 1890–1969: Chronology, Documents, Bibliographical Aids* (Dobbs Ferry, N.Y.: Oceana Publications, 1970).

Electoral Count Act

Federal U.S. legislation passed in 1887 and designed to prevent a disputed national election. The act provided that each state is the final judge over its own electoral returns; Congress must accept returns certified by the authorized state tribunal in accordance with the state's own laws. Congress may intervene only if the state itself is unable to decide or has made an irregular decision. In such cases the two houses of Congress shall decide concurrently. The act resulted from the 1876 presidential election dispute between Samuel J. Tilden and Rutherford B. Hayes.

Further reading: Donald C. Bacon, Roger H. Davidson, and Morton Keller, eds., *The Encyclopedia of the United States Congress* (New York: Simon & Schuster, 1995); John Hampden Dougherty, *The Electoral System of the United States* (New York: G. P. Putnam's Sons, 1906); David A. McKnight, *The Electoral System of the United States: A Critical and Historical Exposition of Its Fundamental Principles in the Constitution and the Acts and Proceedings of Congress Enforcing It* (Littleton, Colo.: F. B. Rothman, 1993).

Electricity Act of 1947, British

Labour government's nationalization on August 13, 1947, of the electric power industry in Great Britain. Part of a broad nationalization policy (see TRANSPORT ACT OF 1947, BRITISH), it was introduced by Prime Minister Clement Attlee's administration to help Britain recover from the disastrous effects of World War II (1939–45) and regain some of her prewar strength. It established the British Electricity Authority "to develop and maintain an efficient, coordinated and economical system of electricity supply for all parts of Great Britain except the North of Scotland district."

Further reading: John C. J. Dalton, *The Electricity Act, 1947* (London: Butterworth, 1948); *History of Electricity Supply in Great Britain: A Chronology* (London: Electricity Council, 1971).

Elementary and Secondary Education Act of 1965, U.S.

Federal legislation signed into law by U.S. president Lyndon B. Johnson on April 11, 1965, improving educational opportunities by providing $1.3 billion in federal aid to schools with large numbers of children from low-income families. The aid was to be available to both private and public schools, and expenditures were to be controlled by public agencies. The law stated that no direct federal aid would go to church-related schools but that needy school children enrolled in such schools could receive "on loan" textbooks and other instructional materials (which would remain the property of the public schools). Federal funds were also provided for supplemental education centers, services, and research; state education departments were strengthened.

Further reading: Donald C. Bacon, Roger H. Davidson, and Morton Keller, eds., *The Encyclopedia of the United States Congress* (New York: Simon & Schuster, 1995); Julie Roy Jeffrey, *Education for Children of the Poor: A Study of the Origins* *and Implementation of the Elementary and Secondary Education Act of 1965* (Columbus: Ohio State University Press, 1978); Leonard W. Levy and Kenneth L. Karst, eds., *Encyclopedia of the American Constitution,* 2d ed. (New York: Macmillan Reference, 2000).

Eleventh Amendment, U.S.

Amendment to the U.S. CONSTITUTION, proposed by Congress in 1794 and ratified by the states in 1798, prohibiting the citizens of one state from suing another state in federal court. The amendment reversed the ruling in CHISHOLM V. GEORGIA, which had raised a furor as a threat to state sovereignty. This restriction of federal judicial power has been tempered by federal laws, such as civil rights legislation, creating rights that can be enforced by suits against a state or a state official.

Further reading: *Dictionary of American History,* rev. ed. (Charles Scribner's Sons, 1976); Clyde W. Jacobs, *The Eleventh Amendment and Sovereign Immunity* (Westport, Conn.: Greenwood Press, 1972); Leonard W. Levy and Kenneth L. Karst, eds., *Encyclopedia of the American Constitution,* 2 ed. (New York: Macmillan Reference, 2000); John V. Orth, *The Judical Power of the United States: The Eleventh Amendment in American History* (New York: Oxford University Press, 1987).

Elgin-Marcy Treaty   See RECIPROCITY TREATY.

Elizabethan Poor Law   See POOR LAW OF 1601.

Elkins Act

Federal U.S. legislation, passed on February 19, 1903, prohibiting railroads from giving rebates to favored shippers engaged in interstate commerce. Supported by antimonopoly reformers and by the railroads, who were being compelled to grant rebates to certain powerful trusts, the act provided for prosecution and punishment of shippers, railroad corporations, agents, and officers who gave or received rebates. It made deviation from the published rates a misdemeanor and gave federal courts the power to issue injunctions against violators. Introduced by Senator Stephen B. Elkins of West Virginia, the act reinforced the INTERSTATE COMMERCE ACT.

Further reading: *Dictionary of American History,* rev. ed. (Charles Scribner's Sons, 1976); Leonard W. Levy and Kenneth L. Karst, eds., *Encyclopedia of the American Constitution,* 2d ed. (New York: Macmillan Reference, 2000).

Emancipation Edict of 1807, Prussian

Edict issued by Prussia's king Frederick William III on October 9, 1807, in the Prussian town of Memel (Klaypeda, Lithuania), through which the Prussian monarchy made its first attempt to reform its semifeudal society. Through the document serfdom was abolished (this provision was to become effective on October 8, 1810); laws requiring members of each class to fill only certain occupations were abolished; laws restricting the purchase and sale of land to individuals within the same class

(i.e., within the noble class or burgher class) were abolished, thus stimulating a freer flow of capital among all classes. Although the edict did not provide for the allotment of land to peasants, it gave them the legal right to own it.

Further reading: Marion W. Gray, *Theodor von Schon and Prussian Reforms, 1806–1808* (Ann Arbor, Mich.: University Microfilms, 1974).

Emancipation Edict of 1861, Russian

Edict issued on March 3 (February 19, Old Style calendar), 1861, by Russian czar Alexander II, providing for the emancipation of the serfs. Through the document, the serfs or peasants obtained their personal freedom and allotments of land. The land, however, was granted them on the condition that the recipient repay the government in installments over a 40-year period (the owners of the land were paid by the government). In addition, the peasants were not to receive the land directly from the government, but from their village, whose officials were obliged to ensure proper distribution of the land. The peasants' acquisition of the land was slow, and although a majority had received their allotments by 1885, most remained in the poorest of circumstances. The required payments were suspended in 1905.

Further reading: Mark A. Kishlansky, ed., *Sources of the West: Readings in Western Civilization,* vol. 2, 4th ed. (New York: Addison Welsey Longman, 2001); Frank N. Magill, ed., *Great Events from History, Modern European Series,* 3 vols. (Englewood Cliffs, N.J.: Salem Press, 1973).

Emancipation Proclamation, U.S.

Edict issued in preliminary form on September 22, 1862, and in final form on January 1, 1863, by U.S. president Abraham Lincoln freeing all slaves in the secessionist Southern states. The proclamation enjoined the freed slaves to refrain from violence, except in self-defense, and opened the armed services to the former slaves. Lincoln, though personally opposed to slavery, had long resisted abolitionist urgings in order to avoid alienating border states. But by 1862 he concluded that emancipation was a military necessity. The final proclamation freed three million slaves (though it had no immediate effect in Confederate-controlled areas), enhanced the Union cause in Europe, infuriated the South, and drew a mixed reaction in the North.

Further reading: Herman Belz, *Emancipation and Equal Rights: Politics and Constitutionalism in the Civil War Era* (New York: Norton, 1978); *Dictionary of American History,* rev. ed. (Charles Scribner's Sons, 1976); Leonard W. Levy and Kenneth L. Karst, eds., *Encyclopedia of the American Constitution,* 2d ed. (New York: Macmillan Reference, 2000); James M. McPherson, *Abraham Lincoln and the Second American Revolution* (New York: Oxford University Press, 1992); Charles L. Phillips and Alan Axelrod, eds., *Encyclopedia of Historical Treaties and Alliances,* 2 vols. (New York: Facts On File, 2001).

Embargo Act of 1807, U.S.

Legislation enacted by the U.S. Congress on December 22, 1807, that prohibited all international trade to and from U.S. ports. The act was designed to deny raw materials to both Great Britain and France, then at war with each other, and to persuade them to cease practices, including the seizure of neutral commercial ships and the impressment of American sailors, that were damaging American commerce. Rather than achieving its goal, the act dramatically lowered American exports, denied merchants and producers of raw materials their income, cost sailors their jobs, and forced the closure of American ports. This unpopular and unsuccessful legislation was repealed on March 1, 1809, and was later replaced by the U.S. NON-INTERCOURSE ACT.

Further reading: Thomas Carson, ed., *Gale Encyclopedia of U.S. Economic History* (Farmington Hills, Mich.: Gale Group, 1999); Leonard W. Levy and Louis Fisher, eds., *Encyclopedia of the American Presidency*, 2 vols. (New York: Simon & Schuster, 1994); Leonard W. Levy and Kenneth L. Karst, eds., *Encyclopedia of the American Constitution*, 2d ed. (New York: Macmillan Reference, 2000); Burton Spivak, *Jefferson's English Crisis: Commerce, Embargo, and the Republican Revolution* (Charlottesville: University Press of Virginia, 1979).

Emergency Banking Relief Act, U.S.

New Deal legislation enacted on March 9, 1933, which gave the U.S. president broad powers over the national banking and monetary systems. The act, quickly passed at a special session of Congress in an atmosphere of economic crisis, validated Roosevelt's BANK HOLIDAY DECLARATION, gave the president control over gold transactions, authorized the Treasury Department to grant or withhold licenses to reopen banks and to appoint conservators for those of questionable soundness, forbade gold hoarding and export, and authorized the issuance of new Federal Reserve banknotes. Qualified banks were permitted to begin reopening on March 13.

Further reading: John Edson Brady, ed., *Banking Act of 1933 and the Emergency Bank Act of 1933* (Cambridge, Mass.: Banking Law Journal, 1933); Benjamin J. Klebaner, *American Commercial Banking: A History* (Boston: Twayne, 1990); Leonard W. Levy and Kenneth L. Karst, eds., *Encyclopedia of the American Constitution*, 2d ed. (New York: Macmillan Reference, 2000); James Francis Thaddeus O'Connor, *The Banking Crisis and Recovery under the Roosevelt Administration* (New York: Da Capo Press, 1971).

Emergency Quota Act, U.S. (Dillingham Immigration Act)

Emergency legislation enacted by Congress on May 19, 1921, establishing the first quota for immigrants to the United States. Sponsored by Senator William P. Dillingham of Vermont, the act set a quota of 357,000 places (aliens); immigrants from a given nation (nationality) were restricted yearly to 3 percent of the population of that nation residing in the United States according to the 1910 census. Immigrants from Asia, already largely excluded by other agreements, and from the Western Hemisphere were exempt from this act, which favored immigrants from the British Isles and northwestern Europe and excluded people from southern and central Europe. This national origins quota system set the pattern for American immigration laws for the first half of the 20th century.

See also: IMMIGRATION QUOTA ACT OF 1924, U.S.

Further reading: *Abstracts of Reports of the Immigration Commission*, 41 vols. (Manchester, N.H.: Ayer, 1978–79).

Emergency Relief Appropriation Act, U.S.

New Deal legislation enacted on April 8, 1935, that transferred direct relief efforts from the U.S. government to state and local governments, and authorized an appropriation of $4.88 billion to establish a massive national public works program to provide employment for jobless workers. President Franklin D. Roosevelt used these funds to create the Works Progress Administration (WPA), which built or improved highways, bridges, public buildings, parks, and airport landing fields. It supported theater, writing, and arts projects. It spent nearly $11 billion and employed 8.5 million workers before it was terminated in 1943. Funding also went to establish the National Youth Administration, which encouraged education and provided jobs for young people, and to support the Public Works Administration and the Civilian Conservation Corps.

Further reading: *Emergency Relief Appropriations Act of 1938 and Public Works Administration Appropriation Act of 1938* (Washington, D.C.: U.S. Government Printing Office, 1938).

Emmet's Proclamation

Proclamation by Irish nationalist Robert Emmet on July 23, 1803, urging the citizens of Dublin to rally around and support the United Irishmen, a movement aimed at bringing freedom to Ireland and an end "to the long career of English oppression." It was made on the same day of Emmet's abortive insurrection, which almost killed the movement and led to Emmet's execution (September 20, 1803). Calling on "every man in whose breast exists a spark of patriotism, or sense of duty" to "impede the march of your oppressors," Emmet requested them to "act with union and concert." He urged those who had been "duped" into supporting Ireland's union with Great Britain in 1801 to "return from the paths of delusion." Finally, recalling the horrors inflicted on his countrymen for over six centuries, he goaded them into action on behalf of their country because, "during public agitation, inaction becomes a crime."

See also: UNION WITH IRELAND, BRITISH ACT OF.

Further reading: Sean McMahon, *Robert Emmet* (Cork, Ireland: Mercier, 2001).

Ems Telegram

July 13, 1870, telegram concerning status of Hohenzollern candidacy to Spanish throne; sent by King

William I of Prussia to Chancellor Otto von Bismarck, who released an edited version to the press to inflame prowar sentiment. In the original telegram from the spa at Ems, William, who opposed Bismarck's attempts to place a Hohenzollern on the Spanish throne, informed him that he had assured the French ambassador, Vincent Benedetti, that Prince Leopold Hohenzollern-Sigmaringen had withdrawn his candidacy; King William also stated that he had refused Benedetti's ill-advised request from Napoléon III to guarantee no future renewal of the candidacy. Bismarck, who wished to humiliate France publicly, released the telegram to the papers and foreign courts, after editing it to give the impression that a curt exchange had occurred between William I and Benedetti. The public reaction led to France's declaration of war on Prussia, July 19.

Further reading: Frank N. Magill, ed., *Great Events from History, Modern European Series*, 3 vols. (Englewood Cliffs, N.J.: Salem Press, 1973); A. A. W. Ramsay, *Idealism and Foreign Policy; a Study of the Relations of Great Britain with Germany and France, 1860–1876* (London: J. Murray, 1925).

Enabling Act of 1933, German

Act proposed by German Chancellor Adolf Hitler and passed on March 23, 1933, by an overwhelming majority of the newly elected German Reichstag (legislative assembly), granting Hitler's government dictatorial powers with respect to legislation and foreign policy. The terms of the act provided that the national cabinet had the right to pass national laws; that such laws did not necessarily need to be in harmony with the constitution; that such laws were to be prepared by the chancellor and were to become effective on the day after their publication; that treaties could be concluded by the German government with foreign powers without the approval of the Reichstag; and that the act was to remain effective until April 1, 1937.

See also: CIVIL SERVICE LAW OF 1933, GERMAN; NÜRNBERG LAWS.

Further reading: Frank N. Magill, ed., *Great Events from History, Modern European Series*, 3 vols. (Englewood Cliffs, N.J.: Salem Press, 1973).

Engel v. *Vitale*

U.S. Supreme Court decision issued June 25, 1962, declaring that religious observances in the public schools were unconstitutional. The case arose when a group of parents and taxpayers in North Hempstead, New York, objected to the daily recitation in the public schools of a prayer written by the New York State Board of Regents. Though the prayer was voluntary and nonsectarian, the Supreme Court, in a six-to-one decision, barred the continuation of the daily recital, declaring that it violated constitutional prohibitions on the establishment of religion. The Court stated: "It is no part of the business of government to compose official prayers for any group of American people to recite as a part of a religious program carried on by government."

Further reading: Walter Berns, *The First Amendment and the Future of American Democracy* (New York: Basic Books, 1976); Leonard W. Levy and Kenneth L. Karst, eds., *Encyclopedia of the American Constitution*, 2d ed. (New York: Macmillan Reference, 2000); William K. Muir, Jr., *Prayer in the Public Schools* (Chicago: University of Chicago Press, 1967).

Enhanced Border Security and Visa Entry Reform Act of 2001, U.S.

Legislation signed into law in May 2002 that mandated tighter controls on non-U.S. citizens entering or leaving the United States. The act was one of many passed in the wake of the terrorist attacks in New York City and Washington, D.C., September 11, 2001. The act charged the Immigration and Naturalization Service (INS) with the responsibility of developing and maintaining an interoperable law enforcement and intelligence data system for tracking foreign nationals. This system was to provide the various federal law enforcement agencies and the intelligence community with a vehicle for sharing information about potential or suspected terrorists. The act also required that INS inspectors check arrival and departure passenger manifests of every aircraft or ship entering or leaving the United States and that the Justice Department establish an electronic means to monitor foreign students. It mandated that visas and passports issued by the State Department include fingerprints and photographs and that those documents be machine-readable by an integrated entry and exit data system to be developed by the INS. Further, it required each State Department overseas mission to maintain a terrorist lookout committee to identify known or potential terrorists. Lastly, it called for a feasibility study of establishing a North American national security program to include the United States, Canada, and Mexico.

Further reading: "Enhanced Border Security and Visa Entry Reform Act of 2001," THOMAS: Legislative Information on the Internet, available online at http://php.auburn.edu/academic/other/International_education/sevp/HR3525_122701.htm; "President Signs Border Security and Visa Entry Reform Act," The White House, available online at http://www.whitehouse.gov/news/releases/2002/05/20020514-4.html.

Enquiry Concerning Human Understanding

See HUME'S TREATISE OF HUMAN NATURE.

Entente Cordiale (Anglo-French Entente)

Anglo-French diplomatic understanding, signed on April 8, 1904. A pivotal event, both in the prewar period and in the relationship of the two countries, the agreement was not a formal alliance; but its public and secret articles resolved most of the long-standing disagreements between the two ancient rivals. In the public articles, France abandoned her Newfoundland fishery rights, acquired by the Treaty of UTRECHT in 1713; in return, she received certain concessions in Africa. Spheres of influence in Siam were identified, and free navigation of the Suez Canal was declared. The final public section resolved the dispute over Egypt and Morocco, with England recognized as having special interests in the former, and France in the latter. The secret clauses, which were not disclosed until 1911, dealt with the fate of Morocco in the eventuality that the sultan's authority collapsed. France agreed to protect British and Spanish interests there, and northern Morocco was promised to Spain. The coast opposite Gibraltar was to remain unfortified.

Further reading: Charles L. Phillips and Alan Axelrod, eds., *Encyclopedia of Historical Treaties and Alliances,* 2 vols. (New York: Facts On File, 2001); P. J. Rolo, *Entente Cordiale: The Origins and Negotiations of the Anglo-French Agreements of April 8, 1904* (New York: Berg Publishing, 1970).

Entente of 1902, Franco-Italian   See FRANCO-ITALIAN ENTENTE OF 1902.

Epistle to the Romans

Lengthy letter written by Saint Paul in Corinth, Greece, in the winter of A.D. 57–58. Part of the Bible's New Testament, it is the deepest expression of Paul's theological views, with a message (his Gospel) that revolved around his words: "For the law of the spirit of life in Jesus Christ hath made me free from the law of sin and death." Addressed to the heathen-Christian community at Home, the epistle emphasizes "righteousness through faith," redemption through Christ, and freedom from the constraint of Judaism's Mosaic Law (see TEN COMMANDMENTS, THE). Included also are exhortations to love one another, to repay evil with good, and to obey the law.

Further reading: Karl Barth, *The Epistle to the Romans* (New York: Oxford University Press, 1968); Douglas J. Moo, *The Epistle to the Romans* (Grand Rapids, Mich.: W. B. Eerdmans, 1996); Pelagius, *Pelagius's Commentary on St. Paul's Epistle to the Romans* (New York: Oxford University Press, 1998).

Equal Employment Opportunities Act, U.S.

Federal legislation signed into law on March 25, 1972, that expanded and strengthened the U.S. government's powers against discrimination in employment. The act gave the Equal Employment Opportunity Commission the power to bring lawsuits in federal district courts to enforce provisions of the CIVIL RIGHTS ACT OF 1964. It expanded protection to people not previously covered—in state and local government, with small employers, and in some educational institutions. It created the Equal Employment Opportunities Coordinating Council to coordinate and monitor the federal government's enforcement efforts against job discrimination.

Further reading: Paul Burstein, *Discrimination, Jobs, and Politics: The Struggle for Equal Employment Opportunity in the United States since the New Deal: With a New Introduction* (Chicago: University of Chicago Press, 1998); U.S. Equal Em-

ployment Opportunity Commission, *The Story of the United States Equal Employment Opportunity Commission: Ensuring the Promise of Opportunity for 35 Years, 1965–2000* (Washington, D.C.: U.S. Government Printing Office, 2000).

Equality of Men and Women, The

Frenchwoman Marie de Gournay's feminist treatise published in 1622, which elevated the debate on the equality of women to a higher level. Continuing in the distinguished tradition of French feminism, de Gournay argued that men and women were basically alike, even though lack of education may cause women to appear inferior. Philosophers, scriptures, and church leaders have long recognized female merits, she noted. Men who did not do likewise, she reasoned, were perhaps intellectually deficient themselves. If women were made in the image of God and allowed to participate in religious rituals, why deny them "the status and privileges of men"? This suggested that men were more "sacred than all these things, and wouldn't that be a grievous blasphemy?" she questioned.

See also: DECLARATION OF THE RIGHTS OF WOMAN AND THE FEMALE CITIZEN; *ON THE ADMISSION OF WOMEN TO CITIZENSHIP.*

Further reading: Sunshine for women, "Marie de Gournay," Sunshine for women, available online at http://www.pinn.net/~sunshine/march 99/gournay2.html; Katharina M. Wilson and Frank J. Warnke, eds., *Women Writers of the Seventeenth Century* (Athens: University of Georgia Press 1989).

Equal Rights Amendment, U.S.

Proposed amendment to the U.S. CONSTITUTION guaranteeing that men and women have equal rights. Supported by the National Woman's Party, the measure was first introduced into Congress in 1923. Opponents, including many progressives, labor unions, and women's organizations, argued that the amendment would invalidate necessary protective legislation for women. The bill was reintroduced many times but failed to pass until 1972. It stated that "equality of rights under the law shall not be denied or abridged . . . on account of sex." By 1979, the deadline for ratification, only 35 of the required 38 states had ratified. Congress extended the deadline until 1982 but no additional states ratified, and the bill died.

Further reading: Mary Frances Berry, *Why ERA Failed: Politics, Women's Rights, and the Amending Process of the Constitution* (Bloomington: Indiana State University Press, 1986); Janet K. Boles, *The Politics of the Equal Rights Amendment* (New York: Longmans, 1979); Joan Hoff-Wilson, ed., *Rights of Passage: The Past and Future of the ERA* (Bloomington: Indiana State University Press, 1986); Leonard W. Levy and Kenneth L. Karst, eds., *Encyclopedia of the American Constitution,* 2d ed. (New York: Macmillan Reference, 2000).

Erfurt, Congress of (Erfurt Program)

Statement of theoretical beliefs and practical goals accepted by German socialists meeting at Erfurt, Germany, in 1891. The meeting followed the repeal in 1890 of the ANTI-SOCIALIST LAW. The theoretical portion of the program preached the Marxian doctrine of class struggle as the major force in history. The Erfurt Program also accepted the Marxian contention that capitalism was an unpleasant, but necessary, transitional form of economy that would eventually and inevitably collapse under its own weight. The practical part of the program, however, attempted to address the concerns of labor in the more immediate future. It called for proportional representation, suffrage for women, replacement of the army by a militia system, complete secularization of education, and an eight-hour day for workers. Both the practical and theoretical portions of the program were actively promoted by the Social Democratic Party in Germany.

Further reading: Karl Kautsky, *The Class Struggle (Erfurt Program)* (New York: Norton, 1971); William S. Sanders, *The Socialist Movement in Germany* (London: Fabian Society, 1913).

Erfurt, Treaty of   Treaty concluded on October 12, 1808, between Russia under Czar Alexander I and France under Emperor Napoléon Bonaparte, in the Thuringian German town of Erfurt; it reconfirmed the friendship established between them in the Treaties of TILSIT. Through the treaty France recognized Russian control over the Danubian principalities of Moldavia and Wallachia and Russia's annexation of Finland; Russians promised France her support should Austria declare war on the latter. Since no agreement was reached regarding the partition of the Ottoman Empire (Russia hoped to secure portions of that disintegrating empire for herself), it was agreed that all remaining Turkish lands would remain under the Ottoman sultan's control. Because France was experiencing difficulties in the Iberian Peninsula and in the Baltic, she was willing to take a conciliatory attitude toward Russia, then her one ally among the major powers.

See also: FREDRIKSHAMM, TREATY OF.

Further reading: Herbert Butterfield, *The Peace Tactics of Napoleon, 1806–1808* (New York: Octagon Books, 1972).

Esch-Cummins Act (Transportation Act of 1920)   U.S. legislation authored by Representative John J. Esch of Wisconsin and Senator Albert B. Cummins of Iowa and enacted on February 28, 1920, returning the railroads to private control on March 1 (see RAILWAY ADMINISTRATION ACT, U.S.) and broadening the powers of the Interstate Commerce Commission (ICC). The act authorized the ICC to consolidate railroads for greater efficiency, exempting the groups from antitrust legislation; to evaluate railroad properties; to set minimum and maximum rates and a fair return to stockholders; and to establish a fund supported by carriers to benefit financially troubled rail lines. The act also created the Railroad Labor Board, composed of employees, company members, and the public, to resolve wage disputes.

Further reading: Leonard W. Levy and Kenneth L. Karst, eds., *Encyclopedia of the American Constitution* 2d ed. (New York: Macmillan Reference, 2000).

Escobedo v. Illinois   U.S. Supreme Court decision issued on June 22, 1964, establishing that a suspect in police custody has a right to consult counsel during an interrogation. Danny Escobedo had been convicted of murder on the basis of a confession he made during an interrogation, prior to his formal indictment, in which he had been denied access to his attorney and had not been advised of his constitutional right to refuse to answer police questions. The Supreme Court ruled that he had therefore been denied his SIXTH AMENDMENT right to the assistance of counsel and that this confession could not be used as evidence against him. The success of a system of criminal justice, the Court said, should not depend on citizens' unawareness of their constitutional rights.

See also: MIRANDA V. ARIZONA.

Further reading: Leonard W. Levy and Kenneth L. Karst, eds., *Encyclopedia of the American Constitution* 2d ed. (New York: Macmillan Reference, 2000).

Escorial, Treaty of   See FAMILY COMPACTS.

Espionage Act of 1917, U.S.   Federal legislation enacted on June 15, 1917, aimed at suppressing treasonable and disloyal activities during World War I (1914–18). It provided that individuals could be fined up to $10,000 and imprisoned for 20 years for such offenses as aiding the enemy, obstructing recruitment, and causing insubordination, disloyalty, or refusal of duty in the military. The U.S. postmaster general was given the power to exclude from the mails newspapers, magazines, and other items deemed treasonable or seditious. The act was extended by the Espionage (or Sedition) Act of 1918 and its constitutionality was upheld by the U.S. Supreme Court in *Schenck* v. *United States* (1919).

Further reading: David M. Kennedy, *Over Here: The First World War and American Society* (New York: Oxford University Press, 1980); Leonard W. Levy and Kenneth L. Karst, eds., *Encyclopedia of the American Constitution,* 2d ed. (New York: Macmillan Reference, 2000); Paul L. Murphy, *World War I and the Origins of Civil Liberties in the United States* (New York: Norton, 1979); Harry N. Scheiber, *The Wilson Administration and Civil Liberties, 1917–1921* (Ithaca, N.Y.: Cornell University Press, 1960).

Espionage and Sabotage Act of 1954, U.S.   Federal U.S. legislation, enacted in 1954 during the cold war, that authorized the death penalty or life imprisonment for acts of espionage or sabotage committed during peacetime as well as wartime. It suspended a federal statute of limitations that had set a 10-year limit on liability for treasonable actions committed during peacetime. The act also required all foreign agents working in the United States to register with the federal government; violators were subject to fines of $10,000 and five years in prison. The law was broadened in 1958 to include acts committed against the United States by American spies overseas.

Further reading: Carl N. Flanders and Stephen A. Flanders, *Dictionary of American Foreign Affairs* (New York: Macmillan, 1993).

Essays (*Essais*)

French courtier Michel Eyquem de Montaigne's collection of essays prompted by the death of his close friend, Etienne de La Boetie; created a new literary genre. Books one and two, published in Bordeaux, France, in 1580, contain 94 chapters written between 1571 and 1580. Montaigne described the work as "a book consubstantial with its author, concerned with my own self, an integral part of my life." Expressing his views on pressing issues such as death, pain, ambition, and inconsistency, Montaigne argued against stoical attitudes toward them. In 1588, Montaigne completed book three (13 chapters) and, together with many additions to the previous two books, published a complete three-book edition. Book three reveals the evolution of Montaigne's ideas and attitudes; its tone is confident, optimistic, and racy. The *Essays* are essentially a self-portrait. He speaks to his reader as if to a friend and that, for many, is the most enduring characteristic of his work.

Further reading: Michel de Montaigne, *The Complete Essays,* trans. Donald M. Frame (Stanford, Calif.: Stanford University Press, 1958); Michel de Montaigne, *The Complete Essays,* trans. M. A. Screech (New York: Penguin, 1993).

Essays on the Principle of Population, Malthus's

Treatises written by British political economist and moral philosopher Thomas Robert Malthus, the first of which was published in 1798 and the second in 1803, containing Malthus's theory on population growth. Malthus argued in both versions that population, in ordinary circumstances, increases in a geometric progression, while the means of subsistence increases in an arithmetic ratio in the best of circumstances. Therefore, Malthus reasoned, checks must exist in order to stem the effects of the high rate of population growth. He identified premature death, crime, checks on birthrate, war, disease, and, in the 1803 version, moral restraint as necessary checks. English naturalist Charles Darwin was influenced by Malthus's theory, traces of which can be seen in the former's concept of the struggle for existence (see ORIGIN OF SPECIES).

Further reading: Frank W. Elwell, *A Commentary on Malthus' 1798 Essay on Population as Social Theory* (Lewiston, N.Y.: Edwin Mellen Press, 2001); Thomas Robert Malthus, *An Essay on the Principle of Population*, ed. Philip Appleman (New York: W. W. Norton, 1976); Thomas Robert Malthus, *An Essay on the Principle of Population*, ed. Geoffrey Gilbert (New York: Oxford University Press, 1999).

Essex Decision

Ruling by the British High Court of Admiralty in 1804 (confirmed on July 23, 1805) concerning the U.S. merchant ship *Essex,* thus aggravating disputes between the United States and Britain that later peaked in the War of 1812. British authorities had seized the *Essex* while she was transporting cargo on a trip from the French West Indies to France, declaring that she had violated the rule of 1756 (which stated that trade not permitted in time of peace could not be permitted in time of war to neutral nations, like America, in this case). U.S. ships had evaded the rule by breaking their trips with stopovers at American ports. The British court ruled that this practice was illegal because it was not really a termination in a continuous journey; U.S. cargo was thus subject to seizure, arousing a storm of protest in the United States, since it strengthened British resolve to seize neutral vessels found trading with France, a wartime enemy then.

Further reading: Burton Spivak, *Jefferson's English Crisis: Commerce, Embargo, and the Republican Revolution* (Charlottesville: University Press of Virginia, 1979).

Estonian Declaration of Sovereignty of 1988

Pronouncement of sovereignty approved by Estonia's Supreme Soviet (parliament) in Tallinn on November 16, 1988. It proclaimed this small Baltic republic's independence in all matters except defense and foreign affairs. The Estonian legislators also approved a constitutional amendment requiring their consent to any new Soviet laws for Estonia (annexed by the Soviet Union in 1940). This unprecedented political challenge to Soviet authority threatened to spread to neighboring Latvia and Lithuania, Soviet-controlled republics since 1940, whose Supreme Soviets claimed the right to veto Soviet laws in 1989 and issued general sovereignty declarations as well. Soviet leader Mikhail Gorbachev's tolerance of the three Baltic republics' push for "self-determination" was, however, offset by his assertion that they must remain in the Soviet confederation of states.

Further reading: A. Kiris, *Restoration of the Independence of the Republic of Estonia: Selection of Legal Acts (1988–1991)* (Tallinn: Ministry of Foreign Affairs of the Republic of Estonia, Estonian Institute for Information, 1991); Anatol Lieven, *The Baltic Revolution: Estonia, Lativa, Lithuania and the Path to Independence*, 2d ed. (New Haven, Conn.: Yale University Press, 1994).

Estrada Doctrine

International legal concept regarding the diplomatic recognition of a new government, articulated in 1930 by Genaro Estrada, foreign minister of Mexico. In contrast to the 1910 TOBAR DOCTRINE, which maintained that no government rising to power through revolution should be recognized, the Estrada Doctrine asserted that new governments should be automatically recognized when they are in political control of the state. The doctrine has been supported by many nations at various times, but Mexico, with certain exceptions, has consistently applied this principle in its recognition policy and has strongly supported it in the Organization of American States (OAS).

Further reading: Rafael H. Valle, "A Contribution Toward the Bibliography of Genaro Estrada," *Hispanic American Historical Review* 18, no. 2 (1938): 243–48.

Établissements de Saint Louis   See LOUIS IX'S LAWS.

Étaples, Treaty of   Anglo-French agreement made at Étaples, France, on November 9, 1492, whereby England's king Henry VII renounced English claims on the duchy of Brittany, following its annexation (1491) by King Charles VIII of France. The treaty ended the war between France and England (aided by Burgundy, Spain, and the Holy Roman Empire) over Brittany. According to its provisons, Charles paid the English monarch the substantial compensation of £159,000 (745,000 gold crowns) in return for a promise not to violate France's territorial integrity. Henry VII, the first Tudor king of England, had thus renounced all historic rights to French lands (except Calais).

See also: SENLIS, TREATY OF.

Further reading: S. B. Chrimes, *Henry VII* (New Haven, Conn.: Yale University Press, 1999).

Eternal Peace of 1686 (Grzymultowski Peace)
Peace treaty and alliance concluded between Poland and Russia at Lvov, Ukraine, on December 22, 1686. Desired by Polish king John III Sobieski, the peace essentially reconfirmed the provisions presented earlier in the 1667 Treaty of ANDRUSOVO, which divided Polish and Russian possession of the Ukraine along the Dnieper River. By brilliant diplomacy, the Russians held on to Kiev. The Cossacks were placed under Russian rule, and the Orthodox Christians in Poland were granted protection by the Russian czar. In return, Poland was promised funds and arms in any war with the Ottoman Turks. The "eternal peace" reflected a decline in Polish political power in relation to Russia.

Further reading: Otton Laskowski, *Sobieski, King of Poland* (Glasgow, Scotland: Polish Library, 1944).

***Ethics*, Spinoza's**   Major work of Dutch philosopher Baruch or Benedict Spinoza, probably written in 1663–65 and published posthumously in 1677. Spinoza divided his work into five parts, dealing with God; nature and origin of the mind; origin and nature of the emotions; human bondage or the strength of the emotions; and power of the intellect or human freedom. Thereby, he sought to lead the reader from the contemplation of God, through a knowledge of the capacities of the human mind and the nature and bondage of the emotions, to the final realization of the power of the intellect, which alone, he believed, could lead man to freedom. Spinoza, a grinder of optical lenses by training, used the geometrical rather than the traditional dialogue form to present his ideas—an attempt to revolutionize the methodology of

philosophy. Over the centuries, his *Ethics* has held a permanent place among the classics in its field.

Further reading: Benedictus de Spinoza, *Spinoza: Ethics,* ed. G. H. R. Parkinson (New York: Oxford University Press, 2000).

Etigny, Treaty of   See MONSIEUR, PEACE OF.

Eu, Agreements of   Anglo-French pact of 1843, renewed in September 1845, resolving the search for a suitable husband for the eligible Spanish infanta Isabella (Queen Isabella II) and her younger sister, Luisa. Prussia and Austria were out of consideration for their pro-Carlist activities, while a Portuguese alliance was rejected by Britain and Portugal. Britain opposed the French candidate (one of King Louis Philippe's sons) while France opposed Prince Leopold of Saxe-Coburg-Gotha, Britain's candidate. At Eu, France, Queen Victoria of Britain and Louis Philippe, aided by their foreign ministers George Aberdeen and François Guizot, agreed to withdraw their respective proposals, exclude the Hapsburgs from consideration, and choose Isabella a husband from among the descendants of King Philip V of Spain. Britain agreed to Luisa's marriage to Louis Philippe's youngest son, the duke of Montpensier, provided Isabella married first and bore children. After much wrangling, Isabella's marriage was finally arranged to her first cousin, Francisco de Asís. The double wedding was celebrated on October 10, 1846.

Further reading: Francis H. Gribble, *The Tragedy of Isabella II* (Boston: R. C. Badger, 1913); Ernest J. Parry, *The Spanish Marriages, 1841–1846; A Study of the Influence of Dynastic Ambition upon Foreign Policy* (London: Macmillan, 1936).

European Coal and Steel Community, Treaty of the
Agreement embodying the SCHUMAN PLAN, signed by representatives of France, West Germany, Italy, and the Benelux countries (Belgium, the Netherlands, and Luxembourg) on April 18, 1951. It established a single market for coal and steel in Western Europe, overseen by a nine-member international "High Authority" with distinct sovereign powers to act independently in the interest of the European community. A special protocol superadded to the treaty explains the code of the Court of Justice, which serves the European communities today; the court's procedures are both written and oral, and matters are referred to the court by petition; hearings can be public; the court's deliberations are secret; and its rulings are made public. Articles 31 to 45 of the treaty (following the protocol) state the structure, work, and proficiency of the Court of Justice.

Further reading: Barry J. Eichengreen, *The Reconstruction of the International Economy, 1945–1960* (Brookfield, Vt.: E. Elgar, 1996); Pascal Fontaine, *A New Idea for Europe: The Schumann Declaration, 1950–2000,* 2d ed. (Luxembourg: Office for Official Publications of the European Communities,

2000); Dirk Spierenburg and Raymond Poidevin, *The History of the High Authority of the European Coal and Steel Community: Supranationality in Operation* (London: Weidenfeld & Nicolson, 1994).

European Convention for the Protection of Human Rights and Fundamental Freedoms

Agreement unanimously approved by the consultative assembly of the council of Europe in August 1950, and signed by the council's committee of ministers in November 1950. Inspired by the UNIVERSAL DECLARATION OF HUMAN RIGHTS, the convention established a European Commission of Human Rights, a European Court of Human Rights, and a Committee on the Elimination of Racial Discrimination. The commission was authorized to examine allegations of human rights violations received from any member and help reach a solution. The court could receive petitions from the commission or individual members; its verdict was binding. If the court was not approached, the committee of ministers could make the final decision. The convention consists of a preamble and 66 articles over five sections and defines human rights and fundamental freedoms.

See also: COUNCIL OF EUROPE, STATUTE OF.

Further reading: Robert Blackburn, *Fundamental Rights in Europe: The European Convention on Human Rights and Its Member States, 1950–2000* (New York: Oxford University Press, 2001); J. G. Merills and A. H. Robertson, *Human Rights in Europe: A Study of the European Convention on Human Rights,* 4th ed. (Manchester, England: Manchester University Press, 2001); A. W. B. Simpson, *Human Rights and the End of Empire: Britain and the Genesis of the European Convention* (New York: Oxford University Press, 2001); Keir Starmer and Iain Byrne, *Blackstone's Human Rights Digest* (London: Blackstone Press, 2001).

European Free Trade Association Agreement

Agreement (November 20, 1959) derived from the Stockholm Convention, establishing the European Free Trade Association (EFTA), a customs union among seven countries (Great Britain, Austria, Portugal, Denmark, Norway, Sweden, and Switzerland); once known as the "Outer Seven" (as opposed to the "Inner Six" of the Common Market). EFTA, which became operative on May 3, 1960, aimed at abolishing trade barriers among members, and encouraging economic progress, full employment, and financial stability. Its agenda included a schedule for the reciprocal elimination of tariffs and a relaxation of quotas for industrial and agricultural products. EFTA's policies are enforced by individual members; there is no supranational authority. Based in Geneva, its ministers meet several times a year and its officers on a weekly basis. EFTA was joined by Finland in 1961 and Iceland in 1970. Britain and Denmark withdrew in 1972 to enter the Common Market or European Economic Community in 1973 (see ROME, TREATIES OF [1957]), with which EFTA signed a Free Trade Agreement in July 1973.

See also: BENELUX ECONOMIC UNION AGREEMENT; SINGLE EUROPEAN ACT.

Further reading: Charles L. Phillips and Alan Axelrod, eds., *Encyclopedia of Historical Treaties and Alliances,* 2 vols. (New York: Facts On File, 2001).

European Recovery Program   See MARSHALL PLAN.

Everson v. Board of Education

U.S. Supreme Court decision issued on February 10, 1947, concerning the separation of church and state. It permitted religious institutions to benefit from government programs that are religiously neutral. A taxpayer had sued the Board of Education in Ewing, New Jersey, for using tax money to provide free transportation for all students attending parochial as well as public schools, claiming the practice violated the U.S. constitutional prohibition against the establishment of religion. In its 5-4 decision, the Supreme Court upheld the Board of Education, arguing that the state must be neutral, not adversarial, in its relations with religious groups. It reaffirmed, however, that the "wall between church and state . . . must be kept high and impregnable."

Further reading: Richard M. Johnson, *The Dynamics of Compliance* (Evanston, Ill.: Northwestern University Press, 1967); Leonard, W. Levy and Kenneth L. Karst, eds., *Encyclopedia of the American Constitution,* 2d ed. (New York: Macmillan Reference, 2000).

Evolutionary Socialism

English translation of influential book (*Die Voraussetzungen des Sozialismus und die Aufgaben der Sozialdemokratie*) written and first published (1899) in German by socialist Eduard Bernstein, whose criticisms of Karl Marx's theories aroused every socialist party in Europe before World War I (1914–18). Bernstein rejected orthodox Marxism with its belief in increasing class warfare and the collapse of capitalism as a result. Instead, the "father of revisionism" (as Bernstein was called) envisaged an increasingly larger middle class (thus offsetting an inevitable proletarian dictatorship, Marx's result of capitalism's collapse), an increasing standard of living for all classes, and a social democracy through "the struggle for the political rights of the working man." Private initiative and the will of the people would help bring a moralistic socialism of the future, Bernstein said.

Further reading: Eduard Bernstein, *Evolutionary Socialism: A Criticism and Affirmation* (New York: Schocken, 1971); Manfred B. Steger, *The Quest for Evolutionary Socialism: Eduard Bernstein and Social Democracy* (New York: Cambridge University Press, 1997).

Exclusion, Act of   See SECLUSION, ACT OF.

Execrabilis of 1460   Pope Pius II's bull of January 18, 1460, seeking to end the practice of appealing to a general church council (see PISA, DECLARATION OF THE COUNCIL OF). The bull, issued at the end of the Congress of Mantua (1459–60), was a striking reversal of Pius's previous stance on the subject, and inflicted the penalty of heresy and treason on those who appealed to a council. It grew out of Pius's conviction that the growing importance of councils had caused a corresponding decline in the influence of the papacy. The death in 1461 of France's king Charles VII, who had vehemently opposed the bull, apparently eased acceptance of the bull, which long remained the supreme expression of the extremist ultramontane position.

See also: UNAM SANCTUM.

Further reading: Paul Halsall, *Medieval Source Book: Pius II: The Decree Execrabilis 1459*, Internet medieval sourcebook, available online at http://www.fordham.edu/halsall/source/p2-execrabilis.html.

Execrabilis of 1530   Pope Clement VII's bull of March 1530, ordering England's king Henry VIII not to remarry until a verdict had been reached on the validity of his first marriage to Catherine of Aragon. Owing to the king's politicking and the pope's indecisions, the bull was not publicized until July 11, 1533, when Clement VII condemned Henry's separation from Catherine and his marriage to Anne Boleyn. Threatening to excommunicate the king, the pope ordered him to take Catherine back. The bull did not address the validity or condition of Henry's first marriage (Henry wanted it declared invalid); it only criticized Henry's actions against the marriage. For the English monarch, this signaled a complete break with Rome.

See also: ANNATES' STATUTES.

Further reading: Pierre Crabites, *Clement VII and Henry VIII* (London: G. Routledge, 1936); Herbert M. Vaughan, *The Medici Popes (Leo X and Clement VII)* (Port Washington, N.Y.: Kennikat Press, 1971).

Execrabilis of 1606   Papal bull of Paul IV in 1606, forbidding the Roman Catholics of England from taking the oath of allegiance required of them by the penal laws of England's king James I. Taking the oath of allegiance meant renouncing the idea that the pope could topple kings, and King James wanted to force this assurance from the Catholics, following the Gunpowder Plot of 1605 (to blow up Parliament and the king), when he thought it necessary to distinguish between loyal and disloyal Catholics.

Further reading: Cecilia M. Ady, *Pius II (Aeneas Silvius Piccolomini): The Humanist Pope* (London: Methuen, 1989); Rosamund J. Mitchell, *The Laurels and the Tiara; Pope Pius II, 1458–1464* (Garden City, N.Y.: Doubleday, 1963); Pope Pius II, *Memoirs of a Renaissance Pope; the Commentaries of Pius II, an Abridgement*, trans. Florence A. Gragg (London: Allen & Unwin, 1960).

Execrabilis of 1809   Pope Pius VII's bull *Quum memoranda*, issued on June 10, 1809, in response to Napoléon's decree of May 17, 1809, announcing France's annexation of the remaining papal states. The bull excommunicated all "robbers of Peter's patrimony," referring generally to all invaders and specifically, though without mentioning him by name, to Emperor Napoléon, who had invaded the Holy See. Napoléon's relations with the Vatican had become strained over Pope Pius VII's refusal to participate in France's continental blockade of England (see FONTAINEBLEAU DECREES; MILAN DECREES). The pope was then arrested and deported, first to Grenoble, then to Savona, and finally to Fontainebleau, his total imprisonment lasting five years.

Further reading: Robin Anderson, *Pope Pius VII, 1800–1823: His Life, Reign and Struggle with Napoleon in the Aftermath of the French Revolution* (Rockford, Ill.: Tan Books, 2001); E. E. Y. Hales, *The Emperor and the Pope: The Story of Napoleon and Pius VII* (New York: Octagon Books, 1978); Margaret M. O'Dwyer, *The Papacy in the Age of Napoleon and the Restoration: Pius VII, 1800–1823* (Lanham, Md.: University Press of America, 1985).

Executive Order 9066, U.S. (Japanese Relocation Order)   Order issued by U.S. president Franklin D. Roosevelt on February 19, 1942, authorizing military commanders to establish special zones from which "any or all persons" might be excluded. The order, prompted by fears of sabotage and espionage following the Japanese attack on Pearl Harbor, allowed the U.S. Army to evacuate persons of Japanese ancestry living on the U.S. West Coast, to inland "relocation centers." On March 21 Congress enacted legislation in support of this order. Some 112,000 people—most of them native-born U.S. citizens—were forced to sell their homes and businesses and remove to bleak internment camps, where most remained until 1945. The U.S. Supreme Court, in *KOREMATSU V. UNITED STATES*, upheld the internment, but in 1983 a federal commission called the program "a grave injustice." In 1988 Congress authorized reparations for Japanese Americans interned during World War II (1939–45), and the following year provided funding for payments of $20,000 for each surviving internee.

Further reading: Maisie Conrat, *Executive Order 9066: The Internment of 110,000 Japanese Americans* (Los Angeles: University of California Press, 1992); Leonard W. Levy and Kenneth L. Karst, eds., *Encyclopedia of the American Constitution*, 2d ed. (New York: Macmillan Reference, 2000); Greg Robinson, *By Order of the President: FDR and the Internment of Japanese Americans* (Cambridge, Mass.: Harvard University Press, 2001).

Ex Parte Endo   U.S. Supreme Court decision issued in December 1944, declaring that the government could not detain in a relocation camp a Japanese American whose loyalty had been established. Misuye Endo, an American citizen of Japanese descent, had reported for internment (see EXECUTIVE OR-DER 9066), then challenged her detention by the War Relocation Authority. In a unanimous opinion, the Court granted her liberty, ruling that Congress had not authorized an indefinite detention program for Japanese Americans declared "loyal"; the Court did not rule on the constitutionality of the program in general. The army ordered the release of all loyal Japanese Americans in January 1945.

Further reading: Kermit Hall et al., eds., *American Legal History: Cases and Materials*, 2d ed. (New York: Oxford University Press, 1996); Kermit L. Hall et al., eds., *The Oxford Companion to the Supreme Court of the United States* (New York: Oxford University Press, 1992); United States Supreme Court, *United States Reports: Cases Adjudged in the Supreme Court at . . . and Rules Announced at . . .* (New York: Banks & Brothers, Law Publishers, 1884–1921; Washington: Government Printing Office, 1922–).

Explanation, Act of (Act of Settlement and Explanation)

English supplementary legislation enacted in 1665 to settle satisfactorily dissenting claims arising from the 1662 Act of SETTLEMENT for Ireland. Because there was not enough Irish land for distribution, adventurers, soldiers, and Cromwellian settlers were asked to give up one-third of their land-grants, thus yielding estates to Irish Catholics as compensation for losses during the Commonwealth (the English interregnum under Oliver Cromwell, from 1649 to 1660). However, dubious land grant decisions were decided in favor of Protestant loyalists, who ultimately held about two-thirds of the profitable lands and estates in Ireland.

Further reading: Christopher Haigh, ed., *The Cambridge Historical Encyclopedia of Great Britain and Ireland* (Cambridge, England: Cambridge University Press, 1985); George Philips and John Jeffreys, *Rules, Orders, and Directions, Appointed by His Majesties Commissioners for Executing the Act of Settlement and the Act of Explanation . . .* (Woodbridge, Conn.: Research Publications, 1974).

Exposition and Protest, Calhoun's (South Carolina Exposition and Protest)

Essay protesting the TARIFF ACT OF 1828, drafted secretly, but not signed, by U.S. vice president John C. Calhoun of South Carolina, and issued by that state's legislature. Calhoun argued that the tariff was "unconstitutional, oppressive, and unjust." He declared that the U.S. CONSTITUTION gave Congress the power to tax only to raise revenues, not the power to protect manufactures, and that the tariff violated these principles. Moreover, he claimed that a state could declare null and void a federal statute that it considered unconstitutional; such nullification could be overridden only by a constitutional amendment. In 1832 SOUTH CAROLINA'S ORDINANCE OF NULLIFICATION was adopted.

Further reading: Irving H. Bartlett, *John C. Calhoun: A Biography* (New York: W. W. Norton, 1993); Henry Steele Commager, ed., *Documents of American History*, 8th ed. (New York: Appleton-Century-Crofts, 1968); Merrill D. Peterson, *The Great Triumvirate: Webster, Clay, and Calhoun* (New York: Oxford University Press, 1987).

Exsurge Domine

Papal bull issued by Pope Leo X on June 15, 1520, rebuking the heresies of Martin Luther, the German leader of the Protestant Reformation. The pope condemned Luther's views and writings and threatened him with excommunication should he fail to comply with orders to recant his opinions. The pope also forbade all Christian believers to communicate with him; if they did not comply, they also risked excommunication. Luther's response to Exsurge Domine, which was sent to him at Wittenberg, Germany, was to burn publicly the bull and the canon law—the first dramatic incident leading to the turmoil of the Reformation. Luther was formally excommunicated in 1521.

See also: NINETY-FIVE THESES, LUTHER'S; WORMS, EDICT OF (1521).

Further reading: Jesuamirtham R. Narchison, *Papal Authority in Exsurge Domine* (Ann Arbor, Mich.: University Microfilms International, 1978).

F

Fabian Essays Classic expression of British socialism in a compendium of lectures on socialism, first published in 1889 under the aegis of the Fabian Society (socialistic society founded in London in 1884). The contributors (George Bernard Shaw, Sidney Webb, William Clarke, Sydney Olivier, Graham Wallas, Annie Besant, and Hubert Bland) were members of the society's executive council and the essays were edited for publication by Shaw. The essays were organized under three main heads: (1) the basis of socialism (exploring the economic, historic, industrial, and moral bases of socialism); (2) the organization of society (discussing property and industry under socialism); and (3) the transition to social democracy (looking ahead to the general outlook during the transition phase). Outlining exhaustive proposals or social legislation and reform, the essays had a tremendous influence on contemporary political thought. They were imbued with the Fabian philosophy of striving for a new order "without breach of continuity or abrupt change of the entire social tissue."

Further reading: Clive E. Hill, *Understanding the Fabian Essays in Socialism (1889)* (Lewiston, N.Y.: Edwin Mellen Press, 1996); George Bernard Shaw, ed., *Fabian Essays in Socialism* (Gloucester, Mass.: Peter Smith, 1967).

Factory Act of 1873, Australian (Workrooms and Factories Act)

Pioneering legislation of June 1873, passed by the government of Victoria (a separate, self-governing British colony in Australia since 1851). The act was intended to protect women and children working in the factories by establishing standards for safe and sanitary working conditions. Revisions in 1884 strengthened the act, which was used as a model by other British colonies in Australia. It was the first law for Australian factory workers.

Further reading: *Anno Tricesimo Septimo Victoriae Reginae, No. 466: An Act for the Supervision and Regulation of Workrooms and Factories and the Employment of Females Therein, 11th November 1873* (Melbourne, Australia: J. Ferres, 1873).

Factory Act of 1833, British (Factories Regulation Act)

In Great Britain, on August 29, 1833, first effective legislation seeking to improve the dreadful working conditions of children in textile factories. Children under nine years of age could not be employed; children between ages nine and 13 were restricted to a 48-hour week or a maximum of nine hours in one day (night shifts being banned for all children); and those between 13 and 18 to a 69-hour week or a maximum of 10 hours in a single day. Children below 13 had to receive compulsory education for two hours every day. A panel of paid inspectors was constituted to ensure that all these provisions were effectively implemented. An improvement on the factory acts of 1802 and 1816 and the precursor of subsequent factory legislation, this act was the result of an agitation for a 10-hour day led by Richard Oastler and Lord Ashley.

See also: HEALTH AND MORALS OF APPRENTICES ACT.

Further reading: *The Factory Act of 1833: Eight Pamphlets, 1833–1834* (New York: Arno Press, 1972).

Factory Laws, Russian   Series of labor laws introduced from 1882 to 1886, which were intended to regulate industrial working conditions. Primarily the work of Nicholas Bunge, Russia's finance minister from 1881 to 1887, the legislation forbade labor for children under 12; limited the working day to eight hours for children between 12 and 15; required employers to allow child workers to attend school; prohibited night work for women and children in the textile industry; regulated employment contracts and payment methods for workers; imposed penalties for striking; and established government inspection. The laws were unpopular with industrialists, and in 1886 Bunge was replaced by the more conservative Ivan Vyshnegradsky, who removed some of his predecessor's restrictions on hours of employment.

Further reading: Frederick C. Giffin, *Russian Factory Legislation in the 1880s* (Ph.D. Dissertation, Emory University, 1965).

Fairfax Resolves   Resolutions drawn up by George Mason and approved by a citizens' assembly in Fairfax County, Virginia, on July 18, 1774. They restated the American colonies' view of the COERCIVE ACTS as unconstitutional and outlined steps to resist them. The resolutions included provisions that supported the nonimportation of goods from Britain; urged giving aid to Boston; recommended that the colonies unite to resist the Coercive Acts; recommended calling an intercolonial congress; and advised nonexportation of tobacco and refusal to grow tobacco crops if the Coercive Acts were not repealed. The Fairfax Resolves were subsequently adopted by the First Continental Congress (September 5–October 26, 1774) in Philadelphia.

See also: SUFFOLK RESOLVES.

Further reading: George Mason, *The Fairfax Resolves* (Fairfax, Va.: Board of Regents, Gunston Hall, 1974); Fletcher H. Shaw, *George Mason, the Fairfax County Resolves, and the American Revolution* (Fairfax, Va.: F. H. Shaw, 1982).

Fair Housing Amendments Act, U.S.   Federal legislation passed by both houses of the United States Congress and signed into law on September 13, 1988, by President Ronald Reagan, including new, more stringent provisions against discrimination in housing. The nation's first such legislation was included in the CIVIL RIGHTS ACT OF 1968. By the 1988 act, discrimination in public and private housing against both the disabled and families with children (except in housing specifically designated as housing for the retired) became illegal. In addition, transgressors would receive substantial fines from the government.

Further reading: *The Fair Housing Amendments Act of 1988* (Washington, D.C.: United States Commission on Civil Rights, 1994); *The New Fair Housing Law: Impact and Analysis* (Washington D.C.: Bureau of National Affairs, 1988).

Fair Labor Standards Act, U.S. (Wages and Hours Act)   Federal U.S. legislation enacted on June 25, 1938, that established a minimum wage of 25¢ per hour (to be increased gradually to 40¢) and a maximum workweek of 44 hours (to be reduced gradually to 40 hours), with time and a half for overtime; prohibited labor by children under age 16; and protected children under 18 from hazardous occupations. The act applied only to businesses engaged in interstate commerce and exempted such occupations as farm, domestic, and professional workers and fishermen. The constitutionality of the act was upheld in *UNITED STATES* V. *DARBY LUMBER COMPANY* (1941). The act has been amended many times to raise the minimum wage and extend coverage to more workers.

Further reading: Ellen C. Kearns and Monica Gallagher, eds., *The Fair Labor Standards Act* (Washington, D.C.: BNA Books, 1999); George E. Paulsen, *A Living Wage for the Forgotten Man: The Quest for Fair Labor Standards, 1933–1941* (Selinsgrove, Penn.: Susquehanna University Press, 1996); Ronnie Steinberg, *Wages and Hours: Labor and Reform in 20th Century America* (New Brunswick, N.J.: Rutgers University Press, 1982); Neal G. Thomas, *Wages and the Fair Labor Standards Act in Everyday Language: Everything You, Your Employee and Your Lawyer Should Know about Your Rights* (Charleston, S.C.: Narwhal Press, 1998).

Falk Laws   See MAY LAWS.

Falloux Law (Loi Falloux)   Enactment of March 15, 1850, ending the state's monopoly over secondary education in France by granting the church a greater role in it. Drafted by an extraparliamentary commission appointed by education minister Frédéric de Falloux, the act spurred the growth of Catholic secondary schools as well as private lay schools and increased clerical representation on higher education councils. Government officials were responsible for all school inspections, and baccalaureate degrees could be awarded only by the state. Anyone above age 25 holding this degree or having five years teaching experience could start a secondary school. Towns were allowed to transfer their public colleges to the clergy. Communes of 800 or more were compelled to have a girls' school, and teachers were guaranteed a minimum wage. Newly created departmental academic councils expanded the prefect's authority over appointments in his school district.

See also: FERRY LAWS; GUIZOT LAW.

Further reading: Alfred Wolff, *La Loi Falloux et son application en Alsace et Lorraine* (Paris: Librairie du Recueil Sirey, 1939).

False Decretals (Isidorian Decretals, Pseudo-Isidorian Decretals)   Collection of ecclesiastical documents, subsequently found to contain many falsified texts, compiled about A.D. 850 by a group of Frankish authors seeking to improve church-state relations and to defend the rights of bishops by quoting relevant texts from the ancient popes. Originally ascribed to St. Isidore of Seville and sometimes to Isidorus Mercator, the compilation can be divided into (1) letters of the anti-Nicene popes, all forged; (2) collection of canons of councils, mainly genuine, except for the forged Donation of CONSTANTINE; and (3) large collection of papal letters, 35 of them forgeries, from Popes Sylvester I (d. 335) to Gregory II (d. 731). During the Middle Ages the decretals were generally believed to be authentic. For instance, Sir Thomas More used them in his defense of the papacy. While the collection's influence on the development of canon law has often been exaggerated, it did succeed in securing some rights for the bishops.

See also: DECRETAL OF GRATIAN; DECRETALS OF 1234.

Further reading: Ernest Harold Davenport, *The False Decretals* (Oxford, England: B. H. Blackwell, 1916).

Family and Medical Leave Act, U.S.

First legislation enacted on February 5, 1993 (effective August 5, 1993), by President Bill Clinton's administration, requiring nonprofit and government organizations and businesses with more than 50 employees to provide their workers with up to 12 weeks of unpaid leave to deal with family and medical emergencies. Further, the employee's health benefits would continue and his or her position (or equivalent) was guaranteed upon return. However, the top 10 percent of a company's workforce, part-time employees, and those with less than one year on the job were exempt. Estimated to cover approximately 50 percent of the nation's workforce, the act would be administered by the U.S. Department of Labor. Some of its provisions overlap with those of the AMERICANS WITH DISABILITIES ACT.

Further reading: The U.S. Equal Employment Opportunity Commission, *The Family and Medical Leave Act, the Americans with Disabilities Act, and Title VII of the Civil Rights Act of 1964*, U.S. Equal Employment Opportunity Commission, available online at http://www.eeoc.gov/docs/fmlaada.html; Barbara Woller, "Family Medical Leave Act Turns 5," Gannett News Service, August 10, 1998.

Family Compacts (Pactes de Famille)

Series of three pacts between the two branches (Spain and France) of the Bourbon family. The first, the Treaty of Escorial (November 7, 1733), signed in Madrid during the War of the Polish Succession (1733–38), helped Spain recover Naples and Sicily. It guaranteed mutual possessions and support for future territorial gains and annulled all previous treaties. The French and Spanish Bourbons agreed not to make separate peace. By the second, the Treaty of Fontainebleau (October 25, 1743), Spain allied herself with France in the War of the Austrian Succession (1740–48). Initial gains were short lived, but the alliance was sealed with the marriage, in December 1744, of

the Spanish infanta Teresa to the dauphin Louis. The third pact (August 15, 1761) included Parma and Naples (see PRAGMATIC SANCTION OF CHARLES III) and aimed at the recovery of Gibraltar from Britain and the preservation of mutual overseas territories. Spain's king Charles III also assured France's king Louis XV of Spanish support for France if Britain rejected Spain's mediation (see ARANJUEZ, CONVENTION OF) and if the Seven Years' War (1756–63) was not resolved by May 1762. All three pacts were betrayed by France.

Further reading: John D. Bergamini, *The Spanish Bourbons: The History of a Tenacious Dynasty* (New York: Putnam, 1974); Desmond Seward, *The Bourbon Kings of France* (New York: Barnes & Noble Books, 1976).

Farm Credit Act, U.S.

New Deal legislation enacted on June 16, 1933, to centralize all farm credit services into the Farm Credit Administration, allowing American farmers to refinance their mortgages on long terms at low interest rates. The legislation completed action begun by President Franklin D. Roosevelt's executive order of March 27, which had consolidated several federal agencies—among them the Federal Farm Board and the Federal Farm Loan Board—dealing with farm credit. It established production credit corporations in 12 regional districts to provide long-term financing for farmers.

Further reading: Murray Benedict, *Farm Policies of the United States, 1790–1950* (New York: Twentieth Century Fund, 1953); Thomas Carson, ed., *Gale Encyclopedia of U.S. Economic History* (Farmington Hills, Mich.: Gale Group 1999); Richard Kirkendall, *Social Scientists and Farm Politics in the Age of Roosevelt* (Ames: Iowa State University Press, 1982).

Farmer's Law, Byzantine   See BYZANTINE AGRARIAN CODE.

Farmer's Letters, Dickinson's (Letters from a Farmer in Pennsylvania to the Inhabitants of the British Colonies)

Series of 14 essays written by John Dickinson, a Philadelphia lawyer, member of the Pennsylvania legislature, and delegate to the Stamp Act Congress of 1765. The letters criticized the TOWNSHEND ACTS enacted by the British Parliament, which imposed import duties on numerous items. Originally published in the *Pennsylvania Chronicle* in 1767 and 1768, the letters argued that while the British Parliament had the right to produce revenue in the course of regulating trade, it could not legally tax the colonies solely for the purpose of raising revenue in America. The letters were reprinted in a pamphlet and circulated throughout the colonies, and the position they enunciated on British taxation in the colonies became widely accepted.

See also: STAMP ACT OF 1765.

Further reading: *Dictionary of American History*, rev. ed. (New York: Charles Scribner's Sons, 1976); Samuel Eliot Morison, *Sources and Documents Illustrating the American Revo-*

lution, 1764–1788, 2d ed. (New York: Oxford University Press, 1965).

Farm Mortgage Moratorium Act, U.S.   See FRAZIER-LEMKE FARM BANKRUPTCY ACT.

Farm Mortgage Refinancing Act, U.S.   New Deal legislation enacted by Congress on January 31, 1934, establishing the Federal Farm Mortgage Corporation (FFMC) to assist in the refinancing of farm debts during the Great Depression. The FFMC was to advance the loan operations of the federal land banks by issuing fully guaranteed, tax-exempt bonds and exchanging the proceeds for land-bank bonds. The FFMC, set up under the Farm Credit Corporation, was authorized to issue up to $2,000,000 in bonds, whose principal and interest were guaranteed.

Further reading: Murray Benedict, *Farm Policies of the United States, 1790–1950* (New York: Twentieth Century Fund, 1953); Richard Kirkendall, *Social Scientists and Farm Politics in the Age of Roosevelt* (Ames: Iowa State University Press, 1982).

Faulkner's "Nobel Prize Speech"   Address delivered by American writer William Faulkner on December 10, 1950, in Stockholm, Sweden, when he received the 1949 Nobel Prize in literature. In it Faulkner argued that it was difficult for the artist in the nuclear age, amid a cold war that threatened human survival, to remember that only "the problems of the human heart in conflict with itself" make for good writing. The "old universal truths" of human feeling remain the basis for literature. Moreover, Faulkner predicted that man will not only endure but prevail, because he has a soul capable of noble action. The writer's task is to help man endure "by lifting his heart, by reminding him of the courage and honor and hope and pride and compassion and pity and sacrifice which have been the glory of his past."

Further reading: William Faulkner, *Essays, Speeches and Public Letters,* James B. Meriwether, ed. (New York: Random House, 1966); *William Faulkner Reads: "The Nobel Prize Acceptance Speech" and Selections from "As I Lay Dying," "A Fable" and "The Old Man"* (audiocassette), (New York: Caedmon, 1992).

February Manifesto   Decree by Russia's czar Nicholas II in February 1899, effectively abrogating the constitution of the autonomous Grand Duchy of Finland, and transferring the legislative responsibility for Finland to the Russian Imperial Council. As a result, Russian laws were given precedence over Finnish laws, and the Finnish Diet was reduced to the status of a provincial assembly. The actions were part of Nicholas's attempted Russification of outlying provinces, beginning in Finland in 1898 with the appointment of General Nicholas Bobrikov as governor general. In 1898, Bobrikov began Russification of the Finnish army, and in 1901, Russian

conscription was introduced into Finland. In 1902, the Russian language was introduced into Finnish schools, and in 1903, the Finnish constitution was suspended. The Finns reacted to these measures with passive resistance. The new laws were not proclaimed in the villages, were ignored by the judicial system, and were not enforced by conscripts. In 1904, Bobrikov was assassinated—a precursor to the Russian Revolution of 1905.

Further reading: Osmo Jussila et al., *From Grand Duchy to a Modern State: A Political History of Finland since 1809* (London: Hurst & Co., 1999).

February Patent   Constitution drawn up under the influence of Austrian minister of the interior Anton von Schmerling and issued by the Austrian government on February 26, 1861, nominally revising the OCTOBER DIPLOMA but in reality representing a new constitution. Like the October Diploma the February Patent provided that the imperial diet was to consist of representatives from the whole Austrian Empire, and that Hungary would retain the degree of autonomy that she had had prior to 1848. The new electoral system, however, provided that the voice of the German bourgeoisie would be dominant; and, although the provincial diets remained, the responsibilities of the imperial diet were significantly enlarged. Other changes included the creation of a central bicameral parliament, and of a separate diet for the Hapsburg lands of the Austrian Empire alone (i.e., without Hungary or Venetia). The nationalists refused to accept the document, and in 1865 it was suspended.

See also: AUSTRIAN CONSTITUTION OF 1867.

Further reading: Paula S. Fichtner, *The Habsburg Empire: From Dynasticism to Multinationalism* (Malabar, Fla.: Krieger, 1997); Pieter M. Judson, *Exclusive Revolutionaries: Liberal Politics, Social Experience, and National Identity in the Austrian Empire, 1848–1914* (Ann Arbor: University of Michigan Press, 1996); Robert A. Kann, *The Multinational Empire; Nationalism and National Reform in the Habsburg Monarchy, 1848–1918* (New York: Octagon Book, 1970).

Federal Communications Act, U.S.   Federal legislation enacted on June 19, 1934, creating the Federal Communications Commission (FCC) to regulate interstate and foreign communications by telegraph, cable, and radio. The FCC replaced the Federal Radio Commission and consolidated regulatory powers formerly vested in the Interstate Commerce Commission and the postal and commerce departments. The commission was to consist of seven members appointed by the U.S. president, with the consent of the Senate. The act authorized new regulations to control the radio broadcasting industry.

Further reading: *Communications by Wire and Radio, a Treatise on the Law of Wire and Wireless Communications in Interstate and Foreign Commerce Based on the Federal Communications Act of June 19, 1934, as Amended, with a Discussion* *of the Rules of Practice and Procedure Before the Federal Communications Commission and the Courts, and Suggested Forms* (Chicago: Callaghan & Co., 1937); Robert L. Hilliard, *The Federal Communications Commission: A Primer* (Boston: Focal Press, 1991).

Federal Emergency Relief Act, U.S.

New Deal legislation enacted by the U.S. Congress on May 12, 1933, that created the Federal Emergency Relief Administration (FERA), with an appropriation of $500 million, to aid millions of unemployed workers and their families, as well as drought victims. Half of this sum was to be given directly to the states; half was to be distributed on the basis of $1 of federal aid for every $3 of state and local relief funds spent. At first the FERA provided food and other essentials to the unemployed. Later it provided public-works jobs for the unemployed under the Civil Works Administration and eventually the Public Works Administration. In 1935 FERA was replaced by the Works Progress Administration.

Further reading: *Federal Emergency Relief and Civil Works Program* (Washington, D.C.: U.S. Government Printing Office, 1934).

Federal "Income Tax" Amendment, U.S.

See SIXTEENTH AMENDMENT, U.S.

Federal Income Tax Law, Canadian

See CANADIAN FEDERAL INCOME TAX LAW.

Federalist No. 10

Essay written by James Madison, first published in the *New York Packet* on November 23, 1787, and probably the most famous of the *FEDERALIST PAPERS*. In it Madison refuted the popular view that republican government was suitable only for small states, arguing that only a large republic with a diverse population and a representative system can safeguard liberty, justice, and stability. Madison believed that republicanism protected against the dangers of "factions," which he defined as citizens "united . . . by some common impulse of passion, or of interest, adverse to the rights of other citizens, or to the permanent and aggregate interests of the community."

Further reading: William B. Allen and Kevin A. Cloonan, *The Federalist Papers: A Commentary* (New York: Peter Lang, 2000); Jacob E. Cooke, ed., *The Federalist* (Middletown, Conn.: Wesleyan University Press, 1961); Alexander Hamilton, James Madison, and John Jay, *The Federalist Papers,* ed. Clinton Rossiter (New York: Mentor Books, 1999); Frederick Quinn, ed., *The Federalist Papers Reader and Historical Documents of Our American Heritage* (Santa Ana, Calif.: Seven Locks Press, 1997).

Federalist Papers

Series of 85 essays written to promote the ratification of the proposed U.S. CONSTITUTION and published in 1787–88. Though all the essays were signed with the pseudonym "Publius," the actual authors were Alexander Hamilton, who wrote most of the essays and emphasized economic issues; John Jay, who dealt with international relations; and James Madison, who discussed political theory. The essays consider the nature of republican government and promote the new federal system as an attempt to preserve state sovereignty and to protect individual liberty. Though widely viewed as a classic work of political philosophy, *The Federalist* (the title under which the essays were collected) probably had little effect on the vote to ratify the Constitution.

See also: FEDERALIST NO. 10.

Further reading: William B. Allen and Kevin A. Cloonan, *The Federalist Papers: A Commentary* (New York: Peter Lang, 2000); Jacob E. Cooke, ed., *The Federalist* (Middletown, Conn.: Wesleyan University Press, 1961, rep., 1982); Alexander Hamilton, James Madison, and John Jay, *The Federalist Papers,* ed. Clinton Rossiter (New York: Mentor Books, 1999); Frederick Quinn, ed., *The Federalist Papers Reader and Historical Documents of Our American Heritage* (Santa Ana, Calif.: Seven Locks Press, 1997).

Federal Reserve Act of 1913, U.S. (Glass-Owen Act)

Federal U.S. legislation drafted by Representative Carter Glass of Virginia and Senator Robert L. Owen of Oklahoma and enacted on December 23, 1913, establishing the Federal Reserve System, a major reform aimed at assuring an elastic currency and more effective supervision of the national banking system, especially its credit procedures. Twelve regional Federal Reserve banks, under the central Federal Reserve Board, were established. All national banks were required to join the system, and state banks were allowed to do so if they met certain requirements. The Federal Reserve banks function as bankers' banks, holding deposits and making loans to member banks. The Federal Reserve Board of Governors, consisting of seven members appointed by the U.S. president, may adjust interest rates that member banks pay for loans and thus influences the availability of credit for individual borrowers.

Further reading: J. Lawrence Broz, *The International Origins of the Federal Reserve System* (Ithaca, N.Y.: Cornell University Press, 1997); James L. Livingston, *Origins of the Federal Reserve System: Money, Class, and Corporate Capitalism, 1890–1913* (Ithaca, N.Y.: Cornell University Press, 1986); Richard T. McCulley, *Banks and Politics During the Progressive Era: The Origins of the Federal Reserve System, 1897–1913* (New York: Garland Publishing, 1992); Robert C. West, *Banking Reform and the Federal Reserve, 1863–1923* (Ithaca, N.Y.: Cornell University Press, 1977).

Federal Trade Commission Act of 1914

National U.S. legislation enacted on September 26, 1914, designed to prohibit "unfair methods of competition" in interstate commerce. It established the bipartisan Federal Trade Commission (FTC), consisting of five members appointed by the U.S. president and approved by the Senate. The FTC was authorized to investigate possible violations of antitrust legislation by all interstate businesses (excepting banks and common carriers, which were governed by other regulations) and to issue cease-and-desist orders (subject to federal judicial review) to eliminate unfair business practices. The act gave the FTC the power to gather information, to require annual or special reports from corporations, and to assure compliance with federal court rulings on such matters.

Further reading: *Federal Trade Commission Act* (Washington, D.C.: U.S. Government Printing Office, 1934); William Stull Holt, *The Federal Trade Commission: Its History, Activities, and Organization* (New York: AMS Press, 1974); Robert V. Labaree, *The Federal Trade Commission: A Guide to Sources* (New York: Garland, 2001).

Federation of the United Provinces of New Granada, Act of

Act of federal congress, meeting in Santa Fe de Bogotá in 1811, that formed the general government of New Granada (Colombia). Delegates from the provinces of Antioquia, Cartagena, Casanare, Chocó, Neiva, Pamplona, Soccoro, Tunja, and Cundinamarca arrived at a pact of federation, drafted principally by the lawyer/independence leader Camilo Torres. It stipulated that each province would retain its own administration, and that the central government, consisting of a congress, would be assigned powers over military matters and foreign affairs. Soon after the federation was formed, however, disagreements over juridical boundaries led to the existence of two opposing governments in New Granada during most of 1811 and 1812.

Further reading: Frank Safford and Marco Palacios, *Colombia: Fragmented Land, Divided Society* (New York: Oxford University Press, 2002).

Ferry Laws (French Primary Education Laws of 1881 and 1882)

Two education bills introduced by French education minister Jules Ferry, making public primary education free, compulsory, and secular. The first, passed on June 16, 1881, made public primary education free. The second, enacted on March 28, 1882, declared primary education compulsory from six to 13 years, and excluded religious instruction from the school timetable. Instead, "moral and civil instruction" was included, with a small paragraph on duties to God. Municipal commissions, prefects, and town mayors were given increased authority over primary education. School principals and officials also had a greater say in administrative matters. Ferry's goal—complete laicization of the teaching staff—was not achieved until 1886. The Ferry Laws encouraged the growth of state-sponsored primary schools, an important step in French primary education.

See also: FALLOUX LAW; GUIZOT LAW.

Further reading: Francois Furet and Jacques Ozouf, *Reading and Writing: Literacy in France from Calvin to Jules Ferry* (New York: Cambridge University Press, 1982); Raymond Grew and Patrick J. Harrigan, *School, State, and Society: The Growth of Elementary Schooling in Nineteenth-Century France: A Quantitative Analysis* (Ann Arbor: University of Michigan Press, 1991).

Fielding Tariff Act (Canadian Preferential Tariff of 1897)

Bill proposed by Canadian minister of finance William S. Fielding and passed by Prime Minister Wilfrid Laurier's government in 1897, granting special lower tariff rates on products imported into Canada from Great Britain. This preferential tariff act provided that a percentage of the duty collected on imported British goods be returned to the British government. The British, who initially remained loyal to the principle of free trade and against protectionism, did not reciprocate in kind until 1919. The liberal politicians who supported the bill hoped that its passage would encourage the United States and Canada to conclude a protective tariff agreement, which they did in 1911—a short-lived reciprocity treaty reducing duties on many Canadian and U.S. manufactures shipped to each other.

See also: RECIPROCITY TREATY (ELGIN-MARCY TREATY).

Further reading: Thomas H. Farrer, *Free Trade, Preferential Tariffs, Canadian Fiscal Policy, . . .* (London: Cobden Club, 1897); Charles B. Ferguson, *Hon. W. S. Fielding*, 2 vols. (Windsor, Nova Scotia: Lancelot Press, 1970).

Fifteenth Amendment, U.S.

Amendment to the U.S. CONSTITUTION proposed in 1869 and ratified by the states in 1870, declaring that the rights of U.S. citizens to vote "shall not be denied or abridged by the United States or by any State on account of race, color or previous condition of servitude." The amendment, urged by radical Republicans to enfranchise black people, was for many years circumvented by white primaries, poll taxes, literacy and property tests, or residence and registration requirements. In 1915 the U.S. Supreme Court disallowed the "grandfather clause," which exempted from these requirements anyone whose ancestor had the right to vote before 1867 (when most blacks were slaves), as a violation of the Fifteenth Amendment, and later decisions have prohibited other discriminatory practices.

Further reading: Thomas Carson, ed., *Gale Encyclopedia of U.S. Economic History* (Farmington Hills, Mich.: Gale Group, 1999); Paul Finkelman, ed., *Encyclopedia of the United States in the Nineteenth Century* (New York: Charles Scribner's Sons, 2001); William Gillette, *The Right to Vote: Politics and the Passage of the Fifteenth Amendment* (Baltimore: Johns Hopkins Press, 1969).

Fifth Amendment, U.S.

Amendment to the U.S. CONSTITUTION, adopted in 1791, that requires grand jury action before a civilian can be subjected to criminal prosecution for a "capital or otherwise infamous crime," protects an accused person from being forced to testify against himself, protects the accused from being tried more than once for the same offense, ensures that no one may be deprived of "life, liberty or property, without due process of law," and provides just compensation if private property is taken for public use.

Further reading: Erwin N. Griswold, *The 5th Amendment Today* (Cambridge, Mass.: Harvard University Press, 1955); Eugene W. Hickok, Jr., ed., *The Bill of Rights; Original Meaning and Current Understanding* (Charlottesville: University Press of Virginia, 1991); A. E. Dick Howard, *The Road from Runnymeade: Magna Carta and Constitutionalism in America* (Charlottesville: University of Virginia Press, 1968).

Fighting Instructions First British handbook of naval tactics, issued in 1653 and used to direct much of Britain's naval warfare during the Anglo-Dutch Wars (1652–54, 1665–67, 1672–78). It declared the line-ahead formation compulsory in battle (a naval formation in which ships proceed one after another); because the Dutch navy was similarly organized, both powers were often equally matched in the wars. Later in the century, when France began to assert her naval strength, the restrictive effects of the British strategies began to be felt. This naval manual was also used as a guide for fighting at sea in the 18th century.

Further reading: Julian Stafford Corbett, ed., *Fighting Instructions, 1530–1816* (Annapolis, Md.: United States Naval Institute, 1971).

Financial Services Modernization Act, U.S. (Gramm-Leach-Bliley Act)
Major overhaul of the regulations governing the American banking and financial services industry, signed on November 12, 1999, by President Bill Clinton, replacing the restrictive and aging Glass-Steagall Banking Act (*see* BANKING ACT OF 1933, U.S.) and the 1956 Bank Holding Company Act. The legislation (Public Law 106-102) freed banks, insurance companies, and brokerage firms—which had heavily lobbied for legal changes for years—to compete across state lines and merge into financial conglomerates. Thus, a single financial institution could now conduct commercial and merchant banking, investment management, securities underwriting, and insurance by operating as a holding company. The legislation expected banks to comply with the Community Reinvestment Act by providing certain levels of credit to members of underserved groups. The law banned financial companies from sharing or selling the personal financial information of their customers without permission. It also forbade acquisition of new thrifts by commercial companies. The legislation was criticized as favoring big business over the average customers.

Further reading: The Region, "Financial Modernization," Woodrow Federal Reserve Bank of Minneapolis, available online at http://minneapolisfed.org/pubs/region/00-03; The United States Senate, "Financial Services Modernization Act Gramm-Leach-Bliley Summary of Provisions," The United States Senate Committee on Banking, Housing, and Urban Affairs, available online at http://www.senate.gov/~banking/conf/grmleach.htm.

First Amendment, U.S.
Amendment to the U.S. CONSTITUTION, adopted in 1791, that prohibits Congress from making any law establishing a national religion and from abridging the free exercise of religion, freedom of speech and of the press, the right of peaceful assembly, and the right to petition the government for the redress of grievances. The U.S. Supreme Court has ruled that freedom of speech under this amendment may be restricted if the speech represents a "clear and present danger" to the public interest. Among the important First Amendment issues that have been raised over the years are prayer in schools, obscenity, and libel.

Further reading: Daniel A. Farber, *The First Amendment* (New York: Foundation Press, 1998); John H. Garvey, ed., *The First Amendment: A Reader* (St. Paul, Minn.: West Publishing, 1996); Donald E. Lively, Dorothy E. Roberts, and Russell L. Weaver, eds., *First Amendment Anthology* (Cincinnati, Ohio: Anderson Publishing, 1994); Paul L. Murphy, *The Meaning of Freedom of Speech: First Amendment Freedoms from Wilson to FDR* (Westport, Conn.: Greenwood Press, 1972).

Five Articles of Perth
Religious restrictions that England's king James I persuaded the Kirk (Presbyterian Church) assembly at Perth, Scotland, to accept in 1618, in an effort to make the form of worship closer to the Church of England. The articles imposed kneeling at communion, private administering of communion and of baptism in extreme cases, confirmation of young people by the bishop, and observance of five holy days (Christmas, Good Friday, Easter, Ascension, and Pentecost). Forty-five clergymen protested, but in 1621 the articles were ratified by Parliament, thanks partly to the efforts of 11 parliamentary bishops.

Further reading: Hugh Watt and Duncan Shaw, eds., *Reformation and Revolution: Essays Presented to the Very Reverend Principal Emeritus Hugh Watt, D.D., D. Litt., on the Sixtieth Anniversary of His Ordination* (Edinburgh, Scotland: Saint Andrew Press, 1967).

Five Knights' Case (Darnel's Case)
Famous decision in British legal history, arising out of the refusal of Sir Thomas Darnel and four fellow knights (John Corbet, Walter Earl, Edmund Hampden, and John Hevingham) to contribute to the forced loans imposed by King Charles I in 1627 to raise revenue for the war against France (Anglo-French War of 1627–28). Eighty members of the gentry refused to pay and were imprisoned. Darnel and the others, however, filed an appeal against the crown before the King's Bench, demanding that they either be charged with a specific offense or released on bail. When their case was argued in November 1627, Chief Justice Hyde refused bail and ruled that they could not be released. They were eventually freed in 1628, but discussion of the decision continued in Parliament despite Charles I's assurance that no subject would be imprisoned for nonpayment of the forced loans. The stalemate was broken with the passage of the PETITION OF RIGHT in 1628.

Further reading: T. B. Howell, ed., *Cobbett's Complete Collection of State Trials* (Ann Arbor: University of Michigan Library, Photoduplication Service, 1978).

Five Mile Act (Oxford Act of 1665)

Fourth and final English law or act of the CLARENDON CODE, prohibiting clergymen who had not subscribed to the Act of UNIFORMITY from coming within five miles of where they had once preached, unless they swore nonresistance to the crown and promised never to try to change the church or the state. Enacted in October 1665, it forbade ejected clergy from teaching or taking in boarders and was intended to cover the evaders of the CONVENTICLE ACT. The provisions of this act were incapable of strict enforcement and were repealed by the TOLERATION ACT OF 1689.

Further reading: Carl Stephenson and Frederick George Marcham, eds., *Sources of English Constitutional History: A Selection of Documents from A.D. 600 to the Present* (New York: Harper & Row, 1937).

Five Power Naval Treaty (Treaty of Washington, Naval Armament Limitation Treaty)

One of three treaties (see FOUR POWER PACIFIC TREATY; NINE POWER PACTS) concluded at the Washington Conference (1921–22); also the first (February 6, 1922) major international arms limitation agreement. The five signatory powers (the United States, Great Britain, Japan, France, and Italy) defined ratios of naval might—the United States and Britain to have five battleships for every three by Japan and 1.75 each by France and Italy. Naval expansion was to be discontinued for a 10-year period and there were to be no further territorial gains in the Pacific. Britain and America agreed not to develop their existing naval bases in Hong Kong and the Philippines, which heightened Japan's importance in the area. While the treaty did not cover small ships and submarines, it was nevertheless very effective in controlling and accelerating the naval race among the powers.

Further reading: Erik Goldstein and John H. Maurer, *The Washington Conference, 1921–22: Naval Rivalry, East Asian Stability and the Road to Pearl Harbor* (Portland, Ore.: Frank Cass, 1994); B. J. C. McKercher, *Arms Limitation and Disarmament: Restraints on War, 1899–1939* (Westport, Conn.: Praeger, 1992).

Fletcher v. Peck

U.S. Supreme Court decision issued on March 16, 1810, concerning a Georgia land fraud case; the ruling was the first to declare a state law void under the U.S. CONSTITUTION. In the Yazoo land fraud case, the Georgia legislature had been bribed, in 1795, into selling 35 million acres to four land companies for $500,000. The following year a new Georgia legislature rescinded the sale on the grounds of fraud and corruption, and a suit concerning land title eventually reached the Supreme Court. In a unanimous opinion written by Chief Justice John Marshall, the Court upheld the 1795 grant, stating that the Court could not inquire into the legislature's motives in passing the original act and that the rescinding act was unconstitutional because it revoked rights previously granted by a contract.

Further reading: Leonard W. Levy and Kenneth L. Karst, eds., *Encyclopedia of the American Constitution*, 2 ed. (New York: Macmillan Reference, 2000); C. Peter Magrath, *Yazoo: Law and Politics in the New Republic. The Case of Fletcher v. Peck* (Providence, R.I.: Brown University Press, 1966).

Florence, Treaty of

Treaty concluded at Florence, Italy, on March 18, 1801, between Napoléon Bonaparte of France and King Ferdinand IV of the Kingdom of Naples during Napoléon's military campaign on the Italian Peninsula. Through previous treaties Napoléon had already gained control of northern and central Italy. Through the Florence treaty Ferdinand agreed to close the ports of his kingdom to British and Turkish vessels; to cede to France his Neapolitan holdings in central Italy, as well as the island of Elba; and to allow Napoléon to station French troops in certain towns, among them Taranto. Before concluding this agreement, Ferdinand had participated in the First and Second Coalitions, together with Austria and Great Britain, against France.

See also: CAMPO FORMIO, TREATY OF; LUNÉVILLE, TREATY OF; TOLENTINO, TREATY OF.

Further reading: R. B. Mowat, *The Diplomacy of Napoleon* (New York: Russell & Russell, 1971).

Flushing Remonstrance

Statement against the persecution of Quakers, written by English settlers at Flushing, Long Island, and addressed to Governor Peter Stuyvesant of New Amsterdam (New York) on December 27, 1657. Stuyvesant had ordered that Flushing "not receive any of those people called Quakers because they are supposed to be, by some, seducers of the people." The settlers remonstrated: "We desire in this case not to judge lest we be condemned, but rather to let every man stand and fall to his own Master." They probably made the first declaration of religious toleration in America. Nonetheless, five recently arrived Quakers at New Amsterdam were deported to Rhode Island.

Further reading: Haynes Trébor, *The Flushing Remonstrance: The Origin of Religious Freedom in America* (Flushing, N.Y.: Bowne House, c. 1957).

Fontainebleau, Edict of

See NANTES, REVOCATION OF THE EDICT OF.

Fontainebleau, Treaty of (1679)

See NIJMEGEN, TREATIES OF.

Fontainebleau, Treaty of (1743)

See FAMILY COMPACTS.

Fontainebleau, Treaty of (1785)

Peace accord concluded between Austria and Holland at Fontainebleau,

France, on November 8, 1785, terminating the fighting between them over the opening of the navigable Scheldt River, located in the Austrian Netherlands. Since the 1648 Peace of WESTPHALIA the Scheldt and its estuary had been generally closed to foreign vessels, free navigation being reserved for the Dutch alone; consequently, many towns had declined in prosperity. It was therefore in Austria's interest to reopen the river to reverse this trend. By the treaty, Austria received control of the Scheldt above Sanftingen and portions of the provinces of Brabant and Limburg, as well as 10 million florins. Austria recognized Dutch possession of the city of Maastricht.

Further reading: Felix Magnette, *Joseph II et la liberté de l'Escaut* (Brussels: Hayez, 1897).

Fontainebleau, Treaty of (1814)

Treaty bestowing a generous settlement on the defeated emperor Napoléon Bonaparte; concluded on April 11, 1814, between him and the Allies after his unconditional abdication (see NAPOLÉON'S ABDICATION DECLARATION). It confirmed Napoléon's complete renunciation of rights over France, Italy, or any other country. From France, Napoléon received the island of Elba "in full sovereignty and proprietorship" and an annual income of 2 million francs of which 1 million was for the Empress Marie Louise. They were allowed to "retain their titles and rank" for life; the emperor's close relatives (including Empress Josephine) were also permitted to keep their titles and shared the sum of 2.5 million francs. Napoléon's followers received 2 million francs among them. The Allies gave Marie Louise the duchies of Parma, Piacenza, and Guastalla; these were to "pass to her son and his descendants in the direct line." The treaty's terms reflect the Allies' guarded respect for Napoléon's extraordinary capacities.

Further reading: R. F. Deidenfield, *Imperial Sunset: The Fall of Napoleon, 1813–1814* (New York: Cooper Square Press, 2001).

Fontainebleau Decrees

French emperor Napoléon Bonaparte's attempts to tighten his control over neutral shipping. An extension of the BERLIN DECREE, the Fontainebleau Decree of October 13, 1807, declared that neutral ships responding to the British government's ORDERS IN COUNCIL OF 1807 would henceforth be treated as English ships. A certificate of origin was to accompany all goods, and even ships that passed through British ports would be confiscated. The second decree (October 18, 1810) authorized the French state to seize and sell any unlicensed colonial goods and to publicly destroy British-made products. It introduced severe penalties—such as branding and up to 10 years of penal servitude—for smugglers. A special tribunal (*cours douanieres*) was set up to try these cases. Revenues soared with the enforcement of this decree, Napoléon's final attempt to achieve his continental blockade.

See also: BAYONNE DECREE; MILAN DECREES; RAMBOUILLET DECREE.

Further reading: James H. Robinson, ed., *The Napoleonic Period* (Philadelphia: Department of History of the University of Pennsylvania, 1895).

Food, Drug, and Cosmetic Act, U.S.

Federal legislation enacted on June 24, 1938, under the congressional power to regulate interstate commerce, that prohibited the sale of foods dangerous to health as well as foods, drugs, and cosmetics packaged in unsanitary or contaminated containers. It required manufacturers of foods, drugs, and cosmetics to list their ingredients on the labels. It prohibited the sale of "poisonous" or "deleterious" substances and broadened the definitions of "adulteration" and "misbranding." The Food and Drug Administration was authorized to enforce the act, and inspection stations were established in several large cities. The act superseded the U.S. PURE FOOD AND DRUG ACT OF 1906.

Further reading: Charles Wesley Dunn, *Federal Food, Drug, and Cosmetic Act: A Statement of Its Legislative Record* (New York: G. E. Stechert & Co., 1938); *Food, Drug and Cosmetic Act* (Washington, D.C.: U.S. Government Printing Office, 1938).

Foote's Resolution

U.S. Senate resolution concerning the sale of public lands, introduced by Senator Samuel A. Foote of Connecticut, on December 29, 1829. Foote's proposal—that Congress consider restrictions on the sale of public lands to new settlers—touched off a historic debate on broader issues of sectionalism and states' rights between Senator Daniel Webster, representing Northern interests, and Senator Robert Y. Hayne, speaking for the South (see WEBSTER'S FIRST AND SECOND REPLIES TO HAYNE). New England manufacturers favored restrictions to protect their supply of cheap labor, while Southerners and Westerners opposed restrictions and wished to encourage Western migration.

Further reading: Herman Belz, ed., *The Webster-Hayne Debate on the Nature of the Union: Selected Documents* (Indianapolis, Ind.: Liberty Fund, 2000); Glenn Clark, ed., *The World's Greatest Debate* (St. Paul, Minn.: Macalester Park Pub. Co., 1940).

Foraker Act

Law sponsored by U.S. Senator Joseph B. Foraker of Ohio and enacted on April 12, 1900, to provide for a civil government in Puerto Rico. After two years of military government following the cession of Puerto Rico to the United States by the 1898 Treaty of PARIS, which ended the Spanish-American War (1898), the act established a presidential-type government in which the governor, his cabinet, and the judges of the supreme court were all to be appointed by the U.S. president. The will of the people of Puerto Rico was represented only in a 35-member House of Delegates. While the act benefited the U.S. economically, since the island was incorporated within the U.S. tariff system, and the free movement of goods between Puerto Rico and the mainland was established, the Foraker Act pleased almost no one in

Puerto Rico, since the island now possessed less autonomy than it had under monarchical Spain.

Further reading: María Dolores Luque de Sánchez, *La ocupación norteamericana y la ley Foraker* (Río Piedras, Puerto Rico: Editorial Universitaria, Univerdiad de Puerto Rico, 1977); Carmen I. Raffucci de García, *El gobierno civil y la ley Foraker: antecedentes históricos* (Río Piedras, Puerto Rico: Editorial Universitaria, Univerdiad de Puerto Rico, 1981).

Force Act of 1833, U.S.   Federal legislation passed by Congress on March 2, 1833, at the request of U.S. president Andrew Jackson, granting the federal government the authority to enforce its revenue laws by the use of military action if necessary. The act was passed after SOUTH CAROLINA'S ORDINANCE OF NULLIFICATION attempted to declare null and void the U.S. TARIFF ACT OF 1828 and TARIFF ACT OF 1832. At the same time that Congress passed the Force Act, however, it also approved the compromise TARIFF ACT OF 1833, which reduced the earlier objectionable levies. While accepting the compromise tariff, South Carolina continued to assert its sovereignty by declaring, on March 18, 1833, the Force Act to be null and void.

Further reading: Richard E. Ellis, *The Union at Risk: Jacksonian Democracy, States' Rights, and the Nullification Crisis* (New York: Oxford University Press, 1987, rep., 1990); Leonard W. Levy and Louis Fisher, eds., *Encyclopedia of the American Presidency*, 2 vols. (New York: Simon & Schuster, 1994).

Force Acts, U.S. (Ku Klux Klan Acts)   Series of three laws passed in 1870–71, by the radical Republicans who controlled Congress, to protect the constitutional rights granted to blacks by the FOURTEENTH AMENDMENT and FIFTEENTH AMENDMENT. The first act imposed severe penalties on anyone preventing qualified citizens (blacks) from voting. The second act provided for federally appointed election supervisors. The third act, aimed particularly at the Ku Klux Klan and other terrorist organizations, empowered the president to suspend the writ of habeas corpus in lawless areas. These laws resulted in martial law in nine South Carolina counties, thousands of indictments, and hundreds of convictions. The Supreme Court later declared various sections of the acts unconstitutional, and most of their provisions were repealed in 1894.

Further reading: Leonard W. Levy and Louis Fisher, eds., *Encyclopedia of the American Presidency*, 2 vols. (New York: Simon & Schuster, 1994); Allen W. Trelease, *White Terror: The Ku Klux Klan Conspiracy and Southern Reconstruction* (New York: Harper & Row, 1971); Lou Falkner Williams, *The Great South Carolina Ku Klux Klan Trials: 1871–1872* (Athens: University of Georgia Press, 1996).

Force Bill of 1890, U.S.   See LODGE BILL.

Fordney-McCumber Act (U.S. Tariff Act of 1922)   Federal U.S. legislation enacted on September 21, 1922, that established high tariff rates to protect farmers and infant industries. It set high duties on grains, meats, sugar, wool, and other farm products, and raised rates on textiles, dyes, ferroalloys, china, and other manufactured goods. Sponsored by Representative Joseph W. Fordney of Indiana and Senator Porter J. McCumber of North Dakota, the act also made the tariff flexible, giving the U.S. president the power to raise or lower rates by 50 percent in order to equalize American and foreign costs of production. The act was succeeded by the SMOOT-HAWLEY TARIFF ACT.

Further reading: Thomas Carson, ed., *Gale Encyclopedia of U.S. Economic History* (Farmington Hills, Mich.: 1999); C. A. Loeffler, comp., *Fordney-McCumber Tariff Bill of 1922: Yea-and-Nay Votes in the United States Senate Sixty-seventh Congress, Second Session, on the Bill and All Amendments Thereto, H.R. 7456 to Provide Revenue, to Regulate Commerce with Foreign Countries, to Encourage the Industries of the United States, and for Other Purposes* (Washington, D.C.: U.S. Government Printing Office, 1922).

Forest, Assize of   See WOODSTOCK, ASSIZE OF.

Forest Reserve Act   U.S. legislation passed on March 3, 1891, codifying many public land laws. The act authorized the U.S. president to reserve certain public lands from the public domain and reversed the previous policy of transferring public lands to private ownership. Though the act failed to specify the purpose of these reserves and to provide for their administration (the Forest Management Act of 1897 did both), President Benjamin Harrison used the authority to reserve 22 million acres, beginning the national forest system. The act was amended in 1907 to forbid the creation or enlargement of national forests in six Western states without congressional action.

Further reading: Charles F. Wilkinson, *Land and Resource Planning in the National Forests* (Washington, D.C.: Island Press, 1987).

"Fort Hill Letter," Calhoun's   Public letter written by U.S. vice president John C. Calhoun and addressed to South Carolina governor James Hamilton, Jr., dated August 28, 1832; it summarized the doctrine that individual states had the constitutional power to nullify, or veto, federal laws. Restating positions established in Calhoun's EXPOSITION AND PROTEST and "ADDRESS TO THE PEOPLE OF SOUTH CAROLINA," the vice president argued that nullification was constitutional, efficient, and peaceable. Since such action was legal, in Calhoun's view, it would not dissolve the ties that bound a state to the union and should not subject the state to forcible intervention.

Further reading: Irving H. Bartlett, *John C. Calhoun: A Biography* (New York: W. W. Norton, 1993); Merrill D. Peterson, *The Great Triumvirate: Webster, Clay, and Calhoun* (New York: Oxford University Press, 1987).

Fort Jackson, Treaty of   Treaty signed on August 9, 1814, ending the Creek War of 1813–14 and ceding to the U.S. government 23 million acres in Mississippi Territory, two-thirds of the lands belonging to the Creek Indians. The war, initiated by the Upper Creeks or "Red Sticks," was fought largely in Tennessee. It was brought to a close after a decisive white victory, led by Major General Andrew Jackson and the Tennessee militia, at Horseshoe Bend. The treaty, signed by only some of the Creeks, forced the tribe to give up rich cotton lands in southern Georgia and central and southern Alabama. It marked the end of Indian resistance in this area and opened it to white settlement after the War of 1812.

Further reading: Charles L. Phillips and Alan Axelrod, eds., *Encyclopedia of Historical Treaties and Alliances*, 2 vols. (New York: Facts On File, 2001).

Fort Laramie, Treaty of (1851)   Agreement between the United States government and the Sioux, Shoshone, Cheyenne, and Arapaho Indians; assigned reservations to each tribe of the northern Great Plains area, granted an annuity of $50,000, and established certain roads and forts within the Indian territory. This effort to ensure peace as whites expanded west of the Mississippi River across Indian lands later failed, and Sioux uprisings began in 1862, continuing until the resolution of the second Treaty of FORT LARAMIE (1868).

Further reading: Ralph Hoyt Case, *Golconda to the Whites, Golgotha to the Sioux!: The Treaty of Fort Laramie, September, 1851* (Cheyenne Agency, S.D.: Cheyenne River Sioux Tribal Council, 1951); Remi A. Nadeau, *Fort Laramie and the Sioux*, rev. ed. (Santa Barbara, Calif.: Crest Publishers, 1997).

Fort Laramie, Treaty of (1868)   Agreement whereby the United States government agreed to halt its efforts to build a road to Bozeman, Montana, across Sioux hunting grounds in the Big Horn Mountains and guaranteed the Sioux exclusive possession of the land in South Dakota west of the Missouri River. The treaty ended a series of uprisings that had begun after the first Treaty of FORT LARAMIE (1851). After the discovery of gold in the Black Hills in the 1870s, the second treaty was largely ignored as thousands of prospectors invaded the Sioux Reservation.

Further reading: Remi A. Nadeau, *Fort Laramie and the Sioux*, rev. ed. (Santa Barbara, Calif.: Crest Publishers, 1997).

Fort Stanwix, Treaty of (1768)   Pact negotiated and concluded by Sir William Johnson, superintendent of Indian affairs, with the Iroquois Confederacy at Fort Stanwix (Rome, New York) on November 5, 1768. It overturned the Proclamation Line of 1763, by which the British had forbade white settlement west of the Appalachian Mountains in order to ward off Indian wars. In exchange for a payment of $10,000, the Indians relinquished their claims to lands in present-day western Pennsylvania, West Virginia, and Kentucky. The ef-

fect of the treaty was to spur whites to settle farther west and encroach on Indian hunting grounds.

Further reading: John F. Luzader, *The Construction and Military History of Fort Stanwix* (Washington, D.C.: U.S. Office of Archeology and Historic Preservation, Division of History, 1969).

Fort Stanwix, Treaty of (1784)   First Indian treaty made by the U.S. government, signed at Fort Stanwix (Rome, New York) on October 22, 1784. It reestablished peace with the Iroquois Indians, many of whom had fought on the British side during the American Revolution (1775–83). Weakened by the war, with their numbers further diminished, the Iroquois agreed reluctantly to cede to the U.S. government extensive territories in western New York, northwestern Pennsylvania, and Ohio. The treaty was rejected by the Ohio tribes, however.

Further reading: John F. Luzader, *The Construction and Military History of Fort Stanwix* (Washington, D.C.: U.S. Office of Archeology and Historic Preservation, Division of History, 1969); Charles L. Phillips and Alan Axelrod, eds., *Encyclopedia of Historical Treaties and Alliances*, 2 vols. (New York: Facts On File, 2001).

Forty-two Articles   Archbishop of Canterbury Thomas Cranmer's original compilation of the doctrines of the Anglican Church, first issued on June 19, 1553, with a mandate from King Edward VI of England requiring all clergymen, schoolmasters, and university graduates to subscribe to them. Drafted mainly by Cranmer on the doctrinal model of the Thirteen Articles of 1538, they were intended to constitute a definition of the Anglican faith. However, since they had not been endorsed by the 1552 Synod of London or by a church convocation, they had no official validity. Mary I's accession to the throne in late 1553 and the return of Roman Catholicism under her rule, temporarily ended any hopes of their being revived. Ten years later, during Queen Elizabeth I's reign, they formed the basis of the THIRTY-NINE ARTICLES, which were adopted by the Anglican Church or Church of England.

Further reading: Gerald L. Bray, *Documents of the English Reformation* (Minneapolis: Fortress Press, 1994).

Four Articles, Bossuet's (Declaration of the French Clergy, Déclaration du Clergé, Déclaration des Quatre Articles, Gallican Articles)   French prelate Jacques-Bénigne Bossuet's compilation of the rights and privileges claimed by the French clergy, fully approved by the Paris Assembly on March 19, 1682. Bossuet, a Roman Catholic preacher and bishop of Meaux, derived his articles from the Sorbonne's controversial Six Articles of 1663. The first article affirmed the French monarch's supremacy in temporal or civil matters, denying the pope's rights to deposition or dispensation. The second article confirmed the decrees of the Council of Constance (1414–18), asserting the authority of the general councils over the pope. The third declared as inviolate the liberties of the French Church. Finally, the pope's judgment in matters of faith was not irrevocable unless it was approved by the church. On March 22, 1682, King Louis XIV published an edict ordering registration of the Four Articles and requiring every French theology student to subscribe to them. Pope Innocent XI promptly decreed (April 2) the articles as invalid, condemning them as a threat to the integrity of the faith.

Further reading: Jacques-Bénigne Bossuet, *Selections: A Prose Anthology* (London: G. G. Harrap, 1962).

Four Bills of 1647 Bills presented to King Charles I on December 24, 1647, by the English Parliament, demanding (1) immediate recall of all declarations and proclamations against Parliament; (2) a 20-year control over the army; (3) the deposition of peers created since the Great Seal was sent to Charles; and (4) adjournment of both houses (Commons and Lords) at will. Meanwhile, on December 26, the king had already signed a secret treaty with the Scots and, two days later, he rejected these four bills.

Further reading: Pauline Gregg, *King Charles I* (London: Phoenix Press, 2000); Derek Wilson, *The King and the Gentleman: Charles Stuart and Oliver Cromwell, 1599–1649* (London: Pimlico, 2000).

"Four Freedoms" Speech, Roosevelt's Address delivered by U.S. president Franklin D. Roosevelt on January 6, 1941, in his annual message to Congress. Roosevelt called for a world founded on "four essential human freedoms": freedom of speech and expression, freedom of worship, freedom from want, and freedom from fear. Urging citizens to relinquish the false security of isolationism, he described a national policy committed to all-inclusive national defense, full support of other nations trying to preserve democracy, and refusal to buy peace at the cost of other people's freedom. He urged the United States to serve as an arsenal—providing ships, planes, tanks, and guns—for those countries already struggling against international aggression during World War II (1939–45).

Further reading: *History Speaks: Franklin D. Roosevelt's Four Freedoms Speech* (Carthage, Ill.: Teaching & Learning Co., 2000); Leonard W. Levy and Louis Fisher, eds., *Encyclopedia of the American Presidency,* 2 vols. (New York: Simon & Schuster, 1994).

Four-Power Agreement of 1972 Comprehensive agreement on the status of Berlin, signed on June 3, 1972, by the ambassadors of Britain, France, and the United States to the Federal Republic of Germany (FRG), and by the Soviet ambassador to the German Democratic Republic (GDR). The four countries, which controlled Berlin, agreed in the preliminary section (signed on September 3, 1971) to help ease the tension in the area, to settle disputes by peaceful means, and

to respect their individual and common rights and obligations. Transit traffic between West Berlin and the FRG (West Germany) would be simplified and expedited, and communications and travel between the city and neighboring GDR (East Germany) improved. Berlin's legal status, however, remained unchanged; the FRG was represented in West Berlin by a permanent liaison agency and the Soviet Union by a consulate-general, both answerable to the three powers. Finally, Britain, France, and the United States reiterated their continued and absolute responsibility for West Berlin.

Further reading: Thomas F. Healy, *1971 Four-Power Berlin Agreement, Increased or Decreased Tensions in the 1970s* (Carlisle Barracks, Penn.: U.S. Army War College, 1972).

Four Power Pacific Treaty (Treaty of Washington) First of three treaties (see FIVE POWER NAVAL TREATY; NINE POWER PACTS) signed on December 13, 1921, during the Washington Conference of 1921–22. Its signatories—Japan, Great Britain, France, and the United States—agreed to assure or guarantee each other's island territories in the Pacific Ocean and to confer with the other party in the event of any disputes. This treaty replaced the ANGLO-JAPANESE TREATY OF 1902, thereby achieving an unstated diplomatic goal for the United States.

Further reading: Charles L. Phillips and Alan Axelrod, eds., *Encyclopedia of Historical Treaties and Alliances,* 2 vols. (New York: Facts On File, 2001).

Four Power Pact of 1933 Pact endorsed on July 15, 1933, under the influence of Italian dictator Benito Mussolini by representatives of Italy, Germany, France, and Great Britain, calling for the revision of certain parts of the general peace settlement concluded at the close of World War I (see VERSAILLES, TREATY OF [1919]). In the draft treaty Mussolini had proposed that the major European powers, rather than all the members of the League of Nations, consider the possible revision of the peace settlements concluded at the Paris Peace Conference of 1919, and in particular of those points involving Germany's frontiers, restrictions on Germany's armed forces, and Germany's colonial possessions. The final treaty, however, excluded all provisions relating to Germany and merely proposed a revision of treaties through international arbitration. The agreement had no effect.

Further reading: Konrad Hugo Jarausch, *The Four Power Pact, 1933* (Madison: State Historical Society of Wisconsin for Dept. of History, University of Wisconsin, 1965); Charles L. Phillips and Alan Axelrod, eds., *Encyclopedia of Historical Treaties and Alliances,* 2 vols. (New York: Facts On File, 2001).

Fourteen Points Speech, Wilson's Address delivered to the U.S. Congress on January 8, 1918, by President Woodrow Wilson, setting forth his program for a just and enduring world peace. These points became the basis for negotiating an end to World War I (1914–18). Wilson called for "open covenants of peace, openly arrived at"; absolute freedom of the seas, in peace and war; equality of trade conditions among nations; reductions of national armaments; impartial adjustment of colonial claims; self-determination for Russia and the peoples of Austria-Hungary; restoration or adjustments of Belgian, French, Italian, Romanian, Serbian, and Montenegrin territories; autonomy for nationalities under Turkish rule but sovereignty for Turkey; opening of the Dardanelles to all nations; establishment of an independent Poland; and formation of an association of nations to guarantee "political independence and territorial integrity to great and small states alike."

Further reading: Leonard W. Levy and Louis Fisher, eds., *Encyclopedia of the American Presidency,* 2 vols. (New York: Simon & Schuster, 1994); Gaddis Smith, *Woodrow Wilson's Fourteen Points After Seventy-Five Years* (New York: Carnegie Council, 1993).

Fourteenth Amendment, U.S.

Amendment to the U.S. CONSTITUTION, adopted in 1868, that granted citizenship to former slaves, required the states to extend due process of law and equal protection of the laws to all persons, and provided for apportionment of members of the U.S. House of Representatives on the basis of the total population (black and white) within a state. The amendment thus overcame the decision of *DRED SCOTT* v. *SANDFORD* and abrogated the constitutional clause establishing that five slaves counted as three whites in apportioning representatives. The amendment has been used to test the constitutionality of state laws and to force the states to extend the same protections that the federal government provides through the U.S. Bill of Rights. In recent years the Supreme Court has used it to invalidate racial segregation and discrimination against women.

Further reading: Raoul Berger, *The Fourteenth Amendment and the Bill of Rights* (Norman: University of Oklahoma Press, 1989); Horace Edgar Flack, *The Adoption of the Fourteenth Amendment* (Gloucester, Mass.: Peter Smith, 1965); Joseph B. James, *The Framing of the Fourteenth Amendment* (Urbana: University of Illinois Press, 1956); William E. Nelson, *The Fourteenth Amendment: From Political Principle to Judicial Doctrine* (Cambridge, Mass.: Harvard University Press, 1988).

Fourth Amendment, U.S.

Amendment to the U.S. CONSTITUTION, adopted in 1791, that protects the people—including their persons, houses, papers, and effects—from unreasonable searches and seizures. Searches are permitted only after the issuance of a specific warrant, describing the place to be searched and the persons or things to be seized; the warrants must be based upon "probable cause," or evidence of a crime or a conspiracy to commit a crime. The Fourth Amendment has been applied to issues of wiretapping and other electronic eavesdropping.

Further reading: Paula Angle Franklin, *The Fourth Amendment* (Englewood Cliffs, N.J.: Silver Burdett Press, 1991); William W. Greenhalgh, *The Fourth Amendment Handbook: A Chronological Survey of Supreme Court Decisions* (Chicago: Criminal Justice Section, American Bar Association, 1995); J. David Hirschel, *Fourth Amendment Rights* (Lexington, Mass.: Lexington Books, 1979); Wayne R. LaFave, *Search and Seizure: A Treatise on the Fourth Amendment,* 4 vols. (St. Paul, Minn.: West Publishing, 1996).

Frame of Government, Penn's (First Frame of Government of Pennsylvania)

Liberal governmental structure drawn up and issued (April 25, 1682) by William Penn, an English Quaker and founder of the proprietary colony of Pennsylvania. It provided for a governor (the proprietor or his deputy), a council (where the governor served as presiding officer and had three votes), and an assembly. The council had 72 members, of whom a third were to be elected by the colony's freemen each year, while the assembly had 200 to 500 members, elected annually by the freemen. The governor and council held broad governing powers, including the initiation of legislation, and the assembly's vote was to ratify or reject legislation. Penn's plan also provided for friendly relations with the Indians and religious freedom.

See also: CHARTER OF LIBERTIES; SHAKAMAXON, TREATY OF.

Further reading: William Penn, *A Collection of the Works of William Penn, to Which Is Prefixed a Journal of His Life with Many Original Letters and Papers Not Before Published* (New York: AMS Press, 1974).

Franck Report

Report to the U.S. secretary of war issued on June 11, 1945, by a panel of seven distinguished scientists, led by German-born American physicist and Nobel laureate James Franck, urging the United States to refrain from using atomic weapons against Japan. Nuclear power, they wrote, "is fraught with infinitely greater dangers than were all the inventions of the past." Warning that U.S. use of a new weapon of indiscriminate destruction against civilians would cost the United States support of other nations and would precipitate a nuclear arms race, the report urged a demonstration of the atomic bomb, before representatives of the United Nations, on a desert or barren island, to pressure Japan into surrendering during World War II (1939–45). The report also proposed an international agreement to prevent nuclear warfare.

See also: TRUMAN'S ANNOUNCEMENT OF THE ATOMIC BOMBING OF HIROSHIMA.

Further reading: Barton J. Bernstein, ed., *The Atomic Bomb: The Critical Issues* (Boston: Little, Brown, 1976); Gene Dannen, *Franck Report, June 11, 1945,* Gene Dannen, Home Page, available online at http://www.dannen.com/decision/franck.html.

Franco-American Convention of 1800 (Treaty of Mortefontaine)

Treaty signed on September 30, 1800, between the United States and France ending an undeclared naval war over French raids on U.S. shipping. The conflict began in 1798, following publication of the "XYZ" REPORT. In 1800 President John Adams sent a delegation to Paris to negotiate with Napoléon. The Convention of 1800 guaranteed neutral rights at sea for the United States and ended the Franco-American Alliance, a mutual assistance pact against Britain established in 1778. The United States relinquished $20 million in spoliation claims against France for the loss of ships and cargoes.

Further reading: Thomas A. Bailey, *A Diplomatic History of the American People,* 10th ed. (Englewood Cliffs, N.J.: Prentice-Hall, 1980); Carnegie Endowment for International Peace, *Documents Relating to the Controversy over Neutral Rights Between the United States and France, 1797–1800* (Buffalo, N.Y.: William S. Hein & Co., 1999).

Franco-American Treaties of 1778   See PARIS, TREATIES OF (1778).

Franco-German Agreement of 1911

Agreement concluded on November 4, 1911, by France and Germany, bringing an end to the so-called second Moroccan crisis (when, in mid-1911, military encounters between these two nations in the region seemed headed for war). Through the agreement France obtained Germany's approval of her freedom of action in the northern African colony of Morocco, even if that were to entail France's erection of a protectorate there; in exchange, Germany obtained from France part of the French Congo, which, connected with additional strips of territory also ceded by France, provided the new German territory with rivers leading to the Atlantic Ocean. The crisis had arisen over Germany's sudden and startling demands for territorial concessions by France in northern Africa, which was due, she claimed, to France's failure to live up to her obligations specified in the ALGECIRAS ACT of 1909.

Further reading: Great Britain Foreign Office, Historical Section, *Cameroon* (London: H.M. Stationery Office, 1920); David G. Herrmann, *The Arming of Europe and the Making of the First World War* (Princeton, N.J.: Princeton University Press, 1996).

Franco-German Agreements of 1956

Three treaties signed in Luxembourg on October 27, 1956, by Foreign Minister Christian Pineau of France and Foreign Minister Heinrich von Brentano of West Germany, bringing an end to the two countries' dispute over possession of the Saar Basin, and establishing agreement between them on certain economic issues. Specifically, the agreements provided for France's return of the Saar—whose inhabitants had throughout the century fluctuated between desiring union with France and Germany—to West Germany by January 1, 1957; and for a gradual integration of the economies of the Saar and West Germany, which would also accommodate French economic

interests. In return, France gained West German support for the canalization of the Moselle River, which was intended to make the transport of goods between the Ruhr Valley and the Lorraine coal and steel industries more economical, as well as the right to use water from the Rhine River at designated areas in certain industrial endeavors. The settlement, in ending a bitter dispute, opened the way for future friendship and cooperation between France and West Germany.

Further reading: *Treaty Between the Federal Republic of Germany and the French Republic for the Settlement of the Saar Question* (Luxembourg: n.p., 1956).

Franco-German Pact of 1938

Pact signed in Paris on December 6, 1938, by Foreign Minister Georges Bonnet of France and Foreign Minister Joachim von Ribbentrop of Germany, proclaiming the two countries' desire to maintain peace. In the document the two parties declared their conviction that the maintenance of peace in Europe was at least partially dependent upon peace between their countries, and, this being so, that it was their intention to work together to foster good relations between them; they declared their recognition of the existing Franco-German border as definitive, pledged to consult with one another on matters of common interest, and pledged to settle any dispute through pacific means. The issue of the pact came at a time when the world was still recovering from Germany's annexation of Austria earlier that year and, not long before, Germany's denunciation of the Locarno Treaties (see LOCARNO, PACT OF) and withdrawal from the League of Nations.

See also: COMPIÈGNE ARMISTICE.

Further reading: John Weitz, *Hitler's Diplomat: The Life and Times of Joachim von Ribbentrop* (New York: Ticknor & Fields, 1992).

Franco-German Treaty of 1963 (Treaty on Franco-German Cooperation)

Treaty and joint declaration signed in Paris on January 22, 1963, by President Charles de Gaulle of France and Chancellor Konrad Adenauer of the Federal Republic of Germany (West Germany), providing for economic, political, military, and scientific cooperation between the two nations. The treaty provided that the two countries' heads of state and foreign ministers would meet at regular intervals to consult with one another on all decisions to be made with regard to East-West relations, the NORTH ATLANTIC TREATY Organization (NATO), the European Economic Community (EEC or the Common Market), European political cooperation, information, and their respective programs in developing countries; that the two countries' defense ministers and authorities in the armed forces would meet regularly to strive to resolve differences in their respective strategical and tactical plans; and that the two countries' ministers of education and heads of the ministry of youth and family would meet in order to promote the teaching of each other's language in their own country, joint scientific research, and the formulation of equivalent standards in education. This joint declaration confirmed the two countries' reconciliation and recognized it as a necessary step toward the goal of a united Europe. The treaty caused some anxiety among other Western European nations and the United States, due to its failure to stress the importance of NATO.

Further reading: David G. Haglund, *Alliance Within the Alliance?: Franco-German Military Cooperation and the European Pillar of Defense* (Boulder, Colo.: Westview Press, 1991); Mairi Maclean and Jean-Marc Trouille, eds., *France, Germany, and Britain: Partners in a Changing World* (New York: Palgrave, 2001).

Franco-Italian Entente of 1902

Agreement concluded by France and Italy in November 1902, providing for a defensive alliance between the two countries, as well as for mutual recognition of their respective interests in northern Africa. Through the treaty, it was agreed that each country would maintain neutrality with respect to the other in the event of an attack on either country by a third party. In addition, France declared her support for Italian interest in Libya, and Italy pledged to support France's endeavors in Morocco. The Franco-Italian entente's significance lay in its stark incompatibility with the 1882 TRIPLE ALLIANCE, through which Italy's alliance with Germany and Austria-Hungary was, in part, directed against France.

Further reading: John F. MacDonald, *Camille Barrere and the Conduct of Delcassian Diplomacy in Italy, 1898–1902* (Ann Arbor, Mich.: University Microfilms International, 1978).

Franco-Russian Agreement of 1891

Diplomatic and political entente between France and Russia, approved on August 27, 1891. The signatories of this vague document only "agreed to agree on measures" in case of a threat to peace. The French were committed to support Russia diplomatically, especially with regard to Constantinople, but the Russians were not pledged to any military action against Germany in support of France. The mutual agreement or entente was therefore a coup for the Russians, who wanted diplomatic support in their competition with England in the Near East, without being drawn into an anti-German military alliance with France.

Further reading: Frank M. Laney, *The Military Implementation of the Franco-Russian Alliance, 1890–1914* (Ann Arbor, Mich.: University Microfilms International, 1978); William L. Langer, *The Franco-Russian Alliance, 1890–1894* (New York: Octagon Books, 1967); Georges Michon, *The Franco-Russian Alliance, 1891–1917* (New York: H. Fertig, 1969).

Franco-Russian Alliance of 1892 (Dual Alliance of 1892)

Military convention agreed to in principle in August 1892, but not officially approved until January 1894. This alliance, unlike the FRANCO-RUSSIAN AGREEMENT OF 1891, was decidedly anti-German in nature, which was a victory for

France. The Russians promised to support the French with roughly a third of their army if the latter were attacked by the Germans. For her part, France agreed to mobilize (though not necessarily fight) if Austria-Hungary mobilized against Russia. The final draft of the treaty, formalized in 1894, was even more anti-German. It provided that if France were attacked by Germany, or by Italy with German support, Russia would attack Germany with all available forces. If Russia were attacked by Germany, or by Austria-Hungary with German assistance, France would turn all available forces against Germany. The alliance was intended as a counterweight to the TRIPLE ALLIANCE OF 1882, and was specifically designated to last as long as the Triple Alliance was in effect.

Further reading: William L. Langer, *The Franco-Russian Alliance, 1890–1894* (New York: Octagon Books, 1967); Georges Michon, *The Franco-Russian Alliance, 1891–1917* (New York: H. Fertig, 1969); Henry S. Robinson, *Great Britain and the Franco-Russian Alliance, 1894–1904* Lanham, Md.: University Press of America, 1987).

Franco-Russian Agreement of 1935

Treaty signed in Paris on May 2, 1935, by Foreign Minister Pierre Laval of France and the Soviet ambassador to France, Vladimir Potemkin; it provided for mutual assistance in the event of aggression toward either signatory power by a European state. Specifically, each party agreed to consult with the other and with the League of Nations in the event of aggression or danger of aggression on either party's territory, and to provide the other with immediate aid in the event of unprovoked aggression. The pact also upheld the validity of agreements concluded with other countries prior to its conclusion, limited France's obligation to assist Russia to Europe, and was to be valid for five years. The pact was a partial realization of France's interwar foreign policy, by which she had hoped to make alliances with countries to her east in order to maintain the status quo.

Further reading: J. Kenneth Brody, *The Avoidable War*, 2 vols. (New Brunswick, N.J.: Transaction Publishers, 1999).

Frankfurt, Treaty of

Peace treaty ending the Franco-Prussian War (1870–71), signed at Frankfurt (Germany) on May 10, 1871. The settlement, ratified by France's provisional National Assembly elected expressly to conduct peace negotiations, signaled the end of the Second French Empire. The treaty called for the victorious German army to occupy parts of France until a war indemnity of 5,000 million francs was paid. (The amount of the indemnity was directly proportional to that levied by Napoléon I on Prussia in 1807.) The province of Alsace, and part of Lorraine, was also ceded to Germany. The treaty did not limit France's armed forces, nor dictate her foreign policy, however. The indemnity was paid by September 16, 1873, at which time the German occupation ended.

Further reading: Charles L. Phillips and Alan Axelrod, eds., *Encyclopedia of Historical Treaties and Alliances,* 2 vols. (New York: Facts On File, 2001).

Frankfurt Constitution
Constitution completed by the diet of the German Confederation on March 27, 1849, in Frankfurt, by which the German statesmen outlined the principles upon which the federal state was to be based, as well as basic human rights to be guaranteed by the government. The constitution upheld centralist sentiments, proposing that control over foreign policy, the military, justice, and commerce would reside in the executive branch of the government; it supported the sovereignty of the individual German states by allowing each to have its own constitution, declared that every German had a right to citizenship and freedom of speech, press, and religion. Finally, the constitution confirmed that all Hapsburg lands, both German and non-German, would be included in the new German state. Support for the constitution and for the democratic movement in general was destroyed several months later, when Prussian king Frederick William IV rejected Germany's imperial seat to which he had been elected, saying that a king by divine right could not accept a crown from an elected assembly (diet).

See also: PILLERSDORF CONSTITUTION.

Further reading: Louis L. Snyder, ed., *Documents of German History* (New Brunswick, N.J.: Rutgers University Press, 1958).

Franklin-Bouillon Agreement
See ANKARA, TREATY OF.

Frazier-Lemke Farm Bankruptcy Act (Farm Mortgage Moratorium Act)
U.S. legislation enacted on June 28, 1934, to assist farmers threatened with foreclosures on their mortgages by enabling them to get credit extensions. Sponsored by Senator Lynn Frazier and Representative William Lemke, the act allowed bankrupt farmers to repurchase their properties at a lower appraised value, with an interest rate of 1 percent paid over a five-year period. Where creditors refused a settlement, the act allowed farmers to retain possession of the properties, at reasonable rents, by suspending bankruptcy proceedings for five years in certain cases. The Supreme Court, in *Louisville Joint Stock Land Bank* v. *Radford* (May 27, 1935), declared the act unconstitutional, but similar legislation was enacted later that year.

Further reading: Irving Henderson Rand, *The Farmer-Debtor* (Portland, Ore.: Stevens-Ness Law Publishing, 1938); William O. Skeels, *Frazier-Lemke Farm Debt Moratorium Act: A Ready Guide* (Oklahoma City, Okla.: Leader Press, 1937).

Frederick the Great's Code
See CODE FRÉDÉRIC.

Fredrikshamm, Treaty of
Treaty of peace concluded at Fredrikshamm (Hamina, Finland) on September 17, 1809, between Sweden and Russia following the latter's conquest of Finland. Through the treaty Sweden recognized Russian annexation of Finland and the Åland Islands; the Russo-Swedish border was set along the Tornio and Muonio Rivers; and Sweden agreed to join Napoléon Bonaparte's Continental System, the members of which were bound not to engage in trade with Great Britain. This latter provision reflected French influence in Russia, which was allied to France through the Treaties of TILSIT and ERFURT. The provision also had the important effect of stimulating trade between Sweden and Russia, which had been interrupted by their recent war.

See also: PARIS, TREATY OF (1810); ST. PETERSBURG, TREATY OF (1812).

Further reading: Erik Hammström, *Freden i Fredrikshamn* (Uppsala, Sweden: Wretmans tryckeri, 1902).

Free Birth Law, Brazilian
See RIO BRANCO LAW.

Freedmen's Bureau Bill
Legislation enacted by the U.S. Congress on March 3, 1865, to establish a "bureau of refugees, freedmen and abandoned lands" to aid some 4 million destitute, newly freed slaves. In 1866 Congress, overriding the veto of President Andrew Johnson, who thought the bureau was unconstitutional and unnecessary, extended its life and scope. Organized under the War Department, the bureau provided relief for the needy—both black and white—assigned homesteads on public lands, supervised labor contracts to protect illiterate former slaves, established hospitals and schools, and protected civil rights for freedmen. By the time the bureau ceased operations in 1872, most of its duties had been abolished or adopted by other agencies.

Further reading: Eric Foner, *Reconstruction: America's Unfinished Revolution, 1863–1877* (New York: HarperCollins, 1988); Leonard W. Levy and Louis Fisher, eds., *Encyclopedia of the American Presidency,* 2 vols. (New York: Simon & Schuster, 1994); Donald G. Nieman, *To Set the Law in Motion: The Freedman's Bureau and the Legal Rights of Blacks, 1865–1868* (Millwood, N.Y.: KTO Press, 1979).

Freedom Charter
Economic credo drawn up in 1955 by black leaders of the African National Congress (ANC), calling for redistribution of South Africa's wealth and nationalization of the banks and major industries (chiefly controlled by whites). Considered socialist by many, the charter was firmly supported by black lawyers Nelson Mandela and Oliver Tambo, who were working to end South Africa's so-called Pass Laws (requirements that blacks carry passes in white neighborhoods) and the country's apartheid system (segregation and discrimination against nonwhites). The ANC, along with the blacks-only Pan-Africanist Congress (PAC), was later banned by the white South African government following the Sharpeville Massacre (1960), in which police fatally shot 69 unarmed blacks during a peaceful antiapartheid demonstration. The Freedom Charter endured to be buttressed by the so-called Harare Declaration, adopted by the

exiled, Zambia-based ANC in 1989, which called for an interim South African government to be set up to abolish all apartheid laws and to prepare for a general election on the basis of one-person, one-vote majority rule.

See also: DE KLERK'S "SEASON OF VIOLENCE IS OVER" SPEECH; GROUP AREAS ACT OF 1950, SOUTH AFRICAN.

Further reading: *The Freedom Charter of South Africa* (New York: United Nations Centre Against Apartheid, 1979); *Selected Writings on the Freedom Charter, 1955–1985* (London: African National Congress, 1985).

Freedom of Information Act (FOIA)

Federal U.S. legislation enacted on July 3, 1966, designed to make federal agencies disclose more information to the public. It stated that all records in the possession of the executive branch, except those specifically exempted by law, must be provided to any person who requests them. Exempted materials included national defense or foreign policy secrets, personnel or medical files, trade secrets or confidential financial information, certain law-enforcement investigatory files, and information concerning private gas or oil wells. The act was amended in 1974 to make information easier, quicker, and cheaper to obtain by requiring agencies to publish uniform fees for providing documents; empowering federal courts to order agencies to comply with the act; setting time limits for agency responses to requests; and requiring annual reports to Congress from agencies and the attorney general on freedom-of-information matters.

Further reading: Herbert N. Foerstel, *Freedom of Information and the Right to Know: The Origins and Applications of the Freedom of Information Act* (Westport, Conn.: Greenwood, 1999); Frank G. Houdek, *Freedom of Information Act: A Comprehensive Bibliography of Law Related Materials* (Austin: University of Texas at Austin, 1985); U.S. House of Representatives, Committee on Government Operations, *A Citizen's Guide on Using the Freedom of Information Act and the Privacy Act of 1974 to Request Government Records* (Washington, D.C.: U.S. Government Printing Office, 1991).

Freeport Doctrine

Position advocated by Stephen A. Douglas in his debate with his opponent for an Illinois senatorial seat, Abraham Lincoln, at Freeport, on August 27, 1858. When Lincoln asked Douglas how he could reconcile the doctrine of popular sovereignty with the Supreme Court's decision in *DRED SCOTT* V. *SANDFORD*, Douglas replied that the people of a territory could lawfully exclude slavery, without banning it, by failing to make laws enforcing and protecting slavery, which "cannot exist a day or an hour anywhere, unless it is supported by local police regulations." The doctrine outraged Southern Democrats and cost Douglas their support in the 1860 presidential election.

Further reading: Paul M. Angle, ed., *The Complete Lincoln-Douglas Debates of 1858* (Chicago: University of Chicago Press, 1991); Robert W. Johannsen, *Stephen A. Douglas* (Urbana: University of Illinois Press, 1997).

Free Trade Speech, Webster's

Speech delivered by Massachusetts congressman Daniel Webster before the U.S. House of Representatives on April 1–2, 1824, in opposition to the protectionist TARIFF ACT OF 1824 and in support of free trade. Representing a merchant constituency that feared losses from restrictions on foreign trade, Webster argued that the effects of the tariff on industries besides manufacturing—particularly shipping, commerce, and agriculture—must be weighed, and the existing protection for manufacturing be evaluated. By 1827, however, Webster changed his position and favored tariff protection for domestic industry.

Further reading: Edwin P. Whipple, ed., *The Great Speeches and Orations of Daniel Webster: With an Essay on Daniel Webster as a Master of English Style* (New York: The Classics of Liberty Library, Division of Gryphon Editions, 1994).

Frémont's Emancipation Order

Proclamation issued at Saint Louis on August 30, 1861, by Major General John Charles Frémont, an ardent abolitionist given command of the Department of the West, declaring martial law in Missouri and confiscating the property and emancipating the slaves of rebels. His actions, praised by abolitionists, embarrassed President Abraham Lincoln, who was trying to retain the loyalty of the border slave states early in the Civil War. Lincoln ordered Frémont to modify his proclamation to conform to the U.S. CONFISCATION ACT OF 1861 and later relieved Frémont of his command.

Further reading: Henry Steele Commager, ed., *Documents of American History*, 8th ed. (New York: Appleton-Century-Crofts, 1968); John C. Fremont, *Memoirs of My Life* (New York: Cooper Square Press, 2001); John P. C. Shanks, *Vindication of Major General John C. Fremont against the Attacks of the Slave Power and Its Allies* (Louisville, Ky.: Lost Cause Press, 1966).

French Additional Act

See ADDITIONAL ACT, FRENCH.

French Agreement on the Independence of Vietnam

Accord signed on March 6, 1946, by Vietnamese leaders Ho Chi Minh and Vu Huong Khanh with the French government official Jean Sainteny. By it, France recognized the Vietnam republic "as a free state" within the Indochinese Federation and the French Union and agreed to accept the Vietnamese decision (by referendum) with regard to the unification of Cochin China, Annam, and Tonkin (south, central, and north Vietnam respectively). The French and Vietnamese would end hostilities and open negotiations about economic, diplomatic, and cultural relations. Ho Chi Minh concluded another peace agreement at Fontainebleau, France, in September 1946, but when an accidental, bloody clash occurred between French and Vietnamese soldiers in north Vietnam two months later, the French Indochina War of 1946–54 broke out.

See also: GENEVA AGREEMENTS OF 1954, VIETNAMESE DEC-LARATION OF INDEPENDENCE.

Further reading: William J. Duiker, *Ho Chi Minh: A Life* (New York: Hyperion, 2002).

French-British Agreement on Oil in the Near and Middle East   See ANGLO-FRENCH AGREEMENT ON OIL IN THE NEAR AND MIDDLE EAST.

French-British Channel Agreement   See ANGLO-FRENCH CHANNEL AGREEMENT.

French Charter of 1830   Revision of the FRENCH CON-STITUTION OF 1814, undertaken by the French Chamber of Deputies after the forced abdication of King Charles X in July 1830 (see JULY ORDINANCES OF 1830). It was solemnly accepted by King Louis-Philippe on August 9, 1830. The preamble, declaring the constitution a gift of the monarch, was dropped, as was the article announcing Roman Catholicism as the state's official religion. Legislative initiative was to be shared by the king and parliament, guarantees were introduced to protect the freedom of the press, and restrictions were imposed on the royal prerogative of issuing ordinances (Article 14). The minimum age for election as deputy was reduced from 40 to 30 and for electors from 30 to 25. The white flag of the Restoration was replaced by the tricolor. The establishment of extraordinary tribunals was banned. The amended constitution was, in effect, a compromise between the demands of the republicans and the constitutional monarchists.

See also: FRENCH CONSTITUTION OF 1848; FRENCH CONSTITUTION OF 1852.

Further reading: Vincent W. Beach, *Charles X of France: His Life and Times* (Boulder, Colo.: Pruett Pub. Co., 1971); Paul H. Beik, *Louis Philippe and the July Monarchy* (Princeton, N.J.: Van Nostrand, 1965); James Mather, *The Constitutions of Great Britain, France, and the United States of America, Consisting of . . . [the French] Constitution of 1830, . . .* (Woodbridge, Conn.: Research Publications, 1980).

French Civil Code   See NAPOLEONIC CODE.

French Constitution of 1791 (Constitution Française)
Revolutionary France's first constitution, among the earliest written constitutions in Europe; completed on September 3, 1791, and approved by King Louis XVI on September 14, 1791. The document, prefaced by the DECLARATION OF THE RIGHTS OF MAN AND OF THE CITIZEN, was drafted over two years by the National Constituent Assembly. Divided into sections called "Titles," the constitution defined citizenship and its rights, outlined the duties of the various branches of gov-

ernment, and pointed to restrictions placed on certain government actions. Title III, the heart of the constitution, is subdivided into 171 articles under the following five chapters: (1) the national legislative assembly; (2) the royalty, regency, and ministers; (3) the exercise of legislative power; (4) the exercise of executive power; and (5) the judicial power. Legislative power was vested in the assembly, executive power in the king. During the uprising of August 10, 1792, this constitution was declared abandoned.

Further reading: John Bell, *French Constitutional Law* (New York: Oxford University Press, 1992).

French Constitution of 1793 (Acte Constitutionnel)
Constitution replacing the monarchism of the previous FRENCH CONSTITUTION OF 1791 with a republican system; ratified on June 24, 1793, by the National Convention and the primary assemblies but never implemented. Drafted by the Jacobins, the constitution granted voting rights to all Frenchmen and any adult foreigner who had worked in France for over a year. The primary assembly became the focal point of French politics. Its 200 to 600 voters directly elected delegates to the National Assembly, justice of the peace, and municipal officers. The National Assembly had sole power to issue decrees (war, welfare, general security), but financial legislation and civil and criminal laws required a referendum. A 24-member executive council, chosen from this assembly, could negotiate treaties, make important appointments, and share (with the legislature) command over the army. Inaugurated in Paris on August 10, it was set aside the next day when Maximilien Robespierre, leader of the Committee of Public Safety, declared that it was not for application. It was officially abandoned on October 10, 1793.

See also: LAW OF THE SUSPECTS; ROBESPIERRE'S SPEECH ON PROPERTY.

Further reading: John Bell, *French Constitutional Law* (New York: Oxford University Press, 1992).

French Constitution of 1795 (Constitution of the Year III)   Third and longest of the French revolutionary constitutions (others in 1791, 1793, 1800, 1802, and 1804); presented to the National Convention on August 22, 1795, and enacted on September 23 and enforced on October 26. It established a bicameral legislature (a 250-member council of elders/ancients and a council of 500) and was prefaced by a Declaration of Rights and Duties of Man. Executive authority was vested in a five-member directory appointed by the legislature and organized to prevent any individual from seizing power. The directory was in charge of maintaining and conducting foreign policies, including decisions of war and peace. The amendment procedure was too complicated and time-consuming and, therefore, hardly used. A supplemental decree stipulated that two-thirds of the original members of the legislature be drawn from the National Convention. Other sections dealt with the legal system (largely unchanged),

finances, public education, and the armed forces. Despite many defects, this constitution lasted for four years, until December 24, 1799.

Further reading: John Bell, *French Constitutional Law* (New York: Oxford University Press, 1992).

French Constitution of 1800 (Constitution of the Year VIII)

Fourth of France's revolutionary constitutions (others in 1791, 1793, and 1795) and the first of the Napoleonic era (others in 1802 and 1804); proclaimed on Christmas Day, 1799, and approved overwhelmingly on February 18, 1800. Drafted by a 25-member committee according to Napoléon's instructions, it did not include a bill of rights or any amendment procedures. It established a conservative senate (80 members appointed for life), which nominated members to a tribunate and legislative corps, as well as nominating the consuls and other senior officers, and enjoyed veto powers over any act. The tribunate, a 100-member body, could discuss, accept, but not amend proposals received from the consuls. The 300-member legislative corps had to vote without discussion on all government proposals. Membership in both assemblies was renewable annually by one-fifth. The constitution also introduced a council of state, amplified in a later decree. Executive power was shared by the three consuls, but unequally, since considerable legislative and executive power was vested in First Consul (chief of state) Napoléon Bonaparte.

Further reading: John Bell, *French Constitutional Law* (New York: Oxford University Press, 1992).

French Constitution of 1802 (Constitution of the Year X)

Two amendments (August 2 and 4, 1802) by the senate (*senatus consulta*) to the FRENCH CONSTITUTION OF 1800, following a plebiscite electing Napoléon consul for life. Recommended by the tribunate and the senate as a gesture of national recognition of Napoléon's achievements (see AMIENS, TREATY OF [1802]), the new constitution increased his salary and gave him a privy council, which assumed the legislative task of discussing and ratifying treaties and alliances. Electoral colleges replaced the famous List of Notables. They were elected by universal male suffrage from among the "most imposing" of the wealthy citizens and could nominate two persons for every vacancy in the tribunate or the legislature. The council of state's membership was increased to 50, the tribunate's reduced to 50. The senate (80 members, 40 being the first consul's appointees) could introduce constitutional amendments, dissolve the two legislative assemblies, and declare illegal the verdicts of the tribunals. Executive power remained with the three consuls.

See also: FRENCH CONSTITUTION OF 1804.

Further reading: John Bell, *French Constitutional Law* (New York: Oxford University Press, 1992).

French Constitution of 1804 (Constitution of the Year XII)

Amendment (*senatus consultum*) of May 18, 1804, transforming the life consulate (see FRENCH CONSTITUTION OF 1802) into a hereditary monarchy and proclaiming Napoléon as emperor of France. The title and the imperial power would be "hereditary in his family." In introducing these changes, "Equality, Liberty, and the rights of the people in their entirety" were ordered protected. The emperor was voted a salary as high as King Louis XVI's in 1790, and a new nobility was created, including 16 marshals of the empire (four of them honorary). The senate's authority was increased, allowing it to appoint two senatorial commissions to protect individual liberties and freedom of the press, respectively. The legislative corps was restored the right to debate in secret. The term of office of members of the tribunate was extended from five to 10 years, their salary from 15,000 to 25,000 livres. A high court of empire was established to investigate crimes against the state. The amendments were widely approved by the public.

See also: FRENCH CONSTITUTION OF 1814.

Further reading: John Bell, *French Constitutional Law* (New York: Oxford University Press, 1992).

French Constitution of 1814 (Louis XVIII's Charter of 1814, French Constitutional Charter of 1814, Chartre Constitutionnelle)

Louis XVIII's charter establishing the principles of his reign as king of France; proclaimed on May 2, 1814, and adopted on June 4, 1814. Beginning with his historical interpretation of events leading to his restoration, the charter then discussed the "Public Rights of the French," promising equality, freedom of person, religion, and speech, inviolability of property rights, abolition of conscription, and a ban on the investigation of pre-restoration opinions or votes. Executive authority rested in the king, commander of the armed forces and supreme head of state, including decisions of war and peace, high-level appointments, promulgation of regulations and ordinances, and the initiation of legislation. The bicameral legislature—the chamber of peers (the king's appointees) and the chamber of deputies (elected by limited franchise, mainly landlords and local notables)—discussed laws proposed by the king; it could recommend laws to him. Majority approval in both legislative houses was necessary for enactment. Despite many crises, the charter endured until 1848.

Further reading: John Bell, *French Constitutional Law* (New York: Oxford University Press, 1992).

French Constitution of 1848 (Constitution of the Second Republic, Constitution de la République)

Constitution of the Second Republic of France, approved overwhelmingly (639 to 30) by the National Constituent Assembly on November 4, 1848. It established a unicameral legislature, consisting of 750 members (including representatives from the colonies and Algeria) elected directly by secret ballot (from electoral district rolls) for a three-year term. Men over 21, with at least six months permanent residence in the country (increased to three years in 1850) and guaranteed civil rights, were entitled to vote. There was a ministerial tier, but its responsibilities were not clearly defined. Executive authority was vested in a president elected by all eligible voters for a four-year term. He could initiate proposals for laws and conclude and endorse treaties, in concordance with the assembly. The assembly subsequently decided not to submit the constitution to popular vote. It was replaced by the FRENCH CONSTITUTION OF 1852.

Further reading: John Bell, *French Constitutional Law* (New York: Oxford University Press, 1992).

French Constitution of 1852 (Constitution of the Second Empire)

New document established by an organic law on January 14, 1852, to replace the FRENCH CONSTITUTION OF 1848. It vastly increased the powers of the executive within a broad republican framework. A brief document (58 articles), its first article reaffirmed the principles of 1789 (see DECLARATION OF THE RIGHTS OF MAN AND OF THE CITIZEN). The chief executive (president) controlled all appointments and dismissals, treaty negotiations, and high-court decisions; he alone could propose and promulgate laws and suggest constitutional amendments through the senate or by plebiscite. The senate had no legislative authority and met in secret at the executive's command. The *corps législatif* (legislative corps), elected for a six-year term by universal manhood suffrage, could vote only for or against the laws proposed by the executive through the *conseil d'etat* (council of state), a ministerial panel appointed by the executive. Meanwhile, a series of decrees amplified and extended the original constitution, which was amended (November 7, 1852) to suit an imperial regime.

Further reading: John Bell, *French Constitutional Law* (New York: Oxford University Press, 1992).

French Constitution of 1875 (Constitution of the Third Republic)

Not a formal constitution, but a series of constitutional laws passed in 1875, establishing a French republic more in fact than in theory. Narrowly passed by the monarchist majority in the provisional National Assembly, the laws called for a strong executive with broadly defined powers, chosen for an initial term of seven years. There was also a 300-member senate, 75 of whom were chosen for life (discontinued 1884), with the remaining 225 chosen for 19-year terms by indirect suffrage. The senate shared the right to initiate legislation (except financial) with the chamber of deputies, which was elected by direct, universal manhood suffrage. The president had the authority to dissolve the chamber of deputies, upon consent of the senate. Versailles was established as the seat of government, rather than republican Paris.

See also: WALLON AMENDMENT.

Further reading: John Bell, *French Constitutional Law* (New York: Oxford University Press, 1992).

French Constitution of 1946 (Constitution of the Fourth Republic)

Constitution establishing the Fourth Republic of France, adopted by the French National Constituent Assembly on September 30, 1946, by 440 to 106 votes. It provided for a bicameral legislature, but the second chamber—the council of the republic—was given limited power. Legislative authority was concentrated in the National Assembly, each of its 626 members elected for a five-year term. Exercising sovereignty on behalf of the people, the assembly set its own rules and schedules. Its permanent commissions studied legislative proposals and directed the debate during sessions. The 315-member council of the republic was elected from local collectives on a six-year mandate. An economic council was created to advise the assembly. The president, elected by both chambers for a seven-year term, had no control over military and civil appointments. His acts had to be countersigned by a minister and by the president of the council (premier). The constitution's preamble reaffirmed the DECLARATION OF THE RIGHTS OF MAN AND OF THE CITIZEN.

Further reading: John Bell, *French Constitutional Law* (New York: Oxford University Press, 1992); R. Malezieux and J. Rousseau, *The Constitution of the Fourth Republic* (Calcutta, India: Das Gupta, 1950).

French Constitution of 1958 (Constitution of the Fifth Republic)

Constitution of the Fifth Republic of France promulgated on October 4, 1958, following its approval in a popular referendum on September 28, 1958. Consisting of a preamble, 92 articles, and several organic laws, the constitution evolved largely under the direction of General Charles de Gaulle (president of the Fifth Republic from 1959 to 1969). It retained the basic structure of the previous constitution (see FRENCH CONSTITUTION OF 1946) but altered the balance of power among the various branches of government. The bicameral legislature (or parliament) was authorized to declare war or extend a siege; the National Assembly could force a government's resignation. Parliamentary representatives could not vote by proxy or introduce financial measures. The premier (head of government, leader of the cabinet) and the president of the republic (head of state) shared executive power, but not equally. In actuality, the president exerted tremendous control over the government and its policies. He appointed the premier and other government members and presided over the council of ministers; he alone could invoke emergency powers.

Further reading: John Bell, *French Constitutional Law* (New York: Oxford University Press, 1992); William Pickles, *The French Constitution of October 4th, 1958* (London: Stevens, 1960).

French Decree Abolishing Feudalism

Legislation by the National Assembly of France abolishing the feudal regime; proposed on August 4, 1789, and enacted, with modifications, on August 11, 1789. "Both feudal and *consuel* rights and dues deriving from real or personal *mainmorte* and personal servitude" were "abolished without indemnity." Some feudal rights were declared redeemable, according to terms established by the National Assembly. Dues not suppressed by the decree would, however, continue to be collected. All civil, military, and religious offices were open to all citizens "without distinction of birth" (see DECLARATION OF THE RIGHTS OF MAN AND OF THE CITIZEN). In actuality, feudalism in its contractual form persisted, since the terms of redemption (set by subsequent decrees) were beyond the reach of most peasants, for whom the act was "a bitter deception." Redemption, a key issue in the negotiations between the aristocracy and the bourgeoisie, resulted in a compromise advantageous only to the feudal landlord and a few peasant proprietors. The peasants' defiance intensified in the French Revolution (1789–92).

Further reading: John Markoff, *The Abolition of Feudalism: Peasants, Lords, and Legislators in the French Revolution* (University Park: Pennsylvania State University Press, 1996).

French Decree on Feudal Rights

Decree approved on July 17, 1793, by the National Convention on Feudal Rights in France, abolishing without compensation "all former seigneurial rights, fixed or casual feudal rights" including those retained by a previous decree. Rents and charges regarded as "purely landrents and not feudal" were exempt from its provisions. Legal proceedings initiated for the recovery of these dues were ordered closed, and all relevant documents were required to be deposited with the municipality within three months. Failure to submit documents could result in a five-year prison term. Charged with the execution of this decree, the municipalities were then asked to "publicly burn" such documents. The French government was not directly involved in its enforcement.

See also: FRENCH DECREE ABOLISHING FEUDALISM.

Further reading: John Markoff, *The Abolition of Feudalism: Peasants, Lords, and Legislators in the French Revolution* (University Park: Pennsylvania State University Press, 1996).

French Decrees of 1848

Series of decrees issued between February 24 and 26, 1848, by a newly proclaimed provisional government in France. The first decree was a commitment guaranteeing "the livelihood of the worker by labor" and promised work for all citizens. Further, it affirmed the rights of workers to "form associations among themselves to enjoy the legitimate profit of their labor." It returned to the workers the sum of 1 million francs received from the civil list. Another decree ordered the return of all pawned goods valued less than 10 francs to their depositors, the expense being borne by the Ministry of Finance. A third decree designated the Tuileries (royal palace in Paris) as a hospital to treat industrial accidents. Finally, it declared the French Republic to be founded on "liberty, equality, and fraternity" and ordered the minister of public works to set up national workshops immediately.

See also: FRENCH CONSTITUTION OF 1848.

Further reading: J. H. Robinson, ed., *Documents of the Revolution of 1848 in France,* Hanover Historical Texts Project, available online at http://history.hanover.edu/texts/fr1848.htm.

French Edict of 1724

See EDICT OF 1724, FRENCH.

French Law of Separation

See COMBES'S BILL.

French Ordinance of 1357

"Great Ordinance" enacted in February 1357 by the estates-general (assembly of the country's estates) to streamline the royal administration of France without undermining the traditional powers of the monarchy. It called for the establishment of a standing committee of the estates to supervise the collection and expenditure of taxes, for relief measures for the poor, for other reforms, and for the estates to meet regularly. It was loosely drafted and without an organized charter of rights; the estates themselves were divided and disorganized, lacking in administrative skill to implement the ordinance. Moreover, France's King John II intervened to prohibit further meetings of the estates and to ban the payment of subsidy (granted by them); thus the ordinance could not be enforced.

Further reading: John B. Henneman, *Royal Taxation in Fourteenth-Century France: The Captivity and Ransom of John II, 1356–1370* (Philadelphia: American Philosophical Society, 1976).

French Primary Education Law of 1833

See GUIZOT LAW.

French Primary Education Laws of 1881 and 1882

See FERRY LAWS.

French Revolutionary Proclamation of 1792

Proclamation issued by France's republican government on December 15, 1792, urging soldiers to carry the revolutionary spirit into other countries. Addressed to those countries' citizens, it can be seen as a justification for unwarranted French aggression, also an assurance of peaceful intent. The French people, it said, having won their liberty now "offer to bring this inestimable blessing to you." Designating the French armies as the official torchbearers of liberty and reform, the government declared that henceforth all the achievements and benefits of the French Revolution (1789–92) would be deemed applicable to its neighbors. "Brothers and friends . . . all are citizens, equal in rights . . . called to govern, to serve, and to defend your country." Europe, suspicious of France's actual intentions, was immediately on the alert.

Further reading: Georges Lefebvre, *The French Revolution*, 2 vols. (New York: Columbia University Press, 1962); John Paxton, *Companion to the French Revolution* (New York: Facts On File, 1988); Samuel F. Scott and Barry Rothaus, eds., *Historical Dictionary of the French Revolution*, 2 vols. (Westport, Conn.: Greenwood Press, 1985).

Freud's *Psychoanalysis* See PSYCHOANALYSIS, A GENERAL INTRODUCTION TO.

Fribourg, Treaty of (Perpetual Peace, La Paix Perpétuelle) Swiss Confederation's treaty with King Francis I of France, signed in Fribourg, Switzerland, on November 29, 1516, a year after the Swiss defeat at the battle of Marignano and the loss of Milan to the French. Based on terms negotiated in November 1515, the Swiss ceded Domodossola (guarding the strategic Simplon Pass) but retained Bellinzona, the Ticino valley, most of Lake Lugano, and the Locarno side of Lake Maggiore. The system of pensions was reintroduced: In return for one million gold crowns and a pension of 2,000 francs per Swiss canton, the Swiss agreed to join forces with the king of France if required to do so. Massimiliano Sforza, duke of Milan, was pensioned off and Francis crowned duke instead. For the 22-year-old, newly crowned French king, this peace treaty was a major achievement, and it lasted until the French Revolution (1789–92).

See also: NOYON, TREATY OF.

Further reading: R. J. Knecht, *Renaissance Warrior and Patron: The Reign of Francis I* (New York: Cambridge University Press, 1994).

Friedwald, Treaty of Secret agreement concluded between Maurice of Saxony and King Henry II of France on January 15, 1552 at the German village of Friedwald (Friedewald). Maurice and other German princes were obliged to show Henry "lifelong gratitude," meaning they would provide him (at his request) with goods, servants, and lands in return for Henry's pledge to provide them with a monthly payment of 100,000 crowns, as well as men and arms, in support of the war they were waging against Holy Roman Emperor Charles V and his brother Ferdinand I.

See also: PASSAU, TREATY OF.

Further reading: Martyn C. Rady, *The Emperor Charles V* (New York: Longman, 1988).

Fufian Caninian Law (Lex Fufia Caninia) Roman law enacted in 2 B.C. on sponsorship by Emperor Augustus (Octavian), restricting the emancipation of slaves. The influx of liberated alien slaves (freedmen) into Italy concerned Augustus, who saw a threat to the native Roman citizens in business and society in general. By law, masters of one or two slaves could free them all, of three to 10 slaves half of them, of 11 to 30 a third, of 31 to 100 a fourth, and of 101 to 300 a fifth; but not more than 100 slaves could be liberated by any one

master. The law was linked with the Aelian Sentian Law (Lex Aelia Sentia) of A.D. 5, which severely limited the slaveholders' lifetime right of manumission, and with a Junian Law of about the same time, which granted a new citizenship status (Latin as opposed to Roman) to former slaves who had been freed by their masters without the proper legal ceremony. These freedman formed the class, of Junian Latins.

Further reading: W. W. Buckland, *The Roman Law of Slavery: The Condition of the Slave in Private Law from Augustus to Justinian* (Union, N.J.: Lawbook Exchange, 2000); Paul Finkelman and Joseph C. Miller, eds., *Macmillan Encyclopedia of World Slavery* (New York: Simon & Schuster Macmillan, 1999); Beryl Rawson and P. R. C. Weaver, eds., *The Roman Family in Italy: Status, Sentiment, Space* (New York: Oxford University Press, 1997).

Fugitive Slave Act of 1793, U.S. Federal legislation enacted on February 12, 1793, providing for the seizure and return, from one state to another, of escaped slaves in the United States. The act authorized the owner or the owner's agent to arrest a runaway in any state and gave federal and state judges the authority to determine whether the fugitive owed the service claimed, based on oral testimony or an affadavit. No jury trial was required to return a fugitive to the state or territory he or she had fled. Any person who harbored a fugitive or obstructed the arrest was liable for a fine of $500. The act, loosely enforced in the North and undermined by the Underground Railroad (a network to help escaping slaves), was reinforced by the FUGITIVE SLAVE LAW OF 1850. Both acts were repealed in 1864.

Further reading: Paul Finkelman, ed., *Encyclopedia of the United States in the Nineteenth Century* (New York: Charles Scribner's Sons, 2001).

Fugitive Slave Bill of 1818, U.S. Bill presented to Congress to strengthen the U.S. FUGITIVE SLAVE ACT OF 1793. The act was supported by representatives of Southern states and by the powerful Speaker of the House Henry Clay; it was opposed by some Northern states on the grounds that it violated the rights of one class of citizens in order to protect the property rights of other citizens. The bill passed the House of Representatives and, after several important amendments, the Senate in 1818. Northern indignation over the bill grew, however, and when it was returned to the House, it was tabled and allowed to die.

Further reading: *A Bill to Amend an Act Entitled An Act Respecting Fugitives from Justice, and Persons Escaping from the Service of Their Masters* (New York: Readex Microprint, 1981).

Fugitive Slave Law of 1850, U.S. Federal law, passed on September 18, 1850, as part of the COMPROMISE OF 1850, that required U.S. marshals to seize runaway slaves and imposed severe penalties on anyone who aided fugitives. The act was a response to abolitionist efforts, especially those of the Underground Railroad, and laws passed by Northern states hindering the enforcement of the 1793 Fugitive Slave Act. The 1850 law required that captured runaways be taken before a federal court or commissioner, denied fugitives a jury trial, and refused to admit fugitives' testimony, though the masters' claims of ownership were accepted as evidence. The law aroused strong antislavery sentiment in the North and abolitionists defied it vigorously. The acts of 1793 and 1850 were repealed in 1864.

Further reading: Stanley W. Campbell, *The Slave Catchers: Enforcement of the Fugitive Slave Laws, 1950–1860* (Chapel Hill: University of North Carolina Press, 1968); John Jordan Crittenden, *The Fugitive Slave Law, Its Character Fairly Stated—Its Constitutionality and Reasonableness Vindicated—and the Duty of Maintaining and Enforcing It Established Against the Misrepresentations, Sophistry, and Seditious Agitations of Demagogues and Abolitionists* (Washington, D.C., Gideon & Co., c. 1950); Samuel J. May, *The Fugitive Slave Law and Its Victims* (New York: Ayer, 1961).

Fulbright Act of 1946   U.S. legislation enacted on August 1, 1946, to initiate and finance international educational and cultural exchange programs, using funds derived from the sale to foreign governments of surplus World War II property. The act was submitted by Senator J. William Fulbright of Arkansas, as an amendment to the Surplus Property Act of 1944, because the task of "increasing our understanding of others and their understanding of us has an urgency that it has never had in the past." It created a large fund that allowed the exchange of thousands of students, teachers, researchers, journalists, government leaders, and others.

Further reading: Donald C. Bacon, Roger H. Davidson, and Morton Keller, eds., *The Encyclopedia of the United States Congress* (New York: Simon & Schuster, 1995); Walter Johnson and Francis J. Colligan, *The Fulbright Program: A History* (Chicago: University of Chicago Press, 1968).

Fullilove v. Klutznick   U.S. Supreme Court decision issued on July 2, 1980, ruling that the Public Works Employment Act, which set aside 10 percent of its available funds for contracts awarded to minority-owned businesses, was constitutional. The case originated over a number of challenges to the law by nonminority businessmen throughout the country who argued that the law constituted reverse discrimination against whites. The court based its decision on its belief that Congress had the authority, first, to conclude that minorities had been discriminated against in the awarding of government contracts and, second, to remedy such injustices through legislation. The ruling marked the first time a high court had supported the allocation of federal funds based upon the race of recipients.

Further reading: Leonard W. Levy and Kenneth L. Karst, eds., *Encyclopedia of the American Constitution* 2d ed. (New York: Macmillan Reference, 2000).

Fundamental Constitutions of Carolina   Plan of government issued for the proprietary colony of Carolina in 1669 to replace the earlier Concessions and Agreements (1665). Drawn up in England by the philosopher John Locke, the scheme combined progressive concepts of government (such as religious toleration, trial by jury, and limited self-government) with an aristocratic form of rule and a feudal social organization. Various ranks were created, based solely on the amount of land possessed. At the top of this social structure were the proprietors, who were hereditary officials, followed by a nobility of landgraves, caciques, and lords of manors. Freeholders, serfs, and slaves filled out the structure, with freeholders eligible to hold minor offices and to elect their representatives to an assembly. The Fundamental Constitutions were subsequently revised but were never accepted by the assembly, so the elaborate scheme was never adopted.

Further reading: The Avalon Project, *The Fundamental Constitutions of Carolina,* Yale Law School, available online at http://www.yale.edu./lawweb/avalon/states/nc05.htm.

Fundamental Law, Persian   See PERSIAN CONSTITUTION OF 1906.

Fundamental Law, Soviet   See STALIN CONSTITUTION.

Fundamental Law of 1921, Turkey's   Law adopted at Ankara on January 20, 1921, by the Grand National Assembly (the Ankara government) led by Mustafa Kemal (to be distinguished from the sultan's government at Constantinople); it declared the exclusive governing role of the Ankara government in Turkey. Specifically, the law proclaimed the nation's name to be "Turkey" ("Türkiye") and declared Turkey's national sovereignty; it declared that the Grand National Assembly represented the only true government in Turkey; that the assembly would be popularly elected; and that Mustafa Kemal (later Kemal Atatürk) would be the president of the new state. The law reflected the nationalists' increased opposition to the sultan's government following the latter's capitulation to Allied demands that he renounce vast amounts of Ottoman and Turkish territory (see SÈVRES, TREATY OF).

See also: NATIONAL PACT, TURKEY'S.

Further reading: Patrick Kinross, *Ataturk* (London: Phoenix, 2001).

Fundamental Laws, Austrian   See AUSTRIAN CONSTITUTION OF 1867.

Fundamental Laws, Russian   See RUSSIAN FUNDAMENTAL LAWS OF 1864; RUSSIAN FUNDAMENTAL LAWS OF 1906.

Fundamental Orders of Connecticut Document recognized as the first constitution in the colonies, composed by Roger Ludlow and voted upon by representatives of Hartford, Windsor, and Wethersfield, Connecticut, on January 14, 1639; used by framers of state constitutions after 1776. It consisted of a preamble and 11 fundamental laws; it recognized no higher authority than the freemen of these three towns and made provision for election of a governor and magistrate, the calling of general assemblies, and qualifications of voters. It exacted the organization of courts, the apportionment of taxes, and the representation of each local unit in a common council. The first constitution for Connecticut, it remained in force until a new constitution, which retained the basic fundamentals, was written in 1818.

See also: CONNECTICUT, CHARTER OF.

Further reading: Charles McLean Andrews, *The Colonial Period of American History*, vol. 2 (New Haven, Conn.: Yale University Press, 1936); Leonard W. Levy and Kenneth L. Karst, eds., *Encyclopedia of the American Constitution*, 2d ed. (New York: Macmillan Reference, 2000).

Funding Act of 1790, U.S. Federal legislation adopted on August 4, 1790, to fund the public debt of the United States. It authorized the president to borrow up to $12 million to discharge the overdue interest and payments on the foreign debt, and to pay off the entire debt, if possible. It also authorized a loan of $21.5 million to pay off state debts for services and supplies incurred during the American Revolution (1775–83). Income from import duties was set aside to pay the interest and principal of the public debt, and proceeds from the sale of public lands in the West were designated to discharge the principal. The act helped to reestablish commerce in the United States.

Further reading: Richard Brookhiser, *Alexander Hamilton, American* (New York: Free Press, 1999); John S. Gordon, *Hamilton's Blessing: The Extraordinary Life and Times of Our National Debt* (New York: Walker, 1997).

Furman v. Georgia U.S. Supreme Court decision issued on June 29, 1972, in which the death penalty was held to constitute "cruel and unusual punishment," in violation of the EIGHTH AMENDMENT and FOURTEENTH AMENDMENT. The decision overturned the death sentences of three black petitioners who had been convicted of capital crimes (murder and rape). Justice William Brennan declared that it is a "denial of human dignity for the State arbitrarily to subject a person to an unusually severe punishment that society . . . does not regard as acceptable and that cannot be shown to serve any penal purpose more effectively than a significantly less drastic punishment." The Supreme Court, noting that the death sentence was disproportionately imposed and carried out on blacks, the poor, and members of unpopular groups, declared that state statutes allowing arbitrary discretion in sentencing were "pregnant with discrimination" and thus violated constitutional guarantees of equal protection of the laws.

Further reading: The United States Supreme Court Case, *Furman v. Georgia, 408 U.S. 238 (1972),* FindLaw, available online at http://laws.findlaw.com/us/408/238.html.

Furuseth Act See LA FOLLETTE SEAMEN'S ACT.

Füssen, Treaty of Peace agreement concluded at Füssen, Germany, on April 22, 1745, between Austria (under Archduchess Maria Theresa) and Bavaria (under the new elector, Maximilian Joseph, son of the recently deceased Holy Roman Emperor Charles VII [the former elector of Bavaria, as Charles Albert]). By the treaty, Austria gave back all territory in Bavaria, which she had seized during the Second Silesian War (1744–45). In return, Maximilian Joseph, who had no desire to become Holy Roman emperor, renounced all claims to the imperial crown and promised to vote for Maria Theresa's husband, Duke Francis Stephen of Lorraine (later Emperor Francis I), in the coming imperial election.

See also: DRESDEN, TREATY OF.

Further reading: Georg Preuss, *Der Friede von Füssen 1745* (Munich: H. Lüneberg, 1894).

G

Gabinian Law (Lex Gabinia)   Roman legislation proposed in 67 B.C. by the tribune Aulus Gabinius to create a commander of consular rank with absolute control of all Roman fleets and of the Mediterranean shores for 50 miles inland. Increased depredations by pirates had checked maritime commerce and instilled much fear at the time. The appointment as commander was to be for three years, and he was to have authority to raise money and recruit sailors and soldiers. Senatorial opposition failed to stop passage of the law by the Assembly (67 B.C.); Gabinius's friend Pompey the Great was named commander and received 500 vessels and a 125,000-man army; within three months he had subdued the pirates. The Senate's power had been eroded seriously by the loss of its prerogative in creating the extraordinary commander.

See also: MANILIAN LAW.

Further reading: Max Radin, "The Roman Law of Delphi and the Lex Gabinia," *Classical Journal* 33, no. 9 (June 1928): 678–82.

Gadsden Purchase Treaty   Agreement negotiated in 1853 by American army officer and diplomat James Gadsden to settle boundary issues between the United States and Mexico arising from the Treaty of GUADALUPE-HIDALGO. Mexico agreed to cede territory in what is now southern Arizona and southern New Mexico in exchange for $15 million. The United States wanted that area for a southern transcontinental railroad route and to protect private U.S. concessions there. The treaty (signed on December 30, 1853) met strong opposition in the U.S. Senate, which cut the payment to Mexico to $10 million and the size of the new territory to about 30,000 square miles, before ratifying the treaty in 1854.

Further reading: Thomas Carson, ed., *Gale Encyclopedia of U.S. Economic History* (Farmington Hills, Mich.: 1999); Paul Neff Garber, *The Gadsden Treaty* (Philadelphia: Press of the University of Pennsylvania, 1923); Charles L. Phillips and Alan Axelrod, eds., *Encyclopedia of Historical Treaties and Alliances,* 2 vols. (New York: Facts On File, 2001).

Gag Rules, U.S.   Series of U.S. congressional bans on the discussion of antislavery petitions, issued between 1836 and 1844 and designed to eliminate the flood of petitions being submitted to Congress by the growing abolitionist movement. While the Senate simply rejected such petitions, the House of Representatives adopted, on May 26, 1836, the first gag rule, which automatically tabled (set aside indefinitely without consideration) all antislavery petitions. Favored by proslavery representatives, it was strongly opposed by John Quincy Adams and others as a violation of the constitutional right to petition the government, and its effect was to increase abolitionist sentiment. The last gag rule was repealed on December 3, 1844.

Further reading: Paul Finkelman and Joseph C. Miller, eds., *Macmillan Encyclopedia of World Slavery* (New York: Simon & Schuster Macmillan, 1998); Junius P. Rodriguez, ed., *Chronology of World Slavery* (Santa Barbara, Calif.: ABC-CLIO, 1999).

Galerius's Edict of Toleration   See EDICT OF TOLERA-TION, GALERIUS'S.

Gallican Articles   See FOUR ARTICLES, BOSSUET'S.

Galloway's Plan of Union (Plan of a Proposed Union Between Great Britain and the Colonies)   Proposal submitted to the First Continental Congress, meeting in Philadelphia on September 28, 1774, by Joseph Galloway of Pennsylvania. Favored by moderates at the congress as a means of resolving the conflict between Britain and the colonies, the plan recommended the establishment of an American legislature coequal with Parliament that would deal with general American affairs. The proposed governmental structure would include a Grand Council whose members would be chosen by the colonial assemblies to serve three-years terms, and a president-general who would be appointed by the king and would have veto power over the council. The colonial legislature would be considered a branch of the British Parliament, and the consent of both bodies would be required to pass legislation. Galloway's plan was defeated by only one vote.

Further reading: Henry Steele Commager, ed., *Documents of American History*, 8th. ed. (New York: Appleton-Century-Crofts, 1968).

Gambetta Note   Joint note from the British and French governments to the Egyptian khedive on January 8, 1882, promising their support should the khedive need it to calm the unrest in his country. The idea for the note came from France's premier, Léon Gambetta, who wanted to prevent a possible Egyptian-Turkish alliance (the khedive having approached the Ottoman Turks for help). The British foreign secretary, Lord Granville, reluctantly agreed. The note did not elaborate on the kind of support being considered, since Granville had already clarified that his government would not commit itself to "material action" unless the situation became drastic. This it did a few months later and, notwithstanding the note, Britain became even more entangled in Egypt's affairs.

See also: GRANVILLE CIRCULAR.

Further reading: J. P. T. Bury, *Gambetta's Final Years: "The Era of Difficulties," 1877–1882* (London: Longman, 1982); Harold Stannard, *Gambetta and the Foundation of the Third Republic* (London: Methuen, 1921).

Gandhi-Irwin Pact   See DELHI PACT OF 1931 GANDHI'S.

Gandhi's Announcement of a *Satyagraha* (Civil Disobedience) Struggle   Mohandas Gandhi's call to the people of India to observe a day of general *hartal* (stoppage of all work-related activities) in protest against the repressive ROWLATT ACTS passed by the government on March 18, 1919. He appealed to the people to treat it as a day of mourning, hold public meetings to voice their opposition, and stop all work. Intended as part of a wider *satyagraha* (civil disobedience) struggle, the *hartal* was originally set for March 30, 1919, but was later postponed to April 6. Copies of previously banned political works (including Gandhi's *Hind Swaraj*) were to be made available. Public response was unprecedented and largely peaceful except in Delhi and the Punjab, where clashes with the police led to many casualties. In Ahmedabad, the crowds turned violent and destructive. Convinced that *satyagraha* was a movement whose time had not yet come, Gandhi devoted his energies to educating the public in the principles of nonviolence.

Further reading: Mahatma Gandhi, *Non-Violent Resistance (Satyagraha)* (Mineola, N.Y.: Dover, 2001).

Gandhi's Call for Nonviolence   Mohandas Gandhi's first call for nonviolent resistance to British imperialist rule in India; made in 1914 following his return from South Africa (where his work as a lawyer resulted in a governmental agreement [1914] to curb discrimination against Indians and other Asians). In India, Gandhi began the passive-resistance political campaign (*satyagraha*) that he had developed in South Africa. He said men, women, and children could use *satyagraha,* meaning a "truth force" independent of physical force or violence, to oppose and change unjust laws. If petitions and lawgivers fail to make reforms, said Gandhi, then suffering in one's own person, by inviting the penalty for the breach of laws, was the remedy; *satyagraha* largely appears as civil disobedience ("civil in the sense that it is not criminal," he said).

See also: ASIATIC REGISTRATION BILL OF 1907, SOUTH AFRICAN.

Further reading: Louis Fischer, ed., *The Essential Gandhi: His Life, Work and Ideas: An Anthology* (New York: Vintage, 1983).

Garibaldi's Proclamation to the Italians   Italian soldier-patriot Giuseppe Garibaldi's fervent plea urging his fellow countrymen to rally to Italy's independence movement; delivered on May 5, 1860, just before he embarked on his Sicilian campaign. Garibaldi reminded every Italian that it was his duty to help the Sicilians, who were fighting "against the enemies of Italy . . . with money, arms, and especially men." He asked the various provinces to join the fray "so as to divide the enemy's forces." Criticizing "those who cram themselves at well-served tables," he urged: "let the more resolute throw themselves into the open country." Garibaldi praised those who had laid down their lives for the country, declaring: "let us fight for our brothers, tomorrow we can fight for ourselves." He envisioned the battle cry "Italy and Victor Emmanuel" reechoing through the countryside, causing "the tottering thrones of tyranny" to "fall to pieces" and the entire country to "rise like one man."

See also: MAZZINI'S INSTRUCTIONS TO YOUNG ITALY; VICTOR EMMANUEL II'S SPEECH OPENING THE ITALIAN PARLIAMENT.

Further reading: Michael Share, "The Unification of Italy (2), Giuseppe Garibaldi's Proclamation for the Liberation of Sicily (1860)," Department of History University of Hong Kong, available online at http://hkuhist2.hku.hk/firstyear/share/shareE11.html.

Garner v. Louisiana et al.   U.S. Supreme Court decision issued on December 11, 1961, overturning a conviction for disturbing the peace by a civil rights sit-in. The state claimed that black protesters, simply by sitting at segregated lunch counters, had disturbed the peace. The Court ruled that because the protesters had behaved in a peaceful and orderly manner, there was no evidence that they had violated the state's breach-of-peace statute and the conviction was therefore a violation of FOURTEENTH AMENDMENT rights to due process. Justice John Marshall Harlan declared that a sit-in was a constitutionally protected form of free expression; in turn, the U.S. CONSTITUTION did not protect demonstrations conducted on private property over the objections of the owner. The Court ruled that the public has constitutional rights in respect to those enterprises that operate in the public interest and domain.

Further reading: United States Supreme Court Case, *Brown* v. *Louisiana*, 383 U.S. 131 (1966), Find Law, available online at http://caselaw.lp.findlaw.com/scripts/getcase.pl?court=US&vol=383&invol=131.

Gastein, Convention of   Agreement concluded between Austria and Prussia at Gastein (Badgastein, Austria) on August 14, 1865, following the war between the Austro-Prussian coalition and Denmark; it provided for the control of the duchies of Schleswig, Holstein, and Laurenburg. (The Peace of Vienna of 1864, which had concluded the war, had delivered the duchies into Austria and Prussia's joint possession.) The convention provided that Austria would administer Holstein; Prussia would gain Laurenburg, paying Austria for this duchy; and Prussia would administer Schleswig, which was located directly south of Denmark and north of Holstein. Prussia's Otto von Bismarck, who was eager to enlarge Prussia territorially, was able to create from the fragile arrangement a pretext for conflict, which was to develop into the Austro-Prussian Seven Weeks' War.

See also: PRAGUE, TREATY OF (1866).

Further reading: Great Britain Foriegn Office, Historical Section, *Slesvig-Holstein* (London: H.M. Stationery Office, 1919).

GATT   See GENERAL AGREEMENT ON TARIFFS AND TRADE.

Gelasius I's Letter to Anastasius I   Famous letter of political doctrine written by Pope Gelasius I to the Roman emperor of the East, Anastasius I, in A.D. 494. The year before,

Theodoric the Great, with his Ostrogothic army, had won control of Italy, and he now sat on the Western imperial throne at Rome. Gelasius declared that the world was ruled by two powers, of which "the sacred authority of the priests" was superior to kingly or royal power. The church had supremacy over the state, according to the Pope, who magisterially insisted upon the "obedience due to the bishop of that See [of Rome] which the Most High ordained to be above all others."

See also: EDICT OF THEODORIC; HENOTIKON.

Further reading: Paul Halsall, *Medieval Sourcebook: Gelasius 1 on Spiritual and Temporal power, 494,* Internet Medieval Source Book, available online at http://www.fordham.edu/halsall/source/gelasius1.html.

General Act of Brussels   See BRUSSELS ACT OF 1890.

General Agreement on Tariffs and Trade (GATT)   Major accord reached on May 15, 1967, by 53 countries during the Kennedy Round (1963–67) of talks on tariff reductions held in Geneva, Switzerland. The final document of the General Agreement on Tariffs and Trade (GATT), signed in Geneva on June 30, 1967, by 46 countries, called for a 33 percent to 35 percent reduction in world industrial tariffs. To be implemented in stages over a five-year period beginning on January 1, 1968, the accord affected nearly 60,000 items and over $40 billion in world trade annually. Among its other provisions were (1) halving of most chemical tariffs of major producers; (2) liberalization of trade in vegetables, fruits, and noncereal products; (3) adjustment of international iron and steel tariffs to an average of 6 percent; (4) reduction of duties on many items to 5 percent or less; (5) supply of 4.5 million metric tons of grain annually to the underdeveloped countries; and (6) lowering of the trade barriers in tropical products, raw materials, and manufactured goods produced by the developing countries.

Further reading: Thomas Carson, ed., *Gale Encyclopedia of U.S. Economic History* (Farmington Hills, Mich.: 1999); Bernard M. Hoekman and Michel M. Kostecki, *The Political Economy of the World Trading System: From GATT to WTO* (New York: Oxford University Press, 1995).

General Law Amendment Act, South African (Sabotage Bill)   South African legislation of May 2, 1963, authorizing the minister of justice to detain arbitrarily (over a 90-day period) anyone who, the police believed, possessed information about subversive activities. Special courts were created to conduct trials on charges of sabotage or subversion. Those who had completed their sentences could be indefinitely detained again. By 1964, over 900 people had been thus detained when the government extended the 90-day period until July 1, 1965. Aimed at suppressing African nationalist organizations, the act introduced the death penalty for advocating the overthrow of the government or for leaving the country to learn about sabotage. The officials could declare any organization illegal, prohibit attendance at meetings, and order a clampdown on publication of views. The act was internationally condemned as being tyrannous.

Further reading: Mary Benson, *Nelson Mandela: The Man and the Movement* (New York: W. W. Norton, 1994).

Geneva, Order of   See COMMON ORDER, BOOK OF.

Geneva Agreements of 1954 (Indochina War Armistice)

Three armistice agreements concluded in Geneva, Switzerland, consisting of a French-Vietnamese agreement signed on July 20, 1954, by General Henri Deltiel, representing French forces in Indochina, and Colonel Ta Quang Buu, defense vice minister of the Vietminh rebel forces; a Vietnamese-Laotian agreement signed on July 21, 1954, by the same signatories (French and Laotian forces were under the same command); and a Vietnamese-Cambodian agreement signed on July 21, 1954, by Ta Quang Buu and Cambodia's defense minister Nhiek Tioulong. By the agreements (which ended the French Indochina War of 1946–54), the signatories agreed upon the division of Vietnam at the 17th parallel into two parts: the north under the communist-led Vietminh and the south under the French-sponsored government of Bao Dai (the chief of state). Elections to create a unified government in Vietnam were to be held within two years under international supervision (Canada, India, and Poland would enforce the armistice in each state), and the Vietminh were to recognize the governments of Laos and Cambodia (Kampuchea) as independent states within the French Union (elections were to be held in both states by 1955). The agreements also provided for the evacuation of French forces from the Red River delta in North Vietnam within 10 months and the evacuation of Vietminh forces from South Vietnam, Laos, and Cambodia.

See also: GENEVA DECLARATION OF 1954.

Further reading: Charles L. Phillips and Alan Axelrod, eds., *Encyclopedia of Historical Treaties and Alliances,* 2 vols. (New York: Facts On File, 2001).

Geneva Convention of 1864 (Convention for the Amelioration of the Wounded in Time of War)

First of many international negotiations conducted in Geneva, Switzerland, at the instance of Jean Henri Dunant, Swiss founder of the International Red Cross. The treaty (signed at Geneva by representatives of 12 nations in 1864) ruled that all places where sick and wounded soldiers were being treated should be spared from attack, that impartial treatment would be guaranteed to all combatants, and that civilians treating the wounded would be given protection. Further, the sign of the Red Cross (a symbol of mercy and neutrality) was to be universally used to identify persons and property covered under the agreement. The Geneva Convention was ratified within three years. Its provisions were revised and extended

by the Second Geneva Convention (1906) and, in 1899 and 1907, by the Hague Convention.

Further reading: Charles L. Phillips and Alan Axelrod, eds., *Encyclopedia of Historical Treaties and Alliances,* 2 vols. (New York: Facts On File, 2001).

Geneva Conventions of 1949

International treaties governing the treatment of wounded and captured combatants as well as civilians during war. The four Geneva Conventions—for the Amelioration of the Condition of the Wounded and Sick in Armed Forces in the Field; for the Amelioration of the Condition of Wounded, Sick, and Shipwrecked Members of the Armed Forces at Sea; Relative to the Treatment of Prisoners of War; and Relative to the Protection of Civilian Persons in Time of War—were developed at an International Red Cross conference in Stockholm, Sweden, on August 23–30, 1948, and ratified by a vast majority of United Nations member states in Geneva, Switzerland, on August 12, 1949. Although international treaties guaranteeing the safety of sick and wounded military personnel and prohibiting the maltreatment of civilians had existed since 1864, the horrors of World War II necessitated the restatement and expansion of their principles. The first two conventions established the neutral status of noncombatant medical personnel, the facilities where sick or wounded combatants are cared for, and the sick and wounded themselves. The third convention provided for the humane treatment of prisoners of war, including their right to adequate food and medical treatment. It also prohibited captors from demanding any information from prisoners other than name, rank, and serial number. The fourth convention prohibited deportation, hostage taking, torture, and execution of civilians, as well as the deliberate destruction of civilian property. The conventions remain in effect today.

Further reading: United Nations Office of the High Commissioner for Human Rights, "International Human Rights Instruments," Office of the High Commissioner for Human Rights, available online at http://www.unhchr.ch/html/intlinst.htm.

Geneva Declaration of 1948

Declaration establishing an international code of medical ethics, adopted by the General Assembly of the World Medical Association at Geneva, Switzerland, in September 1948. Thereby, physicians were to dedicate themselves to the "service of humanity," practice their professions with "conscience and dignity," and maintain the noble traditions of medicine. They were to respect their teachers and human life and not allow "considerations of religion, nationality, race, party politics, or social standing" to intervene between their responsibilities toward their patients. The international code of medical ethics developed these principles even further. Among other requirements, a physician was to respect his patient's right to "absolute secrecy" (laws pertaining to this vary from country to country) and not weaken "the physical or mental resistance of a human being" except in the patient's interests.

Further reading: Charles L. Phillips and Alan Axelrod, eds., *Encyclopedia of Historical Treaties and Alliances,* 2 vols. (New York: Facts On File, 2001).

Geneva Declaration of 1954   Declaration of intention agreed to (by voice vote) by heads of delegations from France, Britain, the United States, mainland China, the Soviet Union, Vietnam, Cambodia (Kampuchea), and Laos, on the final day of the 1954 Geneva Conference (April 26 to July 21). They recognized the just signed armistices ending the fighting in Vietnam, Laos, and Cambodia (see GENEVA AGREEMENTS OF 1954) and agreed "to consult one another on any question which may be referred to them by the International Supervisory Commission" to ensure that the armistices were respected. The declaration significantly stated the intention of the governments of Cambodia, Laos, and Vietnam to hold free general elections within the next two years. It also stated that "the military demarcation line [the 17th parallel] is provisional and should not in any way be interpreted as constituting a political or territorial boundary" in Vietnam. France was ready, the declaration noted, to withdraw her troops from Vietnam, Laos, and Cambodia at the request of the governments concerned.

See also: WHITE PAPER OF 1965, U.S.

Further reading: Ainslie T. Embree, ed., *Encyclopedia of Asian History,* 4 vols. (New York: Charles Scribner's Sons, 1988).

Geneva Declaration of European Resistance   Charter concluded in Geneva, Switzerland, on July 7, 1944, rallying European resistance to Nazi Germany in World War II (1939–45) and seeking to establish "a federal order for the peoples of Europe." This federal order would bring unity and peace, allowing the Germans "to participate in European life," solving boundary problems, saving democratic institutions, restoring economic and commercial stability, and disposing of irresponsible governments (with their armed forces and courts). The declaration was approved by resistance movements in France, Italy, the Netherlands, Denmark, Norway, Poland, Czechoslovakia, and Yugoslavia.

Further reading: D. A. Lande, *Resistance! Occupied Europe and Its Defiance of Hitler* (Osceola, Wis.: MBI, 2000).

Geneva Protocol of 1924 (Protocol for the Pacific Settlement of International Disputes)   Unanimous adoption (October 2, 1924) by the League of Nations Assembly at Geneva, Switzerland, of a scheme intended to promote defensive alliances and lead eventually to gradual disarmament, an issue pending since the post–World War I peace treaties. The signatories of this document were to accept and respect the arbitration of the league's Permanent Court of International Justice. Further, they were to desist from giving military aid to any country suffering from aggression (despite any treaties to the contrary), until the League of Nations Council had called for sanctions against the aggressor. The protocol was never ratified and many of its proposals were amplified in the 1925 Pact of LOCARNO.

Further reading: James W. Garner, "The Geneva Protocol for the Pacific Settlement of International Disputes," *American Journal of International Law* 19 (1925):123–32; James T. Shotwell, *Plans and Protocols to End War* (New York: Carnegie Endowment for International Peace, Division of Intercourse and Education, 1952).

Gentlemen's Agreement of 1907   Secret executive agreement between the United States and Japan to limit Japanese immigration to the United States. The growing Japanese population of California and increasing competition for jobs led to hostility by white laborers, local discriminatory laws, and the possibility of U.S. congressional action to end all Japanese immigration. To protect U.S.-Japanese relations, President Theodore Roosevelt concluded the Gentlemen's Agreement, a policy in which Japan agreed to withhold passports from laborers wishing to immigrate to the United States, except in the case of former U.S. residents, immediate family of residents, and previously settled agriculturists. The Gentlemen's Agreement was first affirmed in a Japanese diplomatic note on February 24, 1907, and later confirmed in another Japanese note on February 18, 1908.

Further reading: Stephen A. Flanders and Carl N. Flanders, *Dictionary of American Foreign Affairs* (New York: Macmillan, 1993); E. P. Hutchinson, *Legislative History of American Immigration Policy, 1798–1965* (Philadelphia: University of Pennsylvania Press, 1981).

"Geographical Pivot of History"   Influential, 24-page paper by the English geopolitician Halford J. Mackinder, first read by him to the Royal Geographical Society in London in 1904. In it he said that Eurasia had become the world's "heartland" and strategic center and "the geographical pivot of history." This had ensued from southern Siberia's industrial growth and from military power on land becoming as formidable as sea power. His concept of political geography was developed further in his short book, *Democratic Ideals and Reality* (1919), in which, he said, Britain and the United States must act as a stabilizing force among powers (notably Germany and Russia) aiming to control the heartland (an idea later adopted by German Nazi geopoliticians).

Further reading: *Geographical Journal* 23, no. 4 (April 1904); W. H. Parker, *Mackinder: Geography as an Aid to Statecraft* (Oxford, England: Clarendon Press, 1982).

Georgia Platform   Set of resolutions drawn up by Charles J. Jenkins and adopted in December 1850 by a state convention at Milledgeville, Georgia, representing the state's response to the COMPROMISE OF 1850. The platform stated that although Georgia did not entirely approve of the compromise, the state would accept its terms in order to preserve the Union. Nonetheless, the resolutions warned that Georgia intended to resist, "even (as a last resort) to a disruption of . . . the Union," and would resist further Congressional action to weaken fugitive slave laws, to suppress the interstate slave trade, to abolish slavery in the District of Columbia or within the slaveholding states, or to disallow slavery in new states and territories.

Further reading: Henry Steele Commager, ed., *Documents of American History*, 8th ed. (New York: Appleton-Century-Crofts, 1968).

German Anti-Socialist Law See ANTI-SOCIALIST LAW, GERMAN.

German Army Bill of 1887 See BISMARCK'S ARMY BILL OF 1887.

German-Austrian Agreement of 1936. See AUSTRO-GERMAN AGREEMENT OF 1936.

German-British Agreement of 1898 See ANGLO-GERMAN AGREEMENT OF 1898.

German-British Naval Agreement of 1935 See ANGLO-GERMAN NAVAL AGREEMENT OF 1935.

German-British Treaty of 1899 See ANGLO-GERMAN TREATY OF 1899.

German Civil Code German codification of civil and criminal code, passed on July 1, 1896, and effective on January 1, 1900. A quarter of a century in the making, the new code was necessary to create a common German written law to replace the disparate laws of the individual German states comprising the new German Empire. The constitution of 1871 gave the federal government the authority to legislate legal procedure. In 1873, a constitutional amendment extended this authority to include all civil and criminal law, and the first laws on civil and criminal procedure were promulgated, becoming effective in 1879. These new laws provided for a complete reorganization of the judicial system, including the standardization of the courts and their procedure, at the local, district, and provincial levels; and the establishment of a federal supreme court in Leipzig as the highest court of appeal. The written civil code required years of work: The first draft was published in 1888, but was criticized for its highly technical language and reliance on Roman law. A revised version of the code was finally approved in 1896, although it was still predominantly "Roman" in character.

Further reading: Walter Loewy, *The Civil Code of the German Empire: As Enacted on August 18, 1896 . . .* (Littleton, Colo.: F. B. Rothman, 1997).

German Civil Service Law of 1933 See CIVIL SERVICE LAW OF 1933, GERMAN.

German Confederation, Act of Act concluded on June 8, 1815, at the Congress of Vienna by representatives of most European powers; established a German state consisting of 38 (later 39) loosely federated states. Through the act it was agreed that each individual state would act in the interests of each state and of the German Confederation as a whole; that any differences between states would be settled amicably in the confederate Diet; that each state would have equal representation in the supreme lawmaking body, with the chief states alone having representation in a second assembly, which served in an advisory capacity; that legislative decisions would require a two-thirds majority vote, while any change in the constitution would require a unanimous vote; that both Prussia and Austria were to occupy leading roles in the confederation, with the more powerful member, Austria, presiding over the Diet. The settlement was a compromise, satisfying those European leaders who refused to allow for a unified German state and those who refused to accept a German state under exclusively Austrian or Prussian rule.

See also: VIENNA, FINAL ACT OF THE CONGRESS OF; GERMAN CONFEDERATION, SIX ARTICLES OF.

Further reading: William Carr, *A History of Germany, 1815–1985*, 3d ed. (London: Edward Arnold, 1987); Wilfred Fest, *Dictionary of German History, 1806–1945* (New York: St. Martin's, 1978); Hajo Holborn, *A History of Modern Germany, 1840–1945* (New York: Knopf, 1969).

German Confederation, Six Articles of Articles written by Austrian statesman Prince Clemens von Metternich and adopted by the Diet of the German Confederation on June 28, 1832; represented Metternich's reactionary response to several incidents of revolutionary unrest in Europe, including Germany. The document asserted that each German state's sovereign had the right and obligation to reject any measures that could limit his sovereignty; that the states were forbidden to use threats in order to bring about changes in the constitution; that legislation was to be in harmony with the goals of the confederation; that a federal commission was to be founded that would prevent the passage of any legislation restricting the rights of the confederation; that the states were required to defend the confederation from any attack or criticism; and that the federal Diet had the right to reject any individual state's legislation. The articles in fact contained no new principles and aimed at strengthening the forces of reaction.

See also: GERMAN CONFEDERATION, ACT OF.

Further reading: William Carr, *A History of Germany, 1815–1985*, 3d ed. (London: Edward Arnold, 1987); Wilfred Fest, *Dictionary of German History, 1806–1945* (New York: St. Martin's, 1978); Hajo Holborn, *A History of Modern Germany, 1840–1945* (New York: Knopf, 1969).

German Empire, Constitution of the   Imperial constitution forming a federal union of 25 German states, adopted on April 16, 1871. It created a legislature with a Reichstag (lower house), whose members were elected by universal manhood suffrage, and a Bundesrat (upper house), whose 58 members represented the various states; Prussia had 17 members (thus 17 votes) in the Bundesrat and could control any changes in the constitution (14 votes made a veto). The federation's presiding officer was the king of Prussia, who became the "German emperor" (see GERMAN EMPIRE, PROCLAMATION OF THE); Prussia's prime minister became chancellor, and Prussian Junkers and officials seemed to gain strong control of the military, taxation, and the judiciary, among other spheres. In this "German Empire" (the name of the federation), clearly dominated by Prussia, the reigning German princes retained considerable power over their domains (states), but civil and criminal law was under the control of the empire.

See also: GERMAN CIVIL CODE.

Further reading: William Carr, *A History of Germany, 1815–1985*, 3d ed. (London: Edward Arnold, 1987); Wilfred Fest, *Dictionary of German History, 1806–1945* (New York: St. Martin's, 1978); Hajo Holborn, *A History of Modern Germany, 1840–1945* (New York: Knopf, 1969).

German Empire, Proclamation of the   German Empire born on January 18, 1871, when King William I of Prussia was proclaimed "German Emperor" by Chancellor Otto von Bismarck in the Hall of Mirrors at Versailles, France, amidst the ruins of the French Second Empire. The official ceremony was held on the 170th anniversary of the coronation of the first king of Prussia, and one month after Bismarck had arranged for a deputation from the North German parliament, along with representatives of the German princes (a sine qua non for William), to beg the king of Prussia to accept the imperial crown. The proclamation read, in part, that the German empire hoped to "be granted the ability to construct a propitious future for the Fatherland under the symbol of its ancient glory," and "to enjoy the fruits of its zealous and self-sacrificing wars in eternal peace," within borders secure against any French aggression.

Further reading: William Carr, *A History of Germany, 1815–1985*, 3d ed. (London: Edward Arnold, 1987); Wilfred Fest, *Dictionary of German History, 1806–1945* (New York: St. Martin's, 1978); Hajo Holborn, *A History of Modern Germany, 1840–1945* (New York: Knopf, 1969).

German Enabling Act of 1933   See ENABLING ACT OF 1933, GERMAN.

German-Italian Alliance of 1939   See STEEL, PACT OF.

German-Italian-Japanese Pact   See AXIS POWERS, PACT OF THE.

German-Italian Pact of 1936   Pact signed on October 25, 1936, by Foreign Minister Galeazzo Ciano of Italy and Foreign Minister Joachim von Ribbentrop of Germany, establishing the Rome-Berlin Axis, the alliance between Fascist Italy and Nazi Germany that was directed against World War I's victors, primarily Britain and France. Through the pact the signatory powers agreed to cooperate in matters relating to the maintenance of peace in Europe, as well as matters of common interest; to protect Europe against forces threatening to her (this was understood to refer to communism); to see that Spanish General Francisco Franco maintained his commanding position in Spain; to collaborate on actions to be taken in the Danubian basin; to work toward the conclusion of a new Locarno pact (see LOCARNO, PACT OF) involving only Western European nations; and to provide Germany with economic concessions in Italy's colonial territory of Ethiopia in return for Germany's recognition of Italy's sovereignty there. The pact thus most important provided each party with an ally determined to revise the post–World War I status quo, with which both powers were dissatisfied.

See also: AUSTRO-GERMAN AGREEMENT OF 1936; AXIS POWERS, PACT OF THE; STEEL, PACT OF.

Further reading: Viktor L. Israelian and L. N. Kutakov, *Diplomacy of Aggression: Berlin-Rome-Tokyo Axis, Its Rise and Fall* (Moscow: Progress Publishers, 1970); Elizabeth Wiskemann, *The Rome-Berlin Axis, a History of the Relations Between Hitler and Mussolini* (New York: Oxford University Press, 1969).

German-Japanese Pact of 1936   See ANTI-COMINTERN PACT.

German Military Bill of 1893   New German military bill enacted on July 15, 1893, in response to the developing FRANCO-RUSSIAN ALLIANCE OF 1892, greatly increasing both the size of Germany's army and the number of younger inductees. The new law, first proposed in November 1892, also reduced the term of service from three years to two, and decreased the term of the army bill from seven years to five. Despite these concessions to the liberals, the Reichstag (legislature) originally rejected the measure. The bill was approved as proposed only after Germany's Chancellor Leo von Caprivi ordered new parliamentary elections, which returned a more conservative legislature, concerned with the possibility of a war on two fronts.

Further reading: John A. Nichols, *Germany after Bismarck, the Caprivi Era, 1890–1894* (New York: W. W. Norton, 1968).

German Naval Laws of 1898 and 1900   Laws greatly increasing the strength of the German navy, which easily passed by the Reichstag (legislature) on March 28, 1898, and June 12, 1900. The architect of the naval expansion was Admiral Alfred von Tirpitz, minister of marine since 1897, who used both direct political pressure and indirect propaganda tactics to achieve his goal of expanding the German navy. The first bill, in 1898, was designed primarily to make the German navy competitive with the French navy. It projected a navy of 19 battleships, 12 heavy cruisers, and 30 light cruisers, or an increase of seven battleships, two heavy cruisers, and seven light cruisers. The second bill, in 1900, increased this total to 38 battleships, eight heavy cruisers, and 24 light cruisers, to be completed by 1917. The avowed purpose of the second bill was to strengthen the German navy enough to pose a threat to the largest (i.e., British) navy, which would theoretically make war with Germany risky. In fact, the Naval Law of 1900 produced the opposite effect, causing an escalating naval armaments race with Great Britain, and increasing international tension.

Further reading: Holger H. Herwig, *"Luxury" Fleet: The Imperial German Navy, 1888–1918* (Amherst, N.Y.: Humanity Books, 1998); Jonathan Steinberg, *Yesterday's Deterrent: Tirpitz and the Birth of the German Battle Fleet* (Aldershot, England: Gregg Revivals, 1992); Gary E. Weir, *Building the Kaiser's Navy: The Imperial Naval Office and German Industry in the von Tirpitz Era, 1890–1919* (Annapolis, Md.: Naval Institute Press, 1992).

German "State Treaty" of 1990

Formal agreement signed by the finance ministers of the two Germanys (East and West) in Bonn on May 18, 1990, binding the two countries into a single economic entity (effective on July 2, 1990). Full political unification of the two Germanys was to come after all-German elections later in the year and when the question of a united Germany's military allegiance was settled. By the treaty, West Germany's deutsche mark would become East Germany's own legal tender; West Germany's central bank (the Bundesbank) would control all monetary affairs; West Germany's pension system would be introduced into East Germany; and the Bonn government would assume responsibility for East German unemployment benefits. East Germany's state property was to be sold to help pay for the reconstruction costs toward a free-market economy. Some charged that the treaty would make the East Germans more impoverished (a bloodless revolution in 1989 had ended four decades of hard-line communist rule over them).

Further reading: Peter Alter, *The German Question and Europe: A History* (London: Arnold, 2000); Jurgen Thomaneck and William J. Niven, *Dividing and Uniting Germany* (New York: Routledge, 2001).

German Unification Treaty (Second "State Treaty")

Treaty signed on August 31, 1990, providing the framework for the legal and political union of the German Democratic Republic (GDR) and the Federal Republic of Germany (FRG), East Germany and West Germany, respectively. It formalized the constitutional accession of GDR's five Länder (territories) and East Berlin to the FRG and essentially incorporated almost the entire GDR system into the West German, including assumption of its state property, international obligations, and domestic debt. The national parliament was expanded to include representation from the new territories. While the FRG's existing treaties and membership in international organizations remained unaffected, most of the GDR's existing treaties were reviewed and terminated. Most of the German Unification Treaty's 45 articles and three annexes detailed the complex legal aspects of unification. For instance, it favored restitution of property seized by the GDR over compensation and provided for the prosecution of criminal offenses committed in the GDR prior to unification. The treaty was ratified on September 21, 1990, and came into force on October 3, 1990.

Further reading: A. Bradley Shingleton et al., eds., *Dimensions of German Unification—Economic, Social and Legal Analyses* (Boulder, Colo.: Westview Press, 1995); Philip Zelikow and Condoleeza Rice, *Germany Unified and Europe Transformed—A Study in Statecraft* (Cambridge, Mass.: Harvard University Press, 1995).

Germany's Four-Year Plan of 1936

See NAZI GERMANY'S FOUR-YEAR PLAN.

Germany's Surrender in World War II

Instrument of unconditional surrender of Germany signed in Rheims, France, at a little red schoolhouse, the forward command post of SHAEF (Supreme Headquarters of the Allied Expeditionary Force, or AEF), on May 7, 1945, by Colonel General Alfred Jodl, chief of staff of the German army; U.S. Lieutenant General Walter B. Smith, for the Supreme Allied Command; General François Savez, for the commander of French forces of the AEF; and General Ivan Susloparov, for the Russian High Command. It provided for an end to German hostilities in World War II (1939–45). The document specified the unconditional surrender of all German forces to the Supreme Allied Command and the Russian High Command; that all forces remain in their present positions; that the German High Command issue a cease-fire at 12:01 A.M. on May 9, 1945; that the German High Command obey all orders issued by U.S. General Dwight D. Eisenhower (supreme commander of the AEF) or the Russian High Command; and that, in the event of German noncompliance with the terms of surrender, the allies would "take such punitive or other action as they deem appropriate."

Further reading: Charles L. Phillips and Alan Axelrod, eds., *Encyclopedia of Historical Treaties and Alliances* 2 vols. (New York: Facts On File, 2001).

Gettysburg Address

Famous and eloquent speech delivered by President Abraham Lincoln on November 19, 1863, at the dedication of a national cemetery at Gettysburg, Pennsylvania, the site of a pivotal Union victory in the Civil War. Lincoln's brief speech, which followed a two-hour oration by

Edward Everett, has been extolled as one of the greatest prose poems in the English language. "Four score and seven years ago," Lincoln said, "our fathers brought forth on this continent, a new nation, conceived in Liberty, and dedicated to the proposition that all men are created equal." The address expressed Lincoln's personal sorrow at the battlefield deaths while offering the resolve that "these dead shall not have died in vain . . . and that government of the people, by the people, for the people, shall not perish from the earth."

Further reading: Garry Wills, *Lincoln at Gettysburg: The Words That Remade America* (New York: Touchstone Books, 1993).

Ghent, Pacification of   Decision on November 8, 1576, in Ghent by the provinces of the Netherlands to bury their national and religious differences and band together to expel the Spanish troops that had overrun the Low Countries after the death of Luis de Requesens, Spanish governor of the Netherlands, in 1576. Result of an emerging nationalist consciousness, the pacification or agreement was also devoted to restoring local and provincial rights and to ending the atrocities committed against the Protestant Calvinists, who were allowed to exercise their faith within their provinces. The religious issue between Catholics and Protestants was to be separately resolved by a representative assembly. The pacification did not involve a formal renunciation of the provinces' allegiance to King Philip II of Spain; however, institutions of national government began to be established. The new governor, John of Austria, was compelled to reconfirm its provisions and to expel the Spanish troops from the provinces. Peace was short lived, since the Spanish troops soon resumed hostilities while, internally, the fragile religious unity was disrupted. The results were the Treaty of ARRAS and the Union of UTRECHT.

See also: ABJURATION, ACT OF.

Further reading: *Netherlands: A Treatise of the Peace . . . Between the States of the Lowe Countries . . . and the Prince of Orange* (New York: Da Capo Press, 1973).

Ghent, Treaty of   Compromise settlement ending the indecisive War of 1812 between the United States and Great Britain, signed in Ghent, Belgium, on December 24, 1814. Both the Americans and the British receded from demands that would have prolonged the war and agreed to a mutual restoration of conquests. Britain gave up her territorial gains in the American Old Northwest; the United States agreed to respect Indian rights. In addition, the treaty provided for joint arbitral commissions to settle fishing rights and boundary disputes (lines) between the United States and Canada and for cooperation between the United States and Britain in suppressing the international slave trade.

See also: LONDON CONVENTION OF 1818; RUSH-BAGOT AGREEMENT.

Further reading: Charles L. Phillips and Alan Axelrod, eds., *Encyclopedia of Historical Treaties and Alliances,* 2 vols. (New York: Facts On File, 2001).

Gibbons v. Ogden   U.S. Supreme Court decision, issued on March 2, 1824, that ended state-granted monopolies on interstate steam navigation and, more generally, gave a broad construction to the constitutional clause granting Congress the power to regulate commerce among the states. Aaron Ogden, who had a New York state license to operate a steamboat between New York and New Jersey, sued Thomas Gibbons, who had a federal but not a state license for a similar operation. Writing for the Supreme Court majority, Chief Justice John Marshall stated that New York's grant of a monopoly was unconstitutional interference with the congressional right to regulate interstate commerce. He defined "commerce" to mean, in addition to buying and selling, transportation and navigation. The decision encouraged the growth of transportation systems and was an important interpretation of federal over state power.

Further reading: Maurice G. Baxter, *The Steamboat Monopoly: Gibbons v. Ogden, 1824* (New York: Knopf, 1972); Leonard W. Levy and Kenneth L. Karst, eds., *Encyclopedia of the American Constitution,* 2d ed. (New York: Macmillan Reference, 2000).

GI Bill of Rights (Servicemen's Readjustment Act)   U.S. legislation enacted on June 22, 1944, authorizing economic and educational assistance for veterans of World War II (1939–45). A veteran or member of the U.S. Armed Forces is called a GI, an abbreviation of "general, or government, issue" for military use. The law provided low-interest, federally guaranteed mortgages for the purchase of new homes, farms, and businesses; allowed substantial unemployment benefits for up to one year and provided assistance to returning veterans in finding jobs; and gave educational and vocational subsidies for up to four years of college, allowing up to $500 a year for tuition and books and $50 a month as a stipend. It also authorized aid for veterans' hospitals and vocational rehabilitation. Some 12 million veterans took advantage of its educational benefits.

Further reading: Thomas Carson, ed., *Gale Encyclopedia of U.S. Economic History* (Farmington Hills, Mich.: 1999); Keith W. Olson, *The GI Bill, the Veterans, and the Colleges* (Lexington: University Press of Kentucky, 1974); David R. B. Ross, *Preparing for Ulysses: Politics and Veterans During World War II* (New York: Columbia University Press, 1969).

Gideon v. Wainwright   U.S. Supreme Court decision issued on March 18, 1963, declaring that accused persons have a constitutional right to representation by counsel in all state criminal trials. Clarence Earl Gideon, a poor, uneducated Florida drifter, wrote his own petition to the Supreme Court appealing a conviction for petit larceny after a trial in which he had been denied the assistance of a lawyer. Twenty-two states filed briefs supporting his position. The Court ruled unanimously that the SIXTH AMENDMENT made the right to counsel a fundamental one, essential to a fair trial, and that the FOURTEENTH AMENDMENT extended this protection to state matters. The decision led to programs to supply counsel to indigent defendants throughout the United States.

Further reading: Leonard W. Levy and Kenneth L. Karst, eds., *Encyclopedia of the American Constitution,* 2d ed. (New York: Macmillan Reference, 2000); Anthony Lewis, *Gideon's Trumpet* (New York: Random House, 1964).

Gillette v. United States

U.S. Supreme Court decision issued on March 8, 1971, limiting conscientious-objector status to those who object to all wars, not to those who oppose a particular war. The case concerned Guy Gillette, who refused to report for induction into the armed forces, claiming conscientious-objector status because he considered the Vietnam War "unjust"; he admitted that he would serve in a war of national defense or an international peacekeeping effort. The Supreme Court declared that the nation's SELECTIVE SERVICE ACT OF 1967, which allowed exemption from service only for those "conscientiously opposed to participation in war in any form," not for those opposed to a particular war, did not violate constitutional protections of the free exercise of religion and prohibitions against the establishment of religion.

Further reading: The United States Supreme Court Case, *Gillette v. United States, 401 US 437 (1971),* FindLaw, available online at http://laws.findlaw.com/us/401/437.html.

Gin Act of 1736

The British Parliament's unsuccessful attempt in 1736 to control the gin trade by levying taxes on retailed gin and increasing the license fees for retailers. Gin consumption had reached addictive proportions, particularly among the poor in London, which had nearly 7,000 unlicensed gin shops. Sir Joseph Jekyll, who proposed the taxes, suggested a duty of 20 shillings for every gallon of gin sold retail and an annual license fee of £50 for retailers. It was not until the GIN ACT OF 1751, however, that Parliament was able to successfully curb the excessive drinking of spirits.

Further reading: *A Short History of the Gin Act . . .* (New Haven, Conn.: Research Publications, 1974); Jessica Warner, "Can Legislation Prevent Debauchery? Mother Gin and Public Health in 18th-Century England," *American Journal of Public Health* 91, no. 3 (March 2001): 375–84.

Gin Act of 1751

Legislation by the British Parliament in 1751 to curb the excessive drinking of spirits (particularly gin, which was cheap) by increasing the taxes on spirits and the license fees for retailers. Public pressure had been aroused by an active campaign depicting the evils of excessive drinking, as in Hogarth's engraving *Gin Lane.* Retail licenses were disallowed in the poorer sections of London and in prisons or correction houses, and penalties for any offense (such as unlicensed selling) were strictly imposed. Distillers and retailers of spirits could not officiate as justices of the peace or shield any offenders.

Further reading: Jessica Warner, "Can Legislation Prevent Debauchery? Mother Gin and Public Health in 18th-Century England," *American Journal of Public Health* 91, no. 3 (March 2001): 375–84.

Gitlow v. People of New York

U.S. Supreme Court decision issued on June 8, 1925, concerning freedom of speech. The case involved the conviction of Benjamin Gitlow and three associates for violation of the New York Criminal Anarchy Act of 1902, for publishing a manifesto that advocated the overthrow of the government by force, violence, or other unlawful means. The Court ruled that the advocacy of anarchy was so dangerous and "inimical to the general welfare" that the state was justified in prohibiting it to preserve the public peace. But the court also established that the free-speech protections of the FIRST AMENDMENT, formerly applied only against congressional action, could not be impaired by the states because of the due-process protections of "liberty" in the FOURTEENTH AMENDMENT.

Further reading: Zechariah Chafee, *Free Speech in the United States* (Cambridge, Mass.: Harvard University Press, 1941); Leonard W. Levy and Kenneth L. Karst, eds., *Encyclopedia of the American Constitution* 2d ed. (New York: Macmillan Reference, 2000).

"Give Me Liberty" Speech

Address delivered by American colonial leader Patrick Henry to the second Virginia Convention, on March 23, 1775, in St. John's Church, Richmond. Henry addressed the reluctance of many in the colonies to confront the probability of armed conflict with Britain. He argued that hope for the peaceful resolution of differences with Britain was futile, pointed to Britain's preparations for war, and urged that the colonists arm and organize themselves without delay. The speech ended with these memorable words: "Is life so dear, or peace so sweet, as to be purchased at the price of chains and slavery? Forbid it, Almighty God! I know not what course others may take; but as for me, give me liberty or give me death!"

Further reading: William Wirt Henry, *Patrick Henry: Life, Correspondence and Speeches* (New York: B. Franklin, 1969); David A. McCants, *Patrick Henry, the Orator* (New York: Greenwood Press, 1990).

Gladstone's Act of 1881

See IRISH LAND ACT OF 1881.

Glamorgan, Treaty of

Treaty concluded between Ireland's Roman Catholics and the earl of Glamorgan (on behalf of England's king Charles I) in 1644, by which the restrictions of POYNINGS'S LAWS were to be withdrawn, a general amnesty granted, and the period of questioning for land titles narrowed down. In addition to these published terms, there was also a secret treaty, which allowed the Catholics the right of public worship in churches not occupied by the state church. In return, the Irish Catholics were to provide 10,000 men for the king's army in England, paid for out of church revenues.

Further reading: John H. Round, *Studies in Peerage and Family History* (Zug, Switzerland: Inter Documentation Co., 1983).

Glass-Owen Act   See FEDERAL RESERVE ACT OF 1913, U.S.

Glass-Steagall Banking Act   See BANKING ACT OF 1933, U.S.

Glen Grey Act   Act by South Africa's Cape Parliament (August 1894) introducing a native policy meant initially for the Glen Grey district of the eastern Cape, but visualized by its author, Cecil Rhodes, as a "Bill for Africa." In 1898, it was extended to the Transkei region. Small individual plots based on the one-man, one-lot principle replaced communal land tenure, leaving many landless and protesting. But plot ownership did not qualify one for a vote in the Cape colony. Anyone not gainfully employed for at least three months in the year had to pay an annual tax of 10 shillings, a provision withdrawn in 1905. District councils were set up to encourage limited African participation in local government. There was widespread resistance to the act, and its application to other areas was restricted. Its importance lay in its creation of segregated African townships that supplied mining and industrial centers in South Africa with a migrant labor force through the first half of the 20th century.

Further reading: Winifred A. Maxwell and J. A. Benyon, *Studies in Local History: Essays in Honour of Professor Winifred Maxwell* (New York: Oxford University Press, 1976); Antony Thomas, *Rhodes* (New York: St. Martin's Press, 1997).

Godunov's Decree of 1597   Official order made by Boris Godunov, chief adviser and brother-in-law of Czar Feodor I of Russia, granting gentry landowners (masters) five years to recover fugitive peasants (serfs) who had escaped within the last five years. It permitted peasants who had fled from their masters five or more years earlier to be free thenceforth. The 1597 decree reflected the insecure status of the peasant (who, as a servant of the state, had no rights) and was reconfirmed several times until the promulgation of the RUSSIAN NEW CODE OF 1649, which revoked all possibility of freedom for peasants.

Further reading: Stephen Graham, *Boris Godunov* (Hamden, Conn.: Archon Books, 1970); S. F. Platonov and John T. Alexander, *Boris Godunov, Tsar of Russia* (Gulf Breeze, Fla.: Academic International Press, 1973).

Golden Bull of 1356   Bull issued by Holy Roman Emperor Charles IV, king of Germany and Bohemia, in 1356, in which he set down guidelines for future elections to the imperial throne. Specifically, he affirmed the validity of election by majority vote, already affirmed in the Declaration of RHENS. In addition, the indivisibility of the electors' territories was declared; the number of electors was fixed at seven; the body was to consist of three clerical and four secular electors; and the place of election and coronation was stated. The issue of papal confirmation of elections was not addressed.

Further reading: Paul Halsall, *Medieval Source Book: The Golden Bull of Charles IV 1356*, internet Medieval sourcebook, available online at http://www.fordham.edu/halsall/source/goldenbull.html.

Golden Bull of Eger (Golden Bull of 1213)   Statement in 1213 by Frederick II, king of Germany and of Sicily, giving control of the German church to Pope Innocent III, who was aiding the former in his ambitions to be crowned Holy Roman Emperor. Frederick renounced all control held by secular authority in Germany over the German clergy, granting to the German Church the free election of bishops and the right of appeal to Rome (the Pope) in case of conflict.

Further reading: David Abulafia, *Frederick II: A Medieval Emperor* (London: Pimlico, 2002); John C. Moore and Brenda Bolton, *Pope Innocent III and His World* (Brookfield, Vt.: Ashgate, 1999).

Golden Bull of Hungary (Golden Bull of 1222, Magna Carta of Hungary)   Charter of liberty issued reluctantly by King Andrew II of Hungary in 1222, guaranteeing rights and privileges to the nobility and clergy and limiting powers of the king. Compared often to England's MAGNA CARTA, the royal charter forced the king to summon a diet (national assembly) every year at which grievances could be heard, prohibited the imprisonment of nobles and clergy without a proper imperial trial, exempted the nobles' and ecclesiastical estates from taxation, and denied foreigners the right to own landed estates (in 1231 a provision was added that forbade Jews and Muslims from holding public offices and lands). In addition, the nobility was not required to assist the king in his military endeavors abroad, but was obligated in cases of foreign invasion. Among several provisions of lesser importance in the charter was the king's right to enter houses and villages of the nobles only at their invitation.

Further reading: Michael J. Horvath, *Golden Bull (Bulla Aurea), 1222, of Hungary and the Magna Carta, 1215; . . .* (College Park: University of Maryland Library, 1972).

Golden Bull of Rimini   Imperial order issued by Holy Roman Emperor Frederick II, king of Sicily, in March 1226, awarding to the grand master of the Teutonic Knights, Hermann von Salza, sovereign rights over the territory of the heathen Prussians. The knights, a Germanic crusading order, were granted Kulmerland in Poland as a territorial base and organized as Christian missionaries on the empire's eastern frontier. Earlier they had been summoned by the Polish duke of Masovia to help protect his lands from pagan

Prussians and others and to aid in the conversion of the pagans to Christianity.

Further reading: Helen Nicholson, trans., School of History and Archaeology, *Documents Relating to the Baltic Crusade, 1199–1266,* Cardiff University, available online at http://www.cf.ac.uk/hisar/people/hn/MilitaryOrders/TEUTONIC.html.

Golden Bull of Sicily

Charter issued by Frederick II, the German king and also king of Sicily, recognizing the political autonomy of Bohemia in 1212. It conferred on Ottokar I and his heirs the title of king of Bohemia, as well as the right to invest the bishop of Prague, the latter having been solely an imperial right. Frederick also renounced his right to ratify each succession to the Bohemian crown. Ottokar was also released from the obligation of attending imperial diets, except when held in certain cities near his western border; in return, he was to supply Frederick with 300 horsemen to accompany him to his coronation at Mainz as king of Germany, an act promoted by Pope Innocent III.

Further reading: David Abulafia, *Frederick II: A Medieval Emperor* (London: Pimlico, 2002); John C. Moore and Brenda Bolton, *Pope Innocent III and His World* (Brookfield, Vt.: Ashgate, 1999).

Golden Law, Brazilian (Lei Aurea)

Law abolishing slavery in Brazil, passed by both houses of the General Assembly and sanctioned by Princess Isabel of Brazil on May 13, 1888. Superseding earlier slavery legislation (see also FREE BIRTH LAW), the Golden Law simply stated that from the date of passage, slavery in Brazil would be eradicated and that all enactments to the contrary would be revoked. From the slaveowners' viewpoint, the law was a practical recognition that ending the slave system was the only viable solution to the national crises sparked by abolitionist unrest; practical or not, bitterness among slave owners (who received no compensation for lost slaves) contributed to the fall of the Brazilian empire 18 months later.

See also: BRAZILIAN CONSTITUTION OF 1891.

Further reading: Paul Finkelman and Joseph C. Miller, eds., *Macmillan Encyclopedia of World Slavery* (New York: Simon & Schuster Macmillan, 1998); Junius P. Rodriguez, ed., *Chronology of World Slavery* (Santa Barbara, Calif.: ABC-Clio, 1999).

Gold Repeal Resolution, U.S.

Joint resolution of the U.S. Congress, passed on June 5, 1933, that canceled the clause in government and private obligations (for example, currency, bonds, and contracts) that called for payment of principal and interest in gold (or dollars with a gold content of 23.22 grains). It marked the nation's break from the gold standard (from tying the money supply to the amount of gold held in reserve by the U.S. Treasury). Contracts and debts were made payable in legal tender.

Further reading: Henry Steele Commager, ed., *Documents of American History,* 8th ed. (New York: Appleton-Century-Crofts, 1968); Barry J. Eichengreen, *The Gold-Exchange Standard and the Great Depression* (Cambridge, Mass.: National Bureau of Economic Research, 1987).

Gold Reserve Act of 1934, U.S.

Federal legislation enacted on January 30, 1934, that removed the United States from a full gold standard and placed it on a modified one. The act empowered the president to reduce the gold content of the dollar to between 50 percent and 60 percent of its former weight, and to change that value within those limits as necessary. It made the government the sole legal owner of monetary gold, prohibiting the domestic use of gold as money, the redemption of dollars in gold, and individual gold holdings (except under federal license for specified purposes). While gold remained the currency reserve, not every dollar had to be fully backed by that metal. The act also established a stabilization fund to balance international payments. On January 31 President Franklin D. Roosevelt used the authority of this act to fix the value of the gold dollar at 59¢.

Further reading: Leonard W. Levy and Kenneth L. Karst, eds., *Encyclopedia of the American Constitution,* 2d ed. (New York: Macmillan Reference, 2000).

Gold Standard Act of 1900, U.S.

Federal legislation of March 14, 1900, that placed the United States on the gold standard, after years of controversy over bimetallism and the coinage of silver. The act declared that the dollar, consisting of 25.8 grains of gold, nine-tenths fine, would be the standard unit of value, and that all forms of money issued or coined by the United States should be maintained at a parity of value with this standard. The act established a gold reserve of $150 million for the redemption of legal tender notes.

Further reading: Thomas Carson, ed., *Gale Encyclopedia of U.S. Economic History* (Farmington Hills, Mich.: Gale Group, 1999).

Goldwater's "Extremism in Defense of Liberty" Speech

Address delivered to the Republican Party convention by U.S. senator Barry Goldwater of Arizona on July 16, 1964, accepting the party's presidential nomination. Goldwater, an economic conservative and staunch anticommunist, responded to accusations that he was a right-wing extremist by declaring that "extremism in the defense of liberty is no vice" and "moderation in the pursuit of justice is no virtue." He blamed the Democratic Party for communist gains in Cuba, Europe, and Southeast Asia, as well as for violence and corruption in the United States. His uncompromising speech set the tone for his campaign, and Goldwater was soundly defeated by Lyndon B. Johnson.

Further reading: Barry M. Goldwater, *With No Apologies: The Personal and Political Memoirs of United States Senator Barry M. Goldwater* (New York: Morrow, 1979).

Gondra Treaty   Treaty proposed by Manuel Gondra (a distinguished jurist) of Paraguay at the Fifth Pan-American Conference held in 1923 at Santiago, Chile. The treaty provided that all inter-American controversies that could not be settled by diplomatic negotiations be submitted to a commission of inquiry for investigation and report. No hostile action was to be taken until six months after the commission's report had been completed. Two such commissions, one to be established in Washington, D.C., and one at Montevideo, were to report within one year from the date of the first meeting; these reports, though not final, would be given serious consideration. Although it attempted to provide a conciliatory organ until such time as the disputing parties could set up a conciliatory commission of their own, the treaty failed to be ratified in many of the participating states.

Further reading: *Fifth Pan American Conference at Santiago, Chile, March 25, 1923* (New York: Chile-American Association, 1923).

Good Friday Agreement (Northern Ireland Peace Agreement)   Momentous accord reached on April 10, 1998 (Good Friday), between Northern Ireland and the Irish Republic (and later overwhelmingly ratified by voters in both), creating a democratic framework for lasting peace in Northern Ireland. Built around the principle of self-determination for the people of Northern Ireland, the agreement proposed modifications in the constitutions of the United Kingdom and the Irish Republic. It established an elected Northern Ireland Assembly, an Equality Commission, a North/South Council, and various other commissions to resolve controversial issues such as police reform, decommissioning, and the release of political prisoners. Also, the European Convention on Human Rights would be deemed applicable to Northern Ireland.

Further reading: Jack Holland, *Hope Against History—The Course of Conflict in Northern Ireland* (New York: Henry Holt, 1999); George J. Mitchell, *Making Peace* (New York: Alfred A. Knopf, 1999).

Good Parliament, Acts of the   Measures taken by England's Good Parliament of April–July 1376, demanding that aging King Edward III's councillors and his mistress, Alice Perrers, be removed because of corruption and that certain royal financiers be duly punished for profiting at public expense. Peter de la Mare, the first elected speaker of the House of Commons, helped prosecute and impeach Perrers and royal officials (Lords Latimer, Lyons, and others) before the House of Lords (the first such impeachment in English history). However, later in 1376, the great council repealed the Good Parliament's acts; Perrers was returned to court; de la Mare was imprisoned; and the new councillors were dismissed. The acts were nullified by the Parliament of 1377, and John of Gaunt (Edward III's fourth son) resumed virtual dominance of England's government.

Further reading: James Bothwell, *The Age of Edward III* (Rochester, N.Y.: York Medieval Press, 2001); F. George Kay, *Lady of the Sun; the Life and Times of Alice Perrers* (New York: Barnes & Noble, 1966); Anil de Silva-Vigier, *This Moste Highe Prince—John of Gaunt, 1340–1399* (Edinburgh, Scotland: Pentland, 1992).

Gorbachev's United Nations Speech of 1988   Speech delivered by Mikhail Gorbachev, leader of the Soviet Union, to the United Nations General Assembly in New York City on December 7, 1988, containing his country's announcement that it would unilaterally and unconditionally reduce the size of its conventional forces in Eastern Europe and Mongolia. Gorbachev stated that the move would consist of a reduction in Soviet military forces by 500,000 troops (of which 50,000 would be withdrawn from Eastern Europe), 10,000 tanks, 8,500 artillery systems, and 800 combat aircraft by 1991. The Soviet leader also expressed the hope that the United States and the Western European nations would respond accordingly; he stated that the forces remaining in Eastern Europe were to become purely defensive in nature. Although the WARSAW PACT outnumbered the NORTH ATLANTIC TREATY Organization in conventional forces, U.S. and Western European authorities welcomed the move, which many analysts saw as a response, at least in part, to the Soviet leadership's realization that the Soviet economy had been less and less able to sustain high military spending.

Further reading: Mikhail Gorbachev, *A Road to the Future: Complete Text of the Dec. 7, 1988 United Nations Address* (Santa Fe, N.M.: Ocean Tree Books, 1991).

Gore-McLemore Resolution   Resolution introduced into the U.S. Congress in February 1916, declaring that all U.S. citizens, to protect their own safety and the national interest, should "forbear to . . . travel as passengers on any armed vessel of any belligerent power" and that the secretary of state should refuse to issue passports to Americans seeking passage on such vessels. The resolution, introduced by U.S. representative Jeff McLemore and Senator Thomas P. Gore following Germany's declaration that it would sink all armed enemy merchant ships without warning, was intended to prevent the United States from being drawn into World War I (1914–18). Under pressure from President Woodrow Wilson, who opposed the measure as an infringement on U.S. rights and sovereignty, the Senate tabled the measure on March 3 and the House followed on March 7.

Further reading: Stephen A. Flanders and Carl N. Flanders, *Dictionary of American Foreign Affairs* (New York: Macmillan, 1993).

"Gospel of Wealth"   See CARNEGIE'S "WEALTH" ARTICLE.

Government of India Act of 1858   British parliamentary legislation of August 2, 1858, by which the British East

India Company (dissolved in 1874) surrendered its administrative duties in India to the crown. India's governor general assumed the additional title of viceroy and had to report directly to the secretary of state for India (he replaced the Board of Control and Court of Directors) in the British cabinet. The secretary was to be assisted by a Council of India, of whose 15 members eight were to be crown appointees and seven elected by the East India Company's directors. The council had to carry out the policies made for India in the United Kingdom. The crown also took over the company's defense forces. Lord Stanley, who had pushed many of these measures through the Commons, was appointed the first secretary of state.

Further reading: Ainslie T. Embree, ed., *Encyclopedia of Asian History,* 4 vols. (New York: Charles Scribner's Sons, 1988).

Government of India Act of 1784 See PITT'S INDIA ACT.

Government of India Act of 1935

Legislation passed by the British Parliament on August 2, 1935, formulating a new constitution for British India on the basis of discussions held during the Round Table Conferences (1930–33). It separated Burma and Aden (South Yemen) from India and divided the rest of India into 11 largely autonomous provinces, each administered by a governor and his executive council (both appointed) and an elected legislature (bicameral in six provinces, unicameral in five) with ministers responsible to it. Centrally, it envisaged the creation of an All-India Federation including these provinces and at least half of the princely states, followed by a Delhi-based bicameral legislature. This would consist of a council of state (34 elected and 26 nominated members) and a legislative assembly (105 members elected by the provincial assemblies and 40 nominated members). Federal ministers would handle all but defense and foreign affairs, which the governor general would continue to control. The act was opposed by India's Congress and the princely states. The British Parliament's longest statute ever, it was the last milestone on the road to Indian independence.

See also: INDIAN INDEPENDENCE ACT, BRITISH.

Further reading: Ainslie T. Embree, ed., *Encyclopedia of Asian History,* 4 vols. (New York: Charles Scribner's Sons, 1988).

Government of Ireland Act (Better Government of Ireland Act)

Law by the British Parliament (1920) that partitioned Ireland to form two self-governing areas (Northern and Southern Ireland), administered by separate parliaments. A newly established Council of Ireland was to address common concerns, while Westminister (British Parliament) would have 42 Irish members. It was an extension of the HOME RULE BILL OF 1913, with partition as an added incentive to appease the Ulster separatists. Following elections in May 1921, the Parliament of Northern Ireland was formally inaugurated on June 22. The act had almost no impact on southern Ireland, where Sinn Fein's boycott of the elections ensured that all its candidates were returned unopposed. Its Parliament was adjourned, since only four Unionist members (representing the colleges) were present. It met again but only to dissolve itself. Prolonged negotiations resulted in the signing of the ANGLO-IRISH TREATY OF 1921.

Further reading: Christopher Haigh, ed., *The Cambridge Historical Encyclopedia of Great Britain and Ireland* (Cambridge, England: Cambridge University Press, 1985); D. J. Hickey and J. E. Doherty, *A Dictionary of Irish History since 1800* (Dublin: Gill & Macmillan, 1980).

Grace, Edict, or Peace, of See ALAIS, PEACE OF.

Grace Commission Report

Report prepared by the U.S. president's Private Sector Survey on Cost Control (headed by New York industrialist J. Peter Grace) and accepted by President Ronald W. Reagan on January 16, 1984; it contained 2,478 recommendations, which, according to the report, could save the U.S. government $424.4 billion over three years simply by eliminating waste and inefficiency. The report stated, for example, that substantial savings could be made by reducing civil service and military retirement benefits, and that the savings could be made without placing an unreasonable burden on recipients because such benefits were already several times higher than the best plans found in the private sector. The report stated further that savings could be made in all government programs, including defense and social welfare programs, without reducing their effectiveness. Many criticized the report because the majority of the proposals required congressional approval, and thus were ineffectual in the short term.

Further reading: William R. Kennedy, Jr., and Robert W. Lee, *A Taxpayer Survey of the Grace Commission Report* (Ottawa, Ill.: Green Hill Publishers, 1984); Charles Levine, *The Unfinished Agenda of Civil Service Reform: Implications of the Grace Commission Report* (Washington, D.C.: Brookings Institution, 1985).

Gramm-Rudman-Hollings Act

U.S. legislation sponsored by Senators Phil Gramm of Texas, Warren Rudman of New Hampshire, and Ernest Hollings of South Carolina and passed by both houses of Congress on December 11, 1985, and then signed into law by President Ronald Reagan, it required the president and Congress to work together to eliminate the budget deficit by 1991. The bill stipulated that the president's administration and Congress agree each year on budget cuts that would meet successively lower targets, which were also specified by the bill. If the cuts were made accordingly, the deficit was to reach zero by 1991. The law also stipulated that, if agreement was not reached, automatic reductions would be implemented. The legislation also set the national debt ceiling at over $2 trillion.

Further reading: Leonard W. Levy and Kenneth L. Karst, eds. *Encyclopedia of the American Constitution,* 2d ed. (New York: Macmillan Reference, 2000); Bernard Reams, Jr., *Deficit Control and the Gramm-Rudman-Hollings Act—The Legislative History of the Balanced Budget and Emergency Deficit Control Act of 1985* (Buffalo, N.Y.: William S. Hein, 1986).

Grand Alliance of 1689

Offensive alliance formed against King Louis XIV of France in Vienna on May 12, 1689, when England and Holland joined the defensive League of Augsburg (formed in 1686), consisting of Austria, Spain, Savoy, Brandenburg, Bavaria, Saxony, and Hanover. Secretly supported by the pope, the alliance was provoked by Louis XIV's invasion of the Palatinate and sought to annul his territorial gains secured by the 1684 Truce of REGENSBURG. It relied heavily on the naval strength of England and Holland to overpower Louis XIV. They were to maintain three naval squadrons—one each in the Mediterranean and Irish Seas and in the English Channel. England was also to position an army of 8,000 in the Netherlands—the chief scene of the land wars. A secret clause supported the Austrian emperor's claims to the Spanish territories after the death of King Charles II of Spain. Louis XIV managed to overpower the allies on land and at sea, and peace was not restored until 1697.

See also: RYSWICK, TREATY OF.

Further reading: Vincent Cronin, *Louis XIV* (Boston: Houghton Mifflin, 1965); Olivier Bernier, *Louis XIV: A Royal Life* (New York: Doubleday, 1987); John B. Wolf, *Louis XIV* (New York: W. W. Norton, 1974).

Grand Alliance of 1701

Alliance of September 7, 1701, among England, Austria, and the Dutch republic (later joined by Prussia, Portugal, and Savoy), mainly to prevent the union of the French and Spanish crowns. According to its terms, the allies were to recover Spanish possessions in the Dutch republic as a protective barrier between France and the republic, seize Spanish territories in the Indies and prevent France from having any trading rights there, and capture the duchy of Milan and its dependencies for the Austrian emperor. Once the War of the Spanish Succession (1701–14) began, no country was allowed to make peace with the enemy unless by a joint effort and until the subjects of Great Britain and the Dutch republic were restored with the "privileges, rights, immunities and franchises of commerce by sea and land," which they had enjoyed during the reign of the former king of Spain. Special precautions were to be taken so that France and Spain would never "be united under the same government, nor that one and the same person shall be king of both kingdoms." This defensive alliance was to be maintained in war and peace and was open to "all kings, princes, and states that please to have a concern for the general peace."

See also: BARRIER TREATIES.

Further reading: Harold V. Livermore, *A History of Spain* (London: George Allen & Unwin, 1966).

Grand Alliance of 1813 (Sixth and Last Coalition against Napoléon)

Alliance of European states against Napoleonic France, beginning with the Treaty of KALISCH in February 1813, which brought together Prussia and Russia with Britain's support, joined later by Sweden, Austria (August 1813), Bavaria, Württemberg, and Saxony (all in October 1813). Pooling their resources, the allies started expelling Napoléon's troops from their territories. Naples and Denmark joined in January 1814. Joseph Bonaparte's defeat in Spain (see BAYONNE, TREATY OF) by the duke of Wellington's forces created an opening for the allies in southern France. Napoléon offered to restore Ferdinand VII to the Spanish throne if Spain remained neutral, but continued his delaying tactics in negotiations with Austria and Prussia. On March 1, 1814, the coalition's big powers renewed their commitments and coordinated their strategies through the Treaties of CHAUMONT. Routed and facing opposition in France and abroad, Napoléon finally abdicated (April 11, 1814) and was exiled to Elba.

Further reading: Georges Lefebvre, *Napoleon: From Tilsit to Waterloo, 1807–1815* (New York: Columbia University Press, 1969); Alan Palmer, *An Encyclopedia of Napoleon's Europe* (New York: St. Martin's, 1984).

Grand Remonstrance

Grievances presented by the English Long Parliament to King Charles I on December 1, 1641, listing in 206 clauses "all the illegal things that had been done by the King from the first hour of his coming to the crown to that minute." Among the grievances were the war against the French Protestants, the cruelties of the Star Chamber and the High Commission, the ship-money duties, the innovations in the church, and the forced imposition of episcopacy on the Scots and the Irish. Drafted by Puritan and parliamentarian leader John Pym, the Remonstrance asked that the appointment of ministers be subject to Parliament's approval and that the church be reformed according to the suggestions of the Westminster Assembly of Divines. It was violently debated in the House of Commons and passed on November 22 by a narrow margin of 159 to 148 votes. The king rejected the charges and tried, without success, to arrest opposition leaders in the Commons. The Parliament and the king drifted even further apart, and this eventually hastened the beginning of the English Civil Wars (1642–51).

Further reading: Sidney R. Brett, *John Pym, 1583–1643: The Statesman of the Puritan Revolution* (London: J. Murray, 1976); Henry L. Schoolcraft, *The Genesis of the Grand Remonstrance from Parliament to King Charles I* (Urbana, Ill.: University Press, 1902).

Granger Laws

Term applied to various state laws, the first among them passed by Illinois, Iowa, Wisconsin, and Minnesota between 1869 and 1874, to regulate railroads and warehouses within their own borders. Many of the laws set or authorized maximum railroad rates and some established state regulatory commissions. Other laws were designed to prevent abuses by warehousers and grain elevator operators. The early laws were followed by stronger legislation in these and most other states by the mid-1870s as the grange movement, uniting farmers against monopolistic business interests, grew. These laws were challenged in court by the railroad companies in the Granger Cases (see *MUNN V. ILLINOIS*).

Further reading: Leonard W. Levy and Kenneth L. Karst, eds. *Encyclopedia of the American Constitution*, 2d ed. (New York: Macmillan Reference, 2000); George Hall Miller, *Railroads and the Granger Laws* (Madison: University of Wisconsin Press, 1971).

Grant's First Inaugural Address

Speech delivered by Ulysses S. Grant on March 4, 1869, at his inauguration as 18th president of the United States. As the Republican nominee, the Civil War hero Grant had campaigned on the slogan "Let us have peace," a theme that he repeated in his inaugural call for a calm approach to settling sectional differences "without prejudice, hate, or sectional pride." He called for payment of government war debts in gold, not the greenback currency issued during the Civil War, and urged a return to a specie basis as soon as possible. He also urged the ratification of the FIFTEENTH AMENDMENT, which prohibited states from denying the vote to blacks.

Further reading: Grolier Incorporated, *Ulysses S. Grant First Inaugural Address, Thursday, March 4, 1869*, Grolier Presents The American Presidency, available online at http://ap.grolier.com/article?assetid=apia022&templatename=/article/article.html.

Grant's Order No. 11

Order issued by General Ulysses S. Grant on December 17, 1862, expelling "Jews, as a class" from the Department of Tennessee. The Jews, expelled without trial or hearing for alleged violations of trade regulations, were ordered to leave within 24 hours. The order was issued in an attempt to stem illicit cotton and gold trade and war profiteering, for which Grant blamed Jewish traders in part. A storm of protest soon erupted in Washington. President Abraham Lincoln ordered the general in chief of the army Henry W. Halleck to cancel the order, which was done on January 6, 1863. (Halleck later noted that the expulsion of Jewish traders, rather than all Jews, would have been acceptable.) The order became an issue again in the election of 1868, when Grant was the Republican nominee for the presidency.

Further reading: The American-Israeli Cooperative Enterprise, *Judaic Treasures of the Library of Congress: Order No. 11*, Jewish Virtual Library, A Division of the American-Israeli Cooperative Enterprise, available online at http://www.us-israel.org/jsource/loc/abe2.html.

Granville Circular

Notice of January 3, 1883, in which the British foreign secretary, Lord (George Leveson-Gower) Granville, outlined (for the benefit of the European powers) Britain's intentions regarding Egypt following her victory over Arabi's Egyptian forces at the battle of Tel-el-Kebir (September 13, 1882). Despite the GAMBETTA NOTE, France had not taken any part in the action. Granville nevertheless proposed a joint Anglo-French supervision over Egyptian affairs. The offer was declined, so Granville drafted the circular expressing Britain's desire to withdraw her forces from Egypt "as soon as the state of the country and the organization of proper means for the maintenance of the khedievial authority will admit of it." As a definition of British policy in the region, it was to remain unchanged for nearly a quarter of a century.

Further reading: Edmond G. Petty-Fitzmaurice, *The Life of Granville: George Leveson Gower, Second Earl Granville, K. G., 1815–1891*, 2d ed. (New York: Longmans, Green, 1979).

Gratian, Decretal of

See DECRETAL OF GRATIAN.

Graves v. New York ex rel. O'Keefe

U.S. Supreme Court decision issued on March 27, 1939, that denied immunity from state taxation to federal employees; it declared that such taxation did not represent an unconstitutional burden upon the federal government. O'Keefe, an employee of the federal Home Owners' Loan Corporation, sought an income tax refund from New York State on the grounds that his salary, paid by the U.S. government, was exempt under a long-standing practice of intergovernmental tax immunity. The Supreme Court stated that the taxpayer is not "clothed with the implied constitutional tax immunity of the government by which he is employed." The decision gave both federal and state governments large potential sources of new revenues.

Further reading: Leonard W. Levy and Kenneth L. Karst, eds., *Encyclopedia of the American Constitution* 2d ed. (New York: Macmillan Reference, 2000).

Great Compromise (Connecticut Compromise)

Plan reported to the United States's Federal Constitutional Convention on July 5, 1787, by the Committee of Eleven. Advanced by Roger Sherman and Oliver Ellsworth, both from Connecticut, the plan was debated, amended, and adopted by the convention on July 16. In its final form, it provided for a bicameral legislature with each state's representation in the lower house to be proportional to its population (and based on the total white population and three-fifths of the black population) and each state having equal representation in the upper house. The Great Compromise largely resolved the differences among the smaller states, which had favored the NEW JERSEY PLAN, and the larger states, whose interests had been reflected in the VIRGINIA PLAN.

Further reading: Irving Brant, *James Madison: Father of the Constitution, 1787–1800* (Indianapolis, Ind.: Bobbs-Merrill, 1950); Leonard W. Levy and Kenneth L. Karst, eds.,

Encyclopedia of the American Constitution, 2d ed. (New York: Macmillan Reference, 2000).

Great Ordinance, French   See FRENCH ORDINANCE OF 1357.

Great Protestation

Protest recorded in the *Journal* of the House of Commons on December 18, 1621, over the refusal of King James I of England to allow Parliament to dictate terms in matters of foreign policy and royal marriages, which were traditionally under his exclusive control. In the hope of annexing Spain, James was trying for a Spanish alliance for his son Charles (later King Charles I), but Parliament wanted him to declare war on Spain and find a Protestant wife for his son. The House of Commons protested "that the arduous and urgent affairs concerning the king, state, and defense of the realm . . . are proper subjects and matter of council and debate in parliament." An incensed King James tore out this protestation from the *Journal*, dissolved Parliament (February 8, 1622), and promptly imprisoned Southampton, Coke, Pym, and Selden (leaders of the opposition).

Further reading: Sidney R. Brett, *John Pym, 1583–1643: The Statesman of the Puritan Revolution* (London: J. Murray, 1976).

Greeley's "Prayer" (The Prayer of Twenty Millions)

Open letter addressed to U.S. president Abraham Lincoln by Horace Greeley, founder and editor of the *New York Tribune*, published in that newspaper on August 19, 1862. An ardent foe of slavery, Greeley exhorted Lincoln to commit himself to emancipation. He urged Lincoln to enforce strictly the provisions of the CONFISCATION ACT OF 1862 and to ignore the influence of proslavery "fossil politicians" from the border states. Greeley argued that the Union's efforts were suffering from mistaken deference to rebel slavery. He opposed any concessions to or temporizing with armed traitors. In reply (see LINCOLN'S LETTER TO GREELEY), the president stressed that his goal was to save the Union.

Further reading: Harlan Hoyt Horner, *Lincoln and Greeley* (Chicago: University of Illinois Press, 1953).

Green v. Frazier

U.S. Supreme Court decision, issued on June 1, 1920, that established a new criterion for determining whether a state tax serves a "public purpose." The case involved North Dakota's use of tax funds to create such publicly owned facilities as banks and grain elevators. Although earlier Supreme Court determinations had been independent of the state agencies, the Court here ruled that where the public purpose of the expenditures was agreed to by the "united action of the people, legislature and court," the federal court could not interfere unless constitutional rights had clearly been violated.

Further reading: Henry Steele Commager, ed., *Documents of American History*, 8th ed. (New York: Appleton-Century-Crofts, 1968); United States Supreme Court, *United States Reports: Cases Adjudged in the Supreme Court at . . . and Rules Announced at . . .* (New York: Banks & Brothers, Law Publishers, 1884–1921; Washington, D.C.: Government Printing Office, 1922–).

Greenville, Treaty of

Agreement signed on August 3, 1795, at Fort Greenville (now Greenville, Ohio) by U.S. general Anthony Wayne and the leaders of 12 Indian tribes; it opened part of the Northwest Territory to white settlement. Indian parties to the agreement included the Delaware, Shawnee, Wyandot, and Miami Confederacy. The treaty followed Wayne's decisive victory over the Indians at the battle of Fallen Timbers the previous year. For a payment of $20,000 in trade goods and an annual sum of $9,500 the Indians ceded to the United States much of present-day Ohio and southeastern Indiana, as well as the sites of Chicago and Detroit. The Indians agreed to move westward and settlers poured into the area.

Further reading: The University of Oklahoma College of Law, *Treaty of Greenville*, The University of Oklahoma law center, available online at http://www.law.ou.edu/hist/greenvil.html.

Gregory VII's Decree Deposing Henry IV

Decree written in February 1076 by Pope Gregory VII, in which the pope excommunicated the German king Henry IV, deposed him, and released all his subjects from obedience to him. Gregory found Henry guilty of communicating with officials who were out of favor with the Roman Catholic Church, of contempt for the pope's warnings, and of disturbing the unity of the Catholic Church through his attacks on the pope in his letter of 1076. Those who had been forced into signing Henry's letter to the pope (see HENRY IV'S REPLY TO GREGORY VII), in which the former had ordered the pope to step down from the papal throne, were given the opportunity to make peace with the church. Those who supported Henry were also excommunicated from communion with the Roman Catholic Church.

Further reading: Ephraim Emerton, trans., *The Correspondence of Pope Gregory VII* (New York: Columbia University Press, 1932, repr., 1990); Friedrich Kempf et al., eds., *The Church in the Age of Feudalism* (New York: Crossroad, 1969, repr., 1982).

Gregory VII's Letter Denouncing Henry IV

Letter written in December 1075 by Pope Gregory VII, which reflected the struggle for power between secular authority and the papacy. In the letter Pope Gregory sharply criticized German king Henry IV's preference for a candidate to the archbishopric of Milan over the pope's own candidate. He went on to accuse Henry of knowingly consorting with excommunicated individuals, and of placing certain individuals in church offices without the approval of Rome. Henry was told to seek absolution and indulgence for his transgressions, until which time he was not to receive either divine or apostolic blessing.

See also: HENRY IV'S REPLY TO GREGORY VII.

Further reading: Ephraim Emerton, trans., *The Correspondence of Pope Gregory VII* (New York: Columbia University Press, 1932, reptd., 1990); Friedrich Kempf et al., eds., *The Church in the Age of Feudalism* (New York: Crossroad, 1969, repr., 1982).

Griswold v. Connecticut

U.S. Supreme Court decision, issued on June 7, 1965, that upheld the right of privacy, declaring unconstitutional a Connecticut statute forbidding the use of contraceptives and the dissemination of medical advice on their use. The ruling overturned the conviction of Estelle T. Griswold, executive director of a New Haven planned-parenthood center, who gave contraceptive information to married couples. In its seven-to-two decision, the Supreme Court declared that although the right to marital privacy was not explicitly protected by the U.S. CONSTITUTION, it fell under the "penumbra" of fundamental constitutional guarantees of freedom of association, privacy of the home, protection against self-incrimination, and due process.

Further reading: Leonard W. Levy and Kenneth L. Karst, eds., *Encyclopedia of the American Constitution,* 2d ed. (New York: Macmillan Reference, 2000); Roy M. Mersky, ed., *A Documentary History of the Legal Aspects of Abortion in the United States: Griswold v. Connecticut* (Fred B. Rothman, 2001).

Group Areas Act of 1950, South African

Legislation announced on April 27, 1950, creating separate areas in and around towns and cities for the different races of South Africa, thus forcing thousands to relocate. The natives were the earliest victims of urban segregation; this act included the "colored" races as well. It recognized three main racial categories—white, native (Bantu), and colored (within this, the Asians had their own subgroups); it periodically declared certain areas reserved for particular groups. During the relocation, many lost their businesses and had to commute long distances, community networks were destroyed, and white speculators made quick profits by selling vacated properties. Modeled on the Asiatic Land Tenure Act (1946), this frequently amended act was also used to prevent a range of multiracial activities. Its passage led to protests and racial riots.

See also: FREEDOM CHARTER; PUBLIC SAFETY LAW OF 1953, SOUTH AFRICAN.

Further reading: Wilmot G. James, *Group Areas and the Nature of Apartheid* (Chicago: American Bar Foundation, 1992); Noor Nieftagodien, *The Making of Apartheid in Springs During the Sixties: Group Areas, Urban Restructuring and Resistance* (Johannesburg, South Africa: University of the Witwatersrand, Institute for Advanced Social Research, 1996);

Summary of the Group Areas Act, 1950 (Pretoria, South Africa: Government Printer, 1950).

Group Areas Act of 1973, South African

Extension of the GROUP AREAS ACT OF 1950 via a state presidential proclamation issued on October 5, 1973, to prevent interracial matches from being played at the Aurora Cricket Club in Pietermaritzburg, South Africa. The Group Areas Act was originally introduced to create separate areas for the different races of South Africa. Through frequent amendments, the act was applied to many other fields of activity. The 1973 amendment followed a government announcement (May 28) of a relaxation in sports apartheid (racial segregation) at the national and international levels, while maintaining it at the local and provincial levels. The announcement was made by sports minister Piet Koornhof to enable South Africans to compete in international sporting events.

Further reading: Douglas Booth, *The Race Game: Sport and Politics in South Africa* (London: F. Cass, 1998).

Grove City College v. Bell

U.S. Supreme Court decision issued on February 28, 1984, declaring that if civil rights laws were broken by an institution in connection with a specific program receiving federal funds, only that portion or department actually breaking the law, and not the entire institution, could be denied federal funding. The case involved Pennsylvania's Grove City College, which had accepted no federal financial aid but had a few students with federal loans or grants. The college administrators had refused to file an "assurance of compliance" with Title IX of the Education Amendments of 1972, which prohibited sex discrimination in education programs obtaining federal aid. Though not officially accused of sex discrimination, the accusation had been leveled at the college. The Supreme Court ruled, six to three, that Title IX was enforceable only on programs that specifically receive federal funds.

See also: CIVIL RIGHTS RESTORATION ACT, U.S.

Further reading: Lee Edwards, *Freedom's College: The History of Grove City College* (Washington, D.C.: Regnery, 2000); United States Supreme Court Case, *Grove City College v. Bell, 465 U.S. 555 (1984),* FindLaw, available online at http://laws.findlaw.com/us/465/555.html.

Grzymultowski Peace

See ETERNAL PEACE OF 1686.

Guadalupe-Hidalgo, Treaty of

Treaty signed in Guadalupe-Hidalgo, Mexico, on February 2, 1848, ending the 1846–48 war (over boundary and annexation issues) between the United States and Mexico. By the terms of the treaty, Mexico relinquished California, Nevada, Arizona, New Mexico, and Utah; Mexico was forced to recognize Texas as United States territory as far south as the Rio Grande. The United States, in turn, withdrew American troops from Mexican soil, and paid an indemnity of $15 million for Mexico's loss of about half of her territory; also, the United States agreed to assume U.S. citizens' claims against Mexico, which amounted to $3.25 million. The vast territory acquired by the United States as a result of this treaty is known as the "Mexican Cession."

Further reading: Charles L. Phillips and Alan Axelrod, eds., *Encyclopedia of Historical Treaties and Alliances,* 2 vols. (New York: Facts On File, 2001).

Guarantees, Law of   Law enacted on May 13, 1871, by the Italian government, defining its relationship with the pope, who had lost his lands and temporal power during the unification of Italy. The law granted the pope full liberty to perform his religious functions, to communicate freely with all Roman Catholic bishops, to receive foreign diplomats, and to have fixed use of the Vatican and other papal palaces; he was also to receive an annual salary of 3,250,000 lire from the Italian government. The state, however, claimed the right to confirm the appointments of all bishops. The pope, Pius IX, rejected the law, considering himself "the prisoner of the Vatican."

See also: VICTOR EMMANUEL II'S SPEECH TO THE ITALIAN PARLIAMENT IN 1871.

Further reading: Antonio C. N. Gallenga, *The Pope and the King: The War Between Church and State in Italy* (Cambridge, England: Chadwyck-Healey Ltd., 1989).

Guatemala Accord   See CENTRAL AMERICAN PEACE PLAN.

Guatemalan Constitution of 1965   Constitution promulgated by the Guatemalan Constituent Assembly on September 15, 1965, opening the way for the return of democratic rule in Guatemala. More specifically, the document provided for a representative government divided into independent legislative, judicial, and executive branches; stipulated that elections for the presidency, vice presidency, and congressional and municipal offices were to be held the following March; reduced the presidential term from six to four years; provided for fundamental rights, including freedom of religion, press, and expression and for equality before the law; and declared the army to be nonpolitical. Although the country's earlier constitutions had had similar provisions and had still not prevented military rule, the elections of March 1966 were successful in producing a civilian government.

Further reading: *Constitution of the Republic of Guatemala, 1965* (Washington, D.C.: Pan American Union, 1966).

Guérande, Treaty of   Treaty concluded at Guérande, France, on April 12, 1365, resolving the War of the Breton Succession (1341–65) in favor of John IV of Montfort, following his victory over Charles of Blois in the battle of Auray (September 29, 1364). The settlement was initiated by King Charles V of France (see CALAIS, TREATY OF) in an effort to reestablish the duchy of Brittany under French control; he

appeased Montfort, the English-supported candidate, by recognizing him as the only duke of Brittany. Montfort was, however, required to pay homage to the French crown. For surrendering her claim to the duchy, Joan of Penthièvre was rewarded with the county of Penthièvre in Brittany and a lifetime interest in the viscounty of Limoges.

See also: MALESTROIT, TRUCE OF.

Further reading: Alfred H. Burne, *The Hundred Years' War: A Military History* (London: Penguin, 2002); Robin Neillands, *The Hundred Years War*, rev. ed. (New York: Routledge, 2001).

Guffey-Snyder Bituminous Coal Stabilization Act (Bituminous Coal Conservation Act)   Federal legislation enacted on August 30, 1935, to stabilize prices and establish government regulation of the coal industry. Supported by the United Mine Workers and sponsored by Senator Joseph F. Guffey and Representative John B. Snyder (both from Pennsylvania), it created the Bituminous Coal Labor Board and the National Bituminous Coal Commission to regulate wages and hours, protect collective bargaining rights, set prices, and control production. It levied a 15 percent excise tax on coal producers, though 90 percent of the tax was remitted to producers who voluntarily complied with its code of fair practices. The U.S. Supreme Court declared the act unconstitutional in *Carter* v. *Carter Coal Company* on May 18, 1936. It was replaced by the Guffey-Vinson Act, which contained similar provisions but omitted the wage and hour regulations.

Further reading: Charles E. Halt, *Joseph F. Guffey, New Deal Politician from Pennsylvania* (Ann Arbor, Mich.: University Microfilms, 1966); *Report on the Constitutionality of the Bituminous Coal Conservation Act of 1935* (N.p.: American Liberty League, National Lawyers Committee, 1935); *Wage Agreements, Bituminous Coal Industry, 1935–1937, Together with Guffey-Snyder Coal Stabilization Act and the Appalachian Agreement* (Indianapolis, Ind.: United Mine Workers of America, 1935).

Guffey-Vinson Bituminous Coal Act, U.S.   Federal legislation sponsored by Senator Joseph F. Guffey of Pennsylvania and Representative Frederick M. Vinson of Kentucky and enacted on April 26, 1937, that reenacted the main provisions of the GUFFEY-SNYDER BITUMINOUS COAL STABILIZATION ACT, except for the wage and hour regulations that the U.S. Supreme Court had declared unconstitutional in *Carter* v. *Carter Coal Company* (1936). The act regulated the output of soft coal, placed a revenue tax of one cent a ton on soft coal, and imposed a 19.5 percent penalty tax on the wholesale price of coal for those coal operators who failed to observe a code of fair competition. The act also established a seven-member commission to fix coal prices.

Further reading: Charles E. Halt, *Joseph F. Guffey, New Deal Politician from Pennsylvania* (Ann Arbor, Mich.: University Microfilms, 1966).

Guinn and Beal v. United States

Decision by the U.S. Supreme Court issued on June 21, 1915, and declaring unconstitutional the "grandfather clause." The grandfather clause, a legal device used extensively in the South, exempted from various financial and educational voting requirements those whose fathers or grandfathers had voted before 1867; it effectively disenfranched most blacks, whose ancestors had then been slaves. The test case arose from an attempt to include such a clause in the Oklahoma constitution and was brought before the Supreme Court by the National Association for the Advancement of Colored People. The Court ruled that the clause violated the purpose and intent of the FIFTEENTH AMENDMENT, which was to assure equal voting rights regardless of race, color, or previous condition of servitude.

Further reading: United States Supreme Court Case, *Guinn v. U.S. 238 U.S. 347 (1915)*, Find Law, available online at http://laws.findlaw.com/us/238/347.html.

Guizot Law (French Primary Education Law of 1833)

French law promulgated on June 28, 1833, providing for the establishment, maintenance, and regulation of a public primary education system. Drafted under the direction of François Guizot, education minister, the law guaranteed a primary school for every commune in France, which even the poorest student could attend, and charged the community and the state with overseeing the school's efforts. It made only passing reference to primary education for girls—suggesting that communities could establish such schools if necessary. Anyone above 18 years of age could start a primary school, and the development of private elementary schools was accepted. Compulsory attendance was not stressed. Fees were based on the parents' ability to pay and were given to the teachers in addition to their fixed salaries. Every department was to operate a normal primary school for training of teachers. "Moral and religious instruction" was declared an essential part of primary elementary instruction.

See also: FALLOUX LAW; FERRY LAWS.

Further reading: Raymond Grew and Patrick J. Harrigan, *School, State, and Society: The Growth of Elementary Schooling in Nineteenth-Century France: A Quantitative Analysis* (Ann Arbor: University of Michigan Press, 1991); Douglas Johnson, *Guizot: Aspects of French History, 1787–1874* (Westport, Conn.: Greenwood Press, 1975); G. W. Sampson, *French and American Republican Issues in Public Education Harmonized by Guizot* (Woodbridge, Conn.: Research Publications International, 1990).

Gulf of Tonkin Resolution

Joint resolution passed overwhelmingly by U.S. Congress on August 7, 1964, giving President Lyndon B. Johnson broad powers to fight communism in Southeast Asia. On August 5 Johnson had announced that he had ordered air strikes against North Vietnam in retaliation for alleged North Vietnamese attacks on U.S. destroyers in the Gulf of Tonkin. The resolution gave Johnson congressional approval for "all necessary measures to repel any armed attack" against U.S. forces and for "all necessary steps" to assist any Southeast Asian ally seeking to defend its freedom. It became the basis for Johnson's escalation of the war in Southeast Asia. A 1968 U.S. Senate investigation raised serious doubts about the alleged Gulf of Tonkin attacks, and the resolution was repealed in May 1970.

See also: PENTAGON PAPERS.

Further reading: Carl N. Flanders and Stephen A. Flanders, *Dictionary of American Foreign Affairs* (New York: Macmillan, 1993); John Galloway, *The Gulf of Tonkin Resolution* (Madison, N.J.: Fairleigh Dickinson University Press, 1970).

Gulistan, Treaty of

Peace treaty concluded at Gulistan (in modern-day Azerbaijan) on October 12, 1813, between Russia and Persia (Iran), ending their war (1804–13), which had arisen over the disputed possession of Transcaucasia. Through the treaty Persia, which was defeated in the war, reluctantly ceded to Russia Daghestan, Georgia, and north Azerbaijan—provinces that included the important cities of Baku, Derbent, and Lenkoran on the Caspian Sea. In addition Russia received naval rights in the Caspian Sea; duty rates were reduced for Russian goods imported to Persia; and each country extended free or exclusive trading privileges to the other. Persia, which did not accept the agreement as final, renewed hostilities in 1825.

See also: TURKMANCHAI, TREATY OF.

Further reading: William Monteith, *Kars and Erzeroum; with the Campaign of Prince Paskiewitch, in 1828 and 1829; and . . . the Treaty of Turcoman Chie and Adrianople* (London: Longman, Brown, Green & Longmans, 1856).

H

Habeas Corpus Act of 1679 Statute passed by Parliament in England (May 1679), making it compulsory for judges to issue a prisoner (at his request) with the habeas corpus writ, which stated that no one could be imprisoned indefinitely without being charged in a court of law. The statue declared that prisoners were to be tried during the first term of their imprisonment and no later than the second. Once the court freed a prisoner, he could not be imprisoned again for the same crime. Judges were ordered to issue writs even when the courts were not in session and any judge who failed to do so faced stiff penalties. The act applied initially only to criminal charges but was amended by the Habeas Corpus Act of 1816 to cover other charges. It is still considered a fundamental protector of personal freedom and the rule of law.

Further reading: William F. Duker, *A Constitutional History of Habeas Corpus* (Westport, Conn.: Greenwood Press, 1980); Richard L. Perry, ed., *Sources of Our Liberties* (New York: American Bar Association, 1959).

Hadrian's Rescript Roman emperor Hadrian's written response (c. A.D. 130) to a query by Serenius Granianus, proconsul of Asia, concerning policy and legal procedures against Christians. Hadrian proposed to administer justice fairly, declaring that "if anybody shall prove an offense against the laws to have been committed by Christians, proceed against them precisely within the law; if the accusation brought against them be mere slander, then punish the accuser as he deserves." The Christians were scornfully tolerated by Hadrian, a pagan, but the Jews were nearly exterminated in Judaea by him in A.D. 136.

Further reading: Lester L. Grabbe, *Judaism from Cyrus to Hadrian* (Minneapolis, Minn.: Fortress Press, 1992); Benedikt Otzen, *Judaism in Antiquity: Political Development and Religious Currents from Alexander to Hadrian*, trans. Frederick H. Cryer (Sheffield, England: JSOT Press, 1990).

Hague, Treaty of The (1720) Treaty signed at The Hague on February 17, 1720, ending the War of the Quadruple Alliance (1718–20) (England, France, Holland, and Austria) against Spain, wresting important concessions from her. The Spanish king, Philip V, finally renounced his claims to the French throne (see UTRECHT, TREATIES OF) and to the Italian provinces, which, together with Flanders, became a part of the Austrian Empire. In return, the Austrian emperor withdrew his claims to the Spanish succession, acknowledged Philip V as the rightful ruler of Spain, and promised to support the candidacy of Charles (eldest son of Philip V and Isabel Farnese) for succession to Parma, Piacenza, and Tuscany. Austria obtained Sicily in exchange for Sardinia, which was awarded to the duke of Savoy along with the title "King of Sardinia."

Further reading: Henry A. F. Kamen, *Philip V: The King Who Reigned Twice* (New Haven, Conn.: Yale University Press, 2001).

Hague Agreement of 1949 (Round Table Conference Agreement)

Agreement signed at The Hague on November 2, 1949, by J. D. Maarseveen, head of the Ministry of Overseas Territories of the Netherlands, and Premier Mohammad Hatta and Sultan Hamid II of the United States of Indonesia, attempting to end the ongoing conflict between the two sides over the independence of Indonesia, a former Dutch colony. The agreement was a modification of the earlier RENVILLE AGREEMENT, which had provided the Netherlands with sovereignty over the entire area in anticipation of the creation of the United States of Indonesia (which would include the Republic of Indonesia, Kalimantan [Borneo], and the Great East). The present document thus provided that sovereignty over the entire area, excluding West New Guinea, would be transferred to the United States of Indonesia no later than December 30, 1949, and that the United States of Indonesia and the Netherlands would unite, under the Dutch monarch, to form a Dutch-Indonesian union. The Indonesians were dissatisfied with the exclusion of West New Guinea from the new state, however, and abrogated the agreement in 1956.

See also: CHERIBON AGREEMENT.

Further reading: *Round Table Conference: Results as Accepted in the Second Plenary Meeting Held on 2 November 1949 in the "Ridderzaal" at The Hague* (The Hague, Netherlands: Secretariat-General of the Conference, 1949).

Haitian Constitution of 1964

Constitution endorsed by a national referendum on June 14, 1964, and proclaimed by the Haitian National Assembly a week later, providing for President François Duvalier's lifelong tenure as president. The importance of the constitution's democratic guarantees, such as universal suffrage and an elected legislature, was greatly diminished by provisions that made Duvalier president-for-life and endowed him with all significant powers of the state. The constitution also changed the colors of the Haitian flag from red and blue to red and black; the new colors were to symbolize Haiti's links with Africa.

Further reading: *Constitution of Haiti, 1964* (Washington, D.C.: Pan American Union, 1968).

Haitian Constitution of 1987

New constitution approved by Haiti's Constitutional Assembly and almost unanimously in a national referendum on March 29, 1987, about 13 months after the ouster of the dictator Jean-Claude Duvalier, who had been proclaimed "president for life" upon the death of his father, François Duvalier, in 1971. An interim military-civilian council governed before the constitution, which provided for a president as head of state, a premier as head of government, and a legislature (to which the premier would be responsible) to share power in the republic. However, the country suffered severe outbreaks of violence (which canceled some elections), waves of strikes, and government displacement through army coups in the late 1980s.

Further reading: Center for Latin American Studies at Georgetown University, *Constitution of Haiti, 1987*, Political Database of the Americas, Available online at http://www.georgetown.edu/pdba/Constitutions/Haiti/haiti1987.html; Nicholas N. Kittrie and James R. Sevick, *The New Constitution of Haiti: November 29, 1987, the Test Begins: A Report* (Washington, D.C.: Washington Institute for Values in Public Policy, 1987).

Halepa, Pact of

Concessions granted to the Greeks on Crete (held by the Ottoman Turks) and signed at Halepa, Crete, by Ottoman Sultan Abd al-Hamid II on October 25, 1878, providing the island with a greater degree of autonomy. The document provided for a general assembly composed of both Christians and Muslims; the use of the Greek language in the assembly and law courts; a five-year term for the office of the governor general (the leading official); a special adviser to the governor general who would be of the opposite religion; and the employment of native Cretans in governmental posts. The Cretans' desire for independence from the repressive rule of the Ottoman Empire and for union with Greece, coupled with international pressure, forced the Ottoman Empire into granting the concessions. The pact was annulled in 1889, and restored in 1896.

Further reading: Great Britain Foreign Office, Historical Section, *Greece with the Cyclades & Northern Sporades* (Woodbridge, Conn.: Research Publications International, 1995).

Half-Way Covenant

Plan approved by an intercolonial ministerial conference in Boston in 1657 to deal with the membership status of the children of first-generation New England Puritans. The parents were full church members owing to their personal experience of conversion (or "regeneration"), but the Half-Way Covenant decreed that the children would be admitted to membership without the privileges of participating in the Lord's Supper or of voting on church affairs until they showed evidence of their own regeneration. The effect of this policy was to maintain a high level of church attendance while keeping power in the hands of the church founders. Ultimately, however, it also tended to blur the distinction between the "elect" and others.

Further reading: David D. Hall, ed., *Puritanism in Seventeenth-Century Massachusetts* (New York: Holt, Rinehart & Winston, 1968); Frank N. Magill, ed., *Great Events from History, American Series*, 3 vols. (Englewood Cliffs, N.J.: Salem Press, 1975); Robert G. Pope, *The Half-Way Covenant: Church Membership in Puritan New England* (Princeton, N.J.: Princeton University Press, 1980); Westminster Conference, *The Puritan Experiment in the New World* (Huntingdon, England: The Conference, 1976).

Halibut Treaty

Treaty concluded by the United States and Canada on March 2, 1923, regulating halibut fishing rights in the Pacific Ocean along Canada's coast. The treaty provided for a suspension of halibut fishing in Canada's coastal waters in the Pacific during the spawning season, which lasted from mid-November to mid-February. More significant, however, was the fact that Canada, for the first time, insisted on signing the document alone with the United States. Up until that time Canada had acquiesced to Great Britain's insistence that she, as a British colony, allow Britain to participate in the conclusion of any commercial treaty to which she was a signatory, despite the fact that Canada had the right to conclude such treaties independently.

See also: WESTMINSTER, STATUTE OF (1931).

Further reading: *Treaty Between Canada and the United States of America for Securing the Preservation of the Halibut Fishery of the North Pacific Ocean* . . . (London: H.M. Stationery Office, 1925).

Hamas Covenant   Publication on August 18, 1988, of the manifesto of HAMAS (acronym of the Arabic name for the Islamic resistance movement—Harakat-al-Muqawama al-Islamiyya), which dramatically altered the organization's relations with Israel. Describing Jews as an "instrument of evil" and the destruction of Israel as its official mission, the covenant said that every Muslim had a "personal obligation" to participate in the holy war against the Zionist. Attaining Palestinian statehood, it said, was a step toward the "Islamization" of the country. Palestine was sacred land, and no one could give it away or negotiate or compromise with the Zionists over it. The Jews, the HAMAS Covenant stated, wanted to expand farther so that their land bordered the Nile and the Euphrates Rivers. The document also affirmed HAMAS's close ties with the Palestine Liberation Organization (PLO).

Further reading: Benny Morris, *Righteous Victims—A History of the Zionist-Arab Conflict, 1881–1999* (New York: Alfred A. Knopf, 1999); Jewish Community Relations Council, "The Covenant of the Hamas—Main Points," Jewish Community Relations Council, available online at http://www.jcrc.org/main/hamas1.htm; Charles L. Phillips and Alan Axelrod, *Encyclopedia of Historical Treaties and Alliances*, 2 vols. (New York: Facts On File, 2001).

Hamburg, Treaty of   Peace agreement concluded between Sweden (ruled by the pro-French Hattar Party [the "Hats"]) and Prussia (under King Frederick II the Great) on May 22, 1762, at Hamburg, Germany. It ended fighting between them during the Seven Years' War (1756–63) and reflected the military stalemate that had occurred. It provided for a return to the status quo antebellum, meaning Prussia's retention of Prussian Pomerania and Sweden's retention of Swedish Pomerania. The Hats had expected an easy victory over Prussia, which had been preoccupied with fighting Russia until the accession of Peter III to the Russian throne in January 1762.

See also: ST. PETERSBURG, TREATY OF (1762).

Further reading: David Fraser, *Frederick the Great: King of Prussia* (London: Penguin Books, 2000).

Hamilton's Plan of Union   Proposal presented by Alexander Hamilton, a New York delegate to the Federal Constitutional Convention, on June 18, 1787, for a constitution to replace the ARTICLES OF CONFEDERATION. Hamilton, who favored a strong central government, proposed a legislature consisting of an assembly, whose members would be elected directly by the people, and a senate, chosen by electors; an executive, chosen by electors; and a chief judiciary of 12 judges. Assembly members would serve for three years; all others would serve during "good behaviour." Hamilton, however, played only a minor role at the convention and his plan had little effect on the final U.S. CONSTITUTION.

Further reading: Clinton Rossiter, *Alexander Hamilton and the Idea of Republican Government* (New York: Harcourt, Brace, 1964); Gerald Stourzh, *Alexander Hamilton and the Idea of Republican Government* (Stanford, Calif.: Stanford University Press, 1970).

Hammer v. Dagenhart   U.S. Supreme Court decision, issued on June 3, 1918, that invalidated the KEATING-OWEN ACT, which forbade interstate shipment of products of child labor. In its five-to-four decision, the Supreme Court ruled that the statute was an unwarranted infringement on state powers, "repugnant to the Constitution," an attempt to extend federal authority over a "purely local matter." In dissent, Justice Oliver Wendell Holmes deplored the "evil of premature and excessive child labor," upheld the federal right to regulate interstate commerce, and noted that the states lacked the power to control child labor. The decision was overturned in *UNITED STATES* V. *DARBY LUMBER COMPANY* in 1941.

Further reading: Stephen Wood, *Constitutional Politics in the Progressive Era: Child Labor and the Law* (Chicago: University of Chicago Press, 1968).

Hammurabi, Code of   Collection of ancient Babylonian laws carved on a diorite stele or slab; developed and promulgated by King Hammurabi of Babylonia around 1700 B.C. Comprised of 3,600 lines of Akkadian cuneiform (a Semitic writing), the laws were Hammurabi's decisions about civil, commercial, criminal, familial, and other matters; they were humanitarian on the whole, but did include some primitive customs (like trial by ordeal) and retributive punishment (i.e., an eye for an eye, a tooth for a tooth). The code's purpose was explained at the start: "Before this portrait [of Hammurabi, at the top of the stele] let every man who has a legal dispute come forward, read the text, and heed its precious words." The stele, which was placed in Babylon's temple of Marduk (the chief god), was taken away by a conquering Elamite king about 1000 B.C.; it was uncovered by Frenchmen at Susa (a ruined city in western Iran) in 1901 and deposited in the Louvre Museum in Paris.

Further reading: M. E. J. Richardson, *Hammurabi's Laws: Text, Translation and Glossary* (Salem, Wis.: Sheffield Academic Press, 2000).

Hanover, Treaty of Defensive treaty of alliance concluded between Great Britain (under King George I), France (under King Louis XV), and Prussia (under King Frederick William I), at Hanover on September 3, 1725. It was formed to counteract the unexpected alliance that Austria (the Hapsburg Empire) and Spain had entered into earlier that same year (see VIENNA, TREATIES OF [1725]). Holland also joined the alliance, which sought to safeguard Britain from Spain's demand to surrender control of Gibraltar and which also opposed Russian aggressions against Hanover (a German electorate under George I, who was accorded the British crown in 1714). The Austro-Spanish alliance, which even imagined the dismemberment of France, collapsed after the start of the Anglo-Spanish War of 1727–29. Prussia withdrew from the Hanover alliance in 1727.

Further reading: James F. Chance, *The Alliance of Hanover; a Study of British Foreign Policy in the Last Years of George I* (London: J. Murray, 1923).

Harare Declaration See FREEDOM CHARTER.

Hardwicke Marriage Act English legislation successfully promoted in 1753 by Philip Yorke, the earl of Hardwicke, "for the better preventing of clandestine marriages," making it mandatory for licenses or banns of matrimony to be published prior to the event. The couple were also required to furnish their full names and addresses and notice of parental approval (if one or both of them were under 21), and the marriage was to be held in the local parish church where one of them resided. Based on the principle of marriage as a civil contract, the act did not apply to royal marriages, to people in Scotland, to Jews and Quakers, or to marriages solemnized overseas.

Further reading: Philip C. Yorke, *The Life and Correspondence of Philip Yorke, Earl of Hardwicke, Lord High Chancellor of Great Britain*, 3 vols. (New York: Octagon Books, 1977).

Harper* v. *Virginia State Board of Elections See TWENTY-FOURTH AMENDMENT, U.S.

Harrison Act (Harrison Narcotic Law) Federal revenue legislation enacted on December 17, 1914, and effective on April 1, 1915; restricted the legal use of narcotics in the United States. The act, as amended, required everyone who imported, manufactured, sold, or dispensed narcotics to register and pay an occupational tax, to render returns, and to sell and exchange all narcotics in accordance with government recording requirements. All narcotics entering into domestic trade had to be tax-stamped. The U.S. Treasury Department was charged with enforcement responsibility. In effect, the act prohibited the legal use of narcotics, particularly opium and its derivatives, and encouraged the growth of the black market in drugs.

Further reading: Steven R. Belenko, *Drugs and Drug Policy in America: A Documentary History* (Westport, Conn.: Greenwood Press, 2000); David F. Musto, *The American Disease: Origins of Narcotics Control*, 3d ed. (New York: Oxford University Press, 1999).

Harrison Land Act See LAND ACT OF 1800, U.S.

Harris Treaty First commercial treaty between Japan and the United States, signed on July 29, 1858. It was negotiated by Townsend Harris, first U.S. consul general to Japan (1855–61), whose arrival was a result of the Treaty of KANAGAWA. An 1857 agreement had opened Nagasaki to U.S. commerce; the 1858 treaty opened additional ports, granted Americans residence rights, and established diplomatic representatives at the capitals of the two nations. The U.S. Senate consented to the treaty on December 15, 1858.

Further reading: Carl Crow, *He Opened the Door of Japan; Townsend Harris and the Story of His Amazing Adventures in Establishing American Relations with the Far East* (Westport, Conn.: Greenwood Press, 1974); Charles E. Hill, *Leading American Treaties* (New York: Macmillan, 1922).

Hartford, Treaty of Agreement signed in 1650 in Hartford, Connecticut, by the commissioners of the United Colonies of New England and Peter Stuyvesant, the governor of New Netherland, in an attempt to resolve various disputes between the English and Dutch. The major issues to be negotiated were the borders between New Netherland and the English colonies to the north and to the west, and Dutch trading rights with the Indians of the Delaware River Valley. By the terms of the treaty, the Dutch agreed to accept a border that ran from Oyster Bay on Long Island through Greenwich, Connecticut, on the mainland, and gave up a large portion of their original holdings around Hartford. The arbitrators accepted Stuyvesant's explanation of his seizure of a Dutch ship in New Haven Harbor, but the treaty left unresolved the issue of the expulsion of English traders along the Delaware River. The English Parliament never ratified the treaty, and 14 years later it became irrelevant when the English occupied New Netherland (which they renamed New York and New Jersey).

Further reading: John J. Chiodo, *The Foreign Policy of Peter Stuyvesant: Dutch Diplomacy in North America, 1647 to 1664* (Ann Arbor, Mich.: University Microfilms International, 1978).

Hartford Convention Resolutions Report issued on January 4, 1815, by New England Federalists, meeting to consider constitutional amendments to resolve regional problems arising from the War of 1812, which the Federalists opposed. The convention, attended by representatives from

Massachusetts, Connecticut, Rhode Island, Vermont, and New Hampshire, met at Hartford, Connecticut, December 15, 1814, to January 5, 1815. The resolutions criticized the Republican administration, supported states' rights, and proposed constitutional amendments to weaken the power of the South in the federal government. The end of the War of 1812 negated the importance of the report.

Further reading: James M. Banner, Jr., *To the Hartford Convention* (New York: Knopf, 1970).

Hat Act   Statute enacted by the British Parliament in 1732 to protect England's hat makers, already threatened by French competition, against further rivalry from the expanding American hat industry. The act (one of the Acts of Trade and Navigation) forbade the exportation of American-manufactured hats (notably felt hats) from the colony in which they were made (either to another colony, to a foreign land, or to England). Each colonial hatter could have two apprentices (but no more and no blacks), and apprenticeships were to be seven years long. The law was not consistently enforced.

See also: MOLASSES ACT.

Further reading: Leonard E. Fisher, *The Hatters* (New York: Benchmark Books, 2001).

Hatch Act of 1887   Federal U.S. legislation introduced by Missouri congressman William H. Hatch that provided federal funds for establishing experimental stations to conduct agricultural research. The act, which supplemented the MORRILL ACT, granted $15,000 annually to each U.S. state "to aid in acquiring and diffusing among the people . . . useful and practical information on subjects connected with agriculture, and to promote scientific investigation and experiment respecting the principles and applications of agricultural science." The amount of the original subsidy was raised by later legislation.

Further reading: *Agricultural Research for a Better Tomorrow: Commemorating the Hatch Act Centennial, 1887–1987* (Washington, D.C.: U.S. Dept. of Agriculture, 1987); Henry Steele Commager, ed., *Documents of American History*, 8th ed. (New York: Appleton-Century-Crofts, 1968).

Hatch Act of 1939   U.S. legislation enacted on August 2, 1939, that prohibited most federal officeholders in the executive branch of government from actively participating in election campaigns, from soliciting or accepting campaign contributions from workers on federal projects, and from using their authority to influence presidential or congressional elections. The act was amended on July 19, 1940, to include state and local government employees whose salaries were derived, in whole or in part, from federal funds. The amendment also limited the annual expenditures of political parties to $3 million and limited individual campaign contributions to $5,000. The act, sponsored by Senator Carl A. Hatch of

New Mexico and following political scandals involving federal relief workers in the 1938 election, was designed to "prevent pernicious political activities."

Further reading: Donald C. Bacon, Roger H. Davidson, and Morton Keller, eds., *The Encyclopedia of the United States Congress* (New York: Simon & Schuster, 1995); James R. Eccles, *The Hatch Act and the American Bureaucracy* (New York: Vantage Press, 1981); Janet Crews Hendershot, *Guide to the Hatch Act: Law and Procedures* (Arlington, Va.: Dewey Publications, 1993).

Hatfield-McGovern (End-the-War) Amendment   Proposal sponsored by U.S. senators George McGovern of South Dakota and Mark Hatfield of Oregon, during widespread domestic unrest over the conduct of the ongoing Vietnam War (1956–75), to bring all U.S. soldiers home from South Vietnam by December 31, 1971. It was narrowly defeated in the Senate on September 1, 1970. In urging its passage, McGovern said, "Every Senator in this chamber is partly responsible for sending 50,000 young Americans to an early grave . . . [and] for human wreckage . . . all across the land." If Congress failed to end "this damnable war," he charged, its victims would "some day curse us for our pitiful willingness to let the Executive carry that burden that the Constitution places on us."

Further reading: *What Pace Withdrawal? The McGovern-Hatfield Amendment* (Washington, D.C.: American Enterprise Institute for Public Policy Research, 1970).

Havana, Act of (Declaration of Reciprocal Assistance and Cooperation for the Defense of the Nations of the Americas)   Declaration adopted on July 29, 1940, at the Havana Conference, a meeting of foreign ministers of the American republics held at Havana, Cuba, July 21–30, 1940. In this act the Latin American nations declared their right to defend European possessions in the Western Hemisphere against foreign aggression if the situation warranted such action. These possessions might be occupied and held in trusteeship until the end of the war (World War II [1939–45]). The act, designed to prevent British, French, and Dutch possessions in the New World from falling into the hands of Nazi Germany, gave pan-American sanction to the traditional No-Transfer Doctrine of the United States.

Further reading: Charles I. Bevans, comp., *Treaties and Other International Agreements of the United States of America, 1776–1949*, 12 vols. (Washington: U.S. Government Printing Office, 1968); Stephen A. Flanders and Carl N. Flanders, *Dictionary of American Foreign Affairs* (New York: Macmillan, 1993).

Havel's Address to Congress   Eloquent speech delivered on February 21, 1990, to the U.S. Congress by Václav Havel, playwright and new president of Czechoslovakia. Lauding the recent "revolutionary change" in the countries of

Eastern Europe, Havel said, paradoxically, that the United States "can help us most of all if you help the Soviet Union on its irreversible but immensely complicated road to democracy." The peoples of Czechoslovakia and other nations suffered "enormous human humiliation" under the Soviet communist totalitarian system, he said, and yet they gained "something positive, a special capacity to look from time to time somewhat further than someone who has not undergone this bitter experience." Eastern Europe and the West have much experience and knowledge to offer each other. Havel concluded by saying the world's salvation lies chiefly in deeds, not words, of human moral responsibility.

Further reading: Vaclav Havel, *The Art of the Impossible: Politics as Morality in Practice: Speeches and Writings, 1990–1996* (New York: Knopf, 1997).

Hawaiian Treaty of 1897

Treaty annexing the Hawaiian Islands to the United States. In 1893 American settlers had engineered the overthrow of the Hawaiian monarchy and installed a provisional government, which negotiated a treaty of annexation. U.S. president Grover Cleveland withdrew this treaty from the Senate, on grounds that the provisional government was illegitimate and without popular support. Pressure for annexation continued, and a second treaty was concluded in 1897. While it was pending in the Senate, the Spanish-American War (1898) broke out. To secure U.S. use of Hawaiian harbors for naval bases, the treaty was adopted by a joint resolution of Congress on July 7, 1898, avoiding the need for a two-thirds vote in the Senate for ratification.

Further reading: Tom Coffman, *Nation Within: The Story of America's Annexation of the Nation of Hawai'i* (Kaneohe, Hawaii: Tom Coffman/EPICenter, 1998); Henry Steele Commager, ed., *Documents of American History*, 8th ed. (New York: Appleton-Century-Crofts, 1968); Thomas J. Osborne, *Annexation Hawaii* (Waimanalo, Hawaii: Island Style Press, 1998); William A. Russ, *The Hawaiian Republic (1894–98): And Its Struggle to Win Annexation* (Selinsgrove, Pa.: Susquehanna University Press, 1992).

Hay-Bunau-Varilla Treaty

Treaty of November 18, 1903, signed in Washington, D.C., and negotiated by U.S. secretary of state John Hay and Philippe Bunau-Varilla, a French engineer associated with the New Panama Canal Company and the Republic of Panama's appointed minister to Washington. The treaty gave the United States the right to build a canal across the Isthmus of Panama; to perpetually use, occupy, and control a zone 10 miles wide; and the right to acquire additional lands as might be needed for the construction, maintenance, sanitation, operation, and protection of the canal. Panama was to receive $10,000,000 along with $250,000 annually beginning nine years after the day the treaty went into effect.

Further reading: Charles I. Bevans, comp., *Treaties and Other International Agreements of the United States of America,* *1776–1949* 12 vols. (Washington, D.C.: U.S. Government Printing Office, 1968); Charles L. Phillips and Alan Axelrod, eds., *Encyclopedia of Historical Treaties and Alliances,* 2 vols. (New York: Facts On File, 2001).

Hay-Herrán Treaty

Treaty signed on January 22, 1903, by U.S. secretary of state John Hay and the Colombian chargé in Washington, Tomás Herrán, granting the United States the authority to build a canal across the Isthmus of Panama. The treaty conferred upon the United States the right to operate the canal for 100 years and the option of extending this time for an indefinite period. Also the United States was to receive the lease of a strip of land three miles wide on each side of the canal. In exchange Colombia was to receive $10,000,000 immediately and an annuity of $250,000 nine years after the treaty's ratification. However, the Colombian senate, hoping to get better terms, did not ratify the treaty.

Further reading: Charles I. Bevans, comp., *Treaties and Other International Agreements of the United States of America,* *1776–1949* 12 vols. (Washington, D.C.: U.S. Government Printing Office, 1968); Stephen A. Flanders and Carl N. Flanders, *Dictionary of American Foreign Affairs* (New York: Macmillan, 1993).

Hay-Pauncefote Treaties

Two treaties concluded between U.S. secretary of state John M. Hay and Lord Julian Pauncefote, Great Britain's ambassador to the United States, on February 5, 1900, and November 18, 1901, providing for exclusive control by the United States over the construction and management of any future isthmian canal in Central America (the Panama Canal). The second treaty, which was definitive (the British Parliament rejected the first treaty), differed from the first in that it contained an added provision granting the United States the right to fortify and defend any such future canal (which was to be open to ships of all countries on equal terms, under a general principle of its neutrality). The treaty thus abrogated the previous British-U.S. agreement (see CLAYTON-BULWER TREATY of 1850) through which both Great Britain and the United States were to share control over the canal. In 1902 the United States chose Panama as the site for the construction of a Central American canal.

Further reading: Charles I. Bevans, comp., *Treaties and Other International Agreements of the United States of America,* *1776–1949* 12 vols. (Washington, D.C.: U.S. Government Printing Office, 1968); Stephen A. Flanders and Carl N. Flanders, *Dictionary of American Foreign Affairs* (New York: Macmillan, 1993).

Hay's Circular Letter of 1899

Letter of September 6, 1899, written by U.S. secretary of state John Hay and announcing the Open Door policy toward China, an attempt to protect American commercial interests at a time when European nations were establishing spheres of influence in China.

Hay's letter instructed U.S. embassies in Germany, Russia, Great Britain, France, Italy, and Japan to seek assurances that those powers would respect the trading rights of other nations within their spheres of influence, that the Chinese treaty tariff would apply to all spheres of influence and would be collected by the Chinese government, and that discriminatory tariffs and fees would not be applied to any nation. Though the various nations gave evasive replies, on March 20, 1900, Hay announced the acceptance of the Open Door policy as "final and definitive."

See also: HAY'S CIRCULAR LETTER OF 1900.

Further reading: Mortimer Adler, ed., *The Annals of America*, 18 vols. (Chicago: Encyclopedia Britannica, 1968); Henry Steele Commager, ed., *Documents of American History*, 8th ed. (New York: Appleton-Century-Crofts, 1968).

Hay's Circular Letter of 1900   Circular telegram sent by U.S. secretary of state John Hay to American embassies and missions in Europe and Japan on July 3, 1900, during the Boxer Uprising (1899–1901) against foreign influence in China. Extending the Open Door policy (see HAY'S CIRCULAR LETTER OF 1899), Hay declared that U.S. policy sought to "bring about permanent safety and peace to China, preserve Chinese territorial and administrative entity, protect all rights guaranteed to friendly powers by treaty and international law, and safeguard for the world the principle of equal and impartial trade with all parts of the Chinese Empire."

Further reading: Henry Steele Commager, ed., *Documents of American History*, 8th ed. (New York: Appleton-Century-Crofts, 1968).

Heads of Proposals   See INSTRUMENT OF GOVERNMENT.

Health Consequences of Smoking   Report issued by the U.S. surgeon general on January 10, 1972, which stated that smoking had detrimental effects on nonsmokers as well as smokers, and which recommended that smoking be banned from public places. The report confirmed earlier studies showing associations among smoking and coronary heart disease, cerebrovascular disease, lung cancer, peptic ulcers, oral disease, and retarded fetal growth (see SMOKING AND HEALTH). *Health Consequences of Smoking* documented claims that tobacco is antigenic to humans and may exacerbate allergies, stated that public exposure to air pollution (especially carbon monoxide) from tobacco smoking may be harmful to the health even of nonsmokers, and identified the harmful constituents of smoke. Although the tobacco industry denounced the report, the document encouraged nonsmokers to insist on a right to a smoke-free environment.

Further reading: National Clearinghouse for Smoking and Health, *The Health Consequences of Smoking: A Report of the Surgeon General, 1972* (Washington, D.C.: U.S. Public Health Service, 1972).

Health and Morals of Apprentices Act   British government's first attempt to regulate the working conditions in the cotton mills and factories, initiated by Sir Robert Peel (himself a manufacturer) "to promote the religious and moral education" of the parish apprentices. The act, effective December 2, 1802, barred apprentices from working more than a 12-hour day and from doing any night shifts. Their living quarters were to be properly ventilated and washed at least twice a year. At least two complete sets of clothing and separate male and female dormitories were to be provided. They were to be instructed in the three R's and in religion, and guaranteed medical coverage especially in case of infectious diseases. The act recommended the appointment of two overseers to check mills and factories for compliance—failure to do so could result in fines ranging from 40 shillings to £5.

Further reading: Norman Gash, *Mr. Secretary Peel: The Life of Sir Robert Peel to 1830* (London: Longman, 1985).

Health Insurance and Portability and Accountability Act (HIPAA), U.S.   Two-part legislation (public law 104–191) signed by President Bill Clinton in 1996, protecting the medical rights of patients and estimating to save the health care industry some $30 billion over 10 years. The first part, probability, ensured that patients with preexisting medical conditions were not denied health insurance coverage. The "accountability" aspect was not addressed until December 2000 when 1,500 pages of applicable rules were released. These rules were ratified in April 2001 and full compliance is expected by April 14, 2003. The legislation prohibits unauthorized persons from accessing private medical data (written, oral, or electronic); violators would be fined $100 per violation up to a maximum of $25,000. Patients would gain access to their medical records and correct any inaccuracies. Companies could not use these data for any purpose without written consent from patients. Also, health care companies would be required to hire a privacy officer who would then train the staff in handling sensitive information.

Further reading: William L. Manning, "Summary of Bill, from HCFA," Health Law Resource, available online at http://www.netreach.net/~wmanning/hr3103.htm; office of the Assistant Secretary for planning and evaluation, "Administrative Simplification," U.S. Department of Health and Human Services, available online at http://aspe.hhs.gov/admnsimp.

Heidelberg Catechism (Palatinate Catechism)   Confession of faith of the German Reformed (Calvinistic) Church compiled chiefly by Kaspar Olevianus and Zacharias Ursinus, theologians in Heidelberg, and accepted by the Rhenish Palatinate Church in Germany in 1563. Elector Frederick III the Pious of the Palatinate had ordered the catechism to be drafted, for he hoped to settle differences among Protestant groups (notably moderate and orthodox Lutherans) through a reformed catechism acceptable to all. The result was a practical and moderate profession of faith (not dogmatic), one mildly stating the controversial doctrine of predestination. Though it did not unite the various Protestant groups, it was sanctioned by several synods.

See also: DORT, CANONS OF.

Further reading: *Heidelberg Catechism: A Short History of the Heidelberg Catechism, Introduction, Tercentenary Text, Selected Bible Passages, Suitable Hymns and Selections from the Scriptures* (St. Louis, Mo.: Eden Publishing House, 1988); Fred H. Klooster, *The Heidelberg Catechism: Origin and History* (Grand Rapids, Mich.: Calvin Theological Seminary, 1981); John W. Nevin, *History and Genius of the Heidelberg Catechism* (Evanston, Ill.: American Theological Library Association, 1990).

Heligoland Agreement

Anglo-German treaty of July 1, 1890, in which Germany made significant concessions in Africa in return for the island of Heligoland or Helgoland in the North Sea. The Germans accepted the British claim to Zanzibar, and restricted their own claims in German East Africa to an area south of the Nile headwaters. In return, the British agreed that South-West Africa could reach the Zambezi River, and allowed German East Africa to touch the Belgian Congo. The British also surrendered Heligoland, which they had acquired from Denmark in 1815. The new German chancellor, General Leo von Caprivi, believed Heligoland would be useful in the defense of the Kiel Canal, which Germany was building across her territory at the base of the Danish peninsula. The German concessions in Africa, however, appeared to be more significant than what the British had given in return, and the treaty was generally regarded as evidence of Germany's interest in accommodating Britain.

Further reading: Paul E. Hubbell, *The Helgoland-Zanzibar Treaty of 1890* (Ann Arbor, Mich.: University Microfilms, 1965).

Helms-Burton Act (Cuban Liberty and Democratic Solidarity [LIBERTAD] Act of 1996)

Legislation enacted by the U.S. Congress that reaffirmed U.S. opposition to Fidel Castro's communist regime in Cuba. Signed into law on March 12, 1996, the act was drafted following the downing of two U.S. civilian aircraft that had entered Cuban airspace without permission. The act's stated intention was to effect an international economic boycott of Cuba that would make living conditions on the island so unbearable that the Cuban people would overthrow Castro. Upon coming to power, Castro's government had seized the property of American corporations and was now leasing it to foreign corporations. Among other things, the act authorized the U.S. government to sue such corporations and to deny their executives or their families permission to enter the United States. This use of economic pressure to influence a foreign government violated international trade law, and the act was condemned by the Organization of American States, the European Union, and the United Nations. It was also denounced in Canada, where many of the corporations targeted by the act were headquartered, and many Canadians called for a tourist boycott of Florida. As for Cubans, the act seemed only to strengthen their suppoort for Castro.

Further reading: Library of Congress, "H.R. 927: Cuban Liberty and Democratic Solidarity (LIBERTAD) Act of 1996," available online at http://thomas.loc.gov/cgi-bin/query/z?c104: H.R.927.ENR:.

Helsinki Accord

Accord (final act) signed on August 1, 1975, by 33 European countries, Canada, and the United States during the Helsinki Conference (July 30–August 1, 1975), held to ratify the agreements of the several Conferences on Security and Cooperation in Europe (CSCE). The accord related to principles of European security, among them: respect for national sovereignty, territorial integrity, human rights and civil liberties, nonintervention, peaceful settlement of disputes, recognition of a country's international obligations, and a policy of cooperation on technical, scientific, economic, and environmental issues. An offshoot of the policy of détente adopted by the superpowers, the Helsinki Accord was not a treaty and had no legal force. However, it was a major document, generally accepted as a standard by which the human rights records of the communist or Eastern bloc countries were judged before these countries threw off their communist-controlled governments and became democratic in 1989 and 1990.

Further reading: Ogor I. Davass, *Human Rights, European Politics and the Helsinki Accord of the Documentary Evolution of the Conference on Security and Co-operation in Europe, 1973–1975* (Buffalo, N.Y.: William S. Hein, 1981); Stephen A. Flanders and Carl N. Flanders, *Dictionary of American Foreign Affairs* (New York: Macmillan, 1993).

Henotikon (Henoticon)

Concordat letter issued in A.D. 482 by Zeno the Isaurian, Roman emperor of the East, in an attempt to resolve an angry dispute between Orthodox Christians and the Monophysites and for a reconciliation between the churches of Constantinople and Alexandria (Egypt). Zeno, probably induced by the Patriarch Acacius of Constantinople, addressed his letter to the church in Egypt, confirming the decisions of the earlier councils of Nicaea and Constantinople (see NICENE CREED) but modifying the results of the Council of Chalcedon (see TOME OF LEO), allowing the opinion that there was but one nature in Jesus Christ. Many Monophysites accepted it, but Pope Felix III condemned it and excommunicated Acacius in A.D. 484, when a church schism began between East and West (Rome), which ended in A.D. 519, when the Eastern Roman (Byzantine) Emperor Justin I revoked the Henotikon.

Further reading: A. A. Luce, *Monophysitism, Past and Present; a Study in Christology* (New York: Macmillan, 1920); John J. Norwich, *Byzantium: The Early Centuries* (New York: Alfred A. Knopf, 1999.

Henrician Articles   Articles agreed to and signed by Henry of Valois on his election to the throne of Poland in May 1573. They required King Henry to swear an oath not to interfere in the Sejm's (diet's) election of his successor; to agree to share authority over legislation with the Sejm; to accept limited powers when raising an army; not to declare war without sanction of the Sejm; and to convene the Sejm at least every two years (between sessions he would be governed by a privy council). The king also agreed to the Compact of WAR-SAW and to the nobles' demand that they be allowed to disobey him should he fail to live up to his vows. All future kings of Poland were required to sign the document and the PACTA CONVENTA OF 1573, which together were later considered one "constitution." Henry became king of France (Henry III) on the death of his brother Charles IX in 1574.

Further reading: Mieczyslaw B. Biskupski and James S. Pula, *Polish Democratic Thought from the Renaissance to the Great Emigration: Essays and Documents* (Boulder Colo.: Eastern European Monographs, 1990).

Henry IV's Reply to Gregory VII   Letter written on January 24, 1076, by German king Henry IV, in response to Pope Gregory VII's sharply critical letter to him (see GREGORY VII'S LETTER DENOUNCING HENRY IV). In January of 1076 Henry held a conference in Worms attended by German bishops, during which it was decided that Gregory should be deposed. Also during the session the letter was composed. In it Gregory was accused, falsely, of adultery, perjury, and of unjust treatment of the office of the bishop. Henry also rejected Gregory's claim to supremacy over his secular authority (see POPE'S DICTATE), ordered him to resign, and released all of his subjects from obedience to him.

Further reading: Joseph H. Dahmus, *A History of Medieval Civilization* (New York: Odyssey Press, 1964); Frank N. Magill, ed., *Great Events from History, Ancient and Medieval*, 3 vols. (Englewood Cliffs. N.J.: Salem Press, 1972).

Henry Letters   Reports written in 1808 by British secret agent John Henry for the governor general of Canada, concerning the unrest and secessionist sentiment in New England generated by the U.S. EMBARGO ACT OF 1807. President James Madison bought the letters for $50,000 and transmitted them to Congress on March 9, 1812, claiming they proved that Great Britain was encouraging resistance to the federal government, particularly in Massachusetts. The actual disclosures in the documents, however, were minor, summarizing only Henry's general impressions without giving names or details about a secessionist movement. Publication of the report deepened American antagonism toward Great Britain, already inflamed by violations of neutral U.S. shipping rights.

Further reading: Henry Adams, *History of the United States During the Administration of Jefferson and Madison*, 10 vols. (New York: H. Adams, 1889–91).

Hepburn Act   Federal U.S. legislation enacted on June 29, 1906, that increased the power of the Interstate Commerce Commission (ICC) to regulate railroads. In strengthening the INTERSTATE COMMERCE ACT, the 1906 act extended the ICC's jurisdiction to include refrigeration and storage facilities, terminals, bridges, and pipelines. It empowered the commission to set reasonable maximum railroad rates and to require uniform accounting methods. It also prohibited railroads from carrying commodities—other than certain products needed for railway operations—produced by companies in which they held a financial interest. The ELKINS ACT prohibiting rebates was also strengthened. The ICC's rulings were made binding without court action, although its decisions could be appealed.

Further reading: Donald C. Bacon, Roger H. Davidson, and Morton Keller, eds., *The Encyclopedia of the United States Congress* (New York: Simon & Schuster, 1995); Thomas Carson, ed., *Gale Encyclopedia of U.S. Economic History* (Farmington Hills, Mich.: Gale Group, 1999); Isaiah L. Sharfman, *The Interstate Commerce Commission*, 4 vols. (New York: Commonwealth Fund, 1931–37).

Heretics, Statute of (De Haeretico Comburendo)   English law enacted upon pressure from the clergy led by the Archbishop of Canterbury, Arundel, in 1401. It aimed at suppressing Lollardy, a heretical movement seeking to revive the spirit and the enthusiasm of the Christian martyrs and the first friars. It declared that any person found to be expounding heretical views was to be arrested and tried in a religious court. If this court pronounced him guilty of heresy, he was to be handed over to the king's officers "to be burnt that such punishment may strike fear to the minds of others." The legislation was not entirely new; previously, the church could force the state to inflict the penalty of being burned alive as dictated by canon law. In 1401 clergyman William Sawtre (a Lollard) was the first to suffer this fate. The law was later repealed by Henry VIII, revived by Mary Queen of Scots, and ultimately repealed by Elizabeth I.

Further reading: John W. Dahmus, *Thomas Arundel, Archbishop of Canterbury, 1396–1414: Churchman and Statesman* (Ann Arbor, Mich.: University Microfilms International, 1984); George M. Trevelyan, *De Haeretico Comburendo, or, The Ethics of Religious Conformity* (Cambridge, England: W. Heffer, 1914).

"Higher Law" Speech, Seward's   Speech given by William Henry Seward on March 11, 1850, in the U.S. Senate, opposing the COMPROMISE OF 1850. A strong opponent of slavery, the Whig senator from New York said that, although he recognized the right of Congress to permit or prohibit slavery in newly acquired U.S. territories, "there is a higher law than the Constitution which regulates our authority over the domain." Seward opposed any concessions to slavery forces and hoped to see the institution abolished everywhere. Seward's speech enraged Southerners, and some Northerners dismissed his appeal to a "higher law."

Further reading: Mortimer Adler, ed., *The Annals of America*, 18 vols. (Chicago: Encyclopedia Britannica, 1968); Nineteenth Century Documents Project of Lloyd Benson, *William Henry Seward's Higher Law Speech*, Furman University, available online at http://www.furman.edu/%7Ebenson/docs/seward.htm.

Highway Act of 1956, U.S.

Federal legislation signed into law on June 29, 1956, that established the National System of Interstate and Defense Highways to upgrade and modernize the road system of the United States. Supported by President Dwight D. Eisenhower, the act set up a 13-year program of highway construction to connect cities and industrial centers across the country for national defense and commercial purposes. To finance the program the act created the Federal Highway Trust Fund, with revenues to come from federal taxes on gasoline, tires, and truck tonnage. The act was expanded by acts in 1968 and 1973.

Further reading: Robert J. Allison, *American Social and Political Movements, 1945–2000: Pursuit of Liberty* (Detroit: St. James Press, 2000); Henry Steele Commager, ed., *Documents of American History*, 8th ed. (New York: Appleton-Century-Crofts, 1968); Henry Moon, *The Interstate Highway System* (Washington, D.C.: Association of American Geographers, 1994); Ray Spangenburg and Diane Moser, *The Story of America's Roads* (New York: Facts On File, 1992).

Hillsborough Agreement

See ANGLO-IRISH ACCORD OF 1985.

Hippocratic Oath

Ethical code of conduct appearing in the writings attributed to Hippocrates (c. 460–c. 377 B.C.), an ancient Greek physician often called the "father of medicine." Probably penned about 430 B.C., the oath embodied the duties and obligations of physicians, who have usually taken it upon entering the practice of medicine. It states, in part, that the physician "will use treatment to help the sick according to my ability and judgment, but I will never use it to injure or wrong them. I will not give poison to anyone . . . Similarly I will not give a pessary to a woman to cause abortion . . . Whatsoever in the course of practice I see or hear (or even outside my practice in social intercourse) that ought never to be published abroad, I will not divulge, but consider such things to be holy secrets."

Further reading: Ruth DeJauregui, *100 Medical Milestones That Shaped World History* (San Mateo, Calif.: Bluewood Books, 1998); Lilian R. Furst, *Medical Progress and Social Reality: A Reader in Nineteenth-Century Medicine and Literature* (Albany: State University of New York Press, 2000); Hippocrates, *The Oath*, Internet Classics Archive, available online at http://classics.mit.edu/Hippocrates/hippooath.html; Frank N.

Magill, *Great Events from History, Ancient and Medieval Series*, 3 vols. (Englewood Cliffs, N.J.: Salem Press, 1972).

Hirabayashi v. *United States*

U.S. Supreme Court decision issued on June 21, 1943, upholding a military curfew established on the West Coast after the Japanese attack on Pearl Harbor. Gordon Hirabayashi, an American-born citizen of Japanese ancestry, refused to obey the 8 P.M. to 6 A.M. curfew and the evacuation order imposed on Japanese-Americans (see EXECUTIVE ORDER 9066), on the grounds that they constituted racial discrimination, in violation of his Fifth Amendment right to due process. In its unanimous decision, the Court refused to consider the evacuation issue but justified the curfew as a temporary, emergency war measure. In 1983 Hirabayashi sued for vindication, charging "prosecutorial misconduct." In 1986 a federal district court struck down his conviction for refusing to obey the evacuation order but declined to reverse the curfew violation.

See also: *KOREMATSU* V. *UNITED STATES*.

Further reading: Henry Steele Commager, ed., *Documents of American History*, 8th ed. (New York: Appleton-Century-Crofts, 1968); Kermit Hall et al., eds., *American Legal History: Cases and Materials* 2d ed. (New York: Oxford University Press, 1996); Kermit L. Hall et al., eds., *The Oxford Companion to the Supreme Court of the United States* (New York: Oxford University Press, 1992); United States Supreme Court, *United States Reports: Cases Adjudged in the Supreme Court at . . . and Rules Announced at . . .* (New York: Banks & Brothers, Law Publishers, 1884–1921; Washington, D.C.: Government Printing Office, 1922–).

Hitler's Berlin Sportpalast Speech (Hitler's Speech on the Munich Crisis)

Infamous speech of invective and belligerence delivered by German chancellor Adolf Hitler at the Sportpalast (sports arena) in Berlin on September 26, 1938. He resolutely made claim to land in Czechoslovakia and attacked that nation's president, Eduard Beneš, who (Hitler falsely said) had set out to destroy and persecute the minority Sudeten Germans of Czechoslovakia. During Hitler's wildly exaggerated account of the ruinous conditions in the Sudetenland, he said his patience was at an end (for the Czech cession of the Sudetenland) and the decision for Beneš was either "peace or war." Beneš was to give the Germans their freedom, or the German people would go and fetch it themselves, concluded Hitler, who had become excited by his own reckless words.

See also: MUNICH AGREEMENT OF 1938.

Further reading: Max Domarus, ed., *Hitler: Speeches and Proclamations, 1932–1945* (Wauconda, Ill.: Bolchazy Carducci, 2000).

Hitler's Last Will and Political Testament

German document written on April 29, 1945, the day before Adolf Hitler committed suicide, and witnessed by Joseph Goebbels,

Wilhelm Burgdorf, Martin Bormann, and Hans Krebs. In this final message, the German Nazi leader blamed World War II on the Jews, "the truly guilty party in this murderous struggle." In it, Hitler also expelled Reich Marshal Hermann Goering and SS Reichsfuehrer Heinrich Himmler from the Nazi Party for their disloyalty and attempts to negotiate a peace with the Allies. Finally, he appointed a new cabinet to continue the war "by all available means." On the same day, Hitler also wrote a personal will, in which he recorded his wish to marry Eva Braun and named Martin Bormann his executor.

Further reading: "Humanitas International home page," Humanitas international, available online at http://www.humanitas-international.org/homepage.htm/.

Hitler's Proclamation on Invading the Soviet Union

Adolf Hitler's highly colored version of the events leading to his invasion of the Soviet Union; issued in a proclamation on June 22, 1941, to the German people. Unable to conquer Britain, he accused her of systematically ruining consolidation attempts in Europe and of misleading the smaller countries into believing that Germany had evil designs on them. Eventually carrying her "encirclement policy against Germany" into the Soviet Union, Britain began mobilizing a strong anti-German coalition. The Soviet Union, violating her pact of friendship with Germany, started piling up troops along her eastern border, invaded Finland and the Baltic states, and threatened Romania. Asked to guarantee Romanian integrity, Hitler agreed "because when the German Reich gives a guarantee . . . it also abides by it. We are neither Englishmen nor Jews." With the continuation of the Anglo-Soviet conspiracies in Romania, Bulgaria, and Yugoslavia, Hitler believed that "to continue as a mere observer would not only be a sin of omission but a crime against the German people—yes, even against the whole of Europe." He, therefore, had decided to go to war with the Soviet Union.

Further reading: Max Domarus, ed., *Hitler: Speeches and Proclamations, 1932–1945* (Wauconda, Ill.: Bolchazy Carducci, 2000).

Hitler's Speech Replying to Roosevelt

Masterful speech of political propaganda justifying his foreign policy, delivered by Germany's chancellor Adolf Hitler to the Reichstag (legislative assembly) in Berlin on April 28, 1939. He defended German occupation of Czechoslovakia, his denunciation of both the German-Polish Non-Aggression Pact of 1934 and the ANGLO-GERMAN NAVAL AGREEMENT OF 1935, and Germany's demands for access to East Prussia and for the return of the German city of Danzig (Gdansk). The Reichstag roared with applause for Hitler's replies to U.S. president Franklin D. Roosevelt, who had asked Hitler and Italian dictator Benito Mussolini (in an April 14 message about the futility of war) to give assurances of nonaggression. Hitler said that Germany had suffered from the unjust 1919 Treaty of VERSAILLES, under unilateral disarmament; saying

Germany was much smaller than the United States, which had unlimited mineral resources and wealth, he compared himself to Roosevelt, who had had "a much easier task" since coming to office in 1933. Hitler had conquered chaos, reestablished order, increased production, united Germans politically, and rearmed them, "without spilling blood."

Further reading: Max Domarus, ed., *Hitler: Speeches and Proclamations, 1932–1945* (Wauconda, Ill.: Bolchazy Carducci, 2000).

Hitler-Stalin Pact   See MOLOTOV-RIBBENTROP PACT.

Holden v. Hardy

U.S. Supreme Court decision of February 28, 1898, upholding a Utah statute regulating the hours of labor for men who worked in underground mines and in the smelting, reduction, and refining of ores or metals. The law was challenged as a violation of the FOURTEENTH AMENDMENT, a denial of due process and equal protection for both employer and employee. The Supreme Court ruled, however, that the state had the right, under its police power, to protect the health of citizens involved in dangerous occupations. It also argued that the state may interfere in a contract when the two parties have unequal bargaining power. The ruling served as a precedent for later state regulation of labor conditions.

Further reading: Henry Steele Commager, ed., *Documents of American History*, 8th ed. (New York: Appleton-Century-Crofts, 1968); Kermit Hall et al., eds., *American Legal History: Cases and Materials*, 2d ed. (New York: Oxford University Press, 1996); Kermit L. Hall et al., eds., *The Oxford Companion to the Supreme Court of the United States* (New York: Oxford University press, 1992); United States Supreme Court, *United States Reports: Cases Adjudged in the Supreme Court at . . . and Rules Announced at . . .* (New York: Banks & Brothers, Law Publishers, 1884–1921; Washington, D.C.: Government Printing Office, 1922–).

Holy Alliance of 1815

Document drafted by Russian czar Alexander I and signed at Paris on September 26, 1815, by Austrian emperor Francis I, Prussian king Frederick William III, and Czar Alexander. It was signed eventually by all the major European powers except Great Britain and the Ottoman Empire. Through the document (a vague declaration of principles), the signatory powers agreed to join together to form a "Holy Alliance," in which they pledged themselves to support policy decisions consistent with Christianity and the principles of love, justice, and peace, and in this way strive to maintain the status quo in Europe, which they had established at the Congress of Vienna in 1815 (see VIENNA, FINAL ACT OF THE CONGRESS OF). Later, the alliance became confused with the QUADRUPLE ALLIANCE OF 1815 and the reactionary policies that the three eastern monarchs came to endorse (Russia, Austria, and Prussia aimed to stem the tide of political freedom, ignited by the French Revolution).

Further reading: Margery Weiner, *The Sovereign Remedy; Europe after Waterloo* (New York: St. Martin's Press, 1973).

"Holy Alliance" Speech, Webster's   See WEBSTER'S SPEECH ON GREEK INDEPENDENCE.

Holy Constitution (La Sainte Constitution)   Imperial ordinance issued by Louis the Pious (Louis I of France) in A.D. 817, making his oldest son, Lothair I, coruler and sole heir to his empire. In addition, Louis gave his younger sons, Pepin I and Louis the German, sovereignty over two dependent kingdoms, Aquitaine and Bavaria, respectively. This created friction, especially after the birth of a fourth son, Charles the Bald (Charles II), by a second marriage and Louis the Pious's awarding of Aquitaine to him following Pepin I's death in A.D. 838 (Charles the Bald was also given Neustria [northwest France]). After the death of their father in A.D. 840, the sons quarreled over the succession until they reached an agreement three years later in the Treaty of VERDUN.

Further reading: Peter Godman and Roger Collins, *Charlemagne's Heir: New Perspectives on the Reign of Louis the Pious (814–840)* (New York: Clarendon Press, 1990).

Homeowners' Loan Act, U.S.   Federal legislation enacted on April 27, 1934, that guaranteed the principal and interest of the $2 billion in bonds that the U.S. HOMEOWNERS' REFINANCING ACT had authorized for refinancing individual home mortgages. The act made available to the Home Owners Loan Corporation additional funds for home maintenance and repair and for federally sponsored savings and loan associations.

Further reading: C. Lowell Harriss, *History and Policies of the Home Owners' Loan Corporation* (New York: National Bureau of Economic Research, 1951).

Homeowners' Refinancing Act, U.S.   New Deal legislation, enacted on June 13, 1933, that established the Home Owners Loan Corporation (HOLC) to refinance individual nonfarm home mortgages in the United States. The act was designed to avert foreclosure and evictions for the many urban families unable to meet existing mortgage payments during the Great Depression. The HOLC, with a revolving fund of $2 billion (raised through bond issues), refinanced home mortgages up to $14,000, at 5 percent interest, for up to 15 years. It was also authorized to grant cash advances for taxes, maintenance, and repair of properties. By the time it was terminated in 1936, the HOLC had extended loans to about a million homeowners.

Further reading: C. Lowell Harriss, *History and Policies of the Home Owners' Loan Corporation* (New York: National Bureau of Economic Research, 1951).

Home Rule Bill of 1886   Bill introduced on April 8, 1886, into Parliament by British prime minister William Gladstone (a Liberal), proposing a subordinate Irish legislature in Dublin, with authority over all matters concerning Ireland. The legislature was to consist of two chambers—one with 28 peers and 75 members elected by and from the propertied class, and the other with 204 elected members. The crown, however, was to have veto right, and the British parliament (which was to have no more Irish members) was to continue to determine all foreign, colonial, and defense policies, as well as matters relating to manufacture, trade, navigation, coinage, customs, and excise. Ireland was to contribute one-fifteenth of her revenue for this proposal. On the bill's second reading in the House of Commons in July 1886, it was defeated by 30 votes when the "Liberal Unionists" (led by Joseph Chamberlain and Lord Hartington) walked out in opposition to it (thus siding with the Conservatives). Parliament was dissolved. Gladstone was defeated in the ensuing elections and resigned.

Further reading: Gary Peatling, *British Opinion and Irish Self-Government, 1865–1925: From Unionism to Liberal Commonwealth* (Dublin: Irish Academic Press, 2001); John E. Redmond, *The Home Rule Bill* (London: Cassell & Co., 1912); Jeremy Smith, *Britain and Ireland: From Home Rule to Independence* (New York: Longman, 2000).

Home Rule Bill of 1913   Bill proposing some measure of self-government for Ireland, the third of its kind, introduced by British prime minister Herbert Asquith on April 11, 1912. It provided for a bicameral Irish legislature (a 40-member senate and a 164-member house of commons) and also for the retention of 42 Irish members in the British House of Commons. In the Protestant province of Ulster, hundreds signed a covenant (see BELFAST COVENANT OF 1912) pledging to resist home rule. In 1913, the bill was passed by the House of Commons on two occasions (January 16 and July 7) but rejected twice by the Lords (January 30 and July 15). On May 26, 1914, it passed the Commons for the third time and received royal sanction on September 18, 1914. Simultaneously, another act delayed its enforcement until the end of World War I, and the British government promised to reconsider the status of Ulster at that time. The bill was never operative and, in 1920, was replaced by the GOVERNMENT OF IRELAND ACT.

Further reading: Frank N. Magill, ed., *Great Events from History, Modern European Series*, 3 vols. (Englewood Cliffs, N.J.: Salem Press, 1973); Gary Peatling, *British Opinion and Irish Self-Government, 1865–1925: From Unionism to Liberal Commonwealth* (Dublin: Irish Academic Press, 2001); Jeremy Smith, *Britain and Ireland: From Home Rule to Independence* (New York: Longman, 2000); Jeremy Smith, *The Tories and Ireland: Conservative Party Politics and the Home Rule Crisis, 1910–1914* (Dublin: Irish Academic Press, 2000).

Homestead Act of 1862   First act passed by the U.S. Congress distributing public lands in the West to settlers. A long-standing demand for such legislation, which was to benefit laborers and tenant farmers, was met only after the

election of a Republican administration in 1860 and the secession of the South, which had opposed the policy, fearing an influx of antislavery homesteaders. The Homestead Act, enacted on May 20, 1862, provided 160 acres of unoccupied public land to any citizen, or intended citizen, who was head of a family or at least 21 years old and who was willing to occupy and cultivate the land for five years. The land was free except for a small filing fee. By 1870 nearly 14 million acres had been homesteaded.

Further reading: Donald C. Bacon, Roger H. Davidson, and Morton Keller, eds., *The Encyclopedia of the United States Congress* (New York: Simon & Schuster, 1995); Paul Wallace Gates, *Free Homesteads for all Americans: The Homestead Act of 1862* (Washington, D.C.: Civil War Centennial Commission, 1962); Lawrence Bacon Lee, *Kansas and the Homestead Act, 1862–1905* (New York: Arno Press, 1979).

Honduran Constitution of 1965   Constitution drawn up by the Honduran Constituent Assembly and adopted on June 5, 1965, containing many democratic elements and designating the assembly's candidate, Colonel Osvaldo López Arellano, the new president, who was to wield great powers. The constitution asserted that power be shared by the legislative, executive, and judicial branches of government; provided for fundamental rights, such as the freedom of speech, press, expression, and religion; and established that the economy was based on the principle of free enterprise. Despite such democratic guarantees, however, the president had the power to suspend certain rights and to declare martial law; the principle of checks and balances among the three governmental branches was not fully put into practice. Honduras was committed, the constitution declared, to the restoration of a federal republic of Central America (see CENTRAL AMERICAN TREATY OF UNION; UNITED PROVINCES OF CENTRAL AMERICA, DECLARATION OF INDEPENDENCE OF THE).

Further reading: Harvey K. Meyer, *Historical Dictionary of Honduras* (Metuchen, N.J.: Scarecrow Press, 1976).

Hoover's "Rugged Individualism" Speech   Speech delivered in New York City by Republican presidential candidate Herbert Hoover on October 22, 1928, toward the close of the election campaign. In this classic example of American conservative philosophy, Hoover condemned the Democratic platform as a misguided attempt to solve the problems of prohibition, farm relief, and electrical power through state socialism; he extolled free, private enterprise and initiative, a system of "rugged individualism," as the foundations of America's "unparalleled greatness." Government entry into commercial business, he argued, would destroy political equality, increase corruption, stifle initiative, undermine the development of leadership, extinguish opportunity, and "dry up the spirit of liberty and progress."

Further reading: Mortimer Adler, ed., *The Annals of America*, 18 vols. (Chicago: Encyclopedia Britannica, 1968); Henry Steele Commager, ed., *Documents of American History*, 8th ed. (New York: Appleton-Century-Crofts, 1968).

Hopewell, Treaty of   Agreement of November 28, 1785, between the Cherokee Indians and the commissioners of the United States, confirming Cherokee rights to most lands held in 1777. The treaty, reached at Hopewell, South Carolina, gave the United States sovereignty over the tribe and control of its trade. It was the first general Indian treaty made by the United States and established definite boundaries for Indian lands. Similar treaties with the Choctaw and Chickasaw Indians were signed at Hopewell the following year.

Further reading: Stephen A. Flanders and Carl N. Flanders, *Dictionary of American Foreign Affairs* (New York: Macmillan, 1993).

Hortensian Law (Lex Hortensia)   Ancient Roman law passed in 287 B.C. by Quintas Hortensius, dictator of Rome, making the decisions of the Tribal Assembly (Comitia Tributa) binding on all citizens (plebeians and patricians alike). The Tribal Assembly, presided over by the tribunes of the plebeians, had earlier passed legislation for relief from debts owed by plebeians, but the patrician-controlled Senate (which acted in the interests of creditors) refused to approve it; the plebs then threatened to secede from the Roman state. The Senate relented and empowered Hortensius, a plebeian, as dictator to resolve the problem. Hortensius thus decreed that, in the future, all resolutions passed by the Tribal Assembly had the force of law without requiring approval of the Senate. The law was a triumph of Roman democracy.

See also: PUBLILIAN LAWS.

Further reading: Frank N. Magill, ed., *Great Events from History, Ancient and Medieval Series*, 3 vols. (Englewood Cliffs, N.J.: Salem Press, 1972); Richard E. Mitchell, *Patricians and Plebeians: The Origin of the Roman State* (Ithaca, N.Y.: Cornell University Press, 1990).

Hossbach Memorandum (Hossbach Minutes)   Record of the führer (German leader) Adolf Hitler's ambitious plans in 1937 to take control of central Europe, written by Hitler's army aide, Lieutenant Colonel Friedrich Hossbach, following a meeting he attended with Germany's military leaders and Foreign Minister Constantin von Neurath. Hossbach said that Hitler's strategy was to prolong the Spanish Civil War of 1936–39 and encourage Italian interest in the Balearic Islands, while Germany confronted France in North Africa. This "tension in the Mediterranean" and possible "war of France and England against Italy" would work favorably for Germany, which then would pick the right, opportune moment to descend on Czechoslovakia and Austria militarily.

Further reading: Keith Eubank, *World War II: Roots and Causes*, 2d ed. (Lexington, Mass.: D.C. Heath, 1992).

"House Divided" Speech, Lincoln's

Abraham Lincoln's speech, delivered on June 16, 1858, accepting the Republican Party nomination for U.S. senator. Commenting on the KANSAS-NEBRASKA ACT and the decision in *DRED SCOTT V. SANDFORD*, Lincoln stated: " 'A house divided against itself cannot stand.' I believe this government cannot endure permanently half slave and half free." He maintained that he did not expect the Union to be dissolved but believed it would cease to be divided: "It will become all one thing, or all the other." Though Lincoln was not the first to use the "house divided" phrase, this speech gave the idea national currency.

Further reading: Don E. Fehrenbacher, ed., *Abraham Lincoln's Speeches and Writings*, 2 vols. (New York: Library of America, 1989).

Housing Act of 1934, U.S.

See NATIONAL HOUSING ACT OF 1934.

Housing Act of 1937, U.S.

See WAGNER-STEAGALL ACT.

Housing Acts, U.S.

See NATIONAL HOUSING ACT OF 1934, U.S.; NATIONAL HOUSING ACT OF 1937, U.S.; NATIONAL HOUSING ACT OF 1965, U.S.

Howe's Letters to Lord John Russell

Four letters written in 1839 by Canadian journalist Joseph Howe of Nova Scotia to the British colonial secretary in Lower Canada, Lord John Russell, in which the author made an eloquent appeal for responsible government. At the time, a British-appointed governor and legislative council could continue to govern with or without the confidence of a popularly elected legislative assembly. Howe, in his letters, sought to reverse this state of affairs by making the government's rule dependent upon the will of the majority. Russell's TEN RESOLUTIONS, which had categorically rejected popular demands for such a reform (see NINETY-TWO RESOLUTIONS, PAPINEAU'S), motivated Howe to write the letters.

See also: DURHAM'S REPORT.

Further reading: Norah Story, *The Oxford Companion to Canadian History and Literature* (Toronto: Oxford University Press, 1967).

Hubertusburg, Treaty of

Peace treaty made between Prussia on one side and Austria (and her ally Saxony) on the other at Hubertusburg or Hubertsburg, a castle in Saxony, on February 15, 1763. It ended the Third Silesian War (1756–63), or Seven Years' War, between them over control of the former Austrian province of Silesia. The treaty reconfirmed Austria's cession of Silesia to Prussia, ratified the 1742 treaties of BRESLAU and BERLIN and 1745 Treaty of DRESDEN, and divided practically all German lands between these two powers. Prussia also vowed to support Austria's archduke Joseph II in the election for the king of the Romans, and returned Saxony to its elector. Austria, whose power declined, agreed to a res-toration of the status quo in Europe, as Prussian power and prestige rose.

See also: BERLIN, PEACE OF.

Further reading: Charles L. Phillips and Alan Axelrod, eds., *Encyclopedia of Historical Treaties and Alliances*, 2 vols. (New York: Facts On File, 2001).

Hudson's Bay Company Charter

Royal charter for incorporating the Hudson's Bay Company, granted on May 2, 1670, by England's king Charles II. It gave this English fur-trading company wide proprietary rights to territory surrounding "Hudson's Bay" and to all lands drained by rivers flowing into it. The charter allowed the company to make laws for the "lands aforesaid" and to send warships and armed men "into any of their [the company's] plantations, forts, factories, or places of trade aforesaid, for the security and defence of the same." Two Frenchmen, Pierre Esprit Radisson and Medard Chouart (Sieur des Groseilliers), who founded the company, had been unable to interest French authorities in the fur-trading route through Hudson Bay and had turned to Prince Rupert, a cousin of Charles II, who secured the charter. The company eventually maintained trading posts throughout Canada and a few forts on U.S. soil; it still exists, but without its original monopolistic, territorial, and administrative rights.

Further reading: Privy Seale, *The Royal Charter for incorporating the Hudson's Bay Company, A.D. 1670*, History of the World, available online at http://www.historyoftheworld.com/canada/docs/hbc_ch~1.htm.

Hull-Alfaro Treaty (General Treaty of Friendship and Cooperation between the U.S.A. and Panama)

Agreement amending the HAY-BUNAU-VARILLA TREATY signed in Washington, D.C., on March 2, 1936, by U.S. secretary of state Cordell Hull and the foreign minister of Panama, Ricardo J. Alfaro. Making substantial concessions to Panama, the United States renounced its guarantee of the independence of Panama, the right to expropriate additional land for Panama Canal use without restrictions, the right of eminent domain in the cities of Panama and Colón, and the unlimited right to defend the canal. Panama's annual annuity of $250,000 was also increased to $430,000. The U.S. Senate approved the treaty in July 1939, only after the United States was assured the freedom to act without consultation in defense emergencies.

Further reading: Charles I. Bevans, comp., *Treaties and Other International Agreements of the United States of America, 1776–1949*, 12 vols. (Washington, D.C.: U.S. Government Printing Office, 1968).

Hülsemann Letter

Letter issued by Austria's chargé d'affaires in the United States, Chevalier Johann von Hülsemann, in 1849, protesting American support for Louis Kossuth, leader of the Hungarian Revolution of 1848–49 against the rule of Austria's emperor Francis Joseph. The angry protest charged that the United States was interfering in Austria's affairs when U.S. president Zachary Taylor's administration authorized (June 1849) A. Dudley Mann, a U.S. diplomat in Europe, to go to Hungary and to consider formal recognition of the revolutionary government, if he thought such a move justified. The revolution fell apart, and Mann never reached Hungary.

See also: WEBSTER'S REPLY TO HÜLSEMANN LETTER.

Further reading: Paul Revere Frothingham, *Edward Everett: Orator and Statesman* (Boston: Houghton Mifflin, 1925).

Humanae Vitae (Of Human Life)

Encyclical issued by Pope Paul VI, published on July 29, 1968, and sent to all the bishops of the Roman Catholic Church, reaffirming the church's official teaching on contraception and its opposition to artificial methods of birth control. The encyclical, which was not issued as an infallible teaching of the church but as a pronouncement expected to be followed by all Catholics, states that only by abstinence or the rhythm method would believers be permitted to practice birth control; it reconfirmed the church's teaching that each act of sexual intercourse was to "remain open to the transmission of life." It added that, in the event of a woman's decision to follow a physician's recommendation to take measures that were necessary to maintain her health and that would also inhibit conception, the woman's action would not be condemned as long as contraception was not willed by her. Finally, the document restated the church's condemnation of abortion and sterilization. The encyclical aroused much opposition among the laity and priesthood alike.

Further reading: Vatican, *Encyclical of Pope Paul VI on the Regulation of Birth July 25, 1968*, Humanae Vitae, available online at http://www.vatican.va/holy_father/paul_vi/encyclicals/index.htm.

Humani Generis Unitas (On the Unity of Mankind)

Lost encyclical denouncing racism and anti-Semitism, secretly drafted in Paris in 1938 by American Jesuit John Lafarge (with fellow Jesuits Gustav Grundlach and Gustave Desbuquois) at the request of Pope Pius XI, the timely publication of which might have altered the course of history. However, Pius XI died before signing it, his successor shelved it, and the encyclical's draft mysteriously disappeared. It was unearthed in 1967 and finally published in France in 1995. The dignity of the human being and the unity of all humankind are violated by racism, the draft argued. However, the encyclical appeared to condone religious anti-Semitism by suggesting that Jews were outcasts, an idea later rejected in the *NOSTRA AETATE*. Although only 14 of its 100 pages dealt with anti-Semitism, it was the Roman Catholic Church's strongest condemnation of this growing trend in Europe at the time.

Further reading: Georges Passelecq and Bernard Suchecky, eds., *The Hidden Encyclical of Pius XI* (Orlando, Fla.: Harcourt Brace, 1997).

Human Nature and Conduct

Major work written by American philosopher and educator John Dewey, published in 1922 and based on three lectures he delivered at Stanford University in the spring of 1918. Subtitled "An Introduction to Social Psychology," the book "sets forth a belief that an understanding of habit and of different types of habit is the key to social psychology while the operation of impulse and intelligence gives the key to individualized mental activity." An introductory chapter is followed by four parts dealing singly with the places of habit, impulse, and intelligence in conduct and a conclusion reflecting upon morality and freedom. Dewey criticized the moralities of the past as being arbitrarily derived rather than developed from a scientific understanding of human nature within the social context. Morality, he argued, consisted of actions developed in response to specific situations; reactions to these became habits. With education man can alter his behavior to suit new situations.

Further reading: John Dewey, *Human Nature and Conduct* (New York: Modern Library, 1957).

Humble Petition and Advice

Petition (first entitled "A Humble Address and Remonstrance") presented to Oliver Cromwell, lord protector, by a parliamentary delegation on March 31, 1657, requesting him to accept the English crown, reestablish the House of Lords, and revive the ancient constitution. Amid strong opposition from some senior members, Cromwell rejected the royal title (king) on May 8, 1657. On May 25, he accepted a revised petition, giving him the power to nominate his successor and members of the upper house (Lords). But control of the membership of the privy council and the admission or exclusion of elected members rested with the triennial two-house parliament. The petition also proposed toleration for trinitarian Christians (excluding Episcopalians and Roman Catholics). This system did not last too long after Cromwell's death in 1658.

See also: INSTRUMENT OF GOVERNMENT.

Further reading: Carl Stephenson and Frederick George Marcham, eds., *Sources of English Constitutional History: A Selection of Documents from A.D. 600 to the Present* (New York: Harper & Row, 1937).

Hume's *Treatise of Human Nature*

Important three-volume treatise by Scottish philosopher-historian David Hume, completed in 1737 when he was age 26. The first volume was published in 1739, the other two in 1740. The treatise (declared Hume on the title page of the first book) was "an attempt to introduce the experimental Method of Reasoning into Moral Subjects." He thus sought to establish the groundwork for a truly empirical science of human nature as opposed to previous philosophies that relied "more upon invention than experience." The titles of the three books are "Of the Understanding"; "Of the Passions"; and "Of Morals"; each book is further subdivided into various parts. The work first received only slight attention, so in 1748 Hume published a more popular version of the first book called *An Enquiry Concerning Human Understanding,* which secured him much recognition.

Further reading: David Hume, *A Treatise of Human Nature,* eds. David Fate Norton and Mary J. Norton (New York: Oxford University Press, 2000).

Humphrey-Hawkins (Full-Employment and Balanced Growth) Act

U.S. legislation signed into law on October 27, 1978, to establish a system by which the federal government, in cooperation with state and local governments and private enterprise, would work to reduce unemployment and inflation and promote steady economic growth. It set a national goal of 3 percent inflation by 1983 and a goal of 4 percent unemployment. Sponsored by Senator Hubert H. Humphrey of Minnesota (who died before its passage) and Representative Augustus F. Hawkins of California, the act required that Congress, the president, and the Federal Reserve Board cooperate in setting policies to achieve full employment with stable prices. It required programs of specific goals in employment, inflation, production, real income, productivity, price levels, balanced growth, trade balance, balanced budget, and federal share of the gross national product.

Further reading: Dennis M. Roth, *Full Employment and Balanced Growth Act of 1978 (The Humphrey-Hawkins Bill)* (Washington, D.C.: Library of Congress, Congressional Research Service, 1978).

Humphrey's Executor v. United States (Rathbun v. United States)

U.S. Supreme Court decision issued on May 27, 1935, restricting the president's power to remove from office members of independent regulatory agencies. In 1933 President Franklin D. Roosevelt had removed William E. Humphrey from the Federal Trade Commission because of differences over policy, claiming that the presidential power to appoint officials implied the power to remove them. Humphrey died, but his executor sued for the deceased's salary. The Supreme Court unanimously ruled in favor of Humphrey and prohibited future dismissals of members of regulatory agencies except for specified causes. The FTC was declared a "quasi-legislative or quasi-judicial" agency, whose officials must be able to make decisions independent of executive control.

Further reading: Leonard W. Levy and Kenneth L. Karst, eds., *Encyclopedia of the American Constitution,* 2d ed. (New York: Macmillan Reference, 2000).

Hungarian Acts of 1848   See MARCH LAWS.

Hungarian Declaration of Democracy

Declaration made in Budapest on October 23, 1989, by Hungarian acting president Matyas Szuros, proclaiming Hungary a free republic. In addition, Szuros declared that the Hungarian Republic would be a democratic state "in which the values of bourgeois democracy and democratic socialism are expressed equally." The declaration most significantly reflected a change in the thinking of Hungary's communist leadership, which for over four decades had denounced all Western values in favor of the Soviet Union's interpretation of communist ideology. The fact that the declaration occurred on the 33rd anniversary of the Hungarian Revolt of 1956, a democratic movement that was crushed by Soviet forces, increased the jubilation of the nation's people.

Further reading: Ruth M. Anderson and J. M. Anderson, *Barbed Wire for Sale: The Hungarian Transition to Democracy, 1988–1991* (Graham, Wash.: Poetic License, 1999); Andras Bozoki, *The Roundtable Talks of 1989: The Genesis of Hungarian Democracy: Analysis and Documents* (Budapest, Hungary: Central European University Press 2002).

Hungarian Declaration of Independence

Declaration drawn up under the influence of Hungarian statesman Louis Kossuth and confirmed by the Hungarian Diet (assembly) on April 14, 1849, in the Hungarian city of Debrecen; it proclaimed the independence of Hungary. The document declared that the autonomous state included Hungary proper as well as Transylvania and Croatia, and that the Austrian Hapsburg ruler and his descendants were deposed from the Hungarian throne. Although the MARCH LAWS of 1848 had provided for Hungarian autonomy (with the Austrian emperor as Hungary's king), the Austrian government had, in a new constitution in March 1849, rendered that document void. The move, however, did not succeed in suppressing Hungarian nationalism, but rather antagonized the revolutionaries, driving them to issue the declaration.

See also: KREMSIER CONSTITUTION.

Further reading: Paul Ignatus, *Hungary* (London: Ernest Benn, 1972); C. A. Macartney, *Hungary: A Short History* (Chicago: Aldine, 1962); Denis Sinor, *History of Hungary* (New York: Praeger, 1959); Otto Zarek, *The History of Hungary* (London: Selwyn & Bleunt, 1939).

Hünkâr Iskelesi (Unkiar Skelessi), Treaty of

Treaty of peace and alliance concluded between Russia and the Ottoman Empire (Turkey) on July 8, 1833, in the Turkish town of Hünkâr Iskelesi or Unkiar Skelessi, near Constantinople (Istanbul). The two powers agreed to aid each other in time of need and to defend the other against invaders. In a secret article of the treaty, Russia agreed to limit her right to Ottoman aid if, in time of war, the Ottomans promised to close the Strait of Dardanelles and the Bosporus to all foreign ships except those of Russia. This provision alarmed other powers, especially Britain, which disliked the supposedly privileged passage of Russian warships through the straits (see STRAITS CONVENTION). The treaty was to remain effective eight years, with the hope that it would be perpetual.

See also: KÜTAHYA, CONVENTION OF; LONDON, TREATY OF (1840).

Further reading: Reeva S. Simon, Philip Mattar, and Richard W. Bulliet, eds., *Encyclopedia of the Modern Middle East*, 4 vols. (New York: Macmillan, 1996).

Hurley v. Irish-American Gay, Lesbian and Bisexual Group of Boston

U.S. Supreme Court decision issued on June 19, 1995, that upheld the right of parade organizers to bar participants whose message they disagree with. The case was brought on behalf of the South Boston Allied War Veterans Council, which for a number of years organized Boston's St. Patrick's Day Parade. In 1993 the council refused a place in the parade to the Gay, Lesbian and Bisexual Group of Boston, which was formed for the sole purpose of marching in the parade as a way for its members to express pride in their Irishness and their homosexuality. The group sued successfully for admission under the provisions of a Massachusetts law that prohibited discrimination on the grounds of sexual orientation in public places. In a unanimous decision, the Supreme Court overturned the state court's ruling. While it did not challenge the constitutionality of the Massachusetts law under which the ruling had been made, it did affirm the right of the parade organizers to include only those groups with whose messages they agreed. The Court noted that the First Amendment's guarantee of freedom of speech also conveys the right to refrain from speaking and to refrain from expressing a view with which the speaker disagrees. Therefore, the government cannot force any person or organization to speak in a way that is politically correct if that person or group does not wish to do so.

Further reading: Peter H. Irons, ed., *May It Please the Court: The First Amendment; Transcripts of the Oral Arguments Made Before the Supreme Court in Sixteen Key First Amendment Cases* (New York: New Press, 1997); Arthur S. Leonard, ed., *Homosexuality, Politics, and Speech* (New York: Garland Pub., 1997).

Hyde Park Declaration

Agreement between U.S. president Franklin D. Roosevelt and Canadian prime minister W. L. Mackenzie King, signed by them at Roosevelt's estate at Hyde Park, New York, on April 20, 1941; provided for shared defense production and for greater U.S. purchases of war materials from Canada, thus creating closer economic ties between the two nations. The agreement continued the pattern of friendship and cooperative defense established by the OGDENSBURG DECLARATION.

Further reading: William L. M. Mackenzie, *The Hyde Park Declaration; Cooperation in Economic Defence . . .* (Ottawa: Edmond Cloutier, Printer to the King's Most Excellent Majesty, 1941).

I

Iglesias Law (Ley Iglesias)   Law authored by the Mexican minister of justice José María Iglesias and signed by President Ignacio Comonfort of Mexico on April 11, 1857, stipulating strict limits on the fees to be paid clergy for their services. Specifically, the law provided that clergy could not charge the poor fees for performing baptisms, marriages, or funerals; that those with moderate incomes were to be charged modest fees; and that clergy who refused to comply with the law would be punished severely. The law was intended to curb clerical abuses, as well as diminish the power of the Roman Catholic Church with respect to the state. As with earlier reforms involving church-state relations (see JUÁREZ LAW; LERDO LAW), the law was condemned by the church. These reforms helped ignite the War of the Reform (1857–60) between conservatives and liberals in Mexico.

See also: MEXICAN CONSTITUTION OF 1857.

Further reading: Ray F. Broussard, *Ignacio Comonfort: His Contributions to the Mexican Reform, 1855–1857* (Ann Arbor, Mich.: Xerox University Microfilms International, 1959); Richard N. Sinkin, *Modernization and Reform in Mexico, 1855–1876* (Ann Arbor, Mich.: Xerox University Microfilms, 1972).

Iguala, Plan of   Plan drawn up in Iguala (state of Guerrero, Mexico) by the Mexican political and military leader Agustín de Iturbide in 1821. After defecting from the Spanish cause in 1820, Iturbide joined the independence movement and, in collaboration with the insurgent Vicente Guerrero, drafted a plan for Mexican independence. This plan, which laid the foundations for the future constitution, had three main provisons: equality under the law for Creoles and Spaniards who settled in Mexico; Roman Catholicism as the only acceptable religion; and the establishment of an independent empire under Ferdinand VII (king of Spain) or a European prince acceptable to Mexico. The plan was generally supported by Mexican independence leaders, although it completely ignored the rights of the lower classes.

See also: CÓRDOBA, TREATY OF.

Further reading: Wallace L. McKeehan, *Plan of Iguala and the Treaty of Cordova*. Mexican Independence, available online at http://www.tamu.edu/ccbn/dewitt/iguala.htm.

Ilbert Bill   Controversial bill introduced by Sir C. P. Ilbert (law member in the executive counsel of India's governor general Lord Ripon) in 1883, seeking to remove racial inequities by allowing Indian judges and magistrates to try Europeans. According to the Criminal Procedure Code of 1873, Europeans could be tried only by European magistrates and judges, except in presidency towns where they could be tried by Indian officials. The British community in India angrily protested against the bill, even boycotting Lord Ripon, who was one of its main supporters. The government finally succumbed to the pressure and fundamentally altered the bill—entitling British citizens to a jury, half of which would be European. It was passed by the Indian Legislative Council on January 25, 1884. In its new form, it incensed the rising middle class in India and helped fan the nationalist fervor that led to the formation of the Indian National Congress in 1885.

Further reading: Ainslie T. Embree, ed., *Encyclopedia of Asian History,* 4 vols. (New York: Charles Scribner's Sons, 1988).

Illinois v. McArthur   U.S. Supreme Court decision issued on February 20, 2001, that gave police the right to prevent a suspect from entering his home until a search warrant to search the home could be obtained. In 1997 Tesa McArthur had two Sullivan, Illinois, policemen accompany her while she removed her belongings from the trailer she had shared with her estranged husband, Charles McArthur. Upon leaving the trailer, she informed the policemen that McArthur kept marijuana under the living room sofa. The officers called McArthur onto the front porch and asked for permission to search the premises. When he refused, one officer kept him from reentering the trailer while the other went to get a search warrant. About two hours later, the second officer returned with a warrant, whereupon the trailer was searched, the marijuana was discovered, and McArthur was arrested. At his trail, McArthur's attorney had the evidence suppressed on the grounds that it had been obtained illegally, McArthur's detention on the porch constituting a violation of his Fourth Amendment rights. In an 8-1 decision, the Supreme Court overturned the lower court's ruling on the grounds that the officers' conduct was reasonable given the information they had received from McArthur's wife, and that McArthur would have destroyed the evidence had he been allowed to reenter the trailer pending the issue of a warrant.

Further reading: Criminal Law and Procedure Decisions, "*Illinois v. McArthur.*" FindLaw for Legal Professionals, available online at http://sol.lp.findlaw.com/2000/mcarthur.html; Robert S. Greenberger, "Court's Decision Bolsters Powers of Police in Conducting Searches," *Wall Street Journal,* February 21, 2001.

Imitation of Christ (Imitatio Christi)   Religious treatise affirming the Christian devotional life, reputedly written by the German-born Dutch monk Thomas à Kempis about 1425. Some scholars hold that the Dutch Roman Catholic reformer Gerard Groote authored the work, which was written in Latin in simple language and style. It is divided into four parts: the first contains "exhortations useful for spiritual living"; the second advocates spiritualism over materialism; the third explains how a Christ-centered soul can find peace; and the fourth shows how human faith is strengthened through the sacrament of the Eucharist or Holy Communion. Various attempts were made to trace its authorship to other earlier writers (St. Bonaventure, John Gerson, and Pope Innocent III, among others) but without success.

Further reading: Joseph H. Dahmus, *A History of Medieval Civilization* (New York: Odyssey Press, 1964); Charles W. Eliot, ed., *The Harvard Classics,* 51 vols. (New York: P. F. Col-

lier and Son, 1937); Frank N. Magill, ed., *Great Events from History, Ancient and Medieval Series,* 3 vols. (Englewood Cliffs, N.J.: Salem Press, 1972).

Immigration Act of 1965, U.S.   Landmark measure signed into law on October 3, 1965, by U.S. president Lyndon B. Johnson at the Statue of Liberty; set annual limits of 120,000 immigrants from the Western Hemisphere, but no national quotas, and set annual limits of 170,000 immigrants from the rest of the world, with a quota (limit) of 20,000 from any single country. The act, which became fully effective within three years, ended the national quota system established under the IMMIGRATION QUOTA ACT OF 1924. It gave priority to immediate relatives of U.S. citizens and resident aliens and to people with special skills. For the first time it set a ceiling on immigration from the Western Hemisphere.

Further reading: Carl N. Flanders and Stephen A. Flanders, *Dictionary of American Foreign Affairs* (New York: Macmillan, 1993); E. P. Hutchinson, *Legislative History of American Immigration Policy, 1798–1965* (Philadelphia: University of Pennsylvania Press, 1981).

Immigration Act of 1990, U.S.   Major law sponsored by Connecticut representative Bruce A. Morrison and signed by U.S. president George H. W. Bush on November 29, 1990, allowing more immigrants into the United States, especially skilled workers (like engineers and scientists) and immediate relatives of U.S. citizens. The new law raised the annual cap on immigration from 530,000 to 700,000 through 1994 and set it at 675,000 each year beginning in 1995. Included in the act were provisions allowing U.S. authorities to deport quickly certain immigrants convicted of aggravated felonies (like violent crimes, political crimes, and money laundering); lift immigration exclusions based on sexual orientation and political views (though the State Department could ban persons considered a threat to foreign policy); and ease medical restrictions.

Further reading: Donald C. Bacon, Roger H. Davidson, and Morton Keller, eds., *The Encyclopedia of the United States Congress* (New York: Simon & Schuster, 1995); Carl N. Flanders and Stephen A. Flanders, *Dictionary of American Foreign Affairs* (New York: Macmillan, 1993); David M. Reimers, *Still the Golden Door: The Third World Comes to America* (New York: Columbia University Press, 1985).

Immigration and Nationality Act of 1952, U.S.   See MCCARRAN-WALTER ACT.

Immigration Quota Act of 1924, U.S. (National Origins Act, Johnson-Reed Act)   Federal U.S. immigration legislation enacted on May 26, 1924, that amended the U.S. EMERGENCY QUOTA ACT by halving the 1921 quota (placing the number of immigrants at 164,447) and by limiting annual immigration for any group to 2 percent of that group's U.S.

population according to the census of 1890. This quota was to apply until 1927, when the limit on immigrants was to be set at 150,000, apportioned by national origin according to the 1920 census. Sponsored by Senator Hiram W. Johnson of California and Senator James A. Reed of Missouri, the act favored immigrants from northern and western Europe. It aroused so much hostility that it was not implemented until 1929.

Further reading: Carl N. Flanders and Stephen A. Flanders, *Dictionary of American Foreign Affairs* (New York: Macmillan, 1993); E. P. Hutchinson, *Legislative History of American Immigration Policy, 1798–1965* (Philadelphia: University of Pennsylvania Press, 1981).

Immigration Reform and Control Act of 1986, U.S.

Legislation signed into law on November 6, 1986, liberalizing regulations for persons residing illegally in the United States and seeking amnesty. It provided a process for legalizing the status of many illegal aliens who entered the United States before January 1, 1982. Under the new law, qualified alien applicants could receive temporary resident status and then, after 18 months' residence in the United States, could apply for permanent resident status. The act also imposed civil and criminal penalties on employers who knowingly hire or help aliens not allowed to work in the United States. Among the many other provisions of the act were the categorization of temporary workers into two groups (agricultural laborers and all others), antidiscrimination rules, and some increases in emigration from colonies of foreign nations.

Further reading: Carl N. Flanders and Stephen A. Flanders, *Dictionary of American Foreign Affairs* (New York: Macmillan, 1993); U.S. Commission on Immigration Reform, *U.S. Immigration Policy: Restoring Credibility* (Washington, D.C.: U.S. Commission on Immigration Reform, 1994).

Immigration Restriction Act of 1902, Australian (White Australia Policy)

Australian legislation by Prime Minister Edmund Barton's Commonwealth Parliament (1901–2) to exclude non-Europeans (particularly Asians) by making it mandatory for prospective immigrants to successfully complete a 50-word dictation test "in any European language." In 1905, this last clause was amended to read "a prescribed language." Passed almost unanimously, the act was part of the White Australia Policy (see IMMIGRATION RESTRICTION ACT OF 1925, AUSTRALIAN), viewing the new immigrants primarily as a threat to the European labor market. While the act did not specify the races or types of people to be excluded, the manner in which the test was administered made it quite evident. The dictation tests were abolished by the Migration Act of 1958.

See also: PACIFIC ISLAND LABORERS' ACT.

Further reading: F. K. Crowley, *Modern Australia in Documents, 1901–1939,* 2 vols. (Melbourne: Wren, 1973).

Immigration Restriction Act of 1925, Australian

Legislative amendment (September 23, 1925) of the IMMIGRATION RESTRICTION ACT OF 1902 to cope with the growing industrial unrest in Australia. It was specifically directed against two British-born Australian leaders of striking seamen, and provided for the deportation of foreign-born agitators. The government could also ban immigrants on the basis of their nationality, class, race, and occupation—referring, apparently, to the large-scale Italian or other European immigration, which, it was feared, might sully Australia's racial purity. The act was bitterly opposed by the Labour Party, which viewed it as an infringement on union and civil liberties. It was never effectively enforced.

Further reading: F. K. Crowley, *Modern Australia in Documents, 1901–1939,* 2 vols. (Melbourne: Wren, 1973).

Immunity Act of 1954, U.S.

See ULLMANN V. UNITED STATES.

Imperialism, a Study

Comprehensive, seminal critique of economic imperialism written by English economist John A. Hobson and first published in London in 1902. Hobson saw imperialism's "taproot" in the financial and profitable interests of capitalists, who sought foreign markets for manufactures and investments because of restricted absorption of goods and capital at home (because of monopolistic behavior by industrial and financial chiefs and lower consuming power by the masses—the result of a maldistribution of income). The growth of economic imperialism was also helped by the spirit of adventure, patriotism, and philanthropy, but it could be checked by social reforms restricting the profits of the capitalist class and raising the income level of the public so that it bought up all manufactures and left none for overseas markets, Hobson said.

Further reading: J. A. Hobson, *Writings on Imperialism and Internationalism,* ed. Peter Cain (London: Routledge/Thoemmes Press, 1992); Mark A. Kishlansky, ed., *Sources of the West: Readings in Western Civilization,* vol. 2, 4th ed. (New York: Longman, 2001).

Impuls 99

Manifesto issued on July 23, 1999, with the endorsement of more than 200 Czech intellectuals from all walks of life, expressing dissatisfaction with politicians and the direction of Czech society at the time. It was drafted by Jana Smidova (former right-wing journalist), Tomáš Halik (priest and disciple of Czech president Václav Havel), and Jiří Pehe (political scientist and Havel's former foreign policy chief) to initiate a public dialogue on the current status and future direction of the Czech Republic. The manifesto sought early membership in the European Union, EU (formerly called the European Community), a less centralized government, improvement in the legal and educational systems, and an end to political dissension. Halik's and Pehe's political associations made the manifesto suspect in the eyes of many politicians; however, the authors insisted that this was just the first of the group's many planned undertakings to revive democracy in the country.

Further reading: Jan Culik, "Culik's Czech Republic No Pulse 99," Central Europe Review, available online at http://www.ce-review.org/99/7culik7.html; "The Disappearing Czech Intellectual," *Economist* (August 21, 1999): 41.

Indemnity and Oblivion, Act of

English act passed in 1660 by the Convention Parliament (the first Parliament after the restoration of monarchical government), giving the power of the law to a clause in the Declaration of BREDA of King Charles II of England. The act included amnesty for all political offenses committed during the Commonwealth (the English government established after the execution of Charles I in 1649 until the restoration of Charles II in 1660); it also included indemnity for all acts of treason and all state offenses committed during this period. However, more than 100 individuals were not forgiven or pardoned, including the Puritan statesman Sir Harry Vane, the parliamentarian General John Lambert, the regicides, and others involved in the revolt against Charles I. Land settlements were made in favor of the original owners.

Further reading: Mary E. Helms, *The Convention Parliament of 1660* (Ann Arbor, Mich.: University Microfilms, 1964); *His Majesties Gracious Speech . . . Concerning the Speedy Passing of the Bill of Indemnity & Oblivion . . .* (Ann Arbor, Mich.: University Microfilms International, 1982).

Independent Treasury Act, U.S.

Federal legislation enacted on August 8, 1846, that established an independent treasury, separate from the national banking and financial system, in Washington, D.C., as well as subtreasuries in various U.S. cities. This system replaced the National Bank of the United States. A similar act, passed in 1840, had been repealed the following year. According to the 1846 measure, the federal treasury would store all public funds and would receive and disburse all federal payments. The act required that such payments be made in gold or silver coin or treasury notes, an effort to remove from circulation unsecured currencies. The act remained in effect until the U.S. Civil War (1861–65).

Further reading: Henry Steele Commager, ed., *Documents of American History*, 8th ed. (New York: Appleton-Century-Crofts, 1968).

Indian Councils Act of 1909

Legislation of May 25, 1909, based on the reforms evolved by John Morley (Britain's secretary of state for India) and Lord Minto (viceroy of India), which increased the membership and power of India's imperial and provincial legislative councils, with the latter now having elected members. It also introduced the system of communal representation for Muslims and other special groups, which created the rift that eventually led to the partition of India. The Supreme Council membership was increased from 16 to a maximum of 60, and membership of the three legislative councils (Bombay, Bengal, and Madras) grew to 50. Fifty members were added to the United Provinces, Assam, and Eastern Bengal, and 30 members to the other provinces. Third and most important of the Indian Council Acts, it became operative on November 15, 1909.

Further reading: E. Major, *Viscount Morley and Indian Reform* (London: J. Nisbet & Co., 1910); Pardaman Singh, *Lord Minto and Indian Nationalism, 1905–1910* (Allahabad, India: Chugh Publications, 1976).

Indian Evidence Act

British parliamentary act passed in 1872, defining the rules of evidence considered admissible in India's courts. The aim was to streamline judicial procedures in the interests of efficiency and uniformity. In India, where intracaste disputes were resolved by appeal to caste councils, the act imposed an alien state system—where a stranger, often unaware of the subtle nuances of the caste systems or the circumstances surrounding the case, adjudicated on the issue. At the caste courts, most of the proceedings were oral and there was often no documentary evidence at all. With the new, stringent rules of evidence in the state courts, litigants sometimes evaded the caste courts and brought their cases here directly. This undermined the hitherto powerful position of the punchayats (caste councils), creating a wide rift between custom and law. Many caste councils continued to conduct their own trials, irrespective of the decisions of the state court.

Further reading: M. Monir and Deoki N. Agarwala, *Principles and Digest of the Law of Evidence: Being a Commentary on the Indian Evidence Act, 1 of 1872*, 2 vols., 11th ed. (Allahabad, India: University Book Agency, 1995).

Indian Independence Act, British

British legislation of July 18, 1947, providing for the formal transfer of power in India to the two new dominions of India and Pakistan on August 15, 1947. Earlier that year, Britain's prime minister Clement Attlee had speeded the process by his bold announcement (February 20) of the British government's definite intention to transfer power into responsible hands no later than June 1948. Taking into account his discussions with the major Indian political parties, Lord Mountbatten (the last British viceroy of India) announced (June 3) plans for the partition of India into two successor states, with Bengal and Punjab divided to give the Muslim-majority areas to Pakistan. Attlee introduced the Indian Independence Bill into the British Parliament on July 4; its passage through both houses was swift. Lord Mountbatten was appointed governor general of India and Muhammad Ali Jinnah (president of the Muslim League) governor general of Pakistan.

Further reading: Manmath N. Das, *Partition and Independence of India: Inside Story of the Mountbatten Days* (New Delhi: Vision Books, 1982); Manik L. Gupta, *Constitutional Development of India: From the Regulating Act (1773) to the*

Indian Independence Act (1947) (New Delhi: Atlantic Publishers & Distributors, 1989); Eric Wakin, *Asian Independence Leaders* (New York: Facts On File, 1997).

Indian National Congress "Independence Day" Resolution

Formal proposal drawn up and adopted (January 20, 1930) by the Indian National Congress in Lahore, setting January 26, 1930, as Independence Day in India (where the growing nationalist movement led by Mohandas K. Gandhi was trying to throw off British rule). The congress's president, Jawaharlal Nehru, ordered wide distribution of the resolution in the provinces. The Indian people, the resolution stated, had "inalienable rights . . . to have freedom to enjoy the fruit of their toil." The British government in India had ruined the country economically, politically, culturally, and spiritually, it further stated, and thus India "must sever the British connection and attain *purna swarajya*, or complete independence." The Indians resolved to prepare for civil disobedience, including nonpayment of taxes and nonviolence to gain their freedom.

Further reading: S. R. Mehrotra, *A History of the Indian National Congress* (New Delhi: Vikas Pub. House, 1995).

Indian Removal Act of 1830, U.S.

Federal legislation enacted on May 28, 1830, authorizing the U.S. president to exchange land west of the Mississippi River for eastern lands held by Indian tribes within the states or territories of the United States. The act codified a policy proposed by President Andrew Jackson to allow increased white settlement in the East. In the following decade some 100,000 Indians were removed to western prairie lands thought to be undesirable to whites. Though many northern tribes were peacefully resettled under this act, the Five Civilized Tribes of the Southeast were forced to migrate by the U.S. military and suffered severely.

Further reading: Charles L. Phillips and Alan Axelrod, eds., *Encyclopedia of Historical Treaties and Alliances,* 2 vols. (New York: Facts On File, 2001); Ronald N. Satz, *American Indian Policy in the Jacksonian Era* (Lincoln: University of Nebraska Press, 1975); S. Lyman Tyler, *A History of Indian Policy* (Washington, D.C.: Department of the Interior, Bureau of Indian Affairs, 1973).

Indian Reorganization Act, U.S.

See WHEELER-HOWARD ACT.

Indies, New Laws of the

See NEW LAWS OF THE INDIES.

Indochina War Armistice of 1954

See GENEVA AGREEMENTS OF 1954.

Indulgence, Declarations of

Declarations of religious toleration issued by the English kings Charles II (in 1662 and 1672) and James II (in 1687 and 1688). In the 1662 declaration, Charles II swore to withdraw the laws against Nonconformists, but Parliament vetoed the idea. Penal laws were suspended by the 1672 declaration; Protestant dissenters were permitted the freedom to worship in public and Roman Catholics to worship in private. Parliament insisted that the royal power should be used to give relief only in specific cases (instead of generally) and forced the king to withdraw the indulgence. In 1673, Parliament countered by passing the TEST ACT. The 1687 indulgence of James II allowed Protestant dissenters and Roman Catholics the freedom to worship in public and announced the dismissal of all penal laws. The terms of the 1688 declaration were identical except for the clause stating that it was to be read aloud in the churches. The clergy protested, leading to the vain trial of seven bishops for seditious libel. The uproar over the last two declarations (which are sometimes called Declarations of Liberty of Conscience) is believed to have helped bring about the Glorious Revolution of 1688: the overthrow of James II and the accession of William and Mary to the English throne.

Further reading: Carl Stephenson and Frederick George Marcham, eds., *Sources of English Constitutional History: A Selection of Documents from* A.D. *600 to the Present* (New York: Harper & Row, 1937).

Industrial Relations Act of 1971, British

Major industrial legislation enacted on August 5, 1971, by Britain's Conservative government following British industry's worst year. The act established a National Industrial Relations Court (NIRC), of High Court status, to implement the proposals of the Commission on Industrial Relations (CIR), to authorize ballots, and to impose "conciliation pauses" of up to 60 days each. It extended the scope of the Industrial Tribunals and entrusted the Industrial Relations Board with drafting standards of employment. Trade unions had to be registered and to conform to certain standards, a requirement that trade unionists bitterly opposed. Fines were introduced against unfair industrial practices (sympathetic strikes, action against nonunion members) and workers were required to vote on strike action. Trade union members were protected against unfair dismissal; under the law, their rights were guaranteed. As a supplement to the act, an advisory code was soon to be published to encourage voluntary methods of industrial relations.

Further reading: Michael Moran, *The Politics of Industrial Relations: The Origins, Life, and Death of the 1971 Industrial Relations Act* (London: Macmillan, 1977); A. W. J. Thomson and Stephen R. Engleman, *The Industrial Relations Act: A Review and Analysis* (London: M. Robertson, 1975); Brian Weekes, *Industrial Relations and the Limits of Law: The Industrial Effects of the Industrial Relations Act, 1971* (Oxford, England: Blackwell, 1975).

Industrial Workers of the World, Preamble of the Constitution of the

Manifesto of the Industrial Workers

of the World (IWW, or Wobblies), a militant labor organization; first issued at the founding convention in Chicago in June 1905. The preamble declared that the "working class and the employing class have nothing in common," and that the mission of the working class is to eliminate capitalism. It stated that the workers must organize to overthrow the capitalists and to form the structure of a new, socialist society. At the organization's fourth convention, in 1908, the preamble was revised by the IWW's radical members in favor of more direct, physical action at the point of production rather than political effort.

Further reading: Henry Steele Commager, ed., *Documents of American History*, 8th ed. (New York: Appleton-Century-Crofts, 1968); *Preamble and Constitution of the Industrial Workers of the World, Organized July 7, 1905* (Chicago: Industrial Workers of the World, 1916).

Indus Waters Treaty   Agreement in Karachi, Pakistan, on September 19, 1960, wherein World Bank mediation helped India and Pakistan resolve the long-standing Indus Basin water dispute; it had resulted from the partition of the Punjab (see INDIAN INDEPENDENCE ACT, BRITISH), when India disconnected (April 1, 1948) the flow of canal waters to Pakistan. The treaty created a fund of $900 million to finance a complex of irrigation projects in Pakistan—with $174 million payable by India; $640 million contributed by Australia, Canada, West Germany, New Zealand, the United Kingdom, and the United States; and $80 million loaned by the World Bank. During the 10-year transition period (extendable by three years) India was to supply Pakistan with waters from the eastern rivers (Ravi, Beas, and the Sutlej) alloted to her. Pakistan was given the western rivers (Indus, Jhelum, and most of the Chenab). The two nations could utilize the services of a neutral expert or a court of arbitration under special circumstances.

Further reading: N. D. Gulhati, *Indus Waters Treaty; an Exercise in International Mediation* (Bombay, India: Allied Publishers, 1973).

In Eminenti   Bull issued by Pope Urban VIII on March 6, 1642, against Roman Catholic theologian Cornelis Jansen and his posthumous work *AUGUSTINUS*, which was declared heretical. The bull, published on June 19, 1643, said that Jansen's views of grace, predestination, and free will were theologically untenable; it also banned the reading of *Augustinus* on the grounds that it had not been cleared with the Holy See before its publication. Pope Urban VIII also criticized Jansen's life work in general.

See also: CLEMENT IX, PEACE OF; CUM OCCASIONE IMPRESSIONIS LIBRI; PROVINCIAL LETTERS.

Further reading: Alexander Sedgwick, *Jansenism in Seventeenth-Century France: Voices from the Wilderness* (Charlottesville: University Press of Virginia, 1977).

In Re Debs   U.S. Supreme Court decision of May 27, 1895, concerning the case of UNITED STATES V. DEBS ET AL. On being sentenced to prison for violating an injunction against interfering with the railroads during the Pullman strike of 1894, Eugene V. Debs sued out a writ of habeas corpus in the Supreme Court. The writ was denied, not on the grounds of the Sherman Anti-trust Act (the basis for the injunction), but on the broader grounds that the federal government's constitutional authority over interstate commerce and the transportation of the mails justified the issuance of such injunctions to prevent forcible obstructions.

Further reading: Mortimer Adler, ed., *The Annals of America*, 18 vols. (Chicago: Encyclopaedia Britannica, 1968); Henry Steele Commager, ed., *Documents of American History*, 8th ed. (New York: Appleton-Century-Crofts, 1968); Kermit Hall et al., eds., *American Legal History: Cases and Materials*, 2d ed. (New York: Oxford University Press, 1996); Nick Salvatore, *Eugene v. Debs: Citizen and Socialist* (Urbana: University of Illinois Press, 1982).

Institutes of the Christian Religion (Institution de la Religion Chrétienne, Christianae Religionis Institutio)   Systematic introduction to biblical theology—John Calvin's authoritative compendium of the Reformed faith (Protestantism). The first edition, published in Basel in Latin (1536), opened with a dedication to Francis I (king of France) and consisted of six chapters discussing the Ten Commandments, the Apostles' Creed, the Lord's Prayer, the controversial sacraments, and church government. The book underwent several revisions and additions before the publication of the definitive editions in 1559 (Latin), 1560 (French), and 1561 (English). Its four books discussed God as Creator, God as Redeemer, the Holy Spirit and Grace, and the Church. The recurrent themes in Calvin's work were his belief in the absolute sovereignty of God, in His Word as evident in the scriptures, and in the need for man to seek salvation through the Grace of God. The most comprehensive guide to Reformed theology, most certainly Calvin's magnum opus, the *Institutes of the Christian Religion*, helped to unify the Reformation movement and prevent its rupture into several individual cults.

See also: COMMON ORDER, BOOK OF; DISCIPLINE, FIRST BOOK OF.

Further reading: Mark A. Kishlansky, ed., *Sources of the West: Reading in Western Civilization*, vol. 1, 4th ed. (New York: Addison Wesley Longman, 2001); Frank N. Magill, ed., *Great Events from History, Modern European Series*, 3 vols. (Englewood Cliffs, N.J.: Salem Press, 1973).

Instruction (Nakaz), Catherine the Great's   Document drawn up by Russia's czarina Catherine II the Great and first published on August 10 (July 30, Old Style calendar), 1767, to serve as a guide for a legislative commission (convened that year by Catherine) to frame a constitution and new code of laws. Although it was rewritten to suit the tastes of her conservative advisers and its ideas were not original, the Instruction addressed the most progressive issues of the Enlightenment and expressed Catherine's support for the concept of an absolute monarchy (ruled by an enlightened sovereign). In her paper, Catherine also condemned the use of torture, opposed capital punishment, supported legislation ensuring the rights of all citizens (granting that serfs were not citizens), and promised to improve the serfs' general situation. The commission's delegates debated the ideas for months but produced nothing new when they adjourned in late 1768. The Instruction was considered overly liberal but influenced future legislation in Russia.

Further reading: Paul Dukes, *Catherine the Great's Instruction (Nakaz) to the Legislative Commission, 1767* (Newtonville, Mass.: Oriental Research Partners, 1977); Paul Dukes *Russia under Catherine the Great*, 2 vols. (Newtonville, Mass.: Oriental Research Publishers, 1977); W. F. Reddaway, ed., *Documents of Catherine the Great; The Correspondence with Voltaire and the Instruction of 1767 in the English Text of 1768* (New York: Russell & Russell, 1971).

Instruction on the Ecclesial Vocation of the Theologian

Vatican decree against public dissent by Catholic theologians; prepared and issued by the Congregation for the Doctrine of the Faith on June 26, 1990. Approved by Pope John Paul II, the document was a response to a "climate of conflict" instigated by dissident theologians, said West Germany's cardinal Joseph Ratzinger, head of the congregation and the pope's main guardian of orthodoxy. The decree upheld punishments given to dissidents in recent years, demanded that theologians vent their dissent on doctrines and moral teachings with the church hierarchy in private (not in the public arena, through the mass media), and affirmed the right of the church to speak out on issues of sexual morality. Theologians unable to resolve their differences should "suffer for the truth in silence and prayer," stated the decree, which received immediate scorn from Catholic academics who viewed it as a response to recent criticism of the pope in the COLOGNE DECLARATION.

Further reading: Catholic Church, *Instruction on the Ecclesial Vocation of the Theologian* (Washington, D.C.: United States Catholic Conference, Office for Publishing and Promotion Services, 1990).

Instrument of Government

First detail-written constitution in England, drafted by John Lambert and the Council of Officers after the Barebones Parliament (1653) had failed, and published on December 16, 1653. The Instrument derived much from Henry Ireton's Heads of Proposals (army proposals for peace in 1647) and provided for Oliver Cromwell's appointment as "lord protector of the Commonwealth" of England, Ireland, and Scotland. He was to be assisted by a council of state (21 members) and was given an annual sum

of £200,000 for administrative use, in addition to funds for an army of 30,000 men, and he also had veto powers over any attempt to alter the Instrument. Parliament, elected under a reformed system of representation, was to meet triennially (each session being at least five months), the first session starting on September 3, 1654. Royalists were to be debarred from the first four parliaments. When Parliament was not in session, the lord protector and the council of state could issue ordinances, but taxes and granting of supplies were left to Parliament to determine. The Instrument of Government was replaced by the HUMBLE PETITION AND ADVICE of 1657.

See also: INDEMNITY AND OBLIVION, ACT OF.

Further reading: Carl Stephenson and Frederick George Marcham, eds., *Sources of English Constitutional History: A Selection of Documents from* A.D. *600 to the Present* (New York: Harper & Row, 1937).

Inter-American Conciliation and Arbitration Treaties of 1929

Two treaties concluded on January 5, 1929, in Washington, D.C., at the close of the special International Conference of American States (a Pan-American conference), by 19 Latin American states and the United States; they provided for the arbitration of disputes and conciliation of adversarial parties. In general, the treaties obliged the signatory powers to submit all disputes of an international nature to arbitration and conciliation commissions, the establishment of which was also provided by the treaties. A majority of the signatory governments eventually ratified the treaties. The treaties were two of many like them concluded during the interwar period (between World Wars I and II).

See also: PARIS, PACT OF.

Further reading: Leslie Bethell, ed., *The Cambridge History of Latin America* (Cambridge, England: Cambridge University Press, 1985); *Convention Between the United States and Other American Republics: Inter-American Conciliation . . .* (Washington, D.C.: U.S. Government Printing Office, 1929); Michael Rheta Martin and Gabriel H. Lovett, *Encyclopedia of Latin American History* (New York: Bobbs-Merrill, 1968).

Inter-American Treaty on Pacific Settlement

See BOGOTÁ, PACT OF.

Inter Caetera

See DEMARCATION, BULL OF.

Intercursus Magnus

Commercial treaty concluded on February 24, 1496, between England and the Netherlands, ending the trade embargo imposed (September 1493) by King Henry VII of England on the Netherlands for sheltering Perkin Warbeck, the pretender to the English throne. Archduke Philip, son of Holy Roman Emperor Maximilian I, initiated the negotiations by renouncing all interest in Henry's enemies and promising to expel the pretender. Henry, on the other hand, was pressured by the powerful Merchant Adventurers, a group of traders whose business had been severely affected by the embargo. The agreement called for a resumption of the prosperous cloth trade between London and Antwerp, and it established fixed duties on all exports and greatly liberalized trade barriers between the English, Dutch, and Flemings.

Further reading: Ian Arthurson, *The Perkin Warbeck Conspiracy, 1491–1499* (Stroud, England: Sutton Publishing, 1997).

Inter Innumeras (Au Milieu des Sollicitudes)

Papal encyclical on February 16, 1892, published in French by Pope Leo XIII; exhorted France's Roman Catholics to reconcile themselves to the anticlerical Third French Republic. The document decreed that any established government was legitimate, and urged French Catholics to join the government in order to modify existing anticlerical legislation. The encyclical provided an impetus to the Ralliement, an attempt to rally the conservative, monarchist, and Catholic elements in society to the cause of the republic. The Ralliement was short lived, however, and had a limited impact on the fundamentally anticlerical nature of the republic.

See also: COMBES'S BILL.

Further reading: Pope Leo XIII, *The Great Encyclical Letters of Pope Leo XIII: Plus Other Documents; Translations from Approved Sources* (Rockford, Ill.: Tan Books, 1995); Alexander Sedgwick, *The Ralliement in French Politics, 1890–1898* (Cambridge, Mass.: Harvard University Press, 1965).

Intermediate Nuclear Forces Treaty (INF Treaty)

Agreement for the elimination of intermediate-range and shorter-range missiles; signed on December 8, 1987, by the American president Ronald W. Reagan and the Soviet general secretary Mikhail S. Gorbachev during their summit in Washington, D.C. Both countries agreed to immediately destroy their land-based missiles having a range from 300 to 3,400 miles (500–5,000 km). The destruction of shorter-range missiles (Soviet SS-12s and SS-23s) would be achieved over 18 months and that of medium-range missiles in two stages over three years. The treaty was accompanied by two protocols. The first described the many ways in which they could destroy their missiles. The second protocol outlined a 13-year verification schedule that included resident and short-notice, on-site inspections of INF bases, storage depots, and repair yards. The acceptance of this condition by the Soviet Union was in itself considered a major achievement in the bilateral arms negotiation process. The treaty had unlimited validity and would be enforced upon ratification.

Further reading: Richard Dean Burns, ed., *Encyclopedia of Arms Control and Disarmament,* 3 vols. (New York: Charles Scribner's Sons, 1993); Carl N. Flanders and Stephen A. Flanders, *Dictionary of American Foreign Affairs* (New York: Macmillan, 1993); Charles L. Phillips and Alan Axelrod, eds., *Encyclopedia of Historical Treaties and Alliances,* 2 vols. (New York: Facts On File, 2001).

Internal Security Act of 1950, U.S.   See MCCARRAN ACT.

International Criminal Court, Rome Statute of (Charter of the International Criminal Court)

Treaty establishing a permanent international court to deal with crimes against humanity, such as war crimes, widespread atrocities, genocide, mass murders, and aggression. The treaty was adopted by 120 member states of the United Nations in Rome in July 1998. By April 2002 it had been ratified by 60 member states, enough to put it into effect as of July 2002. The International Criminal Court (ICC) was established to deter crimes against humanity by putting into place an effective and efficient vehicle for trying perpetrators. Previously, special tribunals had been set up after the crimes had already been committed, as in Germany and Japan after World War II and in Yugoslavia and Rwanda during the late 20th century. The statute established the ICC as an entity independent of the United Nations, to be situated in The Hague, Netherlands. The ICC's powers are limited in that it can only hear cases involving widespread or systematic abuses, not individual acts no matter how horrendous they might be; consequently, the court cannot hear cases involving terrorism or drug trafficking. Further, it can only hear cases that originate after July 2002, when the treaty went into effect. Most important, the ICC cannot hear any case until after the courts in the country in which the abuses have taken place have either refused or are unable to hear it.

Further reading: "The International Criminal Court," Amnesty International: International Justice, available online at http://web.amnesty.org/web/web.nsf/pages/ICChome; "International Criminal Court," Global Issues, available online at http://www.globalissues.org/Geopolitics/ICC.asp; "The International Criminal Court," United Nations, available online at http://www.un.org/News/facts/iccfact.htm.

International Energy Agency Agreement

Agreement establishing the International Energy Agency (IEA) to initiate and supervise oil-sharing, stock-piling, and conservation schemes; concluded on November 18, 1974, between the Organization for Economic Cooperation and Development (OECD) and 16 major oil-consuming nations, including all of Western Europe (except France and Finland), Canada, Japan, Turkey, the United Kingdom, and the United States. If oil supplies fell by 7 percent or more, the 10-year agreement would automatically activate (unless vetoed by 12 countries or more than 60 percent of the vote) an oil-sharing scheme. If the shortfall exceeded 12 percent, members would have to reduce their consumption by 10 percent. They were expected to maintain 60 days' worth of contingency supplies. A total of 148 votes was divided among members according to their consumption; this actively involved them in the decision-making process. The IEA has a governing body, advised by four expert committees.

Further reading: Richard Scott, *The History of the International Energy Agency, 1974–1994: IEA, the First 20 Years* (Washington, D.C.: OECD/IEA, 1994).

International Religious Freedom Act (IRFA), U.S.

Legislation (Public Law 105-292) signed on October 27, 1998, by President Bill Clinton, authorizing him to take action against countries engaged in "systematic, ongoing, and egregious" acts of religious persecution. The act, an amendment of an earlier version passed by the House, recognized two types of violations: "severe violations" (torture, imprisonment without charges, disappearance of persons) and "violations" (curbs on religious advocacy or practice). It established a 10-member bipartisan federal commission and the Office of International Religious Freedom (within the State Department) headed by an ambassador at large; both bodies would submit separate reports on religious freedom worldwide to Congress. After consulting with churches and other nongovernmental organizations, the president would take action ranging from a mild, private protest to harsh economic sanctions against the offending country. If "important national interest" was at stake, he could also waive any penalties.

Further reading: Sean D. Murphy, "Contemporary Practice of the U.S. Relating to International Law," *American Journal of International Law* 94 (January 2000): 102–40; United States Department of State International Information Programs, *One Hundred Fifth Congress of the United States of America at the Second Session*, info USA, available online at http://usinfo.state.gov/usa/infousa/laws/majorlaw/intlrel.htm.

International Working-Men's Association, Manifesto of the   See MANIFESTO OF THE INTERNATIONAL WORKING-MEN'S ASSOCIATION.

Interstate Commerce Act, U.S. (Cullom Act)   Federal
law proposed by U.S. senator Shelby M. Cullom of Illinois and enacted on February 4, 1887, as a result of public outcry over railroad abuses; established the Interstate Commerce Commission (ICC), the first federal administrative agency. The act, which applied only to railroads traveling through two or more states, provided that all railroad charges be "reasonable and just"; prohibited pooling arrangements, rebates, drawbacks, and other discriminatory rates; and made unlawful the practice of charging more for a short haul than a long haul. The ICC, charged with inquiring into railroad management, had the power to call for witnesses and documents and to require annual reports. The commission was strengthened by later legislation.

Further reading: Ari Hoogenboom and Olive Hoogenboom, *A History of the ICC: From Panacea to Palliative* (New York: Norton, 1976); Isaiah L. Sharfman, *The Interstate Commerce Commission* (New York: Commonwealth Fund, 1931).

Interstate Liquor Act of 1913, U.S.   See WEBB-KENYON ACT.

Intolerable Acts   See COERCIVE ACTS.

Iranian Constitution of 1979   Constitution establishing
the Islamic Republic of Iran and affirming the sovereignty of the people, approved in a national referendum in 1979, despite reservations by some groups. It was drafted by the largely clerical, 80-member Assembly of Experts at the behest of Iran's Revolutionary Council, following the overthrow of the shah. An elected president headed the executive branch, but real power lay with the *faqih* (expert in Islamic law, or sharia), the supreme religious leader of Iran's official religion, Shi'a Islam. The *faqih* nominated six of the 12 members of the Council of Guardians, the ranking members of the judiciary, and was the commander of the armed forces. The council exercised veto powers over any legislation passed by the 290-member National Consultative Assembly, or Majlis, which appointed the Council's remaining six members (lawyers). Judicial powers were concentrated in the Supreme Court and the four-member High Council of the Judiciary. The Revolutionary Guard Corps supervised domestic security while the military protected Iran's borders. Adopted on October 24, 1979, and effective on December 3, 1979, the constitution consisted of 12 chapters and 175 articles. In 1988, the Council of Expediency was established to resolve legislative disputes between the Council and the Assembly and advise the *faqih* on national policy matters. On July 28, 1989, 45 constitutional amendments were approved.

Further reading: Asghar Schirazi, *The Constitution of Iran: Politics and the State in the Islamic Republic*, trans. John O'Kane (London: I. B. Tauris, 1997); Manou and Associates, "Islamic Republic of Iran Constitution," Iranian government, available online at http://www.iranonline.com/iran/iran-info/Government/constitution.html.

Iraqi-British Treaty of 1930   See ANGLO-IRAQI TREATY OF 1930.

Ireland Act, Republic of   Bill for independence for Ire-
land (Irish Free State), passed by the Irish Parliament (Dail) on December 21, 1948, thus ending Ireland's membership in the British Commonwealth of Nations (see ANGLO-IRISH TREATY OF 1921). The new Republic of Ireland was formally proclaimed in Dublin on Easter Monday, 1949. The British government responded by passing the Ireland Act (May 17, 1949), acknowledging the independence of the Irish republic but stating emphatically that Northern Ireland would maintain its position within the United Kingdom (see GOVERNMENT OF IRELAND ACT) and that any change in this would have to be determined by the Parliament of Northern Ireland.

Further reading: Christopher Haigh, ed., *The Cambridge Historical Encyclopedia of Great Britain and Ireland*

(Cambridge, England: Cambridge University Press, 1985); D. J. Hickey and J. E. Doherty, *A Dictionary of Irish History since 1800* (Dublin: Gill & Macmillan, 1980).

Ireland's Offenses Against the State Act   See OF-FENSES AGAINST THE STATE ACT, IRELAND'S.

Irish-British Treaty of 1921   See ANGLO-IRISH TREATY OF 1921.

Irish Church Temporalities Act   British act of August 2, 1833, witholding 10 sees (bishop seats) of the Church of Ireland and limiting the revenues of the other five. It reduced the Irish episcopate from four archbishops and 18 bishops to two archbishops and 10 bishops, and utilized the savings for church purposes. Clerical incomes were subjected to a graded tax, to relieve ratepayers from responsibility for parish expenses. Daniel O'Connell, who opposed the bill, was upset that the savings were not used for secular purposes. Intended to appease those who favored the disestablishment of the Church of Ireland, the bill was amended in 1834 and again in 1836.

Further reading: Christopher Haigh, ed., *The Cambridge Historical Encyclopedia of Great Britain and Ireland* (Cambridge, England: Cambridge University Press, 1985); D. J. Hickey and J. E. Doherty, *A Dictionary of Irish History since 1800* (Dublin: Gill & Macmillan, 1980).

Irish Land Act of 1860 (Deasy's Act, Ireland Landlord and Tenant Law Amendment or Act)   Act weighted in favor of the landlord, promoted by Richard Deasy (attorney general for Ireland) in 1860. According to the act, the landlord-tenant relationship was based "on the express or implied contract of the parties and not upon tenure or service." Thus, the landlord could recover his property by not renewing the tenant's lease or by dictating his own terms on renewal. A tenant could be asked to leave for defaulting on rent, nor was he compensated for any improvements he may have made. It was replaced by the IRISH LAND ACT OF 1870.

Further reading: Christopher Haigh, ed., *The Cambridge Historical Encyclopedia of Great Britain and Ireland* (Cambridge, England: Cambridge University Press, 1985); D. J. Hickey and J. E. Doherty, *A Dictionary of Irish History since 1800* (Dublin: Gill & Macmillan, 1980).

Irish Land Act of 1870 (Ireland Landlord and Tenant Act)   Act passed by British prime minister William Gladstone's government on August 1, 1870, to provide a tenant compensation for eviction (except where due to rent default) and for any improvements done by him. It prevented the landlord from freely disposing of his land in Ireland, but did not offer the tenant security of tenure or protection against increased rents and proved difficult to enforce in practice. The BRIGHT CLAUSE enabled a tenant to purchase his holding by

borrowing up to two-thirds of the price, but few tenants took advantage of this. One of numerous Irish land reforms, it failed to recognize the "three F's" (fair rent, fixity of tenure, and freedom to sell), and its enforcement created more problems than it solved. To quell the rioting that ensued, the government was forced to introduce the PEACE PRESERVATION ACT OF 1870.

Further reading: Christopher Haigh, ed., *The Cambridge Historical Encyclopedia of Great Britain and Ireland* (Cambridge, England: Cambridge University Press, 1985); D. J. Hickey and J. E. Doherty, *A Dictionary of Irish History since 1800* (Dublin: Gill & Macmillan, 1980).

Irish Land Act of 1881 (Gladstone's Act of 1881)   British parliamentary legislation of August 1881, passed by Prime Minister William Gladstone to correct the deficiencies of the IRISH LAND ACT OF 1870. The 1881 Land Act legalized the "three F's": fair rents, fixity of tenure (provided the tenant's rent is paid), and freedom to sell by the tenant (the Ulster Custom). The act also provided compensation for improvements and eviction and established a land court and a land commission to mediate between the landlord and the tenant. The Land Court determined the fair rent over 15 years, gave security of tenure to the tenants who paid it, and offered them the right to sell to the highest bidder. It enabled tenants to purchase their holdings, with the Land Commission loaning three-quarters of the amount, repayable at 5 percent over 35 years. Nearly 280,000 tenants were excluded—being either leaseholders or in arrears—and the "land wars" continued in Ireland.

Further reading: Christopher Haigh, ed., *The Cambridge Historical Encyclopedia of Great Britain and Ireland* (Cambridge, England: Cambridge University Press, 1985); D. J. Hickey and J. E. Doherty, *A Dictionary of Irish History since 1800* (Dublin: Gill & Macmillan, 1980).

Irish Land Act of 1885   See ASHBOURNE ACT.

Irish Land Act of 1887   Amendment of Gladstone's IRISH LAND ACT OF 1881, introduced successfully into the British parliament by Arthur J. Balfour in 1887 during his term as chief secretary of Ireland. It extended the benefits of Gladstone's act to cover the leaseholders, reduced the 15-years "fair rent" to three, and gave the tenants protection against arbitrary eviction. This act was passed simultaneously with the CRIMES BILL OF 1887 with the intention of bringing peace to riot-torn Ireland.

Further reading: Christopher Haigh, ed., *The Cambridge Historical Encyclopedia of Great Britain and Ireland* (Cambridge, England: Cambridge University Press, 1985); D. J. Hickey and J. E. Doherty, *A Dictionary of Irish History since 1800* (Dublin: Gill & Macmillan, 1980).

Irish Land Purchase Act of 1903   See WYNDHAM'S LAND PURCHASE ACT OF 1903.

Iron Act   Trade measure enacted by the British Parliament in 1750, restricting the American colonial manufacture of goods made of iron. Manufacturers of iron tools, nails, and wars in Britain had complained of growing competition from the iron-finishing industry in the colonies; they wanted to protect their interests. The act (included among the British laws known as the Acts of Trade and Navigation) allowed only raw pig iron (and bar iron after 1756) from the colonies to enter England duty-free, to be made into finished products there. The construction of new slitting mills, iron furnaces, and plating mills in the colonies was forbidden. Many colonists objected, paying more for iron imports from England, and new ironworks continued to be erected in America.

Further reading: Paul F. Paskoff, *Colonial Merchant-Manufacturers and Iron: A Study in Capital Transformation, 1725–1775* (Ann Arbor, Mich.: University Microfilms, 1976).

Ironclad Oath   Oath prescribed by a congressional act of July 2, 1862, requiring all federal civil or military officials, elected or appointed, honorary or paid, to swear allegiance to the U.S. CONSTITUTION and to declare that they had never voluntarily borne arms against the United States, or aided those who had done so, or supported or held any office under any authority hostile to the United States. Congress applied the oath to its own members in 1864 and to lawyers practicing in federal courts in 1865. States also adopted the ironclad oath. The oath which disqualified many opponents of the radical Republicans, was challenged in the courts on constitutional grounds. It was modified in 1868 and again in 1871, to require only a promise of future loyalty, and was repealed in 1884.

Further reading: Harold M. Hyman, *Era of the Oath: Northern Loyalty Tests during the Civil War and Reconstruction* (New York: Octagon Books, 1978); Harold M. Hyman, *To Try Men's Souls: Loyalty Tests in American History* (Westport, Conn.: Greenwood Press, 1981).

"Iron Curtain" Speech, Churchill's   Widely considered Winston Churchill's most important speech as British leader of the parliamentary opposition (1945–51); delivered on March 5, 1946, at Westminster College in Fulton, Missouri, while accepting an honorary degree awarded him by the college. After elaborating on the many facets of the harmonious Anglo-American relationship and its promise for the future, Churchill expressed alarm and concern at the Soviet Union's aggression in Eastern Europe: "From Stettin in the Baltic to Trieste in the Adriatic, an iron curtain has descended across the Continent." Communist parties, he pointed out, were spreading across the world, constituting "a growing challenge and peril to Christian civilization." He suggested that a united stand from the Western democracies, acting in accordance

with the UNITED NATIONS CHARTER, would help clear "the high-roads of the future . . . for a century to come" for all the peoples of the world.

See also: STALIN'S "COLD WAR" SPEECH.

Further reading: David Cannadine, ed., *Blood, Toil, Tears and Sweat: The Speeches of Winston Churchill* (Boston: Houghton Mifflin, 1989).

Isidorian Decretals   See FALSE DECRETALS.

Israeli-Egyptian Peace Treaty   International treaty signed by Egyptian president Anwar el-Sadat and Israeli prime minister Menachem Begin, and witnessed by U.S. president Jimmy Carter, on March 26, 1979, in Washington, D.C.; it ended a state of war that had existed between the two countries since 1948. The treaty called for the gradual withdrawal of Israeli troops and civilian settlers from the Sinai Peninsula, the deployment of United Nations forces along the border, the establishment of diplomatic relations between Israel and Egypt, free passage through the Suez Canal, Israeli purchase of Sinai oil, and negotiations concerning self-rule for Palestinians on the Israeli-occupied West Bank and Gaza Strip. The treaty was based on accords reached, with Carter's assistance, at a 1978 summit meeting at Camp David, Maryland (see CAMP DAVID ACCORDS).

Further reading: Lawrence Ziring, *The Middle East Political Dictionary* (Santa Barbara, Calif.: ABC-CLIO Information Services, 1984).

Israeli-Jordanian Treaty of 1994   Major accord signed by the prime ministers of Israel and Jordan (Yitzhak Rabin and Abdel Salem al-Majali, respectively) on October 26, 1994, triggered by the OSLO ACCORDS, and sought to resolve key issues of contention and officially end 46 years of hostility between the two countries. The international boundary was defined and agreed upon, without reference to the land won by Israel in 1967. They pledged to create a conference on security and cooperation in the region. The thorny issue of water allocation was resolved by expanding allotments to each. Both countries would cooperate in developing new resources to increase availability, and also in the areas of tourism, energy, transportation, drug control, environmental protection, and economic development. Full diplomatic relations would be established within one month of its ratification.

Further reading: *Facts On File World News Digest* (New York: Facts On File, 1994); Bernard Reich, ed., *An Encyclopedia of the Arab-Israeli Conflict* (Westport, CT.: Greenwood Press, 1996).

Israel's Proclamation of Independence   Proclamation announcing the independence of the newly created state of Israel; read on May 14, 1948, by David Ben-Gurion (who became Israel's first prime minister) at a meeting of the provisional state council in Tel Aviv. The British mandate for Israel terminated that same day. The document stated that "Israel will be open to the immigration of Jews from all countries of their dispersion; will promote the development of the country for the benefit of all its inhabitants; will be based on the principles of liberty, justice and peace as conceived by the Prophets of Israel." The world's Jewish people were called to aid in the task of immigration and development and to support the long-awaited Jewish state in Palestine. It was proclaimed "with trust in Almighty God . . . on the soil of the Homeland . . . on this Sabbath eve, the fifth of Iyar, 5708."

Further reading: Walter Lacqueur and Barry Rubin, eds., *The Israeli-Arab Reader: A Documentary History of the Middle East Conflict* (New York: Viking Penguin, 1969).

Italian Constitution of 1821   Promulgation on March 13, 1821, of the SPANISH CONSTITUTION OF 1812 in Piedmont-Sardinia; granted by regent Charles Albert of Savoy in response to demands from the liberals. He made two important changes in the original constitution. First, he recognized the SALIC LAW (by which females were excluded from succession to the crown). Second, he excluded the article declaring Roman Catholicism as the state's official religion and disallowing other forms of worship.

See also: ITALIAN CONSTITUTIONS OF 1848.

Further reading: Evelyn Martinengo-Cesaresco, *The Liberation of Italy, 1815–1870* (New York: Scribner, 1894); Denis Mack Smith, *Italy: A Modern History* (Ann Arbor: University of Michigan Press, 1959).

Italian Constitution of 1948   New constitution drafted and later adopted by Italy's constituent assembly on December 22, 1947, and effective on January 1, 1948, guaranteeing the citizenry many political, social, and economic liberties and rights. It set up a decentralized government, a popularly elected senate and a chamber of deputies, and a constitutional court having the power of judicial review of legislation. This fundamental law of the Italian Republic recognized both private property and public control of businesses; it proclaimed the country to be a free "democratic Republic founded on work." Other innovations in the constitution were the ideas of republicanism, regional governments, and popular initiative and referendum. The government protected the interests of the Roman Catholic Church by making the LATERAN TREATIES OF 1929 part of the state design.

Further reading: Evelyn Martinengo-Cesaresco, *The Liberation of Italy, 1815–1870* (New York: Scribner, 1894); Denis Mack Smith, *Italy: A Modern History* (Ann Arbor: University of Michigan Press, 1959).

Italian Constitutions of 1848   Series of constitutions granted by various Italian states during 1848. King Ferdinand II of the Two Sicilies was the first to grant a moderately liberal constitution (January 29, 1848). Subsequently, Grand Duke Leopold of Tuscany (February 17), Charles Albert of Savoy (March 4) and Pope Pius IX (March 14) were forced to grant similar constitutions. Charles Albert's *statuto,* not quite as liberal as that of the Second French Republic or the FRENCH CHARTER OF 1830, nevertheless became the basis of the Italian Constitution of 1861. The king was said to rule "by the grace of God and by the will of the Nation." He controlled foreign policy, nominations to the upper house, and decisions of war and peace, and all ministers reported directly to him. The *statuto* could be amended by ordinary legislation and was not submitted to a plebiscite for approval. It established permanent legislative committees to discuss proposed laws and granted suffrage to a mere 2.5 percent of Piedmont-Sardinia's population.

Further reading: Martin Clark, *Modern Italy, 1871–1982* (New York: Longman, 1984); Denis Mack Smith, *Italy: A Modern History* (Ann Arbor: University of Michigan Press, 1959).

Italo-British Agreements   See ANGLO-ITALIAN AGREEMENT OF 1925; ANGLO-ITALIAN AGREEMENTS OF 1891; ANGLO-ITALIAN AGREEMENTS OF 1937 AND 1938.

Italo-German Pact of 1936   See GERMAN-ITALIAN PACT OF 1936.

J'accuse Letter published in January 1898 by novelist Emile Zola, accusing the French War Office of judicial crimes in the Dreyfus affair. Captain (later Major) Alfred Dreyfus, a staff member of the War Office in Paris, had been convicted of selling military secrets in 1894 to the Germans, and had been banished to Devil's Island. Zola's letter, which appeared in George Clemenceau's leftist journal, *L'Aurore,* accused high-ranking army officers of a conspiracy to use Dreyfus, a wealthy Alsatian Jew, as a scapegoat for protecting the real culprit. Zola also called on the president of the Third Republic, Félix Faure, to reopen the case. As a result of his letter, Zola was tried for, and convicted of, criminal libel. He fled to England, but a higher court later overturned his conviction. The Dreyfus case was eventually reopened, revealing a conspiracy and establishing Dreyfus's innocence. In 1899, Dreyfus was returned from Devil's Island and pardoned; not until 1906 was he fully exonerated.

Further reading: Emile Zola, *The Dreyfus Affair: "J'accuse" and Other Writings,* ed. Alain Pages and trans. Eleanor Levieux (New Haven, Conn.: Yale University Press, 1998).

Jackson's Message on Removal of Southern Indians

Section of U.S. president Andrew Jackson's seventh annual message to Congress, delivered on December 7, 1835, promoting the removal of the Cherokee and other Indian tribes from their valuable lands in the southern United States and their resettlement west of the Mississippi. Jackson's support for Indian removal was evident when he refused to enforce the U.S. Supreme Court's decision in *WORCESTER V. GEORGIA,* which ruled that the Cherokees were subject to federal, not state, jurisdiction. Claiming that the removal was "dictated by a spirit of enlarged liberality," Jackson stated that its aim was to "protect and . . . preserve and perpetuate the scattered remnants of this race." The removal was codified in the Treaty of NEW ECHOTA.

Further reading: Ronald N. Satz, *American Indian Policy in the Jacksonian Era* (Lincoln: University of Nebraska Press, 1975).

Jackson's Proclamation to South Carolina   See NULLIFICATION PROCLAMATION.

Jackson's Special Circular   See SPECIE CIRCULAR.

James I's Claim of Divine Right   Postulate that kings were appointed by God, and therefore answerable only to Him for their actions, found its staunchest advocate in King James I (King James VI of Scotland) who ascended the throne of England in 1603. Through his speeches and writings, he proclaimed this view of divine hereditary rights, also relating it to the church government, with the priests seen as the direct representatives of God. Sanction for this was assured in the Church of England's canons of 1604 and the penal laws of 1606. However, the king was unable to appreciate that a new national spirit was gradually pervading the country. His insistence on his royal prerogatives often brought him into

conflict with the Parliament, which was moving toward a more democratic form of government. This view is clearly set forth in the 1689 DECLARATION OF RIGHTS, which gave to the British people the power to choose their king.

Further reading: John A. Butler, *James I and Divine Right* (Tokyo: Renaissance Institute, Sophia University, 1999); Mark A. Kishlansky, ed., *Sources of the West: Readings in Western Civilization*, vol. 2, 4th ed. (New York: Longman, 2001).

James I's Great Contract   Plan devised in 1610 by treasurer Lord Robert Cecil Salisbury, whereby King James I of England would surrender his privileges (profits from feudal rights such as purveyances, wardships, and impositions) in return for a regular income of £200,000 per annum from land tax and excise. Parliament was also expected to pay off the king's accumulated debts of £600,000. Amidst disagreements over sums and the king's reluctance to initiate financial reforms, negotiations broke down and Parliament was dissolved (February 1611) before any agreement could be reached.

Further reading: Eric N. Lindquist, *The Great Contract: Parliament and Royal Finance in the Reign of James I* (Ann Arbor, Mich.: University Microfilms International, 1985).

January, Edict of   Royal decree attempting to stem the religious rioting in France by granting basic concessions to the Huguenots (French Protestants) and formally recognizing their religion (see ROMORANTIN, EDICT OF). Intended as a working agreement pending the decisions of a church council, the edict was signed by the young King Charles IX at St. Germain-en-Laye on January 17, 1562, on the advice of Queen Mother Catherine de Médicis and Chancellor Michel de L'Hospital (L'Hôpital). It authorized Protestants to hold meetings outside the towns and religious services in private homes. Synods were allowed, provided the newly recognized, reformed ministers gave advance notice. The Huguenots were, however, required to restore Roman Catholic property and buildings. The most impressive achievement of Catherine's career, the edict was introduced "to keep our subjects in peace until by God's grace, we may be able to reunite them in one fold." Its rejection by the Catholics helped spark the First War of Religion (1562–63).

See also: AMBOISE, EDICT OF (1563).

Further reading: Mack P. Holt, *The French Wars of Religion, 1562–1629* (New York: Cambridge University Press, 1999); R. J. Knecht, *The French Wars of Religion, 1559–1598*, 2d ed. (New York: Longman, 1996); David Potter, *The French Wars of Religion: Selected Documents* (New York: St. Martin's Press, 1997).

Japanese-British Treaty of 1902   See ANGLO-JAPANESE TREATY OF 1902.

Japanese Constitution of 1946   New constitution drafted at the insistence of U.S. general Douglas MacArthur

(commander of the Allied Forces) following Japan's defeat in World War II (see POTSDAM DECLARATION), approved by Japan's Diet on October 7, 1946, and effective on May 3, 1947. It replaced the Meiji Constitution of 1889. The Matsumoto Committee, appointed by the Japanese prime minister to look into constitutional revisions, basically followed MacArthur's draft except that it created a bicameral diet. The Diet reigned supreme, being responsible for appointing the prime minister and with the cabinet reporting directly to it, instead of to the emperor. The monarchy was stripped of its power but retained as "the symbol of State and of the Unity of the people." Thus, popular sovereignty replaced imperial sovereignty. The Privy Council and all other nonparliamentary decision-making agencies were abolished. It declared as "eternal and inviolate" the fundamental civil and social rights of Japanese citizens, devoting one-third of its articles to the protection of these rights. Then as now, the most controversial part of the new 11-chapter, 103-article constitution is Article 9 whereby Japan formally renounced its "sovereign right" to wage war.

Further reading: Kyoko Inoue, *MacArthur's Japanese Constitution: A Linguistic and Cultural Study of Its Making* (Chicago: University of Chicago Press, 1991); Shoichi Koseki, ed., *The Birth of Japan's Post-war Constitution*, trans Ray A. Moore (Boulder, Colo.: Westview Press, 1998).

Japanese Peace Treaty of 1951   International treaty signed at San Francisco on September 8, 1951, formally ending the war (World War II) with Japan and establishing lenient peace terms. Fifty nations were invited to sign; all but the Soviet Union did so. The treaty recognized Japan's residual sovereignty over her home islands (notably the Ryukyu Islands) and provided for the withdrawal of occupation forces within 90 days after a majority of signatories ratified the treaty. It placed no restrictions on Japan's economic development, war industries, or rearmament. Japan acknowledged Korean independence and relinquished claims to Formosa (Taiwan) and other former island possessions.

See also: U.S.-JAPANESE TREATY OF 1951.

Further reading: Stephen A. Flanders and Carl N. Flanders, *Dictionary of American Foreign Affairs* (New York: Macmillan, 1993); Quincy Howe, *Ashes of Victory: World War II and Its Aftermath* (New York: Simon & Schuster, 1972); Charles L. Phillips and Alan Axelrod, eds., *Encyclopedia of Historical Treaties and Alliances*, 2 vols. (New York: Facts On File, 2001).

Japanese Relocation Order   See EXECUTIVE ORDER 9066, U.S.

Japanese-Soviet Peace Declaration of 1956   See SOVIET-JAPANESE PEACE DECLARATION OF 1956.

Japan's Surrender in World War II   Instrument of surrender of Japan signed aboard the U.S. battleship *Missouri* in

Tokyo Bay on September 2, 1945, by Foreign Minister Shigemitsu Mamoru and General Umezu Yoshijiro for the Japanese General Staff; and by representatives of Australia, China, France, New Zealand, the Netherlands, Great Britain, the Soviet Union, and the United States. It provided for Japan's surrender in World War II (1939–45). The document required the Japanese Imperial Headquarters, the Japanese armed forces, and all forces everywhere under Japan to surrender unconditionally to the Allied powers; required the Japanese Imperial Headquarters to order all forces to surrender unconditionally; required all Japanese officials to enforce the order and to see that all orders given by the supreme command of the Allied powers were carried out; required Japan to accept the POTSDAM DECLARATION in its entirety; required Japan to provide for the liberation and safety of all prisoners of war; and required the Japanese emperor and government to recognize the supreme governing authority of the supreme commander of the Allied powers.

Further reading: Quincy Howe, *Ashes of Victory: World War II and Its Aftermath* (New York: Simon & Schuster, 1972); Charles L. Phillips and Alan Axelrod, eds., *Encyclopedia of Historical Treaties and Alliances*, 2 vols. (New York: Facts On File, 2001).

Japan's Twenty-one Demands   See TWENTY-ONE DEMANDS, JAPAN'S.

Jaruzelski's Martial Law Decree

Formal order declared on December 13, 1981, by Polish communist prime minister General Wojciech Jaruzelski to suppress the growing Solidarity union movement and its call for human rights (see SOLIDARITY CHARTER). Under the decree, Polish borders, airports, and main roads were closed; telephone lines were cut; mail was censored; and all radio and television broadcasts, except two government stations, were shut down. Thousands of Solidarity members were rounded up, Lech Walesa and other union leaders were arrested, and the Solidarity union was officially outlawed. Strikes and marches were organized against martial law but were brutally suppressed; nine coal miners were shot dead by police on December 16, 1981. Martial law was finally lifted on July 22, 1983, although Solidarity was still outlawed.

Further reading: Leopold Labedz, ed., *Poland under Jaruzelski: A Comprehensive Sourcebook on Poland During and after Martial Law* (New York: Scribner, 1984); Amos Lakos, *Polish Crisis: Solidarity and Martial Law: A Bibliography* (Monticello, Ill.: Vance Bibliographies, 1987); Polska Ludowa, "Obwieszczerie," Polska Ludowa.com, available online at http://polskaludowa.com/dokumenty/prawne/stan_wojenny_obwieszczenie.htm/.

Jassy, Treaty of

Peace treaty made at Jassy (Iasi, Romania) on January 9, 1792, between Russia under Czarina Catherine II the Great and the Ottoman Empire under Sultan Selim III, ending the Russo-Turkish War of 1787–92. The treaty established the Dniester River as the Russian-Ottoman border, with Russia retaining all conquered territory east of the river (including the port of Ochakov) and restoring Moldavia and Bessarabia to Ottoman control. The Turkish sultan recognized Russian control of the Crimea and much of the northern Black Sea coast (including the Don River port of Azov), while Catherine accepted Turkish rule over the Balkans.

See also: CATHERINE THE GREAT'S DECREE ANNEXING THE CRIMEA; KUCHUK KAINARDJI, TREATY OF.

Further reading: Bernard Lewis, *The Emergence of Modern Turkey* (New York: Oxford University Press, 1961, repr., 2001); Reeva S. Simon, Philip Mattar, and Richard W. Bulliet, eds., 4 vols. *Encyclopedia of the Modern Middle East* (New York: Macmillan, 1996).

Jaworzno, Treaty of

Secret treaty of alliance concluded at Jaworzno, Poland, on July 11, 1675, between King John III Sobieski of Poland and King Louis XIV of France, obtaining a Polish promise to fight the Holy Roman (Hapsburg) emperor after the conclusion of the ongoing Polish-Turkish war. The Poles were to enter the alliance together with Swedes, Turks, and Hungarians. By the treaty, Poland was to receive 200,000 crowns and French military aid in her struggle against Elector Frederick William of Brandenburg in order to regain control of East Prussia. Poland would also make peace with Sweden and cooperate in anti-Hapsburg activities in Transylvania.

See also: ZURAVNO, TREATY OF.

Further reading: Norman Davies, *God's Playground: A History of Poland*, 2 vols. (New York: Columbia University Press, 1981).

Jay Treaty

Agreement negotiated by John Jay, U.S. chief justice and special envoy, and William Grenville, British foreign secretary, and signed in London, England, on November 19, 1794; it settled outstanding grievances and disputes between their two countries. Britain agreed to evacuate her forts in the Northwest Territory by June 1, 1796, to make monetary amends for seizure of American ships, and to give the United States trading concessions in England and the British East Indies. The Mississippi River was to be accessible to both countries, and commissions were to be set up to fix boundaries between the United States and Canada in the Northwest and Northeast regions. American debts owed to British merchants prior to the American Revolution were to be paid. Though the treaty was unpopular in the United States (not having dealt with British impressment of U.S. seamen), it was ratified by the U.S. Congress in 1795.

Further reading: Charles I. Bevans, comp., *Treaties and Other International Agreements of the United States of America, 1776–1949*, 12 vols. (Washington, D.C.: U.S. Government Printing Office, 1968); Thomas Carson, ed., *Gale Encyclopedia of U.S. Economic History* (Farmington Hills, Mich.: Gale

Group, 1999); Jerald Combs, *The Jay Treaty: Political Background of the Founding Fathers* (Berkeley: University of California Press, 1970); Charles L. Phillips and Alan Axelrod, eds., *Encyclopedia of Historical Treaties and Alliances*, 2 vols. (New York: Facts On File, 2001).

Jefferson's First Inaugural Address   Speech delivered by Thomas Jefferson on March 4, 1801, in Washington, D.C., at his inauguration as third president of the United States. This classic discourse on democratic philosophy stressed the need for limiting government powers, strict construction of the U.S. CONSTITUTION, support for the rights of state governments, economy in national administration, majority rule tempered by recognition of equal rights for minorities, protection of civil liberties, freedom of trade, minimal public debt, and "peace, commerce, and honest friendship with all nations, entangling alliances with none."

Further reading: Philip S. Foner, ed., *Basic Writings of Thomas Jefferson* (New York: Willey Book Co., 1944); A. A. Lipscomb and A. E. Bergh, eds., *The Writings of Thomas Jefferson* 20 vols. (Washington, D.C.: Thomas Jefferson Memorial Association, 1904).

Jerusalem, Assizes of   Comprehensive compilation of feudal law based on the usages and practices prevalent in 12th-century Jerusalem, a remarkable achievement of its Second Kingdom. The original assizes, contained in the *Lettres du Sepulchre* and destroyed during Saladin's capture of Jerusalem in 1187, derived from French Crusade leader Godfrey of Bouillon's questioning of Crusaders regarding the customs in their countries. The customs incorporated in the code were mainly French and covered legal, administrative, trade, and military issues. The assizes, in their existing forms, were compiled in the 13th century by three lawyers (two members of the Ibelin family and Philip of Novara) from Cyprus. They contain a charter of baronial rights and describe the customs of an ideal feudal state. Two separate codes were drawn up: the *Assises de la Haute Cour* for the nobility and the *Assises de la Cour des Bourgeois* for the rest of the country. They underwent frequent revision during the next three centuries.

Further reading: P. W. Edbury, *John of Ibelin and the Kingdom of Jerusalem* (Rochester, N.Y.: Boydell Press, 1997).

Jesuit Estates Act   Act sponsored by Quebec's Premier Honoré Mercier and passed by the Quebec legislature in 1888, providing that the Jesuits receive compensation for the confiscation of their order's estates by the British following Great Britain's conquest of Canada in the 18th century. Mercier had set a value of $400,000 on the estates. By the act, the Jesuits received an indemnity of $160,000 for surrendering all claims to their property; $60,000 went to Protestant schools in Quebec; and the remainder went to Roman Catholic institutions. Because Pope Leo XXII had been invited to arbitrate, the settlement aroused intense opposition within Ontario's Orange

Order, a Protestant nativist organization fearful of any increase in Catholic French Canadian influence in Canada.

Further reading: *The Jesuits' Estate Act: A Speech Delivered in the House of Commons of Canada on the 30th of April, 1890* (Ottawa: Canadian Institute for Historical Microreproductions, 1986).

Jeu de Paume, Oath of the (Tennis Court Oath)   Vow made at Versailles, France, on June 20, 1789, by the Third Estate (common people) and some members of the lower clergy, three days after they formed themselves into the National Assembly of France (June 17). Locked out of their usual meeting hall, they took the oath on a tennis court (jeu de paume) at Versailles, vowing "not to separate, and to reassemble wherever circumstances require until the constitution of the kingdom is established and consolidated upon firm foundations." The oath was one of the most important of the 1789 French Revolution (see DECLARATION OF THE RIGHTS OF MAN AND OF THE CITIZEN; FRENCH DECREE ABOLISHING FEUDALISM); only one member abstained from making the commitment, risking harassment. Overwhelmed by this massive show of resistance, King Louis XVI ordered (June 27) the nobility and higher clergy to join the Third Estate in a truly representative National Assembly.

Further reading: Georges Lefebvre, *The French Revolution: From Its Origins to 1793* (New York: Columbia University Press, 1962); Raymond Postgate, ed., *Revolution from 1789 to 1906* (New York: Harper & Row, 1962).

Jewish Liberties, Charter of   Charter granted by Poland's Boleslaus V the Pious, prince of Kraków, in 1264 to the Jewish community. During this period conditions for Jews were poor in other parts of Europe, particularly where the crusading spirit was prominent. In Poland, Jews were generally tolerated and granted certain privileges, which encouraged them to migrate to Poland. The charter affirmed the Jews' right to travel without molestation, granted them certain trading privileges, allowed for the practice of their religion, and provided for exemption from slavery and serfdom. It did not, however, affirm many other rights possessed by free Christian citizens of Poland.

Further reading: Antony Polonsky et al., *The Jews in Old Poland, 1000–1795* (Oxford, England: Institute for Polish-Jewish Studies, 1993).

Jewish State, The (Der Judenstaat)   Pamphlet written by Hungarian-born Austrian journalist Theodor Herzl and published in Vienna in February 1896; it contained the ideas upon which the Zionist movement were founded. In the work Herzl, a Jew, expressed his conviction that, owing to both anti-Semitism and the Jews' will to survive, assimilation could never be a solution to the Jewish problem. Rather, Herzl saw the only solution in the creation of an independent Jewish state, either in Argentina or in Erez Israel, according to the wishes of the Jewish people. He imagined that the future state would employ the most modern technology and scientific knowledge available and that it would be financed primarily through Jewish banks. The Jews of eastern Europe, in contrast to those of western Europe, embraced the plan enthusiastically. Because of the work Herzl is known as the father of the Zionist movement.

Further reading: Theodor Herzl, *The Jewish State* (Mineola, N.Y.: Dover Books, 1989); Theodor Herzl, *The Jews' State: A Critical English Translation* trans. Henk Overberg (Northvale, N.J.: Jason Aronson, 1997).

Jim Crow Laws   State statutes, passed between the end of Reconstruction (1877) and the beginning of the modern civil rights movement (in the 1950s), that enforced racial segregation, primarily in the southern United States. Named for a minstrel character, Jim Crow laws were designed to deny the civil rights that black people had gained during Reconstruction. Laws prohibited intermarriage and segregated blacks and whites in public transportation, hotels, restaurants, schools, housing, factories, hospitals, and other public institutions. Supreme Court rulings in the U.S. CIVIL RIGHTS CASES OF 1883 and *PLESSY* V. *FERGUSON* upheld these laws. It was not until *BROWN* V. *BOARD OF EDUCATION OF TOPEKA, KANSAS* in 1954 that Jim Crow laws began to be overturned.

Further reading: Thomas Carson, ed., *Gale Encyclopedia of U.S. Economic History* (Farmington Hills, Mich.: 1999); Leon F. Litwack, *Trouble in Mind: Black Southerners in the Age of Jim Crow* (New York: Knopf, 1998).

Johnson Debt Default Act   U.S. legislation enacted on April 13, 1934, that prohibited U.S. citizens and organizations from making private loans to any country that was in default or arrears on its World War I debt payments to the United States. The act also forbade the purchase or sale of securities issued by the governments of such countries in the United States. Violators were subject to a fine up to $10,000 and/or imprisonment up to five years. Sponsored by Senator Hiram Johnson of California, a militant isolationist, the act was intended to aid the struggling U.S. economy but it greatly angered debtor nations.

Further reading: Stephen A. Flanders and Carl N. Flanders, *Dictionary of American Foreign Affairs* (New York: Macmillan, 1993).

Johnson-Reed Act   See IMMIGRATION QUOTA ACT OF 1924, U.S.

Johnson's First Address to Congress   Speech delivered by Lyndon B. Johnson before Congress on November 27, 1963, after he assumed the U.S. presidency in the wake of the assassination of John F. Kennedy. Johnson sought to reassure the nation that the government was in steady hands and that he would continue the policies of his predecessor—in support

for the United Nations, commitment to America's allies, maintenance of military strength, and, particularly, support for civil rights. "No memorial oration or eulogy could more eloquently honor President Kennedy's memory than the earliest possible passage of the civil rights bill for which he fought so long," Johnson said (see: CIVIL RIGHTS ACT OF 1964, U.S.).

Further reading: Lyndon B. Johnson and Howard B. Furer, *Lyndon B. Johnson, 1908– : Chronology–Documents–Bibliographical Aids* (Dobbs Ferry, N.Y.: Oceana Publications, 1971); Bruce J. Schulman, *Lyndon B. Johnson and American Liberalism: A Brief Biography with Documents* (New York: St. Martin's, 1995).

Johnson's Inaugural Address   Speech delivered by Lyndon B. Johnson on January 20, 1965, following his inauguration as president of the United States, reiterating his campaign goal of creating a "Great Society" based on the principles of the American covenant: justice, liberty, and union. "In a land of great wealth," he said, "families must not live in hopeless poverty. In a land rich in harvest, children must not go hungry. In a land of healing miracles, neighbors must not suffer and die unattended. In a great land of learning and scholars, young people must be taught to read and write." Describing the nation as "prosperous, great, and mighty," he welcomed the rapid changes of modern life.

Further reading: Lyndon B. Johnson and Howard B. Furer, *Lyndon B. Johnson, 1908– : Chronology–Documents–Bibliographical Aids* (Dobbs Ferry, N.Y.: Oceana Publications, 1971); Bruce J. Schulman, *Lyndon B. Johnson and American Liberalism: A Brief Biography with Documents* (New York: St. Martin's, 1995).

Johnson's Speech at Johns Hopkins University   Address delivered by U.S. President Lyndon B. Johnson on April 7, 1965, defending U.S. involvement in the Vietnam War (1956–75) in the face of rising domestic criticism. Insisting that the war was a result of North Vietnamese aggression (inspired by Communist China) against South Vietnam, Johnson justified increased U.S. intervention to protect the independence of the south. He advanced the "domino theory," claiming that a communist victory in South Vietnam would lead to similar victories elsewhere in Southeast Asia. Johnson nonetheless declared his readiness to undertake "unconditional discussions" with the North Vietnamese to achieve a peaceful settlement, based on a secure, independent South Vietnam.

Further reading: Lyndon B. Johnson and Howard B. Furer, *Lyndon B. Johnson, 1908– : Chronology–Documents–Bibliographical Aids* (Dobbs Ferry, N.Y.: Oceana Publications, 1971); Bruce J. Schulman, *Lyndon B. Johnson and American Liberalism: A Brief Biography with Documents* (New York: St. Martin's, 1995).

Johnson's United Nations Address of 1963   Address delivered by U.S. president Lyndon B. Johnson before the

United Nations General Assembly on December 17, 1963, mourning the death of his predecessor, John F. Kennedy, and emphasizing Johnson's "unswerving commitment" to world peace. "Peace is a journey of a thousand miles and it must be taken one step at a time," he stated. He said that the United States favored nuclear arms control and an end to the cold war. Johnson reaffirmed America's commitment to the United Nations, to a rule of law, to human rights, and to the elimination of hunger, disease, ignorance, and misery through international aid and international cooperation.

Further reading: Lyndon B. Johnson and Howard B. Furer, *Lyndon B. Johnson, 1908– : Chronology–Documents–Bibliographical Aids* (Dobbs Ferry, N.Y.: Oceana Publications, 1971); Bruce J. Schulman, *Lyndon B. Johnson and American Liberalism: A Brief Biography with Documents* (New York: St. Martin's, 1995).

Jones Act of 1916 (Organic Act of the Philippine Islands)

Legislation enacted by the U.S. Congress on August 29, 1916, reaffirming a U.S. intention to withdraw its sovereignty over the Philippine Islands, which had been acquired from Spain in 1898, and to grant independence "as soon as a stable government can be established therein." The act increased Filipino self-government: It provided a senate and a house of representatives to be elected by Filipino citizens; granted Filipino citizenship to all inhabitants who had been Spanish subjects on April 11, 1899; included a bill of rights; and granted the vote to literate males with a small property qualification. The United States, however, retained the power to appoint the chief executive (the governor general) and to veto legislative acts.

Further reading: Ainslie T. Embree, ed., *Encyclopedia of Asian History*, 4 vols. (New York: Charles Scribner's Sons, 1988).

Jones Act of 1917 (Organic Act for Puerto Rico)

Legislation enacted by the U.S. Congress on March 2, 1917, that made Puerto Rico a U.S. territory, granted U.S. citizenship to its inhabitants, and broadened self-government in the island. The act incorporated a bill of rights that gave Puerto Ricans most of the civil rights enunciated in the U.S. CONSTITUTION, except the right to demand a trial by jury. Male suffrage was granted, and the Puerto Rican senate was made an elective body. Legislative acts were nonetheless subject to veto by the U.S. president, who also retained the power to appoint the governor, the supreme court, and most executive department heads in Puerto Rico.

Further reading: *Documents on the Constitutional History of Puerto Rico* (Washington, D.C.: Office of the Commonwealth of Puerto Rico, 1948).

Journey from St. Petersburg to Moscow (Puteshestvie iz Peterburga v Moskvu)

Book written by Russian social critic and philosopher Aleksandr N. Radishchev and published in Russia in 1790; it related a story about the peasantry and, through it, condemned serfdom as well as the forces in his country that were resisting its reform. The story centered around a traveler who, throughout his journey, encountered the peasantry and who was himself moved to improve their lot. The author portrayed the failure of the reformer and the serf to communicate, thus relating the difficulty of reform even when motivated by good will. The work also contained proposals on how to end serfdom, an attack on censorship, and Radishchev's prediction that failure to end serfdom would bring about revolution. The author's attack on autocracy, which at one point took the form of a portrayal of Czarina Catherine II the Great as hypocritical, vain, and despotic, led to his arrest and exile to Siberia in the same year, 1790. The novel is generally regarded as the beginning of revolutionary literature in Russia.

Further reading: Aleksandr N. Radishchev, *A Journey from St. Petersburg to Moscow*, trans. Leo Weiner and ed. Roderick P. Thaler (Cambridge, Mass.: Harvard University Press, 1969).

Joyeuse Entrée of Brabant   See BRABANT CONSTITUTION.

Juárez Law (Ley Juárez)

Law proposed by Mexico's minister of justice and ecclesiastical affairs Benito Juárez and promulgated by the new liberal Mexican government on November 23, 1855. The law declared that military and ecclesiastical courts would have no jurisdiction in civil cases, but in military and ecclesiastical cases alone. The law therefore effectively abolished special courts and the privilege previously enjoyed by the military and clergy of their being exempt from standing trial in civil courts for civil or criminal offenses. The law was intended to promote social equality, as well as diminish the tremendous power wielded by the Roman Catholic Church in Mexico. The strong opposition of the clergy and military to the law contributed to Mexican president Juan Álvarez's fall from power later that year.

See also: IGLESIAS LAW; LERDO LAW.

Further reading: Brian R. Hammett, *Juarez* (New York: Longman, 1994); Richard N. Sinkin, *Modernization and Reform in Mexico, 1855–1876* (Ann Arbor, Mich.: Xerox University Microfilms, 1972); Elizabeth B. de Trevino, *Juarez, Man of Law* (New York: Farrar, Straus & Giroux, 1974).

Judicature Act of 1873, British (Supreme Court of Judicature Act)

Major constructive reform (August 5, 1873) from the William Gladstone administration, completely overhauling (with amendments in 1876 and 1880) the judicial system of England. The act, drafted by Lord Selborne (lord chancellor), established one supreme court of judicature (to replace a welter of equity and common law courts) with two main branches: the High Court of Justice (including the Queen's Bench, Chancery, and Probate, Divorce, and Admiralty); and the Court of Appeal, whose decision would be binding. In 1876, this court's right to appeal to the House of Lords was reinstituted (by the Benjamin Disraeli administration) by the creation of three law lords tenured for life.

Further reading: Carl Stephenson and Frederick George Marcham, eds., *Sources of English Constitutional History: A Selection of Documents from A.D. 600 to the Present* (New York: Harper & Row, 1937).

Judiciary Act of 1789, U.S.

Federal legislation enacted September 24, 1789, creating the federal court system. The U.S. CONSTITUTION had established a Supreme Court but given Congress the power to organize it and the rest of the judiciary. The 1789 act provided for the Supreme Court to consist of a chief justice and five associates and established three intermediate circuit courts and 13 federal district courts. For each district court a U.S. attorney and deputies were to serve as federal prosecutors, and U.S. marshals were to serve as federal police. The act established an attorney general for the United States to conduct all suits in the Supreme Court and to advise the executive branch. It also gave the Supreme Court the right to hear and decide certain appeals from state courts.

Further reading: Julius Goebel, *History of the Supreme Court of the United States: Antecedents and Beginnings to 1801* (New York: Macmillan, 1971); Leonard W. Levy and Kenneth L. Karst, eds., *Encyclopedia of the American Constitution.* 2nd ed. (New York: Macmillan Reference, 2000); Wilfred J. Ritz, *Rewriting the History of the Judiciary Act of 1789: Exposing Myths, Challenging Premises, and Using New Evidence* (Norman: University of Oklahoma Press, 1990).

Judiciary Act of 1801, U.S.

Federal legislation that reduced the number of Supreme Court justices from six to five and relieved the justices of circuit court duty; created 16 circuit courts and a judgeship for each; and increased the number of federal marshals, attorneys, and clerks. The act was supported by the outgoing Federalist administration of U.S. president John Adams, who filled the newly created positions with the appointment of so-called midnight judges just before he left office. In 1802 Congress, now controlled by the Democratic-Republican Party of Thomas Jefferson, repealed the 1801 act, restoring the U.S. JUDICIARY ACT OF 1789.

Further reading: Leonard W. Levy and Kenneth L. Karst, eds., *Encyclopedia of the American Constitution.* 2nd ed. (New York: Macmillan Reference, 2000).

Judiciary Reorganization Bill, U.S.

Controversial proposal by U.S. president Franklin D. Roosevelt, submitted to Congress on February 5, 1937, to reorganize the federal judiciary. The bill, which represented Roosevelt's response to the U.S. Supreme Court's invalidation of major New Deal legislation, proposed to add to the Supreme Court and to other federal courts one new judge for every judge aged 70 or more who had served at least 10 years and failed to retire. A maximum of 50 additional judges could be appointed, and the Supreme Court could be increased to 15 justices. The bill also proposed procedural reforms to improve efficiency. Characterized as "court packing" by its opponents, the bill was killed in the Senate Judiciary Committee. A greatly modified version, the Judicial Procedure Reform Act, was enacted August 26, 1937; it reformed lower court procedures but did not provide for the appointment of additional judges.

Further reading: James MacGregor Burns, *Roosevelt: The Lion and the Fox* (New York: Harcourt, Brace and World, 1956); William E. Leuchtenburg, *Franklin Roosevelt and the New Deal, 1932–1940* (New York: Harper and Row, 1963).

Julian Law of 90 B.C. (Lex Julia of 90 B.C.)

Roman law successfully proposed by consul Lucius Julius Caesar in 90 B.C., during the Social War of 91–88 B.C. (a revolt of the Italian allies against Rome). Roman citizenship was granted to all allied communities that had remained faithful and not joined the revolt (mostly Etruscans, Umbrians, Latins, and Greek federate allies). A second law, called the Plautian-Papirian Law (Lex Plautia Papiria) in honor of its two tribune sponsors in 89 B.C., extended Roman citizenship to all Italians who could claim it within 60 days, disregarding whether their communities were under arms or not. A third law, the Pompeian Law (Lex Pompeia), the work of consul Gnaeus Pompeius Strabo in 89 B.C., granted citizenship to towns in Cisalpine Gaul (northern Italy) south of the Po River, and privileges to those north of the river. These concessions helped end the war, for the revolting allied peoples had gained the Roman citizenship for which they had taken up arms.

Further reading: Frank N. Magill, ed., *Great Events from History, Ancient and Medieval Series,* 3 vols. (Englewood Cliffs, N.J.: Salem Press, 1972).

Julian Laws of 18 B.C. (Leges Juliae of 18 B.C.)

Major social reform legislation initiated by Roman Emperor Augustus (Octavian) and passed by the Tribal Assembly in 18 B.C., seeking to restore morality and family life in Roman society. (The Julian Laws, of which there were others relating to criminality, slavery, and citizenship, were so named from the Julian clan to which Augustus belonged by adoption.) Most important was the law (18 B.C.) that gave a father, who was a Roman citizen, the right to kill an adulterous daughter and her lover and allowed a husband the right to kill his wife and her lover if he found them committing adultery in his own house. An adulterous woman had to be indicted in court, was banished for life on conviction, forfeited a third of her fortune and half her dowry, and was forbidden from marrying again. A husband could not be charged with adultery by his wife and could visit registered prostitutes. Another law obliged all mature males under 60 and females under 50 to marry. Inheritance penalties of varying degrees were imposed on celibates, widows, divorcees, spinsters, and childless wives. Preeminence was given to the Roman consul with the most children, and in appointments to office, prior favor was given to fathers with large families. A mother of three children gained emancipation from the authority of her husband. Much public criticism of these laws led to mollifying revisions during Augustus's reign (27 B.C.–A.D. 14).

Further reading: Leo F. Raditsa, "Augustus' Legislation Concerning Marriage, Procreation, Love Affairs and Adultery," *Aufstieg und Niedergang der Romischen Welt* 2, no. 13 (1980): 278–339; Pat Southern, *Augustus* (New York: Routledge, 1999); Alban D. Winspear and Lenore K. Geweke, *Augustus and the Reconstruction of Roman Government and Society* (New York: Russell & Russell, 1970).

Julliard v. Greenman   U.S. Supreme Court decision of March 3, 1884, upholding the power of Congress to make U.S. notes legal tender in peacetime as well as wartime. The ruling upheld the constitutionality of an 1878 act providing that Civil War legal tender notes should not be concealed or retired but should be reissued and kept in circulation. The Court argued that the power of Congress to make notes legal tender did not rest solely on its war power but derived from Congress's authority to provide a uniform national currency.

Further reading: Henry Steele Commager, ed., *Documents of American History*, 8th ed. (New York: Appleton-Century-Crofts, 1968); United States Supreme Court, *United States Reports: Cases Adjudged in the Supreme Court at. . . . and Rules Announced at . . .* (New York: Banks & Brothers, Law Publishers, 1884–1921; Washington, D.C.: Government Printing Office, 1922–).

July Ordinances of 1830 (Quatre Ordonnances)

Four ordinances issued on July 25, 1830, by King Charles X of France, sparking the July Revolution that forced his eventual abdication. The first severely restricted the freedom of the press, requiring government authorization for every publication less than 20 pages. Alleging election fraud and invoking Article 14 of the FRENCH CONSTITUTION OF 1814, the king dissolved the newly formed chamber of deputies via the second ordinance. The third once again reduced the number of deputies to 258 (see LAW OF THE DOUBLE VOTE). These, it stipulated, could be elected only by the department electoral colleges, whereas the *arrondissement* colleges were limited to the nomination of candidates. Professional license fees, and door and window taxes, were declared exempt from voter tax qualifications, further shrinking voter groups. The fourth convened a meeting of the electoral colleges for September 6 and 13, and of the chamber for September 28, 1830. Publication of these ordinances galvanized a stunned opposition into revolt.

Further reading: William Hone and Thomas Tegg, *Full Annals of the Revolution in France, 1830: Illegal Ordinances of Charles X . . .* (Cambridge, England: Chadwyck-Healey, 1991); Pamela M. Pilbeam, *The French Revolution of 1830* (New York: St. Martin's Press, 1991).

Junius, Letters of   Series of 69 letters published in the London newspaper *Public Advertiser* at intervals between 1769 and 1772, attacking the Tory government and King George III. Written under the mysterious pen name "Junius," the author sought to unite the opposition by showing the corruption and scandals in the public and private lives of royal and government leaders, most notably the duke of Grafton (whose prime ministry collapsed in 1770), Sir William Blackstone, Lord Mansfield, Lord North, and the duke of Bedford. The letters also supported British politician John Wilkes (see NO. 45 OF THE NORTH BRITON). They were very popular because of their satiric, rational, and eloquent style, and their authorship has been attributed to many persons, including Lord Shelburne, Edward Gibbon, Edmund Burke, John Wilkes, Lord Chesterfield, and Thomas Paine; but they are generally ascribed to the writer Sir Philip Francis.

Further reading: *The Letters of Junius* (New Canaan, Conn.: Readex Microprint, 1987).

Justice, Ordinances of (Ordinanze della Giustizia)

Memorable laws enacted in Florence, Italy, on January 18, 1293, virtually excluding the nobility from the guilds and from participation in the government. In the 1280s Florence's wealthy mercantile class had gained power over the nobility after a protracted struggle; a law of 1282 had allowed only the nobles who joined guilds to be participants in the city government. Now the guilds increased in power; the ordinances imposed harsh punishment and heavy fines on nobles who committed violent crimes; the nobles also had to attest to good behavior. The ruling Guelphs (the propapal faction opposing the proimperial Ghibellines), however, split into two warring groups, the Blacks and the Whites, the former favoring repeal of the ordinances, which were moderated in 1295.

Further reading: Carol Lansing, *The Florentine Magnates: Lineage and Faction in a Medieval Commune* (Princeton, N.J.: Princeton University Press, 1991); John M. Najemy, *Corporatism and Consensus in Florentine Electoral Politics, 1280–1400* (Chapel Hill: University of North Carolina Press, 1982).

Justinian Code (Corpus Juris Civilis)   Body of Roman law codified and annotated by a commission of expert jurists under Trebonian, appointed by Byzantine Emperor Justinian I. It consisted of four parts: (1) the *Codex*, in 10 books, containing all imperial ordinances ("constitutions") of general validity, issued in A.D. 529 (a revised *Codex*, in 12 books, with Justinian's new laws, was issued in A.D. 534); (2) the *Digest* or *Pandects*, in 50 books, containing the opinions of past famous Roman jurists with interpretations, published in A.D. 533; (3) the *Institutes*, in four books designed as manuals for students of civil law, issued in A.D. 533; and (4) the *Novels*, holding Justinian's new ordinances and edicts between A.D. 534 and his death in 565, issued posthumously.

The code (published in Latin except for the fourth part, written in Greek) saliently acknowledged the Roman Christian Church (but proclaimed the emperor's dominion over it), divided all freemen into commoners and men of honor or rank (in which there was a hierarchy), encouraged manumission, legalized serfdom, made the inheritance of property through cognate relatives (not agnate relatives), provided more grounds for divorce, and specified severe punishment for sexual irregularities (death for committing homosexual acts, rape, and most adultery). This conservative code of the Byzantine Empire later became the basis of nearly all modern European states' legal systems, with the notable exception of England (whose common law was nevertheless influenced by the code's principles).

Further reading: J. A. S. Evans, *The Age of Justinian: The Circumstances of Imperial Power* (New York: Routledge, 1996); John Moorhead, *Justinian* (New York: Addison-Wesley, 1994).

K

Kalisch (Kalisz), Treaty of (1343) Peace treaty concluded at Kalisz, Poland, on July 8, 1343, ending the protracted Teutonic Knights' War with Poland of 1309–43. King Casimir III of Poland was compelled to cede to the Teutonic Knights eastern Pomerania (Pomerelia), Chełmno, and Michałowo, giving up his former title of "Lord and Heir of Pomerania." He also renounced indemnity payments, preferring that to Pope Clement VI's confirmation of the treaty, which would have made it more binding yet. Though the Pope had asked that a hearing be held to judge the matter, he had not supported its decision (see PROCESS OF WARSAW, STATEMENTS AT THE), which would have led to a better settlement for Poland. Instead, the treaty was based on the Agreement at VISEGRÁD.

See also: THORN, FIRST PEACE OF; THORN, SECOND PEACE OF.)

Further reading: Norman Davies, *God's Playground: A History of Poland*, 2 vols. (New York: Columbia University, 1982); W. F. Reddaway, ed., *The Cambridge History of Poland to 1696* (Cambridge, England: Cambridge University Press, 1950).

Kalisch (Kalisz), Treaty of (1813) Agreement concluded at Kalisz, Poland, on February 28, 1813, by which the governments of Russia and Prussia allied themselves against France during the Napoleonic Wars (1803–15). French emperor Napoléon's Grand Army was then retreating from Russia, its 1812 invasion having failed. By the treaty, Russia and Prussia agreed on the number of troops to be provided by each in the war against France. In secret articles, they also agreed that much of the territory lost by Prussia since 1806 (see TILSIT, TREATIES OF) would be restored to her, with Russia being compensated with part of Prussia's former Polish possession in the east. The treaty followed the unauthorized decision of Prussian general Ludwig Yorck von Wartenburg to withdraw from the war against Russia (see TAUROGGEN, CONVENTION OF).

Further reading: Michael Glover, *The Napoleonic Wars: An Illustrated History, 1792–1815* (New York: Hippocrene, 1979); Nicholas V. Riasanovsky, *A History of Russia*, 3d ed. (New York: Oxford University Press, 1977).

Kalisz, Treaties of See KALISCH (KALISZ), TREATY OF (1343); KALISCH (KALISZ), TREATY OF (1813).

Kalmar, Union of Accord reached at Kalmar, or Calmar, Sweden, on July 12, 1397, unifying the kingdoms of Denmark, Norway, and Sweden under a sole king, Eric VII of Pomerania. Engineered by Denmark's Queen Margaret I (Eric's great aunt), the union developed from a need to have a united Scandinavian front against threats from Germany and the Hanseatic League. The nature of the union (which created Europe's second-largest unified territory) was defined in two different documents: the Coronation Letter, suggesting a dynastic union with a centralized and hereditary monarchy; and the Union Letter, describing a federation of states with a common monarch, whose office was hereditary unless there was no dynastic heir, in which case he was elected. Each kingdom was to conduct its own legal and administrative affairs, but defense and foreign policy were to be made in common. The Union Letter is seen as the draft of a constitution that never received formal approval. Sweden seceded from the union in 1521 and Norway in 1814.

Further reading: Ingmar Andersson, *A History of Sweden* (New York: Praeger, 1968); T. K. Derry, *A History of Scandinavia* (Minneapolis: University of Minnesota Press, 1979); Stewart Oakley, *A Short History of Denmark* (New York: Praeger, 1972).

Kampala, Treaty of (East African Cooperation Treaty)

Treaty establishing an East African Economic Community and replacing the East African Common Services Organization (established in 1961); signed on June 6, 1967, in Kampala, Uganda, among the presidents of Tanzania (Julius K. Nyerere), Kenya (Jomo Kenyatta), and Uganda (Milton Obote). It sought to strengthen regional cooperation by coordinating rail, postal, and civil aviation services, developing a uniform tariff scale, setting up an area development bank, and enabling free transit of goods within the common market. A transfer tax was instituted to offset unequal development. The East African Community was linked with the European Economic Community in July 1968 (see ROME, TREATIES OF [1957]). The Kampala treaty, implemented on December 1, 1967, was formally abandoned on June 30, 1977, because of economic and political dissension.

See also: CENTRAL AFRICAN CUSTOMS AND ECONOMIC UNION; WEST AFRICAN ECONOMIC COMMUNITY TREATY.

Further reading: Roland Oliver et al. eds., *History of East Africa*, 3 vols. (Oxford, England: Clarendon Press, 1963–76).

Kanagawa, Treaty of

Pact of peace, friendship, and commerce negotiated by U.S. commodore Matthew C. Perry that ended Japan's isolation from the West. In 1853 Perry sailed into Tokyo Bay with a fleet of warships as a show of force to deliver proposals from President Millard Fillmore on establishing commercial relations. When Perry returned the following year with a larger fleet, Japanese officials decided to abandon their policy of seclusion. Signed on March 31, 1854, the treaty opened the Japanese ports of Shimoda and Hakodate to U.S. trade, allowed the United States to establish a consulate at Shimoda, and provided for the protection of shipwrecked U.S. nationals.

Further reading: Charles I. Bevans, comp., *Treaties and Other International Agreements of the United States of America, 1776–1949*, 12 vols. (Washington, D.C.: U.S. Government Printing Office, 1968); Ainslie T. Embree, ed., *Encyclopedia of Asian History*, 4 vols. (New York: Charles Scribner's Sons, 1988); Stephen A. Flanders and Carl N. Flanders, *Dictionary of American Foreign Affairs* (New York: Macmillan, 1993); Charles L. Phillips and Alan Axelrod, eds., *Encyclopedia of*

Historical Treaties and Alliances, 2 vols. (New York: Facts On File, 2001).

Kansas-Nebraska Act

Bill passed by the U.S. Congress in 1854 that established the territories of Kansas and Nebraska, repealed the MISSOURI COMPROMISE of 1820, and established the principle of popular sovereignty, which allowed settlers in the newly organized territories to determine whether or not slavery would be permitted there. Though the bill, sponsored by Democratic senator Stephen A. Douglas and signed into law by President Franklin Pierce on May 30, 1854, aimed to reduce the growing national controversy over the extension of slavery, it actually intensified the conflict. Its passage led to the formation of the Republican Party, which opposed expansion of slavery into the territories. A period of bloodshed between pro- and antislavery factions erupted in Kansas as a precursor to the U.S. Civil War (1861–65).

Further reading: Robert Walter Johannsen, *The Frontier, the Union, and Stephen A. Douglas* (Urbana: University of Illinois Press, 1989); Michael A. Morrison, *Slavery and the American West* (Chapel Hill: University of North Carolina Press, 1997); David M. Potter, *The Impending Crisis, 1848–1861* (New York: Harper & Row, 1976); Gerald W. Wolff, *The Kansas-Nebraska Bill: Party, Section, and the Coming of the Civil War* (New York: Revisionist Press, 1977).

Kappel, Peace of

Second peace accord signed at Kappel, Switzerland, on November 21, 1531 (an armistice in 1529 fell apart), ending the wars between the Protestant canton of Zurich and the Roman Catholic cantons of Uri, Schwyz, Luzern, Unterwalden, and Zug. Zurich's defeat on the battlefield had quashed its zealous Protestantizing efforts in the other Swiss cantons. The accord stated that each canton and lordship could choose its own form of religion; that in cantons where both Protestants and Catholics resided the status quo antebellum was to be maintained; that preaching the Protestant faith in Catholic cantons was forbidden; and that no violence or abuse was to be inflicted upon anyone for religious reasons.

Further reading: E. Bonjour, H. S. Offler, and G. R. Potter, *A Short History of Switzerland* (Oxford, England: Clarendon Press, 1952); William Martin, *Switzerland: From Roman Times to the Present* (London: Elek Books, 1971).

Kardis (Cardis), Treaty of

Peace agreement concluded between Sweden and Russia at the northern Swedish border town of Kardis in July 1661; based on the conditions of the 1617 Treaty of STOLBOVO. By the Kardis treaty, Sweden regained a large part of the Baltic province of Livonia, which the Russians had seized during their 1656 military campaign against Sweden (while the latter was struggling to subjugate Poland in the First Northern War [1655–60]). The status quo antebellum was reconfirmed between Russia and Sweden.

See also: COPENHAGEN, TREATY OF; OLIVA, TREATY OF.

Further reading: Ingmar Andersson, *A History of Sweden* (New York: Praeger, 1968); Andrew A. Stomberg, *A History of Sweden* (New York: Macmillan, 1931).

Karlowitz, Peace of   Peace agreements marking the end of the Austro-Turkish War of 1683–99; concluded at Karlowitz (Sremski Karlovci, Yugoslavia) on January 26, 1699, between Austria, Poland, Venice, and Russia on one side and the Ottoman Empire on the other. The Ottoman Turks recognized Austrian suzerainty over most of Hungary, including Transylvania (except for the Banat of Temesvár), Croatia, and Slavonia. The Turks also recognized Polish suzerainty over Podolia in the Ukraine, as well as over the remaining part of the western Ukraine still held by the Turks. Venetian control over most of Dalmatia, Morea (Peloponnesus), and several Ionian islands was also accepted by the Turks, who retained Belgrade and Serbia but agreed to Russian control over the fortress-city of Azov near the mouth of the Don River. The peace marked the start of the breakdown of the Ottoman Empire.

See also: CONSTANTINOPLE, TREATY OF (1700).

Further reading: Stanford J. Shaw, *History of the Ottoman Empire and Modern Turkey*, vol. 1: *Empire of the Gazis, 1280–1808* (Cambridge, England: Cambridge University Press, 1976).

Kars, Treaty of   Treaty concluded in the Turkish town of Kars on October 13, 1921, by the Turkish nationalist (Ankara) government and the Soviet governments of Armenia, Azerbaijan, and Georgia; brought an end to the conflict between Soviet Russia and Turkey (the Ottoman Empire) over possession of territory in Transcaucasia. The treaty confirmed the Treaty of MOSCOW (1921) concluded by Soviet Russia and Turkey; provided for the mutual recognition of their respective governments; declared their agreement not to recognize any international settlement not recognized by the government concerned; and defined the frontiers of the four parties, with Georgia gaining possession of Batum, Armenia gaining possession of Alexandropol, and with the autonomous province of Nakhichevan being placed under the protection of Azerbaijan. The treaty left the Turkish nationalists free to pursue their war against the allies (particularly Greece), and the Soviets free to tend to the aftermath of their revolution.

See also: ALEXANDROPOL, TREATY OF; BATUM, TREATY OF; LAUSANNE, TREATY OF (1923).

Further reading: Harry N. Howard, *The Partition of Turkey, 1913–1923* (New York: Howard Fertig, 1966).

Katmandu, Treaty of   Truce agreement made during the Anglo-Nepali, or Gurkha, War (1814–16) at Katmandu, Nepal, on December 2, 1815. British Indian forces had advanced, with difficulty, into Nepal to put an end to raids by the Gurkhas (a Hindu people living in Nepal) into northern India. The Gurkhas were forced to cede some of their key territories

(Almora, Dehradun, Garhwal, Nainital, and Simla—the latter becoming the summer capital of British India) to the British and large tracts of their eastern sections to Sikkim, a small kingdom between India and Tibet. The lowland region of Terai remained in dispute. Renewed fighting ensued over provisions of the treaty, which was finally ratified formally by the 1816 Treaty of SAGAULI.

Further reading: Basil C. Hedrick and Anne K. Hedrick, *Historical and Cultural Dictionary of Nepal* (Metuchen, N.J.: Scarecrow Press, 1972).

Keating-Owen Act   Legislation enacted by the U.S. Congress on September 1, 1916; designed to reduce the abuses of child labor in mines, mills, and factories by prohibiting from shipments in interstate commerce products made by children under age 14 or by children 14 to 16 who had worked more than eight hours per day. The act was drafted by Representative Edward Keating of Colorado and Senator Robert L. Owen of Oklahoma. The U.S. Supreme Court, in HAMMER V. DAGENHART, declared the act unconstitutional on the grounds that it was not a regulation of interstate commerce but rather interfered with freedom of contract and a state's right to regulate the conditions of manufacture.

Further reading: Leonard W. Levy and Kenneth L. Karst, eds., *Encyclopedia of the American Constitution*, 2d ed. (New York: Macmillan Reference, 2000); Stephen Wood, *Constitutional Politics in the Progressive Era: Child Labor and the Law* (Chicago: University of Chicago Press, 1968).

Kellogg-Briand Peace Pact   See PARIS, PACT OF (1928).

Kendall v. United States   U.S. Supreme Court decision, issued in 1838, that declared that an administrative officer must conform to the law, not just answer to the president, when performing administrative duties that were not executive or discretionary in nature. The court unanimously rejected the claim by U.S. postmaster general Amos Kendall that he was responsible only to the chief executive, ruling that such a claim would grant the president powers not authorized by the U.S. CONSTITUTION.

Further reading: Kermit L. Hall et al., eds., *The Oxford Companion to the Supreme Court of the United States* (New York: Oxford University Press, 1992); Martin Siegel, *The Taney Court, 1836–1864* (Danbury, Conn.: Grolier Educational Corp., 1995); United States Supreme Court, *United States Reports: Cases Adjudged in the Supreme Court at . . . and Rules Announced at . . .* (New York: Banks & Brothers, Law Publishers, 1884–1921; Washington, D.C.: Government Printing Office, 1922–).

Kenilworth, Dictum of   Pacification agreement of October 31, 1266, between King Henry III of England and his rebellious subjects, and an important constitutional document restoring the monarchy and ending baronial reforms in

England. It declared nullified "the injurious and damnable acts" of Simon de Montfort, who had led the Barons' War (1263–65) and been killed at the decisive battle of Evesham (August 4, 1265). The king promised to "fully protect and observe the liberties of the church, and the charters of liberties, and of the forest" and to pardon all those who had been in arms against him. They could redeem their lands at five times its annual value (or at a rate proportionate to their guilt) or, if they owned no land, pay one half of their goods in ransom. The redeemed property would then be redistributed amongst the king's landless supporters. Crown property was to be immediately restored. The punishment for the late Earl Montfort and his family would be determined by King Louis IX of France. Finally, all were committed to maintaining a "firm peace" and appropriate action would be taken against any violators.

See also: LEWES, MISE OF; OXFORD, PROVISIONS OF; WESTMINSTER, PROVISIONS OF.

Further reading: Carl Stephenson and Frederick George Marcham, eds., *Sources of English Constitutional History: A Selection of Documents from A.D. 600 to the Present* (New York: Harper & Row, 1937).

Kennedy's Address on Removal of Soviet Weapons from Cuba

Televised address by U.S. president John F. Kennedy, on October 22, 1962, explaining the Soviet Union's secret placement of medium- and intermediate-range ballistic missiles in Cuba and the U.S. response. Calling the Soviet action "an explicit threat to the peace and security of all the Americas," Kennedy announced a strict quarantine on all offensive military equipment bound for Cuba and close surveillance of that nation. He declared that any nuclear missile launched from Cuba against any nation in the Western Hemisphere would be considered an attack by the Soviet Union against the United States and would elicit a full retaliatory response upon the Soviet Union. The world stood at the brink of nuclear war until the Soviets, on October 28, agreed to stop building bases in Cuba and to dismantle and remove their offensive weapons there.

See also: U.S.-SOVIET "HOTLINE" AGREEMENT.

Further reading: John F. Kennedy, *The Greatest Speeches of President John F. Kennedy* (Bellingham, Wash.: Titan Publishing, 2000); Theodore C. Sorensen, ed., *"Let the Word Go Forth": The Speeches, Statements, and Writings of John F. Kennedy, 1947 to 1963* (New York: Delacorte, 1988).

Kennedy's Appeal for Nuclear Disarmament

Speech delivered before the United Nations General Assembly by U.S. president John F. Kennedy on September 25, 1961, arguing the folly of war in a nuclear age. Kennedy stated: "Mankind must put an end to war—or war will put an end to mankind." He urged a prompt resumption of nuclear disarmament negotiations, beginning with efforts to achieve a treaty assuring the end of all nuclear testing, under workable controls. He proposed a mutual ban on atmospheric testing, without inspection of controls, to end the dangers of radioactive fallout, as well as a prohibition on weapons of mass destruction in outer space. "The risks inherent in disarmament pale in comparison to the risks inherent in an unlimited arms race," he said.

Further reading: Theodore C. Sorensen, ed., *"Let the Word Go Forth": The Speeches, Statements, and Writings of John F. Kennedy, 1947 to 1963* (New York: Delacorte, 1988).

Kennedy's "Ich bin ein Berliner" ("I am a Berliner") Speech

Address delivered by U.S. president John F. Kennedy in West Berlin on June 26, 1963, after a visit to the Berlin Wall separating the east and west sections of the city. Affirming his support for West Berlin as an island of freedom, Kennedy described the two-year-old wall as an offense against humanity, a demonstration of the failures of the communist system. Although freedom has flaws and democracy is imperfect, he said, "we have never had to put a wall up to keep our people in." To people who believed that communism was the wave of the future or a foundation for economic progress, Kennedy issued a challenge: "Let them come to Berlin!" In 1989 East German officials began opening up travel to West Berlin, allowing sections of the 26-mile-long wall to tumble for the first time since Kennedy's 1963 appeal to tear it down.

See also: GERMAN "STATE TREATY" OF 1990.

Further reading: Stephen A. Flanders and Carl N. Flanders, *Dictionary of American Foreign Affairs* (New York: Macmillan, 1993); John F. Kennedy, *The Greatest Speeches of President John F. Kennedy* (Bellingham, Wash.: Titan Publishing, 2000); Theodore C. Sorensen, ed., *"Let the Word Go Forth": The Speeches, Statements, and Writings of John F. Kennedy, 1947 to 1963* (New York: Delacorte, 1988).

Kennedy's Inaugural Address

Address delivered by John F. Kennedy on January 20, 1961, at his inauguration as 35th president of the United States. Speaking to and for a new generation of Americans, Kennedy announced to the world that the United States would "pay any price, bear any burden, meet any hardship . . . to assure the survival and the success of liberty." He pledged loyalty to old allies, support for the freedom of new ones, and an alliance for progress with Latin America. He offered to America's adversaries a new quest for peace and cooperation, for arms control and inspection. He challenged all Americans to join in a struggle against tyranny, poverty, disease, and war: "Ask not what your country can do for you—ask what you can do for your country."

Further reading: Theodore C. Sorensen, ed., *"Let the Word Go Forth": The Speeches, Statements, and Writings of John F. Kennedy, 1947 to 1963* (New York: Delacorte, 1988).

Kennedy's Message on the Peace Corps

Message to Congress from U.S. president John F. Kennedy on March 1, 1961, seeking the establishment of a permanent Peace Corps, a pool of trained American volunteers to be sent to developing nations to work for social and economic progress. Declaring that the lack of skilled personnel was one of the greatest obstacles to liberation from hunger, ignorance, and poverty, Kennedy argued that volunteers could teach in primary and secondary schools, construct development projects, demonstrate modern methods of sanitation, instruct farmers in modern agricultural techniques, and perform other tasks. Projects would be undertaken in consultation with the host countries. Membership in the Peace Corps would be open to Americans of all ages, and members would receive no salary. Kennedy established the corps on a pilot basis by executive order on March 1; on September 22, 1961, Congress authorized the corps on a permanent basis.

Further reading: Theodore C. Sorensen, ed., *"Let the Word Go Forth": The Speeches, Statements, and Writings of John F. Kennedy, 1947 to 1963* (New York: Delacorte, 1988).

Kennedy's Report on the Berlin Crisis

Report to the American people by President John F. Kennedy, delivered on July 25, 1961; it explained his defiance of Soviet premier Nikita Khrushchev's demand that British, French, and U.S. troops be removed from West Berlin, ending the three-power control and protection of that territory. Declaring the Soviet proposal a threat to peace and freedom, Kennedy stated: "We do not want to fight, but we have fought before . . . We cannot and will not permit the Communists to drive us out of Berlin, either gradually or by force." He asked Congress to appropriate additional funding for the armed forces and for civil defense, to authorize an increase in military personnel, and to increase draft calls. The Soviet response was to build the Berlin Wall, which separated East and West Berlin until 1989.

See also: U.S. NOTE ON BERLIN BLOCKADE AND AIRLIFT.

Further reading: Theodore C. Sorensen, ed., *"Let the Word Go Forth": The Speeches, Statements, and Writings of John F. Kennedy, 1947 to 1963* (New York: Delacorte, 1988).

Kennedy's Speech at American University

Address on world peace delivered by U.S. president John F. Kennedy on June 10, 1963, at American University commencement in Washington, D.C. Kennedy urged a rapprochement with the Soviet Union and a reexamination of America's cold war policy. He argued for a belief that peace is possible, that the Soviet Union and the United States have common interests in "a just and genuine peace" and an end to the arms race, that differences can be resolved, that world law can be achieved through increased understanding and communication. He announced an American, British, and Soviet agreement to begin negotiations on a comprehensive nuclear test ban treaty and, to show good faith, announced a U.S. moratorium on atmospheric testing so long as other states also refrained from such testing.

Further reading: Theodore C. Sorensen, ed., *"Let the Word Go Forth": The Speeches, Statements, and Writings of John F. Kennedy, 1947 to 1963* (New York: Delacorte, 1988).

Kentucky Resolutions (1798)

Resolutions drafted by Thomas Jefferson and passed by the Kentucky legislature on November 16, 1798; they declared the U.S. ALIEN AND SEDITION ACTS to be unconstitutional and expressed a strict constructionist view of the U.S. CONSTITUTION, limiting the power of the national government. Like the VIRGINIA RESOLUTIONS, they outlined a belief that the federal government represented a "compact" between the states and that when the national government exercised powers not specifically granted it by the Constitution, each state had "an equal right to judge for itself" and to determine the mode of redress. These resolutions were amplified by the KENTUCKY RESOLUTIONS of 1799.

Further reading: Donald C. Bacon, Roger H. Davidson, and Morton Keller, eds., *The Encyclopedia of the United States Congress* (New York: Simon & Schuster, 1995); John C. Miller, *The Federalist Era, 1789–1801* (New York: Harper & Row, 1960).

Kentucky Resolutions (1799)

Resolutions drafted by Thomas Jefferson and passed unanimously by the Kentucky legislature on February 22, 1799; they reaffirmed the state's position in the 1798 KENTUCKY RESOLUTIONS concerning the ALIEN AND SEDITION ACTS and added that the states had the right to judge infractions of the U.S. CONSTITUTION and to nullify federal actions that they believed to be in violation of it. These resolutions were passed after several Northern states opposed the principles expressed in the 1798 document and declared the federal judiciary, rather than the states, to be the judge of constitutionality.

Further reading: Donald C. Bacon, Roger H. Davidson, and Morton Keller, eds., *The Encyclopedia of the United States Congress* (New York: Simon & Schuster, 1995); John C. Miller, *The Federalist Era, 1789–1801* (New York: Harper & Row, 1960).

Kerner Commission Report

Report released on February 29, 1968, by the National Advisory Commission on Civil Disorders, appointed by U.S. president Lyndon B. Johnson to investigate a 1967 wave of riots in American inner cities, and headed by Illinois governor Otto Kerner. The 11-member commission concluded that despite civil rights legislation and desegregation, little progress had been made in housing, jobs, educational opportunities, and living conditions for most black Americans. The nation, the report said, was "moving toward two societies, one black, one white—separate but unequal," and white racism was a chief cause of black unrest. A "compassionate, massive, and sustained" program of national action was the required remedy. Such a program was never developed.

Further reading: Irving Herbert Siegel, *The Kerner Commission Report and Economic Policy* (Kalamazoo, Mich.: W. E. Upjohn Institute for Employment Research, 1969); Brian S. Vargus, *The Kerner Commission Report: Black and White in America, A Study Guide* (Bloomington: Indiana University, Bureau of Public Discussion, 1968).

Khrushchev's "Positions of Strength" Speech   Address condemning aggressive Western imperialistic policies (so-called positions of strength), delivered by the Soviet Union's premier Nikita S. Khrushchev on February 15, 1956, before the 20th Party Congress of the Central Committee of the Communist Party. American, British, and French plans for military adventures had initiated the "cold war" against the Soviet Union, China, and other socialist countries, declared Khrushchev, who also claimed that the United States wanted to become the capitalist world's dominant power. The danger of war grew with the "arms race" among nations, and peace was only possible through a united, worldwide labor movement that could influence international events.

Further reading: *Conquest Without War, An Analytical Anthology of the Speeches, Interviews, and Remarks of Nikita Sergeyevich Khrushchev with Commentary by Lenin, Stalin, and Others* (New York: Simon & Schuster, 1961); *Khrushchev Speaks: Selected Speeches, Articles, and Press Conferences, 1949–1961* (Ann Arbor: University of Michigan Press, 1963).

Khrushchev's "Secret Speech"   Private report castigating former Soviet dictator Joseph V. Stalin; delivered by Premier Nikita S. Khrushchev on February 24, 1956, in Moscow during the 20th Party Congress of the Soviet Union's Central Committee of the Communist Party. Labeled "The Personality Cult and Its Consequences," the report attacked Stalin's intolerance, brutality, and abuse of power, notably the many thousands of executions during his "Great Purge" of the Soviet Communist Party (1934–39) and the ruthless excesses of his police force. Khrushchev's denunciations jolted the communist world and effected a "destalinization" program (discrediting of Stalin's one-man rule, policies, and cult of personality). Thousands of Soviet political prisoners were released from forced labor and concentration camps, and relatively more freedom arose than under the tyranny of Stalin, who had died in 1953.

Further reading: *The "Secret" Speech: Delivered to the Closed Session of the Twentieth Congress of the Communist Party of the Soviet Union by Nikita Sergeevich Khrushchev* (Nottingham, England: Spokesman Books for the Bertrand Russell Peace Foundation, 1976).

Kidnapping Act of 1872, British   See PACIFIC ISLANDERS PROTECTION ACT.

Kiel, Treaty of   Peace treaty concluded at Kiel on January 14, 1814, among Denmark, Sweden, and Britain following a successful Swedish military campaign against the Danes in Holstein. By the treaty Denmark ceded Norway (which had belonged to Denmark since 1380) to Sweden; Denmark received from Sweden the Baltic island of Rügen and Swedish (or western) Pomerania and received a subsidy payment to continue the war against Napoleonic France. Denmark retained the Norwegian possessions of Greenland, Iceland, and the Faeroe Islands. Britain returned all conquests of Denmark except the North Sea island of Helgoland. Russia, which had annexed the former Swedish territory of Finland through the 1812 Treaty of ST. PETERSBURG, had promised to support Sweden in her attempt to gain control over Norway. The Norwegians repudiated the settlement, however.

See also: MOSS, CONVENTION OF.

Further reading: Ingmar Andersson, *A History of Sweden* (New York: Praeger, 1968); T. K. Derry, *A History of Scandinavia* (Minneapolis: University of Minnesota Press, 1979); Stewart Oakley, *A Short History of Denmark* (New York: Praeger, 1972); Andrew A. Stomberg, *A History of Sweden* (New York: Macmillan, 1931).

Kiersy (Quierzy), Capitulary of   Capitulary made by Charles the Bald (Charles II) at Kiersy-sur-Oise, France, in June of A.D. 877 to ensure the safe administration of his kingdom (especially by his son, Louis the Stammerer, interim ruler) during the emperor's second Italian expedition, and to reassure the counts accompanying Charles to Italy about the fate of their benefices. The capitulary pledged to confer on the sons of deceased counts or vassals the benefice or office of their fathers; it also prohibited Louis from nominating countships vacated during his father's absence. Charles's capitulary was not intended to establish new inheritance legislation but merely to maintain order.

Further reading: Joseph H. Dahmus, *A History of Western Civilization* (New York: Odyssey Press, 1964).

Kilbourn v. Thompson   U.S. Supreme Court ruling in October 1880 that restricted the powers of Congress to make inquiries of a judicial, rather than legislative, nature. After the banking house of Jay Cooke & Company became bankrupt, while owing the U.S. government considerable money, a congressional committee began an investigation. When Kilbourn, summoned before the committee, refused to answer questions and provide requested documents, the House committed him for contempt. He later sued Thompson, the sergeant-at-arms, for false imprisonment, claiming that the courts, not the House, had jurisdiction to investigate this matter. The Supreme Court ruled that Congress had no "general power of making inquiry into the private affairs of the citizens." Not until 1927 did the Court establish that Congress could investigate for legislative purposes.

Further reading: Donald C. Bacon, Roger H. Davidson, and Morton Keller, eds., *The Encyclopedia of the United States Congress* (New York: Simon & Schuster, 1995).

Kilkenny, Statutes of   Series of 35 statutes passed in February 1366 by an Irish parliament at Kilkenny, summoned by Lionel of Antwerp, first duke of Clarence, who had been made viceroy of Ireland by his father, King Edward III of England. The statutes tried to stabilize English-Irish relations, to abolish the BREHON LAWS, and to prevent "degeneracy" (process of Gaelicization). Some banned alliance by marriage, fosterage, or concubinage; upheld English law, customs, dress, and language; outlawed the presentation of Irishmen to cathedral/collegiate churches; and denied the Irish pasturage on lands. Others banned games such as "hurlings" and "coitings," recommending instead archery, lancing, "and other gentle games which pertain to arms." Englishmen, whether born in England or Ireland, were declared "the English lieges of our lord the king." The remaining statutes dealt with the maintenance of order, legal issues, the rights and liberties of the church, wage and price fixation, and the fees and conduct of royal officials. Actually a codification of existing legislation, the statutes subsequently acquired tremendous significance in medieval history. Frequently reissued, they were repealed in 1613.

Further reading: Christopher Haigh, ed., *The Cambridge Historical Encyclopedia of Great Britain and Ireland* (Cambridge, England: Cambridge University Press, 1985).

Kilmainham Treaty   Informal agreement on May 2, 1882, whereby the William Gladstone–led British government released Charles Parnell, leader of the Irish Home Rule Party, and his followers from the Kilmainham Prison, where they had been imprisoned for opposing Gladstone's IRISH LAND ACT OF 1881. In April 1882 Parnell indicated his willingness to call off the agitation and cooperate with the Liberal government, if it extended the provisions of the Land Act to include the 130,000 tenants in arrears and the 150,000 leaseholders. The government accepted his terms, and Parnell promised to treat the amended act as a settlement of the land problem. However, the treaty did not satisfy the radicals in Parnell's party.

See also: PREVENTION OF CRIMES ACT, BRITISH.

Further reading: Christopher Haigh, ed., *The Cambridge Historical Encyclopedia of Great Britain and Ireland* (Cambridge, England: Cambridge University Press, 1985); D. J. Hickey and J. E. Doherty, *A Dictionary of Irish History since 1800* (Dublin: Gill & Macmillan, 1980).

King's "I Have a Dream" Speech   Address delivered by the Reverend Martin Luther King, Jr., on August 28, 1963, at the Lincoln Memorial, at the culmination of a march on Washington, D.C., for jobs and freedom. In this eloquent, emotionally charged speech, the black civil rights leader described his vision of freedom and equality for all Americans— black and white, Jew and Gentile, Protestant and Catholic. "I still have a dream," he said. "It is a dream deeply rooted in the American dream." It was a dream that the descendants of slaves and slaveowners would live in brotherhood, that free-

dom and justice would replace oppression and injustice, that people would be judged on the basis of character not skin color. King looked forward to the day when all Americans could join in the spiritual refrain: "Free at last. Free at last. Thank God Almighty, we are free at last."

Further reading: Clayborne Carson and Kris Shephard, eds., *A Call to Conscience: The Landmark Speeches of Dr. Martin Luther King, Jr.* (New York: Warner Books, 2001); James Melvin Washington, ed., *I Have a Dream: Writings and Speeches That Changed the World* (San Francisco: Harper, 1992).

King's Peace   See BERGERAC, TREATY OF.

Knights of Labor Constitution   Constitution drawn up in 1878 by the Noble Order of the Knights of Labor, an outgrowth of a secret society of garment cutters organized in Philadelphia in 1869. The Knights, composed of men and women, whites and blacks, skilled and unskilled workers, advocated industrial democracy. The preamble to the constitution stated that a united effort was necessary to protect workers from the "aggression of aggregated wealth." The constitution called for the establishment of cooperatives, weekly pay, equal justice for workers and capitalists, prohibition of child labor, arbitration instead of strikes, an eight-hour day, and equal pay for both sexes for equal work. The Knights flourished until 1886, when labor unrest and violence led to its decline.

Further reading: Henry Steele Commager, ed., *Documents of American History*, 8th ed. (New York: Appleton-Century-Crofts, 1968); Leon Fink, *Workingmen's Democracy: The Knights of Labor and American Politics* (Urbana: University of Illinois, 1985).

Knox's Liturgy   See COMMON ORDER, BOOK OF.

Königsberg, Convention of   Agreement concluded at Königsberg (Kaliningrad) on July 12, 1807, between France under Emperor Napoléon Bonaparte and Prussia under King Frederick William III, the provisions of which were additions to those of the Treaties of TILSIT, concluded a few days earlier. Through the convention France (which had defeated Prussia during the recent hostilities) agreed to evacuate her troops from Prussia, with the stipulation that Prussia first furnish France with a large war indemnity payment. Because the payment could not be made, France acquired the right to maintain a force of 100,000 troops in Prussia.

See also: SCHÖNBRUNN, TREATY OF (1805).

Further reading: R. B. Mowat, *The Diplomacy of Napoleon* (New York: Russell & Russell, 1971).

Königsberg, Treaty of   Agreement made at the Prussian city of Königsberg (Kaliningrad) on January 17, 1656, between Elector Frederick William of Brandenburg and King

Charles X of Sweden, during the latter's war against Poland (First Northern War [1655–60]). When Charles had tried to bring all of Poland under his authority, Frederick William had sought to ally himself with West Prussia, a territory he would have liked to separate from Swedish-occupied Poland. Charles, however, defeated the elector, who was forced to sign the treaty. It required Frederick William to recognize East Prussia as a Swedish fief, to hand over to Sweden half of East Prussia's revenue from customs duties, and to supply the Swedish army with 1,500 men. Sweden retained control of West Prussia.

Further reading: Derek McKay, *The Great Elector* (New York: Longman, 2001).

Koran (Qur'an)

Islamic scriptures sacred to Muslims, recorded in classical Arabic as the revelations that the prophet Muhammad received from Allah (God) between A.D. 610 and A.D. 632 (the year of Muhammad's death). The Koran's canonical text, compiled by Arabic editors around A.D. 651, consists of 114 suras (chapters), which are arranged generally by length, from longest to shortest (and generally in inverse order to their date of origin). The essence of this holy book is that Allah is the only God, the absolute being and creator and ruler. The fate of humankind is wholly in God's hand, and Muslims must pray regularly and abide by laws of marriage and inheritance and ritual practices of fasting and pilgrimage, according to the Koran.

Further reading: Joseph H. Dahmus, *A History of Western Civilization* (New York: Odyssey Press, 1964); Mark A. Kishlansky, ed., *Sources of the West: Readings in Western Civilization*, vol. 1, 4th ed. (New York: Addison Wesley Longman, 2001); Ibn Warraq, *What the Koran Really Says: Language, Text, and Commentary* (Amherst, N.Y.: Prometheus Books, 2002).

Korean War Armistice

Agreement signed at Panmunjom in northern South Korea on July 27, 1953, by Lieutenant General William K. Harrison, Jr., representing the United Nations Command, and by General Nam Il, representing the communist command; it brought an end to the Korean War (1950–53), which had originated over the failure of South and North Korea to agree upon the form of government that a united Korea would take. The armistice provided for the cessation of hostilities and, within 72 hours of that, for the establishment of a neutral demilitarized zone between opposing forces (the North and South Korean borderline, near the 38th parallel); also, for the formation of a military armistice commission consisting of both United Nations and communist representatives of Sweden, Switzerland, Poland, and Czechoslovakia, both of which commissions would be responsible for seeing that the armistice's terms were not violated. The truce also provided for the repatriation of all prisoners of war who desired it and for the future convocation of representatives of both sides at a conference to bring about a peaceful conclusion to the Korean question. No formal peace treaty has ever been signed.

Further reading: Charles L. Phillips and Alan Axelrod, eds., *Encyclopedia of Historical Treaties and Alliances*, 2 vols. (New York: Facts On File, 2001).

Korematsu v. United States

U.S. Supreme Court decision, issued on December 18, 1944, that upheld the constitutionality of the Japanese evacuation program established after Pearl Harbor (see EXECUTIVE ORDER 9066). Fred Korematsu, an American-born citizen of Japanese ancestry, refused to obey the evacuation order on the grounds that it violated his Fifth Amendment rights to due process. In its six-to-three decision, the Court ruled that military authorities were justified in relocating people of Japanese descent without individual hearings because of national security needs. In dissent, Justice Frank Murphy criticized the evacuation program as "legalization of racism." In 1983, when Korematsu sued for vindication on a charge of "prosecutorial misconduct," a federal court vacated his conviction and erased his criminal record.

See also: EX PARTE ENDO.

Further reading: Mortimer Adler, ed., *The Annals of America*, 18 vols. (Chicago: Encyclopaedia Britannica, 1968); Kermit Hall et al., eds., *American Legal History: Cases and Materials*, 2d ed. (New York: Oxford University Press, 1996); Tony Mauro, *Illustrated Great Decisions of the Supreme Court* (Washington, D.C.: CQ Press, 2000); Robert R. Mayer, *The Court and the American Crises, 1930–1952* (Danbury, Conn.: Grolier Educational Corp., 1995).

Koszyce, Charter of

Charter of rights granted at Koszyce, or Košice (Slovakia), to the Polish nobility by Louis I, king of Hungary and Poland, on September 17, 1374, in return for the Polish nobles' agreement to accept one of his daughters as heir to the Polish throne, should he die without a male heir (see KOSZYCE, PACT OF). In the charter Louis affirmed all privileges previously won by the Polish gentry from the Piast kings preceding him; broadened the freedoms of the towns; exempted the nobles from all taxes, except for the payment of an insignificant, symbolic sum; and affirmed that only Poles would occupy the office of royal governor. The charter has many similarities to the 1222 GOLDEN BULL OF HUNGARY.

Further reading: Norman Davies, *God's Playground: A History of Poland*, 2 vols. (New York: Columbia University, 1982); Paul Ignatus, *Hungary* (London: Ernest Benn, 1972); W. F. Reddaway, ed., *The Cambridge History of Poland to 1696* (Cambridge, England: Cambridge University Press, 1950).

Koszyce, Pact of

Pact made by Hungarian king Louis I (who was, as legal heir to King Casimir III the Great, also king of Poland) and the Polish nobility on September 17, 1374, at the Slovakian town of Koszyce (Košice). In order to gain the support of the Polish gentry, the foreign king granted to them many privileges (see KOSZYCE, CHARTER OF). In return Louis, who had not yet had any sons (nor would he) received the right to place one of his daughters upon the Polish throne, in this way ensuring the continuation of his dynasty.

Further reading: Norman Davies, *God's Playground: A History of Poland*, 2 vols. (New York: Columbia University, 1982); Paul Ignatus, *Hungary* (London: Ernest Benn, 1972); W. F. Reddaway, ed., *The Cambridge History of Poland to 1696* (Cambridge, England: Cambridge University Press, 1950).

Kraków, Treaty of

Treaty concluded between King Casimir III the Great of Poland and John of Luxembourg, king of Bohemia, at the Polish city of Kraków in 1338. Casimir ceded to Bohemia suzerainty over Silesia. During the reign of Casimir, Poland faced the threat of the Teutonic Knights in the north, as well as the less grave threat of Bohemia in the south, which had been making claims on Silesia. With the hope of graining an ally in Bohemia who might perhaps support him against the knights, Casimir decided to renounce Poland's control over Silesia. The gamble was not particularly successful.

See also: VISEGRÁD, AGREEMENT AT.

Further reading: Norman Davies, *God's Playground: A History of Poland*, 2 vols. (New York: Columbia University, 1982); W. F. Reddaway, ed., *The Cambridge History of Poland to 1696* (Cambridge, England: Cambridge University Press, 1950).

Kremsier Constitution

Constitution drawn up by the Austrian general Diet and completed on March 1, 1849, in the Moravian town of Kremsier (Kroměříž, Czechoslovakia). The Diet, however, was dissolved by Austria's prime minister Felix Schwarzenberg, and the constitution, which reflected the liberal views of that period of revolutionary fervor in Europe, was replaced by a reactionary document within several days of its completion. The doomed constitution asserted the individual's freedom of religion and his fundamental human rights, as well as the equality of all citizens in the ethnically diverse Austrian Empire; it provided for a legislative body consisting of members representing all nationalities, and limited the powers of the monarch. Its provisions reflected the influence of the U.S. CONSTITUTION and SWISS CONSTITUTION OF 1848.

Further reading: Adolph Schwarzenberg, *Prince Felix zu Schwarzenberg, Prime Minister of Austria, 1848–1852* (New York: AMS Press, 1966).

Kronshtadt Demands

Document prepared by Russian sailors from the naval base at Kronshtadt in the Soviet Union in March 1921, and signed by S. M. Petrichenko (who then became the leader of the vain Kronshtadt Rebellion); it contained the sailors' demands to limit Bolshevik or communist power and provide greater rights to the people. The document included the sailors' demands that new elections to the soviets (district councils) be held by secret ballot; that workers be allowed to form trade unions; that all socialist political prisoners be granted amnesty; that jobs, to be filled by communists only, be abolished; and that all workers receive equal rations. The economic hardship suffered by the masses throughout World War I (1914–18) and the communist-won Russian Civil War of 1918–21 had contributed to the discontent among the sailors. The Soviet authorities responded to the demands by armed attack.

Further reading: Emanuel Pollack, *The Kronstadt Rebellion, the First Armed Revolt Against the Soviets* (New York: Philosophical Library, 1959).

Kruger Telegram

German telegram of January 3, 1896, to Paul Kruger, president of the Transvaal (the South African Republic), which precipitated an Anglo-German diplomatic crisis. The telegram congratulated Kruger on suppressing a raid by the neighboring British Cape Colony on the independent Boer republic of the Transvaal. The congratulatory telegram was the brainchild of Germany's Emperor William II, who wished to intervene militarily, but was persuaded by his advisers not to do so. Germany also tried—and failed—to have France and Russia join her in supporting the Boers. The Germans were apparently hoping to use the incident to threaten Great Britain with a continental bloc against her, thus encouraging her to join the TRIPLE ALLIANCE. In fact, it had the opposite effect: The British took offense at the German action and drifted toward the FRANCO-RUSSIAN ALLIANCE OF 1892.

Further reading: John Fisher, *Paul Kruger: His Life and Times* (London: Secker & Warbureg, 1974).

Kuchuk Kainardji, Treaty of

Peace treaty between the Ottoman Empire and Russia, signed on July 21, 1774 at the town of Kuchuk Kainardji (Kaynardzha, Bulgaria), ending the Russo-Turkish War of 1768–74 and Ottoman domination of the Black Sea. The treaty confirmed Russian possession of the Black Sea coast between the Dnieper and Bug Rivers, the Don River port of Azov, and certain strategic fortresses in the Crimea, including Kerch, Yenikale, and Kinburn. It provided for the return of Wallachia, Moldavia, Bessarabia, Bulgaria, and some Aegean territories to Ottoman control. In addition, the treaty gave the Crimean Tatars freedom to choose their own khan (leader) and gave Russia certain navigational, trading, commercial, and political rights in the Ottoman Empire, on its waters and lands. And the Ottomans were obliged to protect Christians living in their lands, otherwise Russia could intervene on the Christians' behalf as protector.

See also: CATHERINE THE GREAT'S DECREE ANNEXING THE CRIMEA; JASSY, TREATY OF.

Further reading: J. C. Hurewitz, *The Middle East and North Africa in World Politics: A Documentary Record*, 2d ed. (New Haven, Conn.: Yale University Press, 1975); Reeva S.

Simon, Philip Mattar, and Richard W. Bulliet, eds., *Encyclopedia of the Modern Middle East*, 4 vols. (New York: Macmillan, 1996).

Ku Klux Klan Acts   See FORCE ACTS, U.S.

Kütahya, Convention of   Agreement concluded between Pasha Muhammad Ali of Egypt (then a Turkish vassal state) and Sultan Mahmud II of the Ottoman Empire, between April 8 and May 4, 1833. The Ottoman Turks made territorial concessions to the Egyptians, whose army had advanced as far as Kütahya in western Turkey (not far from Constantinople) during the Turko-Egyptian War of 1832–33. Mahmud II agreed to cede Syria to Muhammad Ali for the rest of his life and to make Ali's son Ibrahim tax collector of the Turkish city of Adana. At first Mahmud II hoped to keep Adana province but ceded it under British and French pressure when the Russians began encroaching militarily.

See also: HÜNKÂR ISKELESI, TREATY OF.

Further reading: Stanford Jay Shaw and Ezel Kural Shaw, *History of the Ottoman Empire and Modern Turkey* (New York: Cambridge University Press, 1977); Reeva S. Simon, Philip

Mattar, and Richard W. Bulliet, eds., *Encyclopedia of the Modern Middle East*, 4 vols. (New York: Macmillan, 1996).

Kyoto Protocol   Protocol to the United Nations Framework Convention on Climate Change (UNFCCC), finalized by 160 countries on December 11, 1997, in Kyoto, Japan, setting binding limitations on the emissions of greenhouse gases for 38 developed countries and economies still in industrial transition. Under the protocol, for instance, the United States would reduce its emissions of six greenhouse gases by 7 percent below 1990 levels over the five-year period 2008 to 2012. By May 2002, 84 countries had signed the protocol and 54 had ratified it; however, the protocol could not be implemented unless the major industrialized countries that emit 55 percent of the world's greenhouse gases ratified it. The United States, which accounts for 4 percent of the world's population and 25 percent of its greenhouse emissions, signed the protocol on November 12, 1998, but has yet to ratify it.

Further reading: United Nations Framework Convention on Climate Change, *Kyoto Protocol to the United Nations Framework Convention on Climate Change*, UNFCC, available online at http://www.unfccc.de/resource/docs/convkp/kpeng.html.

L

Laborers, Statute of English parliamentary statute of 1351, by which King Edward III's government fixed wages at the rates prevalent before the 1348–49 plague (the Black Death). Embodying the recommendations of a council of 1349, the repressive legislation forced all able-bodied, landless men below 60 years of age to accept work at these rates and to give their masters just claim on their work. Further, the masters were not allowed to offer more than these standard rates, and prices were to be "reasonable." Penalties for violations included whipping, branding, or imprisonment for the peasants and fines for the masters. Anyone caught fleeing to escape the ordinance was liable to be punished. Its implementation did little to alleviate the labor crisis; rather, it helped accelerate the movement toward greater emancipation of peasant labor in England.

Further reading: Karl De Schweinitz, *England's Road to Social Security, from the Statute of Laborers in 1349 to the Beveridge Report of 1942* (New York: A. S. Barnes, 1972); Paul Halsall, ed., *Statue of Laborers, 1351,* Internet Medieval Source Book, available online at: http://www.fordham.edu/halsall/seth/statute-labourers.html.

Labor-Management Relations Act, U.S. See TAFT-HARTLEY ACT.

Labor-Management Reporting and Disclosure Act, U.S. See LANDRUM-GRIFFIN ACT.

Ladies' Peace See CAMBRAI, PEACE OF.

La Follette Platform of 1924 Presidential campaign platform of U.S. senator Robert M. La Follette of Wisconsin, running on the ticket of the newly formed Progressive Party in the election of 1924. Declaring that the "great issue before the American people today is the control of government and industry by private monopoly," the platform called for government ownership of railroads and water power resources, freedom for farmers and industrial workers to organize and to bargain collectively, the abolition of the use of injunctions in labor disputes, federal protection of children in industry, restrictions on judicial review, and federal tax reform. La Follette received 17 percent of the popular vote in the election, which was won by the Republican candidate, Calvin Coolidge, who received 54 percent of the vote while running a platform of "Coolidge prosperity."

Further reading: David P. Thelen, *Robert M. La Follette and the Insurgent Spirit* (Madison: University of Wisconsin Press, 1976).

La Follette Seamen's Act (Furuseth Act) Federal U.S. legislation approved on March 4, 1915, that aimed to improve the conditions of maritime employment and ensure greater safety on ships. The act, inspired by Seamen's Union president Andrew Furuseth and sponsored by Senator Robert La Follette, protected crews of all ships under U.S. registration and of foreign ships while in U.S. ports. It abolished imprisonment for desertion, reduced penalties for disobedience, regulated the payment of wages and restricted the payment of wage allotments to certain relatives, regulated the hours of work, established minimum daily food requirements, fixed the number and type of lifeboats, specified the percentage of able seamen in the total crew, and required that most of the crew members understand the language spoken by the officers.

Further reading: David P. Thelen, *Robert M. La Follette and the Insurgent Spirit* (Madison: University of Wisconsin Press, 1976).

Lamartine's Manifesto to Europe   French foreign affairs minister Alphonse de Lamartine's circular of March 2, 1848, to French diplomats abroad, acquainting them with the broad guidelines of France's foreign policy. The proclamation of the French Republic, he declared, was "not an act of aggression against any form of government in the world." Urging them to explain the "pacific character" of the present French Republic, as opposed to that of 1792, Lamartine reiterated his country's "desire to advance towards fraternity and peace." Constantly highlighting the differences between the revolutions of 1789 and 1848, Lamartine sought to "prevent involuntary mistakes concerning the character of our Revolution." The French Republic, he announced, wished to obtain modifications of the treaties of 1815 "pacifically and in a regular manner." Further, France would protect "legitimate movements of growth and nationality" elsewhere in Europe. France's foreign policy aims were to unshackle herself from the chains that had bound "her principle and her dignity," to attain her proper rank among European powers and, finally, enter into "alliance and friendship" with all nations.

Further reading: Helen Castelli, *Alphonse de Lamartine: A Reevaluation of His Role in Nineteenth Century French Political Life* (Ann Arbor, Mich.: Xerox University Microfilms, 1975).

Lambeth Articles   Set of nine theological principles drafted at the Lambeth Conference held in England in 1595, under the aegis of the archbishop of Canterbury, John Whitgift. The articles advanced the extreme Calvinist position on many issues. For instance, they reiterated the supralapsarian doctrine, stating that man could attain salvation not through his merit but through God's pleasure alone (predestination) and that his election or nonelection was thus decreed from eternity. Contemporary Puritan opinion in England was inclined toward this thesis, but the articles angered Queen Elizabeth I. The articles never received the official seal of approval and could not be enforced.

See also: THIRTY-NINE ARTICLES.

Further reading: Gerald L. Bray, *Documents of the English Reformation* (Minneapolis: Fortress Press, 1994); V. C. Miller, *The Lambeth Articles: Doctrinal Development & Conflict in 16th Century England* (Oxford, England: Latimer House, 1994); Laurence M. Vance, *The Other Side of Calvinism*, rev. ed. (Pensacola, Fla.: Vance Publications, 1999).

Land Act of 1796, U.S.   First important federal land act, adopted on May 18, 1796, to administer public lands in the western territories of the United States. It established the office of surveyor general and provided for a rectangular survey system, as in the LAND ORDINANCE OF 1785. Lands were to be divided into townships of six miles square. Half of the townships were to be divided into sections of 640 acres, the smallest unit available for sale; the other half of the townships were offered in 5,120-acre blocks. Lands were to be sold at public auction to the highest bidder, with a minimum price of two dollars per acre. The buyer was required to pay in full within a year of purchase. The law was unsuccessful because the minimum price was high and the minimum parcel for sale was large.

Further reading: Paul Wallace Gates, *History of Public Land Law Development* (Washington, D.C.: Zenger Publishing, 1978).

Land Act of 1800, U.S. (Harrison Land Act)   Federal U.S. legislation enacted on May 10, 1800, designed to reduce the national debt and to encourage the settlement of the West by making the purchase of public lands easier than it had been under the LAND ACT OF 1796. The act of 1800, sponsored by William Henry Harrison, retained the minimum price of two dollars per acre but authorized minimum purchases of 320 acres, granted buyers four years to pay, and gave a discount of 8 percent for cash payment. Administrative processes were revised to help the small purchaser. Though modified several times, the act served as the basis for federal land policy until passage of the LAND ACT OF 1820.

Further reading: Paul Wallace Gates, *History of Public Land Law Development* (Washington, D.C.: Zenger Publishing, 1978).

Land Act of 1820, U.S.   Federal U.S. legislation, enacted on April 24, 1820, that abolished the liberal credit system that had allowed purchasers of public lands to pay for their property over a period of several years. The credit system, established by the LAND ACT OF 1796 and extended by the LAND ACT OF 1800, had encouraged widespread land speculation, and many settlers were unable or unwilling to make the required deferred payments. The 1820 reform, intended to help settlers and hinder speculators, reduced the minimum price from $2 to $1.25 per acre, set the minimum purchase at 80 acres, and required that the entire amount be paid at the time of purchase. Payments were still too heavy for most settlers, and speculators again benefited.

Further reading: Paul Wallace Gates, *History of Public Land Law Development* (Washington, D.C.: Zenger Publishing, 1978).

Land Acts, Irish   See IRISH LAND ACTS OF 1860, OF 1870, OF 1881, OF 1885, OF 1887.

Land Apportionment Act of 1930, Rhodesian Legislation (1930) that furthered racial segregation in Rhodesia (Zimbabwe) by reserving more than half the land for Europeans and prohibiting Africans from buying land outside their reserves. Enacted on April 1, 1931, it was based on the recommendations of the Carter Commission and patterned on similar South African legislation (see NATIVES' LAND ACT, SOUTH AFRICAN). The Europeans had access to all the urban areas and prime agricultural land, while the natives, unable to purchase land in the towns, were restricted to their grossly insufficient reserves (8 million acres). Municipalities could, if they wished, set aside areas for African use only. Also described as the "White Man's Magna Carta," it has had a profound impact on race relations in the country to this day.

Further reading: Carol Summers, *From Civilization to Segregation: Social Ideals and Social Control in Southern Rhodesia, 1890–1934* (Athens: Ohio University Press, 1994).

Land Occupation Act of 1861, Australian Act restricting the duration of land leases in the British colony of New South Wales, Australia, to enable the small farmer (selector) to buy small holdings. It was part of a countrywide effort to divide the vast landholdings (when the lease came up for renewal) into smaller units. In practice, the law was widely abused since many selectors acted as mere agents for the big landholders and farmers. After 1910, estates valued over £5,000 were heavily taxed—another measure to help the small farmer—but none of these measures were entirely successful.

Further reading: David Denholm, *Land Usage and Ownership* (Wagga Wagga, Australia: RMIHEARS, 1986); David Denholm, *Some Aspects of Squatting in New South Wales and Queensland, 1847–1864* (Fyshwick, Australia: Microdata, 1970).

Land Ordinance of 1784, U.S. Law establishing procedures for the survey and sale of the territories northwest of the Ohio River and for the admission of new states into the Union. Proposed by Thomas Jefferson and enacted by Congress on April 23, 1784, it divided the West into 16 districts and granted to the settlers in each district the authority to establish a temporary government based on the laws and constitution of one of the original states. A district would be eligible for statehood when its population reached 20,000. Jefferson originally included a clause barring slavery or involuntary servitude in the new states after 1800, but it was rejected by Congress. The ordinance was eventually repealed by passage of the NORTHWEST ORDINANCE OF 1787.

Further reading: Paul Wallace Gates, *History of Public Land Law Development* (Washington, D.C.: Zenger Publishing, 1978).

Land Ordinance of 1785, U.S. Plan enacted by Congress on May 20, 1785, that outlined a systematic survey and subdivision of land in the western territories and provided for clear-cut boundaries and titles. The land was to be divided into townships, each six miles square, which would be further subdivided into 36 lots of 640 acres each. Boundaries were based on meridians of longitude and parallels of latitude with lines running, wherever possible, due north and south by due east and west. Land was sold in 640-acre parcels for $1 an acre. A proportion of the land was reserved for the United States government, and one lot in every township was set aside for public schools. This system of land disposal remained in effect, with a few changes, until the passage of the HOMESTEAD ACT OF 1862.

Further reading: Paul Wallace Gates, *History of Public Land Law Development* (Washington, D.C.: Zenger Publishing, 1978).

Land Ordinance of 1787, U.S. See NORTHWEST ORDINANCE OF 1787.

Land Purchase Act of 1891, Irish Major land reform bill by Arthur J. Balfour, Britain's chief secretary for Ireland, at the end of the "Plan of Campaign" agitation in Ireland (see CRIMES BILL OF 1887). Its most important achievement was the setting up of a Congested Districts Board to deal with land problems in Ireland's economically distressed areas, where there was not enough land to make every peasant or tenant a proprietor or landowner. It established a £33 million fund (advanced at 2½ percent interest) to help tenants purchase their farms at the equivalent of 20 years' rent. However, the act was riddled with so many clauses that only £13.5 million was utilized at that time. After its amendment five years later, it proved more effective.

Further reading: Christopher Haigh, ed., *The Cambridge Historical Encyclopedia of Great Britain and Ireland* (Cambridge, England: Cambridge University Press, 1985); D. J. Hickey and J. E. Doherty, *A Dictionary of Irish History since 1800* (Dublin: Gill & Macmillian, 1980).

Landrum-Griffin Act (Labor-Management Reporting and Disclosure Act) Federal legislation sponsored by U.S. congressmen Phillip M. Landrum of Georgia and Robert P. Griffin of Michigan and enacted on September 14, 1959; intended to reduce corruption in American labor unions and to ensure that union elections follow democratic procedures. It required that unions file public financial statements with the U.S. secretary of labor, and it restricted picketing and strikes to achieve union recognition where a rival union was already established. A bill of rights for union members guaranteed freedom of speech and periodic secret elections. The measure, passed after Senate investigations uncovered improper and illegal practices in some unions, strengthened provisions of the 1947 TAFT-HARTLEY ACT and was opposed by many members of organized labor. In 1962 amendments to the act imposed the bonding of managers of all union pension and welfare funds, with severe penalties for embezzlers of such funds.

Further reading: Christopher L. Tomlins, *The State and the Unions: Labor Relations, Law, and the Organized Labor Movement in America, 1880–1960* (New York: Cambridge University Press, 1985).

Lansing Declaration   U.S. government declaration of sympathy with the Czech and Slovak movement for independence from the Austro-Hungarian Empire during World War I (1914–18). Issued in May 1918 and named for U.S. Secretary of State Robert Lansing, the declaration followed negotiations between Lansing, President Woodrow Wilson, and Czechoslovakian independence leader Thomas G. Masaryk, who was elected (November 14, 1918) the first president of Czechoslovakia and reelected president in 1920, 1927, and 1934.

See also: PITTSBURGH CONVENTION.

Further reading: Robert Lansing, *War Memoirs of Robert Lansing, Secretary of State* (Indianapolis, Ind.: Bobbs Merrill, 1935).

Lansing-Ishii Agreement (U.S.-Japanese Agreement of 1917)   Agreement between the United States and Japan, signed on November 2, 1917, recognizing Japan's special commercial interests in China. Signed by U.S. secretary of state Robert Lansing and Japan's viscount Kikujiro Ishii, the pact, while formally reaffirming the Open Door policy of equal commercial and industrial opportunities for all nations in China, actually accepted Japan's "special interests" in that nation because of its territorial propinquity. The agreement also reaffirmed the territorial sovereignty and integrity of China. The agreement was annulled at a conference in Washington, D.C., in 1923.

Further reading: Charles I. Bevans, comp., *Treaties and Other International Agreements of the United States of America, 1776–1949*, 12 vols. (Washington, D.C.: U.S. Government Printing Office, 1968); Jerry Israel, *Progressivism and the Open Door: America and China, 1905–1921* (Pittsburgh, Pa.: University of Pittsburgh Press, 1971); Edwin O. Reischauer, *The United States and Japan*, 3d ed. (Cambridge, Mass.: Harvard University Press, 1965).

Lapse, Doctrine of   Principle introduced by Lord Dalhousie, governor general of India (1847–56), to determine and regulate the succession in dependent Hindu states where rulers did not have any natural heirs. In such cases, Hindu law permitted adoption and conferred on the adopted son all the rights and privileges of a natural son. By the doctrine of lapse, Dalhousie asserted Britain's right to approve such adoptions and to determine the succession in the absence of adopted heirs. Thus, he dismissed hasty adoptions and merely attached those states without natural or adopted heirs. The states of Satara (1848), Jaitpur and Sambalpur (1849), Baghat (1850), Chhota Udaipur (1852), Jhansi (1853), and Nagpur

(1853) became part of the British Empire in this manner. Though the doctrine affected only the Hindu states, it created much discontent and was a contributing factor in the Indian Mutiny of 1857–58. It was not enforced after 1859.

Further reading: Lawrence James, *Raj: The Making and Unmaking of British India* (New York: St. Martin's Press, 1998); Antony Wild, *The East India Company: Trade and Conquest from 1600* (New York: Lyons Press, 2000).

La Rochelle, Treaty of   See BOULOGNE, EDICT OF.

Lateran Treaties of 1929   Three treaties (the Lateran Treaty, an Italian-papal concordat, and a financial agreement) concluded on February 11, 1929, between Lord Cardinal Pietro Gasparri, representing the papacy, and Prime Minister Benito Mussolini, representing Italy, brought an end to the conflict between the two, which had originated during the Italian unification movement (see PIUS IX'S ENCYCLICAL OF 1871). The terms of the first treaty included Italy's recognition of Roman Catholicism as Italy's state religion; of the Holy See's exclusive control over the Vatican City; and of the Holy See's freedom to administer the Roman Catholic Church without the state's interference. Through the concordat the Holy See agreed to submit to the state for its approval the names of papal appointees to the church's bishoprics and archbishoprics; to require bishops to swear allegiance to the state before assuming their offices; and to forbid the clergy from taking part in politics. In addition the Italian state agreed that marriage, when consummated as a sacrament of the church, would be regarded as legal, and that ecclesiastics would be exempt from military service. Finally, the financial agreement required the Italian state to pay the papacy 750 million lire in cash and one billion in government bonds, as compensation for Italy's annexation of papal territory during the unification movement.

Further reading: Daniel A. Binchy, *Church and State in Fascist Italy* (London: Oxford University Press, 1970); *Treaty and Concordat Between the Holy See and Italy: Official Documents* (Washington, D.C.: National Catholic Welfare Conference, 1929).

Latvian Declaration of Independence of 1990   Measure passed by Latvia's Supreme Soviet (parliament) in Riga on May 4, 1990, restoring independence of the Latvian republic and calling for a gradual break from the Soviet Union. The parliamentary vote, 138–0, occurred 50 years after the Soviet Union had seized Latvia, which now became the final Baltic republic to split from Soviet rule. The Latvian lawmakers approved the start of an unspecified period of transition to full independence, putting Latvia on a similar but cautious secessionist path with neighboring Lithuania and Estonia. Latvia also called for negotiations with Moscow. Soviet leader Mikhail Gorbachev called the declaration "invalid from the moment of its passage" and reserved the right to take political, economic, and administrative measures in response. He issued similar rulings against Estonia's declaration about being an occupied country (March 30) and proclamation of solidarity with her Baltic neighbors (May 8). During a failed hardliner coup against Gorbachev in 1991, Estonia declared its full independence on August 20, followed by Latvia on August 21.

See also: BALTIC STATES DECLARATION OF INDEPENDENCE OF 1991; LITHUANIAN DECLARATION OF INDEPENDENCE OF 1990.

Further reading: International Constitutional Law, "Latvia—Declaration on the Renewal of Independence," International Constitutional Law, available online at http://www.uni-wuerzburg.de/law/lg01000_html.

Laurier's "Political Liberalism" Speech

Speech delivered in Quebec City on June 26, 1877, by Wilfrid Laurier, a Quebec liberal politician, containing his views on liberalism, through which he addressed the conflict between the proclerical members of Quebec's conservatives, who sought to form a Catholic Party, and the far left of his own Liberal Party, who were vehemently opposed to the participation of the clergy in political affairs. In the speech, Laurier said that Canadian liberalism differed markedly from radical European liberalism, with its anti-Catholicism, and resembled reformist British liberalism. He argued against the clergy's insistence on forming a Catholic Party (arguing that religion, which he supported, ought not to be used as a basis for political organization) and against the liberal extremists' insistence that the clergy be barred from participating in politics (arguing that the clergy had the right, as did everyone else, to express their political views). Although both groups initially opposed Laurier's views, his efforts to end the conflict between them were ultimately successful.

Further reading: *Wilfrid Laurier on the Platform: Collection of the Principal Speeches Made in Parliament or Before the People* (Quebec: Turcotte & Menard, 1890).

Lausanne, Treaty of (1912)

Treaty concluded in Lausanne, Switzerland, on October 18, 1912, between Italy and the Ottoman Empire (Turkey), bringing an end to the Italo-Turkish War of 1911–12, which had been waged by the two over the possession of Tripolitania and Cyrenaica (Libya). Turkey agreed to withdraw her forces from Tripoli and to recognize Italy as the ruler of Libya; Italy agreed to withdraw her forces from the Aegean Islands, on the condition that Turkey first complete her withdrawal; and finally, the Italians agreed to the presence of a religious representative of the Turkish sultan in Tripoli. The war had no victor; Turkey's cession of Libya to Italy was due at least in part to the outbreak of the First Balkan War (1912–13).

See also: LONDON, TREATY OF (1913).

Further reading: Charles L. Phillips and Alan Axelrod, eds., *Encyclopedia of Historical Treaties and Alliances,* 2 vols. (New York: Facts On File, 2001).

Lausanne, Treaty of (1923)

Treaty concluded in the Swiss city of Lausanne on July 24, 1923, by the Turkish government in Ankara and the Allies, the primary negotiators of which were representatives of Great Britain, Italy, and France; it settled issues of great political importance that had developed as a result of the victory of Turkey over the Greeks in the Greco-Turkish War of 1921–22, which had been part of the more general war between Turkey and the Allies—virtually over Turkey's existence (see SÈVRES, TREATY OF). Through the treaty Turkey's loss of her non-Turkish territories during World War I (1914–18) was confirmed (she accepted the mandated states of Syria, Palestine, and Iraq). Turkey regained Constantinople (Istanbul), eastern Thrace up to the Maritsa River, Karagatch, and the Aegean islands of Imbros and Tenedos; the Bosporus and Dardanelles Straits were demilitarized; the free passage of vessels through the Straits and the Sea of Marmara during time of peace or Turkish neutrality was declared; the free passage of neutral vessels through these waters when Turkey was at war was also declared; Turkey recognized Italian control of the Dodecanese Islands and British possession of Cyprus and agreed to guarantee the protection of minorities in Turkey; and the Allies agreed to the abolition of capitulations.

See also: ANKARA, TREATY OF; MUDROS, ARMISTICE OF.

Further reading: Charles L. Phillips and Alan Axelrod, eds., *Encyclopedia of Historical Treaties and Alliances,* 2 vols. (New York: Facts On File, 2001).

Law of Germinal (Law of Public Worship)

Law of 19 Germinal of the Year X (April 8, 1802) promulgating the CONCORDAT OF 1801 between Napoléon and Pope Pius VII. It created a stir because it contained 77 organic articles not discussed in the negotiations (see ORGANIC ARTICLES OF APRIL 8, FRENCH). Thereby, Napoléon sought to restore traditional Gallicanism and to limit the freedom of the church. Communications between the Vatican and the French clergy were deliberately restricted. Power was handed down from the government to the episcopate and from them to the lower clergy, who could be dismissed from their posts at the bishop's will. Organic articles were also issued for the Reformed and Lutheran Churches, which generally brought them on par with the Roman Catholic Church. The Vatican strongly objected to the articles and their surreptitious inclusion in the promulgation.

See also: EXECRABILIS OF 1809.

Further reading: Owen Connelly, *Historical Dictionary of Napoleonic France, 1799–1815* (Westport, Conn.: Greenwood Press, 1985); Margaret M. O'Dwyer, *The Papacy in the Age of Napoleon and the Restoration: Pius VII, 1800–23* (Lanham, Md.: University Press of America, 1985).

Law of Indemnity, French

French premier Jean-Baptiste de Villèle's bill proposing the payment of indemnities to those émigrés whose lands had been confiscated during the French

Revolution (1789–92); enacted in April 1825. The issue was first raised in 1814 and again in 1824 by King Louis XVIII, but the bill's passage was delayed because Villèle had suggested converting the compensation into government bonds. Shrouded in controversy, the law's implementation was complicated because half of the nationalized property had already been restored, while some émigrés had recovered their lands directly from the buyers. These properties were estimated at 988 million francs—payable in 3 percent bonds, with 30 million francs to be paid in annuities over five years. Nearly 25,000 indemnity applications were considered from among 700,000 persons. Although the law did not drastically alter the distribution of landed property, those who bought or inherited it were more secure in their ownership now. The liquidation of the indemnity during a major recession later created problems for Villèle's ministry.

Further reading: André Jardin and André-Jean Tudesq, *Restoration and Reaction, 1815–1848,* 2 vols. (Westport, Conn.: Greenwood Press, 1986).

Law of Sacrilege (Loi de Sacrilège)

Legislation introducing penalties against sacrilege, enacted in 1826 (amidst strong opposition) by the Villèle ministry in France. Intended to bolster the Catholic Church following a spate of anticlerical demonstrations, some leading to theft and desecration of church property, the legislation established a penalty scale for different kinds of sacrilege. For desecration of sacred vessels without consecrated elements, the penalty was a lifetime of forced labor; profanation of vessels containing the consecrated host (bread) was punishable by death; and atrocities against the host resulted in execution after the severance of one hand. This was later changed to "honorable amends." In defining sacrilege as an act committed "voluntarily, publicly, and out of hate or scorn for religion," the government rendered the law virtually unenforceable. It thus remained a dead letter.

Further reading: André Jardin and André-Jean Tudesq, *Restoration and Reaction, 1815–1848,* 2 vols. (Westport, Conn.: Greenwood Press, 1986).

Law of the Double Vote (Loi du Double Vote)

French electoral legislation enacted in mid-June 1820 by the Richelieu administration, granting the wealthier sections of society the right to vote in their *arrondissements* as well as in the departmental "higher colleges." Debated continuously from May 15 to June 12, 1820, the bill eventually passed by a vote of 154 to 93. The legislative chamber's membership was increased from 258 to 430 (see JULY ORDINANCES OF 1830), with the proviso that the original 258 seats would be elected by *arrondissement* colleges (subdivisions of departments) consisting of citizens paying 300 francs or more annually in direct taxes. The additional 172 seats would be elected by departmental colleges, representing one-fourth of the department's highest taxpaying electors, who thereby

gained a double vote. Two-fifths of the chamber would thus be chosen by one-fourth of the electorate, a move intended to bolster the strength of the Right. Thousands were deprived of their voting rights through a drastic reduction in taxes, adding to the law's effectiveness.

Further reading: André Jardin and André-Jean Tudesq, *Restoration and Reaction, 1815–1848,* 2 vols. (Westport, Conn.: Greenwood Press, 1986).

Law of the 40 Sous

French law proposed by Georges-Jacques Danton and issued by the Committee of Public Safety on September 5, 1793, decreeing that *sans-culottes* (poor citizens) be paid an indemnity of 40 sous for every assembly they attended. It was intended to encourage participation of true workingmen in the section assemblies and thus prevent the aristocracy from wielding even greater control. Danton also proposed to end the permanence of these assemblies by limiting them to two a week (Thursdays and Sundays). The law stated that those without any other source of income than "their daily manual labor" were entitled to the compensation. Further, it authorized the appointment of commissioners to ascertain "the degree of want experienced by citizens" in the above category and to confirm their actual attendance at the assemblies. The final legislation was too narrow in scope, and often abused. Many citizens even refused the compensation because of the stigma attached to the "forty-sous patriots."

Further reading: Albert Soboul, *The Parisian Sans Culottes and the French Revolution, 1793–4* (Oxford, England: Oxford University Press, 1964).

Law of the Suspects (Loi des Suspects)

Law proposed by Maximilien Robespierre and enacted by France's National Convention on September 17, 1793, during the French Revolution's Reign of Terror (1793–94); it ordered the arrest of "suspected persons." Extending a previous decree proscribing journalists, the act defined six categories of suspects: (1) "partisans of tyranny or federalism and enemies of liberty"; (2) those unable to justify "their means of existence and the performance of their civic duties"; (3) people refused patriotism certificates; (4) public officials suspended/dismissed by the National Convention; (5) direct relatives, agents of émigrés who had not supported the Revolution; and (6) those who emigrated between July 1, 1789, and March 30–April 8, 1792. The watch committees were charged with compiling lists of suspected persons who, on arrest, would be lodged in jails at their own expense. Their names and papers would then be forwarded to the Committee of General Security, which could bring proceedings against any suspect at any time.

Further reading: James Michael Eagan, *Maximilien Robespierre: Nationalist Dictator* (New York: AMS Press, 1970); R. R. Palmer, *Twelve Who Ruled: The Year of the Terror in the French Revolution* (Princeton, N.J.: Princeton University Press, 1969).

Law of 22 Prairial Legislation enhancing the powers of France's revolutionary tribunal and expanding the definition of "enemies of the people"; enacted on 22 Prairial in the Year II (June 10, 1794) by the Great Committee during the Reign of Terror. It reorganized the structure of the tribunal and added considerably to the list of crimes against the people. Under the tribunal, the penalty for all offenses was death; the number of executions thus rose sharply, up to 354 a month. Only the National Convention, the Committees of Public Safety and of General Security, commissioners and the tribunal's public prosecutors could bring cases before the tribunal. Another provision allowed juries to convict without hearing evidence—"if either material or moral proofs exist, apart from the attested proof, there shall be no further hearing of witnesses . . ." This law compounded the evils (see LAW OF THE SUSPECTS) of the Reign of Terror and is considered responsible for Maximilien Robespierre's downfall.

Further reading: R. R. Palmer, *Twelve Who Ruled: The Year of the Terror in the French Revolution* (Princeton, N.J.: Princeton University Press, 1969).

Law on Associations, French (Loi Chapelier, Chapelier Law) Law passed by France's National Assembly on June 14, 1791, suppressing all corporations and guilds in accordance with Article III of the DECLARATION OF THE RIGHTS OF MAN AND OF THE CITIZEN. It forbade their reestablishment "under whatever form or pretext." Citizens of the same profession were not allowed to elect office-bearers or representatives, make notes of their deliberations, or "formulate rules in their alleged common interest." Instigators would be stripped of their civil rights for a year and charged with a 500-livre fine. It was forbidden to entertain petitions from such a body or to employ its members. For publishing threats against workers from outside the locality or against free workers, the punishment was 1,000 livres and three months' imprisonment. Large gatherings of workers organized "against the freedom of laboring" would be considered seditious and punished accordingly.

Further reading: Michelle Vovelle, *The Fall of the French Monarchy, 1787–1792* (Cambridge, England: Cambridge University Press, 1984).

Laws of Reform, Mexican (la Reforma) Series of Mexican laws promulgated by the liberal government of Benito Juárez in July 1859, during the War of the Reform (1857–60). They provided for: the confiscation without compensation of all ecclesiastical property except actual church buildings; the immediate cessation of operation of all monasteries and the closing of all convents at such time as their occupants had died; the nationalizing of all cemeteries; civil registry and civil matrimony; and the division of church estates into small farms and the sale of these farms. In 1873 these laws were incorporated into the MEXICAN CONSTITUTION OF 1857 as amendments.

Further reading: Donald C. Briggs and Marvin Alisky, *Historical Dictionary of Mexico* (Metuchen, N.J.: Scarecrow Press, 1981); Michael C. Meyer and William L. Sherman, *The Course of Mexican History* (Oxford, England: Oxford University Press, 1983).

Layton-Wiggin Report Report issued on August 19, 1931, by an international committee of bankers appointed by the International Bank to assess Germany's immediate and future credit requirements and explore the possibility of converting her short-term credits to long-term loans. Headed by economist Sir Walter Layton of Britain and Albert H. Wiggin of the Chase National Bank, the committee began discussions in Basel, Switzerland, on August 8. It reported that, while Germany needed a long-term loan to help her regain some stability, to secure that Germany would have to improve relations with her European neighbors and try to get her war reparation payments reduced (see VERSAILLES, TREATY OF [1919]) so that they would not "imperil the maintenance of her financial stability." On the same day, a consortium of Germany's creditors extended by six months her short-term credits totaling $1.2 billion, thus averting a major financial collapse.

Further reading: David Hubback, *No Ordinary Press Baron: A Life of Walter Layton* (London: Weidenfeld & Nicolson, 1985); Albert H. Wiggin, *Report of the Committee Appointed on the Recommendation of the London Conference 1931* (London: The Committee, 1931).

League of Nations Covenant Part one of the 1919 Treaty of VERSAILLES, enunciating the goals and the organizational framework of the proposed new international body, the League of Nations. Finalized by an Allied committee on April 28, 1919, the covenant became effective in January 1920, with the creation of the league. Its signatories agreed to protect each other against aggression, to accept mediation in settling their disputes and, for at least three months after an award, to refrain from war. The League of Nations was to consist of the General Assembly (one representative from each member state), the Council (representatives from the five main Allied powers, plus four others chosen by rotation), and the Geneva-based Permanent Secretariat, headed by a Secretary-General. A Permanent Court of International Justice was to be established. Disarmament, labor and health reforms, and international cooperation were other key concerns. In 1946, after World War II, its activities were taken over by the United Nations.

See also: UNITED NATIONS CHARTER.

Further reading: Richard Dean Burns, *Encyclopedia of Arms Control and Disarmament*, 3 vols. (New York: Charles Scribner's Sons, 1993); Theodore Marburg, *Development of the League of Nations Idea: Documents and Correspondence of Theodore Marburg* (New York: Macmillan, 1932); Charles L. Phillips and Alan Axelrod, eds., *Encyclopedia of Historical Treaties and Alliances,* 2 vols. (New York: Facts On File, 2001).

League of Nations Mandates

Authorization stated in Article 22 of the LEAGUE OF NATIONS COVENANT of 1919 charging advanced nations (the mandatory powers) with the administrative and developmental responsibility and authority over territories and colonies (also called mandates) no longer governed as they were before World War I (1914–18). Certain former Turkish territories could be almost provisionally recognized as independent nations, while other mandates (especially in central Africa) needed a power's close supervision to keep public order and to prevent various abuses (like the slave trade and arms trafficking). Some territories in the South Pacific and southwest Africa could possibly be integrated into a mandatory's state under its state law. A permanent commission, which checked each power's required annual report about its mandate, was to advise the League of Nations' Council on all matters relating to the mandates.

Further reading: Theodore Marburg, *Development of the League of Nations Idea: Documents and Correspondence of Theodore Marburg* (New York: Macmillan, 1932).

Lea-McCarran Act

See CIVIL AERONAUTICS ACT, U.S.

Lecompton Constitution

Instrument drafted by a constitutional convention in September 1857 to organize the territory of Kansas as a proslavery state; it was adopted after free-state supporters boycotted a vote on the document. In October Kansas sought admission to the Union under the Lecompton Constitution. Despite the support of President James Buchanan, the measure failed to win congressional approval and was returned for a territorial referendum. In August 1858 Kansas voters rejected the Lecompton Constitution, and three years later Kansas joined the Union as a free state.

Further reading: Calvin C. Chaffee, *The Lecompton Constitution: A Measure to Africanize the Territories of the United States* (Louisville, Ky.: Lost Cause Press, 1986); Th. Goodrich, *War to the Knife: Bleeding Kansas, 1854–1861* (Mechanicsburg, Pa.: Stackpole Books, 1998); *The Lecompton Constitution* (Westport, Conn.: Greenwood Press, Microform Div., 1973).

Ledru-Rollin's Speech on Family and Property

Alexander Ledru-Rollin's response on August 25, 1848, to the charges leveled against him by the French Assembly's investigation committee, for his role in the June Rebellion. Ledru-Rollin, minister of the interior in France's provisional government, began by calling the Red (Socialist) Republic "a mere bogey." He believed that social institutions, rather than another constitution, were necessary to remedy "the profound misery of society today." A true republic, he argued, was founded on "respect for the family, respect for property." He wished the "family to be universal" and demanded property for all, "open and justified by labor," because in France "there

is a place in the sun for all." Ancient and medieval republics, he said, had perished "through the concentration of property," a problem being faced by America at that time. In suggesting that property, like the family, be "infinitely multiplied," Ledru-Rollin said that he was interpreting "the great thought of the Convention." Finally, he reminded the assembly that by "beginning a series of proscriptions," liberty would suffer throughout the world.

Further reading: Alvin R. Calman, "Ledru-Rollin and the Second French Republic," *Studies in History, Economics and Public Law* 103, no. 2 (1922).

Lee's Farewell to His Soldiers

Speech delivered by Robert E. Lee, commander in chief of the Confederate Army, on April 10, 1865, the day after his surrender to Ulysses S. Grant, commander in chief of the Union forces, at Appomattox Court House, at the end of the U.S. Civil War. In an emotional and dramatic scene, Lee bade farewell to his loyal but exhausted and defeated troops soon after the Union army drove Southern forces from Petersburg, Virginia, ensuring the final collapse of the Confederacy. Lee praised his troops for their courage, steadfastness, and devotion to their country, urging them to feel "the satisfaction that proceeds from the consciousness of duty faithfully performed."

Further reading: Mortimer Adler, ed., *The Annals of America*, 18 vols. (Chicago: Encyclopaedia Britannica, 1968); Henry Steele Commager, ed., *Documents of American History*, 8th ed. (New York: Appleton-Century-Crofts, 1968); *Lee's General Order Number Nine* (Chicago: R. R. Donnelly & Sons, 1959).

Lee's Resolutions

Three resolutions introduced in the Continental Congress on June 7, 1776, by Virginia delegate Richard Henry Lee. The first resolution declared "that these United [American] Colonies are and of right ought to be free and independent states"; the second urged the colonies to make foreign alliances; and the third proposed a confederation of the colonies under an approved constitution. The Continental Congress voted to postpone a decision on Lee's Resolutions until July 1, but appointed a committee, consisting of Thomas Jefferson, Benjamin Franklin, John Adams, Robert R. Livingston, and Roger Sherman, to draft a declaration of independence. Final adoption of Lee's Resolutions by the Congress took place on July 2 by a vote of 12–0, with New York abstaining.

See also: DECLARATION OF INDEPENDENCE, AMERICAN.

Further reading: Oliver P. Chitwood, *Richard Henry Lee, Statesman of the Revolution* (Morgantown: West Virginia University Library, 1967); John C. Matthews and Edward M. Riley, *Richard Henry Lee* (Williamsburg: Virginia Independence Bicentennial Commission, 1978); Charles Royster, *Light-Horse Harry Lee and the Legacy of the American Revolution* (Baton Rouge: Louisiana State University Press, 1994).

Lee v. Weisman Case that led to the United States Supreme Court's landmark 5-4 ruling (issued on June 24, 1992) stating that invocations or benedictions by the clergy at public secondary school graduations violated the "establishment of religion" clause of the First Amendment (see U.S. CONSTITUTION). The U.S. Constitution's Fourteenth Amendment declares this clause fully applicable to all states and their school districts. At issue was the decision by Principal Robert E. Lee of Nathan Bishop Middle School (Providence, Rhode Island) to invite a rabbi to offer prayers (as was customary in the district) at the school's graduation exercises on June 29, 1989. Daniel Weisman, father of Deborah Weisman, who was in the graduating class, objected to the inclusion of any kind of prayers at such ceremonies and challenged Lee's decision in court. Ruling in his favor, the Supreme Court noted that although the prayers were brief and nonsectarian in nature and attendance at graduation was not mandatory, any form of state-endorsed religion was prohibited by the above-mentioned clause of the U.S. Constitution.

Further reading: Edward McGlynn Gaffney, Jr., "Prayer at Commencement," *Christian Century* 110 (June 2, 1993): 590–91; Perry A. Zirkel, "A Bedeviling Message from Providence," *Phi Delta Kappan* 74 (October 1992): 183–84.

Legal Tender Act, U.S. Federal legislation passed on February 25, 1862, to finance the Civil War (1861–65). The act authorized the issue of $150 million of "United States notes" (popularly called "greenbacks"), which were not backed by reserve or specie. By the end of the war the government had issued more than $450 million of the controversial paper money. Problems arose because some debts contracted earlier could be repaid in this cheaper currency, while other debts, borrowed in greenbacks, were to be repaid in gold. Several cases in this subject reached the Supreme Court, which finally ruled, in *Knox* v. *Lee* (1871) that the act was a valid exercise of congressional war power. In *Julliard* v. *Greenman* (1884) the court upheld legal tender laws in peacetime.

Further reading: Alonzo Barton Hepburn, *History of Coinage and Currency in the United States and the Perennial Contest for Sound Money* (New York: Greenwood Press, 1968); Arthur Nussbaum, *A History of the Dollar* (New York: Columbia University Press, 1957).

Leges Aureliae See AURELIAN LAWS.

Leges Cornelia See CORNELIAN LAWS.

Leges Juliae of 18 B.C. See JULIAN LAWS OF 18 B.C.

Leges Publiliae See PUBLILIAN LAWS.

Leges Rusticae See BYZANTINE AGRARIAN CODE.

Leinster Declaration Statement issued in 1828 by the third duke of Leinster (Augustus Frederick Fitzgerald), the only duke of Ireland at the time. It urged the Tory-dominated British Parliament to initiate immediately such reforms as would restore peace and unity to Ireland. In particular, Leinster referred to laws that disqualified Roman Catholics from the enjoyment of political and civil rights and the free disposal of their property; he felt these laws were ruining Ireland. His was a moderate approach to winning Catholic freedoms, as opposed to that of the Catholic Association or the Protestant-run Brunswick Clubs (the former, founded in 1823, with the aim of securing for Catholics the same rights as Protestants; the latter, formed in 1828, against the granting of concessions to Catholics).

See also: CATHOLIC EMANCIPATION ACT, BRITISH.

Further reading: Tom Bartlett, *The Fall and Rise of the Irish Nation: The Catholic Question 1690–1830* (Dublin: Gill & Macmillan, 1992); Wendy Hinde, *Catholic Emancipation: A Shake to Men's Mind* (Cambridge, Mass.: Blackwell, 1992); Brian Jenkins, *Era of Emancipation: British Government of Ireland, 1812–1830* (Kingston, Ontario: McGill-Queen's University Press, 1988); Robert C. Shipkey, *Robert Peel's Irish Policy, 1812–1846* (New York: Garland, 1987).

Leith, Treaty of See EDINBURGH, TREATY OF.

Lend-Lease Act, U.S. Federal legislation enacted on March 11, 1941, that authorized the American president to sell, transfer, exchange, lease, or lend arms or other war supplies to any country whose defense he deemed vital to U.S. security. Opposed by those who feared direct U.S. involvement in World War II (1939–45), the controversial legislation enabled the United States to aid the hard-pressed Allies—particularly Great Britain—despite U.S. neutrality laws. Congress promptly appropriated $7 billion for the first installment of the program. By the time the program was terminated, on August 21, 1945, total Lend-Lease aid had exceeded $50 billion.

Further reading: Stephen A. Flanders and Carl N. Flanders, *Dictionary of American Foreign Affairs* (New York: Macmillan, 1993); Charles L. Phillips and Alan Axelrod, eds., *Encyclopedia of Historical Treaties and Alliances*, 2 vols. (New York: Facts On File, 2001).

Lend-Lease Agreement, U.S.-Soviet See U.S.-SOVIET LEND-LEASE AGREEMENT.

Lenin's Land Decree Major distribution of land decreed by Bolshevik leader Vladimir I. Lenin and approved by the Council (Soviet) of Peoples' Commissars on November 8 (October 26, Old Style calendar), 1917. The day before, the Bolsheviks (communists) had seized power from the provisional liberal government, which, six months earlier, had overthrown the Russian czardom. The decree ordered the confiscation and partition of all large estates of private, church, and state owners; the land was to be turned over to volost (local) land committees and distributed among those who worked it—the peasants or farmers—without compensation to the former owners. The radical decree thus ratified the peasants' recent land seizures during the Bolshevik Revolution (Russian Revolution of 1917). The new Soviet government also made sweeping decrees on peace (see LENIN'S PEACE DECREE), nationalization of the banks and property, workers' control in industry, and separation of church and state, among others.

Further reading: V. I. Lenin, *Collected Works,* 47 vols., 4th ed. (New York: Pathfinder Press, 1995).

Lenin's Peace Decree Revolutionary decree on peace proposed by Russian Bolshevik leader Vladimir I. Lenin, demanding an immediate armistice with the Central Powers (Germany, Austria-Hungary, Bulgaria, and Turkey) in World War I (1914–18). On November 6 (October 24, Old Style calendar), 1917, the Bolsheviks (communists), under Lenin's leadership, revolted successfully against Russia's provisional government and formed a new government, the Council (Soviet) of People's Commissars, with the approval of the Second All-Russian Congress of Soviets. Lenin's decree, approved on November 8, 1917, called for all the belligerent powers to make peace on a nonimperialistic basis, "without annexations or indemnities." It also called for political self-determination for all peoples, on the threat of setting off world revolution if not effected. Though Russia made no progress in peace negotiations with Germany, she ceased hostilities and withdrew from the war.

Further reading: V. I. Lenin, *Collected Works,* 47 vols., 4th ed. (New York: Pathfinder Press, 1995).

Leoben, Peace of Armistice concluded between Napoléon Bonaparte (for the French Republic) and the Austrians at Leoben (Austria) on April 18, 1797, following Napoléon's conquest of and withdrawal from Italy. Unrest in Venetia and the Tyrol made Napoléon anxious, causing him to make this preliminary peace with Austria. The Austrians agreed to cede the Austrian Netherlands and Lombardy to the French. Austria was to recognize Lombardy (together with former Venetian territories) as the Cisalpine Republic and, in return, obtained Dalmatia, Istria, and other former Venetian territories between the Po and Oglio Rivers on the Adriatic. In compensation for her losses, Venice received Romagna, Bologna, and Ferrara as territories. These provisions were reconfirmed in the more definitive 1797 Treaty of CAMPO FORMIO

See also: TOLENTINO, TREATY OF.

Further reading: R. B. Mowat, *The Diplomacy of Napoleon* (New York: Russell & Russell, 1971).

Leopoldina See DIPLOMA LEOPOLDINUM.

Leo X's Papal Bull of 1520 See EXSURGE DOMINE.

Leptines, Law of Ancient Athenian decision to raise funds for Athens, financially exhausted at the time (354 B.C.) from warring against other Greek city-states and King Philip II of Macedon. Named for Leptines, an Athenian who proposed the law, it was fully supported by Aristophon, a leader of the ruling imperialist party. The law was designed to abolish all special (especially hereditary) exemptions from taxation previously granted to certain Athenians (especially of rich families) for their public service. The Athenian orator Demosthenes directed a speech against the Law of Leptines in 354 B.C.

Further reading: Demosthenes, *The Speech of Demosthenes Against the Law of Leptines,* ed. John E. Sandys (New York: Arno Press, 1979).

Lerdo Law (Ley Lerdo) Law authored by Mexican minister of finance Miguel Lerdo de Tejada and promulgated in Mexico on June 25, 1856, stipulating restrictive measures on the Roman Catholic Church's ownership of property (church lands). It declared that the church would be required to sell all property not used directly for worship at a discount to tenants and lessees; that if such property were to have no buyers, the government would sell the property at public auction; and that the church would be barred from acquiring land in the future. The law also provided for a tax, to be collected by the government, on each sale. Publicly, the government declared that the law's objective was to increase the real estate holdings of the lower and middle classes, as well as increase state revenues; an underlying motive, however, was the destruction of the enormous political influence of the church in Mexico. The law was condemned by the clergy.

See also: IGLESIAS LAW; JUÁREZ LAW; MEXICAN CONSTITUTION OF 1857.

Further reading: Richard N. Sinkin, *Modernization and Reform in Mexico, 1855–1876* (Ann Arbor, Mich.: Xerox University Microfilms, 1972).

Letters from the Federal Farmer, Lee's Document written by Virginia's Revolutionary War statesman Richard Henry Lee and published in 1787; it opposed ratification of the U.S. CONSTITUTION because it would establish a "consolidated" government and contained no bill of rights. The Letters advocated a reform of the federal system and a strengthening of the state governments. Lee also proposed a more democratic lower house. Lee's main suggestions were incorporated into the U.S. BILL OF RIGHTS.

Further reading: Mortimer Adler, ed., *The Annals of America,* 18 vols. (Chicago: Encyclopaedia Britannica, 1968); Walter H. Bennett, ed., *Letters from the Federal Farmer to the Republican* (Tuscaloosa: University of Alabama Press, 1978); Forrest McDonald, ed., *Empire and Nation: Letters from a Farmer in Pennsylvania, John Dickinson; Letters from the Federal Farmer, Richard Henry Lee* (Englewood Cliffs, N.J.: Prentice-Hall, 1962); Alan Rogers and R. Alan Lawson, *From Revolution* to *Republic: A Documentary Reader* (Cambridge, Mass.: Schenkman Pub., 1976).

Lettres Provinciales, Les   See PROVINCIAL LETTERS.

Leviathan (or the Matter, Form, and Power of a Commonwealth, Ecclesiastical and Civil)   Masterpiece of political philosophy written by English philosopher Thomas Hobbes during the English Civil War of 1648–51. Hobbes, a convert to materialist philosophy while in political exile in Paris (1641–51), believed that man was a series of material particles in motion and that the state was the great Leviathan, an artificial man of many facets and with diverse responsibilities. To maintain peace, it was necessary for men to create a sovereign power, whose pronouncements all men would undertake to obey. Hobbes also argued that of the three types of sovereign power—monarchy, aristocracy, and democracy—monarchy alone was most effective in maintaining peace. Organized into four parts, the first two—"Of Man" and "Of the Commonwealth"—echoed the sentiments of his earlier treatises. In "Of a Christian Commonwealth" and "Of the Kingdom of Darkness," he defended the rights of the monarch amidst attacks from the papists and the Presbyterians. The book (published in 1651) was not well received by the English court in exile.

Further reading: Thomas Hobbes, *Leviathan*. ed. John Plamenatz (Cleveland, Ohio: Meridian Books/World, 1963).

Lewes, Mise of   Agreement of May 15, 1264, imposed on King Henry III of England by Earl Simon de Montfort (see AMIENS, MISE OF) after his baronial rebel forces had unexpectedly defeated the royal army in the battle of Lewes (May 14). By it, Henry guaranteed the MAGNA CARTA, the Charter of the Forests, and the Provisions of OXFORD; he surrendered his castles after ordering the castellans (the castles' wardens) to maintain peace. Further, a mutual renunciation of violence, exchange of prisoners taken at Northampton, and release of Montfort's son occurred. The captured King Henry and his son, Prince Edward, were kept hostage by Montfort, pending fulfillment of the terms. At a specially convened Parliament in June, a group of three electors was entrusted with appointing a council of nine, whose advice the king was to obey. This Parliament drafted the final peace terms, which were to be in force until the mise had been ratified by all parties.

See also: KENILWORTH, DICTUM OF; WESTMINSTER, PROVISIONS OF.

Further reading: John R. Maddicott, *Simon de Montfort* (New York: Cambridge University Press, 1994); R. F. Treharne and E. B. Fryde, *Simon de Montfort and Baronial Reform: Thirteenth-Century Essays* (London: Hambledon Press, 1986).

Lewis's "American Fear of Literature" Speech   Speech delivered by American novelist and social critic Sinclair Lewis on December 12, 1930, following his acceptance of the Nobel Prize in literature in Stockholm, Sweden. Lewis, the first American to receive this award, attacked the conservative American literary establishment as antithetic to the revolutionary nature of the United States. He criticized the withered gentility of American literary values, the separation between American intellectual life and real literary standards, between academic values and actual experience, maintaining that material culture had outstripped intellectual culture. The speech aroused great indignation in the United States.

Further reading: Mark Schorer, *Sinclair Lewis: An American Life* (New York: McGraw-Hill, 1961).

Lex Acilia de Repetundarum   See ACILIAN LAW.

Lex Agraria of 111 B.C.   See ROMAN AGRARIAN LAW OF 111 B.C.

Lex Calpurnia   See CALPURNIAN LAW.

Les Canuleia   See CANULEIAN LAW.

Lex de Imperio Vespasiani   See VESPASIAN IMPERIAL LAW.

Lex Domitia   See DOMITIAN LAW.

Lex Fufia Caninia   See FUFIAN CANINIAN LAW.

Lex Gabinia   See GABINIAN LAW.

Lex Gundobada   See BURGUNDIAN CODE.

Lex Hortensia   See HORTENSIAN LAW.

Lex Julia of 90 B.C.   See JULIAN LAW OF 90 B.C.

Lex Manilia   See MANILIAN LAW.

Lex Ogulnia   See OGULNIAN LAW.

Lex Oppia   See OPPIAN LAW.

Lex Papia Poppaea   See PAPIAN POPPAEAN LAW.

Lex Romana Visigothorum   See BREVIARY OF ALARIC.

Lex Salica   See SALIC LAW.

Lex Sempronia Agraria   See ROMAN AGRARIAN LAW OF 133 B.C.

Lex Titia   See TITIAN LAW.

Lex Vatinia   See VATINIAN LAW.

Ley de Patronato   See PATRONATO LAW.

Leyes Nuevas   See NEW LAWS OF THE INDIES.

Ley Iglesias   See IGLESIAS LAW.

Ley Juárez   See JUÁREZ LAW.

Ley Lerdo   See LERDO LAW.

Liberator   Weekly antislavery newspaper published by militant American abolitionist William Lloyd Garrison between January 1, 1831, and December 29, 1865. This periodical, issued in Boston, decried slavery as a national sin and promoted the immediate, unconditional emancipation of slaves in the United States. Although its paid circulation never exceeded 3,000 subscribers, the *Liberator* had a wide influence, persuading many Northern abolitionists to abandon proposals for more gradual, compensated emancipation, and encouraging Southerners to defend the institution of slavery. The paper ceased publication after ratification of the THIRTEENTH AMENDMENT, ending slavery.

Further reading: William E. Cain, ed., *William Lloyd Garrison and the Fight Against Slavery: Selections from the Liberator* (Boston: Bedford Books of St. Martin's Press, 1995); Henry Steele Commager, ed., *Documents of American History*, 8th ed. (New York: Appleton-Century-Crofts, 1968).

Liberties, Charter of   See CHARTER OF LIBERTIES (CHARTER OF FRANCHISES AND LIBERTIES); CHARTER OF LIBERTIES (CHARTER OF PRIVILEGES).

Lichfield House Compact   Informal alliance between Lord Melbourne and Daniel O'Connell (radical Irish leader), reached at the home of the Earl of Lichfield in March 1835; O'Connell and his Irish nationalist party promised to support the Whigs in their opposition to the Tories and the government of Sir Robert Peel. In return, Lord Melbourne and the Whigs agreed to settle the tithe question and to consider municipal reforms (to help Roman Catholics) when they came to power. Accordingly, Peel's administration fell on April 11. The tithe problem was subsequently solved and, in 1840, a MUNICIPAL CORPORATION REFORM ACT passed. The agreement was honored until the end of Melbourne's administration in 1841.

Further reading: Oliver MacDonagh, *O'Connell: The Life of Daniel O'Connell, 1775–1847* (London: Weidenfeld & Nicolson, 1991); L. G. Mitchell, *Lord Melbourne, 1779–1848* (New York: Oxford University Press, 1997); Maurice R. O'Connell, *Daniel O'Connell: The Man and His Politics* (Blackrock, Ireland: Irish Academic Press, 1990).

Licinian-Sextian Laws (Licinian Rogations)   Traditional Roman reform measures of 367 B.C. attributed to the plebeian tribunes Caius Licinius and Lucius Sextius (consul in 366 B.C.). The laws gave some relief to debtors, limited a person's public-land holdings to no more than 500 iugera (313 acres), restricted the number of cattle and sheep that a person could graze on public land, and prescribed that one of the two consulships (chief magistrates ruling conjointly in the Roman republic) was open to a plebeian (a common person, as opposed to a patrician or aristocrat). The latter provision was observed from 366 to 355 B.C., when again both consulships were filled by patricians, until 342 B.C.; afterward at least one of the consuls each year was a plebeian until 172 B.C., when two plebeians became consuls.

See also: ROMAN AGRARIAN LAW OF 133 B.C.

Further reading: Daniel J. Gargola, *Lands, Laws and Gods: Magistrates and Ceremony in the Regulation of Public Lands in Republican Rome* (Chapel Hill: University of North Carolina Press, 1995); Andrew Stephenson, *Public Lands and Agrarian Laws of the Roman Republic* (New York: Johnson Reprint Corp., 1973).

Lima, Declaration of   Act adopted by 21 American states on December 24, 1938, in Lima, Peru, at an Inter-American conference; the American states demonstrated their solidarity and their firm conviction to defend American principles against foreign intervention. They agreed that in case of any threat to their peace, security, or territorial integrity, there should be a meeting of foreign ministers convened for consultation. This act reaffirmed decisions already reached in a similar conference at Buenos Aires, Argentina, in 1936. At Lima, the United States had wanted a more potent declaration of unity in the Western Hemisphere, to oppose totalitarian Germany and Italy and others.

Further reading: Stephen A. Flanders and Carl N. Flanders, *Dictionary of American Foreign Affairs* (New York: Macmillan, 1993).

Limerick, Treaty of (Pacification of Limerick)   Treaty between the warring English and Irish, marking the final surrender of James II's Irish troops at Limerick in Ireland on October 3, 1691. Its military articles permitted the Irish officers and soldiers to flee to France, even offering them free transportation to do so. The civil articles promised to restore to the Irish Catholics all the liberties they had enjoyed under Charles II. These included the carrying of arms, practicing of their professions, and full amnesty. While the English Parliament confirmed this treaty, the Protestant-dominated Irish Parliament refused to do so until much later (1695) and, in opposition to the terms of the treaty, approved severe anti-Catholic legislation. In England, the promise of religious toleration was broken by the passage of the Penal Codes or Laws against Catholics.

Further reading: John Gerald Simms, *The Treaty of Limerick* (Dundalk, Ireland: Dublin Historical Association/Dundalgan Press, 1961).

Lincoln's First Inaugural Address   Speech delivered by Abraham Lincoln on March 4, 1861, at his inauguration as 16th president of the United States. By this date seven Southern states had seceded from the Union. Lincoln's address was firm but conciliatory toward the South. He reassured Southerners that he would not interfere with the institution of slavery in the states where it existed, but he insisted that the Union was perpetual and secession unlawful. He stated that in defending the Union "there needs to be no bloodshed or violence; and there shall be none, unless it be forced upon the national authority." Lincoln closed: "We are not enemies, but friends. We must not be enemies. Though passion may have strained, it must not break, our bonds of affection." On April 12, the U.S. Civil War began.

Further reading: Roy P. Basler, *Abraham Lincoln: His Speeches and Writings* (New York: Da Capo Press, 1990).

Lincoln's "House Divided" Speech   See "HOUSE DIVIDED" SPEECH, LINCOLN'S.

Lincoln's Last Speech in the Lincoln-Douglas Debates   Seventh and final statement by Abraham Lincoln, Illinois Republican candidate for the U.S. Senate, in the series of joint debates with Democratic candidate Stephen A. Douglas; the speech was delivered on October 15, 1858, in Alton, Illinois. In his strong and eloquent stand against slavery, Lincoln argued that the institution was a moral, social, and political wrong, which, like a cancer, should not be allowed to spread into new territories. He called for a peaceful way of dealing with this wrong, which he described as a threat to the union, to liberty, and to prosperity.

See also: FREEPORT DOCTRINE.

Further reading: Paul M. Angle, ed., *The Complete Lincoln-Douglas Debates of 1858* (Chicago: University of Chicago Press, 1958, repr., 1991); Roy P. Basler, *Abraham Lincoln: His Speeches and Writings* (New York: Da Capo Press, 1990).

Lincoln's Letter to Greeley   Reply by U.S. president Abraham Lincoln, published on August 22, 1862, in the *New York Tribune*, to Horace GREELEY's "PRAYER" for the emancipation of the slaves. In his famous answer, Lincoln explained that his goal was neither to save nor to destroy slavery but to save the Union: "If I could save the Union without freeing *any* slave, I would do it; and if I could save it by freeing *all* the slaves, I would do it; and if I could do it by freeing some and leaving others alone, I would also do that." He noted that this statement represented his view of his official duty and did not alter his personal wish that "all men, everywhere, could be free."

Further reading: Roy P. Basler, *Abraham Lincoln: His Speeches and Writings* (New York: Da Capo Press, 1990).

Lincoln's Proclamation of Amnesty and Reconstruction   Presidential plan issued by Abraham Lincoln on December 8, 1863, offering to pardon most rebels who were willing to take an oath of loyalty to the U.S. CONSTITUTION and to abide by federal laws and proclamations concerning slaves. Lincoln proposed that new state governments could be formed when a number equal to 10 percent of the state's voting population in 1860 took the prescribed oath. The program assumed that reconstruction was a presidential, not congressional, function. Radical Republican opposition led to defeat of this proposal as too moderate, and Congress instead passed the WADE-DAVIS BILL.

Further reading: Roy P. Basler, *Abraham Lincoln: His Speeches and Writings* (New York: Da Capo Press, 1990).

Lincoln's Second Inaugural Address   Speech delivered on March 4, 1865, by Abraham Lincoln at his second presidential inauguration, outlining a philosophy of reconstruction as the U.S. Civil War (1861–65) was drawing to a close. The president appealed to the nation for a spirit of forgiveness, for peace without hatred. In his famous and eloquent closing, Lincoln said, "With malice toward none, with charity for all . . . let us strive on to finish the work we are in, to bind up the nation's wounds . . . to do all which may achieve and cherish a just and lasting peace among ourselves and with all nations." Though Lincoln saw the end of the Civil War, he did not live to implement his plans for reconstruction.

Further reading: Roy P. Basler, *Abraham Lincoln: His Speeches and Writings* (New York: Da Capo Press, 1990).

"Lincoln the Lover" Letters   Fraudulent love letters of correspondence between Abraham Lincoln and Ann Rutledge, published in a series of articles in the *Atlantic Monthly* magazine in 1928. *San Diego Union* columnist Wilma Frances Minor had sent the supposed, newly discovered letters to the magazine's editor, Ellery Sedgwick, who had accepted as true Minor's claim that the letters had been passed down through the family of her mother, Mrs. Cora DeBoyer. Their authenticity was believed by journalist Ida M. Tarbell and poet Carl Sandburg, but the hoax was exposed under the scrutiny of historians and detectives. The forged letters had been written by Mrs. DeBoyer after communicating in a trance with the spirits of Lincoln and Rutledge, Minor said.

Further reading: Paul M. Angle, *The Atlantic Monthly Hoax: Lincoln the Lover by Wilma Frances Miner [i.e., Minor]: Criticism and Exposé* (Self-published: 1928–29).

Linggadjati Agreement   See CHERIBON AGREEMENT.

Linz, Treaty of   Separate peace concluded at Linz, Austria, on December 16, 1645, by Holy Roman Emperor Ferdinand III and Prince George Rákóczy I of Transylvania, three years before the final settlement of the Thirty Years' War (see WESTPHALIA, PEACE OF). Although Transylvania made no territorial gains and remained under imperial authority (Transylvania had hoped to gain independence in her struggle against the

Holy Roman Empire), the treaty guaranteed religious freedom to all Transylvanians, including serfs, thereby annulling the principle that the prince's subjects were obliged to practice his religion (he was a Protestant). Transylvania had had no choice but to come to an agreement: Her Swedish and French allies had refused to provide her with more military aid, and alone she could not have continued to fight the empire.

Further reading: Milton G. Lehrer, *Transylvania, History and Reality* (Silver Spring, Md.: Bartleby Press, 1986).

Lipit-Ishtar, Code of Major ancient code of laws instituted about 1930 B.C. by King Lipit-Ishtar (Lipiteshtar) of Isin, a city in Babylonia in lower Mesopotamia. These Sumerian laws, written in cuneiform and discovered by modern archaeologists, pertain to mainly secular matters in the kingdom, such as line of succession, rights of the citizenry, marriages, property, contracts, and punishments. Also explained are the importance and intent of Lipit-Ishtar's code, which commanded obedience through kindness or foreboding by the king, rather than through the principle of "an eye for an eye and a tooth for a tooth."

See also: HAMMURABI, CODE OF.

Further reading: Francis R. Steele, ed. and trans., *The Code of Lipit-Ishtar* (Philadelphia: University Museum, University of Pennsylvania, 1948).

Lisbon, Treaty of Peace agreement concluded in Lisbon on February 13, 1668, ending the Spanish-Portuguese War of 1657–68 and recognizing Portugal's ruling royal House of Braganza. Spain's regent Mariana de Austria, widow of King Philip IV, acknowledged Portugal's independence from Spain and a sovereign Portuguese crown with the title "majesty." The treaty was largely the result of mediation by King Charles of England and his ambassador to Portugal, following the repeated defeat of Spanish troops by the Portuguese, led by Frederick Herman Schomberg (German soldier of fortune in the service of Portugal) and aided by England and France. The treaty required Portugal to cede Ceuta (an enclave in Morocco on the Strait of Gibraltar) to Spain; all conquered lands were returned, however.

Further reading: William C. Atkinson, *A History of Spain and Portugal* (Harmondsworth, England: Penguin, 1960); Harold V. Livermore, *A New History of Portugal*, 2d ed. (Cambridge, England: Cambridge University Press, 1976).

Lithuanian Declaration of Independence of 1990

Landmark resolution declaring Lithuania independent from the Soviet Union; overwhelmingly approved by the deputies of Lithuania's Supreme Soviet (parliament) in Vilnius on March 11, 1990. It declared the "restoration of the sovereign rights of the Lithuanian state which were taken away in 1940" (when the Soviet Union took control). "From this moment Lithuania has again become an independent state. The territory of Lithuania is one and indivisible. No constitution of

any other state has any jurisdiction on it," the declaration stated. The deputies also changed the territory's name from the Lithuanian Soviet Socialist Republic to the Republic of Lithuania and restored the national coat of arms. Lithuania's sister Baltic republics, Latvia and Estonia, were expected to follow and vote for freedom. Although each of the 15 Soviet republics theoretically had the constitutional right to secede from the Soviet Union, Mikhail Gorbachev, the Soviet leader, declared the Lithuanian declaration illegal and invalid the next day but also urged patience in dealing with the Baltic republics as well as Georgia, where a parliamentary resolution was passed (March 9, 1990) condemning the republic's annexation by the Soviet Union in 1921.

On September 6, 1991, Lithuania gained its full independence after an abortive coup by hard-liners in the Soviet Union (see BALTIC STATES DECLARATION OF INDEPENDENCE OF 1991).

Further reading: Dana M. Ables, *Lithuanian Dissent and the Drive for Independence* (Austin, Tex.: Precision Micrographics, 2001); *Lithuanians Declare Independence March 11, 1990* (Chicago: Lituanus, 1990).

Little Entente Treaties Treaties of alliance concluded at Belgrade on August 14, 1920, by Yugoslavia and Czechoslovakia; at Bucharest on April 23, 1921, by Romania and Czechoslovakia; and at Belgrade on June 7, 1921, by Yugoslavia and Romania; they brought into existence the Little Entente, the objective of which was to maintain the status quo as determined at the Paris Peace Conference (see VERSAILLES, TREATY OF [1919]). Each treaty was to be valid for two years; each contained articles calling for the subsequent conclusion of military conventions to uphold the present treaties; and each required each signatory power to inform the other of any alliance concluded with a third party. In addition, both the Yugoslav-Czechoslovak and Czechoslovak-Romanian treaties obligated each contracting party to come to the aid of the other in the event of an unprovoked attack by Hungary; and the Yugoslav-Romanian treaty obligated each party to come to the aid of the other in the event of an unprovoked attack by Bulgaria. The system of alliances had the support of France, with which Czechoslovakia (in the Franco-Czechoslovak Treaty of 1924) and Romania (in the Franco-Romanian Treaty of 1926) and Yugoslavia (in the Franco-Yugoslav Treaty of 1927) signed similar agreements.

See also: BUCHAREST, TREATY OF (1921).

Further reading: Charles L. Phillips and Alan Axelrod, eds., *Encyclopedia of Historical Treaties and Alliances*. 2 vols. (New York: Facts On File, 2001).

Local Government Act of 1888, British See RITCHIE ACT.

Locarno, Pact of (Locarno Security Treaties) Treaties agreed upon in talks at Locarno, Switzerland, on October

5–16, 1925, and signed in London, England, on December 1, 1925, by representatives of Germany, France, Belgium, Great Britain, Italy, Poland, and Czechoslovakia, providing for the maintenance of peace in post–World War I Europe. The pact included, first, a treaty concluded by Germany, Belgium, France, Great Britain, and Italy through which the signatories mutually guaranteed the German-Belgian and German-French borders and agreed not to attack another signatory power except upon a mandate by the League of Nations; second, two identical arbitration conventions concluded between Germany and Belgium, and between Germany and France, plus two identical arbitration treaties concluded by Germany and Poland, and by Germany and Czechoslovakia, through which the signatories agreed to settle all disputes, if not amicably, then through a procedure involving international commissions and courts; and finally, treaties between France and Poland, and between France and Czechoslovakia, through which the signatories pledged their mutual support in the event of an unprovoked attack by a third power. Significantly, Germany did not specifically pledge not to attack Poland or Czechoslovakia, nor did Great Britain pledge to guarantee those states' frontiers.

See also: GENEVA PROTOCOL OF 1924; MUNICH AGREEMENT OF 1938.

Further reading: Charles L. Phillips and Alan Axelrod, eds., *Encyclopedia of Historical Treaties and Alliances.* 2 vols. (New York: Facts On File, 2001).

Lochner **v.** *New York* U.S. Supreme Court decision of April 17, 1905, invalidating an 1897 New York State law that limited the hours of work in bakeries to not more than 60 hours a week or 10 hours a day. Joseph Lochner, a bakery owner who was convicted of violating the law, challenged it in court. The Supreme Court ruled the law unconstitutional—overstepping the state's own police powers to regulate public safety, health, morals, and general welfare—because the law interfered with the right of contract between an employer and employees and because it violated individual "liberty" under the due process clause of the FOURTEENTH AMENDMENT.

Further reading: United States Supreme Court case, *Joseph Lochner, plff. in Err., v. People of the State of New York*, Lectric Law Library, available online at http://www.lectlaw.com/files/case37.htm.

Locke's *Essay Concerning Human Understanding*
Treatise published in 1690 by John Locke, eminent English empiricist philosopher, venturing to explore, analyze, and define the limits of human understanding "together with the grounds and degrees of belief, opinion and assent" so that "we may learn to content ourselves with what is attainable by us in this state." The treatise grew out of an informal philosophical discussion between Locke and friends, amidst an emerging, new background of scientific outlook and developments. In its four parts, Locke criticized the innate theory of knowledge, developed his hypothesis of knowledge gained through experience, discussed the extent and limitation of such knowledge (and knowledge in general), and elaborated on the nature of words and language. Locke's intention was to lay the groundwork of philosophy by "removing some of the rubbish that lies in the way to knowledge." The *Essay*, however, proved to have a seminal influence on modern empiricist philosophy.

Further reading: John Locke, *An Essay Concerning Human Understanding* (New York: Prometheus Books, 1994).

Locke's "Letter Concerning Toleration" (Espitola de Tolerantia) Tract written by English empiricist philosopher John Locke, fervently pleading for religious toleration; published anonymously in Latin in the city of Gouda in south Holland in 1689. In it Locke envisioned a national English church capable of tolerating individual differences within it. Human understanding, he argued, was too limited for anyone to impose his religious beliefs on another, nor would such an imposition create more than a superficial conformity if it contradicted the individual's free will. This letter and two that followed it in 1690 and 1692 were written in clear, crisp prose, thus greatly enhancing their readability and intrinsic merit. Locke had been debating the subject of religious toleration since his years at Oxford University and continued to champion the cause throughout his career.

Further reading: John Locke, *A Letter Concerning Toleration* (New York: Prometheus Books, 1990).

Locke's *Two Treatises on Civil Government* John Locke's views on the true principles of politics, published in 1690 and partly written in defense of the Glorious Revolution of 1688, which saw the expulsion of King James II from the throne of England. In his first treatise, Locke rationally rejected the commonly held divine right theory of kings. In his renowned second treatise, he developed fully his ideas of the social contract theory. In a free society, Locke suggested, men enter into a social contract, creating a civil government to protect them, their rights, and their property. Therefore, if a government abused the power vested in it by the people (by endangering the security or rights of its citizens), they had the right to dismiss it. Similarly, the government was entitled to punish citizens who violated its laws. This treatise greatly influenced American politicians during the American Revolution (1775–83).

See also: LOCKE'S *ESSAY CONCERNING HUMAN UNDERSTANDING.*

Further reading: Mark Goldie, ed., *Locke: Political Essays* (New York: Cambridge University Press, 1997); Peter Laslett, ed., *Two Treatises of Government* (New York: Cambridge University Press, 1988); John Locke, *The Second Treatise on Civil Government* (New York: Prometheus Books, 1986).

Lodge Bill (Force Bill of 1890)   Proposed federal legislation by U.S. representative Henry Cabot Lodge of Massachusetts that would have provided for federal supervision of national elections in order to protect Southern black voters against state attempts to deprive them of the vote; the bill was passed by the U.S. House of Representatives on July 2, 1890, but defeated by the U.S. Senate in 1891. In the absence of federal protection, state JIM CROW LAWS allowed discrimination and denial of rights to blacks to continue until the mid-20th century.

Further reading: William J. Miller, *Henry Cabot Lodge: A Biography* (New York: James H. Heineman, 1967).

Lodge Corollary (Magdalena Bay Resolution)   Statement of U.S. policy allied to the MONROE DOCTRINE; prepared by Senator Henry Cabot Lodge of Massachusetts and adopted by the Senate on August 2, 1912. The resolution was occasioned by American concern that a Japanese syndicate was trying to obtain control of land on Magdalena Bay in Baja California. It declared that any land in the American continents situated where foreign military or naval occupation "might threaten the communications or safety of the United States" could not pass into possession by a corporation or association controlled by a foreign power. The corollary was the first application of the Monroe Doctrine to an Asian power.

Further reading: Stephen A. Flanders and Carl N. Flanders, *Dictionary of American Foreign Affairs* (New York: Macmillan, 1993).

Lodge Reservations   Series of 14 resolutions proposed by Republican U.S. senator Henry Cabot Lodge of Massachusetts in 1919 to modify the LEAGUE OF NATIONS COVENANT, which had been presented to the Senate for ratification as part of the 1919 Treaty of VERSAILLES. The proposed amendments, designed to protect American interests and national sovereignty, included a key provision for Congress to retain the right to decide the conditions under which the United States would join the league in collective security measures. Democratic U.S. president Woodrow Wilson rejected the reservations, claiming they would nullify rather than ratify the treaty. He especially disliked the Lodge reservation about the permanent territorial borders agreed upon at Versailles. The reservations were defeated in the Senate, as was treaty ratification, in March 1920.

See also: PUEBLO SPEECH, WILSON'S.

Further reading: Stephen A. Flanders and Carl N. Flanders, *Dictionary of American Foreign Affairs* (New York: Macmillan, 1993).

Lodi, Peace of   Treaty made at Lodi, near Milan, Italy, on April 9, 1454, ending the Venetian-Milanese War of 1448–54 and recognizing Francesco Sforza as the duke of Milan. Initiated by Pope Nicholas V and ratified on February 24, 1455, the treaty restored to Venice her northern territories (including Brescia and Bergamo) and secured a precarious 40-year peace between Venice (together with her allies Naples, Savoy, and Montferrat) and Milan (with Florence, Mantua, and Genoa). The pope, seeking support for a crusade against the Turks, provided a counterbalance between the two sides. At the same time, a 25-year mutual defensive pact set up an Italian League (*Lega Italica*) to avert war (not always successfully, because the member states often pursued their own policies against each other); it was abandoned in 1494.

Further reading: W. Carew Hazlitt, *The Venetian Republic: Its Rise, Its Growth and Its Fall*, A.D. 409–1797. 2 vols. (New York: AMS Press, 1966).

***Loewe* v. *Lawlor* (Danbury Hatters' Case)**   U.S. Supreme Court decision of February 3, 1908, that a union boycott constituted a conspiracy in restraint of trade—the first case applying the SHERMAN ANTI-TRUST ACT against organized labor. When the United Hatters of North America organized a national boycott of a nonunion hat manufacturer in Danbury, Connecticut, in 1902, the company sued the members of the local union. As a result of the Supreme Court ruling, the case was retried and in 1912 the hat company was awarded triple damages, amounting to more than $250,000. The ruling, a serious blow to organized labor, helped lead to the passage of the CLAYTON ANTI-TRUST ACT.

Further reading: Leonard W. Levy and Kenneth L. Karst, eds., *Encyclopedia of the American Constitution*. 2d ed. (New York: Macmillan Reference, 2000); Elias Lieberman, *Unions Before the Bar* (New York: Harper & Row, 1960).

Logan Act   Federal U.S. legislation, enacted in 1798, that prohibited private citizens from undertaking diplomatic negotiations with foreign nations that were engaged in a dispute with the United States. The act was passed after Dr. George Logan, a Pennsylvania farmer, began to negotiate with French authorities in 1798 in an effort to improve relations between the two countries following publication of the "XYZ" REPORT. The law, which has not been tested in the courts, authorized a fine up to $5,000 and a jail term up to three years for violations.

Further reading: Stephen A. Flanders and Carl N. Flanders, *Dictionary of American Foreign Affairs* (New York: Macmillan, 1993).

Loi de Sacrilège   See LAW OF SACRILEGE.

Loi des Suspects   See LAW OF THE SUSPECTS.

Loi du Double Vote   See LAW OF THE DOUBLE VOTE.

Loi Falloux   See FALLOUX LAW.

Loi Rivet-Vitet   See RIVET-VITET LAW.

Lois de Septembre   See SEPTEMBER LAWS OF 1835.

Lombard's *Book of Sentences*   See SENTENCES, FOUR BOOKS OF.

Lomé Convention   Comprehensive, five-year economic cooperation pact between the European Economic Community (EEC) (see ROME, TREATIES OF [1957]) and 46 African, Caribbean, and Pacific (ACP) countries; signed on February 28, 1975, in Lomé, Togo. Referred to as a "new model for relations between industrialized and developing countries," the agreement involved all of black Africa and replaced the earlier Arusha and Yaoundé Conventions and the Commonwealth Sugar Agreement. The Lomé Convention granted most ACP products nonreciprocal, duty-free access into the EEC, proposed technical and industrial cooperation, including a scheme to stabilize ACP export earnings, and instituted a $4 billion development fund. The attached sugar protocol guaranteed Britain's Commonwealth sugar suppliers access to the European market on the same terms as EEC farmers. To administer these plans, the ACP states established a secretariat and planned regular ministerial meetings. An important advance in African economic integration, the Lomé Convention inspired the creation of the Economic Community of West African States (ECOWAS) in May 1975.

Further reading: Karin Arts, *Integrating Human Rights into Development Cooperation: The Case of the Lome Convention* (Cambridge, Mass.: Kluwer Law International, 2000); Ellen Frey-Wouters, *The European Community and the Third World: The Lome Convention and Its Impact* (New York: Praeger, 1980); Marjorie Lister, *The European Community and the Developing World: The Role of the Lome Convention* (Brookfield, Vt.: Avebury, 1988); John Ravenhill, *Collective Clientelism: The Lome Conventions and North-South Relations* (New York: Columbia University Press, 1985).

London, Compromise of   See COMPROMISE OF 1107, ENGLISH.

London, Declaration of (1909)   Declaration issued in London in February 1909 by an international committee appointed by the British government to discuss the question of contraband and to draft a code of laws to govern the international naval prize court established at The Hague in 1907. It attempted to reconcile Britain's rights on the seas with "the widest possible freedom for neutrals in the unhindered navigation of the seas." Neutral ships under convoy were not to be searched. Contraband was divided into absolute (intended for use in war) and conditional (goods that the enemy could use in war). Cargo meant for the enemy was allowed, provided a neutral port was cited as its destination. The declaration was strongly criticized in Britain and rejected 145 to 53 by the House of Lords on December 12, 1911. An insufficient number of nations ratified it to put it in force.

Further reading: *Debates in the British Parliament 1911–1912 on the Declaration of London and the Naval Prize Bill* (Wilmington, Del.: Scholarly Resources, 1974); James B. Scott, *The Declaration of London, February 26, 1909: A Collection of Official Papers and Documents . . .* (Buffalo, N.Y.: W. S. Hein, 2000).

London, Declaration of (1990)   Major, 23-point declaration to render the North Atlantic Treaty Organization (NATO) more peaceable and nonaggressive to the Soviet Union; issued by 16 Western leaders of the NATO alliance in London on July 6, 1990. It was designed to help persuade the wary Soviets to accept NATO membership for a reunified Germany. The Western leaders, who invited Soviet leader Mikhail Gorbachev to address a future NATO meeting, also invited representatives of the countries of the collapsing WARSAW PACT to establish regular diplomatic ties with NATO. The use of nuclear weapons in Europe was to be a "last resort," according to the declaration, which also said that Germany would consent to have a specific size for her army following completion of an East-West conventional arms treaty, probably by year's end.

Further reading: George Bush, *NATO Transformed—The London Declaration* (Washington, D.C.: U.S. Dept. of State, Bureau of Public Affairs, 1990); *The Trransformation of an Alliance: The Decisions of NATO's Heads of State and Government: London 1990, Rome 1991* (Brussels: NATO Office of Information and Press, 1992).

London, Treaty of (1818)   See LONDON CONVENTION OF 1818.

London, Treaty of (1827)   Alliance formed among Great Britain, France, and Russia on July 6, 1827, in London to mediate with the Ottoman government on behalf of the Greeks and thus end the hostilities between the Ottoman Turks and the Greeks. The Greeks were to acknowledge the Turkish sultan as their ruler and pay him an annual tribute, the sum of which was to be fixed later. The treaty entitled the Greeks to elect their own leaders, but reserved for the Ottomans the right to make the nominations. Greeks could negotiate to purchase Turkish property on their islands or on the continent. If the Ottomans failed to accept this offer of mediation, the allies warned that they would establish commercial relations with Greece. Similarly, if Greece did not execute her side of the agreement, the allies said they would find other ways to bring peace to the region.

See also: ST. PETERSBURG PROTOCOL OF 1826.

Further reading: Paul Halsall, ed., *The Treaty of London for Greek Independence, July 6, 1827, Excerpts*, Modern History Sourcebook, available online at http://www.fordham.edu/halsall/mod/1827gktreaty.html.

London, Treaty of (1831)   See BELGIAN NEUTRALITY TREATY.

London, Treaty of (1832)   Agreement concluded at London among Britain, France, and Russia on May 7, 1832, formally recognizing the independence of Greece (see ST. PETERSBURG PROTOCOL OF 1826). This issue had been pending since the end of the Battle of Navarino (1827) where the combined British, French, and Russian forces had crushed the Egyptian-Turkish fleet (see LONDON, TREATY OF [1827]). Britain's prime minister, Lord Wellington, had supported Turkish interests and denounced the Greeks as rebels. When his government fell in 1831, Lord Palmerston became Britain's foreign secretary and, accompanied by guarantees from Russia and France, established an independent Greek state, free from Turkish interference. It was to be ruled by a hereditary monarch not chosen from any of the reigning families of Britain, France, or Russia.

Further reading: Kenneth Bourne, *Palmerston, the Early Years, 1784–1841* (New York: Macmillan, 1982).

London, Treaty of (1834)   Treaty signed in London on April 22, 1834, by Britain, France, Spain, and Portugal to bring peace to the Iberian Peninsula by the expulsion of Don Carlos, uncle of Queen Isabella II of Spain, and Don Miguel, uncle of Queen Maria II of Portugal. Lord Palmerston, the British prime minister, sought the help of France in ridding the peninsula of the two "wicked uncles." His aim was to establish in Western Europe a liberal bloc (Quadruple Alliance) to counteract the Holly Alliance of the east. Don Miguel was defeated by Captain Charles Napier and Portuguese forces and left the country, never to return. Carlos, too, left Spain but only briefly and returned to find it in a state of civil war. Palmerston declared the treaty as a personal triumph, but the peace he had achieved did not last long.

Further reading: Kenneth Bourne, *Palmerston, the Early Years, 1784–1841* (New York: Macmillan, 1982).

London, Treaty of (1839) (Belgian Neutrality Treaty)
Treaty formally ending the union of Holland and Belgium and guaranteeing the neutrality and independence of Belgium, signed on April 19, 1839, in London among the five European powers (Austria, France, Great Britain, Prussia, and Russia) and the Netherlands (see PROTOCOL OF THE EIGHT ARTICLES). They also signed a similar agreement with Belgium. Belgium was to consist of the provinces of South Brabant, Liège, Namur, Hainaut, West Flanders, East Flanders, and Antwerp, as well as specified areas of the province of Limburg and the duchy of Luxembourg. The treaty defined Belgium as an "independent and perpetually neutral state" committed "to observe such neutrality towards all other states."

Further reading: Atilio Tamaro, *Il trattato di Londra e le rivendicazioni nazionali* (Milan, Italy: Fratelli Treves, 1918).

London, Treaty of (1840)   Agreement signed in London on July 15, 1840, by representatives of Britain, Austria, Russia, and Prussia, with the Ottoman Empire, pledging themselves to force Muhammad Ali of Egypt to peace terms to end the Turko-Egyptian War of 1839–40. By the treaty, the powers declared their intention to make Ali accept their proposal for a settlement, which offered Egypt and south Syria to Ali for his lifetime; he was to renounce control of Crete, north Syria, Mecca, and Medina—areas he had invaded or held. The powers further stated that they would withdraw the offer of south Syria should Ali not comply within 10 days, and withdraw the offer of Egypt as well should another 10 days pass without his acceptance. Finally, they declared their intention to use arms, if necessary, to bring about the settlement. Ali rejected it and later was defeated.

See also: HÜNKÂR ISKELESI, TREATY OF; STRAITS CONVENTION.

Further reading: Kenneth Bourne, *Palmerston, the Early Years, 1784–1841* (New York: Macmillan, 1982); Henry Dodwell, *The Founder of Modern Egypt: A Study of Muhammad Ali* (New York: AMS Press, 1977); Klahed Fahmy, *All the Pasha's Men: Mehmed Ali, His Army, and the Making of Modern Egypt* (New York: Cambridge University Press, 1997); Afaf L. Sayyid-Marsot, *Egypt in the Reign of Muhammad Ali* (New York: Cambridge University Press, 1984).

London, Treaty of (1867)   Treaty prepared at an international conference in London and signed on September 9, 1867, by representatives of Prussia, France, Russia, and Great Britain, bringing an end to the Franco-Prussian "Luxembourg" crisis, which had resulted from French emperor Napoléon III's plans to purchase the grand duchy of Luxembourg from King William III of the Netherlands, and Prussia's determination to oppose the purchase militarily. The settlement provided that the Prussian fortress in Luxembourg (a onetime member of the former German Confederation) be destroyed; that the Prussian garrison return to Prussia; and that the independence and neutrality of the grand duchy come under the protection of the powers. Napoléon, humiliated by the settlement, looked forward to avenging himself and his country for Prussia's antagonism.

Further reading: Warren F. Spencer, *Edouard Drouyn de Lhuys and the Foreign Policy of the Second Empire* (Ann Arbor, Mich.: University Microfilms, 1955).

London, Treaty of (1871)   Result of the Conference of London, January 1871, in which the Great Powers agreed to abolish the naval restrictions placed on Russia by the Treaty of PARIS (1856). During the Franco-Prussian War (1870–71), Russia had renounced sections of the Treaty of Paris barring Russian warships and naval installations from the Black Sea. The Russian action was secretly supported by German Chancellor Bismarck, who then suggested the London conference to address, specifically and exclusively, the abrogation of the

Black Sea clauses. Bismarck thus mollified the British by supporting the principle that treaties could be altered only by agreement of the signatories, while removing the Franco-Prussian conflict from consideration by the conference.

Further reading: William D. Starnes, *The Diplomacy and European Foreign Policies of Prince Alexander Gorchakov* (Ann Arbor, Mich.: University Microfilms International, 1972).

London, Treaty of (1913)

Treaty concluded in London on May 30, 1913, between the Ottoman Empire (Turkey) and a coalition of the Balkan provinces of Serbia, Montenegro, Bulgaria, and Greece, bringing an end to the First Balkan War (1912–13). Through the treaty, the defeated Ottoman Empire ceded to the Balkan allies all of its European territory west of the Enez-Midye line, reducing the Ottoman's European possessions to Constantinople (Istanbul) and the straits of the Bosporus and the Dardanelles. In addition, it was agreed the Greece would obtain Crete, that parts of Macedonia would go to both Serbia and Bulgaria, and that the fate of Albania and the Aegean Islands would be determined at a later time by the great powers. The Balkan provinces had, since the middle of the 19th century, been attempting to engineer the overthrow of Ottoman rule in their lands. The attempt was finally made in 1912, with the belligerents vying for control over other Ottoman-ruled territories, including Albania, Macedonia, and Crete.

See also: BUCHAREST, TREATY OF (1913), LAUSANNE, TREATY OF (1912); VLORË PROCLAMATION.

Further reading: Charles L. Phillips and Alan Axelrod, eds., *Encyclopedia of Historical Treaties and Alliances,* 2 vols. (New York: Facts On File, 2001).

London, Treaty of (1915)

Secret treaty made in London on April 26, 1915, whereby Great Britain, France, and Russia persuaded Italy to desert Germany and Austria and join forces with them in World War I (1914–18). Italy was promised key Yugoslavian territories (including Northern Dalmatia and most of the Dalmatian Islands), the southern Tyrol up to the Brenner Pass, sovereignty over Rhodes and 11 of the Dodecanese Islands, the naval base of Valona, and a protectorate over Albania. In return, she was to surrender the port of Fiume (Rijeka) to the Yugoslavs and to declare war on the Allies' enemies. The United States refused to accept the treaty, which Russia published in 1917. Italy's occupation of the Slav territories and the creation of Yugoslavia in December 1918, led to further complications and prolonged negotiations, which were ultimately (November 1920) resolved in the Treaty of RAPALLO between Yugoslavia and Italy. Fiume was declared a free city, Istria was divided between the two countries, Zara and some Dalmatian Islands were given to Italy and the rest of Dalmatia to Yugoslavia.

Further reading: Charles L. Phillips and Alan Axelrod, eds., *Encyclopedia of Historical Treaties and Alliances,* 2 vols. (New York: Facts On File, 2001).

London Convention of 1818 (Treaty of London)

Agreement between American and British representatives in London on October 20, 1818, supplementing the provisions of the 1814 Treaty of GHENT. The disputed northern border of the Louisiana Territory (between the United States and Canada) was fixed at the 49th parallel, running between the Lake of the Woods in northern Minnesota to the Rocky Mountains. The Oregon Territory was to be occupied jointly by the United States and Britain and open to the citizens of both countries for a 10-year, renewable period. The treaty also awarded U.S. fishing rights in certain areas off the coasts of Labrador and Newfoundland.

Further reading: Francis M. Carroll, *A Good and Wise Measure: The Search for the Canadian-American Boundary, 1783–1842* (Toronto: University of Toronto Press, 2001).

London Naval Treaty of 1936

Pact concluded on March 25, 1936, among Britain, France, and the United States during the London Naval Conference (December 1935–March 1936), convened to discuss the extension of the FIVE POWER NAVAL TREATY. Japan withdrew from the conference when her demands for full parity with the American and British navies and extension of the common ceiling on expansion were rejected. Britain and the United States agreed to restrict their existing battleships to 35,000 tons each, with specified limits on their armaments. The signatories pledged to continue the ban on construction of heavy cruisers and battleships and to exchange information about their naval expansion plans, if any. Italy and Japan were given the option to join the treaty, whose only positive outcome was the development of a new Anglo-American understanding. Italy and Japan never signed the treaty.

Further reading: Charles I. Bevans, comp., *Treaties and Other International Agreements of the United States of America, 1776–1949,* 12 vols. (Washington, D.C.: U.S. Government Printing Office, 1968); Richard Dean Burns, *Encyclopedia of Arms Control and Disarmament,* 3 vols. (New York: Charles Scribner's Sons, 1993); Stephen A. Flanders and Carl N. Flanders, *Dictionary of American Foreign Affairs* (New York: Macmillan, 1993).

London Protocol of 1829

Protocol signed in London on March 22, 1829, by representatives of Russia, Great Britain, and France; it consisted of a new proposal for the creation of an autonomous Greek state, then still a part of the Ottoman Empire. By the report, the three signatory powers agreed to protect a Greek state with a frontier that would reach as far as the line drawn from the Gulf of Arta to the Gulf of Volo (in the Ionian and Aegean seas respectively), including Negropont (Euboea) and the Cyclades but excluding Crete; they agreed that the new state was to have an autonomous but tributary status and that it was to be ruled by a prince chosen by the three powers. The Greeks rejected the proposal.

See also: LONDON PROTOCOL OF 1830.

Further reading: Kenneth Bourne, *Palmerston, the Early Years, 1784–1841* (New York: Macmillan, 1982).

London Protocol of 1830 Protocol signed in London on February 3, 1830, by representatives of Russia, Great Britain, and France, in which a new proposal for a solution to the question of Greek independence from the Ottoman Empire was agreed upon. Through the document, the three powers agreed that Greece was to be fully independent; that Leopold of Saxe-Coburg was to be prince of the new state; and that the new state was to consist of territory reaching nearly to the Gulf of Corinth. This represented a significant reduction in territory from that proposed in the LONDON PROTOCOL OF 1829 and reflected the powers' view that a smaller, but independent Greece was more favorable than a larger state with a tributary status. Leopold declined the appointment, and the Greeks rejected the proposal.

Further reading: Kenneth Bourne, *Palmerston, the Early Years, 1784–1841* (New York: Macmillan, 1982).

London Protocol of 1852 Agreement signed in London on May 8, 1852, between Denmark and the Great Powers (Great Britain, Russia, France, Austria, and Prussia) regarding the issue of succession and the future status of the duchies of Holstein and Schleswig, which had coexisted under a personal union with Denmark since the 15th century. In 1848, the union between the duchies was dissolved; Schleswig became part of Denmark and Holstein joined the German Confederation. War broke out between Denmark and the confederation. The mediation of Lord Palmerston (Britain) and Czar Nicholas (Russia) temporarily averted further trouble and resulted in the signing of the protocol. This called for the unification of Denmark and the duchies under one king, and favored the succession of Prince Christian of Glücksburg. The feelings of the two duchies were ignored.

Further reading: Great Britain Foreign Office, Historical Section, *Slesvig-Holstein* (London: H.M. Statinery Office, 1919).

London Protocol of 1877 Document signed in London on March 31, 1877, following Serbia's defeat by the Ottoman Turks (February 28, 1877); in it the Great Powers urged the Ottoman empire to demobilize, and to institute reforms in its Christian provinces. The protocol was drafted jointly by the British and the Russians, in an attempt to satisfy Russian demands in the Balkans. The signatories pledged to monitor carefully the promulgation of reforms promised by the new Turkish constitution of December 20, 1876, and warned that the situation would be considered "incompatible with their interests and those of Europe" if the Turks did not effect the promised reforms. The protocol was rejected by the Turks on April 9, and on April 24, Russia declared war on the Ottoman Empire.

Further reading: George D. Campbell, *The Eastern Question from the Treaty of Paris 1856 to the Treaty of Berlin 1878, and to the Second Afghan War* (London: Strahan & Co., 1879); Charles Jelavich, ed., *Russia in the East, 1876–1880* (Leiden, Netherlands: E. J. Brill, 1959); Bruce Menning, *Bayonets Before Bullets: The Imperial Russian Army, 1861–1914* (Bloomington: Indiana University Press, 1992); George H. Rupp, *A Wavering Friendship: Russia and Austria, 1876–1878* (Philadelphia: Porcupine Press, 1976).

London Straits Convention See STRAITS CONVENTION.

Long's "Every Man a King" Speech Great Depression–era slogan—"every man a king, but no man wears a crown"—of Louisiana politician Huey P. Long, who demanded that the U.S. government guarantee a minimum income of $5,000 per year to every family. Long first used the slogan in his successful 1928 campaign for the Democratic gubernatorial nomination in Louisiana. In 1934, Long, then a U.S. senator, used the slogan in a speech before the Senate that outlined his "Share-Our-Wealth" program, a plan to liquidate large personal fortunes and to give each poor family enough money to buy a house, a car, and a radio. It also promised college educations for worthy young men, pensions for the elderly, public works, a national minimum wage, a shorter work week, and a balanced farm program.

Further reading: Alan Brinkley, *Voices of Protest: Huey Long, Father Coughlin, and the Great Depression* (New York: Vintage, 1982); Huey P. Long, *Every Man a King: The Autobiography of Huey P. Long* (New York: Da Capo Press, 1933, repr., 1996); T. Harry Williams, *Huey Long* (New York: Random House, 1969, repr., 1981).

Lorris, Charter of Charter granted to the village of Lorris, near Orléans, by King Louis VII in 1155; it became the basis for similar settlements with other villages in France. The charter guaranteed the villagers freedom, property rights, and some degree of autonomy in government—all of which were unusual in a feudal society. Among its salient provisions were (1) residents were to pay the king a sixpence tax annually for every house and acre of land owned; (2) tallage taxes and subsidies were withdrawn; (3) no *corvée* (forced labor) other than the annual transporting of wine, corn, and wood for the king; (4) exemption from military service; (5) residents were exempt from fees on their own produce; (6) freedom for serfs settled in Lorris for a year and a day; (7) no detainment, if guaranteeing one's presence at judgment; and (8) new provosts were to swear to uphold these regulations. The king continued to dispense justice and gained considerable revenues from the implementation of charters such as this one.

Further reading: Frederic Austin Ogg, ed., *A Source Book of Medieval History: Documents Illustrative of European Life and Institutions from the German Invasion to the Renaissance* (New York: American Book Company, 1908); Paul Halsall, *Urban*

Privileges: Charter of Lorris 1155, Medieval sourcebook, available online at http://www.fordham.edu/halsall/source/lorris.html.

Louis IX's Laws   Series of ordinances issued by France's King Louis IX, or St. Louis, attempting to improve the royal administration in the 1250s. The best known of these, passed in 1254, forced royal officials to swear oaths promising good conduct and forbade them to behave in a dishonest manner. Their subordinates could appeal against their dishonorable conduct. Subsequent amendments prohibited officers from indulging in usury, blasphemy, games of chance, judicial duels, ordeal by battle, and prostitution, and from frequenting inns meant for travellers. Officers were required to seek the king's permission before finalizing the marriage of their daughters or entering into any real estate deals. An influential collection of laws, Établissements de Saint Louis, compiled before 1273, has been mistakenly attributed to St. Louis. In reality, only the first part was devoted to Louis's ordinances; the rest described customs from Touraine-Anjou and Orléans and contained extracts from the Corpus Juris (body of law) of France.

Further reading: Charles Petit-Dutaillis, *The Feudal Monarchy in France and England: From the Tenth to the Thirteenth Century,* trans. E. D. Hunt (New York: Harper & Row, 1964); Sir Maurice Powicke, *The Thirteenth Century, 1216–1307* (London: Oxford University Press, 1962).

Louis IX's Pragmatic Sanction   See PRAGMATIC SANCTION OF ST. LOUIS.

Louis XIII's Edict of 1626   French edict of July 1626, ordering the demolition of castles and fortresses not situated on France's frontier borders. Issued by King Louis XIII on the advice of his first minister, Cardinal de Richelieu (Armand Jean du Plessis), it was part of a strategy to secure greater royal control over the nobility and to suppress any rebellions against the state. The destruction was, however, restricted to certain provinces only, and once the basic policy had been approved by the Assembly of Notables, the actual demolitions and razing were carried out in phases until the end of Louis's reign (1643). The edict is considered to have been the catalyst for an abortive cabal formed against Richelieu by the nobles. French peasants saw the castles as symbols of tyranny and willingly helped in their destruction.

See also: RICHELIEU'S POLITICAL TESTAMENT.

Further reading: Victor L. Tapié, *France in the Age of Louis XIII and Richelieu,* ed. D. M. Locke (Cambridge, England: Cambridge University Press, 1984).

Louis XIV's Letter Accepting the Spanish Succession
French King Louis XIV's letter of November 12, 1700, accepting the Spanish Crown willed to his grandson, Duke Philip of Anjou, by King Charles II of Spain. It sparked the War of the Spanish Succession (1701–14) throughout Europe. Expressing his grief on Charles's death (November 1, 1700), Louis XIV promised to raise "the Spanish Monarchy to the highest pitch of grandeur it has ever arrived at." All Europe awaited his response with bated breath, fearing that the possible union of the French and Spanish crowns (despite provisions to the contrary) might upset the balance of continental power. Louis XIV made no attempt to allay these fears through his letter, nor to come to an arrangement with the European rulers. Rather, he indicated that he would urge his grandson "to maintain forever that peace and perfect good understanding so necessary to the common happiness of our subjects and his own." This signalled the start of a war that was to last over a decade.

See also: UTRECHT, TREATIES OF.

Further reading: Olivier Bernier, *Louis XIV: A Royal Life* (New York: Doubleday, 1987); Vincent Cronin, *Louis XIV* (Boston: Houghton Mifflin, 1965); John B. Wolf, *Louis XIV* (New York: W. W. Norton, 1974).

Louis XVI's Letter to the Prussian King   French King Louis XVI's surreptitious attempt to win support from the king of Prussia for his counterrevolutionary activities; written on December 3, 1791, "when despite my acceptance of the new constitution, the [French] insurgents openly profess a scheme for destroying the remnants of the monarchy." The letter, found after Louis XVI's execution, was one of several asking for help from various European monarchs. He proposed in it "the idea of a congress of the principal powers of Europe, supported by an armed force," as the best way of checking and perhaps even improving the situation and also of preventing the "evil which torments us" from spreading across Europe. In 1792, the French revolutionaries had declared war against the leading European monarchies (see FRENCH REVOLUTIONARY PROCLAMATION OF 1792). Soon, the commander of the enemy armies openly announced his allegiance to the French king, confirming suspicions that Louis XVI had been conspiring with France's enemies, for which he was executed in early 1793—after which the letter was found.

Further reading: Milton Viorst, *The Great Documents of Western Civilization* (Philadelphia: Chilton, 1965); Michelle Vovelle, *The Fall of the French Monarchy, 1787–1792* (Cambridge, England: Cambridge University Press, 1984).

Louis XVIII's Charter of 1814   See FRENCH CONSTITUTION OF 1814.

Louisiana Purchase Treaty   Agreement signed on April 30, 1803, by which the United States purchased from France a vast territory north and west of New Orleans, from the Mississippi River to the Rocky Mountains, for $15,000,000. The purchase of the 828,000-square-mile area doubled the size of the United States. President Thomas Jefferson had initially sought to purchase only New Orleans, a port necessary for western commerce, but Napoléon, troubled by a revolt in Haiti and an impending war with Great Britain, offered to sell the entire Louisiana Territory. The U.S. Senate approved the treaty in October 1803 and the United States took possession of the territory in December. The precise boundaries of the purchase, which were not defined in the treaty, were disputed for many years. All or part of 15 states were created from this area.

Further reading: Everett S. Brown, *The Constitutional History of the Louisiana Purchase, 1803–1812* (Berkeley: University of California Press, 1920); Paul Finkelman, ed., *Encyclopedia of the United States in the Nineteenth Century* (New York: Charles Scribner's Sons, 2001); Charles L. Phillips and Alan Axelrod, eds., *Encyclopedia of Historical Treaties and Alliances*, 2 vols. (New York: Facts On File, 2001).

Lübeck, Peace of   Peace treaty concluded by the German city of Lübeck and Birger Jarl of Sweden in 1251 or 1252. The document reflected the prestige and importance Lübeck had gained as a leader in Hanseatic trade. Through the peace the merchants of Lübeck became exempt from the payment of tolls and taxes on goods brought into Sweden, and were permitted to live according to their own laws. Should a merchant choose to settle in Sweden, however, he would become subject to Swedish law and become a Swedish citizen.

Further reading: Philippe Dollinger, *The German Hansa* (Stanford, Calif.: Stanford University Press, 1970); Johannes Schildhauer, *The Hansa: History and Culture* (London: Dorset Press, 1988).

Lübeck, Treaty of   Peace concluded at Lübeck, Germany, on May 22, 1629, between King Christian IV of Denmark and Holy Roman Emperor Ferdinand II. Christian IV had intervened militarily in Germany, ostensibly on behalf of the Protestants there, but was overcome by imperial forces under the command of Albrecht von Wallenstein. Through the treaty, which temporarily ended hostilities in the region (involving part of the Thirty Years' War [1618–48]), Christian IV was forced to refrain from similar military campaigns in Germany. The treaty did not require him to renounce any of his hereditary lands.

Further reading: Stewart Oakley, *A Short History of Denmark* (New York: Praeger, 1972).

Lublin, Union of   Document signed by the Polish and Lithuanian nobility in Lublin, Poland, on July 1, 1569, formalizing a political and constitutional alliance or union between Poland and Lithuania. It formed a Polish-Lithuanian "republic," in which there would be a commonly elected king, a common Sejm (diet), and one currency. Although the Lithuanians, who feared Polish political and cultural domination, were required to accept Poland's constitution as their own, they were permitted to keep their own administration, army, and laws; Lithuanian nobles were also allowed to retain their traditional titles. The union had been concluded because of Polish and Lithuanian fear of the increasing military and political strength of Muscovite Russia, the Turkish Empire, and Sweden.

Further reading: Harry E. Dembkowski, *The Union of Lublin, Polish Federalism in the Golden Age* (Boulder, Colo.: East European Monographs, 1982).

Lucknow Pact   Agreement between the Indian National Congress and the All-India Muslim League; negotiated, respectively, by Bal Gangadhar Tilak and Muhammad Ali Jinnah, it was approved by the congress (during its Lucknow session) on December 29, 1916, and by the league on December 31. It proposed that four-fifths of India's provincial and central legislatures be directly elected by the voters, and that at least 50 percent of the membership of the executive council (including the Central Executive Council) consist of Indians elected by provincial councils. In 1919, some of these proposals were incorporated in another Government of India Act. The Muslims were allotted separate electorates, with an increased representation in minority areas (except Punjab and Bengal). A bill affecting either community could be blocked if three-quarters of the community opposed it. This new Hindu-Muslim amity greatly strengthened Mohandas Gandhi's Non-Cooperation Movement in 1920–21 against British rule.

Further reading: Rafi Ullah Shebab, *History of Pakistan* (Lahore, Pakistan: Sang-e-Meel Publications, 1989).

Ludlow's Code (Code of 1650)   Body of laws for the commonwealth of Connecticut compiled at the request of the Connecticut General Court by Roger Ludlow, a member of the court who was trained in English law. Ludlow's Code, which was based on Puritan beliefs, began with a strong assertion of the rule of law and the protection of individual rights and went on to deal with such matters as the military obligations of citizens, Indian affairs, the education of children, judicial procedures, church attendance, and financial support of ministers. It was the first codification of the laws of Connecticut.

Further reading: George Brinley, ed., *The Laws of Connecticut: An Exact Reprint of the Original Edition of 1673* (Chicago: Library Resources, 1970).

Lund, Treaty of   See NIJMEGEN (NIMWEGEN), TREATIES OF.

Lunéville, Treaty of   Treaty concluded at Lunéville, France, on February 9, 1801, between Austria and revolutionary France, following French general Napoléon Bonaparte's renewed campaign against and victory over Austria on the Italian peninsula during the French Revolutionary Wars (1792–1802). By this peace treaty, territorial gains in Italy (as far as the Adige River) made by France through the Treaty of CAMPO FORMIO of 1797 were reaffirmed; Austria recognized the French-protected Batavian (Holland), Helvetian (Switzerland), Cisalpine and Ligurian (in Italy) republics; and agreed to cede the grand duchy of Tuscany (thenceforth the kingdom of Etruria) to the duke of Parma, who, through a marital arrangement, was essentially under Napoléon's control.

See also: ALESSANDRIA, ARMISTICE OF.

Further reading: Geoffrey Bruun, *Napoleon and His Empire* (New York: Van Nostrand, 1972); Georges Lefebvre, *Napoleon: From 18 Brumaire to Tilsit, 1799–1807* (New York: Columbia University Press, 1969); Alan Palmer, *An Encyclopedia of Napoleon's Europe* (New York: St. Martin's, 1984).

Lusitania Notes, Wilson's   Set of notes drafted by U.S. President Woodrow Wilson and dated May 13 and June 9, 1915, to the German government, protesting the sinking of the British passenger ship *Lusitania* on May 7 by a German submarine and the resulting deaths of 128 American citizens. The first note demanded that Germany cease unrestricted submarine warfare, calling German attacks on unarmed merchant ships "unlawful and inhumane" and asserting the rights of Americans to sail on the high seas. Holding the German government to a "strict accountability," it sought Germany's disavowal of the attack, reparations, and immediate action to prevent a recurrence. An unsatisfactory reply led to the second note, in which Wilson dismissed German justifications for the attack and again demanded action to prevent similar attacks on merchant ships. Germany later apologized and ended such attacks until 1917.

Further reading: Jean-Baptiste Duroselle, *From Wilson to Roosevelt: Foreign Policy of the United States, 1913–1945* (Cambridge, Mass.: Harvard Unversity Press, 1963); Ross Gregory, *The Origins of American Intervention in the First World War* (New York: Norton, 1971).

Luther's Ninety-five Theses   See NINETY-FIVE THESES, LUTHER'S.

Luther v. Borden   U.S. Supreme Court decision issued in 1849, declaring that Congress and the president, not the courts, have the authority to decide whether a state government is republican in form, the question being political rather than judicial in nature. The case arose from Dorr's Rebellion in 1842, when Thomas W. Dorr attempted to seize control of the government of Rhode Island in order to establish universal manhood suffrage in that state. The Supreme Court ruled that Congress had the constitutional power to guarantee republican government in the states and to recognize the lawful government; in the event of an armed conflict within a state, the president had the authority, under federal legislation, to decide which government was lawful.

Further reading: United States supreme court case, *Luther v. Borden, 48 U.S. 1 (1849)*, supreme court collection legal Information Institute, available online at http://www4.law.cornell.edu/cgi.bin/empower.

Lynch v. Donnelly   U.S. Supreme Court decision on March 5, 1984, deciding that a city-sponsored and funded Christmas Nativity display did not violate the FIRST AMENDMENT doctrine of separation of church and state. The American Civil Liberties Union, supported by the National Council of Churches and the American Jewish Committee, had challenged the city of Pawtucket, Rhode Island, for using public funds (taxes) to erect a life-size Nativity scene (part of a Christmas display, including reindeer, a Santa Claus house, and a Christmas tree, that the city had been setting up for about 40 years in a public park). The Supreme Court ruled, five to four, that the Pawtucket display (with its religious and secular symbols) did not present a "real danger of establishment of a state church" through government recognition and support of religion in general. The court must decide, on a case-by-case basis, whether practices or actions constitute establishment of a religion or mean to do so.

Further reading: The United States supreme court case, *Lynch v. Donnelly, 465 U.S. 668 (1984)*, FindLaw, available online at http://laws.findlaw.com/US/465/668.html.

Lytton Commission Report   Findings of the Lytton Commission (headed by the second Earl of Lytton), appointed by the League of Nations to investigate Japan's invasion of Manchuria (September 18–19, 1931). The report, submitted in September 1932 and approved by the League Assembly on February 24, 1933, declared Japan the aggressor. Japanese action, the commission ruled, was not in self-defense nor was the creation of the dummy state of Manchukuo the result of a "genuine and spontaneous independent movement." It criticized China for creating an anti-Japan climate and urged it to acknowledge Japan's economic interests in the region. It proposed limited autonomy for Manchuria under Chinese supremacy and asked Japan to halt her military activities. Japan spurned the commission's findings and dealt the League of Nations (see LEAGUE OF NATIONS COVENANT) its first major blow by withdrawing her membership on May 27, 1933.

Further reading: Dorothy Borg, *The United States and the Far Eastern Crisis of 1933–1938* (Cambridge, Mass.: Harvard University Press, 1964).

M

Maastricht Treaty (Treaty on European Union) Series of complex agreements elaborating on and amending previous pacts (see SINGLE EUROPEAN ACTS; TREATIES OF ROME on political and monetary union, reached by the 12-member European Community (EC) in Maastricht, the Netherlands, on December 11, 1991. All members (except Britain and Denmark) agreed to establish a common currency (the euro) by 1999. It provided for the implementation of "a common foreign and security policy," the latter managed by the Western European Union. The EC was also given more leverage in social policy issues (Britain was exempted from this provision), and the European Parliament's powers were expanded. The EC also voted to increase aid for its four poorest members. The treaty was ratified on February 7, 1992, and came into force on November 1, 1993. The EC changed its name to the European Union (EU) on January 1, 1994; free movement of people and goods within the EU began in March 1995. Some countries, like Germany and France, wish to increase the pace toward achieving full political union, while others, such as Britain, want to limit the EU's role to economic cooperation and want to be able to choose the programs they prefer to participate in (industry, education, environment, health, and so forth).

Further reading: Dinan, Desmond, ed., *Encyclopedia of the European Union* (Boulder, Colo.: Lynne Rienner Publishers, 1998).

MacArthur's "Old Soldiers Never Die" Speech Address delivered before a joint session of the U.S. Congress by General Douglas MacArthur on April 19, 1951, after President Harry S Truman had relieved him of his command of United States and United Nations forces in Korea (because MacArthur had challenged Truman's instructions to wage only a limited war in Korea). In his speech, MacArthur argued that a surrender to communism in Asia would undermine containment efforts elsewhere. He argued for greater military efforts against the Chinese invasion forces: "in war . . . there can be no substitute for victory." His emotional address ended: "Old soldiers never die. They just fade away . . . I close my military career . . . an old soldier who tried to do his duty as God gave him the light to see that duty."

Further reading: Mortimer Adler, ed., *The Annals of America*, 18 vols. (Chicago: Encyclopaedia Britannica, 1968); Henry Steele Commager, ed., *Documents of American History*, 8th ed. (New York: Appleton-Century-Crofts, 1968); Geoffrey Perret, *Old Soldiers Never Die: The Life of Douglas MacArthur* (New York: Random House, 1996).

McCain-Feingold Bill See BIPARTISAN CAMPAIGN REFORM ACT OF 2002, U.S.

McCarran Act (Internal Security Act of 1950, Subversive Activities Control Act) U.S. legislation enacted on September 23, 1950, over the veto of President Harry S

Truman; intended to control the Communist Party in the United States. Sponsored by Senator Patrick A. McCarran of Nevada, the act required all communist and communist-front organizations to register with the attorney general. It prohibited communists from working in defense plants and prevented them from acquiring passports. It allowed the president, during national emergencies, to authorize the seizure and detention of persons who might engage in espionage or sabotage. The act was widely criticized as a violation of civil liberties, and many of its provisions have been overturned by the courts.

Further reading: Mortimer Adler, ed., *The Annals of America*, 18 vols. (Chicago: Encyclopaedia Britannica, 1968); Henry Steele Commager, ed., *Documents of American History*, 8th ed. (New York: Appleton-Century-Crofts, 1968); Kermit L. Hall, et al., eds., *The Oxford Companion to the Supreme Court of the United States* (New York: Oxford University Press, 1992); *United States Supreme Court, United States Reports: Cases Adjudged in the Supreme Court at . . . and Rules Announced at . . .* (New York: Banks & Brothers, Law Publishers, 1884–1921; Washington, D.C.: Government Printing Office, 1922–).

McCarran-Walter Act (Immigration and Nationality Act)

U.S. legislation enacted on June 30, 1952, that revised and codified immigration laws, continuing the basic quota system established by the U.S. IMMIGRATION QUOTA ACT OF 1924 but adding new provisions to exclude possible subversives and to permit the expulsion of aliens who engage in activities "prejudicial to the public interest." The act was sponsored by Senator Patrick A. McCarran of Nevada and Representative Francis E. Walter of Pennsylvania. It removed the ban on Asian immigrants but set an extremely low quota for them and for southern European immigrants, greatly favoring people from Great Britain and Germany instead. The act was vetoed by U.S. president Harry S Truman as inhumane, discriminatory, and inconsistent with democratic ideals, but it was passed over his veto.

Further reading: Mortimer Adler, ed., *The Annals of America*, 18 vols. (Chicago: Encyclopaedia Britannica, 1968); Henry Steele Commager, ed., *Documents of American History*, 8th ed. (New York: Appleton-Century-Crofts, 1968); M. G. Shimm, et al., *Immigration* (Durham, N.C.: Duke University School of Law, 1956).

McCollum v. Board of Education

U.S. Supreme Court decision issued in 1948, declaring unconstitutional the use of public schools for religious instruction. A released-time program in Champaign, Illinois, allowed public school children, with parental consent, to attend Protestant, Catholic, or Jewish religious instruction during school hours and in the school buildings. Teachers were supervised by the school superintendents but not paid by the schools. The Supreme Court ruled that the use of tax-supported buildings and pub-

lic school administration to provide religious instruction violated the constitutional ban on the establishment of religion and breached the wall separating church and state.

Further reading: Henry Steele Commager, ed., *Documents of American History*, 8th ed. (New York: Appleton-Century-Crofts, 1968).

McCulloch v. Maryland

U.S. Supreme Court decision of March 6, 1819, that confirmed the constitutional doctrine of implied powers. The case involved a tax that the state of Maryland imposed on all banks not chartered by the state; the tax was intended to destroy the second Bank of the United States, chartered by Congress. When the bank refused to pay, Maryland sued to collect the tax. Chief Justice John Marshall, writing for a unanimous Supreme Court, stated that Congress, which had constitutional power over federal fiscal matters, also had the implied power to establish a bank. Moreover, he argued that the state did not have the right to tax a federal agency. The decision greatly expanded federal power.

Further reading: Mortimer Adler, ed., *The Annals of America*, 18 vols. (Chicago: Encyclopaedia Britannica, 1968); Henry Steele Commager, ed., *Documents of American History*, 8th ed. (New York: Appleton-Century-Crofts, 1968); Charles W. Eliot, ed., *The Harvard Classics*, 51 vols. (New York: P. F. Collier & Son, 1937); Kermit L. Hall, et al., eds, *American Legal History: Cases and Materials*, 2d ed. (New York: Oxford University Press, 1996).

McKinley's War Message

Message from President William McKinley to the U.S. Congress on April 11, 1898, requesting the "forcible intervention of the United States" to end the Cuban rebellion against Spain. After publication of the DE LÔME LETTER and the destruction of the U.S. battleship *Maine* in Havana harbor on February 15, 1898, American sentiment for war against Spain increased. McKinley, rejecting Spain's offer of major concessions, justified intervention as a means to end the bloodshed in Cuba, to protect American commercial interests on the island, and to protect the safety and property of American citizens. On April 19 Congress authorized the president to initiate military intervention, and on April 25 the United States declared war on Spain.

See also: TELLER RESOLUTION.

Further reading: Mortimer Adler, ed., *The Annals of America*, 18 vols. (Chicago: Encyclopaedia Britannica, 1968); Henry Steele Commager, ed., *Documents of American History*, 8th ed. (New York: Appleton-Century-Crofts, 1968).

McKinley Tariff Act

Protectionist tariff legislation introduced by Republican congressman William McKinley and passed by Congress in 1890. With the fostering of U.S. industry as its goal, the act established the highest tariff for dutiable imports in U.S. history up to then, with rates averaging 49 percent, effectively barring some foreign-made goods from the United States. For farmers, tariffs were raised on wheat, corn, potatoes, and eggs. When, as a result of the tariff, prices rose faster than wages, the Republicans lost popular support and were defeated in the following elections. The McKinley Tariff Act was replaced by the WILSON-GORMAN TARIFF ACT in 1894.

Further reading: *The Latest Tariff Law: . . . the McKinley Act . . .* (Sanford, N.C.: Microfilming Corp. of America, 1979); *The New Tariff Laws Enacted by the Fifty-First Congress: The Tariff of 1890 . . .* (Sanford, N.C.: Microfilming Corp. of America, 1979).

McNary-Haugen Bill   Farm relief bill designed to control American agricultural surplus and stabilize prices; enacted in 1927 and promptly vetoed by U.S. president Calvin Coolidge. The bill, sponsored by Oregon's senator Charles L. McNary and Iowa's representative Gilbert N. Haugen, called for dual pricing of agricultural products—a fixed domestic price and a free international price for goods sold abroad. It would have established a federal farm board to purchase surpluses at the domestic price and sell them abroad at the prevailing world price. Any government losses through such sales were to be made up by equalization fees, paid by the farmers. In 1928 the bill was again passed and again vetoed by President Coolidge.

Further reading: Mortimer Adler, ed., *The Annals of America*, 18 vols. (Chicago: Encyclopaedia Britannica, 1968); Henry Steele Commager, ed., *Documents of American History*, 8th ed. (New York: Appleton-Century-Crofts, 1968).

Macon Act (Macon's Bill No. 2)   Legislation enacted by the U.S. Congress on May 1, 1810, that restored commerce with Great Britain and France following the suspension of trade under the U.S. EMBARGO ACT OF 1807 and the NON-INTERCOURSE ACT. When the earlier acts failed to halt interference with neutral American shipping by the two European powers (then at war with each other), Congress tried a new strategy. The Macon Act, sponsored by Senator Nathaniel Macon, reopened trade with both nations but provided that if either France or Britain recognized American neutrality and ceased violations on American shipping, the United States would cease trading with the other nation. Trade was restored with France and nonintercourse reimposed on Great Britain in 1811, in a prelude to the War of 1812.

Further reading: Henry Steele Commager, ed., *Documents of American History*, 8th ed. (New York: Appleton-Century-Crofts, 1968).

Madison's War Message   Message delivered by U.S. president James Madison to Congress on June 1, 1812, urging Congress to declare war on Great Britain following the failure of other attempts to end British interference with American shipping (see EMBARGO ACT OF 1807, U.S.; MACON ACT NON-INTERCOURSE ACT). Madison cited as grounds for war the British impressment of American sailors, the violation of American territorial waters and neutral shipping rights, and the blockade of U.S. ports. The House of Representatives approved a declaration of war on June 4; the Senate passed the measure on June 18 and Madison signed it the same day, beginning the War of 1812.

Further reading: Mortimer Adler, ed., *The Annals of America*, 18 vols. (Chicago: Encyclopaedia Britannica, 1968); Henry Steele Commager, ed., *Documents of American History*, 8th ed. (New York: Appleton-Century-Crofts, 1968).

Madrid, Treaty of (1526)   Agreement signed on January 14, 1526, in Madrid by King Francis I of France while imprisoned there by the Hapsburg emperor Charles V (formerly Charles I of Spain) following the battle of Pavia (in which Francis was badly beaten and captured, February 24, 1525). Francis renounced his claims to Italy (both Naples and Milan), surrendered his sovereignty over Artois, Flanders, and Tournai, and conceded the duchy of Burgundy to Charles V. Also, he agreed to pardon Duke Charles of Bourbon (who had turned against Francis and helped defeat him at Pavia) and to restore his titles and lands with the addition of Provence. Francis, a widower, contracted to marry Eleanor, widow of the king of Portugal and sister of Charles V. On signing the treaty, Francis was released and allowed to return home on the guarantee that he would shortly ratify the treaty. Once in France, however, he refused to endorse its terms, saying they had been forced from him. He then began plotting and planning the overthrow of Charles V with help from Italy and the pope, which resulted in the Treaty of COGNAC

See also: CAMBRAI, PEACE OF.

Further reading: Robert J. Knecht, *French Renaissance Monarchy: Francis I and Henry II*, 2d ed. (London: Longman, 1996); Robert J. Knecht, *Renaissance Warrior and Patron: The Reign of Francis I*, rev. ed. (New York: Cambridge University Press, 1994).

Madrid, Treaty of (1715) (Second Peace of Utrecht)   Long-awaited pact of February 6, 1715, representing the final settlement of the Treaties of UTRECHT and ending the war between Spain and Portugal. Portugal returned to Spain the border fortresses captured during the War of the Spanish Succession (1701–14). Spain surrendered the Sacramento colony (across the river from Buenos Aires) to Portugal. The settlement also confirmed the mutual restoration of peninsular conquests as provided for in Portugal's agreement with France. The Madrid treaty, concluded largely through the mediation of Britain (Portugal's ally) and guaranteed by her, was ratified by Portugal on March 9, 1715.

Further reading: Henry A. F. Kamen, *The War of Succession in Spain, 1700–15* (Bloomington: Indiana University Press, 1969).

Madrid, Treaty of (1750)   Treaty between Spain and Portugal signed in 1750, revoking the theoretical line established by the Treaty of TORDESILLAS in 1494, concerning their interests abroad. Instead, two new principles were put into effect: *uti possidetis*, or ownership by occupation rather than by claim; and the recognition of natural boundaries rather than astronomical ones. Although Portugal agreed to relinquish Colônia del Sacramento, she established her claim to much of Amazonia; acquired the territory of the seven missions of Uruguay; reaffirmed her claim to Brazil; and guaranteed her possession of the gold and diamond regions of Minas Gerais, Goiás, and Mato Grosso. Spain gained acceptance of its supremacy in the Rio de la Plata. While the treaty was strongly opposed and never effectively executed, the principle of *uti possidetis* provided the legal basis upon which Brazil based her boundaries thereafter.

Further reading: R. B. Cunninghame-Graham, *A Vanished Arcadia; Being Some Account of the Jesuits in Paraguay, 1607 to 1767* (New York: Haskell House, 1968); Bernard Moses, *The Spanish-Portuguese Treaty of 1750* (Berkeley: University of California Press, 1910).

Madrid, Treaty of (1801)   Treaty signed in Madrid on September 29, 1801, confirming the Peace of Badajoz (June 6, 1801), which ended the War of the Oranges (March–June 1801) between Spain and Portugal; the treaty granted concessions to Spain's ally France (see SAN ILDEFONSO, TREATY OF [1800]). Negotiated by Spanish prime minister Manuel de Godoy, French ambassador to Spain Lucien Bonaparte, and Portuguese minister Pinto de Souza, it ceded the fortress of Olivenza to Spain and a part of Brazil (Portuguese Guiana) to France. Portugal also promised to deny entry to British ships and to open her ports to French and Spanish ships, a major demand of the allies. France also obtained some commercial concessions and an indemnity of 20 million livres. The treaty only mentioned 15 million livres, the balance reportedly divided between Lucien and Godoy. In return, Spain guaranteed the territorial integrity of Portugal.

Further reading: Douglas Hilt, *The Troubled Trinity: Godoy and the Spanish Monarchs* (Tuscaloosa: University of Alabama Press, 1987); Jacques Chastenet, *Godoy: Master of Spain, 1792–1808* (Port Washington, N.Y.: Kennikat Press, 1972).

Magdalena Bay Resolution   See LODGE COROLLARY.

Magdeburg Law   Law originated in Magdeburg, Germany, and soon began to be adopted by other German towns, as well as many towns in Poland, in the mid-13th century. Under its principles, a town had the right to have its own court of law, was obligated to its prince alone for feudal rent payments, and was run by a council and an elected top official. Additional privileges were often granted to these towns. The law became especially prevalent in Poland, whose landowners welcomed settlers from Germany. (The country was at that time recovering from the destruction caused by years of Mongol invasions.) The towns founded in this way were German, and many Polish towns, after the adoption of the law, became Germanized.

Further reading: Wenceslas J. Wagner, ed., *Polish Law Throughout the Ages* (Stanford, Calif.: Hoover Institution Press, 1970).

Magna Carta (Magna Charta)   "Great Charter" of personal and political English liberties demanded by the feudal barons and reluctantly sealed by King John on June 15, 1215, at Runnymede, a meadow in Surrey County, England. The irate barons, vowing to end John's despotism, had drawn up, in November 1214 and with the help of Stephen Langton, archbishop of Canterbury, articles of reform; these articles were then redrafted and issued as the Magna Carta, written in Latin and consisting of a preamble and 63 clauses. Its major points included a "free" English church (clause 1); limitations on the king's exaction of "reliefs," fees paid by heirs to fiefs (clause 2), and of "scutage," a tax paid by knights in lieu of military service (clause 12); letters of summons to the great council to be sent by the king to the nobles and clergymen individually (clause 14); restraints by the barons on "aid" (dues) they had extracted from their vassals (clause 15); and, most importantly, the king's assurance of what is today called "due process of law" (clause 39), which stated: "No freeman shall be arrested or imprisoned, or disseized, or outlawed, or banished, or in any way molested; nor will we set forth against him, nor send against him, unless by the lawful judgment of his peers and by the law of the land." Other clauses granted all men's right to justice, encouraged freedom of trade and travel, and required the king to discharge his foreign mercenaries. On John's appeal, Pope Innocent III declared the charter void, but it was reissued with changes in 1216, 1217, and 1225 and became the basis of modern constitutional government.

Further reading: *American Jurisprudence, Second Edition,* Desk Book N.p.: West Group, 1998); A. E. Dick Howard, *Magna Carta: Text and Commentary,* rev. ed. (Charlottesville: University Press of Virginia, 1998); Frank N. Magill, ed., *Great Events from History: Ancient and Medieval Series,* 3 vols. (Englewood Cliffs, N.J.: Salem Press, 1972); Milton Viorst, *The Great Documents of Western Civilization* (Philadelphia: Chilton Books, 1965).

Magna Carta of Aragón   See ARAGONESE PRIVILEGES OF UNION.

Magna Carta of Denmark   See DANISH GREAT CHARTER.

Magna Carta of Hungary   See GOLDEN BULL OF HUNGARY.

Magna Carta of Ottoman Liberty   See OTTOMAN IMPERIAL EDICT OF 1839.

Magna Carta of Poland   See PIOTRKOW, STATUTE OF.

Magna Carta of Turkey   See OTTOMAN IMPERIAL EDICT OF 1856.

Mahon's Act, Lord   British copyright law promoted by Lord Mahon in 1842, by which an author (or his nominee) retained copyright over his books during life and for seven years afterwards. For 42 years after publication, the copyright would be held in the author's (or his nominee's) name. If, at the end of this period, the author was still alive, he would continue to hold the copyright until his death and for seven years afterward. If the author died before the end of the 42-year period, his nominees could claim copyright for the remainder of the period or for seven years—whichever was longer. Upon publication, a complimentary copy of the book was to be sent to five specified libraries in Great Britain.

Further reading: Catherine Seville, *Literary Copyright Reform in Early Victorian England: The Framing of the 1842 Copyright Act* (New York: Cambridge University Press, 1999).

Majesty, Letter of (Majestätsbrief)   Royal charter issued by the Hapsburg Holy Roman Emperor Rudolf II in July 1609, guaranteeing full religious freedom to his Bohemian subjects. The Protestants of Bohemia had forced him to confirm their "liberties," for Rudolf wished to gain their support (religious sentiment in Bohemia was anti-Rome) and not have Bohemia break away, as Upper and Lower Austria, Hungary, and Moravia had (to accept Matthias, Rudolf's brother, as their ruler). By the charter, the Protestants regained control over the ordination of their clergy, the right to erect their own churches, and control of the University of Prague. But Rudolf's efforts to gain their cooperation, particularly monetarily, were in vain; in 1611 he was forced to give up Bohemia to Matthias.

Further reading: Zdenek V. David and David Holeton, *The Bohemian Reformation and Religious Practice: Papers from the . . . World Congress of the Czechoslovak Society of Arts and Sciences, Bratislava, 1998* (Prague: Academy of Sciences of the Czech Republic, 1998); R. J. W. Evans, *Rudolf II and His World: A Study in Intellectual History, 1576–1612* (London: Thames & Hudson, 1997).

Malayan-British Agreements of 1956 and 1957   See BRITISH-MALAYAN AGREEMENTS OF 1956 AND 1957.

Malestroit, Truce of   Armistice made at Malestroit, France, on January 19, 1343; imposed by papal legates (representatives of Pope Clement VI) between John IV of Montfort and Charles of Blois, both of whom claimed the right of succession to the sovereign duchy of Brittany (see GUÉRANDE, TREATY OF) after the death of Duke John III in April 1341. The issue was complicated because Montfort was backed by England's king Edward III, whereas Blois had the support of France's king Philip VI. According to its terms, Montfort promised never to return to Brittany. He reneged on this soon after, the armistice proved short-lived, and the War of the Breton Succession (1341–65), within the Hundred Years' War (1337–1457), was resumed.

Further reading: Michael Jones, *Some Documents Relating to the Disputed Succession to the Duchy of Brittany, 1341* (London: Royal Historical Society, 1972).

Malthus's *Essays on the Principle of Population*   See ESSAYS ON THE PRINCIPLE OF POPULATION, MALTHUS'S.

Manifesto of the Equals (Manifeste des Egaux)   François Noël (or Gracchus) Babeuf's communistic manifesto (April 1796) declaring that "the time has come to found the REPUBLIC OF EQUALS, that great guesthouse of all mankind." Babeuf, French insurgent leader of the campaign for equality during the Directory, demanded "real equality," not "merely written down in the DECLARATION OF THE RIGHTS OF MAN AND THE CITIZEN," but "in our midst." Railing against the system that forced the masses to work "at the pleasure of a tiny minority," he aimed at a state where everyone would enjoy "one education and one standard of life." Aware that his campaign would anger some privileged members, Babeuf described real equality as "the only state which answers all requirements without making victims or costing sacrifices." He condemned the aristocratic FRENCH CONSTITUTION OF 1791 and the FRENCH CONSTITUTION OF 1795 and praised the FRENCH CONSTITUTION OF 1793 for taking a big step toward real equality. Babeuf and his followers were persecuted for their views, and Babeuf was guillotined on May 27, 1797, at Vendôme, France.

Further reading: Massimo Salvadori, ed., *Modern Socialism* (New York: Harper & Row, 1968).

Manifesto of the International Working-Men's Association   Address at the General Council of the International Working-Men's Association in Paris on May 30, 1871, apprising all association members in Europe and the United States of events leading to the French Civil War of 1871 and the birth of the Paris Commune. Authored by Karl Marx, it praised the workingmen's revolution of March 18 (see PARIS COMMUNE, FIRST PROCLAMATION OF THE) for taking "undisputed sway of Paris" and reiterated the ideals and organization of the commune. Hailing the French working class as "the advanced guard of the modern proletariate," it declared "there can be neither peace nor truce possible between the working men of France and the appropriators of their produce." Their association, it maintained, was an "international bond" between workingmen in the "civilized world," one that could not be destroyed "by any amount of carnage." Finally, the General Council paid tribute to workingmen of Paris and the commune for being "the glorious harbinger of a new society."

Further reading: Frank N. Magill, ed., *Great Events from History: Modern European Series*, 3 vols. (Englewood Cliffs, N.J.: Salem Press, 1973).

Manifesto of the Second World Peace Congress

Pronouncement endorsed by representatives of over 60 countries at the Second World Peace Congress (November 16–20, 1950) at Warsaw, Poland. Embodying the philosophy of the STOCKHOLM RESOLUTION, the manifesto's opening words were: "War is threatening humanity—children, women and men. The United Nations has failed to justify the hopes which the peoples placed in it for the maintenance of peace and tranquility. Human life and the attainments of human culture are in danger!" It went on to urge all to fight for peace and to adopt laws against war propaganda. The communist-inspired Second World Peace Congress provided no specifics for genuine international inspection and control of the destruction of atomic weapons; it overlooked the United Nations' plans for the control of atomic energy.

Further reading: Gordon Schaffer, *We Can Save Peace: Story of the Second World Peace Congress, Warsaw, 1950* (London: British Peace Committee, 1950); World Peace Congress 1950, *Second World Peace Congress, Warsaw, November 16–22, 1950* (N.p.: 1951).

Manila Pact   See SEATO PACT.

Manilian Law (Lex Manilia)

Measure proposed in 66 B.C. by the Roman tribune Caius Manilius to transfer to his friend Pompey the Great complete command of the armies and Asiatic provinces (notably Bithynia and Cilicia) then under Lucullus, a rival commander. The Senate strongly opposed giving additional military power to Pompey, but the law was supported by Marcus Tullius Cicero (or Tully), then a praetor, in an eloquent speech, "For the Manilian Law" (Pro Lege Manilia), in which he favored Pompey and criticized the senatorial oligarchy's apathy about the Asiatic provinces' financial importance to Rome. The measure was passed by the Senate, and Pompey replaced Lucullus in the eastern command.

See also: GABINIAN LAW.

Further reading: Francis P. Donnelly, *Cicero's Manilian Law: A Rhetorical Commentary* (New York: Fordham University Press, 1939).

Manitoba Act of 1870

Act approved by Canada's government on May 2, 1870, providing for Manitoba's admission into the Dominion of Canada as the fifth province, and marking the end of its inhabitants' (the métis') first struggle with the Dominion over control of their land, which the Dominion had intended to annex outright. The act provided that Manitoba, as part of the Dominion, would be represented in the federal legislature in Ottawa and that Manitoba would have its own provincial government. In addition, the distinctive way of life of the métis (half-breeds of white-Indian parentage) would be protected by guarantees that both English and French could be used in provincial government and that both Protestant and Catholic schools would receive governmental support. Despite these gains, the province lost control over its land and natural resources to the Dominion.

See also: BRITISH NORTH AMERICAN ACT; NORTHWEST TERRITORIES ACT OF 1875.

Further reading: Paul L. A. H. Chartrand, *Manitoba's Metis Settlement Scheme of 1870* (Saskatoon, Canada: Native Law Center, University of Saskatchewan, 1991); Thomas Flanagan, *Metis Lands in Manitoba* (Calgary, Canada: University of Calgary Press, 1991).

Mann Act (White Slave Traffic Act)

Legislation enacted by the U.S. Congress on June 25, 1910, prohibiting the interstate transportation of women and girls for "immoral purposes." Named for its sponsor, Representative James Robert Mann of Illinois, the act was intended to curb prostitution. The Mann Act marked an important extension of federal involvement in national social problems, based on Congress's constitutional power to regulate commerce. Though challenged as an unwarranted restriction on interstate commerce, an intrusion into state jurisdiction, and an overstepping of congressional power, the act was upheld by the U.S. Supreme Court.

Further reading: Kermit L. Hall et al., eds., *The Oxford Companion to the Supreme Court of the United States* (New York: Oxford University Press, 1992); United States Supreme Court, *United States reports: Cases Adjudged in the Supreme Court at . . . and Rules Announced at . . .* (New York: Banks & Brothers, Law Publishers, 1884–1921; Washington, D.C.: Government Printing Office, 1922–).

Mann-Elkins Act

Legislation enacted by the U.S. Congress on June 18, 1910, that placed the growing, and previously unregulated, communications industry—including telephone, telegraph, cable, and wireless companies—under the jurisdiction of the Interstate Commerce Commission (ICC). The act, sponsored by Senator Stephen B. Elkins of West Virginia and Representative James Robert Mann of Illinois, also strengthened federal control over railroad rates by giving the ICC power to act on its own initiative, rather than merely in response to formal complaints. The ICC could suspend rate increases pending court decisions and could more effectively enforce provisions preventing carriers from charging more for short hauls than for long ones.

Further reading: Keith L. Bryant, *Railroads in the Age of Regulation, 1900–1980* (New York: Facts On File, 1988); Dewitt C. Moore, *The Law of Interstate Commerce and Federal Regulation Thereof, Including the Mann-Elkins Amendments of 1910 and the Sherman Anti-Trust Act of 1890* (Albany, N.Y.: M. Bender & Company, 1910).

Mann's Twelfth Annual Report Report issued in 1848 by American educational reformer Horace Mann, secretary of the Massachusetts State Board of Education, discussing his pedagogical and social philosophy. Mann argued that universal education was necessary to eliminate ignorance and poverty, to prevent formation of a permanent class of underprivileged people, such as the European lower classes. "Education," he said, "is a great equalizer of the conditions of men,—the balance wheel of the social machinery." He argued that it was the highest duty of the state to advance human welfare and equality, to elevate the downtrodden, relieve suffering, and develop human talent, and that education was the best means to achieve these goals.

Further reading: Mortimer Adler, ed., *The Annals of America*, 18 vols. (Chicago: Encyclopaedia Britannica, 1968); Henry Steele Commager, ed., *Documents of American History*, 8th ed. (New York: Appleton-Century-Crofts, 1968).

Manueline Ordinances See AFONSINE ORDINANCES.

Maori Representation Act See NATIVE REPRESENTATION ACT, NEW ZEALAND'S.

Mao's "Little Red Book" See QUOTATIONS FROM CHAIRMAN MAO TSE-TUNG.

Mapp v. Ohio U.S. Supreme Court decision, issued on June 19, 1961, that extended to state courts the constitutional protections against unreasonable searches and seizures in federal courts. In 1957 police officers in Cleveland, Ohio, seeking a fugitive, broke into the home of Doll Ree Mapp without a search warrant. They found no fugitive but did discover some "lewd and lascivious material," for possession of which Mapp was later convicted. In a five-to-three decision, the Supreme Court overturned the conviction on the grounds that the evidence had been seized in violation of FOURTH AMENDMENT requirements of a search warrant. The exclusion of such evidence, previously binding only in federal courts, was extended to state courts through the FOURTEENTH AMENDMENT.

Further reading: Kermit L. Hall et al., eds., *The Oxford Companion to the Supreme Court of the United States* (New York: Oxford University Press, 1992); *United States Supreme Court, United States Reports: Cases Adjudged in the Supreme Court at . . . and Rules Announced at . . .* (New York: Banks & Brothers, Law Publishers, 1884–1921; Washington, D.C.: Government Printing Office, 1922–).

Marburg, Fifteen Articles of Statements of Protestant belief accepted by Swiss and German theologians and others, after a series of discussions at Marburg, Germany, on October 1–4, 1529. Protestant reformers had split over the question of Christ's presence in the bread and wine of the Eucharist rite. At Marburg, the German theologian Martin Luther said that Christ was literally present at the Eucharist; the Swiss reformer Huldreich Zwingli insisted that His presence was to be understood symbolically. When the talks broke down, Luther drew up the Fifteen Articles of Marburg, in which he stated in the first 14 articles the generally accepted common doctrines of the Swiss and German reformers; the 15th article declared that "at present we are not agreed as to whether the true body and blood [of Christ] are bodily present in the bread and wine."

Further reading: Gerhard Ebeling, *Luther: An Introduction to His Thought*, trans. R.A. Wilson (London: Collins, 1970).

Marbury v. Madison U.S. Supreme Court decision, issued on February 24, 1803, that established the principle of judicial review, whereby the Court could declare unconstitutional and void acts passed by the Congress. In 1801, at the end of his term of office, President John Adams appointed William Marbury to be justice of the peace, but the commission was not delivered promptly. When his successor (and political opponent), President Thomas Jefferson, ordered that the commission be withheld, Marbury asked the Supreme Court, under powers given it by the JUDICIARY ACT OF 1789, to order delivery of the commission. The Court ruled that although Marbury had a right to the commission, the section of the Judiciary Act authorizing the Court to issue such an order was in conflict with the U.S. CONSTITUTION and was therefore void.

Further reading: Mortimer Adler, ed., *The Annals of America*, 18 vols. (Chicago: Encyclopaedia Britannica, 1968); Henry Steele Commager, ed., *Documents of American History*, 8th ed. (New York: Appleton-Century-Crofts, 1968); Kermit L. Hall, et al., eds, *American Legal History: Cases and Materials*, 2d ed. (New York: Oxford University Press, 1996); Kermit L. Hall, et al., eds., *The Oxford Companion to the Supreme Court of the United States* (New York: Oxford University Press, 1992).

March Constitution (Schwarzenberg Constitution) Constitution promulgated on March 4, 1849, by Austrian prince Felix Schwarzenberg, an influential statesman devoted to the extension of imperial power; it provided for the Austrian empire's return to a highly centralized form of government. The constitution called for a representative diet with two chambers and for the temporary, but autocratic, rule of the emperor. Most significant, however, was that this constitution was to be in force throughout the whole empire, thus effectively annulling any degree of self-rule that had been instituted anywhere in the empire, most notably in Hungary, which had had her own constitution (see MARCH LAWS) since 1848. The document replaced the KREMSIER CONSTITUTION, only days old, and reflected the conservative forces' attempt to suppress nationalistic movements that had been springing up throughout the empire. The constitution was abandoned in 1851.

Further reading: Adolph Schwartzenberg, *Prince Felix zu Schwarzenberg, Prime Minister of Austria, 1848–1852* (New York: AMS Press, 1966).

March Laws (April Laws, Hungarian Acts of 1848)

Laws proposed on March 15, 1848, by liberal Hungarian statesman Louis Kossuth; passed by the Hungarian Diet at Pozsony (Bratislava, Czechoslovakia), and confirmed on April 11, 1848, by Austrian emperor Ferdinand. It created a modern and unified Hungarian state. Most significantly, the laws provided that historic Hungarian lands (including Transylvania and Croatia-Slavonia), which had long been governed separately from Hungary, were to be included in the new Hungarian state and the the new state was to be an autonomous entity, whose king was to be the Austrian emperor, ultimately responsible to the Hungarian Diet. In addition, the nobility's exemption from taxation was abolished; peasants were granted ownership of the land they tilled; freedom of religion and abolition of press censorship were proclaimed. The ongoing Hungarian Revolution of 1848 culminated in the confirmation of these laws.

Further reading: Istvan Deak, *Lawful Revolution: Louis Kossuth and the Hungarians, 1848–1849* (London: Phoenix, 2001).

Marcos's Martial Law Decree

Formal order declared on September 21, 1972, with Proclamation 1081 by Philippine president Ferdinand E. Marcos. In response to perceived threats from both communist and Muslim guerrilla movements, the bombing of a Liberal Party rally; and an alleged assassination attempt against the secretary of defense, Marcos declared martial law and suspended civil liberties. Some 30,000 opposition members were arrested, including journalists, union leaders, and politicians. In 1973 Marcos replaced the constitution, created a new National Assembly, and changed the law so that he could be reelected president indefinitely. With a visit from Pope John Paul II scheduled for the summer of 1981, Marcos officially lifted martial law on January 17, 1981, although all of the other orders associated with the decree and thereafter remained in effect.

Further reading: David A. Rosenberg, ed., *Marcos and Martial Law in the Philippines* (Ithaca, N.Y.: Cornell University Press, 1979).

Marquess of Queensberry Rules

Set of 12 boxing rules written in 1865 and first published in 1867 under the patronage of Englishman John Sholto Douglas, ninth marquess of Queensberry (hence their name); they were first used by boxers in London in 1872 and became the basic rules of modern boxing. Drafted by John Graham Chambers (member of the British Amateur Athletic Club), the rules defined the conduct of the game and the kind of equipment to be used. The boxing match was to be conducted in a 24-foot square ring with the contestants wearing standard-size, quality boxing gloves and shoes without springs. Each round was to be three minutes, with a one-minute interval between two rounds. Wrestling or hugging was prohibited. If a contestant fell down, he was given 10 seconds to get up (unassisted) and resume the game; if not, the other man would win it. Every match was to be played to its completion, unless the stakes were withdrawn. In all other respects, the revised rules of the London Prize Ring were deemed applicable.

Further reading: John C. Earl, *Earl's Handbook of Boxing, with the Marquis of Queensberry and Amateur Boxing Association's Rules for the Regulation of Contests with the Gloves* (London: Dean & Son, 1909).

Marshall Plan (European Recovery Program)

Plan first proposed by U.S. secretary of state George C. Marshall in an address at Harvard University on June 5, 1947; it established a U.S.-sponsored program to give financial aid to European countries "willing to assist in the task of recovery" from World War II (1939–45). In Paris, 16 European nations (the Soviet Union and its satellites refused to participate in the plan) drafted a four-year program costing $22.4 billion. In 1948 the U.S. Congress authorized the spending of $5.4 billion the first year; participating European nations then matched the aid they received during the program, which ended in late 1951, a year ahead of schedule, with a final, total cost of some $12 billion. The 16 European nations (plus West Germany), grouped together as the Organization for European Economic Cooperation (OEEC), restored their economic and agricultural production by completing many projects (new roads, bridges, hydroelectric plants, land reclamations, irrigation systems, and large-scale housing, among other undertakings). Along with stimulating trade and creating financial stability, the Marshall Plan also checked and reduced communist influence in Western Europe. Canada and countries in Latin America and other parts of the world also contributed to the plan, some 70 percent of whose cost was paid by the United States.

Further reading: Mortimer Adler, ed., *The Annals of America*, 18 vols. (Chicago: Encyclopaedia Britannica, 1968); Henry Steele Commager, ed., *Documents of American History*, 8th ed. (New York: Appleton-Century-Crofts, 1968); Frank N. Magill, ed., *Great Events from History: Modern European Series*, 3 vols. (Englewood Cliffs, N.J.: Salem Press, 1973); Constantine C. Menges, *The Marshall Plan from Those Who Made It Succeed* (Lanham, Md.: University Press of America, 1999).

Martin v. Hunter's Lessee

U.S. Supreme Court decision of March 20, 1816, that upheld the Court's right to review the decisions of state courts in all cases involving the laws, treaties, and constitution of the United States. The decision, written by Justice Joseph Story, reversed a ruling of the Virginia Court of Appeals affirming the state's right to confiscate British-owned land, a right contrary to the JAY TREATY between the British and U.S. governments, which protected such property from exploration. Virginia argued that the state and federal governments were equal, neither having the power to overrule the other. Story, however, ruled that the Supreme Court had primacy and appellate jurisdiction over state courts in constitutional cases.

Further reading: Kermit L. Hall et al., eds., *The Oxford Companion to the Supreme Court of the United States* (New York: Oxford University Press, 1992); John M. Rogers, *International Law and United States Law* (Brookfield, Vt.: Ashgate/ Dartmouth, 1999).

Maryland Colony Charter   Proprietory rights to what is now the state of Maryland; granted in 1632 to George Calvert, the first Lord Baltimore, who had petitioned King Charles I of England for the land. Upon Calvert's death in April, the grant was passed to his son Cecilius Calvert, the second Lord Baltimore, who was issued the charter for the proprietary colony of Maryland on June 20, 1632. He then sent colonists, about half of whom were fellow Roman Catholics (Cecilius, like his father, had converted to the Catholic faith). The charter gave Cecilius as proprietor the right to collect taxes, appoint administrators, award land grants, and establish churches according to English laws. He thus started the first Roman Catholic colony in America through the charter.

Further reading: Henry Steele Commager, ed., *Documents of American History*, 8th ed. (New York: Appleton-Century-Crofts, 1968); David D. Douglas et al., eds., *English Historical Documents*, 12 vols. (New York: Oxford University Press, 1950–77); William MacDonald, ed., *Select Charters and Other Documents Illustrative of American History, 1606–1775* (New York: Macmillan, 1899).

Massachusetts Bay Colony, Charter of   Royal charter of 1629 that confirmed to a group of influential Puritans, merchants, and others, power to trade and colonize in New England between the Charles and Merrimack Rivers. It gave to the approximately 1,000 immigrants local powers of self-government and general court power to admit new members as a means of limiting the voting in the colony to those of their own religious beliefs—consequently, within a few years transforming the enterprise from a trading company into a theocracy almost void of outside control. Dissent resulted in the voluntary exile of founders of Connecticut and the forced exile of founders of Rhode Island towns.

Further reading: Mortimer Adler, ed., *The Annals of America*, 18 vols. (Chicago: Encyclopaedia Britannica, 1968); Henry Steele Commager, ed., *Documents of American History*, 8th ed. (New York: Appleton-Century-Crofts, 1968); David D. Douglas, et al., eds., *English Historical Documents*, 12 vols. (New York: Oxford University Press, 1950–77).

Massachusetts Bill of Rights   Set of 30 articles, incorporated into the constitution of the commonwealth of Mas-

sachusetts and adopted in 1780, outlining the rights of its inhabitants. Drafted largely by John Adams, the document declared that "all men are born free and equal, and have certain natural, essential, and unalienable rights." It specified the right of the people to bear arms; to assemble; to be free of unreasonable searches; to participate in free elections; to be protected in life, liberty, and property; to obtain justice freely; to have a free press. Declaring that "it is the right as well as the duty of all men . . . to worship the Supreme Being," it granted religious freedom to all Christian denominations.

Further reading: Mortimer Adler, ed., *The Annals of America*, 18 vols. (Chicago: Encyclopaedia Britannica, 1968); Henry Steele Commager, ed., *Documents of American History*, 8th ed. (New York: Appleton-Century-Crofts, 1968).

Massachusetts Body of Liberties   Code of law put forth by the Massachusetts General Court in December 1641 and sent to towns for recommendations. It was based largely on English common law, leaving much authority to the magistrates, yet it contained indications of a growing spirit of colonial independence. The General Court, in response to criticism of the Body of Liberties in 1646, stated "our allegiance binds us not to the laws of England any longer than while we live in England." At the end of a probation period, the Body of Liberties was replaced with *The Book of General Lawes and Libertyes* (1648).

Further reading: Mortimer Adler, ed., *The Annals of America*, 18 vols. (Chicago: Encyclopaedia Britannica, 1968); Charles W. Eliot, ed., *American Historical Documents, 1000–1904: With Introductions and Notes* (Danbury, Conn.: Grolier, 1980); Charles W. Eliot, ed., *The Harvard Classics*, 51 vols. (New York: P. F. Collier & Son, 1937); William MacDonald, ed., *Select Charters and Other Documents Illustrative of American History, 1606–1775* (New York: Macmillan, 1899).

Massachusetts Charter of 1691   Royal charter, granted by England's king William III, that formally united the Massachusetts Bay Colony, Plymouth, and Maine into the royal colony of Massachusetts. Replacing the earlier royal charter granted to the Massachusetts Bay Colony in 1629, which had been revoked in 1684, the charter also provided for a crown-appointed governor, a council to be elected by the General Court subject to the governor's veto, the abolishment of church membership as a requirement for suffrage, royal review of legislation, and appeals to the king in council.

Further reading: Harry C. Allen and Roger Thompson, eds., *Contrast and Connection: Bicentennial Essays in Anglo-American History* (Athens: Ohio University Press, 1976); William MacDonald, ed., *Select Charters and Other Documents Illustrative of American History, 1606–1775* (New York: Macmillan, 1899).

Massachusetts Circular Letter   Document written by American patriot Samuel Adams and approved by the

Massachusetts House of Representatives in 1768 in response to the TOWNSHEND ACTS passed by the British Parliament in the previous year, which imposed duties on selected colonial imports. The letter informed the assemblies of the other 12 colonies of the Massachusetts General Court's denunciation of the Townshend Acts on the grounds that they represented taxation without representation, and it urged a united colonial protest. The British government used the threat of dissolution in an attempt to prevent other legislatures from endorsing the letter and did eventually dissolve the assemblies of Massachusetts, Virginia, and other supporting colonies, thus heightening the tension between the colonies and the British Crown.

Further reading: Mortimer Adler, ed., *The Annals of America*, 18 vols. (Chicago: Encyclopaedia Britannica, 1968); Henry Steele Commager, ed., *Documents of American History*, 8th ed. (New York: Appleton-Century-Crofts, 1968); David D. Douglas et al., eds., *English Historical Documents*, 12 vols. (New York: Oxford University Press, 1950–77).

Massachusetts Government Act

Statute enacted by the British Parliament with royal assent on May 20, 1774, enlarging the British governor's powers in the colony of Massachusetts. One of the COERCIVE ACTS, it nullified the colony's charter, depriving the colonists of their rights and reducing Massachusetts to the status of a crown colony. Appointment or election of various officials passed out of the hands of citizens and their representatives and came under the control of the governor and British king. The act also abolished town meetings, except for the strict purpose of electing municipal officers. It met with intense indignation throughout the colonies in America.

Further reading: Henry Steele Commager, ed., *Documents of American History*, 8th ed. (New York: Appleton-Century-Crofts, 1968); David D. Douglas, et al., eds., *English Historical Documents*, 12 vols. (New York: Oxford University Press, 1950–77).

Massey Commission Report

Report prepared from 1949 to 1951 by the Canadian Royal Commission on National Development in the Arts, Letters and Sciences (which was chaired by Canadian politician Vincent Massey) and published in June 1951; it contained recommendations intended to increase the federal government's support of culture in Canada. Following a discussion of the causes of Canada's "inferiority" in cultural matters (which included Canada's allegedly indiscriminate acceptance of American culture), the report recommended the creation of new museums and cultural institutions; the allocation of federal funds to Canadian universities; and the creation of the Canada Council, which would be responsible for stimulating participation in cultural activities and higher education. In response to the report, federal grants were made available to Canadian universities in 1951, and the Canada Council was established in 1957.

Further reading: Paul Litt, *The Muses, the Masses, and the Massey Commission* (Toronto: University of Toronto Press, 1992); Maria Tippett, *Making Culture: English-Canadian Institutions and the Arts Before the Massey Commission* (Toronto: University of Toronto Press, 1990).

Masulipatam, Treaty of

Peace treaty between the nizam (ruler) of Hyderabad, India, and the British forces, signed on February 23, 1768, in Masulipatam. It was made during the First Mysore War (1767–69) (between the Indian Hindu state of Mysore and the British East India Company) and marked the surrender of the nizam, who was an ally of Mysore and who now accepted the status of being a vassal of the British empire. He also recognized British superiority over Mysore and was made ruler of the district of Balaghat (to appease him). But a year later the British slyly handed the district to Mysore.

Further reading: Praxy Fernandes, *The Tigers of Mysore: A Biography of Hyder Ali and Tipu Sultan*, rev. updated ed. (New York: Viking, 1991).

Mater et Magistra

Pope John XXIII's bold social encyclical of May 15, 1961, commemorating the 70th anniversary of Pope Leo XIII's *RERUM NOVARUM*. Published on July 15, the encyclical broke new ground by exploring man's relationship with society, the state, and communities worldwide. Accepting "socialization" as "an effect and a cause of the growing intervention of the state" in matters intimately affecting man, Pope John reasoned that this did not reduce "men to . . . being merely automatons." As protection against "the potential evils of state control and excessive bureaucracy," he believed that "a healthy view of the public good must be present and operative in men invested with public authority." Secondly, "the numerous intermediate bodies and corporate enterprises" should be completely autonomous. Pope John's tone was gentle, that of a mother (*mater*) and teacher (*magistra*), and his style simple and readable, suitable for the topic. The encyclical thus aroused tremendous interest in the Catholic and secular worlds.

Further reading: Claudia Carlen, comp., *The Papal Encyclicals* (Wilmington, N.C.: McGrath Publishing, 1981); Catholic University of America, eds., *New Catholic Encyclopedia* (New York: McGraw-Hill, 1967); Anne Fremantle, *The Papal Encyclicals in Their Historical Context* (New York: Mentor-Omega Books, 1963); David J. O'Brien and Thomas A. Shannon, eds., *Catholic Social Thought: The Documentary Heritage* (Maryknoll, N.Y.: Orbis Books, 1992).

Max Havelaar

Satiric classic of 19th-century Dutch literature written by Eduard D. Dekker under the pseudonym "Multatuli" and first published in Holland in 1860; it condemned the exploitation of Dutch colonial policy in Indonesia. The story, based on Dekker's own experiences while in office in Indonesia, was about a Dutch official, Max Havelaar, who deplored the exploitation of the native Indonesians by the Dutch and who (like Dekker himself) ultimately was forced to resign his post because of this attempt to expose it. The novel became enormously popular in Holland and abroad and was at least partially responsible for the liberalization of Dutch colonial policy that occurred following its publication.

Further reading: Multatuli, *Max Havelaar, or, the Coffee Auctions of a Dutch Trading Company* (New York: Penguin Books, 1987); Multatuli, *The Stone Cutter's Dream* (Toronto: Aliquando Press, 1994); James Purdy, *No Need to Knock: Stories and Fragments Focusing on Men in Office* (Amsterdam: Ahrend, 1990).

Maximum Prices, Edict of   See EDICT OF MAXIMUM PRICES.

Mayflower Compact   Agreement signed by 41 male passengers (Pilgrims) while aboard the *Mayflower* in Provincetown Harbor, November 11, 1620; it stated that they would submit to the will of the majority in whatever regulations of government were agreed upon. The compact committed them to "frame such just and equal laws . . . as shall be thought most meet and convenient for the general good of the colony . . ." It also bound them to constitute offices for the general good of the proposed colony and to hold in check dissenters who had threatened to strike out for themselves when Pilgrim leaders decided to land in New England (Plymouth) instead of Virginia. It was patterned after their church covenant, which placed religious authority in the congregation. The compact was intended to preserve order, until a patent could be obtained, and remained in force until 1691. A form of democratic government had begun.

Further reading: Mortimer Adler, ed., *The Annals of America*, 18 vols. (Chicago Encyclopaedia Britannica, 1968); *American Jurisprudence, Second Edition*, Desk Book (N.p.: (West Group, 1998); Henry Steele Commager, ed., *Documents of American History*, 8th ed. (New York: Appleton-Century-Crofts, 1968); Charles W. Eliot, ed., *The Harvard Classics*, 51 vols. (New York: P. F. Collier & Son, 1937).

May Laws (Falk Laws)   Series of anticlerical measures known as the Kulturkampf (cultural struggle), which were approved by the Prussian Landtag (diet) in May 1873. The legislation was largely a reaction to the dogma of papal infallibility announced July 18, 1870, and was drafted by the Prussian minister of ecclesiastical affairs and education, Adalbert Falk, with the full support of Chancellor Otto von Bismarck. The laws gave the state veto power over ecclesiastical appointments, which were made dependent on regular attendance at a German high school and university. Candidates for ecclesiastical positions were also required to pass a state-administered examination. Papal jurisdiction over the Roman Catholic Church in Prussia was abolished, and the disciplinary authority of the church was transferred to the state.

Church penalties were regulated, and separation from the church was facilitated. The laws failed to diminish the power of Catholicism in Germany, and the strength of the Catholic Center Party increased.

See also: BREAD-BASKET BILL.

Further reading: Ronald J. Ross, *The Failure of Bismarck's Kulturkampf: Catholicism and State Power in Imperial Germany, 1871–1887)* (Washington, D.C.: Catholic University of America Press, 1998).

Maysville Road Bill   Bill passed by the U.S. Congress in 1830 authorizing a federal stock subscription of $150,000 in the Maysville, Washington, Paris, and Lexington Turnpike Road Company, to aid in the construction of 60 miles of road within the state of Kentucky. The bill was vetoed by President Andrew Jackson on the grounds that the U.S CONSTITUTION did not provide for federal support of internal improvements, and that the road, which was exclusively within the state limits and had no connection with an established transportation network, did not fall under national jurisdiction.

Further reading: Mortimer Adler, ed., *The Annals of America*, 18 vols. (Chicago: Encyclopaedia Britannica, 1968); Henry Steele Commager, ed., *Documents of American History*, 8th ed. (New York: Appleton-Century-Crofts, 1968).

Mazzei Letter   Letter written by Thomas Jefferson to his Italian friend Philip Mazzei, dated April 24, 1796, and first published, in translation, in Florence, Italy, on January 1, 1797. It was republished in English later that year (in the *New York Minerva*, May 1797). The letter, in which Jefferson, leader of America's Democratic-Republican Party, attacked George Washington and other Federalists, led to a permanent split between Washington and Jefferson. To Mazzei, Jefferson described the Federalists as "an anglican, monarchical, and aristocratic party" and their chief leaders as taken in by supposed "heresies" and with "their heads shorn by the harlot England."

Further reading: Margherita Marchione, ed. and trans., *Philip Mazzei: Selected Writings and Correspondence* (Prato, Italy: Edizioni del Palazzo, 1983); Margherita Marchione, *Philip Mazzei: World Citizen (Jefferson's "Zealous Whig")* (Lanham, Md.: University Press of America, 1994.

Mazzini's Instructions to Young Italy   Italian nationalist leader Giuseppe Mazzini's soul-stirring address (1831) to members of the "Young Italy" group he had recently founded, inspiring the emerging Risorgimento (movement for Italian unification) with greater impetus. "Convinced that Italy is destined to become one nation," and believing that this could only be achieved by "constancy and unity of efforts," Young Italy, he said, aimed at "revolution" through a campaign of "national education." Young Italy, he declared, "is republican and unitarian" because the monarchical system was basically flawed, because Europe was gradually moving "toward the enthronement of the republican principle." Decrying federalism, Mazzini stated that "without unity there is no true nation . . . no real strength." Education and insurrection, he believed, were different sides of the same coin "to be adopted simultaneously and made to harmonize with each other."

See also: GARIBALDI'S PROCLAMATION TO THE ITALIANS; VICTOR EMMANUEL II'S SPEECH OPENING THE ITALIAN PARLIAMENT.

Further reading: Frank N. Magill, ed., *Great Events from History: Modern European Series*, 3 vols. (Englewood Cliffs, N.J.: Salem Press, 1973); Milton Viorst, *The Great Documents of Western Civilization* (Philadelphia: Chilton Books, 1965).

Meat Inspection Act of 1906, U.S.
Federal legislation enacted on June 30, 1906, giving the U.S. secretary of agriculture the power to inspect meat and condemn products that are "unsound, unhealthful, unwholesome, or otherwise unfit for human food." The act was intended to correct unsanitary and dangerous practices in the meat-packing industry, such as resulted in the "embalmed beef" scandal, when soldiers in the Spanish-American War (1898) were fed tainted beef. The act allowed for federal inspection of all companies selling meats in interstate commerce.

Further reading: Edward F. Keuchel, "Chemicals and Meat: The Embalmed Beef Scandal of the Spanish-American War," *Bulletin of the History of Medicine* 48 (1974); 249–64.

Mecklenburg Resolves (Mecklenburg "Declaration of Independence")
Resolves or resolutions adopted by the citizens of Mecklenburg County, North Carolina, in which they established a local government at the start of the American Revolution (1775–83) and pronounced the annulment of all laws and commissions enacted by the king and Parliament and declared royal government in their province to be suspended. According to historical facts based on recollections published in the *Raleigh Register* on April 30, 1819, the 20 resolves were advocated on May 20, 1775, and were then handed in trust to the North Carolina delegates to the Second Continental Congress. No copy of "a declaration" was ever found, and accounts from a Charleston newspaper of June 16, 1775, which was found in 1847, mention that a muster of militia and citizens in Charlotte in Mecklenburg County was held on May 31, 1775, and produced the Mecklenburg Resolves, which did not declare independence but ultimately a conditional loyalty to Britain. The Mecklenburg "Declaration of Independence" is generally regarded as a spurious document.

Further reading: Mortimer Adler, ed., *The Annals of America*, 18 vols. (Chicago: Encyclopaedia Britannica, 1968); Henry Steele Commager, ed., *Documents of American History*, 8th ed. (New York: Appleton-Century-Crofts, 1968); Charles W. Eliot, ed., *American Historical Documents, 1000–1904: With Introductions and Notes* (Danbury, Conn.: Grolier, 1980);

Charles W. Eliot, ed., *The Harvard Classics*, 51 vols. (New York: P. F. Collier 8 Son, 1937).

Medicare Catastrophe Coverage Act, U.S.
Major health care plan enacted by U.S. president Ronald Reagan on July 1, 1988, and effective on January 1, 1989. It greatly expanded Medicare (national health insurance for persons aged 65 and over, set up in 1965) in order to safeguard America's elderly against medical bankruptcy in case of catastrophic illness. Among its provisions were free, unlimited hospital care, after a Medicare recipient pays the first $564 annually, and free, unlimited, doctor care after he or she pays the first $1,400 annually. The plan also increased payments for nursing home care. Gradual increases in premiums were to defray the new costs of the plan. However, in 1989, Congress repealed the act because of much controversy and protest over the surtax that the elderly with incomes greater than $16,000 had to pay to finance the increased benefits.

Further reading: U.S. Department of Health and Human Services, *Guide to Health Insurance for People with Medicare, 1989* (Washington, D.C.: Government Printing Office, 1989).

Medicine Lodge, Treaty of
Agreement of October 1867 concluded at Medicine Lodge Creek, Kansas, between the U.S. government and a confederacy of Kiowa, Cheyenne, Comanche, Arapahoe, and Apache Indians; it ended long-standing hostilities over the encroachments of white settlers and displaced eastern Indians into the southwestern Indian Territory. Under terms of the Treaty of Medicine Lodge, the Kiowa and Comanche agreed to relinquish their claims to lands in the Texas Panhandle; they and the other Native American participants also agreed to remove to new reservations in Oklahoma. The continued resistance of some Kiowa culminated in the Red River Indian War of 1874–75, which ended when U.S. troops crushed the Indian forces.

Further reading: Raymond J. DeMallie and Lynn Kickingbird, *The Treaty of Medicine Lodge, 1867, Between the United States and the Kiowa, Comanche, and Apache Indians* (Washington, D.C.: Institute for the Development of Indian Law, 1976); Douglas C. Jones, *The Treaty of Medicine Lodge: The Story of the Great Treaty Council as Told by Eyewitnesses* (Norman: University of Oklahoma Press, 1966).

Medina, Constitution of
Islamic charter promulgated by the prophet Muhammad soon after his flight from Mecca to Medina (the Hegira) in September A.D. 622 (July 16, according to the Arabic date). Based on two mainly political pacts made between Muhammad and the Medinans, it established the *muhajirun* (Muslim refugees who followed Muhammad) as a clan alongside eight clans of Medina (named the *ansar*, helpers or converts); the nine clans together were said to constitute the first Muslim community or *ummah*. Muhammad had authority over one group, not the *ummah*; however, the charter stipulated that disagreements were to "be referred,

under God, to the Prophet," The Jews of Medina were to be free, equal, and protected, provided they formed a commonweal with the Muslims. But Muhammad soon expelled and killed the Jews for mockery of his warlike faith.

See also: KORAN.

Further reading: W. Montgomery Watt, *Islamic Political Thought* (Edinburgh, Scotland: Edinburgh University Press, 1998).

Meditations (Marcus Aurelius Antoninus to Himself)

Roman emperor Marcus Aurelius' private journal, written during the Roman defeat of the Marcomanni (Germanic tribe) in the Danube area (A.D. 170s). An intimate but fragmentary record (not intended for publication) of his observations on life around him, first published in 1558, it reveals the outpourings of a sensitive, serene, and cultured mind, steeped in the austere philosophy of Stoicism but indicative of its transitional phase. "Observe constantly that all things take place by change," he said, "and accustom thyself to consider that the nature of the Universe loves nothing so much as to change the things that are, and to make new things like them." Writing in Greek, Marcus Aurelius Antoninus, perhaps the Western world's only philosopher-king, subjects his every action to scrutiny and continually exhorts himself to higher, almost unattainable standards of conduct. Given the fleeting nature of our life on earth, he reasons that man should rise above the mere physical passions and draw on his inner resources to carry him through life. Consisting of 12 books, *Meditations* is a unique memoranda of moral advice and wisdom.

Further reading: Charles W. Eliot, ed., *The Harvard Classics*, 51 vols. (New York: P. F. Collier & Son, 1937); A. S. L. Farquharson et al., *The Meditations of Marcus Aurelius Antoninus* (Oxford: Oxford University Press, 1998); Pierre Hadot, *The Inner Citadel: The Meditations of Marcus Aurelius* (Cambridge, Mass.: Harvard University Press, 1998).

Meech Lake Accord

Controversial constitutional amendment signed by Canada's prime minister Brian Mulroney and the 10 provincial premiers at a government retreat at Meech Lake, north of Ottawa, on June 3, 1987. It would have transferred extensive new powers to all the provinces (concerning changes in federal institutions, the creation of new provinces, immigration, candidates for the Senate and Supreme Court, and acceptance of new national shared-cost programs). In an effort to win Quebec's support, the amendment designated it a "distinct society" within Canada with the right to assert its French-speaking culture (Quebec had refused to sign the CANADIAN CONSTITUTION ACT OF 1982, saying the act did not recognize the province's distinct character). To become part of the 1982 constitution, the Meech Lake Accord had to be ratified by the federal government and all the provincial legislatures by June 23, 1990. It failed because Newfoundland and Manitoba refused.

Further reading: Deborah M. R. Coyne, *Roll of the Dice: Working with Clyde Wells During the Meech Lake Negotiations* (Toronto: James Lorimer, 1992); C. E. S. Franks, *The Myths and Symbols of the Constitutional Debate in Canada* (Kingston, Canada: Institute of Intergovernmental Relations, Queen's University, 1993); Pierre E. Trudeau, *Pierre Trudeau Speaks Out on Meech Lake* (Toronto: General Paperbacks, 1990).

Megan's Law (Sex Offender Notification Bill)

Amendment to the Violent Crime and Law Enforcement Act of 1994 that was signed on May 17, 1996, by U.S. president Bill Clinton, requiring states to notify the public when convicted sex offenders (on parole or after serving time in prison) moved into their communities. It was modeled on a New Jersey state law passed after seven-year-old Megan Kanka was killed by her new neighbor, Jesse Timmendequas, a convicted sex offender. Her parents had lobbied extensively for the federal legislation, which was sponsored by Representative Dick Zimmer of New Jersey. The new law (Public Law 104–145) required the release of "relevant information" about such offenders, including their address. Failure to establish a system of notification by September 1997 could result in a loss of crime-fighting funds. It closed a loophole in the 1994 law, which had required registration and tracking of convicted sex offenders and notification of local law enforcement agencies and had allowed but not mandated notification of the public.

Further reading: W3 Lawyer, Inc., "Megan's Law," New Jersey Law Network, available online at http://www.njlawnet.com/index.html.

Mein Kampf (My Struggle)

Autobiographical work by Austrian-born, German Nazi leader Adolf Hitler, the first part of which was written in 1924, in the fortress of Landsberg am Lech, a Bavarian prison, and published in 1925; the second part was written after his release from prison, from 1925 to 1927, and published in 1928. Both parts were published by the Nazi publisher Max Amann; they contained Hitler's ideas on the creation of a nationalistic, Aryan state, which would be both self-sufficient and racially pure. In the work Hitler declared that the Aryan race was in fact the "chosen people," a people who were responsible for the advances in science and technology as well as the development of culture. He also argued that the Jews were involved in a conspiracy both to undermine the Aryans' superiority and to spoil their purity by interbreeding with them; he concluded that the only solution was to exclude them from the nationalist state. He also called for Germany's eastward expansion, for conquering the Slavs, for whom Hitler also had great contempt. He condemned France and Bolshevism, both of which, he wrote, were dominated by Jews; he called upon Germans to strive for economic self-sufficiency. The book became the bible of Nazism (National Socialism) and extremely popular, selling more than 5.2 million copies by 1939.

Further reading: Ted Daniels, *A Doomsday Reader: Prophets, Predictors, and Hucksters of Salvation* (New York: New York University Press, 1999); Adolf Hitler, *Mein Kampf*, trans. Ralph Manheim (Boston: Houghlin Mifflin, 1999); Mark A. Kishlansky, ed., *Sources of the West: Readings in Western Civilization*, vol. 2, 4th ed. (New York: Longman, 2001).

Melbourne's Six Acts   Legislation passed during 1835–41 in the second prime ministry of Lord Melbourne of Britain. The Municipal Corporations Reform Act of September 9, 1835, laid the foundation for representative local government in England and Wales, by entrusting elected borough councils with responsibility for local services. The electorate was considerably increased by allowing all householders (who had paid poor rates and lived in the property for at least three years) to vote. In 1836, the Corporation Reform Act was extended to cover Scotland. The New Marriage Law (Civil Marriage Act) of August 17, 1836, legalized marriages solemnized outside the Church of England, by a license from the registrar's office. The Tithe Commutation Act of August 13, 1836, was an attempt to revamp the finances and operations of the Church of England, by enabling tithe payments to be converted into regular rental charges. The POOR LAW OF 1838 revised and extended the provisions of England's POOR LAW OF 1834 to Ireland. The Municipal Corporations Act of 1840 dissolved 58 corporations in Ireland and reconstituted the remaining corporations with selective town councils. The Irish laws were introduced to appease Daniel O'Connell and his Nationalist Party, whose support had helped the Whigs come into power.

Further reading: Frank N. Magill, ed., *Great Events from History: Modern European Series*, 3 vols. (Englewood Cliffs, N.J.: Salem Press, 1973); L. G. Mitchell, *Lord Melbourne, 1779–1848* (New York: Oxford University Press, 1997).

Melfi, Constitutions of (Liber Augustalis)   Series of laws issued by Holy Roman Emperor Frederick II (also king of Sicily) for the kingdom of Sicily in August 1231. The constitutions are significant because, unlike other codes of law issued contemporaneously, Frederick rejected tradition and custom as bases for law and instead referred to Roman law for its basis. Among other things, the laws described the legal relationships between vassal and lord, the process of appointment to secular offices, and how law was to be administered.

See also: WORMS, EDICT OF (1231).

Further reading: Kenneth Pennington, *Popes, Canonists, and Texts, 1150–1550* (Brookfield, Vt.: Variorum, 1993); James M. Powell, trans., *The Liber Augustalis; or, Constitutions of Melfi, Promulgated by the Emperor Frederick II for the Kingdom of Sicily in 1231* (Syracuse, N.Y.: Syracuse University Press, 1971).

Memorial Ajustado   Document prepared by a special committee of 39 citizens, theologians, and jurists appointed by the Argentine government and published in Argentina in 1834 by the government's chief legal officer Pedro Agrelo, establishing guidelines on the Argentine state's relationship with the Roman Catholic Church. The document concluded that the state had the right to exercise its patronal rights (by which the state would assume ultimate control over the affairs of the church). This right most significantly included the right of the state to choose candidates to fill ecclesiastical offices. The document was intended to bring an end to years of dispute between church and state over the nature of national patronage in Argentina.

Further reading: Austen Ivereigh, *Catholicism and Politics in Argentina, 1810–1960* (New York: St. Martin's Press, 1995).

Merchant Marine Act (U.S. Ship Subsidy Act)   Federal U.S. legislation enacted on June 26, 1936, to provide direct subsidies to encourage development of the nation's merchant marine. It established the U.S. Maritime Commission, an independent regulatory agency authorized to offset the differences in construction and operating costs between U.S. and foreign ships. It continued a program of low-interest loans for some construction costs, while the subsidies replaced an earlier system of indirect support for the merchant marine. The act was designed to support domestic shipyards, ensure a supply of new ships, enable U.S. shippers to compete with foreign firms, and promote the national defense.

Further reading: *The Merchant Marine Act, 1936, the Maritime Security Act of 1996, the Shipping Act of 1984, and Related Acts* (Washington, D.C.: Government Printing Office, 1998).

Merchant Shipping Act of 1876, British   Important British parliamentary act of August 15, 1876, seeking to regulate the operations of merchant and passenger ships and improve the working conditions of merchant seamen. It was initiated and promoted by Samuel Plimsoll (1824–98), who secured its passage through Parliament. It authorized the Board of Trade to institute proceedings against those who endangered lives by sending unseaworthy ships to sea, and to temporarily detain defective ships for inspection and repairs in any British port. All vessels were to be fitted with emergency signals and lifeboats. More importantly, the act required that the load-line (Plimsoll line) be marked on the hull of every British merchant ship, showing the maximum safe submergence of a loaded ship allowed by law—a provision that helped save many lives.

Further reading: George H. Peters, *The Plimsoll Line: The Story of Samuel Plimsoll, Member of Parliament for Derby from 1868 to 1880* (Chichester, England: Rose, 1975).

Merryman, Ex Parte   Decision by Chief Justice Roger B. Taney, sitting as a federal circuit court judge in 1861, ruling that President Abraham Lincoln lacked the constitutional authority to suspend habeas corpus even in times of national emergency. The case concerned John Merryman, a Baltimore secessionist, who was imprisoned by military order at Fort McHenry. The commanding general refused to comply with a writ of habeas corpus issued by Taney, on the grounds that the president had suspended the writ. Taney's ruling, which was attacked in the North, stated that only Congress could suspend the writ in case of rebellion or invasion. Lincoln nonetheless continued the practice throughout the U.S. Civil War (1861–65).

Further reading: Henry Steele Commager, ed., *Documents of American History*, 8th ed. (New York: Appleton-Century-Crofts, 1968); Samuel Klaus, ed., *The Milligan Case* (Holmes Beach, Fla.: Gaunt, 1997); William H. Rehnquist, *Civil Liberty and the Civil War* (Washington, D.C.: National Legal Center for the Public Interest, 1996).

Mersen, Capitulary of

Capitulary or ordinance made by Emperor Charles the Bald (Charles II) in A.D. 847 at Mersen (Meerssen, Holland); it stated that every free man was obliged to choose a *seigneur* (lord), to accompany his lord in battle, and to remain with his lord for life. During his rule Charles was able to arrest neither the disintegration of his West Frankish (French) kingdom's territories into fragmentary fiefs nor the displacement of his imperial power into the hands of a number of wealthy landowners. By announcing this capitulary, Charles hoped to restore his subjects' respect as well as some degree of military authority over them; yet he managed only to increase the power of the seigneurs.

Further reading: Norton Downs, *Basic Documents in Medieval History* (New York: Van Nostrand Reinhold, 1959); Margaret Gibson and Janet L. Nelson, *Charles the Bald: Court and Kingdom* (Aldershot, England: Variorum, 1990); J. M. Wallace-Hadrill, *A Carolingian Renaissance Prince: The Emperor Charles the Bald* (London: British Academy, 1980).

Mersen, Treaty of

Partition treaty superseding the Treaty of VERDUN between Charles the Bald (Charles II) and his half-brother Louis the German; signed in A.D. 870 in Mersen (Meerssen, Holland). Following the death of their nephew Lothair II in A.D. 869, the treaty divided Lothair's kingdom between them. Charles was granted the lands roughly corresponding to modern Belgium, the Netherlands and Lorraine; Louis was awarded Alsace, and the left bank of the Lower Rhine. The border between the two kingdoms, marked approximately by the valleys of the Meuse and Moselle and by the Jura, permanently established a common boundary between the Teutonic and Romance races and languages.

Further reading: *The Barbarian Invasions of Western Europe: The Germanic Kingdoms Established in the Roman Empire* (Chicago: Rand McNally, 1994).

Message to [from] Garcia

Romantic legend, based loosely on an incident in the Spanish-American War (1898) and popularized in an essay entitled "A Message to Garcia" by Elbert Hubbard, published in the magazine *Philistine* in March 1899. The essay, which glorifies a persevering subordinate who unquestioningly carries out the orders of his superiors, concerned a fictional message from President William McKinley to be delivered to General Calixto García y Iñigues, a Cuban revolutionary whose whereabouts were unknown. In reality, Lieutenant A. S. Rowan met with García in Cuba in May 1898 and brought information *from* him to Washington, D.C.

Further reading: Mortimer Adler, ed., *The Annals of America*, 18 vols. (Chicago: Encyclopaedia Britannica, 1968).

Methuen Treaties

Two agreements between England and Portugal, negotiated in 1703 by John Methuen (England's envoy to Portugal) and the Portuguese Conde de Alegrete. The first (May 16), declared Portugal's support for the Anglo-Austrian Grand Alliance in the struggle of the Hapsburgs against the Bourbons for the Spanish throne. Portugal was to be used as a landing base for British troops during the War of the Spanish Succession (1701–14). The second (December 27), was a commercial treaty that had important consequences for both countries. Portugal agreed to lift her ban on English textiles; in return, England was to import port wine at a duty one-third of that levied on French wines. The agreement gave the Portuguese king the right to ban imports of British textiles if England reneged and lowered the duties on French wines. The treaty also opened the Brazilian markets to English trade until the reign of George III, when it was restricted to Portuguese companies only. In 1842, the treaty was repealed by another agreement.

Further reading: David D. Douglas et al., eds., *English Historical Documents*, 12 vols. (New York: Oxford University Press, 1950–77).

Metternich's Circular about Troppau

Circular or notice prepared by Austrian statesman Prince Clemens von Metternich and endorsed by representatives of Prussia and Russia on December 8, 1820, at a conference held in the Silesian town of Troppau (Opava). Metternich undertook to explain to the allied powers' diplomatic representatives at diplomatic posts abroad the decisions that had been made by the three powers (Austria, Prussia, and Russia) to suppress all revolutionary movements in the name of the alliance (see TROPPAU PROTOCOL). Metternich felt that Austria could not act against the revolution in Naples, which was part of the Austrian Empire, without the express support of Austria's allies. Great Britain, which had also been represented at the conference, protested against Metternich's Circular and the Troppau Protocol. Austria's intervention in Naples was successful in suppressing the revolution there.

Further reading: Milton Viorst, *The Great Documents of Western Civilization* (Philadelphia: Chilton Books, 1965).

Mexican Constitution of 1824

Constitution adopted by the newly elected Mexican Constitutional Congress on

October 4, 1824; it resembled that of the United States. The constitution provided that the Mexican nation would be divided into 19 states, each of which would elect its own governor and state legislature, and four territories, which would be governed by a national congress. The new government would be divided into independent executive, judicial, and legislative branches; and there would be a bicameral legislature. The Mexican Constitution differed from that of the United States in that the former declared Roman Catholicism the state religion; declared that the military and clergy remain exempt from having to stand trial in civil courts (see JUÁREZ LAW); and accorded that the president and vice president be elected by the state legislatures.

Further reading: Robert J. Knowlton, *The Early Influence of the United States Constitution in the Western Hemisphere: The Cases of the Mexican Constitution of 1824 and Bolivar's Ideas* (Milwaukee: University of Wisconsin–Milwaukee, Center for Latin America, 1987).

Mexican Constitution of 1857
Document adopted by Mexico's Constitutional Congress and promulgated on February 12, 1857 (but not effective until September 16 that year). It granted freedom of speech and of the press, abolished hereditary titles, and prohibited monopolies and the confiscation of property. Provision was also made for an elected judiciary, a unicameral congress (amended in 1874 to provide for a bicameral congress), indirect election of the president, and the abolition of military and ecclesiastical privileges. The constitution, embodying the earlier JUÁREZ LAW and LERDO LAW and representing the merging of liberalism and federalism in Mexico, was a significant step in liberating the common people from the dominance of the privileged classes. Although the church and other conservative elements sought to nullify it and the War of the Reform (1857–60) erupted, the constitution remained in effect (with frequent amendments) until 1917.

See also: IGLESIAS LAW.

Further reading: Hilarion N. Branch, *The Mexican Constitution of 1917 Compared with the Constitution of 1857* (Mexico City: American Chamber of Commerce of Mexico, 1927).

Mexican Constitution of 1917
Constitution drafted at a Constituent Congress (called by Mexico's president Venustiano Carranza) meeting in Querétaro on December 1, 1916, and promulgated on February 5, 1917. Although similar in many respects to the MEXICAN CONSTITUTION OF 1857, the new constitution contained several new and radical provisions. Among these were the following: the Roman Catholic Church was prohibited from holding property; ownership of the land and water was originally vested in the nation, which had the right to transmit ownership to private citizens; workers in industrial or commercial enterprises would have the right to share in the profits of those ventures and be allowed the right to strike; distribution of land among the landless

agricultural class would also occur. Although Carranza was unwilling to carry out this revolution-inspired program, General Alvaro Obregón began putting into effect some of the ideas of the constitution when he became president in 1920.

Further reading: Albert P. Blaustein and Jay A. Sigler, *Constitutions That Made History* (New York: Paragon House Publishers, 1988); Hilarion N. Branch, *The Mexican Constitution of 1917 Compared with the Constitution of 1857* (Mexico City: American Chamber of Commerce of Mexico, 1927); Alberto Trueba Urbina, *The Mexican Constitution of 1917 as Reflected in the Peace Treaty of Versailles of 1919* (New York: n.p. 1974).

Middle East Treaty Organization
See BAGHDAD PACT.

Mid-German Commercial Union
Document signed by the German states of Saxony, electoral Hesse, Hanover, Brunswick, most of the Thuringian states, Hamburg, Bremen, and Frankfurt on September 24, 1828, through which the contracting parties joined to form a customs union, the third major customs union among the German states. Through the document it was agreed that no contracting party was to enter into any other commercial union, nor to conclude separate customs treaties with any state outside the union, for a duration of six years; that transit dues on goods traded among member states were not to exceed those of Saxony. They also declared their commitment to the improvement of communication routes. The objective of the union was to prevent the extension of the Prusso-Darmstadt Customs Union (see PRUSSO-DARMSTADT CUSTOMS TREATY).

Further reading: Rolf H. Dumke, *German Economic Unification in the 19th Century: The Political Economy of the Zollverein* (Munich: Institut für Volkswirtschaftslehre, Unversität der Bundeswehr München, 1994); Rodney Leach, *Europe: A Concise Encyclopedia of the European Union from Aachen to Zollverein*, 3d ed. (Chicago: Fitzroy Dearborn, 2000).

Milan, Edict of
Declaration issued jointly by the Roman coemperors Constantine I the Great and Licinius in Milan, Italy, in early A.D. 313, confirming toleration of the Christians (see EDICT OF TOLERATION, GALERIUS'S). Constantine, master of the West by defeating Maxentius at the Milvian Bridge near Rome (A.D. 312), had converted to Christianity because he had vowed to do so if victorious. The edict proclaimed toleration of and equal rights for all religions and ordered all Christian property confiscated during recent persecutions to be returned. As is sometimes said, Christianity was not made the official religion of the Roman Empire; paganism was, however, degraded.

See also: NICENE CREED.

Further reading: William Bright, *A History of the Church from the Edict of Milan, A.D. 313, to the Council of Chalcedon, A.D. 451* (Oxford, England: J. H. & James Parker, 1979); Everett Ferguson, *Conversion, Catechumenate, and Baptism in the*

Early Church (New York: Garland, 1992); Frank N. Magill, ed., *Great Events from History: Ancient and Medieval Series*, 3 vols. (Englewood Cliffs, N.J.: Salem Press, 1972); Frank S. Mead, *The Ten Decisive Battles of Christianity* (Freeport, N.Y.: Books for Libraries Press, 1970).

Milan Decrees   Two decrees issued on November 23 and December 17, 1807, by French emperor Napoléon Bonaparte to counteract the British government's ORDERS IN COUNCIL OF 1807. They were mainly directed at neutral (American) shipping. The first, an amplification of the BERLIN DECREE and a renewal of the 1807 FONTAINEBLEAU DECREE, ordered confiscation of any ship (and its cargo) that had touched at British ports. Further, all goods had to bear certification proving that they had originated outside Britain and her colonies. The second decree declared as denationalized any neutral vessel responding to British naval orders. Such a vessel would be deemed British property, liable to seizure as a prize of war. Through these decrees Napoléon hoped to break Britain's stranglehold over American shipping and to intensify his blockade of British trade.

See also: BAYONNE DECREE, RAMBOUILLET DECREE.

Further reading: Henry Steele Commager, ed., *Documents of American History*, 8th ed. (New York: Appleton-Century-Crofts, 1968).

Military Selective Service Acts, U.S.   See SELECTIVE SERVICE ACT OF 1917, U.S.; SELECTIVE SERVICE ACT OF 1948, U.S.; SELECTIVE SERVICE ACT OF 1967, U.S.

Millenary Petition   Petition submitted to King James I of England in 1603 and signed by roughly 1,000 (actually 800) ministers of the established national church (hence its name "Millenary"); it called for minor reforms in certain ceremonies and practices of the church. It asked that the clergy be required to subscribe only to the THIRTY-NINE ARTICLES and not the *BOOK OF COMMON PRAYER*, that wearing of surplices be declared optional, that the sign of the cross in baptism, the ring in marriage, and the bowing at the name of Jesus be abolished. The ministers also wanted preaching to be encouraged, pluralism and nonresidence discouraged, and stressed that excommunication be reserved only for the most serious offenses and that it should never be pronounced by laymen. The king responded by convening a meeting of the Puritan ministers and the Anglican bishops in January 1604 (the Hampton Court Conference), where he rebuffed the Puritans.

Further reading: Lawrence A. Sasek, *Images of English Puritanism: A Collection of Contemporary Sources, 1589–1646* (Baton Rouge: Louisiana State University Press, 1989).

Miller v. California   U.S. Supreme Court decision issued on June 21, 1973, that redefined the legal standard for obscenity. Earlier Supreme Court decisions, notably *United*

States v. *One Book Entitled "Ulysses"* (1934) and *Roth* v. *United States* (1957), had defined obscene works as those which, taken as a whole, were intended to sexually arouse their audiences. In 1966 the Court modified this definition by its ruling in *Fanny Hill* v. *Massachusetts*, which declared that an obscene work must be "utterly without redeeming social value"; in other words, the inclusion of a small amount of nonobscene material was enough to render an otherwise obscene work legally acceptable. *Miller* v. *California* marked a return to the earlier definition; however, it offered two additional criteria. In order to be classified obscene, according to the ruling a work must meet three standards: The "average person" must agree that the work as a whole attempts to arouse sexual feelings in its audience, the work must depict or describe in a graphic and offensive manner a specific sexual act as defined by state law, and the work as a whole must lack redeeming social value. These three criteria, the so-called Miller test, remain the legal definition of obscenity in the United States today.

Further reading: Arthur L. Galub, *The Burger Court, 1968–1984* (Danbury, Conn.: Grolier Educational, 1995); Maureen Harrison and Steve Gilbert, *Obscenity and Pornography Decisions of the United States Supreme Court* (Carlsbad, Calif.: Excellent Books, 2000); Peter H. Irons, ed., *May It Please the Court: The First Amendment; Transcripts of the Oral Arguments Made Before the Supreme Court in Sixteen Key First Amendment Cases* (New York: New Press, 1997); Tony Mauro, *Illustrated Great Decisions of the Supreme Court* (Washington, D.C.: CQ Press, 2000).

Milligan, Ex Parte   U.S. Supreme Court ruling on April 3, 1866, that neither the president nor Congress had the power to order trials by military tribunals where civil courts were functioning. The case concerned Lambdin P. Milligan, a civilian charged with fomenting insurrection in 1864, who was tried, convicted, and sentenced to be hanged by a military commission established on the authority of President Abraham Lincoln. The Court ruled unanimously that the president had no power to institute military commissions in areas not in rebellion and where the civil courts were open. A majority opinion denied Congress this power as well. The ruling raised doubts about the constitutionality of congressional reconstruction.

Further reading: Mortimer Adler, ed., *The Annals of America*, 18 vols. (Chicago: Encyclopaedia Britannica, 1968); Henry Steele Commager, ed., *Documents of American History*, 8th ed. (New York: Appleton-Century-Crofts, 1968); Kermit L. Hall, et al., eds., *The Oxford Companion to the Supreme Court of the United States* (New York: Oxford University Press, 1992); Samuel Klaus, ed., *The Milligan Case* (Holmes Beach, Fla.: Gaunt, 1997).

Milner-Scialoja Agreement   See ANGLO-ITALIAN AGREEMENT OF 1925.

Minsk Agreement (Commonwealth Pact) Historic accord (December 8, 1991) among Russia, Ukraine, and Belarus dissolving the Soviet Union and replacing it with a Commonwealth of Independent States (CIS), to be headquartered in Minsk (the capital of Belarus). The pact would retain all the structures of the former Soviet Union and honor its existing international agreements. Soviet national laws, however, would not be applicable. CIS members would work together on radical reforms to create market economies, with the Soviet ruble as the common currency. Also, the military (including nuclear arsenals) would be subject to a common command, with a declared aim toward nuclear disarmament. CIS members would remain neutral and respect one another's sovereignty. Soviet president Mikhail S. Gorbachev denounced the pact. Its proposals were reiterated in the ALMA-ATA DECLARATION and later in the RUSSIAN CONSTITUTION OF 1993.

Further reading: *The Europa World Yearbook 1999* (London: Europa Publications, 1999).

Mint Act, U.S. See COINAGE ACT OF 1792, U.S.

Miranda v. Arizona Landmark U.S. Supreme Court decision issued on June 13, 1966, that extended federal constitutional protections to defendants in state criminal trials. The decision reversed the conviction of accused rapist Ernesto Miranda, who had been questioned by law enforcement officers without being advised of his rights. Citing FIFTH AMENDMENT protection against self-incrimination and SIXTH AMENDMENT right to counsel, the Supreme Court, in a 5–4 decision, ruled that as soon as a suspect is seized by police, he must be told that he has the right to remain silent, that anything he says can and will be used against him in court, that he has the right to consult with an attorney before questioning and to have counsel present during questioning, and, if he is indigent, an attorney will be appointed for him.

See also: *ESCOBEDO* V. *ILLINOIS*.

Further reading: Mortimer Adler, ed., *The Annals of America*, 18 vols. (Chicago: Encyclopaedia Britannica, 1968); Kermit L. Hall et al., eds, *American Legal History: Cases and Materials*, 2d ed. (New York: Oxford University Press, 1996); Kermit L. Hall et al., eds., *The Oxford Companion to the Supreme Court of the United States* (New York: Oxford University Press, 1992); United States Supreme Court, *United States Reports: Cases Adjudged in the Supreme Court at . . . and Rules Announced at . . .* (New York: Banks & Brothers, Law Publishers, 1884–1921; Washington, D.C.: Government Printing Office, 1922–).

Mirari Vos Pope Gregory XVI's reactionary encyclical of August 15, 1832, condemning liberalism and the liberal position of French abbé Félicité de Lamennais without actually mentioning him or his writings. The pope criticized those for whom the sanctity of mysteries and of divine worship had become "an object of censure, profanation, and sacrilegious derision." He lamented the fact that the Roman Catholic Church's divine authority was under attack, "submitted to the contempt of nations and reduced to a shameful servitude," and that the academies and universities had publicly mounted "a horrible and impious war" against the Catholic faith. Heresy and sects, he declared, had emptied into "an ever-approaching revolutionary-abyss of bottomless miseries . . . all that their bosom holds of license, sacrilege and blasphemy." Lamennais responded with *Paroles d'un Croyant* (1834), prompting Pope Gregory to issue another encyclical, *Singulari Nos*, on June 25, 1834.

See also: SYLLABUS OF ERRORS.

Further reading: Claudia Carlen, comp., *The Papal Encyclicals* (Wilmington, N.C.: McGrath Publishing, 1981); Catholic University of America, eds., *New Catholic Encyclopedia* (New York: McGraw-Hill, 1967); Anne Fremantle, *The Papal Encyclicals in Their Historical Context* (New York: Mentor-Omega Books, 1963); Anthony J. Mioni, ed., *Popes Against Modern Errors: 16 Papal Documents* (Rockford, Ill.: Tan Books, 1999).

Misenum, Treaty of Roman pact made among Octavian (Augustus), Sextus Pompey (Pompey the Younger), and Marc Antony at Misenum (Miseno, Italy) in 39 B.C. Sextus, a pirate fleet commander who held Sicily, had wrested Sardinia from Octavian's control and stopped grain-laden ships from reaching Rome, where famine broke out. By the treaty's terms (which were never fully effected), Sextus was to rule Sicily, Sardinia, and Archaea (a region in the northern Peloponnesus) for five years, while agreeing to end his piracy and to carry grain to Rome. Sextus was also to be consul and augur and to have a monetary reward for his late father's (Pompey the Great) property in Rome. Octavian accused Sextus, a supporter of Antony, of breaking the pact, and war again erupted.

See also: BRUNDISIUM, TREATY OF.

Further reading: Moses Hadas, *Sextus Pompey* (New York: AMS Press, 1966).

Mise of Amiens See AMIENS, MISE OF.

Mise of Lewes See LEWES, MISE OF.

Mississippi v. Johnson Suit filed on April 5, 1867, by the state of Mississippi asking the U.S. Supreme Court to enjoin President Andrew Johnson from enforcing the RECONSTRUCTION ACTS of 1867 passed by the Radical Republican Congress. Though Johnson had opposed the acts as unconstitutional, and Congress had passed them over his veto, he nonetheless ordered the U.S. attorney general to fight the Mississippi suit. The Court unanimously denied the petition for lack of jurisdiction, stating that purely executive or purely legislative acts were not subject to judicial restraint.

Further reading: Henry Steele Commager, ed., *Documents of American History*, 8th ed. (New York: Appleton-Century-Crofts, 1968); Robert Fridington, *The Reconstruction Court, 1864–1888* (Danbury, Conn.: Grolier Educational, 1995); Kermit L. Hall et al., eds., *The Oxford Companion to the Supreme Court of the United States* (New York: Oxford University Press, 1992).

Missouri Compromise

Compromise legislation enacted by the U.S. Congress on March 3, 1820, that admitted Maine to the Union as a free state (in 1820) and authorized Missouri to adopt a constitution with no restrictions on slavery. Missouri (acquired through the Louisiana Purchase) was admitted as a slaveholding state in 1821. The compromise prohibited slavery in the remaining territory of the Louisiana Purchase north of 36° 30'. The measure, engineered by House Speaker Henry Clay, was designed to maintain the political balance between free and slave states, which were equal in number in 1819. The compromise marked the beginning of the great national debate over slavery; it postponed but failed to resolve the issue. It was repealed in 1854 by the KANSAS-NEBRASKA ACT.

Further reading: Mortimer Adler, ed., *The Annals of America*, 18 vols. (Chicago: Encyclopaedia Britannica, 1968); Henry Steele Commager, ed., *Documents of American History*, 8th ed. (New York: Appleton-Century-Crofts, 1968); Don E. Fehrenbacher, *Sectional Crisis and Southern Constitutionalism* (Baton Rouge: Louisiana State University Press, 1995; Paul Finkelman, *Dred Scott v. Sandford: A Brief History with Documents* (Boston: Bedford Books, 1997).

Missouri v. Holland

U.S. Supreme Court decision issued on April 19, 1920, upholding the constitutionality of the Migratory Bird Treaty Act (1918) between the United States and Canada and, more broadly, establishing that a treaty could confer powers on Congress that it did not otherwise have under the U.S. CONSTITUTION. The case arose when the state of Missouri attempted to prevent a U.S. game warden from enforcing the treaty act, claiming that the act violated the rights reserved to the states under the TENTH AMENDMENT. In its seven-to-two decision, the Supreme Court upheld the treaty on the grounds that it did not contravene any express constitutional prohibitions and that a treaty may override a state's power. The treaty-making power is not limited by any "invisible radiation" from the terms of the Tenth Amendment, said the Court.

Further reading: Henry Steele Commager, ed., *Documents of American History*, 8th ed. (New York: Appleton-Century-Crofts, 1968); David S. Favre, *Wildlife Law*, 2d ed. (Detroit: Lupus Publications, 1991); Kermit L. Hall et al., eds., *The Oxford Companion to the Supreme Court of the United States* (New York: Oxford University Press, 1992); *United States Supreme Court, United States Reports: Cases Adjudged in the Supreme Court at . . . and Rules Announced at . . .* (New York:

Banks & Brothers, Law Publishers, 1884–1921; Washington, D.C.: Government Printing Office, 1922–).

Molasses Act

Measure enacted by the British Parliament on May 17, 1733, with the aim of protecting sugar planters in the British West Indies from their counterparts in the French and Spanish West Indies. One of the laws known as the Acts of Trade and Navigation, the Molasses Act levied high and prohibitive duties (taxes) on rum, molasses, and sugar imported into the 13 American colonies from non-British-owned islands in the Caribbean area. Parliament hoped to give the British West Indian colonies a trade monopoly, but the North Americans resented it and evaded the act through widespread smuggling. The measure was replaced by the SUGAR ACT OF 1764, which was enforced more successfully.

See also: IRON ACT.

Further reading: Mortimer Adler, ed., *The Annals of America*, 18 vols. (Chicago: Encyclopaedia Britannica, 1968); Henry Steele Commager, ed., *Documents of American History*, 8th ed. (New York: Appleton-Century-Crofts, 1968); David D. Douglas, et al., eds., *English Historical Documents*, 12 vols. (New York: Oxford University Press, 1950–77); William MacDonald, ed., *Select Charters and Other Documents Illustrative of American History, 1606–1775* (New York: Macmillan, 1899).

Molotov-Ribbentrop Pact (Hitler-Stalin Pact, Soviet-German Non-Aggression Treaty of 1939, Nazi-Soviet Pact)

Pact concluded in Moscow on August 23, 1939, by Nazi Germany and the Soviet Union, providing for neutrality and nonaggression between them during both war and peace. Specifically, each party pledged not to attack the other, to remain neutral if either party to the pact were attacked by a third party, and not to join any coalition of powers that did not support the other. In a secret protocol to the pact the two powers agreed upon the division of spheres of interest in the event of a "territorial and political transformation" in the Baltic region (Estonia, Latvia, and Lithuania) and Poland, such that Russia's sphere of interest would constitute all territory roughly to the east of the Narew, Vistula, and San Rivers, while Germany's sphere would constitute all territory roughly to the west of that line. The pact was of the utmost importance to Germany because, confident of Soviet neutrality, she could initiate her eastward expansion, with war threatening her only on her western border. Germany invaded Poland on September 1, 1939.

Further reading: Frank N. Magill, ed., *Great Events from History: Modern European Series*, 3 vols. (Englewood Cliffs, N.J.: Salem Press, 1973); Graham Smith, *The Baltic States: The National Self-determination of Estonia, Latvia, and Lithuania* (New York: St. Martin's Press, 1994); I. Joseph Vizulis, *The Molotov-Ribbentrop Pact of 1939: The Baltic Case* (New York: Praeger, 1990).

Monroe Doctrine   Principles of U.S. foreign policy stated in a message to Congress by President James Monroe on December 2, 1823; they declared U.S. opposition to any further colonization of the Americas by European powers and any European intervention in political affairs of the Western Hemisphere, as well as a U.S. policy of noninterference in existing colonies or in European affairs. The doctrine was prompted by U.S. concern with Russian expansion along the northwest coast of North America and fear that some European powers would seek to reassert colonial control in newly independent Latin American republics. It was modified in 1904 by the ROOSEVELT COROLLARY. Of little importance until the mid-19th century, the doctrine was used to justify U.S. actions in the Cuban missile crisis of 1963 and in the Dominican Republic revolution of 1965.

Further reading: Mortimer Adler, ed., *The Annals of America*, 18 vols. (Chicago: Encyclopaedia Britannica, 1968); *American Jurisprudence, Second Edition*, Desk Book (N.p.: West Group, 1998); Henry Steele Commager, ed., *Documents of American History*, 8th ed. (New York: Appleton-Century-Crofts, 1968); Charles W. Eliot, ed., *The Harvard Classics*, 51 vols. (New York: P. F. Collier & Son, 1937).

Monsieur, Peace of (Paix de Monsieur, Peace of Chastenoy, Treaty of Etigny)   Settlement between Huguenots (French Protestants) and Catholics signed at Chastenoy or Etigny by Monsieur (Francis, duke of Alençon, the king's eldest brother) on May 6, 1576, and promulgated by the Edict of BEAULIEU; it followed the defeat of King Henry III's forces by the Huguenots in the Fifth War of Religion (1575–76). Forced to sign this humiliating treaty at Queen Mother Catherine de Médicis's bidding, Henry III conceded to his brother Monsieur the provinces of Anjou, Touraine, and Berry and an annual pension of 400,000 gold crowns. The Huguenots were granted freedom of worship throughout France except in Paris, given eight cities in which they were to have full political and military control, and made eligible for all public offices. Huguenot leaders were rewarded: Henry I of Condé with the governorship of Picardy and Henry of Navarre with Guienne, among others; charges against Gaspard of Coligny, Gabriel Montgomery, and other principal Huguenots were dropped. But Duke Henry of Guise, desirous of the throne, rejected the terms (which were never carried out) and formed the Catholic Holy League against the Huguenots; the Sixth War of Religion (1576–77) began.

See also: BERGERAC, TREATY OF.

Further reading: Mack P. Holt, *The French Wars of Religion, 1562–1629* (New York: Cambridge University Press, 1999); David Potter, *The French Wars of Religion: Selected Documents* (London: Macmillan, 1997).

Monster Petition   See CHARTIST PETITION OF 1848.

Montcrieff Commission Report   See SCOTT-MONTCRIEFF COMMISSION REPORT.

Montgomerie Charter   Colonial charter of government granted by Governor John Montgomerie (Montgomery) to the city of New York in 1731. It expanded the city's governing powers. The early municipal government empowered by this charter was similar to that of many boroughs (self-governing, incorporated towns) in Britain at the time. New York City's mayor remained an appointed and unsalaried official; the city, however, in addition to gaining some judicial powers, was given control over the establishment of ferries and docks and the construction of public buildings. The charter was in force until 1830.

See also: DONGAN CHARTER.

Further reading: William L. Andrews, *The Bradford Map: The City of New York at the Time of the Granting of the Montgomerie Charter, a Description Thereof* (New York: De Vinne Press, 1893).

Montreal, Treaty of   General peace settlement with the French and the English, ratified by the Iroquois in 1701, that established Iroquois neutrality in conflicts between the English and French. The Five Nation's Iroquois Confederacy (comprising the Mohawk, Oneida, Onondaga, Cayuga, and Seneca) had fought a series of wars with neighboring Indian tribes throughout the 17th century in an effort to guarantee their access to furs, which they traded for metal tools and weapons with the Dutch and English in New York. These wars frequently brought the Iroquois into conflict with the French as well, since the latter were allied with many Iroquois enemies. For the most part official Iroquois neutrality was maintained after 1701.

Further reading: Gilles Havard et al., *The Great Peace of Montreal of 1701: French-Native Diplomacy in the Seventeenth Century* (Montreal: McGill-Queen's University Press, 2001).

Montreal Protocol of 1987   Protocol signed on September 16, 1987, in Montreal by representatives of 24 nations, including Canada, the United States, Japan, and the members of the European Economic Community, calling for a reduction in the production of chlorofluorocarbons (CFCs), chemicals known to destroy the protective ozone layer of the atmosphere. Dependence on CFCs had been widespread; they were used in the production of such common substances as refrigerants, aerosol propellants, and foam insulation. Under the terms of the agreement, production of CFCs was to be frozen in 1990 at their 1986 levels, and production was to be cut by 50 percent by 1999. The international meeting had been sponsored by the United Nations Environment Program.

Further reading: *Handbook for the International Treaties for the Protection of the Ozone Layer: The Vienna Convention (1985); the Montreal Protocol (1987)* (Nairobi, Kenya: Ozone Secretariat, United Nations Environment Programme, 2000).

Montreaux, Treaty of (1936) (Montreaux Straits Convention) Treaty concluded on July 20, 1936, in Montreaux, Switzerland, by Australia, Bulgaria, France, Germany, Great Britain, Greece, Japan, Romania, Turkey, the Soviet Union, and Yugoslavia, returning control of the straits of the Dardanelles and the Bosporus to Turkey. The agreement placed restrictions on the passage of other countries' vessels (excepting those countries with access to the Black Sea via rivers) through the straits; and, in time of war, provided Turkey with the right to permit or refuse passage of warships through the straits. The agreement also granted Turkey the legal right to fortify the straits. The agreement had been concluded in response to Turkey's claim that the Treaty of Lausanne of 1922–23, which allowed for passage of all warships through the straits, could no longer guarantee her security, given that the political climate was then becoming increasingly unstable.

See also: STRAITS CONVENTION.

Further reading: Helen P. Kirkpatrick, *The Montreaux Straits Convention* (Geneva: Geneva Research Center, 1936).

Morey Letter Forged letter first published in the *New York Truth* on October 20, 1880, attempting to damage the U.S. presidential campaign of Republican candidate James A. Garfield. It was allegedly written by Garfield to one "H. L. Morey" of the Employer's Union of Lynn, Massachusetts. According to the letter, Garfield had announced his support of "Chinese cheap labor," a heated issue on the West Coast, where white laborers increasingly agitated for the exclusion of competing Chinese labor. Though the letter was denounced immediately as a fabrication, and the Republican Party platform called for the limitation of Chinese labor, the mere charge that Garfield would support free immigration may have cost him California's electoral votes. He nonetheless won the election.

Further reading: John I. Davenport, *History of the Forged "Morey Letter": A Narrative of the Discovered Facts, Respecting This Great Political Forgery* (New York: J. I. Davenport, 1884).

Mormon, Book of Book of scripture in the Church of Jesus Christ of Latter-day Saints; first published in 1830 in Palmyra, New York. According to Mormon belief, the angel Moroni revealed the book, inscribed on golden tablets, to Joseph Smith, who translated it and founded the church. The *Book of Mormon,* which along with the Bible provides the foundation for the Mormon faith, recounts the history of Hebrews who left Jerusalem about 600 B.C. and migrated to America. They eventually split into two groups: the civilized Nephites, to whom Jesus is said to have appeared after his Resurrection and taught the gospel contained in the *Book of Mormon,* and the savage Lamanites, who destroyed the Nephites and were the ancestors of the American Indians.

Further reading: *The Book of Mormon: Another Testament of Jesus Christ* (Salt Lake City, Utah: Church of Jesus Christ of Latter-day Saints, 1981); Royal Skousen, ed., *The Original Manuscript of the Book of Mormon: Typographical Facsimile of the Extant Text* (Provo, Utah: Foundation for Ancient Research and Mormon Studies, Brigham Young University, 2001).

Morrill Act Federal U.S. legislation passed on July 2, 1862, establishing land-grant colleges through the sale of public lands. Sponsored by Vermont representative Justin S. Morrill, the bill gave to the states federal lands for the establishment of colleges offering programs in agriculture, mechanical sciences, and military science, as well as other scientific and classical subjects. Generally considered one of the most important pieces of educational legislation ever passed, the act spurred the development of state universities, made the federal government an important force in higher education, and helped democratize that education. Each state was granted 30,000 acres for each senator and representative in the U.S. Congress.

Further reading: Henry Steele Commager, ed., *Documents of American History*, 8th ed. (New York: Appleton-Century-Crofts, 1968); Edmund J. James, *The Origin of the Land Grant Act of 1862: The So-called Morrill Act and Some Account of Its Author, Jonathan B. Turner* (Urbana-Champaign, Ill.: University Press, 1984); Allan Nevins, *The Origins of the Land-Grant Colleges and State Universities: A Brief Account of the Morrill Act of 1862 and Its Results* (Washington, D.C.: Civil War Centennial Commission, 1962).

Morrill Tariff Act Protective tariff sponsored by Republican representative Justin S. Morrill of Vermont, which became law on March 2, 1861. The bill had been designed to gain support for the Republican presidential candidate Abraham Lincoln in key industrial states by raising import duties on items such as wool and iron. It substituted specific for ad valorem duties and raised rates overall, from 5 percent to 10 percent. The U.S. House of Representatives passed the bill in May 1860, but the Senate did not approve it until February 1861, after secession had removed many antiprotectionist Southern senators. Subsequent tariffs raised rates much higher.

Further reading: Coy F. Cross II, *Justin Smith Morrill: Father of the Land-Grant Colleges* (East Lansing: Michigan State University Press, 1999).

Morrison v. Olson Important U.S. Supreme Court decision on June 29, 1988, upholding the authority of Congress to investigate alleged criminal actions by certain persons in the executive branch of government. By the Ethics in Government Act, passed by Congress in 1978, a special prosecutor was allowed to be named to investigate alleged criminal illegalities committed by particular high government officials. In the case, Congress claimed to have received false and misleading testimony from some officials of the Justice

Department (part of the executive branch) and hoped a special prosecutor would look into the matter and gain withheld information, too. The Justice Department argued vainly that Congress had assumed authority that properly belonged to the executive branch, citing that the U.S. CONSTITUTION, through the constitutional separation of powers, barred the three branches of government (executive, legislative, and judicial) against ever controlling each other.

Further reading: Kermit L. Hall et al., eds., *The Oxford Companion to the Supreme Court of the United States* (New York: Oxford University Press, 1992); United States Supreme Court, *United States Reports: Cases Adjudged in the Supreme Court at . . . and Rules Announced at . . .* (New York: Banks & Brothers, Law Publishers, 1884–1921; Washington, D.C.: Government Printing Office, 1922–).

Mortefontaine, Treaty of   See FRANCO-AMERICAN CONVENTION OF 1800.

Mortmain, Statute of (Statute de Viris Religiosis)

Legislation of November 14, 1279, by King Edward I of England, prohibiting the purchase, sale, or receipt of lands or tenements liable to come "in any way into mortmain" (dead hand), except with license from the crown. The statute was actually intended to prevent the church—which was a dead hand, since it did not marry, die, or pay succession dues, or perform all the feudal services expected of lay tenants—from acquiring more property. It authorized those "so alienated to enter it within a year from the time of such alienation and hold it in fee and heritably." If such a holder failed to pay the fee within the year, the lord above him in the feudal hierarchy was entitled to gain possession. Violation of the statute led to forfeiture and the enfeoffment (investment) of the land by the crown. In reality, the crown freely gave or sold licenses transferring land to the church.

See also: WESTMINSTER, STATUTES OF.

Further reading: Norman Downs, *Basic Documents in Medieval History* (New York: Van Nostrand Reinhold, 1959).

Mosaic Law   See TEN COMMANDMENTS, THE.

Moscow, Treaty of (1920)

Treaty concluded in Moscow on July 12, 1920, by Soviet Russia and the Baltic state of Lithuania, bringing an end to more than two years of hostilities between the two, which had commenced after Soviet Russia's involuntary renunciation of the province through the Treaty of BREST-LITOVSK. The treaty provided for Soviet Russia's de jure recognition of the independent Lithuanian state; for Lithuania's possession of Vilna (Vilnius); for the establishment of the new Soviet-Lithuanian frontier; for the amnesty of prisoners of war; for Soviet Russia's payment of 3 million rubles to Lithuania; and for the establishment of diplomatic and commercial relations between the two. Despite major Soviet advances into Lithuania, the Soviets had been eager to conclude peace with Lithuanians because they were at the same time at war with Poland, immediately to Lithuania's west.

See also: RIGA, TREATY OF (1920); TARTU, TREATY OF.

Further reading: Bronis J. Kaslas, *The USSR-German Aggression Against Lithuania* (New York: R. Speller, 1973).

Moscow, Treaty of (1921)

Agreement concluded on March 16, 1921, in Moscow between Soviet Russia and Turkey's new nationalist government, settling border disputes and establishing amity between them. The city of Batum (Batumi) on the Black Sea was returned to Russia, while Kars and Ardahan went to Turkey (formerly the Ottoman Empire). Also, the Soviets recognized the Turkish nationalist government under the leadership of Mustafa Kemal (later Kemal Atatürk) and, shortly, provided arms and ammunition to the Turkish nationalists to help maintain their power at home and abroad.

See also: ALEXANDROPOL, TREATY OF; BATUM, TREATY OF; KARS, TREATY OF.

Further reading: Bulent Gokay, *A Clash of Empires: Turkey Between Russian Bolshevism and British Imperialism, 1918–1923* (New York: Tauris Academic Studies, 1997).

Moscow, Treaty of (Soviet-Japanese Non-Aggression Pact of 1941)

Pact signed in Moscow on April 13, 1941, by Foreign Minister Matsuoka Yosuke and Ambassador Tatekawa Yoshitsuou to the Soviet Union (both representing Japan) and Premier Vyacheslav M. Molotov of the Soviet Union, providing for peace and neutrality between the two countries. Through the document, each party pledged to strive to maintain peace between them, to respect the other's territorial integrity and inviolability, and to maintain neutrality in the event that one party were to become involved in a war with a third power or powers. Accompanying the pact was a joint declaration, the Frontier Declaration, through which Japan agreed to respect the territorial integrity and inviolability of the Outer Mongolian People's Republic, dominated by Moscow; the Soviet Union likewise agreed to respect the same of Japan's puppet-state of Manchukuo (Manchuria and Jehol province in China). The document was to become effective upon ratification, which was to occur as soon as possible, and was to remain in force for five years. The treaty was a diplomatic success for Moscow because, while the Soviet Union gained the assurance of Japanese neutrality in the event of a German attack, she remained free to support Nationalist China in the Sino-Japanese War of 1937–45.

Further reading: Jonathan Haslam, *The Soviet Union and the Threat from the East, 1933–41: Moscow, Tokyo, and the Prelude of the Pacific War* (Pittsburgh, Pa.: University of Pittsburgh Press, 1992).

Moscow, Treaty of (Strategic Offensive Reductions Treaty)

Agreement reducing by two-thirds the nuclear arsenals of the United States and Russia. The treaty was signed by U.S. president George W. Bush and Russian president Vladimir Putin on May 24, 2002, in Moscow. It mandated that each nation reduce its deployed strategic nuclear weapons from about 6,000, the number owned by each side in 2002, to no more than 2,200 by December 31, 2012. The treaty left it up to each country to determine which weapons to take out of service and how best to dispose of them, allowing for them to be either destroyed or stored. The treaty was one of several documents signed during a three-day summit meeting in Moscow and St. Petersburg that heralded the indisputable end of the cold war. These documents acknowledged an informal alliance between the United States and Russia and noted the willingness of the two nations to work together to find solutions to other problems of mutual interest.

Further reading: "Text of Strategic Offensive Reductions Treaty," The White House, available online at http://www.whitehouse.gov.news/releases/2002/05/20020524-3.html; "The Treaty of Moscow," NTI: Issues & Analysis, available online at http://www.nti.org/e_research/e3_14a.html.

Moscow Conference Declarations of 1943

Declarations made by the governments of the United States, Great Britain, China, and the Soviet Union at the conclusion of the Moscow Conference (October 19–November 1, 1943) during World War II (1939–45). Fu Ping-chang of China signed the first statement, called the Declaration of the Four States on the Question of General Security; the other signatories were Cordell Hull (United States), Anthony Eden (Britain), and Vyacheslav M. Molotov (Soviet Union). They pledged to continue the war against their respective Axis enemies, to establish an international organization to maintain peace and security, and to cooperate with one another to bring about an agreement to control armaments in the postwar period. A declaration regarding Italy stated that "Fascism and all its evil influences and emanations shall be utterly destroyed" and that the Italian people will have every opportunity to establish a democratic government. A declaration on Austria stated that she be liberated from German domination and reestablished as free and independent.

Further reading: William Arnold-Foster, *Charters of the Peace: A Commentary on the Atlantic Charter and the Declaration of Moscow, Cairo and Teheran* (London: V. Gollancz, 1944); Hugh M. Clokie, *Moscow Conference* (Toronto: Canadian Association for Adult Education and the Canadian Institute of International Affairs, 1943); Henry Steele Commager, ed., *Documents of American History*, 8th ed. (New York: Appleton-Century-Crofts, 1968); Keith Sainsbury, *The Turning Point: Roosevelt, Stalin, Churchill, and Chiang Kai-Shek, 1943: The Moscow, Cairo, and Teheran Conferences* (New York: Oxford University Press, 1986).

Moss, Convention of

Agreement concluded by Sweden and Norway in the Norwegian town of Moss on August 16, 1814, by which Norway renounced her ties to Denmark and took her first steps toward union with Sweden. Through the convention, it was agreed that King Charles XIII of Sweden would assume the title of king of Norway, thus filling the position already vacated by Danish prince Charles Frederick, and that the Swedes would recognize the Norwegians' May Constitution of 1814, which, among other things, denied the king absolute power. The subsequent union between the two states was thus to be based not upon Denmark's cession of Norway as agreed upon in the 1814 Treaty of KIEL but on the two states' acceptance of a common crown.

See also: UNION, ACT OF (UNION OF SWEDEN AND NORWAY).

Further reading: T. K. Derry, *A History of Scandanavia: Norway, Sweden, Denmark, Finland, and Iceland* (Minneapolis: University of Minnesota Press, 1979).

Moynihan's Memorandum for President Nixon

Memorandum on blacks in the United States, written by White House urban-affairs expert Daniel P. Moynihan for President Richard M. Nixon, on January 16, 1970. Moynihan stated that "the time may have come when the issue of race could benefit from a period of benign neglect. The subject has been too much taken over by hysterics, paranoids and boodlers on all sides." He argued that the administration should pay close attention to progress for blacks and should avoid giving either black or white extremists "opportunity for martyrdom, heroics, histrionics or whatever." When the memo was leaked to the press on February 28, 1970, it created a national furor among blacks and white liberals. The phrase "benign neglect" was widely interpreted as an appeal for white racist support.

Further reading: Robert A. Katzmann, *Daniel Patrick Moynihan: The Intellectual in Public Life* (Washington, D.C.: Woodrow Wilson Center Press, 1998).

Mudros, Armistice of

Terms for peace concluded between Great Britain and the Ottoman Empire (Turkey) on October 31, 1918, at Mudros (on the Aegean island of Lemnos), following the latter's defeat in the battle of Megiddo (1918). Acting on behalf of the Allies, Britain forced the Ottomans to cede Hejaz, Yemen, Syria, Mesopotamia, Tripolitania, and Cyrenaica, and also their ports, railways, and natural resources. They were to release Allied prisoners and disband their army. The Allies secured the straits of Dardanelles and Bosporus, Batum, the Taurus tunnel system, and the right to seize, if circumstances warranted, the six Armenian provinces in Anatolia or any strategic region.

See also: ANGLO-FRENCH-RUSSIAN AGREEMENT ABOUT ASIATIC TURKEY; SÈVRES, TREATY OF.

Further reading: Briton C. Busch, *Mudros to Lausanne: Britain's Frontier in West Asia, 1918–1923* (Albany: State University of New York Press, 1976); Roderic H. Davison, *Essays in Ottoman and Turkish History, 1774–1923: The Impact of the West* (Austin: University of Texas Press, 1990).

Muller v. Oregon   U.S. Supreme Court decision of February 24, 1908, upholding a 1903 Oregon law limiting the maximum hours women could work in any factory or laundry to 10 hours a day. The Court denied a claim that the law violated the liberty of contract rights under the FOURTEENTH AMENDMENT. Attorney Louis Brandeis, representing the state of Oregon, submitted an extensive brief consisting of historical, medical, psychological, and statistical information to support his legal arguments. In upholding the state's law, the Court not only ruled that a state could use its police powers in this area, but also set a precedent for considering nonlegal evidence.

Further reading: Henry Steele Commager, ed., *Documents of American History*, 8th ed. (New York: Appleton-Century-Crofts, 1968); Kermit L. Hall et al., eds, *American Legal History: Cases and Materials*, 2d ed. (New York: Oxford University Press, 1996); Kermit L. Hall et al., eds., *The Oxford Companion to the Supreme Court of the United States* (New York: Oxford University Press, 1992); United States Supreme Court, *United States Reports: Cases Adjudged in the Supreme Court at . . . and Rules Announced at . . .* (New York: Banks & Brothers, Law Publishers, 1884–1921; Washington, D.C.: Government Printing Office, 1922–).

Mulligan Letters   Letters written by James G. Blaine, Republican representative from Maine and sometime speaker of the House, to Warren Fisher, Jr., a Boston businessman, between 1864 and 1876; they implicated Blaine in a financial scandal. The letters were revealed by James Mulligan, a bookkeeper for Fisher, testifying on May 31, 1876, during a congressional investigation of the Little Rock and Fort Smith Railroad. Mulligan charged that Blaine had used his influence as speaker to aid the railroad in exchange for financial favors. The charges led to Blaine's loss of the Republican presidential nomination in 1876 and 1880. Blaine was nominated in 1884, but the publication of the letters that year contributed to his loss to Grover Cleveland.

Further reading: *Mr. Blaine and the Mulligan Letters* (Boston: J. S. Cushing & Co., 1884); Kenneth W. Thompson, ed., *Statesmen Who Were Never President* (Lanham, Md.: University Press of America, 1996).

Münchengrätz Agreement   Agreement concluded by Czar Nicholas I of Russia and Emperor Francis I of Austria (through the influence of Austrian statesman Prince Clemens von Metternich) on September 18, 1833, in the Moravian town of Münchengrätz; these eastern powers reconfirmed their commitment to the maintenance of the status quo. In the document the monarchs confirmed their mutual interest in maintaining the integrity of the Ottoman Empire, which, due to nationalistic and revolutionary movements in several of her vassal states, was then threatened with partition; they reconfirmed their opposition to all revolutionary movements, as well as their right to intervene on behalf of any power

experiencing revolutionary unrest, which requested aid of them. The agreement caused alarm in western Europe, particularly in Great Britain and France, because it appeared to express active opposition to liberalism in the West.

Further reading: Alan W. Palmer, *Metternich* (New York: Harper & Row, 1972).

Munich Agreement of 1938   Agreement presented by Italy's dictator Benito Mussolini at a conference in Munich, Germany, attended by himself, Chancellor Adolf Hitler of Germany, Prime Minister Neville Chamberlain of Britain, and Premier Édouard Daladier of France; signed by these four leaders on September 30, 1938, it endorsed Hitler's demand that Germany be permitted to annex the Sudeten area of Czechoslovakia, which had a significant German population. The terms of the document provided for the German army's occupation of the Sudetenland by October 10, 1938, and stipulated that the fate of other areas under dispute would be determined by an international commission. Czechoslovakia was not represented at the conference; she yielded to the terms of the agreement on the same day. The agreement had the effect of destroying the value of the Little Entente (see LITTLE ENTENTE TREATIES) and of facilitating Germany's efforts to continue her territorial expansion. It came to symbolize the western democracies' craven appeasement of Hitler for the purpose of "bringing peace and honor" (the words of Chamberlain); however, the agreement only encouraged Hitler's ambitions on the eve of World War II (1939–45).

See also: AXIS POWERS, PACT OF THE; STEEL, PACT OF.

Further reading: Robert Kee, *Munich: The Eleventh Hour* (London: H. Hamilton, 1988); Frank N. Magill, ed., *Great Events from History: Modern European Series*, 3 vols. (Englewood Cliffs, N.J.: Salem Press, 1973); Louis L. Snyder, *Fifty Major Documents of the Twentieth Century* (Princeton, N.J.: D. Van Nostrand Co., 1955); Norman Stone and Eduard Strouhal, *Czechoslovakia: Crossroads and Crises, 1918–88* (New York: St. Martin's Press, 1989).

Municipal Corporations Reform Act of 1835   See MELBOURNE'S SIX ACTS.

Munn v. Illinois   Decision of the U.S. Supreme Court, issued on March 1, 1877, concerning the validity of one of the GRANGER LAWS passed by the state of Illinois to regulate maximum grain storage charges. In 1872 the Chicago storage company of Munn and Cott was found guilty of violating that law. The company appealed the decision, claiming that fixing maximum rates violated the FOURTEENTH AMENDMENT by confiscating private property without due process of law. The Supreme Court ruled that because the warehouses were "affected with a public interest," their rates were subject to public regulation. The principle thus established led to further public regulation of private businesses serving the public interest.

Further reading: Mortimer Adler, ed., *The Annals of America*, 18 vols. (Chicago: Encyclopedia Britannica, 1968); Henry Steele Commager, ed., *Documents of American History*, 8th ed. (New York: Appleton-Century-Crofts, 1968); Kermit L. Hall et al., eds, *American Legal History: Cases and Materials*, 2d ed. (New York: Oxford University Press, 1996); Kermit L. Hall et al., eds., *The Oxford Companion to the Supreme Court of the United States* (New York: Oxford University Press, 1992).

Münster, Treaty of   One of the treaties that became part of the Peace of WESTPHALIA, signed on October 24, 1648, at the Westphalian town of Münster (Germany) by France, the German Catholic Estates, and the Holy Roman Empire, bringing an end to the Thirty Years' War (1618–48). The negotiations were attended by Roman Catholics, who sided with either the empire or France. The treaty confirmed France's control over Alsace (except Strasbourg), part of Lorraine, and several Rhenish fortress towns. The German Estates were granted full sovereignty, and the emperor's power concerning taxes, waging wars, and making new laws was limited.

See also: OSNABRÜCK, TREATY OF.

Further reading: Alison M. Kettering, *Gerard ter Borch and the Treaty of Munster* (The Hague: Mauritshuis, 1998); Frank N. Magill, ed., *Great Events from History: Modern European Series*, 3 vols. (Englewood Cliffs, N.J.: Salem Press, 1973).

Murchison Letter   Hoax letter published on October 24, 1888, and intended to damage the reelection campaign of Democratic U.S. president Grover Cleveland. The letter, purporting to be from a naturalized Englishman named Charles F. Murchison (actually George A. Osgoodby, a California Republican), was sent to the British minister to the United States, Lionel Sackeville-West, seeking his advice on how to vote in the upcoming election. Sackeville-West advised a vote for Cleveland. When the Republicans published the correspondence, the public outcry against foreign interference in U.S. elections, particularly among Irish Americans, cost the Democrats many votes. Republican Benjamin Harrison won the 1888 election, narrowly defeating Cleveland.

Further reading: Charles F. Murchison, *A Letter Addressed to Lord (Sackcloth) West* (Sanford, N.C.: Microfilming Corp. of America, 1979).

Mussolini's Doctrine of Fascism   Principles advocated by Italian Fascist dictator Benito Mussolini, published in the *Enciclopedia Italiana* (vol. 14) in June 1932. Mussolini's "Fundamental Ideas" are commonly ascribed to philosopher Giovanni Gentile, Mussolini's first minister of public instruction. "The man of Fascism is the individual who is nation and fatherland, which is a moral law, binding together individuals and the generations into a tradition and mission." Fascism acts qualitatively and spiritually within a nation through the will of a few for the benefit of all, Mussolini said. He became more jumbled tracing the development of Fascism with his "Political and Social Doctrine." But he clearly said: "Before everything, Fascism believes neither in the possibility nor in the utility of perpetual peace . . . Only war brings all human energies to a maximum tension and imprints a mark of nobility upon the peoples who have the virtue to face it."

Further reading: Frank N. Magil, ed., *Great Events from History: Modern European Series*, 3 vols. (Englewood Cliffs, N.J.: Salem Press, 1973).

Mutiny Act of 1689   Bill passed by Parliament in England in 1689, legalizing the standing army, providing for its maintenance, and authorizing punishment for desertion and mutiny. It was necessitated by a mutiny that broke out among troops at Ipswich, England, and was the first of many such acts, initially enacted every six months and then annually by Parliament from 1689 to 1879 (no such act was passed between 1697 and 1701). Military offenders could be arrested and court-martialed by military authority, independent of the civil courts. The Mutiny Act was replaced (1879) by the Army Discipline and Regulation Act, which was repealed by the Army and Air Force (Annual) Acts in 1917.

Further reading: Arthur Swinson, *A Register of the Regiments and Corps of the British Army: The Ancestry of the Regiments and Corps of the Regular Establishment* (London: Archive Press, 1972).

Mutual Assistance, Draft Treaty of   Draft proposal for mutual assistance among European countries; presented by France before the League of Nations Assembly in September 1923. The proposal, prepared by Colonel Edouard Réquin, Lord Robert Cecil, and others, envisaged a series of defensive pacts accompanied by a process of gradual deduction of armaments. Belgium, Czechoslovakia, and France backed the plan but Great Britain opposed it, and the League Assembly rejected it (September 1923). The following year, France and England collaborated in drafting another plan that resulted in the passage of the GENEVA PROTOCOL OF 1924.

Further reading: Charles de Visscher, *The Stabilization of Europe: Lectures on the Harris Foundation, 1924* (Chicago: University of Chicago Press, 1924).

Myers v. United States   U.S. Supreme Court decision, issued on October 25, 1926, that upheld the right of the president to remove from office an appointed official without the consent of the Senate. While the U.S. CONSTITUTION requires the "advice and consent" of the Senate for presidential appointments, it says nothing about the president's right to remove such appointees from office. In 1920 President Woodrow Wilson fired Frank S. Myers, postmaster of Portland, Oregon. Myers sued, claiming that an 1876 congressional act called for senatorial approval of dismissals of postmasters. In a 6-3 decision, the Supreme Court ruled that the 1876 act was an unconstitutional violation of the president's executive authority.

Further reading: Henry Steele Commager, ed., *Documents of American History*, 8th ed. (New York: Appleton-Century-Crofts, 1968); Kermit L. Hall et al., eds., *The Oxford Companion to the Supreme Court of the United States* (New York: Oxford University Press, 1992); James Hart, *Tenure of Office under the Constitution: A Study in Law and Public Policy* (Baltimore: Johns Hopkins Press, 1930); United States Supreme Court, *United States Reports: Cases Adjudged in the Supreme Court at . . . and Rules Announced at . . .* (New York: Banks & Brothers, Law Publishers, 1884–1921; Washington, D.C.: Government Printing Office, 1922–).

N

NAACP v. Alabama   U.S. Supreme Court decision, issued in 1958, protecting the right to privacy of association by ruling that an organization may not be required to divulge its membership lists as a condition of doing business in a state. Alabama, attempting to hamper the civil rights work of the National Association for the Advancement of Colored People (NAACP) through a corporate registration requirement, sought to compel the association to reveal the names and addresses of its members in Alabama. The organization, fearing social, economic, and physical reprisals against its members, refused. The Supreme Court stated that Alabama's requirement would violate the constitutional rights of members to associate lawfully in support of common beliefs.

Further reading: Henry Steele Commager, ed., *Documents of American History*, 8th ed. (New York: Appleton-Century-Crofts, 1968); Kermit L. Hall et al., eds., *The Oxford Companion to the Supreme Court of the United States* (New York: Oxford University Press, 1992); United States Supreme Court, *United States Reports: Cases Adjudged in the Supreme Court at . . . and Rules Announced at . . .* (New York: Banks & Brothers, Law Publishers, 1884–1921; Washington: Government Printing Office, 1922–).

Nagoda   See CROATIAN-HUNGARIAN COMPROMISE OF 1868.

Nagyvárad, Treaty of   Secret peace accord negotiated by Croatian-Hungarian statesman George Martinuzzi, ending the prolonged fighting between Austria's archduke Ferdinand and Hungary's John Zápolya for the Hungarian throne in 1538. Ferdinand and Zápolya had each been elected king of Hungary by separate diets in 1526. By the treaty, Ferdinand recognized Zápolya's claim to the Hungarian crown and to rule Transylvania (the central portion of Hungary). In return, Zápolya accepted Ferdinand's control over western Hungary and Croatia and agreed that Ferdinand would be his royal successor when he died.

Further reading: Miklos Molnar, *A Concise History of Hungary* (New York: Cambridge University Press, 2001).

Nakaz   See INSTRUCTION (NAKAZ), CATHERINE THE GREAT'S.

Namibian Agreement of 1988   Peace pact initiating an independence plan for Namibia (South West Africa), signed at the United Nations on December 22, 1988, by the foreign ministers of South Africa, Angola, and Cuba (Roelof [Pik] Botha, Afonso Van Dunem, and Isidoro Malmierca Peoli, respectively). A starting date for the independence of Namibia (ruled by South Africa since 1915) was set for April 1, 1989. Simultaneous with this U.S.-mediated pact was a separate agreement, signed by Cuba and Angola, for withdrawal of Cuban troops from Angola by July 1, 1991 (this was a South African condition for consenting to Namibian independence). The Cubans were helping Marxist-oriented Angola battle guerrillas of the National Union for the Total Independence of Angola (UNITA), a faction backed by South Africa and the United States.

Further reading: Anthony Feinstein, *In Conflict* (Windhoek, Namibia: New Namibia Books, 1998); Iurii I. Gorbunov, *Namibia, a Struggle for Independence: A Collection of Articles, Documents, and Speeches* (Moscow: Progress Publishers, 1988); B. Harlech-Jones, *A New Thing? The Namibian Independence Process, 1989–1990* (Windhoek, Namibia: Ecumenical Institute for Namibia, University of Namibia, 1997); Robert S. Jaster, *The 1988 Peace Accords and the Future of South-western Africa* (London: Brassey's for the International Institute for Strategic Studies, 1990).

Nanking, Treaty of   Treaty signed on August 29, 1842, ending the Opium War (1839–42) between Britain and China, and opening up Chinese markets to British traders for the first time. China paid an indemnity of £21 million, surrendered Hong Kong (which she had captured in January 1841), and declared five ports (Canton, Amoy, Foochow, Nangpo, and Shanghai) open to British traders. A uniform import duty of 5 percent ad valorem was levied and trade was to be conducted under the supervision of the consular offices. On the British side, the treaty was negotiated by Sir Henry Pottinger. Another treaty, signed in 1843, declared that Chinese laws were not binding on British citizens.

Further reading: Peter W. Fay, *The Opium War, 1840–1842: Barbarians in the Celestial Empire in the Early Part of the Nineteenth Century and the War by Which They Forced Her Gates Ajar* (Chapel Hill: University of North Carolina Press, 1997); John Ouchterlony, *The Chinese War: An Account of All the Operations of the British Forces from the Commencement to the Treaty of Nanking* (New York: Praeger Publishers, 1970); Cornelia Spencer, *Ancient China* (New York: John Day Co., 1964); Ssu-yu Teng, ed., *Chang Hsi and the Treaty of Nanking, 1842* (Chicago: University of Chicago Press, 1944).

Nantes, Edict of   Edict issued at Nantes in Brittany on April 13, 1598, by France's king Henry IV, ending the protracted Wars of Religion; it gave the Huguenots (French Protestants) equal political rights with the Catholics but did not establish complete freedom of worship. Certain Huguenot nobles and citizens could practice their religion in certain towns and cities. But the edict prohibited this freedom in and around Paris, in episcopal cities, and at the king's court. Huguenots could hold public offices and sat in mixed Catholic-Protestant *parlements* set up at Paris, Bordeaux, Grenoble, and Toulouse. The edict provided for more than 100 fortified places of safety for Huguenots in France—a situation considered politically dangerous to the Catholic majority, which constantly attacked the Huguenot's privileges.

See also: NANTES, REVOCATION OF THE EDICT OF.

Further reading: Richard L. Goodbar and Jotham Parsons, *The Edict of Nantes: Five Essays and a New Translation* (Bloomington, Minn.: National Huguenot Society, 1998); Mark A. Kishlansky, ed., *Sources of the West: Readings in Western Civilization*, vol. 2, 4th ed. (New York: Longman, 2001); Frank N. Magill, ed., *Great Events from History: Modern European Series*, 3 vols. (Englewood Cliffs, N.J.: Salem Press, 1973); Milton Viorst, ed., *The Great Documents of Western Civilization* (Philadelphia: Chilton Books, 1965).

Nantes, Revocation of the Edict of (Edict of Revocation, Edict of Fontainebleau)   Decree issued by France's king Louis XIV at Fontainebleau on October 18, 1685, repealing Henry IV's Edict of NANTES of 1598, which had granted the Huguenots (Protestants) freedom of worship and other concessions. Arguing that the unity of the country was at stake, Louis XIV banned the exercise of the reformed faith, ordered its churches to be demolished, and decreed that henceforth children were to be educated in the Roman Catholic faith only. The revocation, which recreated the situation as it had existed before 1598, aroused the anger of Protestants all over Europe. Despite his ban on emigration, thousands of families fled the country and some 600 French soldiers joined forces with William of Orange (later, England's William III) against Louis XIV.

Further reading: Frank N. Magill, ed., *Great Events from History: Modern European Series*, 3 vols. (Englewood Cliffs, N.J.: Salem Press, 1973); Elisabeth I. Perry, *From Theology to History: French Religious Controversy and the Revocation of the Edict of Nantes* (The Hague: M. Nijhoff, 1973); Milton Viorst, ed., *The Great Documents of Western Civilization* (Philadelphia: Chilton Books, 1965).

Napoleonic Code (Code Napoléon)   Codification of French laws in five codes (a sixth, the Rural Code, was not enacted); completed and enacted between 1804 and 1810, during Napoléon Bonaparte's reign as emperor of France and sometimes with his active participation. Together, they had a pioneering influence on the legal codes of many countries. The first, the Civil Code of France promulgated on March 21, 1804, consists of three books, dealing with "persons," "goods and the various kinds of property," and with "various modes in which property is acquired." Drafted by a committee of four lawyers (Tronchet, Portalis, Preameneu, and Maleville), it went through elaborate revisions, is noted for its equity and common sense, and bears the stamp of Napoléon's dynamism. The Code of Civil Procedure, approved in April 1806, simplified and streamlined civil judicial proceedings. The Criminal Code (October 1808) incorporated some of Napoléon's plans to decentralize criminal justice. The Penal Code (February 2, 1810), a complete revision of the Penal Code of 1791, is stringent, sometimes harshly so. Completed in August 1807, the Commercial Code defined France's commercial laws; of all codes, it has been subject to the most modifications. The Napoleonic Code eliminated conflicting provincial statutes and made the law consistent throughout France.

Further reading: Bryant Barrett, ed., *The Code Napoleon, Verbally Translated from the French . . .* (Holmes Beach, Fla.: Gaunt, 1999); *Code Napoleon, or, the French Civil Code*

(Washington, D.C.: Beard Books, 1999); Xavier Martin, *Human Nature and the French Revolution: From the Enlightenment to the Napoleonic Code* (New York: Berghahn Books, 2001).

Napoléon's Abdication Declaration

Statement of unconditional abdication of the French throne, forced by the Allies from Emperor Napoléon Bonaparte on April 11, 1814, as a precondition to the signing of the Treaty of FONTAINE-BLEAU of 1814. Therein, Napoléon renounced "for himself and his heirs the thrones of France and Italy," declaring that there was "no personal sacrifice, even were it of life itself" that he would not make in "the interest of France." Earlier, Napoléon had offered to abdicate in his son's favor or to establish a Napoleonic regency, but both his proposals were rejected. The Allies refused to accept anything other than an unconditional surrender. The same day, the Allies concluded their peace settlement with Napoléon in the Treaty of Fontainebleau.

Further reading: Robert B. Asprey, *The Rise and Fall of Napoleon*, 2 vols. (London: Little, Brown, 2001); R. F. Delderfield, *Imperial Sunset: The Fall of Napoleon, 1813–1814* (New York: Cooper Square Press, 2001); Louis L. Snyder, ed., *Fifty Major Documents of the Nineteenth Century* (Princeton, N.J.: D. Van Nostrand Company, 1955).

Napoléon's Mediation Constitution (Act of Mediation)

Constitutional instrument drafted on September 30, 1802, and finalized on February 19, 1803, by Napoléon Bonaparte, replacing the Helvetic Republic with the loosely constituted Swiss Confederation. Each of the country's 19 Swiss cantons had its own constitution, legislature, chancery, and president. The federal Diet, moving annually through each of the six designated cities, was presided over by a Landammann, Napoléon's appointee. The country was declared a free-trade zone, requirements for citizenship were relaxed, feudal bonds eliminated, and torture abolished. The act provided for the separation of church and state; many monasteries were closed down, incentives introduced for education, and marriage declared a civil contract. Additionally, it established a federal army and foreign policy and codified laws. Another provision entitled France to enlist up to 16,000 Swiss soldiers. This Napoleonic document created an 11-year peace and also made the Swiss Confederation France's satellite state.

Further reading: Dieter Fahrni, *An Outline History of Switzerland: From the Origins to the Present Day* (Zurich: Pro Helvetia, 1984); James Murray Luck, *A History of Switzerland: The First 100,000 Years: Before the Beginnings to the Days of the Present* (Palo Alto Calif.: Society for the Promotion of Science & Scholarship, 1985).

Napoléon's Order Dissolving the Holy Roman Empire

Order or decree made by Emperor Napoléon Bonaparte of France in 1806, by which the Holy Roman Empire formally ceased to exist. Napoléon's announcement (made by his representative before the Diet of the Holy Roman Empire on August 1, 1806) that he no longer recognized the empire was followed by Holy Roman Emperor Francis II's renunciation of his imperial title and crown and assumption of the title of Emperor Francis I of Austria, on August 6, 1806. Napoléon's withdrawal of recognition of the empire followed the creation of the Confederation of the Rhine, an empire, under French protection, consisting of German states previously united with the Hapsburg Empire of Austria.

Further reading: Louis L. Snyder, ed., *Fifty Major Documents of the Nineteenth Century* (Princeton, N.J.: D. Van Nostrand Company, 1955; Maiken Umbach, *Federalism and Enlightenment in Germany, 1740–1806* (London: Hambledon Press, 2000); Milton Viorst, ed., *The Great Documents of Western Civilization* (Philadelphia: Chilton Books, 1965).

Napoléon's Statement of 18 Brumaire

Napoléon Bonaparte's version of his coup d'état of 18 Brumaire (November 9, 1799), issued in a statement to the French people the following day. Altering the events of the day to suit his purpose, Napoléon's highly fictionalized account succeeded in convincing the public of the "zeal of a soldier of liberty, of a citizen devoted to the republic." Graphically describing the prevailing anarchy and the Council of Elders' appeal to him to "accept the command," Napoléon then painted a rather heroic picture of himself standing up to the armed assassins who had apparently invaded the assemblies at Saint-Cloud (suburb of Paris). Intimidated by the grenadiers, the "seditious" fled, leaving the assembly to deliberate on proposals for public safety and to draft the "salutary resolution" instituted as "the new and provisional law of the republic." Having thus established his sincerity and valor, Napoléon concluded by hoping that France would recognize his merits through a leadership role.

Further reading: Georges Lefebvre, *Napoleon, from 18 Brumaire to Tilsit, 1799–1807*, trans. Henry F. Stockhold (New York: Columbia University Press, 1969); Milton Viorst, ed., *The Great Documents of Western Civilization* (Philadelphia: Chilton Books, 1965).

Napoléon III's Treaty with Austria

Secret treaty concluded on July 12, 1866, between Emperor Napoléon III of France and Emperor Francis Joseph of Austria, providing terms for French neutrality during the Austro-Prussian Seven Weeks' War, the outbreak of which was imminent. The two powers agreed that, in return for French neutrality, Austria would cede her Italian province of Venetia to France, which in turn would cede it to Italy, regardless of the outcome of the war; and that, in the event of an Austrian victory, Austria's right to effect whatever changes in Germany that she might desire would be subject to French approval. Austria was defeated in the war.

See also: PRAGUE, TREATY OF (1866); VIENNA, TREATY OF (1866); VILLAFRANCA, TREATY OF.

Further reading: Fenton S. Bresler, *Napoleon III: A Life* (New York: Carroll & Graf, 1999); Frank N. Magill, ed., *Great Events from History: Modern European Series*, 3 vols. (Englewood Cliffs, N.J.: Salem Press, 1973); E. Ann Pottinger, *Napoleon III and the German Crisis, 1865–1866* (Cambridge, Mass.: Harvard University Press, 1966); Geoffrey Wawro, *The Austro-Prussian War: Austria's War with Prussia and Italy in 1866* (New York: Cambridge University Press, 1996).

Narcisse (Préface de Narcisse)   Polemic written in 1752 by Jean-Jacques Rousseau and prefaced to his first play, *Narcisse* (c. 1741). At the time compiling an anthology of his writings, Rousseau used the preface to express his views on the state of contemporary French music in particular, and art in general, lamenting the lack of originality, vigor, and freshness. Responding to charges that his own works (music and writings) directly contradicted the statements in his own prize-winning essay "Discourse on the Arts and Sciences" (1750), Rousseau declared that since he was unable to offset or arrest the corrupting influence of the arts, he was seeking to use them to expose themselves and thus prove his assertion. The preface is much longer than the play itself, which revolves around the self-obsessed Narcisse. Rousseau, perhaps the most controversial of the French philosophers, was severely criticized and even persecuted for these views.

See also: DISCOURSE ON THE ORIGIN OF INEQUALITY.

Further reading: Timothy O'Hagan, *Rousseau* (New York: Routledge, 1998); Philip E. J. Robinson, *Jean-Jacques Rousseau's Doctrine of the Arts* (New York: P. Lang, 1984).

National Bank Act of 1863, U.S.   Federal legislation, enacted on February 25, 1863, and amended on June 3, 1864, that established a national banking system that lasted until the passage of the FEDERAL RESERVE ACT OF 1913. To provide a sounder currency than state banks then offered and to increase the sales of government bonds to finance the Civil War, the 1863 and 1864 acts organized federally chartered banks that were required to invest at least one-third of their capital in U.S. bonds. These banks could then issue national bank notes (paper money) up to 90 percent of their bond holdings. The acts regulated capital requirements, loans, and reserves, and provided for the supervision and examination of banks and the protection of noteholders.

Further reading: Henry Steele Commager, ed., *Documents of American History*, 8th ed. (New York: Appleton-Century-Crofts, 1968); Frank N. Magill, ed., *Great Events from History: American Series*, 3 vols. (Englewood Cliffs, N.J.: Salem Press, 1975).

National Covenant, Scottish   See SOLEMN LEAGUE AND COVENANT OF 1638.

National Environmental Policy Act, U.S.   Federal legislation enacted in 1969 and effective on January 1, 1970, requiring federal agencies to include an environmental impact statement in every recommendation or report on proposed federal action or legislation significantly affecting the U.S. environment. The statement must identify any unavoidable, adverse environmental effects, alternatives to the proposed action, the relationship between local short-term use of the environment and the maintenance of long-term productivity, and any irreversible commitments of resources that the action would involve. The act declared as national policy "a productive harmony between man and his environment" and established the Council on Environmental Quality to advise the U.S. president on environmental issues.

Further reading: Ronald E. Bass et al., *The NEPA Book: A Step-by-Step Guide on How to Comply with the National Environmental Policy Act* (Point Area, Calif.: Solano Press Books, 2001); Matthew J. Lindstorm and Zachary A. Smith, *The National Environmental Policy Act: Judicial Misconstruction, Legislative Indifference, and Executive Neglect* (College Station: Texas A&M University Press, 2001); Emmett B. Moore, *The Environmental Impact Statement Process and Environmental Law* (Columbus, Ohio: Battelle Press, 2000); Thomas F. P. Sullivan and Christopher L. Bell, *Environmental Law Handbook* (Rockville, Md.: Government Institute, 2001).

National Health Service Act, British   Legislation of November 6, 1946, establishing a comprehensive state-controlled public health scheme in Great Britain. Promoted by Health Minister Aneurin Bevan, the act offered complete medical and dental coverage (including hospitalization and specialists' services) regardless of ability to pay. Local health authorities were made responsible for maternity and pediatric care and ambulance facilities and for providing home nurses and health visitors. Participating doctors and dentists were also allowed private practice and the option to withdraw from the scheme. Implemented in July 1948, the act was based on the NATIONAL INSURANCE ACT OF 1911 and the Maternity and Child Welfare Act of 1918. It was funded through general taxes. By 1950, 88 percent of the medical practitioners and 95 percent of the population were enrolled in the scheme, which was supervised by a Central Health Services Council.

Further reading: Roger Ormrod and Harris Walker, *The National Health Service* (London: Butterworth, 1950); S. R. Speller, *The National Health Service Act, 1946, Annotated; Together with Various Orders and Regulations Made Thereunto* (London: Lewis, 1948).

National Housing Act of 1934, U.S.   New Deal legislation enacted on June 28, 1934, that established the Federal Housing Administration (FHA) to insure mortgage loans made by banks, trust companies, and other lending institutions on new and existing private homes. The act was intended to aid homeowners, to stimulate the depressed housing industry, to improve housing standards, and to establish sound home financing. It authorized the FHA to underwrite loans for new construction, repairs, alterations, and improvements. It also encouraged the modernization of farms and small manufacturing facilities in the United States.

Further reading: Joseph B. Mason, *History of Housing in the U.S., 1930–1980* (Houston: Gulf Publishing, 1982); Gail Radford, *Modern Housing for America: Policy Struggles in the New Deal Era* (Chicago: University of Chicago Press, 1996).

National Housing Act of 1937, U.S. See WAGNER-STEAGALL ACT.

National Housing Act of 1965, U.S.
Federal omnibus housing legislation enacted on August 10, 1965, providing loans and grants of $7.8 billion over a four-year period to build housing for some 500,000 low-income families living in substandard homes in the United States. Construction would be done by private companies with mortgage money insured either by the U.S. government or private sources. Some low-income families would pay 25 percent of their total income for rent, and the government would pay the rest. The law also stated that the U.S. government would match funds provided by states and localities for the construction of water and sewer facilities and community centers in urban low-income areas. Money would also be provided for low-rent, farm-labor housing, for college housing, and for housing for the elderly at lower interest rates. Middle-income home buyers were eligible for federal insurance in some cases.

Further reading: Jeffrey W. Helsing, *Johnson's War/Johnson's Great Society: The Guns and Butter Trap* (Westport, Conn.: Praeger, 2000); Joseph B. Mason, *History of Housing in the U.S., 1930–1980* (Houston: Gulf Publishing, 1982).

National Industrial Recovery Act, U.S.
Federal U.S. legislation enacted on June 16, 1933, intended to improve industrial and business activity, to reduce unemployment, to foster fair competition, and to provide for the construction of public works. The centerpiece of President Franklin D. Roosevelt's New Deal legislation, the NIRA created the National Recovery Administration to supervise industrial self-regulation under codes of fair competition. The codes, which had the force of law, gave workers the right to organize and bargain collectively and set minimum wages, maximum hours, and other working conditions. The act gave the president broad powers to manage the national economy. It also created the Public Works Administration to increase employment and business activity by building roads, public buildings, and other works.

Further reading: Mortimer Adler, ed., *The Annals of America*, 18 vols. (Chicago: Encyclopaedia Britannica, 1968); Henry Steele Commager, ed., *Documents of American History*, 8th ed. (New York: Appleton-Century-Crofts, 1968); Frank N. Magill, ed., *Great Events from History: American Series*, 3 vols. (Englewood Cliffs, N.J.: Salem Press, 1975); T. H. Wat-

kins, *The Hungry Years: A Narrative History of the Great Depression in America* (New York: Henry Holt, 1999).

National Insurance Act of 1911, British
Landmark act of December 16, 1911, climaxing a series of social reforms and laying the foundations of the British welfare state. Its main feature was the formulation of a national health scheme, which for 10 shillings a week covered all workers against ill-health and job disability and provided maternity benefits. Workers between 16 and 65 years of age with an annual property income lower than £26 were required to take health insurance. Lloyd George, chancellor of the exchequer, authored this scheme. Home Secretary Winston Churchill introduced the unemployment insurance scheme—providing a maximum benefit of 15 weeks—initially for the 2¼ million workers in the building and engineering trades, later extended to all manual workers. Both schemes were contributory—a clause that caused some dissension in the Labour Party—with the state, employers, and employees paying their compulsory dues. The importance of this act was not appreciated until many years later.

Further reading: William H. Dawson, *Social Insurance in Germany, 1883–1911: Its History, Operation, Results, and a Comparison with the National Insurance Act, 1911* (Westport, Conn.: Greenwood Press, 1979); Frank N. Magill, ed., *Great Events from History: Modern European Series*, 3 vols. (Englewood Cliffs, N.J.: Salem Press, 1973).

Nationality and Flag Act, South African
Legislation passed on November 11, 1927, settling the bitter controversy over the design of the new national flag in South Africa. The controversy centered around the inclusion (or otherwise) of Britain's Union Jack in the new flag. The final design, approved after months of intense negotiations, incorporated the orange, white, and blue vertical stripes of the Van Riebeeck flag (flown by the Netherlands during the Cape settlement), with three small flags (the Union Jack, the Vierkleur of the Transvaal, and the flag of the Orange Free State) in the center. This and the Union Jack were declared "the flags of the Union." The Union Jack could be flown only in certain places and always with the national flag. Operative May 31, 1928, the act was subsequently (1957) amended to delete any mention of the Union Jack, declaring the South African flag to be the national flag.

Further reading: Harry Saker, *The South African Flag Controversy, 1925–1928* (Cape Town, South Africa: Oxford University Press, 1980).

National Labor Relations Act, U.S. (Wagner-Connery Act)
New Deal legislation, enacted on July 5, 1935, that created the National Labor Relations Board (NLRB) and guaranteed workers the right to organize and to bargain collectively through their chosen representatives. Sponsored by Senator Robert F. Wagner of New York and Representative

William P. Connery, Jr., of Massachusetts, the act authorized the NLRB to investigate complaints, issue cease-and-desist orders against unfair labor practices in interstate commerce, protect the right to collective bargaining, and arbitrate labor disputes. It prohibited employers from interfering with workers' rights to organize or to join independent unions, from promoting company unions, from discriminating in employment because of union membership, from punishing employees who file charges or testify under the act, and from refusing to negotiate with an elected union.

Further reading: Henry Steele Commager, ed., *Documents of American History*, 8th ed. (New York: Appleton-Century-Crofts, 1968); Frank N. Magill, ed., *Great Events from History: American Series*, 3 vols. (Englewood Cliffs, N.J.: Salem Press, 1975); National Labor Relations Board, *Legislative History of the National Labor Relations Act, 1935* (Washington, D.C.: Government Printing Office, 1985); T. H. Watkins, *The Hungry Years: A Narrative History of the Great Depression in America* (New York: Henry Holt, 1999).

National Labor Relations Board v. Jones & Laughlin Steel Corporation

U.S. Supreme Court decision, issued on April 12, 1937, that upheld the constitutionality of the U.S. NATIONAL LABOR RELATIONS ACT. The case arose when the NLRB found the Jones & Laughlin Steel Corporation guilty of unfair labor practices (discriminating against union members in hiring and job tenure and trying to prevent employees from joining a union); the company challenged the act granting the NLRB the right to issue a cease-and-desist order. In its five-to-four ruling, the Supreme Court declared that the act was a valid exercise of the congressional power to regulate interstate commerce, particularly labor relations.

Further reading: Henry Steele Commager, ed., *Documents of American History*, 8th ed. (New York: Appleton-Century-Crofts, 1968); Kermit L. Hall et al., eds., *The Oxford Companion to the Supreme Court of the United States* (New York: Oxford University Press, 1992); Robert R. Mayer, *The Court and the American Crises, 1930–1952* (Danbury, Conn.: Grolier Educational, 1995); United States Supreme Court, *United States Reports: Cases Adjudged in the Supreme Court at . . . and Rules Announced at . . .* (New York: Banks & Brothers, Law Publishers, 1884–1921; Washington, D.C.: Government Printing Office, 1922–).

National Organization for Women, Inc. v. Scheidler

Civil suit filed in October 1986 by the National Organization for Women (NOW) and two abortion clinics against pro-life advocates Joseph Scheidler, Tim Murphy, and Andy Scholberg for their intimidatory tactics at the clinics; its determination had important consequences for the pro-life movement in the country. In April 1998, a jury found the three defendants (a fourth defendant, Randall Terry of Operation Rescue, had previously settled with NOW) guilty under the federal Racketeer Influenced and Corrupt Organizations Act, or RICO

LAW. On July 16, 1999, a judge ordered the defendants to pay $257,780 in damages to the clinics and post a $440,000 bond with the court pending their appeal. Also, the three individual defendants and two organization, Pro-Life Action League and Operation Rescue, were prohibited from interfering with clinic operations and threatening doctors and patients for the next 12 years. The suit's class action status meant that other abortion clinics could claim damages as well.

Further reading: Robert G. Blakey, "The RICO Racket," *National Review* 46 (May 16, 1994): 61–63; National Organization for Women Foundation, "*Now v. Scheidler* Racketeering lawsuit," National Organization for Women Foundation, available online at http://now.org/issues/abortion/scheidr.html.

National Origins Act of 1924, U.S.

See IMMIGRATION QUOTA ACT OF 1924, U.S.

National Pact, Turkey's

Pact concluded at Ankara on September 13, 1920, by the Turkish nationalists, led by Mustafa Kemal (Atatürk), and adopted on January 28, 1920, by the Turkish government at Constantinople (Istanbul); it declared the independence of Turkey, which was then threatened by the Allied Powers' plan to detach all non-Turkish territory from the former Ottoman Empire (see also SÈVRES, TREATY OF). The document, consisting of six articles, declared the indivisibility of Turkey; pledged to uphold minorities' rights; confirmed the opening of the Straits of the Dardanelles and Bosporus on the condition that the security of Constantinople be guaranteed; declared the abolition of capitulations; and guaranteed the right of the inhabitants of western Thrace and of Arabs inhabiting territory formerly part of the Ottoman Empire but now under occupation to choose in freedom their nationality.

See also: FUNDAMENTAL LAW OF 1921, TURKEY'S; LAUSANNE, TREATY OF (1923).

Further reading: Gulzar Ahmed, *Turkey: Rebirth of a Nation; A Short History of the Turkish War of Independence* (Karachi, Pakistan: Ma'Aref, 1961); A. L. Macfie, *The End of the Ottoman Empire; 1908–1923* (New York: Longman, 1998).

National Progressive Republican League's Declaration of Principles

Founding philosophy for an organization of Republican Party reformers who opposed the PAYNE-ALDRICH TARIFF; written by Republican senator Robert M. La Follette of Wisconsin and issued on January 21, 1911. According to the declaration, the league's purpose was "the promotion of popular government and progressive legislation." It advocated the direct election of U.S. senators; direct primaries for the nomination of elective officials; direct election of delegates to national presidential conventions; amendment of state constitutions to provide for initiatives, referendums, and recalls; and a comprehensive corrupt-practices act.

Further reading: Henry Steele Commager, ed., *Documents of American History*, 8th ed. (New York: Appleton-Century-Crofts, 1968); Nancy C. Unger, *Fighting Bob La Follette: The Righteous Reformer* (Chapel Hill: University of North Carolina Press, 2000).

National Prohibition Act, U.S. See VOLSTEAD ACT.

National Reclamation Act, U.S. See NEWLANDS ACT.

National Security Act of 1947, U.S.
Federal legislation enacted on July 26, 1947, that coordinated the formerly separate departments of the U.S. Army, Navy, and Air Force within a single, unified command called the National Military Establishment. The agency was headed by a secretary of defense, who was made a member of the U.S. president's cabinet. The purpose of the act was to eliminate overlapping authority and to make national defense efforts more efficient and effective. In 1949 the department was reorganized, with greater authority for the secretary of defense to enforce cooperation among the services, and was renamed the Department of Defense.

Further reading: Henry Steele Commager, ed., *Documents of American History*, 8th ed. (New York: Appleton-Century-Crofts, 1968); Victor H. Krulak, *Organization for National Security: A Study* (Washington, D.C.: United States Strategic Institute, 1983); Frank N. Magill, ed., *Great Events from History: American Series*, 3 vols. (Englewood Cliffs, N.J.: Salem Press, 1975).

National Theatre Act, British
Legislation passed by the British Parliament in 1949, establishing a national theater in Britain with a promised grant of £1 million toward building costs. The project did not get off the ground, being repeatedly postponed by successive British governments. In 1963, the government reaffirmed its commitment to financing a national theater, by setting up the Old Vic as its temporary site and appointing Sir Laurence Olivier as its director. Three years later, the government and the Greater London Council decided to share the construction costs of a building (with two auditoriums) in London.

Further reading: Tim Goodwin, *Britain's Royal National Theatre: The First 25 Years* (London: National Theatre in Association with Nick Hern, 1988).

Native Land Acts, New Zealand's
Two land acts passed by the New Zealand Government (1862 and 1865) to regulate the sale of Maori lands, thereby encouraging both legal settlement and native development. By the Native Land Act of 1862, the government renounced its right to preemption of native lands (see WAITANGI, TREATY OF) and forbade transfer of such properties until the ownership had been determined. The 1865 legislation established a Maori Land Court with powers to investigate and individualize Maori land

titles. European settlers were then allowed to buy the lands directly from the owners; by 1892, most of the good land was purchased by them. The cornerstone of land legislation in New Zealand, the act was significantly amended in 1867.

Further reading: Dora Alves, *The Maori and the Crown: An Indigenous People's Struggle for Self-Determination* (Westport, Conn.: Greenwood Press, 1999); Graham V. Butterworth, *Maori Affairs* (Wellington, New Zealand: GP Books, 1990); Paul Havemann, ed., *Indigenous Peoples' Rights in Australia, Canada, & New Zealand* (New York: Oxford University Press, 1999); Alan Ward, *National Overview* (Wellington, New Zealand: GP Publication, 1997).

Native Land Husbandry Act, Rhodesian
Major legislation enacted in Rhodesia (Zimbabwe) in 1951; aimed at revolutionizing the native agricultural system through a series of measures. Primarily, it sought to convert communal tenure in the reserves to individual ownership, thereby assuring security of tenure. However, it did not comcomitantly alter the LAND APPORTIONMENT ACT OF 1930 so that the urban African, deprived of his stake in the reserves, was not compensated by secure tenure in the townships. The act divided the arable land in the reserves into smaller, more economic units, but despite the increased allocation under the act (from 2.2 to 3.5 million acres), there were not enough units to go around and many were forced to seek employment in the towns. This legislation was also aimed at reducing excessive stock and improving crop quality and harvests through modern husbandry methods.

Further reading: Mary E. Bulman, *The Native Land Husbandry Act of Southern Rhodesia: A Failure in Land Reform* (Salisbury: Tribal Areas of Rhodesia Research Foundation, 1975).

Native Representation Act, New Zealand's (Maori Representation Act)
New Zealand legislation of 1867 that gave the Maori (an aboriginal people of New Zealand) direct political representation by dividing the self-governing British colony into four Maori electoral areas, each electing one member to the colony's House of Representatives. Five years later, two chiefs were nominated to the Upper House. This was intended as a temporary measure since the Maori were to be incorporated into the general electoral rolls following the conversion of their holdings from tribal to individual ownership. The holdings, however, were found to be not easily divisible and the act became permanent in 1876. The act also gave the Maori universal male suffrage—more than a decade before the European colonists received theirs.

Further reading: Dora Alves, *The Maori and the Crown: An Indigenous People's Struggle for Self-Determination* (Westport, Conn.: Greenwood Press, 1999); Graham V. Butterworth, *Maori Affairs* (Wellington, New Zealand: GP Books, 1990); Paul Havemann, ed., *Indigenous Peoples' Rights in Australia, Canada, & New Zealand* (New York: Oxford University Press, 1999); Alan Ward, *National Overview* (Wellington, New Zealand: GP Publications, 1997).

Natives' Land Act, South African

Law passed by the government of South Africa on June 16, 1913, prohibiting black Africans from owning or leasing land outside their existing reserves and thus further extending the government's policy of racial segregation. Intended to establish a uniform land policy, the act demoted many African farmers to the status of wage laborers and created a source of cheap labor for the white landowners. It proposed to extend the existing reserves and appointed the Beaumont Commission to examine the situation. However, even with the additional land released by the Native Trust and Land Act of 1936, its distribution was still inequitable—four million Africans had access to a mere 12 percent to 13 percent of the land, while the rest was reserved for whites. The act also provided for the eviction of squatters in the Orange Free State. It did not apply to the Cape, where African land rights were linked to qualified franchise, which was not abolished until 1936.

Further reading: Shula Marks and Richard Rathbone, *Industrialisation and Social Change in South Africa: African Class Formation, Culture, and Consciousness, 1870–1930* (New York: Longman, 1982); R. W. Msimang, *Natives Land Act 1913: Specific Cases of Evictions and Hardships, Etc.* (Cape Town: Friends of South Africa Library, 1996).

Natives' Trust and Land Act, South African

South African land and labor legislation (June 1936) reinforcing the segregationist policies of the James Hertzog—Jan Smuts coalition government. It greatly increased the size of the native reserves (see NATIVES' LAND ACT, SOUTH AFRICAN) by releasing 15.3 million acres of land, far less than the Beaumont Commission had recommended. A corporation was established to purchase land for native settlements. Though the native population exceeded the whites by a three to one margin, they were allowed control over only 12 percent of the land. The act also required labor tenants to work for 180 days and squatters to be registered and licensed. Its intention was to gradually end squatting over a 30-year period. There was widespread resistance against these provisions, particularly in the Transvaal, and they could not be fully implemented in many areas.

Further reading: Marj Brown et al., *Land Restitution in South Africa: A Long Way Home* (Cape Town, South Africa: IDASA, 1998); Essy M. Letsoalo, *Land Reform in South Africa: A Black Perspective* (Johannesburg, South Africa: Thorold's Africana Books, 1987).

Naturalization Act of 1795, U.S.

Federal legislation enacted on January 29, 1795, that allowed free white aliens to apply to the courts for U.S. citizenship after five years of residence. Such aliens were required to swear to uphold the U.S. CONSTITUTION, to show themselves to be of good character, and to renounce all hereditary titles and foreign allegiance. The act modified a 1790 naturalization law, which required only two years of residence, because increasing unrest in Europe led some Americans to fear an influx of aristocratic political refugees from France.

See also: NATURALIZATION ACT OF 1798, U.S.

Further reading: Frank G. Franklin, *The Legislative History of Naturalization in the United States* (New York: Arno Press, 1969); James H. Kettner, *The Development of American Citizenship, 1608–1870* (Chapel Hill: University of North Carolina Press, 1978).

Naturalization Act of 1798, U.S.

Federal legislation enacted on June 18, 1798, that changed the required period of residence for admission to U.S. citizenship from five to 14 years. Aliens had to declare their intention five years before they applied for citizenship. As one of the ALIEN AND SEDITION ACTS, this law postponed citizenship, and thus voting privileges, for European refugees who supported the Jeffersonian Republicans. The act was repealed by the Republicans in 1802, when the U.S. NATURALIZATION ACT OF 1795 was reinstated.

Further reading: Henry Steele Commager, ed., *Documents of American History*, 8th ed. (New York: Appleton-Century-Crofts, 1968); Frank G. Franklin, *The Legislative History of Naturalization in the United States* (New York: Arno Press, 1969); James H. Kettner, *The Development of American Citizenship, 1608–1870* (Chapel Hill: University of North Carolina Press, 1978); Frank N. Magill, ed., *Great Events from History: American Series*, 3 vols. (Englewood Cliffs, N.J.: Salem Press, 1975).

Naval Armament Limitation Treaty

See FIVE POWER NAVAL TREATY.

Naval Defense Act of 1889, British

British parliamentary legislation of May 31, 1889, introducing the Two-Power Standard into the British Navy to ensure that its battleship strength would be twice that of the next two powers combined. Promoted by Britain's prime minister, Lord Salisbury, to counteract the growing naval might and collaborative efforts of France and Russia, it initiated a naval expansion plan costing £21.5 million, which involved the construction of 10 new battleships, nine large cruisers, and 33 smaller ones. The existing docks were to be improved, as were the training schemes (regular maneuvers and gunnery practice). The naval fleets were to be reorganized to provide a competent, fully-equipped naval force within a 30-mile radius. This was the beginning of an expensive modernization program that soon had to contend with the rapidly growing naval strength of Germany, Japan, and the United States, also.

Further reading: Frank N. Magill, ed., *Great Events from History: Modern European Series*, 3 vols. (Englewood Cliffs, N.J.: Salem Press, 1973); Jon T. Sumida, *In Defence of Naval*

Supremacy: Finance, Technology, and British Naval Policy, 1889–1914 (Boston: Unwin Hyman, 1989); John E. Tashjean, *The Two-Power Standard and the Risk Navy: Some Recent Literature* (Arlington, Va.: Economic & Political Studies Division, Institute for Defense Analyses, 1965).

Naval Expansion Act, U.S. See VINSON NAVAL ACT.

Navigation Act of 1650, English

First of a series of laws, known as the Navigation Acts, enacted by the English Parliament between 1650 and 1696. These acts stemmed from the doctrine of mercantilism, which had as its objective the creation of a powerful and economically self-sufficient national state, and were intended to protect English shipping against Dutch and other foreign competition. The Navigation Act of 1650 specifically prohibited foreign ships from trading in the colonies without a special license. Subsequent acts went on to provide a legal monopoly to Englishmen and English ships on trade between various colonial ports and between colonial ports and England. (American colonists were considered Englishmen.)

Further reading: Mortimer Adler, ed., *The Annals of America*, 18 vols. (Chicago: Encyclopaedia Britannica, 1968); David D. Douglas et al., *English Historical Documents*, 12 vols. (New York: Oxford University Press, 1950–77); William MacDonald, ed., *Select Charters and Other Documents Illustrative of American History, 1606–1775* (New York: Macmillan, 1899); Frank N. Magill, ed., *Great Events from History: American Series*, 3 vols. (Englewood Cliffs, N.J.: Salem Press, 1975).

Nazi Germany's Four-Year Plan

Plan proclaimed on September 9, 1936, by Chancellor Adolf Hitler of Nazi Germany at the Nuremberg Rally of the National Socialist, or Nazi, Party, formalizing Hitler's intention to make Germany economically independent within a four-year period. The economic independence to be attained would be characterized by an equality of consumption and production in Germany of all materials that could conceivably be produced through German chemical, machine, and mining industries, such that any dependence upon foreign sources would cease to exist. The implementation of the plan was placed with Hermann Göring, who later became minister of economics. Although the plan failed to produce the desired results, it was continued throughout the war years under Göring's control.

Further reading: Beauftrager fur den Vierjahresplan (Delegate for the Four-Year Plan), *Goering's Atlas* (Berlin: U.S. Army Forces in the European Theater, 1946); Erich Gritzbach, *Hermann Goring: The Man and His Works*, trans. Gerald Griffin (New York: AMS Press, 1973); David Irving, *Goering: A Biography* (London: Macmillan London, 1989); Guido Knopp, *Hitler's Henchman*, trans. Angus McGeoch (Stroud, England: Sutton, 2000).

Nazi-Soviet Pact of 1939 See MOLOTOV-RIBBENTROP PACT.

Neagle, In Re

U.S. Supreme Court decision of April 14, 1890, asserting the supremacy of federal over state law. David Neagle, a deputy U.S. marshal, was ordered by the attorney general to accompany and protect Supreme Court Justice Stephen J. Field against a threatened attack. In California Field was assaulted by David Terry, whom Neagle shot and killed. Neagle was arrested and charged with murder by state authorities. He was brought before the U.S. circuit court on writ of habeas corpus and was set free on the ground that he was being held in custody for "an act done in pursuance of a law of the United States." The Supreme Court upheld his release.

Further reading: Howard B. Furer, *The Fuller Court, 1888–1919* (Danbury, Conn.: Grolier Educational, 1995); Kermit L. Hall, et al., eds., *The Oxford Companion to the Supreme Court of the United States* (New York: Oxford University Press, 1992); United States Supreme Court, *United States Reports: Cases Adjudged in the Supreme Court at . . . and Rules Announced at . . .* (New York: Banks & Brothers, Law Publishers, 1884–1921; Washington, D.C.: Government Printing Office, 1922–).

Near v. Minnesota

U.S. Supreme Court decision, issued on June 1, 1931, that upheld the right of the press to criticize public officials. It invalidated a Minnesota statute, known as the "gag law," that allowed the courts to suppress a "malicious, scandalous and defamatory" periodical as a public nuisance. Under this statue, the state had banned further publication of the weekly *Saturday Press* (edited by J. M. Near) because it had published a series of articles charging corruption among law enforcement officers. In its 5-4 decision, the Court ruled the law unconstitutional, maintaining that the state could not exercise prior restraint by closing down a newspaper, although it could prosecute for criminal libel after publication of objectionable material.

Further reading: Kermit L. Hall et al., eds., *The Oxford Companion to the Supreme Court of the United States* (New York: Oxford University Press, 1992); Maureen Harrison and Steve Gilbert, *Freedom of the Press Decisions of the United States Supreme Court* (San Diego, Calif.: Excellent Books, 1996); United States Supreme Court, *United States Reports: Cases Adjudged in the Supreme Court at . . . and Rules Announced at . . .* (New York: Banks & Brothers, Law Publishers, 1884–1921; Washington, D.C.: Government Printing Office, 1922–); Stanley N. Worton, comp., *Freedom of Speech and Press* (Rochelle Park, N.J.: Hayden Book Co., 1975).

Nebbia v. New York

U.S. Supreme Court decision, issued on March 5, 1934, that accepted the validity of a state statute regulating milk prices and broadened the definition of businesses "affected with a public interest." In 1933 New York state had established the Milk Control Board, empowered to fix minimum and maximum retail prices. Nebbia, a grocery store proprietor who was convicted of underselling, appealed on the grounds that the law violated the FOURTEENTH AMENDMENT right to due process. In its five-to-four decision, the Court reaffirmed that the state had the right to regulate industries for the public welfare, and ruled that "there is no closed class or category of businesses affected with a public interest."

Further reading: Henry Steele Commager, ed., *Documents of American History*, 8th ed. (New York: Appleton-Century-Crofts, 1968); Kermit L. Hall et al., eds., *The Oxford Companion to the Supreme Court of the United States* (New York: Oxford University Press, 1992); Robert R. Mayer, *The Court and the American Crises, 1930–1952* (Danbury, Conn.: Grolier Educational, 1995); United States Supreme Court, *United States Reports: Cases Adjudged in the Supreme Court at . . . and Rules Announced at . . .* (New York: Banks & Brothers, Law Publishers, 1884–1921; Washington, D.C.: Government Printing Office, 1922–).

Nehru-Liaquat Pact (Delhi Pact of 1950)

Agreement made on April 8, 1950, between the prime ministers of India (Jawaharlal Nehru) and Pakistan (Liaquat Ali Khan), seeking to ease the communal tension that had led to a massive interchange of inhabitants, notably Hindus from East Pakistan (now Bangladesh) and Muslims from West Bengal crossing borders in 1950. India and Pakistan acknowledged their responsibility in protecting the rights of minorities and promised to ensure "equality of citizenship" and "a full sense of security." The pact outlined steps for the protection of refugees and the normalization of conditions in the areas; it appointed minority commissions to implement these provisions. Returning refugees were allowed to recover their property and forced conversions were not recognized. Many took advantage of the protection offered and returned home. The pact temporarily healed the Muslim-Hindu rift highlighted by the partition of India.

See also: INDIAN INDEPENDENCE ACT, BRITISH.

Further reading: M. Rafique Afzal, ed., *Speeches and Statements of Quaid-i-Millat Liaquat Ali Khan, 1941–1951* (Lahore: Research Society of Pakistan, University of the Punjab, 1967); B. R. Nanda, *Jawaharlal Nehru: Rebel and Statesman* (New Delhi, India: Oxford University Press, 1998); Amrik Singh, ed., *The Partition in Retrospect* (New Delhi, India: Anamika Publishers and Distributors, 2000).

Nehru Report for a Constitution

Draft by the Nehru Committee for a New Indian Constitution, presented to the British Parliament on August 10, 1928. As a first step, the committee (chaired by Pandit Motilal Nehru) demanded dominion status for India. It proposed a bicameral legislature, consisting of a senate and house of representatives, to which the governor-general and his executive council would be accountable. Joint electorates were proposed, with reserved seats for minorities (except in Bengal and Punjab), though they could also contest other seats. The rights of Muslims would be protected and consideration given to the creation of Muslim-majority provinces on a linguistic basis. The report also suggested the inclusion of 19 fundamental rights in the constitution. The Muslim League demanded some amendments to this draft but, as Britain's Lord Birkenhead had envisioned, there was eventually little consensus among the Indian political parties and the matter was left to further deliberations.

Further reading: D. C. Goswami et al., eds., *Pandit Motilal Nehru, a Great Patriot* (New Delhi, India: National Forum of Lawyers & Legal Aid, 1976); Ravinder Kumar and D. N. Panigrahi, eds., *Selected Works of Motilal Nehru* (New Delhi, India: Vikas, 1982); Shan Muhammad, *The Indian Muslims: A Documentary Record* (Meerut, India: Meenakshi Prakashan, 1980); Motilal Nehru, *The Nehru Report: An Anti-Separatist Manifesto* (New Delhi, India: Michiko & Panjathan, 1975).

Nemours, Treaty of

Treaty made on July 7, 1585, marking King Henry III's humiliating surrender at Nemours, France, before the feudalists of the Catholic Holy League. Its signatories were Queen Mother Catherine de Médicis (on the French king's behalf) and Cardinal Charles de Bourbon on the one side and Duke Henry of Guise, his brother Louis the Cardinal, and Duke Charles III the Great for the Holy League. Catherine was forced to denounce her policy of French unity and religious freedom, to condemn the Huguenots (Protestants), whom she had tried to protect throughout her long career, and to surrender fortresses and cities. The treaty committed Henry III to fighting against the Huguenots, who were led by Henry of Navarre (later King Henry IV). By an edict issued on July 18, 1585, which the Paris Parlement was pressured into approving, Henry III officially condemned the Huguenots and the Calvinistic clergy, revoked all concessions made to them, and ordered them to renounce their faith or to leave the country under penalty of confiscation of goods or death.

See also: BEAULIEU, EDICT OF; BERGERAC, TREATY OF.

Further reading: Mack P. Holt, *The French Wars of Religion, 1562–1629* (New York: Cambridge University Press, 1995); R. J. Knecht, *Catherine de Medici* (New York: Longman, 1998); R. J. Knecht, *The French Wars of Religion, 1559–1598* (New York: Longman, 1996); David Potter, ed. and trans., *The French Wars of Religion; Selected Documents* (New York: St. Martin's Press, 1997).

Neuilly, Treaty of

Pact signed between Bulgaria and the Allied powers at Neuilly-sur-Seine, France, on November 27, 1919, following the Allied victory in World War I (1914–18). Operative August 9, 1920, Bulgaria was to surrender four areas on her western border to Yugoslavia, and a small area in the Rhodope Mountains and most of western Thrace to Greece. This cut off her access to the Aegean Sea and displaced 300,000 people; she was allowed to retain her merchant navy fleet. The Bulgarian army was reduced to 20,000 regulars, 10,000 gendarmes, and 3,000 frontier guards. Bulgaria's monetary compensation was fixed at £80 million, but 75 percent of it was later forgiven with the balance to be paid over 60 years.

Further reading: Georgi P. Genov, *Bulgaria and the Treaty of Neuilly* (Sofia, Bulgaria: H. G. Danov & Co., 1935).

Neutrality Act of 1794, U.S.

Federal legislation, enacted on June 5, 1794, that prohibited U.S. citizens from enlisting in the service of a foreign power and prohibited the fitting out of foreign armed ships in U.S. ports. The act codified George Washington's 1793 PROCLAMATION OF NEUTRALITY. Designed to avoid U.S. entanglement in the ongoing war between France and Great Britain, the act only partially relieved tension between the United States and Britain.

Further reading: Mortimer Adler, ed., *The Annals of America*, 18 vols. (Chicago: Encyclopaedia Britannica, 1968); Henry Steele Commager, ed., *Documents of American History*, 8th ed. (New York: Appleton-Century-Crofts, 1968).

Neutrality Act of 1937, U.S.

Federal legislation enacted on May 1, 1937, to keep the United States from becoming embroiled in international conflicts, particularly the Spanish Civil War of 1936–39. The act strengthened earlier congressional resolutions (1935–37) by placing an embargo on the export of arms, ammunition, and other war materials to belligerents in civil wars or wars between two or more foreign powers; by prohibiting loans or credit to belligerents; by forbidding American vessels to carry arms to belligerents; and by restricting the use of U.S. ports as a base of supply by such nations. American merchant vessels were prohibited from being armed. The act created the National Munitions Control Board to enforce its provisions.

Further reading: Raymond L. Buell, *The Neutrality Act of 1937* (New York: Foreign Policy Association, 1937); Henry Steele Commager, ed., *Documents of American History*, 8th ed. (New York: Appleton-Century-Crofts, 1968); Frank N. Magill, ed., *Great Events from History: American Series,* 3 vols. (Englewood Cliffs, N.J.: Salem Press, 1975); John N. Petrie, *American Neutrality in the 20th Century: The Impossible Dream* (Washington, D.C.: Institute for National Strategic Studies, National Defense University, 1995).

Neutrality Act of 1939, U.S.

Federal legislation enacted on November 4, 1939, that repealed the arms embargo established by the U.S. NEUTRALITY ACT OF 1937. Passed after the eruption of World War II in Europe, the act restated a U.S. policy of neutrality but allowed England and France to buy arms and munitions on a "cash and carry" basis: They would have to pay cash and to transport the war materials themselves. The act prohibited U.S. citizens from sailing on belligerent ships and U.S. ships from sailing to belligerent ports; it authorized the U.S. president to forbid ships to enter combat zones. It also prohibited the arming of merchant vessels. In November 1941, Congress repealed the restrictions on the arming of merchant vessels and allowed such ships to carry cargoes to belligerent ports.

Further reading: Paxton Blair, *Breach of Contract due to War* (New York: Baker, Voorhis, 1940); Frank N. Magill, ed., *Great Events from History: American Series*, 3 vols. (Englewood Cliffs, N.J.: Salem Press, 1975); John N. Petrie, *American Neutrality in the 20th Century: The Impossible Dream* (Washington, D.C.: Institute for National Strategic Studies, National Defense University, 1995); Ronald E. Powaski, *Toward an Entangling Alliance: American Isolationism, Internationalism, and Europe, 1901–1950* (New York: Greenwood Press, 1991).

Newburgh Addresses

Two addresses outlining grievances of American Revolutionary War army officers concerning their pay and pensions; issued on March 10 and 12, 1783, at George Washington's encampment near Newburgh, New York. Written by Major John Armstrong but circulated anonymously, the first address urged the officers to pressure Congress strongly and invited them to meet on March 11 to consider coercive action. Washington forbade the meeting but proposed further discussion. The second address, issued the following day, bore a less defiant tone. On March 15 Washington met with the officers and counseled patience and confidence in Congress. The officers responded with resolutions affirming their patriotism and condemning the addresses.

Further reading: Mortimer Adler, ed., *The Annals of America*, 18 vols. (Chicago: Encyclopaedia Britannica, 1968); Henry Steele Commager and Richard B. Morris, eds., *The Spirit of 'Seventy Six: The Story of the American Revolution as Told by Participants* (New York: Harper & Row, 1967); Amos E. Corning, *Washington at Temple Hill* (Newburgh, N.Y.: Lanmere, 1932); Don Higginbotham, *The War of American Independence: Military Attitudes, Policies, and Practice, 1763–1789* (Boston: Northeastern University Press, 1983).

Newcastle Program

British charter of policy aims approved by the National Liberal Federation Council at its Newcastle Conference in October 1891 and enunciated by William Gladstone in his conference speech. Irish Home Rule was topmost on the agenda, but Gladstone also tried to woo a broad section of voters by talking about the disestablishment of the church in Scotland and Wales, reforms in land laws and local government, fixing liability for accidents on the employers, triennial parliaments, and a ban on the local consumption of alcohol. To appease the radicals in the party, he stressed free education, reform or abolition of the House of Lords, and a withdrawal of duties on staple foods. In practice, the Liberal Party could not implement most of these reforms and, after its defeat in the 1895 election, it dissociated itself from this charter.

Further reading: Alan O'Day, *Irish Home Rule, 1867–1921* (Manchester, England: Manchester University Press, 1998); H. C. G. Matthew, *Gladstone 1809–1898* (New York: Oxford University Press, 1997).

Newcastle Proposals (Propositions of Newcastle)

Parliamentary conditions for a peace settlement and for the return of England's king Charles I (a prisoner of the Scots in Newcastle during the Great English Civil War) to the throne; submitted to the king on July 14, 1646. The king was to take the Covenant, abolish episcopacy and reform the church, and allow Parliament to control army and foreign policy for 20 years. His supporters were to be punished. The king dallied with his reply, hoping that the Presbyterians in Parliament and Independents in the army would split on the issue, but he finally rejected the conditions.

See also: SOLEMN LEAGUE AND COVENANT OF 1643.

Further reading: Mark C. Fissel, *The Bishops' Wars: Charles I's Campaigns Against Scotland, 1638–1649* (New York: Cambridge University Press, 1994); Peter Gaunt, *The English Civil War: The Essential Readings* (Malden, Mass.: Blackwell Publishers, 2000); Derek A. Wilson, *The King and the Gentleman: Charles Stuart and Oliver Cromwell, 1599–1649* (New York: St. Martin's Press, 1999).

New Echota, Treaty of

Agreement signed on December 29, 1835, by which the Cherokee Indians gave up their capital at New Echota, Georgia, and ceded all their lands east of the Mississippi River to the United States in exchange for $5,000,000 and 7 million acres of land in Indian Territory. The discovery of gold on Cherokee land in Georgia had intensified white desire for Indian land. The treaty, though signed by only a small faction of Cherokees and repudiated by the majority, bound the entire nation to move west of the Mississippi within three years. Thousands of Cherokee perished during the removal, which was accomplished by military force in 1838–39 and became known as the Trail of Tears.

See also: *CHEROKEE NATION V. GEORGIA; WORCESTER V. GEORGIA.*

Further reading: William L. Anderson, ed., *Cherokee Removal: Before and After* (Athens: University of Georgia Press, 1991); John Ehle, *Trail of Tears: The Rise and Fall of the Cherokee Nation* (New York: Doubleday, 1988); Thomas E. Mails, *The Cherokee People: The Story of the Cherokees from Earliest Origins to Contemporary Times* (New York: Marlowe, 1996).

New England Confederation, Articles of

Agreement establishing a union of the English colonies of Massachusetts Bay, Plymouth, Connecticut, and New Haven, adopted on May 19, 1643. The United Colonies of New England, organized largely for mutual protection against hostile Indians and other colonial powers, represented the first alliance among American colonies. The 12 articles of confederation set up a governing board of eight commissioners (two from each col-ony) who were to be chosen by the colonial general courts. The commissioners had the power to declare offensive and defensive war and had jurisdiction over disputes among the colonies, fugitives, and Indian affairs. Six votes were required for legal action. The union was dissolved in 1684.

Further reading: Mortimer Adler, ed., *The Annals of America*, 18 vols. (Chicago: Encyclopaedia Britannica, 1968); Henry Steele Commager, ed., *Documents of American History*, 8th ed. (New York: Appleton-Century-Crofts, 1968); Frederick K. Lister, *The Early Security Confederations: From the Ancient Greeks to the United Colonies of New England* (Westport, Conn.: Greenwood Press, 1999); Frank N. Magill, ed., *Great Events from History: American Series*, 3 vols. (Englewood Cliffs, N.J.: Salem Press, 1975).

New Granada Treaty

See BIDLACK TREATY.

New Jersey Plan (Paterson Plan)

Proposal submitted to the U.S.'s Federal Constitutional Convention on June 15, 1787, by William Paterson of New Jersey, a delegate aligned with the states' rights faction at the convention, as opposed to the nationalist faction. In opposition to the VIRGINIA PLAN, Paterson's proposal called for a unicameral legislature similar to the Articles of Confederation Congress in that each state would have equal representation. The plan also included provisions that would strengthen the national government: Congress would have the power to tax and to regulate interstate and foreign commerce; a federal executive and judiciary branch would be created; and the treaties and acts of Congress would be the supreme law in the states. The New Jersey Plan was rejected by the convention, which instead approved the GREAT COMPROMISE.

Further reading: Mortimer Adler, ed., *The Annals of America*, 18 vols. (Chicago: Encyclopaedia Britannica, 1968); Henry Steele Commager, ed., *Documents of American History*, 8th ed. (New York: Appleton-Century-Crofts, 1968); Frank N. Magill, ed., *Great Events from History: American Series*, 3 vols. (Englewood Cliffs, N.J.: Salem Press, 1975); John E. O'Connor, *William Paterson, Lawyer and Statesman, 1745–1806* (New Brunswick, N.J.: Rutgers University Press, 1979).

Newlands Act (Newlands Reclamation Act, U.S. National Reclamation Act)

Federal legislation written by U.S. senator Francis G. Newlands of Nevada and enacted on June 17, 1902; it created, within the U.S. Interior Department, the Bureau of Reclamation to develop irrigation projects in arid states. The proceeds from the sale of public lands financed the construction and maintenance of the projects. Settlers were to repay construction costs, thus creating a permanent revolving fund for irrigation works. As a result of the act, an extensive system of water resources, including the Hoover Dam in Nevada, has been created.

Further reading: Lawrence B. Lee, *Reclaiming the American West: An Historiography and Guide* (Santa Barbara, Calif.:

ABC-Clio, 1980); Lawrence J. MacDonnell, *From Reclamation to Sustainability: Water, Agriculture, and the Environment in the American West* (Niwot: University Press of Colorado, 1999); William D. Rowley, *Reclaiming the Arid West: The Career of Francis G. Newlands* (Bloomington: Indiana University Press, 1996).

New Laws of the Indies (New Laws of the Indies for the Good Treatment and Preservation of the Indians)

Laws decreed by the Spanish Crown in 1542, aimed at easing the lot of Indians in the Spanish colonies in America. The government provided that all *encomiendas* (feudal estates) were to cease at the death of the holders and be returned to the crown, and that no new ones would be granted; clerics and public officials were to surrender their *encomiendas* immediately; slavery was to be abolished; also, the laws were to be published in the major Indian languages. The New Laws (Leyes Nuevas) aroused such violent opposition among Spanish colonists that their main provisions were later repealed; the *encomienda* system in Latin America prospered until the 18th century.

Further reading: Fred W. Lucas and Henry Stevens, *The New Laws of the Indies for the Good Treatment and Preservation of the Indians . . . A Facsimile Reprint of the Original Spanish Edition, Together with a Literal Translation into the English Language* (New York: AMS Press, 1971); Frank N. Magill, ed., *Great Events from History: Modern European Series*, 3 vols. (Englewood Cliffs, N.J.: Salem Press, 1973).

Newport, Treaty of

Agreement between the Presbyterians in Parliament and King Charles I of England; made at Newport (on the Isle of Wight) on September 18, 1648, after the end of the Great English Civil War. Parliament was keen on reaching an understanding with the king and disregarded the army and the Vote of No Addresses (parliamentary vote forbidding addresses to the king, i.e., attempts at reconciliation). Meanwhile, the Independents, with the army's support, seized the king (on December 1) and imprisoned him at Hurst Castle, rendering the agreement useless. Shortly after (December 6 and 7), Colonel Thomas Pride, under orders from the army council, forcibly threw out (Pride's Purge) 96 Presbyterian members and other royalist sympathizers from what came to be known as the Rump Parliament (so-called as the supposed, inferior remnant of the Long Parliament, 1640–53).

See also: CHARLES, DEATH WARRANT OF.

Further reading: Maurice Ashley, *Charles I and Oliver Cromwell: A Study in Contrasts and Comparisons* (London: Methuen, 1987); Peter Gaunt, *The English Civil War: The Essential Readings* (Malden, Mass.: Blackwell Publishers, 2000); Derek A. Wilson, *The King and the Gentleman: Charles Stuart and Oliver Cromwell, 1599–1649* (New York: St. Martin's Press, 1999).

New Provinces Act

New Zealand legislation of 1858, framed by the ministry of E. W. Stafford for the creation of new provinces upon the petition (see NEW ZEALAND'S CONSTITUTION ACT OF 1852) of three-fifths of the electorate (minimum 150) in any district a half million to 3 million acres in size. It was passed after loud complaints of neglect and underrepresentation from settlers in remote areas, particularly Hawke's Bay—the first province to be so established. Marlborough (October 1859), Southland (1861–70), and Westland (1873) were similarly created. The superintendent of these new provinces was elected by the Provincial Council; he could not pass amendments or endorse bills and had only a negative vote. New Zealand's central government gradually gained control over the provincial system until the Provinces Act was abolished in 1876.

Further reading: Angela Caughey, *Pioneer Families: The Settlers of Nineteenth-Century New Zealand* (Glenfield, New Zealand: D. Bateman, 1994); Matthew Wright, *Hawke's Bay: The History of a Province* (Palmerston North, New Zealand: Dunmore Press, 1994).

New York Sons of Liberty, Resolutions of the

Declarations voted on and accepted by a group of patriots in New York City on November 29, 1773, denouncing the TEA ACT and declaring anyone who imported, transported, sold, or bought tea (while it was subject to duty by act of British Parliament) to be "an enemy of the liberties of America." These anti-Britishers also agreed to associate under the name "sons of liberty of New York"; they warned harbor pilots against guiding tea-carrying British ships into New York harbor. As a result of the resolutions, many consignments for the sale of tea in New York were either turned down or given up.

Further reading: Mortimer Adler, ed., *The Annals of America*, 18 vols. (Chicago: Encyclopaedia Britannica, 1968); Henry Steele Commager, ed., *Documents of American History*, 8th ed. (New York: Appleton-Century-Crofts, 1968); Henry B. Dawson, *The Sons of Liberty in New York* (New York: Arno Press, 1969).

New York State Club Association v. City of New York

U.S. Supreme Court decision issued on June 20, 1988, upholding a New York City law requiring women to be admitted to large, private, business-oriented clubs. The New York law, covered under the city's human rights laws, prohibited discrimination by private clubs having more than 400 members, supplying regular meal service, and being used for business and professional purposes by members and nonmembers. According to the unanimous Supreme Court ruling, the New York law did not affect "the ability of individuals to form associations that will advocate public or private viewpoints," but some private club members argued that their right of freedom of association under the FIRST AMENDMENT was violated by the New York law, which served to open up private men's clubs to women and minorities.

Further reading: Kermit L. Hall et al., eds., *The Oxford Companion to the Supreme Court of the United States* (New York: Oxford University Press, 1992); United States Supreme Court, *United States Reports: Cases Adjudged in the Supreme Court at . . . and Rules Announced at . . .* (New York: Banks & Brothers, Law Publishers, 1884–1921; Washington, D.C.: Government Printing Office, 1922–).

New York Times Company v. Sullivan

New York Times Company v. Sullivan　U.S. Supreme Court decision issued on March 9, 1964, ruling that the constitutional protections of freedom of speech and the press limit a state's power to award damages in a libel action brought by a public official. L. B. Sullivan, an elected commissioner of Montgomery, Alabama, had sued the *New York Times* for having published an advertisement alleging that Alabama officials had harassed black civil rights workers. In its unanimous decision, the Supreme Court ruled that the FIRST AMENDMENT and FOURTEENTH AMENDMENT guaranteed Americans the right to criticize the official conduct of their public officials. Defamatory statements, even errors of fact, were not punishable unless "actual malice" could be proved.

Further reading: Kermit L. Hall, et al., eds., *The Oxford Companion to the Supreme Court of the United States* (New York: Oxford University Press, 1992); Maureen Harrison and Steve Gilbert, *Freedom of the Press Decisions of the United States Supreme Court* (San Diego, Calif.: Excellent Books, 1996); Anthony Lewis, *Make No Law: The Sullivan Case and the First Amendment* (New York: Random House, 1991); United States Supreme Court, *United States Reports: Cases Adjudged in the Supreme Court at . . . and Rules Announced at . . .* (New York: Banks & Brothers, Law Publishers, 1884–1921; Washington, D.C.: Government Printing Office, 1922–).

New Zealand's Constitution Act of 1852

New Zealand's Constitution Act of 1852　By the British Parliament in 1852, an act creating a new constitution for New Zealand (the New Zealand Company having been dissolved a year earlier). The country was divided into six provinces, each administered by an elected superintendent and a provincial council (four-year term for members). The country would be presided over by a governor, assisted by a general assembly consisting of a legislative council (nominated) and a house of representatives (24 to 42 members, elected every five years). Only propertied males above the age of 21 were entitled to vote. Provincial governments (subservient to the general assembly) were not allowed to determine issues pertaining to customs duties, currency, the legal system, postal services, and marriage; the governor could veto their legislation. The governor controlled native affairs, while the foreign policy was dictated by the British government.

Further reading: John L. Robson, ed., *New Zealand: The Development of Its Laws and Constitution* (London: Stevens, 1967).

New Zealand's Native Land Acts

New Zealand's Native Land Acts　See NATIVE LAND ACTS, NEW ZEALAND'S.

New Zealand's Native Representation Act

New Zealand's Native Representation Act　See NATIVE REPRESENTATION ACT, NEW ZEALAND'S.

New Zealand's New Provinces Act

New Zealand's New Provinces Act　See NEW PROVINCES ACT.

Nicene Creed

Nicene Creed　Formal statement of Christian belief, promulgated at the First Council of Nicaea in A.D. 325; in a revised form, known as the Niceno-Constantinopolitan Creed, promulgated by the First Council of Constantinople in A.D. 381. Roman emperor Constantine I the Great had summoned the Christian bishops to meet at Nicaea in Asia Minor to settle a major doctrinal dispute between the priest Arius, who said that Jesus Christ the Son was subordinate to and not consubstantial with God the Father, and the bishop Athanasius of Alexandria, who said Christ and God were of the same substance. The Nicaea council laid down the formula or creed implying the same doctrine adopted later at Constantinople—that Christ was of the same substance (Greek, *homo-ousios*) as God, begotten but not created, which was (and is) the tenet of Western Christendom. The council anathematized Arius, who was then exiled by Constantine. The opening words of the creed are "I believe in one God the Father Almighty, maker of heaven and earth, and of all things visible and invisible, and in one Lord Jesus Christ."

See also: ATHANASIAN CREED.

Further reading: Virginia Burrus, *"Begotten, Not Made": Conceiving Manhood in Late Antiquity* (Stanford, Calif.: Stanford University Press, 2000); Catholic University of America, eds., *New Catholic Encyclopedia* (New York: McGraw-Hill, 1967); Frank N. Magill, ed., *Great Events from History: Ancient and Medieval Series*, 3 vols. (Englewood Cliffs, N.J.: Salem Press, 1972); Thomas F. Torrance, *The Trinitarian Faith: The Evangelical Theology of the Ancient Catholic Church* (Edinburgh, Scotland: T. & T. Clark, 1988).

Nicholas II's Abdication Manifesto

Nicholas II's Abdication Manifesto　Czar Nicholas II's formal letter of abdication, written on March 2, 1917, in Pskov, Russia, at the request of the members of the Duma (national assembly). It was published the following day in the "Izvestia of the Committee of Petrograd Journalists." Asked to abdicate in favor of his son but "not wishing to be separated" from him, he stepped down in favor of his brother Grand Duke Michael, urging him "to govern in union and harmony with the representatives of the people." Referring to the February Revolution (1917) as "a new and painful trial" in the midst of Russia's "great struggle against a foreign foe," he deemed it best "to lay down the Supreme Power" in his country's interests. Finally, Nicholas called on the Russian people to cooperate with the czar and the Duma in leading Russia toward "victory, well-being, and glory." Grand Duke

Michael refused the crown, which then lapsed, thus ending the Romanov dynasty, which had ruled Russia since 1613.

Further reading: Nikolai A. Bazili, *The Abdication of Emperor Nicholas II of Russia: A Memoir* (Princeton, N.J.: Kingston Press, 1984); D. C. B. Lieven, *Nicholas II: Twilight of the Empire* (New York: St. Martin's Press, 1994); Robert D. Warth, *Nicholas II: The Life and Reign of Russia's Last Monarch* (Westport, Conn.: Praeger, 1997); Richard Wortman, *Scenarios of Power: Myth and Ceremony in Russian Monarchy* (Princeton, N.J.: Princeton University Press, 1995).

Nicholas II's Declaration of Policy

Declaratory speech made by Czar Nicholas II of Russia on January 17, 1895, to representatives of the elective provincial assemblies (zemstvos). Delivered shortly after his accession, the speech was to set the tone for a continuance of the reactionary policies of his father, Czar Alexander III. In his talk, he characterized any thoughts that the zemstvos would be allowed to participate in the administration of internal affairs as "senseless dreams." Czar Nicholas also announced that he intended "to uphold the principle of autocracy as firmly and unflinchingly" as his father. The declaration embittered Russian liberals and revolutionaries, who had hoped the new regime might pursue a more enlightened policy.

Further reading: Marc Ferro, *Nicholas II: The Last of the Tsars,* trans. Brian Pearce (New York: Oxford University Press, 1993); D. C. B. Lieven, *Nicholas II: Twilight of the Empire* (New York: St. Martin's Press, 1994); Robert D. Warth, *Nicholas II: The Life and Reign of Russia's Last Monarch* (Westport, Conn.: Praeger, 1997); Milton Viorst, ed., *The Great Documents of Western Civilization* (Philadelphia: Chilton Books, 1965).

Nicholas II's Decree Dissolving the First Duma

Czar Nicholas II's decree of July 21, 1906, dissolving the first Duma (Russian national assembly), following its attempts to impose restrictions on his absolute authority. Alleging that Russia's representatives "have strayed into spheres beyond their competence" rather than applying themselves to "productive legislation," Nicholas declared that he would "impose our imperial will on the disobedient by all the power of the State." He urged "all well-disposed Russians" to cooperate in the restoration of peace and claim in the country and proposed that the peasant be provided "with legitimate and honest means for enlarging his holdings." Declaring his faith in the assembly as an institution, he announced March 5, 1907, as the inauguration date of the new Duma. He expressed the hope that the new Duma would fulfill "the requirements of a regenerated Russia," and urged his countrymen to strive with him toward that end.

Further reading: Marc Ferro, *Nicholas II: The Last of the Tsars,* trans. Brian Pearce (New York: Oxford University Press, 1993); D. C. B. Lieven, *Nicholas II: Twilight of the Empire* (New York: St. Martin's Press, 1994); Frank N. Magill,

ed., *Great Events from History: Modern European Series*, 3 vols. (Englewood Cliffs, N.J.: Salem Press, 1973); Milton Viorst, ed., *The Great Documents of Western Civilization* (Philadelphia: Chilton Books, 1965).

Nicholsburg, Treaty of

Treaty concluded at Nicholsburg (Mikulov, Czechoslovakia) on December 31, 1621, by Holy Roman Emperor Ferdinand II and Transylvanian prince Gabriel Bethlen after Transylvania's military struggle, born of nationalistic sentiments, against the Hapsburgs. Bethlen, who had been elected (though not crowned) king of Hungary by the Hungarian Protestants a year and a half earlier, agreed in the treaty to renounce this title. This was the only real concession he made. In return for his renunciation of Hapsburg Hungary, which he had gained in the recent hostilities, he received the duchies of Oppeln and Ratibor. The treaty turned out to be a temporary settlement during the Thirty Years' War (1618–48).

See also: LINZ, TREATY OF.

Further reading: Ronald G. Asch, *The Thirty Years' War: The Holy Roman Empire and Europe, 1618–48* (New York: St. Martin's Press, 1997).

Nicholson Non-Importation Act

See NON-IMPORTATION ACT OF 1806.

Nicias, Peace of

Treaty of peace negotiated in 421 B.C. during the Great Peloponnesian War (431–404 B.C.) between Athens and Sparta; signed by the new Athenian leader Nicias and the Spartan King Plistoanax. The peace was to last 50 years, and each signatory was to return all the captives and territories taken during the war. Athens was to retain Pylos (a harbor in Messenia) and Sparta was to keep Amphipolis (a city in Macedonia). Boeotia and Megara (enemies of Athens) and other city-states refused to sign the treaty because they either wished to hold on to captured lands or gained no benefits from it. The truce came apart when the unscrupulous Athenian politician Alcibiades forged Athenian alliances with Argos, Mantinea, and Tegea (former allies of Sparta).

Further reading: Donald Kagan, *A New History of the Peloponnesian War* (Ithaca, N.Y.: Cornell University Press, 1989); Donald Kagan, *The Peace of Nicias and the Sicilian Expedition* (Ithaca, N.Y.: Cornell University Press, 1981).

Nicola Proposal

Plan put forward in May 1782 by Colonel Lewis Nicola, proposing that George Washington serve as king of the United States. Lewis, an Irish immigrant and commander of a Pennsylvania regiment of the home guard, sent his proposal to Washington, arguing that a monarchy was necessary to establish an efficient government and secure the rights of the American people. Nicola professed to speak for the army, which he claimed would support such a plan. Washington sternly rejected the proposal, describing it as "big with the greatest mischiefs, that could befall my Country." The plan was thereafter abandoned.

Further reading: Louise B. Dunbar, *A Study of Monarchial Tendencies in the United States, from 1776 to 1801* (Urbana, Ill.: n.p., 1922); James T. Flexner, *Washington, the Indispensable Man* (Boston: Little, Brown, 1974); Don Higginbotham, *The War of American Independence: Military Attitudes, Policies, and Practice, 1763–1789* (Boston: Northeastern University Press, 1983).

Nicomachean Ethics (Ethica Nicomachea)   Greek philosopher Aristotle's (384–322 B.C.) authoritative lectures on ethics (in 10 books), dedicated to his son Nicomachus and edited from his notes in the first century B.C. Book one defines ethics as a practical science devoted to the study of human happiness, the ultimate goal of conduct, and distinguishes between the intellectual and moral virtues. Book two defines moral virtue as the ability to find the "mean" between extremes of conduct, while books three and four tabulate and analyze each moral virtue with its vices of excess and defect. Book five contains a separate essay on justice. Book six discusses the intellectual virtues, while book seven—actually an appendix to the chapters on moral virtue—is concerned with weakness of will. Books eight and nine constitute an essay of friendship and book 10 analyzes pleasure. Contemplation is the highest form of activity, concluded Aristotle, who was a pupil of Plato (see REPUBLIC, THE). Most of the Western conception of ethics comes from Aristotle's work.

Further reading: Antonina Alberti and Robert W. Sharples, eds., *Aspasius: The Earliest Extant Commentary on Aristotle's Ethics* (New York: W. de Gruyter, 1999); Roger Crisp, trans. and ed., *Nicomachean Ethics* (Cambridge, England: Cambridge University Press, 2000); Gerald J. Hughes, *Routledge Philosophy Guidebook to Aristotle on Ethics* (New York: Routledge, 2001).

Nieszawa, Statute of (Nieszawa Privilege)   Charter by which King Casimir IV of Poland made certain concessions to the kingdom's gentry (upper class, though not of noble rank) in November 1454, at Nieszawa, Poland. Seeking to repossess all of Pomerania from the Teutonic Knights, Casimir enlisted troops, but the gentry agreed to help only if the king pledged never to impose a mass levy (of troops or money), introduce new laws, or declare war without the consent of the provincial assemblies. The king agreed, and thus the statute significantly reduced the power of the Polish nobility in relation to the gentry.

Further reading: Michael Burleigh, *Prussian Society and the German Order: An Aristocratic Corporation in Crisis c. 1410–1466* (New York: Cambridge University Press, 1984).

Nietzsche's *Beyond Good and Evil*   See BEYOND GOOD AND EVIL.

Night and Fog Decree (Nacht und Nebel Erlass)   Secret order issued on December 7, 1941, by Chancellor Adolf Hitler of Germany, ordering the Gestapo and the SD (Sicherheitsdienst), the Nazi Party's intelligence and security force, to capture all individuals throughout Germany and German-occupied territory who were believed to be a threat to German security. It was intended that such individuals would be made to disappear into the "night and fog." In addition, questions about the prisoners' fate were forbidden. General Wilhelm Keitel, chief of staff of the German armed forces' high command in World War II (1939–45), was put in charge of carrying out the decree.

Further reading: Walter Gorlitz, ed., *The Memoirs of Field-Marshal Wilhelm Keitel* (New York: Cooper Square Press, 2000); Walter Gorlitz, ed., *In the Service of the Reich* (New York: Stein & Day, 1979); William L. Shirer, *The Rise and Fall of the Third Reich: A History of Nazi Germany* (New York: Simon & Schuster, 1960).

Nijmegen (Nimwegen), Treaties of   Series of six separate peace agreements (four of them signed at Nijmegen, or Nimwegen, Holland) concluded by France with Spain, Holland, Austria (Holy Roman emperor), Denmark, and Sweden, ending the Franco-Dutch War or Third Dutch War (1672–78). By the first treaty, with Holland (August 10, 1678), France returned Maastricht and withdrew oppressive levies (1667) against the Dutch (a great boost to Holland's commerce and maritime power). Spain surrendered (September 17, 1678, treaty) Franche-Comté, Artois, and 16 border fortresses in Flanders, while France ceded some frontier territories in the Spanish Netherlands. Austria retained (February 5, 1679, treaty) Philippsburg but surrendered Freiburg im Breisgau, including free access to it from Breisach (French-held). Austria also returned captured territories to Sweden, France's ally. Another treaty at Nijmegen (October 12, 1679) confirmed the status quo between Holland and Sweden. By a treaty signed at Fontainebleau (September 2, 1679), France forced Denmark to restore all her Swedish conquests. And finally, at Lund, Sweden (September 26, 1679), Denmark permitted Sweden to retain possession of all she had at the start of the war. The duke of Lorraine rejected conditions for his reinstatement, and French occupation continued. Although these treaties clearly showed France's supremacy, they contained the seeds of an anti-French coalition.

See also: RYSWICK, TREATY OF.

Further reading: J. A. H. Bots ed., *The Peace of Nijmegen 1676–1678/79* (Amsterdam: Holland Universiteits Pers, 1980).

Nile River Distribution Agreement   Agreement (November 8, 1959) between Egypt and the Republic of Sudan regarding the distribution of the waters of the Nile River. Negotiations began when the new Sudanese government (see ANGLO-EGYPTIAN SUDAN TREATY OF 1953) rejected the 1929 agreement in search of a more equitable arrangement. Following year-long negotiations, it was decided to grant Sudan a compensation of 15 million Egyptian pounds in lieu of the area flooded by Lake Nasser and a one-third share of the total Nile flow once the Aswan High Dam Project went into operation. The two countries also signed a program of technical cooperation. The agreement is intended to be valid until 2059.

Further reading: Abd el-Fattah Ibrahim el-Sayed Baddour, *Sudanese-Egyptian Relations: A Chronological and Analytical Study* (The Hague: M. Nijhoff, 1960); Husayn Dhu al-Faqar Sabri, *Sovereignty for Sudan* (London: Ithaca Press, 1982); John Waterbury, *The Nile Basin: National Determination of Collective Action* (New Haven, Conn.: Yale University Press, 2002).

Nimwegen, Treaties of   See NIJMEGEN, TREATIES OF.

Nine Power Pacts (Treaties of Washington)   Agreements concluded on February 6, 1922, among nine nations at the Washington Conference (1921–22), affirming the new "open door" policy of China and reflecting a consensus of opinion in their relations toward China. The signatories (the United States, Britain, France, Japan, Italy, Belgium, the Netherlands, China, and Portugal) recognized the independence of China and agreed to help stabilize her government, to encourage joint commercial ventures, and not to claim special privileges by exploiting her instability. Despite this, Britain, France, and Japan maintained their existing spheres of influence in China, while the United States claimed the right to seek equal benefits. The signatories were not bound to defend China's territorial integrity. Another pact increased China's tariff rates (see ANGLO-CHINESE TREATY OF 1928) and expanded her administrative authority regarding customs duties and collections. A commission was appointed to deliberate on the issue of extraterritoriality in China.

See also: FIVE POWER NAVAL TREATY; FOUR POWER PACIFIC TREATY.

Further reading: Henry Steele Commager, ed., *Documents of American History*, 8th ed. (New York: Appleton-Century-Crofts, 1968); Erik Goldstein and John H. Maurer, *The Washington Conference, 1921–22: Naval Rivalry, East Asian Stability and the Road to Pearl Harbor* (Portland, Ore.: Frank Cass, 1994); Frank N. Magill, ed., *Great Events from History: American Series*, 3 vols. (Englewood Cliffs, N.J.: Salem Press, 1975); Westel W. Willoughby, *China at the Conference; a Report* (Westport Conn.: Greenwood Press, 1972).

Nineteen Propositions   Propositions from the English Long Parliament to King Charles I at York on June 2, 1642, demanding that he relinquish his rights of appointment in government and accept parliamentary proposals for the reformation of the church. The king was asked to sign the militia bill and hand over fortified sites to officers approved by Parliament. Further, Parliament was to be given the power to hire and fire royal ministers and guardians for the king's children and to exclude from the House of Lords all peers created after that date. The king rejected these proposals outright.

Further reading: Maurice Ashley, *Charles I and Oliver Cromwell: A Study in Contrasts and Comparisons* (London: Methuen, 1987); Peter Gaunt, *The English Civil War: The Essential Readings* (Malden, Mass.: Blackwell Publishers, 2000); Derek A. Wilson, *The King and the Gentleman: Charles Stuart and Oliver Cromwell, 1599–1649* (New York: St. Martin's Press, 1999).

Nineteenth Amendment, U.S.   Amendment to the U.S. CONSTITUTION passed by Congress in 1919 and ratified by the states in 1920 giving women the right to vote. The amendment, the culmination of decades of crusading by women suffragists, gained support during World War I (1914–18), when women increasingly entered business and industry and otherwise contributed to the war effort. Several states had already enfranchised women by 1918, when U.S. president Woodrow Wilson declared himself in favor of a national amendment. Though the amendment doubled the number of Americans entitled to vote, voting patterns did not change drastically, as some reformers had expected.

Further reading: Alan Brinkley, *American History: A Survey*, 10th ed. (Boston: McGraw-Hill College, 1999); Kermit L. Hall, et al., eds., *The Oxford Companion to the Supreme Court of the United States* (New York: Oxford University Press, 1992); June Hannam, et al., *International Encyclopedia of Women's Suffrage* (Santa Barbara, Calif.: ABC-Clio, 2000); Frank N. Magill, ed., *Great Events from History: American Series*, 3 vols. (Englewood Cliffs, N.J.: Salem Press, 1975).

Ninety-five Theses, Luther's   Formal propositions composed by the German religious reformer Martin Luther, who was an ordained Roman Catholic priest, and nailed by him to the door of the castle church in the Saxon town of Wittenberg, Germany, on October 31, 1517. Written in Latin but immediately translated into German, the theses challenged the excesses and abuses of the Roman Catholic Church, particularly the shameless sale of indulgences (pardons of temporal punishment due for sin). And Luther questioned the pope's right to forgive sin. Luther had been angered by the German Dominican preacher Johann Tetzel's sale of indulgences (granted by Pope Leo X) for the erection of St. Peter's Church. Among the most important of the theses was Luther's thorough and harsh repudiation of the promotion of indulgences, his strong belief that no priest was required to mediate between man and God, and his doctrine of justification by faith alone. The Ninety-five Theses subsequently became a declaration of independence for Protestantism, fueling the fire of the Reformation to reform Catholicism.

See also: EXSURGE DOMINE.

Further reading: Charles W. Eliot, ed., *The Harvard Classics*, 51 vols. (New York: P. F. Collier & Son, 1937); Frank

N. Magill, ed., *Great Events from History: Modern European Series*, 3 vols. (Englewood cliffs, N.J.: Salem Press, 1973); Louis L. Snyder, ed., *Documents of German History* (New Brunswick, N.J.: Rutgers University Press, 1958); Milton Viorst, ed., *The Great Documents of Western Civilization* (Philadelphia: Chilton Books, 1965).

Ninety-two Resolutions, Papineau's Resolutions prepared by a committee of the Legislative Assembly in Lower Canada (Quebec), led by French-Canadian rebel leader Louis Joseph Papineau and passed by the assembly in February 1834; they consisted of grievances and a series of demands for increased power and constitutional changes. The document contained demands for "responsible government," whereby the executive, which consisted of British-appointed officials, would be responsible to the popularly elected Legislative Assembly and responsible for greater application of the elective principle and for the legislature's control of revenues. British rejection of the resolutions in 1837 (see TEN RESOLUTIONS, RUSSELL'S) intensified the resentment of the French Canadians against the British.

See also: DURHAM'S REPORT.

Further reading: Claude Baribeau and Bruce G. Wilson, *Papineau, His Life and Times*, rev. ed. (Ottawa: National Archives of Canada, 1987); Fernand Ouellet, *Louis-Joseph Papineau, a Divided Soul* (Ottawa: Canadian Historical Association, 1972).

Ninth Amendment, U.S. Amendment to the U.S. CONSTITUTION, ratified in 1791, declaring that the particular "enumeration in the Constitution of certain rights" of the people should not be construed to mean that other rights are being denied or disparaged. Citing this amendment as law, the U.S. Supreme Court later upheld the citizen right to engage in political activity, which is now safeguarded by court decision.

See also: BILL OF RIGHTS, U.S.

Further reading: Alan Brinkley, *American History: A Survey*, 10th ed. (Boston: McGraw-Hill College, 1999); Marshall L. DeRosa, *The Ninth Amendment and the Politics of Creative Jurisprudence: Disparaging the Fundamental Right of Popular Control* (New Brunswick, N.J.: Transaction Publishers, 1996); Kermit L. Hall et al., eds., *The Oxford Companion to the Supreme Court of the United States* (New York: Oxford University Press, 1992); Calvin R. Massey, *Silent Rights: The Ninth Amendment and the Constitution's Unenumerated Rights* (Philadelphia: Temple University Press, 1995).

Nissa, Treaty of Peace treaty sought by Russia with the Ottoman Empire (Turkey) and signed on October 3, 1739, at Nissa (Niš, Serbia, Yugoslavia), concluding the Russo-Turkish War of 1736–39 (see BELGRADE, TREATY OF). Russia's territorial ambitions and her underestimation of the Turks' ability to counter Russian aggression had caused the war. By the treaty, Russia restored portions of Moldavia and Bessa-rabia, including the city of Khotin, to the Turks. The Russians also promised to dismantle the fortifications at Azov, which they had captured and were allowed to retain, and they agreed not to maintain naval vessels in the Black Sea. The Ottomans agreed to give the Russians some trading privileges in their empire.

Further reading: Jane Burbank and David L. Ransel, eds., *Imperial Russia: New Histories for the Empire* (Bloomington: Indiana University Press, 1998); Justin McCarthy, *The Ottoman Turks: An Introductory History to 1923* (New York: Longman, 1997); Donald Quataert, *The Ottoman Empire, 1700–1922* (New York: Cambridge University Press, 2000).

Nixon's "Checkers" Speech Television address delivered by U.S. Republican vice presidential candidate Richard M. Nixon on September 23, 1952, refuting charges that he had benefited from a secret "slush fund" established by California millionaires. Threatened with losing his position on the Republican ticket, Nixon made an emotional appeal to voters, denying any impropriety and claiming that the fund was used for legitimate political purposes. He described his wife's "plain Republican cloth coat" and stated that he had received only one gift—a cocker spaniel dog named Checkers—which he vowed to keep. Nixon also challenged Democratic candidates to reveal their finances. The speech won Nixon public support and probably saved his political career.

Further reading: Irwin F. Gellman, *The Contender: Richard Nixon: The Congress Years, 1946–1952* (New York: Free Press, 1999); *Great Speeches of the 20th Century*, vol. 1 (sound recording): *The Political Arena* (Santa Monica, Calif.: Rhino Records, 1991); Irving J. Rein, comp., *The Relevant Rhetoric; Principles of Public Speaking Through Case Studies* (New York: Free Press, 1969).

Nixon's Inaugural Address Speech delivered by Richard M. Nixon on January 20, 1969, at his inauguration as 37th president of the United States. Nixon stated that although America was engaged in a war, the nation was ready to assume the role of peacemaker in the world. Appealing to a national concern for law and order, he said that America had suffered from inflated, bombastic, and angry rhetoric that promised more than it could deliver, fanned discontent into hatred, and postured rather than persuaded. "We cannot learn from one another until we stop shouting at one another," he said, claiming that his administration would "strive to listen in new ways." He argued that the nation must enlist the efforts of all the people, not just the government, to achieve the goals of full employment, fair housing, excellent education, rebuilding the cities, improving rural areas, and protecting the environment.

Further reading: *Great Speeches of the 20th Century*, vol. 1 (sound recording): *The Political Arena* (Santa Monica, Calif.: Rhino Records, 1991); Joan Hoff, *Nixon Reconsidered* (New

York: Basic Books, 1994); Melvin Small, *The Presidency of Richard Nixon* (Lawrence: University Press of Kansas, 1999).

Nixon's Resignation Speech

Address to the nation delivered by U.S. president Richard M. Nixon on August 8, 1974, announcing his resignation from office, effective the following day. Facing impeachment and trial for obstruction of justice in the Watergate scandal, abuse of presidential power, and defying congressional subpoenas for evidence, Nixon became the first U.S. president to resign. Nixon admitted that he no longer had political support in Congress and declared that the country needed a full-time president, not one largely occupied with self-vindication. He expressed regret for possible errors in judgment but admitted no wrongdoing, stating that he had tried to act in the best interests of the nation. He hoped that his resignation would begin "the process of healing which is so desperately needed in America."

Further reading: *Great Speeches of the 20th Century*, vol. 1 (sound recording): *The Political Arena* (Santa Monica, Calif.: Rhino Records, 1991); Joan Hoff, *Nixon Reconsidered* (New York: Basic Books, 1994); Melvin Small, *The Presidency of Richard Nixon* (Lawrence: University Press of Kansas, 1999).

Nixon's Speech Announcing a Freeze on Prices and Wages

Address delivered by U.S. president Richard M. Nixon on August 15, 1971, announcing a new economic policy to control rampant inflation, high unemployment, and international monetary speculation. To halt the rise in the cost of living, he ordered an immediate 90-day freeze on all prices and wages, an unprecedented measure in peacetime, and appointed a Cost of Living Council to oversee wage and price controls after the freeze ended. To stabilize the American dollar, Nixon suspended the free convertibility of dollars into gold, and to make American goods more competitive, he imposed an additional 10 percent import tax. He also asked Congress to enact jobs development legislation and urged tax reductions, to be offset by cuts in federal spending and foreign aid. The announcement was followed by the formal devaluation of the dollar in December.

Further reading: Joan Hoff, *Nixon Reconsidered* (New York: Basic Books, 1994); Melvin Small, *The Presidency of Richard Nixon* (Lawrence: University Press of Kansas, 1999).

Noble Edict of the Rose Chamber

See OTTOMAN IMPERIAL EDICT OF 1839.

No Child Left Behind Act (U.S. Education Reform Act of 2002)

Legislation enacted by the U.S. Congress to improve public education in the United States. The act was a sweeping reform of the ELEMENTARY AND SECONDARY EDUCATION ACT OF 1965, U.S., and redefined the federal government's role in educating students from kindergarten through high school. The act's main goals were to improve the aca-

demic performance of minority and disadvantaged students, make all students fluent in the English language, improve math and science skills in general, boost the quality of teachers, promote innovative learning programs, involve parents to a greater degree in their children's education, and improve the safety of schools. The act imposed stringent accountability procedures to ensure that all goals would be met; states that met all goals would be rewarded with additional federal funds, while those that did not would have their federal funding cut back. The act was signed into law on January 8, 2002, by President George W. Bush, its chief architect, who had pledged during the Election of 2000 to make education reform a top priority of his administration.

Further reading: U.S. Department of Education, "No Child Left Behind—Executive Summary," available online at http://www.ed.gov/inits/nclb/part2.html.

No. 45 of *The North Briton*

Famous issue (no. 45) of John Wilkes's periodical *The North Briton*, published on April 23, 1763, in which Britain's king George III and his prime minister, Lord Bute, were vilified. Wilkes, a member of Parliament, insulted the king and charged him with making falsehoods in a recent speech from the throne, concerning peace negotiations in Paris (see PARIS, TREATY OF [1763]). Wilkes was arrested on a general warrant for seditious libel, but was soon released on grounds that his arrest violated his rights as a member of Parliament (from which he was later expelled in 1764).

See also: JUNIUS, LETTERS OF.

Further reading: *The North Briton* (New York: AMS Press, 1976); George F. E. Rude, *Wilkes and Liberty; a Social Study of 1763 to 1774* (Oxford, England: Clarendon Press, 1962); Peter D. G. Thomas, *John Wilkes, a Friend to Liberty* (New York: Clarendon Press, 1996).

Non-Importation Act of 1806 (Nicholson Non-Importation Act)

U.S. legislation sponsored by Representative Joseph Hopper Nicholson of Maryland and enacted on April 18, 1806, prohibiting the importation of certain British goods. The purpose of the act was to force Great Britain, then at war with France, to cease her practices of seizing neutral American commercial vessels engaged in trade with the French and of impressing American sailors under the claim that they were deserters from the British navy or British subjects, forcing them into royal service. The act, suspended on December 19, 1806, was followed by the U.S. EMBARGO ACT OF 1807.

Further reading: Louis M. Sears, *Jefferson and the Embargo* (New York: Octagon Books, 1978).

Non-Intercourse Act, U.S.

Federal legislation signed by U.S. president Thomas Jefferson on March 1, 1809, and effective on March 15, repealing the U.S. EMBARGO ACT OF 1807 and restoring trade with all foreign countries except Great

Britain and France. The act authorized the president to allow resumption of trade with those two nations when they stopped violating neutral rights by seizing U.S. commercial ships and impressing U.S. sailors. When the act failed to end French and British interference with America shipping, it was replaced by the MACON ACT.

Further reading: Ralph K. Beebe, *Thomas Jefferson, the Embargo, and the Decision for Peace* (Menlo Park, Calif.: Addison-Wesley Publishing, 1972); Henry Steele Commager, ed., *Documents of American History*, 8th ed. (New York: Appleton-Century-Crofts, 1968); Louis M. Sears, *Jefferson and the Embargo* (New York: Octagon Books, 1978).

Norris–La Guardia Anti-Injunction Act   U.S. legislation, enacted on March 23, 1932, that forbade the use of federal court injunctions to preserve antiunion employment contracts or to restrain strikes, boycotts, or picketing, except where such strikes affected the public safety. Sponsored by Senator George W. Norris of Nebraska and Representative Fiorello La Guardia of New York, it protected workers' rights to join a union by prohibiting "yellow dog" contracts (agreements by which employers required their workers not to join unions and not to participate in any strike against the employers).

Further reading: Henry Steele Commager, ed., *Documents of American History*, 8th ed. (New York: Appleton-Century-Crofts, 1968); Lawrence Elliott, *Little Flower: The Life and Times of Fiorello La Guardia* (New York: Morrow, 1983); Howard Zinn, *La Guardia in Congress* (New York: Norton, 1969); Norman L. Zucker, *George W. Norris; Gentle Knight of American Democracy* (Urbana: University of Illinois Press, 1966).

North American Air Defense Agreement   Pact made by Canada and the United States on August 1, 1957, providing for the creation of a North American Air Defense (NORAD) through the integration of the two countries' air defense operations. By the agreement, formally ratified on May 14, 1958, NORAD would be responsible for the air defense of the continental United States, Alaska, and Canada; it would be responsible for developing joint U.S.-Canadian plans and procedures for emergency situations; would be headed by an American commander and a Canadian deputy; and would be headquartered in Colorado Springs, Colorado. NORAD's combat operations center would be built inside Cheyenne Mountain, Colorado, and would announce the first warning of an attack. The agreement was intended to be seen as an extension of NATO's objectives for the security of North America. NORAD was activated in 1961.

Further reading: David Cox, *Canada and NORAD, 1958–1978: A Cautionary Retrospective* (Ottawa: Canadian Centre for Arms Control and Disarmament, 1985); Ann D. Crosby, *Dilemmas in Defence Decision-Making: Constructing Canada's Role in NORAD, 1958–96* (New York: St. Martin's Press,

1998); Lewis Hertzman, et al., *Alliances and Illusions; Canada and the NATO-NORAD Question* (Edmonton, Canada: Hurtig, 1969); Joseph T. Jockel, *No Boundaries Upstairs: Canada, the United States, and the Origins of North American Air Defence, 1945–1958* (Vancouver: University of British Columbia Press, 1987).

North American Free Trade Agreement (NAFTA)
Pact signed on December 17, 1992, between the United States, Canada, and Mexico to create a free trade zone in North America. It was the culmination of years of negotiations between the governments of U.S. president George H. W. Bush, Canadian prime minister Brian Mulroney, and Mexican president Carlos Salinas de Gortari. By gradually reducing and eventually removing tariffs, customs charges, and other barriers to trade as the European Community (European Union) had previously done (see MAASTRICHT TREATY), NAFTA would expand trade and stimulate the region's economies. Also, U.S. and Canadian companies would have increased access to Mexican markets in service industries (banking, insurance, advertising), telecommunications, and trucking. Actually, the United States and Canada had signed their own free trade agreement in 1988, so NAFTA represented an extension of this agreement to Mexico. NAFTA was approved (after much debate) by the legislatures of the three countries in 1993 and went into effect January 1, 1994.

See also: EUROPEAN FREE TRADE ASSOCIATION AGREEMENT.

Further reading: Jim Landers, "Five Years of NAFTA: The Road Ahead," *Dallas Morning News*, January 30, 1999; The Tech, "Index of/Bulletins/Nafta," Massachusetts Institute of Technology, available online at http://www-tech.mit.edu/Bulletins/Nafta.

Northampton, Assize of   English legislation of King Henry II at the Council of Northampton in January 1176, confirming and revising many provisions of the Assize of CLARENDON. Drafted as a set of instructions for the six groups of judges assigned to newly defined circuits, it greatly increased their powers and also introduced more stringent penalties for various offenses. Those convicted by the king's justices would henceforth lose a right hand (in addition to a foot) and be expelled from the country within 40 days. All men were required to swear loyalty to the king in the county courts. No one could entertain a stranger for more than one night unless he could also vouchsafe for him. A freeholder's fief passed to his heirs; if denied, the matter would be determined at an inquest. Fugitives who failed to obey the royal summons were outlawed. The judges were ordered to act entirely in the king's interests while discharging their duties.

See also: ARMS, ASSIZE OF; DARRIEN PRESENTMENT, ASSIZE OF; WOODSTOCK, ASSIZE OF.

Further reading: Robert Bartlett, *England under the Norman and Angevin Kings, 1075–1225* (Oxford, England: Clarendon Press, 1999); James C. Holt, *Colonial England, 1066–*

1215 (Rio Grande, Ohio: Hambledon Press, 1997); Ralph V. Turner, *Judges, Administrators and the Common Law in Angevin England* (Rio Grande, Ohio: Hambledon Press, 1994); Patrick Wormald, *The Making of English Law: King Alfred to the Twelfth Century* (Malden, Mass.: Blackwell Publishers, 1999).

Northampton, Treaty of

Agreement of May 4, 1328, indicating England's recognition of Scotland's independence; concluded between King Edward III's regency government (Queen Isabella and Sir Roger Mortimer) and Robert Bruce of Scotland. Thereby, Scotland was to pay £20,000 and be released "from all exaction, right, claim or demand" of overlordship on England's part and "from any homage" to be paid to the English monarchs. The treaty also acknowledged Robert Bruce as king of Scotland and restored Scotland's frontiers to those during the reign of King Alexander III (1249–86). Further, five-year-old David Bruce (Robert's son) was betrothed to Edward's younger sister, Joan of the Tower. The proposed return of the Stone of Scone to the Scots was, however, disallowed by the abbot of Westminster and prominent Londoners. Unhappy with these concessions, Edward III tried to salvage his position after the death of Robert Bruce in 1329.

Further reading: Colm McNamee, *The Wars of the Bruces: Scotland, England and Ireland, 1306–1328* (East Linton, Scotland: Tuckwell Press, 1997); Raymond C. Paterson, *For the Lion: A History of the Scottish Wars of Independence* (Edinburgh, Scotland: J. Donald, 1996); Bruce Webster, *Medieval Scotland: The Making of an Identity* (New York: St. Martin's Press, 1997).

North Atlantic Treaty (North Atlantic Pact)

Security pact established on April 4, 1949, by countries of the North Atlantic region, forming the North Atlantic Treaty Organization (NATO), a military and political alliance intended to counteract the Soviet Union's increasing military presence and expansionist moves in Eastern and Western Europe. Successor to the BRUSSELS TREATY OF 1948, it was endorsed by Belgium, Britain, Canada, Denmark, France, Iceland, Italy, Luxembourg, the Netherlands, Norway, Portugal, and the United States, and later joined by Greece, Turkey, and West Germany. The treaty, initiated by the United States, bound its signatories to help each other in the event of aggression (an attack on one was to be regarded as an attack on all) and "to safeguard the freedom, common heritage and civilization of their peoples founded on the principles of democracy, individual organization, liberty and the rule of law." NATO has standing military forces in Europe and operates chiefly through its council (made up of representatives from the member nations).

See also: WARSAW PACT.

Further reading: Mortimer Adler, ed., *The Annals of America*, 18 vols. (Chicago: Encyclopaedia Britannica, 1968); Henry Steele Commager, ed., *Documents of American History*, 8th ed. (New York: Appleton-Century-Crofts, 1968); Frank

N. Magill, ed., *Great Events from History: Modern European Series*, 3 vols. (Englewood Cliffs, N.J.: Salem Press, 1973); Louis L. Snyder, ed., *Fifty Major Documents of the Twentieth Century* (Princeton, N.J.: D. Van Nostrand Company, 1955.

Northern Securities Company v. United States

U.S. Supreme Court decision of March 14, 1904, that ordered the dissolution of the Northern Securities Company, a holding company formed in 1901, which controlled the Great Northern, Northern Pacific, and Chicago, Burlington, and Quincy railroads and monopolized rail transportation westward from the Great Lakes. President Theodore Roosevelt ordered the U.S. attorney general to file suit under the SHERMAN ANTI-TRUST ACT. The court, by a 5-4 decision, ruled that the holding company was in illegal restraint of trade, since it eliminated competition.

Further reading: Henry Steele Commager, ed., *Documents of American History*, 8th ed. (New York: Appleton-Century-Crofts, 1968); Howard B. Furer, *The Fuller Court, 1888–1919* (Danbury, Conn.: Grolier Educational, 1995); Kermit L. Hall, et al., eds., *The Oxford Companion to the Supreme Court of the United States* (New York: Oxford University Press, 1992); United States Supreme Court, *United States Reports: Cases Adjudged in the Supreme Court at . . . and Rules Announced at . . .* (New York: Banks & Brothers, Law Publishers, 1884–1921; Washington, D.C.: Government Printing Office, 1922–).

Northwest Ordinance of 1787 (Land Ordinance of 1787)

U.S. law, enacted by Congress on July 13, 1787, that provided for the organization and government of the Northwest Territory and laid out procedures for the admission of new states to the Union. Based on and replacing the LAND ORDINANCE OF 1784, the plan was written principally by Massachusetts jurist Nathan Dane. It stipulated that the Northwest Territory would initially be governed by a governor, secretary, and three judges, who would be appointed by Congress, and that a representative bicameral legislature was to be created when the colony included 5,000 adult free males. The territory could ultimately be divided into three to five states, and a population of 60,000 free inhabitants was necessary for statehood. Slavery was forbidden in the Northwest Territory, and freedom of worship, trial by jury, and public support of education were guaranteed. The Northwest Ordinance is considered the most significant achievement of the Congress of the ARTICLES OF CONFEDERATION.

Further reading: Mortimer Adler, ed., *The Annals of America*, 18 vols. (Chicago: Encyclopaedia Britannica, 1968); *American Jurisprudence, Second Edition*, Desk Book (N.p.: West Group, 1998); Henry Steele Commager, ed., *Documents of American History*, 8th ed. (New York: Appleton-Century-Crofts, 1968); Frank N. Magill, ed., *Great Events from History: American Series*, 3 vols. (Englewood Cliffs, N.J.: Salem Press, 1975).

Northwest Territories Act of 1875   Federal legislation passed by the Canadian government in 1875, containing provisions relating to the administration of Canada's northwestern region (the Northwest Territories, consisting of lands acquired by Canada from the Hudson Bay Company in 1870). The act provided that the territory would be governed by a council and governor appointed by the federal government in Ottawa and that these appointed officials would gradually be replaced by elected officials as the territory's population increased. In addition, the bill guaranteed the existence of both Protestant and Roman Catholic schools. The legislation replaced the Northwest Territories Act of 1869, through which the governor of Manitoba was to administer the territory.

Further reading: R. C. Brown and M. E. Prang, eds., *Canadian Historical Documents Series*, vol. 3: *Confederation to 1949* (Scarborough, Canada: Prentice-Hall of Canada, 1966); Kenneth Coates, *Canada's Colonies: A History of the Yukon and Northwest Territories* (Toronto: J. Lorimer, 1985).

Norwegian-Swedish Treaty of Separation   Treaty prepared by members of both the Swedish and Norwegian parliaments, agreed to by both parliaments on September 24, 1905, and endorsed by Swedish king Oscar II on October 26, 1905, declaring the end of the union of the two crowns, which had come into being less than a century earlier (see UNION, ACT OF [UNION OF SWEDEN AND NORWAY]). Through the treaty, Norway gained independence from Sweden; a neutral zone, running along the two countries' common border, was established; Sweden received the right to use the ice-free port of Narvik, on Norway's northern coast, for export of certain commodities; and it was agreed that any future disagreements were to be referred to an arbitration court at The Hague.

See also: KIEL, TREATY OF.

Further reading: Raymond E. Lindgren, *Norway-Sweden: Union, Disunion, and Scnadanavian Integration* (Princeton, N.J.: Princeton University Press, 1959); Frank N. Magill, ed., *Great Events from History: Modern European Series*, 3 vols. (Englewood Cliffs, N.J.: Salem Press, 1973).

Nostra Aetate (Declaration on the Relation of the Church to non-Christian Religions)   The Second Vatican Council's proclamation, issued by Pope Paul VI on October 28, 1965, acknowledging the commonality of the search for the absolute truth by peoples of all religious backgrounds (Hinduism and Buddhism were mentioned, for example) and rejecting any discrimination based on race, color, status, or religion. Referring to the historically close but sometimes contentious relationship among Christianity, Islam, and Judaism, it exhorted their followers to work toward promoting mutual understanding, peace, and freedom for all humanity. Sweeping in its scope and influential in its impact, the document was drafted by John M. Osterreicher, an Austrian Jew who converted to Christianity and eventually joined the priesthood.

Further reading: *The Documents of Vatican II* (New York: America Press, 1966).

Nöteborg, Treaty of   Agreement concluded at Nöteborg (Petrokrepost, Russia) in 1323 between Sweden and Russia, establishing the Finnish-Russian border. The Swedish magnates (ranking nobles) had taken control and elected (1319) three-year-old King Magnus VII of Norway (recent inheritor of that crown) as Sweden's king Magnus II. They ruled during the king's minority (until 1332) and negotiated the treaty, which expanded advantageously Sweden's territorial rule and power over Norway, Finland, and other areas.

Further reading: Anssi Paasi, *Territories, Boundaries, and Consciousness: The Changing Geographies of the Finnish-Russian Border* (Chichester, England: J. Wiley & Sons, 1996).

Nova Scotia's General Assembly, Proclamation for   Summons issued by Governor Charles Lawrence of Nova Scotia on May 20, 1758, forming Canada's first elective assembly, which met in Halifax later that year. Lawrence acted on instructions from Britain and under pressure from immigrant colonists from England and New England who insisted on the "rights of Englishmen" and self-government. The proclamation established a 16-member general assembly. To be elected, a member could not be a "Popish Recusant" or under the age of 21; he also had to own a "Freehold Estate within the District for which he shall be elected, or shall vote."

Further reading: J. M. Beck, *The Government of Nova Scotia* (Toronto: n.p., 1957); Charles B. Ferguson, *The Origin of Representative Government in Canada* (Halifax, Canada: Committee on Bicentenary of Representative Government, 1958); Archibald M. MacMechan, *The 200th Anniversary of Representative Government in Canada: 1758–1958* (Halifax, Canada: Committee on Bicentenary of Representative Government, 1958); P. B. Waite, ed., *Canadian Historical Documents Series*, vol. 2: *Pre-Confederation* (Scarborough, Canada: Prentice-Hall of Canada, 1965).

November Treaty (Pact of Guarantee, November Pact)   Treaty concluded on November 21, 1855, by Great Britain, France, and Sweden, confirming the western powers' support for the territorial integrity of Sweden. Specifically, France and Great Britain pledged to come to the aid of Sweden in the event that she was faced with Russian demands for territorial concessions; Sweden in turn pledged not to yield to any such demands. The treaty was concluded during the Crimean War (1853–56), in which Russia and the Ottoman Empire (supported by France and Great Britain) were fighting over supremacy in the Balkans, among other things. The western powers, through the treaty, sought to deter Russian aggression on Russia's northwestern frontier, in the Baltic region.

See also: PARIS, TREATY OF (1856); VIENNA FOUR POINTS; VIENNA NOTE OF 1853.

Further reading: Herbert Paul, ed., *Famous Speeches* (London: I. Pittman, 1911).

Novgorod, Treaty of   Treaty concluded on June 3, 1326, bringing to an end a hostile, decades-long conflict between Russia (specifically, the principality of Novgorod) and Norway over a border dispute. The disputed area, located in the extreme north of present-day Norway, was called Finnmark. Instead of determining a specific border between the two countries, it was decided that the region would be shared in common by the Norwegians, Swedes, Finns, and Russians, while formally under the control of Norway. It also provided for taxing and fishing rights to those four peoples. The accord lasted until the present-day Russian-Norwegian border was secured in 1826.

Further reading: Henrik Birnbaum, *Lord Novgorod the Great: Essays in the History and Culture of a Medieval City-State* (Columbus, Ohio: Slavica Publishers, 1981); Janet Martin, *Medieval Russia, 980–1584* (New York: Cambridge University Press, 1995); Vilhelm L. P. Thomsen, *The Relations Between Ancient Russia and Scandanavia, and the Origin of the Russian State* (New York: B. Franklin, 1964).

Novum Organum (New Instrument)   Philosophical work written in Latin by English philosopher Francis Bacon and published in 1620, presenting the author's argument that the natural world was to be understood inductively from experience. In the work Bacon proposed that if one were first to observe the natural world, arrange the observations systematically, and then compare the data, one could discover general laws governing the natural world. A general theory could ultimately be derived from a series of laws. In the work he also denounced other methods, such as the deductive method of Aristotelian scholasticism, because they had no practical application. In contrast, Bacon argued, his method contributed directly to scientific and technical advancement. Perhaps somewhat inconsistently, Bacon also maintained that knowledge of the supernatural world must be attained through revelation.

Further reading: Francis Bacon, *The New Organon*, eds. Lisa Jardine and Michael Silverthorne (New York: Cambridge University Press, 2000); Charles W. Eliot, ed., *The Harvard Classics*, 51 vols. (New York: P. F. Collier & Son, 1937); Frank N. Magill, ed., *Great Events from History: Modern European Series*, 3 vols. (Englewood Cliffs, N.J.: Salem Press, 1973); Alvin Snider, *Origin and Authority in Seventeenth-Century England: Bacon, Milton, Butler* (Toronto: University of Toronto Press, 1994).

Noyon, Treaty of   Agreement concluded by King Charles I of Spain and King Francis I of France at Noyon, France, on August 13, 1516, resolving their main differences in the face of a common threat, the Ottoman Turks. France renounced her claim to Naples but was allowed to keep Milan. Francis's daughter, Louise, was to be betrothed to Charles, bringing Naples as her dowry. Holy Roman Emperor Maximilian I (grandfather of Charles I), who later ratified the treaty, restored Brescia and Verona to Venice in lieu of financial compensation. The treaty, an exercise in European diplomacy that involved Pope Leo X, helped to strengthen Charles's supremacy in Europe (he was chosen Holy Roman emperor in 1519).

See also: BOLOGNA, CONCORDAT OF; FRIBOURG, TREATY OF.

Further reading: R. J. Knecht, *Renaissance Warrior and Patron: The Reign of Francis I* (New York: Cambridge University Press, 1994); Frank N. Magill, ed., *Great Events from History: Modern European Series*, 3 vols. (Englewood Cliffs, N.J.: Salem Press, 1973); William Roscoe, *The Life and Pontificate of Leo the Tenth* (New York: AMS Press, 1973).

Nuclear Non-Proliferation Treaty of 1968   Agreement adopted by the United Nations General Assembly on June 12, 1968, to prevent the proliferation of nuclear weapons. Thereby, the transfer of nuclear weapons and devices to another country was banned, as was the acquiring of such by nonnuclear weapon countries, whose nuclear systems would be subject to verification. However, the development, manufacture, and use of nuclear energy for peaceful purposes, and international cooperation in this regard—ensuring that any benefits accruing from peaceful applications of nuclear technology could be passed on to nonnuclear-weapon states—would be encouraged. The signatories pledged to continue negotiations for ending the nuclear arms race at an early date. Subject then to ratification by the Soviet Union, the United Kingdom, the United States, and 40 other countries, the treaty was to be reviewed every five years.

See also: INTERMEDIATE NUCLEAR FORCES TREATY; NUCLEAR TEST BAN TREATY OF 1963; STRATEGIC ARMS LIMITATION TREATY OF 1972; STRATEGIC ARMS LIMITATION TREATY OF 1979.

Further reading: William M. Evan and Ved P. Nanda, eds., *Nuclear Proliferation and the Legality of Nuclear Weapons* (Lanham, Md.: University Press of America, 1995); David A. Koplow, *Nuclear Testing and the Non-Proliferation Treaty* (Washington, D.C.: Lawyers Alliance for World Security, 1992); Mohamed I. Shaker, *The Nuclear Non-Proliferation Treaty: Origin and Implementation, 1959–1979* (New York: Oceana Publications, 1980); John Simpson and Darryl A. Howlett, eds., *The Future of the Non-Proliferation Treaty* (New York: St. Martin's Press, 1995).

Nuclear Test Ban Treaty of 1963   Treaty by the United Kingdom, the United States, and the Soviet Union in Moscow on August 5, 1963, prohibiting the testing of nuclear weapons in the atmosphere, outer space, or underwater. Underground testing was allowed. There were no provisions for on-site inspection, control posts, or international supervision, nor did it address issues such as reduction in nuclear stockpiles, stopping the production of nuclear weapons, or limiting their employment during war. The signatories, however, intended it as the first step on the road to complete disarmament. Before enforcement (October 10, 1963), more than 100 countries had endorsed it—France and the People's Republic of China being the two major exceptions. The approval of the three original signatories and of the majority of the other countries was required to pass any amendments to the treaty, but the three countries could veto any amendment.

Further reading: Mortimer Adler, ed., *The Annals of America*, 18 vols. (Chicago: Encyclopaedia Britannica, 1968); Henry Steele Commager, ed., *Documents of American History*, 8th ed. (New York: Appleton-Century-Crofts, 1968); Mary M. Lepper, *Foreign Policy Formulation; a Case Study of the Nuclear Test Ban Treaty of 1963* (Columbus, Ohio: C. E. Merrill Publishing, 1971); Kendrick Oliver, *Kennedy, Macmillan, and the Nuclear Test-Ban Debate, 1961–63* (New York: St. Martin's Press, 1998).

Nullification Proclamation (Jackson's Proclamation to South Carolina)

Proclamation issued by U.S. president Andrew Jackson on December 10, 1832, concerning the constitutional issues of state nullification of federal statutes. Prepared in response to SOUTH CAROLINA'S ORDINANCE OF NULLIFICATION, which declared null and void the TARIFF ACT OF 1828 and the TARIFF ACT OF 1832, Jackson's proclamation called nullification unconstitutional and an "impractical absurdity." The president maintained the supremacy of the federal government: No state could refuse to obey federal laws. He warned that "disunion by armed force" was treason.

See also: SOUTH CAROLINA'S REPLY TO JACKSON'S PROCLAMATION.

Further reading: Mortimer Adler, ed., *The Annals of America*, 18 vols. (Chicago: Encyclopaedia Britannica, 1968); Henry Steele Commager, ed., *Documents of American History*, 8th ed. (New York: Appleton-Century-Crofts, 1968); Frank N. Magill, ed., *Great Events from History: American Series*, 3 vols. (Englewood Cliffs, N.J.: Salem Press, 1975).

Nürnberg, Peace of

Truce concluded by Holy Roman Emperor Charles V and German Protestant princes; signed in Nürnberg (Nuremberg), Germany, on June 23, 1532. It provided for a temporary end to hostilities between Roman Catholics and Protestants and suspension of the 1530 imperial decree by the Diet of Augsburg against the Protestants, who were allowed freedom of worship until the next imperial Diet (when a solution to the religious conflict could perhaps be decided). In return, the Protestant princes agreed to contribute arms and men to the defense of the Holy Roman Empire against the Turkish invaders. The interim truce lasted 15 years and was needed, if the emperor hoped to drive back the Turks.

Further reading: Martyn C. Rady, *The Emperor Charles V* (New York: Longman, 1988).

Nürnberg Laws

Laws decreed in Nürnberg (Nuremberg, Germany) on September 15, 1935, by the German Reichstag (assembly) at the annual Nürnberg Rally of the National Socialist, or Nazi, Party; the laws deprived Jews (and those of at least quarter-Jewish extraction) of the status of being German citizens. The first law provided that only those individuals of German or racially related blood, and who had also proven themselves to be true servants of the German Reich (state), would be granted German citizenship; those not fulfilling the criteria were thenceforth servants, or state members, of the Reich. A second law prohibited marriage between Jews and Germans or German citizens of racially related blood; offenders would be punished by imprisonment or penal servitude. Increasingly severe laws were enacted as the Nazi obsession with Jews developed.

Further reading: Ingeborg Hecht, *Invisible Walls: A German Family under the Nuremberg Laws* (Evanston, Ill.: Northwestern University Press, 1999); Amy Newman, *The Nuremberg Laws: Institutionalized Anti-Semitism* (San Diego, Calif.: Lucent Books, 1999); Louis L. Snyder, ed., *Fifty Major Documents of the Twentieth Century* (Princeton, N.J.: D. Van Nostrand Company, 1955; Louis L. Snyder, ed., *Documents of German History* (New Brunswick, N.J.: Rutgers University Press, 1958).

Nurses Act of 1919, British

Parliamentary legislation introduced to regulate the profession of nursing, which had seen a sudden upsurge since the end of World War I (1914–18). The act created a General Nursing Council for England and Wales with authority to conduct examinations and maintain a register of qualified nurses. Similar legislation was passed in Scotland (1919) and Northern Ireland (1922). Later these nursing laws were joined in new legislation in 1949, which formed regional boards to help improve nursing schools in Britain.

Further reading: Brian Abel-Smith, *A History of the Nursing Profession* (London: Heinemann, 1975).

Nymphenburg, Treaty of

Secret treaty of alliance made between France and Bavaria at Nymphenburg palace, near Munich, on May 18, 1741; soon joined by Spain (May 28, 1741) and later by Saxony and Prussia (1742). The alliance was formed in opposition to the expansionist policy of Austrian archduchess Maria Theresa, the successor to the Hapsburg dominions, at the beginning of the War of the Austrian Succession (1740–48). France pledged financial and military assistance to Bavaria in the latter's claims to the Hapsburg throne. In return for Spanish subsidy payments, Bavaria pledged to recognize Spain's king Philip V's claims to Austrian lands in Italy. The sudden alliance reflected the general belief in Austria's inability to defend herself.

See also: BRESLAU, TREATY OF; PRAGMATIC SANCTION OF 1713.

Further reading: M. S. Anderson, *The War of the Austrian Succession, 1740–1748* (New York: Longman, 1995); Reed Browning, *The War of the Austrian Succession* (New York: St. Martin's Press, 1993).

Nyon Agreement   Agreement to effect a system of patrol zones to combat "piracy" on the Mediterranean Sea; concluded by Britain, France, Russia, and six Mediterranean countries during a conference (September 10–14, 1937) held at the Swiss town of Nyon. It was decided that Britain and France would organize a patrolling system for the Mediterranean to detect and attack any unidentifiable submarines. This became necessary when Italy violated the "Gentleman's Agreement" (see ANGLO-ITALIAN AGREEMENTS OF 1937 AND 1938) by launching random attacks on neutral shipping in the region. When the Italian attacks stopped, negotiations began on the other thorny issue—the presence of Italian volunteers (troops) in Spain—and were successfully concluded in the 1938 Anglo-Italian Agreement. Britain was to recognize Italian control over Ethiopia, Italy was to withdraw some volunteers from Spain and abstain from hostile agitation in the Near East, and both nations were to maintain the status quo in the Red Sea.

Further reading: Nyon Conference, 1937, "The Nyon Arrangement, September 14 and 17, 1937," *American Journal of International Law* 31 (1937): 179–82; Norman J. Padelford, "Foreign Shipping During the Spanish Civil War," *American Journal of International Law* 32 (1938): 264–79.

Nystadt, Treaty of   Peace treaty between Russia and Sweden, concluded on August 30, 1721 at the Finnish town of Nystadt; it marked the end of the Great Northern War (1700–1721), during which these two countries struggled for hegemony in the Baltic region. By the agreement, Sweden ceded to Russia the territories of Livonia, Ingermanland, part of Karelia, and several Baltic islands. Russia gave back to Sweden a large part of Finland and made an indemnity payment of 2 million rix-dollars. The treaty marked the end of Sweden's bid for supremacy in the Baltic and the beginning of Russia's influence in European power politics.

Further reading: Robert I. Frost, *The Northern Wars: War, State, and Society in Northeastern Europe, 1558–1721* (New York: Longman, 2000); Frank N. Magill, ed., *Great Events from History: Modern European Series*, 3 vols. (Englewood Cliffs, N.J.: Salem Press, 1973); Andrew Rothstein, *Peter the Great and Marlborough: Politics and Diplomacy in Converging Wars* (London: Macmillan, 1986).

O

Ocala Platform   Set of demands adopted by the National Farmers' Alliance and Industrial Union, meeting at Ocala, Florida, in December 1890. The platform demanded the abolition of national banks, the establishment of subtreasuries to provide low-interest loans, an increase in circulating money, the prohibition of futures dealings on agricultural and mechanical production, free and unlimited coinage of silver, a graduated income tax, elimination of tax on the necessities of life, government control and supervision of public communication and transportation, and the direct election of U.S. senators. The meeting, drawing agrarian leaders from across the United States, represented a landmark in the formation of a national farmers' movement.

Further reading: Henry Steele Commager, ed., *Documents of American History*, 8th ed. (New York: Appleton-Century-Crofts, 1968); Theodore R. Mitchell, *Political Education in the Southern Farmers' Alliance, 1887–1900* (Madison: University of Wisconsin Press, 1987).

Occasional Conformity Bill   British act finally passed in 1711, preventing dissenters (nonconformists) from simply taking one communion in the Anglican Church to satisfy and evade the TEST ACT OF 1673 and so qualify for civil and military office. Anyone attending nonconformist services after receiving the Anglican sacrament was fined £40 and disqualified from office. The bill was promoted by the Whigs as a ploy to get support from the Nottingham group of Tories against the government's peace efforts with France. However, it was never strictly enforced and was finally repealed in 1719.

See also: TOLERATION ACT OF 1689.

Further reading: William Gibson, ed., *Religion and Society in England and Wales, 1689–1800* (London: Leicester University Press, 1998); E. Gordon Rupp, *Religion in England, 1688–1791* (New York: Oxford University Press, 1986); Joel H. Wiener, ed., *Great Britain—The Lion at Home: A Documentary History of Domestic Policy 1689–1973*), 4 vols. (New York: Chelsea House, 1974).

October Diploma   Constitution issued by Austrian emperor Francis Joseph on October 20, 1860, providing for a centralized government as well as a greater degree of autonomy for the individual provinces within the ethnically diverse Austrian Empire. The document provided that the imperial diet (assembly) would consist of representatives from the whole empire; that the imperial diet would be responsible for matters involving the empire as a whole, such as foreign policy and the military, while the individual provincial diets would be responsible for their own affairs; and that Hungary would regain the autonomy that she had possessed prior to 1848. Although the document represented a positive development with respect to the preceding 12 years, to the nationalist federalists, represented largely by Czech, Polish, and Magyar nobles, it was not far-reaching enough. The German centralists on the other hand felt it had compromised too much, and within months it was replaced by the FEBRUARY PATENT, a new constitution.

Further reading: Steven Beller, *Francis Joseph* (New York: Longman, 1996); Anatol Murad, *Franz Joseph I of Austria and His Empire* (New York: Twayne Publishers, 1968); Alan Palmer, *Twilight of the Habsburgs: The Life and Times of Emperor Francis Joseph* (New York: Grove Press, 1995).

October Manifesto

Decree issued on October 30, 1905, by Czar Nicholas II, effectively transforming Russia into a constitutional monarchy. The embryonic constitution guaranteed civil liberties; provided for a legislative duma elected by indirect but nearly universal manhood suffrage; and created a council of ministers, whose president, Count Sergei Witte, was comparable to a prime minister. The manifesto was an attempt to stem the tide of the Russian Revolution of 1905, which in October had culminated in a 10-day general strike and the formation in Moscow of a workers' soviet, or council, to coordinate and direct strike activities. The manifesto succeeded in neutralizing the opposition, which split over the question of whether the proposed constitution was satisfactory: The liberals and moderates proclaimed their support, but the radicals of both the right and the left were dissatisfied.

See also: RUSSIAN FUNDAMENTAL LAWS OF 1906.

Further reading: Abraham Ascher, *The Revolution of 1905* (Stanford, Calif.: Stanford University Press, 1988–92); Frank N. Magill, ed., *Great Events from History: Modern European Series*, 3 vols. (Englewood Cliffs, N.J.: Salem Press, 1973); Andrew M. Verner, *The Crisis of Russian Autocracy: Nicholas II and the 1905 Revolution* (Princeton, N.J.: Princeton University Press, 1990); Milton Viorst, ed., *The Great Documents of Western Civilization* (Philadelphia: Chilton Books, 1965).

October Revolution, Proclamation of the

Proclamation issued in Petrograd (St. Petersburg) on November 7 (October 25, Old Style calendar), 1917, by the executive committee of the Petrograd Soviet, or Council of Workers' and Soldiers' Deputies; it declared the overthrow of the provisional government, which had been called into being by the czarist government eight months earlier, and marked the beginning of the Russian October (November) Revolution. The issue of the proclamation had been preceded on November 6 by the provisional government's attempt to close down the Bolshevik newspapers, an act that the Bolsheviks feared would develop into a general anti-Bolshevik movement. The Petrograd Soviet then called for troops to defend the soviet, and they ended up occupying most government buildings. The next evening, following the issue of the proclamation, the troops under Bolshevik leadership captured the ministers of the provisional government and occupied its headquarters. The All-Russian Congress of Soviets the following day acknowledged the beginning of the revolution.

See also: ORDER NO. 1, PETROGRAD SOVIET'S.

Further reading: Frank N. Magill, ed., *Great Events from History: Modern European Series*, 3 vols. (Englewood Cliffs, N.J.: Salem Press, 1973); David R. Marples, *Lenin's Revolution: Russia, 1917–1921* (New York: Longman, 2000); Milton Viorst, ed., *The Great Documents of Western Civilization* (Philadelphia: Chilton Books, 1965); Rex A. Wade, *The Russian Revolution, 1917* (New York: Cambridge University Press, 2000).

Ofen, Treaty of

Agreement concluded between King Béla IV of Hungary and King Ottocar II of Bohemia in 1254 at Ofen (German for Buda, now a part of Budapest). It marked an end to a territorial conflict between them over possession of the Babenberg lands in Austria. King Ottocar had a dynastic claim to the powerful Babenberg throne because he was married to Margaret, sister of the last Babenberg ruler of the lands, Duke Frederick II of Austria and Styria, who had died in 1246. King Béla's claim rested on his status as victor in battle over Duke Frederick. By the treaty, Ottocar was allowed to rule Austria, and Béla received Styria.

Further reading: A. W. A. Leeper, *A History of Medieval Austria*, eds. R. W. Seton-Watson and C. A. Macartney (New York: AMS Press, 1978); Imre Lukinch, *A History of Hungary in Biographical Sketches* (Freeport, N.Y.: Books for Libraries Press, 1968).

Offenses Against the State Act, Ireland's

Legislation of December 4, 1970, by which the government of the Republic of Ireland invoked Section 2 of the Offenses Against the State Act of 1940, allowing it to intern, without trial, suspected enemies of the state. Irish prime minister John Lynch reportedly introduced the measure following rumors of a "secret conspiracy" involving plans to rob banks, kidnap or assassinate government officials, and create general lawlessness. The government did not mention any of the alleged conspirators by name; however, it was assumed that the Irish Republican Army (IRA) and the Saor Eire (Free Ireland) were the groups responsible. Under the act, the government opened detention centers and acquired emergency powers to deal with the expected crisis.

Further reading: J. Bowyer Bell, *The IRA, 1968–2000: Analysis of a Secret Army* (Portland, Ore.: Frank Cass, 2000); T. G. Fraser, *Ireland in Conflict, 1922–1998* (New York: Routledge, 2000); Eunan O'Halpin, *Defending Ireland: The Irish State and Its Enemies* (New York: Oxford University Press, 1999).

Ogdensburg Declaration

Statement issued by U.S. president Franklin D. Roosevelt and Canadian prime minister W. L. Mackenzie King at Ogdensburg, New York, on August 18, 1940, announcing the establishment of the Permanent Joint Board of Defense, to plan for the cooperative defense of North America in case of any foreign attack. The board, with members from both Canada and the United States, was to investigate mutual sea, land, and air defense problems, including personnel and matériel. Soon after the declaration, Canada served as a mediator between the United States and Great Britain for the DESTROYERS-FOR-BASES AGREEMENT.

Further reading: *The Canada–United States Permanent Joint Board on Defence* (Ottawa: External Information Programs Division, Department of External Affairs, 1982); Henry Steele Commager, ed., *Documents of American History*, 8th ed. (New York: Appleton-Century-Crofts, 1968); J. L. Granatstein, *Mackenzie King: His Life and World* (New York: McGraw-Hill Ryerson, 1977).

Ogulnian Law (Lex Ogulnia)   Ancient Roman law enacted in 300 B.C., granting to the plebeians (common people) access to the higher priesthoods (governed then by the patricians). Earlier, in 368 B.C., the plebes (admitted to all other offices) were granted half the increased (from two to 10 persons) membership on the board in charge of public sacred books and religious ceremonies. By the law of 300 B.C., the number of pontifices (priests in the pontifical college) increased by four to nine, and the college of augures (religious interpreters of omens) increased by five to nine members. The law also required the new places in the colleges to be filled by plebeians. It ended obstruction of plebeian political activity through patrician control of the priesthood.

See also: DOMITIAN LAW.

Further reading: Paul F. Girard, *A Short History of Roman Law* (Union, N.J.: Lawbook Exchange, 2000).

Oil Pollution Act of 1990, U.S. (OPA90)   Enactment of August 18, 1990, by U.S. president George H. W. Bush that tightened federal laws pertaining to oil spills and cleanups following the *Exxon-Valdez* oil spill of March 1989. It required vessel and facility owners to submit detailed emergency response plans including cleanup contracts. Cargo owners were spared liability for spills, while spillers faced unlimited liability for gross negligence, deliberate misconduct, violation of national operating and safety guidelines, or failure to report spills or participate in cleanup efforts. A $1 billion liability fund was established. The U.S. Coast Guard was ordered to explore use of improved navigational aids to reduce spills, consider banning tankers from certain areas, and reexamine tug escort laws. Also, states could pass stricter laws if they wanted to, and two regional citizens' advisory councils were created in Alaska.

Further reading: Thomas A. Birkland, "In the Wake of the Exxon Valdez—How Environmental Disasters Influence Policy," *Environment* 40, no. 7 (September 1998): 4ff.

Oléron, Judgments of (Code or Laws of Oléron)   Codification (c. 1150) of commercial maritime decisions generally ascribed to King Richard I of England. It was mainly a recompilation of the judgments decreed by the judges of Oléron Island (off the west coast of France). Backed by royal authority, the 47-article code quickly gained acceptance as the standard maritime law of the Atlantic coast, paralleling the law of the Mediterranean, Consolato del Mare. It required that a master consult the crew before setting out in inclement weather and recompense any damage that occurred if he failed to heed their advice. Sick sailors were to be sent ashore with an attendant and without loss of pay unless the injury was caused by drunkenness or quarrels. It clearly specified the liability of the master, the crew, and the merchants in various types of accidents and introduced severe penalties against dishonest owners, inefficient pilots, and wrecking lords. During the reign of King Edward III (1327–77), the admirality used it as the basis for resolving maritime disputes in England.

Further reading: *The Federal Cases [with appendix comprising the Laws of Oleron]*, 30 vols. (New York: Hein, 1995); Louis F. Middleton, *The Laws of Oleron, or, The Judgements of the Sea*, A.D. 1375: *From Black Book of the Admiralty* (Mystic, Conn.: Marine Historical Association, 1935).

Oliva, Treaty of   Treaty concluded at the monastery of Oliva (Oliwa) near Danzig (Gdansk, Poland) on May 3, 1660, by King John II Casimir of Poland and representatives from Sweden (King Charles X of Sweden had died unexpectedly in February). Through the treaty Poland agreed to cede to Sweden the disputed Baltic region of Livonia (except for a small southeastern portion); Casimir agreed to renounce his claims to the Swedish crown, although he retained until his death the title of king of Sweden; Brandenburg, which had supported the Austro-Polish alliance against Sweden with men and arms, was granted sovereignty over East Prussia. The treaty brought to an end the First Northern War (1655–60), in which Sweden had attempted to gain mastery over Poland and various Baltic Areas.

See also: WEHLAU, TREATY OF.

Further reading: Robert I. Frost, *The Northern Wars: War, State and Society in Northeastern Europe, 1558–1721* (New York: Longman, 2000); Wladyslaw Konopczynski, *Poland and Sweden* (Torun, Poland: The Baltic Institute, 1935); Margaret Shennan, *The Rise of Brandenburg-Prussia* (New York: Routledge, 1995).

Olive Branch Petition   Statement written by John Dickinson and adopted by the Second Continental Congress on July 5, 1775, after the first armed clashes between the American colonists and the British at Bunker Hill, Concord, and Lexington. The petition was a last attempt to settle the colonists' differences with Britain by means short of war. It restated the grievances of the colonists but expressed their attachment to the king and asked his aid in preventing further conflict. Its conciliatory intent was also demonstrated by the fact that the delegates signed the petition as individuals rather than as a united group, and that they sent as their messenger Richard Penn, descendant of William Penn and a loyalist.

King George III, however, refused to see Penn or to receive the petition on grounds that the Americans were disloyal and in revolt.

Further reading: N. E. Evans, ed., *The Olive Branch Petition* (London: H.M. Stationery Office, 1972); Paul Sparer and Jack Curtis, eds., *Literature of Revolutionary America* (New York: Lexington, 1962); Cornelius W. Wickersham and Gilbert H. Montague, eds., *The Olive Branch, Petition of the American Congress to George III . . .* (New York: New York Public Library, 1954).

Olmstead v. United States

U.S. Supreme Court decision, issued on June 4, 1928, that allowed the admission of wiretapping evidence in court. Federal prohibition agents had used recorded conversations obtained from wiretapping to secure convictions of suspected bootleggers. The case was appealed on the grounds that wiretapping constituted an unreasonable search and seizure, prohibited by the FOURTH AMENDMENT to the U.S. CONSTITUTION. In a 5-4 decision, the court stated that wiretapping was permitted because it was not physical entry; even though wiretapping was illegal in the state of Washington, where the acts occurred, the evidence was admissible in federal court. In dissent, Justice Oliver Wendell Holmes called wiretapping a "dirty business" in which the government should not engage.

Further reading: Alan Barth, *Prophets with Honor: Great Dissents and Great Dissenters in the Supreme Court* (New York: Knopf, 1974); Kermit L. Hall et al., eds, *American Legal History: Cases and Materials*, 2d ed. (New York: Oxford University Press, 1996); Kermit L. Hall et al., eds., *The Oxford Companion to the Supreme Court of the United States* (New York: Oxford University Press, 1992); *United States Supreme Court, United States Reports: Cases Adjudged in the Supreme Court at . . . and Rules Announced at . . .* (New York: Banks & Brothers, Law Publishers, 1884–1921; Washington, D.C.: Government Printing Office, 1922–).

Olmütz, Punctation of

Agreement concluded by Prime Minister Otto von Manteuffel of Prussia and Prince Felix Schwarzenberg of Austria on November 29, 1850, at Olmütz (Olomouc, Czechoslovakia), bringing an end to a conflict between the two states that had nearly resulted in civil war. Through the document it was agreed that Prussia would abandon her plan to unite Germany under her leadership, and that at a meeting of German princes to be held in Dresden from December 1850 to March 1851 a revision of the federal constitution would be prepared. The conflict had arisen over Prussia's desire to unite all the German states under a new constitution through the leadership of Prussia, and over Austria's determination to prevent any such development, as she wished to maintain her historic position as the leader in the German world. The agreement was considered by Prussians to be the "humiliation of Olmütz."

See also: FRANKFURT CONSTITUTION; MARCH CONSTITUTION.

Further reading: John Breuilly, *The Formation of the First German Nation-State, 1800–1871* (New York: St. Martin's Press, 1996); James J. Sheehan, *German History, 1770–1866* (New York: Oxford University Press, 1989); W. G. Shreeves, *Nationmaking in Nineteenth Century Europe: The National Unification of Italy and Germany 1815–1914* (Walton-on-Thames, England: Nelson, 1984); Louis L. Snyder, ed., *Documents of German History* (New Brunswick, N.J.: Rutgers University Press, 1958).

Olney Doctrine

Corollary to the Monroe Doctrine propounded by U.S. Secretary of State Richard Olney in 1895. Intervening in a dispute between Great Britain and Venezuela over a boundary in British Guiana, Olney demanded that Britain submit the dispute to arbitration. In a broad interpretation of the Monroe Doctrine, he argued that British pressure on Venezuela would constitute an unacceptable extension of European colonization in the Americas. His dispatch read: "Today the United States is practically sovereign on this continent, and its fiat is law upon the subjects to which it confines its interposition." To avoid the possibility of war with the United States, Britain agreed to arbitration. The dispute was settled in 1899.

Further reading: Samuel F. Bemis, *The American Secretaries of State and Their Diplomacy*, 8 vols. (New York: Cooper Square Publishers, 1963); Gerald G. Eggert, *Richard Olney: Evolution of a Statesman* (University Park: Pennsylvania State University Press, 1974); Henry James, *Richard Olney and His Public Service* (Boston: Houghton Mifflin, 1923); Jai N. Singh, *Diplomacy or War: The Guyana-Venezuela Border Controversy* (Georgetown, Guyana: J. N. Singh, 1982).

Olney-Pauncefote Treaty

British-American arbitration agreement, drafted by U.S. secretary of state Richard Olney and British ambassador to the United States Sir Julian Pauncefote in 1896. The agreement (signed on January 11, 1897, at Washington, D.C.) made financial and most other nonterritorial disputes entirely arbitrable. It made territorial disputes and certain important principles arbitrable but subject to an appeal to a six-member court; if more than one member of the court dissented, the decision was not binding. Though the British Parliament ratified the treaty, the U.S. Senate failed to do so.

Further reading: Samuel F. Bemis, *The American Secretaries of State and Their Diplomacy*, 8 vols. (New York: Cooper Square Publishers, 1963); Gerald G. Eggert, *Richard Olney: Evolution of a Statesman* (University Park: Pennsylvania State University Press, 1974); Henry James, *Richard Olney and His Public Service* (Boston: Houghton Mifflin, 1923); Robert B. Mowat, *The Life of Lord Pauncefote, First Ambassador to the United States* (Boston: Houghton Mifflin, 1929).

Olynthiacs   Three eloquent orations delivered by Athenian statesman Demosthenes in 349 B.C., urging his fellow Athenians to aid the Olynthians against King Philip II of Macedon. Olynthus, a Greek city-state on the Chalcidice Peninsula, was under attack by Philip's forces, and Demosthenes tried to arouse Athens, which had an alliance with Olynthus. Despite his stirring speeches and the Olynthians' appeals, the Athenians gave no active aid, and Olynthus was seized by Philip in 348 B.C., razed to the ground, and the citizens sold as slaves.

See also: PHILIPPICS.

Further reading: J. R. Ellis and R. D. Milns, *The Spectre of Philip; Demosthenes' First Philippic, Olynthiac and Speech On the Peace; a Study in Historical Evidence* (Sydney, Australia: Sydney University Press, 1970); E. I. McQueen, ed., *Olynthiacs/Demosthenes* (Bristol, England: Bristol Classical, 1986); John E. Sandys, ed., *The First Philippic and the Olynthiacs of Demosthenes* (New York: Arno Press, 1979); J. H. Vince et al., trans., *Demosthenes*, 7 vols. (Cambridge, Mass.: Harvard University Press, 1984–92).

Omaha Platform   Platform drafted by the newly formed People's (Populist) Party at its first national convention, held at Omaha, Nebraska, in July 1892. In its preamble, the platform described America as verging on "moral, political, and material ruin." Representing the demands of the agrarian protest movement, the Populist program called for free coinage of silver, a graduated income tax, a subtreasury plan for low-interest loans, an increase in the supply of paper money, reclamation of unneeded lands from railroads and other corporations, the prohibition of alien land ownership, and government ownership of the railroads, telegraph, and telephone.

Further reading: Gene Clanton, *Populism: The Humane Preference in America, 1890–1900* (Boston: Twayne Publishers, 1991); Henry Steele Commager, ed., *Documents of American History*, 8th ed. (New York: Appleton-Century-Crofts, 1968); Sheldon Hackney, comp., *Populism: The Critical Issues* (Boston: Little, Brown, 1971); Frank N. Magill, ed., *Great Events from History: Modern European Series*, 3 vols. (Englewood Cliffs, N.J.: Salem Press, 1973).

Omnibus Crime Control and Safe Streets Act of 1968, U.S.   Federal legislation signed into law on June 19, 1968, to provide federal assistance to state and local law enforcement agencies in order to reduce street crime. The act created the Law Enforcement Assistance Administration to aid state and local agencies in funding programs for police, courts, corrections, control of organized crime, civil disorders, and related crime problems; it authorized $400 million in grants to develop programs over a two-year period. It prohibited interstate traffic in handguns and their sale to minors. Its most controversial provisions sanctioned eavesdropping and wiretapping by federal, state, and local officials, specify-

ing when and how they may be authorized. These provisions have been criticized as violations of rights to privacy.

Further reading: Lawyers' Committee for Civil Rights under Law, *Law and Disorder III: State and Federal Performance under Title I of the Omnibus Crime Control and Safe Streets Act of 1968* (Washington D.C.: n. p., 1973); *Title I: The Omnibus Crime Control and Safe Streets Act of 1968 (Public Law 90–351) . . .* (Washington, D.C.: U.S. Department of Justice, 1986).

On the Admission of Women to Citizenship (Sur l'admission des Femmes au Droit de Cité)   French philosopher Marie-Jean de Caritat, marquis de Condorcet's groundbreaking pamphlet advocating voting rights for women in 1790. "They have the same qualities as men," so "either no one truly has any rights or all have the same ones," he argued. Women's physical limitations were no more debilitating than men's annual bouts of cold and gout, he continued, while their inferior social status and lack of education had made them more emotional and less reasonable. He believed that basically women's intellectual capacities were the same as men's except in science and philosophy and that they should run for any public office other than the military. Further, enfranchisement would enhance women's life experiences and make them better "fitted to be mothers and wives."

See also: DECLARATION OF THE RIGHTS OF WOMAN AND THE FEMALE CITIZENSHIP; *VINDICATION OF THE RIGHTS OF WOMAN.*

Further reading: Lynn Hunt, ed. and trans., *The French Revolution and Human Rights: A Brief Documentary History* (Boston: Bedford, 1996); J. Selwyn Schapiro, *Condorcet and the Rise of Liberalism* (New York: Harcourt, Brace, 1934.

On the Crown (De Corona)   Celebrated speech given in 330 B.C. by the Athenian statesman Demosthenes during a public trial or debate with his arch political rival, Aeschines. Earlier Aeschines had attacked Ctesiphon for proposing that a golden crown be awarded to Demosthenes for his public service and patriotism. In 330 B.C. Aeschines prosecuted Ctesiphon on technical grounds and confronted Demosthenes, who defended Ctesiphon and his own conduct and character in response to Aeschines's accusations of cowardice, bribe-taking, and indecision. Before a jury of more than 500 citizens, Demosthenes delivered "On the Crown," defending his career and policies for the past 20 years as leader of a strong anti-Macedonian party (see PHILIPPICS) and scathingly contrasting his policies with those of Aeschines, portrayed as contemptible and treacherous and as a tool of King Philip II of Macedon. The jury acquitted Ctesiphon, Aeschines was exiled, and Demosthenes won great popular approval.

Further reading: James J. Murphy, *Demosthenes' On the Crown: A Critical Study of a Masterpiece of Ancient Oratory* (New York: Random House, 1967); S. Usher, trans., *On the Crown/Demosthenes* (Warminster, England: Aris & Phillips,

1993); J. H. Vince et al., trans., *Demosthenes*, 7 vols. (Cambridge, Mass.: Harvard University Press, 1984–92).

On the Law of War and Peace (De Jure Belli ac Pacis)

Legal treatise written by Dutch jurist and statesman Hugo Grotius (Latinized version of Huigh de Groot) between 1620 and 1625 while in exile in Paris; published in 1625, it contained a discussion of principles that he felt should govern the relations between sovereign states. Prevalent throughout the entire work was the author's abhorrence for war. Although he conceded the legitimacy of a just war, he held a very limited few of such a war, condemning, for example, the wars of religion that had occurred so frequently during the Middle Ages. He argued that war ought to be avoided at all costs and challenged states to negotiate in order to bring about an end to conflict. In the event of war, the author urged combatants to spare innocent noncombatants, and challenged victors to treat the conquered with mercy. At the time of the work's publication, the stability of medieval Europe, which had been the result of the uncontested power of the Roman Catholic Church and the Holy Roman emperor, had been destroyed and was being replaced by wars among kingdoms, principalities, and religious groups. Grotius's work thus provided Europe with a new foundation for international relations.

Further reading: Edward Dumbauld, *The Life and Legal Writings of Hugo Grotius* (Norman: University of Olkahoma Press, 1969); John Dunn and Ian Harris, eds., *Grotius* (Lyme, N.H.: Elgar, 1997); Friedrich Heer, *Great Documents of the World: Milestones of Human Thought* (New York: McGraw-Hill, 1977); L. E. van Holk and C. G. Roelofsen, eds., *Grotius Reader: A Reader for Students of International Law and Legal History* (The Hague: T. M. C. Asser Instituut, 1983).

On Liberty

Treatise written by English philosopher and economist John Stuart Mill and published in 1859; it contained his ideals of personal liberty (particularly freedom of speech, thought, and association). He opposed despotism of all kinds. A significant portion of the work was devoted to a discussion on individuality, with regard to which he argued that even eccentricity would be more desirable than conformity because the former had, at the very least, the potential to contribute to the growth of society. Mill also argued that the threat to personal freedom was greater in democratic societies than in authoritarian ones, since in the former public opinion was highly effective in suppressing the opinions of minority groups. Largely because of this work Mill is now held to be one of the greatest spokesmen in support of civil liberties, popular education, and liberalism.

Further reading: Charles W. Eliot, ed., *The Harvard Classics*, 51 vols. (New York: P. F. Collier & Son, 1937); Mark A. Kishlansky, ed., *Sources of the West: Readings in Western Civilization*, vol. 2, 4th ed. (New York: Longman, 2001); Frank N. Magill, ed., *Great Events from History: Modern European Series*, 3 vols. (Englewood Cliffs, N.J.: Salem Press, 1973); G. W. Smith, ed., *John Stuart Mill's Social and Political Thought: Critical Assessments* (New York: Routledge, 1998).

On the Motion of the Heart and Blood in Animals (De Motu Cordis et Sanguinis in Animalibus)

Scientific treatise written by English physician and anatomist William Harvey and published in 1628, containing his description of the circulation of the blood through the body, which he derived from his own observations and experiments. He traced the circulation of blood from the heart to the body and its organs via arteries, and its return to the heart via veins, as well as the flow of blood between the heart and lungs. He described the heart as a pump that, during contraction, expelled blood and during expansion became filled with it. He explained that the valves in the heart maintained the unidirectional flow of blood and that the valves in the veins functioned similarly in contributing to the blood's return to the heart. His work dispelled the centuries-old belief that blood was produced in the liver and ultimately excreted. His discoveries challenged men to see his body in mechanical and scientific terms.

Further reading: Charles W. Eliot, ed., *The Harvard Classics*, 51 vols. (New York: P. F. Collier & Son, 1937); Kenneth J. Franklin, trans., *The Circulation of the Blood: Two Anatomical Essays by William Harvey . . .* (Oxford, England: Blackwell Scientific Publications, 1958); Robert Willis, trans., *The Works of William Harvey* (Philadelphia: University of Pennsylvania Press, 1989).

On the Nature of Things (De Rerum Natura)

Didactic work (poem) by the first-century B.C. poet Lucretius, introducing the Roman world to the atomist-materialist theories of the Greek philosopher Epicurus, who had lived two centuries earlier. Dedicated to Memmius (a Roman official), it opened with an invocation to Venus and was divided into six books. Lucretius eulogized Epicurus as being the "first to break through the tight locks of nature's portals" and, in the first two books, explained the basic principles of Epicurus's atomist theories. Book three elaborated on the composition of atoms and discussed the mortality of the soul. The fourth book was concerned with thought, senses, and body functions, and ended with a condemnation of sexual passion. In books four and five, Lucretius discussed creation, evolution, and wondrous phenomena such as thunder and lightning. The poem concluded with the somber images of the plague at Athens. One of the masterpieces of classical literature, the poem helped liberate humankind from superstition and the fear of death.

Further reading: Bonnie A. Catto, *Selections from De Rerum Natura* (Wauconda, Ill.: Bolchazy-Carducci Publishers, 1998); John Godwin, *Selections from the De Rerum Natura* (Bristol, England: Bristol Classical Press, 2000); Frank N. Magill, ed., *Great Events from History: Ancient and Medieval*

Series, 3 vols. (Englewood Cliffs, N.J.: Salem Press, 1972); Martin F. Smith, trans., *On the Nature of Things* (Indianapolis, Ind.: Hackett Publishers, 2001).

On the Navy Boards Famous speech given by the Athenian statesman Demosthenes before the ecclesia (legislative assembly) in ancient Athens in 354 B.C. With logic and eloquence, Demosthenes addressed the supposed threat to Athens from Persia to the east. He skillfully reasoned that Athens should not launch an attack, but definitely be ready to wage war if attacked; other Greek city-states would ally with Athens then, knowing she had not initiated the fighting with the Persians. Demosthenes swayed the Athenians to strengthen their navy to meet the rumored danger to their freedom and independence; he suggested a reform of the taxation by which funds for shipbuilding were collected from the rich.

See also: PHILIPPICS.

Further reading: J. H. Vince et al., trans., *Demosthenes*, 7 vols. (Cambridge, Mass.: Harvard University Press, 1984–92); Ian Worthington, ed., *Demosthenes: Statesman and Orator* (New York: Routledge, 2000).

On the Revolutions of the Heavenly Bodies (De Revolutionibus Orbium Coelestium) Scientific treatise written by Polish astronomer Nicolaus Copernicus in 1530 and first published in Nuremberg, Germany, in 1543, containing his revolutionary model of the solar system. The treatise described the order of the planets from the sun, which, he had concluded, was the body around which the planets rotated; it also described mathematically the motion of the Earth, Moon, and remaining planets. Copernicus concluded that the universe was much larger than formerly supposed; he showed that Aristotle's theory stating that objects fall to the ground because they are attracted to the center of the universe was inaccurate. The treatise's most significant effect on Western thought was that the Earth could no longer be considered the center of the universe, a conclusion that aroused the staunchest opposition among leaders in the church and scientific community alike. Since the second century the Ptolemaic view, which held that planets rotated around the Earth, had served as the unchallenged model of the universe.

Further reading: Charles W. Eliot, ed., *The Harvard Classics*, 51 vols. (New York: P. F. Collier & Son, 1937); John W. Knedler, Jr., ed., *Masterworks of Science: Digests of 13 Great Classics*, 3 vols. (New York: McGraw-Hill, 1973); Frank N. Magill, ed., *Great Events from History: Modern European Series*, 3 vols. (Englewood Cliffs, N.J.: Salem Press, 1973); Edward Rosen, *Copernicus and the Scientific Revolution* (Malabar, Fla.: Krieger, 1984).

Oppian Law (Lex Oppia) Ancient Roman law restricting female extravagance in dress, successfully sponsored by the tribune Caius Oppius in 215 B.C. because of public insis-

tence on the need for conservation (Rome was then engaged in the Second Punic War [218–202 B.C.] against Carthage, led by Hannibal). The law prohibited any woman from wearing parti-colored garments and more than half an ounce of gold. In addition, no woman could ride in a chariot more than a mile unless she was observing a religious rite or other solemn celebration or festivity. In 195 B.C. the law was repealed, and in 181, 161, and 143 B.C. other attempts to pass sumptuary laws failed.

Further reading: Alexandra Croom, *Roman Clothing and Fashion* (Charleston, S.C.: Tempus, 2000); Alan Hunt, *Governance of the Consuming Passions: A History of Sumptuary Laws* (New York: St. Martin's Press, 1996).

Order No. 1, Petrograd Soviet's (Proclamation of March 14, 1917) Document issued to the Petrograd garrison on March 14 (March 1, Old Style calendar), 1917, by the Petrograd Soviet (Council of Workers' and Soldiers' Deputies), declaring that elected committees take charge of the military units, thus depriving the officers of their authority over the soldiers. Specifically, the order called for the election of representative committees by all naval and military units; the appearance of a representative of every company at a meeting to be held on the following day; the submission of all military units to the Petrograd Soviet; the control of all arms by the elected committees, rather than by the officers; freedom of the soldiers and sailors from military etiquette while not on duty; and the proper treatment of soldiers by their officers. The issue of the order had been demanded by the soldiers in order to gain support against the officers for their already mutinous and disrespectful behavior, which had accompanied the growing Bolshevik Revolution (1917) in Russia; the revolution saw both the fall of the czarist government and the formation of a provisional government (March–November 1917) in Petrograd (St. Petersburg).

See also: APRIL THESES; OCTOBER REVOLUTION, PROCLAMATION OF THE.

Further reading: Gregory L. Freeze, ed., *Russia: A History* (New York: Oxford University Press, 1997); David R. Marples, *Lenin's Revolution: Russia, 1917–1921* (New York: Longman, 2000); Robert Service, *The Russian Revolution, 1900–1927* (New York: St. Martin's Press, 1999); Rex A. Wade, *The Russian Revolution, 1917* (New York: Cambridge University Press, 2000).

Orders in Council of 1807 Specific regulations issued by the British king on the advice of the privy council and promulgated by the British government in 1807 during the Napoleonic Wars (1803–15) to counteract French emperor Napoléon's 1806 BERLIN DECREE, which prohibited trade with the British Isles. The first order (January 7, 1807) forbade neutral ships from trading between French ports. Two other orders (November 11 and 25, 1807) declared that any ship with a cargo bound for France or a French-controlled port would first be required to unload its cargo, pay a duty, and then obtain a special license from the British before being allowed to continue to its destination. Napoléon responded with the 1807 MILAN DECREES, stating that ships complying with these orders lost their neutral status and would be treated as British vessels.

Further reading: Henry Steele Commager, ed., *Documents of American History*, 8th ed. (New York: Appleton-Century-Crofts, 1968).

Ordinance of Nullification, South Carolina's See SOUTH CAROLINA'S ORDINANCE OF NULLIFICATION.

Ordinance of Secession, South Carolina's Resolution passed unanimously by a convention meeting at Charleston, South Carolina, on December 20, 1860, by which the state seceded from the Union in a prelude to the Civil War (1861–65). The Charleston convention, its members chosen by popular vote, was called by the state legislature immediately after the election of Abraham Lincoln as president of the United States. In its "Declaration of Causes of Secession" of December 24, South Carolina affirmed state sovereignty and cited Northern opposition to slavery, the accession of power of a sectional party, and the election of a president hostile to slavery. South Carolina, the first state to secede, was soon followed by the six other states of the lower South.

Further reading: Mortimer Adler, ed., *The Annals of America*, 18 vols. (Chicago: Encyclopedia Britannica, 1968); Henry Steele Commager, ed., *Documents of American History*, 8th ed. (New York: Appleton-Century-Crofts, 1968); Charles H. Lesser, *Relic of the Lost Cause: The Story of South Carolina's Ordinance of Secession* (Columbia: South Carolina Department of Archives & History, 1990); Frank N. Magill, ed., *Great Events from History: American Series*, 3 vols. (Englewood Cliffs, N.J.: Salem Press, 1975).

Ordinances of the Holy Apostles Through Clement See APOSTOLIC CONSTITUTIONS.

Ordonnance Cabochienne See CABOCHIEN ORDINANCE.

Oregon Boundary Treaty Agreement between the United States and Great Britain, ratified by the Senate on June 15, 1846; ended a long-standing and heated border controversy by setting the boundary between Canada and the United States at the 49th parallel. The compromise treaty replaced an 1818 agreement for joint occupancy of the area between the 42nd and 54th parallels. The treaty also provided for free navigation rights of both nations in the channel between Vancouver Island and the mainland and in Fuca's Straits, and gave the British navigation rights in the Columbia River south of the boundary.

Further reading: Henry Steele Commager, ed., *Documents of American History*, 8th ed. (New York: Appleton-Century-

Crofts, 1968); Frank N. Magill, ed., *Great Events from History: American Series*, 3 vols. (Englewood Cliffs, N.J.: Salem Press, 1975); David M. Pletcher, *The Diplomacy of Annexation; Texas, Oregon, and the Mexican War* (Columbia: University of Missouri Press, 1973).

Organic Act for Puerto Rico See JONES ACT OF 1917.

Organic Act of 1883 British-supported legislation of May 1, 1883, reorganizing Egypt's administrative and constitutional system according to the DUFFERIN PROPOSALS. It set up a two-tiered legislature on the national level. The legislative council would consist of 30 members, 14 appointed and the others elected by the provincial councils. Of the 82-member legislative assembly, 46 would be elected and the rest taken from the council and the ministers. In the provinces, local affairs would be administered by a consultative council. The legislature had only limited advisory powers, the final authority resting with the khedive and, through him, with the British resident.

Further reading: Alfred C. Lyall, *The Life of the Marquis of Dufferin and Ava* (London: J. Murray, 1979); Peter Mansfield, *The British in Egypt* (New York: Holt, Rinehart & Winston, 1972); John Marlowe, *A History of Modern Egypt and Anglo-Egyptian Relations, 1800–1953* (New York: Praeger, 1954); William M. Welch, *No Country for a Gentleman: British Rule in Egypt, 1883–1907* (New York: Greenwood Press, 1988).

Organic Act of the Philippine Islands See JONES ACT OF 1916.

Organic Articles of April 8, French Articles drawn up by First Consul Napoléon Bonaparte of France as new religious legislation; promulgated in Paris on April 8, 1802. The new laws undermined the agreement that Napoléon and Pope Pius VII had made in the CONCORDAT OF 1801. The articles asserted the state's supremacy over the Roman Catholic Church and its right to reject any documents issued by the papacy; the precedence that civil marriage had over marriage in the church; the equality of all religious faiths; the principle of freedom of conscience; and the state's right to control such matters as the titles, dress, and salaries of clergymen. The articles were kept secret from the pope until their promulgation along with the 1801 concordat. Napoléon's presentation of such issues was necessary, if he hoped to maintain the support of the powerful French revolutionaries.

See also: LAW OF GERMINAL.

Further reading: Edward E. Y. Hales, *The Emperor and the Pope: The Story of Napoleon and Pius VII* (New York: Octagon Books, 1978); Douglas Hilt, *Ten Against Napoleon* (Chicago: Nelson-Hall, 1975); Margaret M. O'Dwyer, *The Papacy in the Age of Napoleon and the Restoration: Pius VII, 1800–1823* (Lanham, Md.: University Press of America, 1985).

Organization for Economic Cooperation and Development, Pact of the

Charter establishing international OECD, acronym for the organization, signed on December 14, 1960, to encourage trade and economic expansion. Successor to the Organization for European Economic Cooperation (OEEC), which had been set up in 1948 under the MARSHALL PLAN, the OECD was strengthened by the participation of Canada and the United States in addition to the 20 European members of the OEEC. It sought to help members (25 countries worldwide today) attain a consistently high level of economic growth and employment, while maintaining financial stability and contributing to a better world economy. It also proposed to aid underdeveloped countries. Decisions taken by the OECD are not binding on its members. Based in Paris, the OECD consists of a council (each member sends a permanent delegate) and a secretariat headed by a secretary-general elected for a five-year term.

Further reading: Henry W. Degenhardt, ed., *Treaties and Alliances of the World*, 4th ed. (Detroit: Gale Research, 1986).

Organization of African Unity, Charter of the

Charter establishing the Organization of African Unity (OAU), an association to promote African interests; signed on May 25, 1963, in Addis Ababa, Ethiopia. It outlined the founding principles of the OAU: noninterference in another state's internal matters; respect for the equality, sovereignty, and territorial integrity of other states; and a commitment to the independence of all African colonies. The charter advocated a policy of nonalignment with any bloc and peaceful settlement of disputes, and condemned subversive political activities. It defined the OAU's principal organs as an assembly of heads of state and government, a council of ministers, and a general secretariat. Fifty independent African states (South Africa and Morocco being the two exceptions) belonged to the OAU, which also created a number of specialized commissions and a commission of mediation, conciliation, and arbitration, to help it achieve its goals. The OAU also drafted the African Charter on Human and People's Rights. In July 2001 in Zambia, African leaders held the last summit of the OAU, a meeting that ended with the formal acceptance of a treaty for a new African union.

Further reading: Henry W. Degenhardt, ed., *Treaties and Alliances of the World*, 4th ed. (Detroit: Gale Research, 1986); P. Olisanwuche Esedebe, *Pan-Africanism: The Idea and Movement, 1776–1991* (Washington, D.C.: Howard University, 1994); Gino J. Naldi, *The Organization of African Unity: An Analysis of Its Role* (New York: Mansell, 1999); J. A. S. Grenville and Barnard Wasserstein, *The Major International Treaties since 1945: A History and Guide with Texts* (New York: Methuen, 1987).

Organization of American States, Charter of the

Document signed in Bogotá, Colombia, on April 30, 1948, at the close of the Ninth Pan-American Conference, by representatives of 21 American states (excluding, notably, Canada) attending the conference, it founded the Organization of American States (OAS), laid down its fundamental principles, and described its structure. Through the document the signatories agreed to settle all disputes through peaceful means; to work together to promote economic, social, and cultural progress among them; and to respect the right of each state to govern itself in its own way. In addition, the charter described the structure of the OAS, and laid down a meeting schedule to be followed by representatives to the OAS. While not explicitly stated, the OAS was anticommunist in its orientation.

Further reading: Henry W. Degenhardt, ed., *Treaties and Alliances of the World*, 4th ed. (Detroit: Gale Research, 1986); J. A. S. Grenville and Barnard Wasserstein, *The Major International Treaties since 1945: A History and Guide with Texts* (New York: Methuen, 1987); Frank N. Magill, ed., *Great Events from History: American Series*, 3 vols. (Englewood Cliffs, N.J.: Salem Press, 1975); O. Carlos Stoetzer, *The Organization of American States*, 2d ed. (Westport, Conn.: Praeger, 1993).

Organization of Petroleum Exporting Countries, Pact of the

Agreement made at Baghdad, Iraq, on November 14, 1960, by five oil-producing nations—Venezuela (the pact's initiator), Iran, Iraq, Kuwait, and Saudi Arabia—to promote economic and technical cooperation and establish a unified petroleum policy for the sale of oil to consumer nations. The pact's signatories became known as the Organization of Petroleum Exporting Countries (OPEC). Based initially in Geneva and now in Vienna, OPEC is administered by a board of governors (elected by member countries), a chairman (elected by a conference of representatives), and a secretariat for administration and research. OPEC was joined by the nations of Qatar, Indonesia, Libya, Abu Dhabi (forming in 1971 part of the United Arab Emirates), Algeria, Nigeria, Ecuador, and Gabon. The organization's policies, formulated during its biannual conferences, have been to raise the price of oil, but volatile situations in the Middle East have made it difficult. OPEC producers have periodically agreed to take part in worldwide production cuts to support prices. Increased demand for oil by 2000 enabled OPEC to better enforce its production quotas, despite the West's attempt to reduce its dependence on OPEC oil.

Further reading: Albert L. Danielson, *The Evolution of OPEC* (New York: Harcourt Brace Jovanovich, 1982); Henry W. Degenhardt, ed., *Treaties and Alliances of the World*, 4th ed. (Detroit: Gale Research, 1986); J. A. S. Grenville and Barnard Wasserstein, *The Major International Treaties since 1945: A History and Guide with Texts* (New York: Methuen, 1987); Pierre Terzian, *OPEC, the Inside Story* (London: Zed Books, 1985).

Organized Crime Control Act of 1970, U.S.

Federal legislation enacted on October 17, 1970, that sought to eradicate organized crime by strengthening legal tools for gathering evidence, by establishing new penal prohibitions, and by providing stronger sanctions in dealing with unlawful activities. The act declared that organized crime drained billions of dollars from the U.S. economy, used money and power to infiltrate legitimate businesses and labor unions, and corrupted the democratic process. It provided for special grand juries to report to federal courts, issuance of general immunity to compel witnesses to testify, and increased sentences for dangerous special offenders. Its provisions covered a wide range of offenses besides organized crime, including passing bad checks, burglary, and conspiracy.

See also: RICO LAW.

Further reading: *Legislative History: Organized Crime Control Act, 1970, PL 91–452* (Englewood, Colo.: Microcard Editions, 1974).

Origin of Species

Scientific work written by English naturalist Charles Darwin and first published in London on November 24, 1859, containing his theory "On the Origin of Species by Means of Natural Selection, or the Preservation of Favored Species in the Struggle for Life" (the work's full title). Darwin sought to explain, on the basis of his experiments with animals and plants, that one species developed into another species by inheriting a collection of particular biological variations that rendered the organism better able to survive in the environment. Nature favored the survival only of the fittest. Darwin's theory of natural selection explained the evolution of an advanced species from a low one; he thus agreed that man and the ape had had a common ancestor. Because of this conclusion, the work was bitterly challenged by theologians and conservative scientists alike.

Further reading: Charles W. Eliot, ed., *The Harvard Classics*, 51 vols. (New York: P. F. Collier & Son, 1937); Steve Jones, *Darwin's Ghost: The Origin of Species Updated* (New York: Random House, 2000); John W. Knedler, Jr., ed., *Masterworks of Science: Digests of 13 Great Classics*, 3 vols. (New York: McGraw-Hill, 1973); Frank N. Magill, ed., *Great Events from History: Modern European Series*, 3 vols. (Englewood Cliffs, N.J.: Salem Press, 1973).

Orkhon Inscriptions (Turkish Runes)

Oldest known Turkish script found by the Russian explorer N. M. Yadrinstev in 1889 in the Orkhon (Orhon) River valley near ancient Karakorum, Mongolia. Inscribed on two large monuments built in A.D. 732 and 735, the writings (some of which are in Chinese) were deciphered by the Danish philologist Vilhelm L. Thomsen in 1893; he called them the "Turkish Runes." The inscriptions tell about the nomadic Turks' origins, early heyday, control by the Chinese, and freedom under the Turkish chieftains Kül and his brother Bilge Kagan. The Turks seemed fairly advanced linguistically from the writings.

Further reading: Tuncer Gulensoy, *The First Turkish Inscriptions and the Turkish Language* (Kayseri, Turkey: Bizim Genclik Yayiniari, 1994); Talat Tekin, *A Grammar of Orkhon Turkic* (Bloomington: Indiana University, 1968).

Oslo Accords

Several clandestine agreements between Israel and the Palestine Liberation Organization (PLO) that set the basis for future negotiations, mediated by Norway, with the crucial "Declaration of Principles" (DOP) signed on September 13, 1993, in Washington, D.C. Previously, in "Letters of Mutual Recognition," Israel acknowledged the "PLO as a representative of the Palestinian people," while the PLO recognized Israel's right to exist, accepted U.N. Security Council Resolutions 242 and 338, and disavowed terrorism. According to the DOP, Israel would begin withdrawing troops from Gaza and the West Bank (excluding the city of Hebron) within three weeks. A Palestinian Interim Self-Government Authority (PA) would temporarily (no more than five years) assume legislative and executive powers in these areas, except for foreign affairs. Israel would release 5,000 Palestinian prisoners but disclaimed all financial responsibility for claims regarding acts prior to the transfer of power. Both parties agreed to a temporary international presence in the region and to establish a Joint Israeli-Palestinian Liaison Committee to supervise the implementation of the agreement. They invited cooperation from Jordan (see ISRAELI-JORDANIAN TREATY OF 1994) and Egypt. These provisions necessitated further intensive negotiations, hence several protocols and agreements later became part of this historic accord.

Further reading: Benny Morris, *Righteous Victims—A History of the Zionist-Arab Conflict, 1881–1999* (New York: Alfred A. Knopf, 1999); N. J. Rengger, with John Campbell, *Treaties and Alliances of the World* (London: Cartermill International, 1995).

Osnabrück, Treaty of

One of the treaties that made up the Peace of WESTPHALIA, ending the Thirty Years' War, concluded at Osnabrück (Germany) on October 24, 1648, by Sweden, the German Protestant Estates, and the Holy Roman Empire. At the talks the German Protestants sided with either Sweden or the empire. By the treaty, Sweden gained control over western Pomerania and received an indemnity payment from the Germans; in return for its loss of western Pomerania, Brandenburg received the archbishopric of Magdeburg as a duchy and several secular territories; the German Estates won full sovereignty and, in relation to the emperor, greatly increased their authority in regulating their internal affairs (like making new laws and levying more taxes).

See also: MÜNSTER, TREATY OF.

Further reading: Derek Croxton, *Peacemaking in Early Modern Europe: Cardinal Mazarin and the Congress of Westphalia, 1643–1648* (Selinsgrove, Pa.: Susquehanna University Press, 1999); Charles W. Kegley, *Exorcising the Ghost of Westphalia: Building World Order in the New Millennium* (Upper

Saddle River, N.J.: Prentice-Hall, 2002); Frank N. Magill, ed., *Great Events from History: Modern European Series*, 3 vols. (Englewood Cliffs, N.J.: Salem Press, 1973); Thomas Cussans, ed., *The Times Atlas of European History* (New York: HarperCollins Publishers, 1994).

Ostend Manifesto   Secret memorandum from three U.S. diplomats to Secretary of State William L. Marcy in 1854 urging the United States to purchase Cuba from Spain or to seize it by force. The U.S. ministers to Spain, Great Britain, and France—Pierre Soule, James Buchanan, and John Y. Mason, respectively—issued their expansionist dispatch from Ostend, Belgium. The document argued that if Spain refused to sell Cuba, the United States would be justified in seizing the island by force. Publication of the manifesto aroused a furor in Spain and in the United States, where antislavery forces viewed it as an attempt to acquire new territory for slavery. Marcy promptly repudiated the memorandum.

Further reading: Mortimer Adler, ed., *The Annals of America*, 18 vols. (Chicago: Encyclopaedia Britannica, 1968); Frederick M. Binder, *James Buchanan and the American Empire* (Selinsgrove, Pa.: Susquehanna University Press, 1994); Henry Steele Commager, ed., *Documents of American History*, 8th ed. (New York: Appleton-Century-Crofts, 1968); Ivor D. Spencer, *The Victor and the Spoils: A Life of William L. Marcy* (Providence, R.I.: Brown University Press, 1959).

Oswego, Treaty of   Indian-British peace treaty signed at Oswego, New York, in April 1766, ending a rebellion of confederated Indian tribes under the Ottawa chief Pontiac. Pontiac's Rebellion began at the end of the French and Indian War (1754–63) and was rooted in Pontiac's hostility to the British (he had sided with the French in the war) and in the Indians' fear of losing their lands to the English settlers. The Indians captured every western fort except Forts Pitt, Niagara, and Detroit. Faced with defections among his allies and growing British strength, Pontiac reluctantly submitted at Oswego to British authority and was pardoned.

Further reading: Nathaniel C. Hale, *Pontiac's War: the Great Indian Uprising Against the English in 1763* (Wynnewood, Pa.: Hale House, 1973); William R. Nester, *"Haughty Conquerors": Amherst and the Great Indian Uprising of 1763* (Westport, Conn.: Praeger, 2000); Francis Parkman, *The Oregon Trail; The Conspiracy of Pontiac* (New York: Literary Classics of the United States, 1991); Howard H. Peckham, *Pontiac and the Indian Uprising* (New York: Russell & Russell, 1970).

Otis's Speech Opposing Writs of Assistance   Legal argument by Boston attorney James Otis, dated February 24, 1761, against the issuance by the British court of exchequer of writs of assistance (general search warrants that gave British customs officers the power to search any house for smuggled items without showing cause). Though no formal record of the speech exists, it is known from notes taken by John Adams. Representing a group of Boston merchants, Otis argued (before the Superior Court of Massachusetts) that such writs were unconstitutional and void because they violated natural law (that a man is "as secure in his house, as a prince in his castle"). Otis's speech is often, perhaps erroneously, credited as the source of the slogan "Taxation without representation is tyranny." He lost the case in court but became an influential pamphleteer.

See also: RIGHTS OF THE BRITISH COLONIES ASSERTED AND PROVED, OTIS'S.

Further reading: Mortimer Adler, ed., *The Annals of America*, 18 vols. (Chicago: Encyclopaedia Britannica, 1968); Henry Steele Commager, ed., *Documents of American History*, 8th ed. (New York: Appleton-Century-Crofts, 1968); Maurice H. Smith, *The Writs of Assistance Case* (Berkeley: University of California Press, 1978).

Ottoman Empire Constitution, First   First comprehensive Ottoman constitution, prepared with the approval of Turkish sultan Abd al-Hamid II and proclaimed on December 23, 1876, by Midhat Pasha, an influential Turkish statesman; it declared the institution of certain democratic reforms in the Ottoman Empire (Turkey). The document provided for a two-chamber parliament, with elected lower house members and nominated upper house members; for equality before the law; for freedom of conscience; and for the maintenance of the territorial integrity of the Ottoman Empire. Freedom of the press and equality of taxation were also proclaimed in the constitution. Despite these concessions to democratic ideals, the sultan in fact ruled almost autocratically.

Further reading: Joan Haslip, *The Sultan: The Life of Abdul Hamid II* (London: Weidenfeld & Nicolson, 1973); Justin McCarthy, *The Ottoman Turks: An Introductory History to 1923* (New York: Longman, 1997); Ali Haydar Mithat; *The Life of Midhat Pasha* (New York: Arno Press, 1973); Donald Quataert, *The Ottoman Empire, 1700–1922* (New York: Cambridge University Press, 2000).

Ottoman Imperial Edict of 1839 (Hatt-i Serif of Gülhane, Noble Edict of the Rose Chamber, Magna Carta of Ottoman Liberty)   Reform decree issued on November 3, 1839, by Ottoman sultan Abd al-Majid, who had been persuaded to introduce some modernization in the Ottoman Empire (Turkey). One of the best known of the Tanzimat (name for the reforms then), the 1839 edict declared that all the empire's subjects were guaranteed individual liberty, freedom from oppression, and equality before the law. It also stated that taxes would be exacted and collected in a fair and equal manner and that the military would be improved. Many European countries, particularly Britain and France, were critical of these democratic Ottoman principles, claiming that they were endorsed merely to raise popular opinion in the West at a time when the Ottoman Empire was at war with Egypt and thus in need of Western aid.

Further reading: Justin McCarthy, *The Ottoman Turks: An Introductory History to 1923* (New York: Longman, 1997); Donald Quataert, *The Ottoman Empire, 1700–1922* (New York: Cambridge University Press, 2000).

Ottoman Imperial Edict of 1856 (Hatt-i Hümayun, Magna Carta of Turkey)

Reform edict issued on February 18, 1856, by Sultan Abd al-Majid at the end of the Crimean War (1853–56). It granted full civil and religious freedom to Christians in the Ottoman Empire (Turkey); they obtained the right to life and dignity and to own property and to control their own churches and schools. Class distinctions were eliminated; all subjects won liberty of conscience and the right to occupy all civil and military offices. Torture and beatings were curbed. Taxation was made progressive. Commerce was to be open and free. Some ownership of property by foreigners was allowed. There was strong Turkish opposition to these reforms, which had been pressed on the sultan by Britain, France, and Austria (the Ottoman Empire's allies against Russia during the war). The 1856 edict was one of the most important of the Tanzimat (a series of Ottoman reforms of that period).

Further reading: Justin McCarthy, *The Ottoman Turks: An Introductory History to 1923* (New York: Longman, 1997); Donald Quataert, *The Ottoman Empire, 1700–1922* (New York: Cambridge University Press, 2000); N. M. Vaporis, *Witnesses for Christ: Orthodox Christian Meomartyrs of the Ottoman Period, 1437–1860* (Crestwood, N.Y.: St. Vladimir's Seminary Press, 2000).

Ottoman New Regulations of 1793

Reforms enacted by Turkish sultan Selim III in 1793, setting forth guidelines for the modernization of the military and changes in the tax system of the Ottoman Empire (Turkey). Specifically, the newly created army was fashioned after European armies in terms of both the types of modern weapons used and strategic planning; and taxes were to be collected from parts of the society until then protected from taxation. The reforms stimulated industrial production, and Selim created a small, potent army.

Further reading: Justin McCarthy, *The Ottoman Turks: An Introductory History to 1923* (New York: Longman, 1997); Donald Quataert, *The Ottoman Empire, 1700–1922* (New York: Cambridge University Press, 2000); Stanford J. Shaw, *Between Old and New: the Ottoman Empire under Sultan Selim III, 1789–1807* (Cambridge, Mass.: Harvard University Press, 1971).

Ouchy Convention

Convention concluded at Ouchy (the port city of Lausanne, Switzerland) on July 19, 1932, by Belgium, Luxembourg, and the Netherlands, providing for incentives to increase trade among the three countries. Specif-ically, the signatory powers agreed to reduce import and export duties by one-half over a period of four years. The three countries thus hoped to stimulate their economies, which were suffering as a result of the stagnation of the general European economy in post–World War I Europe. The convention had no effect, however, owing to British and U.S. opposition.

Further reading: Derek H. Aldcroft, *Studies in the Interwar European Economy* (Brookfield, Vt.: Ashgate, 1997); Patricia Clavin, *The Great Depression in Europe, 1929–1939* (New York: St. Martin's Press, 2000); C. H. Feinstein, et al., *The European Economy Between the Wars* (New York: Oxford University Press, 1997).

Outer Space Treaty of 1966

Treaty regulating the use of outer space for exploration and research purposes; drafted under the supervision of the United Nations (U.N.) in December 1966, and signed by 63 countries on January 27, 1967. Primarily a reiteration of the U.N. General Assembly's 1963 resolutions on the subject, the treaty's salient points on outer space were (1) free and equal access for all countries and international cooperation encouraged; (2) no sovereignty claims whether through use or occupation; (3) conformation with international law, to foster peace and understanding; (4) ban on use of destructive weapons; (5) astronauts to help each other and to be helped to land safely; (6) space exploration is government's responsibility, even when conducted by a private company; (7) the launching country is responsible for any damages; (8) dissemination of information regarding space activities; and (9) all space vehicles subject to open inspection.

Further reading: Henry W. Degenhardt, ed., *Treaties and Alliances of the World*, 4th ed. (Detroit: Gale Research, 1986); Gabriel Lafferranderie and Daphne Crowther, *Outlook on Space Law over the Next 30 Years: Essays Published for the 30th Anniversary of the Outer Space Treaty* (Boston: Kluwer Law International, 1997); United Nations, *The United Nations Treaties on Outer Space* (New York: United Nations, 1984).

Oxford, Provisions of

Articles of reform issued by the so-called Mad Parliament (Easter Parliament) at Oxford in 1258 and accepted reluctantly by England's king Henry III. A 24-man royal committee was created to handle governmental and religious problems; a permanent 15-man council (dominated by barons) was to advise the king and have veto power over his decisions; three annual parliaments were to be called by the king, who was to converse with a group of 12 representing the barons. The chancellor, justiciar, and treasurer were to be named yearly by the council, and the king and officers of the realm were to swear loyalty to the provisions (considered England's first written constitution), which were to be in effect for 12 years but were nullified permanently by the Dictum of KENILWORTH in 1266.

See also: AMIENS, MISE OF; WESTMINSTER, PROVISIONS OF.

Further reading: Ernest F. Jacob, *Studies in the Period of Baronial Reform and Rebellion, 1258–1267* (Oxford, England: Clarendon Press, 1925); Frank N. Magill, ed., *Great Events from History: Ancient and Medieval Series*, 3 vols. (Englewood Cliffs, N.J.: Salem Press, 1972); H. G. Richardson and G. O. Sayles, *The Provisions of Oxford: A Forgotten Document and Some Comments* (Manchester, England: Manchester University Press, 1933).

Oxford Act of 1665   See FIVE MILE ACT.

Oxford Propositions (Oxford Negotiations)   Proposals for a peace settlement put forward by a group of parliamentary commissioners (led by the earl of Northumberland) at a meeting with England's king Charles I in Oxford in March 1643. The commissioners wanted episcopacy to be abolished, penal laws against the Roman Catholics to be implemented more rigorously, and leading royalists to be punished. The king responded by asking for the shifting of Parliament from Westminster to a more neutral place, for the return of all fortified sites, and for the breakup of parliament's forces. The discussions ended in deadlock.

Further reading: Maurice Ashley, *Charles I and Oliver Cromwell: A Study in Contrasts and Comparisons* (London: Methuen, 1987); Peter Gaunt, *The English Civil War: The Essential Readings* (Malden, Mass.: Blackwell Publishers, 2000); Derek A. Wilson, *The King and the Gentleman: Charles Stuart and Oliver Cromwell, 1599–1649* (New York: St. Martin's Press, 1999).

Oxford Tracts   See *TRACTS FOR THE TIMES*.

P

Pacem in Terris (Peace on Earth) Eighth encyclical written by Roman Catholic pope John XXIII, signed by him at the Vatican on April 9, 1963, and dated April 11, Holy Thursday; it called upon not only the Catholic clergy and faithful but also "all men of good will" to work for peace in the world. The document's main points included the pope's plea to reduce nuclear armaments; his warning that the continued existence of these weapons could have disastrous consequences; his support for the United Nations; his call to all nations to work together to solve the world's problems, which had become so complex as to be beyond the abilities of nations in isolation; his call to governments to protect the rights of individuals, and especially of minorities; his support for the rights acquired by the working class and women, evidence that the world was becoming more just; and his plea to both the communist and capitalist nations to work together for peace.

Further reading: Claudia Carlen, comp., *The Papal Encyclicals* (Wilmington, N.C.: McGrath Publishing, 1981); Catholic University of America, eds., *New Catholic Encyclopedia* (New York: McGraw-Hill, 1967); Anne Fremantle, *The Papal Encyclicals in Their Historical Context* (New York: Mentor-Omega Books, 1963); David J. O'Brien and Thomas A. Shannon, eds., *Catholic Social Thought: The Documentary Heritage* (Maryknoll, N.Y.: Orbis Books, 1992).

Pacification, Edict of See AMBOISE, EDICT OF.

Pacific Islanders Protection Act (Kidnapping Act of 1872, British) British law in 1872 seeking to regulate the indenturing of Kanakas (Pacific Islanders), recruited to ease the acute labor shortage on the cotton and sugar plantations in the Fiji Islands and Queensland, Australia. These laborers were often kidnapped, initially from the Solomon Islands, and sold by unscrupulous traders to the plantation owners for £7 each. The laborers were treated no better than slaves. To prevent this exploitation, Britain banned recruiting by British ships and on British colonies and protectorates. The act also defined proper recruiting procedures and set up licensing guidelines, but the exploitation of the Kanaka did not effectively cease until a few decades later.

See also: PACIFIC ISLAND LABORERS' ACT; WESTERN PACIFIC ORDER IN COUNCIL.

Further reading: O. W. Parnaby, *Aspects of British Policy in the Pacific: The 1872 Pacific Islanders Protection Act* (Melbourne, Australia: Brown, Prior, Anderson Pty. 1957); O. W. Parnaby, *Britain and the Labor Trade in the Southwest Pacific* (Durham, N.C.: Duke University Press, 1964).

Pacific Island Laborers' Act Australian legislation (March 1, 1901) prohibiting the recruitment of Kanakas (Pacific islanders) for work in the sugar plantations of Queensland, after March 1904. From 1864 onward, nearly 57,000 islanders had been recruited, many by force, for this purpose (see PACIFIC ISLANDERS PROTECTION ACT). To relieve the Australian sugar industry from its excessive dependence on foreign labor, the new federal government ordered the gradual and humane repatriation of all islanders by March 1904, and introduced protectionist tariffs on sugar. Additional legislation exempted those islanders who had arrived in Australia before October 1879, or had resided continuously for more than 20 years or who owned land. Eventually, only 3,642 islanders were repatriated. Together with the IMMIGRATION RESTRICTION ACT OF 1902, this was intended to fulfil government's White Australia Policy.

Further reading: O. W. Parnaby, *Britain and the Labor Trade in the Southwest Pacific* (Durham, N.C.: Duke University Press, 1964).

Pacific Railroad Act   Federal U.S. legislation passed in 1862 that provided land grants and loans for the first transcontinental railroad. The act and its subsequent amendments authorized the Union Pacific Railroad to build a rail line west from Omaha, Nebraska, and the Central Pacific Railroad to build east from Sacramento, California, until the two met. For each mile of track laid the companies were to receive loan bonds in varying amounts, depending on the type of terrain. The rail lines were also granted tracts of land along their rights of way. The Second Pacific Railway Act (1864) doubled the size of the land grants and allowed the companies to sell their own bonds. The two lines joined at Promontory Point, Utah, in 1869.

Further reading: Henry Steele Commager, ed., *Documents of American History*, 8th ed. (New York: Appleton-Century-Crofts, 1968); Frank N. Magill, ed., *Great Events from History: American Series*, 3 vols. (Englewood Cliffs, N.J.: Salem Press, 1975).

Pacta Conventa of 1355   Agreement made between King Louis I the Great of Hungary and the Polish nobility in 1355. As early as 1335 Casimir III the Great, king of Poland, had made arrangements to be succeeded by Louis of Hungary (his nephew) if he should die without an heir. The arrangement had been renewed several times, eventually with the nobility taking part in the negotiations. Thus the future king (Louis) gained the support of the Polish nobility, but not without ceding to them certain privileges. Specifically, the nobility won the right to refuse the king its obedience should he appoint foreigners to secular offices; the king's promise not to impose any new taxes; and the king's promise to pay for military service.

Further reading: S. B. Vardy et al., eds., *Louis the Great: King of Hungary and Poland* (Boulder, Colo.: East European Mnographs, 1986).

Pacta Conventa of 1573   Conditions presented to Henry of Valois, elected king of Poland, by the Polish nobility in 1573, to which he was required to agree before his coronation. The conditions consisted of his pledge to conclude a political alliance and a trade agreement with France; to pro-

vide Poland with a fleet in the Baltic, at his own expense; to maintain Poland's dominion in the Baltic; to pay off Poland's debt, which had been accrued by his predecessor Sigismund II Augustus; to provide for the education of 100 Polish nobles in France; and to aid in the financing of the education of foreigners invited to study in Poland. At the time these conditions were separate from the HENRICIAN ARTICLES, to which he was also required to agree before his coronation. Later on, the terms of the Pacta Conventa and Henrician Articles were used interchangeably.

Further reading: Mieczyslaw B. Biskupski and James S. Pula, *Polish Democratic Thought from the Renaissance to the Great Emigration: Essays and Documents* (Boulder, Colo.: Eastern European Monographs, 1990).

Pactes de Famille   See FAMILY COMPACTS.

Pact of Guarantee   See NOVEMBER TREATY.

Pains and Penalties, Bill of   Measure introduced into the British Parliament on July 5, 1820, to deprive the queen, Caroline of Brunswick, of her royal title by declaring her marriage to King George IV null and void. The two had married in 1795 but led separate lives soon after, he in England and she on the Continent. Soon after George became king in 1820, she returned to claim her rights as queen. To prevent that, the British government put forth the bill; it passed the House of Lords by a margin of nine votes but later was dropped (November 10) to avoid almost certain defeat in the House of Commons. The queen was given a royal residence but was not allowed to participate in the king's coronation. Bills of Pains and Penalties have been used to accuse persons of treason or felony and to inflict hardship and punishment beyond the English common law.

Further reading: Thea Holme, *Caroline: A Biography of Caroline of Brunswick* (London: H. Hamilton, 1979); Steven Parissien, *George IV: The Grand Entertainment* (London: John Murray, 2001); Joanna Richardson, *The Disastrous Marriage: A Study of George IV and Caroline of Brunswick* (Westport, Conn.: Greenwood Press, 1975).

Paix de Dieu   See PEACE OF GOD.

Paix des Dames   See CAMBRAI, PEACE OF.

Paix Malheureuse   See CATEAU-CAMBRÉSIS, TREATY OF.

Pakistan Constitution of 1962   Pakistan's second constitution, announced on March 1, 1962, and put into effect on June 8, 1962; it ended martial law and established a strong presidential system of government. It provided for a 156-seat national assembly (75 members each from East and West Pakistan, plus six women representatives elected by the provincial councils) and two 150-seat provincial assemblies.

Islamabad was declared the new capital and Dacca the seat of the national assembly. Bengali and Urdu became the national languages, with English to be accepted until 1972. The initial three-year term of the president and the legislators would later be extended to a five-year term. The Republic of Pakistan would have a Muslim president, restricted to a maximum of two terms extendable only through the approval of the national and provincial assemblies. Civil rights would be restored and an independent judiciary installed. The presidential veto could be overruled by a two-thirds majority of the national assembly.

Further reading: M. Mahmood, *The Constitution of the Islamic Republic of Pakistan, 1973; a Comprehensive and Detailed Commentary with a Comparative Study of the Constitution of Pakistan, 1956 and 1962* (Lahore, Pakistan: Pakistan Law Times Publications, 1973); Shaukat Mahmood, *The Second Republic of Pakistan: An Analytical and Comparative Evaluation of the Constitution of Pakistan, 1962*, 3d rev. ed. (Lahore, Pakistan: Ilmi Kitab Khana, 1964); Muhammad Munir, *Constitution of the Islamic Republic of Pakistan, Being a Commentary on the Constitution of Pakistan, 1962* (Lahore, Pakistan: All Pakistan Legal Decisions, 1965).

Palatinate Catechism   See HEIDELBERG CATECHISM.

Palestine National Charter (Palestine National Covenant)   Document issued by the Palestine Liberation Organization (PLO) setting forth its goals and declaring the independence of Palestinian Arabs. The charter was written by Ahmad Shuqayri and adopted at a meeting of the First Palestine National Council in Jerusalem in June 1964. Consisting of 29 articles, the charter declared the PLO's commitment to liberate the Palestinian homeland and destroy Israel, the Jewish state that occupied Palestine. In addition to defining the territorial boundaries of Palestine and Palestinian "citizenship," it declared the partition of Palestine in 1947 and the creation of Israel "entirely illegal . . . because they were contrary to the will of the Palestinian people and its natural right to its homeland, and inconsistent with the general principles embodied in the UNITED NATIONS CHARTER, particularly the right of self-determination" (see UNITED NATIONS RESOLUTION 181). The charter was revised in July 1968 to make it clear that the Palestinians are a nation, not a collection of refugees, and that the problem of Palestinian statelessness demands a solution. In 1989, PLO leaders such as Yasir Arafat expressed a willingness to declare the charter null and void in return for official recognition by the Israeli government and the opening of negotiations between the Israelis and the PLO.

Further reading: Bernard Reich, *Arab-Israeli Conflict and Conciliation: A Documentary History* (Westport, Conn.: Greenwood Press, 1995); Mark Tessler, *A History of the Israeli-Palestinian Conflict* (Bloomington: Indiana University Press, 1994).

Pan-African Congress Resolutions of 1919   Resolutions passed by the Second Pan-African Congress, meeting in Paris in 1919, calling for improved colonial governments in the African countries. The congress, arranged by U.S. black scholar W. E. B. Du Bois, resolved that the allied powers create an international law code for the protection of African natives, that a special League of Nations bureau be formed to oversee the application of the code, and that black Africans gain ownership of much land, be free from outside capitalistic exploitation and slavery, be educated to read and write in their own native language and that of their trustee nation at public expense, and participate in local, tribal, and state governments. Independence for the African colonies was not demanded until the Fifth Pan-African Congress, held at Manchester, England, in 1945.

Further reading: Adi Hakim et al., *The 1945 Manchester Pan-African Congress Revisited*, 3d ed. (London: New Beacon Books, 1995); George Padmore, ed., *History of the Pan-African Congress: Colonial and Coloured Unity, a Programme of Action*, 2d ed. (London: Hammersmith Bookshop, 1963).

Panama, Declaration of   Declaration issued at the Pan-American Conference on Neutrality, held in Panama from September 23 to October 3, 1939; signed on October 3, 1939; it stated that the American republics would create a safety zone around the continent, exclusive of Canada, which was to present a united front against aggressors; and in this zone, varying from 250 miles to 1,250 miles in width, no aggressor would be permitted to commit a hostile act. The area would be policed by the navies of the United States and the Latin American countries. The declaration, however, quickly became ineffective, being violated in the fighting between German and British warships during World War II (1939–45). In January 1940, England and Germany refused to recognize the zone.

Further reading: Henry Steele Commager, ed., *Documents of American History*, 8th ed. (New York: Appleton-Century-Crofts, 1968); J. A. S. Grenville and Bernard Wasserstein, *The Major International Treaties since 1945: A History and Guide with Texts* (New York: Methuen, 1987).

Panama Canal Treaties of 1978   Two treaties—the Panama Canal Treaty and the Neutrality Treaty—signed in Washington, D.C., by U.S. president Jimmy Carter and Panama's chief of government Brigadier General Omar Torrijos on September 7, 1978; they granted Panama control of the Panama Canal at the end of 1999 and guaranteed the permanent neutrality of the canal. In addition, the first treaty provided that the United States and Panama would control the operation and oversee the security of the canal jointly, until 1999, with increasing control being given to the Panamanians as 1999 approached. The Neutrality Treaty further provided that both the United States and Panama were responsible for defending the canal, maintaining its neutrality, and keeping the canal open to the ships of the world. Shipping of all countries was to be guaranteed passage through the canal on a nondiscriminatory basis. U.S. forces would have the right to act after 2000 to ensure that the canal remain open and secure. The treaties were concluded after 14 years of negotiation, and replaced the HAY-BUNAU-VARILLA TREATY of 1903.

Further reading: Henry W. Degenhardt, ed., *Treaties and Alliances of the World*, 4th ed. (Detroit: Gale Research, 1986); Mark Falcoff, *Panama's Canal: What Happens When the United States Gives a Small Country What It Wants* (Washington, D.C.: AEI Press, 1998); K. Larry Storrs and Rosemary P. Jackson, *Panama Canal Treaties* (Washington, D.C.: Library of Congress, Congressional Research Service, 1978); U.S. Congress House Committee on Banking and Financial Services, Subcommittee on Domestic and International Monetary Policy, *The Financial and Commercial Impact of the Panama Canal Treaty* (Washington, D.C.: Government Printing Ofice, 2000).

Panamanian Constitution of 1904   Constitution adopted on February 13, 1904, by the government of Panama, containing many democratic elements as well as a provision authorizing United States intervention in Panamanian affairs. The constitution provided for a government consisting of independent legislative, executive, and judicial branches; for an elected legislature and president; and for fundamental rights, such as the freedom of religion, expression, assembly, and equality of all Panamanians and foreigners before the law. More significant, however, was a provision giving the United States the power to intervene in Panama to maintain order there—provided a U.S.-Panamanian treaty were concluded that guaranteed Panama's independence and sovereignty. America's special interest in Panama was due to her plans to build a canal within Panama's territory.

See also: HAY-BUNAU-VARILLA TREATY; HAY-HERRÁN TREATY; HAY-PAUNCEFOTE TREATIES.

Further reading: Henry Steele Commager, ed., *Documents of American History*, 8th ed. (New York: Appleton-Century-Crofts, 1968); *Constitution of the Republic of Panama* (Panama City: Imp. "Star and Herald," 1904).

Pan-German Creed of Lebensraum   Statement of belief in the need for Lebensraum (living space) for the German-speaking peoples; notably publicized in Berlin, Germany, in 1904. German geographer Friedrich Ratzel's essay "Lebensraum" (1901) helped stimulate the pan-German movement (led by Ernst Hasse, Karl Wolf, and others), which sought to unify all the German peoples in one political state. The creed stated that the rapid growth of Germany's population had made her boundaries "dangerously narrow" and that Germans must "once again move full of freedom and fresh energy" and have "wholesome light and air in plenty" for their children. It cried out "We must have lands, new lands!" The concept of Lebensraum was later misused by the Nazis under Adolf Hitler.

Further reading: James M. Hunter, *Perspective on Ratzel's Political Geography* (Lanham, Md.: University Press of America, 1983); Ihor Kamenetsky, *Secret Nazi Plans for Eastern Europe; a Study of Lebensraum Politics* (New York: Bookman Associates, 1961); Harriet G. Wanklyn, *Friedrich Ratzel* (Cambridge, England: Cambridge University Press, 1961).

Pangkor Engagement (Treaty of Pangkor)   Agreement (1874) by which the British government gained a foothold in the Malay state of Perak, leading eventually (1914) to domination over the entire Malay Peninsula. At the invitation of Governor Andrew Clarke of the Straits Settlements (British crown colony on the Strait of Malacca), British, Chinese, and Malay officials met at Pangkor Island (off the coast of Perak) in January 1874 to discuss issues relating to the controversial Perak succession and the embattled Chinese secret societies. The absent contender from Upper Perak was summarily retired with a pension, and Raja Abdullah (ignored in the 1871 succession) was chosen as the new ruler of Perak. In return, Abdullah was forced to have a British resident stationed at his court and to solicit the resident's advice on all important matters—a stipulation that angered the local chiefs. The Chinese secret society issue was separately settled by the CHINESE ENGAGEMENT. Subsequently, other Malay states signed similar treaties, thus bringing the entire peninsula under British control.

Further reading: Frederick S. Clark, *Men of Malaya* (London: Eldon Press, 1942); Richard J. Wilkinson and Cuthbert W. Harrison, *Papers on Malay Subjects/History*, 4 vols. (Kuala Lumpur, Malaysia: F.M.S. Government Press, 1970).

Papian Poppaean Law (Lex Papia Poppaea)   Roman reforms enacted in A.D. 9 to moderate the JULIAN LAWS OF 18 B.C. and also halt the degenerate trends of the Augustan Age (27 B.C.–A.D. 14). Sponsored by the two Roman consuls (who gave it their names), the law relaxed the conditions of inheritance for celibates, for widows and divorcees (who had twice the time to remarry in order to inherit), and for childless heirs (who received more). Also, the larger the family, the lower the age at which a male member of that family could seek public office. The law also granted priority to fathers among the candidates seeking the various offices.

Further reading: James Bryce, *Studies in History and Jurisprudence*, 2 vols. (Oxford, England: Clarendon Press, 1901); Paul F. Girard, *A Short History of Roman Law* (Union, N.J.: Lawbook Exchange, 2000).

Papineau's Ninety-two Resolutions   See NINETY-TWO RESOLUTIONS, PAPINEAU'S.

Papists' Disabling Act (Test Act of 1678)   Law in September 1678 to exclude Roman Catholics from Parliament, after the scare over the Popish Plot (alleged Jesuit-guided plan to kill King Charles II and to restore England to the pope); it required each member of either house of Parliament to swear oaths of allegiance and supremacy, declare his belief in transubstantiation, and denounce the invocation of saints and the sacrifice of mass as "superstitious and idolatrous." Any member above the age of 21 in England, Scotland, or Ireland, who offended the above provisions, was to be treated as a popish recusant convict, "disabled to hold or execute any office or place of profit or trust, civil or military . . . and to sit or vote in either House of Parliament." The act also covered sworn servants of the king or queen, with the fine for every willful offense placed at £500. Natural-born subjects of the king of Portugal and women (sworn servants of the queen) were exempt, as was the duke of York.

See also: TEST ACT OF 1673, ENGLISH.

Further reading: T. A. Birrell, ed., *The History of English Persecution of Catholics and the Presbyterian Plot*, 2 vols. (London: J. Whitehead & Son, 1953–55); John L. Miller, *Popery and Politics in England 1660–1688* (Cambridge, England: Cambridge University Press, 1973).

Paris, Convention of (1858)

European convention held in Paris to determine, among other things, the future organization of the Danubian principalities of Moldavia (now Moldova) and Wallachia (now part of Romania) as provided for in the 1856 Treaty of PARIS. The final convention or agreement was signed on August 19, 1858, after years of deliberation, by Austria, France, Great Britain, Prussia, Russia, Sardinia, and the Ottoman Empire (Turkey). Thereby, the principalities gained autonomous status under Turkish sovereignty, and were guaranteed equality and individual liberty before the law. Each principality would be headed by a *hospodar* (governor) elected for life by the legislative assembly. A 16-member central commission (eight from each principality) was established to propose laws to the assemblies. The convention also provided for one high court, and a common blue pennant to be displayed prominently on each flag. Though the convention failed to achieve the union of the two principalities, it sowed the seeds for the eventual union.

Further reading: William G. East, *The Union of Moldavia and Wallachia, 1859; an Episode in Diplomatic History* (New York: Octagon Books, 1973); Charles D. Hazen, et al., *Three Peace Congresses of the Nineteenth Century* (Cambridge, Mass.: Harvard University Press, 1917); Fred L. Israel, ed., *Major Peace Treaties of Modern History, 1648–1967*, 4 vols. (New York: Chelsea House, 1967).

Paris, Pact of (1928) (Kellogg-Briand Peace Pact)

Multinational treaty signed by 15 nations in Paris on August 27, 1928, that aimed to outlaw war as an instrument of national policy and to settle international disputes through peaceful means. The treaty, first proposed by French foreign minister Aristide Briand and supported by U.S. secretary of state Frank B. Kellogg, was eventually signed by 62 countries. The treaty condemned "recourse to war for the solution of international controversies." It was ineffective, however, because most nations reserved the right to engage in war in self-defense and because the pact contained no sanctions against violators other than the moral force of international opinion.

Further reading: Henry Steele Commager, ed., *Documents of American History*, 8th ed. (New York: Appleton-Century-Crofts, 1968); Henry W. Degenhardt, ed., *Treaties and Alliances of the World*, 4th ed. (Detroit: Gale Research, 1986); Robert H. Ferrell, *Peace in Their Time: The Origins of the Kellogg-Briand Pact* (New Haven, Conn.: Yale University Press, 1953); Fred L. Israel, ed., *Major Peace Treaties of Modern History, 1648–1967*, 4 vols. (New York: Chelsea House, 1967).

Paris, Treaties of (1778)

Two Franco-American treaties signed on February 6, 1778, in Paris by French foreign minister Charles Gravier, count de Vergennes, and American commissioners Silas Deane and Benjamin Franklin. The first established a formal alliance, directed toward continuing the war against the common enemy (Britain) until American independence was "formally or tacitly assured" and vowing not to make separate peace. France granted America the rights to Bermuda and all British colonies on the mainland, reserving to herself the rights to Britain's territories in the West Indies. By the second, a treaty of amity and commerce, both countries received the "most-favored-nation" status in each other's ports. Climaxing several years of French aid to America, the treaties ensured its continuation during the American Revolution (1775–83), when France provided both manpower and financial resources. The treaties were ratified by the American Congress on May 4, 1778.

See also: FRANCO-AMERICAN CONVENTION OF 1800.

Further reading: Mortimer Adler, ed., *The Annals of America*, 18 vols. (Chicago: Encyclopaedia Britannica, 1968); Henry Steele Commager, ed., *Documents of American History*, 8th ed. (New York: Appleton-Century-Crofts, 1968); Jonathan R. Dull, *A Diplomatic History of the American Revolution* (New Haven, Conn.: Yale University Press, 1985); Frank N. Magill, ed., *Great Events from History: American Series*, 3 vols. (Englewood Cliffs, N.J.: Salem Press, 1975).

Paris, Treaties of (1947)

Satellite treaties, after World War II (1939–45), forced by the Allies on the Axis states (Italy, Romania, Hungary, Bulgaria, and Finland), in Paris on February 10, 1947. Italy's pact took away her North African colonies, curtailed her armed forces, required the surrender of some border areas to France, made Trieste into a free state, and asked that Italy pay compensation to war victims. Romania, Bulgaria, and Hungary also had to pay war reparations and agree to a reduction in armaments. Romania retained Transylvania but ceded Bessarabia and northern Bukovina to the Soviet Union. Bulgaria surrendered western Thrace to

Greece, but kept southern Dobruja. Hungary handed over areas in southern Slovakia to Czechoslovakia. Finland had to pay $300 million to the Soviet Union, which also obtained the power to interfere in Finnish internal affairs. The border between the two countries was fixed according to an agreement of 1940. All the countries, other than Finland, tried to get their treaties revised.

Further reading: Henry W. Degenhardt, ed., *Treaties and Alliances of the World*, 4th ed. (Detroit: Gale Research, 1986); Pieter N. Drost, *Contracts and Peace Treaties; the General Clause on Contracts in the Peace Treaties of Paris 1947 and in the Peace Treaty of Versailles 1919* (The Hague: M. Nijhoff, 1948); J. A. S. Grenville and Bernard Wasserstein, *The Major International Treaties since 1945: A History and Guide with Texts* (New York: Methuen, 1987).

Paris, Treaty of (1229)   Pact of April 11, 1229, at Paris, ending the Albigensian Crusade (1208–29) in France, with King Louis IX's imposition of a harsh settlement on Count Raymond VII of Toulouse (after the royal army had defeated the count's forces in Languedoc). Raymond retained Toulouse, Agenais, Rouergue, Quercy, and northern Albigeois, while the king assumed the seneschalships of Beaucaire-Nîmes and Carcassonne-Béziers, territories conquered by Simon and Amaury of Montfort. Raymond's daughter Joan was to marry Louis IX's brother, Alphonse of Poitiers. If the marriage was issueless, Toulouse would revert to the crown after their deaths. The treaty provided for the establishment of a university at Toulouse and called for the extirpation of heresy from the region. The peace process was initiated by the papal legate and its terms dictated mainly by Queen Mother Blanche of Castile. It succeeded in subduing the feudal French barons of the south.

Further reading: Margaret W. Labarge, *Saint Louis: The Life of Louis IX of France* (London: Eyre & Spottiswoode, 1968); Frank N. Magill, ed., *Great Events from History: Ancient and Medieval Series*, 3 vols. (Englewood Cliffs, N.J.: Salem Press, 1972); Jean Richard, *Saint Louis: Crusader King of France*, ed. Simon Lloyd, trans. Jean Birrell (New York: Cambridge University Press, 1992); W. A. Silby and M. D. Silby, trans., *The History of the Albigensian Crusade* (Woodbridge, England: Boydell, 1998).

Paris, Treaty of (1259)   Treaty made in Paris between Louis IX of France and Henry III of England on December 4, 1259, regularizing the latter's somewhat ambiguous position in France. Henry surrendered his claims to Normandy, Anjou, Maine, Touraine, and Poitou, while Louis recognized Henry's feudal lordship in Bordeaux, Bayonne, and Gascony, making him a peer of France and a vassal of the French king. Henry was generously compensated, with resources to support 500 knights for two years, and was promised reversionary rights in Agenais, Quercy, and Saintonge after the death of Alphonse of Poitiers (see PARIS, TREATY OF [1229]). The 1259 treaty,

initiated by Louis as part of his European peace mission (see CORBEIL, TREATY OF), was bitterly criticized by the nobles in both countries. However, its long-drawn-out negotiations kept the two countries from war, and the new amity enabled Louis to mediate in Henry's dispute with his barons.

See also: AMIENS, MISE OF.

Further reading: David Carpenter, *The Reign of Henry III* (London: Hambledon Press, 1996); Margaret W. Labarge, *Saint Louis: The Life of Louis IX of France* (London: Eyre & Spottiswoode, 1968); Jean Richard, *Saint Louis: Crusader King of France*, ed. Simon Lloyd, trans. Jean Birrell (New York: Cambridge University Press, 1992).

Paris, Treaty of (1327)   Humiliating English settlement with the French, concluded in Paris on March 31, 1327, between King Charles IV of France and Queen Isabella and Sir Roger Mortimer of England (regents for young Edward III). Edward was required to do homage to the French king. England was forced to surrender Agenais and Bazadais and pay a £60,000 indemnity; she retained Ponthieu and a greatly reduced Aquitaine. Subjects who had fled their lands during the recent Anglo-French conflict were allowed to return, while the punishment for eight Gascon loyalists who had supported England was reduced from a death sentence to banishment. The treaty, which did not address key issues of conflict, was a moral victory for Charles IV and the high point of his reign.

Further reading: Michael Prestwich, *The Three Edwards: War and Peace in England, 1272–1377* (London: Weidenfeld & Nicolson, 1980).

Paris, Treaty of (1763)   Diplomatic peace agreement signed by Great Britain, France, and Spain on February 10, 1763, ending the Seven Years' War (1756–63). It was followed by the Treaty of HUBERTUSBURG between Austria and Prussia on February 15. Britain added much to her imperial stature territorially—receiving Canada, Nova Scotia (including Cape Breton), Senegal in West Africa, Minorca in the Mediterranean, and the West Indian islands of Grenada, St. Vincent, Dominica, and Tobago from France, and receiving Florida and concessions in Honduras from Spain. France regained Belle Isle and St. Pierre and Miquelon in the Gulf of St. Lawrence, Gorée Island off West Africa, the West Indian islands of Guadeloupe, Martinique, Marie-Galante, and St. Lucia, and her trading stations in India; she also agreed to destroy the fortifications at Dunkirk. But her fishing rights off Newfoundland and in the St. Lawrence Gulf remained intact, thereby causing discord. Spain recovered Manila in the Philippines and Havana in Cuba from Britain, and Lousiana from France (all other territory east of the Mississippi River was ceded to Britain).

See also: SAN ILDEFONSO, TREATY OF (1762).

Further reading: William MacDonald, ed., *Select Charters and Other Documents Illustrative of American History, 1606–1775* (New York: Macmillan, 1899); Frank N. Magill, ed.,

Great Events from History: Modern European Series, 3 vols. (Englewood Cliffs, N.J.: Salem Press, 1973); Zenab E. Rashed, *The Peace of Paris, 1763* (Liverpool, England: University Press, 1951).

Paris, Treaty of (1783) (Treaty of Versailles)

Peace agreement concluded at Versailles, near Paris, France, on September 3, 1783, between Great Britain and the United States (the 13 colonies), officially ending the American Revolution (1775–83). Britain also signed separate treaties with France and Spain. Britain recognized American independence and agreed to withdraw her troops. The boundaries of the United States were established: the Mississippi River as the western boundary (navigation on the river was open), Canada as the northern, and Florida as the southern (Spain reacquired Florida and the island of Minorca in her treaty with Britain, which retained Gibraltar). The United States and Britain agreed that creditors of either side could collect just debts. The former promised also to press several states to return property confiscated from Loyalists (colonial Tories) during the revolution. The Americans were given fishing rights off Newfoundland, too. In her treaty with France, Britain returned the islands of St. Lucia and Tobago (both in the West Indies) and St. Pierre and Miquelon (in the Gulf of St. Lawrence); France returned the West Indian islands of Grenada and the Grenadines, St. Vincent, Dominica, St. Kitts-Nevis, and Montserrat. In West Africa, in exchange for Fort James and the Gambia River, Britain ceded the Senegal River and the forts of St. Louis, Podor, Galam, Arguin, and Portendic; Gorée Island was returned to France, too. The French won some territories in India (Mahe, Surat, and others) and received trading rights there; they gave up some fishing rights in Newfoundland but retained those in the Gulf of St. Lawrence.

Further reading: Henry Steele Commager, ed., *Documents of American History*, 8th ed. (New York: Appleton-Century-Crofts, 1968); Jonathan R. Dull, *A Diplomatic History of the American Revolution* (New Haven, Conn.: Yale University Press, 1985); Charles W. Eliot, ed., *The Harvard Classics* (New York: P. F. Collier & Son, 1937); Frank N. Magill, ed., *Great Events from History: American Series*, 3 vols. (Englewood Cliffs, N.J.: Salem Press, 1975).

Paris, Treaty of (1796)

Treaty of May 15, 1796, between Napoléon Bonaparte (then general of the French army) and the king of Sardinia (Piedmont) after the battle of Mondovi (April 22, 1796), Napoléon's successful start of his first Italian campaign. Signed in Paris, on the basis of preliminaries conducted at Cherasco and Turin (April 23–28, 1796), it was the first of Napoléon's many diplomatic triumphs. The treat called for the cessation of hostilities, for "peace, amity, and good understanding," and for Sardinia to withdraw from the armed coalition against France. The Sardinian king renounced his claims over Savoy and Nice, allowed French couriers passage through his country, denied refuge to French émigrés, and ceded Conti, Tortone, and Alexandrie to France, which agreed to mediate in settling Sardinia's differences with Genoa. The Batavian Republic (the Netherlands) was also included in the deliberations. Trade relations were restablished, and France and Sardinia agreed to enter into a commercial pact.

See also: CHERASCO, ARMISTICE OF.

Further reading: Elijah Adlow, *Napoleon in Italy, 1796–1797* (Boston: W. J. Rochfort, 1948); Spenser Wilkinson, *The Rise of General Bonaparte* (Brookfield, Vt.: Ashgate, 1991).

Paris, Treaty of (1810)

Treaty concluded in Paris on January 6, 1810, between France under Emperor Napoléon Bonaparte and Sweden under King Charles XIII, bringing Sweden (which had previously been allied with Great Britain) into an alliance with France. Through the treaty Sweden regained control over Swedish Pomerania and the Baltic island of Rügen, which France had seized from her earlier, during the Napoleonic Wars (1803–15). In return Sweden agreed to join the Continental System, the members (the French Empire and her allies) of which had pledged to cease all trade with Great Britain. This latter provision had also been included in the Treaty of FREDRIKSHAMM, which Sweden had concluded with Russia. Russia (which had mediated the Paris treaty) had been France's ally since 1807.

See also: BERLIN DECREE.

Further reading: Alan W. Palmer, *Bernadotte: Napoleon's Marshall, Sweden's King* (London: Murray, 1990).

Paris, Treaty of (1814) (First Peace of Paris)

Peace accord made in Paris on May 30, 1814 (after Emperor Napoléon's April 11 abdication), between France's king Louis XVIII and the allied powers of Europe (Britain, Russia, Austria, and Prussia). France was allowed to keep her boundaries of 1792, which included areas (Avignon, Venaissin, parts of Savoy and Belgium, some German lands) she did not possess in 1789. Britain returned all the French colonies she had seized during the French Revolutionary Wars (1803–15) and Napoleonic Wars (1803–15), except Mauritius, St. Lucia, and Tobago. The British also retained Malta, the Ionian Islands, and the Cape of Good Hope. In return, France recognized the independence of the Netherlands, the German states, Switzerland, and the Italian states, and also promised to abolish the slave trade within five years. The Allies exacted no war indemnities, showing extraordinary leniency overall. It was also decided to refer unresolved questions to a congress at Vienna, to be held later the same year.

Further reading: Tim Chapman, *The Congress of Vienna: Origins, Processes and Results* (New York: Routledge, 1998); Charles D. Hazen, et al., *Three Peace Congresses of the Nineteenth Century* (Cambridge, Mass.: Harvard University Press, 1917); Frank N. Magill, ed., *Great Events from History:*

Modern European Series 3 vols. (Englewood Cliffs, N.J.: Salem Press, 1973).

Paris, Treaty of (1815) (Second Peace of Paris)

Peace treaty ending the Napoleonic Wars (1803–15), concluded at Paris on November 20, 1815, between King Louis XVIII of France and the allied powers of Europe. Unlike the 1814 Treaty of PARIS, it imposed severe and humiliating terms on France, which was compelled to cede the strategic fortresses of Philippeville and Marienburg to the Netherlands, Saarlouis and Saarbrucken to Prussia, and Landau to the German Confederation; the French also ceded territory as far as the Lauter River to Bavaria, and the district of Haute-Savoie to Savoy. Eighteen French fortresses on the north and east frontier were to be occupied by 150,000 troops of the Allies for not more than five years and at French expense. France, which lost all gains on her borders since 1790, had to pay a war indemnity of 700,000,000 francs and had to restore the art treasures she had seized from all over Europe to their rightful owners. The Allies—Britain, Russia, Austria, and Prussia—renewed their Quadruple Alliance on the same day as the treaty.

Further reading: Tim Chapman, *The Congress of Vienna: Origins, Processes and Results* (New York: Routledge, 1998); Charles D. Hazen, et al., *Three Peace Congresses of the Nineteenth Century* (Cambridge, Mass.: Harvard University Press, 1917); Fred L. Israel, ed., *Major Peace Treaties of Modern History, 1648–1967*, 4 vols. (New York: Chelsea House, 1967); Frank N. Magill, ed., *Great Events from History: Modern European Series*, 3 vols. (Englewood Cliffs, N.J.: Salem Press, 1973).

Paris, Treaty of (1856)

Peace treaty concluded on March 30, 1856, at the close of the Congress of Paris between Britain, France, Austria, Sardinia, and the Ottoman Empire (Turkey) on one side and Russia on the other, ending the Crimean War (1853–56) and marking the Ottoman Empire's entrance into the European family of nations. The war had originated as a conflict between Russia and the Ottoman Empire over supremacy in the Balkans and the status of the sultan's Orthodox Christian subjects, whose rights Russia claimed the duty to protect. Through the treaty the powers pledged to maintain the territorial integrity and independence of the Ottoman Empire; Russia ceded part of Bessarabia to the Ottomans, renounced control over the mouth of the Danube River, and agreed to the neutralization of the Black Sea. Safe navigation on the lower Danube was guaranteed by an international commission; the Black Sea was not open to warships, only merchant ships; and Russian and Ottoman borders in Asia returned to their prewar status. The Danubian principalities of Moldavia and Wallachia, as well as the rights of the sultan's Christian subjects, were thenceforth guaranteed collectively by the powers.

See also: OTTOMAN IMPERIAL EDICT OF 1856; VIENNA FOUR POINTS; VIENNA NOTE OF 1853.

Further reading: Henry W. Degenhardt, ed., *Treaties and Alliances of the World*, 4th ed. (Detroit: Gale Research, 1986); Charles D. Hazen, et al., *Three Peace Congresses of the Nineteenth Century* (Cambridge, Mass.: Harvard University Press, 1917); Frank N. Magill, ed., *Great Events from History: Modern European Series*, 3 vols. (Englewood Cliffs, N.J.: Salem Press, 1973); Louis L. Snyder, ed., *Fifty Major Documents of the Nineteenth Century* (Princeton, N.J.: D. Van Nostrand, 1955).

Paris, Treaty of (1898)

Treaty signed on December 10, 1898, ending the Spanish-American War (1898). According to the treaty terms, Spain abandoned her claim to Cuba and ceded Puerto Rico, Guam, and the Philippine Islands to the United States in exchange for $20 million. The U.S. acquisition of the Philippines sparked a controversy in the Senate over American imperialism. Treaty supporters, including U.S. president William McKinley, hoped to help the people of the Philippines and to establish a base for Far East trade. Opponents decried U.S. control of distant people as a violation of self-determination. The Senate ratified the treaty by a narrow margin on February 6, 1899.

Further reading: Mortimer Adler, ed., *The Annals of America*, 18 vols. (Chicago: Encyclopedia Britannica, 1968); Henry Steele Commager, ed., *Documents of American History*, 8th ed. (New York: Appleton-Century-Crofts, 1968); Charles W. Eliot, ed., *The Harvard Classics* (New York: P. F. Collier & Son, 1937); Frank N. Magill, ed., *Great Events from History: Modern European Series*, 3 vols. (Englewood Cliffs, N.J.: Salem Press, 1973).

Paris Commune, First Proclamation of the

Declaration made on March 29, 1871, from the Hôtel de Ville in Paris, announcing the inauguration of the Paris Commune following victory in the March 26 elections, which climaxed a short-lived, successful revolution. It reminded French citizens that they were "masters" of their own fate, having established "a constitution which defies all attack" and assured them that, with their support, their representatives would "repair the destruction caused by the fallen authorities" in the fields of commerce, industry, and labor. The proclamation outlined the republic's immediate agenda—decisions on rent and moratorium, and the reorganization of all public services and the National Guard. Its accompanying decrees ended conscription, declared the National Guard to be the only military force in Paris, and called on all able-bodied citizens to join it. Finally, the proclamation called on "the support of its confidence to assure the triumph of the Republic."

Further reading: Frank N. Magill, ed., *Great Events from History: Modern European Series*, 3 vols. (Englewood Cliffs, N.J.: Salem Press, 1973); Robert Tombs, *The Paris Commune, 1871* (New York: Longman, 1999).

Paris Commune, Program of the   Agenda (dated April 19, 1871) of the newly proclaimed Paris Commune, directed toward "the recognition and consolidation of the Republic." It sought "absolute autonomy of the Commune extended to all parts of France," all communes being bound contractually into an association to secure "French Unity." It defined a commune's rights as (1) individual liberty and liberty of conscience; (2) voting on communal budget; (3) fixing taxation; (4) directing local services; (5) organizing educational, magistracy, and police services; and (6) administering communal property. The commune's leaders sought, from France's central government, guarantees for these rights and "the realization and practice of the same principles." However, they reserved the right to enact any reforms "in accordance with the needs of the moment, the wishes of those interested and the results of experience." Hailing the communal revolution as the beginning of "a new era of experimental positive and scientific politics," its leaders rededicated themselves to accomplishing "the modern Revolution, the greatest and most fruitful of all that have illumined history."

Further reading: Frank N. Magill, ed., *Great Events from History: Modern European Series*, 3 vols. (Englewood Cliffs, N.J.: Salem Press, 1973); Robert Tombs, *The Paris Commune, 1871* (New York: Longman, 1999).

Parliament Act of 1911, British   British Minister Herbert Asquith's proposals for parliamentary reform made in 1910, following the rejection of his People's Budget by the House of Lords. Passed on August 18, 1911, the act withdrew from the House of Lords its right of veto except on bills meant to extend the parliamentary term. It limited Parliament to a maximum five-year tenure. The Lords were allowed to postpone decisions on money bills for one year, and on other matters for two years. All bills would become law after passing in the House of Commons but failing in the Lords three times in two years. The 1911 act also allowed for the payment of salaries to members of Parliament. The act was passed after Asquith threatened to create more liberal peers to facilitate its passage.

Further reading: Randolph L. Braham, ed., *Documents on Major European Governments* (New York: Knopf/Borzoi, 1966); David D. Douglas, et al., eds., *English Historical Documents*, 12 vols. (New York: Oxford University Press, 1950–77); Frank N. Magill, ed., *Great Events from History: Modern European Series*, 3 vols. (Englewood Cliffs, N.J.: Salem Press, 1973); Joel H. Wiener, ed., *Great Britain—The Lion at Home: A Documentary History of Domestic Policy (1689–1973)*, 4 vols. (New York: Chelsea House, 1974).

Parliament Act of 1949, British   Statute of December 16, 1949, restricting the delaying powers of the House of Lords (to veto legislation) from two years to one. The bill had a tortuous passage in the British Parliament, with the House of Lords rejecting it thrice, November 29, 1949, being the third time. However, since it had passed the House of Commons it was sent for royal approval, which was easily won. The upper house was thus overruled for the third time since the PARLIAMENT ACT OF 1911—the HOME RULE BILL OF 1913 and the WELSH DISESTABLISHMENT BILL OF 1914 being the other two times it had been overruled.

Further reading: Randolph L. Braham, ed., *Documents on Major European Governments* (New York: Knopf/Borzoi, 1966).

Parnell Commission Report   Report released on February 2, 1890, by a special parliamentary commission of three judges (Judges Hansen, Day, and Smith), appointed by the British government in September 1888 to investigate all the charges brought by *The Times* (see PARNELLISM AND CRIME) against Charles S. Parnell and other Irish leaders. Earlier, parliament had refused Parnell's request for a select committee hearing. Before the commission could investigate the specific case of an incriminating letter (allegedly written by Parnell), Sir Charles Webster (his legal counsel) put into the witness box an old and impoverished journalist named Richard Pigott, who confessed to having forged it. Parnell was instantly acclaimed as a hero. A year later, the commission's report formally cleared him of all blame, while condemning the militant activities of some of his other colleagues.

Further reading: David D. Douglas et al., eds., *English Historical Documents*, 12 vols. (New York: Oxford University Press, 1950–77); Special Commission to Inquire into Charges and Allegations Against Certain Members of Parliament and Others, *A Verbatim Copy of the Parnell Commission Report: With Complete Index and Notes* (London: Irish Loyal & Patriotic Union, 1890).

Parnellism and Crime   Series of articles published by the *Times* of London during 1887–88, accusing Charles S. Parnell and his followers of inciting and abetting the violence during the Land War (1879–82) in Ireland. The first article appeared on March 7, 1887, but it was the second (April 18) that started the controversy (see PARNELL COMMISSION REPORT) that almost destroyed Parnell's reputation and his alliance with the Liberals. It was a letter, allegedly in Parnell's handwriting, condoning the Phoenix Park murders of May 6, 1882 (see KILMAINHAM TREATY). Parnell denied having written it but, since he took no other action, the attacks continued. Meanwhile, the *Times* published another series on the same subject, based on material gathered by Henri Le Caron and written by Robert Anderson. In February 1890, a parliamentary commission declared Parnell innocent—the real culprit having been already identified. The *Times* was saddled with damages of £200,000 and a broken reputation.

Further reading: Donal McCartney, ed., *Parnell: The Politics of Power* (Dublin: Wolfhound Press, 1991).

Pascendi Gregis   Encyclical letter (*De pascendi dominici gregis,* or *Pascendi gregis*) of September 8, 1907, in which Pope Pius X condemned modernism. Catholic modernists wished to reconcile modern scientific findings with the teachings of the Roman Catholic Church. Reviling modernism as "the synthesis of all heresies," the encyclical called for measures to combat it, including censoring of written works, and disciplinary measures to be used in the training of priests. The letter also condemned agnosticism and vital immanence, as well as the emancipation of exegesis from dogma, and of politico-religious movements from ecclesiastical authority.

Further reading: Claudia Carlen, comp., *The Papal Encyclicals* (Wilmington, N.C.: McGrath Publishing, 1981); Catholic University of America, eds., *New Catholic Encyclopedia* (New York: McGraw-Hill, 1967); Anne Fremantle, *The Papal Encyclicals in Their Historical Context* (New York: Mentor-Omega Books, 1963); Anthony J. Mioni, ed., *Popes Against Modern Errors: 16 Papal Documents* (Rockford, Ill.: Tan Books, 1999).

Passarowitz, Treaty of   Peace treaty ending the Venetian-Turkish War of 1714–18 and the Austro-Turkish War of 1716–18; made at Passarowitz, Serbia, on July 21, 1718, among the Holy Roman Empire, the Ottoman Empire, and Venice through the mediation of the Dutch and British. By the treaty, the Ottoman Turks gave up to the Austrians the Banat of Temesvár (the remaining portion of Hungary that they had kept after the 1699 Peace of KARLOWITZ), northern Serbia and Belgrade, and portions of the provinces of Bosnia and Wallachia. The Venetians lost control of Morea (Peloponnesus), handing over this southern Greek peninsula to the Turks.

Further reading: Fred L. Israel, ed., *Major Peace Treaties of Modern History, 1648–1967,* 4 vols. (New York: Chelsea House, 1967); John J. Norwich, *A History of Venice* (New York: Vintage Books, 1989); Nancy A. Walker, *The Peace of Passarowitz, 1714–1718* (Ann Arbor, Mich.: Xerox University Microfilms, 1976).

Passau, Treaty of (Convention of Passau)   Religious peace treaty concluded between Maurice, elector of Saxony, and Ferdinand I, king of Bohemia and Hungary (who represented his brother, Holy Roman Emperor Charles V), at Passau, Bavaria, on August 7, 1552. The Protestants (led by Maurice) and Roman Catholics (led by Ferdinand and Charles) agreed to stop warring until their religious disputes could be settled at the next imperial Diet. Maurice secured freedom of worship for Protestants and the release of captive Protestant princes, including Philip of Hesse, and the elector agreed to assist Ferdinand against the Turks.

See also: AUGSBURG, PEACE OF; FRIEDWALD, TREATY OF.

Further reading: Martyn C. Rady, *The Emperor Charles V* (New York: Longman, 1988).

Passfield Report (Passfield White Paper)   Statement of British foreign policy issued as a white paper on October 20, 1930, by the Colonial Office of the British government, which was headed by Lord Passfield (Sidney Webb); it set forth the government's recommendations on the immigration of the Jews to Palestine within the context of the 1929 Arab attacks against the Jews. The report stated that the government's obligation to support the establishment of a Jewish national home (see BALFOUR DECLARATION) must in no way interfere with its obligation to uphold the rights of the non-Jewish population in Palestine; recommended that the acquisition of new land by Jews already in Palestine be postponed while landless Arabs remained; and recommended that the immigration of Jews to Palestine cease while Arabs remained unemployed. The report caused an uproar within the Jewish community.

See also: CHURCHILL WHITE PAPER OF 1922.

Further reading: Cyrus Adler et al., *Lectures, Selected Papers, Addresses* (Philadelphia: Priv. print., 1933).

Pass Laws, South African   See FREEDOM CHARTER.

Patriot Act, U.S.   See USA-PATRIOT ACT.

Paterson Plan   See NEW JERSEY PLAN.

Patronato Law (Ley de Patronato)   Law of ecclesiastical patronage (*patronato,* in Spanish) passed by the National Congress of Greater Colombia (New Granada, Venezuela, and Quito) on July 28, 1824, providing for the state's right to control the actions and decisions of the Roman Catholic Church, a right previously claimed and exercised for centuries by the kings of Spain. Specifically, the law provided for the right of the state to nominate candidates to ecclesiastical sees, to control the formation of new dioceses, to regulate the collection of tithes, and to pass laws affecting the exercise of patronage. The law also established the union of church and state in Greater Colombia.

Further reading: J. Lloyd Mecham, *Church and State in Latin America: A History of Politicoecclesiastical Relations,* rev. ed. (Chapel Hill: University of North Carolina Press, 1966); Austen Ivereigh, *The Politics of Religion in an Age of Revival: Studies in Nineteenth-Century Europe and Latin America* (London: Institute of Latin American Studies, 2000).

Payne-Aldrich Tariff Act (U.S. Tariff of 1909)   Tariff revision act, passed by the U.S. Congress on August 5, 1909, which reduced overall rates from the high levels of the DINGLEY TARIFF to about 38 percent but raised the levies on coal and iron ore. The act, a compromise between protectionism and the 1908 Republican Party platform promise to lower tariffs, was cosponsored by Republican senator Nelson W. Aldrich of Rhode Island and representative Sereno Elisha Payne of New York. It left more than a thousand tariff schedules unchanged, lowered 650, and raised 220. Its largely protectionist features became a major political issue, resulting in Republican defeat in the election of 1910.

Further reading: Mortimer Adler, ed., *The Annals of America*, 18 vols. (Chicago: Encyclopaedia Britannica, 1968); Henry Steele Commager, ed., *Documents of American History*, 8th ed. (New York: Appleton-Century-Crofts, 1968); Edward S. Kaplan and Thomas W. Ryley, *Prelude to Trade Wars: American Tariff Policy, 1890–1922* (Westport, Conn.: Greenwood Press, 1994); Paul Wolman, *Most Favored Nation: The Republican Revisionists and U.S. Tariff Policy, 1897–1912* (Chapel Hill: University of North Carolina Press, 1992).

Peace Manifesto (Perpetual Peace: A Philosophical Essay)

Immanuel Kant's prescription for perpetual peace among nations, published in 1795. A synthesis of Kant's various philosophies, it consists of two sections, two supplements, and two appendixes. Kant, the renowned German metaphysical philosopher of the Enlightenment, called for the invalidation of peace treaties that "tacitly reserved matter for a future war," for an end to one state's domination of another, for noninterference in another's constitutional affairs, and for the abolition of standing armies. The state of peace, he believed, "is not the natural state," but one that "must be established" through a republican constitution, an enlightened public, the founding of the law of nations "on a federation of free states," and by limiting the law of world citizenship to "conditions of universal hospitality." Describing nature, "that great artist," as the guarantor of peace, Kant urged nations to secretly consult philosophers on matters of public peace. Finally, Kant discussed the harmony between politics and morality, concluding that perpetual peace was a gradually attainable goal.

See also: CRITIQUE OF PURE REASON.

Further reading: Friedrich Heer, *Great Documents of the World: Milestones of Human Thought* (New York: McGraw-Hill, 1977); Manfred Kuehn, *Kant: A Biography* (New York: Cambridge University Press, 2001); M. Campbell Smith, trans., *Perpetual Peace; a Philosophical Essay* (New York: Macmillan, 1917).

Peace of God (Pax Ecclesiae, Paix de Dieu)

Decrees declared by the Roman Catholic Church at three synods in the late 10th century, the first in A.D. 989, in an attempt to abolish feudal violence and encourage peace. In general it forbade violence committed against ecclesiastical buildings, clergyman, pilgrims, merchants, women, and peasants, as well as against livestock and agricultural equipment. Individuals embracing its provisions were obliged to swear to its observance and enforcement. Those who performed acts not in keeping with the peace were subject to excommunication. The peace was never particularly effective.

See also: TRUCE OF GOD.

Further reading: Catholic University of America, eds., *New Catholic Encyclopedia* (New York: McGraw-Hill, 1967); George Duby, *The Chivalrous Society*, trans. Cynthia Postan (London: Arnold, 1977).

Peace of the Church   See CLEMENT IX, PEACE OF.

Peace on Earth   See PACEM IN TERRIS.

Peace Preservation Act of 1870, British

Act passed by the British government on April 4, 1870, giving the Irish administration special emergency powers to control the agrarian crimes in Ireland, particularly in County Mayo where the agitation was widespread against British repressive powers. Four kinds of agrarian crime were recognized: against person, property, public peace, and written intimidation or threats. Between 1800 and 1921, 105 Peace Preservation Acts (also called Coercion Acts) were enacted in Britain.

Further reading: Alvin Jackson, *A History of Ireland, 1778–1998* (Oxford, England: Blackwell, 1999); I. S. Leadam, *Coercive Measures in Ireland, 1830–1880* (London: National Press Agency, 1880).

"Peace Without Victory" Speech, Wilson's

Address delivered by President Woodrow Wilson to the U.S. Senate on January 22, 1917, calling for an end to World War I (1914–18) and outlining his ideas for the basis of an enduring world peace. Wilson sought a peace that would protect the rights of both sides, a "peace without victory," between nations equal in rights if not in power. This peace must be guaranteed by an international organization, "the organized major force of mankind." He argued that peace must be based on the principle of government by the consent of the governed, that all nations must have free access to the seas and the paths of commerce, that no nation should seek to extend its powers over another, that nations should avoid entangling alliances, and that armaments must be limited. These points were developed further in Wilson's FOURTEEN POINTS SPEECH.

Further reading: Mortimer Adler, ed., *The Annals of America*, 18 vols. (Chicago: Encyclopaedia Britannica, 1968); Henry Steele Commager, ed., *Documents of American History*, 8th ed. (New York: Appleton-Century-Crofts, 1968); Laurence W. Martin, *Peace Without Victory; Woodrow Wilson and the British Liberals* (Port Washington, N.Y.: Kennikat Press, 1973).

Peasants' Manifesto, German (Twelve Articles)

Document drawn up by the German peasants and addressed to "the Christian reader" in March 1524; in it they put forth their claims for freedom based on religious principles and scriptural texts. Among the most important of their claims were the demands that all tithes be dropped (except for the grain tithe, which they felt had biblical sanction); that they be permitted to hunt and fish freely; that the ownership and use of forests return to the community; that they be guaranteed a fair price for their labor; and that a fair price be charged them for rent. Martin Luther, the German leader of the Protestant Reformation, backed the peasants' demands at first, but soon opposed them when the Peasants' Revolt (1524–25) endangered his religious movement through wanton depredations. The nobles crushed the revolt, Luther lost much popular appeal, and the manifesto was ineffective.

Further reading: Mark A. Kishlansky, ed., *Sources of the West: Readings in Western Civilization*, vol. 2, 4th ed. (New York: Longman, 2001); Frank N. Magill, ed., *Great Events from History: Modern European Series*, 3 vols. (Englewood Cliffs, N.J.: Salem Press, 1973); Louis L. Snyder, ed., *Documents of German History* (New Brunswick, N.J.: Rutgers University Press, 1958); Milton Viorst, ed., *The Great Documents of Western Civilization* (Philadelphia: Chilton Books, 1965).

Peerage Act of 1963   British legislation of July 31, 1963, allowing peers to renounce permanently their peerages within one year (one month for members of the House of Commons) in order to stand election for public office, without this affecting the course of the peerage. For instance, Lord Home resigned his peerage, was elected to the British Parliament as Sir Alexander Frederick Douglas-Home, and later (October 1964) became prime minister. Promoted by Viscount Stangate (later Minister Anthony Wedgwood Benn), the act canceled the elections for Scottish representative peers and admitted all Scottish peers into parliament (see UNION, ACT OF [UNION OF ENGLAND AND SCOTLAND]). Also, female hereditary peers became members of the House of Lords, and some of the disabilities of the Irish peers were withdrawn.

Further reading: Randolph L. Braham, ed., *Documents on Major European Governments* (New York: Knopf/Borzoi, 1966); *Peerage Act, 1963: Eliz. 2. 1963 Ch. 48* (H.M. Stationery Office, 1963); Nicole Smith, *Reform of the House of Lords* (London: Constitution Unit, 1996); Joel H. Wiener, ed., *Great Britain—The Lion at Home: A Documentary History of Domestic Policy (1689–1973)*, 4 vols. (New York: Chelsea House, 1974).

Peerage Bill   British legislation of 1719, seeking to restrict the appointment of new peers, thereby ensuring a permanent Whig majority. Since the Restoration (the return of Charles II as king in 1660), peerages had been awarded in recognition of political services; at the end of the 17th century, there were nearly 220 peers. The 1719 bill tried to limit the number of new peerages (excluding princes) to six and named 25 hereditary Scottish Lords of Parliament instead of 16. The bill passed the House of Lords but was rejected by the House of Commons following an exposé of its constitutional and political pitfalls by Sir Robert Walpole.

Further reading: Jeremy Black, *Robert Walpole and Politics in Early-Eighteenth Century Britain* (Basingstroke, England: Macmillan Education, 1990); John F. Naylor, *The British Aristocracy and the Peerage Bill of 1719* (New York: Oxford University Press, 1968); Joel H. Wiener, ed., *Great Britain—The Lion at Home: A Documentary History of Domestic Policy (1689–1973)*, 4 vols. (New York: Chelsea House, 1974).

Peking, Peace of   Pact between the Chinese emperor and joint Anglo-French forces (signed on October 24, 1860, with Britain and the next day with France), after the burning of the emperor's summer palace in Peking (Beijing) in protest over China's imprisonment of English diplomat Sir Harry Parkes and other peace envoys. Its terms were dictated largely by Lord Palmerston (British prime minister), who secured for Britain trading rights in opium and other goods, free access to Peking and Canton for all Westerners, and possession of the Kowloon Peninsula across from Hong Kong. French Catholic missions gained the right to buy property. Both France and Britain also received indemnities from China. General Nikolai Ignatiev (noted Russian diplomat and a mediator of this pact) was rewarded on November 14, 1860, by the maritime province of Vladivostock (see PEKING, TREATY OF).

See also: TIENTSIN, TREATY OF.

Further reading: Muriel E. Chamberlain, *Lord Palmerston* (Washington, D.C.: Catholic University of America Press, 1987).

Peking, Treaty of (1860)   Pact signed between China and Russia on November 14, 1860, by which the latter gained control of a long strip of Pacific coastline—a maritime province where the Russians founded the naval port of Vladivostok in 1860–61. By the treaty, concluded in Peking (Beijing), China ceded to Russia territories east of the Ussuri River and north and east of the Amur River. Consequently Manchuria became a sphere of Russian influence. The Treaty of Peking officially confirmed the 1858 Treaty of Aigun, whose terms were similar in the cessions.

See also: PEKING, PEACE OF.

Further reading: John L. Evans, *Russian Expansion on the Amur, 1848–1860: The Push to the Pacific* (Lewiston, N.Y.: Edwin Mellen Press, 1999); S. C. M. Paine, *Imperial Rivals: China, Russia, and Their Disputed Frontier* (Armonk, N.Y.: M. E. Sharpe, 1996).

Pendleton Act (Pendleton Civil Service Act)   Legislation passed on January 16, 1883, establishing the U.S. Civil Service Commission and thus ending a long political battle over civil service reform. The act was passed after the 1881 assassination of U.S. president James A. Garfield by a disgruntled office seeker dramatized the need for reform. It established the merit system for federal employment, replacing the spoils system whereby jobs were granted to party loyalists without regard to their competence. Sponsored by Senator George H. Pendleton of Ohio, the legislation provided for a bipartisan three-man commission to administer competitive examinations for civil service appointments. Though the act originally affected only a small percentage of federal employees, it has been broadened considerably over the years.

Further reading: Henry Steele Commager, ed., *Documents of American History*, 8th ed. (New York: Appleton-Century-Crofts, 1968); Frank N. Magill, ed., *Great Events from History: American Series*, 3 vols. (Englewood Cliffs, N.J.: Salem Press, 1975); David H. Rosenbloom and Mark A. Emmert, eds., *Centenary Issues of the Pendleton Act of 1883: The Problematic Legacy of Civil Service Reform* (New York: M. Dekker, 1982).

Pennsylvania, Charter of Patent granted by England's king Charles II to William Penn in 1681, establishing Pennsylvania as the last of Britain's proprietary colonies. Reportedly granted in lieu of a debt owed to Penn's father, the charter made Penn proprietor of the area between 43° N and 40° N, through five degrees in longitude running west from the Delaware River, but placed certain limits on his powers. It called for establishment of an assembly with the power to approve legislation as well as a privy council, which could disallow such legislation within five years; provided that the courts of the province could make appeals to the crown; and mandated the king's right to impose taxes by act of Parliament. The Penn family's proprietorship continued until the American Revolution, but a strong colonial assembly also developed in Pennsylvania.

Further reading: Mortimer Adler, ed., *The Annals of America*, 18 vols. (Chicago: Encyclopaedia Britannica, 1968); Henry Steele Commager, ed., *Documents of American History*, 8th ed. (New York: Appleton-Century-Crofts, 1968); David D. Douglas, et al., eds., *English Historical Documents*, 12 vols. (New York: Oxford University Press, 1950–77); William MacDonald, ed., *Select Charters and Other Documents Illustrative of American History, 1606–1775* (New York: Macmillan, 1899).

Pentagon Papers (History of U.S. Decision-Making Process on Vietnam Policy) Secret U.S. Defense Department history of the U.S. role in Southeast Asia, from World War II to May 1968; prepared in 1967–68. It was leaked to the press by Daniel Ellsberg, a Pentagon consultant, and information therein began to be published by the *New York Times* on June 13, 1971. Justice Department attempts to prevent further publication were overruled on June 30 by the U.S. Supreme Court, which declared that FIRST AMENDMENT guarantees of a free press applied. Charges of espionage, theft, and conspiracy against Ellsberg were eventually dropped because of government misconduct. The papers, which documented a growing commitment to a noncommunist South Vietnam and clandestine military activities, aroused a storm of controversy over the origins and conduct of the Vietnam War (1956–75). They revealed major disparities between declared government policies and the real intentions of American leaders.

Further reading: Maureen Harrison and Steve Gilbert, *Freedom of the Press Decisions of the United States Supreme Court* (San Diego, Calif.: Excellent Books, 1996); New York Times, eds. *The Pentagon Papers, as Published by the New York Times* (New York: Bantam Books, 1981); Stanley N. Worton, comp., *Freedom of Speech and Press* (Rochelle Park, N.J.: Hayden Book Co., 1975).

Peonage Abolition Act, U.S. Act passed by Congress on March 2, 1867, that abolished peonage in the Territory of New Mexico and elsewhere in the United States. Designed to help enforce the THIRTEENTH AMENDMENT, the act declared that holding any person to service or labor under the peonage system was unlawful and forever prohibited. It defined peonage as the "voluntary or involuntary service or labor of any persons . . . in liquidation of any debt or obligation." Violations were punishable by fines and imprisonment.

Further reading: Erlinda Gonzales-Berry and David Maciel, *The Contested Homeland: A Chicano History of New Mexico* (Albuquerque: University of New Mexico Press, 2000); Roxanne D. Ortiz, *Roots of Resistance: Land Tenure in New Mexico, 1680–1980* (Los Angeles: Chicano Studies Research Center Publications, 1980); Alvin R. Sunseri, *Seeds of Discord: New Mexico in the Aftermath of the American Conquest, 1846–1861* (Chicago: Nelson-Hall, 1979).

People, Agreement of the See AGREEMENT OF THE PEOPLE.

People's Charter (Chartist Petition of 1838) British charter having six points or articles, drafted in May 1838 by William Lovett and Francis Place (both of the London Workingmen's Association) to highlight the demands of the working classes for parliamentary reform. The focus of the Chartist movement (1838–48), the People's Charter called for (1) annual parliaments, (2) universal male suffrage, (3) equal electoral districts, (4) abolition of the property qualification for members of parliament, (5) election by ballot, and (6) payment for members of Parliament. During the next decade, Chartism developed into a strong, nationwide movement addressing itself to the issues facing the working class people of Britain and led by men such as Feargus O'Connor and James Bronterre O'Brien.

Further reading: Mark A. Kishlansky, ed., *Sources of the West: Readings in Western Civilization*, vol. 2, 4th ed. (New York: Longman, 2001); Frank N. Magill, ed., *Great Events from History: Modern European Series*, 3 vols. (Englewood Cliffs, N.J.: Salem Press, 1973); Joel H. Wiener, ed., *Great Britain— The Lion at Home: A Documentary History of Domestic Policy (1689–1973)*, 4 vols. (New York: Chelsea House, 1974).

Pepin, Donation of Document recognizing papal rule over lands in central Italy, establishing the Roman Catholic

Church's temporal domain in A.D. 756. Earlier, Pope Stephen II had turned to the Frankish King Pepin the Short for help against the Lombards, who threatened to seize Rome; in return for Stephen's personal anointment of Pepin as king (January, A.D. 754), Pepin promised then to subdue the Lombards and give their conquered Italian lands to Stephen. Pepin was successful and donated to the papcy the exarchate of Ravenna, the duchies of Rome and Perugia, and the Pentapolis (five Italian Adriatic cities: Rimini, Pesaro, Fano, Senigallia, and Ancona). Pepin's son and successor, Charlemagne, confirmed the "Donation" in A.D. 774, acknowledging the role of protector of the church and papal lands (states). The popes were not divested of their lands until the 1850s, when Italy was being unified.

Further reading: Louis Duchesne, *The Beginnings of the Temporal Sovereignty of the Popes, A.D. 754–1073*, trans. Arnold H. Mathew (New York: B. Franklin, 1972); Frank N. Magill, ed., *Great Events from History: Ancient and Medieval Series*, 3 vols. (Englewood Cliffs, N.J.: Salem Press, 1972); Thomas F. X. Noble, *The Republic of St. Peter: The Birth of the Papal State, 680–825* (Philadelphia: University of Pennsylvania Press, 1984).

Pericles' Funeral Oration

Eloquent speech in praise of the fallen Athenian soldiers, delivered by the statesman Pericles at the end of the first year of the Great Peloponnesian War (431–404 B.C.) between the rival Greek city-states of Athens and Sparta. In the oration, recorded by the Greek historian Thucydides, Pericles said the soldiers died in battle to preserve the virtues and democracy of Athens, for which every citizen "should gladly toil on her behalf." He appealed to all Athenians, rich and poor, to take interest in public affairs, to not neglect the state, to acquire knowledge before acting, but foremostly to act vigorously and courageously so that their democratic way of life could not be taken from them..Greek culture reached its zenith under the leadership of Pericles, who died of plague in 429 B.C. His funeral oration influenced Abraham Lincoln's GETTYSBURG ADDRESS.

Further reading: Charles W. Eliot, ed., *The Harvard Classics* (New York: P. F. Collier & Son, 1937); Frank J. Frost, ed., *Domocracy and the Athenians; Aspects of Ancient Politics* (New York: Wiley, 1969); Donald Kagan, *Pericles of Athens and the Birth of Democracy* (New York: Free Press, 1991); Thucydides, *The Speeches of Pericles*, trans. H. G. Edinger (New York: F. Ungar Publishing, 1979).

Perpetual Edict (Praetorian Perpetual Edict, Edictum Perpetuum)

Compilation and rearrangement of all the various edicts of preceding Roman praetors (magistrates engaged chiefly in the administration of justice), carried out by the jurist Salvius Julianus by order of the Roman emperor Hadrian and published as a general code of civil law in A.D. 131. It replaced the variable yearly edicts of the praetors, divided Italy outside of Rome into four districts (each under a consular-ranked legal official named by the emperor), and thus weakened the Roman Senate's control of Italy. The praetors' sometimes unusual legal procedures ended, and the emperor's edicts became the mainspring of Roman law.

Further reading: Bryan Walker, ed., *The Fragments of the Perpetual Edict of Salvius Julianus* (Cambridge, England: Cambridge University Press, 1877).

Perpetual Peace (1516)   See FRIBOURG, TREATY OF.

Perpetual Peace: A Philosophical Essay   See PEACE MANIFESTO.

Persian-British Agreements   See ANGLO-PERSIAN AGREEMENT OF 1919; ANGLO-PERSIAN AGREEMENT OF 1933.

Persian Constitution of 1906

Fundamental law of Persia (renamed Iran in 1935) drafted by the Majlis (national assembly) and approved by Muzaffar ad-Din Shah on December 30, 1906. It established the rights and obligations of the Majlis, defined the check on its authority, and stipulated the procedures for the drafting of legislation and the formation of the senate. The Majlis secured wide-ranging powers, including control over important economic, financial, and budgetary matters and foreign policy decisions. Thus, the Majlis had the authority to conclude treaties and covenants, grant state loans, permit the establishment of public companies, and approve road and railroad construction projects. Any alteration in the country's frontiers or any proposal to sell or transfer its resources could not be accomplished without the assembly's permission. This new-found authority of the Majlis was severely undermined by the new shah of Persia (Muhammad Ali) and his Russian allies, but the struggle to restore it began almost immediately.

See also: AFGHAN CONSTITUTION OF 1923.

Further reading: Janet Afary, *The Iranian Constitutional Revolution, 1906–1911: Grassroots Democracy, Social Democracy & the Origins of Feminism* (New York: Columbia University Press, 1996); Houri Berberian, *Armenians and the Iranian Constitutional Revolution of 1905–1911: The Love for Freedom Has No Fatherland* (Boulder, Col.: Westview Press, 2001).

Peruvian Agrarian Reform Law of 1964

Law promulgated by Peru's president Fernando Belaúnde Terry on May 22, 1964, providing for the redistribution of land to Indians and landless peasants working the land. In addition to land, the recipients were also to receive credits and technical aid. The land to be expropriated included both state- and church-owned property; land used for the production of sugar, a major source of foreign exchange, was exempt. The law was passed in order to increase the amount of land under cultivation, which was then about 2 percent. Experts believed that up to 11 percent could be cultivated.

Further reading: Steven E. Hendrix, *Property Law Innovations in Latin America, with Recommendations* (Madison: Land Tenure Center, University of Wisconsin–Madison).

Petition of Right

Bill incorporating the four resolutions presented to King Charles I of England by both the House of Lords and the House of Commons when the new Parliament met in May–June 1628 to decide on the grant of subsidies. It forbade benevolences (forced loans) and taxation without Parliament's consent, billeting of soldiers in private homes, enforcement of martial law in peacetime by the military and imprisonment without specific charges. The king, then desperately in need of money, was forced to give his assent to the bill. However, he continued to extort customs duties without permission.

Further reading: Randolph L. Braham, ed., *Documents on Major European Governments* (New York: Knopf/Borzoi, 1966); David L. Brooks, *From Magna Carta to the Constitution: Documents in the Struggle for Liberty* (San Francisco: Fox & Wilkes, 1993); Frank N. Magill, ed., *Great Events from History: Modern European Series*, 3 vols. (Englewood Cliffs, N.J.: Salem Press, 1973); Milton Viorst, ed., *The Great Documents of Western Civilization* (Philadelphia: Chilton Books, 1965).

Petrópolis, Treaty of

Treaty negotiating a boundary settlement between Brazil and Bolivia; signed by representatives of the two countries on November 17, 1903, in the Brazilian city of Petrópolis. The dispute was over the Acre territory, a poorly surveyed, rubber-rich area on the Brazil-Bolivia-Peru borders, an area that both signatory countries attempted to develop. The treaty stipulated that Bolivia was to cede Acre (73,000 square miles) to Brazil; Brazil was to cede lands bordering the Madeira River to Bolivia; Brazil was to construct the Madeira-Mamoré railroad; and Brazil would pay Bolivia a $10 million indemnity. Brazil fulfilled her treaty obligations, obtained agreeable decisions regarding other disputed areas, and profited by rubber revenues. Bolivia lost a province but gained financial reimbursement and, through the railroad, a passage to world markets.

Further reading: *Brazil and Bolivia Boundary Settlement . . . Signed at Petropolis, November 17, 1903; . . .* (New York: Knickerbocker Press, 1904).

Peutinger Table (Tabula Peutingeriana, Theodosian Table)

Old parchment copy of an ancient map showing the military roads of the Roman Empire during Theodosius I the Great's reign (A.D. 379–95). The copy was made by an Alsatian monk in Colmar in 1265, found by the German scholar Conradus Celtes in a Benedictine monastery in upper Bavaria in 1494, and left to his friend Konrad Peutinger, an antiquarian of Augsburg, Germany, for publication. Peutinger died (1547) before it could be published (in 1598). The itinerarium (road map), elongated in shape and multicolored, stretches east-west distances and squeezes north-south lengths. It is a valuable, extant relic now resting in Austria's National Library in Vienna.

Further reading: Willem P. Blocksman and Wolfram Fischer, *Centers of Invention*, 1st American ed. (Danbury, Conn.: Grolier Educational, 1994).

Philippics

Three famous condemnatory orations delivered by the Athenian statesman Demosthenes against King Philip II of Macedon. Demosthenes first warned Athens and other Greek city-states against Philip's plans to conquer them and overthrow their independence in 351 B.C., in his so-called First Philippic. He vainly urged the Athenians to join the Locrians against Philip, whose boldness could be matched by the Athenians on the battlefield if the latter so desired; he challenged Athens's seeming want of courage. Philip moved toward Chalcidice and the city-state of Olynthus, which appealed for aid (see OLYNTHIACS). In 344 B.C., in the "Second Philippic," Demosthenes again courageously denounced the Macedonian menace, stating that Philip was scheming to pit the Greek city-states against one another. Though Philip had signed the Peace of Philocrates (346 B.C.) with Athens, Demosthenes charged him with perfidy and said the Athenian leaders, notably Aeschines, had been duped and should fear for their safety. In his "Third Philippic," in 341 B.C., Demosthenes successfully stirred Athens to take resolute action against Philip's encroachments. War was renewed with Philip, who eventually defeated Athens and her allies at the battle of Chaeronea in 338 B.C.

See also: ON THE CROWN.

Further reading: J. R. Ellis and R. D. Milns, *The Spectre of Philip; Demosthenes' First Philippic, Olynthiac and Speech On the Peace; a Study in Historical Evidence* (Sydney, Australia: Sydney University Press, 1970); John E. Sandys, ed., *The First Philippic and the Olynthiacs of Demosthenes* (New York: Arno Press, 1979); J. H. Vince et al., trans., *Demosthenes*, 7 vols. (Cambridge, Mass.: Harvard University Press, 1984–92).

Philippics, Cicero's

Series of 14 vituperative orations delivered by Marcus Tullius Cicero, fiercely attacking Marc Antony as well as responding to Antony's abusive words against him in the Roman Senate in 44 B.C. Cicero's speeches, called PHILIPPICS in imitation of Demosthenes's earlier orations against Philip II of Macedon, were voiced in the Senate, the Assembly, and the public forum (propaganda pieces). The first oration (September 2, 44 B.C.) was principally a defense of the Roman republic, as was the second; the others became excoriations of Antony's public policies and private life. After Cicero's last oration (April 21, 43 B.C.), Antony put him high on his enemies list and later had him beheaded (December 7, 43 B.C.).

See also: TITIAN LAW.

Further reading: D. R. Shackleton Bailey, ed. and trans., *Philippics/Cicero* (Chapel Hill: University of North Carolina Press, 1986); Frank N. Magill, ed., *Great Events from History:*

Ancient and Medieval Series, 3 vols. (Englewood Cliffs, N.J.: Salem Press, 1972).

Philippine Constitution of 1987

New constitution for the Philippines accepted by Filipino voters in a plebiscite on February 2, 1987; it provided for a bicameral national legislature (congress), a presidency with specified limits of power, and a judiciary to be named free of political influence. It confirmed Corazon C. Aquino as president until mid-1992 (thereafter presidents would be elected for six-year terms and could not be reelected). Aquino had abrogated the previous constitution after succeeding deposed dictatorial President Ferdinand Marcos in 1986. The new bicameral congress (Marcos had abolished the old one in 1973) consisted of a 24-member senate and a 250-member house of representatives. Despite the new document and land reform, the political situation remained unstable in the Philippines, where some military officers and communists were especially hostile.

Further reading: Edmundo R. Abigan, *Focus: The Philippine Constitution of 1986* (Manila, Philippines: self-published, 1987); Joaquin G. Bernas, *The 1987 Philippine Constitution: A Reviewer-Primer*, 3d ed. (Manila, Philippines: Rex Book Store, 1997); Criselda S. Martin, *The Continuing Revolution: Human Rights and the Philippine Constitution: An Assessment of the Current State of Human Rights in the Light of the 1987 Constitution* (Quezon City, Philippines: Institute of Human Rights, University of the Philippines Law Center 1996).

Philippine Government Act (Organic Act) of 1902

Legislation enacted by the U.S. Congress on July 1, 1902, making the Philippine Islands an unincorporated U.S. territory and making its inhabitants citizens of the Philippines, not the United States. The islands had become a U.S. possession through the Treaty of PARIS (1898), ending the Spanish-American War. An uprising begun in 1899 was put down by U.S. troops, and civil government, under William Howard Taft, was established in 1901. The 1902 act confirmed the Taft Commission as the governing body of the Philippines.

Further reading: Norbert Lyons and George H. Fairchild, *The Philippine Problem Presented from a New Angle: With an Appendix Containing Complete Texts of the Philippine Organic Act* (Manila, Philippines: n.p., 1924); Stuart C. Miller, *"Benevolent Assimilation": The American Conquest of the Philippines, 1899–1903* (New Haven, Conn.: Yale University Press, 1982); Daniel B. Schirmer and Stephen R. Shalom, eds., *The Philippines Reader: A History of Colonialism, Neocolonialism, Dictatorship, and Resistance* (Boston: South End Press, 1987).

Philippine Trade Act of 1946, U.S.

See BELL TRADE ACT.

Picquigny, Treaty of

Pact concluded at Picquigny, France, on August 29, 1475, by King Louis XI of France with England's Edward IV; Louis was attempting to break up Ed-ward's alliance (July 25, 1474) with Charles the Bold, duke of Burgundy, an alliance aimed at conquering France. As a surety against war, Louis promised Edward 75,000 gold crowns immediately on condition that the English troops withdraw from France. For the duration of the seven-year truce, Edward was guaranteed 50,000 gold crowns annually. At Louis's request, Edward released his prisoner, Margaret of Anjou, for an additional sum of 50,000 crowns. Finally, Louis sealed the pact by proposing the marriage of Edward's daughter, Princess Elizabeth, to his son the dauphin (later King Charles VIII). Separate treaties were subsequently concluded with the duke of Burgundy and other French dukes. The Picquigny truce also led to the signing of a commercial treaty restoring normal trade between the two countries.

Further reading: Gila Falkus, *The Life and Times of Edward IV* (London: Weidenfeld and Nicolson, 1981); Emmanuel Le Roy Ladurie, *The Royal French State, 1460–1610*, trans. Juliet Vale, (Cambridge, Mass.: Blackwell Publishers, 1994); David Potter, *A History of France, 1460–1560* (New York: St. Martin's Press, 1995); Joseph M. Tyrrell, *Louis XI* (Boston: Twayne, 1980).

Pierce v. *Society of the Sisters* (Oregon Parochial School Case)

U.S. Supreme Court decision, issued on June 1, 1925, that overturned a 1922 Oregon statute requiring all children between the ages of eight and 16 years to attend public schools. The statue was challenged by the Society of the Sisters of the Holy Names of Jesus and Mary, which operated Roman Catholic primary and high schools in the state. The Supreme Court unanimously ruled that the statute violated the due process clause of the FOURTEENTH AMENDMENT by unreasonably interfering with the rights of parents to direct the education of their children and the rights of the owners and teachers in such schools to conduct their business.

Further reading: Henry Steele Commager, ed., *Documents of American History*, 8th ed. (New York: Appleton-Century-Crofts, 1968); Kermit L. Hall et al., eds., *The Oxford Companion to the Supreme Court of the United States* (New York: Oxford University Press, 1992); Donald P. Kommers and Michael J. Wahoske, eds., *Freedom and Education: Pierce v. Society of Sisters Reconsidered* (Notre Dame, Ind.: Center for Civil Rights, University of Notre Dame Law School, 1978); United States Supreme Court, *United States Reports: Cases Adjudged in the Supreme Court at . . . and Rules Announced at . . .* (New York: Banks & Brothers, Law Publishers, 1884–1921; Washington, D.C.: Government Printing Office, 1922–).

Pillar Edicts, Aśoka's

Buddhist principles of the right life (dharma) inscribed on pillars and rocks at sites all over India during Emperor Aśoka's reign, from about 265 B.C. to about 238 B.C. Aśoka had converted to Buddhism, lamenting the suffering he had caused by his bloody armed conquest of almost the whole of India. He began engraving on rocks statements and edicts regarding his belief in peace and nonviolence and respect for all life and truth. The inscriptions also provided information about Aśoka's own life; they were written in the local dialects for the benefit of the common folk.

See also: TIPITAKA.

Further reading: Benimadhab Barua, *Inscriptions of Asoka: Translation and Glossary*, 2d ed., ed. Binayendra N. Chaudhury (Calcutta, India: Sanskrit College, 1990); Dineschandra Sircar, *Asokan Studies* (Calcutta, India: Indian Museum, 1979); Dineschandra Sircar, *Inscriptions of Asoka*, 3d rev. ed. (New Delhi, India: Publication Division, Ministry of Information and Broadcasting, Government of India, 1975).

Pillersdorf Constitution (April Constitution of 1848, Austrian Constitution of 1848)

Constitution proclaimed by the newly formed Austrian cabinet, under the influence of the Austrian liberal Baron Franz von Pillersdorf, on April 25, 1848, in response to the revolutions in Vienna and Paris and to the general unrest in several parts of the Austrian Empire. The new constitution was to be valid only in those parts of the Austrian Empire included in the Germanic Confederation, plus Galicia, thus excluding Hungary and the Italian provinces. To the moderates' liking, the document declared that the diet was to be composed of two chambers, one consisting of princes and aristocrats, the other consisting of qualified taxpayers. The emperor had the right to veto any legislation and to dissolve the diet. In addition to the many provisions detailing the rights of all citizens, the constitution provided for the "inviolability of all citizens' nationality and language." Radicals subsequently protested, claiming that it was not liberal enough. The cabinet lacked the skill to put its principles into effect, and thus it came to no more result than the FRANKFURT CONSTITUTION OF 1849.

Further reading: David Ward, *1848: The Fall of Metternich and the Year of Revolution* (New York: Weybright & Talley, 1970).

Pillnitz, Declaration of

Statement issued by Holy Roman Emperor Leopold II and Prussia's king Frederick William II following their meeting on August 27, 1791, at Pillnitz (part of Dresden, Germany) to discuss the French Revolution (1789–92) and its disquieting effect on their monarchies. Signed by them and other dignitaries in attendance, the declaration asked all European powers to join together to restore order and the monarchy (King Louis XVI) to France, a monarchy that would be both friendly to their own governments and responsive to the needs of the French nation. If necessary, armed force would be used against revolutionary France, and intervention in French affairs would occur only with the complete consent of all powers (then impossible, because of British unconcern for French internal matters). France interpreted the document as a veiled threat of interference, a possible war threat, and she declared war on Austria less than eight months after its publication.

Further reading: Oscar Browning, *The Conference of Pillnitz* (London: Transactions of the Royal Historical Society, 1897).

Pinckney Treaty (Treaty of San Lorenzo)

Agreement signed at San Lorenzo, Spain, on October 27, 1795, to resolve long-standing disputes between the United States and Spain over the southern and western boundaries of the United States, over Spanish encouragement of Indian discontent, and over free navigation of the Mississippi River for Americans. The terms of the treaty, negotiated by Thomas Pinckney, special U.S. commissioner to Spain, were favorable to the United States: Spain recognized the Mississippi River and the 31st parallel as the U.S. boundaries, gave Americans free navigation of the Mississippi and the right to deposit goods for shipment at New Orleans, and promised more peaceful relations with the Indians.

Further reading: Samuel F. Bemis, *Pinckney's Treaty; America's Advantage from Europe's Distress, 1783–1800* (New Haven, Conn.: Yale University Press, 1960); Henry Steele Commager, ed., *Documents of American History*, 8th ed. (New York: Appleton-Century-Crofts, 1968); Frank N. Magill, ed., *Great Events from History: American Series*, 3 vols. (Englewood Cliffs, N.J.: Salem Press, 1975).

Pinerolo, Pacification of (Treaty of Pinerolo)

Agreement made by Duke Charles Emmanuel II of Savoy and the French, stopping the persecution of Charles's Vaudois (Waldenses) subjects in October 1655. The Italian marquis of Piacenza had recently attacked the Vaudois, a Protestant sect, as had French Catholics, resulting in a protest from England's Lord Protector Oliver Cromwell. The treaty at Pinerolo (in northwest Italy) set aside areas where the Vaudois could worship without being harmed; but Duke Charles could celebrate mass wherever he wanted. France agreed to expel England's king Charles II, who had fled there after his defeat by Cromwell in 1651.

Further reading: Giorgio Tourn et al., *You Are My Witnesses: The Waldensians Across 800 Years* (Turin, Italy: Claudiana, 1989).

Piotrków, Statute of (Magna Carta of Poland)

Constitution agreed upon in 1496 by John Albert (Jan Olbracht), first elected king of Poland, and the Polish gentry and nobility, whose political and social positions were strengthened as a result. To the advantage of the nobility and gentry, the statute bound the peasants more fully to the land and their masters (landowners). Only one son of a peasant could leave the land in order to learn a trade. Townspeople (burghers) were not allowed to buy or own land. Furthermore, certain offices were reserved strictly for the sons of nobles. The king had agreed to the statute because the gentry and nobles had the means to provide for an army to defend Poland against the invading Turks—an army for which the king did not have the funds to pay.

Further reading: Jacek Jedruch, *Constitutions, Elections, and Legislatures of Poland, 1493–1993: A Guide to Their History* (New York: EJJ Books, 1998).

Pisa, Declaration of the Council of   Declaration made by the General Council of Pisa in March–April 1409, asserting the right of the "united college of cardinals" to convene such a council "especially now when there is a detestable schism." Having already deposed the popes reigning at Avignon and Rome and appointed a third pope, the cardinals (claiming to be "representing the universal Church") sought to turn the papal schism to their advantage by undermining papal power and declaring the supremacy of the council in ecclesiastical affairs. The council also called upon the deposed popes "to come and hear the final decision . . . pronounced, or to give a good and sufficient reason why such sentence should not be rendered." An act of clerical defiance, the council's declaration was not recognized by either of the deposed popes. Subsequently, the papacy tried to undermine the growing influence of church councils (see EXECRABILIS OF 1460).

See also: UNAM SANCTUM.

Further reading: Catholic University of America, eds., *New Catholic Encyclopedia* (New York: McGraw-Hill, 1967); Frank N. Magill, ed., *Great Events from History: Ancient and Medieval Series*, 3 vols. (Englewood Cliffs, N.J.: Salem Press, 1972); Milton Viorst, ed., *The Great Documents of Western Civilization* (Philadelphia: Chilton Books, 1965).

Pittsburgh Convention   Declaration of support by U.S. Czechs and Slovaks for the formation of a united Czechoslovakian state; signed on May 31, 1918. The document was drawn up at a meeting in Pittsburgh, Pennsylvania, of emigré societies and Czechoslovakian independence leader Thomas G. Masaryk. It called for considerable home rule for Slovaks, including a separate legislature, judicial system, and administration, and supported the preservation of the Slovak language. Failure to achieve the degree of autonomy outlined in this declaration later led to Slovak nationalist dissent within the newly unified state of Czechoslovakia.

See also: LANSING DECLARATION.

Further reading: T. G. Masaryk, *T. G. Masaryk, His Life and Thought* (New York: Masaryk Institute, 1960).

Pitt's India Act (Government of India Act of 1784, British East India Company Act of 1784)   Bill introduced into Parliament by Britain's prime minister William Pitt in 1784, seeking to amend the inequities of the REGULATING ACT OF 1773. The act created a new government department called the Board of Control (which included the chancellor of the exchequer, the secretary of state, and four others from the king's privy council) "to superintend, direct, and control all acts, operations, and concerns" relating to civil and military government in India. Thus, while the Board of Control had power over the Court of Directors of the British East India Company, it left the company to manage the daily affairs of India. Its president had the casting vote and could represent India in the British Parliament. The British governor general's authority in India was extended to cover Bombay and Madras. Company officials could not enter into any hostilities except on advice from the Court of Directors, and the British crown had the power to appoint or remove the governor-general or members of his executive council.

Further reading: John Keay, *The Honourable Company: A History of the English East India Company* (London: Harper-Collins, 1991); Philip Lawson, *The East India Company: A History* (New York: Longman, 1993).

Pius IX's Encyclical of 1871   Encyclical written by Pope Pius IX and sent to the Roman Catholic higher clergy in May 1871; it denounced the Italian government's capture of Rome from the papacy, which had until then exercised temporal power over the city for centuries. The encyclical contained the pope's condemnation of the Italian action and his declaration that reconciliation with the Italian government was impossible. The Italian action had occurred during the Italian unification movement, the leaders of which had intended to make Rome the capital of the new state, and after the outbreak of the Franco-Prussian War (1870–71), which had required France to pull her garrison out of Rome, thus removing all protection of the city from the Italian nationalists. The two parties were not reconciled until 1929 (see LATERAN TREATIES OF 1929).

See also: GUARANTEES, LAW OF; VICTOR EMMANUEL II'S SPEECH TO THE ITALIAN PARLIAMENT IN 1871.

Further reading: Claudia Carlen, comp., *The Papal Encyclicals* (Wilmington, N.C.: McGrath Publishing, 1981); Catholic University of America, eds., *New Catholic Encyclopedia* (New York: McGraw-Hill, 1967); Frank J. Coppa, *Pope Pius IX, Crusader in a Secular Age* (Boston: Twayne Publishers, 1979); Milton Viorst, ed., *The Great Documents of Western Civilization* (Philadelphia: Chilton Books, 1965).

Pius XI's Encyclical of 1931   See QUADRAGESIMO ANNO.

Planned Parenthood v. Casey   Another landmark U.S. abortion rights case (see ROE V. WADE), wherein a group of abortion service providers challenged the constitutionality of several provisions of the Pennsylvania Abortion Control Act of 1982 (amended 1988 and 1989). Pennsylvania governor Robert Casey was named defendant. The federal district court had declared the provisions (counseling, mandatory waiting period, parental [if minor] or husband's consent, and reporting the details of the abortion to authorities) unconstitutional, but the Circuit Court of Appeals had reversed that decision, upholding all but one provision (husband notification). In a high-impact 5-4 plurality ruling based on the doctrine of stare decisis, the U.S. Supreme Court in 1992 reaffirmed "the essential holding" of *Roe,* while replacing its strict judicial scrutiny standard with that of "undue burden," which allowed state and local laws to place deterrents on a woman's right to choose provided they were not excessively burdensome. Seven of the nine justices allowed some limitations on abortion rights; for instance, they recognized that the woman's freedom to seek abortion "gives way at some point to the rights of the fetus," and here "viability" was key. By bringing abortion under the protection of the FOURTEENTH AMENDMENT, the Court made the decision almost irreversible. Simultaneously, by upholding four of the five challenged provisions (the fifth one was invalidated) the court also weakened women's rights.

Further reading: Leslie Friedman Goldstein, *Contemporary Cases in Women's Rights* (Madison: University of Wisconsin Press, 1994); National Foundation for Life Organization, *"Planned Parenthood of Southeast Pennsylvania v. Casey,"* National Foundation for Life Litigation Project, available online at http:www.nffllp.org/casey.htm.

Pläswitz, Armistice of

Truce signed at Pläswitz, or Poischwitz, on June 4, 1813, by the French emperor Napoléon Bonaparte with the combined coalition of Russia and Prussia, following France's narrow victory over the latter powers at the battles of Lützen and Bautzen. Austria (still formally allied with France) had mediated between the two sides, but France had refused to accept the lenient terms that she proposed. The three countries therefore settled for the armistice, which was to last until July 26 but was later extended until August 16, 1813. At that time it was unknown to Napoléon (whose army needed the truce less than did the Allies) that Austria had promised to join the allied coalition should France refuse to accept her terms (see REICHENBACH, CONVENTION OF).

Further reading: J. P. Riley, *Napoleon and the World War of 1813: Lessons in Coalition Warfighting* (Portland, Ore.: Frank Cass, 2000).

Platt Amendment

Amendment designed to regulate the relations between the United States and Cuba and originally attached to the Army Appropriations Bill of 1901. Named after U.S. senator Orville H. Platt of Connecticut (chairman of the Committee on Relations with Cuba), the amendment prohibited Cuba from signing any treaties that might jeopardize her independence; it stipulated that Cuba would leave naval bases to the United States; and it sanctioned United States intervention in Cuba whenever there existed a danger to life, property, or individual freedom. Under pressure from the United States, Cuba reluctantly incorporated the amendment into her 1901 constitution. In effect until 1934, the amendment was finally abrogated under Franklin D. Roosevelt's Good Neighbor Policy.

See also: CUBAN CONSTITUTION OF 1901.

Further reading: Mortimer Adler, ed., *The Annals of America,* 18 vols. (Chicago: Encyclopedia Britannica, 1968); Henry Steele Commager, ed., *Documents of American History,* 8th ed. (New York: Appleton-Century-Crofts, 1968); Louis A. Perez, *Cuba under the Platt Amendment, 1902–1934* (Pittsburgh, Pa.: University of Pittsburgh Press, 1986).

Pledge of Allegiance, U.S.

Memorable patriotic promise apparently written by the Reverend Francis Bellamy and first published in a Boston magazine, *The Youth's Companion,* on September 8, 1892. A socialist Baptist minister who joined the magazine in 1891, Bellamy composed the pledge while the magazine was campaigning to sell U.S. flags for the 400th anniversary of Columbus's voyage to America. The original pledge read: "I pledge allegiance to my flag and to the republic for which it stands: one nation, indivisible, with liberty and justice for all." In 1923 the words "my flag" were changed to "the flag of the United States of America" since immigrant children could suppose they were vowing to some other flag. The words "one nation" became "one nation under God" on President Dwight D. Eisenhower's request in 1954.

Further reading: *"I Pledge Allegiance . . .": Bilingual—English/Spanish* (Washington, D.C.: U.S. Department of Justice, Immigration & Naturalization Service, 1990); Margarette S. Miller, *I Pledge Allegiance* (Boston: Christopher Publishing House, 1946); *The Pledge of Allegiance* (New York: Scholastic, 2001).

Plessy v. *Ferguson*

U.S. Supreme Court decision of May 18, 1896, upholding the doctrine of "separate but equal" facilities for blacks and whites, thus legitimizing JIM CROW LAWS. Homer Plessy, a light-skinned mulatto, challenged the constitutionality of an 1890 Louisiana statute requiring railroads to provide "equal but separate accommodations" for the two races. Ruling eight to one against Plessy, the Supreme Court declared that the FOURTEENTH AMENDMENT guaranteed equality before the law, not social equality, that the statute was reasonable, and that separate facilities were not a "badge of inferiority" for blacks. This segregationist doctrine was overturned in *BROWN* V. *BOARD OF EDUCATION OF TOPEKA* in 1954.

Further reading: Mortimer Adler, ed., *The Annals of America,* 18 vols. (Chicago: Encyclopedia Britannica, 1968); Henry Steel Commager, ed., *Documents of American History,* 8th ed. (New York: Appleton-Century-Crofts, 1968); Kermit L. Hall et al., eds., *American Legal History: Cases and Materials,* 2d ed. (New York: Oxford University Press, 1996); Kermit L. Hall et al., eds., *The Oxford Companion to the Supreme Court of the United States* (New York: Oxford University Press, 1992).

Pliny the Younger's *Letters*

Private letters written between about A.D. 97 and 112 by Roman statesman Pliny the Younger and published in 10 books, showing the social, literary, and political life of the early Roman Empire.

Carefully composed, they contain brief sketches of Emperors Domitian, Nerva, and Trajan, historian Tacitus, poet Statius, and other leading Romans, as well as diverse accounts about places, events, problems, and administrative policies. Each letter concerns a single subject and frequently reveals the good, kind, and honorable nature of Pliny, whose most important letter perhaps is that sent by him to Trajan concerning the treatment of Christians (whose religion had been proclaimed illicit); both Pliny and Trajan's correspondence indicates their sense of fairness and humanity (see TRAJAN'S RESCRIPT).

Further reading: Charles W. Eliot, ed., *The Harvard Classics*, 51 vols. (New York: P. F. Collier & Son, 1937); Helen H. Tanzer, ed., *The Letters of Pliny the Younger* (New York: G. E. Stechert, 1936); Milton Viorst, ed., *The Great Documents of Western Civilization* (Philadelphia: Chilton Books, 1965).

Plombières, Agreement of

Secret pact of July 20, 1858, whereby Emperor Napoléon III of France and Count Camillo Cavour, prime minister of Piedmont-Sardinia, pledged to effect Austria's complete withdrawal from Italy. Concluded during a private meeting at Plombières, France, the agreement opened the final chapter of the Risorgimento in Italy. France would help Sardinia in expelling the Austrians from the Italian peninsula provided Austria could be seen as having initiated the war. Napoléon III promised to help Sardinia acquire Lombardy, Venetia, and a part of central Italy after the war. He envisioned an Italian federation presided over by the pope. France, in return, would receive Nice and Savoy (see VICTOR EMMANUEL II'S SPEECH OPENING THE ITALIAN PARLIAMENT). Napoléon's cousin, Prince Napoléon (Plon-Plon), was to wed Clotilde, daughter of the Sardinian king Victor Emmanuel II. In January 1859, the Treaty of Turin confirmed these agreements and precipitated the crisis leading to the Franco-Sardinian-Austrian War (Italian War of Independence of 1859–61).

Further reading: Frank N. Magill, ed., *Great Events from History: Modern European Series*, 3 vols. (Englewood Cliffs, N.J.: Salem Press, 1973); Mack Walker, ed., *Plombieres: Secret Diplomacy and the Rebirth of Italy* (New York: Oxford University Press, 1968).

Plymouth Rock Speech, Webster's

Historical address delivered by Daniel Webster on December 22, 1820, at the 200th anniversary of the settlement of Plymouth, Massachusetts. The speech, characterized by the eloquence and grand style that brought Webster fame, discussed the civil and religious foundations of New England and the growth and expansion of the United States. It reflected his nationalistic position and his conservative views that power follows property. The speech was enthusiastically received and was the first of several historical addresses that gave him a reputation as an extraordinary orator. It was published a year after its delivery.

Further reading: Craig R. Smith, *Defender of the Union: The Oratory of Daniel Webster* (New York: Greenwood Press, 1989); Edwin P. Whipple, ed., *The Great Speeches and Orations of Daniel Webster* (Boston: Little, Brown, 1923); Charles M. Wiltse, ed., *The Papers of Daniel Webster: Speeches and Formal Writings*, vol. 1: *1800–1833* (Hanover, N.H.: University of New England, 1986).

Point Four Program

U.S. program outlined in a message sent to Congress on June 24, 1949, by President Harry S Truman, proposing technical, scientific, and managerial assistance to raise the living standards of underdeveloped nations, and encouragement of private capital investment to benefit their economic development. The Point Four Program, so named because it was mentioned as the fourth point in TRUMAN'S INAUGURAL ADDRESS, was intended to win the support of underdeveloped nations in the cold war against communism. The program was enacted by Congress on June 5, 1950, and functioned until 1953, when it was merged with other foreign aid programs.

Further reading: Mortimer Adler, ed., *The Annals of America*, 18 vols. (Chicago: Encyclopaedia Britannica, 1968); Henry Steele Commager, ed., *Documents of American History*, 8th ed. (New York: Appleton-Century-Crofts, 1968); Dennis K. Merrill, ed., *Documentary History of the Truman Presidency*, 20 vols. (Bethesda, Md.: University Publications of America, 1995); Sergei Y. Shenin, *The United States and the Third World: The Origins of the Postwar Relations and the Point Four Program* (Huntington, N.Y.: Nova Science Publishers, 2000).

Poitiers, First Edict of
See BOULOGNE, EDICT OF.

Poitiers, Peace, or Edict, of
See BERGERAC, TREATY OF.

Poland, Treaties of Partition of
See AUSTRO-RUSSIAN AND RUSSO-PRUSSIAN TREATY OF 1795; RUSSO-PRUSSIAN TREATIES OF 1973; ST. PETERSBURG, TREATY OF (1772).

Polaniec, Manifesto of

Declaration issued by General Thaddeus Kosciusko on May 7, 1794, in the Polish town of Polaniec, suspending serfdom and proclaiming freedom for the peasantry in Poland. Kosciusko hoped, through the manifesto, to motivate more peasants to join his army in Poland's fight for independence against the occupying powers of Prussia, Russia, and Austria. In the document, he announced governmental protection of the peasants against their landlords and the right of peasants to own land. He also pledged to reduce state taxes by one-half for the peasantry and to cut in half the feudal servitude of villeins (half-free peasants or serfs).

See also: AUSTRO-RUSSIAN AND RUSSO-PRUSSIAN TREATIES OF 1795.

Further reading: Mieczyslaw B. Biskupski and James S. Pula, *Polish Democratic Thought from the Renaissance to the*

Great Emigration: Essays and Documents (Boulder, Colo.: Eastern European Monographs, 1990); Andrzej Walicki, *The Enlightenment and the Birth of Modern Nationhood: Polish Political Thought from Noble Republicanism to Tadeusz Kosciuszko* (Notre Dame, Ind.: University of Notre Dame Press, 1989).

Polish Constitution of 1791

Constitution drafted by King Stanislaus II of Poland and ratified by a majority in the Polish Diet on May 3, 1791. The constitution was based upon democratic ideals inspired by the American Revolution (1775–83). Through the constitution the destructive *liberum veto* (through which legislation could be blocked by a single vote) was abolished in favor of majority rule; the monarchy became hereditary, by which Poland could avoid the problems accompanied by the election of foreign kings; legislative power was to reside in an assembly made up of two chambers, one of which was to propose laws, the second of which was to approve them. The document also included articles regarding the relationship between serf and noble; the powers of the king; the practice of religion; and the election and appointment of officials.

See also: AUSTRO-RUSSIAN AND RUSSO-PRUSSIAN TREATIES OF 1795; RUSSO-PRUSSIAN TREATY OF 1793.

Further reading: Mieczyslaw B. Biskupski and James S. Pula, *Polish Democratic Thought from the Renaissance to the Great Emigration: Essays and Documents* (Boulder, Col.: Eastern European Monographs, 1990); Albert P. Blaustein and Jay A. Sigler, eds., *Constitutions That Made History* (New York: Paragon House Publishers, 1988); Samuel Fiszman, *Constitution and Reform in Eighteenth-Century Poland: The Constitution of 3 May 1791* (Bloomington: Indiana University Press, 1997); Jacek Jedruch, *Constitutions, Elections, and Legislatures of Poland, 1493–1993: A Guide to Their History* (New York: EJJ Books, 1998).

Polish Constitution of 1807

Constitution granted to the duchy of Warsaw, then under French protection, by Emperor Napoléon Bonaparte of France on July 22, 1807; it was based upon that of France. Through the constitution religious freedom was guaranteed to all; the state accepted the Roman Catholic faith as the religion of the Polish people, while asserting its authority over the church; the king was granted the right to nominate the members of the Senate, the decisions of which, together with the king's, were to have precedence over those of the popular chamber (which was elected by the people but with weight given to the nobles' vote); the Diet was to be convoked at the king's discretion (theoretically this was to take place every two years), but had no legislative powers; finally, France reserved the right to install her own representative, who ultimately became responsible for the foreign policy of the duchy. The French protectorate came to an end in 1815.

See also: POLISH CONSTITUTION OF 1815; VIENNA, FINAL ACT OF THE CONGRESS OF.

Further reading: Mieczyslaw B. Biskupski and James S. Pula, *Polish Democratic Thought from the Renaissance to the Great Emigration: Essays and Documents* (Boulder, Col.: Eastern European Monographs, 1990); Jacek Jedruch, *Constitutions, Elections, and Legislatures of Poland, 1493–1993: A Guide to Their History* (New York: EJJ Books, 1998).

Polish Constitution of 1815

Constitution of the kingdom of Poland drafted by Polish prince Adam Czartoryski and endorsed by Russian czar Alexander I on November 27, 1815. The 165-article document provided that the Russian czar and his descendants were to hold the Polish crown; that legislative power was to reside in a diet, which was to meet twice a year and consist of two chambers; that the king had the right to veto legislation and to convoke and adjourn the diet as he saw fit; that the kingdom's foreign policy was to be directed by Russia's Ministry of Foreign Affairs; that the kingdom's official language was to be Polish; that only citizens were to be permitted to hold public and military posts; and that freedom of the press and religious liberty were to be guaranteed to every individual. The kingdom of Poland became part of the Russian Empire in 1815 through the Final Act of the Congress of VIENNA.

Further reading: Mieczyslaw B. Biskupski and James S. Pula, *Polish Democratic Thought from the Renaissance to the Great Emigration: Essays and Documents* (Boulder, Col.: Eastern European Monographs, 1990); Adam Gielgud, ed., *Memoirs of Prince Adam Czartoryski* (New York: Arno Press, 1971); Jacek Jedruch, *Constitutions, Elections, and Legislatures of Poland, 1493–1993: A Guide to Their History* (New York: EJJ Books, 1998); W. H. Zawadzki, *A Man of Honour: Adam Czartoryski as a Statesman of Russia and Poland, 1795–1831* (New York: Oxford University Press, 1993).

Polish–East German Agreements of 1950 (Warsaw Agreements)

Pact, including a border agreement, several economic agreements, and a protocol on cultural affairs, concluded in Warsaw on June 7, 1950, by East Germany and Poland, bringing the two countries into closer relations. The border agreement provided for the two countries' recognition of the Oder-Neisse line as the definitive East German–Polish border. The economic accords included an agreement calling for a 60 percent increase in trade between them; an agreement through which Poland would provide East Germany with a credit for an undisclosed amount; an agreement to exchange production methods in order to expedite technological growth; and an agreement to conclude a long-term commercial agreement by September of that year. Finally, a protocol provided for cultural exchanges between the two countries. The border agreement achieved notoriety because the western powers, and West Germany in particular, were adamantly opposed to it.

Further reading: Phillip A. Buhler, *The Oder-Neisse Line: A Reappraisal under International Law* (Boulder, Colo.: East European Monographs, 1990); J. A. S. Grenville and Bernard Wasserstein, *The Major International Treaties since 1945: A History and Guide with Texts* (New York: Methuen, 1987).

Polish Organic Statute of 1832

Organic statute promulgated on February 14, 1832, by the reactionary Russian czar Nicholas I, who also ruled the kingdom of Poland. The document, which contained measures curtailing many of Poland's freedoms acquired through the POLISH CONSTITUTION OF 1815, was issued after the abortive Polish Rebellion of 1830–31. The document included mandates requiring the Polish army to become part of the Russian army; the Russian language to become the official political language of the Polish government; Russians alone to occupy positions in higher educational institutions and in the government; and the repeal of all electoral rights. Poland retained a limited degree of autonomy, which was meaningless when considered together with the restrictive measures.

Further reading: Mieczyslaw B. Biskupski and James S. Pula, *Polish Democratic Thought from the Renaissance to the Great Emigration: Essays and Documents* (Boulder, Colo.: Eastern European Monographs, 1990); Frank N. Magill, ed., *Great Events from History: Modern European Series*, 3 vols. (Englewood Cliffs, N.J.: Salem Press, 1973).

Politeia

See REPUBLIC, THE.

Political Interference Act, South African

One of several 1968 South African measures (including the Separate Representation of Voters Amendment Act and the Coloured Persons Representative Council Amendment Act) politically segregating the colored peoples from the whites. It was based on the recommendations of a parliamentary committee and recognized the four racial categories laid down in the GROUP AREAS ACT OF 1950. It forbade any mixing of the races in political party memberships and banned interference by one racial group in the political affairs of another. Consequently, members of one group could not speak at political meetings where most of the audience belonged to another group. Political parties were not allowed to receive money from outside South Africa to promote their aims. Penalties for offenders were stiff. The act thus strengthened the political isolation of the colored peoples.

Further reading: Peter Joyce, *The Rise and Fall of Apartheid: The Chronicle of a Divided Society as Told Through South Africa's Newspapers* (Cape Town, South Africa: Struik, 1990); Paul Maylam, *South Africa's Racial Past: The History and Historiography of Racism, Segregation, and Apartheid* (Aldershot, England: Ashgate, 2001); Tim Nuttall, *From Apartheid to Democracy: South Africa, 1948–1994* (Pietermaritzburg, South Africa: Shuter & Shooter, 1998).

Politics Drawn from the Very Words of Holy Scripture (Politique Tirée des Propres Paroles de l'Ecriture Sainte)

Treatise written by French bishop Jacques Bénigne Bossuet for the eldest son of King Louis XIV of France and updated in the 1690s for publication; it presented a discussion in defense of the divine right of kings. In the work (published in final form in 1709) Bossuet claimed that a sovereign's authority was derived from God himself and that obedience to the monarch was therefore a religious obligation. He also emphasized the monarch's responsibility to his subjects to use his power in a way fitting for one created in God's image. The treatise was Bossuet's response to the decline, at the close of the Middle Ages, of the omnipotent power of the pope in political affairs, and the subsequent rise in the monarch's power. His ideas were thus originally understood to be a means of justifying civil authority; only later did his ideas come to be understood as a defense for absolutism.

Further reading: Jacques Benigne Bossuet, *Politics Drawn from the Very Words of Holy Scripture*, ed. Patrick Riley (New York: Cambridge University Press, 1999); Richard Lockwood, *The Reader's Figure: Epideictic Rhetoric in Plato, Aristotle, Bossuet, Racine and Pascal* (Geneva: Librairie Droz, 1996); Ernest E. Reynolds, *Bossuet* (Garden City, N.Y.: Doubleday, 1963).

Polk's First Message to Congress (Polk Doctrine)

Message delivered to Congress on December 2, 1845, by U.S. president James K. Polk; most notable for its elaboration of the MONROE DOCTRINE. Polk stated that the people of North America alone have the right to decide their own destiny, that European powers may not interfere in the affairs of independent and sovereign North American nations, and that no future European colony or dominion may be established on this continent. The message also recommended tariff revision, the restoration of an independent treasury so that the government could hold its own funds rather than deposit them in state banks, and measures to protect the U.S. claim to Oregon.

Further reading: Paul H. Bergeron, *The Presidency of James K. Polk* (Lawrence: University Press of Kansas, 1987); Henry Steele Commager, ed., *Documents of American History*, 8th ed. (New York: Appleton-Century-Crofts, 1968).

Polk's Inaugural Address

Address delivered by James K. Polk on March 4, 1845, at his inauguration as 11th president of the United States. In the speech Polk, a Democrat and an expansionist, reaffirmed his party platform's call for the annexation of Texas and the occupation of Oregon. He described the annexation as a contract between two independent powers, a peaceful reacquisition of territory that was formerly part of the United States, and a way to avoid future conflict. He called the U.S. title to Oregon "clear and unquestionable," despite British claims to the contrary.

Further reading: Mortimer Adler, ed., *The Annals of America*, 18 vols. (Chicago: Encyclopedia Britannica, 1968); Paul H. Bergeron, *The Presidency of James K. Polk* (Lawrence: University Press of Kansas, 1987); Henry Steele Commager, ed., *Documents of American History*, 8th ed. (New York: Appleton-Century-Crofts, 1968).

Polk's Message on War with Mexico

Message from President James K. Polk, dated May 11, 1846, to the U.S. Congress, requesting that body to declare war against Mexico, a result of the dispute over the U.S. annexation of Texas. In the message Polk traced the origins of the conflict and claimed that Mexico had invaded American territory "and shed American blood upon the American soil" in her April 24 attack on U.S. troops in territory between the Rio Grande and the Nueces River. Though this territory, despite Polk's claim, was not undisputedly part of the United States, Congress declared war two days later.

Further reading: Paul H. Bergeron, *The Presidency of James K. Polk* (Lawrence: University Press of Kansas, 1987); Henry Steele Commager, ed., *Documents of American History*, 8th ed. (New York: Appleton-Century-Crofts, 1968); Frank N. Magill, ed., *Great Events from History: American Series*, 3 vols. (Englewood Cliffs, N.J.: Salem Press, 1975).

Pollock v. Farmers' Loan and Trust Company

U.S. Supreme Court decision of May 20, 1895, invalidating the income tax provision of the WILSON-GORMAN TARIFF ACT. That provision, which applied a tax of 2 percent on all income over $4,000, was challenged when Charles Pollock, a stockholder in the Farmers' Loan and Trust Company of New York, sued to stop the bank from paying tax on its income. In a 5-4 decision, the Supreme Court ruled that the income tax was unconstitutional because it was a direct tax and therefore was required to be apportioned among the states according to population. Widespread dissatisfaction with the decision ultimately led to the passage of the SIXTEENTH AMENDMENT.

Further reading: Howard B. Furer, *The Fuller Court, 1888–1910* (Danbury, Conn.: Grolier Educational, 1995); Kermit L. Hall, et al., eds., *American Legal History: Cases and Materials*, 2d ed. (New York: Oxford University Press, 1996); Kermit L. Hall, et al., eds., *The Oxford Companion to the Supreme Court of the United States* (New York: Oxford University Press, 1992); United States Supreme Court, *United States Reports: Cases Adjudged in the Supreme Court at . . . and Rules Announced at . . .* (New York: Banks & Brothers, Law Publishers, 1884–1921; Washington, D.C.: Government Printing Office, 1922–).

Poll Tax of 1990, British

Controversial law enacted by British prime minister Margaret Thatcher's conservative government to take effect on April 1, 1990, in England and Wales. It was designed to replace a local property tax (a single household tax based on property values) with a head levy or poll tax, making almost all persons over 18 pay a per capita amount set by local authorities and based on the cost of government services in their localities. Under the system, a lord in a 100-room mansion would pay as much as a grocer in a cottage, if they reside in the same borough. The tax aroused much anger, ignited protests that turned into riots, and mobilized a majority of Britons in opposition to Thatcher, who lost the prime ministry to her chancellor of the exchequer, John R. Major, in late November 1990.

Further reading: John Campbell, *Margaret Thatcher* (London: Jonathan Cape, 2000); Christopher Collins, ed., *Margaret Thatcher: Complete Public Statements, 1945–1990*, CD-ROM (Oxford, England: Oxford University Press, 1999).

Polyanov (Polianovka), Peace of

Treaty concluded by the Russian state and the Polish-Lithuanian republic near the river Polyanov or Polianovka in June 1634. The terms of the treaty were similar to those of the Treaty of DEULINO of 1618. Poland's Prince Ladislaus IV (who was later king) agreed to renounce his claim to the Russian throne, which had been pledged to him during the Russian "Time of Troubles" (1604–13) by a group of Russian boyars (aristocrats). He also agreed to hand over to Russian Czar Michael Romanov the official document endorsing his claim to the Russian throne. In return Russia agreed to the Polish-Lithuanian republic's possession of the Smolensk region and other territories captured from Russia during the Russo-Polish War of 1632–34.

Further reading: Richard Butterwick, *The Polish-Lithuanian Monarchy in European Context: c. 1500–1795* (New York: Palgrave, 2001).

Pomeroy Circular

Letter issued and distributed secretly in January 1864 by the National Executive Committee of Radical Republicans, proposing U.S. secretary of the treasury Salmon P. Chase as the 1864 Republican presidential candidate and criticizing incumbent Abraham Lincoln. The circular, signed by Kansas senator Samuel C. Pomeroy, chairman of the committee, was made public by the *National Intelligencer* on February 22. Pomeroy argued that Chase would more vigorously prosecute the Civil War. The letter outraged Republican loyalists, and support for Chase collapsed after his own Ohio party organization announced for Lincoln.

Further reading: John C. Waugh, *Reelecting Lincoln: The Battle for the 1864 Presidency* (New York: Crown Publishers, 1997).

Poona Pact of 1932

Pact made on September 24, 1932, wherein Dr. Bhimrao Ramji Ambedkar, leader of India's depressed classes (untouchable Hindus), conceded to the demand of other Hindu leaders by agreeing to the withdrawal of the "separate electorates" provided in the British government's communal award (August 4, 1932). The concession was almost forced from him when Mohandas Gandhi (one of the Hindu leaders) began a fast unto death on September 18, to protest against the alienation of the depressed classes from the larger Hindu community. Ambedkar, who knew that the British award would be more beneficial to his group, settled instead for increased representation for the depressed classes within the general constituencies for a 10-year period. Later, he complained of having been coerced into making these concessions. The Poona Pact (concluded in and named for Poona, India) is often viewed as the first in a series of national campaigns against untouchability.

Further reading: Jadagisa C. Mandala, *Poona Pact and Depressed Classes* (Calcutta, India: Sujan Publications, 1999); Valerian Rodrigues, ed., *The Essential Writings of B. R. Ambedkar* (Delhi, India: Oxford University Press, 2001); Stanley Wolpert, *Gandhi's Passion: The Life and Legacy of Mahatma Gandhi* (Oxford, England: Oxford University Press, 2001).

Poor Law of 1601 (Elizabethan Poor Law)

Bill passed in the last Parliament of Queen Elizabeth I of England charging the government with the responsibility of providing for the needy. In every parish, it authorized a group (consisting of the churchwarden and two to four householders appointed by the justices of peace) to levy a tax on the land and use the income to employ able, unemployed men and children. The incapacited and those who had no one to support them were exempt. Pauper children were to be apprenticed to trades. Houses of correction were to be built to reform vagabonds. A landmark law, its principles were never repealed in subsequent legislation.

Further reading: A. L. Beier, *The Problem of the Poor in Tudor and Early Stuart England* (New York: Methuen, 1983); Paul Slack, *The English Poor Law, 1531–1782* (Basingstroke, England: Macmillan Education, 1990).

Poor Law of 1834 (Poor Law Amendment Act)

British legislation passed on August 14, 1834, encouraging the able-bodied poor to seek work (in workhouses set up for that purpose). It withdrew the concessions offered to them since the Elizabethan Poor Law of 1601 and its subsequent amendments. However, aged and infirm paupers continued to receive charitable assistance. It established 600 unions of parishes to be managed by boards of guardians (elected by the taxpayers), who were entrusted with the administration of relief measures for the local poor. This law was enacted on the recommendation of the report presented by the Royal Commission on Poor Laws in 1834.

Further reading: Felix Driver, *Power and Pauperism: The Workhouse System, 1834–1884* (New York: Cambridge University Press, 1993); David Englander, *Poverty and Poor Law Reform in Britain: From Chadwick to Booth, 1834–1914* (New York: Longman, 1998); Frank N. Magill, ed., *Great Events from History: Modern European Series*, 3 vols. (Englewood Cliffs, N.J.: Salem Press, 1973); Joel H. Wiener, ed., *Great Britain— The Lion at Home: A Documentary History of Domestic Policy (1689–1973)*, 4 vols. (New York: Chelsea House, 1974).

Poor Law of 1838

British legislation passed on July 31, 1838, introducing the new poor law (see POOR LAW OF 1834)

into Ireland—its implementation there being drafted by George Nicholls, an English Poor Law commissioner. The system was to be administered by a central board (based in Dublin), reporting to the English Board of Poor Law Commissioners. The country was divided into unions, each with an elected board of guardians. They were responsible for setting up the workhouse, managing it, and raising funds for its upkeep. Initial opposition to the act (notably from Daniel O'Connell and many Irish landlords) fizzled out and Ireland's first organized relief system for the poor became operative.

Further reading: Helen Burke, *The People and the Poor Law in 19th Century Ireland* (Littlehampton, England: George Philip Services, 1987); Michael Farrell, *The Poor Law and the Workhouse in Belfast, 1838–1948* (Belfast: Public Record Office of Northern Ireland, 1978).

Pope's Dictate (Dictatus Papae)

Decree written in March 1075, in which Pope Gregory VII affirmed the supremacy of the spiritual authority of the Roman Catholic Church over all other authority, including that of monarchs. Among the more salient features was the declaration that the pope alone would be permitted to depose or reinstate bishops or emperors, and could establish new laws; that he was to be judged by no man; that no one was to call himself Catholic unless he was in agreement with the Roman Church; that the Roman Church had never erred nor would it ever do so. Many of these claims had already been considered canonical, but it was under Gregory that they began to be enforced.

Further reading: Catholic University of America, eds., *New Catholic Encyclopedia* (New York: McGraw-Hill, 1967); Norton Downs, ed., *Basic Documents in Medieval History* (New York: Van Nostrand Reinhold, 1959); Frank N. Magill, ed., *Great Events from History: Ancient and Medieval Series*, 3 vols. (Englewood Cliffs, N.J.: Salem Press, 1972); Milton Viorst, ed., *The Great Documents of Western Civilization* (Philadelphia: Chilton Books, 1965).

Portsmouth, Treaty of

Peace treaty ending the Russo-Japanese War of 1904–5; mediated by U.S. president Theodore Roosevelt and signed at Portsmouth, New Hampshire, on September 5, 1905. The terms of the treaty reflected Japan's surprisingly complete victory over Russia. Although not required to pay an indemnity, Russia was forced to acknowledge Korea as a Japanese sphere of influence; to lease to Japan the areas of Port Arthur and Talien, as well as adjacent territorial waters; to cede to Japan railway and coal mines between Changchun and Port Arthur, plus the southern portion of the island of Sakhalin; and to grant Japanese fishing rights along the coasts of Russian possessions in the Sea of Japan, Sea of Okhotsk, and Bering Sea. In addition, both countries agreed to evacuate Manchuria and to use the railroad there for commercial purposes only. Also, both agreed to grant each other most-favored-nation status.

Further reading: Fred L. Israel, ed., *Major Peace Treaties of Modern History, 1648–1967*, 4 vols. (New York: Chelsea House, 1967) ; Frank N. Magill, ed., *Great Events from History: Modern European Series*, 3 vols. (Englewood Cliffs, N.J.: Salem Press, 1973); Eugene P. Trani, *The Treaty of Portsmouth; an Adventure in American Diplomacy* (Lexington: University of Kentucky Press, 1969).

Positive Philosophy See *COURSE OF POSITIVE PHILOSOPHY.*

Potsdam, Edict of Decree issued at Potsdam (East Germany) on November 8, 1685, by Elector Frederick William of Brandenburg, granting asylum to all Huguenots driven out of France by King Louis XIV. Religious and political persecution of the Huguenots (French Protestants) increased following Louis's Revocation of the Edict of NANTES in October 1685. The Potsdam edict led to about 20,000 Huguenots emigrating from France to Brandenburg and East Prussia. The influx stimulated Prussian industrial growth and increased the size of the Prussian army.

Further reading: C. Edmund Maurice, *Life of Frederick William, the Great Elector of Brandenburg* (Westport, Conn.: Greenwood Press, 1981).

Potsdam Declaration Allied powers' declaration on July 26, 1945, of their plans for the future of Germany; made at the Potsdam Conference (July 17–August 2, 1945). There, outside Berlin, the United States (President Harry S Truman), Great Britain (Prime Minister Winston Churchill, later replaced by Clement Attlee) and the Soviet Union (Premier Joseph Stalin) discussed further the provisions of the YALTA AGREEMENT. Their intention, they clarified, was not "to destroy or enslave the German people" but to ensure that Germany would never again threaten world peace. Therefore, they sought to abolish Germany's armed forces and prohibit the manufacture of armaments, bring war criminals to trial, destroy Nazism and its institutions, and give German education new direction. Germany was divided into four zones, administered by France and the three big powers. She had to surrender territory to Poland and the Soviet Union; war reparations payable to the Allies were also discussed. Her economy would be decentralized and industrial strength severely limited. A council of foreign ministers was formed to negotiate settlements with Italy, Bulgaria, Romania, Hungary, and Finland.

See also: PARIS, TREATIES OF (1947).

Further reading: Henry W. Degenhardt, ed., *Treaties and Alliances of the World*, 4th ed. (Detroit: Gale Research, 1986); Frank N. Magill, ed., *Great Events from History: Modern European Series*, 3 vols. (Englewood Cliffs, N.J.: Salem Press, 1973); Louis L. Snyder, ed., *Documents of German History* (New Brunswick, N.J.: Rutgers University Press, 1958); Louis L. Snyder, ed., *Fifty Major Docuemnts of the Twentieth Century* (Princeton, N.J.: D. Van Nostrand, 1955).

Poynings's Act of 1494 See DROGHEDA, STATUTE OF.

Poynings's Laws Legislation enacted between December 1494 and April 1495 by the Irish Parliament during the Drogheda session, under the leadership of Sir Edward Poynings, lord deputy of Ireland (1494–95) for England's king Henry VII. Including the famous DROGHEDA STATUTE, 49 acts—most of them minor and insignificant—were passed, covering financial, legal, defense, and constitutional matters. Laws of importance included (1) 12-pence levy on all merchandise; (2) control over all alienated crown lands; (3) reenactment and confirmation of all previous statutes (in England and Ireland) against papal provisions; (4) cancellation of all acts of pretender Lambert Simnel, recently crowned king of Ireland; (5) imprisonment on charges of treason, for the earl of Kildare; (6) compensation for Poynings's army; (7) no peace or war except with the governor's consent; (8) high-level appointments only at the king's pleasure; (9) invalidation of all acts of the 1493 Drogheda parliament; and (10) extension of all English public welfare laws to Ireland.

Further reading: W. N. Osborough, ed., *The Irish Statutes: Edward II to the Union AD 1310–1800* (Portland, Ore.: Round Hall Press, 1995).

Praemunire, Statute of Statute enacted in 1353 by England's Edward III to protect the rights of the crown from papal interference. It prohibited, upon penalty, the practice of appealing to courts outside England in matters that were within the jurisdiction of the crown. Not entirely new legislation, it merely improved the legal procedures for checking any such appeals made to the papal curia. The statute was passed in response to public pressure, but Edward remained wary of its enforcement. It was reissued several times (notably in 1365 and by Richard II in 1393) and was also used by Henry VIII, Elizabeth I, and James I to serve different purposes. Together with the Statute of PROVISORS, it apparently helped set the scene for the Church of England's subsequent break with Rome.

Further reading: Catholic University of America, eds., *New Catholic Encyclopedia* (New York: McGraw-Hill, 1967); Edgar B. Graves, *The Legal Significance of the Statute of Praemunire of 1353* (Cambridge, Mass.: Houghton Mifflin, 1929); Frank N. Magill, ed., *Great Events from History: Ancient and Medieval Series*, 3 vols. (Englewood Cliffs, N.J.: Salem Press, 1972); Charles H. Taylor and John L. La Monte, eds., *Anniversary Essays in Mediaeval History* (New York: Houghton Mifflin, 1929).

Pragmatic Sanction of 1713 State decree first drafted in 1703 by Holy Roman Emperor Leopold I and later amended and published in 1713 by his son, Holy Roman Emperor Charles VI, the brother and successor of Emperor Joseph I. Charles, without a male heir and with Joseph's daughters having formally renounced their claims to the

Hapsburg throne, sought to ensure the indivisibility of Austria's Hapsburg dominions and the continuation of the Hapsburg ruling dynasty. The instrument of 1713, which was eventually guaranteed by most of the European sovereigns, decreed that if Charles left no male descendants, his daughters should inherit his crown and states; that if Charles left no male or female descendants, the crown and states should pass to Joseph's descendants; and that the unity of the Hapsburg lands was to be guaranteed. Elector Charles Albert of Bavaria, the next male heir to Charles's dominions, rejected the Pragmatic Sanction, which led to the War of the Austrian Succession (1740–48), after Charles's death in 1740, and the hereditary succession of his crown and states to his eldest daughter, Maria Theresa, that same year.

Further reading: M. S. Anderson, *The War of the Austrian Succession, 1740–1748* (New York: Longman, 1995); Jeremy Black, ed., *The Origins of War in Early Modern Europe* (Atlantic Highlands, N.J.: Humanities Press, 1987); Charles Ingrao et al., *The Habsburg Dominions under Maria Theresa: A Commemorative Issue Marking the Two Hundredth Anniversary of Maria Theresa's Death* (Washington, Pa.: Washington & Jefferson College, 1980); John P. Spielman, *Leopold I of Austria* (London: Thames & Hudson, 1977).

Pragmatic Sanction of Bourges   Decree issued in the name of King Charles VII by a French synod (assembly of higher clergy and nobility) at Bourges, France, on July 7, 1438; it marked the beginning of the French church's independence from the Church of Rome. The sanction, referring to the civil government's settlement of ecclesiastical issues, authorized the supremacy of national church councils over the papacy, abolished most of the papal revenues from France (annates and other papal taxations), restricted the effect of excommunication and interdicts by the Roman Catholic Church, and asserted the freedom of France's Gallican Church (established by the monarchy). The sanction also limited papal patronage and judicial appeals to Rome and insisted on the free election of French abbots and bishops. It was revoked by King Louis XI in 1461, later briefly reintroduced, and finally replaced by the Concordat of BOLOGNA in 1516.

Further reading: Catholic University of America, eds., *New Catholic Encyclopedia* (New York: McGraw-Hill, 1967); Frank N. Magill, ed., *Great Events from History: Ancient and Medieval Series*, 3 vols. (Englewood Cliffs, N.J.: Salem Press, 1972); Milton Viorst, ed., *The Great Documents of Western Civilization* (Philadelphia: Chilton Books, 1965).

Pragmatic Sanction of Charles III   King Charles III's resolution of the issue of succession to the Two Sicilies (kingdoms of Naples and of Sicily), following his accession to the Spanish throne on the death (August 10, 1759) of his half-brother Ferdinand VI. Before an assembly of Spanish and Italian nobles, Charles III declared that he was renouncing the throne of Naples (where he had reigned as king since 1735)

in favor of his third son, eight-year-old Ferdinand (Ferdinand I), realizing that "all Europe desires the separation of the Spanish power from that of Italy." He also appointed a regency council to manage affairs until Ferdinand came of age. Thus began the Neapolitan branch of the Bourbon family. Charles III also disinherited his eldest son Philip, an imbecile, and named his second son, Charles, prince of the Asturias and heir to the Spanish throne.

Further reading: Harold M. M. Acton, *The Bourbons of Naples, 1734–1825* (London: Methuen, 1956); Charles Petrie, *King Charles III of Spain; an Enlightened Despot* (London: Constable, 1971).

Pragmatic Sanction of Rhens   See RHENS, DECLARATION OF.

Pragmatic Sanction of St. Louis   French ordinance, issued in March 1269, prohibiting irregular clerical appointments and the levying of taxes on the French clergy to benefit the Roman Curia (papal court) in its struggle against the Holy Roman emperor. Attributed to King Louis IX (St. Louis), it is now known to be a forged document invented in 1438 by the followers of King Charles VII, who were seeking a precedent to justify their own religious policies. The aim was to restrict external or papal influence in appointments to bishoprics and abbeys, and to prevent gold from leaving France. The document's spurious nature is evident from its date, because by 1269 Louis had already reached a contradictory understanding with the Holy See (to the disadvantage of the French Church).

Further reading: M. G. A. Vale, *Charles VII* (London: Methuen, 1974).

Prague, Compacts of (Basel Compacta)   Document consisting of four articles accepted by the Hussites (followers of Jan Hus, a Czech religious martyr) in July 1436; ratified in 1437 by the Council of Basel. It represented a compromise between the conservative Catholics and the liberal Hussites. It asserted that Communion was to be given freely to Christians who practiced the Hussite form of worship; that proper punishment of sin would be enforced; that priests must renounce all wordly possessions; and that the teaching of the Gospel would be limited to priests and deacons. The articles originally proposed by the Hussites were much more radical. They were based upon the demands made in the Four Articles of PRAGUE.

Further reading: Thomas A. Fudge, *The Magnificent Ride: The First Reformation in Hussite Bohemia* (Brookfield, Vt.: Ashgate, 1998); John M. Klassen, *Warring Maidens, Captive Wives and Hussite Queens: Women and Men at War and Peace in Fifteenth Century Bohemia* (Boulder, Colo.: East European Monographs, 1999).

Prague, Four Articles of   Declarations made by the Hussite Union in 1420, several years after the Decrees of the Council of CONSTANCE. A Czech religious reform group, the union made demands for the ministry of both bread and wine to the laity; for the laity's freedom to teach the word of God; for the priests' renunciation of all extravagance and inordinate control over the laity; as well as for the proper punishment of all sin. These demands were made with the hope of abolishing the many abuses within the Roman Catholic Church, which had been a cause for dispute since the period leading up to the Jan Hus controversy in the early 1400s.

Further reading: Thomas A. Fudge, *The Magnificent Ride: The First Reformation in Hussite Bohemia* (Brookfield, Vt.: Ashgate, 1998); John M. Klassen, *Warring Maidens, Captive Wives and Hussite Queens: Women and Men at War and Peace in Fifteenth Century Bohemia* (Boulder, Colo.: East European Monographs, 1999).

Prague, Peace of   Peace concluded by Elector John George of Saxony and Holy Roman Emperor Ferdinand II on May 30, 1635, essentially annulling the provisions of the Edict of RESTITUTION, through which German Protestants would have lost a substantial amount of secularized land to Roman Catholics. The peace said that all church property that had been secularized before 1552 should remain in the hands of its possessor (rather than revert to the pre-1552 possessors, the majority of whom were Roman Catholic), and that amnesty was to be given to all individuals involved in the conflict. In addition the Saxon elector received the region of Lusatia, and the archbishopric of Magdeburg was reserved for his son. A majority of German Protestant estates agreed to the peace treaty, through which Ferdinand's ambitious designs to counter the spread of Protestantism were checked.

Further reading: Robert Bireley, *Religion and Politics in the Age of the Counterreformation: Emperor Ferdinand II, William Lamormaini, S. J., and the Formation of Imperial Policy* (Chapel Hill: University of North Carolina Press, 1981); Frank N. Magill, ed., *Great Events from History: Modern European Series*, 3 vols. (Englewood Cliffs, N.J.: Salem Press, 1973).

Prague, Treaty of (1866)   Treaty concluded in Prague on August 23, 1866, between Prussia and Austria, providing for a settlement to the Austro-Prussian Seven Weeks' War (1866), which had ensued over Prussian Premier Otto von Bismarck's grandiose plans to make Prussia the leader in the German world. Austria's defeat (and the subsequent Treaty of Prague) resulted in her loss of Venetia to Italy (see NAPOLÉON III'S TREATY WITH AUSTRIA; PRUSSIAN-ITALIAN ALLIANCE OF 1866); her loss of the duchy of Holstein to Prussia (see GASTEIN, CONVENTION OF); her obligation to make war indemnity payments to Prussia; and her acknowledgment of the dissolution of the German Confederation (see GERMAN CONFEDERATION, ACT OF) and of the subsequent creation of a North German Confederation from which she was excluded.

In addition, Austria's south German allies (Bavaria, Württemberg, Baden, and Hesse-Darmstadt) were obliged to make indemnity payments to Prussia; and Hanover and Hesse-Kassel were annexed by Prussia. Of lasting importance was the ascendancy of Prussia in the German world, and the decline of Austria as a great power.

See also: VIENNA, TREATY OF (1866).

Further reading: Fred L. Israel, ed., *Major Peace Treaties of Modern History, 1648–1967*, 4 vols. (New York: Chelsea House, 1967); Frank N. Magill, ed., *Great Events from History: Modern European Series*, 3 vols. (Englewood Cliffs, N.J.: Salem Press, 1973); Louis L. Snyder, ed., *Documents of German History* (New Brunswick, N.J.: Rutgers University Press, 1958); Milton Viorst, ed., *The Great Documents of Western Civilization* (Philadelphia: Chilton Books, 1965).

Prayer of Twenty Millions, The   See GREELEY'S "PRAYER."

Preamble to the U.S. Constitution   Introduction to the U.S. CONSTITUTION, stating the purposes underlying the document and identifying "the people of the United States" as the source of its authority. Adopted and ratified with the main body of the Constitution in 1788, the Preamble declares the purposes of the Constitution to be "to form a more perfect union, establish justice, insure domestic tranquillity, provide for the common defense, promote the general welfare, and secure the blessings of liberty" to the people of the nation. The phrase "to promote the general welfare" has been used by Congress in the 20th century to justify social programs such as federal aid to education and Social Security.

Further reading: Mortimer Adler, ed., *The Annals of America*, 18 vols. (Chicago: Encyclopaedia Britannica, 1968); Henry Steele Commager, ed., *Documents of American History*, 8th ed. (New York: Appleton-Century-Crofts, 1968); Charles W. Eliot, ed., *The Harvard Classics*, 51 vols. (New York: P. F. Collier & Son, 1937); Kermit L. Hall et al., eds., *American Legal History: Cases and Materials*, 2d ed. (New York: Oxford University Press, 1996).

Pre-Emption Act of 1841, U.S.   Federal legislation enacted on September 4, 1841, that permitted western settlers to claim up to 160 acres of surveyed public lands and, after a period of residence, to purchase that land from the U.S. government at a minimum price of $1.25 per acre, before it was put up for public auction. The act was favored by western states to encourage settlement rather than land speculation but was opposed by the East, which feared a loss of its labor supply. Eastern support was gained with the addition of a plan to distribute revenues from the sale of public lands among the states, based on population. Though the distribution provisions were repealed in 1842, the preemption act remained in effect until 1891, when abuses led to its repeal.

Further reading: Mortimer Adler, ed., *The Annals of America*, 18 vols. (Chicago: Encyclopaedia Britannica, 1968); Henry Steele Commager, ed., *Documents of American History*, 8th ed. (New York: Appleton-Century-Crofts, 1968); Frank N. Magill, ed., *Great Events from History: American Series*, 3 vols. (Englewood Cliffs, N.J.: Salem Press, 1975).

Preobrazhenskoe, Treaty of   Agreement made between Russia's czar Peter I the Great and Poland's king Augustus II (the latter in his capacity as elector of Saxony, Frederick Augustus I) in the Russian town of Preobrazhenskoe in November 1699. It was made prior to the Great Northern War (1700–1721), in which Sweden strove to maintain hegemony in the Baltic area while Russia sought access to the Baltic Sea. Sweden's policies represented an immediate threat to Saxony, which entered into an offensive alliance with Russia. By the treaty, both powers agreed to wage war against Sweden, with Saxony invading the Baltic provinces of Livonia and Estonia, and Russia invading Karelia and Izhora. Both also agreed not to conclude a separate peace with Sweden. Through the treaty, Poland (then in union with Lithuania) became implicated in the war.

Further reading: Lindsey Hughes, *Russia in the Age of Peter the Great* (New Haven, Conn.: Yale University Press, 1998).

Presidential Succession Law, U.S.   Various plans adopted to ensure succession to the U.S. presidency in the event of a vacancy in that office. The U.S. Constitution provided that the vice president should succeed if the presidency is vacated or the president is unable to discharge his duties. A 1792 law provided that the order of succession, after the vice president, should be the president pro tempore of the Senate and the speaker of the House. An act of 1886 altered this order, providing that, after the vice president, the successors should be the cabinet members in the order in which their departments were established. In 1947 this act was amended to place the speaker of the House and the president pro tempore of the Senate before the cabinet members. The TWENTY-FIFTH AMENDMENT allowed for the vice president to serve as acting president if the president is incapacitated.

Further reading: Alan Brinkley, *American History: A Survey*, 10th ed. (Boston: McGraw-Hill College, 1999); John D. Feerick, *The Twenty-Fifth Amendment: Its Complete History and Applications*, 2d ed. (New York: Fordham University Press, 1992); Robert E. Gilbert, ed., *Managing Crisis: Presidential Disability and the Twenty-Fifth Amendment* (New York: Fordham University Press, 2000); Vance R. Kincaid, *Heirs Apparent: Solving the Vice Presidential Dilemma* (Westport, Conn.: Praeger, 2000).

Pressburg, Treaty of (1491)   Agreement made in Pressburg (Bratislava) between Hungary's king Uladislaus II and Maximilian of Hapsburg (later Holy Roman Emperor Maximilian I) on November 7, 1491. By its terms, Maximilian recognized Uladislaus as king of Hungary and, in return, regained control of Austria, Styria, and Carinthia—provinces that the former Hungarian king, Matthias Corvinus, had taken in 1486. Uladislaus also promised his crown to Maximilian if he died without a male heir (which he did not do). Hungary's Diet refused to ratify the treaty because the Hapsburg association was unwelcome.

Further reading: Gerhard Benecke, *Maximilian I (1459–1519): An Analytical Biography* (Boston: Routledge & Kegan Paul, 1982).

Pressburg, Treaty of (1805)   Treaty concluded at Pressburg (Bratislava) on December 26, 1805, between Austria, under Emperor Francis I, and France, under Emperor Napoléon Bonaparte; it followed the Russo-Austrian defeat at Austerlitz. Through this peace treaty, Austria was forced to cede all her Venetian possessions, including Dalmatia and Istria, to the newly formed Italian Republic (formerly the Cisalpine Republic), of which Napoléon was now recognized as king. Austria also ceded to France the Italian provinces of Piedmont, Parma, and Piacenza. To Württemberg and Bavaria (which were thenceforth kingdoms) and to Baden (thenceforth a grand duchy) Austria ceded large portions of her Hapsburg territories, including the Tyrol and Vorarlberg. Finally, Austria agreed to pay France an indemnity of 40 million francs. The treaty marked the territorial destruction of the Holy Roman Empire.

See also: SCHÖNBRUNN, TREATY OF (1805).

Further reading: Fred L. Israel, ed., *Major Peace Treaties of Modern History, 1648–1967*, 4 vols. (New York: Chelsea House, 1967).

Prevention of Crimes Act, British   Act passed by the British Parliament in July 1882, in an attempt to restrain the activities of the Irish extremists who were suspected of being involved in the brutal Phoenix Park murders. (Lord Frederick Cavendish, the newly appointed secretary for Ireland, and Thomas A. Burke, the undersecretary, were stabbed to death on May 6, 1882, by Irish extremists seeking independence; the two had been taking a daytime walk in Phoenix Park, Dublin.) The act strengthened the powers of the lord lieutenant and authorized trials without jury. The police were allowed to search premises and arrest anyone on suspicion.

See also: KILMAINHAM TREATY.

Further reading: Thomas H. Corfe, *The Phoenix Park Murders; Conflict, Compromise and Tragedy in Ireland, 1879–1882* (London: Hodder & Stoughton, 1968); David D. Douglas et al., eds., *English Historical Documents*, 12 vols. (New York: Oxford University Press, 1950–77).

Priests (Ordination of Women) Measure   Measure passed on November 11, 1992, by the General Synod of the Church of England providing "for the ordination of women as priests, and for connected purposes." Approved by the British Parliament in 1993, the measure received royal consent on November 5, 1993. The first women priests were ordained on March 12, 1994; however, male priests and parishes could refuse to accept women as priests, and those who resigned on this account were entitled to compensation as part of an accompanying measure. The Parochial Church Councils could declare that they did not wish to appoint women priests or have them perform certain duties (for example, presiding at the Eucharist or pronouncing absolution). The Anglican Church in Australia also passed a similar measure in 1993.

Further reading: F. L. Cross and E. A. Livingstone, eds., *The Oxford Dictionary of the Christian Church* (Oxford, England: Oxford University Press, 1997); Her Majesty's Stationery Office, "Priests (Ordination of Women) Measure 1993 (No. 2)," Her Majesty's Government UK online, available online at http://www.hmso.gov.uk/measures/ukcm_19930002_en_1.htm#end.

Prince, The (Il Principe)

Political treatise written by Italian political theorist Niccolò Machiavelli in 1513, containing advice to the ruler of a state on how to retain power over his subjects and maintain his territorial conquests. Through a series of historical examples, Machiavelli advised the ruler that, in order to maintain his power, he must utilize his ability to be cunning (cruel when necessary), despotic, and forceful, while at the same time striving to maintain a virtuous reputation. The author thus rejected the medieval view that a prince must possess the virtues of justice, generosity, and mercy, endorsing instead the more practical view that a prince must do whatever necessary, regardless of whether it would be deemed a virtue or vice, in order to maintain his power as well as the strength of the state. In the final chapter, Machiavelli called upon the Italian princes to drive the barbarians out of Italy, over which the latter had seized control.

Further reading: Charles W. Eliot, ed., *The Harvard Classics*, 51 vols. (New York: P. F. Collier & Son, 1937); Mark A. Kishlansky, ed., *Sources of the West: Readings in Western Civilization*, vol. 1, 4th ed. (New York: Longman, 2001); Frank N. Magill, ed., *Great Events from History: Modern European Series*, 3 vols. (Englewood Cliffs, N.J.: Salem Press, 1973).

Principia (Philosophiae Naturalis Principia Mathematica)

Magnum opus of English mathematician Sir Isaac Newton, having a seminal influence on the development of the science of physics. Written in Latin and published in 1687 (financed by his friend Edmund Halley), Newton's work is split into three parts. Book one is devoted to Newton's three laws of motion and to an analysis of orbital motion. In book two, Newton carefully studied the motion of fluids and discussed the inadequacy of René Descartes's vortex model in explaining how celestial bodies move. In book three, devoted to the system of the world, Newton proposed his theory that gravity is proportional to mass. He also showed how the the-

ory was applicable to planetary orbits, including the irregular motion of the moon and the trajectories of comets. The *Principia* is also known for its pioneering approach in the use of the scientific method to help understand natural phenomena in the world around us.

Further reading: Charles W. Eliot, ed., *The Harvard Classics*, 51 vols. (New York: P. F. Collier & Son, 1937); Desmond King-Hele and A. R. Hall, eds., *Newton's Principia and Its Legacy: Proceedings of Royal Society Discussion Meeting Held on 30 June, 1987* (London: Royal Society, 1988); John W. Knedler, Jr., *Masterworks of Science: Digests of 13 Great Classics*, 3 vols. (New York: McGraw-Hill, 1973); I. Bernard Cohen, trans., *The Principia: Mathematical Principles of Natural Philosophy* (Berkeley: University of California Press, 1999).

Principia Mathematica

Monumental three-volume treatise coauthored by the British mathematicians and philosophers Bertrand Russell and Alfred North Whitehead, and published in 1910–13; it aimed to prove that mathematics could be explained in terms of self-evident, logical principles. The two men collaborated brilliantly, with Russell handling many philosophical problems, such as developing a theory of logical types, and writing out most of the book. Whitehead partly invented the notation in which the "official" text was written and partly borrowed it from Giuseppe Peano, a contemporary Italian mathematician and linguist. The work covered many topics in logic (like proposition and theories of quantification, classes, and relations) and in mathematics (like cardinal arithmetic and theories of ordinals, relation-numbers, series, and measurement). A culmination of previous research, it served as the basis for the development of logic as a discipline in the 20th century.

Further reading: Bernard Linsky, *Russell's Metaphysical Logic* (Stanford, Calif.: CSLI Publications, 1999); W. V. Quine, *The Logic of Sequences: A Generalization of Principia Mathematica* (New York: Garland, 1990); A. Pampapathy Rao, *Understanding Principia and Tractatus: Russell and Wittgenstein Revisited* (San Francisco: International Scholars Publications, 1998); Alfred North Whitehead and Bertrand Russell, *Principia Mathematica* (New York: Cambridge University Press, 1997).

Principles of Psychology, The

Major two-volume work on psychology written by American philosopher William James over 12 years; published in 1890 and condensed into a textbook two years later. An immediate success (because of its thoroughness, accuracy, and easy style), it was then translated into French, German, Italian, and Russian. A Harvard University professor, James related psychological ideas to the life of his student (reader), without conveying the impression that psychology could furnish all the answers. Among the subjects covered in his work were brain function, habit, "the automation-theory," stream of thought, the self, attention, association, the perception of time, memory, sensation, imagination, perception, reasoning, voluntary movement, instinct, emotions, will, and hypnotism. The work had a great influence on the development of psychology, particularly in providing a way of analyzing, rather than describing human behavior.

Further reading: William James, *The Principles of Psychology* (Bristol, England: Thoemmes, 1998); Michael G. Johnson and Tracy B. Henley, eds., *Reflections on The Principles of Psychology: William James after a Century* (Hillsdale, N.J.: L. Erlbaum Associates, 1990).

Process of Warsaw, Statements at the   Statements made by 126 witnesses from all levels of Polish society at a hearing convened at Pope Clement VI's request and held in Warsaw from February 4 to September 15, 1339. During the session, Polish citizens were asked to testify about the devastation done to Poland by the Teutonic Knights. The judges concluded that eastern Pomerania (Pomerelia), Kujawia, and Dobrzyń should all be returned to Poland and that the Teutonic Knights should make a large indemnity payment. The verdict, however, was not accepted by the pope, and King Casimir III of Poland was forced to conclude the 1343 Treaty of KALISCH on the basis of the less favorable Agreement at VISEGRÁD.

Further reading: Diana Wood, *Clement VI: The Pontificate and Ideas of an Avignon Pope* (New York: Cambridge University Press, 1989).

Proclamation of 1763, British   Royal order issued by Britain's king George III on October 7, 1763, in an effort to placate the Indians in the American colonies after the French and Indian War (1756–63). It organized the British American territories into four governments—for East and West Florida, Grenada, and Quebec—and established the lands west of the Appalachian Mountains as a vast Indian reservation barred to colonial white settlers (those already there were ordered to leave). Land titles secured from western Indians were revoked, and the profitable Indian fur trade was placed under royal license. The proclamation was strongly denounced by many colonists.

See also: PARIS, TREATY OF (1763).

Further reading: Mortimer Adler, ed., *The Annals of America*, 18 vols. (Chicago: Encyclopaedia Britannica, 1968); Henry Steele Commager, ed., *Documents of American History*, 8th ed. (New York: Appleton-Century-Crofts, 1968); David D. Douglas, et al., eds., *English Historical Documents*, 12 vols. (New York: Oxford University Press, 1950–77); William MacDonald, ed., *Select Charters and Other Documents Illustrative of American History, 1606–1775* (New York: Macmillan, 1899).

Proclamation of March 14, 1917   See ORDER NO. 1, PETROGRAD SOVIET'S.

Proclamation of Neutrality, Washington's   Proclamation issued by U.S. president George Washington on April 22, 1793, after France had declared war on Great Britain; it stated that the United States would "adopt and pursue a conduct friendly and impartial toward the belligerent powers" and warned U.S. citizens to avoid aiding any hostile nations, under threat of punishment. Washington's statement carefully avoided the word "neutrality" in hopes of securing British maritime concessions in exchange for a U.S. promise to remain neutral. The proclamation, which was strictly enforced and was codified in the NEUTRALITY ACT OF 1794, set important precedents in international law and American policy toward foreign wars.

Further reading: Mortimer Adler, ed., *The Annals of America*, 18 vols. (Chicago: Encyclopaedia Britannica, 1968); Henry Steele Commager, ed., *Documents of American History*, 8th ed. (New York: Appleton-Century-Crofts, 1968).

Progressive Party Platform of 1924   See LA FOLLETTE PLATFORM OF 1924.

Progressive Republicans' Declaration of Principles, U.S.   See NATIONAL PROGRESSIVE REPUBLICAN LEAGUE'S DECLARATION OF PRINCIPLES.

Property Qualification Act (Landed Property Qualification Act; Parliamentary Qualification Act)   British statute of 1711, ruling that any person who sat or voted in the House of Commons should be possessed of estates in land, failing which the election would be void. The annual value of the estate was placed at £600 or more for every knight of a shire and £300 or more for every citizen, burgess, or baron of a cinque port. It also declared that the eldest son or heir-apparent of any peer or lord of Parliament or any person qualified by the terms of this act to serve as knight of the shire, could be elected as a member of the House of Commons in any Parliament. Elected representatives of the two universities (Oxford and Cambridge) were exempt from the provisions of the act, which was intended to exclude merchants, financiers, and industrialists from Parliament. It was repealed in 1866.

Further reading: Joel H. Wiener, ed., *Great Britain—The Lion at Home: A Documentary History of Domestic Policy (1689–1973)*, 4 vols. (New York: Chelsea House, 1974).

Protocol for the Pacific Settlement of International Disputes   See GENEVA PROTOCOL OF 1924.

Protocol of the Eight Articles   Protocol outlining the fundamental conditions for the union of Holland and the Belgian provinces as the Netherlands; adopted by the Allied powers on June 21, 1814 on the basis of proposals submitted by Prince William VI of Orange (later King William I of the Netherlands). It served as a working guideline for the half-

Dutch, half-Belgian royal commission entrusted with adapting the Dutch Constitution of 1814 to the new situation. The staggering Dutch debts were to be amalgamated with the miniscule Belgian debts and religious freedom was ensured, conditions offensive to Catholic Belgium. A bicameral legislature was proposed—the first chamber consisting of appointed members, the second of 110 members (elected on a limited franchise) with equal representation from both countries (even though Belgium's population was considerably more). Approved by Holland but rejected by Belgium, the constitution passed despite Belgium's opposition since all abstentions were considered as favorable votes.

Further reading: Adriaan J. Barnouw, *The Pageant of Netherlands History* (New York: Longmans, Green, 1952).

Protocols of the Elders of Zion

Invidious, spurious, anti-Semitic document first printed, partially, in 1903 in a Russian newspaper in St. Petersburg and included in 1905 in a Russian religious booklet by Serge Nilus, a civil servant of Czar Nicholas II. According to the document, Jewish elders and Freemasons allegedly conspired at meetings held in Basel, Switzerland, in 1897 to destroy Christendom through subversion and sabotage and subsequently to dominate the world. Its words were virulent: "Poison the spirit by destructive theories, weaken human bodies by inoculation with microbes, foment international hatreds and prepare for universal bankruptcy and concentration of gold in the hands of the Jews." The protocols' fraudulence was first revealed in 1921 by English journalist Philip Graves, who showed how close they were in language and ideas to a 1864 French satire by Maurice Joly, *Dialogue aux Enfers entre Machiavel et Montesquieu* (*Dialogue in Hell Between Machiavelli and Montesquieu*). Later inquiry showed that the czar's secret police probably were forgers, devising the document from a novel entitled *Biarritz* (1868) by Hermann Goedsche (a German who used the pen name Sir John Retcliffe), as well as from Joly's satire and other works.

Further reading: Norman R. C. Cohn, *Warrant for Genocide: The Myth of the Jewish World Conspiracy and the Protocols of the Elders of Zion* (London: Serif, 1996); B. W. Segel and Richard S. Levy, *A Lie and a Libel: The History of the Protocols of the Elders of Zion* (Lincoln: University of Nebraska Press, 1995).

Provincial Letters (Les Lettres Provinciales)

Eighteen letters written by French mathematician and theologian Blaise Pascal (using the pseudonym of Louis de Montalte) between January 23, 1656, and March 24, 1657, in support of noted Jansenist controversialist Antoine Arnauld, who was on trial for his views before the Sorbonne's faculty of theology. Only six of the letters actually addressed the immediate issue; in the other 12, Pascal criticized the Jesuit theories of grace (molinism) and moral theology (probabilism). He attacked the casuistry and lax morality of the Jesuit teachings, contrasting this with the strict morality and austere discipline of the Jansenists. The tone of the last two letters was more conciliatory and paved the way for the Peace of CLEMENT IX. Written in an easy, fluent style, which greatly influenced modern French prose, *Les Lettres Provinciales* were condemned by the Congregation of the Index in 1657.

See also: *AUGUSTINUS*; CUM OCCASIONE IMPRESSIONIS LIBRI; *IN EMINENTI*.

Further reading: Richard Lockwood, *The Reader's Figure: Epideictic Rhetoric in Plato, Aristotle, Bossuet, Racine and Pascal* (Geneva: Librairie Droz, 1996); Walter E. Rex, *Pascal's Provincial Letters: An Introduction* (London: Hodder & Stoughton, 1977).

Provisors, Statute of

One of two English antipapal statutes (see PRAEMUNIRE, STATUTE OF) introduced during King Edward III's reign (1327–77). Passed in 1351, the Statute of Provisors denied the right of papal provisors to fill vacant benefices, declaring that appointment to church offices in England should be by free election and presentation by those entitled to do so. By superseding the traditional rights of patrons, it sought to prevent the papacy from appointing foreign clergy to benefices left vacant on the death or the promotion of the previous holder. If a patron failed to exercise his right, the king could make the appointment. Papal appointees were subject to severe penalties as a further discouragement. Though the statute was renewed several times, it was not enforced.

Further reading: Fredric Cheyette, *Kings, Courts, Cures and Sinecures: The Statute of Provisors and the Common Law* (New York: Fordham University Press, 1963).

Prussian Emancipation Edict of 1807

See EMANICIPATION EDICT OF 1807, PRUSSIAN.

Prussian-Italian Alliance of 1866

Treaty concluded on April 8, 1866, by Prussia and Italy through the influence of French emperor Napoléon III; it provided for an alliance between the two powers against Austria, in preparation for the war between Austria and Prussia (Seven Weeks' War), which was in fact imminent. The two powers agreed, in the event that war should break out between Austria and Prussia within three months, that Italy would join Prussia against Austria; and that Prussia would support Italy's bid for Austrian-controlled Venetia. The treaty was part of a grander scheme developed by Prussia's premier, Otto von Bismarck, to bring about Prussian supremacy in the German world.

See also: GASTEIN, CONVENTION OF; NAPOLÉON III'S TREATY WITH AUSTRIA; PRAGUE, TREATY OF (1866); VIENNA, TREATY OF (1866).

Further reading: H. M. Hozier, *The Seven Weeks' War: Its Antecedents and Its Incidents* (Minneapolis: Absinthe Press, 1997); Frank N. Magill, ed., *Great Events from History: Modern European Series*, 3 vols. (Englewood Cliffs, N.J.: Salem Press,

1973); Geoffrey Wawro, *The Austro-Prussian War: Austria's War with Prussia and Italy in 1866* (New York: Cambridge University Press, 1997).

Prusso-Darmstadt Customs' Treaty   Treaty concluded by the German states of Prussia and Hesse-Darmstadt on February 28, 1828, in which the two partners agreed to enter into a commercial union. The treaty provided that Hesse-Darmstadt would share equally with Prussia in the responsibility of forming tariff laws and of determining how revenues should be divided. The two partners were compelled to enter into the union because they feared that the recently formed Bavaro-Württemberg Customs' Union in the southwest would adversely affect their trade. The treaty was to remain effective for six years; it proved to be profitable for both partners. It initiated the Zollverein, a customs' union of German states, which eventually spread throughout central Europe and which served to unify the German states economically (a major step toward their eventual political unification).

See also: MID-GERMAN COMMERCIAL UNION.

Further reading: Rolf H. Dumke, *German Economic Unification in the 19th Century: The Political Econony of the Zollverein* (Munich: Institut für Volkswirtschaftslehre, Universität der Bundeswehr München, 1994); Frank N. Magill, ed., *Great Events from History: Modern European Series*, 3 vols. (Englewood Cliffs, N.J.: Salem Press, 1973).

Pruth, Treaty of   Agreement concluded on July 21, 1711, near the Pruth River (on the present-day eastern border of Romania), between Russia and the Ottoman Empire, ending the Russo-Turkish War of 1710–11. After Russian forces were encircled by Turks on the Pruth, Czar Peter I the Great was obliged to accept the treaty, which required him to give back to the Turks the fortress of Azov; destroy other strategic forts near the Turkish border; allow safe passage to Sweden for Swedish king Charles XII (who had found refuge in Turkish Moldavia after his army suffered defeat in Russia during the Great Northern War [1700–1721]); make peace with Sweden; and maintain peaceful relations with Poland and the Cossacks in the Ukraine.

Further reading: Robert K. Massie, *Peter the Great: His Life and World* (London: Gollancz, 1981); Edward J. Phillips, *The Founding of Russia's Navy: Peter the Great and the Azov Fleet, 1688–1714* (Westport, Conn.: Greenwood Press, 1995).

Pseudo-Isidorian Decretals   See FALSE DECRETALS.

Psychoanalysis, A General Introduction to (Vorlesungen zur Einführung in die Psychoanalyse)   Premier introductory textbook to the study of psychoanalysis, written by Sigmund Freud in 1915–16 and based on 28 lectures delivered by him at the University of Vienna during the winter semesters of those years. It covered three topics: the psychopathology of everyday life, dreams, and neuroses.

The first two topics were meant for students with no knowledge of the subject, while the third (the psychoanalysis of neuroses) presupposed a basic grounding in the subject, was more technical, and was intended for a more advanced student. Part one of the book is mainly a general introduction and a discussion of the psychology of errors; part two explores the features and techniques of dream interpretation; and part three deals with various types of neuroses and analytic therapy. The book (or lectures), frank and conversational in tone, summarized three decades of arduous research by Freud, an Austrian neurologist and founder of psychoanalysis.

Further reading: Joan Riviere, trans., *A General Introduction to Psychoanalysis*, 26th printing (New York: Pocket Books, 1975); James Strachey, trans. and ed., *The Standard Edition of the Complete Psychological Works of Sigmund Freud: Early Psycho-Analytical Publications* (London: Vintage, 2001).

Public Health Act of 1848, British   Government's first attempt to tackle the issue of public health, by creating a General Board of Health reporting directly to the British Parliament. The board was authorized to appoint local boards on the petition of at least 10 percent of the taxpayers or if the death rate exceeded 21 per 1,000. The local boards could appoint a medical officer of health; they were charged with the maintenance of proper drainage, sewage, clean streets, cemeteries, public parks, with water supplies and regular inspection of public lodgings. Funds were to be raised by increasing the rates and by borrowing. It was the culmination of a lengthy agitation for better public health facilities (inspired by Sir Edwin Chadwick's efforts) and was passed amidst news of a cholera epidemic. Scotland was not covered until 1867. The board was neither very popular nor, with its limited powers, very effective and was abolished in 1858.

Further reading: Christopher Hamlin, *Public Health and Social Justice in the Age of Chadwick: Britain, 1800–1854* (New York: Cambridge University Press, 1998); Rosemary Rees, *Poverty and Public Health, 1815–1948* (Oxford, England: Heinemann, 2001); Benjamin W. Richardson, ed., *The Health of Nations: A Review of the Works of Edwin Chadwick* (London: Dawsons, 1965); Joel H. Wiener, ed., *Great Britain—The Lion at Home: A Documentary History of Domestic Policy (1689–1973)*, 4 vols. (New York: Chelsea House, 1974).

Public Health Act of 1875, British   Comprehensive British public health policy (August 11, 1875), widely considered one of Prime Minister Benjamin Disraeli's major achievements. Codified from previous legislation by Richard Cross (Home Office), it introduced the element of compulsion into public health legislation. It vested greater authority in the local boards by charging them with the provision and maintenance of proper sewage and drainage facilities, garbage collection, and control of water supply. They were to report and control the spread of infectious diseases and destroy any food that was harmful to public health. Regulations were tightened to prevent unhealthy overcrowding of houses and inhaling of factory smoke (ventilation of factories and long chimneys was required). The act was initially judged as interfering with individual liberties. Retrospectively, it is considered the greatest act of the century for Great Britain.

Further reading: David D. Douglas et al., eds., *English Historical Documents*, 12 vols. (New York: Oxford University Press, 1950–77); Anne Hardy, *Health and Medicine in Britain since 1860* (New York: Palgrave, 2001); Rosemary Rees, *Poverty and Public Health, 1815–1948* (Oxford, England: Heinemann, 2001); Joel H. Wiener, ed., *Great Britain—The Lion at Home: A Documentary History of Domestic Policy (1689–1973)*, 4 vols. (New York: Chelsea House, 1974).

Public Order (Temporary Measures) Act of 1970, Canadian

Act introduced by Canada's prime minister Pierre Elliott Trudeau on November 2, 1970, and passed by the House of Commons on December 1, 1970; it replaced the WAR MEASURES ACT, which Trudeau had invoked in mid-October and which many had opposed for being too harsh, with less stringent emergency measures designed to deal with the Front de Libération du Québec (FLQ), a terrorist organization that had kidnapped two government officials in its effort to achieve the political separation of Quebec from Canada. Under the new act, membership in this FLQ remained illegal, although attending one or very few meetings was no longer enough to determine membership; in addition, detention of arrested persons became limited to seven days, rather than 21 days as under the previous order; and detainees were guaranteed the right to immediate legal counsel. The act expired on April 30, 1971.

Further reading: D. G. Loomis, *Not Much Glory: Quelling the F.L.Q.* (Toronto: Deneau, 1985).

Public Safety (Emergency Powers) Law of 1927, Irish

In Ireland, last of a series of public safety acts introduced between 1923 and 1927 to stem the violence resulting from the lawless activities of the Irish Republican Army. The act of 1927 was passed following the brutal murder of Kevin O'Higgins who, as Ireland's minister of justice, had sponsored the earlier laws. It banned organizations engaged in the use of arms or in subversive, antigovernment activities and imposed stiff penalties on their members. Authorities were given added powers to search and detain suspects, and a special court was set up to determine the punishment (even life imprisonment or the death penalty) for someone caught with the illegal possession of arms. The act remained in operation until December 1928.

Further reading: Tim P. Coogan, *The IRA*, rev. and updated ed. (London: HarperCollins, 2000); Terence De Vere White, *Kevin O'Higgins* (Dublin: Anvil, 1986).

Public Safety Law of 1953, South African

Legislation (February 24, 1953) enabling the South African government to declare a state of emergency if it felt that public order or safety was at risk. The act was provoked by the race riots stemming from the nonviolent resistance organized by the African and Indian National Congresses in late 1952. Demands for a judicial inquiry into the riots were rejected and in February 1953 Parliament speedily passed this legislation. Thereby the government could issue regulations on any subject other than Parliament, industrial unrest involving nonnative workers, and compulsory military service. It could also arrest and detain any person under these regulations.

Further reading: Tim Nuttall, *From Apartheid to Democracy: South Africa, 1948–1994* (Pietermaritzburg, South Africa: Shuter & Shooter, 1998).

Public Schools Act of 1866, Australian

British parliamentary legislation of 1866 that laid the foundation of the system of compulsory education in New South Wales, Australia. Drafted by Sir Henry Parkes, colonial secretary of New South Wales, the act abolished the National and the Denominational Schools Boards, replacing them by a five-member council of education. The council was entrusted with the management of finances, with establishing and maintaining public schools (including appointment and training of teachers and drafting of the curriculum), and with the disbursement of aid to certified denominational schools. It was to fix a scale of fees for both types of schools, and no child was to be denied admission for financial reasons. In the public schools, four hours a day were to be devoted to secular instruction and one hour for religious instruction. Rather than creating a uniform educational system, the act led to bitter protests from the Roman Catholics, who later established their own schools.

Further reading: G. T. Reynolds, *Public Schools Act of 1866, Rules and Regulations (Amended): For the Guidance of Teachers in the Colony of New South Wales* (Batemans Bay, Australia: Possum Printing, 1992).

Public Utility Holding Company Act, U.S.

See WHEELER-RAYBURN ACT.

Publilian Laws (Leges Publiliae)

Two separate measures enlarging the political power of the plebeians in ancient Rome. The first law, passed about 471 B.C. through the work of Volero Publilius, authorized the Tribal Assembly (Comitia Tributa), instead of the centuries, to elect the tribunes; the plebs thus had the right to initiate laws. About 339 B.C. the Roman consul Quintus Phililius Philo successfully sponsored three laws: at least one censor (census-taking magistrate) had to be a plebeian; legislation approved by the Tribal Assembly had the force of law, provided it received either previous or subsequent consent by the Senate; and legislation handed to the centuries needed prior consent of the Curiae, Rome's great assembly.

See also: HORTENSIAN LAW; TWELVE TABLES, LAW OF THE.

Further reading: Richard E. Mitchell, *Patricians and Plebeians: The Origin of the Roman State* (Ithaca, N.Y.: Cornell University Press, 1990); Thomas Collett Sandars, *The Institutes of Justinian, with English Introduction, Translation, and Notes*, 7th ed. (Westport, Conn.: Greenwood Press, 1970).

Pueblo Speech, Wilson's   Address delivered by U.S. president Woodrow Wilson at Pueblo, Colorado, on September 25, 1919, was part of his national tour to gather support for ratification of the Covenant of the League of Nations (see WILSON'S EXPOSITION OF THE LEAGUE OF NATIONS). The "heart of the covenant" was Article 10, he said: "that no member of the League . . . shall impair the territorial integrity or the political independence of any other member of the League." As in other speeches on the tour, Wilson declared that the covenant was essential to preserve international peace and to give meaning to the sacrifices made by American soldiers in World War I (1914–18). Shortly after the speech, Wilson collapsed, suffering a stroke that ended his tour and effectively ended all hopes for ratification.

See also: LODGE RESERVATIONS.

Further reading: Mortimer Adler, ed., *The Annals of America*, 18 vols. (Chicago: Encyclopedia Britannica, 1968); John M. Cooper, *Breaking the Heart of the World: Woodrow Wilson and the fight for the League of Nations* (New York: Cambridge University Press, 2001); Ralph A. Stone, ed., *Wilson and the League of Nations: Why America's Rejection?* (New York: Holt, Rinehart & Winston, 1967).

Puerto Rican Constitution of 1952   Constitution ratified by popular vote in Puerto Rico on March 3, 1952; later approved by a resolution of the U.S. Congress signed by President Harry S Truman on July 3, 1952. It provided for self-rule for the newly established Commonwealth of Puerto Rico. Although the United States retained certain rights with regard to Puerto Rico (such as the right of the U.S. armed forces to enter the island in the event of invasion or rebellion), the constitution (effective on July 25, 1952) abolished the right of the United States to repeal insular laws and the right to appoint auditors and Supreme Court justices. In addition, the Puerto Rican governor (since 1948 an elected official) could no longer suspend the right of habeas corpus, and thenceforth the Puerto Rican legislature could override the governor's veto.

Further reading: *Constitution of the Commonwealth of Puerto Rico* (San Juan, Puerto Rico: Department of Education Press, 1953); Jorge Heine and Juan M. Garcia-Passalacqua, *The Puerto Rican Question* (New York: Foreign Policy Association, 1984).

Pujo Committee, Report of the   Report on the concentration of control of money and credit in the United States; issued on February 28, 1913, by the House of Representatives Committee on Banking and Currency. The committee, headed by Arsène P. Pujo, found evidence of a "money trust," a "vast and growing concentration of control of money and credit in the hands of a comparatively few men." This concentration was achieved through the consolidation of banks and trusts, the purchase of competitors' stocks, interlocking directorates, extension of control into diverse industries, and joint purchase of security issues. The report led to passage of the FEDERAL RESERVE ACT AND THE CLAYTON ANTITRUST ACT.

Further reading: Mortimer Adler, ed., *The Annals of America*, 18 vols. (Chicago: Encyclopedia Britannica, 1968); Henry Steele Commager, ed., *Documents of American History*, 8th ed. (New York: Appleton-Century-Crofts, 1968).

Purandhar, Treaty of   Agreement made between the peshwa (leader) of the Marathas (Hindu people in India) and the chief governing body of the British East India Company in Calcutta, India, on March 1, 1776. It canceled the peshwa's earlier Treaty of Surat (March 7, 1775), in which the company's Bombay government had supported Raghunatha Rao's claim to the peshwa title, in exchange for control of Salsette Island and Bassein. The Purandhar treaty, however, forced the peshwa into retirement at Kopargaon, on a monthly pension of 25,000 rupees, with certain servants and a retinue of 1,000 horses. The British kept Salsette Island and the revenues from Broach (Gujarat state in India). The Bombay government condemned this treaty and renewed its support for the peshwa in 1778–79. In London, the authorities concurred with Bombay, and so peace was not obtained until the 1782 Treaty of SALBAI.

Further reading: Stewart Gordon, *Marathas, Marauders, and State Formation in Eighteenth-Century India* (Delhi, India: Oxford University Press, 1998).

Pure Food and Drug Act of 1906, U.S.   Federal legislation enacted on June 30, 1906, that prohibited the manufacture, sale, or transportation of adulterated or fraudulently labeled foods and drugs shipped in foreign or interstate commerce. Among the items prohibited were confectionery that contained dangerous colorings or flavorings and food composed of filthy or decomposed animal matter, or containing poisonous ingredients, or adulterated to conceal inferior goods. Labels of proprietary medicines were required to indicate the percentages of narcotics, stimulants, or other potentially harmful ingredients. The act has been strengthened many times.

Further reading: Mortimer Adler, ed., *The Annals of America*, 18 vols. (Chicago: Encyclopedia Britannica, 1968); Lorine S. Goodwin, *The Pure Food, Drink, and Drug Crusaders, 1879–1914* (Jefferson, N.C.: McFarland, 1999); Frank N. Magill, ed., *Great Events from History: American Series*, 3 vols. (Englewood Cliffs, N.J.: Salem Press, 1975).

Putin's Statement of Principles (Joint Statement by the Presidents of the United States of America and the Russian Federation on Principles of Strategic Stability)

Statement issued on June 4, 2000, at the U.S.-Russia Summit in Moscow by U.S. president Bill Clinton and Russian president Vladimir Putin. The summit had been requested by the United States shortly after Putin assumed office to help secure Russia's ratification of the START-II TREATY, which limited the proliferation of strategic nuclear weapons. The statement declared both presidents' intentions to maintain each nation's capability for deterrence while reducing strategic forces in a way that "advances both countries' interests and security." Noting that "the international community faces a dangerous and growing threat of proliferation of weapons of mass destruction and their means of delivery," the statement stressed the presidents' "desire to reverse that process." The joint statement effectively laid to rest the United States's fear that Putin would repudiate past strategic arms treaties and renew the cold war.

Further reading: The White House, Office of the Press Secretary, "Joint Statement," Coalition to Reduce Nuclear Dangers, available online at http://www.clw.org/coalition/summit060400strategic.htm.

Pyrenees, Treaty of the   Peace treaty between King Louis XIV of France and King Philip IV of Spain, ending the Franco-Spanish War of 1648–59; signed on November 7, 1659, on the Isle of Pheasants in the Bidassoa River. It signaled the end of Spanish supremacy in Europe and the rapid rise of French power. Spain ceded parts of Roussillon and Cerdagne (Cerdaña) in the Pyrenees Mountains, which were fixed as the French-Spanish border; in the north Spain made other territorial concessions to France, including part of Artois, Conflans, Hainaut, and Luxembourg, as well as fortresses in Flanders. Louis XIV received in marriage Maria Theresa, eldest daughter of Philip IV, accompanied by a dowry of 500,000 Spanish crowns for surrendering her claims to any inheritance for herself and any children of the marriage. The French prince of Condé was reinstated, and the duke of Lorraine, a Spanish ally, regained some of his privileges, while France obtained Bar and Clermont and right of passage for her troops. By the treaty, England gained control of Dunkirk on the North Sea.

See also: WESTPHALIA, PEACE OF.

Further reading: Francois Bluche, *Louis XIV* (Oxford, England: Basil Blackwell, 1990); Fred L. Israel, ed., *Major Peace Treaties of Modern History, 1648–1967*, 4 vols. (New York: Chelsea House, 1967); Frank N. Magill, ed., *Great Events from History: Modern European Series*, 3 vols. (Englewood Cliffs, N.J.: Salem Press, 1973).

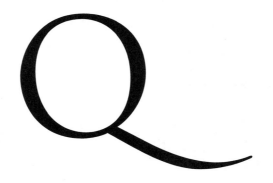

***Quadragesimo Anno* (Pius XI's Encyclical of 1931)**
Encyclical issued on May 25, 1931, by Pope Pius XI, commemorating the 40th anniversary of Pope Leo XIII's encyclical *RERUM NOVARUM*; it addressed, as did the earlier document, the conditions of modern society, and criticized the proposed solutions of extremists, such as the communists. After stating the papacy's observation that exploitation of workers by owners was still present in society, the pope criticized both the endorsement of unrestrained competition and the communist regime's replacement of private enterprise with the state itself and its employment of any means, including violent ones, to attain its ends. Ultimately the document represented the pope's plea to his readers to work toward a more just worker-owner relationship, and to recognize communism's rejection of fundamental human values and rights.

Further reading: Claudia Carlen, comp., *The Papal Encyclicals* (Wilmington N.C.: McGrath Publishing, 1981); Catholic University of America, eds., *New Catholic Encyclopedia* (New York: McGraw-Hill, 1967); Anne Fremantle, *The Papal Encyclicals in Their Historical Context* (New York: Mentor-Omega Books, 1963); David J. O'Brien and Thomas A. Shannon, eds., *Catholic Social Thought: The Documentary Heritage* (Maryknoll, N.Y.: Orbis Books, 1992).

Quadruple Alliance of 1815   Document signed by representatives of Russia, Austria, Prussia, and Great Britain on November 20, 1815, through which the four powers pledged to strive to maintain peace in post-Napoleonic Europe. Spe-

cifically, the powers agreed to be prepared to challenge any attempt on Napoléon's part to return to power in France; to ensure that France's borders remained confined to those established in the Second Peace of Paris (see PARIS, TREATY OF [1815]); to maintain their occupational forces and to supply additional forces should France violate any of the terms of the Second Peace of Paris; and to meet together on a regular basis to discuss issues common to all European nations, the object of which was to maintain peace in Europe. The alliance was to remain in effect for 20 years.

See also: HOLY ALLIANCE OF 1815.

Further reading: Frank N. Magill, ed., *Great Events from History: Modern European Series*, 3 vols. (Englewood Cliffs, N.J.: Salem Press, 1973); Louis L. Snyder, ed., *Fifty Major Documents of the Nineteenth Century* (Princeton, N.J.: D. Van Nostrand, 1955).

Quadruple Alliance of 1718   Peace alliance or league formed on August 2, 1718, when Austria joined the Triple Alliance (Britain, the Dutch republic, and France) in an attempt to force Spain to adhere to the provisions of the Treaty of UTRECHT. Instigated by his wife, Elizabeth Farnese of Parma, and her adviser, Giulio Alberoni, King Philip V of Spain had captured Sardinia and Sicily (these belonged to Austria and Savoy, respectively, as per the terms of the Utrecht treaty). With the support of the Quadruple Alliance, the British navy transported Austrian troops to Sicily and the French troops invaded northern Spain. After trying to subjugate Austrian power in Italy and to support the Jacobite uprisings in England, Spain finally gave in to the allied pressure. By the Treaty of The Hague signed on February 17, 1720, Philip V gave up his claims in Italy, and Victor Amadeus II of Savoy exchanged Sicily for Sardinia with Austria.

See also: TRIPLE ALLIANCE OF 1717.

Further reading: Derek McKay, *Allies of Convenience: Diplomatic Relations Between Great Britain and Austria, 1714–1719* (New York: Garland, 1986).

Quartering Act of 1765

Act passed by the British Parliament in March 1765, requiring the American colonists to provide British soldiers with living quarters wherever barracks were not available. It stated that troops could be housed in public and private barns, empty houses, and taverns, and that persons who supplied the quarters were entitled to payment from their colonial authorities. Actually an amendment to the annual Mutiny Acts (see MUTINY ACT OF 1689), the act was necessitated by escalating defense costs; it met intense opposition, was allowed to lapse in 1770, and later was replaced by the QUARTERING ACT OF 1774.

See also: SUSPENDING ACT OF 1767.

Further reading: Henry Steele Commager, ed., *Documents of American History*, 8th ed. (New York: Appleton-Century-Crofts, 1968); William MacDonald, ed., *Select Charters and Other Documents Illustrative of American History, 1606–1775* (New York: Macmillan, 1899).

Quartering Act of 1774

Statute passed by the British Parliament on June 2, 1774, as part of a punitive policy against the colonies in America. One of the COERCIVE ACTS, it ordered that British troops be provided with quarters (lodging), whenever necessary, in private homes, as well as in public houses and inns, without the consent of their owners. Unlike the other Coercive Acts, the Quartering Act applied to all the colonies.

Further reading: Mortimer Adler, ed., *The Annals of America*, 18 vols. (Chicago: Encyclopaedia Britannica, 1968); David D. Douglas, et al., eds., *English Historical Documents*, 12 vols. (New York: Oxford University Press, 1950–77); William MacDonald, ed., *Select Charters and Other Documents Illustrative of American History, 1606–1775* (New York: Macmillan, 1899).

Quatre Ordonnances

See JULY ORDINANCES OF 1830.

Quebec, Treaty of

Peace agreement between France and the Iroquois Confederacy signed in 1667; it put a temporary end to hostilities between them. Beginning with an attack on an Iroquois group in 1607 by French explorer Samuel de Champlain, who was allied with Indian tribes inimical to the Iroquois, the tribes of the confederacy had harassed and endangered the settlements of New France (Quebec). By defeating the Huron and other tribes, the Iroquois had also drastically reduced the quantity of furs available to the French for trade. The French colonial settlement finally gained enough military strength to resist the hostile tribes and negotiate the agreement.

Further reading: Bruce E. Johansen and Barbara A. Mann, *Encyclopedia of the Haudenosaunee (Iroquois Confederacy)* (Westport, Conn.: Greenwood Press, 2000).

Quebec Act

Law enacted by the British Parliament on June 22, 1774, establishing a permanent civil government for Quebec (or Canada). The act created a highly centralized administration, with legislative power vested in a crown-appointed council, and guaranteed political and religious freedom for Quebec's Roman Catholic French Canadians (this alarmed American Protestants). The act also extended Quebec's southern boundary to the Ohio River and her western boundary to the Mississippi, thus ignoring western land claims by the colonies of Massachusetts, Connecticut, New York, and Virginia. American colonists regarded the act as a punitive measure, as one of the COERCIVE ACTS, although the British had not so intended, seeking simply to improve administrative efficiency.

Further reading: Henry Steele Commager, ed., *Documents of American History*, 8th ed. (New York: Appleton-Century-Crofts, 1968); Peter M. Doll, *Revolution, Religion, and National Identity: Imperial Anglicanism in British North America, 1745–1795* (Madison, N.J.: Fairleigh Dickinson University Press, 2000); Hilda Neatby, *The Quebec Act: Protest and Policy* (Scarborough, Canada: Prentice-Hall of Canada, 1972); Prentice-Hall of Canada, eds., *Canadian Historical Document Series*, 3 vols. (Scarborough, Canada: Prentice-Hall of Canada, 1965–66).

Quebec Resolutions (Seventy-two Resolutions, Canadian)

Resolutions adopted on October 27, 1864, in Quebec City by 33 delegates from the British North American provinces of Canada, Nova Scotia, New Brunswick, Prince Edward Island, and New Foundland attending the Quebec Conference; it outlined a plan for the provinces' union. The document called for a bicameral federal parliament with members of a House of Commons being elected on the basis of representation by population; stipulated that the federal government provide each province with an annual grant determined according to the size of its population; allowed each province to have both its own government and constitution; and proposed the creation of an intercontinental railway linking the provinces. The document ultimately gained legislative approval from the provinces of Canada, Nova Scotia, and New Brunswick and became the basis for the BRITISH NORTH AMERICA ACT OF 1867.

Further reading: *British North America Act and Amendments, 1867–1927* (Ottawa, Canada: F. A. Acland, 1929).

Queiroz Law   Law sanctioned by Emperor Pedro II of Brazil on September 4, 1850, and intended to supplement and strengthen the antislave trade law of November 7, 1831 (which had ordered the liberation of all slaves entering Brazil from that time forward). The legislation, named after Minister of Justice Eusébio de Queiroz, declared the slave trade to be piracy; it also provided that Brazilian ships and all foreign vessels encountered in Brazilian waters that were known to be involved in slave trading were to be seized by Brazilian authorities. Moreover, the law sanctioned severe punishment for the owners and officers of such ships and their accomplices onshore. The Queiroz law was the result of decades of British pressure against the Brazilian slave trade.

Further reading: Celia M. M. de Azevedo, *Abolitionism in the United States and Brazil: A Comparative Perspective* (New York: Garland, 1995); Joaquim Nabuco, *Abolitionism: The Brazilian Antislavery Struggle* (Urbana: University of Illinois Press, 1977); Junius P. Rodriguez, ed., *Chronology of World Slavery* (Santa Barbara, Calif.: ABC-Clio, 1999).

Quicumque Vult   See ATHANASIAN CREED.

Quotations from Chairman Mao Tse-tung   Book of quotations of Chinese communist leader Mao Zedong (Mao Tse-tung) first published in 1964, containing selections of his thought. The quotations included his call to the army to carry out a cultural revolution, praise for the masses and young people, and his call to all to embrace correct thinking, which would bring about positive change in Chinese society. The campaign to study Mao's thought began in the early 1960s and was carried out by Defense Minister Lin Biao. The campaign gathered momentum throughout the decade, and reached its peak during the first few years of China's Cultural Revolution (1966–69). Reports of millions of Red Guards marching through cities and traveling throughout the country brandishing copies of Mao's "Little Red Book" were not uncommon.

Further reading: Mao Zedong, *Quotations from Chairman Mao Tse-tung* (San Francisco, Calif.: Foreign Language Press, 1990); Philip Short, *Mao: A Life* (New York: Henry Holt, 1999); Jonathan Spence, *Mao Zedong* (New York: Penguin Putnam 1999).

R

Race Relations Bill of 1968, British Act passed on April 23, 1968, prohibiting racial discrimination "in the provision of goods, facilities or services, in employment, in organizations of employers or workers, and in the disposal of housing accommodation or other land" in Great Britain. The publication of racially discriminatory advertising was also declared illegal. Enacted following the Commonwealth Immigration Act of 1965 (which rendered nearly 150,000 East African Asians stateless), the act of 1968 extended the scope of the Race Relations Board (created by the act of 1965). Local conciliation committees were established to handle complaints of discrimination, and a community relations commission constituted to encourage racial harmony. A civil suit could be filed if it could be proved that the discrimination was based on "colour, race, or ethnic or national origins," but the act stressed conciliation instead.

Further reading: Simon Abbott, ed., *The Prevention of Racial Discrimination in Britain* (New York: Oxford University Press, 1971); E. J. B. Rose et al., *Colour and Citizenship: A Report on British Race Relations* (New York: Oxford University Press, 1969); Richard Rose, comp., *Policy-Making in Britain: A Reader in Government* (New York: Free Press, 1969); Edward Scobie, *Black Britannia: A History of Blacks in Britain* (Chicago: Johnson Publishing, 1972).

Racketeer Influenced and Corrupt Organizations Act See RICO LAW.

Radom, Constitution of Constitution favorably voted on by the Sejm (national diet) in June 1505 at the walled town of Radom in east-central Poland. It made the Sejm the supreme legislative body, which was elected by the nobles at their provincial assemblies and consisted of the senate and the chamber of envoys. It ruled that new laws needed the Sejm's consent to be enacted. The supremacy of the chamber of envoys over the senate was confirmed, a move that revoked concessions granted to the senate earlier through the Union of Mielnik in 1501. The constitution reflected the growing power of the Polish nobles over other social groups.

Further reading: Mieczyslaw B. Biskupski and James S. Pula, *Polish Democratic Thought from the Renaissance to the Great Emigration: Essays and Documents* (Boulder, Colo.: Eastern European Monographs, 1990); Jacek Jedruch, *Constitutions, Elections, and Legislatures of Poland, 1493–1993: A Guide to Their History* (New York: EJJ Books, 1998).

Railway Administration Act, U.S. Emergency legislation enacted by the U.S. Congress on March 21, 1918, that provided for the operation of the nation's railroads by the federal government for the duration of World War I (and a reasonable period thereafter) and for just compensation to the owners. The U.S. government had taken control of railroads in December 1917 to prevent a rail crisis following the outbreak of the war. The act guaranteed stockholders and bondholders compensation equal to the average annual net operating income between 1914 and 1917. It also established a regional system of administration. The railroads were returned to private ownership in 1920 under the ESCH-CUMMINS TRANSPORTATION ACT.

Further reading: Keith L. Bryant, Jr., ed., *Railroads in the Age of Regulation, 1900–1980* (New York: Facts On File, 1988); Henry Steele Commager, ed., *Documents of American History*, 8th ed. (New York: Appleton-Century-Crofts, 1968).

Railway Labor Act of 1926, U.S.   See WATSON-PARKER ACT.

Raleigh Letter, Clay's   Letter written by Whig politician Henry Clay and published in the *National Intelligencer* on April 17, 1844, opposing the immediate annexation of Texas to the United States, a heated issue in the upcoming presidential campaign. In this letter Clay, the probable Whig candidate, argued that annexation, favored by the South, did not represent the desire of the American people and would certainly lead to a calamitous war with Mexico and perhaps her European allies. He stated that the United States should concentrate on developing her own strengths and resources before adding foreign territory. Clay also considered the annexation a threat to the integrity of the Union, as it embodied the dispute between the slave-holding and the free states. His letter supported the existence of Texas as an independent republic.

See also: ALABAMA LETTERS.

Further reading: Calvin Colton et al., eds., *The Works of Henry Clay, Comprising His Life, Correspondence and Speeches*, 10 vols. (New York: G. P. Putnam's Sons, 1904); Henry Steele Commager, ed., *Documents of American History*, 8th ed. (New York: Appleton-Century-Crofts, 1968); James E. Hopkins and Mary W. M. Hargreaves, eds., *The Papers of Henry Clay*, 10 vols. (Lexington: University of Kentucky Press, 1959); Merrill D. Peterson, *The Great Triumvirate: Webster, Clay, and Calhoun* (New York: Oxford University Press, 1987).

Rambouillet Decree   Legislation extending the provisions of the BAYONNE DECREE, promulgated at Rambouillet, France, on March 23, 1810, by French emperor Napoléon Bonaparte. A retaliatory gesture against the U.S. NON-INTERCOURSE ACT (1809), it ordered the capture and sale of any American ship (and its cargo) found in French territorial waters whether or not it had violated any previous Napoleonic decrees (see FONTAINEBLEAU DECREES; MILAN DECREES). The United States later pressed for compensation for losses sustained under this and other decrees.

Further reading: David S. Heidler and Jeanne T. Heidler, *Encyclopedia of the War of 1812* (Santa Barbara, Calif.: ABC-Clio, 1997).

Randolph Plan   See VIRGINIA PLAN.

Rapallo, Treaty of (1920)   Treaty concluded at Rapallo, Italy, on November 12, 1920, by Italy and Yugoslavia, represented by foreign ministers Carlo Sforza and Ante Trumbić, respectively; it brought an end to the two countries' dispute over their common border, and particularly over possession of the Adriatic port of Fiume (Rijeka). Through the treaty, Fiume became a free state; Italy received the city of Zara (Zadar) and the Dalmatian islands of Creš (Cherso), Lussino (Losinj), and Lastovo; and Italy renounced all claims on what remained of Dalmatia. The dispute, which had arisen over Italy's dissatisfaction with the settlement reached at the Paris Peace Conference of 1919 (which awarded Fiume to Yugoslavia), was resumed several years later during Fascist leader Benito Mussolini's rule, when the Italians once again expressed dissatisfaction with the status quo.

Further reading: Carlo Sforza, *Diplomatic Europe since the Treaty of Versailles* (New Haven, Conn.: Yale University Press, 1928); Denis Mack Smith, *Modern Italy: A Political History* (Ann Arbor: University of Michigan Press, 1997).

Rapallo, Treaty of (1922)   Treaty signed at Rapallo, Italy, on April 16, 1922, by German foreign minister Walther Rathenau and Soviet commissar of foreign affairs Georgi V. Chicherin, representing the Weimar Republic of Germany and Soviet Russia, respectively; ratified at Berlin on January 31, 1923; it provided each party with its first alliance with a major power in post–World War I Europe. Through the treaty both parties agreed to renounce all claims for compensation for expenses incurred in connection with the war; to resume diplomatic relations; to establish commercial relations on a most-favored-nation basis; and to cooperate in economic matters to their mutual advantage. The treaty of alliance remained effective until Germany's invasion of Soviet Russia in 1941.

Further reading: E. J. Feuchtwanger, *From Weimar to Hitler: Germany, 1918–33* (New York: St. Martin's Press, 1993); Gabriel Gorodetsky, *Soviet Foreign Policy, 1917–1991: A Retrospective* (Portland, Ore.: Frank Cass, 1994).

Rastatt, Treaty of   Agreement between France's king Louis XIV and Holy Roman Emperor Charles VI, made at Rastatt, Germany, on March 7, 1714; it helped end the War of the Spanish Succession (1701–14), along with the Treaties of BADEN and UTRECHT. France's borders were preserved, and she received Alsace. The Holy Roman Empire regained control over all territories east of the Rhine River and received Naples, Sardinia, Milan, and the Netherlands (all taken from Spain). Charles continued to refuse to recognize Philip V as king of Spain, maintaining his claim to that throne. Likewise, Philip refused to recognize imperial possession of former Spanish lands.

Further reading: Linda Frey, *The Treaties of the War of the Spanish Succession: An Historical and Critical Dictionary* (Westport, Conn.: Greenwood Press, 1995); Fred L. Israel, ed., *Major Peace Treaties of Modern History, 1648–1967*, 4 vols. (New York: Chelsea House, 1967); Heinz-Joachim Mullenbrock, *The Culture of Contention: A Rhetorical Analysis of the Public Controversy about the Ending of the War of the Spanish Succession, 1710–1713* (Munich: Fink, 1997).

Rathbun v. United States   See HUMPHREY'S EXECUTOR V. UNITED STATES.

Ratisbon, Truce of   See REGENSBURG, TRUCE OF.

Ratisbon Interim   Provisional arrangement between Roman Catholics and Lutherans at Ratisbon (Regensburg, Germany), devised and declared by Holy Roman Emperor Charles V on February 25, 1541. It reflected Charles's effort, at a time when the Turkish threat demanded his full attention, to settle matters in dispute between Catholics and Protestants. Charles declared that the clergy could make reforms on their own and could not be deprived of revenues due them. By the interim, three Catholics and three Lutherans were named to prepare provisions of religious understanding between them. An accord was reached on all issues except the sacraments and the authority of the church.

See also: AUGSBURG INTERIM.

Further reading: Karl Brandi, *The Emperor Charles V: The Growth and Destiny of a Man and of a World-Empire* (London: Harvester, 1980); Catholic University of America, eds., *New Catholic Encyclopedia* (New York: McGraw-Hill, 1967).

Ravenna, Decree of   Decree issued in 1232 by Holy Roman Emperor Frederick II, king of Sicily, against the organization of all communes, leagues, councils, and the placement of officials in public office without his approval. The decree was not particularly effective, for the emperor resided in Italy (and thus could not see to its enforcement) and his son Henry, king of Germany, actively supported the towns and would occasionally issue edicts to their advantage. Thus the towns continued to prosper and to grow in power.

Further reading: David Abulafia, *Frederick II: A Medieval Emperor* (London: Allen Lane The Penguin Press, 1988); Georgina Masson, *Frederick II of Hohenstaufen: A Life* (London: Secker & Warburg, 1973).

Rawalpindi, Treaty of   Agreement of August 8, 1919, ending the Third Anglo-Afghan War (1919) and Britain's sovereignty over Afghanistan. Neither side was winning the war and the Afghans finally called for an armistice on May 28, 1919. After prolonged negotiations at Rawalpindi, Pakistan, both sides committed themselves to maintaining peace in the region. Britain confiscated the arrears in subsidy and discontinued further subsidies to the Afghan government. The import of arms through India was halted, and it was agreed to establish an Afghan mission (after six months) to discuss matters of mutual interest and renew friendship. Afghanistan was forced to accept the Durand Line as the Indo-Afghan border,

with a proviso that her unmarked areas would be settled later by a British boundary commission. The commission's verdict, Afghanistan was assured, would not affect her internal or external independence.

Further reading: N. D. Ahmad, *The Survival of Afghanistan, 1747–1979: A Diplomatic History with an Analytic and Reflective Approach* (Lahore, Pakistan: Institute of Islamic Culture, 1990); Erik Goldstein, *Wars and Peace Treaties, 1816–1991* (New York: Routledge, 1992).

Reagan's First Inaugural Address   Speech delivered by Ronald W. Reagan on January 20, 1981, at his inauguration as 40th president of the United States. Stressing his belief that big government was the cause of America's economic problems, not the solution to those problems, Reagan announced his intention to "curb the size and influence of the federal establishment." "Government must provide opportunity, not smother it; foster productivity, not stifle it," he stated. To create a healthy economy, he sought to lighten the tax burden. He also demanded recognition of the distinction between the powers granted by the U.S. CONSTITUTION to the federal government and those reserved to the states.

Further reading: *Inaugural Addresses of the Presidents of the United States from George Washington 1789 to George Bush 1989*, bicentennial ed. (Washington, D.C.: Government Printing Office, 1989); Davis N. Lott, *The Presidents Speak: The Inaugural Addresses of the American Presidents from Washington to Clinton* (New York: H. Holt, 1994); Ronald Reagan, *Speaking My Mind: Selected Speeches* (New York: Simon & Schuster, 1989); Halford Ryan, ed., *The Inaugural Addresses of Twentieth-Century American Presidents* (Westport, Conn.: Praeger, 1993).

Rebellion Losses Bill, Canadian   Bill passed by both houses of Parliament of the province of Canada in 1849, providing for financial compensation to those in the administrative district of Canada East (Quebec) whose property had been damaged during Papineau's Rebellion of 1837 (a rebellion by French Canadians under Louis Joseph Papineau against British rule in Quebec). The significance of the bill lay in the fact that Canada's governor general, Lord Elgin, in spite of his own reluctance and the vehement opposition of conservatives in the government, signed the bill into law on the advice of his ministers. His signature thus indicated the government's acceptance of the principle of "responsible government," the principle that the governor, a British-appointed official, was responsible to the will of the majority.

Further reading: Phillip A. Buckner, *The Transition to Responsible Government: British Policy in British North America, 1815–1850* (Westport, Conn.: Greenwood Press, 1985); James Knight, ed., *The Formative Years; Canada 1812–1871* (Toronto: Ryerson Press, 1968).

Reciprocal Tariff Act, U.S. (Trade Agreements Act)

Federal legislation enacted on June 12, 1934, that authorized the U.S. president to negotiate agreements to reduce tariff rates, up to 50 percent, with foreign countries that would reciprocate with similar concessions for American goods. The act allowed such agreements to take effect without congressional ratification. They were to be based on the most-favored-nation principle: If the United States negotiated a treaty with one nation to lower the tariff on one item, other countries—so long as they did not discriminate against the United States—could enjoy equal terms.

Further reading: Mortimer Adler, ed., *The Annals of America*, 18 vols. (Chicago: Encyclopaedia Britannica, 1968); Abraham Berglund, "Reciprocal Trade Agreements Act of 1934," *American Economic Review* 25, no. 3 (September 1935).

Reciprocity Treaty (Elgin-Marcy Treaty)

Reciprocal trade agreement in 1854 between the United States and Canada, in which the United States greatly reduced or eliminated tariffs on Canadian produce in exchange for fishing and navigation rights along the Saint Lawrence River. Lord Elgin (James Bruce), governor general of Canada, and William L. Marcy, U.S. secretary of state, handled the negotiations leading to the treaty (June 5, 1854), which was the first pact in which U.S. tariffs were reduced in exchange for reciprocal concessions from a foreign nation. The pact helped to assure a steady flow of commerce between the two nations for 12 years. Renewal failed in 1866 as a result of Canadian tariffs on manufactured goods, U.S. protectionist pressures in some Northern states, and alleged pro-Confederate sentiment in Canada and Britain.

Further reading: Mortimer Adler, ed., *The Annals of America*, 18 vols. (Chicago: Encyclopaedia Britannica, 1968); Donald C. Masters, *The Reciprocity Treaty of 1854: Its History, Its Relation to British Colonial and Foreign Policy and to the Development of Canadian Fiscal Autonomy* (Toronto: McClelland and Stewart, 1969); Charles C. Tansill, *The Canadian Reciprocity Treaty of 1854* (Baltimore: Johns Hopkins Press, 1922).

Reconstruction Acts, U.S.

Series of four related acts, passed over vetoes by President Andrew Johnson between March 1867 and March 1868; they divided the former Confederate states (except for Tennessee, which had already been readmitted to the Union) into five military districts and gave to the military commanders control of all civil functions, including the power to organize new governments, control registration and voting, and appoint and remove state officials. The first act required ratification of the FOURTEENTH AMENDMENT before a state could be readmitted to the Union. The last act provided that a majority of votes cast was sufficient to ratify a new state constitution. Between 1868 and 1870 all of the Southern states were readmitted.

Further reading: Mortimer Adler, ed., *The Annals of America*, 18 vols. (Chicago: Encyclopaedia Britannica, 1968); Henry Steele Commager, ed., *Documents of American History*, 8th ed. (New York: Appleton-Century-Crofts, 1968); David H. Donald, et al., *The Civil War and Reconstruction* (New York: Norton, 2001); Michael Perman, ed., *Major Problems in the Civil War and Reconstruction*, 2d ed. (Boston: Houghton Mifflin, 1998).

Recusancy Laws

Legislation reintroduced in July 1604 by King James I of England to penalize recusants, dissenting persons who willfully refused to attend the services of the Church of England, mainly Roman Catholics. Popish recusants were also punished for hearing, saying, and assisting at Mass. Various recusancy laws had been passed in the reign of Queen Elizabeth I (from 1558 onward) but they were not always fully enforced. However, the Main and Bye Plots of 1603 (simultaneous conspiracies to dethrone or imprison James) and political, Puritan pressure within Parliament forced the king to revive these penal laws, where punishment was usually in the form of fines or confiscation of property or imprisonment in some cases.

Further reading: Brian Magee, *The English Recusants; A Study of the Post-Reformation Catholic Survival and the Operation of the Recusancy Laws* (London: Burns, Oates & Washbourne, 1938).

Redistribution (of Seats) Act of 1885, British

Complete revision of the electoral map effected by British prime minister William Gladstone's administration in June 1885 to complement its REFORM ACT OF 1884. The last in a series of parliamentary reforms, it maintained the county-borough separation, but provided for their subdivision into single-member constituencies (36 boroughs lost one member), except in the city of London and in cities and boroughs with populations between 50,000 and 165,000. Universities retained two members. Boroughs with populations less than 15,000 (72 in all) were incorporated into surrounding counties. Additional representation was given to London (37), Liverpool (6), Birmingham (4), Glasgow (4), Yorkshire (16), and Lancashire (15). In Ireland, all the peasants secured the vote. Thus, the individual became the basis of electoral representation and "one vote, one value" its master principle.

Further reading: Randolph L. Braham, ed., *Documents on Major European Governments* (New York: Knopf/Borzoi, 1966; Frank N. Magill, ed., *Great Events from History: Modern European Series*, 3 vols. (Englewood Cliffs, N.J.: Salem Press, 1973); Joel H. Wiener, ed., *Great Britain—The Lion at Home: A Documentary History of Domestic Policy (1689–1973)* (New York: Chelsea House, 1974).

Reed Treaty

See U.S.-CHINESE TREATY OF 1858.

Reflections on the Revolution in France Treatise written and published by Edmund Burke, Irish-born British philosopher, politician, and orator, in November 1790, wherein he attacked the principles of the French Revolution (accurately predicting the instability and violence it would lead to) and discussed how political change could be achieved within the constitutional framework. A brilliant exposition of conservative thought, it explores Burke's view of man as an organism whose character is shaped by its history, with all its members bound to each other by invisible influences. Burke's recognition of the unconscious and historical elements in human life is his greatest contribution to political thought. Its weakness is Burke's inability to see the revolution as a nation's revolt against suffering and oppression. The publication of the treatise led to Burke's separation from the Whigs and their leader, Charles Fox.

Further reading: J. C. D. Clark, ed., *Reflections on the Revolution in France* (Stanford, Calif.: Stanford University Press, 2001); Charles W. Eliot, ed., *The Harvard Classics*, 51 vols. (New York: P. F. Collier & Son, 1938); Mark A. Kishlansky, ed., *Sources of the West: Readings in Western Civilization*, 4th ed., vol. 2 (New York: Longman, 2001).

Reform Act of 1832, British Measure enacted on June 4, 1832, in Britain by the Whig government of Prime Minister Charles Grey. The bill altered the allotment of electoral seats and the eligibility for voting. Fifty-six English boroughs were disenfranchised, 30 lost one member; the seats so released were redistributed in areas with little or no previous representation. In England, 22 new two-member boroughs and 19 single-member boroughs were created; extra seats were created in Wales (5), Ireland (5), and Scotland (8). Voting rights were conferred (in the counties) to freeholders of property worth 40 shillings a year, £10 copyholders, £50 short-lease holders and tenants, and (in the boroughs) to £10 householders. This measure increased the electorate by 50 percent. Intended to quell the wave of unrest in the country, the bill shifted the balance of power to a new industrial and commercial class, while still leaving the poor without a vote.

Further reading: Frank N. Magill, ed., *Great Events from History: Modern European Series*, 3 vols. (Englewood Cliffs, N.J.: Salem Press, 1973); *The Reform Act of 1832* (Crewe, England: Historical Discovery, 1991); Louis L. Snyder, ed., *Fifty Major Documents of the Nineteenth Century* (Princeton, N.J.: D. Van Nostrand, 1955); Joel H. Wiener, ed., *Great Britain— The Lion at Home: A Documentary History of Domestic Policy (1689–1973)* (New York: Chelsea House, 1974).

Reform Act of 1867, British (Representation of the People Act) Landmark bill passed by the British Parliament on August 15, 1867, extending the franchise to all householders and ratepayers (paying £10 per annum) in the boroughs and to £5 leaseholders and £12 occupiers in the counties. The electorate thus doubled—increasing by 938,000 voters. Drafted by Benjamin Disraeli, chancellor of the exchequer, and supported by the conservative government of Prime Minister Lord Derby, the act significantly redistributed 45 parliamentary seats—nine new boroughs were created, 25 extra members allotted to the counties, and a third member each to Manchester, Birmingham, Liverpool, and Leeds. The boroughs of Salford and Merthyr were given a second member, while boroughs with a population less than 10,000 were restricted to one instead of two members each. A personal triumph for Disraeli and a boost for political democracy, the act's weakness lay in its denial of the vote to laborers in the counties, where the landed gentry continued to wield power.

Further reading: Catherine Hall et al., *Defining the Victorian Nation: Class, Race, Gender and the Reform Act of 1867* (Cambridge, England: Cambridge University Press, 2000); Frank N. Magill, ed., *Great Events from History: Modern European Series*, 3 vols. (Englewood Cliffs, N.J.: Salem Press, 1973); Louis L. Snyder, ed., *Fifty Major Documents of the Nineteenth Century* (Princeton, N.J.: D. Van Nostrand, 1955); Joel H. Wiener, ed., *Great Britain—The Lion at Home: A Documentary History of Domestic Policy (1689–1973)* (New York: Chelsea House, 1974).

Reform Act of 1884, British (Representation of the People Act) Legislation by William Gladstone's government on December 6, 1884, which extended the household franchise to the rural classes in Britain, thus rectifying a glaring omission in the REFORM ACT OF 1867. It increased the electorate from 3 to 5 million, leaving only the domestic help, bachelors living with their families, and the homeless without a vote. The bill passed the House of Commons but the Lords refused to consider it, unless accompanied by a corresponding redistribution of parliamentary seats. Gladstone conceded this demand and, in 1885, the Redistribution Act was passed. By this, universities and towns with a population between 50,000 and 165,000 retained two members each, whereas the rest of the country was redivided into single-member constituencies. Boroughs with fewer than 15,000 people lost their representation, those between 15,000 to 50,000 were allowed one member each, and the counties allotted one member for every 50,000 voters.

Further reading: Frank N. Magill, ed., *Great Events from History: Modern European Series*, 3 vols. (Englewood Cliffs, N.J.: Salem Press, 1973); Louis L. Snyder, ed., *Fifty Major Documents of the Nineteenth Century* (Princeton, N.J.: D. Van Nostrand, 1955); Joel H. Wiener, ed., *Great Britain—The Lion at Home: A Documentary History of Domestic Policy (1689–1973)* (New York: Chelsea House, 1974).

Reform Act of 1868, Irish Legislation of July 13, 1868, supplemental to Britain's REFORM ACT OF 1867, lowering the borough voting rights in Ireland to householders paying a minimum of £4. However, the British Parliament left unchanged the Irish county franchise and the number of parliamentary seats allotted to Ireland. William Gladstone, leader of Britain's Liberal Party, espoused the parliamentary reforms of 1867 and 1868, which had passed under the prime ministries of Lord Derby and his successor, Benjamin Disraeli, leaders of the Conservative Party; at the end of 1868 the general elections gave the Liberals control and Gladstone the prime ministry.

See also: DISESTABLISHMENT ACT OF 1869.

Further reading: Joel H. Wiener, ed., *Great Britain—The Lion at Home: A Documentary History of Domestic Policy (1689–1973)* (New York: Chelsea House, 1974).

Reform Act of 1868, Scottish

Act of July 13, 1868, by which the British Parliament conferred voting rights on all rate-paying male householders in the boroughs and on occupiers paying £14 in the counties of Scotland. An extension of Britain's REFORM ACT OF 1867, it also gave Scotland seven more seats in the British Parliament—the universities secured their representation, Glasgow received a third member, and Dundee a second.

See also: REFORM ACT OF 1868, IRISH.

Further reading: Joel H. Wiener, ed., *Great Britain—The Lion at Home: A Documentary History of Domestic Policy (1689–1973)* (New York: Chelsea House, 1974).

Refugee Relief Act of 1953, U.S.

Emergency federal U.S. legislation enacted on August 7, 1953, that allowed a total of 214,000 German, Italian, Greek, Far Eastern, and other refugees (186,000 of them victims of communist persecution, the remainder in specified categories) to enter the United States, outside regular immigration quotas, over the following three years. An accelerated program, adopted in 1956 in response to the Soviet suppression of the Hungarian Revolution of 1956, allowed the entry of 21,500 Hungarian refugees into the United States. By a U.S. law in 1958, Hungarian immigrants could become resident aliens if they lived in the country for two years.

See also: IMMIGRATION ACT OF 1965, U.S.

Further reading: Gil Loescher, *Calculated Kindness; Refugees and America's Half-Open Door, 1945 to the Present* (New York: Free Press, 1986); U.S. Department of State, Public Services Division, *The Refugee Relief Act of 1953; What It Is, How It Works* (Washington, D.C.: Government Printing Office, 1954).

Regensburg, Truce of (Truce of Ratisbon)

French king Louis XIV's 20-year truce with Spain and the Holy Roman Emperor Leopold I, concluded at Regensburg in Bavaria on August 15, 1684, following Louis's successful invasion of Catalonia and the Low Countries. Also known as the Truce of Ratisbon, after the Diet of Ratisbon (where its preliminary articles were drafted), it allowed the French king to retain all the territories he had secured by reunion prior to August 1,

1681. In addition, he was given Strasbourg, Kehl, Luxembourg, and a number of villages in the Netherlands for 20 years. A war-weary and financially exhausted Spain was forced to agree to the terms, as was the Emperor Leopold, who was preoccupied with the advancing Ottoman Turks.

Further reading: Ian Dunlop, *Louis XIV* (New York: St. Martin's Press, 2000); John P. Spielman, *Leopold I of Austria* (New Brunswick, N.J.: Rutgers University Press, 1977).

Regnans in Excelsis

Papal bull excommunicating and deposing England's queen Elizabeth I, issued by Pope Pius V on February 25, 1570. Denouncing her as "that servant of iniquity . . . pretended Queen of England," as an usurper and a heretic who had rejected the true religion restored by her predecessor (Mary I), the decree released her subjects from their oaths of allegiance (see SUPREMACY, ACT OF [1559]), instructing them to disobey her laws instead. Further, for appointing "ignoble and heretical persons" as her counsellors and for authorizing the publication of books that taught "the impious constitutions and atrocious mysteries of Calvin," Elizabeth was "wholly deprived of her pretended right to the . . . kingdom." The last such papal decree ever issued on a reigning monarch, it upset France, Spain, and the Holy Roman Empire, caught the English Catholics in an uneasy bind, and eventually led to the passage of the Elizabethan penal laws against Catholics (imprisonment or fines for those who did not attend Anglican services, continued to celebrate Mass and recognize papal supremacy, and aided Jesuits expelled from England).

Further reading: Catholic University of America, eds., *New Catholic Encyclopedia* (New York: McGraw-Hill, 1967); Anne Fremantle, *The Papal Encyclicals in Their Historical Context* (New York: Mentor-Omega Books, 1963); Frank N. Magill, ed., *Great Events from History: Modern European Series*, 3 vols. (Englewood Cliffs, N.J.: Salem Press, 1973).

Regula Monachorum   See BENEDICTINE RULE.

Regulating Act of 1773, British

Parliamentary legislation in 1773, empowering the government of Britain to regulate the British East India Company's lands and affairs in India, especially in Bengal, where the company's mismanagement had nearly led to its bankruptcy. Introduced by Lord North, the act appointed a governor general based in Fort William (Bengal), with authority over the presidencies of Bengal, Madras, and Bombay; while assisted by a council of four, the governor general had only a casting vote but no veto power. In Calcutta, a supreme court of four English judges was set up for all British subjects. In Britain, instead of the annual election of 24 company directors, six judges were to be elected for four-year terms each. The act prohibited company officials from engaging in trade and receiving presents from natives. It was amended in 1784 (see PITT'S INDIA ACT), but it was an important first step in the British government's eventual complete takeover of the East India Company in 1858.

Further reading: *British Parliamentary Papers: House of Commons Sessional Papers of the Eighteenth Century, George III, East India Company, 1767 to 1773* (Delhi, India: Amar Prakashan, 1985); H. V. Bowen, *Revenue and Reform: The Indian Problem in British Politics, 1757–1773* (New York: Cambridge University Press, 1991); Manik L. Gupta, *Constitutional Development of India: From the Regulating Act (1773) to the Indian Independence Act (1947)* (New Delhi, India: Atlantic Publishers & Distributors, 1989).

Reichenbach, Convention of (1790)
Agreement concluded at Reichenbach, Germany (Dzierzoniów, Poland), on July 27, 1790, preventing war between Prussia under King Frederick William II and Austria under Holy Roman Emperor Leopold II. Austria had reluctantly entered the Russo-Turkish War of 1787–92 as Russia's ally and had rightly become fearful of Prussian expansionist ambitions to the south (Prussia had made a pact with the Ottoman Turks). In exchange for peace with Prussia, Austria agreed to negotiate for peace with the Turks and to return territory won in the war. Prussia agreed to certain territorial readjustments advantageous to Austria, provided the latter consented to a future territorial settlement advantageous to Prussia. That "future settlement" was the second partition of Poland (see RUSSO-PRUSSIAN TREATY OF 1793).

Further reading: David Blackbourn, *The Long Nineteenth Century: A History of Germany, 1780–1918* (New York: Oxford University Press, 1998); Charles W. Ingrao, *The Habsburg Monarchy, 1618–1815* (New York: Cambridge University Press, 2000).

Reichenbach, Convention of (1813)
Agreement concluded at Reichenbach (Dzierzoniów, Poland) on June 27, 1813, between Austria (formally, still allied with France) and Prussia and Russia, in which the three powers made arrangements for Austria's entrance into the war against France, together with Prussia and Russia. Through the convention Austria promised to enter the war against France should the latter fail to agree, before the conclusion of the armistice then in effect, to the following terms: the partition of the Grand Duchy of Warsaw among the three contracting powers; France's renunciation of conquered territory in northern Germany; and the restoration of Illyria (territory along the Dalmatian coast) to Austria. In addition, the contracting parties agreed on the number of troops to be provided by each. Austria declared war on France following the latter's rejection of the terms.

See also: PLÄSWITZ, ARMISTICE OF.

Further reading: David Blackbourn, *The Long Nineteenth Century: A History of Germany, 1780–1918* (New York: Oxford University Press, 1998); Charles W. Ingrao, *The Habs-*

burg Monarchy, 1618–1815 (New York: Cambridge University Press, 2000).

Reichenbach, Treaties of (1813)
Treaties concluded at Reichenbach (Dzierzoniów, Poland) in 1813 between Prussia and Great Britain (June 14) and between Russia and Great Britain (June 15), in which the powers made arrangements for their common defense against the armies of Emperor Napoléon Bonaparte of France at the close of the Napoleonic Wars (1803–15). Through the treaties Great Britain agreed to provide Russia and Prussia with subsidy payments for each to continue the war against France. In addition, the number of troops that each was to provide was stipulated; and each party agreed not to negotiate separately with Napoléon. The treaties preceded the 1813 Convention of REICHENBACH, in which Austria made arrangements to join the coalition (later known as the Sixth Coalition) against France.

Further reading: David Blackbourn, *The Long Nineteenth Century: A History of Germany, 1780–1918* (New York: Oxford University Press, 1998); Clive Emsley, *Britain and the French Revolution* (New York: Longman, 2000); Wendy Hinde, *Castlereagh* (London: Collins, 1981); Charles W. Ingrao, *The Habsburg Monarchy, 1618–1815* (New York: Cambridge University Press, 2000).

Reichstadt Agreement
Austro-Russian agreement of July 8, 1876, concerning disposition of territory in the Balkans prior to the end of the Turko-Serbian war of 1876–78. If the Turks were victorious, the two powers would insist on the status quo antebellum, and demand institution of the reforms described in the BERLIN MEMORANDUM. If the Ottoman empire (Turkey) were defeated, Russia was to take southern Bessarabia, with access to the mouth of the Danube; and Austria would claim the major portion of Bosnia and Herzegovina, with the remainder going to Serbia and Montenegro (the relative portions assigned to Austria, Serbia, and Montenegro differed between the Austrian and Russian texts of the agreement). If the Ottoman Empire collapsed, Bulgaria and Rumelia were to become autonomous states or independent principalities, Greece would acquire some territory, and Constantinople would be declared a free city. The Reichstadt Agreement was superseded by the BUDAPEST CONVENTION of January 15, 1877.

Further reading: Barbara Jelavich, *Russia's Balkan Entanglements, 1806–1914* (New York: Cambridge University Press, 1991); R. W. Seton-Watson, *The Southern Slav Question and the Habsburg Monarchy* (New York: H. Fertig, 1969).

Reinsurance Treaty
Russo-German treaty signed on June 18, 1887, exactly six years after the THREE EMPERORS' ALLIANCE, from which it evolved. Like the earlier treaty, this one also reaffirmed the principle of the closure of the Straits (of the Bosporus and Dardanelles), with Germany pledged to benevolent neutrality and diplomatic support if Russia found it

necessary to defend the entrance to the Black Sea. The main provision, however, was a promise of benevolent neutrality if either party were at war with a third power, unless Germany attacked France, or Russia attacked Austria. In addition, Russia's special interest in Bulgaria was recognized, and a secret protocol promised German assistance in restoring internal order in that Balkan country. The three-year treaty was not renewed by Germany, after Otto von Bismarck resigned as German chancellor in 1890, because of the potential conflict with the German commitments to the TRIPLE ALLIANCE OF 1882 and FRANCO-RUSSIAN ALLIANCE OF 1892.

Further reading: *The Background of the War; History and Texts* (Boston: World Peace Foundation, 1918); Louis L. Snyder, ed., *Documents of German History* (New Brunswick, N.J.: Rutgers University Press, 1958); Louis L. Snyder, ed., *Fifty Major Documents of the Nineteenth Century* (Princeton, N.J.: D. Van Nostrand, 1955).

Religious Land Use and Institutionalized Persons Act, U.S.

Legislation (Public Law 106–274) "to protect religious liberty" enacted on September 22, 2000. It banned government (state or local) from imposing land-use regulations (for example, zoning) that created "a substantial burden on the religious exercise of a person, including a religious assembly or institution" unless it could establish that the imposition promoted "a compelling government interest" in the "least restrictive" manner possible. Similarly, the law also protected the religious exercise of people in institutions (hospitals, prisons, residential facilities). They could seek redress in court. It forbade the use of such regulations to discriminate against religious institutions and denominations, or to exclude and limit religious groups from certain areas. It was sponsored by U.S. representative Charles T. Canady of Florida as an amendment to the Religious Freedom Restoration Act of 1993, certain provisions of which had been struck down in a controversial 1997 decision by the U.S. Supreme Court.

Further reading: Library of Congress, *The Religious Land Use and Institutionalized Persons Act*, Thomas Legislative Information on the Internet, available online at http://thomas.locgov/bss/d106/d106laws.html.

Remonstrance of Grievances

List of Irish grievances (consisting of 16 articles) submitted to England's Parliament in 1640. Among these were complaints about the arbitrary decisions of the lord deputy, the perversion of law by the judges, and the tremendous power vested in the Court of Commission. The Irish also protested against the lack of security for life or property, against the punishment given to those who spoke out freely, against the increase in monopolies and the outrageous fees charged by the clergy.

Further reading: Martyn Bennett, *Historical Dictionary of the British and Irish Civil Wars, 1637–1660* (Chicago: Fitzroy Dearborn, 2000); Aidan Clarke, *The Old English in Ireland, 1625–42* (Portland, Ore.: Four Courts Press, 2000).

Remonstrance of 1610

Petition with five articles of faith accepted by the Arminians (followers of the late Jacobus Arminius, a Dutch theologian), presented to the states-general of Holland in 1610. The Arminians (also called Remonstrants because of the document) opposed the strict Calvinist conception of predestination (man's salvation foreordained by God) and were less dogmatic and more liberal in their Protestant doctrine. The five articles were (1) predestination is conditional, not absolute, (2) universal atonement; (3) regeneration of man through the Holy Spirit; (4) divine grace may be resisted, yet is needed for man to think and do good; and (5) sin or fall from grace can be resisted through the help of the Holy Spirit. Under the leadership of Simon Episcopius, the Arminians presented the Remonstrance for Holland and West Friesland.

See also: DORT, CANONS OF.

Further reading: Laurence M. Vance, *The Other Side of Calvinism*, rev. ed. (Pensacola, Fla.: Vance Publications, 1999).

Reno v. American Civil Liberties Union

Law case (521 U.S. 844, 117 S.Ct. 2329 1997) filed by the American Civil Liberties Union (ACLU) challenging two provisions of the Communications Decency Act (CDA) of 1996 and resulting in a landmark decision issued on June 26, 1997—the Supreme Court's first case pertaining to free speech and online communications. The CDA provisions declared the display or distribution of "indecent" and "patently offensive" materials to minors (under 18 years of age) through online networks a crime and punishable as such. In a 7-2 ruling, the Court acknowledged that while it was in the national interest to protect minors from access to pornographic materials, it agreed with the three-judge district court in Philadelphia that the CDA violated an individual's rights to free speech. Further, the CDA was "so vague that it violates the Fifth Amendment." It might prevent the dissemination of useful health-related information online because it could be construed as unsuitable for children. Finally, in the opinion of the Court, until new technology made it possible to verify when minors were accessing such materials, the law could not be enforced.

Further reading: American Civil Liberties Union, "Supreme Court of the United States," Courts American Civil Liberties Union Freedom Network, available online at http://www.aclu.org/court/renovacludec.html.

Rense, Declaration of

See RHENS, DECLARATION OF.

Renville Agreement

Truce signed on board the U.S. warship *Renville* at Batavia (Jakarta) on January 17, 1948, by Raden Abdul Kadur Widjojoatmodjo, representing the Netherlands, and Premier Amur Sjarifudin of the Republic of Indonesia; it brought an end to the conflict between the two sides over the independence of Indonesia, a former Dutch colony. The agreement provided for Dutch sovereignty over the Republic of Indonesia until the United States of Indonesia, which would consist of the republic, Kalimantan (Borneo), and the Great East, was formed (see CHERIBON AGREEMENT); and for the Netherlands's possession of territory gained during the war, which included Java's eastern plantation coast and Sumatra's oil fields. Indonesia's sole gain was the promise that a plebiscite would be held in those areas then occupied by the Dutch to determine if their residents wished to become part of the republic or to form a separate state. Less than a year passed before conflict broke out again.

See also: HAGUE AGREEMENT OF 1949.

Further reading: Philip Dorling and David Lee, *Australia & Indonesia's Independence: The Renville Agreement: Documents 1948* (Canberra: Australian Government Publishing Service, 1996).

Report on the Lands of the Arid Region of the United States

Study of the arid regions of the western United States issued by Major John Wesley Powell in 1878. Powell, a geologist and ethnologist who led a series of exploratory expeditions of the Rocky Mountain region for the federal government between 1869 and 1875, later became the first director of the U.S. Bureau of Ethnology. His 1878 report is considered a pioneering effort in conservation. Powell argued that the land system that had applied in the eastern United States was unsuitable in the arid western areas, where irrigation, and therefore access to water, was the critical concern. His recommendations eventually became part of the nation's land policy.

Further reading: Mortimer Adler, ed., *The Annals of America*, 18 vols. (Chicago: Encyclopedia Britannica, 1968); Henry Steele Commager, ed., *Documents of American History*, 8th ed. (New York: Appleton-Century-Crofts, 1968); Frank N. Magill, ed., *Great Events from History: American Series*, 3 vols. (Englewood Cliffs, N.J.: Salem Press, 1975); Peter Wild and Dean Saxton, *The Desert Reader: Descriptions of America's Arid Regions* (Salt Lake City: University of Utah Press, 1991).

Report on Manufactures

Report submitted by U.S. secretary of the treasury Alexander Hamilton to Congress on December 5, 1791, proposing federal aid to infant industries through protective tariffs. Hamilton argued that the national welfare required the federal government to encourage manufacturing, in order to increase the national income and provide a dependable home market for agriculture. Hamilton's views were influenced by Adam Smith's *WEALTH OF NATIONS* (1776), but he rejected Smith's laissez-faire view that the state must not direct economic processes. Congress took no action on the report.

Further reading: Mortimer Adler, ed., *The Annals of America*, 18 vols. (Chicago: Encyclopedia Britannica, 1968); Jacob E. Cooke, ed., *The Reports of Alexander Hamilton* (New York: Harper & Row, 1964); Peter McNamara, *Political Economy and Statesmanship: Smith, Hamilton, and the Foundation of the*

Commercial Republic (DeKalb: Northern Illinois University Press, 1998).

Report on the Public Credit, First

Report submitted to the U.S. Congress by Secretary of the Treasury Alexander Hamilton on January 14, 1790, outlining his fiscal program. With the goal of establishing public credit domestically and abroad, and of strengthening the central government at the expense of the states, Hamilton recommended that the United States fund the foreign and domestic debt at full value, allowing creditors to replace depreciated securities with new interest-bearing bonds at face value, and that the federal government assume the debts incurred by the states during the American Revolution (1775–83) (see ASSUMPTION ACT, U.S.). The foreign debt was set at $11 million, the domestic debt at $40 million; the state debts were estimated at $25 million.

Further reading: Mortimer Adler, ed., *The Annals of America*, 18 vols. (Chicago: Encyclopedia Britannica, 1968); Jacob E. Cooke, ed., *The Reports of Alexander Hamilton* (New York: Harper & Row, 1964); John S. Gordon, *Hamilton's Blessing: The Extraordinary Life and Times of Our National Debt* (New York: Walker & Co., 1997); Frank N. Magill, ed., *Great Events from History: American Series*, 3 vols. (Englewood Cliffs, N.J.: Salem Press, 1975).

Republic, The (Politeia)

Plato's best-known dialogue (c. 380 B.C.) and perhaps the most complete introduction to his general philosophy. It has had a seminal influence on Western philosophical thought and is organized into 10 books or chapters and written as a dialogue between Socrates (teacher and friend of Plato) and various Athenian citizens. The Greek philosopher Plato used the question-and-answer technique to express his ideas on man and the state, on the role of art in society, and his theories of knowledge and form. Exploring the question "What is justice?" in all its ramifications, Socrates argued in favor of the just life. Art, Plato believed, had a corrupting influence on society; he recommended censorship of some of the tales of Hesiod and Homer (two earlier Greek poets). An ideal state is described as one in which philosophers rule and share in the community life. According to Plato, abstract forms are the ultimate reality, and realization of the vision of the Form of Good, the ultimate aspiration of every human soul.

Further reading: Bernard Bosanquet, *A Companion to Plato's Republic* (Bristol, England: Thoemmes, 1999); Daryl H. Rice, *A Guide to Plato's Republic* (New York: Oxford University Press, 1998); Sean Sayers, *Plato's Republic: An Introduction* (Edinburgh, Scotland: Edinburgh University Press, 1999).

Rerum Novarum

Encyclical issued by Pope Leo XIII on May 15, 1891, providing a Roman Catholic response to the social issues of the day, particularly with respect to the working class and the poor. In the document, the pope addressed issues that had arisen in society as a result of the Industrial Revolution, including the rise of the power of the few over the masses in industry, and the latter's subsequent exploitation. He criticized the socialists' proposed solution to destroy private ownership, as well as their repudiation of religion; proposed that the state accept the obligation to protect the poor against exploitation; and entreated faithful Catholics to apply the Christian principle of social justice in their own lives. The document was considered to be revolutionary by many.

Further reading: Claudia Carlen, comp., *The Papal Encyclicals* (Wilmington N.C.: McGrath Publishing, 1981); Catholic University of America, eds., *New Catholic Encyclopedia* (New York: McGraw Hill, 1967); Anne Fremantle, *The Papal Encyclicals in Their Historical Context* (New York: Mentor-Omega Books, 1963); David J. O'Brien and Thomas A. Shannon, eds., *Catholic Social Thought: The Documentary Heritage* (Maryknoll, N.Y.: Orbis Books, 1992).

Resht, Treaty of   Agreement concluded between Russia and Persia (Iran) on January 21, 1732, in the Persian town of Resht (Rasht); it reversed the territorial acquisitions made by Russia in the 1723 Treaty of ST. PETERSBURG. It provided that Russia would return to Persia the provinces of Gilan, Mazanderan, and Astrabad (Gorgan); that the Russian forces then occupying those areas would be withdrawn; that the Kura River (rising in northeast Turkey and flowing into the Caucasus region) would serve as the new boundary between the two countries; and that Russia was to enjoy certain trading privileges in Persia.

Further reading: Percy M. Sukes, *A History of Persia*, 3d ed. (New York: Barnes & Noble, 1969).

Restitution, Edict of   Edict issued by Holy Roman Emperor Ferdinand II on March 6, 1629. It proclaimed that all ecclesiastical property in Germany confiscated by the Protestants since 1552 was to be restored to the Roman Catholic Church; that Catholic clergy were to be reinstated to ecclesiastical offices in those areas; that Protestants could be legally expelled from Catholic territories; and that Protestant groups not adhering to the AUGSBURG CONFESSION in its original form were prohibited. According to Ferdinand, the Protestants had illegally gained possession of church lands, and he sought to reverse the injustice. The document alarmed Protestants (in 1552 the Catholics had repossessed much property, which by 1555 was again under Protestant control [see PASSAU, TREATY OF]); assent to the edict was highly unlikely, and by 1648 it was fully nullified.

See also: PRAGUE, PEACE OF.

Further reading: Frank N. Magill, ed., *Great Events from History: Modern European Series*, 3 vols. (Englewood Cliffs, N.J.: Salem Press, 1973).

Restraining Act for New England, British   Law enacted by British Parliament on March 30, 1775, before the outbreak of the American Revolution (1775–83), in retaliation for the colonial boycott of British goods (initiated by the First Continental Congress in 1774 as a protest against British taxes and repression). The act restricted the trade of the New England colonies to England, Ireland, and the British West Indies and prohibited New England fishermen from fishing in North Atlantic waters.

See also: RESTRAINING ACT OF 1775, BRITISH.

Further reading: William MacDonald, ed., *Select Charters and Other Documents Illustrative of American History, 1606–1775* (New York: Macmillan, 1899);

Restraining Act of 1775, British (American Prohibitory Act)   British parliamentary act passed on December 22, 1775, declaring that "all manner of trade and commerce is and shall be prohibited" with the American colonies. It further stated that American ships found trading at any port would be captured and the cargoes distributed among the British crew members. The act was intended as a retaliatory gesture against those in the colonies who had expressed open defiance against the authority of the British king and Parliament. However, instead of suppressing the rebellion, the act only strengthened the colonies' resolve to free themselves from British rule, leading ultimately to their DECLARATION OF INDEPENDENCE in 1776.

See also: RESTRAINING ACT FOR NEW ENGLAND, BRITISH.

Further reading: David D. Douglas et al., *English Historical Documents*, 12 vols. (New York: Oxford University Press, 1950–77); William MacDonald, ed., *Select Charters and Other Documents Illustrative of American History, 1606–1775* New York: Macmillan, 1899).

Resumption Act, U.S.   See SPECIE RESUMPTION ACT, U.S.

Revenue Act of 1935, U.S.   See WEALTH-TAX ACT, U.S.

Rex Pacificus   See DECRETALS OF 1234.

Reykjavík Agreement of 1986   Agreement between the United States and the Soviet Union following talks in Reykjavík, Iceland, on October 11–12, 1986, concerning the reduction of nuclear armaments. Concerned that the cold war was bankrupting his country, USSR general secretary Mikhail S. Gorbachev proposed that each side reduce its nuclear weapons by 50 percent. Furthermore, he proposed the withdrawal of all intermediate-range nuclear weapons from Europe, offered to limit Soviet missiles in Asia to 100 warheads, and promised to abide by the ANTI-BALLISTIC MISSILE TREATY for at least 10 years. He also agreed to on-site verifications and to discuss human rights in future summit meetings. In return, he insisted that the U.S. Strategic Defense Initiative (SDI), a multibillion-dollar, space-based weapons system known as

"Star Wars," be confined to the laboratory. U.S. president Ronald Reagan countered the 50 percent reduction by suggesting a ceiling be placed on warheads and missiles, and he offered to confine SDI to research and testing for 10 years. Reagan's proposal concerning SDI was unacceptable to Gorbachev, and the talks ended without any agreement other than to try again. The proposals and counterproposals concerning arms reduction formed the basis for the Strategic Arms Reduction Talks (START) and helped end the cold war (see START I TREATY).

Further reading: Frances Fitzgerald, *Way Out There in the Blue: Reagan, Star Wars and the End of the Cold War* (New York: Simon & Schuster, 2000); Jay Winik, *On the Brink: The Dramatic Behind-the-Scenes Saga of the Reagan Era and the Men and Women Who Won the Cold War* (New York: Simon & Schuster, 1996).

Reynolds v. Sims

U.S. Supreme Court decision issued on June 15, 1964, ruling that members of both houses of the state legislatures must be elected from equal population districts. In establishing the principle of "one person/one vote," the Court assumed a basic standard of equality among voters and invoked the principles of representative government, majority rule, and equal protection of the laws. Chief Justice Earl Warren wrote: "Legislators represent people, not trees or acres. Legislators are elected by votes, not farms or cities or economic interests." Unequal districting, he said, debases a citizen's right to vote.

Further reading: Henry Steele Commager, ed., *Documents of American History*, 8th ed. (New York: Appleton-Century-Crofts, 1968); Kermit L. Hall et al., eds., *The Oxford Companion to the Supreme Court of the United States* (New York: Oxford University Press, 1992); United States Supreme Court, *United States Reports: Cases Adjudged in the Supreme Court at . . . and Rules Announced at . . .* (New York: Banks & Brothers, Law Publishers, 1884–1921; Washington, D.C.: Government Printing Office, 1922–.

Reynolds v. United States

U.S. Supreme Court decision of October 1878 concerning the constitutional separation of church and state. The case raised the question of whether a U.S. statute prohibiting polygamy could be applied to a Mormon, whose religion encouraged a man to marry more than one wife. The Court, in deciding whether "religious belief can be accepted as a justification of an overt act made criminal by the law of the land," unanimously upheld the statute. The Court ruled that Congress had the authority to enact such a law and that the statute must be applied to everyone, without regard to religious convictions; to excuse from compliance some individuals would be to punish others for not subscribing to the same beliefs.

Further reading: Kermit L. Hall et al., eds., *American Legal History: Cases and Materials*, 2d ed. (New York: Oxford University Press, 1996); Kermit L. Hall et al., eds., *The Oxford Companion to the Supreme Court of the United States* (New York: Oxford University Press, 1992); United States Supreme Court, *United States Reports: Cases Adjudged in the Supreme Court at . . . and Rules Announced at . . .* (New York: Banks & Brothers, Law Publishers, 1884–1921; Washington, D.C.: Government Printing Office, 1922–).

Rhens (Rense), Declaration of (Pragmatic Sanction of Rhens)

Declaration made by six German electors in 1338 at Rhens, or Rense, near Koblenz, Germany, affirming the validity of a royal/imperial election by majority vote without confirmation of the pope. It was made because of a dispute over the succession to Henry VII, king of Germany and Holy Roman emperor; Bavaria's duke Louis of Wittelsbach successfully waged war against Austrian duke Frederick the Fair to claim the title king and emperor, which was sealed by majority vote but declared invalid by Pope Benedict XII at Avignon (the final choice was a Roman papal right, upset by the Avignonese papacy or the so-called Babylonian exile of the papacy [1309–78], when all popes were French and under the control of French kings). The electors' declaration, made to avoid future conflicts, confirmed the elected German king as the ex officio emperor of the Holy Roman Empire, with or without the pope's sanction, and without the prerequisite of being crowned in Rome.

Further reading: G. Barraclough, *The Origins of Modern Germany* (New York: W. W. Norton, 1984).

Rhode Island and Providence Plantations, Charter of

Royal charter granted on July 8, 1663, by England's king Charles II to the confederation of Rhode Island and Providence Plantations. Secured by John Clarke, acting as Rhode Island's colonial agent, the charter replaced an earlier grant made in 1644. The 1663 charter established Rhode Island's western border, long disputed with Connecticut, at the Pawcatuck River; guaranteed religious freedom; and provided for an elected governor, deputy governor, assistants, and general assembly, with suffrage to be determined by the colony. The charter was kept throughout the colonial period and continued as Rhode Island's state constitution until 1842.

Further reading: *Constitution & Royal Charter of 1663* (Providence, R.I.: Office of the Secretary of State, 1987); William MacDonald, ed., *Select Charters and Other Documents Illustrative of American History, 1606–1775* (New York: Macmillan, 1899).

Rhodesian Native Land Husbandry Act

See NATIVE LAND HUSBANDRY ACT, RHODESIAN.

Richelieu's *Political Testament (Testament Politique)*

Highly personalized document conveying the views of cardinal de Richelieu (principal minister in the councils of King Louis XIII of France) on a variety of subjects, expressing in one volume his basic social and political ideologies; first published in France in 1688. Actually, it is a loosely held anthology of pieces written by Richelieu and was amateurishly assembled after his death (1642). It purports to be a manual for Louis XIII "for the regulation and guidance of your realm"; Richelieu claimed to have "no other motive than the interests of the state and the advantage of your person." Despite his disclaimer, Richelieu was obviously also seeking to record his achievements for posterity and to vindicate some of his policies. Strewn with pithy maxims, the book's enduring qualities are to be found in its general policy recommendations and pieces on statesmanship. It first appeared in England in 1695 as *The Compleat Statesman* and was reprinted several times.

See also: LOUIS XIII'S EDICT OF 1626.

Further reading: Henry B. Hill, trans., *Political Testament* (Madison: University of Wisconsin Press, 1961); Mark A. Kishlansky, ed., *Sources of the West: Readings in Western Civilization*, 4th ed., vol. 2 (New York: Longman, 2001); Milton Viorst, ed., *The Great Documents of Western Civilization* (Philadelphia: Chilton Books, 1965).

RICO Law (Racketeer Influenced and Corrupt Organizations Act)

Federal U.S. legislation, effective on October 15, 1970, that defined racketeering and set strict penalties. The law was aimed at organized criminal activity that was operated as a business or that affected a legitimate business. Racketeering included bribery, counterfeiting, theft from interstate commerce, embezzlement of labor union and benefit fund monies, extortionate credit transactions, mail and wire fraud, gambling offenses, unlawful welfare-pension fund payments, security frauds, and similar offenses. Penalties could include a fine up to $25,000 and a prison term up to 20 years. The act also provided civil penalties, such as forfeiture of all interests in the racketeer-influenced organization, divestiture, and corporate dissolution and reorganization.

Further reading: John E. Floyd, *RICO State by State: A Guide to Litigation under the State Racketeering Statute* (Chicago: American Bar Association, 1998); John C. Fricano, ed., *Guide to RICO: A Practical Guide for the Corporate Counselor* (Washington, D.C.: Bureau of National Affairs, 1986); Patricia M. Hynes, *Civil RICO* (New York: Practicing Law Institute, 1984).

Riga, Treaty of (1920)

Treaty concluded in Riga, Latvia, on August 11, 1920, by Soviet Russia and the Baltic state of Latvia, bringing an end to the hostilities between the two, which had arisen over Soviet Russia's determination to regain possession of the Latvian state, which had once been part of the Russian Empire (see BREST-LITOVSK, TREATY OF). The treaty provided for Soviet Russia's de jure recognition of an independent Latvia, with newly defined frontiers; the inhabitants' right to choose their nationality within a fixed period of time; the amnesty of prisoners of war; Soviet Russia's payment of 4 million rubles to Latvia; the establishment of commercial and diplomatic relations between the two countries; and for each country's pledge to forbid the existence of groups antagonistic to the other within its territory.

See also: MOSCOW, TREATY OF (1920); TARTU, TREATY OF.

Further reading: *Treaty of Peace Between Latvia and Soviet Russia* (Stockholm, Sweden: Latvian National Foundation, 1985).

Riga, Treaty of (1921)

Treaty definitively concluded at Riga on March 18, 1921, by Poland and Soviet Russia, bringing an end to the Russo-Polish War of 1919–20. By the treaty, both parties pledged not to interfere in the internal affairs of the other; not to press for reparations; agreed to a general amnesty for prisoners and émigrés; agreed on a new Soviet-Polish border, more favorable to Poland than the previous one arranged at the Paris Peace Conference (see VERSAILLES, TREATY OF [1919], to run from the city of Polotsk in the north to the Dniester River in the south; and agreed to the independence of Belorussia and the Ukraine. Poland's aggressive ambitions to extend her eastern border farther east had led to the war.

See also: MOSCOW, TREATY OF (1920).

Further reading: Norman Davies, *White Eagle, Red Star: The Polish-Soviet War, 1919–20* (London: Orbis, 1983); Thomas C. Fiddick, *Russia's Retreat from Poland, 1920: From Permanent Revolution to Peaceful Coexistence* (Houndmills, England: Macmillan, 1990); Fred L. Israel, ed., *Major Peace Treaties of Modern History, 1648–1967*, 4 vols. (New York: Chelsea House, 1967).

Rights of Man, Dutch

Proclamation of the rights of man and burgher issued on January 31, 1795, by the "Provisional Representatives of the People of Holland" in the newly constituted Batavian Republic (the Netherlands). Among its salient features were (1) the revocation of the Synod of Dort (see DORT, CANONS OF) and all disabilities for Roman Catholics and dissenters withdrawn; (2) the abolition of heredity for dignities and offices; (3) no more torture and hanging on wayside gallows; (4) nobles and gentry stripped of their hunting rights, patrimonial jurisdiction, and their privilege of displaying coats-of-arms on carriages and church pews; and (5) the rechristening of towns whose names evoked their aristocratic heritage. The document confirmed that all persons are created with equal rights, can worship as they choose, and can have the rulers they so desire to elect.

Further reading: Gerald Newton, *The Netherlands: An Historical and Cultural Survey, 1795–1977* (Boulder, Colo.: Westview Press, 1978).

Rights of Man, The

Pamphlet written by Anglo American radical political theorist Thomas Paine and published in England in 1791–92, praising the French Revolution (1789–92) and republican principles and denouncing monarchism. It was soon reprinted in America and was widely distributed. In this two-part work Paine argued that there are natural rights common to all people, and that these rights can be guaranteed only by democratic institutions. Paine analyzed the problems of poverty, illiteracy, unemployment, and war, and outlined a plan for education, aid to the poor, pensions for the elderly, and public works for the jobless. The pamphlet was suppressed in England and Paine was indicted for treason; he fled to France before he was arrested.

Further reading: Bruce Kuklick, ed., *Political Writings/ Thomas Paine* (New York: Cambridge University Press, 2000); Mark Philp, ed., *Rights of Man; Common Sense; and Other Political Writings/Thomas Paine* (New York: Oxford University Press, 1995).

Rights of the British Colonies Asserted and Proved, Otis's

Pamphlet written by pre–American Revolutionary War leader James Otis and published in 1764, denying the authority of the British Parliament to tax the American colonies. The tract, a protest against the SUGAR ACT OF 1764, argued against taxation without representation. Otis proposed parliamentary representation for the colonies, which he compared with Ireland. He also declared that parliamentary acts in violation of natural law or the British Constitution were void.

See also: OTIS'S SPEECH OPPOSING WRITS OF ASSISTANCE.

Further reading: Mortimer Adler, ed., *The Annals of America*, 18 vols. (Chicago: Encyclopedia Britannica, 1968); Bernard Bailyn, *The Ideological Origins of the American Revolution*, enlarged ed. (Cambridge, Mass.: Harvard University Press, 1992); Alan Rogers and Alan Lawson, eds., *From Revolution to Republic: A Documentary Reader* (Cambridge, Mass.: Schenkman Publications, 1976).

Rijswijk, Treaty of

See RYSWICK (RIJSWIJK), TREATY OF.

Rio Branco Law (Free Birth Law)

Law adopted in Brazil on September 28, 1871, under Emperor Pedro II, freeing the newborn children of slave women. The law, named after Viscount Rio Branco, who was responsible for its approval by the parliament, also included the following major provisions: It created an emancipation fund for the annual liberation of slaves in all the provinces; it gave slaves the right to buy their freedom; it freed government-owned, inherited, or abandoned slaves; and it ordered nationwide registration of all slaves. While the Free Birth Law failed to produce significant results for a decade after passage, it helped to prepare the way for the abolitionist movement of the 1880s.

Further reading: Junius P. Rodriguez, ed., *Chronology of World Slavery* (Santa Barbara, Calif.: ABC-Clio, 1999).

Rio Declaration

Major declaration signed on June 14, 1992, by 172 countries at the Earth Summit (June 3–14, 1992) in Rio de Janeiro, Brazil, calling upon nations to "equitably meet developmental and environmental needs." Originally intended as a more ambitious "Earth Charter," its 27 principles define the rights and obligations of states to achieve more environmentally sustainable patterns of development, which demanded the scaling-down of "unsustainable patterns of production and consumption" and the promoting of "appropriate demographic policies." Also, while countries had the right to "exploit their own resources," it stipulated that they could not destroy the environment of other nations. Reducing the worldwide disparity in living standards and eradicating poverty were "indispensable" to attaining the declaration's goals. Also important was improved access to information and full citizen (especially women's) participation.

Further reading: Nicholas Low et al., eds., *Consuming Cities: the Urban Environment in the Global Economy after the Rio Declaration* (London: Routledge, 2000); "The Rio Declaration on Environment and Development, 1992," *UN Chronicle* 29 (September 1992): 66–67.

Riot Act of 1715, British

Statute enacted in 1715 by the British Whigs following Jacobite unrest and the growing unpopularity of Britain's new Hanoverian king, George I. It declared that if 12 or more persons assembled riotously, to disturb the public peace, and refused to disperse on order from a local official (hence called "reading the Riot Act"), they were guilty of a felony and could be punished by death. The officials, who acted on behalf of the king, included magistrates and soldiers. By the act, local riots were separated legally from the purview of the treason law.

Further reading: Joel H. Wiener, ed., *Great Britain—The Lion at Home: A Documentary History of Domestic Policy (1689–1973)* (New York: Chelsea House, 1974).

Rio Treaty (Rio Pact, Inter-American Treaty of Reciprocal Assistance)

Collective security pact drafted at the Inter-American Conference for the Maintenance of Peace and Security; held near Rio de Janeiro, Brazil, from August 15 to September 2, 1947. The treaty, signed by the United States and 18 Latin American countries, went into effect in 1948 after is ratification by two-thirds of the American states. Among its major provisions, the treaty asserted that an armed attack by one state against another American state would be considered as an attack against all American states, and that a consulting body would meet immediately to decide upon measures to be taken. A meeting of the consulting body would also be held if the integrity or sovereignty of any American state were affected by any situation that might endanger the peace of the Western Hemisphere. The Rio Treaty has been invoked in a number of instances since 1948, notably during the Cuban missile crisis of 1962.

See also: CHAPULTEPEC, ACT OF.

Further reading: Henry W. Degenhardt, ed., *Treaties and Alliances of the World*, 4th ed. (Detroit: Gale Research, 1986); J. A. S. Greenville and Bernard Wasserstein, *The Major International Treaties since 1945: A History and Guide with*

Texts (New York: Methuen, 1987); *Inter-American Treaty of Reciprocal Assistance* (Washington, D.C.: Pan American Union, 1965).

Ripon, Treaty of   Peace treaty concluded between King Charles I of England and the Scots at Ripon in northern England on October 26, 1640, following Charles's defeat at Newburn-on-Tyne in the Second Bishops' War. By the pact, Northumberland and Durham were occupied by the Scots, and the king agreed to pay the Scottish army £850 a day pending a permanent settlement. This financial obligation compelled the king to convene the Long Parliament, which then sat for 13 years for redress of grievances.

Further reading: David Stevenson, *The Scottish Revolution, 1637–1644; the Triumph of the Covenanters* (New York: St. Martin's Press, 1974).

Ritchie Act (Local Government Act of 1888, Country Councils Act)   British act of August 13, 1888, drafted by Charles Thomson Ritchie (president of the Local Government Board), introducing significant administrative reforms at the county level. It entrusted elected county councils with all the administrative tasks (except licensing) of the justices of the peace in the newly created 62 counties. Large towns were converted into county boroughs (62 in all) with full county powers. Police forces were withdrawn from boroughs with population less than 10,000; elsewhere, they were supervised by a joint standing committee of county councillors and magistrates. The county councils were allotted a part of specific national revenues. In London, four counties were incorporated into the London County Council, with the city of London retaining its autonomous status. The act did not affect the boards of guardians or the parish vestries.

Further reading: C. Harold Carter, *Handbook on the Local Government Act, 1888* (London: Butterworth, 1924); Joel H. Wiener, ed., *Great Britain—The Lion at Home: A Documentary History of Domestic Policy (1689–1973)* (New York: Chelsea House, 1974).

Rives's Treaty   Treaty between France and the United States, signed on July 4, 1831, to settle French spoliation claims. Negotiated by William C. Rives, U.S. minister to France, the treaty dealt with more than $12 million in claims arising largely from French seizures and confiscations of American ships during the Napoleonic Wars (1803–15), as well as with French counterclaims. Under the treaty, France agreed to pay 25 million francs and the United States $1.5 million, in six annual installments beginning a year after ratification. When France failed to pay the first installment by 1836, war nearly erupted; hostilities were prevented by British mediation. All six installments were eventually paid.

Further reading: Henry Blumenthal, *France and the United States: Their Diplomatic Relation, 1789–1914* (Chapel Hill: University of North Carolina Press, 1970); Beckles Willson,

America's Ambassadors to France (1777–1927): A Narrative of Franco-American Diplomatic Relations (London: J. Murray, 1928).

Rivet-Vitet Law (Loi Rivet-Vitet)   Legislation of August 31, 1871, conferring the title "President of the French Republic" on the "chief of the executive power" but also making him answerable to France's National Assembly. Based on Louis Vitet's amendment of Baron Rivet's original proposal (a three-year presidential term was dropped), the bill passed the Assembly by a vote of 491 to 94. The legislation recognized the existence of a republic but retained the "provisional" status of institutions and affirmed the Assembly's "constituent power." Thus, Adolphe Thiers, the new president of the republic, also simultaneously became the president of the Council of Ministers and an Assembly member. He was entitled to promulgate laws passed by the Assembly, supervise their implementation, and appoint and dismiss ministers, who were, however, "responsible to the Assembly." The president could address the Assembly after receiving the speaker's permission. All his acts were to "be countersigned by a minister." And the presidential term was to last as long as the Assembly lasted.

Further reading: J. P. T. Bury and Robert Tombs, *Theirs, 1797–1877: A Political Life* (Boston: Allen & Unwin, 1986); William Fortescue, *The Third Republic in France, 1870–1940: Conflicts and Continuities* (New York: Routledge, 2000).

Robespierre's Speech on Property   Maximilien Robespierre's discussion of the principles governing property rights, in a speech before France's National Convention on April 24, 1793. Robespierre, one of the most implacable leaders of the French Revolution (1789–92), argued that property was a social institution with "moral responsibilities" and that it was necessary to "define its nature and its legitimacy." Charging that the DECLARATION OF THE RIGHTS OF MAN AND OF THE CITIZEN was not made for "ordinary men," Robespierre redefined property rights, proposed progressive taxation, and issued a new Declaration of the Rights of Man. Property, he held, was the right of every citizen, limited only by respect for the property of others and that any violation of another's property was "unlawful and immoral." Finally, he urged recognition of the brotherhood binding all nations and their right to mutual assistance; he condemned kings, aristocrats, and tyrants as slaves rebelling against the human race and nature.

See also: VENTÔSE DECREES.

Further reading: Norman Hampson, *The Life and Opinions of Maximilien Robespierre* (London: Duckworth, 1974); John Hardman, *Robespierre* (New York: Wesley Addison Longman, 1999).

Robinson-Patman Act (Federal Anti-Price Discrimination Act)   Federal legislation enacted on June 20, 1936, that made illegal prices that were unreasonably low and thus tended to destroy competition and promote monopolies in the United States. It was directed against those chain stores engaged in interstate commerce that, by virtue of their large purchasing volume, could demand lower wholesale prices than could smaller, independent stores. Sponsored by Senator Joseph T. Robinson of Arkansas and Representative John William Wright Patman of Texas, the act prohibited discrimination in prices or terms of sale as well as certain brokerage or advertising allowances. The U.S. Federal Trade Commission was authorized to enforce its provisions.

Further reading: Earl W. Kintner, *A Robinson-Patman Primer: Guide to the Law Against Price Discrimination* (New York: Macmillan, 1979); *A Primer on the Federal Price Discrimination Laws: A General Review of the Robinson-Patman Act for Business Managers* (Chicago: American Bar Association, 1992); Robinson-Patman Act Editorial Committee, *The Robinson-Patman Act—Policy and Law* (Chicago: American Bar Association, 1980).

Rock Edicts   See PILLAR EDICTS, AŚOKA'S.

Rockingham Memorial, Webster's   Paper addressed to U.S. president James Madison and written by Daniel Webster in August 1812, expressing opposition to the War of 1812. Prepared for and adopted by a large convention in Rockingham County, New Hampshire, the memorial reviewed the policies that had led to the war, explained the reasons for opposition to the conflict, opposed an alliance with France, urged improved naval preparations and defense, and recommended a speedy restoration of peace and commerce. It reaffirmed fidelity to the national union, while pointing out that the war endangered that union. The memorial gave impetus to Webster's political career, and the Rockingham convention nominated him for a congressional seat, which he won.

Further reading: Edwin P. Whipple, ed., *The Great Speeches and Orations of Daniel Webster* (Birmingham, Ala.: Gryphon Editions, 1989); Charles M. Wiltse, ed., *The Papers of Daniel Webster: Speeches and Formal Writings*, 2 vols. (Hanover, N.H.: University of New England, 1986).

Roe v. Wade   Controversial, landmark U.S. Supreme Court decision issued on January 22, 1973, ruling that the FOURTEENTH AMENDMENT gave an adult woman the right to terminate her pregnancy during the first trimester without any government interference, and that during the second trimester the state may limit that right only to safeguard the woman's health. The case involved "Jane Roe" (a pseudonym), an impoverished Texas woman who wished to terminate a pregnancy resulting from a rape. In its 7-2 decision, the Supreme Court declared unconstitutional a Texas antiabortion statute, as a violation of a woman's right to personal privacy. It stated that the fetus was not a person within the meaning of the Fourteenth Amendment and said that the state had no "compelling interest" in protecting prenatal life until

viability. The decision did not decide the question of when life actually begins. The ruling aroused a storm of controversy and led to proposals for a constitutional amendment to prohibit abortions.

Further reading: Marian Faux, *Roe v. Wade: The Untold Story of the Landmark Supreme Court Decision That Made Abortion Legal* (New York: Cooper Square Press, 2001); Kermit L. Hall, et al., eds., *American Legal History: Cases and Materials*, 2d ed. (New York: Oxford University Press, 1996); Kermit L. Hall et al., eds., *The Oxford Companion to the Supreme Court of the United States* (New York: Oxford University Press, 1992); United States Supreme Court, *United States Reports: Cases Adjudged in the Supreme Court at . . . and Rules Announced at . . .* (New York: Banks & Brothers, Law Publishers, 1884–1921; Washington, D.C.: Government Printing Office, 1922–).

Roman Agrarian Law of 133 B.C. (Sempronian Law of 133 B.C., Lex Sempronia Agraria)   Major land reform measure proposed by the Roman tribune Tiberius Sempronius Gracchus, reenacting and altering land laws of 367 B.C. that had fallen into disuse. Enacted in 133 B.C. despite some opposition by the senatorial aristocracy, the law raised the previous limit of 500 iugera (313 acres) of public lands per person by allowing an additional 250 iugera for each of two sons. Landholders were not liable to tax or rental in perpetuity, but all occupied public land in excess of the legal limit had to be ceded to the state. Surplus land was assigned to peasants in small allotments, for which they paid a nominal rental fee to the state. Later that year, Tiberius tried (contrary to law) to be reelected tribune and was murdered, allegedly by reactionary aristocrats, during a riot.

See also: LICINIAN-SEXTIAN LAWS.

Further reading: Alvin H. Bernstein, *Tiberius Sempronius Gracchus: Tradition and Apostasy* (Ithaca, N.Y.: Cornell University Press, 1978); Frank N. Magill, ed., *Great Events from History: Ancient and Medieval Series*, 3 vols. (Englewood Cliffs, N.J.: Salem Press, 1972).

Roman Agrarian Law of 111 B.C. (Lex Agraria of 111 B.C.)   Reactionary land reform measures enacted in 111 B.C., when the old Roman Republic's existence was being threatened by invading Germanic tribes in Gaul and about to move on Italy. The earlier reforms of the brothers Tiberius and Caius Sempronius Gracchus were ruined by these new enactments, which legalized private possession of public domains, made all landholdings private property, ended all land distributions and rental land allotments (making them capable of being transferred to new owners), and forbade squatting on public lands. The Senate's consent to the sale of land by new tenants led to the rich buying up much land, thus undoing the Sempronian Law of 123 B.C., a renewal by tribune Caius Gracchus of a similarly named land law of 133 B.C. (see ROMAN AGRARIAN LAW OF 133 B.C.).

Further reading: Ernest G. Hardy, *Roman Laws and Charters, and Three Spanish Charters and Other Documents* (New York: Arno Press, 1975).

Romanian Organic Statutes of 1832

Laws or principles prepared by Russian-sponsored Wallachian and Moldavian noblemen and endorsed by federal assemblies consisting of wealthy landowners and high-ranking clergy, in 1832. The statutes actually served as the constitutions of the two Danubian principalities of Moldavia and Wallachia, which were each to have an assembly of noblemen that was to be responsible for the legislation and administration of the state. The assemblies were to elect the ruling prince, who was to serve for life, and the prince was to have extensive power over the noblemen (he could adjourn the assembly without the noblemen's consent, for example), although effective power ultimately resided in the Russian consul general. The Russians, who had defeated the Ottoman Turks in the Russo-Turkish War of 1828–29, had occupied the principalities (which formally still belonged to the Ottoman Empire) jointly with the Ottomans since the end of the war.

Further reading: W. Gordon East, *The Union of Moldavia and Wallachia, 1859; an Episode in Diplomatic History* (New York: Octagon Books, 1973).

Rome, Treaties of (1957)

Two treaties concluded in Rome on March 25, 1957, creating the European Economic Community (EEC), known as the Common Market and now called the European Union, and the European Atomic Energy Community (EURATOM). Established by France, Belgium, the Netherlands, Luxembourg, Italy, and West Germany, the EEC's aim was to remove trade barriers among members; present a unified commercial policy toward nonmembers; coordinate transport systems and agricultural and economic policies; repeal any legislation restricting free competition; and ensure the easy flow of labor, capital, and entrepreneurship. The European Union operates chiefly through its commission, its council of ministers, the European Court of Justice, and the European Parliament—the last two also serving the European Coal and Steel Community (see SCHUMAN PLAN) and EURATOM. Besides several special committees, it is also served by the European Investment Bank, the European Social Fund, and the European Development Fund. Plans for an EEC were formulated during discussions held in Messina in 1955; it became operative on January 1, 1958. The United Kingdom, Denmark, and Ireland became members in 1973.

See also: BENELUX ECONOMIC UNION AGREEMENT; EUROPEAN FREE TRADE ASSOCIATION AGREEMENT; SINGLE EUROPEAN ACT.

Further reading: Henry W. Degenhardt, ed., *Treaties and Alliances of the World*, 4th ed. (Detroit: Gale Research, 1986); J. A. S. Grenville and Bernard Wasserstein, *The Major International Treaties since 1945: A History and Guide with Texts* (New York: Methuen, 1987); *The Rome, Maastricht and Amsterdam Treaties: The Treaty on European Union (The Treaty of Rome)* (Brussels: Euroconfidential, 1999).

Rome Protocols of 1934

Three protocols signed in Rome on March 17, 1934, by Italian dictator Benito Mussolini, Austrian chancellor Engelbert Dollfuss, and Hungarian premier Julius von Gömbös, providing for closer economic and diplomatic relations among the three countries. The first of the three protocols provided that the three states would consult with one another on matters of common concern, with the aim of maintaining peace in Europe. The second, an economic agreement, called for the conclusion, by May 15, of commercial agreements designed to increase trade; in addition, a committee was to be established to monitor the three states' economic relations with the object of improving them. A third protocol, concluded by Austria and Italy alone, contained proposals for the improvement of economic relations between the two states. The protocols represented largely an Italian effort to counter the Little Entente (see LITTLE ENTENTE TREATIES) and to replace France as Austria's protector against Germany.

Further reading: Gerhard Schachter, *Central Europe and the Western World* (New York: H. Holt & Co., 1936).

Romorantin, Edict of

French law issued at Romorantin, France, in May 1560, entrusting heresy trials to church tribunals; announced by French chancellor Michel de L'Hospital (L'Hôpital) at the instance of Queen Mother Catherine de Médicis. It authorized these tribunals to punish illegal assemblies if found "seditious"; nonseditious assemblies remained within the jurisdiction of the secular courts (*presidiaux*). The 1560 Edict of Amboise prevented these courts from conducting heresy trials; hence, cases condemned by the church tribunals could not be tried and the new edict remained inapplicable in its most intolerant aspect. Deliberately ambiguous, the edict (signed by France's king Francis II at Romorantin Castle) was intended to appease the cardinal Inquisitors, Rome and Spain, while actually freeing the Huguenots (French Protestants) from the Inquisition.

See also: AMBOISE, EDICT OF; CHÂTEAUBRIANT, EDICT OF; JANUARY, EDICT OF.

Further reading: Seong-Hak Kim, *Michel de L'Hopital: The Vision of a Reformist Chancellor During the French Religious Wars* (Kirksville, M.: Sixteenth Century Journal Publishers, 1997).

Roncaglia, Decrees of

Decrees issued by Emperor Frederick I (Frederick Barbarossa, king of Germany) in November 1158, at Roncaglia, Italy, claiming for the Holy Roman Empire the royal rights that had gradually been taken over by the Lombard towns in Italy during the preceding period. Stipulations authoritatively declared that no man would be permitted to sell or pledge the sale of any portion of land held in fief without the permission of the lord to which it belonged; that the division of any duchy or county was prohibited; that a lord's fief would be confiscated if he should fail to provide the required payments during a levy; and that the emperor had control over all appointments to public office.

Further reading: G. Barraclough, *The Origins of Modern Germany* (New York: W. W. Norton, 1984); Marcel Pacaut, *Frederick Barbarossa*, trans. A. J. Pomerans (New York: Scribner, 1970).

Roosevelt Corollary

Expansion of the MONROE DOCTRINE, enunciated by U.S. president Theodore Roosevelt on December 6, 1904. To ward off a threat to U.S. interests in the Caribbean, Roosevelt stated that the United States would intervene in any Latin American country that engaged in "chronic wrongdoing" or that was unable to preserve the "ties of civilized society." Since the Monroe Doctrine prohibited European nations from intervention in Latin America, the United States would exercise "international police power." An example of Roosevelt's "big stick" diplomacy, the corollary led to intervention in Santo Domingo, Haiti, Nicaragua, and Cuba.

Further reading: Henry Steele Commager, ed., *Documents of American History*, 8th ed. (New York: Appleton-Century-Crofts, 1968); James C. Humes, *My Fellow Americans: Presidential Addresses that Shaped History* (New York: Praeger, 1992).

Roosevelt-Litvinov Correspondence

Exchange of communications between U.S. president Franklin D. Roosevelt and Soviet foreign affairs commissar Maxim M. Litvinov on November 16, 1933; they signed agreements to establish diplomatic relations between their two countries and to grant American nationals within the Soviet Union (immediately upon the establishment of relations) the right to "free exercise of liberty of conscience and religious worship" and rights of business and legal protection. Americans in Russia won protection from "persecution on account of their faith or worship" and the right "to lease, erect or maintain in convenient situations" churches or other buildings suitable for religious purposes. The Soviets reserved, however, the right to refuse visas to Americans wishing to enter on personal grounds. The Soviets waived all their claims arising out of U.S. military activities in Siberia after January 1, 1918. Roosevelt and Litvinov were to negotiate a consular convention on these matters in the immediate future.

Further reading: Mortimer Adler, ed., *The Annals of America*, 18 vols. (Chicago: Encyclopaedia Britannica, 1968); Donald G. Bishop, ed., *Soviet Foreign Relations: Documents & Readings* (Syracuse, N.Y.: Syracuse University Press, 1952); Henry Steele Commager, ed., *Documents of American History*, 8th ed. (New York: Appleton-Century-Crofts, 1968).

Roosevelt's "Confession of Faith" Speech

Acceptance speech delivered on August 6, 1912, by Theodore Roosevelt, U.S. presidential candidate of the newly formed Progressive Party, at its Chicago convention. As in ROOSEVELT'S "NEW NATIONALISM" SPEECH OF 1910, the candidate set forth his program for social and economic justice. Roosevelt decried the corruption, insincerity, and reactionary nature of both the Democratic and Republican Parties and declared that the time was ripe for a genuine national progressive moment. He urged new measures to make government more truly representative, nationally mandated presidential primaries, direct election of senators, and national regulation of interstate corporations.

Further reading: John A. Gable, *The Bull Moose Years: Theodore Roosevelt and the Progressive Party* (Port Washington, N.Y.: Kennikat Press, 1978); Theodore Roosevelt, *Theodore Roosevelt's Confession of Faith Before the Progressive National Convention, August 6, 1912* (New York: Stoddard-Sutherland Press, 1912).

Roosevelt's Conservation Message

Part of President Theodore Roosevelt's seventh annual message to the U.S. Congress, delivered on December 3, 1907, calling for the conservation of America's natural resources. Roosevelt urged the nation to plan for orderly development rather than strive for immediate profit. He proposed the creation of a system of national water highways on America's rivers, the development of dams and waterpower systems, and the establishment of irrigation programs. Contradicting the view that America's national resources were inexhaustible, he sought the preservation and protection of public lands, mineral resources, soil, and forests.

Further reading: Henry Steele Commager, ed., *Documents of American History*, 8th ed. (New York: Appleton-Century-Crofts, 1968); Lewis L. Gould, *The Presidency of Theodore Roosevelt* (Lawrence: University Press of Kansas, 1991); Judson King, *The Conservation Fight from Theodore Roosevelt to the Tennessee Valley Authority* (Washington, D.C.: Public Affairs Press, 1959).

Roosevelt's First Inaugural Address

Speech delivered by Franklin Delano Roosevelt on March 4, 1933, at his inauguration as 32nd president of the United States. His address, coming at the height of the Great Depression, offered reassurance to the nation and the promise of prompt, vigorous action. Stating that "the only thing we have to fear is fear itself," Roosevelt castigated the nation's bankers for their "stubbornness and . . . incompetence" in the face of the economic crisis and broadly outlined his plan for recovery. The greatest task, he stated, was to put people to work, to be accomplished in part by direct government employment. He called for strict supervision of banking, credit, and investment, a sound currency, and an end to speculation. In international relations he proposed a good-neighbor policy.

Further reading: Mortimer Adler, ed., *The Annals of America*, 18 vols. (Chicago: Encyclopaedia Britannica, 1968);

Henry Steele Commager, ed., *Documents of American History*, 8th ed. (New York: Appleton-Century-Crofts, 1968); *Inaugural Addresses of the Presidents of the United States from George Washington 1789 to George Bush 1989*, bicentennial ed. (Washington, D.C.: Government Printing Office, 1989); Davis N. Lott, *The Presidents Speak: The Inaugural Addresses of the American Presidents from Washington to Clinton* (New York: H. Holt & Co., 1994).

Roosevelt's "Hands Off the Western Hemisphere" Speech

Pan-American Day address delivered by President Franklin D. Roosevelt on April 14, 1939, that proclaimed the solidarity of the American nations against outside attack, whether military or economic, and at the same time recognized the interrelationship between the New World and the Old. In the face of increasing German, Italian, and Japanese expansionism, Roosevelt declared that the United States was prepared to defend the sovereignty and independence of "the American family of nations." He also stated: "The truest defense of the peace of our hemisphere must always lie in the hope that our sister nations beyond the seas will break the bonds . . . of perpetual warfare."

Further reading: Henry Steele Commager, ed., *Documents of American History*, 8th ed. (New York: Appleton-Century-Crofts, 1968); George McJimsey, *The Presidency of Franklin Delano Roosevelt* (Lawrence: University Press of Kansas, 2000).

Roosevelt's "New Nationalism" Speech of 1910

Speech delivered by former U.S. president Theodore Roosevelt at Osawatomie, Kansas, on August 31, 1910, outlining his progressive "New Nationalism" program. Breaking with conservatives in his own Republican Party, Roosevelt called for a strong national government, federal regulation of the corporate system, and the protection of human rights over property rights. He argued for the "square deal," for equal opportunity for all citizens, for fair wages and working conditions, for government free of control by special interests, for prohibitions on corporate funding of political activity. "The object of government," he said, "is the welfare of the people."

Further reading: Mortimer Adler, ed., *The Annals of America*, 18 vols. (Chicago: Encyclopaedia Britannica, 1968); Henry Steele Commager, ed., *Documents of American History*, 8th ed. (New York: Appleton-Century-Crofts, 1968).

Roosevelt's "Quarantine the Aggressors" Speech

Address delivered by U.S. president Franklin D. Roosevelt in Chicago on October 5, 1937, in response to expansionist policies of Germany, Italy, and Japan, particularly the Japanese invasion of China. Arguing against isolationism and for collective security, Roosevelt warned that if aggression triumphed elsewhere in the world, the United States too was endangered. To fight the spreading "epidemic of world lawlessness," he stated, the international community had to join in a "quarantine of the patients in order to protect the health of the community" from the disease. The speech was well received by the public and encouraged a U.S. boycott of Japanese products.

Further reading: Mortimer Adler, ed., *The Annals of America*, 18 vols. (Chicago: Encyclopaedia Britannica, 1968); George McJimsey, *The Presidency of Franklin Delano Roosevelt* (Lawrence: University Press of Kansas, 2000).

Roosevelt's Second Inaugural Address ("One-Third of a Nation" Speech)

Address delivered by the U.S. president Franklin D. Roosevelt in Washington, D.C., on January 20, 1937, as he began his second term in office (he was the first president to be inaugurated on this day, set by the TWENTIETH AMENDMENT. In stressing his goal of social justice, Roosevelt stated that the nation faced the challenge of "tens of millions of its citizens . . . [who] are denied the greater part of what the very lowest standards of today call the necessities of life . . . I see one-third of a nation ill-housed, ill-clad, ill-nourished." He spoke, said the president, not in despair but in hope, "because the Nation, seeing and understanding the injustice in it, proposes to paint it out."

Further reading: *Inaugural Addresses of the Presidents of the United States from George Washington 1789 to George Bush 1989*, bicentennial ed. (Washington, D.C.: Government Printing Office, 1989); Davis N. Lott, *The Presidents Speak: The Inaugural Addresses of the American Presidents from Washington to Clinton* (New York: H. Holt & Co., 1994); Halford Ryan, ed., *The Inaugural Addresses of Twentieth-Century American Presidents* (Westport, Conn.: Praeger, 1993); *Great Speeches of the 20th Century*, vol. 1 (sound recording): "The Political Arena" (Santa Monica, Calif.: Rhino Records, 1991).

Roosevelt's Statement on North African Policy

Statement issued by U.S. president Franklin D. Roosevelt on November 17, 1942, defending the political arrangements made by General Dwight D. Eisenhower, commander of the Allied invasion forces in North Africa, in securing an armistice with Vichy French forces during World War II (1939–45). Eisenhower had accepted the assistance of French admiral Jean-François Darlan, vice premier of Vichy France and widely disliked in the United States for his pro-Nazi stance. Roosevelt defended the action as a "temporary expedient, justified solely by the stress of battle" against the Axis powers, and declared that it did not represent U.S. support for a future Vichy government in France.

Further reading: Henry Steele Commager, ed., *Documents of American History*, 8th ed. (New York: Appleton-Century-Crofts, 1968); Frank N. Magill, ed., *Great Events from History: Modern European Series*, 3 vols. (Englewood Cliffs, N.J.: Salem Press, 1973).

Roosevelt's "Strenuous Life" Speech

Celebrated speech given by New York governor Theodore Roosevelt to the Hamilton Club of Chicago on April 10, 1899. He firmly asserted that "the strenuous life, the life of toil and effort" was examplary, that idleness did not befit those desiring to do serious work, and that self-respect and success in life meant endeavoring, "not to shirk difficulties, but to overcome them." This applied to the United States as well, Roosevelt said, which cannot be timid and shrink from responsibilities at home and abroad, from "a legacy of duty" left to the American people after the Spanish-American War (1898). Hawaii, Cuba, Puerto Rico, and the Philippines presented new, difficult problems, which America could solve through upholding the "qualities of courage, of honesty, and of good judgment." Roosevelt became U.S. president in 1901.

Further reading: William D. Johnston, *T.R., Champion of the Strenuous Life; A Photographic Biography of Theodore Roosevelt* (New York: Farrar, Straus & Cudahy, 1958); Theodore Roosevelt, *The Strenuous Life; Essays and Addresses by Theodore Roosevelt* (New York: The Century Co., 1901).

Roosevelt's War Message ("Day of Infamy" Speech)

Address to a joint session of the U.S. Congress delivered by President Franklin D. Roosevelt on December 8, 1941, the day after the surprise Japanese naval and air attack on the U.S. naval base at Pearl Harbor, Hawaii. Calling December 7 "a date which will live in infamy," Roosevelt announced that Japanese forces had also attacked other Pacific targets—Malaya, Hong Kong, Guam, the Philippines, Wake Island, and Midway Island. He asked Congress to declare war on Japan because of this "unprovoked and dastardly attack." Within an hour Congress complied, with only one dissenting vote, and the United States entered World War II (1939–45).

See also: U.S. DECLARATION OF WAR ON NAZI GERMANY.

Further reading: Mortimer Adler, ed., *The Annals of America*, 18 vols. (Chicago: Encyclopaedia Britannica, 1968); Henry Steele Commager, ed., *Documents of American History*, 8th ed. (New York: Appleton-Century-Crofts, 1968); George McJimsey, *The Presidency of Franklin Delano Roosevelt* (Lawrence: University Press of Kansas, 2000); Louis L. Snyder, ed., *Fifty Major Documents of the Twentieth Century* (Princeton, N.J.:D. Van Nostrand, 1955).

Root and Branch Bill (Root and Branch Petition)

Petition signed by nearly 15,000 Londoners, dated December 11, 1640, and sent to the Long Parliament of King Charles I; it demanded the abolition of episcopal government "with all its dependencies, roots and branches." The petition, particularly over the question of bishops, was violently debated in February 1641 and was introduced into the House of Commons on May 27, 1641. It proposed the abolition of archbishops, bishops, deans, archdeacons, prebendaries, and canons and suggested that a joint commission of clergy and laymen be appointed to control church affairs in each county.

The bill was dropped when the parliamentary leaders realized that it might cause a religious split in the opposition to King Charles I.

Further reading: Kenneth Fincham, *The Early Stuart Church: 1603–1642* (Stanford, Calif.: Stanford University Press, 1993); Tom Webster, *Godly Clergy in Early Stuart England: The Caroline Puritan Movement, c. 1620–1643* (New York: Cambridge University Press, 1997).

Root-Takahira Agreement

Executive agreement reached on November 30, 1908, between U.S. secretary of state Elihu Root and Japanese ambassador Takahira Kogoro, announcing the intent of their two nations to encourage free and peaceful development of commerce in the Pacific region, to maintain the "existing status quo" there, to uphold the Open Door policy of equal commercial opportunity for all nations in China, to respect each other's territorial possessions, and to support peacefully the independence and integrity of China. The agreement helped reduce tensions between the two nations, particularly over Japanese expansion in Asia and U.S. immigration policies (see GENTLEMEN'S AGREEMENT OF 1907).

Further reading: Carnegie Endowment for International Peace, Division of Intercourse and Education, *The Imperial Japanese Mission, 1917; A Record . . . Together with the Exchange of Notes Embodying the Root-Takahira Understanding . . .* (Washington, D.C.: Press of B. S. Adams, 1918); Henry Steele Commager, ed., *Documents of American History*, 8th ed. (New York: Appleton-Century-Crofts, 1968); *The United States and Japan* (New York: American Association for International Conciliation, 1918).

Rosen-Nishi Agreement (Russo-Japanese Agreement of 1898)

Convention concluded on April 25, 1898, in Tokyo by Foreign Minister Nishi Tokujiro of Japan and Foreign Minister Roman Romanovich Rosen of Russia, providing terms for the two powers' future behavior with respect to Korea. The agreement provided for Russia's recognition of Japan's special interest in Korea, and that neither power would send military or financial advisers to Korea without first consulting with the other. Since the conclusion of the 1894–95 Sino-Japanese War, Russia had taken China's place as Japan's rival in Korea. Relations began to deteriorate when Russia obtained a lease of the Liaotung Peninsula from China, a lease that the great powers had denied Japan three years earlier. The negotiations and subsequent agreement reflected the attempt to ease tensions between the two countries.

See also: RUSSO-CHINESE TREATY OF 1896.

Further reading: Morinosuke Kajima, *The Diplomacy of Japan, 1894–1922* (Tokyo: Kajima Institute of International Peace, 1976); Morinosuke Kajima, *The Emergence of Japan as a World Power, 1895–1925* (Rutland, Vt.: C. E. Tuttle Co., 1968).

Rosetta Stone   Slab of black basalt containing inscriptions in Egyptian hieroglyphic and demotic writing and in Greek; found in August 1799 near the town of Rosetta (Rashid), Egypt, by a French army captain named Boussard or Bouchard. It was apparently inscribed by ancient priests of Memphis, who recounted the generous deeds of Ptolemy V Epiphanes, king of ancient Egypt (205–180 B.C.). The hieroglyphics and demotics were indecipherable until English physicist Thomas Young and French Egyptologist Jean-François Champollion succeeded (c. 1819–22) in translating the scripts and establishing the key principles of understanding the ancient Egyptian writing.

Further reading: R. B. Parkinson, *Cracking Codes: The Rosetta Stone and Decipherment* (Berkeley: University of California Press, 1999); Robert Sole and Dominique Valbelle, *The Rosetta Stone: The Story of the Decoding of Hieroglyphics* (London: Profile, 2001).

Roskilde, Treaty of   Peace concluded at Roskilde or Roeskilde, Denmark, on February 27, 1658, by King Frederick III of Denmark and King Charles X of Sweden. During the First Northern War (1655–60), Sweden had invaded and subjugated Poland, causing Denmark to help the Poles and consequently Sweden to invade and overrun Danish lands. Frederick sued for peace. By the treaty, the Danish-held lands in southern Sweden were ceded to Charles, together with the island of Bornholm and the Norwegian area of Trondheim. Frederick, who also promised to close the Öresund (Danish Sound, through which ships had access to the Baltic) to Sweden's enemies, failed to abide by the treaty, as did Charles, and the war continued.

See also: COPENHAGEN, TREATY OF.

Further reading: *An Exact Relation of All the Transactions and Proceedings . . . from the Treaty at Rottshild, Concluded February 26. 1657/1658 . . .* (Ann Arbor, Mich.: University Microfilms International, 1986).

Roth v. United States   U.S. Supreme Court decision issued on June 24, 1957, that upheld the constitutionality of obscenity laws, declaring that obscenity is not a form of free speech protected by the FIRST AMENDMENT because it is "utterly without redeeming social importance." The Court specified a test for obscene material: "whether to the average person, applying contemporary community standards, the dominant theme of the material taken as a whole appeals to prurient interest." The case involved the federal prosecution of American publisher Samuel Roth for sending alleged pornographic and obscene material through the mails. Government censorship was broken, for the decision required courts to examine carefully offensive materials before allowing their condemnation.

Further reading: Kermit L. Hall et al., eds., *The Oxford Companion to the Supreme Court of the United States* (New York: Oxford University Press, 1992); Maureen Harrison and Steve Gilbert, eds., *Obscenity and Pornography Decisions of the United States Supreme Court* (Carlsbad, Calif.: Excellent Books, 2000); Maureen Harrison and Steve Gilbert, eds., *Landmark Decisions of the United States Supreme Court* (Beverly Hills, Calif.: Excellent Books, 1991); United States Supreme Court, *United States Reports: Cases Adjudged in the Supreme Court at . . . and Rules Announced at . . .* (New York: Banks & Brothers, Law Publishers, 1884–1921; Washington, D.C.: Government Printing Office, 1922–).

Rousseau's *Social Contract*   See SOCIAL CONTRACT.

Rowell-Sirois Report   See SIROIS COMMISSION REPORT.

Rowlatt Acts   In India, two antisedition acts passed on March 18, 1919, despite the united opposition of the Indian members of the Imperial Legislative Council. Based on the recommendations of the Rowlatt Sedition Committee (headed by Justice Sidney Rowlatt), they were an extension of the DEFENSE OF INDIA ACT and were introduced to deal with suspected antigovernment crimes and terrorism. The first act tightened the government's control over the press. The second allowed judges to try political cases without juries and authorized imprisonment without trial. Massive protests were organized all over the country; Mohandas Gandhi declared a day of fasting and ordered people to stop work. Clashes between the rioters and the police led to the horrendous Amritsar Massacre (April 13, 1919) and to the beginning of Gandhi's noncooperation movement. The Rowlatt Acts were never implemented.

Further reading: *Rowlatt Sedition Committee Report* (Calcutta, India: New Age Publishers, 1973); Stanley Wolpert, *Gandhi's Passion: The Life and Legacy of Mahatma Gandhi* (New York: Oxford University Press, 2001); Stanley Wolpert *Jinnah of Pakistan* (New York: Oxford University Press, 1989).

Royal Marriage Act, British   Act passed by the British Parliament in 1772, at the insistence of King George III (whose two brothers had recently married commoners without his consent); it required all descendants of George II below 25 years of age to obtain the sovereign's consent before marrying, failing which the marriage would be declared null and void. The children of princesses marrying into foreign families were exempt. Parliament inserted a second clause stating that descendants above 25 could get married, even without the king's approval, by giving a one-year notice to the Privy Council to allow both houses of Parliament to register their objections (if any) to the marriage. Anyone officiating at, attending, or participating in a marriage where the royal permission had not been obtained, could be punished.

Further reading: John J. Dillon, *Considerations on the Royal Marriage Act* (London: J. Ridgway, 1811); Christopher

Hibbert, *George III: A Personal History* (New York: Basic Books, 1988).

Royal Titles Act of 1876, British

British legislation in April 1876, proclaiming Queen Victoria the "empress of India." The formal proclamation was made by Viceroy Lord Lytton (Edward Robert Bulwer-Lytton) at a colorful "durbar" (formal reception) in Delhi, India, on January 1, 1877. The idea had been proposed by Prime Minister Benjamin Disraeli to convey to the Indian people the closeness of their relationship with the sovereign and was passed soon after the visit of the Prince of Wales to India in 1875–76. It was widely criticized in England as being "un-English," but the pomp and pageantry of the event found an enthusiastic audience in India. It was agreed that the title would not be used in England.

Further reading: Christopher Hibbert, *Queen Victoria: A Personal History* (New York: Basic Books, 2000); Mary Lutyens, *The Lyttons in India: An Account of Lord Lytton's Viceroyalty, 1876–1880.* (London: J. Murray, 1979).

Rueil, Treaty of

Truce between the regent government of young King Louis XIV of France and the Parlement of Paris, concluded at Rueil on March 30, 1649, after some of the Parlement's demands were conceded. The Paris Parlement, supported by court magistrates and enraged nobles, had detailed its demands in 27 articles. Among the major demands conceded by the treaty were discontinuation of the office of intendant (provincial administrator), lowering of the taille (royal tax from which the nobles and clergy were exempt), and reestablishment of normal judicial channels for the registration of financial edicts in the Parlement. A general amnesty was granted to the rebellious parliamentarians (frondeurs) and their leaders. The treaty, however, did not end the Parlement's opposition and its attempt to limit the French Crown's authority during the so-called Wars of the Fronde (1648–53).

Further reading: Frank N. Magill, ed., *Great Events from History: Modern European Series*, 3 vols. (Englewood Cliffs, N.J.: Salem Press, 1973); A. Lloyd Moote, *The Revolt of the Judges: The Parlement of Paris and the Fronde, 1643–1652* (Princeton, N.J.: Princeton University Press, 1971); J. H. Shennan, *The Parlement of Paris*, 2d ed. (Phoenix Mill, England: Sutton Publications, 1998).

Runyon v. McCrary et al.

U.S. Supreme Court decision issued on June 25, 1976, declaring that private schools may not refuse admission to students solely because of their race. The decision applied to private, commercially operated, nonsectarian schools. The case arose when the parents of Michael McCrary and Colin Gonzales, who were black students, sued Russell and Katheryne Runyon, proprietors of a private school in Arlington, Virginia, for denying admission to the students. In a 7-2 decision, the Supreme Court declared that the school violated the CIVIL RIGHTS ACT OF 1866 by refusing to extend to black people, solely because of their race, the same opportunities to make contracts that white people have.

Further reading: Kermit L. Hall et al., eds,. *The Oxford Companion to the Supreme Court of the United States* (New York: Oxford University Press, 1992); United States Supreme Court, *United States Reports: Cases Adjudged in the Supreme Court at . . . and Rules Announced at . . .* (New York: Banks & Brothers, Law Publishers, 1884–1921; Washington, D.C.: Government Printing Office, 1922–.

Rush-Bagot Agreement

Convention concluded in Washington, D.C., on April 28–29, 1817, between Great Britain and the United States for mutual disarmament on the Great Lakes and Lake Champlain. The correspondence between acting U.S. secretary of state Richard Rush and British minister to the U.S. Charles Bagot brought about the agreement, under which their respective countries consented to restrict their construction and use of naval forces on these inland waters (each side agreed to maintain only three armed ships in the Great Lakes and only one on Lake Champlain). The agreement could be annulled by either side, giving the other a six-month advance notice to that effect. The U.S. Senate approved it about a year later, thus beginning a policy (later extended to the land) of a relatively unfortified U.S.-Canadian border.

See also: GHENT, TREATY OF.

Further reading: James M. Callahan, *The Neutrality of the American Lakes and Anglo-American Relations* (New York: Johnson Reprint Corp., 1973); Henry Steele Commager, ed., *Documents of American Hsitory*, 8th ed. (New York: Appleton-Century-Crofts, 1968); Charles W. Eliot, ed., *The Harvard Classics*, 51 vols. (New York: P. F. Collier & Sons, 1938).

Russell's Ten Resolutions

See TEN RESOLUTIONS, RUSSELL'S.

Russian-British Convention of 1755

See ANGLO-RUSSIAN CONVENTION OF 1755.

Russian-British Entente of 1907

See ANGLO-RUSSIAN ENTENTE OF 1907.

Russian Constitution of 1993

Draft of a new constitution for the Russian Federation (see ALMA-ATA DECLARATION; MINSK AGREEMENT), finalized by the Constitutional Conference in November 1993 and approved in a nationwide referendum in December 1993. The president, elected by popular vote for a four-year term, was head of state and commander in chief of the armed forces and also had executive powers. Power in the ethnically diverse and democratic federation was divided among the executive, judiciary, and legislative branches, all of them independent. The bicameral Federal Assembly consisted of the 178-member Federal

Council (Upper House) and the 450-member State Duma (Lower House). The federation comprised 21 republics (see CHECHNYAN DECLARATION OF INDEPENDENCE), one autonomous oblast (region), 49 administrative oblasts, six *krais* (provinces), and 10 autonomous *okrugs* (districts). Moscow and St. Petersburg enjoyed special status.

Further reading: *The Europa World Yearbook, 1999* (London: Europa Publications, 1999).

Russian Decree of 1597   See GODUNOV'S DECREE OF 1597.

Russian Emancipation Edict of 1861   See EMANCIPATION EDICT OF 1861, RUSSIAN.

Russian Fundamental Laws of 1864

Legal reforms promulgated after two years of preparation (by an ad hoc commission) on November 20, 1864, under the influence of Russian czar Alexander II; they provided for the reformation of the judicial system in Russia. Based on European models, a new Russian judiciary was set up with modernized court procedures for both civil and criminal prosecutions. The judiciary was split into two branches: justices of the peace, newly elected by zemstvos (district assemblies), who dealt with minor cases; and regular civil and criminal courts under judges appointed by the state. Through the laws, all men became equal before the law, no longer being considered according to class (the old system of class courts was abolished); a man could not be convicted of any crime without due process; the practice of trial by jury was implemented (in courts open to the public); and separation of the judicial branch of the government from all other was effected. The reform of the laws had been necessary in order to accommodate the new legal status of the recently emancipated serf (see EMANCIPATION EDICT OF 1861, RUSSIAN).

Further reading: Stephen Graham, *Tsar of Freedom, the Life and Reign of Alexander II* (Hamden, Conn.: Archon Books, 1968); David Saunders, *Russia in the Age of Reaction and Reform 1801–1881* (New York: Longman, 1993).

Russian Fundamental Laws of 1906

Imperial proclamation of May 6, 1906, detailing the structure of Russia's constitutional monarchy established by the OCTOBER MANIFESTO. Under the new laws, the czar or emperor retained control of the executive and all its ministers, including exclusive authority over the armed forces, foreign policy, the succession to the throne, the imperial court and lands. The czar also continued as head of the Russian Orthodox Church. He had the authority to call and disband the Duma, to veto legislation, and, when the Duma was not in session, to issue ukazes with the authority of laws, subject to the subsequent approval of the next session of the Duma. The Duma had limited legislative and budgetary rights: Nearly 40 percent of the state budget was excluded from its fiscal responsibility, including state loans and the budgets of the army, navy, and the imperial court. Moreover, if the Duma did not pass the annual budget, the amount for the previous year was automatically reenacted. The state council, an advisory body of dignitaries established by Czar Alexander I in 1810, became the conservative upper legislative chamber, equal in rights to the Duma.

Further reading: Albert P. Blaustein and Jay A. Sigler, eds., *Constitutions That Made History* (New York: Paragon House Publishers, 1988); Anna Geifman, ed., *Russia under the Last Tsar: Opposition and Subversion* (Malden, Mass.: Blackwell Publishers, 1999); Frank N. Magill, ed., *Great Events from History: Modern European Series*, 3 vols. (Englewood Cliffs, N.J.: Salem Press, 1973).

Russian (Muscovite) Code of 1497 (Sûdebnik)

Code of laws compiled in 1497 by order of Ivan III the Great, grand duke of Moscow, describing the rights of the various Russian social classes. It repeated the important provision found earlier in the RUSSIAN TRUTH, namely that a person became a slave by selling oneself, by marrying a slave, or by turning into a servant. But included also were new provisions making slavery more difficult. The law code also stated that a peasant could relocate, provided he paid his landowner (master) a fee; however, he could leave only during two fixed weeks of the year—the week before and the week after St. George's Day (November 25), at the beginning of the inclement Russian winter! The code was revised in 1550 by Grand Duke Ivan IV the Terrible.

Further reading: Richard Hellie, *Slavery in Russia, 1450–1725* (Chicago: University of Chicago Press, 1982); Daniel H. Kaiser, *The Growth of the Law in Medieval Russia* (Princeton, N.J.: Princeton University Press, 1980).

Russian New Code of 1649 (Sobornoe Ulajenie)

First comprehensive compilation of laws in Muscovite Russia, dealing principally with social relationships; prepared by a governmental assembly in 1649 by order of Czar Alexis. The code forced individuals into fixed classes according to their livelihoods or the needs of the state. Peasants were officially made the property of landowners, were held responsible for the debts of bankrupt landlords, and were not permitted to speak against their owners even in court (except when the latter was acting against the interests of the state). Every individual, free or unfree, was required (under penalty of death) to inform the authorities of "anti-governmental plots." The code became the basis of the czarist regime in Russia until the late 19th century.

Further reading: Joseph T. Fuhrmann, *Tsar Alexis, His Reign and His Russia* (Gulf Breeze, Fla.: Academic International Press, 1981).

Russian Truth (Ruskaya Pravda)

Compilation of a series of early Russian legal pronouncements made by private persons from the 11th to the 13th century. Slavery was the subject most often addressed; the captor of a runaway slave was to receive a large reward; an abettor of a fugitive slave was to be punished severely. And a person became a slave in three ways: by selling oneself, marrying a slave, or appearing as a servant. There were pronouncements about a person borrowing money from a wealthy landowner, requiring him thenceforth to do whatever work the landowner requested of him and forbidding him to testify against his creditor in court. And should the borrower flee, he would become the landowner's slave if caught. Statements were also made concerning the right of inheritance (a concern not enjoyed by lower-class members, even when free).

Further reading: Gregory L. Freeze, ed., *Russia: A History* (New York: Oxford University Press, 1997).

Russo-Chinese Treaties of 1945, 1950, and 1954

See SINO-SOVIET TREATY OF 1945; SINO-SOVIET TREATY OF 1950; SINO-SOVIET TREATY OF 1954.

Russo-Chinese Treaty of 1896

Pact secretly concluded in Moscow between Russia and China on June 3, 1896, providing for a 15-year-long defensive alliance against Japan. The treaty provided that Russia would protect China in the event of a Japanese attack. In return, Russia gained the right to construct the Chinese Eastern Railway, which would run from Russia's Siberia, through Manchuria (which belonged to China), to Vladivostok on the Pacific coast. The railway was to be owned by Russia and operated by Russians. The railway, ostensibly required in order to ensure the speedy arrival of Russian forces in China's defense, would thus be much shorter—and less expensive—than any railway running its full course through Russian territory would have been. The treaty followed the conclusion of the 1894–95 Sino-Japanese War, in which China was defeated.

See also: ROSEN-NISHI AGREEMENT.

Further reading: Geoffrey Drage, *Russian Affairs* (London: J. Murray, 1904); Ernest B. Price, *The Russo-Japanese Treaties of 1907–1916 Concerning Manchuria and Mongolia [appendices include an English translation of the Russo-Chinese Treaty of 1896]* (New York: AMS Press, 1971).

Russo-German Tariff Treaty of 1894

Treaty signed on March 16, 1894, at the conclusion of a customs war between the two countries; it lowered import duties and heralded a new spirit of cooperation between them. The tariff war had resulted from high import duties in both countries. Germany had instituted protective tariffs in 1879; and in the 1880s, Russia had increased duties on imported industrial goods and raw materials. In 1890 and 1891, Russia imposed two large tariff increases, which triggered the customs war. Although the treaty with Russia was only one of several Germany concluded with her continental trading partners, it was a particularly significant one, in that it signaled a foreign policy shift away from Great Britain. The agreement also demonstrated Russia's desire for better relations with Germany; however, it did not prevent the former from concluding the anti-German Franco-Russian defensive alliance later in the year.

Further reading: George W. Buchanan et al., *Reports on Tariff Wars Between Certain European States* (London: Harrison & Sons, 1904).

Russo-Japanese Agreement of 1898

See ROSEN-NISHI AGREEMENT.

Russo-Japanese Agreement of 1910

Agreement concluded by Japan and Russia on July 4, 1910, expanding upon the Russo-Japanese Convention of July 30, 1907, which was concerned with the two powers' interests in the Far East. The treaty reconfirmed the two powers' agreement to uphold the integrity of China, in accordance with the great powers' policies. Secretly however, the treaty included their agreement that, in the event that territory within their respective spheres of influence (which included Outer Mongolia and northern Manchuria for Russia, and Inner Mongolia and southern Manchuria for Japan) were threatened by another power, the two allies would act together to carry out measures agreed upon in common. The accord was one of several Russo-Japanese agreements concluded after the close of the Russo-Japanese War of 1904–5, when Russia and Japan gradually began to strengthen their alliance with the hope of expanding their influence in the Far East.

Further reading: Ernest B. Price, *The Russo-Japanese Treaties of 1907–1916 Concerning Manchuria and Mongolia* (New York: AMS Press, 1971).

Russo-Prussian Treaty of 1793 (Second Treaty of Partition of Poland)

Agreement concluded on January 23, 1793, between Russia's czarina Catherine II the Great and Prussia's king Frederick William II, thwarting Polish constitutional reforms by partitioning Poland for a second time (see ST. PETERSBURG, TREATY OF [1772]). By the treaty, Russia acquired most of the western Ukraine (Ruthenia) and most of Lithuania, while Prussia received Danzig (Gdańsk), Thorn (Toruń), and Great Poland, as well as some of Mazovia. Poland was to be governed by her old constitution (through which the obstructive *liberum veto* [which allowed legislation to be vetoed by a single vote in the Diet] was operative). Politically and economically disorganized, Poland could not defend herself against her powerful neighbors, which were eager to make new conquests.

See also: AUSTRO-RUSSIAN AND RUSSO-PRUSSIAN TREATIES OF 1795.

Further reading: Robert H. Lord, *The Second Partition of Poland; a Study in Diplomatic History* (New York: AMS Press, 1969); Jerzy Lukowski, *The Partitions of Poland: 1772, 1793, 1795* (New York: Longman, 1999); Frank N. Magill, ed., *Great Events from History: Modern European Series*, 3 vols. (Englewood Cliffs, N.J.: Salem Press, 1973).

Rutan v. Republican Party of Illinois   Landmark U.S. Supreme Court decision issued on June 21, 1990, barring the political patronage-based hiring, promoting, and transferring of most public employees. The Court's five-to-four ruling grounded on the First Amendment's protection for free speech and free association, was a broad extension of two Supreme Court decisions—*Elrod* v. *Burns* (1976) and *Branti* v. *Frankel* (1980)—which prohibited government officials from firing anyone solely because of their political affiliation, unless party loyalty is an appropriate requirement. The 1990 ruling was the result of a lawsuit by five Illinois residents (including Cynthia B. Rutan, a rehabilitation counselor) against the Illinois Republican Party and top state officials, alleging that they had been denied state jobs, promotions, and transfers because they had not been supporters of Governor James Thompson and Illinois's other Republican leaders.

Further reading: Kermit L. Hall et al., eds., *The Oxford Companion to the Supreme Court of the United States* (New York: Oxford University Press, 1992); United States Supreme Court, *United States Reports: Cases Adjudged in the Supreme Court at . . . and Rules Announced at . . .* (New York: Banks & Brothers, Law Publishers, 1884–1921; Washington, D.C.: Government Printing Office, 1922–).

Ryswick (Rijswijk), Treaty of   Treaty wherein the allies (England, Spain, Holland, and the Holy Roman emperor) signed an agreement with France to conclude the War of the Grand Alliance (1688–97). Negotiations began on May 9, 1697, with William III of England and Louis XIV of France bargaining on the main issues. The status quo was reestablished in the French and British colonies, and Louis acknowledged William (who had seized power in 1688) as the rightful heir to the English throne. The French and the Dutch worked out a more acceptable commercial pact, agreeing to lift the ban on Dutch salted herring and to return to the tariffs of 1664. Spain received Catalonia, Luxembourg, and some of the territories in the Spanish Netherlands, and the Holy Roman Empire received many fortified areas along the Rhine. Alsace and Lorraine (without Strasbourg, which France kept) were returned to Duke Leopold. According to the treaty, the Dutch troops were to guard the main fortresses in the Spanish Netherlands and Roman Catholicism was to be retained in the areas given to the empire. In return for commercial gains, the Dutch gave up Pondicherry in India to the French East India Company. The treaty was primarily negotiated at Ryswick or Rijswijk, Holland, and signed by England, France, Spain, and Holland on September 20, 1697, and by the Holy Roman emperor on October 30, 1697; it was designed to serve as a check on French offensives, but it was more a temporary settlement rather than a long-lasting peace effort.

See also: BARRIER TREATIES.

Further reading: Fred L. Israel, ed., *Major Peace Treaties of Modern History, 1648–1967*, 4 vols. (New York: Chelsea House, 1967); William MacDonald, ed., *Select Charters and Other Documents Illustrative of American History, 1606–1775* (New York: Macmillan, 1899).

S

Sabotage Bill See GENERAL LAW AMENDMENT ACT, SOUTH AFRICAN.

Sagauli, Treaty of British-Gurkha settlement ending the Anglo-Nepali or Gurkha War (1814–16); signed at Sagauli in northern India on March 4, 1816. The Gurkha leaders of Nepal accepted the 1815 Treaty of KATMANDU and ceded to the British Indian government the disputed Terai region and conquered territories west of the Kali River as far as the Sutlej River. Nepal remained independent and agreed to have a British resident officer (like an ambassador) in its capital, Katmandu. The treaty is important in that it virtually defined the borders of present-day Nepal. After the Indian Mutiny (1857–58), the British rewarded the loyal Gurkha forces of Nepal by restoring some lands from the Terai region.

Further reading: Kiranchandra Chaudhuri, *Anglo-Nepalese Relations, from the Earliest Times of the British Rule in India till the Gurkha War* (Calcutta, India: Modern Book Agency Private, 1960); Kanchanmoy Mojumdar, *Anglo-Nepalese Relations in the Nineteenth Century* (Calcutta, India: Firma K. L. Mukhopadhyay, 1973).

St.-Clair-sur-Epte, Treaty of Agreement between King Charles III (Charles the Simple) of France and Rollo, leader of the Norsemen (Northmen), at St.-Clair-sur-Epte, France, in A.D. 911; it legalized the settlement of the Norsemen along the lower Seine River. Seeking to stop the influx of Scandinavian invaders, the French king had initiated negotiations after his troops defeated Norsemen at Chartres earlier in the year. Rollo submitted to Charles's authority and agreed to convert to Christianity and to help defend the country against attack. In return, Charles endowed him with the counties of Rouen, Lisieux, Evreux, and the land between the Epte and Bresle Rivers and the sea, the territory later known as Normandy. The treaty, while it regulated the Norse or Viking settlement in the Normandy area, established a precedent in that Vikings arriving in the Loire River region began to demand a similar settlement.

Further reading: David Bates and Anne Curry, *England and Normandy in the Middle Ages* (Rio Grande, Ohio: Hambledon Press, 1994); Joseph H. Dahmus, *A History of Medieval Civilization* (New York: Odyssey Press, 1964); Eleanor Searle, *Predatory Kinship and the Creation of Norman Power, 840–1066* (Berkeley: University of California Press, 1988).

St.-Germain, Treaty of (1632) Settlement in 1632 between France and England, serving to resolve territorial ambiguities left by the 1629 Treaty of SUSA. Under the terms of the treaty, which was concluded at St.-Germain-en-Laye, France, all territory in New France (Canada) and Acadia (Nova Scotia, including Cape Breton Island, and New Brunswick) that had been occupied or seized by the English in the course of past war was restored to French control. Included in the areas returned were the important trading colonies at Quebec and Port Royal (Annapolis Royal, Nova Scotia).

Further reading: W. J. Eccles, *The French in North America, 1500–1783*, 3d ed. (East Lansing: Michigan State University Press, 1998).

St.-Germain, Treaty of (1679)

Agreement signed at St.-Germain-en-Laye (near Paris) on June 29, 1679, restoring peace between Sweden (France's ally) and Brandenburg and helping end the Third Dutch War (1672–78) and the Danish-Swedish War of 1675–79. The elector of Brandenburg returned to Sweden most of his conquests in Pomerania. The powerful King Louis XIV of France ensured that Swedish interests were not compromised: Sweden paid a small indemnity and returned East Friesland to Brandenburg. This settlement was followed on August 23, 1679, by the Treaty of Fontainebleau, a peace accord among France, Denmark, and Sweden, whereby Denmark was compelled to return all her Swedish conquests.

See also: NIJMEGEN, TREATIES OF.

Further reading: Carl J. Ekburg, *The Failure of Louis XIV's Dutch War* (Chapel Hill: University of North Carolina Press, 1979); J. R. Jones, *The Anglo-Dutch Wars of the Seventeenth Century* (New York: Longman, 1996).

St.-Germain, Treaty of (1919)

Allies' pact at St.-Germain-en-Laye, France, September 10, 1919, with Austria, after the defeat of the Austro-Hungarian Empire in World War I (1914–18). Operative July 16, 1920, Austria's Sudeten areas, comprising 3.5 million Germans, became part of Czechoslovakia, while the southern Tyrol, with 250,000 Germans, was allotted to Italy—in utter disregard for the principle of self-determination that the Allies had earlier avowed. Austria's independence was acknowledged on the condition that she would not surrender it except with the permission of the League of Nations Council (see VERSAILLES TREATY OF [1919]). Carinthia was given to Austria, as were the westernmost regions of three Hungarian provinces (see TRIANON, TREATY OF); a 1921 plebiscite restored Sopron (Ödenburg) to Hungary. Austria's army was limited to 30,000 volunteers, while her naval fleet was distributed among the Allies. She was forced to accept responsibility for the damages of the war, but no financial compensation was actually claimed.

Further reading: Nina Almond and Ralph H. Lutz, eds., *The Treaty of St. Germain: A Documentary History* (Stanford, Calif.: Stanford University Press, 1935); Fred L. Israel, ed., *Major Peace Treaties of Modern History, 1648–1967*, 4 vols. (New York: Chelsea House, 1967); Lawrence Martin, *The Treaties of Peace, 1919–1923* (New York: Carnegie Endowment for International Peace, 1924).

St. Lawrence Seaway Treaties

Treaties concluded by the United States and Canada in 1932 and 1941 and, definitively, on August 18, 1954, in Ottawa; they provided for the joint construction of a modern inland seaway along the St. Lawrence River. According to the latter treaty, the seaway would extent from Montreal to the Great Lakes and would consist of a series of canals, some deepened and others newly created, as well as dams and power stations. The seaway, once completed, would thus provide the two countries with approximately 2,300 miles of waterways capable of supporting the transportation of modern vessels, as well as being a source of hydroelectric power. The seaway was opened to traffic in 1959. Canada had been prepared to build the seaway alone, because of past U.S. failure to ratify a treaty; Canada's decision to do so (May 6, 1954) propelled the United States to authorize construction, three months after the Canadian government had approved it.

Further reading: William H. Becker, *From the Atlantic to the Great Lakes: A History of the U.S. Army Corps of Engineers and the St. Lawrence Seaway* (Washington, D.C.: Government Printing Office, 1984); Gennifer Sussman, *The St. Lawrence Seaway: History and Analysis of a Joint Water Highway* (Montreal: C.D. Howe Research Institute, 1978).

St.-Ouen, Declaration of

Proclamation made by King Louis XVIII of France, brother of the guillotined French king Louis XVI, in St.-Ouen (outside Paris) on May 2, 1814, upon his reentry into France from Britain. Although the Senate had, prior to his arrival, adopted a constitution upholding the right of the French people to elect their king, a right that the king was required to swear to defend, the declaration stated that the king would draw up a new constitution, which would be liberal in its provisions. The new king had thus acquired the old monarchical privilege of rule not dependent on popular consent.

Further reading: Philip Mansel, *Louis XVIII*, rev. ed. (Stroud, England: Sutton, 1999); Pamela M. Pilbeam, *The Constitutional Monarchy in France, 1814–1848: Revolution and Stability* (Harlow, England: Longman, 1999).

St. Petersburg, Treaty of (1723)

Treaty of alliance concluded on September 23, 1723, at St. Petersburg between Russia and Persia (Iran). It was proposed to check expansionist ambitions of the Ottoman Turks to the east. Terms of the treaty, which was never ratified by the Persian government, were that Persia would cede to Russia the cities of Derbent and Baku (ports on the Caspian Sea) along with the southern and western Caspian shoreline and the surrounding provinces of Gilan, Mazanderan, and Astrabad (Gorgan, Iran) and that Russia would supply Persia with arms and soldiers against threatening Afghans and Turks.

Further reading: Guive Mirfendereski, *A Diplomatic History of the Caspian Sea: Treaties, Diaries, and Other Stories* (New York: Palgrave, 2001).

St. Petersburg, Treaty of (1762)

Treaty of peace made between Czar Peter III of Russia and King Frederick II the Great of Prussia on May 5, 1762, at St. Petersburg, ending the hostilities between them, which were part of the larger Seven

Years' War (1756–63). The treaty, which kept Frederick from almost certain defeat, provided for an "eternal peace" between the two states; for Russia to return east Prussian and east Pomeranian territory to Prussia; and for Russia's aid in bringing about a settlement between Sweden and Prussia (foes in the war). In July 1762, Peter (a devotee of Frederick) was deposed and assassinated and succeeded by his wife, Czarina Catherine II the Great, who broke the treaty with Prussia but did not resume the war.

See also: HAMBURG, TREATY OF.

Further reading: Carol S. Leonard, *Reform and Regicide: The Reign of Peter III of Russia* (Bloomington: Indiana University Press, 1993); Karl W. Schweizer, *England, Prussia, and the Seven Years War: Studies in Alliance Policies and Diplomacy* (Lewiston, Maine: E. Mellen Press, 1989).

St. Petersburg, Treaty of (1772) (First Treaty of Partition of Poland)

Agreement drawn up by Prussian king Frederick II the Great and signed by Prussia, Russia, and Austria on August 5, 1772, in which the three powers arranged for the first partition of Poland. Frederick had sought to strengthen Prussia while controlling Russian and Austrian advances. By the treaty, Russias obtained the lands east of the Dvina and Dnieper Rivers (White Russia); Austria received the territory south of the Vistula River and the kingdom of Galicia; and Prussia received Polish or west Prussia, excluding Danzig (Gdańsk) and Thorn (Toruń). Poland consequently lost about a third of her territory and a half of her inhabitants. Poland's Diet ratified the treaty in 1775, though this act was merely ornamental.

See also: RUSSO-PRUSSIAN TREATY OF 1793.

Further reading: Herbert H. Kaplan, *The First Partition of Poland* (New York: AMS Press, 1972); Jerzy Lukowski, *The Partitions of Poland: 1772, 1793, 1795* (New York: Longman, 1999); Frank N. Magill, ed., *Great Events from History: Modern European Series*, 3 vols. (Englewood Cliffs, N.J.: Salem Press, 1973).

St. Petersburg, Treaty of (1805)

Agreement between Britain and Russia signed at St. Petersburg on April 8, 1805, for the formation of a third coalition of European nations against France's emperor Napoléon I in order to restore peace and the balance of power during the Napoleonic Wars (1803–15). They agreed to free North Germany, Holland, Switzerland, and Italy from French control and to strengthen Holland, Switzerland, and Prussia against French attacks. In addition to maintaining her own troops, Britain agreed to pay £1,250,000 annually for every 100,000 soldiers sent by the European powers against France, and to return British conquests in the East and West Indies. Sardinia was to receive Piedmont, and Russia was to send 115,000 troops besides those guarding her borders.

Further reading: H. T. Dickinson, ed., *Britain and the French Revolution, 1789–1815* (Basingstroke, England: Mac-

millan Education, 1989); John H. Rose, ed., *Select Dispatches from the British Foreign Office Archives, Relating to the Formation of the Third Coalition Against France, 1804–1805* (London: Royal Historical Society, 1904).

St. Petersburg, Treaty of (1812)

Agreement concluded at St. Petersburg on April 5, 1812, between Sweden and Russia at a time when both powers were threatened by Napoleonic France. Through the treaty Sweden renounced all claims upon Finland, formerly a Swedish territory, which Russia had annexed in 1808 and later secured through the Treaty of FREDRICKSHAMM; Sweden promised to send troops to northern Germany in order to fight the French; and Russia promised to support Sweden's anticipated attempt to annex Norway, a Danish possession. The treaty was concluded on the eve of Napoleon's invasion of Russia, and after France's reoccupation of Sweden's island of Rügen and Swedish Pomerania.

See also: ÅBO, TREATY OF (1812); PARIS, TREATY OF (1810).

Further reading: Alan W. Palmer, *Bernadotte: Napoleon's Marshall, Sweden's King* (London: Murray, 1990).

St. Petersburg, Treaty of (1875)

Treaty concluded at St. Petersburg on May 7, 1875, between Russia and Japan, providing for the recognition of the two countries' territorial possessions in the Far East. Through the treaty Japan recognized Russia's control over the island of Sakhalin, located north of Japan, off Russia's eastern coast; in return, Japan's possession of all of the Kuril Islands, located to the east of Sakhalin (the two countries had possessed a half each of the Kurils until then), was recognized by Russia. With regard to Sakhalin, the treaty merely confirmed the status quo, as the Russians had, by 1875, come into almost complete occupation of the island, and the Japanese were incapable of reversing the situation. The Russian cession of her half of the Kuril Islands was a measure largely taken to ease Russo-Japanese tensions, which had increased because of the Russian occupation of Sakhalin.

Further reading: James W. Morley, *Japan's Foreign Policy, 1868–1941: A Research Guide* (New York: Columbia University Press, 1974); M. S. Vysokov, *A Brief History of Sakhalin and the Kurils* (Yuzhno-Sakhalinsk, Russia: Sakhalin Book Publishing House, 1996).

St. Petersburg, Treaty of (1881)

Treaty concluded at St. Petersburg on February 24, 1881, between Russia and China, bringing an end to the 1879–81 "Ili Crisis" over possession of Ili, a river-valley area located in northern Chinese Turkistan, near Russian Turkistan. Through the treaty Russia agreed to return most of Ili to China and to reduce the number of Russian consulates in the area to two; China was required to make a heavy indemnity payment to Russia and to allow Russia to open new consulates in central Asia. Russia had occupied the territory in 1871 at a time of instability in the region. Contrary to her promises to withdraw she continued to occupy Ili, and the situation deteriorated even further when China was tricked into signing away most of the territory in the Treaty of Livadia (September 15, 1879), which gave Ili to China in name only and left the Russians in control with the right to set up consulates in seven key places. China threatened to go to war, but the crisis was resolved with the intervention of Western diplomats to bring about the 1881 peace.

Further reading: S. C. M. Paine, *Imperial Rivals: China, Russia, and Their Disputed Frontier* (Armonk, N.Y.: M. E. Sharpe, 1996); A. D. Voskresenskii, *The Sino-Russian St. Petersburg Treaty of 1881: Diplomatic History* (Commack, N.Y.: Nova Science, 1995).

St. Petersburg Protocol of 1826   Agreement between the duke of Wellington (Great Britain) and Czar Nicholas I (Russia) to try to obtain for Greece an autonomous status within the Ottoman Empire; signed on April 4, 1826, during a diplomatic conference at St. Petersburg. After the Ottoman Turks laid siege to the Greek fortress of Missolonghi in 1825, the Greek Assembly formally requested the British government to mediate between the Turks and Greeks (during the Greek War of Independence [1821–32]). Britain sent Wellington to St. Petersburg to prevent the czar from threatening war with the Turks; by the protocol, Britain and Russia agreed to use their good offices to settle the war and establish self-government for Greece.

See also: LONDON, TREATY OF (1827).

Further reading: David Brewer, *The Greek War of Independence, 1821–1833* (New York: Overlook Press, 2001).

Salary Grab Act, U.S.   Congressional act passed on March 3, 1873, raising the salaries of U.S. government officials: for the president, an increase from $25,000 to $50,000; chief justice, $8,500 to $10,500; vice president, cabinet members, associate justices, and speaker of the House, $8,000 to $10,000; senators and representatives, $5,000 to $7,500. The increase for members of Congress was made retroactive for two years, giving them "back pay" of $5,000 each. Public furor made the legislation an election issue, and most congressmen, of both parties, refused to accept the increase, returned it, or donated it to charity. On January 20, 1874, Congress repealed the law except for the increases for the president and Supreme Court justices.

Further reading: William S. Robinson, *The Salary Grab: A History of the Passage of the Act* (Boston: Lee & Shepard, 1873).

Salbai, Treaty of   Peace pact made between the Marathas (Hindu people in India) and the British on May 17, 1782, ending the first war between them (1775–82) and establishing, beyond doubt, the supremacy of the British in India. It was achieved through the mediation of Mahadaji Sindhia, a Hindu leader. The Bombay government secured two decades

of peace with the Marathas and sent Raghunatha Rao (the peshwa whom they had supported) into retirement. The two parties agreed to keep peace between them and their respective allies. All conquests after the Treaty of PURANDHAR were to be restored, along with some revenue from the Gujarat state of Broach. Hyder Ali, Muslim ruler of Mysore who had allied with the Marathas in the war, returned the lands he had seized from the British and the nawab (viceroy) of Arcot. He died before the treaty could be ratified, and the peshwa minister Nana Fadnavis delayed its ratification until February 20, 1783.

Further reading: Praxy Fernandes, *The Tigers of Mysore: A Biography of Hyder Ali & Tipu Sultan*, rev. and updated ed. (New York: Viking, 1991); J. F. Michaud, *Michaud's History of Mysore, under Hyder Ali & Tippoo Sultan*, trans. V. K. Raman Menon (New Delhi, India: Asian Educational Services, 1985).

Salic Law (Lex Salica)   Code of laws introduced by the Salian or Merovingian Franks into Gaul (France) about A.D. 507–11 (the last years of the reign of Clovis I, the first Merovingian king). First written in Latin, reportedly by four venerable leaders, the code stated primarily the penalties (fines) for committing various civil offenses and crimes (unpaid debts, theft, assault, battery, and murder, among others). Trial was generally by compurgation (the legal clearing of an accused person by witnesses testifying to his innocence) or by ordeal (guilt or innocence determined by the effect of fire, water, fatigue, or other trying experience on the accused) or by combat (the guilty lost in battle, according to God's judgment). The code's most famous article read: "Of Salic land no portion of the inheritance shall go to a woman." At the time only men could inherit Salic lands given for military service. Women in medieval France, however, held large landed estates, but in the 1300s they were excluded from succession to the French throne by the arbitrary extension of the "Salic principle" to the crown. In Spain, between 1713 and 1833, the throne could pass only through the males because this Salic Law of Succession was applied also.

Further reading: Joseph H. Dahmus, *A History of Medieval Civilization* (New York: Odyssey Press, 1964); Katherine F. Drew, *The Laws of the Salian Franks* (Philadelphia: University of Pennsylvania Press, 1991); Louis L. Snyder, ed., *Documents of German History* (New Brunswick, N.J.: Rutgers University Press, 1958).

SALT I and II   See STRATEGIC ARMS LIMITATION TREATY OF 1972 (SALT I); STRATEGIC ARMS LIMITATION TREATY OF 1979 (SALT II).

Salvadoran Constitution of 1962   Constitution signed on January 8, 1962, by members of El Salvador's ruling Civil-Military Directorate and cabinet, containing several reforms in addition to a large part of the Salvadoran Constitution of

1950, which it replaced. The 1962 constitution provided for a government consisting of independent legislative, executive, and judicial branches; for fundamental rights, including equality before the law, freedom of religion, expression, and asylum, and the right of habeas corpus; and for elections of the legislature and president. Among the reforms was a provision reducing the presidential term from six to five years. The constitution also stipulated that a president could not succeed himself, and provided for the right of insurrection in the event of violation of this principle. As in other Central American constitutions (see HONDURAN CONSTITUTION OF 1965), the Salvadoran document declared the nation's obligation to promote the restoration of a republic of Central America (see CENTRAL AMERICAN TREATY OF UNION; UNITED PROVINCES OF CENTRAL AMERICA, DECLARATION OF INDEPENDENCE OF THE).

Further reading: *Constitution of the Republic of El Salvador, 1962* (Washington, D.C.: General Secretariat, Organization of American States, 1971).

Samoa Act   See BERLIN ACT OF 1889.

Samoan Treaty   See ANGLO-GERMAN TREATY OF 1899.

Sanaa, Treaty of   Treaty of friendship and mutual cooperation between Great Britain and Yemen; concluded on February 11, 1934, and ratified at Sanaa (San'a, North Yemen) on September 4, 1934. Thereby, Britain acknowledged the independence of Yemen, and both countries agreed not to violate the existing border situation between them in the region—the demarcation of the frontiers between Yemen and the British protectorate of Aden (South Yemen). Therefore the key issue remained unresolved and was deferred to future negotiations. The two countries were now free to enter into economic and commercial agreements, being accorded "most-favored nation" status in each other's countries and ports. Neither country was to participate in wrecking, or conniving to do so, this harmonious relationship. The treaty was valid for 40 years.

Further reading: Harvey Sicherman, *Aden and British Strategy, 1839–1968* (Philadelphia: Foreign Policy Research Institute, 1972).

San Germano, Peace of   Treaty concluded by Holy Roman Emperor Frederick II, king of Sicily, and Pope Gregory IX on July 23, 1230, at San Germano (Cassino, Italy); it represented a temporary halt to a power struggle between them. Frederick's independence in his kingdom of Sicily and accord with the Turkish sultan were unacceptable to Gregory, who raised an army and invaded Sicily, but was defeated by Frederick's forces. The treaty reflected generally a return to the status quo: papal acceptance of Frederick's sovereignty in Sicily and the Holy Roman Empire, and the emperor's promise

to safeguard papal domains and to accept the pope's authority over the clergy in all matters in Sicily.

Further reading: David Abulafia, *Frederick II: A Medieval Emperor* (New York: Oxford University Press, 1992).

San Ildefonso, Treaty of (1762)   Secret treaty signed at San Ildefonso, Spain, on November 3, 1762, whereby France fulfilled her obligations of alliance (1761) with Spain (see FAMILY COMPACTS). The treaty was concluded simultaneously with the preliminaries of their 1763 Treaty of PARIS with Britain. France surrendered to Spain the Isle of Orleans (New Orleans) and Louisiana west of the Mississippi River. These gains, together with those of the Treaty of Paris, strengthened Spain's position in the New World and later brought her into direct conflict with Britain.

See also: ARANJUEZ, CONVENTION OF.

Further reading: Joseph G. Tregle, Jr., ed., *The History of Louisiana; Translated from the French of M. Le Page du Pratz* (Baton Rouge: Louisiana State University Press, 1975); John P. Moore, *Revolt in Louisiana: The Spanish Occupation, 1766–1770* (Baton Rouge: Louisiana University Press, 1976).

San Ildefonso, Treaty of (1777)   Accord between Spain and Portugal signed in 1777, settling hostilities between those countries in South America and establishing boundaries in the so-called debatable lands. By this treaty, Spain returned Santa Catarina to the Portuguese and recognized essentially the same boundaries established by the Treaty of MADRID in 1750. However, the seven Christian missions of Banda Oriental (Uruguay) were awarded to Spain. In addition, Portugal ceded Colônia del Sacramento as well as her claim to a frontier on the Río de la Plata, while Spain was left in control of the bulk of the Plata region.

Further reading: Bernard Moses, *South America on the Eve of Emancipation; the Southern Spanish Colonies in the Last Half-Century of their Dependence* (New York: Cooper Square Publishers, 1966); Mark D. Szuchman and Jonathan C. Brown, *Revolution and Restoration: The Rearrangement of Power in Argentina, 1776–1860* (Lincoln: University of Nebraska Press, 1994).

San Ildefonso, Treaty of (1796)   Offensive and defensive Franco-Spanish alliance directed against Britain; signed on August 19, 1796, at San Ildefonso, Spain. Negotiated mainly by Spanish prime minister Manuel de Godoy, it committed them to defend each other's territories (if attacked) through naval and military support. When both powers were directly involved in war, peace was to be negotiated "only by mutual consent." A commercial pact, granting each country "most-favored nation status" in ally ports, was to be concluded soon. The treaty's secret clauses called for the Batavian Republic (the Netherlands) to be included in the alliance (June 28, 1797), banned French émigrés from Spanish naval and military forces, promised to force Portugal to close her

ports to England, and allowed warships and privateers of both countries free access in each other's New World colonies. For Spain, the alliance was not a wise one since it exposed her American colonies to Britain and the United States.

See also: SAN ILDEFONSO, TREATY OF (1800).

Further reading: Douglas Hilt, *The Troubled Trinity: Godoy and the Spanish Monarchs* (Tuscaloosa: University of Alabama Press, 1987).

San Ildefonso, Treaty of (1800)

Secret treaty concluded at San Ildefonso, Spain, on October 1, 1800, between King Charles IV of Spain and Napoléon Bonaparte of France, reestablishing the French colonial empire in America. Charles IV surrendered Louisiana (see PARIS, TREATY OF [1763]) and Spain's share in Santo Domingo to France, receiving in return the expanded kingdom of Tuscany (designated "kingdom of Etruria") for his son-in-law. Thus, Charles's brother Ferdinand, the reigning duke of Parma, was deposed. Spain was also to present France with six warships. Subsequently (January 20, 1801), Spain joined France in sending an ultimatum to Portugal, ordering her to withdraw from the English alliance and to allow Spanish troops to occupy part of her territory as surety for England's capture of Spanish possessions. Portugal's refusal led to the War of the Oranges (1801) (see MADRID, TREATY OF [1801]). The terms of the treaty of San Ildefonso were confirmed by the Convention of Aranjuez of March 21, 1801.

Further reading: Avalon Project, *Treaty of San Ildefonso: October 1, 1800*, Avalon Project at the Yale Law School, available online at http://www.yale.edu/lawweb/avalon/ildefens.htm.

San Lorenzo, Treaty of   See PINCKNEY TREATY.

San Luis Potosí, Plan of

Revolutionary program issued in San Luis Potosí, Mexico, in November 1910 by Francisco I. Madero (a wealthy liberal opposition leader) in which he called for the overthrow of President Porfirio Díaz of Mexico. In the plan Madero declared the recent presidential, judicial, and congressional elections null and void and named November 20, 1910, as the starting date of the revolution. Although he disavowed the Díaz regime, he agreed to recognize obligations contracted by the government before November 20. Denouncing the fact that many small landowners, mainly Indians, had been robbed of their lands by abuse of the surveying laws, he offered to restore such lands to the original owners and to pay them an indemnity. Finally, Madero demanded effective suffrage and no reelection. Díaz finally capitulated, and Madero assumed the presidency on December 11, 1911.

Further reading: Charles C. Cumberland, *Mexican Revolution: Genesis under Madero* (Austin: University of Texas Press, 1974); Enrique Krauze, *Mexico: Biography of Power: A History of Modern Mexico, 1810–1996* (New York: Harper-

Perennial, 1998); David G. LaFrance, *The Mexican Revolution in Puebla, 1908–1913: The Maderista Movement and the Failure of Liberal Reform* (Wilmington, Del.: SR Books, 1989).

San Remo Agreements

Decisions made at the San Remo Conference in Italy (April 18–26, 1920), where allied foreign ministers met to discuss problems arising from World War I (1914–18) and to ratify understandings reached at the 1919 Paris Peace Conference. Various territorial problems were discussed by the British, French, Italians, Japanese, Greeks, and Belgians at the coastal city of San Remo. The basic features of the Turkish peace treaty were endorsed (see SÈVRES, TREATY OF); control over the city of Fiume (Rijeka) was left to Italy and Yugoslavia (see RAPALLO, TREATY OF [1920]); and Class A mandates in the Middle East were assigned (the mandates were trusteeships for the administration of former Turkish provinces). Iraq and Palestine became British-administered mandate territories, while Syria and Lebanon became French mandates; by 1949 these four mandate territories had won complete independence.

See also: VERSAILLES, TREATY OF (1919).

Further reading: Henry H. Cumming, *Franco-British Rivalry in the Post-War Near East: The Decline of French Influence* (Westport, Conn.: Greenwood Press, 1986); Isaiah Friedman, *The Rise of Israel: Riots in Jerusalem, San Remo Conference, April, 1920* (New York: Garland Publications, 1987); Jacob Stoyanovsky, *The Mandate for Palestine: A Contribution to the Theory and Practices of International Mandates* (Westport, Conn.: Hyperion Press, 1976).

San Sebastián, Pact of

Formal coalition signed at San Sebastián, Spain, on August 17, 1930, by antimonarchist parties seeking primarily the overthrow of the monarchy; it set the stage for a revolutionary movement in Spain. By the pact, Castilian and Catalan republicans agreed to end their differences and work toward the establishment of a Spanish republic in which the Catalans, Galicians, and the Basques had some measure of autonomy (see SPANISH CONSTITUTION OF 1931). A major concession from the republicans, this later led to controversial interpretations. A revolutionary committee was elected to coordinate activities, and various commissions were established to draw other parties (socialists, communists, anarcho-syndicalists, and the military) into the fray. In securing Catalonian cooperation in Spain's overall revolutionary plan, the republicans effectively neutralized any opposition from that quarter. The pact was thus an important step in Spain's long process toward a unified republican form of government.

Further reading: Raymond Carr, *Spain: 1808–1939* (Oxford, England: Clarendon Press, 1966); Robert Kern, *Red Years/Black Years: A Political History of Spanish Anarchism, 1911–1937* (Philadelphia: Institute for the Study of Human Issues, 1978); Kenneth McRoberts, *Catalonia: Nation Building Without a State* (New York: Oxford University Press, 2001).

San Stefano, Treaty of

Peace treaty concluding the Russo-Turkish War of 1877–78; signed on March 3, 1878, at San Stefano (Yesilkoy, Turkey), but overturned by the Treaty of BERLIN. The victorious Russians exacted a large indemnity from the Turks, in addition to important border concessions in the Caucasus. They also received southern Bessarabia from their ally, Romania, thereby violating a prior Russo-Romanian military convention that guaranteed Romania's territorial integrity; Romania was compensated with her independence, plus territory south of the Danube delta. Serbia and Montenegro also gained territory and their independence, while Bosnia and Herzegovina were promised some autonomy and reforms. The major sticking point, however, was the establishment of an autonomous Bulgarian state reaching to the Aegean Sea, a prospect that was anathema to both Austria-Hungary and Great Britain.

See also: BUDAPEST CONVENTIONS OF 1877.

Further reading: Anita P. Burdett, *The Historical Boundaries Between Bosnia, Croatia, Serbia: Documents and Maps 1815–1945* (Southampton, England: Hobbs the Printers of Southampton, 1995); Fred L. Israel, ed., *Major Peace Treaties of Modern History, 1648–1967*, 4 vols. (New York: Chelsea House, 1967); Frank N. Magill, ed., *Great Events from History: Modern European Series*, 3 vols. (Englewood Cliffs, N.J.: Salem Press, 1973).

Santiago, Declaration of

Declaration made on August 18, 1959, in Santiago, Chile, at the conclusion of a conference there by the foreign ministers of 21 American states; it affirmed the principles of democracy and denounced dictatorship. Among the document's more salient points were its support for free elections, separation of powers in the government, and for fundamental human rights and freedoms; its condemnation of dictatorship; its proclamation that regimes based on antidemocratic principles represented a "violation of the principles on which the OAS was founded" (see ORGANIZATION OF AMERICAN STATES, CHARTER OF THE); and its condemnation of the attempt of any one country to force democracy on another. The declaration was prepared following several years of tension between democratic and antidemocratic forces in the region.

Further reading: Henry W. Degenhardt, ed., *Treaties and Alliances of the World*, 4th ed. (Detroit: Gale Research, 1986).

Saraiva Law

Law named for Brazilian senator José Antônio Saraiva and enacted on January 9, 1881, reforming the electoral process in Brazil (then an empire under Pedro II). It provided for direct popular elections for government members (deputies), replacing the previous process of electing electors, who in turn had voted directly; for the creation of electoral districts; and for less stringent requirements on voters' eligibility, the objective of which was to increase the electorate. Despite the reform, the electorate remained about 1 percent of the population, and the holding of honest elections depended upon strong leadership (like Saraiva's), which was not always the case in the future.

Further reading: Roderick J. Barman, *Citizen Emperor: Pedro II and the Making of Brazil, 1825–1891* (Stanford, Calif.: Stanford University Press, 1999).

Sarbanes-Oxley Act

Legislation that aimed to eliminate fraudulent accounting practices by U.S. corporations. The act was prompted by a number of cases of corporate fraud that negatively affected investor confidence in publicly held companies in general. It was the most far-reaching reform of business practices since the 1930s, when the Securities and Exchange Commission was established. The act created a public company accounting oversight board, as part of the SEC, with the power to regulate, investigate, and discipline public accounting firms. The act prohibited public accounting firms from offering accounting services to those companies that it audited. It required corporate executive and financial officers to certify the accuracy of their financial reports, made them directly liable for false statements and misstatements concerning their company's financial condition, and imposed penalties of up to 25 years in prison for noncompliance. The act prohibited executives from selling personally held company stock during certain periods and from receiving company loans not available to nonexecutives, and forced them to report their trades of company stock within two days. Lastly, it protected whistleblowers who disclosed corrupt accounting practices in their company. Sponsored by Senator Paul Sarbanes and Representative Mike Oxley, the act was signed into law on July 30, 2002.

Further reading: "Summary of Sarbanes-Oxley Act of 2002," AICPA Online, available online at http://www.aicpa.org/info/sarbanes_oxley_summary.htm; "Transcript of Bush Remarks at Signing of Sarbanes-Oxley Act," U.S. Newswire, available online at http://www.usnewswire.com/topnews/prime/0730-115.html.

Savoy Declaration

Statement of faith drawn up at a convocation of English Congregationalists when they met at the Savoy, London, on September 29, 1658. It differs from the Presbyterians' WESTMINSTER CONFESSION OF FAITH in the democratic nature of its church government. According to the declaration, the Church of England would be governed by Parliament and the bishops, with assistance from the deans and ecclesiatics. The presbyter and a group of elders would govern the Presbyterian Church, whereas the Independents or Congregationalists would leave the governing to the discretion of each individual congregation.

Further reading: Gerald L. Bray, *Documents of the English Reformation* (Minneapolis:Fortress Press, 1994); Robert E. Davis and David F. Wells, *The Savoy Declaration of Faith with Scripture Footnotes from the Saybrook Platform; also Containing the Heads of Agreement* (Millers Falls, Mass.: First

Congregational Church, 1998); *The Savoy Declaration of Faith and Order, 1658* (London: Evangelical Press, 1971).

Saxon Mirror (Sachsenspiegel)

Most famous and important of the German medieval legal texts—a private compilation of custom law written between 1220 and 1230 by the Saxon knight and judge Eike von Repkow (or Repgow). Composed originally in Latin and later in German, it consisted of two books: the *Landrecht,* concerned with territorial law, and the *Lehnrecht,* devoted to feudal law and applicable mainly to the region known as Ostphalia (eastern Saxony). Criminal and civil laws and procedures were included within the *Landrecht.* Repkow's compilation was soon elevated to the status of a statute book in the Saxon courts, translated, revised, and even published with an accompanying commentary. Subsequently, it became the accepted model on which many towns based their codes and constitutions. Despite attacks from theologians and a condemnation of some articles in 1372, it remained the sourcebook of legal literature and civil law in Germany until the 19th century. It prompted the compilation (c. 1280) of a similar text, the *Swabian Mirror (Schwabenspiegel)*, applying to the local laws of Swabia in southwest Germany.

Further reading: Maria Dobozy, trans., *The Saxon Mirror: A Sachsenspiegel of the Fourteenth Century* (Philadelphia:University of Pennsylvania Press, 1999).

Schecter Poultry Corporation v. United States

U.S. Supreme Court decision, issued on May 27, 1935, that declared the U.S. NATIONAL INDUSTRIAL RECOVERY ACT (NIRA) unconstitutional on the grounds that it improperly delegated legislative power to the executive branch, lacked constitutional authority, and regulated purely intrastate (not interstate) commerce, which was outside the authority of Congress. The case arose from alleged violations by a New York slaughterhouse of the city's code for fair competition for the live poultry industry—a code, established under the NIRA, that regulated hours, wages, and local sales practices. In its unanimous decision, the Supreme Court ruled that "extraordinary conditions [the Great Depression] do not create or enlarge constitutional powers."

Further reading: Henry Steele Commager, ed., *Documents of American History*, 8th ed. (New York: Appleton-Century-Crofts, 1968); Kermit L. Hall et al., eds., *American Legal History: Cases and Materials*, 2 ed. (New York: Oxford University Press, 1996); Kermit L. Hall et al., eds., *The Oxford Companion to the Supreme Court of the United States* (New York: Oxford University Press, 1992); United States Supreme Court, *United States Reports: Cases Adjudged in the Supreme Court at . . . and Rules Announced at . . .* (New York: Banks & Brothers, Law Publishers, 1884–1921; Washington, D.C.: Government Printing Office, 1922–).

Schenck v. United States

U.S. Supreme Court decision issued on March 3, 1919, upholding the ESPIONAGE ACT OF 1917 and ruling that freedom of speech, though guaranteed by the FIRST AMENDMENT, may be suppressed if it creates a "clear and present danger" of bringing about "substantive evils." Charles T. Schenck, a member of the American Socialist Party, had been convicted under the Espionage Act of distributing a pamphlet urging draft resistance during World War I (1914–18). The Supreme Court unanimously held that the pamphlet might cause insubordination and obstruction to military service, which represented a "clear and present danger" in wartime. In arguing the limits of free speech, Justice Oliver Wendell Holmes wrote: "The most stringent protection of free speech would not protect a man in falsely shouting fire in a theatre and causing a panic."

Further reading: Henry Steele Commager, ed., *Documents of American History*, 8th ed. (New York: Appleton-Century-Crofts, 1968); Kermit L. Hall et al., eds., The *Oxford Companion to the Supreme Court of the United States* (New York: Oxford University Press, 1992); Tony Mauro, *Illustrated Great Decisions of the Supreme Court* (Washington, D.C.: CQ Press, 2000); United States Supreme Court, *United States Reports: Cases Adjudged in the Supreme Court at . . . and Rules Announced at . . .* (New York: Banks & Brothers, Law Publishers, 1884–1921; Washington, D.C.: Government Printing Office, 1922–).

Schism Act

Bill passed by the fifth Parliament of Britain's Queen Anne in 1714, seeking to deprive the dissenters of their schools and academies by limiting teaching posts to those licensed by the Anglican bishops of their diocese. It was introduced into Parliament by Lord Bolingbroke, the Tory leader, in an effort to undermine the social and political influence of the Whigs and dissenters (who were supported by the Whigs). The act also applied to Ireland. With the death of Anne, the Whigs came into power, diluting the effectiveness of the act. It was repealed in January 1718.

Further reading: Edward Gregg, *Queen Anne* (London: Routledge & Kegan Paul, 1980); Jonathan Swift, *The History of the Four Last Years of the Queen* (Oxford, England: Basil Blackwell, 1951); Joel H. Wiener, ed., *Great Britain—The Lion at Home: A Documentary History of Domestic Policy (1689–1973)*, 4 vols. (New York: Chelsea House, 1974).

Schleitheim Confession

Articles of faith drawn up at a meeting of Anabaptists at Schleitheim, northern Switzerland, on February 24, 1527. As the first recorded Anabaptist confession, it stated that only persons who believed in Christ's sacrifice had the right to receive baptism, and only believers had the right to partake of the bread and wine during Eucharist (Holy Communion). The confession also included prohibitions against swearing and associating with the "wicked" and the threat of excommunication for those whom fell into sin. Swiss, German, Dutch, and other Anabaptists were persecuted by orthodox Protestants because of their distinct tenets of faith and their desire to form a separate church, different from the Catholic or Protestant.

Further reading: Lewis W. Spitz, *The Protestant Reformation* (Englewood Cliffs, N.J.: Prentice-Hall, 1966); J. C. Wenger, *The Doctrines of the Mennonites* (Scottsdale, Pa.: Mennonite Publishing House, 1950); John H. Yoder, *The Schleitheim Confession* (Scottsdale, Pa.: Herald Press, 1977).

Schmalkaldic Articles   Articles of faith written by the theologian Martin Luther and adopted by the Protestants in the town of Schmalkalden (Smalkald), Germany, in 1537. In them, Luther affirmed his belief in the traditional Christian doctrines, as well as upheld his controversial views and teachings (e.g., his justification by faith alone, condemnation of the pope, rejection of the Mass as a sacrifice, and his eristic understanding of the sacraments). His views were uncompromising in the articles, which were never officially accepted, either by a general council or by the Schmalkaldic League (alliance of German Protestant princes and towns formed in 1531), although they were later signed by numerous theologians who endorsed them as an expression of their own personal faith.

Further reading: William R. Russell, *Luther's Theological Testament: The Schmalkald Articles* (Minneapolis: Fortress Press, 1995); William R. Russell, trans., *The Schmalkald Articles* (Minneapolis: Fortress Press, 1995).

Schönbrunn, Treaty of (1805)   Treaty concluded on December 15, 1805, in Vienna (at the royal palace of Schönbrunn) between Prussia under King Frederick William III and France under Emperor Napoléon Bonaparte; it followed the famous allied defeat by the French at Austerlitz (December 2, 1805). By the treaty, Prussia entered into a defensive and offensive alliance with France against the allied powers (including Great Britain, Russia, and Austria); Prussia was required to cede Ansbach, Cleves, and Neuchâtel to France; and Napoléon promised Prussia control over Hanover, a German state to which the British also had claims. Through this latter provision Napoléon succeeded in creating enmity between Prussia and Britain. Prior to the battle at Austerlitz, Prussia, after 10 years of neutrality, had contemplated joining the allies against France; upon their defeat, Prussia opted for the alliance with France.

See also: PRESSBURG, TREATY OF (1805).

Further reading: Alistair Horne, *How Far from Austerlitz?: Napoleon, 1805–1815* (New York: St. Martin's Press, 1996).

Schönbrunn, Treaty of (1809) (Treaty of Vienna)   Peace concluded in Vienna at the Schönbrunn Palace on October 14, 1809, between Austria under Francis I and France under Emperor Napoléon Bonaparte; it followed the Austrian defeat in the battle of Wagram (July 5–6, 1809). Through the treaty Austria ceded Salzburg, Berchtesgaden, the Innviertel,

and half of Hausrückviertel to France's ally Bavaria. To the Grand Duchy of Warsaw, which was under French protection, Austria ceded West Galicia; to Russia, which was allied to France through the Treaties of TILSIT and ERFURT, she ceded part of East Galicia; and to France, she ceded her possessions beyond the Save River, which included Istria and Dalmatia. In addition, Austria was required to join the Continental System, the members of which had ceased all trade with Great Britain.

See also: BERLIN DECREE; CAMPO FORMIO, TREATY OF; LUNÉVILLE, TREATY OF; PRESSBURG, TREATY OF (1805).

Further reading: Robert M. Epstein, *Napoleon's Last Victory and the Emergence of Modern War* (Lawrence: University Press of Kansas, 1994); Fred L. Israel, ed., *Major Peace Treaties of Modern History, 1648–1967*, 4 vols. (New York: Chelsea House, 1967); Francis L. Petre, *Napoleon and the Archduke Charles: A History of the Franco-Austrian Campaign in the Valley of the Danube in 1809* (Novato, Calif.: Presidio Press, 1991).

Schopenhauer's *World as Will and Idea*   See WORLD AS WILL AND IDEA, THE.

Schuman Plan   Proposal announced on May 9, 1950, by Robert Schuman, the French foreign minister, for the integration of the Western European coal and steel industries under one "supranational authority." Authored by French economist Jean Monnet, it envisaged uniform pricing and wage policies, production quotas, and the abolition of customs duties. France hoped thereby to create a permanent economic collaboration with Germany, thus reducing the threat of German militarism and ensuring regular supplies of Ruhr coal for her steel industry. Britain did not respond, but on June 3, 1950, Italy and the Benelux countries joined France and Germany in the negotiations for a coal-steel pool. By a treaty signed on April 18, 1951, the European Coal and Steel Community was formed. In 1957, these countries created the European Economic Community (Common Market). Britain did not gain entry until 1973.

See also: EUROPEAN COAL AND STEEL COMMUNITY, TREATY OF THE; ROME, TREATIES OF (1957); SINGLE EUROPEAN ACT.

Further reading: Pascal Fontaine, *A New Idea for Europe: The Schuman Declaration, 1950–2000*, 2d ed. (Luxembourg: Office for Official Publications of the European Communities, 2000); J. A. S. Grenville and Bernard Wasserstein, *The Major International Treaties since 1945: A History and Guide with Texts* (New York: Methuen, 1987).

Schwarzenberg Constitution   See MARCH CONSTITUTION.

Scott-Montcrieff Commission Report   Recommendations of the commission appointed in 1901 by Lord Curzon, British viceroy in India, to draft a comprehensive irrigation scheme for the whole of India. Chaired by Sir Colin Campbell Scott-Montcrieff, the commission presented its report to the viceroy in 1903. It proposed specific schemes to irrigate an additional 6.5 million acres at a cost of £30 million, mainly in the Punjab area. The commission also recommended previous plans to irrigate the lower Bari Doab and the scheme for a series of canals to transport the waters of the Jhelum River to the lower Bari Doab. These proposals were accepted by the government in 1905 and became the cornerstone of India's irrigation policy.

Further reading: Nayana Goradia, *Lord Curzon: The Last of the British Moghuls* (New York: Oxford University Press, 1993).

Seabury Commission Report

Report issued in June 1932 by American lawyer Samuel Seabury, summarizing the results of extensive investigations into corruption in the New York City government of Democratic mayor James J. Walker. Seabury, a former supreme and appellate court judge in New York State, was chief counsel for the probe of the powerful Tammany Hall Democratic organization, launched by the Republican-controlled state legislature. The investigation uncovered widespread corruption throughout the city government, and Seabury's report detailed 15 charges of malfeasance, misfeasance, and nonfeasance against Walker. Faced with removal from office, Walker resigned on September 1, 1932.

Further reading: Herbert Mitgang, *Once upon a Time in New York: Jimmy Walker, Franklin Roosevelt, and the Last Great Battle of the Jazz Age* (New York: Free Press, 2000); Herbert Mitgang, *The Man Who Rode the Tiger: The Life and Times of Judge Samuel Seabury* (New York: Fordham University Press, 1996).

SEATO Pact (Southeast Asia Defense Treaty, Manila Pact)

Pact made on September 8, 1954, in Manila, the Philippines, creating the Southeast Asia Treaty Organization (SEATO) to counteract the growing communist influence in the Far East. Signed by Britain, France, the United States, Australia, New Zealand, the Philippines, Pakistan, and Thailand, the treaty became operative on February 19, 1955. SEATO's role was mainly to provide consultation during an emergency; unlike NATO (see NORTH ATLANTIC TREATY) it did not command standing forces. Its activities were directed (from its Bangkok, Thailand, headquarters) by a secretary-general advised by his council. The absence of India, Indonesia, and Burma and the exclusion of Vietnam, Laos, and Cambodia undermined SEATO's effectiveness in the region. After losing Pakistan in 1973 (following the creation of Bangladesh) and France in 1974, SEATO's signatories decided in September 1975 to gradually phase out operations in view of the changing regional picture. SEATO was formally dissolved on June 30, 1977.

Further reading: Francis A. Beer, comp., *Alliances: Latent War Communities in the Contemporary World* (New York: Holt, Rinehart & Winston, 1970); Henry Steele Commager, ed., *Documents of American History*, 8th ed. (New York: Appleton-Century-Crofts, 1968); Henry W. Degenhardt, ed., *Treaties and Alliances of the World*, 4th ed. (Detroit: Gale Research, 1986); J. A. S. Grenville and Bernard Wasserstein, *The Major International Treaties since 1945: A History and Guide with Texts* (New York: Methuen, 1987).

Seclusion, Act of (Act of Exclusion)

Law approved on May 4, 1654, by the Dutch assembly of Holland, excluding members of the House of Orange from ruling power. Actually an implementation of a secret clause in the 1654 Treaty of WESTMINSTER, which ended the First Dutch War (1652–54) against England, the act was forced on the Hollanders and directed against the young Prince William of Orange (later King William III of England), whom the Dutch republican elite sought to debar from the office of stadtholder (chief magistrate) of Holland. Jan de Witt, Holland's grand pensionary and republican leader, was the chief advocate of the act. With the restoration of King Charles II to the throne of England in 1660, the act was revoked in favor of Charles's nephew, the prince of Orange. De Witt, however, continued to oppose the young prince's appointment to office.

Further reading: Bryan Bevan, *King William III: Prince of Orange, the First European* (London: Rubicon Press, 1997).

Securities Act of 1933, U.S. (Truth-in-Securities Act)

New Deal legislation enacted on May 27, 1933, designed to ensure full disclosure to purchasers of all stocks and bonds offered for public sale (with the exception of certain government bonds, railroad securities, and securities of some nonprofit institutions). The securities were to be registered with the U.S. Federal Trade Commission; the registration had to include accurate and complete financial and other relevant information, as well as a prospectus. The prospectus was required to be given to every potential investor. The act imposed stiff penalties for the sale of misrepresented or unregistered securities.

Further reading: Jack S. Ellenberger and Ellen P. Mahar, *Legislative History of the Securities Act of 1933 and Securities Exchange Act of 1934* (South Hackensack, N.J.: F. B. Rothman, 1973).

Securities Exchange Act, U.S.

Federal legislation enacted on June 6, 1934, that established the Securities and Exchange Commission (SEC) to regulate America stock exchanges and to enforce the U.S. SECURITIES ACT OF 1933. The SEC, consisting of five members appointed by the president and approved by the Senate, was authorized to license stock exchanges and regulate securities trading. To prevent unfair and deceptive practices, the act required that current information about corporations whose securities were traded be made available to investors and required that each security traded must be registered with the SEC. The Federal Reserve Board was authorized to regulate margin requirements in securities trading so as to reduce speculation.

Further reading: Jack S. Ellenberger and Ellen P. Mahar, *Legislative History of the Securities Act of 1933 and Securities Exchange Act of 1934* (South Hackensack, N.J.: F. B. Rothman, 1973); Joel Seligman, *The Transformation of Wall Street: A History of the Securities and Exchange Commission and Modern Corporate Finance* (Boston: Northeastern University Press, 1995).

Security, Act of   Act passed by the Scottish Parliament during Queen Anne's reign in 1703, stating that it was not bound to accept the Protestant succession provided for by the 1701 English Act of SETTLEMENT. Scotland thereby issued an ultimatum that if the issues of her "rights, liberties and independence" were not satisfactorily settled during the current reign, she would, on the death of the present queen, consider appointing a successor different from the successor to the English throne. This eventually led to the Act of UNION with Scotland in 1707.

Further reading: P. W. J. Riley, *The Union of England and Scotland: A Study in Anglo-Scottish Politics of the Eighteenth Century* (Totowa, N.J.: Rowman & Littlefield, 1978).

Sedition Act of 1798, U.S.   Federal legislation enacted on July 14, 1798, that gave the U.S. government broad powers to repress treasonable activities. One of the U.S. ALIEN AND SEDITION ACTS OF 1798, it prohibited citizens or aliens from conspiring against the operation of federal laws; from preventing federal officials from executing their duties; and from aiding any insurrection, riot, or unlawful assembly. It outlawed the publication of any "false, scandalous and malicious writing" against the government and any effort to incite opposition to the government. Twenty-five Republican editors or printers were arrested and 10 were convicted under this law. Opposition to the act, expressed in the VIRGINIA RESOLUTIONS and the KENTUCKY RESOLUTIONS, led to the decline of the Federalist Party. The act expired in 1801.

Further reading: Mortimer Adler, ed., *The Annals of America*, 18 vols. (Chicago: Encyclopaedia Britannica, 1968); Henry Steele Commager, ed., *Documents of American History*, 8th ed. (New York: Appleton-Century-Crofts, 1968); John C. Miller, *Crisis in Freedom: The Alien and Sedition Acts* (Boston: Little, Brown, 1951).

Sedition Act of 1918, U.S.   Legislation enacted by the U.S. Congress on May 16, 1918, amending the ESPIONAGE ACT OF 1917 and drastically curtailing freedom of speech and the press during World War I (1914–18). The act established severe penalties for making or conveying false statements that interfered with military or naval operations, that promoted enemy successes, that obstructed military recruitment or the

sale of U.S. bonds, or that incited military insubordination, disloyalty, or refusal of duty. It prohibited "disloyal, profane, scurrilous, or abusive language" about the form of the U.S. government, the U.S. CONSTITUTION, the flag, and the military and naval forces; it outlawed urging the curtailment of essential war production. It also punished the advocating, teaching, defending, or suggesting of any of these actions.

Further reading: Henry Steele Commager, ed., *Documents of American History*, 8th ed. (New York: Appleton-Century-Crofts, 1968); John G. Hunt, *The Dissenters: America's Voices of Opposition* (New York: Gramercy, 1993).

Selective Service Act of 1917, U.S.   Federal legislation enacted on May 18, 1917, establishing registration and classification for military service of all men between the ages of 21 and 30, inclusive. Local civilian draft boards were given responsibility for administering the draft. Exemptions were allowed for alienage, physical unfitness, and conscientious objections on religious grounds. The act was amended by the Man Power Act, passed on August 31, 1918, which required registration of all men from age 18 to 45. More than 24 million men were registered over the course of World War I (1914–18). Conscription was halted after the war.

Further reading: Mortimer Adler, ed., *The Annals of America*, 18 vols. (Chicago: Encyclopaedia Britannica, 1968); Michael Pearlman, *To Make Democracy Safe for America: Patricians and Preparedness in the Progressive Era* (Urbana: University of Illinois Press, 1984).

Selective Service Act of 1948, U.S.   Federal U.S. legislation enacted on June 24, 1948, that provided for the military registration of all male citizens and U.S. residents between the ages of 18 and 26; only those between 19 and 26 were liable for training and service, which was limited to 21 months. The act replaced the BURKE-WADSWORTH ACT of 1940, which had expired in 1947. This 1948 arrangement for a peacetime draft grew out of cold war tensions. In 1950 the act was extended for another year. U.S. legislation providing for the military draft was in effect continuously until Congress abolished the draft in 1973.

Further reading: Henry Steele Commager, ed., *Documents of American History*, 8th ed. (New York: Appleton-Century-Crofts, 1968).

Selective Service Act of 1951, U.S.   See UNIVERSAL MILITARY TRAINING AND SERVICE ACT, U.S.

Selective Service Act of 1967, U.S.   Federal U.S. legislation enacted on June 20, 1967, that provided for full-time college students to receive deferments from military service. Passed during the Vietnam War (1956–75), the act allowed deferments until students (enrolled in any institute of higher instruction) completed their baccalaureate degrees, failed to continue satisfactorily full-time studies, or attained the age of

24, whichever occurred first. There were also deferments for graduate students in medicine and other fields, as well as for fathers, extreme hardship cases, sole surviving sons, ministers, some agricultural and industrial workers, and persons with physical, mental, and moral problems, among others. The act, which expired on June 30, 1971, was followed by the Selective Service Act of 1971, whose draft-induction authority expired on June 30, 1973.

Further reading: George Q. Flynn, *Lewis B. Hershey, Mr. Selective Service* (Chapel Hill: University of North Carolina Press, 1985); "Military Selective Service Act of 1967," *Selective Service Law Reporter* 1 (1968).

Selective Training and Service Act, U.S.   See BURKE-WADSWORTH ACT.

Self-Renouncing Ordinance (Self-Denying Ordinance)

Measure passed on April 3, 1645, declaring that no member of the English Parliament (either house) could hold any office, civil or military, during the civil war. The proposal was moved by Zouch Tate and seconded by Sir Harry Vane with the intention of removing from command ineffective generals such as the third earl of Essex and others like him. The ordinance got its name from Tate's proposal, which said that the only way to end so many evils was "for everyone freely to renounce himself." After it was passed, the earls of Essex, Warwick, and Manchester resigned, and Thomas Fairfax was appointed captain-general with Oliver Cromwell (as a member of Parliament, he ought to have been excluded but was cited for his brilliant achievements) as lieutenant-general. Cromwell, who had seen that the aristocracy were only half-hearted in the war, was the brains behind the ordinance. It was initially rejected by the House of Lords but later passed. After the death of the earl of Essex in 1647, the ordinance fell into disuse.

Further reading: Christopher Durston, *Cromwell's Major-Generals: Godly Government During the English Revolution* (Manchester, England: Manchester University Press, 2001).

Sempach, Convention of

Truce negotiated in 1393 by the Swiss, backed by the Swabian League (a confederation of towns in southwest Germany), and the Austrian Hapsburgs, who had suffered defeat in the Austro-Swiss War of 1385–88, notably at Sempach, Switzerland, in 1386 when their Duke Leopold III was killed. The Swiss towns had joined forces with the hope of shaking off the control wielded over them by the duke's authority. By the end of the war the Hapsburgs had lost much power and sought a confederation. In the convention many Swiss towns gained independence; if some were required to continue to pay certain sums to the Hapsburgs, they were often granted the freedom to administer their own government themselves.

Further reading: James M. Luck, *A History of Switzerland: The First 100,000 Years: Before the Beginnings to the Days of the Present* (Palo Alto, Calif.: Society for the Promotion of Science & Scholarship, 1985); William Martin, *Switzerland, from Roman Times to the Present* (New York: Praeger, 1971).

Sempronian Law of 133 B.C.   See ROMAN AGRARIAN LAW OF 133 B.C.

Senatus Consultum Ultimum of 49 B.C.

Decree of martial law (or "last decree") passed by the Roman Senate on January 7, 49 B.C., authorizing the consuls and other magistrates to use any means to protect the Roman republic from Gaius Julius Caesar, who was declared a public enemy at the same time. Pompey the Great had grown jealous over Caesar's military success and gained the support of the Senate, which had illegally decreed him sole consul in 52 B.C. Fearful of Caesar's power and popularity, the Senate vainly ordered (January 1, 49 B.C.) Caesar to give up his command. Upon hearing news of the "last decree," Caesar uttered the words *"alea jacta est"* (the die is cast), crossed the Rubicon (a stream separating his province [Cisalpine Gaul] from Italy), and marched southward with his forces to Rome; the Great Roman Civil War (49–44 B.C.) had begun upon Caesar's breaking the law that forbade a commander to lead an army out of his assigned province.

Further reading: P. A. L. Greenhalgh, *Pompey: The Republican Prince* (London: Weidenfeld & Nicolson, 1981); Ramon L. Jimenez, *Caesar Against Rome: The Great Roman Civil War* (Westport, Conn.: Praeger, 2000); A. J. Langguth, *A Noise of War: Caesar, Pompey, Octavian, and the Struggle for Rome* (New York : Simon & Schuster, 1994).

Senatus Consultum Ultimum of 63 B.C.

Proclamation of martial law, so-called Cicero's Last Decree, to use any means whatsoever to preserve the state; issued by the Roman Senate on October 22, 63 B.C., after the detection of the conspiracy of Catiline (Lucius Sergius Catilina) to overthrow the government by armed force. Defeated for election as a consul in 65 and 63 B.C., Catiline was bitterly opposed by Marcus Tullius Cicero, who induced the Senate to pass the "last decree" against Catiline (a menace to the welfare of the state), declaring him a public enemy and ordering Cicero's colleague Caius Antonius to crush him in battle. Catiline and many followers were killed by Antonius's forces near Pistoria in early 62 B.C.

See also: CICERO'S ORATIONS AGAINST CATILINE.

Further reading: Ernest G. Hardy, *The Catilinarian Conspiracy in Its Context: A Re-Study of the Evidence* (New York: AMS Press, 1976).

Seneca Falls Declaration and Resolutions   See WOMEN'S RIGHTS, DECLARATION OF.

Senlis, Treaty of

Pact made on May 23, 1493, at Senlis, France, between Maximilian I, Holy Roman emperor, and

Charles VIII, king of France, following the latter's defeat in the battle of Salins (at the end of the Austrian Netherlands Civil War of 1477–92 and the Franco-Austrian War of 1477–93). The French king, who had reneged on his promise to marry Margaret of Austria (Maximilian's daughter), had to return her dowry (Artois and Franche-Comté) to Maximilian. France retained the important duchy of Burgundy.

See also: ARRAS, TREATY OF (1482).

Further reading: Gerhard Benecke, *Maximilian I (1459–1519): An Analytical Biography* (Boston: Routledge & Kegan Paul, 1982); John S. C. Bridge, *A History of France from the Death of Louis XI* (New York: Octagon Books, 1978).

Sentences, Four Books of (Sententiarum Libri IV)

French bishop Peter Lombard's summing-up (1148–51) of the Christian faith—a systematic collection of the teachings of the Catholic Church and of medieval masters; it became the prescribed theological text of the Middle Ages (see DECRETAL OF GRATIAN; DECRETALS OF 1234). Book one was devoted to a discussion of God, the Trinity, divine guidance, evil, and predestination. Book two was concerned with angels, demons, man's fall from grace, and sin. Book three dealt with the reincarnation of Jesus Christ, virtues, the forgiveness of sins, and the TEN COMMANDMENTS. In book four, Lombard discussed the sacraments, death, judgment, hell, and heaven. Lombard's organization of the material was skillful and original, as was his interpretation of complex theological issues. The *Sentences* became the focal point of all theological study and sparked over 250 commentaries, some by well-known scholars. It earned Lombard the title *magister sententiarum*, "master of the sentences."

Further reading: Catholic University of America, eds. *New Catholic Encyclopedia* (New York: McGraw-Hill, 1967); Steven J. Livesay, ed., *Theology and Science in the Fourteenth Century: Three Questions on the Unity and Subalternation of the Sciences from John of Reading's Commentary on the Sentences* (New York: E. J. Brill, 1989).

Separate Amenities Act, South African

Major legislation enacted in South Africa in 1953, allowing segregation of blacks in public facilities ranging from restaurants to libraries to buses. It gave municipal and town governments and privately owned businesses the right to reserve facilities, such as parks, swimming pools, hotels, toilets, and recreation areas, for whites only. Later, public facilities in major cities like Johannesburg, Cape Town, and Durban were integrated, but segregated facilities remained in smaller towns and villages until South Africa's parliament, on June 19, 1990, repealed the law, which did not apply to schools and neighborhoods. The change angered some conservative whites.

See also: GROUP AREAS ACT OF 1950, SOUTH AFRICAN.

Further reading: *Report of the Technical Committee of Enquiry into the Group Areas Act, 1966, the Reservation of Separate Amenities Act, 1953, and Related Legislation* (Pretoria, South Africa: Government Printer, 1983).

September Convention of 1864

Agreement made on September 15, 1864, between the Italian government of Premier Mario Minghetti and Emperor Napoléon III of France, whereby the former promised to protect and preserve the territorial integrity of Rome, while France vowed to withdraw her troops from Rome within two years. Meanwhile, Italy agreed to the Vatican's proposal of setting up its own army of volunteers, provided it remained a defensive force and did not attack Italian territory. Italy also contracted to pay some of the debts of the Roman state. A secret annex obliged Italy to move her capital from Turin to another city, just to prove that Rome was not being considered as the future capital. The convention would be operative once the transfer was announced. Florence was thus designated the new capital. Approved by the chamber of deputies in Turin, the convention aroused much controversy, led to Minghetti's overthrow, and prompted a sharp response from Pope Pius IX in his encyclical *Quanta Cura*.

See also: SYLLABUS OF ERRORS.

Further reading: Lynn M. Case, *Franco-Italian Relations, 1860–1865; the Roman Question and the Convention of September* (New York: AMS Press, 1970); Ivan Scott, *The Roman Question and the Powers, 1848–1865* (The Hague: Martinus Nijhoff, 1969).

September Laws of 1835 (Lois de Septembre)

Series of laws passed by the French government following the assassination attempt (July 28, 1835) on King Louis Philippe by Giuseppe Fieschi and his supporters. The fracas left many dead or wounded and an emergency session of the legislative chambers was hastily convened in August 1835. The resulting measures, passed in September and known as the "September Laws," can be summarized as follows: (1) the assize courts and the guidelines for judging seditious acts were revamped; (2) juries were to vote in secret, with a reduction in majority required for condemnation; (3) tighter controls were put on the press; (4) the print and other media (especially engravings) were to be prosecuted for offenses; (5) a ban was put on challenging the principle of the regime; and (6) the profession of republicanism was outlawed. These repressive laws led to the closure of many Republican newspapers, to stricter juries, and to the temporary end of the Republican Party in France.

Further reading: T. E. B. Howarth, *Citizen-King; the Life of Louis-Philippe* (London: Eyre & Spottiswoode, 1961).

Septennate, Law of the

Ordinance of November 20, 1873, proclaiming Marshal Marie Edme MacMahon president of France for a term of seven years. MacMahon, a monarchist, was named by the monarchist majority in the provisional National Assembly elected in 1871 to conclude a peace treaty with Germany. The monarchists hoped that by end of the seven-year period, the Orleanist and legitimist factions would reach a compromise. Meanwhile, MacMahon was charged with framing a constitution that could be adapted to a monarchy. Ironically, this constitution became the constitution of France's third republic.

See also: FRENCH CONSTITUTION OF 1875; WALLON AMENDMENT.

Further reading: William Fortescue, *The Third Republic in France, 1870–1940: Conflicts and Continuities* (New York: Routledge, 2000); Noel M. MacMahon, trans. and ed., *Here I Am, Here I Stay!: Marshal MacMahon, 1808–1893* (Whitegate, Ireland: Ballinakella Press, 1993); Charles Sowerwine, *France since 1870: Culture, Politics and Society* (New York: Palgrave, 2001).

Septennial Act British act passed on May 7, 1716, originally to postpone the general election of 1718 as required by the TRIENNIAL ACT. It set the maximum duration (term) of a Parliament at seven years (instead of three) and the interval between two Parliaments at no longer than four years. Promoted partly because of the Jacobite uprisings of 1715 and to maintain the upper hand of the Whigs, the act was operative until 1911 when the Parliament Act reduced the term to five years. The Septennial Act ultimately created more stability in government and greater authority for the House of Commons.

Further reading: Joel H. Wiener, ed., *Great Britain—The Lion at Home: A Documentary History of Domestic Policy (1689–1973)*, 4 vols. (New York: Chelsea House, 1974).

Serbian Constitution of 1835 Constitution prepared by a group of Serbian nobles in 1835, and accepted, under duress, by the autocratic Serbian Prince Milosh Obrenovich; through it the authors attempted to curb the dictatorial rule of the prince by introducing democratic reforms. The constitution provided for the establishment of a senate, which was to have legislative, executive, and judicial powers, and for the establishment of a general assembly, which was to be responsible for the state's budget. It was drawn up under the influence of France and Great Britain, both of which espoused the doctrine that independent and democratically governed east European states would serve to block Russian expansion. The constitution was abrogated in 1838.

See also: SERBIAN CONSTITUTION OF 1838.

Further reading: Gale Stokes, *Politics as Development: The Emergence of Political Parties in Nineteenth-Century Serbia* (Durham, N.C.: Duke University Press, 1990).

Serbian Constitution of 1838 Charter or constitution promulgated by Ottoman sultan Mahmud II on December 24, 1838, replacing the more liberal SERBIAN CONSTITUTION OF 1835. A senate, composed of 17 members from the Serbian nobility and higher clergy, was to replace Prince Milosh Obrenovich (who was too autocratic for the Turks and Russians)

as the dominant political power in Serbia, and it was to be responsible for all legislation, including taxes. Ministers of finance, home affairs, and justice made up the executive. The document also abolished serfdom and restrictions on foreign trade, and some democratic changes were made in fundamental legal rights. The Ottoman sultan, however, remained the ultimate arbiter in all matters of importance.

Further reading: Gale Stokes, *Politics as Development: The Energence of Political Parties in Nineteenth-Century Serbia* (Durham, N.C.: Duke University Press, 1990).

Sermon on the Mount Discourse spoken by Jesus Christ about A.D. 25 at the foot of a mountain near the Sea of Galilee, later recorded in the Gospels of Matthew (chapters 5–7) and Luke (chapter 6). It was addressed to a crowd of people, including a small band of disciples, who heard a joyful, spiritual message proclaiming that the "kingdom of heaven" (Matthew) or the "kingdom of God" (Luke) is realized by those whom Jesus called "blessed" (a biblical teaching called the Beatitudes). Found also in the sermon's teachings are the Lord's Prayer and the Golden Rule. Jesus, who left not a single written document himself, delivered a new kind of message for living, based on love, justice, and simplicity.

Further reading: Catholic University of America, eds., *New Catholic Encyclopedia* (New York: McGraw-Hill, 1967); Friedrich Heer, *Great Documents of the World: Milestones of Human Thought* (New York: McGraw-Hill, 1977); *The Holy Bible, Containing the Old and New Testaments, Authorized (King James) Version* (Philadelphia: National Bible Press, 1944); Mark A. Kishlansky, ed., *Sources of World History: Readings for World Civilization*, vol. 1, 2d ed. (Belmont, Calif.: West/Wadsworth, 1999)

Servicemen's Readjustment Act, U.S. See GI BILL OF RIGHTS.

Settlement, Act of (1662) Social legislation to control vagrancy, passed by the Cavalier Parliament in England in 1662. It authorized parish overseers to force anyone who was not born in their parish or had no land or work there, to return to his native parish. The poor were eligible for aid only from their own parishes, and the homeless poor, such as unwed mothers, were sometimes evicted to prevent their offspring from being a charge on the parish. The act curbed the mobility of the poor but was amended in 1795 primarily to cover those applying for relief.

See also: EXPLANATION, ACT OF.

Further reading: Tim Hitchcock et al., eds., *Chronicling Poverty: The Voices and Strategies of the English Poor, 1640–1840* (New York: St. Martin's Press, 1997); Thomas Mackay, *The English Poor* (New York: Garland Publications, 1984).

Settlement, Act of (Succession Act) Landmark act (June 12, 1701) of the British Parliament, which ruled that if

King William III and Queen Anne were to die without any heirs, the throne would pass to Princess Sophia of Hanover (granddaughter of James I) or her Protestant heirs. It was promoted by both parties to eliminate the possibility of a Catholic Stuart pretender ascending to the throne and has since been the basis of the British succession. According to the provisions of the act, future monarchs were to take communion within the Anglican Church and not travel abroad or use English funds to defend foreign territories without Parliament's approval. Judges were to be appointed on the basis of their work rather than by the sovereign's whim. Foreigners were not eligible for election to either house of Parliament, the Privy Council, other high offices or to a pension. Two other clauses (excluding all officeholders from the House of Commons and limiting the crown's advisers to privy councillors) were amended before the act was passed. The act further strengthened Parliament's control over the crown.

Further reading: Randolph L. Braham, ed., *Documents on Major European Governments* (New York: Knopf/Borzoi, 1966); Gerald L. Bray, *Documents of the English Reformation* (Minneapolis: Fortress Press, 1994); Frank N. Magill, ed., *Great Events from History: Modern European Series*, 3 vols. (Englewood Cliffs, N.J.: Salem Press, 1973); Joel H. Wiener, ed., *Great Britain—The Lion at Home: A Documentary History of Domestic Policy (1689–1973)*, 4 vols. (New York: Chelsea House, 1974).

Settlement for Ireland, Act of (1653)

Act passed by Oliver Cromwell ("lord protector" of England) in 1653 for the settlement of confiscated estates in Ireland. It provided for the confiscation of all the land of Irish owners who participated in the massacre of 1641 (Irish Catholics killed many English settlers and destroyed their homes and property in Ulster) and two-thirds of the estates belonging to those who had joined King Charles I in the English Civil War. The balance was divided among soldiers on duty before Cromwell's time, adventurers who had loaned money in return for Irish land and Cromwell's own army. One county was reserved for Cromwell himself. All the officers of the Catholic army in Ireland were dismissed. Catholics were restricted to the right bank of the river Shannon.

Further reading: T. C. Barnard, *Cromwellian Ireland: English Government and Reform in Ireland 1649–1660)* (New York: Oxford University Press, 2000); Jane H. Ohlmeyer, ed., *Ireland from Independence to Occupation, 1641–1660* (New York: Cambridge University Press, 1995); John P. Pendergast, *The Cromwellian Settlement of Ireland* (London: Constable, 1996).

Settlement for Ireland, Act of (1662)

Parliamentary act announced by King Charles II of England to reduce the hardships inflicted on the Irish by the Act of SETTLEMENT FOR IRELAND of 1653 and enable Protestant loyalists to regain their estates in Ireland. By this law, adventurers and soldiers kept their lands, and "innocent" Protestants (those who had not rebelled against Charles), who had not been compensated, were promised their lands back. Innocent Catholics were to be treated likewise but the provisions were narrowly interpreted and many were excluded from the settlement of 1662.

Further reading: L. J. Arnold, *The Restoration Land Settlement in County Dublin, 1660–1688: A History of the Administration of the Acts of Settlement and Explanation* (Blackrock, Ireland: Irish Academic Press, 1993).

Seven Lamps of Architecture, The

Selection of essays written by John Ruskin, English art critic, and published in April 1849. In them, he sought to revive interest in the elements of Gothic architecture and thereby influence Victorian builders. The seven "lamps" Ruskin discussed (in separate chapters) were sacrifice, truth, power, beauty, life, memory, and obedience. A critic pointed out that he had omitted the lamp of industry. While the Gothic revival is now history, Ruskin's work is still regarded as an eloquent treatise of art criticism, based on Ruskin's view of art as a fundamental concern of human life rather than as an embellishment that only a privileged few can appreciate. As a critic, Ruskin was a major influence on the public taste of his time.

Further reading: John Ruskin, *The Seven Lamps of Architecture* (New York: Farrar, Straus, & Giroux, 1988).

Seven Parts, Code of the (Seven Divisions of Law, Codigo de las Siete Partidas, Libro de las Leyes)

Spanish medieval law code compiled from 1256 to 1265 at the instance of Alfonso X, the king of Castile and León, to establish a uniform legal system throughout the country. Written in Castilian, it drew upon Castile and León's municipal charters and customs, from canon law, and from Roman jurisprudence and commentaries. It was divided into seven parts (hence its name), dealing with administrative powers and duties, legal justice, religious life, marriage, contracts, wills, and crime and punishment. It contained severe restrictions against the Moors, the Jews, and heretics. The code, which projected a hierarchical society headed by a monarch who derived his authority directly from God, was never imposed as common law but, in 1348, Alfonso XI promulgated it along with his Ordenamiento and the local fueros (laws). A standard university text, it was also carried by the Spanish to their colonies abroad and rapidly incorporated there into local legal systems.

Further reading: Jerry R. Craddock et al., eds., *The Text and Concordance of Las Siete Partidas de Alfonso X* (Madison, Wis.: Hispanic Seminary of Medieval Studies, 1989); Marie R. Madden, *Political Theory and Law in Medieval Spain* (New York: Fordham University Press, 1930).

Seventeen Article "Constitution"

Collection of 17 moral injunctions for Japan's ruling class, issued in A.D. 604 by Crown Prince Shotoku Taishi to end disorder among the clans. Inspired by Confucian ethics, Buddhism, and China's idea of central imperial authority, the articles emphasized harmony in the community, obedience to rulers, responsibility and decorum by officials, and nonpatronage in public offices (to be filled on the basis of merit). Local officials were prohibited from levying taxes upon the people, since taxation by the sovereign government was presumably enough. There were also exhortations against flattery, laziness, neglect, and anger. The moral code was a turning point, serving as an ideological basis for a new state with a centralized imperial government.

Further reading: Mark A. Kishlansky, ed., *Sources of World History: Readings for World Civilization*, vol. 1, 2d ed. (Belmont, Calif.: West/Wadsworth, 1999).

Seventeenth Amendment, U.S.   Amendment to the U.S. CONSTITUTION, ratified in 1913, that provided for the direct election of senators, rather than election by state legislatures. In the late 19th and early 20th centuries the Senate had developed a reputation as a reactionary body representing monied interests. The growth of a progressive movement led to a demand for the more democratic method of election to make the Senate more responsive to the popular will. An amendment to effect this change passed the House of Representatives as early as 1893 but the measure did not clear the Senate until 1912.

Further reading: Alan Brinkley, *American History: A Survey*, 10th ed. (Boston: McGraw-Hill College, 1999); Kermit L. Hall et al., eds., *American Legal History: Cases and Materials*, 2d ed. (New York: Oxford University Press, 1996); Kermit L. Hall et al., eds., *The Oxford Companion to the Supreme Court of the United States* (New York: Oxford University Press, 1992); C. H. Hoebeke, *The Road to Mass Democracy: Original Intent and the Seventeenth Amendment* (New Brunswick, N.J.: Transaction Publishers, 1995).

Seventh Amendment, U.S.   Amendment to the U.S. CONSTITUTION, adopted in 1791, providing the right of trial by jury "in suits at common law, where the value in controversy shall exceed twenty dollars." In addition, it stated that no decision by a jury can be overridden by a court or judge except "according to the rules of the common law." The amendment's main purpose was to keep the powers of the jury and the judge separate, in accordance with the traditional British legal system.

See also: BILL OF RIGHTS, U.S.

Further reading: Alan Brinkley, *American History: A Survey*, 10th ed. (Boston: McGraw-Hill College, 1999); Kermit L. Hall et al., eds., *American Legal History: Cases and Materials*, 2d ed. (New York: Oxford University Press, 1996); Kermit L. Hall et al., eds., *The Oxford Companion to the Supreme Court of the United States* (New York: Oxford University Press, 1992).

"Seventh of March" Speech, Webster's   Powerful, eloquent speech given by Senator Daniel Webster on March 7, 1850, in support of the COMPROMISE OF 1850. Webster spoke "not as a Massachusetts man, not as a Northern man, but as an American . . . for the preservation of the Union." Though he considered slavery inherently evil and had misgivings over the FUGITIVE SLAVE LAW OF 1850, Webster feared a civil war even more. He argued that it was unnecessary to prohibit slavery in new U.S. territory ceded by Mexico because the West was geographically unsuitable for the plantation system. His speech outraged abolitionists and members of his own Whig Party, but it helped the compromise to pass and thus delayed the outbreak of the war.

Further reading: Mortimer Adler, ed., *The Annals of America*, 18 vols. (Chicago: Encyclopedia Britannica, 1968); Herbert D. Foster, *Webster's Seventh of March Speech and the Secession Movement, 1850* (Sanford, N.C.: Microforming Corp. of America, 1983); Robert V. Remini, *Daniel Webster: The Man and His Time* (New York: W. W. Norton, 1997).

Seville, Treaty of (1729)   Treaty made in Seville, Spain, on November 9, 1729, concluding Spain's War with Britain and France (1727–29). By its terms, Spain recognized British control of Gibraltar and granted trading rights (the *asiento*) in her colonies to Britain and France, which in return permitted Spain to send 6,000 soldiers to Italy to ensure the succession of young Charles (son of King Philip V of Spain) in the Farnese duchies of Parma, Piacenza, and Tuscany. The terms of the agreement were later revised in the 1731 Treaty of VIENNA.

See also: UTRECHT, TREATIES OF.

Further reading: Stetson Conn, *Gibraltar in British Diplomacy in the Eighteenth Century* (New Haven, Conn.: Yale University Press, 1942); Richard Lodge, "The Treaty of Seville (1729)," *Transactions of the Royal Historical Society* 16, no. (1933): 1–43.

Sèvres, Treaty of   Allied-framed pact signed at Sèvres (a suburb of Paris) on August 10, 1920, by members of the Ottoman government, leading to the dissolution of the Ottoman Empire. Turkey (the Ottoman Empire) was thereby forced to surrender all claims over Arab Asia and North Africa and grant independence to Armenia and autonomy to Kurdistan. Greece was to receive most of eastern Thrace and have control over the Aegean Islands guarding the Straits of the Dardanelles, the Anatolian west coast, and to administer Smyrna (Izmir) and the surrounding area for five years. Some parts of the straits to the Black Sea were declared international zones and were demilitarized. Led by Mustafa Kemal, the Turkish Nationalists rejected the treaty. In July 1923, it was replaced by the Treaty of LAUSANNE.

See also: ANGLO-FRENCH-RUSSIAN AGREEMENT ABOUT ASIATIC TURKEY; MUDROS, ARMISTICE OF.

Further reading: *Armenia, the Continuing Tragedy* (New York: Commission of the Churches on International Affairs, World Council of Churches, 1984); Fred L. Israel, ed., *Major Peace Treaties of Modern History, 1648–1967*, 4 vols. (New York: Chelsea House, 1967); Lawrence Martin, *The Treaties of Peace, 1919–1923* (New York: Carnegie Endowment for International Peace, 1924); James T. Shotwell, *Turkey at the Straits; a Short History* (New York: Macmillan, 1940).

Seward's "Higher Law" Speech   See "HIGHER LAW" SPEECH, SEWARD'S.

Sex Discrimination Act, British   Legislation of December 29, 1975, declaring illegal discrimination on the basis of sex or marital status and in all matters pertaining to employment, education, and the provision of professional, recreational, banking, insurance, and credit services in Great Britain. Thus, it was unlawful for any establishment employing a woman (except where her sex was an occupational qualification), or for a school or college to deny admission to a girl unless it was a single-sex institution. The act incorporated the Equal Pay Act of 1970, which had introduced in Britain the policy of equal pay for men and women doing the same job. A victim of discrimination could file a civil suit and claim compensation for injury to feelings. An Equal Opportunities Commission was created to help fight discrimination and promote equal opportunity for all. The act represented an important step in the gradual emancipation of women in the country.

Further reading: Jean Coussins, *The Equality Report: One Year of the Equal Pay Act, the Sex Discrimination Act, the Equal Opportunities Commission* (London: National Council for Civil Liberties, 1976); Patricia Hewitt, *Rights for Women: A Guide to the Sex Discrimination Act, the Equal Pay Act, Paid Maternity Leave, Pension Schemes and Unfair Dismissal* (London: National Council for Civil Liberties, 1975); Michael Nash, *The Sex Discrimination Act, a Guide for Managers* (London: Institute of Personnel Management, 1975); D. J. Walker, *Sex Discrimination: A Simple Guide to the Provisions of the Sex Discrimination Act 1975* (London: Shaw, 1975).

Shakamaxon, Treaty of   Famous friendly agreement made between William Penn, founder of the proprietary colony of Pennsylvania, and the chiefs of the Delaware Indians (Leni-Lenape); signed on June 23, 1683, at Shakamaxon (Shackamaxon), a site now occupied by a small park in Philadelphia. There, according to tradition, this "Great Treaty" (as it is sometimes called) was negotiated beneath the so-called Treaty Elm. By its terms, Penn bought some of the Indians' lands (what is now southeastern Pennsylvania) and entered into a long-lasting peace and friendship to benefit both the white settlers and the Indians.

See also: FRAME OF GOVERNMENT, PENN'S.

Further reading: Peter S. Du Ponceau and Joshua F. Fisher, *A Memoir on the History of the Celebrated Treaty Made by William Penn with the Indians: Under the Elm Tree at Shackamaxon, in the Year 1682* (Philadelphia: M'Carty & Davis, 1836); Willis M. Rivinus, *The Red Man in Bucks County* (New Hope, Pa.: Willis M. Rivinus, 1978).

Shanghai Communiqué   See U.S.-CHINESE COMMUNIQUÉ OF 1972.

Shaw v. Reno   Lawsuit filled against the state and federal governments by five white residents (including Ruth O. Shaw) of North Carolina, claiming that the creation of two minority-majority districts constituted racial gerrymandering and violated the equal protection clause of the U.S. Constitution's FOURTEENTH AMENDMENT. The state's original redistricting plan submitted to the Justice Department in accordance with Section 5 of the VOTING RIGHTS ACT OF 1965 had one such district (the First). North Carolina was then ordered to create another minority-majority district, which it did (the Twelfth). In a close 5-4 ruling issued on June 28, 1993, the U.S. Supreme Court sided with the appellants, arguing that irregularly shaped districts could be considered as unconstitutional gerrymandering, even if the intent was to increase minority representation. Focusing on the bizarre shapes of the districts, and without requiring plaintiffs to show proof of injury as a result of the redistricting, the Court said that the reapportionment plan "bears an uncomfortable resemblance to political apartheid." A three-judge district court had earlier dismissed the claim against the state but said it had no jurisdiction in the case against the federal government.

Further reading: NCBVP, Inc., "*Shaw v. Reno*," National Coalition on Black Voter Participation, Inc., available online at http://www.bigvote.org/bigvote/sec4.html; Jamin B. Raskin, "Supreme Court's Double Standard," *Nation*, 260 (February 6, 1995): 167–69.

Shays-Meehan Bill   See BIPARTISAN CAMPAIGN REFORM ACT OF 2002, U.S.

Shelley's *Declaration of Rights*   Pamphlet written by English poet and reformer Percy Bysshe Shelley and printed in Ireland in 1812; it expressed his discontent with the political and social conditions of the day. In the tract's 31 articles, which were called "inflammatory and seditious," Shelley said that "government has no rights" but "is devised for the security of rights." Among man's rights were "unrestricted liberty of discussion" and "an equal share in the benefits and burdens of government." Yet, Shelley said, principles of morality must above all govern man's actions and duties. "Titles are tinsel, power a corruptor, glory a bubble, and excessive wealth a libel on its possessor," declared Shelley, who urged

men to oppose governmental tyranny and find their rights for the sake of happiness and freedom.

Further reading: H. Buxton Forman, ed., *The Works of Percy Bysshe Shelley in Verse and Prose* (London: Reeves & Turner, 1983); Percy Bysshe Shelley, *The Necessity of Atheism; and Declaration of Rights* (Charlottesville, Va.: Patrick Henry Literary Society, 1952); Louis L. Snyder, ed., *Fifty Major Documents of the Nineteenth Century* (Princeton, N.J.: D. Van Nostrand, 1955).

Shell Manifesto   American address written by Benjamin Tillman, a Democrat and leader of the agrarian movement in South Carolina; published over the signature of G. W. Shell, president of the Farmers' Association of South Carolina, during Tillman's successful campaign for the governorship in 1890. The document combined disdain for the "aristocratic coterie" governing the state and elements of agrarian reform with a call for the preservation of white supremacy. The manifesto demanded greater economy and efficiency in government, cheaper and more practical education for farmers and mechanics, and protection of agricultural interests from greedy phosphate miners and fertilizer companies.

Further reading: Henry Steele Commager, ed., *Documents of American History*, 8th ed. (New York: Appleton-Century-Crofts, 1968); Francis B. Simkins, *The Tillman Movement in South Carolina* (Gloucester, Mass.: P. Smith, 1964).

Sheppard-Towner Act   First federal welfare legislation in the United States, cosponsored by Senator John Morris Sheppard of Texas and Representative Horace M. Towner of Iowa and enacted on November 23, 1921; it provided federal money to the states for maternal and infant health care and hygiene. It authorized annual federal appropriations of $1 million to be apportioned among the states; this "humanizing" law operated only in cooperation with the states. Opponents considered it an unwarranted intrusion on state jurisdiction, and some states refused to accept its provisions. The act lapsed in June 1929.

Further reading: Henry Steele Commager, ed., *Documents of American History*, 8th ed. (New York: Appleton-Century-Crofts, 1968); James L. Nolan, Jr., *The Therapeutic State: Justifying Government at Century's End* (New York: New York University, 1998).

Sheridan's Begums Speech   Famous parliamentary speech given by British dramatist and Whig politician Richard Brinsley Sheridan on February 7, 1787, bringing before the House of Commons the third charge in the impeachment proceedings against Warren Hastings. During his tenure as governor-general of India (1774–85), Hastings was said to have clandestinely extorted the rich treasuries of the begums of Oudh (two Muslim princesses) to repay the debt owed to the British East India Company by their son and grandson (vizier of Oudh, India). Sheridan began his speech at 6:30 P.M., focusing attention on the cruel treatment of the begums and appealing eloquently to the "Great God of Justice," and he ended around midnight, to tumultuous applause.

Further reading: *The Speeches of the Right Honorable Richard Brinsley Sheridan* (New York: Russell & Russell, 1969).

Sherman Anti-Trust Act   First federal U.S. legislation, enacted on July 2, 1890, to regulate trusts. Introduced by Republican senator John Sherman, it declared illegal "every contract, combination in the form of trust or otherwise, or conspiracy, in restraint of trade or commerce among the several States, or with foreign nations." The legislation, based on Congress's constitutional power to regulate interstate commerce, grew out of public dissatisfaction with the abuses of business trusts and corporations controlling various commodities. While Supreme Court decisions weakened its effectiveness, it was used successfully in President Theodore Roosevelt's "trust-busting" campaigns and later actions. The law was strengthened and clarified by the CLAYTON ANTITRUST ACT of 1914.

Further reading: Mortimer Adler, ed., *The Annals of America*, 18 vols. (Chicago: Encyclopedia Britannica, 1968); Henry Steele Commager, ed., *Documents of American History*, 8th ed. (New York: Appleton-Century-Crofts, 1968); Frank N. Magill, ed., *Great Events from History: American Series*, 3 vols. (Englewood Cliffs, N.J.: 1975); William H. Taft, *The Anti-Trust Act and the Supreme Court* (New York: Kraus Reprint Co., 1970).

Sherman Silver Purchase Act   Federal legislation enacted on July 14, 1890, requiring the U.S. government to purchase 4.5 million ounces of silver per month at the prevailing market price. It also required the U.S. Treasury to issue, in payment, legal tender notes redeemable in gold or silver coin. The bill was a compromise between free-silver advocates and gold supporters, both groups being dissatisfied with the BLAND-ALLISON ACT. The act, named for Republican Senator John Sherman, failed to raise the price of silver and seriously weakened the federal gold reserve by increasing the circulation of redeemable paper currency. In 1893 President Grover Cleveland called a special session of Congress to repeal the act.

Further reading: Henry Steele Commager, ed., *Documents of American History*, 8th ed. (New York: Appleton-Century-Crofts, 1968); J. Laurence Laughlin, *The History of Bimetallism in the United States*, 4th ed. (New York: Greenwood Press, 1968).

Shimonoseki, Treaty of   Settlement concluded in Shimonoseki, Japan, on April 17, 1895, ending the Sino-Japanese War of 1894–95, in which Japan defeated China. Negotiated by Ito Hirobumi (Japan) and Li Hung-Chang (China), it demanded major concessions from China. Among these were (1) recognition of Korea's independence; (2) cession of the

Liaotung Peninsula (Soviet, French, and German pressure later forced Japan to withdraw this demand), Taiwan, and the Pescadores; (3) compensation of 200 million taels (later increased by 30 million) to be paid over seven years; and (4) the conclusion of a commercial treaty granting Japanese traders favorable terms, similar to those enjoyed by merchants from Western countries, and the opening of seven new treaty ports. The treaty, ratified by both countries in May 1895, helped boost Japan's expansionist aims in the region and set the scene for her exploitation of China on several fronts.

Further reading: Samuel C. Chu and Liu Kwang-Ching, *Li Hung-Chang: Diplomat and Modernizer* (Armonk, N.Y.: M. E. Sharpe, 1990); Geoffrey Drage, *Russian Affairs* (London: J. Murray, 1904); Kengi Hamada; *Prince Ito* (Washington, D.C.: University Publications of America, 1979); Fred L. Israel, ed., *Major Peace Treaties of Modern History, 1648–1967*, 4 vols. (New York: Chelsea House, 1967).

Ship Subsidy Act, U.S. See MERCHANT MARINE ACT.

Siebener Concordat (Siebenerkonkordat, Agreement of Seven) Concordat concluded by seven liberal Swiss cantons (Zurich, Bern, Lucerne, Solothurn, St. Gall, Aargau, and Thurgau) on March 17, 1832; it reflected the cantons' determination to take a stand against the conservative forces within their cantons and against the conservative cantons within the Swiss Confederation. Specifically, the document declared the solidarity of the cantons in their efforts to maintain their new, liberal constitutions. The move was a reaction to events during the period of 1830–31, when many cantons began to liberalize their constitutions. In three cantons violent conflict arose between nationalists and liberals; the seven signatory cantons hoped, through the document, to prevent the possibility of any opposition to their programs within their cantons.

Further reading: Gordon A. Craig, *The Triumph of Liberalism: Zurich in the Golden Age, 1830–1869* (New York: Scribner, 1988).

Siete Partidas, Código de las See SEVEN PARTS, CODE OF THE.

Silver Purchase Act of 1934, U.S. Federal legislation enacted on June 19, 1934, to inflate the price of silver, to establish a mixed gold and silver monetary standard, and to issue silver certificates to increase the currency. According to the act, domestic silver stocks were nationalized and the U.S. government agreed to buy unlimited quantities of silver at artificially high prices, until the price of silver rose to $1.29 per ounce or until federal silver holdings equaled one-third the value of federal gold holdings. The Treasury Department was authorized to issue silver certificates to cover the costs of these purchases. A 50 percent profits tax was imposed on certain silver transactions to prevent speculation. The act ben-

efited U.S. silver producers but damaged the currency systems of China and Mexico.

Further reading: *Silver Purchase Act of 1934* (Englewood, Colo.: Information Handling Services, 1956); *To Repeal the Silver Purchase Act of 1934* (Washington, D.C.: Government Printing Office, 1940).

Simon & Schuster v. New York State Crime Victims Board Case challenging New York State's 1977 "Son of Sam" law (Section 632a) and seeking an injunction to prevent the state's Crime Victims Board (CVB) from enforcing it, in which the U.S. Supreme Court's unanimous decision (issued on December 10, 1991) in favor of the plaintiff struck a blow to similar criminal antiprofit laws nationwide. The "Son of Sam" law, enacted to prevent criminals from profiting from their actions by writing books or other works, required any such money to be deposited in escrow with the CVB for payment to any victims of the crime and creditors. The CVB had tried to recover from publisher Simon & Schuster the money it had contracted to pay Henry Hill (a witness in the Federal Protection Program), who had been the principal source for its hugely successful book *Wiseguy: Life in a Mafia Family* and the film *Goodfellows*. When the publisher sued, both the district court and the Second Circuit court of appeals decided in favor of the CVB. The Supreme Court, however, agreed that the state law violated the FIRST AMENDMENT by placing an undue burden on protected speech that it did not place on any other speech or income. It declared that the law was, therefore, overinclusive.

Further reading: United States Supreme Court Case, *Simon & Schuster, Inc., Petitioner v. Members of the New York State Crime Victims Board, et al.*, Office of the Solicitor General, available online at http://www.usdoj.gov/osg/briefs/1990/sg900197.txt.

Single European Act Major amendment to the 1957 Treaties of ROME, signed on March 1, 1986, by the 12-member national governments of the European Community (Belgium, France, the Netherlands, West Germany, Italy, Luxembourg, Denmark, the United Kingdom, Ireland, Greece, Spain, and Portugal; the latter two became members at the start of 1986). Adoption of this act, which went into effect in July 1987, stimulated the program to develop a single European internal market by 1992 (with a European central bank and a common currency). The act gave the EC's Council of Ministers (representing the 12 member-states) more decision-making authority, on a majority vote basis and not subject to a single country's veto. The act also increased the power of the directly elected European Parliament in decision making, while enlarging its consultative rights. The act was finally approved by all member states, despite some opposition due to fears of dilution of national sovereignty in furthering European political cooperation and union.

Further reading: Michael Burgess, *Federalism and European Union: The Building of Europe, 1950–2000* (New York: Routledge, 2000); Henry W. Degenhardt, ed., *Treaties and Alliances of the World*, 4th ed. (Detroit: Gale Research, 1986); Moshe Kaniel. *The Exclusive Treaty-Making Power of the European Community: Up to the Period of the Single European Act* (Boston: Kluwer Law International, 1996).

Sinn Fein Proclamation of 1916   Proclamation issued by members of the Sinn Fein (Irish political society) upon their seizure of public buildings in Dublin, beginning the Easter Rebellion (April 24–May 1, 1916) for Ireland's independence from Britain. It summoned the men, women, and children of Ireland to strike for freedom, which the Irish Republican Brotherhood heralded at that moment, confident of victory. The Irish rebels, supported by "exiled children in America and by gallant allies in Europe," proclaimed the Irish Republic as a sovereign independent state, which would guarantee religious and civil liberty and equal rights and opportunities to all its citizens. A provisional government would administer civil and military affairs until the establishment of a national government. The British suppressed the rebellion after a week of fighting; signers of the proclamation were arrested and hanged.

See also: DE VALERA'S LETTER ON IRISH GRIEVANCES.

Further reading: Michael Laffan, *The Resurrection of Ireland: The Sinn Fein Party, 1916–1923* (New York: Cambridge University Press, 1999); Brendan O'Brien, *The Long War: The IRA and Sinn Fein*, 2d ed. (Syracuse, N.Y.: Syracuse University Press, 1999).

Sino-Soviet Agreement of 1923   See SUN-JOFFE MANIFESTO.

Sino-Soviet Treaty of 1945   Treaty concluded on August 14, 1945, by the Nationalist government of China and the Soviet Union, providing for a military alliance between them, as well as the Soviet Union's recognition of the Nationalists' government in return for certain concessions. Specifically, the signatory powers agreed to combine their efforts in the war against Japan; not to conclude a separate peace with Japan; to assist one another militarily in the event of a renewed Japanese attack upon either of the signatory powers; and to work together after the war to promote economic reconstruction in both their countries. In two notes and four agreements accompanying the treaty the Soviet Union pledged to support the Nationalists' government, as opposed to the communists', as well as the former's sovereignty over Manchuria. In return, China agreed to the independence of Outer Mongolia in the event that a majority of the residents were to vote in its favor; to the joint ownership of the Manchurian railway; to the joint use of the Port Arthur (Lu-shun) naval base; to free trade at the port of Dairen (Dalian); and

to Soviet authority in military matters for the duration of the war in Manchuria.

See also: SINO-SOVIET TREATY OF   .

Further reading: Raymond L. Garthoff, ed., *Sino-Soviet Military Relations* (New York: F. A. Praeger, 1966); J. A. S. Grenville and Bernard Wasserstein, *The Major International Treaties Since 1945: A History and Guide with Texts* (New York: Methuen, 1987).

Sino-Soviet Treaty of 1950   Treaty signed in Moscow on February 14, 1950, by Foreign Minister Andrei Y. Vishinsky of the Soviet Union and Premier and Foreign Minister Zhou Enlai of the People's Republic of China; it provided for a 30-year political and military alliance between the two countries. Through the treaty each party pledged to assist the other in the event of an attack on one party either by Japan alone or by Japan with another power, and to direct their efforts toward ending strife. An agreement accompanying the treaty provided for the Soviet Union's return to China of the Chinese Changchun railway, without compensation to the Soviets, plus the withdrawal of Soviet troops from Port Arthur (Lushun), both of which were to occur following the conclusion of a peace treaty with Japan. A second agreement provided China with a loan of $300 million from the Soviet Union, at interest with a five-year term.

See also: SINO-SOVIET TREATY OF 1945; SINO-SOVIET TREATY OF 1954; SOVIET-JAPANESE PEACE DECLARATION OF 1956

Further reading: Raymond L. Garthoff, ed., *Sino-Soviet Military Relations* (New York: F. A. Praeger, 1966); J. A. S. Grenville and Bernard Wasserstein, *The Major International Treaties since 1945: A History and Guide with Texts* (New York: Methuen, 1987); *Sino-Soviet Treaty and Agreements, Signed in Moscow on February 14, 1950* (Peking: Foreign Language Press, 1950).

Sino-Soviet Treaty of 1954   Treaty concluded on October 11, 1954, by the Soviet Union and the People's Republic of China, consolidating the alliance between the two countries that had been initiated with the SINO-SOVIET TREATY OF 1950. Most significant, the document contained the two powers' agreement on the withdrawal of Soviet forces from the Port Arthur (Lushun) naval base area by May 31, 1955, as well as on the transfer of all installations there to China without compensation to the Soviets. In addition, it was agreed that the Soviet Union would provide China with financial assistance and equipment totaling over 920 million rubles; that the Soviet Union would return to China full ownership of the joint Sino-Soviet companies; that both countries would share scientific information and personnel; and that a second railway line connecting the Soviet Union and China would be built. With regard to foreign policy, the two governments agreed to work together to maintain peace in the Far East and throughout the world; agreed that a conference would be held to consider the situation in Korea; stated their desire to see their relations with Japan improve; demanded that foreign troops be removed from Japanese territory; and expressed their opposition to the continued American presence in Taiwan as well as American support for the Chinese Nationalists.

Further reading: Francis A. Beer, comp., *Alliances: Latent War Communities in the Contemporary World* (New York: Holt, Rinehart & Winston, 1970); Raymond L. Garthoff, ed., *Sino-Soviet Military Relations* (New York: F. A. Praeger, 1966).

Sintra, Convention of British-French agreement concluded at Torres Vedras, near Lisbon, Portugal, on August 30, 1808, providing for the evacuation of French troops from Portugal during the Peninsular War (1808–14). It was thought to have been signed at Sintra (Cintra), 13 miles away, from where it was sent, dated, to England. In Portugal, British-Portuguese forces under General Sir Arthur Wellesley had defeated (August 21, 1808) French troops under General Androche Junot at Vimeiro, forcing the latter to negotiate the agreement with the British General Sir Hew Dalrymple (Wellesley disliked the treaty—although he signed it with Dalrymple—and requested to be recalled). The British agreed to provide their ships to transport the French troops home. Though realizing shortly that the French had pulled off a diplomatic coup to avoid certain defeat, a British court of inquiry approved the terms of the Sintra Convention a few months later.

Further reading: William Wordsworth, *Convention of Cintra: A Facsimile of the 1809 Tract* (Provo, Utah: Brigham Young University Press, 1983).

Siricius, Decretals of Oldest surviving papal decrees or epistles about Catholic doctrine; issued by Siricius, bishop (pope) of Rome from A.D. 384 to 398. Among the most significant are dictates sent to Bishop Himerius of Tarragona, Spain, in A.D. 385–86, replying to ecclesiastical questions. Siricius commanded strict obedience to the "decrees of the Apostolic See [church of Rome] and the venerable decisions of the canons" by "all our brethren" (bishops and priests). A church order of celibacy for clergymen (the first such on the subject) was also addressed to Himerius. The decretals show the pope to be the supreme authority of the Catholic Church in the West.

Further reading: Catholic University of America, eds., *New Catholic Encyclopedia* (New York: McGraw-Hill, 1967); Frank N. Magill, ed., *Great Events from History: Ancient and Medieval Series*, 3 vols. (Englewood Cliffs, N.J.: Salem Press, 1972); Milton Viorst, ed., *The Great Documents of Western Civilization* (Philadelphia: Chilton Books, 1965).

Sirois Commission Report (Rowell-Sirois Report) Report prepared from 1937 to 1940 by Canada's Royal Commission on Dominion-Provincial Relations (which was chaired initially by Newton Rowell and later by Joseph Sirois),

and in 1940 presented to the Canadian government; it recommended that the federal government assume certain fiscal responsibilities then held by the provincial governments. If implemented, the recommendations were intended to alleviate the economic stagnation that had developed during the post–World War I period. The commission recommended that Canada's federal government assume responsibility for the agricultural sector during emergency situations; responsibility for all provincial debts and for the unemployed; and control over taxation, in return for providing the provinces with annual grants. Because of the opposition of several provincial governments as well as Canada's entry into World War II, the recommendations were not implemented.

Further reading: R. C. Brown and M. E. Prang, eds., *Canadian Historical Documents Series*, 3 vols. (Scarborough, Canada: Prentice-Hall of Canada, 1966); Donald V. Smiley, *The Rowell-Sirois Report: An Abridgement of Book I of the Royal Commission Report on Dominion-Provincial Relations* (Toronto: Macmillan of Canada, 1978).

Sistova, Peace of Separate peace concluded on August 4, 1791, at Sistova (Svishtov, Bulgaria) between Austria and the Ottoman Empire (Turkey), ending the state of war between them. Austria had been fighting together with Russia in order to bring about a partition of the Ottoman Empire in which Russia would have received Turkish territories in the Caucasus and Danube River basin, and Austria would have received territories in the Balkans. Through the peace Austria returned to the Ottomans the Serbian capital of Belgrade, which Austria had captured from them in 1789; in return the Turks ceded to Austria part of northern Bosnia. The Austrians had withdrawn from the war through Prussian influence; Prussia, fearful of Russia and Austria's growing influence in the south, had become allied with the Ottoman Empire.

See also: JASSY, TREATY OF.

Further reading: Michael R. Hickok, *Ottoman Military Administration in Eighteenth-Century Bosnia* (New York: Brill, 1997).

Six Acts of 1819, British Statutes introduced by Lords Sidmouth, Castlereagh, and Eldon into the British Parliament to curb radical agitation and public disturbances; hastily enacted in late November and December 1819, after the Peterloo Massacre (see COERCION ACTS OF 1817). The first act (Eldon's) expedited trials in cases of misdemeanors. The next three acts (Sidmouth's) banned the training of persons in the use of arms, authorized magistrates (during a 27-month period) to confiscate dangerous arms found in certain counties, and punished blasphemous and seditious libel, respectively (these acts were to continue until 1822). The fifth and sixth acts (Castlereagh's) restricted public meetings (for five years) to a maximum of 50 local citizens (who were forbidden to carry arms or flags or engage in sedition) and levied stamp duties on newspapers or periodicals that cost less than six pence and were published more than once every 26 days. The radicals and Whigs denounced the Six Acts.

Further reading: Joel H. Wiener, ed., *Great Britain—The Lion at Home: A Documentary History of Domestic Policy (1689–1673),* 4 vols. (New York: Chelsea House, 1974).

Six Articles, Act of   English statute instigated by King Henry VIII to reverse the progress of the Protestant Reformation by forcing his people to accept the Roman Catholic doctrine on six important issues. The six were necessity of transubstantiation, communion of one kind for laymen, celibacy for the clergy, strict adherence to vows of chastity, continuation of private masses, and auricular confession. The bill, introduced into the English Parliament by the duke of Norfolk, stipulated that rejection of any of the above positions constituted heresy. Henry sought thereby to rebuild his continental alliances in Europe and strengthen his conservative base at home. Known as the "whip with six strings" or the "bloody statute," the act (June 1539) was accepted by most of the clergy (Bishop Hugh Latimer of Worcester resigned in protest) and all the lay peers. However, it was not strictly enforced and, in fact, was generally ignored. It was repealed in 1547.

Further reading: Gerald L. Bray, *Documents of the English Reformation* (Minneapolis: Fortress Press, 1994); Frank N. Magill, ed., *Great Events from History: Modern European Series,* 3 vols. (Englewood Cliffs, N.J.: Salem Press, 1973); Lewis W. Spitz, *The Protestant Reformation* (Englewood Cliffs, N.J.: Prentice-Hall, 1966).

Six Edicts, Turgot's   Six administrative measures introduced in January 1776 by France's comptroller general Robert Jacques Turgot, the sixth being directly responsible for his downfall in May 1776. They were (1) suppression of all dues on grain, cereals, and pulses in Paris; (2) abolition, with compensation, of many petty offices in Parisian docks and markets; (3) abolition of the Caisse de Poissy (financing institution of the meat and cattle trade) and introduction of new rate structures; (4) reorganization of the taxes levied on suet; (5) dissolution of the old trade guilds, complete restructuring of the trades; and (6) suppression of the *corvés* (forced, unpaid road labor), with a small tax levied proportionately on all landowners instead. These funds would be audited and administered by the provinces. Turgot's condemnation of the system of privileges, which had fostered and abused the *corvées,* aroused opposition of these classes. Although the edicts were finally registered after much debate on March 12, Turgot was successfully dislodged from power by destroying the king's confidence in him. After he resigned (May 12), his reforms were gradually abandoned.

See also: TURGOT'S "LETTERS ON THE FREEDOM OF THE GRAIN TRADE"; TURGOT'S LETTER TO LOUIS XVI.

Further reading: Malcolm Hill, *Statesman of the Enlightenment: The Life of Anne-Robert Turgot* (London: Othila Press,

1999); Robert P. Shepherd, *Turgot and the Six Edicts* (New York: B. Franklin, 1971).

Six-Power Agreement of 1948   Draft agreement announced on December 28, 1948, in London for the establishment of an International Ruhr Authority through which Britain, France, Belgium, the Netherlands, Luxembourg, and the United States could exert their control over Germany's coal, coke, and steel industry in the Ruhr region of West Germany). The United States, Britain, France, and Germany had three votes each in the Ruhr Authority (Germany's votes being divided among the other three until the formation of her new government) while Belgium, the Netherlands, and Luxembourg had one vote each. The authority was to divide the production of coal, coke, and steel between German consumption and export and ensure that the other countries secured their requirement of these vital products. It was also to cooperate with the Military Security Board in the disarmament and demilitarization of Germany and remain in charge until the final German peace settlement was signed.

Further reading: Louis H. Pink, *An International Authority for the Ruhr* (New York: Citizens Conference on International Economic Union, 1949).

Sixteenth Amendment, U.S.   Amendment to the U.S. CONSTITUTION, passed by Congress in 1909 and ratified by the states in 1913, that authorized the federal government to levy taxes on incomes, without apportionment among the states. The amendment was adopted after the U.S. Supreme Court, in *Pollock* v. *Farmers' Loan & Trust* (1895), invalidated an income tax law as unconstitutional. The amendment was an attempt to redress inequalities in the distribution of national income as well as to provide additional monies for the federal government.

Further reading: Alan Brinkley, *American History: A Survey,* 10th ed. (Boston: McGraw-Hill College, 1999); Kermit L. Hall et al., eds., *American Legal History: Cases and Materials,* 2d ed. (New York: Oxford University Press, 1996); Kermit L. Hall et al., eds., *The Oxford Companion to the Supreme Court of the United States* (New York: Oxford University Press, 1992); Frank N. Magill, ed., *Great Events from History: American Series,* 3 vols. (Englewood Cliffs, N.J.: Salem Press, 1975).

Sixth Amendment, U.S.   Amendment to the U.S. CONSTITUTION, adopted in 1791, that grants people accused in criminal cases the right to a "speedy and public trial, by an impartial jury"; to be informed of the nature and cause of the accusation; to confront their accusers; to obtain witnesses in their behalf; and to have the assistance of defense counsel. In *GIDEON* V. *WAINWRIGHT* (1963), the Supreme Court ruled that representation by counsel is required in all state criminal trials; states must supply counsel to indigent defendants.

Further reading: Alan Brinkley, *American History: A Survey*, 10th ed. (Boston: McGraw-Hill College, 1999); Kermit L. Hall et al., eds., *American Legal History: Cases and Materials*, 2d ed. (New York: Oxford University Press, 1996); Kermit L. Hall et al., eds., *The Oxford Companion to the Supreme Court of the United States* (New York: Oxford University Press, 1992); Fred Ramen, *The Rights of the Accused* (New York: Rosen Publishing Group, 2001).

Sixty-seven Theses, Zwingli's

Doctrine of 67 conclusions or articles, written and presented publicly by Swiss reformer Huldreich Zwingli in Zurich in 1523; they described the fundamental beliefs held by himself and his Swiss Protestant followers, called Zwinglians. While reciting the many beliefs that all Christians shared, Zwingli also criticized numerous doctrines propounded by the Roman Catholic Church, particularly those based upon tradition rather than upon biblical texts. He specifically condemned the Catholic Church's belief in the mass as a sacrifice and its contention that some believers may be considered "high priests" and therefore superior to laymen, and that believers require a mediator between themselves and God. He also flatly rejected the authority of the pope, the doctrine of transubstantiation, the worship of saints, the belief in purgatory, and mandatory fasting.

Further reading: Arthur C. Cochrane, ed., *Reformed Confessions of the 16th Century* (Philadelphia: Westminster Press, 1966); Carl S. Meyer, trans., *Luther's and Zwingli's Propositions for Debate: The Ninety-Five Theses of 31 October 1517 and the Sixty-Seven Articles of 19 January 1523: In the Original Version and Contemporary Translations* (Leiden, Netherlands: E. J. Brill, 1963); Lewis W. Spitz, *The Protestant Reformation* (Englewood Cliffs, N.J.: Prentice-Hall, 1966).

Slaughterhouse Cases

First U.S. Supreme Court decision, issued on April 14, 1873, interpreting the FOURTEENTH AMENDMENT. In 1869 the Louisiana state legislature granted a monopoly to a New Orleans slaughterhouse. Other slaughterhouse operators sued, claiming that the monopoly abridged their "privileges and immunities" as U.S. citizens, denied them equal protection of the laws, and deprived them of property without due process of law, all in violation of the Fourteenth Amendment. In a 5-4 decision, the Court upheld the monopoly, ruling that the amendment was not intended to deny the states legal jurisdiction over their citizens, that its purpose was to protect the civil rights of blacks, not the property rights of businesspeople. By narrowly defining the rights protected by the amendment, the decision limited federal protection of black civil rights.

Further reading: Mortimer Adler, ed., *The Annals of America*, 18 vols. (Chicago: Encyclopedia Britannica, 1968); Henry Steele Commager, ed., *Documents of American History*, 8th ed. (New York: Appleton-Century-Crofts, 1968); Kermit L. Hall et al., eds., *American Legal History: Cases and Materials*,

2d ed. (New York: Oxford University Press, 1996); Kermit L. Hall et al., eds., *The Oxford Companion to the Supreme Court of the United States* (New York: Oxford University Press, 1992).

Slave Codes, U.S.
See BLACK CODES, U.S.

Slave Emancipation Act, Brazilian
See BRAZILIAN SLAVE EMANCIPATION ACT.

Slave Emancipation Act, French

Legislation abolishing the slave trade in France, passed on March 29, 1815, by Napoléon Bonaparte during his 100-day regime, a desperate attempt to win British favor after his isolation in Europe (see VIENNA, DECLARATION OF [1815]). During the Vienna Congress, Britain had forced the European allies to sign a declaration condemning the slave trade as "repugnant to the principles of humanity and universal morality." Further, they had concurred in the "wish of putting an end to a scourge which has so long desolated Africa, degraded Europe, and afflicted humanity." Slavery had been abolished in France's West Indian colonies during the Reign of Terror (1793–94), only to be reintroduced by Napoléon in 1802.

Further reading: Seymour Drescher, *From Slavery to Freedom: Comparative Studies in the Rise and Fall of Atlantic Slavery* (New York: New York University Press, 1999); Paul M. Kielstra, *The Politics of Slave Trade Suppression in Britain and France, 1814–48: Diplomacy, Morality and Economics* (New York: St. Martin's Press, 2000).

Slave Emancipation Act of 1807, British

Act by the British Parliament banning the African slave trade (effective on May 1, 1807) and declaring as unlawful "all manner of dealing and trading in the purchase, sale, barter or transfer of slaves" (directly or indirectly) in Africa, the West Indies, and America. Violators in Britain or British-ruled areas could incur fines of £100 for each slave and also forfeit the property in which the slave trade was transacted. It prohibited the insurances on slave transactions and directed that slaves on captured ships should be made over to the government, freed from slavery, and allowed to enter the armed forces or be apprenticed for 14 years.

Further reading: Roger Anstey, *The Atlantic Slave Trade and British Abolition, 1760–1810* (Brookfield, Vt.: Ashgate Publications, 1992); Seymour Drescher, *From Slavery to Freedom: Comparative Studies in the Rise and Fall of Atlantic Slavery* (New York: New York: University Press, 1999); Judi Jennings, *The Business of Abolishing the British Slave Trade, 1783–1807* (Portland, Ore.: F. Cass, 1997); Junius P. Rodriguez, ed., *Chronology of World Slavery* (Santa Barbara, Calif.: ABC-Clio, 1999).

Slave Emancipation Act of 1833, British

Act abolishing slavery in the British colonies, carried through Parliament by Edward Stanley, colonial secretary, on August 23, 1833. Children under six were to be freed immediately, and those over six apprenticed for a certain period. This last clause was later withdrawn. Slave owners were to receive compensations of £20 million. This act was the culmination of a long campaign waged by the abolitionists, led by William Wilberforce, which intensified after the abolition of the slave trade (see SLAVE EMANCIPATION ACT OF 1807, BRITISH).

Further reading: Seymour Drescher, *From Slavery to Freedom: Comparative Studies in the Rise and Fall of Atlantic Slavery* (New York: New York University Press, 1999); Paul M. Kielstra, *The Politics of Slave Trade Suppression in Britain and France, 1814–48: Diplomacy, Morality and Economics* (New York: St. Martin's Press, 2000); Frank N. Magill, ed., *Great Events from History: Modern European Series*, 3 vols. (Englewood Cliffs, N.J.: Salem Press, 1973).

Slavery Compromise, U.S. (Three-Fifths Compromise)   Agreement reached at the federal constitutional convention of 1787 to resolve the dispute over apportioning direct taxes and representation in the House of Representatives, where representation is based on population. Northern states argued that slaves were property and should not be counted for apportionment purposes. Southern states claimed that slaves should be counted. Under the terms of the compromise, spelled out in Article One of the U.S. CONSTITUTION, each slave counted as three-fifths of a person for purposes of apportionment.

Further reading: Mortimer Adler, ed., *The Annals of America*, 18 vols. (Chicago: Encyclopedia Britannica, 1968); Henry Steele Commager, ed., *Documents of American History*, 8th ed. (New York: Appleton-Century-Crofts, 1968); Charles W. Eliot, ed., *The Harvard Classics*, 51 vols. (New York: P. F. Collier & Son, 1937); Kermit L. Hall et al., eds., *American Legal History: Cases and Materials*, 2d ed. (New York: Oxford University Press, 1996).

Slaves, Act to Prohibit Importation of (Slave Trade Abolition Act of 1807)   U.S. legislation enacted by Congress on March 2, 1807, that prohibited the importation of "any negro, mulatto, or person of colour" as a slave into the United States on and after January 1, 1808. (Article One of the U.S. CONSTITUTION had forbidden Congress from interfering with the international slave trade prior to 1808.) Violations of the law were punishable by forfeiture of the vessel and its cargo. The state in which the vessel was seized would determine the disposal of the slaves on board. Although the act authorized the U.S. president to use armed ships to interdict the slave trade, slave smuggling continued until 1860.

Further reading: Mortimer Adler, ed., *The Annals of America*, 18 vols. (Chicago: Encyclopedia Britannica, 1968); Henry Steele Commager, ed., *Documents of American History*, 8th ed. (New York: Appleton-Century-Crofts, 1968); Paul Finkelman, *Slavery and the Founders: Race and Liberty in the Age of*

Jefferson, 2d ed. (Armonk, N.Y.: M. E. Sharpe, 2001); Junius P. Rodriguez, ed., *Chronology of World Slavery* (Santa Barbara, Calif.: ABC-Clio, 1999).

Smith Act   See ALIEN REGISTRATION ACT, U.S.

Smith-Connally Anti-Strike Act (War Labor Disputes Act)   U.S. legislation sponsored by Representative Howard W. Smith of Virginia and Senator Thomas T. Connally of Texas and enacted on June 25, 1943, that authorized the president to seize any plant or industry in which a labor dispute might interfere with war production. Anyone promoting a strike after such seizure was subject to criminal prosecution, and unions were liable to damage suits if they failed to give 30 days' notice of intention to strike in war industries. The act was opposed by organized labor and was vetoed by President Franklin D. Roosevelt, but Congress overrode the veto. The president used the act in December 1943 to take temporary possession of U.S. railroads threatened by a strike. The law expired in 1947.

Further reading: Merlyn S. Pitzele and Raymond S. Smethurst, *What to Expect in Labor Legislation: National Service—the Smith-Connally Act* (New York: Kraus Reprint Corp., 1967).

Smith-Hughes Act   Legislation enacted by the U.S. Congress on February 23, 1917, to advance vocational education. It was named for its sponsors, Senator Hoke Smith and Representative Dudley M. Hughes, two Democrats from Georgia. The act provided for federal grants-in-aid to promote training in agriculture, the trades and industries, commerce, home economics, and vocational instruction. The grants were to be matched by state and/or local contributions. The act also established the Federal Board of Vocational Education.

Further reading: Gladys A. Branegan, *Home Economics Teacher Training under the Smith-Hughes Act, 1917 to 1927; A Study of Trends in the Work of Seventy-One Institutions Approved under the National Vocational Education Act* (New York: AMS Press, 1972); National Society for Vocational Education, *Lessons of the War, the States and the Smith-Hughes Act* (New York: Press of Clarence S. Nathan, 1919).

Smith-Lever Act   Federal U.S. legislation enacted on May 8, 1914, that established a national agricultural extension system under the U.S. Department of Agriculture, in cooperation with the land-grant colleges. The system provided county agents and demonstrators to teach farmers and their families the latest agricultural and home economics techniques. Federal grants-in-aid were to be matched by equal state contributions to support the program. The goal was to extend the benefits offered by the land-grant colleges (see MORRILL ACT) and the agricultural experiment stations (see HATCH ACT OF 1887). Later, the act helped to increase food production during World War I (1914–18).

Further reading: *Hearings, Report, and Debate: Smith-Lever Act of 1914* (Blacksburg, Va.: Virginia Agricultural Extension Service, 1959); *Recognizing the 75th Anniversary of the Smith-Lever Act: Report* (Washington, D.C.: Government Printing Office, 1989).

Smith v. Allwright

U.S. Supreme Court decision issued on April 3, 1944, overturning a Texas Democratic Party policy that excluded black citizens from membership in the party and therefore prevented them from voting in the party primary elections. Lonnie E. Smith, a black, challenged the policy, suing election judge S. E. Allwright on the grounds that Smith was excluded from voting in the primaries because of his race. Reversing its decision in *Grovey v. Townsend* (1935), the Supreme Court ruled that party primaries could not be considered private matters and that the party was acting as an agency of the state. The discrimination against blacks was therefore prohibited by the FIFTEENTH AMENDMENT

Further reading: Kermit L. Hall et al., eds., *The Oxford Companion to the Supreme Court of the United States* (New York: Oxford University Press, 1992); Tony Mauro, *Illustrated Great Decisions of the Supreme Court* (Washington, D.C.: CQ Press, 2000); United States Supreme Court, *United States Reports: Cases Adjudged in the Supreme Court at . . . and Rules Announced at . . .* (New York: Banks & Brothers, Law Publishers, 1884–1921; Washington, D.C.: Government Printing Office, 1922–); United States Supreme Court, *Leading Decisions of the United States Supreme Court* (San Francisco, Calif.: Chandler Publications, 1965).

Smoking and Health

Report issued on January 11, 1964, by the Advisory Committee to the U.S. surgeon general, concluding that cigarette smoking was "a health hazard of sufficient importance in the United States to warrant appropriate remedial action." Cigarette smoking was found to be associated with lung cancer, coronary artery disease, chronic bronchitis, and emphysema; pipe smoking was associated with lip cancer. As a result of *Smoking and Health*, and despite tobacco industry opposition, Congress in 1965 passed the Federal Cigarette Labeling and Advertising Act, which required that health warnings be printed on every cigarette package sold from 1966 on. The Public Health Cigarette Smoking Act of 1970 banned cigarette advertising on radio and television and strengthened warnings on packages.

See also: HEALTH CONSEQUENCES OF SMOKING.

Further reading: Harold S. Diehl, *Tobacco & Your Health: The Smoking Controversy* (New York: McGraw-Hill, 1969); Kenneth M. Friedman, *Public Policy and the Smoking-Health Controversy: A Comparative Study* (Lexington, Mass.: Lexington Books, 1975); Jacob Sullum, *For Your Own Good: The Anti-Smoking Crusade and the Tyranny of Public Health* (New York: Free Press, 1998); Tobacco Institute, *Smoking and Health, 1964–1979: The Continuing Controversy* (Washington, D.C.: The Institute, 1979).

Smoot-Hawley Tariff Act

Federal legislation enacted on June 17, 1930, that raised import duties to the highest level in U.S. history. Sponsored by Republican senator Reed Smoot of Utah and Republican representative Willis C. Hawley of Oregon, this protective tariff represented a congressional compromise, raising rates on both agricultural products, as favored by the Senate, and manufactured goods, as supported by the House of Representatives. Despite widespread opposition, President Herbert Hoover signed the act into law. Foreign nations passed retaliatory legislation, which damaged U.S. foreign trade and worsened the worldwide depression.

Further reading: Douglas A. Irwin, *The Smoot-Hawley Tariff: A Quantitative Assessment* (Cambridge, Mass.: National Bureau of Economic Research, 1996); Gail E. Makinen, *The Smoot-Hawley Tariff and the Great Depression of 1929–1933* (Washington, D.C.: Congressional Research Service, Library of Congress, 1994).

Social Contract (Du Contrat Social)

Influential work written by French philosopher Jean-Jacques Rousseau, published in Amsterdam and distributed in 1762; it contained the author's views on the role of the citizen and the government in society. According to Rousseau, all members of society were equal and, therefore, shared equal obligations to the society at large. From this premise Rousseau argued that each individual was therefore obligated to surrender all his rights to the general will, which would be represented by the state, which, in turn, would be headed by a responsible monarch. Rousseau held that such an arrangement was ideal as all citizens would retain equality with respect to one another, as well as ultimate power since they had the right to remove the king from power at will. Despite the work's repeated support for individual liberty, it was blamed for supporting despotism and collectivism. Yet all government, Rousseau insisted, must depend upon the consent of the governed.

Further reading: G. D. H. Cole, trans., *The Social Contract; and, The Discourses* (London: D. Campbell, 1993); Victor Gourevitch, ed. and trans., *The Social Contract and Other Later Political Writings* (New York: Cambridge University Press, 1997); Mark A. Kishlansky, ed., *Sources of the West: Readings in Western Civilization*, 4th ed., vol. 2 (New York: Longman, 2001); Christopher W. Morris, ed., *The Social Contract Theorists: Critical Essays on Hobbes, Locke, and Rousseau* (Lanham, Md.: Rowman & Littlefield, 1999).

Social Security Act, U.S.

New Deal legislation enacted by the U.S. Congress on August 14, 1935, to provide old-age retirement insurance, unemployment insurance, survivors' and disability insurance, and public assistance. It created the Social Security Board to administer the programs. The act granted federal subsidies to state assistance programs for the needy elderly and created a federally administered annuity for retired workers aged 65 and over, based on previous wages and funded by payroll taxes paid by employers and employees. It set up a cooperative federal-state unemployment insurance program financed by a payroll tax on employers. The act also furnished grants to states for aid to dependent children, maternal and child welfare, the blind, vocational rehabilitation, and public health work. The act originally covered only industrial and commercial workers, but it has been amended many times to extend coverage and include new programs.

Further reading: Mortimer Adler, ed., *The Annals of America*, 18 vols. (Chicago: Encyclopedia Britannica, 1968); Henry Steele Commager, ed., *Documents of American History*, 8th ed. (New York: Appleton-Century-Crofts, 1968); Frank N. Magill, ed., *Great Events from History: American Series*, 3 vols. (Englewood Cliffs, N.J.: 1975); Charles McKinley, *Launching Social Security; a Capture-and-Record Account, 1935–1937* (Madison: University of Wisconsin Press, 1970).

Soil Conservation Act, U.S. (Soil Erosion Act)

Federal legislation enacted on April 27, 1935, that established the Soil Conservation Service as a permanent section within the U.S. Department of Agriculture. Its purpose was to prevent and control soil erosion, which had devastated large areas of the Great Plains in the 1930s and created the Dust Bowl. The act aimed to preserve natural resources, control floods, prevent damage to reservoirs, maintain river and harbor navigation, protect public health and public lands, and relieve unemployment. It was succeeded by the SOIL CONSERVATION AND DOMESTIC ALLOTMENT ACT of 1936.

Further reading: Mortimer Adler, ed., *The Annals of America*, 18 vols. (Chicago: Encyclopaedia Britannica, 1968); Henry Steele Commager, ed., *Documents of American History*, 8th ed. (New York: Appleton-Century-Crofts, 1968).

Soil Conservation and Domestic Allotment Act, U.S.

New Deal legislation enacted on February 29, 1936, to control not only soil erosion but also agricultural production, in order to prevent the accumulation of unmarketable surpluses. After the judicial invalidation of the U.S. AGRICULTURAL ADJUSTMENT ACT OF 1933, the 1936 act used indirect control of production, by authorizing benefit payments to farmers who practiced soil conservation under government programs. The programs shifted millions of acres from the cultivation of soil-depleting crops (such as corn, cotton, tobacco, wheat, and oats, which had also contributed to the production surpluses) to soil-conserving crops (such as clover and soybeans) or soil-building efforts.

Further reading: Douglas Helms, *The History of Soil and Water Conservation* (Washington, D.C.: Agricultural History Society, 1985); Brad D. Lookingbill, *Dust Bowl, USA: Depression America and the Ecological Imagination, 1929–1941* (Athens: Ohio University Press, 2001).

Solemn League and Covenant of 1638 (National Covenant)

Bonds of agreement drawn up and signed by leading Presbyterian ministers at Edinburgh, Scotland, on February 28, 1638, wherein the Scottish Presbyterians promised to resist ecclesiastical innovations unless the General Assembly had approved them. The issue came up for discussion when the 1636 *Book of Canons* had insisted that each minister indicate his acceptance of the *Book of COMMON PRAYER* (for the Church of England) and episcopacy. Then, in 1637, when King Charles I of England attempted to enforce on Scotland the *Book of Common Prayer*, there was much opposition to it and riots broke out in Edinburgh. The Scottish opponents of the book organized themselves into the committee of the "Tables" and issued the National Covenant. At its meeting in November 1638, the Presbyterian-controlled General Assembly abolished the episcopacy, discarded the *Book of Canons* of 1636 and the *Book of Common Prayer*, and excommunicated some bishops.

See also: SOLEMN LEAGUE AND COVENANT OF 1643.

Further reading: William L. Mathieson, *Politics and Religion; a Study in Scottish History from the Reformation to the Revolution* (Glasgow, Scotland: J. Maclehose, 1902); David Stevenson, *The Scottish Revolution, 1637–1644; the Triumph of the Covenanters* (New York: St. Martin's Press, 1974).

Solemn League and Covenant of 1643

Anglo-Scottish agreement initiated by the English parliamentarian statesman John Pym during the Great English Civil War; signed by 25 peers and 288 members of the House of Commons on September 25, 1643. A modification of the Solemn League and Covenant of 1638, it agreed to reform the churches of England, Scotland, and Ireland "according to the Word of God and the example of the best reformed churches." The Westminster Assembly of Divines was appointed to bring the churches into a uniformity of faith, worship, and government. The league promised to maintain the purity of the Scottish church and, as compensation for this and a monthly payment of £30,000, the Scots agreed to send an army to fight for the English parliamentarians in the war against the royalists. Civil and military personnel were required to sign the covenant; nearly 2,000 clergymen refused and lost their jobs.

Further reading: Gerald L. Bray, *Documents of the English Reformation* (Minneapolis: Fortress Press, 1994); W. Fred Graham, *Later Calvinism: International Perspectives* (Kirksville, Mo.: Sixteenth Century Publishers, 1994); William L. Mathieson, *Politics and Religion; a Study in Scottish History from the Reformation to the Revolution* (Glasgow: J. Maclehose, 1902); David Stevenson, *The Scottish Revolution, 1637–1644; the Triumph of the Covenanters* (New York: St. Martin's Press, 1974).

Solidarity Charter

Formal document issued in 1979 as a Charter of Workers' Rights by the Workers' Defense Council, a group of Polish dissident intellectuals who assisted the families of workers on strike. In 1980, a series of massive strikes at the Lenin Shipyards in Gdansk, Poland, led to the creation of the Interfactory Strike Committee headed by Lech Walesa. In August the committee presented the government with a list of demands, largely derived from the Charter of Workers' Rights, which called for independent unions and freedom of political and religious expression. An agreement was reached between the Polish government and the committee to allow independent unions. In September of 1980, 36 regional trade unions formed Solidarity, a national union led by Walesa, which soon had some 10 million members across Poland.

See also: JARUZELSKI'S MARTIAL LAW DECREE.

Further reading: Timothy Garton Ash, *The Polish Revolution: Solidarity, 1980–1982* (New York: Scribner, 1984); Robert Eringer, *Strike for Freedom: The Story of Lech Walesa and Polish Solidarity* (New York: Dodd Mead, 1982).

Sollicitudo Rei Socialis   Encyclical letter by Pope John Paul II in February 1988, reiterating the "Social Concerns of the Church" (the document's title in English) for the poor, underdeveloped nations (the Third World) while updating Pope Paul VI's 1967 encyclical *Populorum Progressio* (*Development of Peoples*). Significantly the ideological struggle between the East (Marxism) and the West (capitalism) was directly blamed by the pope for obstructing social and economic progress in the Third World, where both Marxism and capitalism harbor "a tendency toward imperialism" and profit by their "structures of sin." The pope called for "impartial aid from all the richer and more developed countries" to solve the Third World's problems.

Further reading: J. Michael Miller, ed., *The Encyclicals of John Paul II* (Huntington, Ind.: Our Sunday Visitor, 2001); David J. O'Brien and Thomas A. Shannon, eds., *Catholic Social Thought: The Documentary Heritage* (Maryknoll, N.Y.: Orbis Books, 1992); George Weigel and Robert Royal, *Building the Free Society: Democracy, Capitalism, and Catholic Social Teaching* (Grand Rapids, Mich.: Eerdmans, 1993).

Solon, Laws of   Legislative reforms initiated by Solon after he was elected sole archon (chief magistrate) of the Greek city-state of Athens in 594 B.C. Traditionally known as the "first Athenian constitution," these laws are only fragmentary today and found only as quotations in the works of later Greek writers. Solon made several changes in the laws relating to property, such as abolishing all debts, freeing all enslaved debtors, and giving farmers ownership of land they formerly tilled for nobles. His constitutional reforms included the creation of the Council of 400 as a deliberative body to initiate all legislation and the division of the citizenry into four classes by income. His judicial reforms included the establishment of a court for all citizens, where Athenians could sue and appeal a verdict.

Further reading: Friedrich Heer, *Great Documents of the World: Milestones of Human Thought* (New York: McGraw-Hill, 1977); C. Hignett, *A History of the Athenian Constitution to the End of the Fifth Century B.C.* (Oxford, England: Clar-

endon Press, 1952); Frank N. Magill, ed., *Great Events from History: Ancient and Medieval Series*, 3 vols. (Englewood Cliffs, N.J.: Salem Press, 1972).

Solzhenitsyn's Harvard Speech   Commencement address (entitled "A World Split Apart") given by exiled, Nobel Prize–winning Soviet author Aleksandr I. Solzhenitsyn at Harvard University on June 8, 1978. He pointed to the Western world's "decline in courage" . . . "particularly noticeable among the ruling groups and the intellectual elite," and its need to overcome a "loss of will power" and "psychological weakness" seemingly rooted in "a society raised in the cult of material well-being." A crisis or split in the world has occurred, he said in Russian (translated then into English for the audience), with the West suffocated by "commercial interests" and the East destroyed by political rulers' "machinations." The times demanded a "spiritual upsurge" from us all, concluded Solzhenitsyn, whose views were disputed by many upset by his criticism of the West.

Further reading: Irina I. Alberti, trans., *A World Split Apart: Commencement Address Delivered at Harvard University, June 8, 1978* (New York: Harper & Row, 1978); Ronald Berman, ed., *Solzhenitsyn at Harvard: The Address, Twelve Early Responses, and Six Later Reflections* (Washington: Ethics and Public Policy Center, 1980).

"Some Reflections on Marriage"   British feminist Mary Astell's essay on marriage in 1700, prompted by questions of marital authority raised in the scandalous case of the duchess of Mazarin and composed in one afternoon. Astell supported a woman's right to determine her own fate by choosing to stay single, a state she considered preferable to living in servility with a man who has such "a contemptible Opinion of her and her Sex." Men married out of ulterior motives, she argued, needing a housekeeper and someone to bear and rear their children, and "no man can endure a Woman of Superior Sense," according to Astell. Also, a woman had no real choice except "to Refuse or Accept what is offer'd." Nevertheless, Astell (a committed monarchist) believed that a married woman owed her husband the same loyalty that a subject owed the king.

Further reading: Mary Astell, *Some Reflections Upon Marriage*, sunshine for women, available online at http://www.pinn.net/~sunshine/book-sum/astell2.htm; Ruth Perry, *The Celebrated Mary Astell—An Early English Feminist* (Chicago: University of Chicago Press, 1986.

"So Much Owed" Speech, Churchill's   Speech delivered on August 20, 1940, before Britain's House of Commons by Prime Minister Winston Churchill as the Battle of Britain raged in the air (see CHURCHILL'S "THEIR FINEST HOUR" SPEECH). Describing the current war as very different from the previous one, he pointed out that it was "well-suited to the genius and the resources of the British nation," which would

"enforce a strict blockade" of all the countries under German control. He expressed disappointment in the French decision to abandon the struggle, blaming it on the Vichy regime. Britain and Canada had offered the United States use of their defense facilities "against the unmeasured dangers of the future," he informed his audience. In a glowing tribute to the Royal Air Force for "turning the tide of the war," he said, "Never in the field of human conflict was so much owed by so many to so few."

Further reading: David Cannadine, ed., *Blood, Toil, Tears and Sweat: The Speeches of Winston Churchill* (Boston: Houghton Mifflin, 1989).

Somnauth Proclamation   Declaration by Lord Ellenborough, governor general of India (1841–44) during the British conquest of Sind in 1843, announcing that he would restore to the Temple of Somnauth (a sacred shrine of the Hindus) its sandalwood gates, which had been stolen 80 years earlier. It was a foolish declaration because the gates were in ruins and were promised to people who had converted to Islam. Thus, the donation was more an insult than an honor. For the Hindus, the gift was equally unacceptable, not only because it was the symbol of their subjugation but also because it had been prophesized that the restoration of the gates would gradually lead to the end of the Sikh Empire. Lord Ellenborough was hastily recalled to England in 1844.

Further reading: Reginald C. A. Colchester, ed., *History of the Indian Administration of Lord Ellenborough, . . .* (London: R. Bentley and Son, 1874).

Sons of Liberty of New York, Resolutions of the   See NEW YORK SONS OF LIBERTY, RESOLUTIONS OF THE.

South Africa Act of 1909   British legislation passed on September 20, 1909, approving the draft constitution for the union of the four British colonies (Cape, Natal, Orange River, and Transvaal) in South Africa, as proposed by the National Convention in Durban in 1908. Drafted by Jan Smuts (colonial secretary of the Transvaal) using the model of the Australian Constitution (1900), it incorporated the color bar by preventing the Cape African and colored people from electing their own candidates to the parliament. It provided for a "color-blind" franchise subject to amendment by a two-thirds majority in both houses and concentrated power in the all-white parliament. It was hoped that the benefits resulting from the union would far exceed the embarrassment caused by the descriminatory clauses in the constitution. The Union of South Africa was formally inaugurated on May 31, 1910, with Herbert Gladstone as its first governor general and Louis Botha as its first prime minister.

Further reading: Robert H. Brand, *The Union of South Africa* (Oxford, England: Clarendon Press, 1909); Hugh E. Egerton, *Federations and Unions within the British Empire* (Oxford, England: Clarendon Press, 1924); "The South Africa Act, 1909," *American Journal of International Law*, v. 4 (1910), supp.

South African Citizenship Act   Law passed on September 2, 1949, creating for the first time a separate citizenship of South Africa (see BRITISH NATIONALITY AND NEW ZEALAND CITIZENSHIP BILL) and thus replacing the joint British citizenship South Africans shared with other British Commonwealth citizens. Under the new law, citizenship could be acquired by birth, descent, registration, resumption, and naturalization. All citizens enjoyed equal rights. However, citizenship acquired by naturalization or registration could be withdrawn for conviction of certain crimes or for a continuous seven-year absence from the country after receiving citizenship. A South African woman marrying a foreigner retained her citizenship while an alien woman marrying a South African citizen acquired citizenship only by naturalization. Immigrants from the Commonwealth were now required to wait for five years before receiving citizenship.

See also: BRITISH NATIONALITY ACT OF 1948; NATIONALITY AND FLAG ACT, SOUTH AFRICAN.

Further reading: Maxine Reitzes, *Insiders and Outsiders: The Reconstruction of Citizenship in South Africa* (Johannesburg: Center for Policy Studies, 1995).

South African Constitution of 1983   Controversial new constitution approved in a referendum by a two-thirds majority of South Africa's white electorate on November 2, 1983, and effective on September 4, 1984. It restructured the parliament (previously reserved for whites only) into three separately elected chambers: a white House of Assembly (with 178 members, like the old parliament), a Coloured House of Representatives (85 members of mixed African and European or Asian descent), and an Asian House of Deputies (45 members). Each was to handle its constituents' "own affairs" (education, housing, welfare, and so on), while "general affairs" (foreign policy, defense, and finance) were to be voted on by the three chambers separately. The chambers were to choose the head of government (executive state president) through an electoral college, with whites in the majority. Although Prime Minister P. W. Botha (who was elected president) said the constitution was the basis of a new national unity, black opposition strongly denounced it as slyly maintaining the system of apartheid (racial separation), without considering the black majority politically.

See also: DE KLERK'S "SEASON OF VIOLENCE IS OVER" SPEECH.

Further reading: D. A. Basson and H. P. Viljoen, *South African Constitutional* Law (Cape Town: Juta & Co., 1988); *Republic of South Africa Constitution Act, No. 110, 1983* (Pretoria: Department of Foreign Affairs and Information, 1983).

South African Group Areas Acts See GROUP AREAS ACT OF 1950, SOUTH AFRICAN; GROUP AREAS ACT OF 1973, SOUTH AFRICAN.

South African Nationality and Flag Act See NATIONALITY AND FLAG ACT, SOUTH AFRICAN.

South African Natives' Land Act See NATIVES' LAND ACT, SOUTH AFRICAN.

South African Natives' Trust and Land Act See NATIVES' TRUST AND LAND ACT, SOUTH AFRICAN.

South African Political Interference Act See POLITICAL INTERFERENCE ACT, SOUTH AFRICAN.

South African Public Safety Law of 1953 See PUBLIC SAFETY LAW OF 1953, SOUTH AFRICAN.

South African Separate Amenities Act See SEPARATE AMENITIES ACT, SOUTH AFRICAN.

South African Truth and Reconciliation Commission Report See TRUTH AND RECONCILIATION COMMISSION REPORT, SOUTH AFRICAN.

South Carolina Exposition and Protest See EXPOSITION AND PROTEST, CALHOUN'S.

South Carolina's Ordinance of Nullification Statute passed on November 24, 1832, by a special convention called by the South Carolina legislature; it declared null and void the TARIFF ACT OF 1828 and the TARIFF ACT OF 1832 within the state. South Carolina considered these protectionist tariffs unconstitutional, oppressive, and not binding upon the people of that state. The ordinance prohibited the collection of the tariff in South Carolina from February 1, 1833, forbade appeals to the federal courts, and required most state officials to take an oath to support the ordinance. It declared that the federal use of force to impell compliance with the tariffs would be cause for secession. U.S. president Andrew Jackson responded to the ordinance with his NULLIFICATION PROCLAMATION.

Further reading: Mortimer Adler, ed., *The Annals of America*, 18 vols. (Chicago: Encyclopaedia Britannica, 1968); Henry Steele Commager, ed., *Documents of American History*, 8th ed. (New York: Appleton-Century-Crofts, 1968); William W. Freehling, *Prelude to Civil War: The Nullification Controversy in South Carolina, 1816–1836* (New York: Harper & Row, 1968); Frank N. Magill, ed., *Great Events from History: American Series*, 3 vols. (Englewood Cliffs, N.J.: Salem Press, 1975).

South Carolina's Ordinance of Secession See ORDINANCE OF SECESSION, SOUTH CAROLINA'S.

South Carolina's Reply to Jackson's Proclamation Set of resolutions adopted by the South Carolina legislature and issued on December 20, 1832, in answer to U.S. president Andrew Jackson's NULLIFICATION PROCLAMATION, which had denounced the principle of state nullification of federal laws. The state's reply asserted that the president had no constitutional authority to interfere in the affairs of a state or to proclaim the repeal of state statutes, and that states had the right to secede peaceably from the union. South Carolina called Jackson's proclamation "subversive to the rights of the states and liberties of the people."

Further reading: Mortimer Adler, ed., *The Annals of America*, 18 vols. (Chicago: Encyclopaedia Britannica, 1968); Henry Steele Commager, ed., *Documents of American History*, 8th ed. (New York: Appleton-Century-Crofts, 1968); William W. Freehling, *Prelude to Civil War: The Nullification Controversy in South Carolina, 1816–1836* (New York: Harper & Row, 1968); Frank N. Magill, ed., *Great Events from History: American Series*, 3 vols. (Englewood Cliffs, N.J.: Salem Press, 1975).

Southern Manifesto on Integration Declaration issued on March 12, 1956, and signed by 101 southern members of the U.S. Senate and House of Representatives, condemning the U.S. Supreme Court decision in *BROWN V. BOARD OF EDUCATION OF TOPEKA, KANSAS*, and stating that they would try to overturn it. It called the decision "a clear abuse of judicial power" and urged the use of "all lawful means to bring about a reversal of this decision which is contrary to the Constitution." It encouraged states to resist the Supreme Court's mandate to desegregate public schools.

Further reading: Hubert H. Humphrey, ed., *Integration vs. Segregation* (New York: Crowell, 1964); Elizabeth Jacoway and C. Fred Williams, *Understanding the Little Rock Crisis: An Exercise in Remembrance and Reconciliation* (Fayetteville: University of Arkansas Press, 1999).

South Sea Bubble Act See BUBBLE ACT.

Soviet-British Agreement of 1941 See ANGLO-SOVIET AGREEMENT OF 1941.

Soviet Constitutional Amendments of 1990 Major plan for a multiparty system, headed by an executive presidency, approved by the Soviet Union's Congress of People's Deputies (parliament) in Moscow on March 13, 1990. Proposed and pushed by Soviet leader Mikhail S. Gorbachev by parliamentary maneuvering, the amendments (adopted in a single vote) removed the Communist Party's leading role from the Soviet Constitution, legalized some forms of private property, and established presidential powers, which included the right to propose legislation, negotiate treaties, veto laws and decisions of the council of ministers and other state bodies if they violate the constitution, appoint a cabinet, declare a state of emergency or martial law with approval by the Supreme Soviet, and declare war if the country is attacked. The next day, March 14, the deputies decided that the country's first executive president would be elected by them, as Gorbachev wanted, and not by nationwide popular ballot. Gorbachev narrowly won the required two-thirds majority of votes from the 2,250 deputies, to whom he had said before they voted: "This is a major step in favor of democracy and the protection of democracy."

Further reading: Anthony D'Agostino, *Gorbachev's Resolution, 1985–1991* (Basingstroke, England: Macmillan, 1998); Mark Galeotti, *Gorbachev and His Revolution* (New York: St. Martin's Press, 1997); Thomas F. Remington, *The Russian Parliament: Institutional Evolution in a Transitional Regime, 1989–1999* (New Haven, Conn.: Yale University Press, 2001).

Soviet Constitution of 1918 (Russian Constitution of 1918)

Constitution of the Russian Soviet Federated Socialist Republic prepared by a special commission of the party chaired by Bolshevik leader Vladimir Lenin, and adopted on July 10, 1918, by the Fifth All-Russian Congress of Soviets. It contained six sections in which the citizens' rights and obligations and the structure of the government were outlined. The constitution proclaimed that each citizen had the right to participate in the administration of the state, that the Soviet state was a free union of nations, that private ownership would be abolished and banks nationalized, and that the state would abolish all forms of exploitation. The document also determined that supreme power would rest with the All-Russian Congress of Soviets, the delegates of which would be chosen by the provincial congresses of soviets, who in turn would be chosen by the provincial congresses of soviets, who in turn would be elected by the people. Despite the idealistic assurances however, the right to vote was limited to the Soviet worker, and supreme governing authority in reality rested with the Communist Party. The Constitution of 1918 was the first Soviet constitution and served as a model for future constitutions of the other Soviet republics.

Further reading: Albert P. Blaustein and Jay A. Sigler, eds., *Constitutions That Made History* (New York: Paragon House Publishers, 1988); *The Russian Constitution: . . . Adopted July 10, 1918* (New York: Nation Press, 1919); Sidney Webb and Beatrice P. Webb, *Soviet Communism: A New Civilization?* 2d ed. (New York: Scribner, 1938).

Soviet Constitution of 1936   See STALIN CONSTITUTION.

Soviet Constitution of 1977

Constitution replacing (but basically the same as) the 1936 STALIN CONSTITUTION; endorsed on May 27, 1977, by the Presidium of the Supreme Soviet (highest legislative body), which approved it on Oc-

tober 7, 1977. The soviets (councils) of people's deputies became the political basis of the Soviet Union, with the Communist Party as the "leading and guiding force of Soviet society" and politics. The document also defined foreign policy goals; created the post of first vice president of the 39-member Presidium; ensured freedom of speech, the press, and assembly, declaring them "inseparable from the performance by citizens of their duties"; and guaranteed the right to work, education, leisure, medical and geriatric care, and housing. Deputies elected to the Supreme Soviet were to serve five-year terms. Formal power was vested in the Presidium of the Supreme Soviet, which was to meet biannually and elect a Council of Ministers (vested with executive authority). The Soviet economy was to be based on the "Socialist ownership of the means of production."

See also: SOVIET NEW PARTY PLATFORM OF 1990.

Further reading: E. M. Chekharin, *The Fundamental Law of the Country: On the 10th Anniversary of the USSR Constitution* (Moscow: Novosti Press Agency Publishing House, 1987); *Constitution (Fundamental Law) of the Union of Soviet Socialist Republics: Adopted . . . on October 7, 1977* (Moscow: Novosti Press Agency, 1985); F. J. M. Feldbrugge, *The Constitutions of the USSR and the Union Republics: Analysis, Texts, Reports* (Germantown, Md.: Sijthoff & Noordhof, 1979).

Soviet Five-Year Plan, First

Plan adopted by the Central Committee of the Soviet Union in April 1929 (although officially it was effective from October 1928), calling for the attainment of specific goals in industry and agriculture within a five-year period. Consistent with the Soviet leaders' emphasis on developing heavy industry, the plan called for a 250 percent increase in industrial output. In addition, agricultural output and the production of consumer goods were to increase significantly, and one-fifth of all peasant farms were to be collectivized. Because the level of production was dictated by the government rather than determined by demand and available resources, and because of the government's primary concern with industrial production, the Soviet economy was soon marked by tremendous shortages in consumer goods. By December 1932, when Soviet leader Joseph Stalin declared that the first Five-Year Plan had met its goals, there had indeed been a significant increase in industrial production.

Further reading: Paul R. Gregory, *Before Command: An Economic History of Russia from Emancipation to the First Five-Year Plan* (Princeton, N.J.: Princeton University Press, 1994); Peter Kenez, *A History of the Soviet Union from the Beginning to the End* (New York: Cambridge University Press, 1999); Donald W. Treadgold, *Twentieth Century Russia*, 8th ed. (Boulder, Colo.: Westview Press, 1995); Chris Ward, *The Stalinist Dictatorship* (New York: Oxford University Press, 1998).

Soviet-German Non-Aggression Treaty of 1939   See MOLOTOV-RIBBENTROP PACT.

Soviet-Japanese Non-Aggression Pact of 1941   See MOSCOW, TREATY OF.

Soviet-Japanese Peace Declaration of 1956   Declaration signed in Moscow on October 19, 1956, by Premier Nikolai Bulganin and Dmitri Shepilov of the Soviet Union, and Premier Hatoyama Ichiro, Kono Ichiro, and Dr. Matsumoto Shunichi of Japan, bringing an end to the state of war that had commenced between them a week before Japan's surrender during World War II (1939–45). The declaration provided that the war between the two powers would end upon the document's entry into force; that diplomatic and consular relations between them would be reestablished; that the Soviet Union would support Japan's application for membership in the United Nations; that their relations would be based upon the principles contained in the UNITED NATIONS CHARTER; that all Japanese citizens, including prisoners of war, still in the Soviet Union, would be released and repatriated; that agreements providing for the development of trade between them would be concluded; that talks would be continued to conclude a formal peace treaty; that the Soviet-Japanese Fisheries Convention would come into effect upon the present declaration's ratification; and that the Soviet Union would return to Japan the islands of Habomai and Shikotan after the conclusion of the formal peace.

Further reading: Kimie Hara, *Japanese-Soviet/Russian Relations since 1945: Difficult Peace* (New York: Routledge, 1998); Donald C. Hellmann, *Japanese Foreign Policy and Domestic Politics: The Peace Agreement with the Soviet Union* (Berkeley: University of California Press, 1969).

Soviet Law on Freedom of Conscience   Landmark statute passed by the Supreme Soviet (parliament) in Moscow on October 1, 1990, granting all citizens the right to worship in a religion of their choice. Successive communist regimes had previously confiscated churches and mosques, severely restricted religious instruction, and made the Soviet Union virtually an atheist nation (see SOVIET LAW ON RELIGIOUS BODIES). Under the leadership of Mikhail S. Gorbachev, the government had relaxed its stance against religion in the late 1980s. The new law prohibited the state from interfering in religious matters, from financing any particular religion, and from fostering atheism. All religions were legally equal; religious discrimination was prohibited; religious organizations were permitted; and religious teaching in homes, places of worship, and private schools was allowed. But with freedom came problems (notably lack of money and clergy), and serious sectarian conflicts, long repressed, began to heat up among religious factions.

Further reading: Michael Bourdeaux, *Gorbachev, Glasnost & the Gospel* (London: Hodder & Stoughton, 1990); Nathaniel Davis, *A Long Walk to Church: A Contemporary History of Russian Orthodoxy* (Boulder, Colo.: Westview Press, 1995); Niels C. Nielsen, *Christianity after Communism: Social, Polit-*

ical, and Cultural Struggle in Russia (Boulder, Colo.: Westview Press, 1994); John Witte and Michael Bourdeaux, *Proselytism and Orthodoxy in Russia: The New War for Souls* (Maryknoll, N.Y.: Orbis Books, 1999).

Soviet Law on Religious Bodies   State legislation passed in the Soviet Union on April 8, 1929, dramatically restricting the freedom of religious organizations. The new law required all religious communities of greater than 20 persons to register themselves with the local authorities within one year; prohibited religious organizations from becoming involved with charitable causes, or social and cultural activities; allowed preachers to participate in the religious activities of their own communities but no other; and prohibited communities from assisting one another financially. The law was passed in response to the communists' allegations that increasing numbers of people were joining religious groups, and their subsequent fear that such a trend could turn into a mass movement.

Further reading: Gerald Buss, *The Bear's Hug: Christian Belief and the Soviet State, 1917–86* (Grand Rapids, Mich.: W. B. Eerdmans Publishing, 1987).

Soviet Law on State Enterprise   Major economic reform legislation passed by the Soviet Union's Supreme Soviet (parliament) on June 30, 1987, and effective on January 1, 1988. Initiated by Soviet leader Mikhail Gorbachev, who hoped to encourage glasnost (openness) and perestroika (restructuring) to produce economic improvements, the law reduced central planning and control over industries, pricing, and distribution of goods; endorsed individual responsibility and competition in state-owned enterprises; and permitted citizens to sue erring officials. Factories no longer had to fulfill Moscow-dictated quotas by producing goods with little regard for cost, efficiency, quality, or demand. The reforms, however, threatened many bureaucrats (who might lose authority as well as their jobs) and like-minded people (who did not want to work very hard). Two months earlier (May 1) another new law had gone into effect that allowed individuals to establish private businesses but not to hire labor; they had to obtain licenses and pay income tax on gross earnings.

Further reading: Terry Cox, *From Perestroika to Privatisation: The Politics of Property Change in Russian Society, 1985–1991* (Brookfield, Vt.: Avebury, 1996); Anthony D'Agostino, *Gorbachev's Revolution, 1985–1991* (Basingstroke, England: Macmillan, 1998); Michael Ellman and Vladimir Kontorovich, eds., *The Destruction of the Soviet Economic System: An Insiders' History* (Armonk, N.Y.: M. E. Sharpe, 1998); Mark Galeotti, *Gorbachev and His Revolution* (New York: St. Martin's Press, 1997);

Soviet New Party Platform of 1990   Document approval by the Soviet Communist Party's policy-making body, the Central Committee, in Moscow on February 7, 1990, permitting alternative political parties to compete for control in the Soviet Union. It was presented by Soviet president Mikhail S. Gorbachev, who had been struggling for almost five years to transform his country from an authoritarian to a democratic state. The platform called for the abolition of Article 6 of the constitution, which guaranteed the communists a monopoly on power in Soviet society (see SOVIET CONSTITUTION OF 1977). The 249-member Central Committee, with some 700 other officials, debated heavily for three days over Gorbachev's proposal before voting on it. The Soviet Union had followed the lead of the Eastern European countries, where communists had recently bowed to democratic pressure and given up their legal guarantee of political control.

Further reading: G. P. Armstrong, *The End of Ideology: The Soviet Communist Party Platform of February 1990* (Ottawa, Canada; Department of National Defence, Operational Research and Analysis Establishment, 1990); Anthony D'Agostino, *Gorbachev's Revolution, 1985–1991* (Basingstroke, England: Macmillan, 1998); Mark Galeotti, *Gorbachev and His Revolution* (New York: St. Martin's Press, 1997).

Spanish Constitution of 1812

Liberal and idealized constitution drafted in 1812 in Cádiz, Spain, by the Spanish Cortes (representative assembly), declaring the supremacy of the people over the crown and the church. It established a unicameral legislature (Cortes)—one representative then for every 60,000 people—and conferred voting rights on all Spanish males above 25 years of age. Executive power was vested in the constitutional monarch, but all his decrees had to be approved by ministers answerable to the Cortes, which had the power to enact laws and to veto important royal decisions. All Spaniards, including colonials, were declared equal before the law, tax exemptions abolished, and a bill of rights formulated. The document struck a conservative note in declaring Roman Catholicism as "the only true faith" and in forbidding "the practice of any other." When Ferdinand VII returned as king in 1814 (see BAYONNE, TREATY OF), he denounced the constitution as invalid. Nevertheless, it remained the touchstone of liberal Spanish and European politics for several decades.

Further reading: Albert P. Blaustein and Jay A. Sigler, eds., *Constitutions That Made History* (New York: Paragon House Publishers, 1988).

Spanish Constitution of 1834 (Estatuto Real)

Royal constitution promulgated on April 10, 1834, by the Martínez regime in Spain, changing the single-chamber Cortes into a bicameral legislature. Unlike the SPANISH CONSTITUTION OF 1812, it was not founded on the concept of popular sovereignty. The crown reserved for itself the right to summon or dismiss the two chambers and also the right to dictate the issues under discussion. The House of Notables (upper chamber) was to consist of the aristocracy, the clergy, and royal appointees. Election to the lower house, the House of Proc-

tors, was indirect and based on property qualifications. This "octroyee" constitution was loosely modeled on Louis XVIII's FRENCH CONSTITUTION OF 1814 and did not satisfy the Carlists or the radicals. It served as the model for the Constitution of 1845.

Further reading: Carlos Marichal, *Spain, 1834–1844: A New Society* (London: Tamesis Books, 1977).

Spanish Constitution of 1931

Constitution adopted on December 9, 1931, establishing in Spain "a democratic republic of workers of all classes," without an official religion and guaranteeing freedom and equality to all citizens. The unicameral Cortes (national legislature) proposed and approved laws through various presidential commissions, before sending them to the head of state, the chief executive, who operated through a council of ministers led by his appointee, the prime minister. There was also a 16-member council of the realm and a national council. A federation of autonomous regions was openly rejected, but the Cortes could confer a statute of autonomy upon provinces seeking it (see SAN SEBASTIAN, PACT OF). Members of both sexes above 23 could vote, the church was disestablished, the clergy banned from teaching or trade, the Society of Jesus stripped of its property and outlawed, civil marriages and divorce recognized, and primary education made compulsory. Finally, the Law for the Defense of the Republic gave the Spanish government emergency powers to suppress publications, the right of assembly, and an individual's freedom.

Further reading: Manley O. Hudson, "The Spanish Constitution of 1931," *American Journal of International Law* 26 (1932): 579–82; Frank N. Magill, ed., *Great Events from History: Modern European Series*, 3 vols. (Englewood Cliffs, N.J.: Salem Press, 1973); Rhea M. Smith, *The Day of the Liberals in Spain* (Philadelphia: University of Pennsylvania Press, 1938).

Specie Circular (Jackson's Special Circular)

Circular issued by President Andrew Jackson on July 11, 1836, requiring the U.S. Treasury to accept only specie (gold or silver), not paper money, as payment in the sale of public lands. The circular was intended to protect federal revenues and to curb high inflation and rampant land speculation in the West. Its effect was to create an increased demand for specie that many banks could not accommodate; bank failures, reduction of credit, and increased unemployment resulted, producing an economic crisis known as the Panic of 1837. The circular was repealed on May 21, 1838.

Further reading: Donald B. Cole, *The Presidency of Andrew Jackson* (Lawrence: University Press of Kansas, 1993); Henry Steele Commager, ed., *Documents of American History*, 8th ed. (New York: Appleton-Century-Crofts, 1968); Reginald C. McGrane, *Panic of 1837: Some Financial Problems of the Jacksonian Era* (Chicago: University of Chicago Press, 1993);

Robert V. Remini, *The Life of Andrew Jackson* (New York: Harper & Row, 1988).

Specie Resumption Act, U.S. (Resumption Act)

Federal legislation passed on January 14, 1875, providing for a return to specie payment and reducing the amount of greenbacks (legal-tender notes not backed by gold) in circulation from $382 million in 1874 to $300 million (see LEGAL TENDER ACT). The act represented a victory for "hard money" supporters over "soft money" proponents, who favored the continued use of the greenbacks that had been introduced during the Civil War. The act directed the secretary of the treasury to redeem in coin legal-tender notes presented on and after January 1, 1879. When people were thus reassured that the notes were backed by gold, they readily accepted the use of greenbacks as more convenient in many ways.

Further reading: Henry Steele Commager, ed., *Documents of American History*, 8th ed. (New York: Appleton-Century-Crofts, 1968).

Speransky's Plan

Plan prepared by the Russian deputy minister of justice, Michael Speransky (Mikhail Speranski); begun in 1809 and completed in 1812. The plan proposed a reform of Russia's political life and governmental structures. Specifically, the country's political affairs were to be handled by three separate branches: a reformed senate, in charge of legal matters; a reformed ministry, responsible for carrying out all executive tasks; and a duma or assembly, in charge of legislation. All were answerable to the czar or emperor, or to the emperor's advisory council of state. The division of power among these separate branches was to exist on all levels, from that of the central government down to that of village governmental bodies. The plan in its entirety was never carried into effect; the council of state alone was created in 1810.

Further reading: Marc Raeff, *Michael Speransky, Statesman of Imperial Russia, 1772–1839* (Westport, Conn.: Hyperion Press, 1979).

Speyer, Decree of the Diet of (1526)

Decree made at the imperial Diet of Speyer (Spires) in 1526 by a majority of German princes present; they resolved to request Holy Roman Emperor Charles V to call a general council to settle religious differences stirred up by Martin Luther, German leader of the Protestant Reformation. Each German prince was to regulate his own subjects' church matters as he felt was justifiable "before God and the Imperial Majesty." Emperor Charles, who wished to extirpate Lutheranism, had been unable to attend the diet because of unstable political relationships with France and the papacy; this allowed for a more liberal decision to be made at Speyer, Germany.

See also: SPEYER, DECREE OF THE DIET OF (1529); WORMS, EDICT OF (1521).

Further reading: Frank N. Magill, ed., *Great Events from History: Modern European Series*, 3 vols. (Englewood Cliffs, N.J.: Salem Press, 1973).

Speyer, Decree of the Diet of (1529)

Decree accepted by the majority of ruling German princes at the imperial Diet of Speyer (Spires) in 1529, revoking and declaring to be illegal the moderate resolutions made at the Diet of Speyer in 1526 and ordering that Holy Roman Emperor Charles V's stand against heretics be enforced. It declared that the German rulers and their subjects were thenceforth obliged to accept the 1521 Edict of WORMS. In addition, it mandated that the Gospels could be preached only in the way sanctioned by the Roman Catholic Church. The German Lutheran princes made a strong protest (from which the term *Protestant* derives) against the diet's decision and Charles V's anti-Lutheran position.

Further reading: Frank N. Magill, ed., *Great Events from History: Modern European Series*, 3 vols. (Englewood Cliffs, N.J.: Salem Press, 1973).

Spinoza's *Ethics*   See ETHICS, SPINOZA'S.

Spooner Act (Spooner Amendment to the U.S. Army Appropriations Act of 1901)

Federal U.S. legislation introduced by Senator John C. Spooner of Wisconsin and enacted on June 28, 1902, authorizing President Theodore Roosevelt to purchase from the French New Panama Canal Company, for $40 million, a concession to build a canal across the Isthmus of Panama, a part of Colombia at the time. The act stipulated that Colombia grant to the United States perpetual control over the right of way. If Colombia refused, Congress authorized the U.S. president to initiate negotiations with Nicaragua for the construction of a canal. When Colombia refused to accept the U.S. terms, the province of Panama revolted and declared its independence. The United States recognized the new Republic of Panama in November and negotiated the HAY-BUNAU-VARILLA TREATY, granting the United States sovereignty over the Panama Canal Zone.

See also: HAY-HERRÁN TREATY.

Further reading: Dwight C. Miner, *The Fight for the Panama Route; the Story of the Spooner Act and the Hay-Herran Treaty* (New York: Octagon Books, 1971).

Stalin Constitution (Soviet Constitution of 1936, Soviet Fundamental Law)

Constitution of the Soviet Union endorsed by the Eighth All-Union Congress of Soviets on December 5, 1936; drafted by Nikolai I. Bukharin (shortly before he was secretly arrested) and a commission under the chairmanship of dictator Joseph V. Stalin. It heralded a new socialist democracy in which the people exercised power over the state (but in practice the constitution's rights and liberties were mere words). It stated the territorial composition of the Soviet Union, made all votes in elections secret and equal (granting universal suffrage), and made election to the higher soviets (legislative bodies) direct. The top Supreme Soviet was established, replacing the Congress of Soviets and consisting of two chambers—the Soviet of the Union (elected on the basis of population) and the Soviet of Nationalities (elected by the national groups). A Presidium (administrative cabinet) was to exercise powers between sessions of the Supreme Soviet, which appointed the Presidium members. The discrepancy between the constitution (which guaranteed civil and economic rights, including the right to work) and the realities of Soviet life was symbolized by the Communist Party, the country's only political party, which directed all nominations and elections and crushed opposition. A thorough revision of the Stalin Constitution was approved by the Supreme Soviet on February 26, 1947.

Further reading: Donald G. Bishop, ed., *Soviet Foreign Relations: Documents & Readings* (Syracuse, N.Y.: Syracuse University Press, 1952); Randolph L. Braham, ed., *Documents on Major European Governments* (New York: Knopf/Borzoi, 1966); Louis L. Snyder, ed., *Fifty Major Documents of the Twentieth Century* (Princeton, N.J.: D. Van Nostrand, 1955).

Stalin's "Cold War" Speech

Speech delivered by Soviet dictator Joseph V. Stalin on February 9, 1946, the day before the first general elections for the Supreme Soviet since 1937 (the authorized list of candidates was reelected). Stalin reaffirmed the Marxist-Leninist dogma and stated that the "unevenness of development of the capitalist countries" could cause "violent disturbance," with the resultant division of the "capitalist world in to two hostile camps and war between them." He called for the Soviet people's forbearance, urging more basic industrialization and collectivization of agriculture. World peace was unthinkable to Stalin, whose words soon stirred up U.S. leaders and engendered the hostility that became the "cold war" between the Western powers and the Soviet-led Communist bloc.

See also: "IRON CURTAIN" SPEECH, CHURCHILL'S.

Further reading: John Gimbel and John C. Hennessy, comps., *From Coalition to Confrontation: Readings on Cold War Origins* (Belmont, Calif.: Wadsworth Publishing, 1972); Vojtech Mastny, *The Cold War and Soviet Insecurity: The Stalin Years* (New York: Oxford University Press, 1998).

Stalin's Decree of December 1, 1934

Order issued by Soviet dictator Joseph V. Stalin on December 1, 1934; promulgated in the name of the Congress of Soviets and signed (on Stalin's instructions) by the secretary of the Presidium. Earlier that same day Sergei M. Kirov, a close friend and potential rival of Stalin, was assassinated in Leningrad (St. Petersburg); Stalin probably plotted Kirov's murder to initiate a bloody purge of anti-Stalinists (counterrevolutionaries) from the Communist Party. The decree authorized speedy trials of those accused of criminal and terrorist acts; the execution of death sentences was not to be delayed by

judicial courts considering the possibility of pardon or appeal (because the Presidium disallowed receiving these kinds of petitions). Many thousands of innocent people were executed or deported to concentration camps in Stalin's reign of terror to "liquidate" all opposition within the Communist Party (1934–39).

Further reading: Isaac Deutscher and Tamara Deutscher, *The Great Purges* (New York: Blackwell, 1984); J. Arch Getty, *Origins of the Great Purges: The Soviet Communist Party Reconsidered, 1933–1938* (New York: Cambridge University Press, 1987); Amy W. Knight, *Who Killed Kirov?: The Kremlin's Greatest Mystery* (New York: Hill & Wang, 1999).

Stamp Act of 1712

British legislation passed in 1711 and enforced in June 1712, introducing financial restrictions on the press to suppress its growing authority. The first of many such enactments, the act imposed the following taxes on periodicals: (1) halfpenny on periodicals a half-sheet (two pages) or less; (2) one penny per printed copy for pamphlets exceeding a half-sheet but less than one whole sheet; (3) two shillings per sheet for pamphlets larger than one whole sheet, up to a maximum of six octavo sheets, 12 quarto sheets, or 20 folio sheets. Duties were levied on paper and a surcharge of 12 pence on every advertisement appearing in dailies or weeklies. Government publications and stationery were exempt from these provisions. While some newspapers succumbed to the financial pressures, generally these "taxes on knowledge" had no more than a passing impact on the press.

Further reading: Joel H. Wiener, ed., *Great Britain—The Lion at Home: A Documentary History of Domestic Policy (1689–1973)*, 4 vols. (New York: Chelsea House, 1974).

Stamp Act of 1765

Act passed by the British Parliament to go into effect on November 1, 1765, directly for the raising of revenue to pay the costs of governing and protecting the American colonies. Supported by George Grenville, Britain's chancellor of the exchequer, it required stamps to be placed on all legal and commercial documents (licenses, liquor permits, newspapers, pamphlets, almanacs, advertisements) and various articles (dice, playing cards). Not only did the colonists refuse to buy and use the stamps, they also burned them, harassed the stamp distributors, and rioted. The British government repealed the act on March 18, 1766, replacing it that same day with the DECLARATORY ACT OF 1766.

Further reading: Mortimer Adler, ed., *The Annals of America*, 18 vols. (Chicago: Encyclopaedia Britannica, 1968); Henry Steele Commager, ed., *Documents of American History*, 8th ed. (New York: Appleton-Century-Crofts, 1968); William MacDonald, ed., *Select Charters and Other Documents Illustrative of American History, 1606–1775* (New York: Macmillan, 1899); Frank N. Magill, ed., *Great Events from History: American Series*, 3 vols. (Englewood Cliffs, N.J.: Salem Press, 1975).

Standard Oil Company of New Jersey et al. v. United States

U.S. Supreme Court decision issued on May 15, 1911, upholding the dissolution of the Standard Oil Company, a powerful monopolistic trust, on the grounds that it represented an "unreasonable" restraint of trade under the SHERMAN ANTI-TRUST ACT. The decision resulted from a lawsuit initiated by the federal government in 1906, charging Standard Oil and others with conspiring to restrain trade and commerce in petroleum and related products. The Supreme Court, in upholding a 1909 U.S. circuit court ruling that the company had to divest itself of numerous subsidiaries, declared that the Sherman act should be applied according to the "rule of reason."

Further reading: Mortimer Adler, ed., *The Annals of America*, 18 vols. (Chicago: Encyclopaedia Britannica, 1968); Henry Steele Commager, ed., *Documents of American History*, 8th ed. (New York: Appleton-Century-Crofts, 1968); Kermit L. Hall et al., eds., *The Oxford Companion to the Supreme Court of the United States* (New York: Oxford University Press, 1992); United States Supreme Court, *United States Reports: Cases Adjudged in the Supreme Court at . . . and Rules Announced at . . .* (New York: Banks & Brothers, Law Publishers, 1884–1921; Washington, D.C.: Government Printing Office, 1922–).

Stans, Covenant of the Diet of

Agreement reached on December 22, 1481, by the member states of the Swiss Confederation, which had been threatened with disruption because of conflict between its rural cantons (Uri, Schwyz, Unterwalden, Zug, and Glarus) and its urban cantons (Luzern, Bern, and Zürich). The two canton groups had organized themselves into private alliances, and the conflict had become very serious when the urban cantons sought to include two other cities (Fribourg and Solothurn) in the confederation. At Stans (in central Switzerland), a diet drew up a covenant through the mediation of Niklaus von der Flüe, a religious hermit; the eight cantons agreed to renounce private alliances, to admit Fribourg and Solothurn into the confederation, and to distribute fairly all territory and plunder acquired. The covenant regulated the Swiss Confederation and was confirmed officially every five years until 1798.

Further reading: John C. Schaad, *Nicholas of the Flue, the Savior of the Swiss Republic: A Dramatic Poem in Five Acts* (Washington, D.C.: McGill & Witherow, 1989).

START I Treaty (Treaty on the Reduction and Limitation of Strategic Offensive Arms)

First of many arms reduction agreements (see START II) between the United States and the Soviet Union that stipulated actual cuts in their strategic nuclear arsenals, signed on July 31, 1991, by U.S. president George H. W. Bush and Soviet leader Mikhail S. Gorbachev in Moscow. The main treaty's 19 articles specify cuts in all areas; for instance, the Soviet Union agreed to cut its ballistic-missile warheads by about half (leaving it with 6,500) and the United States agreed to a 35 percent cut (leaving it with 8,500) within seven years of ratification. Subsequently, both countries announced even more sweeping reductions. Ratification was delayed by the dissolution of the Soviet Union late that year. On May 23, 1992, the United States, Belarus, Kazakhstan, Russia, and Ukraine signed the Lisbon Protocol, which made them signatories to this treaty.

Further reading: John Pike, "START-1 Strategic Arms Reduction Talks," Federation of American Scientists Weapons of Mass Destruction, available online at http://www.fas.org/mike/control/start1/text/

START II Treaty (Memorandum of Joint Understanding on Nuclear Arms Reductions)

Unexpected agreement reached on June 16, 1992, in Washington, D.C., by United States president George H. W. Bush and Russian president Boris Yeltsin, providing for deeper cuts in their nuclear arsenals than the START I TREATY had envisaged. The two-phased reduction would leave Russia and the United States with 3,000 and 3,500 nuclear warheads, respectively, by 2003. Both countries also agreed to destroy their land-based multiple warhead missiles. The United States promised a 50 percent reduction in its submarine-launched ballistic-missile warheads. The agreement came about after Yeltsin conceded the issue of strategic parity, a major sticking point in the negotiations until then. On June 17, both leaders agreed to formalize this memorandum into a treaty, which was signed by Presidents Bill Clinton and Yeltsin in Moscow on January 3, 1993. In a protocol signed on September 26, 1997, in New York, the deadlines were extended to the end of 2007. Implementation would begin upon ratification, which the U.S. Senate overwhelmingly approved (87-4) on January 26, 1996. Russian ratification of the treaty and the protocol came on April 14, 2000. The United States has yet to ratify the protocol.

Further reading: Bob Aldridge, "The START-2 Treaty," Pacific Life Research Center, available online at http://www.nuclearfiles.org/plrc/01/START-2%20treaty2.pdf; Daniel C. Diller, ed., *Russia and the Independent States* (Washington, D.C.: Congressional Quarterly Books, 1993).

State and Revolution (Gosudarstvo i Revolyutsiya)

Political pamphlet written by Russian revolutionary leader Vladimir I. Lenin in August and September 1917, and first published in Petrograd (St. Petersburg) in May 1918; it contained the author's theories on the nature of the state, revolution, and the state's development from socialism to communism. Using the theories of German philosophers Karl Marx and Friedrich Engels as starting points, Lenin argued in support of their views on the nature of the proletarian state (which would ultimately effect great social and economic reform) and the inevitable overthrow of the bourgeoisie by the proletariat. In contrast to their views, however, Lenin argued that the state's transformation to true communism could never be free of all-out revolution or destruction of the bourgeois state. However, the communist leaders, acting in behalf of the proletariat, would end that capitalism and the exploitation of man by man (while monopolizing power). The work had a major influence on the development of the communists' ideology in Soviet Russia and abroad.

Further reading: V. M. Gavrilov, *Lenin's "The State and Revolution,"* trans. Jane Sayer (Moscow: Progress Publishers, 1988); Robert Service, *Lenin: A Biography* (Cambridge, Mass.: Harvard University Press, 2000); James D. White, *Lenin: The Practice and Theory of Revolution* (New York: Palgrave, 2001).

Steel, Pact of (German-Italian Alliance of 1939)

Pact concluded in Berlin, Germany, on May 22, 1939, by Foreign Minister Joachim von Ribbentrop of Germany and Foreign Minister Galeazzo Ciano of Italy, providing for a strengthened alliance between the two countries (see GERMAN-ITALIAN PACT OF 1936, ANTI-COMINTERN PACT). The pact provided that the two parties would remain in constant communication on issues of common concern and would consult and collaborate with one another on actions to be taken to defend their common interests; that, in the event that one party were threatened militarily by a third party, the other would come to its assistance both politically and diplomatically; and that, in the event that one party should find itself at war with one or more powers, the other would come to its assistance militarily. The pact was to remain in effect for 10 years.

See also: AXIS POWERS, PACT OF THE.

Further reading: Ray Moseley, *Mussolini's Shadow: The Double Life of Count Galeazzo Ciano* (New Haven, Conn.: Yale University Press, 1999); Lewis B. Namier, *Europe in Decay: A Study in Disintegration, 1936–1940* (London: Macmillan, 1950); Mario Toscano, *The Origins of the Pact of Steel* (Baltimore: Johns Hopkins Press, 1968).

Stevenson's Acceptance Speech

Address delivered by Illinois governor Adlai E. Stevenson at the Democratic National Convention in Chicago on July 26, 1952, accepting the Democratic Party's presidential nomination. Stevenson, considered a liberal reformer, warned the convention that "the ordeal of the twentieth century . . . is far from over." He urged the party to "talk sense to the American people," to explain that progress may be painful. "We are now on the eve of great decisions, not easy decisions," he said, challenging the Democrats to attack the great problems of "war, poverty and tyranny—and the assaults upon human dignity which are the most grievous consequences of each." He called for morality, vision, and the courage of truthfulness to overcome the ignorance and mistrust that hinder progress.

Further reading: Mortimer Adler, ed., *The Annals of America,* 18 vols. (Chicago: Encyclopaedia Britannica, 1968); Jill Kneerim, ed., *Adlai Stevenson's Public Years, with Text from*

His Speeches and Writings (New York: Grossman Publishers, 1966); Porter McKeever, *Adlai Stevenson: His Life and Legacy* (New York: Morrow, 1989).

Stevenson's "Nature of Patriotism" Speech

Address delivered by U.S. Democratic presidential candidate Adlai E. Stevenson at the American Legion Convention in New York City on August 27, 1952, in which Stevenson defined patriotism as a sense of national responsibility, of "putting country before self." He challenged the patriotism of special interests who placed their needs above the nation's; of racial or religious bigots who violated the principles of liberty and equality; and especially of overzealous anticommunists who, in trying to protect America from a communist menace, actually threatened American liberty. Stevenson called for freedom to think and inquire. Patriotism, he said, "is not the fear of something; it is the love of something . . . of the ideal of liberty of man and mind."

Further reading: Jill Kneerim, ed., *Adlai Stevenson's Public Years, with Text from His Speeches and Writings* (New York: Grossman Publishers, 1966); Porter McKeever, *Adlai Stevenson: His Life and Legacy* (New York: Morrow, 1989).

Steward Machine Company v. Davis

U.S. Supreme Court decision, issued on May 24, 1937, that upheld the tax provisions of the U.S. SOCIAL SECURITY ACT. The case challenged provisions in the unemployment compensation section of the act that established a federal payroll tax on employers, to be paid into the federal treasury. The act allowed a credit, up to 90 percent, for any amount paid into a federally approved state unemployment compensation system. The Steward Machine Company paid the tax but sued for a refund. In its 5-4 decision, the Supreme Court denied the company's claim that the tax provisions were an unconstitutional attempt by Congress to coerce the states or to usurp their powers; it declared that the provisions merely gave the states a compelling "inducement" to establish unemployment compensation.

Further reading: Henry Steele Commager, ed., *Documents of American History,* 8th ed. (New York: Appleton-Century-Crofts, 1968); Kermit L. Hall et al., eds., *The Oxford Companion to the Supreme Court of the United States* (New York: Oxford University Press, 1992); Robert R. Mayer, *The Court and the American Crises, 1930–1952* (Danbury, Conn.: Grolier Educational, 1995); United States Supreme Court, *United States Reports: Cases Adjudged in the Supreme Court at . . . and Rules Announced at . . .* (New York: Banks & Brothers, Law Publishers, 1884–1921; Washington, D.C.: Government Printing Office, 1922–   ).

Stockholm, Treaties of

Agreements signed by Sweden in an effort to avoid a complete rout in the Great Northern War (1700–21). By means of the first treaty, with Great Britain–Hanover on November 20, 1719, Frederick I of Sweden tried to win British military support for his ongoing war with Russia, in return for many commercial advantages and the two territories of Bremen and Verdun, which he ceded to Hanover (belonging to George I of England). According to the terms of the second treaty with Prussia (February 1720), Frederick surrendered Swedish Pomerania between the Oder and the Peene Rivers, including the port of Stettin (Szczecin), for payment. In the Treaty of Fredericksborg with Denmark (June 1720), he paid Denmark an indemnity to vacate the Swedish lands she had been occupying and yielded Sweden's right to free passage through the Sound between Denmark and Sweden. Britain gave financial aid but no military support and the war finally ended on September 10, 1721 with the Treaty of NYSTADT.

Further reading: R. Nisbet Bain, *Charles XII and the Collapse of the Swedish Empire, 1682–1719* (New York: Putnam's Sons, 1914); Robert I. Frost, *The Northern Wars: War, State, and Society in Northeastern Europe, 1558–1721* (New York: Longman, 2000).

Stockholm Resolution

International petition or statement of peaceful aims drawn up in Stockholm, Sweden, in 1950; it appealed for a pact of peace among the five great powers (Great Britain, France, the United States, the Soviet Union, and China). It called for the elimination and prohibition of the atomic bomb, universal disarmament, and control over the enforcement of these actions. Signed by more than 500 million people within two years, the petition was used by the Soviet Union and the communists to help promote their own deceptive definition of peace and their own propaganda labeling the western governments as untrustworthy (see MANIFESTO OF THE SECOND WORLD PEACE CONGRESS).

Further reading: Donald G. Bishop, ed., *Soviet Foreign Relations: Documents & Readings* (Syracuse, N.Y.: Syracuse University Press, 1952).

Stockholm Security Conference Treaty

Agreement to reduce the risk of accidental war, adopted by 35 nations on September 21, 1986, in Stockholm, Sweden, at the conclusion of almost three years of negotiations during the Conference on Confidence- and Security-Building Measures and Disarmament in Europe. The treaty, involving conventional armed forces and not nuclear weapons, established a system of notification and verification of military activities by members of the WARSAW PACT and the NORTH ATLANTIC TREATY Organization. Each nation was to notify all the others about its military maneuvers ahead of time and was to invite foreign observers to monitor movements of more than 17,000 troops. Each nation was also required to allow up to three military verification inspections a year; the Soviet Union granted on-site inspections for the first time. The treaty was to be in force on January 1, 1987, subject to ratification by the signatory nations.

Further reading: Henry W. Degenhardt, ed., *Treaties and Alliances of the World*, 4th ed. (Detroit: Gale Research, 1986); Alexander L. George, et al., *U.S.-Soviet Security Cooperation: Achievements, Failures, Lessons* (New York: Oxford University Press, 1988); J. A. S. Grenville and Bernard Wasserstein, *The Major International Treaties since 1945: A History and Guide with Texts* (New York: Methuen, 1987).

Stolbovo, Treaty of

Peace treaty concluding the Russo-Swedish War of 1613–17, signed at the Russian town of Stolbovo (Stolbova) on January 26, 1617. Sweden agreed to return Novgorod and other areas in northern Russia, whose international political instability had contributed to its losses. But Sweden retained Karelia and Ingria, thus cutting Russia off from the Baltic Sea (Sweden had possession of all territories on the Gulf of Finland). Russia had to pay a 20,000-ruble indemnity to Sweden, whose Prince Philip agreed to give up his claim to the Russian throne.

See also: KARDIS, TREATY OF.

Further reading: Robert I. Frost, *The Northern Wars: War, State, and Society in Northeastern Europe, 1558–1721* (New York: Longman, 2000)

Stolypin's Agrarian Reform Act

Legislation introduced in November 1906 by Russia's prime minister Peter Stolypin and designed to develop independent peasant-farmers and undermine the peasant communes established by the EMANCIPATION EDICT OF 1861. The law encouraged the secession of individual peasants from the commune. Stolypin reasoned that among the newly enfranchised peasant class, independent peasants would be more conservative than the communes. The legislation allowed peasants to gain title to their plots of communally owned land and provided for redistribution of scattered plots in order to consolidate them into a single farm, if so requested by the owner. The new peasant-farmers retained their communal rights to meadow and forest land, which, in 1911, were also partitioned. Peasants could also vote to abolish their commune, and over the following decade commune dissolutions affected 130,000 households.

Further reading: Richard Hennessy, *The Agrarian Question in Russia 1905–1907: The Inception of the Stolypin Reform* (Giessen, Germany: W. Scmitz, 1977); George L. Yaney, *The Urge to Mobilize: Agrarian Reform in Russia, 1861–1930* (Urbana: University of Illinois Press, 1982).

Straits Convention (London Straits Convention)

Agreement signed on July 13, 1841, by Britain, France, Russia, Prussia, Austria, and the Ottoman Empire (Turkey), closing the Black Sea straits (the Dardanelles and Bosporus). It superseded the 1833 Treaty of HÜNKÂR ISKELESI. At the London convention, the signatory powers agreed that no foreign warships would be permitted to pass through the straits as long as the Ottoman Empire was at peace and that, even if the Ottoman sultan should request it, passage of foreign warships would be forbidden without the consent of the other five signatory powers. The agreement safeguarded Russia's position in the Black Sea in peacetime.

See also: LONDON, TREATY OF (1840).

Further reading: James T. Shotwell and Francis Deak, *Turkey at the Straits: A Short History* (New York: Macmillan, 1940); *Treaties and Other Documents Relating to the Black Sea, the Dardanelles, and the Bosphorus: 1535–1877* (London: Harrison & Sons, 1878).

Stralsund, Treaty of   Peace agreement concluded at the German Baltic port of Stralsund on May 24, 1370, marking an end to the conflict between King Waldemar IV of Denmark and the Hanseatic League (a group of chiefly German coastal towns united by common commercial and political interests). The conditions of the treaty required Waldemar to grant certain concessions. Specifically, the league received the right to trade freely throughout Danish territory, to sail freely throughout Danish waters, and to have the control of four coastal fortresses in Scania. In addition, the league received confirmation of all earlier commercial rights, as well as veto power in the election of Waldemar's future successor unless he renewed the league's trade monopoly in the Baltic area.

Further reading: David K. Bjork, *The Peace of Stralsund* (Cambridge, Mass.: Mediaeval Academy of America, 1932); Louis L. Snyder, ed., *Documents of German History* (New Brunswick, N.J.: Rutgers University Press, 1958).

Strangford Treaty   Accord signed in 1810 between the exiled Portuguese crown, then residing in Brazil, and Great Britain, represented by Lord Strangford, British minister at the Portuguese court. The treaty provided for the export of Brazilian agricultural products to Great Britain and the import of British manufactured goods into Brazil. Also, British warships were permitted to use Brazilian ports to replenish their supplies. English Protestants were given the right to worship freely in Brazil. Finally, British nationals in Brazil had the option to be tried only by magistrates appointed by the British government. According to the agreement, no other nations were to be allowed the commercial privileges granted to Great Britain. While the treaty dealt a severe blow to the new Brazilian manufacturing industries, it contributed significantly to the economic development of the country.

Further reading: Kirsten Schultz, *Tropical Versailles: Empire, Monarchy, and the Portuguese Royal Court in Rio de Janeiro, 1808–1821* (New York: Routledge, 2001).

Strasbourg (Strassburg), Oaths of   Oaths sworn on the plain of Strasbourg in A.D. 842, sealing the alliance between Louis the German and Charles the Bald during a dynastic dispute with their brother, Lothair, over who would succeed their father, Louis the Pious (A.D. 814–840), to the Carolingian throne. Lothair laid claim to the entire empire as well as the imperial title; his brothers hoped that their alliance would force Lothair into a more equitable arrangement. The dispute ended peaceably with the empire partitioned among the three brothers (see VERDUN, TREATY OF). The oaths (an exchange of oaths by the kings and their armies and subjects) are famous for being the first documents in the history of France and Germany to be written in the vernacular.

Further reading: Norton Downs, ed., *Basic Documents in Medieval History* (New York: Van Nostrand Reinhold, 1959); Louis L. Snyder, ed., *Documents of German History* (New Brunswick, N.J.: Rutgers University Press, 1958); Milton Viorst, ed., *The Great Documents of Western Civilization* (Philadelphia: Chilton Books, 1965).

Strategic Arms Limitation Treaty of 1972 (SALT I)
Five-year interim agreement and protocol signed on May 26, 1972, in Moscow by the U.S. president Richard M. Nixon and Soviet general secretary Leonid I. Brezhnev, for a reduction in strategic offensive weapons. No new land-based, intercontinental ballistic missile (ICBM) launchers would be built after July 1, 1972. Submarine-launched ballistic missiles (SLBMs) and other modern ballistic missiles launched from submarines would be restricted to those already in use or under construction, but these could be modernized or replaced. Technical verification was allowed and interference in this process was condemned. The Standing Consultative Commission (established by the treaty, limiting antiballistic missile systems) would assist in implementing the provisions of this agreement. Negotiations would continue for further reduction in strategic offensive weapons. The protocol specified the number of SLBM launchers (710, United States; 950, Soviet Union) and ballistic missile submarines (44, United States; 62, Soviet Union) each country was allowed.

See also: INTERMEDIATE NUCLEAR FORCES TREATY; NUCLEAR NON-PROLIFERATION TREATY OF 1968; NUCLEAR TEST BAN TREATY OF 1963; STRATEGIC ARMS LIMITATION TREATY OF 1979.

Further reading: Robert G. Bell, *Implications of Extending the SALT I Interim Agreement* (Washington, D.C.: Library of Congress, Congressional Research Service, 1977); Henry W. Degenhardt, ed., *Treaties and Alliances of the World*, 4th ed. (Detroit: Gale Research, 1986); J. A. S. Grenville and Bernard Wasserstein, *The Major International Treaties since 1945: A History and Guide with Texts* (New York: Methuen, 1987); Roger P. Labrie, *SALT Handbook: Key Documents and Issues, 1972–1979* (Washington, D.C.: American Enterprise Institute for Public Policy Research, 1979).

Strategic Arms Limitation Treaty of 1979 (SALT II)
Complex arms reduction pact signed on June 18, 1979, by U.S. president Jimmy Carter and Soviet president Leonid I. Brezhnev in Vienna, Austria. Its salient features were (1) each country limited to 2,250 strategic missiles/bombers by the end of 1981, 2,400 within six months of the treaty's implementation; (2) no more than 1,320 of the preceding to be

equipped with multiple warheads or Cruise missiles and no more than 1,200 land- or sea-based or air-to-surface ballistic missiles; limit of 820 land-based intercontinental ballistic missiles (ICBMs) with multiple warheads; (3) Soviet Union to halt production and use of the SS16 strategic missile; (4) each country allowed one new type of strategic missile; (5) maximum number of warheads on any new missile—10 per land-based and 14 per sea-based missile; (6) Cruise missiles restricted to a range of 366 miles; and (7) the ABM treaty of 1972 to continue in effect. SALT II's protocol banned the use of land-based mobile ICBMs, sea-launched and ground-launched strategic Cruiser missiles, and ICBMs transported in aircraft, until 1981. Technical verification procedures were permitted. Upon ratification, the treaty would remain in force until December 31, 1985, unless superseded. It was not ratified by the U.S. Senate.

See also: INTERMEDIATE NUCLEAR FORCES TREATY; NUCLEAR NON-PROLIFERATION TREATY OF 1968; NUCLEAR TEST BAN TREATY OF 1963; STRATEGIC ARMS LIMITATION TREATY OF 1972.

Further reading: Davi D'Agostino, *SALT II: An Article-by-Article Summary* (Washington, D.C.: Library of Congress, Congressional Research Service, 1979); Henry W. Degenhardt, ed., *Treaties and Alliances of the World*, 4th ed. (Detroit: Gale Research, 1986); J. A. S. Grenville and Bernard Wasserstein, *The Major International Treaties since 1945: A History and Guide with Texts* (New York: Methuen, 1987); Roger P. Labrie, *SALT Handbook: Key Documents and Issues, 1972–1979* (Washington, D.C.: American Enterprise Institute for Public Policy Research, 1979).

Subversive Activities Control Act, U.S.   See MCCARRAN ACT.

Succession, Act of (1534)

First of several such acts ordaining succession; passed in March 1534 in England during the reign of King Henry VIII, requiring his subjects to swear an oath declaring his marriage to Anne Boleyn as "undoubted, true, sincere, and perfect" and recognizing *their* children as the rightful heirs to the throne. The oaths would be administered throughout the country by the king's commissioners, and anyone who refused—Lord Chancellor Sir Thomas More was the most prominent dissident—was imprisoned. The act thus sidelined Mary, Henry's daughter by his first wife, Catherine. Henry's several marriages resulted in similar acts being passed in 1536 and again in 1543.

Further reading: Karen Lindsey, *Divorced, Beheaded, Survived: A Feminist Reinterpretation of the Wives of Henry VIII* (Reading, Mass.: Addison-Wesley; 1995); D. M. Loades, *The Politics of Marriage: Henry VIII and His Queens* (Stroud, England: Alan Sutton, 1994); Alison Weir, *Henry VIII: The King and His Court* (New York: Ballantine Books, 2001).

Suez Canal Convention (Constantinople Convention)

Treaty regulating use of the Suez Canal, signed at Constantinople (Istanbul) on October 29, 1888, by Austria-Hungary, France, Germany, Great Britain, Italy, the Netherlands, Russia, Spain, and the Ottoman Empire (Turkey). The canal was to be open in times of peace and war to military and commercial vessels of all nations, and acts of hostility in its waters were forbidden. Great Britain, however, signed the document after stipulating that its provisions would apply only insofar as they were compatible with "the present transitory and exceptional condition of Egypt," which country the British considered a special sphere of influence. In addition, the British declared they intended to abide by the terms of the convention only when those terms were not a hindrance to their occupation of Egypt. Great Britain officially relinquished these restrictions in 1904, upon signing the Anglo-French Entente or ENTENTE CORDIALE and accepted the Constantinople Convention in its entirety.

Further reading: Henry W. Degenhardt, ed., *Treaties and Alliances of the World*, 4th ed. (Detroit: Gale Research, 1986); Donald C. Watt, *Britain and the Suez Canal* (London: Royal Institute of International Affairs, 1956).

Suffolk Resolves

Set of resolutions written by Dr. Joseph Warren and presented at a convention in Suffolk County, Massachusetts, on September 9, 1774. The meeting was one of many convened in Massachusetts to protest the COERCIVE ACTS. The Suffolk Resolves declared the Coercive Acts unconstitutional and refused obedience to them; urged withholding taxes from the royal government until the Coercive Acts were repealed, and recommended that, in the interim, the people of Massachusetts form a government with the power to collect taxes; advised the formation of an armed militia; and recommended the imposition of economic sanctions against Britain. Adopted unanimously by the convention, the resolutions were immediately carried by Paul Revere to the First Continental Congress, which was meeting in Philadelphia. They were endorsed by that body on September 17, 1774.

Further reading: *The Suffolk Resolves, 1774: Reproduced from the Columns of the Boston Gazette, September 19, 1774* (Boston: Society of Printers, 1976); Mary P. Webster and Charles R. Morris, *The Story of the Suffolk Resolves* (Milton, Mass.: Historical Commission, 1973).

Sugar Act of 1764 (Sugar Revenue Act)

Legislation imposed in 1764 by the British Parliament on the American colonies to raise revenue, tacitly to defray the cost of the colonial government and armed forces. The act raised duties on foreign refined sugar and other foreign goods, such as wines and fabrics, but it reduced duties on foreign molasses to discourage smuggling sugar from the French and Dutch West Indies and to ensure a monopoly for the British West Indies. The act, which also provided for strict collection of the duties, angered the colonists because they were taxed without their consent.

See also: STAMP ACT OF 1765.

Further reading: William MacDonald, ed., *Select Charters and Other Documents Illustrative of American History, 1606–1775* (New York: Macmillan, 1899).

Summa Theologica   Philosophical treatise written by Roman Catholic theologian and philosopher Saint Thomas Aquinas from approximately 1265 to 1274; it summarized Christian theology in its entirety. The work was divided into three parts, with the first treating the existence and nature of God; the second, ethical and moral questions; and the third, Christ, the Sacraments, and the salvation of man's soul. Throughout the work Aquinas's arguments were aided by the methodology of Aristotelian logic, whereby ultimate causes were deduced from facts based on experience. At the same time, Aquinas relied on divine revelation, or the Holy Scriptures, for his ultimate conclusions about the Christian faith. The work has been the basis, up to the present day, for the teachings of the Roman Catholic Church.

Further reading: Catholic University of America, eds., *New Catholic Encyclopedia* (New York: McGraw-Hill, 1967); Mark A. Kishlansky, ed., *Sources of World History: Readings for World Civilization*, vol. 1, 2d ed. (Belmont, Calif.: West/ Wadsworth, 1999); Peter Kreeft, ed., *A Summa of the Summa: The Essential Philosophical Passages of St. Thomas Aquinas' Summa Theologica* (San Francisco, Calif.: Ignatius Press, 1990); Frank N. Magill, ed., *Great Events from History: Ancient and Medieval Series*, 3 vols. (Englewood Cliffs, N.J.: Salem Press, 1972).

Sun-Joffe Manifesto   Manifesto issued at Shanghai, China, on January 26, 1923, by Chinese nationalist leader Sun Yixian (Sun Yat-sen) and Soviet diplomat Adolf A. Joffe, representative of the Soviet foreign ministry; it provided a basis upon which the Soviet Union and Sun's Guomindang (Nationalist Party, or Kuomintang) could develop their relationship. The manifesto contained the two parties' agreement that communism would not be a suitable avenue of reform for China to take; that the Soviet Union would provide the Guomindang with military and political assistance; and that the Soviet Union would renegotiate the unfair treaties concluded by China and imperial Russia. In return, Sun agreed to admit the Chinese communists—as individuals, however, and not as a party—into the Guomindang; and to permit the Soviets to remain in Outer Mongolia. The document reflected the Soviet Union's policy of supporting a country's legitimate government (the USSR believed that the Chinese nationalists would be victorious in the civil war) in order to protect her commercial and territorial interests, while simultaneously supporting communist elements in order to spread worldwide revolution.

Further reading: Hsieh Jan-chih, *The Kuomintang: Selected Historical Documents, 1894–1969* (New York: St. John's University, 1970); Kuei Chung-chi, *The Kuomintang-Communist Struggle in China, 1922–1949* (The Hague: M. Nijhoff, 1970).

Sun Yixian's Three People's Principles   Three principles—nationalism, democracy, and socialism—formulated for the Chinese people by revolutionary leader Sun Yixian (Sun Yat-sen) and first put into writing in 1905. Periodically modified by Sun, the principles' final version appeared as a series of lectures published in Guangzhou (Canton), China, in 1924. The principles provided Sun with an ideology throughout his political career. Nationalism was the most important of the three principles. Initially inspiring those in favor of overthrowing the Manchu dynasty, nationalism later (in the 1920s) inspired members of the coalition between the Chinese Nationalist Party, or Guomindang (Kuomintang), and the Communist Party, who were against imperialism and in favor of self-determination. Democracy was originally understood as it is in the West; although Sun later continued to support the people's political rights, he also increasingly supported a government with strongly centralized power. Finally, socialism evolved from the ideal of land ownership for all, to the principle of state ownership of certain industrial enterprises. Today both the communists of the People's Republic of China as well as the regime in Nationalist China, or Taiwan, claim the principles as their own.

Further reading: Sun Yat-sen, *San Min Chu I: The Three Principles of the People*, trans. Frank W. Price, (Taipei: China Publishers, 1960).

Supremacy, Act of (1534)   Royal parliamentary statute in 1534 that declared the English sovereign and his successors "Protector and only Supreme Head of the Church and Clergy of England." Designed to exclude papal authority, the act recognized King Henry VIII as supreme head of the independent Church of England; Henry had just broken with the Roman Catholic Church and the pope, who had refused Henry's request to annul his marriage to Catherine of Aragon and had excommunicated him. Refusal to sign Henry's supremacy oath was considered high treason, of which Sir Thomas More, lord chancellor, was convicted and then beheaded (1535). The English Reformation had begun.

Further reading: Gerald L. Bray, *Documents of the English Reformation* (Minneapolis: Fortress Press, 1994); Frank N. Magill, ed., *Great Events from History: Modern European Series*, 3 vols. (Englewood Cliffs, N.J.: Salem Press, 1973); Mark A. Noll, *Turning Points: Decisive Moments in the History of Christianity* (Grand Rapids, Mich.: Baker Books, 1997); Milton Viorst, ed., *The Great Documents of Western Civilization* (Philadelphia: Chilton Books, 1965).

Supremacy, Act of (1559)   Queen Elizabeth I's first legislation (1559) on assuming office, a revised version of King

Henry VIII's 1534 Act of SUPREMACY, abolishing the pope's supremacy and declaring the queen as the "only Supreme Governor of this realm . . . in all spiritual or ecclesiastical things or causes, as temporal." Public officials and clergymen in England were required to swear obedience to the crown; anyone refusing to do so, as all the bishops did, lost his job for a first offense. Anyone continuing to assert the pope's supremacy was initially fined; repetition of the offense involved life imprisonment, while a third offense meant death. The act was widely opposed in Parliament and all over the country.

Further reading: Randolph L. Braham, ed., *Documents on Major European Governments* (New York: Knopf/Borzoi, 1966); Gerald L. Bray, *Documents of the English Reformation* (Minneapolis: Fortress Press, 1994); Lewis W. Spitz, *The Protestant Reformation* (Englewood Cliffs, N.J.: Prentice-Hall, 1966).

Susa, Treaty of   Pact between England and France signed on April 24, 1629; it addressed territorial issues arising from conflicts between English and French fur trading companies in New France (Canada). According to the treaty, places and property captured before peace was concluded would be retained by the conqueror, but those captured later were to be returned. Consequently, the seizure of the French trading post and settlement of Quebec in July 1629 by an English fleet under the command of David Kirke was nullified. Kirke and his French Huguenot associates nonetheless dominated the fur trade in the region for the next three years.

See also: ST.-GERMAIN, TREATY OF (1632).

Further reading: W. J. Eccles, *The French in North America, 1500–1783*, 3d ed. (East Lansing: Michigan State University Press, 1998); R. C. Brown and M. E. Prang, *Canadian Historical Documents Series*, 3 vols. (Scarborough, Canada: Prentice-Hall of Canada, 1966).

Suspending Act of 1767   First of the four TOWNSHEND ACTS passed by the British Parliament in June 1767, suspending the New York assembly because of its defiance of the QUARTERING ACT OF 1765. The act prohibited the assembly from carrying on any more business until it met the expenses of the many British soldiers quartered in New York, as required by the Quartering Act. Many colonists viewed the act as a serious threat to self-government—one of the causes leading to the American Revolution.

Further reading: Mortimer Adler, ed., *The Annals of America*, 18 vols. (Chicago: Encyclopaedia Britannica, 1968); Henry Steele Commager, ed., *Documents of American History*, 8th ed. (New York: Appleton-Century-Crofts, 1968).

Sussex Pledge   Pledge issued by the German government on May 4, 1916, stating that it would abandon its previous policy of unrestricted submarine warfare, which had allowed for the destruction of merchant and passenger ships during World War I (1914–18). Specifically, the Germans agreed to provide passenger and merchant ships with due warning before initiating attack, and to take measures to ensure the safety of all passengers. The concession was extracted from the Germans upon the United States' issue of a threat to break off diplomatic relations with the Germans if the latter continued to be guided by the policy of unrestricted submarine warfare. The United States, in issuing the threat, was reacting to the recent sinking of an unarmed French passenger ship, the *Sussex,* by a German submarine's torpedo in the English Channel, with the loss of several American lives (March 24, 1916). Unrestricted submarine warfare was resumed in February 1917.

Further reading: Henry Steele Commager, ed., *Documents of American History*, 8th ed. (New York: Appleton-Century-Crofts, 1968).

Swabian Mirror   See SAXON MIRROR.

Swedish Constitution of 1720   New instrument of government approved by the Swedish Riksdag (parliament) in 1720, drastically altering the balance of power in Sweden. It divided the power among the king, his ministerial council, and the Riksdag (see UNITY [UNION] AND SECURITY, ACT OF). The king was required to abide by the Riksdag's decisions and to accept the majority vote of the council (governing body) when outvoted. He had the tie-breaking vote on the council and the right to appoint civil and military personnel. Considerable power was vested in the Riksdag, including reviewing the council's performance, electing new councillors, enacting new legislation, introducing taxes, and declaring war or peace. When the Riksdag was not in session, the king and council ruled jointly. Otherwise, important decisions were made by a secret committee consisting of members of the three higher estates (nobility, clergy, and burghers). The peasants, the lowest estate, were to be consulted on tax issues. The new constitution climaxed several years of disillusionment with the royal absolutism of King Charles XII (died 1718).

Further reading: Michael Roberts, *On Aristocratic Constitutionalism in Swedish History, 1520–1720* (London: Athlone Publishers, 1966).

Swedish-Norwegian Treaty of Separation   See NORWEGIAN-SWEDISH TREATY OF SEPARATION.

Swiss Constitution of 1848   Federal constitution adopted by the Swiss cantons on September 12, 1848, following the 1847 revolution, which left the nationalist faction in power. The constitution replaced the SWISS FEDERAL PACT OF 1815. Through the new constitution the executive branch of the government, the responsibilities of which included the formation of foreign policy, the supervision over the cantons' domestic policies, and the regulation of customs controls, was to consist of a seven-member council, which included a chairman who was to be elected by the legislative branch. The legislative branch, responsible for all federal legislation, was to consist of two chambers, one equally representing each canton in numerical terms, the other representing each canton based on the size of its population. The constitution was inspired by that of the United States.

Further reading: Albert P. Blaustein and Jay A. Sigler, eds., *Constitutions That Made History* (New York: Paragon House Publishers, 1988).

Swiss Federal Pact of 1815

Swiss Federal Pact of 1815   Federal pact, concluded by the Diet of the Swiss Confederation in September 1815 in Zurich, through which the powers of the central government were greatly restricted. The document provided, for example, that only with a two-thirds majority could the Diet make decisions on foreign policy. On the other hand, the Swiss cantons could conclude alliances with foreign powers as they saw fit (as long as such alliances would not be harmful to the confederation as a whole). Restricting the freedom of the cantons were provisions prohibiting the formation of alliances *within* the confederation and requiring each canton to contribute fixed sums, in proportion to the size of the population, to the federal government. The pact was concluded following the Napoleonic era, when states feared giving too much power to the federal government.

Further reading: James H. Hutson, *The Sister Republics: Switzerland and the United States from 1776 to the Present*, 2d ed. (Washington, D.C.: Library of Congress, 1991); William D. McCracken, *The Rise of the Swiss Republic: A History*, 2d ed. (New York: H. Holt & Company, 1908).

Sykes-Picot Agreement

Sykes-Picot Agreement   See ANGLO-FRENCH-RUSSIAN AGREEMENT ABOUT ASIATIC TURKEY.

Syllabus of Errors (Syllabus Errorum)

Syllabus of Errors (Syllabus Errorum)   Pope Pius IX's anthology detailing and condemning "the principal errors of our time"; issued along with his encyclical *Quanta Cura* on December 8, 1864. It contained 80 errors distributed unevenly over 10 headings: (1) pantheism, naturalism, and absolute rationalism; (2) moderate rationalism; (3) indifferentism, latitudinarianism; (4) socialism, communism, secret societies, Bible societies, liberal-clerical societies; (5) church and its rights; (6) civil society and its relation to the church; (7) natural and Christian ethics; (8) Christian marriage; (9) the temporal power of the pope; and (10) modern liberalism. The 80th error became controversial: "The Roman Pontiff can and ought to reconcile himself to, and agree with, progress, liberalism and civilization as lately introduced." Compiled by a commission from Pius IX's earlier pronouncements, the publication was hailed by orthodox Catholics and condemned

by the liberals. The French government briefly banned its transmission from bishops to clergy. Subsequently, Bishop Dupanloup of Orléans issued a reinterpretation of the papal theses, which was more widely appreciated.

See also: SEPTEMBER CONVENTION OF 1864.

Further reading: Claudia Carlen, comp., *The Papal Encyclicals* (Wilmington N.C.: McGrath Publishing, 1981); Catholic University of America, eds., *New Catholic Encyclopedia* (New York: McGraw-Hill, 1967); Anne Fremantle, *The Papal Encyclicals in Their Historical Context* (New York: Mentor-Omega Books, 1963); Anthony J. Mioni, ed., *Popes Against Modern Errors: 16 Papal Documents* (Rockford, Ill.: Tan Books, 1999).

Szatmar, Peace of

Szatmar, Peace of   Peace treaty concluded at Szatmar (Satu-Mare, Hungary) on May 1, 1711, between Holy Roman Emperor Joseph I (who was also king of Hungary and Bohemia) and Hungarian rebel John Pálffy and other followers of Francis II Rákóczy, who had led a violent (but vain) revolt to gain independence for Transylvania. By the treaty, the emperor promised amnesty for all rebels, including freedom, and upheld the Hungarian constitution, with a promise to convene a diet. Rákóczy, vexed by Austrian rule over Hungary and Transylvania, rejected the treaty and fled to Poland and eventually to the Ottoman Empire (Turkey).

Further reading: Ladislaus Hengelmuller von Hengervar, *Hungary's Fight for National Existence: Or the History of the Great Uprising Led by Francis Rakoczi II, 1703–1711* (London: Macmillan, 1913); Agnes R. Varkonyi, *"Ad Pacem Universalem": The International Antecedents of the Peace of Szatmar* (Budapest: Akademiai Klado, 1980).

Szegedin, Treaty of

Szegedin, Treaty of   Peace agreement concluded at Szegedin (Szeged, Hungary) in August 1444, between the Ottoman Sultan Murad II and Hungarian General John Hunyadi; it recognized the independence of Serbia and ceded Wallachia to Hungary. The sultan had offered peace to Hunyadi, whose strong army had won campaigns against the Turks but not decisively defeated them. Aid promised to Hunyadi from other European powers did not materialize, and the last real crusade (the Crusade of Varna) against the Turks, undertaken a few months after the signing of the treaty, was a complete failure.

See also: ADRIANOPLE, TREATY OF (1444).

Further reading: Oskar Halecki, *The Crusade of Varna, A Discussion of Controversial Problems* (New York: Polish Institute of Arts and Sciences in America, 1943); Camil Muresanu, *John Hunyadi: Defender of Christendom* (Iasi, Romania: Center for Romanian Studies, 2001).

T

Taff Vale Case Court case concerning an unofficial strike at the Taff Vale Railway Company in England; highlighted when the House of Lords issued a controversial verdict on July 22, 1901, in the company's favor. It declared the union (Amalgamated Society for Railway Servants) responsible for damages resulting from the strike, thus reversing an earlier decision given by the Court of Appeal. The decision created quite a stir because, until then, it had been assumed that union funds were protected under the TRADE UNION ACT OF 1871. In this particular case, the union had to pay damages amounting to £32,000. The hostility generated by this decision lasted until 1906, when the TRADE DISPUTES ACT overturned it.

Further reading: David D. Douglas et al., *English Historical Documents*, 12 vols. (New York: Oxford University Press, 1950–77); Joel H. Wiener, ed., *Great Britain—The Lion at Home: A Documentary History of Domestic Policy (1689–1973)*, 4 vols. (New York: Chelsea House, 1974); Christine Woodland and Richard Storey, *The Taff Vale Case: A Guide to the ASRS Records* (Coventry, England: University of Warwick Library, 1978).

Tafna, Treaty of Treaty marking Algeria's recognition of "the sovereignty of France in Africa"; signed on May 30, 1837, at Tafna, Algeria, by General Thomas R. Bugeaud, commander of the French forces in Oran, and Emir Abd al-Kadir, the Algerian nationalist leader. The treaty's French and Arabic texts differed significantly and, unknown to anyone, Bugeaud had made secret commitments to al-Kadir. France kept the cities of Mostaganem, Mazagran, Oran, and Arzew in Oran province, and Algiers, the Sahel area, and the Mitija plain in Algiers province. Al-Kadir received Tlemcen, most of Oran (except the above-mentioned cities), Titterji, and part of Algiers. The treaty guaranteed the religious rights of the Arabs living in French territory but denied al-Kadir any control over them. Al-Kadir undertook to supply grain and cattle to the French army, to buy his arms and ammunition from France, to guarantee the freedom of French properties in his lands, and not to cede any coastal area to any other power without France's clearance.

See also: TANGIER, TREATY OF.

Further reading: Wilfrid Blunt, *Desert Hawk: Abd el Kader and the French Conquest of Algeria* (London: Methuen, 1947).

Taft-Hartley Act (Labor-Management Relations Act) U.S. legislation passed by Congress on June 23, 1947, that placed restrictions on organized labor in labor-management disputes. The act, sponsored by Senator Robert A. Taft of Ohio and Representative Fred A. Hartley of New Jersey, and passed over the veto of President Harry S Truman, amended the U.S. NATIONAL LABOR RELATIONS ACT of 1935. It restructured the National Labor Relations Board; prohibited closed shops, secondary boycotts, featherbedding, excessive dues, and union contributions to political campaigns; permitted employers to sue unions over broken contracts and damage done during strikes; required the filing of union financial statements and a 60-day "cooling off" period before strikes; authorized an 80-day injunction against strikes that affect national health or safety; and required union leaders to affirm that they were not members of the Communist Party. It established the independent Federal Mediation and Conciliation Service outside the U.S. Department of Labor.

Further reading: Mortimer Adler, ed., *The Annals of America*, 18 vols. (Chicago: Encyclopedia Britannica, 1968); Henry Steele Commager, ed., *Documents of American History*, 8th ed. (New York: Appleton-Century-Crofts, 1968); R. Alton Lee, *Truman and Taft-Hartley: A Question of Mandate* (Westport, Conn.: Greenwood Press, 1980); Benjamin J. Taylor and Fred Witney, *Labor Relations Law*, 6th ed. (Englewood Cliffs, N.J.: Prentice-Hall, 1992).

Taft's "Equal Justice Under Law" Speech   Controversial address given by U.S. Senator Robert A. Taft of Ohio at Kenyon College in Gambier, Ohio, on October 5, 1946. Reverence for the Anglo-Saxon legal principle of "equal justice under law" (words written over the entrance of the U.S. Supreme Court building in Washington, D.C.) had "steadily lost strength in recent years," said Taft, who criticized recent U.S. government price and wage controls and the Supreme Court regarding itself as a maker of executive policy (thus not commanding "respect for impartial dispensation of justice"). Most startling was Taft's discomfort over the recently tried and convicted German Nazi leaders, the hanging of whom, he said, would show "the spirit of vengeance, and vengeance is seldom justice." The press, in general, upbraided Taft, whose speech remains as an eloquent appeal to the "ingrained belief in fairness, impartiality, and justice."

Further reading: Arthur A. Ekirch, ed., *Voices in Dissent: An Anthology of Individualist Thought in the United States* (New York: Citadel Press, 1964).

Taiwanese Declaration of 1991   Declaration of May 1, 1991, by President Lee Teng-Hui, which ended Taiwan's state of emergency and led to key democratic reforms. He announced the abolition of the "Period of National Mobilization for the Suppression of the Communist Rebellion," promulgated in 1948 in Nanking (Nanjing) by then President Jiang Jieshi (Chiang Kai-shek). The declaration indicated formal renunciation of Taiwan's claim to represent all of China and a unilateral end to its civil war against the communist government. Also, the restrictive temporary provisions appended to Taiwan's constitution were terminated, thereby removing the ban on political parties and on dissent within the political sphere.

Further reading: Keith Maguire, *The Rise of Modern Taiwan* (Aldershot, England: Ashgate Publishing, 1998); Murray A. Rubinstein, ed., *Taiwan—A New History* (Armonk, N.Y.: M. E. Sharpe, 1999).

Take Your Choice!   Pamphlet written by the English parliamentary reformer Major John Cartwright in 1776, urging the people to choose between long Parliaments and slavery or annual Parliaments and liberty. Long Parliaments, he reasoned, made elected representatives "assume the carriage and haughtiness of despotic masters; to think themselves unaccountable for their conduct; and to neglect their duty." The evils perpetrated by corrupt ministers, he added, were trivial when compared to the "one great evil of a long parliament." Cartwright proposed "a reformation, both as to the length, and as to the constituting of your parliaments." People, he said, should trust not in princes or ministers but in themselves and in representatives chosen by them.

Further reading: F. D. Cartwright, ed., *The Life and Correspondence of Major Cartwright*, 2 vols. (New York: B. Franklin, 1972); Joel H. Wiener, ed., *Great Britain—The Lion at Home: A Documentary History of Domestic Policy (1689–1973)*, 4 vols. (New York: Chelsea House, 1974).

Tallmadge Amendment   Proposed amendment to the Missouri Enabling Bill in the U.S. Congress, admitting the Territory of Missouri to statehood in 1819; it prohibited further importation of slaves into Missouri and provided that all children born of slaves in Missouri after admission should become free when they reached the age of 25. Introduced by New York representative James Tallmadge, the amendment generated a bitter debate that reflected sectional divisions over the expansion of slavery. The amendment passed the House of Representatives but not the Senate. The question was settled by the MISSOURI COMPROMISE.

Further reading: Henry Steele Commager, ed., *Documents of American History*, 8th ed. (New York: Appleton-Century-Crofts, 1968); Don E. Fehrenbacher, *Sectional Crisis and Southern Constitutionalism* (Baton Rouge: Louisiana State University Press, 1995); Frank N. Magill, ed., *Great Events from History: American Series*, 3 vols. (Englewood Cliffs, N.J.: 1975).

Talmud   Traditionary source of Jewish civil and religious law, consisting of the Mishna (canonical collection of early rabbinical decisions and traditions) and the Gemara (extended commentary on the Mishna). Rabbi Judah ha-Nasi codified (c. A.D. 180) the Mishna, compiling most of it from accumulated writings of the ancient Jewish scribes and sages, especially Hillel, Shammai, and Akiba ben Joseph. The Mishna, written in Hebrew, is the oral doctrine of the Jews. The Gemara, the second part of the Talmud and written mainly in Aramaic, consists of two separate collections of commentaries: the Palestinian or Jerusalem Talmud (completed about A.D. 400) and the much larger Babylonian Talmud (codified about A.D. 500), both of which are accepted as authority by orthodox Jews. The Talmud also contains the halakah (legal discussions) combined with the haggadah (edifying, nonlegal literature, such as fables and proverbs).

Further reading: Donald H. Akenson, *Surpassing Wonder: The Invention of the Bible and the Talmuds* (New York: Harcourt Brace, 1998); Hyam Maccoby, *Philosophy of the Talmud* (Richmond, England: Curzon, 2000); Frank N. Magill, ed., *Great Events from History: Ancient and Medieval Series*, 3 vols. (Englewood Cliffs, N.J.: 1972); Jacob Neusner and Noam M. M. Neusner, eds., *The Book of Jewish Wisdom: The Talmud of the Well-Considered Life* (New York: Continuum, 1996).

Tanaka Memorial   Summary of Japanese imperialist ambitions, published by the Chinese in 1929 and purportedly written by Tanaka Giichi, Japan's premier and foreign minister, immediately after a conference on Far Eastern affairs in Tokyo, which he had attended (June 27–July 7, 1927). It stated that, since World War I (1914–18), the Japanese had failed to realize their "acquired" privileges and rights in Manchuria and Mongolia and had "to lay plans for the colonization of the Far East." Through use of the Japanese-built South Manchuria Railway, Japan could secure control over and tap the rich natural resources of North Manchuria. The document went on to say that the United States must be crushed and China conquered in order that Japan's trade can grow and strengthen, but mainly so that Japan can "proceed to conquer India, the Archipelago, Asia Minor, Central Asia, and even Europe." Part of Japan's subsequent expansionism followed in this vein, giving authenticity to the document, which the Japanese labeled a forgery.

Further reading: Carl Crow, ed., *Japan's Dream of World Empire; the Tanaka Memorial*, 2d ed. (New York: Harper, 1942); Louis L. Snyder, ed., *Fifty Major Documents of the Nineteenth Century* (Princeton, N.J.: D. Van Nostrand, 1955).

Tangier, Convention and Statute of   Order incorporating the decisions of the Tangier Conference convened to discuss the future of Tangier, Morocco; drafted by England and France on December 18, 1923, and signed by them and Spain on February 7, 1924, and subsequently by all the signatories of the Act of ALGECIRAS, except Austria, Germany, Russia, and the United States. Tangier and its hinterland, a 170-square-mile zone, was placed under an international administration and declared permanently neutral. The port of Tangier was demilitarized and an open-door trade policy established. Moroccans in the zone, legally subjects of the Moroccan sultan, actually came under the jurisdiction of a committee of control (consular representatives of the signatories). A 1928 amendment designated Italy as a major controlling power with England, France, and Spain. The statute also established a mixed court of European judges and an international legislative assembly (17 Europeans, 9 Moroccans). The Moroccan protectorates ended in 1956, as did the statute, but a royal charter extended its provisions until the transfer of power was completed.

Further reading: *The International Problem of Tangier*, (New York: Foreign Policy Associatin, 1926); Graham H. Stu-

art, *The International City of Tangier*, 2d ed. (Stanford, Calif.: Stanford University Press, 1955).

Tangier, Treaty of   French-Moroccan peace treaty signed on September 10, 1844, in Tangier, Morocco, after General Thomas Bugeaud's forces had defeated the Moroccan army at the battle of Isly (August 14, 1844). Humiliated, Sultan Abd ar-Rahman of Morocco was forced to accept the French presence in Algeria and agree to the construction of fortresses along an arbitrarily set boundary between Algeria and Morocco. Also, he agreed to remain neutral and not "accord any assistance nor help to any enemy of France." This was a a reference to the sultan's support of the Algerian nationalist leader, Abd al-Kadir, who had sought refuge in Morocco in 1843 (see TAFNA, TREATY OF). The sultan was to expel al-Kadir or to hand him over to the French if he ever entered Morocco again.

Further reading: J. F. A. Ajayi, *Africa in the Nineteenth Century until the 1880s* (Berkeley: University of California Press, 1989); C. R. Pennell, *Morocco since 1830: A History* (New York: New York University Press, 2000).

Tanis, Table of   See CANOPUS, DECREE OF.

Tao Te Ching (Daodeching)   Taoist "scripture" traditionally (but dubiously) attributed to Laozi (Lao Tzu) (b. 604? B.C.), a shadowy Chinese sage first identified as its author by historian Sima Qian (Ssu-ma Ch'ien) (145–90? B.C.). This book contains 81 short chapters, written in a contemplative, lyrical style, and centers on the concept of Tao (the way nature and the universe function). In the text, selfish, unrestrained rulers are censured, as well as social activism in general. Happiness is said to come through a tranquillity and harmony with nature, whose effortless regularity of phenomena should be accepted fully if man is to find accord with the Tao. Each must renounce all striving ("Do nothing and everything is done") and contemplate mystically alone to achieve freedom from desire and simplicity.

Further reading: Friedrich Heer, *Great Documents of the World: Milestones of Human Thought* (New York: McGraw-Hill, 1977); Mark A. Kishlansky, ed., *Sources of World History: Readings for World Civilization*, vol. 1, 2d ed. (Belmont, Calif.: West/Wadsworth, 1999); Lao Tzu, *Tao Te Ching: The Classic Book of Integrity and the Way*, trans. Victor H. Mair (New York: Quality Paperback Book Club, 1998).

Tariff Act of 1789, U.S.   First tariff act passed by the U.S. Congress. The act levied a duty on imported goods such as hemp, nails, glass, and earthenware, as well as on coffee, cocoa, tea, and sugar. The main purpose of the tariff was to raise money to support the U.S. government, but it also was intended to encourage and protect manufactures to some extent. The act generally applied specific duties, using ad valorem rates for only a few items. It was passed on July 4, to become effective on August 1, 1789.

Further reading: Sidney Ratner, *The Tariff in American History* (New York: Van Nostrand, 1972); F. W. Taussig, *The Tariff History of the United States* (Woodbridge, Conn.: Research Publications, 1991).

Tariff Act of 1816, U.S.

Legislation enacted on April 27, 1816, that established the first protective tariff in the United States. Passed to protect "infant industries" that had developed when the United States could not import British manufactured goods during the War of 1812, the tariff placed a duty of 25 percent on most woolen, cotton, and iron manufactures. It set a minimum valuation of 25 cents per square yard on cotton cloth, virtually eliminating cheap cotton imports. An ad valorem rate of 30 percent was applied to certain paper and leather goods and hats; a 15 percent rate applied to other commodities. The tariff was opposed by New England shipping and commercial interests.

Further reading: Sidney Ratner, *The Tariff in American History* (New York: Van Nostrand, 1972); Edward Stanwood, *American Tariff Controversies in the Nineteenth Century* (Boston: Houghton, Mifflin, 1904); F. W. Taussig, *The Tariff History of the United States* (Woodbridge, Conn.: Research Publications, 1991).

Tariff Act of 1824, U.S.

Federal U.S. legislation enacted on May 22, 1824, increasing tariff protection on wool, iron, lead, glass, silk, linens, cutlery, hemp, and cotton bagging. The 25 percent minimum levy on cotton and woolens set by the TARIFF ACT OF 1816 was increased to 33⅓ percent. The 1824 measure, favored by American manufacturers seeking protection from foreign competition, was opposed by New England shippers and commercial interests and by the South. Agitation for even greater protection led to the TARIFF ACT OF 1828.

Further reading: Lars Magnusson, *Free Trade and Protectionism in America: 1822–1890* (New York: Routledge, 2000); Sidney Ratner, *The Tariff in American History* (New York: Van Nostrand, 1972); Edward Stanwood, *American Tariff Controversies in the Nineteenth Century* (Boston: Houghton, Mifflin, 1904); F. W. Taussig, *The Tariff History of the United States* (Woodbridge, Conn.: Research Publications, 1991).

Tariff Act of 1828, U.S. (Tariff of Abominations)

High protective tariff passed by the U.S. Congress in 1828. Supporters of President John Quincy Adams proposed a high duty on foreign manufactures to protect New England industries; the South opposed the plan. Adams's opponents, supporters of Andrew Jackson, added to the tariff a high duty on imported raw materials, which New England was expected to oppose; they hoped to defeat the bill and discredit Adams, it nonetheless passed, with support from New England and the West, but it proved very unpopular and contributed to Jackson's victory over Adams in the presidential election of 1828.

See also: EXPOSITION AND PROTEST, CALHOUN'S.

Further reading: Henry Steele Commager, ed., *Documents of American History*, 8th ed. (New York: Appleton-Century-Crofts, 1968); Frank N. Magill, ed., *Great Events from History: American Series*, 3 vols. (Englewood Cliffs, N.J.: 1975); Lars Magnusson, *Free Trade and Protectionism in America: 1822–1890* (New York: Routledge, 2000); F. W. Taussig, *The Tariff History of the United States* (Woodbridge, Conn.: Research Publications, 1991).

Tariff Act of 1832, U.S.

Tariff law passed by the U.S. Congress on July 14, 1832, that lowered somewhat the high protective tariff rates that had been established by the controversial TARIFF ACT OF 1828. Opposed by Southerners as a sectional measure, the 1832 act eliminated some features that Eastern manufacturers and commercial interests disliked. It also increased the levy on woolens but allowed free admission to cheap raw wool and flax. Along with the Tariff Act of 1828, it was declared null and void by SOUTH CAROLINA'S ORDINANCE OF NULLIFICATION. The controversy was resolved by the compromise TARIFF ACT OF 1833.

Further reading: Frank N. Magill, ed., *Great Events from History: American Series*, 3 vols. (Englewood Cliffs, N.J.: 1975); Lars Magnusson, *Free Trade and Protectionism in America: 1822–1890* (New York: Routledge, 2000); Sidney Ratner, *The Tariff in American History* (New York: Van Nostrand, 1972); F. W. Taussig, *The Tariff History of the United States* (Woodbridge, Conn.: Research Publications, 1991).

Tariff Act of 1833, U.S. (Compromise Tariff)

Federal U.S. legislation enacted on March 2, 1833, that resolved the national controversy over the protective TARIFF ACT OF 1828 and OF 1832 and SOUTH CAROLINA'S ORDINANCE OF NULLIFICATION, which attempted to nullify them. The compromise, proposed by Henry Clay, systematically reduced the high protective duties until July 1, 1842, when a uniform 20 percent rate was to be set. The compromise was acceptable to Northern manufacturers, who wanted protection from foreign imports, and to Southerners, who generally opposed such taxes.

Further reading: Lars Magnusson, *Free Trade and Protectionism in America: 1822–1890* (New York: Routledge, 2000); Sidney Ratner, *The Tariff in American History* (New York: Van Nostrand, 1972); Edward Stanwood, *American Tariff Controversies in the Nineteenth Century* (Boston: Houghton, Mifflin, 1904); F. W. Taussig, *The Tariff History of the United States* (Woodbridge, Conn.: Research Publications, 1991).

Tariff Act of 1846, U.S.

See WALKER TARIFF ACT.

Tariff Act of 1857, U.S.

Federal act, dated March 3, 1857, lowering protectionist tariffs to a general level of about

20 percent, the lowest rate since 1850, and enlarging the free list. The 1857 Democratic-supported tariff, made possible because the government's income exceeded its needs, superseded the COMPROMISE TARIFF OF 1833, the Whig Tariff of 1842, which raised import duties, and the Democratic WALKER TARIFF ACT of 1846, which lowered them and divided imports into several tariff classes with graduated duties.

Further reading: Lars Magnusson, *Free Trade and Protectionism in America: 1822–1890* (New York: Routledge, 2000); Sidney Ratner, *The Tariff in American History* (New York: Van Nostrand, 1972); Edward Stanwood, *American Tariff Controversies in the Nineteenth Century* (Boston: Houghton, Mifflin, 1904); F. W. Taussig, *The Tariff History of the United States* (Woodbridge, Conn.: Research Publications, 1991).

Tariff Act of 1909, U.S. See PAYNE-ALDRICH TARIFF ACT.

Tariff Act of 1913, U.S. See UNDERWOOD-SIMMONS TARIFF ACT.

Tariff Act of 1922, U.S. See FORDNEY-MCCUMBER ACT.

Tariff Law of 1879, German General protective tariff voted by the German Reichstag on July 12, 1879, which levied duties of 5 percent to 10 percent on all imports. The import duties were part of Bismarck's new economic program, which also relied heavily on indirect taxation. Prompted in part by a severe economic recession in 1873, the protective tariff was supported by both industrialist and agrarian producers, but the duties on corn and other agricultural staples were very unpopular with urban residents. The new tariff was also supported by the National Liberal Party, although a free-trade policy was a hallmark of liberals in other countries. The tariff contributed significantly to Germany's rapid industrialization and urbanization during the following quarter-century.

Further reading: Ivo N. Lambi, *Free Trade and Protection in Germany, 1868–1879* (Wiesbaden: F. Steiner, 1963).

Tartu, Treaty of Treaty concluded in the Estonian town of Tartu (Dorpat in German) on February 2, 1920, by Soviet Russia and the Baltic state of Estonia, bringing an end to more than two years of hostilities between the two, which had arisen over Soviet Russia's involuntary renunciation of Estonia through the Treaty of BREST-LITOVSK. The treaty provided for Russia's formal recognition of Estonia's independence; Russia's agreement to make an indemnity payment of 15 million rubles to Estonia; the establishment of diplomatic relations between the two countries; the establishment of certain commercial arrangements, including Soviet Russia's right to use docks in Estonian ports; and the establishment of the new Soviet-Estonian frontier.

See also: MOSCOW, TREATY OF (1920); RIGA, TREATY OF (1920).

Further reading: Endel Krepp, *The Estonian War of Independence, 1918–1920* (Stockholm, Sweden: Estonian Information Centre, 1980); *Treaty of Peace Between Russia and Esthonia* (London: H. J. Ryman Printers, 1920).

Tashkent Agreement Pact ending the 17-day Indo-Pakistani border war of August-September 1965 in Kashmir; signed on January 10, 1966, in Tashkent by India's prime minister Lal Bahadur Shastri and Pakistan's president Ayub Khan. Their meeting had been proposed by Soviet premier Alexei Kosygin following a ceasefire arranged by the United Nations (UN) on September 27, 1965. Thereby, all troops were to be withdrawn to their pre-August 1965 status, prisoners exchanged, and diplomatic relations resumed. Both India and Pakistan agreed to a policy of noninterference and to initiate high-level discussions of issues of mutual interest (economic, refugee status, etc). Without any guarantees against future aggression, however, it proved to be a temporary truce rather than a permanent settlement. A subsequent military agreement (February 16, 1966) set the troop withdrawal at the 1949 level, under UN supervision.

Further reading: J. A. S. Grenville and Bernard Wasserstein, *The Major International Treaties since 1945: A History and Guide with Texts* (New York: Methuen, 1987); Fred L. Israel, ed., *Major Peace Treaties of Modern History, 1648–1967*, 4 vols. (New York: Chelsea House, 1967); Gulab Mishra, *Indo-Pakistan Relations: From the Tashkent Agreement to the Simla Agreement* (New Delhi, India: Ashish Publishing House, 1987).

Tauroggen, Convention of Agreement of neutrality concluded at Tauroggen (Taurage, Lithuania) on December 30, 1812, between the Prussian general Ludwig Yorck von Wartenburg and the Russian general Ivan Diebitsch during the retreat of Napoleon's Grand Army from Russia. Up until this point Prussia had been fighting alongside France against Russia. Through the convention General Yorck, along with his force of 17,000 troops, withdrew from the war against Russia and declared his army's neutrality. Although Yorck was dismissed and the Prussian government repudiated the agreement (General Yorck had not consulted his government before signing the document), a truce (see KALISCH, TREATY OF) was concluded by the Russian and Prussian governments less than two months later.

Further reading: Peter Paret, *Yorck and the Era of the Prussian Reform, 1807–1815* (Princeton, N.J.: Princeton University Press, 1966).

Taxation No Tyranny Major political pamphlet written by Samuel Johnson, English author and critic, and published in March 1775, supporting Britain's right to tax her subjects in the American colonies. It had been prompted by the actions of the American First Continental Congress in 1774, which effected an economic boycott of Britain. Johnson, a pro-Tory conservative, denounced the commonly held view that taxing the colonies was a means of oppressing them (tyranny) and discussed how the founding charters of the colonies led logically to their "being subject to English government, and chargeable by English taxation." Provincial charters, he argued in his pamphlet, did not exempt them from parliamentary taxes, nor could Americans claim voting rights when they had renounced them to live abroad. But, in concluding, Johnson took a softer stand and admitted that Britain might have to settle for peace on equal terms.

Further reading: Donald J. Greene, ed., *Political Writings/ Samuel Johnson* (Indianapolis, Ind.: Liberty Fund, 2000); Samuel Johnson, *Taxation No Tyranny* (New York: Grolier Club, 1990).

Taxpayer Relief Act of 1997, U.S.   Legislation enacted by the U.S. Congress and signed into law by President Bill Clinton on August 5, 1997. Its 824 code changes substantially reduced the amount of federal income taxes owed by most Americans. The act's major provisions affecting individual taxpayers were a child tax credit, education incentives, modifications to the codes concerning individual retirement accounts (IRAs), lower capital gains rates, and increases in estate and gift tax credits. The child tax credit gave taxpayers $400 per child under age 17. The HOPE Scholarship credit allowed the deduction of up to $1,500 per year of college tuition payments for their children, while the Lifelong Learning credit allowed the deduction of up to $1,000 for taking courses that improved job skills. The Education IRA provided a tax-exempt tool for financing college in the future, while the Roth IRA provided a nondeductible IRA with greater flexibility than previous deductible IRAs had offered. The maximum rate paid on capital gains was lowered from 28 percent to 20 percent, and the amount of capital gains tax to be paid on the sale of a personal residence was greatly reduced. The maximum value of tax-exempt estates and gifts was raised from $600,000 to $1 million. The act's business provisions included extending the research and work opportunity credits, repealing the corporate alternative minimum tax for small businesses, and increasing the deductions for health insurance paid by the self-employed.

Further reading: William H. Manz, *Taxpayer Relief Act of 1997: A Legislative History* (Buffalo, N.Y.: W. S. Hein, 2001); Taxpayer Relief Act of 1997, available online at http://www .filetax.com/97taxact.html.

Tea Act   Legislation enacted by the British Parliament on April 27, 1773, that gave the British East India Company, which possessed a huge surplus of tea, a monopoly on all tea exported to America. The company was allowed duty-free export of tea to America (though the import tax was retained) and could sell directly through its own agents. Thus, the company could undercut the prices of both legitimate colonial merchants and smugglers. In Massachusetts, protests against the company's monopoly culminated in the Boston Tea Party (December 16, 1773), which led to punitive measures by Britain and increasing colonial hostility to the mother country.

Further reading: Mortimer Adler, ed., *The Annals of America*, 18 vols. (Chicago: Encyclopaedia Britannica, 1968); Henry Steele Commager, ed., *Documents of American History*, 8th ed. (New York: Appleton-Century-Crofts, 1968); David D. Douglas, et al., *English Historical Documents*, 12 vols. (New York: Oxford University Press, 1950–77); William MacDonald, ed., *Select Charters and Other Documents Illustrative of American History, 1606–1775* (New York: Macmillan, 1899).

Teller Resolution   Amendment proposed by U.S. Senator Henry M. Teller of Colorado to the war resolutions adopted by Congress on April 20, 1898, on the eve of the Spanish-American War. The three war resolutions recognized Cuba's independence from Spain, demanded the withdrawal of Spanish armed forces, and authorized the president to use the army and navy to enforce these demands. The Teller (or fourth) resolution disclaimed any U.S. intention to exercise "sovereignty, jurisdiction or control" over Cuba once that island gained its independence. Following the war, however, the United States occupied and administered Cuba until the establishment of a republic in 1902.

See also: PARIS, TREATY OF (1898).

Further reading: Henry Steele Commager, ed., *Documents of American History*, 8th ed. (New York: Appleton-Century-Crofts, 1968); Elmer Ellis, *Henry Moore Teller, Defender of the West* (Caldwell, Idaho: Caxton Printers, 1941).

Tell Leilan Tablets   Collection of ancient Mesopotamian clay tablets in Akkadian cuneiform script, inscribed about 1740–1725 B.C. and discovered by an American archaeological expedition under professor Harvey Weiss of Yale University in a palace at Tell Leilan in northeastern Syria in September–October 1987. The approximately 1,100 tablets and seal impressions, made around the time of the Code of HAMMURABI, record the day-to-day life of an ancient Syrian kingdom, mentioned in cuneiform documents found in 1933 by French archaeologists at the ancient city of Mari, some 175 miles south of Tell Leilan. The tablets describe the deployment of horse-mounted soldiers against outlaws and of scouts or spies to investigate activities, as well as business dealings (like the distribution of the wine supply) and communication between kings, among other matters.

Further reading: Claudine A. Vincente, *The 1987 Tell Leilan Tablets Dated by the Limmu of Habil-kinu* (Ann Arbor, Mich.: University Microfilms International, 1994).

Ten Commandments   Set of injunctions attributed to the Hebrew leader Moses, delivered to him from God on Mount Sinai around 1300 B.C.; they constitute the moral code that is the basis of the Mosaic Law (or Law of Moses), which the Jews call the Torah. These precepts, adopted by Christianity, are recorded in the Pentateuch (the first five books of the Old Testament), chiefly in Exodus and Deuteronomy. Early Christian theologians called the commandments the "Decalogue," a Greek term meaning "ten words," and numbered them as we use them today: Thou shalt have no other gods [I am the Lord thy God]; Thou shalt not make thee idols; Thou shalt not take the name of the Lord thy God in vain; Remember to keep the Sabbath day holy; Thou shalt honor thy father and mother; Thou shalt not kill; Thou shalt not commit adultery; Thou shalt not steal; Thou shalt not bear false witness; Thou shalt not covet thy neighbor's house.

Further reading: Catholic University of America, eds., *New Catholic Encyclopedia* (New York: McGraw-Hill, 1967); Alan M. Dershowitz, *The Genesis of Justice: Ten Stories of Biblical Injustice That Led to the Ten Commandments and Modern Law* (New York: Warner Books, 2000); Benjamin W. Farley, ed. and trans., *John Calvin's Sermons on the Ten Commandments* (Grand Rapids, Mich.: Baker Books, 2000); Friedrich Heer, *Great Documents of the World; Milestones of Human Thought* (New York: McGraw-Hill, 1977).

Tennessee Valley Authority Act

Federal U.S. legislation enacted on May 18, 1933, establishing the Tennessee Valley Authority (TVA), an independent public corporation whose purpose was to control floods, improve navigation, provide electric power, and develop—socially and economically—the Tennessee Valley region. It was empowered to produce, distribute, and sell electricity and nitrogen fertilizers in the region; nitrogen not needed for fertilizer was to be made into explosives for the federal government. It was authorized to construct dams, transmission lines, and power plants, and to undertake rural electrification programs. The TVA took over the operation of a large federally owned hydroelectric plant and two munitions factories at Muscle Shoals, Alabama.

Further reading: Mortimer Adler, ed., *The Annals of America*, 18 vols. (Chicago: Encyclopedia Britannica, 1968); Henry Steele Commager, ed., *Documents of American History*, 8th ed. (New York: Appleton-Century-Crofts, 1968); *A History of the Tennessee Valley Authority* (Knoxville, Tenn.: Tennessee Valley Authority, 1983); Frank N. Magill, ed., *Great Events from History: American Series*, 3 vols. (Englewood Cliffs, N.J.: Salem Press, 1975).

Ten Resolutions, Russell's

Resolutions proposed by Lord John Russell, British colonial secretary of Lower Canada (Quebec), and on March 6, 1837, passed by the British Parliament, rejecting the demands of the French majority in Lower Canada as represented in the popularly elected legislative assembly (see NINETY-TWO RESOLUTIONS, PAPINEAU'S). Most significantly, the document spelled out the British rejection of the French demands for an elected legislative council (which then consisted of British-appointed officials) and for "responsible government" (the responsibility of the executive government to the popularly elected legislative assembly). Responsible government, Russell judged, meant granting independence to Lower Canada. The failure of the British to meet demands of French Canadians ultimately led to Papineau's Rebellion of 1837 (see DURHAM'S REPORT).

See also: HOWE'S LETTERS TO LORD JOHN RUSSELL.

Further reading: R. C. Brown and M. E. Prang, eds., *Canadian Historical Documents Series*, 3 vols. (Scarborough, Canada: Prentice-Hall of Canada, 1966); Paul Scherer, *Lord John Russell: A Biography* (London: Associated University Presses, 1999).

Tenth Amendment, U.S.

Amendment to the U.S. CONSTITUTION adopted in 1791, reserving substantial governmental authority and rights for the states or the people. The states (or people) have the "powers not delegated to the United States by the Constitution, nor prohibited by it to the states." The federal government thus gave the states much control over education, health care, and marital and criminal laws, among other matters.

See also: BILL OF RIGHTS, U.S.

Further reading: Ellen Alderman and Caroline Kennedy, *In Our Defense: The Bill of Rights in Action* (New York: Bard, 1998); Alan Brinkley, *American History: A Survey* (Boston: McGraw-Hill College, 1999); Kermit L. Hall et al., eds, *American Legal History: Cases and Materials*, 2d ed. (New York: Oxford University Press, 1996); Kermit L. Hall et al., eds., *The Oxford Companion to the Supreme Court of the United States* (New York: Oxford University Press, 1992).

Tenure of Office Act, U.S.

Legislation passed by Congress on March 2, 1867, over the veto of President Andrew Johnson, that required consent of the Senate before the president could remove from office anyone appointed by and with the advice and consent of the Senate, including members of his own cabinet. Violation of the law was made a high misdemeanor. In 1868, when Johnson defied the act and tried to fire Secretary of War Edwin M. Stanton, he was impeached in the House of Representatives; the Senate failed by one vote to convict him. The act was never again enforced and was repealed in 1887. The Supreme Court ruled it unconstitutional retroactively in 1926.

Further reading: Henry Steele Commager, ed., *Documents of American History*, 8th ed. (New York: Appleton-Century-Crofts, 1968); Chester G. Hearn, *The Impeachment of Andrew Johnson* (Jefferson, N.C.: McFarland & Co., 2000); Frank N. Magill, ed., *Great Events from History: American Series*, 3 vols. (Englewood Cliffs, N.J.: Salem Press, 1975); Gene Smith, *High Crimes and Misdemeanors: The Impeachment and Trial of Andrew Johnson* (New York: Morrow, 1976).

Teplitz, Treaty of

Treaty of alliance concluded at Teplitz (Teplice, Czechoslovakia) on September 9, 1813, by Russia, Prussia, and Austria, which served to consolidate the wartime efforts of this eastern core of the Sixth Coalition against

Napoleonic France. It was this sixth and final coalition that was eventually to be victorious over France. Through the treaty each party promised not to conclude a separate peace with France, and the sizes of the armies to be provided by each power were stipulated. Secretly it was agreed that Austria and Prussia, both of which had suffered territorially during the Napoleonic Wars (1803–15) (in contrast to Russia), would regain territories lost since 1805 through the treaties of PRESSBURG, SCHÖNBRUNN (1805, 1809), and TILSIT.

Further reading: Alistair Horne, *How Far from Austerlitz?: Napoleon, 1805–1815* (New York: St. Martin's Press, 1996).

Terrorism Act of 2000, British   Legislation enacted by the British Parliament to give law enforcement officials throughout Great Britain greater and more uniform powers in the fight against terrorism. The act, which went into force on February 19, 2001, replaced a number of temporary and emergency acts applicable variously to England, Wales, Scotland, and Northern Ireland. It proscribed 14 terrorist organizations, all of which were actively engaged in terrorism in Northern Ireland, and made it a crime to belong to these organizations, associate with their members, speak at meetings attended by their members, or speak or write in support of these organizations. The act gave officials the power to arrest suspected terrorists without first obtaining a warrant, allowed suspects to be detained in special interrogation centers without being charged for up to seven days, gave officials the right to overhear conversations between suspects and their attorneys, and provided suspects with juryless, one-judge trials. Although the act was clearly aimed at stopping terrorism in Northern Ireland, its provisions were worded loosely enough to cause concern about potential abuses. By defining terrorism as the use or threat of violence to advance a political, religious, or ideological cause, it opened the door for its being used against demonstrators protesting virtually any cause.

Further reading: United Kingdom Home Office, "The Terrorism Act 2000," HM Government online, available online at http://www.homeoffice.gov.uk/terrorism/; Clive Walker, *Blackstone's Guide to the Terrorism Act 2000* (London: Blackstone, 2001).

Teschen, Treaty of   Peace treaty made between Austria and Prussia (allied with Saxony) at Teschen (Cieszyn, Silesia, Poland) on May 13, 1779, ending the War of the Bavarian Succession (1778–79), which had begun over Prussian opposition to Austrian expansion into Bavaria. The treaty abrogated the 1778 Treaty of VIENNA, by which Austria had obtained Bavaria's support for her claims to Bavarian lands. Austria renounced all claims to the Bavarian succession and agreed to Prussian rule over the margravates of Ansbach and Bayreuth; Austria retained only the lower Bavarian district of Burghausen (along the Inn River). The Bavarian succession reverted to the elector of the Palatinate, Charles Theodore, to whom it had fallen upon the demise of the Bavarian line in

1777. Saxony received some formerly disputed sovereign rights and 9 million rix-dollars.

Further reading: Marvin E. Thomas, *Karl Theodor and the Bavarian Succession, 1777–1778* (Lewiston, Maine: E. Mellen Press, 1989).

Test Act of 1673, English   Law passed by the Cavalier Parliament in England, requiring all civil or military officers to receive the Anglican sacrament, to swear oaths of supremacy and allegiance, and to make a declaration against the Roman Catholic practice of transubstantiation. It was a more comprehensive version of the CORPORATION ACT and, while it was not repealed until 1828, it was virtually invalidated by the annual indemnity bills passed (after 1689) to legalize the acts of magistrates who had not conformed while in office to the Anglican faith (the Church of England). The act forced Charles II, the king, to abandon his toleration of non-Anglicans.

See also: PAPISTS' DISABLING ACT.

Further reading: Gerald L. Bray, *Documents of the English Reformation* (Minneapolis: Fortress Press, 1994).

Test Act of 1678, English   See PAPISTS' DISABLING ACT.

Testament Politique   See RICHELIEU'S *POLITICAL TESTAMENT*.

Tetrapolitan Confession   Protestant sacramentarian confession of faith submitted on July 9, 1530, by representatives of four German cities (Strasbourg, Memmingen, Lindau, and Constance) to Holy Roman Emperor Charles V. Modeled on the AUGSBURG CONFESSION, the Tetrapolitan Confession was drafted by Martin Bucer and Wolfgang F. Capito at the Diet of Augsburg (1530) to convey the south German response to humanist Philip Melanchthon's Eucharistic doctrine. The confession also aimed at reducing doctrinal arguments with the Roman Catholic Church (Rome) and at preserving the unity of German Protestantism or Lutheranism.

Further reading: Arthur C. Cochrane, ed., *Reformed Confessions of the 16th Century* (Philadelphia: Westminster Press, 1966).

Teusina, Peace of   Peace treaty concluded between Russia and Sweden at Teusina (Tayssina, Tyavzino, Tiavzino) in May 1595, by which Russia regained territory that she had lost to Sweden at the close of the Livonian War (1558–83). The war involved not only Sweden and Russia but Poland and Denmark as well, each of which had conflicting territorial claims in the Baltic region. Through the peace Sweden agreed to Russia's repossession of the towns of Yam, Korela, and Koporye; in return Russia agreed to limit her international trade to the ports of Vyborg and Reval (Tallinn, Estonia), on the Gulf of Finland, thus giving Sweden a degree of control over

Russian commerce. The dispute was renewed several years later.

See also: STOLBOVO, TREATY OF.

Further reading: Robert I. Frost, *The Northern Wars: War, State, and Society in Northeastern Europe, 1558–1721* (New York: Longman, 2000).

Texas Declaration of Independence

Declaration drawn up by Anglo-American settlers convened at Washington, Texas, and issued on March 2, 1836, proclaiming Texas to be independent of Mexico. The convention also prepared a constitution, based on the U.S. CONSTITUTION, establishing the Republic of Texas. The formal declaration of independence superseded a preliminary proclamation that had been issued in November 1835, soon after the outbreak of the revolution against Mexico. Describing the Mexican government as a despotic military rule, and the country in a state of anarchy, the declaration claimed the right to create a new government. Independence was actually achieved after the decisive battle of San Jacinto on April 21, 1836.

Further reading: Henry Steele Commager, ed., *Documents of American History*, 8th ed. (New York: Appleton-Century-Crofts, 1968); *Documents from Texas History* (Austin: Texas State Library, 1976); Frank N. Magill, ed., *Great Events from History: American Series*, 3 vols. (Englewood Cliffs, N.J.: Salem Press, 1975).

Texas v. Johnson

U.S. Supreme Court decision issued on June 21, 1989, declaring that burning the American flag, as a form of symbolic speech, was an action protected by FIRST AMENDMENT guarantees of free speech. In its 5-4 decision, the Court ruled that the government "may not prohibit the expression of an idea simply because society finds the idea itself offensive or disagreeable." The case involved Gregory Johnson, a member of a communist youth organization, who was convicted of defiling the flag after he burned one during the 1984 Republican Party convention in Dallas, Texas. The ruling invalidated state and federal laws against desecrating the flag and led to proposals for a U.S. constitutional amendment to prohibit flag-burning.

Further reading: Robert J. Goldstein, *Flag Burning and Free Speech: The Case of Texas v. Johnson* (Lawrence: University Press of Kansas, 2000); Kermit L. Hall et al., eds., *The Oxford Companion to the Supreme Court of the United States* (New York: Oxford University Press, 1992); Tony Mauro, *Illustrated Great Decisions of the Supreme Court* (Washington, D.C.: CQ Press, 2000); United States Supreme Court, *United States Reports: Cases Adjudged in the Supreme Court at . . . and Rules Announced at . . .* (New York: Banks & Brothers, Law Publishers, 1884–1921; Washington, D.C.: Government Printing Office, 1922–).

Texas v. White

U.S. Supreme Court decision in 1869 that upheld the indissolubility of the Union and the authority of Congress to reconstruct the states. The Reconstruction governor of Texas sued to prevent payment on U.S. bonds that the secessionist Texas government had disposed of to pay for Confederate supplies. He contended that the secessionist state government had been illegal and therefore its disposition of bonds had been illegal. The Court agreed, ruling that secession had been invalid and that the Union was perpetual and indissoluble. While not ruling on the validity of specific U.S. RECONSTRUCTION ACTS, the Court stated that Congress had the duty to guarantee republican governments in the states.

Further reading: Mortimer Adler, ed., *The Annals of America*, 18 vols. (Chicago: Encyclopedia Britannica, 1968); Henry Steele Commager, ed., *Documents of American History*, 8th ed. (New York: Appleton-Century-Crofts, 1968); Robert Fridington, *The Reconstruction Court, 1864–1888* (Danbury, Conn.: Grolier Educational, 1995); Kermit L. Hall et al., eds., *The Oxford Companion to the Supreme Court of the United States* (New York: Oxford University Press, 1992).

"Their Finest Hour" Speech, Churchill's

British prime minister Winston Churchill's rousing speech of unity delivered on June 18, 1940, before the House of Commons and in a same-day radio broadcast, after French resistance collapsed at the start of World War II. "To open a quarrel between the past and the present" would mean risking the future, he cautioned. The events in France will not affect "the resolve of Britain and the British Empire to fight on," and the British forces were more than capable and ready to meet the new military threat, upon which "the survival of Christian civilization" depends, while failure would mean sinking "into the abyss of a Dark Age." He concluded with a call to action so that posterity would say of the British Empire: "This was their finest hour."

See also: CHURCHILL'S "SO MUCH OWED" SPEECH.

Further reading: David Cannadine, ed., *Blood, Toil, Tears and Sweat: The Speeches of Winston Churchill* (Boston: Houghton Mifflin, 1989); Lewis Copeland and Lawrence W. Lamm, eds., *The World's Great Speeches*, 3d ed. (New York: Dover, 1973).

Theodoric, Edict of

See EDICT OF THEODORIC.

Theodosian Code (Codes Theodosianus)

Collection of imperial edicts and rescripts constituting the existing administrative law of the Roman Empire between A.D. 312 and 447. This recueil or collection of some 262 Roman laws was codified by order of Theodosius II, the eastern emperor, who first promulgated it in A.D. 438 and whose western colleague, Valentinian III, issued a similar version nine years later. The codex (code of law) consists of 16 books with numerous subdivisions covering legal practices. Included significantly are the edicts of Constantine I the Great, the first Christian Roman emperor, whose decree in A.D. 319 gave Christian clergymen a privileged social status by exempting them from taxation and other public burdens. In A.D. 321 Constantine granted the Christian Church the right to receive legacies and thus to acquire enormous wealth; another edict by Constantine that year granted all Roman citizens the right not to work on Sunday (a Christian practice). Ruthless laws against heretics appeared in the Theodosian Code, which influenced the legal thought of Western Europe into the Middle Ages.

See also: MILAN, EDICT OF; NICENE CREED.

Further reading: Jill Harris and I. N. Wood, *The Theodosian Code: Studies in the Imperial Law of Late Antiquity* (London: Duckworth, 1993); John Matthews, *Laying Down the Law: A Study of the Theodosian Code* (New Haven, Conn.: Yale University Press, 2000); Clyde Pharr, *The Theodosian Code and Novels and the Sirmondian Constitutions* (New York: Greenwood Press, 1952); Milton Viorst, ed., *The Great Documents of Western Civilization* (Philadelphia: Chilton Books, 1965).

Theodosian Table   See PEUTINGER TABLE.

Theological Declaration of Barmen   See BARMEN DECLARATION.

Thirteenth Amendment, U.S.   Amendment to the U.S. CONSTITUTION, adopted by Congress and ratified by the states in 1865, that abolished slavery and involuntary servitude, "except as a punishment for crime whereof the party shall have been duly convicted," in the United States. Along with the FOURTEENTH AMENDMENT and FIFTEENTH AMENDMENT, it is one of the so-called Civil War Amendments. Though the CONFISCATION ACT OF 1861 and OF 1862 and the EMANCIPATION PROCLAMATION had already freed some slaves, the institution of slavery was not abolished permanently and throughout the nation until passage of this amendment.

Further reading: Alan Brinkley, *American History: A Survey* (Boston: McGraw-Hill College, 1999); Robert Fridington, *The Reconstruction Court, 1864–1888* (Danbury, Conn.: Grolier Educational Corp., 1995); Kermit L. Hall, et al., eds., *American Legal History: Cases and Materials*, 2d ed. (New York: Oxford University Press, 1996); Kermit L. Hall, et al., eds., *The Oxford Companion to the Supreme Court of the United States* (New York: Oxford University Press, 1992).

Thirty-nine Articles   Anthology of doctrinal statements first issued in 1563, defining the Church of England's official position in regard to the religious controversies of the period. Derived from Thomas Cranmer's FORTY-TWO ARTICLES, they were adopted by a church convocation in 1571 after Queen Elizabeth I herself had made some alterations. The clergy were then required to swear allegiance to the 39 Articles, many of which were deliberately ambiguous. The articles tried to clarify the Anglican Church's viewpoint regarding orthodox Roman Catholic doctrine, Calvinism (see INSTITUTES OF THE CHRISTIAN RELIGION), and the teachings of the Ana-

baptists. They recognized baptism and the eucharist as the only two sacraments (transubstantiation was excluded) and discussed the Anglican Church's relations with the sovereign and the civil government. Since 1865, Anglican clergy are required only to declare that the doctrine of the articles is "agreeable to the Word of God."

Further reading: Gerald L. Bray, *Documents of the English Reformation* (Minneapolis: Fortress Press, 1994); Philip E. Hughes, *Theology of the English Reformers*, 3d ed. (Abington, Pa.: Horseradish, 1997); Frank N. Magill, ed., *Great Events from History: Modern European Series*, 3 vols. (Englewood Cliffs, N.J.: Salem Press, 1973); Oliver O'Donovan, *On the Thirty Nine Articles: A Conversation with Tudor Christianity* (Exeter, England: Paternoster Press, 1986).

Thomas Aquinas's *Summa Theologica*   See SUMMA THEOLOGICA.

Thomson-Urrutia Treaty (Treaty of Bogotá)   Treaty between the United States and Colombia signed at Bogotá on April 6, 1914, intended to resolve a dispute over U.S. support for Panamanian independence from Colombia. In the original document Colombia recognized the independence of Panama and the United States expressed regret that a dispute had arisen between the two countries, agreed to give Colombia special commercial transportation privileges in the Panama Canal, and agreed to pay $25 million in reparations to Colombia. Colombia quickly ratified this treaty, but the U.S. Senate refused to do so until April 20, 1921, and then only after the expression of U.S. regret was deleted. The treaty's primary name derived from the two who signed it: Thaddeus Austin Thomson, U.S. minister plenipotentiary to Colombia, and Francisco José Urrutia, Colombian minister for foreign affairs.

Further reading: Norman Thomson, *Colombia and the United States: A Juridical Study of Another "Scrap of Paper" and Its Supersession by the Colombian Indemnity Treaty for the Settlement of the Panama Question* (London: N. Thomson & Co., 1914).

Thorn (Toruń), First Peace of   Peace agreement concluded at Thorn (Toruń, Poland) on February 1, 1411, between the Teutonic Knights and Poland following the famous battle of Grünwald (Tannenberg) (1410). Although Poland had been victorious, she gained through the treaty only indemnity payments and the right to keep the region of Samogitia until the deaths of Polish king Ladislaus II (1350?–1434) and Lithuanian duke Witold (1350–1430), after which time its possession was to revert to the knights.

Further reading: Michael Burleigh, *Prussian Society and the German Order: An Aristocratic Corporation in Crisis c. 1410–1466* (New York: Cambridge University Press, 1984); Eric Christiansen, *The Northern Crusades: The Baltic and the Catholic Frontier, 1100–1525* (London: Macmillan, 1980); William L. Urban, *Tannenberg and After: Lithuania, Poland,*

and the Teutonic Order in Search of Immortality (Chicago: Lithuanian Research & Studies Center, 1999).

Thorn (Toruń), Second Peace of

Peace treaty concluded between Poland and the Teutonic Knights at the city of Thorn (Toruń, Poland) on October 19, 1466, ending a long, bitter struggle in the 1400s between the two powers over who would control the Baltic provinces. The peace established that the Teutonic Knights' grand master was to become a vassal of Poland and that Poland was to gain possession of Pomerania, including Danzig (Gdansk) and Marienburg (Malbork)—essentially West Prussia, thus granting Poland access to the Baltic Sea. The grand master was able to retain Königsburg (Kaliningrad, Russia) and to hold East Prussia as a fief of Poland.

Further reading: Michael Burleigh, *Prussian Society and the German Order: An Aristocratic Corporation in Crisis c. 1410–1466* (New York: Cambridge University Press, 1984); Eric Christiansen, *The Northern Crusades: The Baltic and the Catholic Frontier, 1100–1525* (London: Macmillan, 1980); William L. Urban, *Tannenberg and After: Lithuania, Poland, and the Teutonic Order in Search of Immortality* (Chicago: Lithuanian Research & Studies Center, 1999).

Thoughts on the Cause of the Present Discontents

Famous pamphlet written by British political writer Edmund Burke, published in April 1770; it charged the Tory government with suppression of public opinion. In it, Burke, who was elected a Whig member of Parliament in 1774, criticized King George III for trying to wrest more authority for the crown at the expense of the political parties. He justified the value of the party system, which he considered a vital constitutional link between the king and Parliament, and argued for public approval through Parliament of the choice of ministers. The electorate, he said, should participate more forcefully and actively in the political process. Though some of his claims were later disputed, his persuasive style was widely acknowledged.

Further reading: Catherine Macauley, *Observations on a Pamphlet, Entitled, Thoughts on the Cause of the Present Discontents*, 2d. ed. (Ann Arbor, Mich.: University Microfilms, 1974); David Womersley, ed., *A Philosophical Enquiry into the Origin of Our Ideas of the Sublime and Beautiful, and Other Pre-Revolutionary Writings* (New York: Penguin Books, 1998).

Three Baskets of the Law   See TIPITAKA.

Three Emperors' Alliance (Dreikaiserbund)

Alliance signed on June 18, 1881, representing a final attempt by Germany, Russia, and Austria to promote their common monarchical and conservative interests, despite intense competition in the Balkans between the latter two. The agreement, concluded for an initial period of three years, provided that if one of the three powers went to war with a fourth power, the remaining two would maintain a benevolent neutrality. The document also stipulated that the status quo in the Ottoman Empire (Turkey) could be altered only by agreement among the signatories, and reaffirmed the principle of closure of the Straits (Dardanelles and Bosporus) as stated in the 1878 Treaty of BERLIN. Any violation of this principle by Turkey in favor of a belligerent power would be considered a declaration of war against the aggrieved power. Bosnia and Herzegovina could be annexed to Austria at the latter's convenience, and Bulgaria and Eastern Rumelia could be reunited eventually. The treaty was renewed for a second three-year period of 1884, but foundered the following year in a dispute over Bulgarian internal affairs.

Further reading: James Y. Simpson, ed. and trans., *The Saburov; or Bismarck & Russia; Being Fresh Light on the League of the Three Emperors, 1881* (New York: Macmillan, 1929); Louis L. Snyder, ed., *Documents of German History* (New Brunswick, N.J.: Rutgers University Press, 1958): Louis L. Snyder, ed., *Fifty Major Documents of the Nineteenth Century* (Princeton, N.J.: D. Van Nostrand, 1955).

Three-Fifths Compromise   See SLAVERY COMPROMISE, U.S.

Tientsin, Treaty of

Agreement made between China and Great Britain (Lord Elgin) on June 26, 1858, after the defeat of the Chinese by Anglo-French forces in the Second Opium War (1856–60). The two contracting parties agreed to the residence of ambassadors at each other's court—in Peking (Beijing) and London—and freedom of trade. In the next few days, France, Russia, and the United States signed similar treaties (all of which supplemented earlier agreements) at Tientsin (Tianjin), which opened 10 new ports in China to foreign trade, as well as the Yangtze River, and provided for foreign legations in Peking and Christian missionaries and travelers to journey into China's interior. The Tientsin agreement was ratified by the Peace of PEKING two years later.

Further reading: Jules Davids, comp., *American Diplomatic and Public papers: The United States and China: Series 1: The Treaty System and the Taiping Rebellion, 1842–1860* (Wilmington, Del.: Scholarly Resources, 1973); Immanuel C. Hsu, *The Rise of Modern China*, 5th ed. (New York: Oxford University Press, 1995); Fred L. Israel, ed., *Major Peace Treaties of Modern History, 1648–1967*, 4 vols. (New York: Chelsea House, 1967); Catherine Lamour and Michel R. Lamberti, *The Second Opium War* (London: Lane, 1974).

Tilsit, Treaties of

Peace treaties concluded at Tilsit (Sovetsk) in 1807 between Russia and France (July 7) and between Prussia and France (July 9) following successive French victories over the Prussians and Russians during the Napoleonic Wars (1803–15). Through the treaties Prussia and Russia agreed to the territorial changes made by French emperor Napoléon Bonaparte: Territory between the Rhine and Elbe

Rivers ceded by Prussia, together with Hesse, was to constitute the kingdom of Westphalia, to be governed by Jérôme Bonaparte; Polish territory acquired by Prussia since 1792 (except the city of Bialystok, which Russia received) was to become the Grand Duchy of Warsaw, under French protection; Danzig (Gdańsk) became a free city once again; Cottbus, formerly part of Prussia, joined Saxony. In addition the two defeated powers recognized the Confederation of the Rhine (an association of German states formed in 1806 under French protection), the kingdom of Naples under Joseph Bonaparte, and Holland under Louis Bonaparte.

See also: KÖNIGSBERG, CONVENTION OF.

Further reading: Fred L. Israel, ed., *Major Peace Treaties of Modern History, 1648–1967*, 4 vols. (New York: Chelsea House, 1967); Georges Lefebvre, *Napoleon from 18 Brumaire to Tilsit, 1799–1807* (London: Routledge & Kegan Paul, 1969); Georges Lefebvre, *Napoleon from Tilsit to Waterloo, 1807–1815* (London: Routledge & Kegan Paul, 1969).

Timber Culture Act, U.S.

Legislation enacted by the U.S. Congress on March 3, 1873, authorizing any person who kept 40 acres of timber land in good condition to acquire title to 160 acres of such land. It made available 10 million acres of federal lands for forestation of the Great Plains in hopes of reducing erosion, retaining rainfall, and improving the climate. In 1878 the minimum tree-growing requirement was reduced to 10 acres. Little permanent tree growth resulted on the arid land, but land speculation was widespread. Extensive abuse of the act by cattlemen and speculators, at the expense of settlers, led to its repeal by the FOREST RESERVE ACT of 1891.

Further reading: C. Barron McIntosh, "Use and Abuse of the Timber Culture Act," *Annals of the Association of American Geographers* 65, no. 3 (September 1975): 347–62.

Tipitaka (Three Baskets of the Law)

Oldest surviving Buddhist scripture and law, originally compiled orally about 240 B.C. and finally written down in the Pali sacred language about 80 B.C. It is the foundation of Buddhism, a religion founded by the Enlightened One (Buddha), whose real name was Prince Siddhartha Gautama (c. 550–c. 480 B.C.). The documents fall into three "baskets" (collections): the *Sutta Pitaka* (or legendary discourses of Buddha), the *Vinaya Pitaka* (the regulations of monasticism), and the *Abhidharma Pitaka* (the scholasticism). They consist of teaching dialogues between Buddha and his followers, espousing self-renunciation and denial of worldly lusts and cares in order to find nirvana (a cessation of suffering). Basic to Buddhism are its "four noble truths" (proclaimed by Buddha in a sermon at Benares [Varanasi], India): that all existence is suffering; that suffering has a cause; that knowledge and purification can remove suffering; and that the "Eightfold Way" brings an end to suffering.

See also: PILLAR EDICTS, AŚOKA'S.

Further reading: Friedrich Heer, *Great Documents of the World: Milestones of Human Thought* (New York: McGraw-Hill, 1977); Nyanatiloka, comp. and trans., *The Word of the Buddha; an Outline of the Teaching of the Buddha in the Words of the Pali Canon* (Kandy, Sri Lanka: Buddhist Publications Society, 1968).

Tirana, Treaty of

Treaty concluded in the Albanian capital city of Tirana (Tiranë) on November 27, 1926, by representatives of Albania and Italy, providing terms for an alliance between the two that would render Albania's status as that of an Italian protectorate. Through the treaty both parties agreed that it was in their best interests to maintain the status quo in Albania; that neither party would conclude political or military agreements with a third power that would be harmful to the other; and that they would settle all disputes through pacific means. The treaty was to remain effective for five years. However, on November 22, 1927, Italy and Albania signed the Second Treaty of Tirana, a 20-year defensive alliance between them. In return for large monetary loans, Albania granted Italy important rights, notably in oil, road building, military affairs, and education. Albania became practically an Italian protectorate.

See also: VLORË PROCLAMATION.

Further reading: *Albania: The Problem of the Adriatic* (New York: Foreign Policy Association, 1927); Eugene Staley, *Italy's Financial Stake in Albania* (New York: Foreign Policy Association, 1932).

Tithe Commutation Act of 1836

See MELBOURNE'S SIX ACTS.

Titian Law (Lex Titia)

Roman tribunician law of November 27, 43 B.C., legalizing the formation of the Second Triumvirate, a coalition of Marc Antony, Octavian (Augustus), and Marcus Aemilius Lepidus. After the assassination of Julius Caesar in 44 B.C., the above trio managed a reconciliation of differences and had themselves appointed triumvirs to administer jointly the Roman republic for a term of five years. Antony, Octavian, and Lepidus (who constituted a commission with public dictatorial powers) secured control of Italy by proscriptions, executions of enemies, and confiscations; they also divided the Roman provinces among themselves.

See also: BRUNDISIUM, TREATY OF; PHILIPPICS, CICERO'S.

Further reading: Miriam Greenblatt, *Augustus Caesar and Imperial Rome* (Tarrytown, N.Y.: Benchmark Books, 2000); Frank N. Magill, ed., *Great Events from History: Ancient and Medieval Series*, 3 vols. (Englewood Cliffs, N.J.: Salem Press, 1972); Richard D. Weigel, *Lepidus: The Tarnished Triumvir* (New York: Routledge, 1992).

Tobacco Companies Settlement Agreement (Master Settlement Agreement)

National agreement between the four largest U.S. cigarette manufacturers and 46 states that were suing them to recover Medicaid expenses for treating patients with health conditions related to smoking. On November 14, 1998, Philip Morris, R. J. Reynolds, Lorillard, and Brown & Williamson agreed to pay $206 billion in total to the 46 states (Florida, Minnesota, Mississippi, and Texas had settled their claims earlier for $40 billion total). The companies agreed to pay $12 billion by 2003 and spread the rest of the payments over the next 22 years. The companies also agreed to spend $1.7 billion on research and on programs designed to keep young people from smoking and to limit their advertising efforts. The agreement prohibited tobacco companies from advertising on billboards and public transportation, banned them from selling clothing and merchandise with procigarette messages or logos, prohibited them from using cartoon characters in advertisements, and required them to stop advertising in magazines with a predominantly teenage readership. Despite these terms, the agreement was a victory of sorts for the tobacco companies. The original settlement sought by the states had demanded $368 billion and would have penalized the companies further if the number of underage smokers did not decrease, a provision that was not part of the final agreement.

Further reading: Byron Robinson, "States Announce Settlement with Tobacco Companies," court tv online, available online at http://www.courttv.com/trials/tobacco/national/111698_ctv.html.

Tobar Doctrine

Proposed in 1907 by Ecuadoran diplomat Carlos R. Tobar; this was a policy of collective nonrecognition aimed at denying legitimacy to governments that rise to power by nondemocratic means in Latin American countries. The Tobar Doctrine attempted to reduce the threat of revolution, civil war, and coup d'état as methods of assuming power. Tobar maintained that it was in the interest of all existing governments that they collectively seek to establish constitutionalism and the democratic process as the means for achieving political change in the hemisphere. Although the Tobar Doctrine was incorporated into the Central American peace treaties of 1907 and 1923, it was eventually challenged by the ESTRADA DOCTRINE in 1930.

Further reading: Charles L. Stansifer, *Applications of the Tobar Doctrine to Central America* (Washington, D.C.: Academy of American Franciscan History, 1967).

Tolentino, Treaty of

Peace agreement made between Pope Pius VI and Napoléon Bonaparte (for the French Republic) at Tolentino, Italy, on February 19, 1797, following successful French military campaigns in Italy during the French Revolutionary Wars (1792–1802). Fearful of revolutionary France's future plans for the Roman Catholic Church and helpless in the face of Napoléon's military force, Pope Pius made large payments to Napoléon in exchange for truces with him and, when Napoléon began marching toward Rome in February 1797, the pope concluded the treaty. He ceded important territory in north central Italy—Romagna, Bologna, and Ferrara—and granted certain rights and an indemnity to Napoléon.

Further reading: *History of the Pontificate and Captivity of Pius the Sixth: Together with a Glance at the Catholic Church* (New York: P. O'Shea, 1858).

Toleranzpatent   See EDICT OF TOLERATION OF 1781.

Toleration Act of 1649 (Act Concerning Religion)

Act passed by the Maryland Assembly, upon pressure from Lord Baltimore (Cecilius Calvert), guaranteeing religious freedom to all Christians. It sought to absolve Maryland, a colony seen as a haven for Roman Catholics (see MARYLAND COLONY CHARTER) from the charge of intolerance toward Protestantism. As Protestant groups became more numerous in Maryland, religious disturbances became frequent and bitter, and with the rise of Cromwell in England in 1642, anti-Catholic feeling intensified among Maryland's Puritans. The act stated that no person within the province "professing to believe in Jesus Christ shall be troubled, molested or discountenanced for or in respect of his or her religion, or in the free exercise thereof." It also stated that no one shall be forced to the belief or exercise of any other religion against his conscience; however, it applied only to orthodox Christians who accepted the doctrine of the Trinity.

Further reading: Henry Steele Commager, ed., *Documents of American History*, 8th ed. (New York: Appleton-Century-Crofts, 1968); Gerald W. Johnson, *The Maryland Act of Religious Toleration: An Interpretation* (Baltimore: Committee for the 300th Anniversary of the Maryland Act of Religious Toleration, 1949); Frank N. Magill, ed., *Great Events from History: American Series*, 3 vols. (Englewood Cliffs, N.J.: Salem Press, 1975).

Toleration Act of 1689

English statute of May 24, 1689, withdrawing the penalties imposed on Protestant dissenters for failing to attend the services of the Anglican Church (or Church of England)—subject to their taking the oaths of allegiance and supremacy. They were allowed the freedom to worship in their own places and to choose their own teachers and preachers. The social and political restrictions caused by the TEST ACT OF 1673 and CORPORATION ACT remained in effect, as did the existing penal laws against Roman Catholics and Unitarians. Ministers were required to swear allegiance to those of the THIRTY-NINE ARTICLES that did not deal with church government. The act gave an impetus to the Glorious Revolution in England: the deposition of King James II (a Catholic) and the accession of William and Mary (Protestant daughter of James) to the throne in 1689.

See also: DECLARATION OF RIGHTS, ENGLISH.

Further reading: Gerald L. Bray, *Documents of the English Reformation* (Minneapolis: Fortress Press, 1994); Joel H. Wiener, ed., *Great Britain—The Lion at Home: A Documentary*

History of Domestic Policy (1689–1973), 4 vols. (New York: Chelsea House, 1974).

Tome of Leo Doctrinal letter sent in A.D. 449 by Pope Leo I the Great to Patriarch Flavian of Constantinople, rejecting the teachings of deposed heretic Eutyches, a Monophysite abbot of Constantinople, and defining precisely and systematically the two natures and one person of Jesus Christ. Eutychianism held that Christ had only one nature, a blend of his divine and human. Leo formulated the Catholic orthodox doctrine of Christ's Incarnation (how human form is assumed perfectly by a divine being) and of the union and coexistence of both of Christ's natures. In A.D. 451 the Council of Chalcedon upheld Leo's formulation as "the voice of Peter," declaring that Christ is of two distinct natures, one divine and one human. Disturbances occurred in Egypt, Palestine, and other Near Eastern lands because of the council's ruling, called the *Definition*.

See also: HENOTIKON.

Further reading: T. Herbert Bindley and F. W. Green, eds., *The Oecumenical Documents of the Faith* (Westport, Conn.: Greenwood Press, 1980); Catholic University of America, eds., *New Catholic Encyclopedia* (New York: McGraw-Hill, 1967); Edward R. Hardy, *Christology of the Later Fathers* (Philadelphia: Westminster Press, 1977); Frank N. Magill, ed., *Great Events from History: Ancient and Medieval Series*, 3 vols. (Englewood Cliffs, N.J.: Salem Press, 1972).

Tonkin Gulf Resolution See GULF OF TONKIN RESOLUTION.

"Too Proud to Fight" Speech, Wilson's Address delivered by U.S. president Woodrow Wilson on May 10, 1915, in Philadelphia, after the outbreak of World War I in Europe and the May 7 sinking of the British passenger ship *Lusitania* by a German submarine (see LUSITANIA NOTES, WILSON'S). In a continuing attempt to promote his policy of unarmed neutrality and to avoid U.S. involvement in the war, the president stated, "There is such a thing as a man being too proud to fight. There is such a thing as a nation being so right that it does not need to convince others that it is right." Events later forced Wilson to change that policy.

Further reading: Patrick Devlin, *Too Proud to Fight: Woodrow Wilson's Neutrality* (New York: Oxford University Press, 1975).

Topeka Constitution Instrument drafted by a constitutional convention held in October–November 1855 at Topeka and intending to establish the territory of Kansas as a free state. The document, prepared in opposition to the proslavery territorial government, prohibited slavery and declared invalid black indentures executed in other U.S. states; it was approved by voters in December. A bill to admit Kansas under this constitution passed the U.S. House of Representatives the

following year but failed in the Senate. A period of violence followed. The LECOMPTON CONSTITUTION represented the next attempt to establish the state.

Further reading: Frank N. Magill, ed., *Great Events from History: American Series*, 3 vols. (Englewood Cliffs, N.J.: Salem Press, 1975).

Torah See TEN COMMANDMENTS.

Tordesillas, Treaty of Agreement between Portugal and Spain, signed in Tordesillas, Spain, on June 7, 1494, redefining the maritime spheres of the two countries. The treaty superseded four papal bulls (most notably *Inter Caetera*) issued by Pope Alexander VI for the purpose of dividing Columbus's newly found territories between Spain and Portugal. With each successive bull increasing Spain's holdings, however, John II, king of Portugal, felt his maritime activity restricted and his dream of a sea route to India destroyed. Unable to secure redress from the pope, the king resorted to direct diplomacy. By the terms of the treaty, Spain moved the line of demarcation farther west, placing all of Africa and India (and later Brazil) under Portugal's control.

See also: DEMARCATION, BULL OF.

Further reading: Henry Steele Commager, ed., *Documents of American History*, 8th ed. (New York: Appleton-Century-Crofts, 1968); Paul Gottschalk, trans., *The Earliest Diplomatic Documents on America; the Papal Bulls of 1493 and the Treaty of Tordesillas* (Berlin: P. Gottschalk, 1927); George E. Nunn, *The Diplomacy Concerning the Discovery of America* (Jenkintown, Pa.: Tall Tree Library, 1948).

Torgau, Book of Confession of faith drawn up by Jakob Andreä and other German theologians at Torgau, Saxony (Prussia), in June 1576. It consisted essentially of the private writings and fundamental doctrines of Martin Luther, the German leader of the Protestant Reformation. Presented as authoritative doctrine, the document's contents received mixed reactions, with many believing that the less controversial views of Philip Melanchthon, a German humanist and follower of Luther, and others should be included. A compromising point of view was finally agreed on, and in June 1580 it was presented as the Formula of Concord (or Consensus), which became the Lutheran Church's "constitution."

Further reading: Dennis L. Slabaugh, *Jakob Andreae, Lutheran Orthodoxy, and Anabaptism in the Late Sixteenth Century* (Ann Arbor, Mich.: University Microfilms International, 1987).

Toruń, Peace of See THORN (TORUŃ), FIRST PEACE OF; THORN (TORUŃ), SECOND PEACE OF.

Townsend Plan Old-age pension proposal advanced by Dr. Francis E. Townsend in 1934, to aid the elderly poor and encourage national recovery from the Great Depression.

Townsend, a California physician, sought payments of $200 per month to all persons aged 60 and over (except for criminals), so long as the recipients retired from gainful employment (thus creating jobs for younger workers) and agreed to spend the sum within a month in the United States (stimulating the economy). The payments were to be financed by a 2 percent federal transaction (sales) tax, to be paid into a revolving fund. Opposed as unworkable and inequitable by labor unions and manufacturers, as well as socialist and conservative organizations, the plan nevertheless gained considerable popular support, but all congressional bills to enact it were defeated.

Further reading: Mortimer Adler, ed., *The Annals of America*, 18 vols. (Chicago: Encyclopedia Britannica, 1968); Alan Brinkley, *Voices of Protest: Huey Long, Father Coughlin, and the Great Depression* (New York: Knopf, 1982); Morgan J. Dorman, *Age before Booty* (New York: G. P. Putnam's Sons, 1936); *The Townsend Crusade; an Impartial Review of the Townsend Movement and the Probable Effects of the Townsend Plan* (New York: Committee on Old Age Security of the Twentieth Century Fund, 1936).

Townshend Acts

Four acts sponsored by Britain's chancellor of the exchequer Charles Townshend and passed by the British Parliament between June 15 and July 2, 1767, in an effort to exercise greater royal authority over the American colonies and to levy new taxes. The SUSPENDING ACT was the first; it forbade the New York Assembly from functioning until the financial requirements of the Quartering Act of 1765 had been met. The second act, sometimes called the American Import Duties Act, levied import duties on glass, lead, paint, tea, and paper sent into the colonies. The third act set up a rigorous and arbitrary method of tax collection in the colonies, under the supervision of a Boston-based Board of Custom Commissioners. Custom officers had unlimited authority to search warehouses and homes and to seize contraband. The fourth Townshend Act withdrew British commercial duties on tea imported into the colonies. The acts were viewed as undue interference in colonial affairs and caused deep resentment and widespread resistance. In March 1770, the British government repealed the first three acts, temporarily averting a major British-American colonial crisis.

Further reading: Henry Steele Commager, ed., *Documents of American History*, 8th ed. (New York: Appleton-Century-Crofts, 1968); William MacDonald, ed., *Select Charters and Other Documents Illustrative of American History, 1606–1775* (New York: Macmillan, 1899); Frank N. Magill, ed., *Great Events from History: American Series*, 3 vols. (Englewood Cliffs, N.J.: Salem Press, 1975); Paul Sparer and Jack Curtis, eds., *Literature of Revolutionary America* (New York: Lexington, 1962).

Townshend's Champagne Speech

See CHAMPAGNE SPEECH, TOWNSHEND'S.

Tract No. 90, Newman's

Last and most controversial of the TRACTS FOR THE TIMES, written in 1841 by John Henry Newman, founder of the Oxford Movement. In this, Newman set out to show that the Thirty-nine Articles (of the English Prayer Book) were not in conflict with the teachings of the undivided church. On this basis, he argued for a more harmonious relationship between the Anglican and the Roman Catholic Church. He also decried the political supervision of the church and wrote that if religious changes were to be effective, they should be "the act of the whole body" and not "the mere act of a majority." Publication of this tract offended many religious sensibilities and the bishop of Oxford even called for its suspension. In 1845, Newman and many of his supporters embraced Roman Catholicism.

Further reading: Rune Imberg, *Tracts for the Times: A Complete Survey of All the Editions* (Lund, Sweden: Lund University Press, 1987); Peter B. Nockles, *The Oxford Movement in Context: Anglican High Churchmanship, 1760–1857* (New York: Cambridge University Press, 1994); Stephen Thomas, *Newman and Heresy: The Anglican Years* (New York: Cambridge University Press, 1991); Joel H. Wiener, ed., *Great Britain—The Lion at Home: A Documentary History of Domestic Policy (1689–1973)*, 4 vols. (New York: Chelsea House, 1974).

Tracts for the Times (Oxford Tracts)

Series of 90 religious tracts or pamphlets written between 1833 and 1841, expounding the principles of the Oxford Movement (Tractarianism), which was a strong influence within the Church of England from 1833 to 1845. Among the chief leaders of the movement were John Keble, James Froude, Edward Pusey, and John Henry Newman (who edited the entire series and wrote 24 of the tracts, of which *TRACT NO. 90* is the most famous). The Tractarians rejected the Protestant element in the Anglican Church, advocating instead a return to the teachings of the undivided Roman Catholic Church. They stressed church authority, tradition, ritual, and ceremony, as well as patristic Christianity and sacramentalism; they moved away from liberalism and rationalism of the times.

Further reading: Rune Imberg, *Tracts for the Times: A Complete Survey of All the Editions* (Lund, Sweden: Lund University Press, 1987); Peter B. Nockles, *The Oxford Movement in Context: Anglican High Churchmanship, 1760–1857* (New York: Cambridge University Press, 1994); Stephen Thomas, *Newman and Heresy: The Anglican Years* (New York: Cambridge University Press, 1991); Joel H. Wiener, ed., *Great Britain—The Lion at Home: A Documentary History of Domestic Policy (1689–1973)*, 4 vols. (New York: Chelsea House, 1974).

Trade Act of 1988, U.S.

Omnibus trade legislation aimed at expanding U.S. trade abroad, signed into law by President Ronald W. Reagan on August 23, 1988. Alleged unfair trading practices by some foreign nations and increased imports (at the expense of U.S. companies) helped win passage of the legislation, which enlarged and redefined U.S. trade policy. The new law allowed the president to negotiate international agreements to expand markets for U.S. products, to carry on trade inquiries in response to Senate and House committee resolutions, and to authorize a U.S. trade representative to make decisions in certain trade matters, among other things. Also, the patents and copyrights of U.S. firms gained added protection from international thievery. Overseas reaction to the new law was generally hostile, with Japan, South Korea, Taiwan, France, and other countries criticizing the U.S. for turning toward trade protectionism.

Further reading: Bernard D. Reams and Mary Ann Nelson, *Trade Reform Legislation 1988: A Legislative History of the Omnibus Trade and Competitiveness Act of 1988* (Buffalo, N.Y.: W. S. Hein, 1991); Susan C. Schwab, *Trade-Offs: Negotiating the Omnibus Trade and Competitiveness Act* (Boston: Harvard Business School Press, 1994).

Trade Agreements Act, U.S.   See RECIPROCAL TARIFF ACT, U.S.

Trade Disputes Act of 1906, British   British legislation of December 21, 1906, reversing the Taff Vale judgment of 1901, wherein the trade union was asked to compensate for the losses incurred during its strike at the Taff Vale Railway Company. This act exempted the unions from any liability for losses resulting from strikes. It also provided a new definition of peaceful picketing and approved the use of strikes for contract-breaking.

See also: TAFF VALE CASE.

Further reading: Bernard Shillman, *Trade Unionism and Trade Disputes in Ireland* (Dublin: Dublin Press, 1960); Joel H. Wiener, ed., *Great Britain—The Lion at Home: A Documentary History of Domestic Policy (1689–1973)*, 4 vols. (New York: Chelsea House, 1974).

Trade Disputes and Trade Unions Act of 1927, British   British legislation of July 29, 1927, against the general strike of 1926 (by trade unionists in sympathy with striking coal miners); the act restricted the activities of Britain's trade unions and declared general and sympathetic strikes as illegal. In an attempt to curtail the funds available to the Labour Party, the act amended the 1913 legislation by imposing "contracting in" for political levy. It also prohibited civil servants from registering in Trade Union Congress-affiliated unions. Even though the provision outlawing general strikes was never invoked, the act was widely condemned and brought about the eventual downfall of the Conservatives and the rise to power of the Labour Party. It was repealed in 1946.

Further reading: Frank N. Magill, ed., *Great Events from History: Modern European Series*, 3 vols. (Englewood Cliffs, N.J.: Salem Press, 1973); Joel H. Wiener, ed., *Great Britain—*

The Lion at Home: A Documentary History of Domestic Policy (1689–1973), 4 vols. (New York: Chelsea House, 1974).

Trade Union Act of 1884, French   Law authorizing the formation of labor unions, or *syndicats*, in 1884. The legalization of unions was significant not just for its social implications, but also because unions thereby enjoyed a privileged status in France, where associations of more than 20 people required governmental approval. The newly formed unions were vehemently opposed by employers, however, and state employees and railroad workers were prohibited from joining them. For these reasons, the progress of union membership was slow, and was marked by strikes and violence.

See also: ASSOCIATIONS LAW, FRENCH.

Further reading: Frank N. Magill, ed., *Great Events from History: Modern European Series*, 3 vols. (Englewood Cliffs, N.J.: Salem Press, 1973).

Trade Union Act of 1871, British   Bill passed on June 29, 1871, which legalized the status of the British trade unions as recommended by the Majority Report of the Royal Commission of 1867–69. It also gave protection to trade union funds and put the internal affairs of a union beyond the jurisdiction of the courts. The act legalized strikes, but declared peaceful picketing illegal. For registration, a trade union was required to submit a copy of its rules along with the names of at least seven members. This act was accompanied by the Criminal Law Amendment Act, which sought to impose stiff penalties on trade unions indulging in violent and intimidating activities.

Further reading: William Guthrie, *The Law of Trade Unions in England and Scotland under the Trade Union Act, 1871* (Edinburgh, Scotland: Edmonston & Douglas, 1873); George Howell, *A Handy-Book of the Labour Laws: Being a Popular Guide to the . . . Trade Union Acts, 1871, . . .* , 3d ed. (Woodbridge, Conn.: Research Publications, 1989); Joel H. Wiener, ed., *Great Britain—The Lion at Home: A Documentary History of Domestic Policy (1689–1973)*, 4 vols. (New York: Chelsea House, 1974).

Trajan's Rescript   Written response in A.D. 112 by Roman emperor Trajan to correspondence from Pliny the Younger, who had been dispatched to govern, investigate, and end confusion and corruption in the province of Bithynia in northwest Asia Minor. Pliny had asked for instructions about legal proceedings against Christians and received Trajan's lenient response: "They [Christians] must not be sought out; if they are denounced and convicted, they must be punished, yet with this limitation, that any one who denies that he is a Christian and proves his denial by deed . . . shall earn pardon by repentance."

See also: PLINY THE YOUNGER'S *LETTERS*.

Further reading: Frank N. Magill, ed., *Great Events from History: Ancient and Medieval Series*, 3 vols. (Englewood

Cliffs, N.J.: Salem Press, 1972); Milton Viorst, ed., *The Great Documents of Western Civilization* (Philadelphia: Chilton Books, 1965).

Transcontinental Treaty   See ADAMS-ONÍS TREATY.

Transport Act of 1947, British

Bold and comprehensive British legislation of August 6, 1947, nationalizing the railways, docks, road transport undertakings, and most other means of transport in the country. Of all the nationalization bills (see ELECTRICITY ACT OF 1947, BRITISH) passed by the Labour government, this was the most hotly contested—perhaps because the takeover was estimated at a staggering $4 billion. The idea was to streamline operations, cut waste, and put the British economy back on the road to recovery. The British Transport Commission was created as a central agency to administer the various transport systems after the date of acquisition (January 1, 1948).

Further reading: Michael R. Bonavia, *The Nationalisation of British Transport: The Early History of the British Transport Commission, 1948–53* (New York: St. Martin's Press, 1987); H. F. R. Sturge and T. D. Corpe, *Road Haulage Law and Compensation* (London: Sweet & Maxwell, 1948); Joel H. Wiener, ed., *Great Britain—The Lion at Home: A Documentary History of Domestic Policy (1689–1973),* 4 vols. (New York: Chelsea House, 1974).

Transport Act of 1968, British

British legislation passed in 1968, reorganizing the nationalized transport industry, the most comprehensive law since the TRANSPORT ACT OF 1947. It established the National Freight Corporation to assume charge of, and coordinate, the cargo and freight services offered by the railways and government-owned road companies, and tightened controls over private cargo enterprises. Long-distance bus services were entrusted to the newly-formed National Bus Company, while passenger services (rail and road) in the large urban areas were to be coordinated by another new government agency, the Public Transport Authorities. The legislation also enabled the nationalized transport companies to diversify into ancillary manufacturing (equipment for bus and railway workshops, for export) and service industries (providing, for instance, gas stations and garages near railway car parks).

Further reading: Kenneth J. Button, *The 1968 Transport Act and After* (Loughborough, England: University of Loughborough, Department of Economics, 1974); Vincent Powell-Smith, *The Transport Act of 1968* (London: Butterworths, 1969).

Transportation Act of 1920, U.S.   See ESCH-CUMMINS ACT.

Travendal, Treaty of

Peace treaty signed on August 18, 1700, at Travendal (in Holstein); forced on King Frederick IV of Denmark by King Charles XII of Sweden. It led to Denmark's withdrawal from the tripartite (with Russia and Poland) anti-Swedish coalition, which had started the Great Northern War (1700–21) against Sweden. Responding to Denmark's invasion (March 1700) of Holstein-Gottorp, Sweden marched into Zealand (Sjaelland, Denmark) and threatened (aided by England and Holland) to besiege Copenhagen. Thus overpowered, Frederick IV readily accepted Sweden's peace terms. He agreed to respect the independence of the duke of Holstein Gottorp and to allow him to build a string of fortresses in Schleswig as a guarantee against future Danish aggression. Further, the duke's right to maintain his own army and fortresses was confirmed, and he was reimbursed for all his military expenses during the war. Finally, Denmark restored the status quo by promising not to participate in any hostilities against Sweden.

Further reading: Frank N. Magill, ed., *Great Events from History: Modern European Series,* 3 vols. (Englewood Ciffs, N.J.: Salem Press, 1973).

"Treaty Elm"   See SHAKAMAXON, TREATY OF.

Treaty of Arbitration with China

Agreement between the United States and the Republic of China signed in Washington, D.C., on September 15, 1915; it established that any disputes between the two nations that could not be settled through ordinary diplomatic proceedings would be submitted to a permanent, five-member international commission for investigation. Both parties agreed to forgo any acts of force for one year, to allow the commission time to report. After the report was issued, each nation reserved the right to decide on its course of action. Ratifications of the treaty were exchanged on October 22, 1915. This agreement was one of 30 similar treaties concluded by U.S. secretary of state William Jennings Bryan with various nations.

Further reading: Henry Steele Commager, ed., *Documents of American History,* 8th ed. (New York: Appleton-Century-Crofts, 1968).

Treaty on the Final Settlement with Respect to Germany (Two-Plus-Four Treaty)

Formal agreement signed on September 12, 1990, in Moscow by the foreign ministers of the two Germanys (West and East), Britain, France, the United States, and the Soviet Union. It cleared the way to restoring full sovereignty to a united Germany after 45 years of division following the Allied powers' defeat of Nazi Germany in World War II. The treaty required Britain, France, the United States, and the Soviet Union to relinquish their occupation rights over Berlin and German territory (see POTSDAM DECLARATION), including their right to maintain certain air corridors to Berlin and their right to approve Germany's borders. The two Germanys agreed that their unified nation (which came into being on October 3, 1990) would be a member of the NORTH ATLANTIC TREATY Organization; would never possess nuclear, biological, or chemical weapons;

would limit the size of her armed forces to 370,000 troops; and would have "no territorial claims whatsoever against other states" (Germany was also to sign a treaty with Poland guaranteeing her current border). The seven-page treaty also called for the withdrawal of the Soviet Union's 370,000 troops from East Germany by the end of 1994 (as part of a side agreement, West Germany agreed to give the Soviets nearly $10 billion in aid).

See also: CHARTER OF PARIS FOR A NEW EUROPE; GERMAN "STATE TREATY" OF 1990; GERMAN UNIFICATION TREATY.

Further reading: Imanuel Geiss, *The Question of German Unification: 1806–1996*, trans. Fred Bridgman (New York: Routledge, 1997); Hans D. Genscher, *Rebuilding a House Divided: A Memoir by the Architect of Germany's Reunification*, trans. Thomas Thornton (New York: Broadway Books, 1998); Jurgen Thomaneck, *Dividing and Uniting Germany* (New York: Routledge, 2001).

Trent, Decrees of the Council of   See TRIDENTINE DECREES.

Trianon, Treaty of   Delayed post–World War I agreement of June 4, 1920, thrust by the Allies on Hungary, drastically reducing Hungary to one-third of her former size. Signed at the Grand Trianon Palace in Versailles, France, the treaty forced Hungary to cede key territories to Romania (Transylvania and most of Banat), to Yugoslavia (the remainder of Banat, Bacska, the Prekmurje, and all of Croatia-Slavonia), to Czechoslovakia (Slovakia and sub-Carpathian Ruthenia), to Austria (part of western Hungary), and to the Allied powers (Fiume). This caused the displacement of nearly 3 million Magyars from their homeland and proved to have far-reaching consequences for central European peace. The Hungarian armed forces were limited to 35,000 men but the monetary compensation payable by Hungary was not defined.

See also: ST.-GERMAIN, TREATY OF (1919).

Further reading: Francis Deak, *Hungary at the Paris Peace Conference; the Diplomatic History of the Treaty of Trianon* (New York: Columbia University Press, 1942); Fred L. Israel, ed., *Major Peace Treaties of Modern History, 1648–1967*, 4 vols. (New York: Chelsea House, 1967); Bela K. Kiraly and Laszlo Veszpremy, eds., *Trianon and East Central Europe: Antecedents and Repercussions* (New York: Columbia University Press, 1995); Lawrence Martin, *The Treaties of Peace, 1919–1923* (New York: Carnegie Endowment for International Peace, 1924).

Tridentine Decrees (Decrees of the Council of Trent)
Authoritative pronouncements by the famous council held at Trent, in Tyrol (in northern Italy), intermittently from 1545 to 1563. This council of the Catholic or Counter-Reformation redefined and reconfirmed the doctrines of the Roman Catholic Church, particularly those religious tenets that had been attacked by the Protestants. It condemned the Protestant Ref-

ormation and stated precisely many of the present Catholic doctrines. The decrees significantly reaffirmed the pope's authority as supreme, the church's doctrine as formulated and understood according to the tradition of St. Thomas Aquinas and the Jesuits, the existence of purgatory, the mediation of saints with God on man's behalf, and the church's authority to decide how Holy Communion was to be practiced. In addition, certain recommendations were made with regard to the improvement of the education of the Roman Catholic laity and clergy.

Further reading: Catholic University of America, eds., *New Catholic Encyclopedia* (New York: McGraw-Hill, 1967); Frank N. Magill, ed., *Great Events from History: Modern European Series*, 3 vols. (Englewood Cliffs, N.J.: Salem Press, 1973); H. J. Schroeder, trans., *Canons and Decrees of the Council of Trent* (Rockford, Ill.: Tan Books & Publishers, 1978); Milton Viorst, ed., *The Great Documents of Western Civilization* (Philadelphia: Chilton Books, 1965).

Triennial Act   Bill passed by the Long Parliament of King Charles I of England in 1641 (reluctantly signed by the king), making it compulsory for the king to meet with Parliament for a minimum of 50 days every three years. If the king ignored the act, the lord chancellor and lord keeper could summon Parliament by issuing writs. It was replaced by the Triennial Act of 1664 (Parliament to meet at least once in three years, at the king's discretion), which was, in turn, repealed by the Triennial Act of 1694 (Parliaments not to sit longer than three years).

Further reading: Joel H. Wiener, ed., *Great Britain—The Lion at Home: A Documentary History of Domestic Policy (1689–1973)*, 4 vols. (New York: Chelsea House, 1974).

Trieste Agreement   Agreement initialed in London on October 5, 1954, by representatives of Britain, the United States, Italy, and Yugoslavia, ending the conflict between Yugoslavia and Italy over possession of the Adriatic port of Trieste and surrounding territory. The agreement provided that Italy would gain possession of Trieste, plus a coastal strip, which represented most of "Zone A" of the Free Territory, and that Yugoslavia would gain possession of "Zone B," the remainder of the Free Territory, plus additional territory in the south of Zone A that included several small villages whose inhabitants were primarily Slovenian. In addition, Italy and Yugoslavia pledged to see that human rights were not violated, to forbid nationalistic and racial antagonism, and to enforce the just treatment of their ethnic minorities. The port of Trieste, long desired by Italy and acquired by her in 1919, had been alternately occupied later in the century by Germany and Anglo-American and Yugoslav forces. In 1947 the Free Territory was created. The 1954 agreement proved to be permanent.

Further reading: Glenda Sluga, *The Problem of Trieste and the Italo-Yugoslav Border: Difference, Identity, and Sovereignty in Twentieth-Century Europe* (Albany: State University of New York Press, 2001).

Tripartite Pact of 1940   See AXIS POWERS, PACT OF THE.

Tripartitum

ion of ancient Hungarian customs and royal decrees, compiled by jurist and statesman Stephen Werböczi and ratified by Hungary's king Uladislaus II in 1514. This constitution stated that the Hungarian realm belonged to the Holy Crown and consisted of three interdependent parts: the land, nation, and king (none could have absolute power over the others). Yet, while it ensured against the rise of an absolutist monarchy, it deprived the peasants (serfs) of liberty and landownership and excluded them from the "nation," which consisted exclusively of nobles. The constitution proclaimed equality of all nobles, great and small, and exempted them from taxation. It also limited church authority and forbid the distribution of papal benefices in Hungary. In short, national interests were now identified with the nobility.

Further reading: Gyula Andrassy, *The Development of Hungarian Constitutional Liberty*, trans. Charles A. Ginever and Ilona Ginever (London: K. Paul, Trench, Trubner, 1908); Anthony Endrey, *The Holy Crown of Hungary*, 2d ed. (Melbourne, Australia: Hungarian Institute, 1978).

Triple Alliance of 1668

Diplomatic treaty made among England, Sweden, and the Dutch Republic (Holland) on January 23, 1668. It was negotiated and concluded by England's Sir William Temple and John De Witt, pensionary of Holland, and was to check the growing ambitions of King Louis XIV of France in the Low Countries (the Netherlands, Belgium, and Luxembourg). However, Louis soon secured an agreement with King Charles II of England, thus ending the brief alliance (see DOVER, TREATY OF). The Triple Alliance also induced Louis to accept the 1668 Treaty of AIX-LA-CHAPELLE.

Further reading: Christopher Lindenov, *The First Triple Alliance* (New Haven, Conn.: Yale University Press, 1947); Frank N. Magill, ed., *Great Events from History: Modern European Series*, 3 vols. (Englewood Cliffs, N.J.: Salem Press, 1973).

Triple Alliance of 1717

Treaty formed and signed by France, and the Dutch Republic at The Hague on January 4, 1717, as a joint front against Spain and to safeguard the provisions of the Treaties of UTRECHT, particularly with regard to the order of the succession to the French and British thrones. France agreed to expel the Old Pretender (James, son of King James II) for life and to destroy the fortifications and canals at Dunkirk and Mardyke. The allies were to support each other in the event of an outside attack and to ensure that the crown of France and the Protestant succession of Great Britain remained undisturbed. The alliance signaled the end of the traditional Whig foreign policy of treating France as Britain's natural enemy. The Triple Alliance of 1717 became the QUADRUPLE ALLIANCE when Austria joined the group in 1718.

Further reading: Derek McKay, *Allies of Convenience: Diplomatic Relations Between Great Britain and Austria, 1714–1719* (New York: Garland Publishers, 1986).

Triple Alliance of 1788

Agreement by Great Britain, Prussia, and the Netherlands (the Dutch Republic) to defend and maintain peace in Europe. Promoted by William Pitt, the British prime minister, to revive Britain's sagging position in the European world, its importance was eclipsed by the French Revolution (1789). In a treaty with the Dutch signed at The Hague on April 15, 1788, Pitt broke France's maritime alliance with the Netherlands by guaranteeing the stadtholder's (William V) position in the House of Orange. Prussia and the Netherlands concluded a similar agreement in Berlin on the same day. Britain entered into a defensive pact with Prussia on June 13, 1788. The alliance served as a powerful and calming influence on European affairs until its split in 1792. It settled a Baltic conflict, Britain's dispute with Spain over the Nootka Sound, returned the Belgian Netherlands to Austria, and achieved peace between Russia and the Ottomans and between Austria and the Ottomans.

Further reading: Oscar Browning, *The Flight to Varennes, and Other Historical Essays* (London: Swan Sonnenschein & Co., 1892).

Triple Alliance of 1882

Five-year treaty signed on May 20, 1882, by Germany, Austria, and Italy, which was intended primarily as a defensive alliance against France. An unprovoked French attack against Italy would require Germany and Austria to come to the latter's aid with all their forces. If French aggression were directed against Germany, Italy was pledged to provide full military support. In addition, if one or two signatories were attacked by two or more great powers, the other member or members of the alliance were bound to provide mutual support; and if one or more of the signatories were provoked to declare war on another great power, the allies were pledged to maintain a benevolent neutrality. Renewed regularly until 1915, the alliance protected Austria's back door, ended Italian diplomatic isolation, and gave Germany some protection against France.

Further reading: Frank N. Magill, ed., *Great Events from History: Modern European Series*, 3 vols. (Englewood Cliffs, N.J.: Salem Press, 1973); Bernadotte E. Schmitt, *Triple Alliance and Triple Entente* (New York: H. Fertig, 1971); Louis L. Snyder, ed., *Documents of German History* (New Brunswick, N.J.: Rutgers University Press, 1958): Louis L. Snyder, ed., *Fifty Major Documents of the Nineteenth Century* (Princeton, N.J.: D. Van Nostrand, 1955).

Troppau Protocol

Protocol drawn up and concluded under the influence of Austrian statesman Prince Clemens von Metternich, between Russian czar Alexander I, Austrian emperor Francis I, and Prussian king Frederick William III on

November 19, 1820, during a long conference in the Silesian town of Troppau (Opava, Czechoslovakia). The document declared that any state that submitted to revolutionary forces and subsequently altered its form of government would be expelled from the European alliance and that the allied powers would have the right to intervene, forcibly if necessary, should any such state threaten other states belonging to the alliance. The document was concluded following the outbreak of revolutionary movements in Spain and in the Austrian dominion of Naples, thus endorsing Austria's right of intervention in Naples. Great Britain refused to sign the document.

See also: METTERNICH'S CIRCULAR ABOUT TROPPAU.

Further reading: Milton Viorst, ed., *The Great Documents of Western Civilization* (Philadelphia: Chilton Books, 1965).

Troyes, Treaty of (1420)

Agreement among King Charles VI of France, King Henry V of England, and Duke Philip the Good of Burgundy, concluded at Troyes, France, on May 21, 1420, during the Hundred Years' War (1337–1457). Charles, under Burgundian influence and suffering from recurrent insanity, disinherited the dauphin (his eldest son) through the treaty, which declared Henry regent and heir to the throne of France. Henry was allowed to keep his conquests in northern France and was married to Charles's daughter, Catherine of Valois (June 2, 1420). Afterward Henry began subjugating France until his sudden death (1422), followed shortly by Charles VI's. The dauphin then assumed the royal title as King Charles VII.

See also: ARRAS, TREATY OF (1435).

Further reading: R. C. Famiglietti, *Royal Intrigue: Crisis at the Court of Charles VI, 1392–1420* (New York: AMS Press, 1986); James N. Loehlin, *Henry V* (New York: St. Martin's Press, 2000); Richard Vaughan, *Philip the Good: the Apogee of Burgundy* (New York: Barnes & Noble, 1970).

Troyes, Treaty of (1564)

Amicable settlement of the long-standing Anglo-French dispute over Calais; concluded at Troyes, France, on April 12, 1564, between Queen Mother Catherine de Médicis, regent of France, and Queen Elizabeth I of England. Le Havre was restored to France and, in exchange for 222,000 crowns, England surrendered her claims to Calais. France also paid England a ransom of 120,000 crowns for the release of French hostages. The Treaty of CATEAU-CAMBRÉSIS of 1559 was not discussed. Trade and economic relations between the two countries were normalized. The French queen even commissioned poet laureate Pierre de Ronsard to compose a piece to commemorate the new friendship. The treaty, however, was intended merely as a stepping-stone to future alliances.

Further reading: George A. C. Sandeman, *Calais under English Rule* (Oxford, England: B. H. Blackwell, 1908).

Truce of God (Treuga Dei)

Decree made by the Roman Catholic Church about 1027, similar to the PEACE OF GOD but more specific in its prohibitions of war. It limited fighting to certain days, by 1042 forbidding warfare from sundown on Wednesday to sunrise on Monday and on church festivals (Christmas, Easter, and Lent). It also forbade anyone from harming a man working in the fields and decreed banishment or death for anyone breaking the truce, which was reaffirmed by many church councils but was not particularly successful. By the 13th century it had more or less lost all importance as an effort to impose feudal self-regulation.

Further reading: Catholic University of America, eds., *New Catholic Encyclopedia* (New York: McGraw-Hill, 1967); Joseph H. Dahmus, *A History of Medieval Civilization* (New York: Odyssey Press, 1964); Milton Viorst, ed., *The Great Documents of Western Civilization* (Philadelphia: Chilton Books, 1965).

True Laws of Free Monarchy (Basilikon Doron, or "His Majesty's Instructions to His Dearest Sonne Henry the Prince")

Treatise written by King James VI of Scotland (later King James I of England) in Scots (Scottish dialect of English) in the summer of 1598 and first printed in the spring of 1599 by Robert Waldegrave in Edinburgh; it contained the author's advice to his son on the role of the king. The advice given by James was consistent with earlier works on kingship. He viewed the person of the king as having acquired that position by divine right, explaining that God had made the king a "little God" to rule over men. This imposed upon the king the great responsibility of ruling justly, respecting the law and its institutions, and condemning evil. When James became king of England the tract was translated into several European languages and made available abroad.

Further reading: *Baskilion Doron, or, King James's Instructions to His Dearest Sonne, Henry the Prince* (Ann Arbor, Mich.: University Microfilms International, 1977); Mark A. Kishlansky, ed., *Sources of the West: Readings in Western Civilization*, 4th ed., 2 vols. (New York: Longman, 2001).

Truman Doctrine

Doctrine enunciated by U.S. president Harry S Truman in a speech to Congress on March 12, 1947, proclaiming a U.S. commitment to aid noncommunist countries to resist expansion by the Soviet Union. Truman, announcing this plan to contain communism, declared that American policy was "to help free peoples to maintain their free institutions and their national integrity against aggressive movements that seek to impose upon them totalitarian regimes." He asked Congress for $400 million to defend Greece and Turkey from Soviet aggression. Congress approved the request in May 1947, signaling a departure from the former policy of noninvolvement in European affairs.

Further reading: Mortimer Adler, ed., *The Annals of America*, 18 vols. (Chicago: Encyclopaedia Britannica, 1968); Henry Steele Commager, ed., *Documents of American History*, 8th ed. (New York: Appleton-Century-Crofts, 1968); Dennis K. Merrill, ed., *Documentary History of the Truman Presidency*, 30 vols. (Bethesda, Md.: University Publications of America, 1995); Louis L. Snyder, ed., *Fifty Major Documents of the Twentieth Century* (Princeton, N.J.: D. Van Nostrand, 1955).

Truman Loyalty Oath

Executive Order 9835 issued by U.S. president Harry S Truman on March 21, 1947, to tighten the federal government's loyalty procedures. It required loyalty investigations for all civilian employees of the executive branch and all its job applicants, and created the Loyalty Review Board, within the Civil Service Commission, to coordinate loyalty policies. Disloyalty was defined to include espionage, sabotage, disclosure of confidential documents, and "membership in, affiliation with or sympathetic association with" organizations that the attorney general designated as totalitarian, fascist, communist, subversive, or advocating force, violence, or the use of unconstitutional means to alter the government.

Further reading: Mortimer Adler, ed., *The Annals of America*, 18 vols. (Chicago: Encyclopaedia Britannica, 1968); Henry Steele Commager, ed., *Documents of American History*, 8th ed. (New York: Appleton-Century-Crofts, 1968); Donald R. McCoy, *The Presidency of Harry S. Truman* (Lawrence: University Press of Kansas, 1984).

Truman's Announcement of the Atomic Bombing of Hiroshima

Statement issued by U.S. president Harry S Truman on August 6, 1945, announcing that the United States had dropped a single atomic bomb on the Japanese city of Hiroshima earlier that day. Truman described the bomb as a revolutionary new force for destruction, harnessing the basic power of the universe and having more force than 20,000 tons of TNT. More than 70,000 people were killed. The U.S. president warned that if the Japanese continued to refuse to surrender unconditionally, "they may expect a rain of ruin from the air, the like of which has never been seen on this earth." On August 9, the United States dropped a second atomic bomb, on Nagasaki.

See also: FRANCK REPORT, JAPAN'S SURRENDER IN WORLD WAR II; POTSDAM DECLARATION.

Further reading: Mortimer Adler, ed., *The Annals of America*, 18 vols. (Chicago: Encyclopaedia Britannica, 1968); Donald R. McCoy, *The Presidency of Harry S. Truman* (Lawrence: University Press of Kansas, 1984); Milton Viorst, ed., *The Great Documents of Western Civilization* (Philadelphia: Chilton Books, 1965).

Truman's Inaugural Address

Speech delivered by Harry S Truman on January 20, 1949, at his inauguration as president of the United States. In it Truman noted the dangers of world communism and outlined a four-point program on which, he argued, American foreign policy should rest. These points were: support for the United Nations, continuation of programs for world economic recovery (see MARSHALL PLAN), strengthening collective security through a North Atlantic alliance (implemented in March 1949 as the North Atlantic Treaty Organization, or NATO), and a "bold new program" for technical assistance to underdeveloped nations (which became known as the POINT FOUR PROGRAM).

Further reading: Mortimer Adler, ed., *The Annals of America*, 18 vols. (Chicago: Encyclopaedia Britannica, 1968); *Inaugural Addresses of the Presidents of the United States from George Washington 1789 to George Bush 1989*, bicentennial ed. (Washington, D.C.: Government Printing Office, 1989); Davis N. Lott, *The Presidents Speak: the Inaugural Addresses of the American Presidents from Washington to Clinton* (New York: H. Holt, 1994); Halford Ryan, ed., *The Inaugural Addresses of Twentieth-Century American Presidents* (Westport, Conn.: Praeger, 1993).

Truman's Statement on Fundamentals of American Foreign Policy

Address delivered by U.S. president Harry S Truman on October 27, 1945, outlining a 12-point policy program based on U.S. military strength as a means to preserve world peace; to enforce peace terms ending World War II; to fulfill obligations to the United Nations; to protect the integrity and independence of the Western Hemisphere; and to defend the United States. He stated that the United States sought no territorial expansion; wanted sovereignty and self-government for all people; believed in the freedom of the seas and equal access to trade for all nations; believed in economic cooperation among nations; hoped to improve living conditions and establish "freedom from fear and freedom from want"; would promote freedom of expression and religion; and supported the United Nations. He announced a U.S. willingness "to use force if necessary to insure peace."

Further reading: Mortimer Adler, ed., *The Annals of America*, 18 vols. (Chicago: Encyclopaedia Britannica, 1968); Henry Steele Commager, ed., *Documents of American History*, 8th ed. (New York: Appleton-Century-Crofts, 1968); Donald R. McCoy, *The Presidency of Harry S. Truman* (Lawrence: University Press of Kansas, 1984); Dennis K. Merrill, ed., *Documentary History of the Truman Presidency*, 30 vols. (Bethesda, Md.: University Publications of America, 1995).

Truth and Reconciliation Commission Report, South African

Report of the commission established to investigate crimes committed in South Africa between March 1, 1960, when apartheid went into effect, and May 10, 1994, when Nelson Mandela became president of South Africa. Chaired by Desmond Tutu, Anglican archbishop of Johannesburg, the commission sought to provide "as complete a picture as possible of the nature, causes and extent of gross violations of human rights," and made recommendations regarding reparations, punishments, and amnesty. The 3,500-page report, published in October 1998, condemned the state of South Africa as the "primary perpetrator" of racially motivated human rights violations, but it also indicted black militant groups such as the African National Congress, of which Mandela had been the leader, and the Inkatha Freedom Party for "killing . . . civilians," both black and white. The report recommended that South African corporations be taxed in proportion to their market capitalization and the proceeds used to ease the poverty of South African blacks. It recommended prosecution of individuals who had committed gross violations of human rights, but it also suggested that amnesty be granted to "those who make full disclosure of all the relevant facts relating to acts associated with a political objective committed in the course of the conflicts of the past."

Further reading: BBC News, "Truth Report: Key Points," BBC Online Network, available online at http://news.bbc.co.uk/hi/english/special_report/1998/10/98.

Turgot's "Letters on the Freedom of the Grain Trade" (Lettres sur la Liberté du Commerce des Grains)

Seven letters written in October–December 1770 by Robert-Jacques Turgot, intendant (administrator) of Limoges, France, to French comptroller general Abbé Terray in defense of freedom in the grain trade. He was responding to Terray's circular ordering a ban on the export of corn when its price reached eight livres per quintal. The letters, written during Turgot's inspection tour of famine-stricken Limoges, reflect a tremendous vitality and spontaneity, a sound economic basis, and a conviction that restoration of free trade was essential to rescue the starving peasants from their misery. Turgot, a liberal economist and a distinguished member of the Physiocrats, blamed the government's practice of buying grain for Paris as having inflamed the uproar against free trade. Apparently, Terray never read the letters and, on December 23, 1770, promulgated legislation abolishing the internal and external freedom of trade.

See also: SIX EDICTS, TURGOT'S; TURGOT'S LETTER TO LOUIS XVI.

Further reading: Peter D. Groenewegen, ed. and trans., *The Economics of A.R.J. Turgot* (The Hague: Martinus Nijhoff, 1977); Malcolm Hill, *Statesman of the Enlightenment: The Life of Anne-Robert Turgot* (London: Othila Press, 1999).

Turgot's Letter to Louis XVI

Robert-Jacques Turgot's famous letter of August 24, 1774, to King Louis XVI, outlining his proposed plan of action as France's newly appointed comptroller general. The letter strikes a cautious, almost paternal tone since Turgot did not want to alienate the young, inexperienced king by proposing radical reforms, nor was he certain of his authority to implement such policies. Reiterating three basic principles—"No bankruptcy. No increase of taxes. No loans"—Turgot stressed that the solution was "to reduce expenditure below the revenue, and sufficiently below it" and apply these savings toward the "redemption of old debts." Turgot realized that these and other measures would make him unpopular and perhaps cause him to lose the confidence of the king (see SIX EDICTS, TURGOT'S). In that case, "I shall not regret losing a place which I never solicited. I am ready to resign it . . ." Finally, thanking the king for entrusting him with this tremendous responsibility, "a burden perhaps beyond my strength," he promised to do his best.

See also: TURGOT'S "LETTERS ON THE FREEDOM OF THE GRAIN TRADE."

Further reading: Peter D. Groenewegen, ed. and trans., *The Economics of A.R.J. Turgot* (The Hague: Martinus Nijhoff, 1977); Malcolm Hill, *Statesman of the Enlightenment: The Life of Anne-Robert Turgot* (London: Othila Press, 1999); Milton Viorst, ed., *The Great Documents of Western Civilization* (Philadelphia: Chilton Books, 1965).

Turgot's Six Edicts   See SIX EDICTS, TURGOT'S.

Turin, Treaty of (1381)

Peace pact concluded at Turin, Italy, on August 8, 1381, ending the War of Chioggia (1378–81) between Venice and Genoa and the Hungarian-Venetian War of 1378–81. The treaty was mediated by Count Amadeus VI of Savoy, who received the island of Tenedos and agreed (with Genoa) not to trade at the Crimean port of Sudak for two years. Venice, victorious against the Genoese but not the Hungarians, relinquished control of the entire Dalmatian area to the latter and the city of Trieste to Duke Leopold III of Austria. Venice also abolished privateering in Dalmatian ports, agreed to compensate the Hungarians with 1,000 ducats annually for ceasing their salt manufacture in the area, and regained trading privileges at Constantinople (Istanbul). Genoa's maritime greatness began to wane.

Further reading: Eugene L. Cox, *The Green Count of Savoy, Amadeus VI and Transalpine Savoy in the Fourteenth Century* (Princeton, N.J.: Princeton University Press, 1967).

Turin, Treaty of (1696)

Secret treaty concluded at Turin, Italy, on June 29, 1696, by Duke Victor Amadeus II of Savoy with King Louis XIV of France, after the duke deserted the GRAND ALLIANCE OF 1689 for not satisfying his demands. Its terms (unpublicized until July–August 1696) were drafted by Count R. de Fromlay Tessé (French military commander) and Count Giambattista Gropello (Savoy's minister of finance). Louis XIV extended himself to secure this crucial alliance by returning all the French conquests (Casale, Pinerolo, Nice, and Suza) to Victor Amadeus in exchange for his neutrality in the War of the League of Augsburg or Grand Alliance (1688–97). Together, their forces compelled the mighty alliance into evacuating Italy and guaranteeing her neutralization during the war. Louis XIV sealed the peace by arranging the marriage of his grandson, the duke of Burgundy, to the duke of Savoy's daughter.

Further reading: Geoffrey Symcox, *Victor Amadeus II: Absolutism in the Savoyard State 1675–1730* (London: Thames & Hudson, 1983).

Turin, Treaty of (1796).   See PARIS, TREATY OF (1796).

Turkey's Fundamental Law of 1921   See FUNDAMENTAL LAW OF 1921, TURKEY'S.

Turkey's National Pact   See NATIONAL PACT, TURKEY'S.

Turkish Constitution of 1982

New constitution for Turkey approved by an overwhelming majority of the voters in a referendum on November 7, 1982, providing for a single-chamber parliament (to be elected every five years) and for an executive branch (to be headed by a president elected by parliament). However, General Kenan Evren, head of state since a military takeover in 1980, was made president of the Turkish republic for a seven-year-term under provisions of the constitution, which had been drafted by a constituent assembly consisting of the six-member National Security Council (commanders of the armed forces) and members nominated by them. The constitution also established a cabinet responsible to parliament and an independent judiciary; it banned Marxist, totalitarian, trade-union, and religious fundamentalist politics. The military government gave up power after parliamentary elections in 1983, when the conservative Motherland Party won 212 of the 400 seats in parliament, the Populist Party won 117, and the National Democracy Party finished last with 71 seats.

Further reading: *The Constitution of the Republic of Turkey* (Ankara, Turkey: Prime Ministry, Directorate General of Press & Information, 1982); Metin Heper and Ahmet Evin, *State, Democracy, and the Military: Turkey in the 1980s* (New York: W. de Gruyter, 1988).

Turkmanchai, Treaty of

Treaty concluded at Turkmanchai, or Torkaman, on February 22, 1828, between Russia and Persia, ending the war (1825–28) between the two powers over possession of strategic sites in Transcaucasia. The dispute originated in the 18th century. Through the treaty, Persia accepted once again the terms already agreed upon in the 1813 Treaty of GULISTAN, notably Russia's possession of Daghestan, Georgia, and northern Azerbaijan and Persia's retention of southern Azerbaijan. (The Aras River marked the Russo-Persian boundary in general.) In addition, the treaty required Persia to recognize Russian annexation of eastern Armenia and several khanates in the Caucasus, and Persia agreed to pay Russia a large indemnity.

Further reading: William Monteith, *Kars and Erzeroum;*

with the Campaign of Prince Paskiewitch, in 1828 and 1829; and . . . the Treaty of Turcoman Chie and Adrianople (London: Longman, Brown, Green & Longmans, 1856).

Tuxtepec, Plan of

Proclamation at Tuxtepec, Mexico, by Mexican general Porfirio Díaz on January 1, 1876, signaling the beginning of an armed rebellion against President Sebastián Lerdo de Tejada of Mexico. Among the document's principal points were the call for the president's resignation, effective suffrage, and an end to presidential reelections. Although Díaz was finally installed as Mexico's constitutional president in 1877, the effective suffrage and no reelection issues were, ironically, rallying cries in forcing Díaz's resignation in 1910.

Further reading: Paul H. Garner, *Porfirio Diaz* (New York: Longman, 2001); Frank A. Knapp, *The Life of Sebastian Lerdo de Teja 1823–1889: A Study of Influence and Obscurity* (New York: Greenwood Press, 1968).

Twain's "Horrors of the German Language" Speech

Celebrated, humorous after-dinner speech given by American author Mark Twain (Samuel Clemens) to the Vienna Press Club in Austria on November 21, 1897. Then lecturing abroad to clear his heavy debts, Twain displayed his sense of self-mockery and irony with mastery. "The German language speak I not good," he said, delivering the entire speech as if it had been translated from German (keeping the cumbrous German word order in English). Syntactic reforms were needed, "then will you an elegant language possess, and afterward, when you some thing say will, will you at least yourself understand what you said had." Despite their "mile-long" sentences, the hospitable people of Vienna made "a foreigner" (Twain) welcome, he said at the end.

Further reading: Mark Twain, *Speeches* (New York: Oxford University Press, 1996).

Twain's "To a Person Sitting in Darkness"

Letter written by American author Mark Twain (Samuel Clemens) and published in the *North American Review* of February 1901, scathingly attacking imperialism. Twain asked: "Shall we go on conferring our Civilization upon the peoples that sit in darkness . . . Shall we bang right ahead in our old-time, loud, pious way . . . or shall we sober up and sit down and think it over first?" The game of exporting "the Blessings of Civilization" is the ruination of many countries, for it is done under the West's pretext of Christian magnanimity, love, mercy, and protection of the weak, when in fact "there is more money in it, more territory, more sovereignty, and other kinds of emolument, than there is in any other game that is played," Twain said.

Further reading: Mark Twain, *Huck Finn; Pudd'nhead Wilson; No. 44; The Mysterious Stranger; and Other Writings* (New York: Library of America, 2000); Mark Twain, *Following the*

Equator and Anti-Imperialist Essays (New York: Oxford University Press, 1996); Mark Twain, *The Family Mark Twain* (New York: Dorset Press, 1988).

Twelfth Amendment, U.S.   Amendment to the U.S. CONSTITUTION, passed by Congress in 1803 and ratified by the states the following year, stipulating that the electors in a presidential election cast one set of ballots for president and a separate set of ballots for vice president. Previously each elector had cast two votes without differentiating between the two offices; the candidate winning the most votes became president, while the person with the next highest number became vice president. The original system proved unsatisfactory after the development of political parties. The amendment was motivated by the election of 1800, which had resulted in a tie vote in the electoral college and had been resolved, after much political maneuvering, by the House of Representatives.

Further reading: Alan Brinkley, *American History: A Survey* (Boston: McGraw-Hill College, 1999); Kermit L. Hall et al., eds, *American Legal History: Cases and Materials*, 2d ed. (New York: Oxford University Press, 1996); Kermit L. Hall et al., eds., *The Oxford Companion to the Supreme Court of the United States* (New York: Oxford University Press, 1992); Frank N. Magill, ed., *Great Events from History: American Series*, 3 vols. (Englewood Cliffs, N.J.: Salem Press, 1975).

Twelve Articles, German   See PEASANTS' MANIFESTO, GERMAN.

Twelve Tables, Law of the   Fundamental code of law of ancient Rome, blazoned on 12 tablets (probably wooden) about 450 B.C. This compilation of the customary civil and criminal laws (only scattered quotations have survived) was mostly the work of an appointed commission of 10 magistrates (the decemviri), who responded to the plebeians' demand for written laws in order to end discrimination by patrician judges (who knew the laws orally). The 12 tables, which were a major legal source until the second century A.D., contained rules for lawsuits, thievery, loans, rights of paterfamilias, rights of guardians, property, trespassing and damages, estates, citizen rights, funeral rites, religious rites, and marriages. For example, sanction was given to the arrest and imprisonment of defaulting debtors, who could be sold into slavery by their creditors if there was no other way of recovering the debt. Sanction was also given to the patrician refusal to accept the legitimacy of intermarriage with plebeians and others. And no law could be enacted affecting the status of a citizen except by Rome's "greatest" assembly (probably the Curiae then).

See also: PUBLILIAN LAWS.

Further reading: Charles S. Lobingier, *The Evolution of the Roman Law from Before the Twelve Tables to the Corpus Juris*, 2d ed. (Omaha, Nebr.: Self-published 1923); Frank N. Magill,

ed., *Great Events from History: Ancient and Medieval Series*, 3 vols. (Englewood Cliffs, N.J.: Salem Press, 1972); S. P. Scott, ed., *The Civil Law, Including the Twelve Tables* New York: AMS Press, 1973).

Twelve Years' Truce (Truce of Antwerp)   Truce in 1609 temporarily ending the hostilities in the Eighty Years' War (1568–1648) between Spain and the United Provinces of the Netherlands. Dictated by mutual political and financial considerations, it represented a major setback for Spain, which was forced to accept (though not formally) the independence and sovereignty of the seven northern Dutch states (United Provinces) and to retract Spanish claims on behalf of the Dutch Catholics. The truce (1609–21) was a triumph for the chief Dutch negotiator, Johan van Oldenbarnevelt, who had played an important role in the Union of UTRECHT in 1579, though the fact that he represented only the province of Holland was to create serious dissensions within the Dutch republic of the northern Netherlands.

See also: ABJURATION, ACT OF; ARRAS, TREATY OF (1579); UTRECHT, UNION OF.

Further reading: John L. Motley, *History of the United Netherlands, from the Death of William the Silent to the Twelve Years' Truce, 1609* (New York: AMS Press, 1973); Paul Zumthor, *Daily Life in Rembrandt's Holland* (New York: Macmillan, 1963).

Twentieth Amendment, U.S.   Amendment to the U.S. CONSTITUTION, ratified in 1933, that provided that the terms of U.S. senators and representatives would begin on January 3 and the terms of the president and vice president would begin on January 20 following the national elections. Congress was also required to convene on January 3. Previously, these officials were elected in November of an even-numbered year and took office on March 4 following their election; and members of Congress met annually in December, more than a year after their election. By shortening the period between the election and the time the newly elected officials took office, the amendment reduced the terms of "lame ducks," officials who had not been reelected in November and presumably no longer represented their constituencies.

Further reading: Alan Brinkley, *American History: A Survey* (Boston: McGraw-Hill College, 1999); Kermit L. Hall et al., eds, *American Legal History: Cases and-Materials*, 2d ed. (New York: Oxford University Press, 1996); Kermit L. Hall et al., eds., *The Oxford Companion to the Supreme Court of the United States* (New York: Oxford University Press, 1992); Robert R. Mayer, *The Court and the American Crises, 1930–1952* (Danbury, Conn.: Grolier Educational, 1995).

Twenty-fifth Amendment, U.S.   Amendment to the U.S. CONSTITUTION, ratified in 1967, that provided for succession to office in the event of presidential or vice presidential death or disability. When the office of vice president is vacant, the president may appoint a new vice president, subject to confirmation by both houses of Congress. (This section of the amendment was first used in 1973, when Vice President Spiro T. Agnew resigned and President Richard M. Nixon appointed Gerald R. Ford as his successor.) The vice president may become acting president when the president declares himself incapacitated or when the vice president and other executive officials or a congressionally mandated body declare the president to be "unable to discharge the powers and duties of his office." The president resumes his office when he is no longer incapacitated.

Further reading: Alan Brinkley, *American History: A Survey* (Boston: McGraw-Hill College, 1999); Robert E. Gilbert, ed., *Managing Crisis: Presidential Disability and the Twenty-Fifth Amendment* (New York: Fordham University Press, 2000); Kermit L. Hall et al., eds, *American Legal History: Cases and Materials*, 2d ed. (New York: Oxford University Press, 1996); Kermit L. Hall et al., eds., *The Oxford Companion to the Supreme Court of the United States* (New York: Oxford University Press, 1992).

Twenty-first Amendment, U.S.

Amendment to the U.S. CONSTITUTION, passed by Congress and ratified in 1933, that repealed the EIGHTEENTH AMENDMENT, thus ending 14 years of national prohibition. The regulation of alcoholic beverages was thereby returned to the states. Even before ratification, Congress passed the so-called Beer Act, which permitted the manufacture of beverages containing no more than 3.2 percent alcohol. The Twenty-First Amendment was the first that Congress submitted to ratification by state conventions, rather than state legislatures.

Further reading: Alan Brinkley, *American History: A Survey* (Boston: McGraw-Hill College, 1999); Kermit L. Hall et al., eds, *American Legal History: Cases and Materials*, 2d ed. (New York: Oxford University Press, 1996); Kermit L. Hall et al., eds., *The Oxford Companion to the Supreme Court of the United States* (New York: Oxford University Press, 1992); Robert R. Mayer, *The Court and the American Crises, 1930–1952* (Danbury, Conn.: Grolier Educational, 1995).

Twenty-five Articles of Religion

Set of statements written by English evangelical preacher John Wesley for the formal organization of the Methodist Episcopal Church in America in 1784. Wesley's creed was adopted at a conference of American Methodist preachers in Baltimore, Maryland. It was a simpler and more liberal version of the creed of the Church of England. However, Wesley's articles made no mention of specific English theologics and of the Calvinist doctrine of predestination that said that salvation will come to only the deserving.

Further reading: Henry Wheeler, *History and Exposition of the Twenty-Five Articles of Religion of the Methodist Episcopal Church* (New York: Eaton & Mains, 1908).

Twenty-fourth Amendment, U.S.

Amendment to the U.S. CONSTITUTION, passed by Congress in 1962 and ratified by the states in 1964, that provided that the right to vote in a federal primary or general election cannot be denied because a voter fails to pay a poll tax or other tax. Poll taxes had served for many years to disenfranchise black and poor white voters, and corrupt candidates sometimes paid the taxes in exchange for voting support. After passage of the amendment, four states retained the poll tax for state elections, but in 1966 the Supreme Court, in *Harper v. Virginia State Board of Elections,* struck down such taxes as unconstitutional.

Further reading: Alan Brinkley, *American History: A Survey* (Boston: McGraw-Hill College, 1999); Kermit L. Hall et al., eds, *American Legal History: Cases and Materials*, 2d ed. (New York: Oxford University Press, 1996); Kermit L. Hall et al., eds., *The Oxford Companion to the Supreme Court of the United States* (New York: Oxford University Press, 1992); Arnold S. Rice, *The Warren Court, 1953–1969* (Danbury, Conn.: Grolier Educational, 1995).

Twenty-one Demands, Japan's

Demands presented by Japan to Premier Yuan Shikai (Yuan Shih-k'ai) of China on January 18, 1915, demanding that China accept conditions that would reduce her status to that of a Japanese vassal. The demands, separated into five groups, included China's agreement to the transfer of control in Shantung, including Kiaochow Bay, from Germany to Japan; the extension of Japan's lease on Port Arthur (Lushun) and Dairen (Dalian), with control of the South Manchurian and Antung-Mukden railways for 99 years, and Japan's control over southern Manchuria and eastern Inner Mongolia; Japan's possession of half of the interest in the Chinese Han Yeg-ping Company (which had iron, coal, and steel concerns); Japanese control over the Fukien coast, including islands off the coast; and employment of Japanese as political, military, and financial advisers. While this final demand was later withdrawn and others modified, Japan's influence in China was significantly increased through these demands.

Further reading: Frederick R. Dickinson, *War and National Reinvention: Japan in the Great War, 1914–1919* (Cambridge, Mass.: Harvard University Press, 1999); Noriko Kawamura, *Turbulence in the Pacific: Japanese-U.S. Relations during World War I* (Westport, Conn.: Praeger, 2000); Ge-Zay Wood, *The Twenty-One Demands, Japan versus China* (New York: Fleming H. Revell, 1921).

Twenty-second Amendment, U.S.

Amendment to the U.S. CONSTITUTION, passed by Congress in 1947 and ratified in 1951, that declared that no president could serve more than two full terms of office (and that no vice president who succeeded to the presidency and served more than two years of his predecessor's term could serve more than one full term). The amendment was passed after President Franklin D. Roosevelt broke the two-term tradition and was elected to four successive terms. Designed to limit presidential ambitions and prevent the rise of a popular autocrat, the amendment also precludes continued service by an experienced president and may weaken the authority of a president at the end of a second term.

Further reading: Alan Brinkley, *American History: A Survey* (Boston: McGraw-Hill College, 1999); Kermit L. Hall et al., eds, *American Legal History: Cases and Materials*, 2d ed. (New York: Oxford University Press, 1996); Kermit L. Hall et al., eds., *The Oxford Companion to the Supreme Court of the United States* (New York: Oxford University Press, 1992); Robert R. Mayer, *The Court and the American Crises, 1930–1952* (Danbury, Conn.: Grolier Educational, 1995).

Twenty-sixth Amendment, U.S.   Amendment to the U.S. CONSTITUTION, ratified in 1971, that gave U.S. citizens 18 years of age or older the right to vote in all elections—local, state, and federal. Previously the minimum voting age was 21. The amendment gained support during unrest connected with the Vietnam War (1956–75), which was fought largely by young men under the voting age. Public opinion was swayed by the discrepancy between requiring men to fight for their country and denying them the right to vote.

Further reading: Alan Brinkley, *American History: A Survey* (Boston: McGraw-Hill College, 1999); Arthur L. Galub, *The Burger Court, 1968–1984* (Danbury, Conn.: Grolier Educational, 1995); Kermit L. Hall et al., eds, *American Legal History: Cases and Materials*, 2d ed. (New York: Oxford University Press, 1996); Kermit L. Hall et al., eds., *The Oxford Companion to the Supreme Court of the United States* (New York: Oxford University Press, 1992).

Twenty-third Amendment, U.S.   Amendment to the U.S. CONSTITUTION, ratified in 1961, that gave residents of Washington, D.C., the right to vote in national elections for president and vice president. The district is entitled to as many electors as it would have if it were a state, though no more than the least populous state. The amendment did not, however, grant district residents voting representation in Congress.

Further reading: Alan Brinkley, *American History: A Survey* (Boston: McGraw-Hill College, 1999); Kermit L. Hall et al., eds, *American Legal History: Cases and Materials*, 2d ed. (New York: Oxford University Press, 1996); Kermit L. Hall et al., eds., *The Oxford Companion to the Supreme Court of the United States* (New York: Oxford University Press, 1992); Arnold S. Rice, *The Warren Court, 1953–1969* (Danbury, Conn.: Grolier Educational, 1995).

Two-Plus-Four Treaty   See TREATY ON THE FINAL SETTLEMENT WITH RESPECT TO GERMANY.

Two Thousand Words   Proclamation challenging the communist government of Czechoslovakia to carry out more democratic reforms; written by Czech journalist Ludvik Vaculik, signed by 70 prominent Czech citizens, and published in four Prague newspapers on June 27, 1968. Although conceding that many governmental officials were trying to rectify past grievances of citizens, the document argued that non–Communist Party members must take part in the reform process and that all Czech citizens must have a say in public and economic policy matters, elections, government composition, and human rights. In the document's closing statement, the signatories pledged to support the government in the event of foreign intervention; they were unfortunately so challenged on August 20–21, 1968, when Czechoslovakia was invaded and occupied by Soviet and other WARSAW PACT forces, thus effectively bringing an end to the "Prague Spring," which had seen a brief relaxation of oppression.

See also: CHARTER 77, CZECH.

Further reading: Miklos Kun, *Prague Spring, Prague Fall: Blank Spots of 1968* (Budapest, Hungary: Akademiai Kiado, 1999); Ludvik Vaculik, *A Cup of Coffee with My Interrogator: The Prague Chronicles of Ludvik Vaculik* (London: Readers International, 1987).

Tydings-McDuffie Act   U.S. legislation, sponsored by Senator Millard E. Tydings of Maryland and Representative John McDuffie of Alabama and enacted on March 24, 1934, that promised full independence for the Philippine Islands by 1946 and authorized the Philippine legislature to prepare a constitution. The Philippines were to become an autonomous commonwealth for the intervening period. A successor to the Hawes-Cutting Act of 1933, the Tydings-McDuffie measure also provided for the removal of U.S. military bases and for negotiations concerning U.S. naval bases. The Philippine legislature ratified the act on May 1, 1934, and the islands became independent on July 4, 1946.

Further reading: Henry Steele Commager, ed., *Documents of American History*, 8th ed. (New York: Appleton-Century-Crofts, 1968); Pio Duran, *Philippine Independence and the Far Eastern Question* (Manila: Community Publishers, 1935); Filemon Poblador, *Important Documents Illustrative of Philippine Independence* (Manila: Mrs. P. Auraullo Poblador, 1936); Carlos P. Romulo, *Mother America, a Living Story of Democracy* (Westport, Conn.: Greenwood Press, 1974).

Type (Typos)   Decree promulgated in A.D. 648 by the Byzantine emperor Constans II, flatly forbidding any religious discussion about the divine and human nature of Jesus Christ and the doctrine of monothelitism (see ECTHESIS). Like his predecessor, Emperor Constantine III, Constans II continued to support the monothelite heresy, but Pope Martin I denounced it at a Lateran Council he convened in A.D. 649. Constans later had the pope banished from Rome to the Crimea. The Type, favorable to monophysites, decreed that monothelites and orthodox Christians withhold all dissenting religious opinions in the hope of ending the controversy. Monothelitism eventually faded after the Council of Constantinople of A.D. 680–81 repudiated it.

Further reading: Catholic University of America, eds., *New Catholic Encyclopedia* (New York: McGraw-Hill, 1967).

U

Ubi Primum See BENEDICT XIV'S ENCYCLICAL OF 1740.

Uccialli, Treaty of Pact concluded by Italy at Uccialli (Acciali or Wichale, Ethiopia) on May 2, 1889, with Emperor Menelik II of Ethiopia, bringing an end to the Italo-Ethiopian War of 1887–89, which had originated over Italian premier Francesco Crispi's devotion to expanding Italian influence in northern Africa. Through the treaty Italy promised to provide Menelik with arms in order to defeat his rivals for the Ethiopian throne, which he had obtained only two months earlier; in return Menelik agreed to Italy's occupation of territory bordering Ethiopia and the Red Sea, today known as Eritrea. The Italians, however, interpreted the treaty to also mean that Italy had acquired a protectorate over Ethiopia. Menelik's declaration less than six months later that the Italians had misinterpreted the treaty and that there was no protectorate at all caused Italy great humiliation.

    See also: ADDIS ABABA, TREATY OF (1896).

    Further reading: Lapiso G. Dilebo, *The Italo-Ethiopian War of 1887–1896: From Dogali to Adwa* (Addis Ababa, Ethiopia: Artistic Printing Enterprise, 1996); Harold G. Marcus, *The Life and Times of Menelik II: Ethiopia, 1844–1913* (Lawrencevile, N.J.: Red Sea Press, 1995).

Ukraine Disarmament (Denuclearization) Accord

Trilateral agreement signed (January 14, 1994) in Moscow by the presidents of the United States, Russia, and Ukraine, establishing a schedule for the dismantling of Ukraine's nuclear arsenal (see MINSK AGREEMENT). Ukraine was given 10 months to deactivate all its modern strategic missiles and to ship 200 warheads from older missiles to Russia for dismantling. Russia would provide Ukraine with nuclear fuel for its civil nuclear reactors, pardon some of its oil and gas debts, and provide financial assistance worth almost $1 billion for disarmament. Russia would receive $60 million from the United States through bilateral trade deals. Over a seven-year period, Ukraine's remaining warheads would be similarly disposed of. Russia and the United States gave security assurances. The United States promised Ukraine $900 million in aid during 1994–95 for economic restructuring, food and oil imports, and transportation.

    Further reading: *Facts On File Cumulative News Digest* (New York: Facts On File, 1994).

Ukrainian Declaration of Sovereignty of 1990

Statement issued by the Ukrainian Supreme Soviet (parliament) in Kiev on July 16, 1990, declaring the "supremacy, independence, absolute authority, and indivisibility" of the Ukrainian republic's laws over national Soviet law. Much more radical than the recently adopted sovereignty decree in the neighboring Russian republic, the Ukrainian decree asseverated "independence and equal rights in external relations" and a "neutral government, which does not take part in military blocs." It also asserted the right to establish Ukrainian armed forces, citizenship, currency, and a banking system in the republic, the second most populous (with more than 51 million people) in the Soviet Union (the Russian republic was first, with more than 147 million residents).

Further reading: Roma Hadzewycz, trans., *Declaration on the State Sovereignty of Ukraine: Kiev, July 16 1990* (Ellicott City, Md.: Smoloskyp Publishers, 1990).

Ullmann v. United States

U.S. Supreme Court decision issued on March 26, 1956, upholding the Immunity Act of 1954, under which witnesses could be forced to testify in national security cases—in courts, grand juries, or congressional committees—by granting them immunity from prosecution for criminal actions they might admit. Ullmann, pleading the FIFTH AMENDMENT, had refused to testify about an espionage ring when questioned by a grand jury and a congressional committee. He was later granted immunity but argued that he could lose his job, his union membership, and eligibility for a passport, and could be subjected to public censure if he admitted any subversive activity. The Supreme Court ruled that the Fifth Amendment did protect against such noncriminal penalties.

Further reading: Kermit L. Hall et al., eds., *The Oxford Companion to the Supreme Court of the United States* (New York: Oxford University Press, 1992); United States Supreme Court, *United States Reports: Cases Adjudged in the Supreme Court at . . . and Rules Announced at . . .* (New York: Banks & Brothers, Law Publishers, 1884–1921; Washington, D.C.: Government Printing Office, 1922–).

Unabomber Manifesto (Industrial Society and Its Future)

Document written by American Ted Kaczynski, an antisocial recluse, calling for the violent overthrow of modern industrial society. Between 1978 and 1995, Kaczynski mailed 16 homemade bombs that killed three people and injured 23. Because his initial victims were professors of computer science or engineering and airline executives, he was dubbed "the Unabomber," *una* standing for "universities 'n' airlines." He eluded the Federal Bureau of Investigation (FBI) for 18 years, the longest manhunt in U.S. history. In 1995, he promised to detonate no more bombs if the *Washington Post* and the *New York Times* would print his manifesto in its entirety. They agreed, after much urging by the FBI's director and the U.S. attorney general; the manifesto ran in both papers that same year. The rambling, 35,000-word document claimed that industrial and technological developments "destabilized society [and] . . . made life unfulfilling." It claimed that the "restriction of freedom is unavoidable in industrial society," that "the 'bad' parts of technology cannot be separated from the 'good' parts," and that the system cannot be reformed, only destroyed. Shortly after the manifesto's publication, Kaczynski was captured and imprisoned for life without parole when his brother recognized the writing style and contacted the FBI.

Further reading: Public Access Networks Corporation, "The Unabomber's Manifesto," Panix.com, available online at http://www.panix.com/~clays/Una/index.html.

Unam Sanctam

Pope Boniface VIII's bull of November 18, 1302, directed against France's king Philip IV the Fair, asserting the supremacy of the church and, through it, of the pontiff in both spiritual and temporal matters. Declaring "there is one holy Catholic Apostolic Church" and that "outside of her there is no salvation or remission of sins," Boniface then used the analogy of the two swords to discuss the relationship between temporal and spiritual power. Both swords, he argued, "are in the power of the church," making the temporal authority necessarily subject to the spiritual, "for the truth itself declares that the spiritual power must establish the temporal power and pass judgment on it if it is not good." The final sentence, affirming "that submission on the part of every man to the bishop of Rome is altogether necessary for his salvation," greatly angered the French court and provoked Philip into attempting to imprison Boniface VIII.

See also: EXECRABILIS OF 1460; PISA, DECLARATION OF THE COUNCIL OF.

Further reading: Catholic University of America, eds., *New Catholic Encyclopedia* (New York: McGraw-Hill, 1967); Norton Downs, ed., *Basic Documents in Medieval History* (New York: Van Nostrand Reinhold, 1959); Anne Fremantle, *The Papal Encyclicals in Their Historical Context* (New York: Mentor-Omega Books, 1963); Milton Viorst, ed., *The Great Documents of Western Civilization* (Philadelphia: Chilton Books, 1965).

Uncle Tom's Cabin; or, Life Among the Lowly

Novel about the evil of slavery in the United States, written by American author Harriet Beecher Stowe and published serially in the antislavery weekly *Washington National Era* from June 1851 to April 1852, and published in book form in March 1852 by John P. Jewett & Co. in Boston. The central figure of the story, which was set in Kentucky and Louisiana, was Uncle Tom, an old slave who was faithful and obedient to his master, who was also a good man. The story related Tom's misfortunes, which included his sale by his master who was experiencing financial difficulties, his mistreatment by a Yankee overseer, and his eventual death, as well as the misfortunes of several other slaves. Throughout Stowe sought to show the cruelty and injustice of slavery as a system. Although her opponents argued that the story did not reflect the system accurately, the book was enormously popular, having sold more than 1 million copies by 1860, and was regarded as a major contribution to the abolitionist movement.

Further reading: Mortimer Adler, ed., *The Annals of America*, 18 vols. (Chicago: Encyclopaedia Britannica, 1968); Frank N. Magill, ed., *Great Events from History: American Series*, 3 vols. (Englewood Cliffs, N.J.: Salem Press, 1975); *Uncle*

Tom's Cabin by Harriet Beecher Stowe (New York: Bantam Books, 1981).

Underwood-Simmons Tariff Act (Underwood Act, U.S. Tariff of 1913)

Federal legislation cosponsored by Congressman Oscar W. Underwood and Senator Furnifold M. Simmons and passed on October 33, 1913, lowering the average tariff duties to about 26 percent of the value of an imported item and putting iron, steel, and raw wool on the free list; sugar was added to the free list in 1916. Succeeding the PAYNE-ALDRICH TARIFF, the Underwood Simmons Act was called a "competitive tariff" and was supported by the Democratic Party. Its benefits, however, were swamped by the economic effects of World War I (1914–18).

Further reading: Henry Steele Commager, ed., *Documents of American History*, 8th ed. (New York: Appleton-Century-Crofts, 1968); F. W. Taussig, *The Tariff History of the United States*, 6th ed. (New York: G. P. Putnam's Sons, 1914).

Uniformity, Act of

English law passed in May 1662, as the second act of the CLARENDON CODE. It required clergymen and schoolmasters to swear loyalty to the *Book of COMMON PRAYER*, to censure rebellion and renounce the SOLEMN LEAGUE AND COVENANT OF 1643. Clergymen with livings (benefices) were to be ordained, and schoolmasters licensed, by a bishop. Penalty for a first offense was three months imprisonment and, for a second offense, imprisonment with a fine of £5. Dissenters received no concessions. For failing to comply with the provisions of the act, 1,760 ministers and 150 dons and schoolmasters were ejected from their posts, creating the nonconformist clergy. The TOLERATION ACT OF 1689 eased the situation for Protestant dissenters, but the Roman Catholics had to wait until the acts of 1791 and 1829.

Further reading: Gerald L. Bray, *Documents of the English Reformation* (Minneapolis: Fortress Press, 1994); John Chandos, *In God's Name: Examples of Preaching in England from the Act of Supremacy to the Act of Uniformity, 1534–1662* (Indianapolis, Ind.: Bobbs-Merrill, 1971); George Gould and Peter Bayne, *Documents Relating to the Settlement of the Church of England by the Act of Uniformity of 1662* (London: W. Kent, 1979).

Uniformity, Acts of

Series of acts (1549–1662) enforcing various services of the reformed church in England (the Anglican Church). The first, enacted on January 21, 1549, by King Edward VI, made the use of the first *Book of COMMON PRAYER* compulsory in Mass and in all public services. These services were to be conducted in English except at universities. Noncompliance or denigration of the book was punished. Edward's second uniformity act (March 9–April 14, 1552) substituted a revised version of the book and introduced penalties for nonattendance at church or public services. On June 24, 1559, Queen Elizabeth I imposed a modified form of the 1552 Prayer Book, abolished the Catholic Mass,

restored the Protestant communion service, reinstated the Protestant clergy (deprived during the reign of Mary I), and increased the penalties for noncompliance. By the fourth act (May 19, 1662), King Charles II required all ministers, pastors, schoolmasters, and lecturers to subscribe to the Prayer Book revised recently by a church convocation, to denounce rebellion against the king, and to reject the Solemn League and Covenant. Clergymen not properly ordained lost their livings as did over 2,000 ministers who refused to conform, creating the nonconformist clergy.

See also: CLARENDON CODE; TEST ACT OF 1673; TOLERATION ACT OF 1689.

Further reading: Gerald L. Bray, *Documents of the English Reformation* (Minneapolis: Fortress Press, 1994); John Chandos, *In God's Name: Examples of Preaching in England from the Act of Supremacy to the Act of Uniformity, 1534–1662* (Indianapolis, Ind.: Bobbs-Merrill, 1971); George Gould and Peter Bayne, *Documents Relating to the Settlement of the Church of England by the Act of Uniformity of 1662* (London: W. Kent, 1979); Lewis W. Spitz, *The Protestant Reformation* (Englewood Cliffs, N.J.: Prentice-Hall, 1966).

Unigenitus (1713)

Pope Clement XI's bull *Unigenitus Dei Filius* issued on September 8, 1713; it condemned 101 propositions from Jansenist Pasquier Quesnel's 40-year-old *Réflexions Morales sur le Nouveau Testament* and also denounced Cornelis Jansen's AUGUSTINUS. Intended to settle the Jansenist controversy (see IN EMINENTI; CUM OCCASIONE IMPRESSIONIS LIBRI) by issuing a final condemnation of its basic doctrines, the bull (instigated by France's king Louis XIV) only inflamed it since the French clergy and the *parlements* refused to accept it except conditionally. On February 15, 1714, Louis XIV forced the Parlement of Paris to register the decree. The archbishop of Paris refused and was condemned (March 28, 1714). Opposition to the bull intensified after the king's death in 1715, and the Jansenist leaders referred the issue to a general council. The pope reacted by excommunicating (August 28, 1718) the "appellants." Parlement finally registered the bull (December 4, 1720), after inserting a provision guaranteeing the liberties of the French church. The controversy continued, however.

See also: UNIGENITUS (1730).

Further reading: Catholic University of America, eds., *New Catholic Encyclopedia* (New York: McGraw-Hill, 1967); Anne Fremantle, *The Papal Encyclicals in Their Historical Context* (New York: Mentor-Omega Books, 1963); B. Robert Kreiser, *Miracles, Convulsions, and Ecclesiastical Politics in Early Eighteenth-Century Paris* (Princeton, N.J.: Princeton University Press, 1978).

Unigenitus (1730)

King Louis XV's declaration on March 24, 1730, recognizing the 1713 *UNIGENITUS* as a law of France and requiring all clergymen to accept it unreservedly. Promulgated to reestablish law and order and respect for authority, it condemned the recent religious disturbances, proposing instead a different interpretation of the bull. Clergy who did not sign the formulary on Jansenism would not be ordained or given benefices, nor would they receive redress from the secular courts. Parlement, viewing it as authoritarian and an infringement on the traditional Gallican liberties, was nevertheless compelled to register the decree though it mounted a campaign of confrontation against the crown. Elsewhere, bishops rampantly persecuted, and sometimes even suspended, dissident clergy. The Parlement of Paris's support for the ousted clergy set the bishops against it, escalating the multifaceted confrontation that continued intermittently through the next two decades.

Further reading: B. Robert Kreiser, *Miracles, Convulsions, and Ecclesiastical Politics in Early Eighteenth-Century Paris* (Princeton, N.J.: Princeton University Press, 1978).

Union, Act of (Union of England and Scotland)

Successful legislation initiated in England by Sidney Godolphin, Robert Harley, and the Whigs for the formal union of Scotland with England on May 1, 1707, under the common flag of Great Britain. The separate Scottish Parliament was dissolved, with Scotland to be represented by 16 peers in the House of Lords and 45 members in the House of Commons. The measure was introduced because Scotland had been overlooked in the 1701 English Act of SETTLEMENT and there was always the risk that it might choose its own king and engage in policies running counter to English interests, particularly during the War of the Spanish Succession (1701–14). The Scottish national debt was liquidated and shareholders in the Company of Scotland paid off. Scotland retained her law and church. The adoption of free trade and uniform coinage, weights, measures, and fiscal systems brought great advantages to both countries and the Anglo-Scottish union remained remarkably free of the bitterness that characterized England's relations with Ireland and the American colonies.

Further reading: Randolph L. Braham, ed., *Documents on Major European Governments* (New York: Knopf/Borzoi, 1966); John Clerk, *History of the Union of Scotland and England* (Edinburgh, Scotland: Pillans & Wilson, 1993); Brian P. Levack, *The Formation of the British State: England, Scotland, and the Union, 1603–1707* (New York: Oxford University Press, 1987); Joel H. Wiener, ed., *Great Britain—The Lion at Home: A Documentary History of Domestic Policy (1689–1973)*, 4 vols. (New York: Chelsea House, 1974).

Union, Act of (Union of Sweden and Norway)

November 4, 1814, act ratified by the Norwegian and Swedish assemblies on July 31 and August 1, 1815, respectively, thus endorsing the union between the two states provided by the Convention of MOSS. Specifically, the act confirmed the election of Swedish king Charles XIII to the Norwegian throne and confirmed that the union between the two states was based upon the agreement of two independent and equal states to share the Swedish crown in common. The act thus obscured the fact that the Swedes had invaded Norway and had all but forced them to agree to a union with Sweden. Following the union, the Norwegians were not really to enjoy complete sovereignty, particularly with respect to foreign affairs.

See also: KIEL, TREATY OF.

Further reading: Raymond E. Lindgren, *Norway-Sweden: Union, Disunion, and Scandanavian Integration* (Princeton, N.J.: Princeton University Press, 1959); Fridtjof Nansen, *Norway and the Union with Sweden* (New York: Macmillan, 1905).

Union, Act of (Union of Upper and Lower Canada)

Act passed by the British Parliament on July 23, 1840, and proclaimed in Montreal on February 10, 1841, providing for the union of Lower Canada (Quebec) and Upper Canada (Ontario). Through the act these two provinces were united to form the Province of Canada, and a single government, consisting of a governor, an appointed legislative council, and popularly elected legislative assembly, was provided for. In addition, English was made the language of official use in government, and provision was made for meeting the government's administrative costs. The act followed Lord Durham's recommendations (see DURHAM'S REPORT) for union, which, Durham believed, would reduce racial tensions by facilitating the assimilation of French-speaking Canadians into an English-speaking culture. The act was opposed by both conservatives and French Canadians.

See also: HOWE'S LETTERS TO LORD JOHN RUSSELL; NINETY-TWO RESOLUTIONS, PAPINEAU'S; TEN RESOLUTIONS, RUSSELL'S.

Further reading: R. C. Brown and M. E. Prang, eds., *Canadian Historical Documents Series*, 3 vols. (Scarborough, Canada: Prentice-Hall of Canada, 1966); J. Fernand Tanguay, *Canada 125, Its Constitutions 1763–1992: Evolution of a Democracy* (Montreal: Canada Communications Group, 1992).

Union, Acts of (Union of Wales and England)

Statutes in 1536 and 1543 during King Henry the VIII's reign, introducing major English administrative changes in Wales and bringing it under parliamentary control. The first act destroyed the authority of the Welsh Marcher lords in the east and south by incorporating their 136 self-governing lordships into seven new counties (in addition to the six already existing in the principality of North Wales). Each county secured representation in the English Parliament at Westminster. All 13 counties in Wales were then reorganized according to the English model—governed by justices of the peace and sharing the same taxation and common law systems. English was declared the official language. The act of 1543 abolished the Marcher system completely, created four courts of Great Sessions with a permanent judiciary, and strengthened the earlier legislation. Together, the acts gradually helped bring a measure of political stability to Wales.

Further reading: John A. Andrews and David J. L. Davies, eds., *Welsh Studies in Public Law* (Cardiff: University of Wales, 1970); Glanmor Williams, *Wales and the Act of Union* (Bangor, Wales: Headstart History, 1992).

Union and Security, Act of   See UNITY (UNION) AND SECURITY, ACT OF.

Union with Ireland, British Act of   Legislation, effective on January 1, 1801, passed by the British and Irish parliaments for the formal unification of Great Britain (England, Wales, and Scotland) and Ireland as the United Kingdom. Proposed by British prime minister William Pitt as a possible solution to the Irish problem (Catholic Irish political inequality and desire for independence), it provided for the abolition of the Irish Parliament and the formation of one parliament— the Parliament of the United Kingdom—at which Ireland would be represented by four spiritual peers or lords (attending by rotation), 28 representative peers, and 100 Irish members of the House of Commons. The churches of Ireland and Britain were to be merged into one Protestant Episcopalian church. Irish resistance to the union was overcome by promises of concessions to Roman Catholics. But Britain's king George III refused to honor these, and thus Pitt resigned on February 3, 1801. The union broke up on January 14, 1922.

Further reading: Desmond Bowen, *The Protestant Crusade in Ireland, 1800–70: A Study of Protestant-Catholic Relations Between the Act of Union and Disestablishment* (Dublin: Gill & Macmillan, 1978); Randolph L. Braham, ed., *Documents on Major European Governments* (New York: Knopf/Borzoi, 1966); Patrick M. Geoghegan, *The Irish Act of Union: A Study in High Politics, 1798–1801* (New York: St. Martin's Press, 1999); Frank N. Magill, ed., *Great Events from History: Modern European Series*, 3 vols. (Englewood Cliffs, N.J.: Salem Press, 1973).

United Nations Charter   Charter signed on June 26, 1945, formally establishing the United Nations (UN), a new international peace organization to succeed the League of Nations (see LEAGUE OF NATIONS COVENANT). The UN officially came into existence when the required number of nations (29) ratified the charter on October 24, 1945. Finalized during the San Francisco Conference (April 25–June 26, 1945) on the basis of previous discussions, the charter's preamble defined the principles of the UN: to prevent war and maintain peace and security, foster friendly relations between nations, and create a climate of cooperation to help resolve pressing international problems. Human rights, justice, social progress, and better living standards were also emphasized as UN purposes. The charter, endorsed originally by 51 members (countries), consisted of 19 chapters and 111 articles. It declared that the UN would operate principally through its six organs: the Security Council, the General Assembly, the Trusteeship Council, the International Court of Justice, the Economic and Social Council, and the Secretariat. The UN's permanent home is in New York City.

See also: YALTA AGREEMENT.

Further reading: Mortimer Adler, ed., *The Annals of America*, 18 vols. (Chicago: Encyclopedia Britannica, 1968); *American Jurisprudence*, 2d ed., Desk Book (N.p.: West Group, 1998); Louis L. Snyder, ed., *Fifty Major Documents of the Twentieth Century* (Princeton, N.J.: D. Van Nostrand, 1955); Milton Viorst, ed., *The Great Documents of Western Civilization* (Philadelphia: Chilton Books, 1965).

United Nations Convention Against Torture (and other Cruel, Inhuman or Degrading Treatment or Punishment)   Agreement adopted by the General Assembly of the United Nations on December 10, 1984 (implemented June 26, 1987), prohibiting torture (defined in Article 1) under any circumstances and by any person whatsoever. Signatory states would take measures to prevent such "acts of torture" in the future by treating them as criminal offenses and punishing them accordingly. Also, law enforcement officials would be educated in this regard. The convention established a Committee Against Torture (10 experts elected by secret ballot for a two-year term), which would examine complaints and submit its report within 12 months. Countries could propose amendments or denounce the convention (ratified or acceded to by 130 states as of August 21, 2002) through the UN secretary general.

Further information: Office of the High Commissioner for Human Rights, "Convention against Torture and other Cruel, Inhuman or Degrading Treatment or Punishments," Office of the High Commissioner for Human Rights, available online at http//:www.unhchr.ch/html/menu3/b/h_cat39.htm.

United Nations Convention on the Law of the Sea   Convention (acronym UNCLOS) establishing an international law of the sea; signed on December 10, 1982, in Montego Bay, Jamaica, by 119 nations. It defined four maritime boundaries and proposed the creation of the International Sea-Bed Authority to develop the resources of the area beyond the continental shelf. An antimonopoly clause was inserted to prevent any one nation from obtaining a disproportionately large share of the seabed. The signatories were bound to protect marine life, take steps to prevent and control marine pollution, and participate in drafting international standards of environmental protection. Peaceful scientific research would be allowed in the exclusive economic zone (EEZ) and on the continental shelf with the permission of the coastal states. UNCLOS, not signed by the United Kingdom, the United States, and the Federal Republic of Germany, also provided for the development and transfer of marine technology and for a peaceful settlement of disputes.

Further reading: Henry W. Degenhardt, ed., *Treaties and Alliances of the World*, 4th ed. (Detroit: Gale Research, 1986); *Everyone's United Nations: A Handbook on the Work of the*

United Nations (New York: United Nations, 1986); J. A. S. Grenville and Bernard Wasserstein, *The Major International Treaties since 1945: A History and Guide with Texts* (New York: Methuen, 1987; New York: United Nations, 1997).

United Nations Declaration of Commitment on HIV/AIDS

Nonbinding declaration adopted on June 27, 2001, by consensus by the 189-member General Assembly of the United Nations, establishing specific targets to be achieved in the fight against HIV/AIDS. The 16-page declaration concluded a special three-day session, the first ever convened by the United Nations on a health issue. Member countries agreed to develop and integrate, by 2003, national education and preventive strategies and funding plans for them. Among the goals to be achieved by 2005 were a 25 percent reduction in HIV/AIDs cases and improved access to information for at least 90 percent of those 15 to 24 years old, a "supportive" working environment for AIDS patients, 20 percent reduction (50 percent by 2010) in infant infections, services to at least 80 percent of pregnant women, improved access to preventive services for migrant workers, programs that encourage responsible sexual behavior, "including abstinence and fidelity," and annual expenditures of $7 to $10 billion on these programs by developing countries. It called for legislation to end discrimination against HIV/AIDS patients and women (especially violent and abusive practices) and for creating "on an urgent basis" a global HIV/AIDS fund to help combat the severe AIDS crisis in Africa and the Caribbean.

Further reading: United Nations Department of Public Information, "Global Crisis–Global Action Special Sessions Bulletin No 1," United Nations Special Session on HIV/AIDS, available online at http://www.un.org/ga/aids/bulletin_1.htm.

United Nations Declaration of January 1, 1942

Joint declaration by which 26 signatory nations affirmed the purposes and principles of the ATLANTIC CHARTER and were united in fighting the Axis countries of Germany, Italy, and Japan, and each nation pledged not to make a separate peace with them. The Atlantic Charter had affirmed the common fight of the United States and Britain against Nazi Germany and called for the abandonment of the use of force to settle international disputes and for a general disarmament, pending the "establishment of a wider and permanent system of general security." Signed in Washington, D.C., on New Year's Day 1942, the declaration "may be adhered to by other nations which are, or which may be, rendering material assistance and contributions in the struggle for victory over Hitlerism." It served as a forerunner to the later formation of the United Nations organization (see UNITED NATIONS CHARTER).

Further reading: Avalon Project at the Yale Law School, "Declaration by the United Nations. January 1, 1942," Avalon Project website, available online at http://www.yale.edu/lawweb/avalon/decade/decade03.htm/; Louis L. Snyder, ed.,

Fifty Major Documents of the Twentieth Century (Princeton, N.J.: Van Nostrand/Anvil, 1956).

United Nations Declaration on Decolonization

Part of Resolution 1514-XV, called "Declaration on the Granting of Independence to Colonial Countries and Peoples," sponsored by 43 African and Asian countries and adopted by the United Nations General Assembly in December 1960. Directed primarily against Spain, Portugal, South Africa, and Southern Rhodesia, the declaration censured colonialism and urged immediate action in trust and non-self-governing territories "to transfer all powers to the peoples . . . without any conditions or reservations, in accordance with their freely expressed will and desire, without any distinction as to race, creed or color." The resolution was adopted by a vote of 89 to 0, nine countries abstaining. The following year, another U.N. resolution (1654-XVI) established a 17-member committee to study and report on the implementation of Resolution 1514. In 1962, seven more members were added and the Committee of Twenty-four became the United Nations' watchdog on decolonization.

Further reading: Henry W. Degenhardt, ed., *Treaties and Alliances of the World*, 4th ed. (Detroit: Gale Research, 1986); *Everyone's United Nations: A Handbook on the Work of the United Nations* (New York: United Nations, 1986); A. G. Mezerik, ed., *Colonialism and the United Nations: Decolonization Declaration* (New York: International Review Service, 1964); *The United Nations and Decolonization: Summary of the Work of the Special Committee of Twenty-Four* (New York: United Nations, 1965).

United Nations Resolution 181

Resolution 181-II passed on November 29, 1947, by the United Nations General Assembly, providing for the partition of Palestine into two separate states. It established an Arab state (11,000 sq. km.), a Jewish state (14,000 sq. km.), and an internationally administered *corpus separatum* consisting of Jerusalem, Bethlehem, and their suburbs. Thus, the proposed Jewish state, containing one-third of Palestine's total population, was allotted more than 56 percent of the land. The resolution appointed a five-member commission to oversee the transition period. It also guaranteed human, civil, political, economic, and religious rights for all Palestinians. The decision, based on the report of the United Nations Special Committee on Palestine (UNSCOP), was immediately rejected by the Arabs. Thirty-three member countries voted in favor, 10 abstained, and 14 voted against the resolution (Egypt, Iran, Lebanon, Pakistan, Saudi Arabia, and Syria refused to recognize the partition). Implementation of the plan sparked anew the Arab-Israeli conflict, which remains unresolved today.

See also: BALFOUR DECLARATION; WHITE PAPER OF 1939, BRITISH; WOODHEAD REPORT.

Further reading: *Everyone's United Nations: A Handbook on the Work of the United Nations* (New York: United Nations,

1986); Bernard Reich, ed., *Arab-Israeli Conflict and Conciliation: A Documentary History* (Westport, Conn.: Greenwood Press, 1995).

United Nations Resolution 212 Resolution 212 passed by the General Assembly of the United Nations on November 19, 1948, calling for the creation of an administrative body to initiate and coordinate relief efforts for over a half million Palestinian refugees and for the appointment of a director to oversee these efforts. Adopted unanimously, the resolution also approved the establishment of a $30 million fund for this purpose, envisaging that most of the money would be raised through voluntary contributions from member countries. The secretary general of the United Nations was requested to immediately advance $5 million from the working capital fund, so that the campaign for contributions could begin. Finally, the United Nations was urged to seek the active cooperation of other international organizations such as the World Health Organization, the Food and Agriculture Organization, and the International Refugee Organization.

Further reading: *Everyone's United Nations: A Handbook on the Work of the United Nations* (New York: United Nations, 1986); Benjamin Schiff, *Refugees unto the Third Generation: UN Aid to Palestinians* (Syracuse, N.Y.: Syracuse University Press, 1995).

United Nations Resolution 242 Resolution 242 "concerning principles for a just and lasting peace in the Middle East," passed unanimously by the Security Council of the United Nations on November 22, 1967. This British proposed resolution expressed concern about the "grave situation" in the region, emphasized the "inadmissibility of the acquisition of territory by war," declared that Israel should withdraw her forces from the occupied territories (taken by Israeli forces during the Arab-Israeli War of 1967 [Six-Day War, June 5–10]), and urged the "termination of all claims or states of belligerency" as well as recognition of every state's right to live in peace "free from threats or acts of force." Affirming the need to guarantee freedom of navigation through international waterways, to resolve the Palestinian refugee issue, and to guarantee "the territorial inviolability and political independence of every state in the area," the resolution requested the United Nations' secretary general to appoint a special representative to coordinate peace efforts in the Middle East and to report on progress to the Security Council.

Further reading: Adnan Abu Odeh, *UN Security Council Resolution 242 :The Building Block of Peacemaking* (Washington, D.C.: Washington Institute for Near East Policy, 1993); Jody Boudreault, et al., *U.S. Official Statements Regarding UN Resolution 242* (Washington, D.C.: Institute for Palestine Studies, 1992); *Everyone's United Nations: A Handbook on the Work of the United Nations* (New York: United Nations, 1986); Bernard Reich, ed., *Arab-Israeli Conflict and Conciliation: A*

Documentary History (Westport, Conn.: Greenwood Press, 1995).

United Nations Resolution 338 Resolution 338 adopted by the Security Council of the United Nations on October 22, 1973, attempting to end the ongoing Arab-Israeli War of 1973 (October War). It called on all parties "to cease all firing and terminate all military activity immediately" within 12 hours of the resolution's adoption. Following a cease-fire, the parties were to begin implementing in full the UNITED NATIONS RESOLUTION 242, adopted by the Security Council in 1967. Resolution 338 also proposed that peace negotiations be conducted simultaneously "between the parties concerned under appropriate auspices aimed at establishing a just and durable peace in the Middle East." But fighting continued until a ceasefire agreement was signed on November 11, 1973.

Further reading: Ahron Bregman, *Israel's Wars, 1947–93* (New York: Routledge, 2000); *Everyone's United Nations: A Handbook on the Work of the United Nations* (New York: United Nations, 1986); Bernard Reich, ed., *Arab-Israeli Conflict and Conciliation: A Documentary History* (Westport, Conn.: Greenwood Press, 1995).

United Nations Resolution 661 Resolution 661, adopted by the Security Council of the United Nations on August 6, 1990, called for a worldwide economic embargo on Iraq for invading and occupying Kuwait (August 2, 1990). It reaffirmed Resolution 660 in its condemnation of Iraq, which had "usurped the authority of the legitimate Government of Kuwait." The sanctions of Resolution 661 prohibited all members of the United Nations from buying oil from either Iraq or occupied Kuwait and from having virtually any other commercial, financial, or military dealings with them. But "supplies intended strictly for medical purposes and, in humanitarian circumstances, foodstuffs" were items exempted from the resolution, which passed by a vote of 13 to 0, with Yemen (the only Arab nation among the council's 10 rotating members) and Cuba abstaining. The council's five permanent members—Britain, France, the United States, China, and the Soviet Union (all of which have veto power)—supported the resolution. U.S. president George H. W. Bush then ordered American naval and land forces to Saudi Arabia to defend the oilfields there from an Iraqi attack and to enforce the embargo with a blockade; Iraq's president Saddam Hussein responded by annexing Kuwait.

Further reading: Patrick Clawson, *How Has Saddam Hussein Survived? Economic Sanctions, 1990–93* (Washington, D.C.: Institute for National Strategic Studies, National Defense University, 1993); Musallam Ali Musallam, *The Iraqi Invasion of Kuwait: Saddam Hussein, His State and International Power Politics* (New York: British Academic Press, 1996).

United Nations Resolution 678 Resolution of the United Nations (UN) Security Council calling for the forcible expulsion of the military forces of Iraq from Kuwait. On August 2, 1990, Iraq invaded Kuwait and began taking control of the country, including its extensive oil wells. That same day, the UN Security Council issued Resolution 660, which condemned the invasion and demanded that Iraqi forces withdraw to the positions they had held before the invasion. When this and further resolutions failed to achieve Iraqi withdrawal, on November 29, 1990, the Security Council adopted Resolution 678. This resolution called on Iraq to withdraw completely from Kuwait by January 15, 1991. If Iraq failed to comply, the resolution authorized and called upon member states to use "all necessary means . . . to restore international peace and security in the area." On January 12, 1991, the U.S. Congress passed a joint resolution authorizing the use of U.S. military force to enforce Resolution 678, thus leading to the involvement of the United States and its allies in the Persian Gulf War of 1991.

Further reading: University of Minnesota Human Rights Center, "United Nations Security Council Resolution 660," Peace Resource Center, Available online at http://www1 .umn.edu/humanrts/peace/docs/scres660.html; University of Minnesota Human Rights Center, "United Nations Security Council Resolution 678," Peace Resource Center, available online at http://www1.umn.edu/humanrts/peace/docs/scres 678.html.

United Nations Resolution 1373 Resolution of the United Nations (UN) Security Council that presented the UN strategy for fighting international terrorism in the wake of the terrorist attacks of September 11, 2001, on the United States. Passed on September 28, 2001, the resolution called on UN member states to fight terrorism within their borders by seizing or freezing the assets of terrorist organizations, refusing to offer any help or sanctuary whatsoever to terrorist groups, and actively prosecuting terrorists. It called on member states to cooperate with one another by sharing information concerning terrorist activities, by apprehending suspected terrorists wanted in another state, and by preventing the movement of terrorists from one state to another. It urged member states to ratify and implement as soon as possible the existing UN conventions and protocols concerning international terrorism. It also created a committee of the Security Council to monitor the implementation of the measures called for in the resolution and ordered it to report within 90 days as to how member states were responding.

Further reading: United Nations Security Council, "Security Council Unanimously Adopts Wide-Ranging Anti-Terrorism Resolution; Calls for Suppressing Financing, Improving International Cooperation," Information Technology Section, Department of Public Information, United Nations, available online at http://www.un.org/News/Press/ docs/2001/sc7158.doc.htm.

United Nations Resolution 1402 Resolution passed on March 30, 2002, by the United Nations Security Council condemning developments in the Middle East. In early 2002, a series of suicide bombings protesting Israeli actions in territory under the nominal control of the Palestinian Authority terrorized several Israeli cities. In retaliation, the Israeli government sent troops to surround the headquarters of Yasir Arafat, the head of the Palestinian Authority, in Ramallah. The resolution called for the Israelis to withdraw their troops from Ramallah. It also called upon both sides to negotiate an immediate cease-fire and to work with the special envoy the United Nations was dispatching to the region. It reaffirmed UNITED NATIONS RESOLUTION 242 and UNITED NATIONS RESOLUTION 338, which called for "a just and lasting peace in the Middle East," and Resolution 1397 which demanded an immediate end to "all acts of terror, provocation, incitement and destruction." Most notably, the resolution expressed "grave concern" over the suicide bombings, the closest the Security Council had ever come to condemning terrorist attacks against Israel.

Further reading: "Resolution 1402 (2002)," United Nations and Israel, available online at http://christianaction forisrael.org/un/1402.html.

United Nations Resolution 3236 Resolution adopted on November 22, 1974, by the United Nations General Assembly, expressing "grave concern" over the question of Palestine, which "continues to endanger international peace and security." It was passed soon after Chairman Yasir Arafat of the Palestine Liberation Organization (PLO) addressed the General Assembly. One of many resolutions (see UNITED NATIONS RESOLUTION 181; UNITED NATIONS RESOLUTION 242) dealing with this issue, it reaffirmed the Palestinian "right to self-determination without external interference," and their "inalienable right" of return to their homes and property. Without "full respect for and realization of" these rights and the inclusion of the Palestinians as a "principal party," there could not be "a just and lasting peace" in the region. It urged the world community to support the Palestinian struggle and asked the Secretary General of the United Nations to open dialogue with the PLO and to report on it at the General Assembly's next session.

Further reading: George J. Tomeh, ed., *United Nations Resolutions on Palestine and the Arab-Israeli Conflict*, vol. 1: *1947–1974* (Washington, D.C.: Institute for Palestine Studies, 1975).

United Nations Resolution 3379 Resolution 3379-XXX adopted by the General Assembly of the United Nations on November 10, 1975, declaring Zionism as "a form of racism and racial discrimination." Part of an apparent effort by the United Nations and other organizations to end racial discrimination worldwide, it passed by a vote of 72 to 35, with 32 member countries abstaining and three members absent. The General Assembly recalled its earlier resolutions: 1904-XVIII of November 20, 1963, condemning any form of racial discrimination, and 3151G-XXVIII of December 14, 1973, condemning "the unholy alliance between South African racism and zionism." It also noted similar declarations issued earlier that year by the World Conference of the International Women's Year, the Conference of Non-Aligned Countries, the Organization of African Unity, and other groups. Prominent among the countries opposing Resolution 3379 were Israel, the United States, Canada, Australia, New Zealand, and countries of the European Economic Community (Common Market), now known as the Euroepan Union, or EU.

Further reading: Michael Curtis, *The United Nations, Zionism and Racism* (Dollard des Ormeaux, Canada: Dawn Publications, 1987); *Everyone's United Nations: A Handbook on the Work of the United Nations* (New York: United Nations, 1986); Yohanan Manor, *To Right a Wrong: The Revocation of the UN General Assembly Resolution 3379 Defaming Zionism*, 2d ed. (New York: Shengold, 1997).

United Provinces of Central America, Declaration of Independence of the

Document concluded on July 24, 1823, in Guatemala City by a national constituent assembly consisting of representatives from the provinces of Central America (Costa Rica, Guatemala, Honduras, Nicaragua, and El Salvador), declaring the provinces' collective independence from Mexico and the establishment of the United Provinces of Central America. (In 1821 the Central American provinces had achieved independence from Spain and agreed, with the exception of El Salvador, to a union with Mexico.) The new country promulgated a constitution on November 22, 1824, and elected its first president, Manuel José Arce. The union lasted until 1839, after which many unsuccessful attempts were made to restore it.

See also: CENTRAL AMERICAN TREATY OF UNION.

Further reading: Leslie Bethell, *Central America since Independence* (New York: Cambridge University Press, 1991); Lowell Gudmundson and Hector Lindo-Fuentes, *Central America, 1821–1871: Liberalism Before Liberal Reform* (Tuscaloosa: University of Alabama Press, 1995); Ralph L. Woodward, *Rafael Carrera and the Emergence of the Republic of Guatemala, 1821–1871* (Athens: University of Georgia Press, 1993).

United Provinces of the Río de la Plata, Declaration of Independence of the

Document signed by 29 delegates of the Congress of Tucumán on July 9, 1816, declaring the independence of the provinces of Río de la Plata (which consisted of all present-day Argentine provinces except three, plus four provinces of present-day Bolivia). The declaration patently stated that the United Provinces were independent of the rule of Spain's king Ferdinand VII and his successors and that the United Provinces would rule themselves as one nation. The delegates also conferred the newly created office of supreme dictator upon Juan Martín de Pueyrredón, who collaborated with José de San Martín, commander of the rebel army of the Andes. It was a period of internal anarchy, when the Spanish sought to regain control of their colonial possessions in Latin America.

Further reading: Mark D. Szuchman and Jonathan C. Brown, *Revolution and Restoration: The Rearrangement of Power in Argentina, 1776–1860* (Lincoln: University of Nebraska Press, 1994).

United Public Workers v. Mitchell

U.S. Supreme Court decision, issued on February 10, 1947, that upheld the HATCH ACT OF 1939, limiting the political speech of government employees by forbidding them to participate actively in political management or campaigns. Employees of the federal executive branch had sued for an injunction to prevent the Civil Service Commission from enforcing the act, claiming that it infringed on their constitutional right to free speech. In its 4-3 decision rejecting the suit, the Supreme Court declared that it must balance "the guarantee of freedom against congressional enactment to protect the democratic society against the supposed evil of political partisanship" by government employees.

Further reading: Kermit L. Hall et al., eds., *The Oxford Companion to the Supreme Court of the United States* (New York: Oxford University Press, 1992); United States Supreme Court, *United States Reports: Cases Adjudged in the Supreme Court at . . . and Rules Announced at . . .* (New York: Banks & Brothers, Law Publishers, 1884–1921; Washington, D.C.: Government Printing Office, 1922–).

United States Relations with China

See WHITE PAPER OF 1949, U.S.

United States v. Butler et al. (Hoosac Mills Case)

U.S. Supreme Court decision, issued on January 6, 1936, that invalidated the AGRICULTURAL ADJUSTMENT ACT OF 1933 on the grounds that it infringed on rights reserved to the states under the U.S. CONSTITUTION because the act was intended to regulate and control agricultural production. The case arose when Butler, the receiver for a bankrupt cotton processor (Hoosac Mills), refused to pay the processing tax authorized by the act. In its six-to-three decision, the Supreme Court declared that the processing tax was unconstitutional "coercion by economic pressure" because it was not really a tax but was an indirect method to force farmers to control agricultural production. Congress responded to the decision by passing the SOIL CONSERVATION AND DOMESTIC ALLOTMENT ACT.

Further reading: Kermit L. Hall et al., eds., *American Legal History: Cases and Materials*, 2d ed. (New York: Oxford

University Press, 1996); Kermit L. Hall et al., eds., *The Oxford Companion to the Supreme Court of the United States* (New York: Oxford University Press, 1992); Robert R. Mayer, *The Court and the American Crises, 1930–1952* (Danbury, Conn.: Grolier Educational, 1995); United States Supreme Court, *United States Reports: Cases Adjudged in the Supreme Court at . . . and Rules Announced at . . .* (New York: Banks & Brothers, Law Publishers, 1884–1921; Washington, D.C.: Government Printing Office, 1922–).

United States v. Curtiss-Wright Export Corporation

U.S. Supreme Court decision, issued on December 21, 1936, that confirmed the federal government's power to conduct foreign relations and the U.S. president's exclusive authority to exercise that power. The case arose when the Curtiss-Wright Corporation violated an embargo (authorized by a joint congressional resolution and issued by the president on May 28, 1934) on the shipment of arms to Bolivia. In its 7-1 decision, the Supreme Court ruled that the powers to conduct international relations are "vested in the federal government as necessary concomitants of nationality" and that the president has "plenary and exclusive power . . . as the sole organ of the federal government" in such matters.

Further reading: Henry Steele Commager, ed., *Documents of American History*, 8th ed. (New York: Appleton-Century-Crofts, 1968); Kermit L. Hall et al., eds., *The Oxford Companion to the Supreme Court of the United States* (New York: Oxford University Press, 1992); Robert R. Mayer, *The Court and the American Crises, 1930–1952* (Danbury, Conn.: Grolier Educational, 1995); United States Supreme Court, *United States Reports: Cases Adjusted in the Supreme Court at . . . and Rules Announced at . . .* (New York: Banks & Brothers, Law Publishers, 1884–1921; Washington, D.C.: Government Printing Office, 1922–).

United States v. Darby Lumber Company

U.S. Supreme Court decision, issued on February 3, 1941, that upheld the constitutionality of the U.S. FAIR LABOR STANDARDS ACT and overruled *HAMMER V. DAGENHART*. In its unanimous decision the Supreme Court ruled that Congress has the right, in its regulation of commerce, to prohibit interstate shipment of goods produced in violation of its wages and hours standards and to prohibit employment of workers in the production of such goods. The decision also rejected the doctrine of mutually exclusive spheres of state and federal authority.

Further reading: Henry Steele Commager, ed., *Documents of American History*, 8th ed. (New York: Appleton-Century-Crofts, 1968); Kermit L. Hall et al., eds., *The Oxford Companion to the Supreme Court of the United States* (New York: Oxford University Press, 1992); *Leading Decisions of the United States Supreme Court* (San Francisco, Calif.: Chandler Publications, 1965); United States Supreme Court, *United States Reports: Cases Adjudged in the Supreme Court at . . . and Rules Announced at . . .* (New York: Banks & Brothers,

Law Publishers, 1884–1921; Washington, D.C.: Government Printing Office, 1922–).

United States v. Debs et al.

Contempt proceedings against Eugene V. Debs, president of the American Railway Union, and others for violations of sweeping injunctions prohibiting the obstruction of the railroads and U.S. mail during the Pullman strike of 1894, when railway workers disrupted rail transportation nationwide in protest of wage cuts. The blanket injunctions were issued under the SHERMAN ANTI-TRUST ACT, on the argument that the union was an illegal combination in restraint of trade. After federal troops broke the strike, Debs was arrested, convicted of violating the injunction, and sentenced to jail. The case was carried to the Supreme Court on a writ of habeas corpus (see IN RE DEBS).

Further reading: Henry Steele Commager, ed., *Documents of American History*, 8th ed. (New York: Appleton-Century-Crofts, 1968); Kermit L. Hall et al., eds., *The Oxford Companion to the Supreme Court of the United States* (New York: Oxford University Press, 1992); United States Supreme Court, *United States Reports: Cases Adjudged in the Supreme Court at . . . and Rules Announced at . . .* (New York: Banks & Brothers, Law Publishers, 1884–1921; Washington, D.C.: Government Printing Office, 1922–).

United States v. Earl Caldwell

U.S. Supreme Court decision issued on June 29, 1972, stating that news reporters had the same obligations as other citizens to comply with grand jury subpoenas and give testimony. The case concerned Earl Caldwell, a *New York Times* reporter who had refused to enter a grand jury room to be questioned about information he had obtained from Black Panther Party members. The Supreme Court, in a 5-4 decision, ruled that the public interest in possible future news did not outweigh the public interest in pursuing and prosecuting crimes that had been reported to the press. The American Society of Newspaper Editors called the decision "a direct blow at the right of the people to be fully informed without hindrance by the government."

Further reading: United States Supreme Court, *United States Reports: Cases Adjudged in the Supreme Court at . . . and Rules Announced at . . .* (New York: Banks & Brothers, Law Publishers, 1884–1921; Washington, D.C.: Government Printing Office, 1922–).

United States v. E.C. Knight Company (Sugar Trust Case)

First U.S. Supreme Court interpretation of the SHERMAN ANTI-TRUST ACT, issued on January 21, 1895, and a serious setback to its enforcement. E. C. Knight, a holding company that controlled the American Sugar Refining Company, had purchased competing sugar refineries, securing a near monopoly on the manufacture of refined sugar in the United States. The government charged that the purchases were a combination in restraint of trade. In its 8-1 decision against the government, the Supreme Court ruled that the Sherman Anti-Trust Act applied only to interstate commerce, narrowly defined, not to intrastate manufacturing, even of articles made for export to another state.

Further reading: Henry Steele Commager, ed., *Documents of American History*, 8th ed. (New York: Appleton-Century-Crofts, 1968); Kermit L. Hall et al., eds., *American Legal History: Cases and Materials*, 2d ed. (New York: Oxford University Press, 1996); Kermit L. Hall et al., eds., *The Oxford Companion to the Supreme Court of the United States* (New York: Oxford University Press, 1992); United States Supreme Court, *United States Reports: Cases Adjudged in the Supreme Court at . . . and Rules Announced at . . .* (New York: Banks & Brothers, Law Publishers, 1884–1921; Washington, D.C.: Government Printing Office, 1922–).

United States v. Lanza   U.S. Supreme Court decision, issued on December 11, 1922, concerning the "double jeopardy" provision of the U.S. CONSTITUTION. The EIGHTEENTH AMENDMENT had given Congress and the states concurrent jurisdiction in the enforcement of prohibition. In this case, which arose in the state of Washington, the lower courts denied the federal government the right to try offenders already tried in state courts. Supreme Court Chief Justice William Howard Taft ruled that a second trial could be held without violating the FIFTH AMENDMENT prohibition on double jeopardy. He stated that the defendants had "committed two different offenses by the same act," one offense against the state and another offense against the United States.

Further reading: Kermit L. Hall et. al. eds., *The Oxford Companion to the Supreme Court of the United States* (New York: Oxford University Press, 1992); United States Supreme Court, *United States Reports: Cases Adjudged in the Supreme Court at . . . and Rules Announced at . . .* (New York: Banks & Brothers, Law Publishers, 1884–1921; Washington, D.C.: Government Printing Office, 1922–).

United States v. Seeger   U.S. Supreme Court decision, issued on March 8, 1965, that defined qualifications for exemption from military service on grounds of conscientious objection. The case involved three young men who claimed exemption but were not members of traditional religious groups and did not declare a belief in a Supreme Being. Interpreting the BURKE-WADSWORTH ACT of 1940, the Supreme Court ruled that the statutory requirement for belief in a Supreme Being could be met by anyone who had a "sincere and meaningful belief" that occupied in the life of its possessor a place "parallel to that filled by the orthodox belief in God." It defined "Supreme Being" as a broad concept of a power "to which all else is subordinate or upon which all else is ultimately dependent." The Court excluded exemption based solely on a personal moral code that is in no way related to a Supreme Being.

Further reading: United States Supreme Court, *United States Reports: Cases Adjudged in the Supreme Court at . . . and Rules Announced at . . .* (New York: Banks & Brothers, Law Publishers, 1884–1921; Washington, D.C.: Government Printing Office, 1922–).

Unity (Union) and Security, Act of (Act of Safety)

Constitutional amendment introduced (February 20, 1789) during a meeting of the estates by King Gustavus III of Sweden, granting him virtually absolute control over the country's affairs. Approved by the three lower estates (clergy, burghers, and peasants) despite the opposition of the nobility, it received royal sanction on April 3, 1789. It enabled the king to dispense with the council (a 500-year-old Swedish institution), assume charge of the bureaucracy, collect grants, and declare war. While the nobility lost many privileges (related to land- and officeholding), the three lower estates obtained the right to occupy most public offices (except the highest), including half the seats in the newly constituted Supreme Court, and purchase land anywhere except within the immediate neighborhood of a nobleman's house. These concessions, proposed by Gustavus III himself (albeit selfishly), were impressive for their time; in France, similar concessions were not granted until after the French Revolution (1789–92).

Further reading: Alice M. Baldwin, *Gustavus III of Sweden: A Study of the Enlightened Despotism of the Eighteenth Century in Europe* (Ithaca, N.Y.: Photo Services of Cornell University, 1975).

Universal Declaration of Human Rights

First section of an International Bill of Human Rights adopted (by a vote of 48 to 0) and announced by the United Nations General Assembly in Paris on December 10, 1948. Nine members (the Soviet Bloc countries, Saudi Arabia, and South Africa) abstained. The declaration proclaimed fundamental freedoms and rights as a "common standard of achievement for all peoples and all nations" and the United Nations secretary general was requested to have it disseminated all over the world in various languages. Its 30 articles took the Commission on Human Rights nearly three years to draft. In 1948, the commission began preparing the other two sections of the International Bill of Human Rights—a Convention of Human Rights and its implementation policies. During 1948, the General Assembly also adopted a CONVENTION ON THE PREVENTION AND PUNISHMENT OF THE CRIME OF GENOCIDE.

See also: UNITED NATIONS CHARTER.

Further reading: Mortimer Adler, ed., *The Annals of America*, 18 vols. (Chicago: Encyclopaedia Britannica, 1968); Henry W. Degenhardt, ed., *Treaties and Alliances of the World*, 4th ed. (Detroit: Gale Research, 1986); J. A. S. Grenville and Bernard Wasserstein, *The Major International Treaties since 1945: A History and Guide with Texts* (New York: Methuen, 1987); Louis L. Snyder, ed., *Fifty Major Documents of the Twentieth Century* (Princeton, N.J.: D. Van Nostrand, 1955).

Universal Military Training and Service Act, U.S.

Federal U.S. legislation, enacted on June 19, 1951, that extended the draft, lowered the age of military service to 18.5 years, and set the period of service at 24 months (see SELECTIVE SERVICE ACT OF 1948, U.S.). Passed during the Korean War (1950–53), the act allowed deferments for medical, occupational, and other reasons, and permitted high school and college students to perform their service after graduation. It required conscientious objectors to perform civilian work. The Selective Service System was made a permanent agency. The act, renewed regularly through 1963, was followed by the SELECTIVE SERVICE ACT OF 1967.

Further reading: *The Cost of Conscription: A Critical Review of the Universal Military Training and Service Act* (Washington, D.C.: National Council Against Conscription, 1959); *Universal Military Training and Service Act, as Amended, with Analysis* (Washington, D.C.: Government Printing Office, 1966); Rowland Watts, *The Draftee and Internal Security; a Study of the Army Military Personnal Security Program and Its Effect upon Persons Inducted under the Provisions of the Universal Military Training and Service Act* (New York: Workers Defense League, 1955).

Universities Tests Act, English

British parliamentary legislation of Prime Minister William Gladstone, enacted on June 16, 1871, abolishing religious tests for lay students and for certain lay offices in the universities of Oxford, Cambridge, and Durham. Students need not take religious tests in order to obtain university degrees and some university positions. The legislation did not otherwise alter the system of religious instruction prevalent in these universities or the requirements for divinity students.

Further reading: Joel H. Wiener, ed., *Great Britain—The Lion at Home: A Documentary History of Domestic Policy (1689–1973)*, 4 vols. (New York: Chelsea House, 1974).

University of California Regents v. Allan P. Bakke

U.S. Supreme Court decision, issued on June 28, 1978, that ordered Allan P. Bakke to be admitted to the University of California Medical School at Davis because the school's racial quota plan was inflexibly and unjustifiably biased against white applicants like him. At the same time, in another five-to-four decision, the Court upheld the constitutionality of college admissions' affirmative actions to give advantage to blacks and other minorities to redress past discrimination against them. Bakke had sued the university, claiming "reverse discrimination" after being rejected for admission twice, though his grade average exceeded that of some "disadvantaged students" who had been admitted. The university first lost in the California Supreme Court and then appealed the case to the U.S. Supreme Court.

Further reading: Arthur L. Galub, *The Burger Court, 1968–1984* (Danbury, Conn.: Grolier Educational, 1995); Kermit L. Hall et al., eds., *The Oxford Companion to the Su-* *preme Court of the United States* (New York: Oxford University Press, 1992); Maureen Harrison and Steve Gilbert, eds., *Landmark Decisions of the United States Supreme Court* (Beverly Hills, Calif.: Excellent Books, 1991); United States Supreme Court, *United States Reports: Cases Adjudged in the Supreme Court at . . . and Rules Announced at . . .* (New York: Banks & Brothers, Law Publishers, 1884–1921; Washington, D.C.: Government Printing Office, 1922–).

Unkiar Skelessi, Treaty of

See HÜNKÂR ISKELESI, TREATY OF.

Uphaus v. Wyman

U.S. Supreme Court decision issued on June 8, 1959, affirming the right of a state to investigate possible subversives. The Court upheld the civil contempt conviction of the Reverend Willard Uphaus for refusing to divulge, to a legislative committee investigating subversive activities in the state, the names of persons who had attended a World Fellowship camp in New Hampshire. In its five-to-four decision, the Court ruled that the state's interest in "self-preservation" outweighed individual rights to privacy in association. The dissenting justices argued that the investigation was "exposure for exposure's sake" and violated constitutional rights to privacy in relation to freedom of speech and association.

Further reading: Henry Steele Commager, ed., *Documents of American History*, 8th ed. (New York: Appleton-Century-Crofts, 1968); United States Supreme Court, *United States Reports: Cases Adjudged in the Supreme Court at . . . and Rules Announced at . . .* (New York: Banks & Brothers, Law Publishers, 1884–1921; Washington, D.C.: Government Printing Office, 1922–); Willard E. Uphaus, *Commitment* (New York: McGraw-Hill, 1963).

Uruguayan Constitution of 1830

First constitution after the official establishment of Uruguayan independence in 1828. The constitution, drafted by a committee appointed by the Uruguayan Assembly, called for a unitary, representative republican regime with a division of powers among the executive, the legislative, and the judiciary. It also stipulated that the Banda Oriental state of Uruguay would consist of nine departments. Although it provided for a restricted suffrage, it guaranteed many civil rights; and while it established Roman Catholicism as the official state religion, it guaranteed freedom of religion. Among Latin America's most durable charters, the constitution survived all proposals for its reform until 1918.

Further reading: Philip Bates Taylor, *Government and Politics of Uruguay* (Westport, Conn.: Greenwood Press, 1984).

Uruguayan Constitution of 1919

New constitution put in force in Uruguay on March 1, 1919, greatly diluting the power of the president and disestablishing the Roman Catholic Church. Baltasar Brum was inaugurated as Uruguay's new president on the same day. Governmental power would be shared by the president, who was to be popularly elected and serve a four-year term, and a newly created national council of administration, which was to consist of nine members elected by popular vote from the country's two opposition parties. The document also provided for the separation of church and state, granted increased power to municipalities, and liberalized electoral procedure. Prior to 1919 the country had been ruled by a dictatorship.

See also: URUGUAYAN CONSTITUTION OF 1830.

Further reading: Philip Bates Taylor, *Government and Politics of Uruguay* (Westport, Conn.: Greenwood Press, 1984).

USA-PATRIOT Act (Uniting and Strengthening America by Providing Appropriate Tools Required to Intercept and Obstruct Terrorism Act)

Legislation enacted by the U.S. Congress in response to the terrorist attacks of September 11, 2001. Signed into law by President George W. Bush on October 26, 2001, the act made "countering and investigating terrorist activity . . . the number one priority for both law enforcement and intelligence agencies." The act changed the laws governing information-sharing so that the Federal Bureau of Investigation, the Central Intelligence Agency, and other law enforcement agencies could legally exchange data concerning suspected terrorists. It allowed government surveillance of e-mails, the Internet, and cell phones, and it made federal search warrants valid throughout the United States, not just in the district in which they are issued. The act gave the government greater leeway in seizing the financial assets of suspected terrorist groups, deporting known terrorists and their supporters, and detaining suspected terrorists indefinitely without a trial or hearing. It lengthened the statute of limitations on terrorist acts and increased the penalties for such acts. The act was attacked by civil liberties advocates because it allowed the government to brand virtually any protest group as terrorist sympathizers and act against them accordingly.

Further reading: MacNeil/Lehrer Productions, "President Bush Signs Anti-Terrorism Bill," online News Hour, available online at http://www.pbs.org/newshour/bb/terrorism/bush terrorismbill.htm.

U.S. Articles of Confederation

See ARTICLES OF CONFEDERATION, U.S.

U.S.-Canadian Convention of 1903

Agreement between the United States and Great Britain on January 24, 1903, establishing a joint commission to settle a dispute over the boundary between the Alaskan Panhandle and British Columbia. The dispute arose over water routes to the gold fields discovered in the Klondike in 1896. The six-person commission, consisting of American, Canadian, and English representatives, supported the U.S. claims, with the two Canadians dissenting from the majority opinion.

Further reading: R. C. Brown and M. E. Prang, eds., *Canadian Historical Documents Series*, 3 vols. (Scarborough, Canada: Prentice-Hall of Canada, 1966).

U.S.-Canadian Free Trade Agreement of 1988

Agreement signed on January 2, 1988, in Palm Springs, California, by President Ronald Reagan of the United States and in Ottawa by Prime Minister Brian Mulroney of Canada, containing provisions designed to promote free trade between the two countries. This landmark treaty provided that remaining tariffs on most items would be eliminated within a 10-year period, and on some items as early as January 1989; that regulations governing cross-border banking and investing would be relaxed; that trade disputes would be submitted to U.S.-Canadian commissions for arbitration; and that restrictions on trade of crude oil and natural gas would be eliminated.

Further reading: Marc Gold and David Leyton-Brown, eds., *Trade-Offs on Free Trade: The Canada-U.S. Free Trade Agreement* (Toronto: Carswell, 1988); Donald M. McRae and Debra P. Steger, eds., *Understanding the Free Trade Agreement* (Halifax, Canada: Institute for Research on Public Policy, 1988); Peter Morici, ed., *Making Free Trade Work: The Canada-U.S. Agreement* (New York: Council on Foreign Relations Press, 1990).

U.S.-China "Hotline" Agreement

Agreement between the United States and the People's Republic of China to establish a secure direct communications link similar to the one between the United States and Russia (see U.S.-SOVIET "HOTLINE" AGREEMENT). It was signed on April 29, 1998, in Beijing, China, by U.S. secretary of state Madeleine Albright and Tang Jiaxuan, China's foreign minister. The hotline consisted of two satellite circuits and one wire telegraph circuit connected to facsimile and teletype equipment. Via the hotline, the leaders of the two countries could converse with each other by telephone during a crisis or send printed messages and graphic material such as charts, drawings, and maps. The agreement furthered the normalization of relations between the two superpowers, which had been strained by issues such as human rights, trade, the proliferation of nuclear weapons, and Taiwan. After communicating via the hotline in June 1998, U.S. president Bill Clinton and Chinese president Jiang Zemin agreed to call for an international conference to discuss the acquisition of nuclear arms by nations such as India and Pakistan.

Further reading: John Pike, "Hotline Agreements," FAS: Weapons of Mass Destruction, available online at http://www.fas.org/nuke/control/hotline/.

U.S.-Chinese Communiqué of 1972 (Shanghai Communiqué)

Joint communiqué issued by the United States and the People's Republic of China on February 27, 1972, at the conclusion of U.S. president Richard M. Nixon's historic visit to China; it announced progress in normalizing relations between the two countries after decades of hostility. Both nations wished to reduce the danger of international military conflict, stating that "international disputes should be settled . . . without resorting to the use or threat of force." They agreed that no nation should seek hegemony in the Asia-Pacific region and that major powers should not divide the world into spheres of influence. While admitting that differences remained, particularly over Taiwan, both nations stressed their belief in state sovereignty and territorial integrity, nonagression, noninterference in internal affairs, and peaceful coexistence. They agreed to explore mutual educational, cultural, and economic exchanges.

Further reading: Winberg Chai et al., *Chinese Mainland and Taiwan: A Study of Historical, Cultural, Economic and Political Relations, with Documents*, 2d ed. (Dubuque, Iowa: Kendall/Hunt, 1996); J. A. S. Grenville and Bernard Wasserstein, *The Major International Treaties since 1945: A History and Guide with Texts* (New York: Methuen, 1987); Yu-ming Shaw, *ROC-U.S. Relations, a Decade after the "Shanghai Communique"* (Taipei, Taiwan: Asian & World Institute, 1983); *Sino-American Relations: From the Shanghai Communique to the Present: Report* (Washington, D.C.: Government Printing Office, 1980).

U.S.-Chinese Treaty of 1858 (Reed Treaty)

Agreement reached at Tientsin (Tianjin) on June 18, 1858, after the Anglo-French War against China (1857–58), in which the United States abstained from hostilities but engaged in diplomatic maneuvering. At the end of the war China opened up 11 additional treaty ports to foreign trade and residence and provided for extraterritorial protection (exemption from local jurisdiction) of foreign nationals traveling and trading throughout China. In the treaty bearing his name, U.S. Minister to China William B. Reed secured the same treatment for U.S. citizens as other foreigners had obtained through their peace treaties.

Further reading: Jules Davids, comp., *American Diplomatic and Public Papers: The United States and China, Series 1: The Treaty System and the Taiping Rebellion, 1842–1860* (Wilmington, Del.: Scholarly Resources, 1973).

U.S. Constitution

Instrument of government embodying the fundamental law and principles of the United States. Drafted by the Federal Constitutional Convention in 1787 and ratified by the required nine states in 1788, the document replaced the ARTICLES OF CONFEDERATION and went into effect on March 4, 1789. It consists of the PREAMBLE, seven articles, and 26 amendments. It established a new federal republic, granting certain powers to the national government while reserving other powers to the states. The first three articles establish the three branches of government: the legislature, or Congress (consisting of the Senate and the House of Representatives); the executive, or President and Vice President; and the judiciary, or Supreme Court, with provisions for Congress to establish lower federal courts. The fourth article outlines the relations between the various states and between the national government and the states. Article 5 sets the procedures for amending the Constitution. Article 6 defines the Constitution as the "supreme law of the land," binding on all federal and state officials. The last article provides for ratification of the Constitution.

See also: BILL OF RIGHTS, U.S.; ELEVENTH AMENDMENT, U.S.; TWELFTH AMENDMENT, U.S.; THIRTEENTH AMENDMENT, U.S.; [AND SO ON, TO] TWENTY-SIXTH AMENDMENT, U.S..

Further reading: Mortimer Adler, ed., *The Annals of America*, 18 vols. (Chicago: Encyclopaedia Britannica, 1968); Henry Steele Commager, ed., *Documents of American History*, 8th ed. (New York: Appleton-Century-Crofts, 1968); Charles W. Eliot, ed., *The Harvard Classics* (New York: P. F. Collier & Son, 1937); Kermit L. Hall et al., eds, *American Legal History: Cases and Materials*, 2d ed. (New York: Oxford University Press, 1996).

U.S. Constitution, Preamble to the

See PREAMBLE TO THE U.S. CONSTITUTION.

U.S.-Danish Treaty of 1916

Treaty signed on August 4, 1916, by which the United States purchased the Virgin Islands from Denmark for $25 million. The United States hoped thereby to prevent Germany from acquiring the islands as a result of World War I and establishing a naval base in the Caribbean. The treaty was negotiated by U.S. secretary of state Robert Lansing and Danish ambassador to the United States Constantin Brun. A plebscite held on the islands showed that the inhabitants favored the transfer, which was formally accomplished on March 31, 1917. The Virgin Islands became an unincorporated U.S. territory, to be administered by a governor appointed by the U.S. president.

Further reading: Charles C. Tansill, *The Purchase of the Danish West Indies* (Baltimore: Johns Hopkins Press, 1932).

U.S. Declaration of Independence

See DECLARATION OF INDEPENDENCE, AMERICAN.

U.S. Declaration of War on Nazi Germany

Joint congressional resolution of December 11, 1941, formally declaring that a state of war existed between the governments of Germany and the United States. The action immediately followed Germany's declaration of war against the United States. The unanimous resolution authorized the U.S. president to use all of the nation's resources to carry on the war and bring it to a successful conclusion. A similar war resolution against Italy was passed on the same date.

See also: ROOSEVELT'S WAR MESSAGE.

Further reading: Steven Casey, *Cautious Crusade: Franklin D. Roosevelt, American Public Opinion, and the War Against Nazi Germany* (New York: Oxford University Press, 2002);

Henry Steele Commager, ed., *Documents of American History*, 8th ed. (New York: Appleton-Century-Crofts, 1968).

U.S. Executive Order 9066   See EXECUTIVE ORDER 9066, U.S.

U.S.-German Peace Treaty of 1921 (Treaty of Berlin)

Agreement between the United States and Germany drawn up during a conference in Berlin, Germany, in August 1921, and ratified by the U.S. Senate on October 18, formally establishing peace between the two nations nearly three years after the end of World War I (1914–18). This agreement was based on the 1919 Treaty of VERSAILLES, which the U.S. Senate had twice rejected. It accepted most of the Versailles provisions, including those regarding colonies, disarmament, reparations, and responsibility for the war, but excluded U.S. participation in the League of Nations and the International Labor Organization (formed in 1919 as part of the league and now an agency of the United Nations).

Further reading: Henry Steele Commager, ed., *Documents of American History*, 8th ed. (New York: Appleton-Century-Crofts, 1968); *Treaty Between the United States and Germany. Restoring Friendly Relations. Signed at Berlin, August 25, 1921* (Washington, D.C.: Government Printing Office, 1922).

U.S.-Japanese Agreement of 1917   See LANSING-ISHII AGREEMENT.

U.S.-Japanese Treaty of 1951

Mutual security pact between the United States and Japan, signed in San Francisco on September 8, 1951, the same date as the JAPANESE PEACE TREATY OF 1951. The agreement gave the United States the right to maintain armed forces in Japan and provided a defensive shield for that nation in case of attack. Japan needed U.S. consent to allow any other nation to have military forces or bases there. However, the United States was required to consult with Japan before bringing atomic weapons onto American bases in Japan. In 1960 the treaty was renewed for 10 years.

Further reading: J. A. S. Grenville and Bernard Wasserstein, *The Major International Treaties Since 1945: A History and Guide with Texts* (New York: Methuen, 1987).

U.S.-Japanese Treaty of 1990

Major trade accord concluded between the United States and Japan on June 28, 1990, in Tokyo, aiming to close the trade gap and ease trading friction between the two nations. Japan agreed to spend $1 trillion more on public works in the 1990s (in the Japanese consumers' interests), to increase penalties for violating antimonopoly laws, to crack down on corrupt business practices, and to relax restrictions on retail sales to allow more imports, among other reforms. The United States agreed to increase its tax revenues (to fight the budget deficit), to enact laws to help increase U.S. savings and investments, and to develop pro-

grams to promote exports. These and other measures were designed to cut the $49 billion U.S. trade deficit with Japan.

Further reading: Robert Howe, *Japan-U.S. Economic Relations: Selected References, 1990–1992* (Washington, D.C.: Congressional Research Service, Library of Congress, 1992); Wayne M. Morrison and M. Angeles Villareal, *Japan-U.S. Trade: A Chronology of Major Events, 1980–1990* (Washington, D.C.: Congressional Research Service, Library of Congress, 1991).

U.S. Note on Berlin Blockade and Airlift

Note by U.S. secretary of state George C. Marshall on July 6, 1948, to the Soviet Union, protesting that nation's June 24 halting of all land and water traffic between West Germany and the city of West Berlin. Soviet officials, declaring that Berlin (located more than 100 miles inside Soviet-occupied Germany) was an integral part of the Soviet zone, refused to permit the Western occupying powers access to the Western zones of the city. Marshall's note called the blockade a violation of the recent Four-Power Agreement on Berlin. Maintaining that Berlin was an international, not Soviet, zone of occupation, he demanded restoration of free access. The Soviet blockade, however, lasted until May 12, 1949; during that period the Western nations airlifted more than 2 million tons of food, clothing, and other necessities into the city.

Further reading: Henry Steele Commager, ed., *Documents of American History*, 8th ed. (New York: Appleton-Century-Crofts, 1968); J. A. S. Grenville and Bernard Wasserstein, *The Major International Treaties since 1945: A History and Guide with Texts* (New York: Methuen, 1987); Frank N. Magill, ed., *Great Events from History: American Series*, 3 vols. (Englewood Cliffs, N.J.: Salem Press, 1975); Frank N. Magill, ed., *Great Events from History: Modern European Series*, 3 vols. (Englewood Cliffs, N.J.: Salem Press, 1973).

U.S. Policy on "Open Door" for Oil in the Near and Middle East

Note presented by the U.S. ambassador to Great Britain, John W. Davis, to the British foreign secretary, Lord George Curzon, on May 12, 1920, protesting the British government's seemingly quiet preparations "for exclusive control of the oil resources" in Palestine and Mesopotamia (Iraq). The United States mentioned the building of pipelines, railways, and refineries, as well as possible favored treatment granted to British subjects and companies. This placed American citizens and companies at a disadvantage. The United States asked Britain to adhere strictly to principles of fairness and equitable treatment and "no monopolistic concessions be granted for exploitation of economic resources or other privileges."

See also: ANGLO-FRENCH AGREEMENT ON OIL IN THE NEAR AND MIDDLE EAST; SAN REMO AGREEMENTS.

Further reading: E. L. Woodward and Rohan d'O. Butler, eds., *Documents on British Foreign Policy 1919–1939*, 21 vols. (London: H.M. Stationery Office, 1947).

U.S.-Soviet "Hotline" Agreement

Treaty signed by the United States and the Soviet Union on June 20, 1963, agreeing to establish a direct communications link (so-called hotline) between the two governments for use in times of emergency. The need for such direct, speedy communications had become apparent during the Cuban missile crisis of 1962; it was to reduce the possibility of accidental war between the two nations. The hotline, a direct, 4,883-mile cable telephone line between the White House and the Kremlin, was functional on August 30, 1963; it began operating via satellite in 1978.

See also: KENNEDY'S ADDRESS ON REMOVAL OF SOVIET WEAPONS FROM CUBA; U.S.-CHINA "HOTLINE" AGREEMENT.

Further reading: Aleksandr Fursenko and Timothy J. Naftali, *One Hell of a Gamble: Krushchev, Castro, Kennedy and the Cuban Missile Crisis, 1958–1964* (London: Pimlico, 1999); J. .A. S. Grenville and Bernard Wasserstein, *The Major International Treaties since 1945: A History and Guide with Texts* (New York: Methuen, 1987).

U.S.-Soviet Lend-Lease Agreement

Agreement negotiated by U.S. president Franklin D. Roosevelt and Soviet foreign minister Vyacheslav M. Molotov; effective on July 1, 1942, it supplemented earlier Lend-Lease protocols. On October 1, 1941, the United States had agreed to Russian requests for materials to conduct the war against Germany, and on November 6, 1941, had granted the Soviet Union Lend-Lease credit of $1 billion. The 1942 agreement provided that U.S. materials or information would not be transferred to other parties without U.S. consent and that any materials available after the war would be returned to the United States. Some $11 billion of Lend-Lease aid eventually went to the Soviet Union. The program was terminated at the end of World War II (1939–45).

Further reading: Mortimer Adler, ed., *The Annals of America*, 18 vols. (Chicago: Encyclopaedia Britannica, 1968); Donald G. Bishop, ed., *Soviet Foreign Relations: Documents & Readings* (Syracuse, N.Y.: Syracuse University Press, 1952).

U.S.-Taiwanese Pact of 1954

Mutual defense treaty signed on December 2, 1954, between the United States and the Republic of China (Nationalist China), with its government located on (Formosa Taiwan). The treaty promised U.S. assistance if the communist government of the mainland attacked Taiwan or the nearby Pescadores islands; it did not, however, apply to the Chinese Nationalist–held islands of Quemoy (Jinmen) and Matsu (Mazu), which were close to the mainland coast and had recently been under communist attack. Nationalist leader Jiang Jieshi (Chiang Kai-shek) agreed not to attack the mainland unilaterally. In January 1955, Congress gave President Dwight Eisenhower the authority to use U.S. armed forces, if necessary to defend Taiwan and the Pescadores.

Further reading: J. A. S. Grenville and Bernard Wasserstein, *The Major International Treaties since 1945: A History and Guide with Texts* (New York: Methuen, 1987); John C. Kuan, *A Review of U.S.-ROC Relations, 1949–1978* (Taipei, Taiwan: Asia & World Institute, 1980).

Utrecht, Treaties of (Peace of Utrecht)

Peace agreements signed at Utrecht and Maastricht, Holland, between France and other European countries (April 11, 1713–September 7, 1714) and between Spain and other powers (July 13, 1713–June 26, 1714), ending the War of the Spanish Succession (1701–14). France recognized Britain's Queen Anne as rightful sovereign and agreed to discontinue support for the son of James II, the deposed British king. France also ceded to Britain Acadia (Nova Scotia), Newfoundland, the Hudson Bay area, and St. Kitts in the Caribbean, and promised to demolish the fortifications at Dunkirk. The French allowed the Netherlands to annex part of Gelderland and to keep some fortresses in the Spanish Netherlands (Belgium and Luxembourg), which was given to Austria. In return for recognizing Prussian king Frederick I's royal title and his claim to Neuchâtel and southeast Gelderland, France received the principality of Orange (on the Rhône). The French recognized Savoy's duke Victor Amadeus II as king of Sicily, and they acknowledged Portugal's control of the banks of the Amazon River; also the French colony of Guiana was reduced in size. Spain ceded Gibraltar and Minorca to Britain, which wrung a 30-year exclusive right to supply Spanish America with black slaves from Africa. Victor Amadeus II renounced his claims to the Spanish throne for the Sicilian kingdom. Holy Roman Emperor Charles VI made peace with France by the 1714 Treaties of RASTATT and BADEN and with Spain by the 1720 Treaty of The HAGUE. Philip V, grandson of King Louis XIV of France, was recognized as king of Spain, provided that the Spanish and French crowns never be united.

See also: MADRID, TREATY OF (1715).

Further reading: Henry W. Degenhardt, ed., *Treaties and Alliances of the World*, 4th ed. (Detroit: Gale Research, 1986); William MacDonald, ed., *Select Charters and Other Documents Illustrative of American History, 1606–1775* (New York: Macmillan, 1899); Louis L. Snyder, ed., *Documents of German History* (New Brunswick, N.J.: Rutgers University Press, 1958); Milton Viorst, ed., *The Great Documents of Western Civilization* (Philadelphia: Chilton Books, 1965).

Utrecht, Union of

Treaty of alliance concluded on January 23, 1579, by seven northern Protestant provinces (Holland, Zeeland, Utrecht, Gelderland, Overijssel, Friesland, and Groningen) of the Netherlands, to counter the pro-Spanish alliance (the Union of Arras) organized by the southern provinces. The Utrecht Union, later the basis of the Dutch constitution, was aimed at continuing the opposition against Spanish rule and maintaining the religious and civil liberties of its citizens. The provinces would share a common foreign policy, while maintaining their autonomy in internal affairs. The provincial stadholders (governors) assumed leadership roles, and a military league was formed to overthrow the Spaniards. Calvinism became the dominant faith, replacing the religious truce achieved by the 1576 Pacification of GHENT. Negotiated by John of Nassau and Johan van Oldenbarnevelt (see TWELVE YEARS' TRUCE) of Holland, the Union of Utrecht foreshadowed the 1581 Act of ABJURATION.

See also: ARRAS, TREATY OF (1579).

Further reading: Jonathan I. Israel, *The Dutch Republic: Its Rise, Greatness and Fall, 1477–1806* (Oxford, England: Clarendon Press, 1995); Lucy M. Salmon, "The Union of Utrecht," *American Historical Association Annual Report . . . for the Year 1893* (1894): 135–48).

Uxbridge Propositions (Uxbridge Treaty) English Parliament's terms after discussion at Uxbridge (borough now part of Hillingdon, England) in January–February 1645, between the commissioners of King Charles I (led by the duke of Richmond) and the Parliament's commissioners (led by Scotland's lord chancellor Loudoun). Parliament demanded control over the armed forces, Irish and foreign affairs, and top appointments of the state. It also insisted on the abolition of episcopacy and punishment of specified royalists. The king was not willing to give up "the church, my crown and my friends" and the discussions ended in a stalemate on February 22, 1645. The Great English Civil War (1642–46) resumed with battles between the royalists and parliamentarians.

Further reading: *A True Copy of the Propositions of the King's Commissioners: Presented to the Commissioners of the Lords and Commons of the Parliament of England, Now Assembled at Uxbridge* (Ann Arbor, Mich.: University Microfilms International, 1978).

Valentinian III's Edict   Declaration issued by Valentinian III, Roman emperor in the West, in A.D. 445 recognizing the primacy of the bishop of Rome (the pope) over the provincial churches. In gratitude to Pope Leo I the Great's support in stemming barbaric invaders of the Roman Empire, Valentinian decreed that the bishops of Gaul and other provinces "shall attempt nothing counter to ancient custom without the authority of the venerable father of the Eternal City. Whatever shall be sanctioned by the authority of the Apostolic See shall be law to them and to everyone else."

See also: TOME OF LEO.

Further reading: J. Michael Miller, *The Shepherd and the Rock: Origins, Development, and the Mission of the Papacy* (Huntington, Ind.: Our Sunday Visitor, 1995); Stephen K. Ray, *Upon This Rock: St. Peter and the Primacy of Rome in Scripture and the Early Church* (San Francisco, Calif.: Ignatius Press, 1999); Milton Viorst, ed., *The Great Documents of Western Civilization* (Philadelphia: Chilton Books, 1965).

Vandenberg Resolution   Resolution adopted by the U.S. Senate on June 11, 1948, that reaffirmed U.S. support of the United Nations as the guardian of world peace yet asserted the right of member nations to form regional arrangements for collective self-defense. Introduced by Senator Arthur H. Vandenberg of Michigan, the resolution grew out of fears of Soviet aggression and a request for support of an alliance formed by Britain, France, Belgium, the Netherlands, and Luxembourg. The resolution supported U.S. association with such arrangements based on "continuous and effective self-help and mutual aid, and . . . national security." The resolution was a forerunner of the NORTH ATLANTIC TREATY.

Further reading: Mortimer Adler, ed., *The Annals of America*, 18 vols. (Chicago: Encyclopaedia Britannica, 1968); Henry Steele Commager, ed., *Documents of American History*, 8th ed. (New York: Appleton-Century-Crofts, 1968); Henry W. Degenhardt, ed., *Treaties and Alliances of the World*, 4th ed. (Detroit: Gale Research, 1986); J. A. S. Grenville and Bernard Wasserstein, *The Major International Treaties since 1945: A History and Guide with Texts* (New York: Methuen, 1987).

Vanhorne's Lessee v. Dorrance   Decision by the U.S. Circuit Court in April 1795 that, in declaring invalid a Pennsylvania statute, because it was in conflict with the state constitution, set an important precedent for the principle of judicial review. The case involved a dispute between residents of Connecticut and Pennsylvania over the title to lands in Pennsylvania. In this decision U.S. Supreme Court Justice William Paterson, then sitting in the Circuit Court of Pennsylvania, stated that "every act of the Legislature repugnant to the Constitution is absolutely void." This principle was later applied in *MARBURY V. MADISON*.

Further reading: George J. Lankevich, *The Federal Court, 1787–1801* (Danbury, Conn.: Grolier Educational, 1995).

Vanzetti's Final Court Statement   Last formal statement made by Bartolomeo Vanzetti, on April 9, 1927, shortly before his execution (along with Nicola Sacco) for the 1920 murder of two shoe-factory employees in the course of a robbery. Maintaining his innocence, Vanzetti restated a belief—widely held by liberals about this cause célèbre—that he and Sacco had been judged guilty at their 1921 trial not because of the evidence against them but because they were foreign-born and avowed anarchists: "I am suffering because I am a radical and . . . because I [am] an Italian." After numerous appeals, a blue-ribbon panel sustained the verdict, and Sacco and Vanzetti were electrocuted on August 23, 1927.

Further reading: Mortimer Adler, ed., *The Annals of America*, 18 vols. (Chicago: Encyclopaedia Britannica, 1968); Henry Steele Commager, ed.; *Documents of American History*, 8th ed. (New York: Appleton-Century-Crofts, 1968); Brian Jackson, *The Black Flag: A Look Back at the Strange Case of Nicola Sacco and Bartolomeo Vanzetti* (Boston: Routledge & Kegan Paul, 1981); *The Sacco-Vanzetti Case; Transcript of the Record of the Trial of Nicola Sacco and Bartolomeo Vanzetti in the Courts of Massachusetts and Subsequent Proceedings 1920–7* (Mamaroneck, N.Y.: P. P. Appel, 1969).

Värälä, Treaty of   Peace agreement signed in the Finnish town of Värälä (Wereloe, Werela, or Varela) on August 15, 1790, ending the Russo-Swedish War of 1788–90 between Sweden's king Gustavus III and Russia's czarina Catherine II the Great over possession of the region of Karelia and that portion of Finland retained by Russia through the 1743 Treaty of ÅBO. It restored the status quo antebellum, leaving the Finnish territory and Karelia in Russian hands. Russia promised not to interfere in Swedish politics. During the war, Denmark had suddenly joined Russia and attacked Sweden, thus leaving Russia in an advantageous position diplomatically to bring about an agreement favorable for her.

Further reading: Alice M. Baldwin, *Gustavus III of Sweden: A Study of the Enlightened Despotism of the Eighteenth Century in Europe* (Ithaca, N.Y.: Photo Services of Cornell University, 1975); Carolly Erickson, *Great Catherine* (New York: St. Martin's Griffin, 1995).

Vasvár, Treaty of   Peace agreement concluding the Austro-Turkish War of 1663–64; made between Holy Roman Emperor Leopold I and the Ottoman Turks on August 10, 1664, at Vasvár, Hungary. It came shortly after the stunning imperial victory over the Turks at St. Gotthard, Hungary, and seemed to reflect the emperor's unwillingness to defend Transylvania. The peace, which lasted for 20 years, reconfirmed Turkish suzerainty over Transylvania, and Leopold recognized Michael I Apafi, a weak Szekler, as prince of Transylvania. In addition, the Turks retained all the lands they recently conquered, including the strategic fortress of Nagyvarad, and the sultan received a payment of 200,000 talers (former German silver coins).

Further reading: John P. Spielman, *Leopold I of Austria* (New Brunswick, N.J.: Rutgers University Press, 1977).

Vatinian Law (Lex Vatinia)   Measure proposed by Roman plebeian Tribune Publius Vatinius in 59 B.C. to confer upon consul Gaius Julius Caesar the combined provinces of Cisalpine Gaul (northern Italy) and Illyricum (bordering the east Adriatic coast). Despite vigorous senatorial opposition, Caesar had formed (60 B.C.) the private First Triumvirate (coalition of Pompey the Great, Marcus Licinius Crassus, and Caesar, exercising governmental authority) and pushed through laws distributing Roman public lands in Italy among Pompey's veterans and opening for colonization the state-held land in Campania. The Vatinian law, passed by the Tribal Assembly, gave Caesar Cisalpine Gaul and Illyricum (with a garrison of three legions) for a period of five years (unprecedented) ending on March 1, 54 B.C. Prompted by Pompey (whose eastern dispositions the Senate had confirmed), the Senate added Transalpine Gaul and another legion to Caesar's command.

Further reading: Ernie D. S. Bradford, *Julius Caesar: The Pursuit of Power* (New York: Morrow, 1984); Charles W. C. Oman, *Seven Roman Statesmen of the Later Republic: The Gracchi, Sulla, Crassus, Cato, Pompey, Caesar* (Freeport, N.Y.: Books for Libraries Press, 1971).

Venice, Peace of   Holy Roman Emperor Frederick I's recognition (1177) of Pope Alexander III's rightful authority, after the former's defeat by the Lombards at the battle of Legnano (1176). Receiving the kiss of peace from the pope in front of the Church of St. Mark's in Venice, Frederick I or Frederick Barbarossa promised to withdraw his support from the antipope (Victor IV), restore the church property he had illegally seized, and reinstate the bishops whom he had deposed because of their loyalty to Pope Alexander III. The pope promised to give the antipope an abbey and restore his cardinals to their original offices, and presented Frederick with the heritage of Countess Matilda as a fiefdom for 15 years. Publicly admitting having "inflicted serious harm upon the Church," the emperor declared he was returning "to the bosom of that Church" by concluding peace with it, the king of Sicily, and the Lombards. It was ratified at the Third Lateran Council (1179). The formal treaty with the Lombards was signed in 1283.

Further reading: Geoffrey Barraclough, *The Origins of Modern Germany* (New York: W. W. Norton, 1984); Thomas Carson, *Barbarossa in Italy* (New York: Italica Press, 1994); G. M. Ellis, trans., *Boso's Life of Alexander III* (Totowa, N.J.: Rowman & Littlefield, 1973); John J. Norwich, *A History of Venice* (New York: Vintage Books, 1989).

Ventôse Decrees   French legislation proposed during the Reign of Terror by Louis de Saint-Just and Maximilien Robespierre of the Committee of Public Safety; two decrees were eventually passed by the National Convention, on 8 and 13 Ventôse in the Year II (February 26 and March 3, 1794). The first authorized the confiscation of the property of enemies of the state, the customary practice of revolutionary governments (see ROBESPIERRE'S SPEECH ON PROPERTY). The second called for the distribution of the confiscated lands among the landless peasants, based on names compiled and forwarded by the communes of the republic to the Committee of Public Safety. Intended to win popular support, this radical decree was not properly drafted. For instance, it did not undertake a survey of the needy peasants for whom food was the most pressing necessity. Also, many of the state's enemies were themselves landless. Never enforced, the Ventôse Decrees were repealed in August 1794.

See also: MANIFESTO OF THE EQUALS.

Further reading: Norman Hampson, *Saint-Just* (Oxford, England: Basil Blackwell, 1991); John Hardman, *Robespierre* (New York: Longman, 1999).

Verdun, Treaty of   Partition treaty, concluded at Verdun in A.D. 843, settled the dynastic dispute among Louis the Pious's sons by dividing Charlemagne's Frankish empire into three parts. Louis the German ruled the eastern section (later Germany); Charles the Bald (Charles II) was granted the western section (later France); Lothair I both retained the imperial title and received the central section (Alsace, Lorraine, Burgundy, Provence, the Low Countries, and most of Italy). One of the most monumental events in world history, the partition of the empire at Verdun signaled the end of an era; as national boundaries were drawn (and later disputed), political unity would no longer exist in Western Europe.

See also: HOLY CONSTITUTION.

Further reading: G. Barraclough, *The Origins of Modern Germany* (New York: W. W. Norton, 1984); Norton Downs, ed., *Basic Documents in Medieval History* (New York: Van Nostrand Reinhold, 1959); Louis L. Snyder, ed., *Documents of German History* (New Brunswick, N.J.: Rutgers University Press, 1958); Milton Viorst, ed., *The Great Documents of Western Civilization* (Philadelphia: Chilton Books, 1965).

Vereeniging, Treaty of   Agreement made on May 31, 1902, between the Boers and the British in Pretoria, South Africa, ending the Great Boer War (1899–1902). Routed, the Boers initiated peace talks, which were conducted at Vereeniging on the Vaal River, where the delegates voted 54 to 6 to accept the British terms. According to the treaty, the Boers agreed to surrender their arms and accept Britain's sovereignty. In return, Britain promised them eventual self-government "as soon as the circumstances permitted" and, following that, agreed to consider granting franchise to the natives. English was declared the official language, but Dutch was allowed in schools and law courts. The Boers were given an immediate grant of £3 million to rebuild their farms. The treaty strengthened British supremacy in the region.

Further reading: Fred L. Israel, ed., *Major Peace Treaties of Modern History, 1648–1967*, 4 vols. (New York: Chelsea House, 1967); H. L. Wesseling, *Divide and Rule: The Partition of Africa, 1880–1914* (Westport, Conn.: Praeger, 1996).

Vergara, Convention of (Embrace of Vergara)   Agreement between the rival Spanish generals Rafael Maroto and Baldomero Espartero at Vergara, Spain, concluding (August 31, 1839) the First Carlist War (1834–39). Espartero guaranteed that Maroto's Carlist officers would be pardoned and that their grades, decorations, and salaries would be adjusted and confirmed. The result was that Spain had one officer for every six or seven soldiers—the highest ratio of any country. Don Carlos (first Carlist pretender to the Spanish throne) was granted the status, rights, and privileges of an *infante* and retired to France. There was no discussion of any dynastic marriage proposals. The government generally agreed to respect the *fueros* (rights) of the Basques and the Navarese, "without prejudice to the constitutional unity of the monarchy." The Basques retained their autonomous status and were declared exempt from Spanish customs levies and from national conscription.

Further reading: Gilbert G. Fernandez, *The Making of Spain's First Caudillo: The Life and Career of General Baldomero Fernandez Espartero Through the First Carlist War, 1793–1840* (Ann Arbor, Mich.: Xerox University Microfilms, 1975); Frank N. Magill, ed., *Great Events from History: Modern European Series*, 3 vols. (Englewood Cliffs, N.J.: Salem Press, 1973).

Veritatis Splendor (The Splendor of Truth)   Pope John Paul II's 10th and most complex encyclical, issued on August 6, 1993, examining the religious and philosophical bases of the Roman Catholic Church's ethical teachings. During society's "crisis of truth," he believed that Christ was "the true and final answer to the problem of morality." The encyclical's first chapter ponders the meaning of life and search for happiness attainable through the teachings of Christ. Chapter two attributes the shortcomings of the current modern trends in moral theology to the failure to appreciate the connection between freedom and truth. The last chapter discusses how Catholic moral precepts can renew and enrich both the church and society.

Further reading: Michael J. Miller, ed., *The Encyclicals of Pope John Paul II* (Huntington, Ind.: Our Sunday Visitor Publishing, 1996).

Vermont Civil Union Act (An Act Relating to Civil Unions)   Legislation enacted by the Vermont state legislature permitting eligible couples of the same sex to be joined in civil union. Having their relationship legally sanctioned as a civil union provided the couple with "all the same benefits, protections and responsibilities under Vermont law . . . as are granted to spouses in a marriage." To be joined together in a civil union, a couple had to obtain a license from a town clerk and exchange vows before a justice of the peace or a member of the clergy. The controversial act, the first of its kind in the United States, was enacted on April 25, 2000, by a narrow margin in both houses and went into effect the following July 1. A year later the lower house voted 72–69 to eliminate civil unions and replace them with "reciprocal partnerships," which would not require a license and which would not be afforded all the benefits provided a civil union. The state senate failed to take action on the proposed changes during the 2001 session.

Further reading: "The Civil Union Process Step by Step," Vermont Civil Union, available online at http://www.civilunion.4t.com; "No. 91. An Act Relating to Civil Unions," Acts of the 1999–2000 Vermont Legislature, available online at http://www.leg.state.vt.us/docs/2000/acts/act091.htm.

Verona, Mandate of the Congress of   Last of the post–Napoleonic War conferences, convened (September-December 1822) in Verona, Italy, to formulate a joint plan of action against the ongoing Spanish Civil War of 1820–23; it entrusted France with a mandate to intervene and restore King Ferdinand VII to the Spanish throne (see BAYONNE, TREATY OF). The issue sorely tested allied unity since Britain refused to sanction intervention in the internal affairs of another country, while Russia offered to send her troops into Spain and the French government saw it as an opportunity to extend her influence into the Iberian Peninsula. Eventually, the conference decided in favor of French intervention—a decision supported by Austria, Prussia, and Russia, while Britain registered her protest and refused to endorse the mandate. By late 1823, French troops had successfully ended the civil war and restored Ferdinand VII to the throne.

Further reading: Frank N. Magill, ed., *Great Events from History: Modern European Series*, 3 vols. (Englewood Cliffs, N.J.: Salem Press, 1973); Irby C. Nichols, *The European Pentarchy and the Congress of Verona, 1822* (The Hague: Nijhoff, 1971).

Versailles, Edict of   See EDICT OF TOLERATION OF 1787, FRENCH.

Versailles, Treaty of (1715)   Subsidy treaty concluded at Versailles on April 3, 1715, between France and Sweden, intended to serve mutual political ends. Financially exhausted by the Great Northern War (1700–1721) (see TRAVENDAL, TREATY OF), King Charles XII of Sweden accepted the subsidy offer of King Louis XIV of France, guaranteeing him nearly £135,000 annually. The compensation was meant to help the Swedish king defend his German territories (Swedish Pomerania, Bremen, and Verden). Louis XIV, however, refused to invade Rhenish Prussia on Sweden's behalf and his death a few months later considerably compromised Sweden's position in Germany.

Further reading: R. Nisbet Bain, *Charles XII* (New York: AMS Press, 1980); Ragnhild M. Hatton, *Charles XII* (London: Historical Association, 1974).

Versailles, Treaty of (1783)   See PARIS, TREATY OF (1783).

Versailles, Treaty of (1919)   Allies' "dictated peace" with Germany, signed on June 28, 1919, at Versailles, France, to take effect January 10, 1920. The first part embodied the LEAGUE OF NATIONS COVENANT; the rest involved German war reparations, among these: give three small areas to Belgium; free Luxembourg from German control; demilitarize all of Germany west of the Rhine and a strip east of it; establish a temporary government in Saarland; return Alsace-Lorraine to France; affirm the independence of the future Austria, unless the League of Nations Council declared otherwise (see ST.-GERMAIN, TREATY OF [1919]); cede Poznań and most of West Prussia to Poland; demolish the Heligoland fortresses; cancel the BREST-LITOVSK TREATY; recognize Czechoslovakia; and agree to plebiscites to determine German frontiers with Denmark and Poland. The League of Nations Council would distribute "mandates" over the German colonies. The German army and navy were drastically curtailed, and the air force abolished. A special tribunal was to be created to indict the former German emperor and bring the other war criminals to trial. An Allied Reparation Commission would attend to the financial compensation. Other sections discussed the status of prisoners and graves, adjustment of the German debt, and guarantees for the implementation of the treaty.

See also: WORLD WAR I ARMISTICE.

Further reading: Mortimer Adler, ed., *The Annals of America*, 18 vols. (Chicago: Encyclopaedia Britannica, 1968); Louis L. Snyder, ed., *Fifty Major Documents of the Twentieth Century* (Princeton, N.J.: D. Van Nostrand, 1955); Louis L. Snyder, ed., *Documents of German History* (New Brunswick, N.J.: Rutgers University Press, 1958); Milton Viorst, ed., *The Great Documents of Western Civilization* (Philadelphia: Chilton Books, 1965).

Vervins, Treaty of   Agreement signed at Vervins, France, on May 2, 1598, between envoys of King Henry IV of France and King Philip II of Spain, ending the Ninth War of Religion (1589–98) in which Spain had joined the Catholic Holy League against Henry. Spain formally recognized Henry IV as the legitimate ruler of France and restored to France all the territories bordering the Netherlands. Philip II promised the Spanish Netherlands to his daughter Isabella and her future husband Archduke Albert, provided sovereignty was conferred on them. The provinces would revert to Spain if there was no issue from this marriage. By a secret arrangement, the archduke agreed to let Spanish troops hold the cities of Antwerp, Ghent, and Cambrai. France agreed not to interfere in Spain's war against the Netherlands. The treaty was a reconfirmation of Spanish supremacy and the 1559 Treaty of CATEAU-CAMBRÉSIS.

See also: NANTES, EDICT OF; NEMOURS, TREATY OF.

Further reading: R. J. Knecht, *The French Wars of Religion, 1559–1598*, 2d ed. (New York: Longman, 1996); Michael W. Lodwick, *The Enforcement of the Peace of Vervins: French and English Relations with the Spanish World Empire, 1598–1604* (Ann Arbor, Mich.: University Microfilms International, 1981); Frank N. Magill, ed., *Great Events from History: Modern European Series*, 3 vols. (Englewood Cliffs, N.J.: Salem Press, 1973).

Vespasian Imperial Law (Lex de Imperio Vespasiani)

Roman law conferring on Emperor Vespasian all the imperial powers in one lump; passed by the Roman Senate on December 22, A.D. 69, and soon ratified by the Assembly. Earlier in A.D. 69, Vespasian had been proclaimed emperor by his soldiers in Syria and later by the Senate. Only a fragment of the law still exists, and it seems to confer almost autocratic authority on Vespasian, giving him all of the explicit (and more) powers accumulated by his predecessors (notably Emperors Octavian and Claudius I). Vespasian restored order to Roman society and to the empire's finances.

Further reading: Fred B. R. Hellems, *Lex de Imperio Vespasiani; a Consideration of Some of the Constitutional Aspects of the Principate at Rome* (Chicago: Scott, Foresman, 1902); Barbara Levick, *Vespasian* (New York: Routledge, 1999).

Viborg Manifesto

Denunciation of Russia's czarist regime, issued in Viborg, Finland, immediately following Czar Nicholas II's dissolving of the first Duma on July 21, 1906. Approximately 200 members of the Constitutional Democratic Party (Cadets) and the Labor Party signed the manifesto, alleging certain irregularities in the dissolution of the Duma, and appealing to the Russian people to refuse taxes and military service and to withdraw deposits from savings accounts, until the Duma was reconvened. There was no response from the Russian people to this call for passive resistance, but the government responded by sentencing those who signed the manifesto to three months in jail, and forbidding them to be candidates for future Dumas.

Further reading: Ann E. Healy, *The Russian Autocracy in Crisis, 1905–1907* (Hamden, Conn.: Archon Books, 1976); S. S. Oldenburg, *Last Tsar: Nicholas II, His Reign & His Russia*, 4 vols., trans. and ed. Leonid I. Mihalap and Patrick J. Rollins (Gulf Breeze, Fla.: Academic International Press, 1975); V. V. Shulgin, *The Years: Memoirs of a Member of the Russian Duma, 1906–1917*, trans. Tanya Davis (New York: Hippocrene Books, 1991).

Victor Emmanuel II's Speech Opening the Italian Parliament

Speech by King Victor Emmanuel II of Sardinia, made in Turin in April 1860, to "the representatives of right and of the hopes of the nation," midway through the campaign for the unification of Italy, after the Austrian invasion had been repelled. Graciously attributing these successes to France, "a magnanimous ally," to the soldiers of both countries, to "the self-abnegation of the volunteers, and to the harmony of the various peoples and . . . to God," Victor Emmanuel reminded the people that they still had "many difficulties to overcome." As a gesture of gratitude to France, he announced that he had agreed to a treaty restoring Savoy and the district of Nice to France. Reiterating his respect for "the supreme head of our religion," he nevertheless warned of action "should the ecclesiastical authority resort to spiritual arms in support of its temporal interests." Finally, he assured the people that he would draw strength from a "pure conscience and the traditions of my forefathers" in order "to maintain civil liberty and my authority."

See also: GARIBALDI'S PROCLAMATION TO THE ITALIANS; MAZZINI'S INSTRUCTIONS TO YOUNG ITALY.

Further reading: Lynn M. Case, *Franco-Italian Relations, 1860–1865; the Roman Question and the Convention of September* (New York: AMS Press, 1970); Denis M. Smith, *Victor Emmanuel, Cavour and the Risorgimento* (New York: Oxford University Press, 1971); Milton Viorst, ed., *The Great Documents of Western Civilization* (Philadelphia: Chilton Books, 1965).

Victor Emmanuel II's Speech to the Italian Parliament in 1871

Address to the first meeting of the Italian Parliament in Rome, delivered by Victor Emmanuel II, first king of a united Italy (1861–78), who had entered the city as sovereign on July 2, 1871. During the Franco-Prussian War (1870–71), Napoléon III's troops withdrew from Rome, allowing Italian forces to enter; Pope Pius IX, deprived of his temporal rule, refused to recognize the Italian kingdom and Rome as its capital (which had been transferred there from Florence). In his speech, Victor Emmanuel accepted the "absolute independence" and "respected seat of the Pontificate" in Rome. Despite the attainment of "national unity," he stressed the need to overcome regional differences and rivalries and to develop the "productive forces of the nation." He knew that unification had not ended social and economic problems, which would be surmounted as "banks multiply, as do the commercial institutions, the expositions of the products of art and industry, and the congresses of the learned." He was certain of a "brilliant future" for the "glorious names of Italy and Rome."

See also: PIUS IX'S ENCYCLICAL OF 1871.

Further reading: Denis M. Smith, *Victor Emmanuel, Cavour and the Risorgimento* (New York: Oxford University Press, 1971); Milton Viorst, ed., *The Great Documents of Western Civilization* (Philadelphia: Chilton Books, 1965).

Vienna, Concordat of

Concordat concluded by Pope Nicholas V and Holy Roman Emperor Frederick III in February 1448, establishing the principles that were to govern the relations between the papacy and the Holy Roman Empire until the empire's demise. The concordat provided that imperial cathedral chapters had the right to elect their own bishops, without intervention by the papacy, but that the papacy had the right of confirmation; that the princes were to have a share in episcopal taxation; and that profits were to be shared by the papacy, emperor and princes. These provisions reflected the papacy's triumph over the conciliar movement, the proponents of which wished to make the people, as expressed through church councils, the authoritative voice in ecclesiastical affairs.

Further reading: John B. Toews, *Emperor Frederick III and His Relations with the Papacy from 1440 to 1493* (Ann Arbor, Mich.: University Microfilms International, 1978).

Vienna, Declaration of (1815)

Declaration outlawing deposed French emperor Napoléon Bonaparte after his return from exile on the island of Elba; issued on March 13, 1815, jointly by the eight European allies during their Vienna Conference. In violating "world repose," the Allies said, Napoléon "had exposed himself to public indictment (*vindicte*)." Further, they asserted, "Napoleon Bonaparte had placed himself outside the pale of civil and social relations." Together, the eight nations (Austria, France, Great Britain, Sweden, Spain, Portugal, Prussia, and Russia) promised to assist in the restoration of peace and tranquility to France. In a desperate attempt to curry favor, Napoléon abolished slavery (see SLAVE EMANCIPATION ACT, FRENCH), introduced a constitutional supplement (see ADDITIONAL ACT, FRENCH), and tried diplomatic tactics to break up the coalition strengthening against him.

Further reading: Alan Schom, *One Hundred Days: Napoleon's Road to Waterloo* (New York: Oxford University Press, 1993).

Vienna, Final Act of the Congress of

Document signed on June 9, 1815, in Vienna at the Congress of Vienna by representatives of most European countries; it embodied all the individual settlements recently made there. The Congress of Vienna was convened (1814–15) at the close of the Napoleonic Wars (1803–15). Through the document, Lombardy, Venetia, the Illyrian provinces, Salzburg, the Tyrol, and West Galicia were restored to Austria; Prussia received Posen (Poznán), Danzig (Gdansk), Swedish Pomerania, and the Baltic island of Rügen, with Denmark being indemnified elsewhere (see KIEL, TREATY OF); Sweden's possession of Norway was reaffirmed; the Netherlands, Switzerland, and the German Confederation were recognized as independent; Russia received most of the Grand Duchy of Warsaw; Great Britain retained Malta and several former French and Dutch colonies; France retained most of her colonial possessions abroad, but on the continent her borders were returned approximately to those of 1792.

See also: CHAUMONT, TREATIES OF; PARIS, TREATY OF (1814); PARIS, TREATY OF (1815).

Further reading: Tim Chapman, *The Congress of Vienna: Origins, Processes and Results* (New York: Routledge, 1998); Hilde Spiel, *The Congress of Vienna* (Philadelphia: Chilton Books, 1968); Charles K. Webster, *The Congress of Vienna, 1814–1815* (London: Thames & Hudson, 1963); Frank N. Magill, ed., *Great Events from History: Modern European Series*, 3 vols. (Englewood Cliffs, N.J.: Salem Press, 1973).

Vienna, Treaties of (1725)

Treaties of alliance concluded in Vienna between Austria and Spain on April 30, May 1, and November 5, 1725, bringing an end to the animosity that had been between them since the beginning of the War of the Spanish Succession (1701–14). By the first treaty, Spain agreed to support the PRAGMATIC SANCTION OF 1713. The second treaty provided that Holy Roman Emperor Charles VI of Austria would support Spain in her attempt to gain control over Gibraltar and Minorca, as well as to help develop commerce in the Austrian Netherlands (formerly the Spanish Netherlands). By the third treaty, marriages between two Austrian archduchesses and two Spanish royal infants were arranged. The rapprochement between these two powers, both of which had wielded great influence in Europe during the preceding century, caused alarm among other powers and helped bring on the 1725 Treaty of HANOVER among Britain, France, Holland, and Prussia.

Further reading: Penfield Roberts, *The Quest for Security, 1715–1740* (New York: Harper and Brothers, 1947); *Treaty of Peace between His Imperial and Catholick Majesty Charles VI, and His Royal Catholic Majesty Philip V, Concluded at Vienna the 30th of April 1725 [and] May 1, 1725* (New Haven, Conn.: Research Publications, 1974).

Vienna, Treaty of (1606)

Peace treaty concluded in Vienna by Matthias, viceroy of Hapsburg Hungary and brother of Holy Roman Emperor Rudolf II, and delegates of Stephen Bocskay, prince of Transylvania, on June 23, 1606. Bocskay had led a Protestant rebellion against the emperor's attempts to impose Roman Catholicism on Hungary, of which Transylvania was a part. Bocskay defeated the Hapsburgs and secured the treaty, by which he was recognized as sovereign of Transylvania and the religious freedom of Transylvanian (and other) Protestants was guaranteed. The treaty also legalized the partition of Hungary among the Hapsburgs (Rudolf and Matthias), the Ottoman sultan, and Bocskay; it represented the first major struggle won by the Hungarians against the Hapsburgs.

Further reading: Francois F. Roget, *The Huguenots of Hungary* (Geneva: H. Robert, 1926); Graeme Murdock, *Calvinism on the Frontier, 1600–1660: International Calvinism and the Reformed Church in Hungary and Transylvania* (New York: Oxford University Press, 2000).

Vienna, Treaty of (1656) Treaty of alliance concluded in Vienna on December 1, 1656, by Austria and Poland-Lithuania. Through the treaty Leopold I of Austria and Hungary pledged to send an army of 4,000 men to Poland to clear the country of Swedish forces, which had, with the aid of Transylvanian prince George Rákóczy, occupied the country. Austria and Sweden had long been enemies, for religious as well as political reasons. Swedish king Charles X's bid for control of the Baltic became a threat to Austria, although not as immediate, as well as Poland in the First Northern War (1655–60).

Further reading: Richard Butterwick, *The Polish-Lituanian Monarchy in European Context c. 1500–1795* (New York: Palgrave, 2001); John P. Spielman, *Leopold I of Austria* (London: Thames & Hudson, 1977).

Vienna, Treaty of (1731) Agreement made in Vienna on March 16, 1731, among Britain's king George II, the Holy Roman Emperor Charles VI, and the Dutch Republic (Holland) to promote "a firm, sincere, and inviolable friendship." The British and Dutch promised to guarantee Charles's 1731 Pragmatic Sanction (Maria Theresa's female succession right to Austrian territories), and Charles, Maria Theresa's father, agreed to the peaceful induction of 6,000 Spanish soldiers into the Farnese Italian duchies of Tuscany, Parma, and Piacenza (see SEVILLE, TREATY OF [1729]). Charles also agreed to dissolve the Ostend Company, which had been formed as a rival to the Dutch and English in the East Indies trade. All parties were to meet again in Antwerp to ratify the terms of the Barrier Treaty of 1715 (see BARRIER TREATIES) and conclude a new commercial pact.

Further reading: Penfield Roberts, *The Quest for Security, 1715–1740* (New York: Harper & Brothers, 1947).

Vienna, Treaty of (1735) Preliminary peace concluded in Vienna on October 5, 1735, by Poland, France, Spain, and Austria, bringing the War of the Polish Succession (1733–38) nearly to an end (the definitive Treaty of Vienna was ratified on November 18, 1738). The war had been instigated by the Russo-Austrian coalition's armed attempt to enforce the election to the Polish throne of their Saxon candidate, Augustus III, against the French-supported Polish candidate, Stanislaus I Leszczyński. The treaty provided for Leszczyński's renunciation of the Polish throne and his acquisition of the duchies of Lorraine and Bar; for Duke Francis Stephen of Lorraine's acquisition of Tuscany; for Austria's cession of Naples, Sicily, and several other Italian provinces to Spain; for Austria's acquisition of Parma and Piacenza in Italy; for France's acceptance and guarantee of the PRAGMATIC SANCTION OF 1713. The most significant of the treaty's results was Poland's loss of freedom (to Russia) in electing her own king.

Further reading: Penfield Roberts, *The Quest for Security, 1715–1740* (New York: Harper & Brothers, 1947); J. H. Shennan, *International Relations in Europe, 1689–1789* (New York:

Routledge, 1995); John L. Sutton, *The King's Honor & the King's Cardinal: The War of the Polish Succession* (Lexington: University Press of Kentucky, 1980).

Vienna, Treaty of (1778) Secret agreement made in Vienna on January 15, 1778, between Holy Roman Emperor Joseph II of Austria and Elector Charles Theodore of the Palatinate branch of the House of Wittelsbach. By the treaty, Charles Theodore, who had inherited the duchy of Bavaria in 1777, agreed to recognize old Austrian rights to lower Bavaria and some of the upper Palatinate, in return for Austria's agreement to make provisions for the granting of royal status in the Holy Roman Empire to children the elector might have. The treaty's public disclosure led to the War of the Bavarian Succession (1778–79) and caused anxiety in Prussia and France, both of which opposed Austrian expansion into Germany.

See also: TESCHEN, TREATY OF.

Further reading: Marvin E. Thomas, *Karl Theodor and the Bavarian Succession, 1777–1778* (Lewiston, Maine: E. Mellen Press, 1989).

Vienna, Treaty of (1809) See SCHÖNBRUNN, TREATY OF (1809).

Vienna, Treaty of (1864) Peace treaty concluded between Denmark and the Austro-Prussian coalition in Vienna on October 30, 1864, bringing an end to the brief Schleswig-Holstein War (1864) between the two parties. The peace provided that the victors, Austria and Prussia, would gain joint possession of the Danish-held duchies of Schleswig, Holstein, and Laurenburg. The war had arisen over Danish king Frederick VII's annexation of the duchy of Schleswig to his country and his intervention in the internal affairs of Holstein. The move led to heightened tensions among Denmark and Prussia and Austria, because there existed a previous agreement declaring the inseparability of Schleswig and Holstein. The intervention in Holstein, a member of the German Confederation, had also aroused indignation.

See also: GASTEIN, CONVENTION OF.

Further reading: William Carr, *The Origins of the Wars of German Unification* (New York: Longman, 1991); Fred L. Israel, ed., *Major Peace Treaties of Modern History, 1648–1967*, 4 vols. (New York: Chelsea House, 1967); Keith A. P. Sandiford, *Great Britain and the Schleswig-Holstein Question, 1848–64: A Study in Diplomacy, Politics, and Public Opinion* (Toronto: University of Toronto Press, 1975); Louis L. Snyder, ed., *Documents of German History* (New Brunswick, N.J.: Rutgers University Press, 1958).

Vienna, Treaty of (1866) (Austro-Italian Treaty of Venetia) Treaty of peace concluded between Austria and Italy in the Austrian capital of Vienna on October 12, 1866, reconfirming, this time directly to Italy, Austria's cession of Venetia to Italy. The cession had already been definitively arranged between Austria and France prior to the outbreak of the 1866 Austro-Prussian Seven Weeks' War (see NAPOLÉON III'S TREATY WITH AUSTRIA). Italy had become involved in the war, which was essentially a war between Austria and Prussia over ascendancy in the German world, through Prussia's recruitment of Italy to join her against Austria (see PRUSSIAN-ITALIAN ALLIANCE OF 1866).

See also: PRAGUE, TREATY OF (1866).

Further reading: Fred L. Israel, ed., *Major Peace Treaties of Modern History, 1648–1967*, 4 vols. (New York: Chelsea House, 1967); Frank N. Magill, ed., *Great Events from History: Modern European Series*, 3 vols. (Englewood Cliffs, N.J.: Salem Press, 1973).

Vienna Declaration and Program of Action

Plan adopted on June 25, 1993, by delegates from 171 states at the World Conference on Human Rights (June 14–25, 1993) in Vienna, Austria, to promote and bolster human rights activities worldwide. While reaffirming the principles established in the 1948 UNIVERSAL DECLARATION OF HUMAN RIGHTS, this declaration sought to extend human rights actions and programs "to make the enjoyment of human rights a reality for every human being." In recognizing the close relationship between democracy, development, and human rights, it stressed the cooperative nature of all human rights work. The document recommended creating a rapporteur on Violence Against Women, universal ratification of the Convention on the Rights of the Child, and proclamation of an international decade of all the indigenous peoples of the world. It proposed creating the office of a High Commissioner for Human Rights (established on December 20, 1993) and increasing financial support for the Center for Human Rights to strengthen the United Nations's monitoring capacity.

Further reading: Office of the United Nations High Commission for Human Rights, "World Conference on Human Rights," office of the High Commissioner for Human Rights, Available online at http://www.unhchr.ch/html/menu5/wchr.htm.

Vienna Four Points

Document endorsed by Great Britain, France, and Austria on August 8, 1854, confirming their agreement on issues pertaining to Russo-Turkish jurisdictional disputes, which had brought on the Crimean War (1853–56). It proposed that a settlement between the two parties would have these conditions: (1) Russia's renunciation of her claims to Serbia and the Danubian principalities, plus the collective guarantee of these territories by the signatory powers; (2) the free navigation of the Danube River; (3) the revision of the STRAITS CONVENTION to accommodate the present European political climate; (4) Russia's renunciation of her claims to be the protector of the Ottoman sultan's Orthodox Christian subjects, and the powers' collective guarantee of the rights of all Christians in the Ottoman Empire,

without infringing upon the sultan's sovereign rights. Russia rejected the conditions.

See also: OTTOMAN IMPERIAL EDICT OF 1856; PARIS, TREATY OF (1856); VIENNA NOTE OF 1853.

Further reading: David M. Goldfrank, *The Origins of the Crimean War* (New York: Longman, 1994); Norman Rich, *Why the Crimean War? A Cautionary Tale* (New York: McGraw-Hill, 1991); Alexis S. Troubetzkoy, *The Road to Balaklava: Stumbling into War with Russia* (Toronto: Trafalgar Press, 1986).

Vienna Note of 1853

Note prepared at a conference held in Vienna under the influence of French emperor Napoléon III and Austrian foreign minister Count Buol; endorsed by Prussia and Great Britain, and on July 28, 1853, presented to Russian czar Nicholas I, proposing terms upon which a settlement to the Russo-Turkish disputes could be reached. The disputes, which were soon to develop into the Crimean War (1853–56), originated over the Ottoman Empire's refusal to meet Russia's demand that the sultan extend the same privileges to the sultan's Orthodox Christian subjects that had been extended to the Roman Catholic Christians (supported by France). In the note, which was vaguely worded, the four powers hoped to create terms to which both France and Russia could agree, without offending the sultan. Although the Russians accepted the note, the Turks demanded that the Christian subjects' security depend solely on them, which the Russians would not concede. The war broke out in October 1853.

Further reading: David M. Goldfrank, *The Origins of the Crimean War* (New York: Longman, 1994); Norman Rich, *Why the Crimean War? A Cautionary Tale* (New York: McGraw-Hill, 1991); Alexis S. Troubetzkoy, *The Road to Balaklava: Stumbling into War with Russia* (Toronto: Trafalgar Press, 1986).

Vietnamese Declaration of Independence

Declaration of independence of the Democratic Republic of Vietnam; proclaimed by Ho Chi Minh, communist political leader of the Vietminh (Vietnamese nationalists and communists), on September 2, 1945, at Hanoi in Tonkin (north Vietnam). Recalling the American DECLARATION OF INDEPENDENCE and France's DECLARATION OF THE RIGHTS OF MAN AND OF THE CITIZEN, it declared that "all men are created equal," have "certain inalienable rights," and "must always remain free and have equal rights." Since 1940 the Vietnamese people had been "subjected to the double yoke of the French and Japanese," whose surrender to the Allies (1945) had enabled the Vietnamese to regain their national sovereignty. The declaration further stated that the Vietnamese, "animated by a common purpose, are determined to fight to the bitter end against any attempt by the French colonialists to reconquer their country."

See also: FRENCH AGREEMENT ON THE INDEPENDENCE OF VIETNAM; GENEVA AGREEMENTS OF 1954.

Further reading: William J. Duiker, *Ho Chi Minh* (New York: Hyperion, 2000); Mark A. Kishlansky, ed., *Sources of World History: Readings for World History*, vol. 2, 2d ed. (Belmont, Calif.: West/Wadsworth, 1999); *Ho Chi Minh: Selected Writings, 1920–1969* (Hanoi, Vietnam: Foreign Languages Publishing House, 1973).

Vilayet Law Law enacted in 1864 in the Ottoman Empire (Turkey), providing for the reorganization of local administration within the empire. The empire was redivided into larger administrative provinces, called vilayets, each of which consisted of several of the formerly arranged provinces. These vilayets were under the increased authority of governors and were subdivided into districts, called sanjaks, each with elective councils and tribunals. The aim was to extend greater power to local government and to lessen that of the central government. One of the first vilayets established enjoyed considerable success, its leader providing for the improvement of transportation, the educational system, and commerce.

Further reading: Halil Sahillioglu, *Studies on Ottoman Economics and Social History* (Istanbul: Organization of the Islamic Conference Research Centre for Islamic History, Art & Culture, 1999).

Villafranca, Treaty of Treaty concluded between Emperor Napoléon III of France and Emperor Francis Joseph of Austria at Villafranca, Italy, on July 11, 1859, ending the war between Austria and the Franco-Piedmontese coalition. The war originated over Piedmont's (Sardinia) determination to gain independence from Austria, and France's decision to ally herself with Piedmont and her cause. Through the treaty both parties agreed that Austria would cede most of Lombardy (without Mantua and Peschiera) to France, which in turn would cede it to Piedmont; that Austria would retain Venetia; and that the former Italian princes would regain their thrones, on the condition that they pardon those who had risen up against them during the war. Although the Franco-Piedmontese coalition had been successful against Austria, France desired peace largely because she had grown fearful that Prussia might mobilize her forces in alliance with Austria.

See also: ZURICH, TREATY OF (1859).

Further reading: Arnold Blumberg, *A Carefully Planned Accident: The Italian War of 1859* (Selinsgrove, Pa.: Susquehanna University Press, 1990); Frank N. Magill, ed., *Great Events from History: Modern European Series*, 3 vols. (Englewood Cliffs, N.J.: Salem Press, 1973).

Vincennes, Treaty of Agreement signed at Fort Wayne, Indiana Territory, on June 7, 1803, whereby nine Indian tribes ceded approximately 2,000 square miles of territory around the city of Vincennes to the U.S. government. Negotiated by the governor of the territory, William Henry Harri-

son, and the Shawnee, Potawatomi, Miami, Wea, Eel River, Delaware, Piankashaw, Kaskaskia, and Kickapoo Indians, the treaty provided millions of acres for white settlement. A supplementary treaty, signed at Vincennes on August 7, 1803, ceded additional tracts in Indian territory to build way stations for settlers and traders moving west.

Further reading: Gary W. Pond, *William Henry Harrison and United States Indian Policy in the Northwest and Indiana Territories, 1783–1813* (Ann Arbor, Mich.: University Microfilms International, 1997).

Vindication of the Rights of Woman Mary Wollstonecraft's seminal work (1792) advocating equal rights for women, considered the cornerstone of the modern feminist movement, inspired by events in France (see DECLARATION OF THE RIGHTS OF WOMAN AND THE FEMALE CITIZEN; *ON THE ADMISSION OF WOMEN TO CITIZENSHIP*), and published to widespread criticism. Wollstonecraft attributed women's ignorance and submissiveness to a "false system of education" and to their upbringing rather than to any inherent deficiencies. Arguing that no God would create a separate morality for men and women, she suggested that the "divine right of husbands" should be challenged just like the "divine right of kings." Women should have equal educational and employment opportunities, enjoy "a civil existence in state," and end their economic dependence on men. The time was ripe "to effect a revolution in female manners" so that women, "by reforming themselves," could "reform the world."

Further reading: Eleanor Flexner, *Mary Wollstonecraft—A Biography* (Baltimore: Penguin Books, 1973); Mary Wollstonecraft, *A Vindication of the Rights of Woman*, Bartleby.com. Great Books online, available online at http://www.bartleby.com/144/.

Vinson Naval Act (U.S. Naval Expansion Act) Federal legislation enacted on May 17, 1938, that authorized a $1.09 billion expansion of U.S. naval forces to establish a "two-ocean navy" over the next 10 years. It was formulated by Representative Carl Vinson of Georgia, who was chairman of the House Naval Affairs Committee. It allowed for an increase in capital ships to a maximum of 660,000 tons, in cruisers to 412,500 tons, and in aircraft carriers to 175,000 tons. Japan's invasion of China (beginning the Sino-Japanese War of 1937–45) and growing threats of war in Europe had prompted Congress to act.

Further reading: Samuel E. Morison, *The Two Ocean War, a Short History of the United States Navy in the Second World War* (Boston: Little, Brown, 1963).

Virginia Bill of Rights (Virginia Declaration of Rights) Document written principally by colonial American statesman George Mason and adopted by the Virginia Constitutional Convention on June 12, 1776. It was eventually drawn on by Thomas Jefferson in his formulation of the opening paragraphs of the DECLARATION OF INDEPENDENCE and served as the basis of the BILL OF RIGHTS in the U.S. CONSTITUTION. Mason's document asserted such ideas as the "inherent rights" of all men, the right to "reform, alter, or abolish" ineffective or contrary governments, the separation of powers, the right to trial by jury, and "the free exercise of religion."

See also: FAIRFAX RESOLVES.

Further reading: Mortimer Adler, ed., *The Annals of America*, 18 vols. (Chicago: Encyclopaedia Britannica, 1968); *American Jurisprudence 2d ed., Desk Book* (N.p.: West Group, 1998); Albert P. Blaustein and Jay A. Sigler, eds., *Constitutions That Made History* (New York: Paragon House Publishers, 1988); Henry Steele Commager, ed., *Documents of American History*, 8th ed. (New York: Appleton-Century-Crofts, 1968).

Virginia Plan (Randolph Plan)

Proposal submitted to the Federal Constitutional Convention on May 29, 1787, by Edmund Randolph, governor of Virginia, on behalf of his state's delegation. The plan went beyond mere revision of the ARTICLES OF CONFEDERATION and proposed the creation of a new national government. Its 15 resolutions included such features as a bicameral legislature with the lower house elected directly by the people and the upper house elected by the lower from nominees submitted by the state legislatures; an executive officer and a national judiciary, both to be elected by Congress; and a "council of revision" composed of the executive and members of the judiciary, with an absolute veto over all legislation. The Virginia Plan served as the convention's basis for debate and, like the NEW JERSEY PLAN, was eventually rejected in favor of the GREAT COMPROMISE (CONNECTICUT COMPROMISE).

Further reading: Mortimer Adler, ed., *The Annals of America*, 18 vols. (Chicago: Encyclopaedia Britannica, 1968); Lance Banning, *The Sacred Fire of Liberty: James Madison and the Founding of the Federal Republic* (Ithaca, N.Y.: Cornell University Press, 1995); Henry Steele Commager, ed., *Documents of American History*, 8th ed. (New York: Appleton-Century-Crofts, 1968).

Virginia Resolutions (1798)

Resolutions drafted by James Madison and adopted by the Virginia state legislature on December 24, 1798; they declared the U.S. ALIEN AND SEDITION ACTS OF 1798 to be unconstitutional and appealed to the other states to make similar declarations. Like the 1798 KENTUCKY RESOLUTIONS, the Virginia document expressed loyalty to the Union and urged Congress to repeal the acts. It claimed that the federal government represented a "compact" between the states and therefore held only those powers specifically delegated to it by the states; passage of the Alien and Sedition Acts exceeded those powers. Though Congress took no action, the resolutions, contributed to the defeat of the Federalist Party in the election of 1800.

Further reading: Mortimer Adler, ed., *The Annals of America*, 18 vols. (Chicago: Encyclopaedia Britannica, 1968); Henry Steele Commager, ed., *Documents of American History*, 8th ed. (New York: Appleton-Century-Crofts, 1968); James R. Sharp, *American Politics in the Early Republic: The New Nation in Crisis* (New Haven, Conn.: Yale University Press, 1993).

Virginia Resolves

Set of resolutions, in reaction to the TOWNSHEND ACTS, that were written by George Mason and introduced in the Virginia House of Burgesses on May 16, 1769. Supported by a unanimous vote, they proclaimed that only the governor and the provincial legislature could impose taxes in Virginia and, by implication, criticized the British ministry for denouncing the Massachusetts and Virginia circular letters. They also condemned the British proposal that American dissidents be brought to England for trial. Governor Botetourt (Norborne Berkeley) dissolved the assembly the next day, but the members continued to meet informally and went on to support the Virginia Association of ex-Burgesses.

Further reading: George R. Johnson, *The Will of the People: The Legacy of George Mason* (Fairfax, Va.: George Mason University Press, 1991); William MacDonald, ed., *Select Charters and Other Documents Illustrative of American History, 1606–1775* (New York: Macmillan, 1899).

Visegrád, Agreement at

Settlement reached at Visegrád, near Budapest, Hungary, among the kings of Poland, Bohemia, and Hungary (Casimir III the Great, John of Luxembourg, and Charles Robert of Anjou, respectively) in November 1335. It concerned the outcome of the Teutonic Knights' War with Poland of 1309–43, establishing, tentatively, that the regions of Kujawia and Dobrzyn should be returned to Poland and that Pomerania should be given to the Teutonic Knights as an alm by the Polish king. Casimir, who had conceded much to the other two kings, had hoped for a more favorable settlement; he stalled for several years before agreeing formally to a solution (see KALISCH, TREATY OF [1343]).

Further reading: Paul W. Knoll, *The Foreign Policy of Casimir the Great of Poland, 1333–1370* (Ann Arbor, Mich.: University Microfilms, 1969).

Vlorë Proclamation

Proclamation of an independent Albanian state issued on November 28, 1912, in the Albanian town of Vlorë (Valona) by the nationalist Albanian leader Ismail Kemal Bey, before a group of 83 delegates from throughout Albania. In addition to the proclamation of independence, the document called for the formation of a provisional government, the election of a senate, and the formation of a commission whose task it would be to travel to foreign governments to gain support for Albanian rights. The proclamation was made just after a coalition of Balkan states declared war on the Ottoman Empire (Turkey) and during their armies' advance into Albania, the objective of which was to secure as much of Albania for themselves as possible. The major European powers nevertheless supported Albania's independence, which they formally recognized on July 29, 1913.

See also: LONDON, TREATY OF (1913).

Further reading: Sommerville Story, ed., *The Memoirs of Ismail Kemal Bey* (London: Constable, 1920); Abdul B. Sula, *Albania's Struggle for Independence* (New York: Self-published, 1967).

Voeslau, Treaty of   Secret treaty concluded on August 26, 1867, in the town of Voeslau, or Vöslau, near Vienna, between Serbia under the leadership of Prince Michael Obrenovich and Greece under King George I; it provided terms for their alliance and anticipated an uprising against the Ottoman Empire (Turkey). The contracting parties agreed that, in the event of a successful uprising against the Turks, which was then planned for March 1868, Serbia would receive Bosnia and Herzegovina, while Greece would receive Epirus and Thessaly; in the event of a Turkish attack on either of the two powers, each pledged the other its support. The Greco-Serbian alliance was the most important of several such alliances (see BALKAN TREATIES OF 1866–68).

Further reading: Walter Christmas, *King George of Greece*, trans. A. G. Chater (New York: McBride, Nast & Co., 1914); *Greek-Serbian Cooperation, 1830–1908: Collection of Reports from the Second Greek-Serbian Symposium, 1980* (Belgrade: Serbian Academy of Science and Arts, Institute for Balkan Studies, 1982).

Volstead Act (National Prohibition Act)   Federal U.S. legislation passed on October 28, 1919, to enforce the EIGHTEENTH AMENDMENT, establishing Prohibition. The act, introduced by U.S. Representative Andrew J. Volstead of Minnesota and passed over the veto of President Woodrow Wilson, defined intoxicating liquor as any beverage containing more than 0.5 percent alcohol by volume. It went into effect on January 16, 1920, and gave federal agents, under the Bureau of Internal Revenue, the power to investigate violations; it also prescribed penalties. Strict enforcement proved impossible, however, and the act became void after the TWENTY-FIRST AMENDMENT repealed the Eighteenth.

Further reading: Arthur W. Blakemore, *National Prohibition, The Volstead Act Annotated* (Albany, N.Y.: M. Bender, 1927); Henry Steele Commager, ed., *Documents of American History*, 8th ed. (New York: Appleton-Century-Crofts, 1968); Frank N. Magill, ed., *Great Events from History: American Series*, 3 vols. (Englewood Cliffs, N.J.: Salem Press, 1975); *Prohibition: The 18th Amendment, the Volstead Act, the 21st Amendment* (Washington, D.C.: National Archives & Records Administration, 1986).

Voting Rights Act of 1965, U.S.   Landmark federal U.S. legislation enacted on August 6, 1965, intended to eliminate racial discrimination in voting in the United States, thus enforcing the FIFTEENTH AMENDMENT. The act suspended the use of literacy, educational, moral, and other tests in areas where they had been used to deny the right to vote on account of race or color; authorized the appointment of federal examiners in such areas to register voters; provided criminal penalties for intimidating, threatening, or coercing any person for voting or attempting to vote; and abolished the poll tax. The U.S. Supreme Court upheld the constitutionality of the act in *South Carolina* v. *Katzenbach* (1966) and *Katzenbach* v. *Morgan* (1966).

Further reading: Howard Ball et al., *Compromised Compliance: Implementation of the 1965 Voting Rights Act* (Westport, Conn.: Greenwood Press, 1982); Chandler Davidson and Bernard Grofman, eds., *Quiet Revolution in the South: The Impact of the Voting Rights Act, 1965–1990* (Princeton, N.J.: Princeton University Press, 1994); David M. Hudson, *Along Racial Lines: Consequences of the 1965 Voting Rights Act* (New York: P. Lang, 1998); Garrine P. Laney, *The Voting Rights Act of 1965, as Amended: Its History and Current Issues* (Washington, D.C.: Congressional Research Service, Library of Congress, 1995).

Vulgate   Latin translation of the Bible prepared primarily by St. Jerome, a noted biblical scholar, between A.D. 382 and 405, and accepted, with some modifications, as the authorized version by the Roman Catholic Church. Pope Damasus I commissioned St. Jerome to write an agreeable, useful Latin version of the Bible to replace the *Itala*, an old Latin translation from the Greek. He first revised the Gospels of the New Testament (A.D. 382–83) and ended by carefully translating (with help from several rabbis) the entire Old Testament from Hebrew. Jerome's translation became popular in the West after the fifth century and, by the Middle Ages, was used by Roman Catholics everywhere. In 1546 the Council of Trent declared the Vulgate the Catholics' biblical Latin authority, and in 1592 Pope Clement VIII promulgated the so-called Clementine Vulgate, his edition, which became the exclusive biblical text of the church. In 1965 the Second Vatican Council appointed a commission to carry on a revision.

See also: BIBLE, AUTHORIZED (KING JAMES) VERSION OF THE.

Further reading: Catholic University of America, eds., *New Catholic Encyclopedia* (New York: McGraw-Hill, 1967); Frank N. Magill, ed., *Great Events from History: Ancient and Medieval Series*, 3 vols. (Englewood Cliffs, N.J.: Salem Press, 1972); Richard Marsden, *The Text of the Old Testament in Anglo-Saxon England* (New York: Cambridge University Press, 1995).

W

Wabash, St. Louis and Pacific Railroad Company v. Illinois (Wabash Case) U.S. Supreme Court decision of October 25, 1886, concerning the legality of an Illinois statute prohibiting long-and-short-haul clauses in transportation contracts. The Wabash Railroad had charged different shippers different rates for carrying items. The state of Illinois charged the railroad with gross discrimination in freight rates, fined it $5,000, and allowed the aggrieved shipper to recover heavy damages. The U.S. Supreme Court overturned the state statue, claiming that it infringed on Congress's exclusive control over interstate commerce. The decision weakened the ruling in MUNN V. ILLINOIS and helped lead to the passage of the INTERSTATE COMMERCE ACT.

Further reading: Henry Steele Commager, ed., *Documents of American History*, 8th ed. (New York: Appleton-Century-Crofts, 1968); Robert Fridington, *The Reconstruction Court, 1864–1888* (Danbury, Conn.: Grolier Educational, 1995); Kermit L. Hall et al., eds., *The Oxford Companion to the Supreme Court of the United States* (New York: Oxford University Press, 1992); United States Supreme Court, *United States Reports: Cases Adjudged in the Supreme Court at . . . and Rules Announced at . . .* (New York: Banks & Brothers, Law Publishers, 1884–1921; Washington, D.C.: Government Printing Office, 1992–).

Wade-Davis Bill Severe reconstruction plan passed by the U.S. Congress on July 2, 1864, that provided for the governmental reorganization of a seceded state only after a majority of white male citizens had taken an oath of allegiance and after a constitution acceptable to the president and Congress had been adopted. The bill was sponsored by Senator Benjamin F. Wade of Ohio and Representative Henry W. Davis of Maryland and supported by other Radical Republicans, who believed reconstruction was a congressional function. When Lincoln refused to sign the bill, killing it by pocket veto on July 4, 1864, its sponsors issued the Wade-Davis Manifesto, attacking the president's "studied outrage" and defiance of congressional authority. The manifesto appeared in the *New York Tribune* on August 5, 1864, and was the harshest Republican criticism of Lincoln ever.

Further reading: Mortimer Adler, ed., *The Annals of America*, 18 vols. (Chicago: Encyclopaedia Britannica, 1968); Henry Steele Commager, ed., *Documents of American History*, 8th ed. (New York: Appleton-Century-Crofts, 1968); Frank N. Magill, ed., *Great Events from History: American Series*, 3 vols. (Englewood Cliffs, N.J.: Salem Press, 1975).

Wadgaon, Convention of Agreement made between Bombay-based British forces and the Maratha (Mahratta) army at Wadgaon (23 miles from Poona [Pune]), India, on January 13, 1779. In the First Mahratta War (1775–82), the Marathas had surrounded the British troops, forcing them to accept certain conditions. They demanded the recall of the advancing, Bengal-based British army and the return of all their territories seized since 1773, including Salsette Island. Maratha leader Mahadaji Sindhia wanted part of the British revenues from the Broach district. The Marathas also claimed an indemnity of 41,000 rupees along with two hostages as surety. The Bombay forces withdrew, but the order recalling the Bengal army was suspended. Disgraced, the British authorities in Bengal refused to honor these terms, except the promise made to Sindhia, and so the war continued.

See also: SALBAI, TREATY OF.

Further reading: N. G. Rathod, *The Great Maratha Mahadaji Sindia* (New Delhi, India: Sarup & Sons, 1994); Sailendra N. Sen, *Anglo-Maratha Relations During the Administration of Warren Hastings, 1772–1785* (Bombay, India: Popular Prakashan, 1994); S. P. Varma, *A Study in Maratha Diplomacy; Anglo-Maratha Relations, 1772–1783 A.D.* (Agra, India: Shiva Lal Agrawala, 1956).

Wages and Hours Act, U.S.   See FAIR LABOR STANDARDS ACT, U.S.

Wagner-Connery Act   See NATIONAL LABOR RELATIONS ACT, U.S.

Wagner-Steagall Act (National Housing Act of 1937)
U.S. legislation enacted on September 1, 1937, that established the U.S. Housing Authority (USHA), under the Department of the Interior, to improve housing conditions for low-income people. Sponsored by Senator Robert F. Wagner of New York and Representative Henry B. Steagall of Alabama, the act provided for low-interest, long-term loans to local public agencies for slum clearance and public housing. It authorized subsidies to assist local authorities in setting rents for low-income tenants.

Further reading: Henry Steele Commager, ed., *Documents of American History*, 8th ed. (New York: Appleton-Century-Crofts, 1968).

Waitangi, Treaty of   Agreement made on February 6, 1840, at the settlement of Waitangi (on New Zealand's North Island), by which a group of Maori chiefs (numbering nearly 500) accepted British sovereignty in return for a guarantee of protection of their lands. Intended to protect British traders and missionaries, the pact gave Britain the sole right to purchase Maori property (this article later contributed to racial tension) and conferred on the Maoris the full rights of British subjects. The treaty eventually became the basis for Britain's annexation of New Zealand in May 1840 (South Island having been won, ostensibly, by virtue of discovery), when Captain William Hobson (governor-designate) proclaimed British sovereignty from the new capital at Auckland.

Further reading: Dora Alves, *The Maori and the Crown: An Indigenous People's Struggle for Self-Determination* (Westport, Conn.: Greenwood Press, 1999); Ian Brownlie, *Treaties and Indigenous People* (New York: Oxford University Press, 1992); Paul G. McHugh, *The Maori Magna Carta: New Zealand Law and the Treaty of Waitangi* (New York: Oxford

University Press, 1991); Paul Moon, *The Origins of the Treaty of Waitangi* (Auckland, New Zealand: Birdwood Publications, 1994).

Wales, Statute of   English king Edward I's statute issued on March 19, 1284, from Rhuddlan, providing for the annexation and union of Wales to England and establishing the legal and administrative framework of Welsh territory. It followed the defeat in December 1282 of Llewelyn ap Gruffydd's Welsh forces by Edward's army. Snowdonia, Llewelyn's land, was divided into three counties—Anglesey, Caernarfon, and Merioneth—governed by a justice of North Wales. Another county, Flint, became part of the earldom of Chester. The king also extended his control over two counties in South West Wales—Cardigan and Carmarthen—by reconstituting them under the supervision of the justice of West Wales. The Welsh counties were patterned after their English counterparts and shared certain legal practices (for instance, women were granted "dower" and allowed to inherit property), but they did not have representation in the English Parliament and were not governed by the central courts at Westminster. The Welsh Marchers (inhabitants of English-Welsh border lands) were left untouched by this legislation.

See also: UNION, ACTS OF (UNION OF WALES AND ENGLAND).

Further reading: John E. Morris, *The Welsh Wars of Edward I* (Stroud, England: Sutton, 1998).

Walker Law   First major law governing the sport of boxing in the United States; enacted in New York State under sponsorship of James J. Walker, speaker of the state senate (later mayor of New York City), in 1920. It legalized professional boxing in New York and established a code of rules (drawn mainly from English boxing promoter William Gavin), which greatly influenced legislation in other states (each U.S. state has different boxing rules, as does each country of the world). The Walker Law also established the New York State Athletic Commission, an independent body.

Further reading: Gene Fowler, *Beau James: The Life & Times of Jimmy Walker* (New York: Viking Press, 1949).

Walker Tariff Act (U.S. Tariff Act of 1846)   Federal U.S. legislation enacted on July 30, 1846, that established a moderate protective and revenue-generating tariff. Named for U.S. Secretary of the Treasury Robert J. Walker, the Democratic-sponsored bill lowered rates set by the Tariff of 1842 from an average of about 33 percent to about 25 percent. It also dropped the minimum valuation principle and allowed some commodities to be imported duty-free. The act helped foreign trade and improved relations with Great Britain. It was superseded by the TARIFF ACT OF 1857.

Further reading: Mortimer Adler, ed., *The Annals of America*, 18 vols. (Chicago: Encyclopaedia Britannica, 1968); Lars Magnusson, *Free Trade and Protectionism in America: 1822–*

1890 (New York: Routledge, 2000); Sidney Ratner, *The Tariff in American History* (New York: Van Nostrand, 1972); F. W. Taussig, *The Tariff History of the United States* (Woodbridge, Conn.: Research Publications, 1991).

Wallon Amendment   Proposal by Henri Wallon to formalize the method of electing the French head of state; was passed 353 to 352 by the provisional National Assembly on January 30, 1875. The bill declared that the president of France's republic would be elected (and could be reelected) for a term of seven years, by an absolute majority of the senate and the chamber of deputies, sitting as the National Assembly. Although its ostensible purpose was to establish the process of choosing a successor to Marshal MacMahon, its effect was to transform the provisional government from a temporary expedient into a permanent institution. In doing so, it cleared the way for (and was included in) a subsequent series of constitutional laws that established the Third Republic.

See also: FRENCH CONSTITUTION OF 1875; SEPTENNATE, LAW OF.

Further reading: William Fortescue, *The Third Republic in France, 1870–1940; Conflicts and Continuities* (New York: Routledge, 2000); Noel M. MacMahon, trans. and ed., *Here I Am, Here I Stay!: Marshal MacMahon, 1808–1893* (Whitegate, Ireland: Ballinakella Press, 1993); Charles Sowerwine, *France since 1870: Culture, Politics and Society* (New York: Palgrave, 2001).

Walsh-Healey Government Contracts Act, U.S.
Federal legislation enacted on June 30, 1936, that specified working conditions and wages for employees of companies that had U.S. government contracts greater than $10,000. Sponsored by Representative Arthur D. Healey of Massachusetts and based on earlier work by deceased Senator Thomas J. Walsh of Montana, the act provided that such employees must be paid at least the prevailing minimum wage, as set by the secretary of labor, and may not be required to work more than eight hours a day or 40 hours a week. The act also prohibited child labor (for boys under age 16 and girls under 18) and convict labor in government contracts.

Further reading: Dean Acheson, *Administrative Procedures in Government Agencies* (Washington, D.C.: Government Printing Office, 1940); Leslie E. Sanders, *The Walsh-Healey Act (the Government Contracts Act): A Manual for Department Heads and Foremen* (New York: National Foremen's Institute, 1942).

Waltham Black Act   See BLACK ACT.

Wanghia, Treaty of   Treaty signed on July 3, 1844, at Wanghia, China (near Macao), between the United States and China; opened certain Chinese ports to American trade and gave Americans the right of extraterritoriality, or exemption from the jurisdiction of Chinese laws and courts (Americans accused of crimes were to be tried by American consular officials). The treaty was negotiated by U.S. commissioner Caleb Cushing, and the U.S. Senate consented to it on January 8, 1845. As in other treaties concluded with Great Britain and France during this period, China herein granted a foreign power most-favored-nation status, guaranteeing trading equality. The Wanghia agreement led to increased American trade and the influx of Christian missionaries into China.

Further reading: Jules Davids, comp., *American Diplomatic and Public Papers: The United States and China*, Series 1: *The Treaty System and the Taiping Rebellion, 1842–1860* (Wilmington, Del.: Scholarly Resources, 1973); Fred L. Israel, ed., *Major Peace Treaties of Modern History, 1648–1967*, 4 vols. (New York: Chelsea House, 1967).

Wannsee Protocol   Infamous document prepared during the Wannsee Conference (January 20, 1942) convened by Reinhard Heydrich (head of Germany's Nazi security police) and his supervisor Heinrich Himmler to coordinate the efforts of all the Nazi agencies in planning and implementing "the final solution to the Jewish question" (Endlösung der Judenfrage). This was deemed necessary because the first two strategies involving "the expulsion of Jews from every sphere of life of the German people" and "from the living space (Lebensraum) of the German people" had been deemed insufficient and had failed at containing Europe's 11 million Jews; hence, this third, final strategy, described chillingly by author Adolf Eichmann: the ostensible relocation of thousands of Jews for work, a cover for their deportation to forced labor in prison or to death camps. The last part of the document presents the conference's views on genetics and racial mixing and outlines in stark detail the fate of those Germans (described as half-breeds and quarter-breeds) tainted with Jewish blood through mixed marriages.

Further reading: Office of Strategic Services, *The Wannsee Protocol and a 1944 Report on Auschwitz* (New York: Garland Publishing, 1982); Remember.org, "Wannsee Protocol January 20, 1942; Translation," Remember.org, available online at http://remember.org/wannsee.html.

Ware* v. *Hylton   U.S. Supreme Court decision of 1796 establishing that a national treaty superseded a state law. Under the 1783 Treaty of PARIS the U.S. government agreed that all prewar debts to British creditors would be paid in full. A Virginia statute of 1777, however, provided that Americans could discharge their debts to British subjects by payments to the state treasury. With some $2 million of Virginia debts at stake, British creditors sued. The Supreme Court ruled that a national treaty must take precedence over a state law, so that the federal government could deal effectively with foreign powers without fear that the states would nullify national treaties.

Further reading: Kermit L. Hall et al., eds., *The Oxford Companion to the Supreme Court of the United States* (New

York: Oxford University Press, 1992); George J. Lankevich, *The Federal Court, 1787–1801* (Danbury, Conn.: Grolier Educational, 1995).

War Labor Disputes Act, U.S. See SMITH CONNALLY ANTI-STRIKE ACT.

War Measures Act, Canadian

Legislation passed by the Canadian Parliament in August 1914, providing the government with the authority to implement emergency powers "during time of war, invasion or insurrection, real or apprehended." Among the powers granted the federal government in such times of crisis were the authority to suspend the writ of habeas corpus, to deport individuals from Canada without trial, to govern by decree, and to abrogate decisions made by the provincial governments. The act was invoked during both world wars, and only once during peacetime, during the 1970 Quebec crisis (see CANADIAN PUBLIC ORDER ACT OF 1970).

Further reading: R. C. Brown and M. E. Prang, eds., *Canadian Historical Documents Series*, 3 vols. (Scarborough, Canada: Prentice-Hall of Canada, 1966); *Copies of Proclamations, Orders in Council and Documents Relating to the European War* (Ottawa: Government Printing Bureau, 1915).

War and Peace

Novel written between 1863 and 1869 by Russian author Count Leo Tolstoy and published in 1869; relates a story embracing more than 500 characters from all social strata and centers around Napoléon's 1812 invasion of Russia. The novel followed the history of the Rostov family, of which Natasha, characterized by an instinctual approach to life, was a principal character; and the Bolkonsky family, of which Prince Andrey, who sought the meaning of life through his intellect, played a major role. A third major character, Prince Bezukhov, lived according to simple wisdom, and in the end was portrayed as having been able to embrace a larger view of life because of it. The characters are depicted from youth to maturity, and thus Tolstoy shows the development of human personality with masterful insight, while sharing views on life's meaning throughout. In Tolstoy's philosophical conception of history, events such as battles and wars are of little importance; instead, he sees history as determined by a multitude of separate actions, any of which is capable of being controlled by one individual.

Further reading: Kathryn B. Feuer, *Tolstoy and the Genesis of "War and Peace"* (Ithaca, N.Y.: Cornell University Press, 1996); George Gibian, ed., *War and Peace: The Maude Translation, Backgrounds and Sources, Criticism* (New York: Norton, 1996); David Holbrook, *Tolstoy, Woman, and Death: A Study of War and Peace and Anna Karenina* (Madison, N.J.: Fairleigh Dickinson University Press, 1997); Harold Bloom, ed., *Leo Tolstoy's War and Peace* (New York: Chelsea House Publishers, 1988).

War Powers Act of 1973, U.S.

Federal legislation passed by the U.S. Congress on November 7, 1973 (over the October 24 veto by President Richard M. Nixon), that restricted the right of the president to use his powers as commander in chief to introduce U.S. armed forces into foreign wars or situations abroad where hostilities were imminent. The act required the president to consult with Congress before and during any direct involvement of U.S. forces in hostilities abroad. It limited the commitment of armed forces by the president to 60 days (plus a possible 30-day extension) unless Congress declared war or authorized the continued use of forces in the situation. In the absence of a declaration of war or statutory authorization, Congress was given the right, by adopting a concurrent resolution, to order the removal of such forces. The act was a result of congressional frustration over the conduct of the Vietnam War (1956–75).

See also: GULF OF TONKIN RESOLUTION.

Further reading: Richard H. Kohn, *Military Laws of the United States from the Civil War Through the War Powers Act of 1973* (New York: Arno Press, 1979).

Warren Commission Report

Report prepared by a seven-member commission, appointed by U.S. president Lyndon B. Johnson and chaired by Chief Justice Earl Warren, on its investigation into the assassination of President John F. Kennedy in Dallas, Texas, on November 23, 1963, and of his accused slayer, Lee Harvey Oswald, the following day; the report was published on September 27, 1964. After evaluating thousands of reports from federal and local sources and questioning hundreds of witnesses, the commission concluded that Oswald had acted alone, shooting the president with a high-powered rifle from the Texas School Book Depository Building, and that there was no prior connection between Oswald and Jack Ruby, who killed Oswald in a Dallas police station (November 24). Many critics have attacked the commission's procedures and conclusions, arguing that a conspiracy, either foreign or domestic, was responsible for the assassinations.

Further reading: Mortimer Adler, ed., *The Annals of America*, 18 vols. (Chicago: Encyclopaedia Britannica, 1968); Henry Steele Commager, ed., *Documents of American History*, 8th ed. (New York: Appleton-Century-Crofts, 1968); New York Times, eds., *Report of the Warren Commission on the Assassination of President Kennedy* (New York: Bantam Books, 1964); Arnold S. Rice, *The Warren Court, 1953–1969* (Danbury, Conn.: Grolier Educational, 1995).

Warsaw, Compact of (Pax Dissidentium)

Compact or covenant signed by all members of the Polish Sejm (diet) on January 28, 1573, granting absolute freedom of worship to persons of all faiths, notably to all non-Roman Catholics in Poland. The Polish Catholic nobles consented to the compact to secure Poland's throne for their choice, Henry of Valois (later France's king Henry III), whose election (1573) had been opposed by Polish Protestants because of Henry's help in plotting the 1572 St. Bartholomew's Day Massacre, in which thousands of Protestants were slain. The compact gave equal rights to all Polish nobles and, at royal elections for the next 150 years, was signed by every king of Poland until it was formally abolished in 1736.

See also: HENRICIAN ARTICLES; PACTA CONVENTA OF 1573.

Further reading: Mieczyslaw B. Biskupski and James S. Pula, *Polish Democratic Thought from the Renaissance to the Great Emigration: Essays and Documents* (Boulder, Colo.: Eastern European Monographs, 1990).

Warsaw Agreements of 1950   See POLISH-EAST GERMAN AGREEMENTS OF 1950.

Warsaw Pact   Mutual defense organization formed by eight European Communist countries—the Soviet Union, Albania, Bulgaria, Czechoslovakia, East Germany, Hungary, Poland, and Romania—on May 14, 1955, in response to West Germany's admittance into NATO (see NORTH ATLANTIC TREATY). Albania withdrew in 1968 because of ideological differences. Like its Western counterpart NATO, the Warsaw Pact considered an attack against one member an attack on all; it boasted of combined military troops estimated at 6 million. The treaty allowed the Soviet Union to station her troops within the other member countries, thereby insidiously maintaining her control over them. In some countries, Poland and Hungary, for instance, the Soviet presence led to hostile clashes. According to the pact's provisions, the Warsaw Pact would lapse with the signing of an East-West collective security agreement. The democratization of Eastern Europe in 1989–90 led to the Soviet Union's commitment to withdraw troops from the former East bloc countries; Hungarians, Czechs, and others proposed an end to the "obsolete" Warsaw Pact, which was officially dissolved on April 1, 1991.

Further reading: Francis A. Beer, comp., *Alliances: Latent War Communities in the Contemporary World* (New York: Holt, Rinehart & Winston, 1970); Henry Degenhardt, ed., *Treaties and Alliances of the World*, 4th ed. (Detroit: Gale Research, 1986); J. A. S. Grenville and Bernard Wasserstein, *The Major International Treaties since 1945: A History and Guide with Texts* (New York: Methuen, 1987); Gerard Holden, *The Warsaw Pact: Soviet Security Policy and Bloc Politics* (New York: B. Blackwell, 1989).

Washington, Treaties of (1922)   See NINE POWER PACTS.

Washington, Treaty of (1842)   See WEBSTER-ASHBURTON TREATY.

Washington, Treaty of (1871)   Agreement between the United States and Great Britain, concluded on May 8, 1871, in Washington, D.C.; it settled the *Alabama* claims issue and other differences between the two nations by submitting them to an international arbitration tribunal. The treaty, negotiated by U.S. secretary of state Hamilton Fish, dealt primarily with U.S. claims for Civil War damages to the Northern merchant marine by the Confederate warships, especially the *Alabama*, built and outfitted by British interests despite Britain's neutrality. The treaty expressed British regret for the warships' escape from British ports and incorporated three rules of maritime neutrality, especially a rule asserting that neutral governments must exercise "due diligence" to maintain absolute neutrality. In 1872 the tribunal awarded the United States $15.5 million for Britain's failures as a neutral nation.

Further reading: Henry Steele Commager, ed., *Documents of American History*, 8th ed. (New York: Appleton-Century-Crofts, 1968); Charles E. Hill, *Leading American Treaties* (New York: Macmillan, 1922); Fred L. Israel, ed., *Major Peace Treaties of Modern History, 1648–1967*, 4 vols. (New York: Chelsea House, 1967); Frank N. Magill, ed., *Great Events from History: American Series*, 3 vols. (Englewood Cliffs, N.J.: Salem Press, 1975).

Washington, Treaty of (1921)   See FOUR POWER PACIFIC TREATY.

Washington, Treaty of (1922)   See FIVE POWER NAVAL TREATY.

Washington's Address to the Atlanta Exposition
Controversial speech delivered by African-American educator Booker T. Washington in Atlanta, Georgia, on September 18, 1895, that accepted a socially subordinate position for blacks in the South. While calling for economic opportunity for his people, Washington stated that African Americans must begin at the bottom of the economic ladder, not the top. He urged Southern whites to encourage and educate African-American laborers while maintaining social separation, and called agitation for social equality "the extremest folly." Blacks, he argued, must earn and prepare for social "privileges." The speech gained national acclaim from whites, but many black leaders denounced Washington's position.

Further reading: Mortimer Adler, ed., *The Annals of America*, 18 vols. (Chicago: Encyclopaedia Britannica, 1968); Frank N. Magill, ed., *Great Events from History: American Series*, 3 vols. (Englewood Cliffs, N.J.: Salem Press, 1975); Stephen Mansfield, *Then Darkness Fled: The Liberating Wisdom of Booker T. Washington* (Nashville, Tenn.: Cumberland House, 1999); Diane Ravitch, ed., *The American Reader: Words That Moved a Nation* (New York: Harper-Perennial, 1991).

Washington's Farewell Address   Address to the American people, dated September 17, 1796, and published two days later in Philadelphia's *American Daily Advertiser;* in it George Washington explained his resolution not to run for a third presidential term and offered advice on national policy.

The address, which was never publicly read, was prepared in part as early as 1792 and was written with the help of Alexander Hamilton. It warned against regional divisiveness and urged a strong union of the states, enumerated the dangers of a political party system, advised that the public credit be carefully preserved and wisely disbursed, and counseled against permanent alliances with foreign nations and for "temporary alliances for extraordinary emergencies." The document exerted a great influence on American policy.

Further reading: Mortimer Adler, ed., *The Annals of America*, 18 vols. (Chicago: Encyclopaedia Britannica, 1968); Henry Steele Commager, ed., *Documents of American History*, 8th ed. (New York: Appleton-Century-Crofts, 1968); *American Jurisprudence 2nd ed., Desk Book* (N.p.: West Group, 1998); Charles W. Eliot, ed., *The Harvard Classics*, 51 vols. (New York: P. F. Collier & Sons, 1938).

Washington's First Inaugural Address

Speech delivered to both houses of Congress by George Washington on April 30, 1789, in New York City's Federal Hall, at his inauguration as first president of the United States. Washington opened his address with a modest disclaimer of his qualifications, stating that he had been summoned from his longed-for retreat at Mount Vernon by the voice of his country. He spoke hopefully about a government without local prejudices or party animosities, of honesty and magnanimity in conjunction with public prosperity, of "the enlarged views, the temperate consultations, and the wise measures" on which he believed the success of the American government would depend. He noted that "the preservation of the sacred fire of liberty and the destiny of the republican model of government are . . . staked on the experiment intrusted to the hands of the American people."

Further reading: Mortimer Adler, ed., *The Annals of America*, 18 vols. (Chicago: Encyclopaedia Britannica, 1968); Henry Steele Commager, ed., *Documents of American History*, 8th ed. (New York: Appleton-Century-Crofts, 1968); Charles W. Eliot, ed., *The Harvard Classics*, 51 vols. (New York: P. F. Collier & Sons, 1938); *Inaugural Addresses of the Presidents of the United States from George Washington 1789 to George Bush 1989*, bicentennial ed. (Washington, D.C.: Government Printing Office, 1989).

Watauga Articles of Association

First written constitution "ever adopted west of the [Appalachian] mountains, or by a community of American-born freemen," the basis of a government formed in 1772 by early white settlers along the Watauga River, the first permanent colony in Tennessee. The articles, which took as a guide the laws of Virginia and were intended to offer protection against outlaws and horse thieves, established manhood suffrage and freedom of worship. A body of 13 representatives (one from each of the 13 "stations" or forts of the colony) was selected, which in turn elected a five-member commission with administrative and legislative powers. The Watauga colony, which became the nucleus for later settlements in Tennessee and Kentucky, also aided the defense of the West against the British and their Indian allies during the American Revolution (1775–83).

Further reading: Mary F. Caldwell, *Tennessee: The Dangerous Example; Watauga to 1849* (Nashville, Tenn.: Aurora Publishers, 1974).

Water Power Act of 1920, U.S.

Federal legislation enacted on June 10, 1920, that established the Federal Power Commission to conserve water power reserves on U.S. public lands and on navigable streams. The commission, consisting of the secretaries of war, interior, and agriculture, was authorized to issue licenses for the construction and operation of facilities, such as powerhouses, dams, and reservoirs, to improve navigation and develop power. Leases were limited to 50 years, with the U.S. government maintaining the right to take over the facilities when the leases expired. The commission was empowered to regulate rates. The act also stated that neighboring states or cities would have the first opportunity to use power sites.

Further reading: Milton Conover, *The Federal Power Commission; Its History, Activities and Organization* (New York: AMS Press, 1974).

Water Quality Act, U.S.

Federal U.S. legislation enacted on October 2, 1965, that required the states to set standards of water quality for interstate streams within their borders, subject to federal approval and federal action if the states failed to carry out this mandate. A discharge of matter into interstate waters or their tributaries that reduced water quality below set standards was made subject to federal abatement procedures. The act established the Federal Water Pollution Administration within the U.S. Department of Health, Education, and Welfare. The act was strengthened by the Clean Water Restoration Act of 1966, which provided federal funding to help states install sewers and build sewage-treatment plants.

Further reading: U.S. Senate Committee on Public Works, Subcommittee on Air and Water Pollution, *Water Quality Act of 1965* (Washington, D.C.: Government Printing Office, 1965).

Watson-Parker Act (U.S. Railway Labor Act of 1926)

Federal U.S. legislation sponsored by Senator James E. Watson of Indiana and Representative James S. Parker of New York and enacted on May 20, 1926; established the U.S. Board of Mediation to mediate railroad labor disputes. This board replaced the Railroad Labor Board set up by the ESCH-CUMMINS ACT. The new, independent agency contained five members appointed by the U.S. president and could enter disputes on its own initiative. In the event of an impasse, the board could ask the president to authorize an investigation and to declare a 30-day "cooling-off" period, during which no strike could occur. The act was amended by the Railway Labor Act of 1934, which covered workers' rights to organize and bargain collectively on railroads and airlines and created a board to hear disputes about existing labor contracts.

Further reading: Benjamin Aaron et al., *The Railway Labor Act at Fifty: Collective Bargaining in the Railroad and Airline Industries* (Washington, D.C.: National Mediation Board, 1977); Michael H. Campbell and Edward C. Brewer, *The Railway Labor Act of 1926: A Legislative History* (Buffalo, N.Y.: W. S. Hein, 1988); John W. Gohmann, comp. and ed., *Air and Rail Labor Relations: A Judicial History of the Railway Labor Act* (Dubuque, Iowa: Kendall/Hunt Publishing, 1979).

Watson Report   Recommendations for reforms in Britain's Gold Coast colony (Ghana) made in June 1948 by the Watson Commission (headed by Aiken Watson), appointed to investigate the serious riots that rocked the colony in February–March 1948. The report approved the government's handling of the riots but blamed its economic policies for having caused them. It proposed the establishment of regional councils in the colony in place of the chiefs and native authorities; the councils would have executive powers and could make by-laws. Other recommendations included better public relations for the government and an acceleration in educational progress in the colony, which became in 1957 the first African colony to gain independence, in large part due to the self-governing measure initiated by the British after the Watson Report.

Further reading: Andrew Aiken Watson, *Report 1948* (London: H.M. Stationery Office, 1948).

Wealth of Nations, An Inquiry into the Nature and Causes of the   Work written by Scottish political economist Adam Smith and published in London, England, in 1776; contained a discussion on how to stimulate economic development and on the dynamics of a competitive market. Smith based his theories upon the premise that the amount of consumable goods, rather than reserves of gold or silver, determined the wealth of a nation. This was due to the fact that the existence of surplus goods would lead to trade among nations, with the greatest profits being accrued by the nation that produced the greatest amount of goods. It followed, he argued, that stimulating self-interest was a sure way to increase production. The *Wealth of Nations* also contained a theory of price, which, he argued, was not determined by any one individual but by all consumers collectively. Smith's work is recognized as marking the beginning of economics as a separate field of study.

Further reading: Charles W. Eliot, ed., *The Harvard Classics*, 51 vols. (New York: P. F. Collier & Sons, 1938); Mark A. Kishlansky, ed., *Sources of the West: Readings in Western Civilization*, 2 vols., 4th ed. (New York: Longman, 2001); Cheng-chung Lai, ed., *Adam Smith Across Nations: Translations and Receptions of The Wealth of Nations* (New York:

Oxford University Press, 2000); Frank N. Magill, ed., *Great Events from History: Modern European Series*, 3 vols. (Englewood Cliffs, N.J.: Salem Press, 1973).

Wealth-Tax Act, U.S. (Revenue Act of 1935)   New Deal legislation enacted on August 30, 1935, that increased estate, gift, and capital stock tax rates, levied an excess profits tax, and raised the surtax rate on individual incomes over $50,000 to the highest rates in U.S. history. It established a modest graduated tax on corporations in place of the existing uniform tax, lowering the rate for small corporations and raising the rates for corporations with incomes above $50,000. It raised federal taxes by $250 million. The act represented a watered-down version of U.S. president Franklin D. Roosevelt's controversial proposed program to redistribute wealth and economic power.

Further reading: Carlton Fox, *Revenue Act of 1935: Legislative History of Public Law 74–407*, 3 vols. (Washington: n.p., 1937).

Webb-Kenyon Act (U.S. Interstate Liquor Act of 1913)   Legislation cosponsored by Representative Edwin Y. Webb of North Carolina and Senator William S. Kenyon of Iowa and enacted by the U.S. Congress on March 1, 1913, forbidding the interstate shipment of intoxicating liquor into states where its sale or use was illegal. Intended to allow more effective enforcement of state prohibition laws, the act was vetoed by President William Howard Taft on the grounds that it gave to the states a power reserved to the federal government; Congress overrode the veto, and the U.S. Supreme Court later upheld the law on January 8, 1917. It represented the first federal victory of the Anti-Saloon League.

Further reading: Jack S. Blocker, *Retreat from Reform: The Prohibition Movement in the United States, 1890–1913* (Westport, Conn.: Greenwood Press, 1976); K. Austin Kerr, *Organized for Prohibition: A New History of the Anti-Saloon League* (New Haven, Conn.: Yale University Press, 1985).

Webb-Pomerene Act   Federal U.S. legislation cosponsored by Representative Edwin Y. Webb of North Carolina and Senator Atlee Pomerene of Ohio and enacted on April 10, 1918, that exempted exporters from antitrust laws enough to allow them to organize business combinations or associations for export trade. It also prohibited unfair methods of competition. Following a 1924 Federal Trade Commission ruling that such associations could fix prices and allott export orders, these associations grew dramatically.

Further reading: Wilbur L. Fugate, *Foreign Commerce and the Antitrust Laws* (Boston: Little, Brown, 1958); Milton Gilbert and Paul D. Dickens, *Export Prices and Export Cartels* (New York: AMS Press, 1971).

Webster-Ashburton Treaty (Ashburton Treaty, Treaty of Washington)   Agreement between the United States and Great Britain signed in Washington, D.C., on August 9, 1842; fixed the northeastern boundary between the United States and Canada, thus ending a long-standing and heated dispute. Negotiated by U.S. secretary of state Daniel Webster and British minister Alexander Baring, First Lord Ashburton, the treaty set the present boundary between Maine and New Brunswick, giving the United States 7,000 of the 12,000 square miles of disputed territory; adjusted the boundaries of Vermont and New York; settled a border conflict in the Great Lakes region; and assured U.S. navigation rights along the St. John River. It also provided for joint efforts in suppressing the African slave trade and for mutual extradition of criminals. The treaty led to greatly improved Anglo-American relations.

Further reading: Henry Steele Commager, ed., *Documents of American History*, 8th ed. (New York: Appleton-Century-Crofts, 1968); Charles W. Eliot, ed., *The Harvard Classics*, 51 vols. (New York: P. F. Collier & Sons, 1938); Charles E. Hill, *Leading American Treaties* (New York: Macmillan, 1922); Frank N. Magill, ed., *Great Events from History: American Series*, 3 vols. (Englewood Cliffs, N.J.: Salem Press, 1975).

Webster's First and Second Replies to Hayne

Replies by Daniel Webster of Massachusetts in a U.S. senatorial debate with Robert Y. Hayne of South Carolina, in January 1830, supporting nationalism over states' rights. This important debate, which began over the FOOTE RESOLUTION, ranged broadly over the issues of tariff, slavery, sectionalism, state nullification of federal statutes, the U.S. CONSTITUTION, and the nature of the national union. In the first reply (January 20) Webster defended New England against charges of selfish regionalism. In the second reply (January 26–27) Webster declared that the Union was the creation of the American people, not the states, and that the government was answerable only to the people. It contains his call for nationalism: "Liberty and Union, now and for ever, one and inseparable."

Further reading: Mortimer Adler, ed., *The Annals of America*, 18 vols. (Chicago: Encyclopaedia Britannica, 1968); Herman Belze, ed., *The Webster-Hayne Debate on the Nature of the Union* (Indianapolis, Ind.: Liberty Fund, 2000); Craig R. Smith, *Defender of the Union: The Oratory of Daniel Webster* (New York: Greenwood Press, 1989); Edwin P. Whipple, ed., *The Great Speeches and Orations of Daniel Webster* (Boston: Little, Brown, 1923).

Webster's Free Trade Speech

See FREE TRADE SPEECH, WEBSTER'S.

Webster's Plymouth Rock Speech

See PLYMOUTH ROCK SPEECH, WEBSTER'S.

Webster's Reply to Hülsemann Letter

Letter issued by U.S. Secretary of State Daniel Webster on December 21, 1850, in reply to the HÜLSEMANN LETTER, protesting U.S. interference in Austria's affairs. In his stern rebuke to Austria, Webster defended U.S. interest in European revolutions and asserted the right to seek information and form independent opinions about such events. He stated that these revolutions appear to have a foundation in the ideas of popular and responsible government exemplified by the American Revolution (1775–83). He also boasted that compared with the extensive, powerful, and rich United States, Austria was "but a patch on the earth's surface." This bombastic comparison appealed to the public temper of the time and won praise from both parties, Whigs and Democrats.

Further reading: Mortimer Adler, ed., *The Annals of America*, 18 vols. (Chicago: Encyclopaedia Britannica, 1968); Robert V. Remini, *Daniel Webster: The Man and His Time* (New York: W. W. Norton, 1997).

Webster's Rockingham Memorial

See ROCKINGHAM MEMORIAL, WEBSTER'S.

Webster's "Seventh of March" Speech

See "SEVENTH OF MARCH" SPEECH, WEBSTER'S.

Webster's Speech on the Deaths of Thomas Jefferson and John Adams

Eulogy delivered by Massachusetts congressman Daniel Webster in Boston on August 2, 1826, in honor of Thomas Jefferson and John Adams, both of whom had died on July 4, 1826. Webster praised the two former presidents and reviewed their contributions to their country. In the most famous section of this speech, Webster wrote a hypothetical answer that Adams, a proponent of independence from England, might have given to an opponent of that view in 1776. Though the ideas about the necessity of independence were consistent with Adams's views, the words were Webster's, a fact that caused much confusion for years.

Further reading: Edwin P. Whipple, ed., *The Great Speeches and Orations of Daniel Webster* (Boston: Little, Brown, 1923); Robert V. Remini, *Daniel Webster: The Man and His Time* (New York: W. W. Norton, 1997).

Webster's Speech on Greek Independence ("Holy Alliance" Speech)

Address delivered before the U.S. Congress by Massachusetts representative Daniel Webster on January 19, 1824, urging the United States to recognize Greek independence from the Ottoman Empire, a movement that had generated much sympathy in America. He also hoped to persuade members of the "Holy Alliance" (or "Great Powers," consisting of Russia, Prussia, and Austria) to support the Greek revolt against Turkish rule. Webster criticized the alliance for promoting the principles that constitutional rights are merely grants from the crown, not inherent rights, and that nations may forcibly intervene in the affairs of other nations, particularly in suppressing rebellions against existing governments.

Further reading: Mortimer Adler, ed., *The Annals of America*, 18 vols. (Chicago: Encyclopaedia Britannica, 1968); Robert V. Remini, *Daniel Webster: The Man and His Time* (New York: W. W. Norton, 1997); Edwin P. Whipple, ed., *The Great Speeches and Orations of Daniel Webster* (Boston: Little, Brown, 1923).

Webster v. Reproductive Health Services   U.S. Supreme Court decision issued on July 3, 1989, ruling that a 1986 Missouri state law, which restricted the availability of abortions, was constitutional. The case originated over a challenge to the Missouri law by Reproductive Health Services, a state-run clinic whose services included performing abortions. The Missouri law was defended by Missouri attorney general William Webster. The Missouri law specifically denied the right of a woman to an abortion performed by public employees in public facilities if her life was not in danger; it required the physician, before performing an abortion on a fetus of 20 weeks or more, to determine if the fetus could survive outside the mother's womb. The ruling was a major setback for pro-choice advocates, who feared that more states would adopt laws similar to the Missouri law, and that the 1973 landmark case ROE V. WADE was in danger of being overturned.

Further reading: Stephanie Guitton and Peter Irons, eds., *May It Please the Court: Arguments on Abortion* (New York: New Press, 1995); Kermit L. Hall et al., eds., *The Oxford Companion to the Supreme Court of the United States* (New York: Oxford University Press, 1992); Maureen Harrison and Steve Gilbert, eds., *Abortion Decisions of the United States Supreme Court* (Beverly Hills, Calif.: Excellent Books, 1993); United States Supreme Court, *United States Reports: Cases Adjudged in the Supreme Court at . . . and Rules Announced at . . .* (New York: Banks & Brothers, Law Publishers, 1884–1921; Washington, D.C.: Government Printing Office, 1922–).

Wehlau (Welawa), Treaty of   Treaty concluded at the east Prussian town of Wehlau or Welawa on September 19, 1657, between King John II Casimir of Poland and Elector Frederick William of Brandenburg—through the influence of Leopold I of Austria and Hungary, who sought the elector's vote in the coming imperial election (for Holy Roman emperor). Through the document John Casimir reluctantly agreed to Frederick William's control over the Baltic province of East Prussia. In return the elector agreed to abandon his Swedish alliance, and to provide Poland with a force of 6,000 men to fight the Swedes. At this time Austrian forces had already entered Poland to help drive out the Swedes, making an ultimate Swedish victory unlikely. The settlement therefore could not have been more advantageous to Frederick William. The treaty was ratified on May 3, 1660, at Oliva (a monastery near present-day Gdansk, Poland).

See also: OLIVA, TREATY OF; VIENNA, TREATY OF (1656).

Further reading: Richard Butterwick, *The Polish-Lituanian Monarchy in European Context c. 1500–1795* (New York: Palgrave, 2001); John P. Spielman, *Leopold I of Austria* (London: Thames & Hudson, 1977); Wladyslaw Konopczynski, *Poland and Sweden* (Toruń, Poland: The Baltic Institute, 1935).

Weimar Constitution   Constitution of the Weimar Republic (new German republic formed by a national assembly at Weimar), promulgated on August 11, 1919, and containing many democratic principles, which made it appear to be one of the most liberal constitutions in the world. The constitution guaranteed equality of all citizens before the law, without discrimination on the basis of sex, religious belief, or spoken language. The parliament was to be composed of the Reichstag, the members of which would be chosen by proportional representation, and the Reichsrat, whose members would represent the states, or Länder. The president was to be elected directly by the people for a seven-year term and would have broad powers, including the power, with the Reichstag's approval, to concluded treaties and to declare war and peace. Despite his responsibility to the Reichstag however, the president had the power to dissolve it and present its laws to a referendum. The democratic nature of the constitution was further undermined by the infamous "article 48," which allowed the president to abrogate all rights guaranteed by the constitution in a national emergency, which he also had the authority to declare. The Weimar Republic was dissolved in 1933.

Further reading: Frank N. Magill, ed., *Great Events from History: Modern European Series*, 3 vols. (Englewood Cliffs, N.J.: Salem Press, 1973); Anthony J. Nicholls and Erich Matthias, *German Democracy and the Triumph of Hitler; Essays in Recent German History* (New York: St. Martin's Press, 1972); Louis L. Snyder, ed., *Documents of German History* (New Brunswick, N.J.: Rutgers University Press, 1958); Louis L. Snyder, ed., *Fifty Major Documents of the Twentieth Century* (Princeton, N.J.: D. Van Nostrand, 1955).

Welsh Disestablishment Bill of 1914   British law of September 18, 1914, for the disestablishment and disendowment of the Anglican Church in Wales, to appease its largely nonconformist membership. The bill, which had failed on two previous occasions (1894–95 and 1909), was reintroduced on April 23, 1912, and twice rejected by the House of Lords (February 13 and July 20, 1913), It passed the House of Commons for a third time (May 19, 1914) and received royal approval on September 18. A suspensory bill delayed its implementation until six months after the end of World War I. Operative in 1920, it separated the four Welsh dioceses from the Church of England (Anglican Church) and turned them into self-governing organizations. Some funds were diverted to the University of Wales and the county councils. A later amendment (1919) modified these terms even further. The law also ended the tenure of the Welsh bishops in the House of Lords.

Further reading: P. M. H. Bell, *Disestablishment in Ireland and Wales* (London: S.P.C.K. for the Church Historical Society, 1969); Kenneth O. Morgan, *Freedom or Sacrilege? A History of the Campaign for Welsh Disestablishment* (Penarth, Wales: Church in Wales Publications, 1966); D. T. W. Price, *A History of the Church in Wales in the Twentieth Century* (Penarth, Wales: Church in Wales Publications, 1990); Joel H. Wiener, ed., *Great Britain—The Lion at Home: A Documentary History of Domestic Policy (1689–1973)*, 4 vols. (New York: Chelsea House, 1974).

"We Remember: A Reflection on the Shoah"

The Vatican's long-awaited statement (see DECLARATION OF REPENTANCE) on its role during the Holocaust (Shoah, Hebrew for "catastrophe") finally published on March 16, 1998. Drafted by the Vatican's Commission for Religious Relations with Jews (headed by Cardinal Edward Cassidy), its 14 pages were divided into five sections prefaced by a letter from Pope John Paul II hoping that it would "help to heal the wounds of past misunderstandings and injustices." It stated that this "unspeakable tragedy" occurred "in countries of long-standing Christian civilization" but then blames the horrors on "a thoroughly modern neopagan regime." Although genuinely contrite in tone, this declaration of *teshuvah* (repentance), however, did not address the central issue of the church's not-so tacit complicity in some of the atrocities committed during the Shoah—an omission that, critics argued, greatly diluted its strength.

See also: NOSTRA AETATE.

Further reading: Commission for Religious Relations with the Jews, *We Remember: A Reflection on the Shoah*, Roman world, available online at http://www.vatican.va/roman_curia/pontifical_councils/chrstun; James A. Rudin, "Reflections on the Vatican's Reflection on the Shoah," *Cross Currents* 48 (Winter 1998–99): 518–31.

"We Shall Never Surrender" Speech, Churchill's (Churchill's Speech after Dunkirk)

Speech by Britain's prime minister Winston Churchill on June 4, 1940, before the House of Commons, informing it of the disastrous setbacks faced by the British Expeditionary Force in Belgium and France and the recent evacuation from Dunkirk following the German attack. With the enemy advancing closer to British shores, the possibility of an Allied defeat loomed large in the first year of World War II (1939–45). But Churchill stirred the country's passions with his masterful oratory—"We shall go on to the end . . . We shall never surrender." He said that even if Britain was "subjugated and starving" he was confident that "our empire beyond the seas . . . would carry on the struggle, until, in God's good time, the New World, with all its power and might, steps forth to the rescue and the liberation of the old." Under his leadership, the nation once again rose to meet the challenge.

Further reading: David Cannadine, ed., *Blood, Toil, Tears, and Sweat: The Speeches of Winston Churchill* (Boston: Houghton Mifflin, 1989); Robert R. James, ed., *Winston S. Churchill: His Complete Speeches, 1897–1963* (New York: Chelsea House Publishers, 1974); Stephen Mansfield, *Never Give In: The Extraordinary Character of Winston Churchill* (Nashville, Tenn.: Cumberland House, 2001).

West African Economic Community Treaty

Pact signed on April 16, 1973, by the Ivory Coast, Mali, Mauritania, Niger, Senegal, and Upper Volta, now called Burkina Faso (former French colonies in West Africa), creating the West African Economic Community (whose French acronym is CEAO) to encourage regional trade and economic cooperation (Togo later became the seventh member of what became the West African Economic and Monetary Union). Implemented on January 1, 1974, the treaty proposed a free-trade zone, the coordination of the economic policies of the six countries, and cooperation with the EEC or European Economic Community (see ROME, TREATIES OF [1957]). Benin participates in the CEAO as an observer. The CEAO reportedly came into existence with French and EEC backing, partly to counteract Nigeria's growing regional power and partly as an alternative to the weakening African-Malagasy-Mauritius Common Organization (OCAM).

See also: CENTRAL AFRICAN CUSTOMS AND ECONOMIC UNION; KAMPALA, TREATY OF.

Further reading: E. C. Edozien and E. Osagie, eds., *The Economic Integration of West Africa* (Ibadan, Nigeria: Ibadan University Press, 1982); Samuel A. Oshisanya, *The Ultimate End of Pan-Africanism* (Lagos, Nigeria: self-published, 1983).

West Coast Hotel Company v. Parrish

U.S. Supreme Court decision, issued on March 29, 1937, that upheld the validity of a Washington state law setting a minimum wage for women and minors. Elsie Parrish, a chambermaid, sued her employer when she received less than $14.50 for 48 hours of work. The hotel challenged the minimum-wage statute as a violation of constitutional rights to due process, depriving employers and employees of freedom of contract, as the Supreme Court had held in ADKINS V. CHILDREN'S HOSPITAL. The five-to-four ruling in the West Coast Hotel case overturned the Adkins decision and declared that minimum-wage statutes were a valid exercise of the police power of the state.

Further reading: Kermit L. Hall et al., eds, *American Legal History: Cases and Materials*, 2d ed. (New York: Oxford University Press, 1996); Kermit L. Hall et al., eds., *The Oxford Companion to the Supreme Court of the United States* (New York: Oxford University Press, 1992); Robert R. Mayer, *The Court and the American Crises, 1930–1952* (Danbury, Conn.: Grolier Educational, 1995); United States Supreme Court, *United States Reports: Cases Adjudged in the Supreme Court at . . . and Rules Announced at . . .* (New York: Banks & Brothers,

Law Publishers, 1884–1921; Washington, D.C.: Government Printing Office, 1922–).

Western European Union Accord

Agreement creating on May 6, 1955, the Western European Union (WEU), an association to promote European integration; economic, social, and cultural cooperation; and a coordinated defense policy among Belgium, France, Great Britain, West Germany, Italy, the Netherlands, and Luxembourg. The WEU consisted of a council (to draft policies and discuss matters of general concern), a secretariat, an agency for the control of armaments (of member nations), a standing armaments committee (working with the North Atlantic Treaty Organization to create a climate of cooperation and understanding), and an assembly, which shared membership with the consultative assembly of the council of Europe (see COUNCIL OF EUROPE, STATUTE OF). In 1960, the council of Europe assumed charge of the WEU's social and economic committees.

See also: BRUSSELS TREATY OF 1948.

Further reading: *The Assembly of Western European Union, 1955–1960* (Strasbourg, France: The Union, 1961); Paul Borcier, *The Assembly of Western European Union: Its Contribution to the Defence and Building of Europe since 1955* (Paris: Office of the Clerk of the Assembly of WEU, 1975); Henry Degenhardt, ed., *Treaties and Alliances of the World*, 4th ed. (Detroit: Gale Research, 1986).

Western Pacific Order in Council

British government order in 1877 creating the office of the High Commissioner for the Western Pacific, to afford protection to British nationals and ships in the islands of the western Pacific. This was achieved by extending the jurisdiction of the governor of Fiji (annexed in 1874) to include New Guinea, the Solomon Islands, Vanuatu, Tonga, Samoa, the Gilbert and Ellice Islands (Kiribati and Tuvalu), and various other island groups in the region. The high commissioner's office was to handle matters of civil and criminal justice, under the supervision of Fiji's judiciary. In the individual island groups, specially-appointed deputy commissioners were entrusted with roles similar to county court judges or stipendiary magistrates in England.

Further reading: Deryck Scarr, *Fragments of Empire: A History of the Western Pacific High Commission, 1877–1914* (Honolulu: University of Hawaii Press, 1968).

West German Bundestag Election Law

See BUNDESTAG ELECTION LAW.

West German Constitution

See BASIC LAW OF 1949, WEST GERMAN.

West German Peace Contract

Series of agreements signed at Bonn on May 26, 1952, by Foreign Minister Anthony Eden of Britain, Secretary of State Dean Acheson of the United States, Foreign Minister Robert Schuman of France,

and Chancellor Konrad Adenauer of the Federal Republic of Germany, bringing an end to the Allied occupation of West Germany. The principal agreement provided for the revocation of the Allied Occupation Statute (1949), for a change in the status of Allied forces from occupying troops to that of defensive forces, and for the internal independence of West Germany. The independence of Germany was, however, qualified by the four powers' agreement that certain existing rights of the Western powers would be retained. These included, most importantly, the three powers' right (British, French, and American) to call for a state of emergency in the event of a threat to the democratic order in West Germany or of an attack upon Berlin. Other issues touched upon the establishment of an arbitration tribunal to settle any disputes between West Germany and the three Western powers, the amount of aid that West Germany would grant Berlin, and the amount West Germany would pay for the maintenance of the allied forces on her territory after the end of the occupation.

See also: TREATY ON THE FINAL SETTLEMENT WITH RESPECT TO GERMANY.

Further reading: Alfred Grosser, *The Colossus Again: Western Germany from Defeat to Rearmament* (New York: Praeger, 1955).

Westminister, Provisions of

Radical legal, administrative and political reforms granted on October 13, 1259, by England's king Henry III and his Council of Oxford (barons) to the Community of Bachelors (knights and lesser landowners in baronial households), who had protested that the barons had not fulfilled their charter of reforms (see OXFORD, PROVISIONS OF). Prince Edward (later King Edward I) heeded this appeal and supported the new demands. Accordingly, the powers of the Council of Fifteen and of the Commission of Twelve were expanded. Councillors were appointed to accompany circuit judges and receive complaints. Also, the provisions stipulated that the king should have two or three councillors of "middle rank . . . in constant attendance" from one Parliament to the next. In every county, four knights were to choose the sheriff (usually from among themselves) and to review his actions. The circuit judges were authorized to try seigneurial officials. The legal resolutions mainly introduced common law reforms.

See also: KENILWORTH, DICTUM OF.

Further reading: Noel Denholm-Young, *Collected Papers on Mediaeval Subjects* (Oxford, England: B. Blackwell, 1946); A. G. Little et al., *Essays in Medieval History Presented to Thomas Frederick Tout* (Freeport, N.Y.: Books for Libraries Press, 1967).

Westminster, Statute of (1931)

British act passed on December 11, 1931, in Parliament (Westminister Palace, London), conferring legislative independence on the self-governing dominions of Canada, Australia, New Zealand, the Union of South Africa, the Irish Free State, and Newfoundland, thus implementing the decisions taken at the Imperial conferences of 1926 and 1930. They became "autonomous communities within the British Empire, equal in status . . . and freely associated as members of the British Commonwealth of Nations," with the freedom to determine their own foreign policies and, except for Newfoundland, apply for membership to the League of Nations. The act reiterated their allegiance to the British Crown and required that their consent be obtained before the laws pertaining to the crown and the succession could be altered.

Further reading: Henry Degenhardt, ed., *Treaties and Alliances of the World*, 4th ed. (Detroit: Gale Research, 1986); G. G. Edgar, ed., *Craies on Statute Law*, 7th ed. (London: Sweet & Maxwell, 1971); Frank N. Magill, ed., *Great Events from History: Modern European Series*, 3 vols. (Englewood Cliffs, N.J.: Salem Press, 1973); Louis L. Snyder, ed., *Fifty Major Documents of the Twentieth Century* (Princeton, N.J.: D. Van Nostrand, 1955).

Westminster, Statutes of   Three important statutes enacted during King Edward I's reign in England. The first (1275), issued by the "general" Parliament, provided for (1) jury trial for criminal cases; (2) protection of church property from king and nobility; (3) free, fair election of sheriff and coroner; and (4) implementation of the provisions of the MAGNA CARTA. The second (1285), also known as *De Donis Conditionalibus,* preserved the estate tail (limit) in land to restrict its alienation, deemed land an asset in paying judgment debts, improved the law to manage assets on death, and eased the restrictions on appeal to high circuit courts. The third (1290), *Quia Emptores,* considered England's first conveyancing legislation, prohibited anyone but the crown from granting new feudal rights and allowed the free transfer of land held in fee simple (without limit of ownership) by barring claims from relatives or feudal lords. The second and third statutes, passed by Parliaments attended only by the lords and councillors, unintentionally dealt feudalism a severe blow.

See also: MORTMAIN, STATUTE OF.

Further reading: Frank N. Magill, ed., *Great Events from History: Ancient and Medieval Series*, 3 vols. (Englewood Cliffs, N.J: Salem Press, 1973).

Westminster, Treaty of (1654)   Peace treaty between England and the Netherlands signed at Westminster (part of London) on April 5, 1654, ending the First Anglo-Dutch War (1652–54). The Dutch, who had been humbled but not defeated militarily, agreed to salute the English on the high seas, to pay annual fishing rights in English waters, to abide by the Navigation Act of 1651, and to pay compensation for the Amboina Massacre of 1623 (the Dutch had killed English spice traders and ruined their factory on the Molucca island of Amboina in the East Indies). England also obtained a secret agreement from the province of Holland to exclude all members of the house of Orange from the post of stadtholder (chief magistrate of the Netherlands).

Further reading: D. R. Hainsworth and Christine Churches, *The Anglo-Dutch Naval Wars, 1652–1674* (Stroud, England: Sutton, 1998); J. R. Jones, *The Anglo-Dutch Wars of the Seventeenth Century* (New York: Longman, 1996).

Westminster, Treaty of (1674)   Peace agreement between England and the Netherlands, signed at Westminster (London) on February 19, 1674, bringing the Third Anglo-Dutch War (1672–78) to a partial resolution. The English had not succeeded in obtaining a share of the East Indies spice trade; growing public opposition to the war and Parliament itself forced King Charles II of England to negotiate with the Dutch. The latter agreed to pay an indemnity and to return the colonies of Albany, New Jersey, New York, and western Long Island, which had been taken from England during the war in 1673.

Further reading: D. R. Hainsworth and Christine Churches, *The Anglo-Dutch Naval Wars, 1652–1674* (Stroud, England: Sutton, 1998); J. R. Jones, *The Anglo-Dutch Wars of the Seventeenth Century* (New York: Longman, 1996).

Westminster, Treaty of (1756) (Convention of Westminster)   Treaty of neutrality made by Britain's king George II (who was also elector of Hanover) with Prussia's king Frederick II the Great on January 16, 1756, at Westminster (London). The French and Indian War (1754–63) had erupted in North America between the British and French, preceding the outbreak of the worldwide Seven Years' War (1756–63), and the British feared a French attack on Hanover. By the treaty, Britain obtained Prussia's agreement to bar access into and through Germany of any foreign forces. In return for Prussian help in case of a French invasion of Hanover (in Germany), the British agreed to aid Frederick if the Austrians invaded Silesia. The treaty, concluded shortly after the ANGLO-RUSSIAN CONVENTION OF 1755, caused a break between Britain and Russia, and also helped bring about an Austro-French defensive alliance in 1756.

Further reading: Frank N. Magill, ed., *Great Events from History: Modern European Series*, 3 vols. (Englewood Cliffs, N.J.: Salem Press, 1973).

Westminster Confession of Faith   Declaration of faith drafted by the Westminster Assembly of Divines (an assembly convoked by the Long Parliament to reconstruct the Church of England) in 1646. The Westminster Assembly met between 1643 and 1649, and the 33 articles that contain the declaration are an exposition of the Calvinistic doctrine and set the standards in the Presbyterian churches of the country. But the confession of faith is of no value in the Church of England because it failed to win royal approval.

Further reading: Gerald L. Bray, *Documents of the English Reformation* (Minneapolis: Fortress Press, 1994); Alasdair

I. C. Heron, ed., *The Westminster Confession in the Church Today: Papers Prepared for the Church of Scotland Panel on Doctrine* (Edinburgh: Saint Andrew Press, 1982); John H. Leith, *Assembly at Westminster; Reformed Theology in the Making* (Richmond, Va.: John Knox Press, 1973); Holmes Rolston, *John Calvin Versus the Westminster Confession* (Richmond, Va.: John Knox Press, 1972).

Westphalia, Peace of   Peace treaties ending the Thirty Years' War (1618–48), concluded on October 24, 1648, by France, Sweden, the German Estates, and the Holy Roman Empire. The peace consisted of the Treaty of OSNABRÜCK and the Treaty of MÜNSTER, wherein some specific territorial agreements were made with individual parties (the cities of Münster and Osnabrück are in Westphalia, a former Prussian province; hence the name of the peace). In addition, the peace endorsed Calvinism as an official form of religion; allowed Protestants to attend the imperial diet along with Roman Catholics; annulled the Peace of PRAGUE and the Edict of RESTITUTION, made January 1, 1624, the date by which ownership of ecclesiastical property would be determined; extended a general amnesty to all; provided for the territorial sovereignty of all imperial estates; and recognized the United Netherlands (Holland) and Switzerland as independent of the Holy Roman Empire. The treaty effectively ended this period of general European war over territorial, dynastic, and religious issues.

Further reading: Derek Croxton, *Peacemaking in Early Modern Europe: Cardinal Mazarin and the Congress of Westphalia, 1643–1648* (Selinsgrove, Pa.: Susquehanna University Press, 1999); Fred L. Israel, ed., *Major Peace Treaties of Modern History, 1648–1967*, 4 vols. (New York: Chelsea House, 1967); Frank N. Magill, ed., *Great Events from History: Modern European Series*, 3 vols. (Englewood Cliffs, N.J.: Salem Press, 1973); Louis L. Snyder, ed., *Documents of German History* (New Brunswick, N.J.: Rutgers University Press, 1958).

West Virginia Board of Education v. Barnette   U.S. Supreme Court decision issued on June 14, 1943, invalidating—as a violation of First Amendment rights—a state requirement that public school children salute and pledge allegiance to the flag. The regulation, which stated that children who refused could be expelled and their parents fined, was challenged by Walter Barnette, a Jehovah's Witness. In its six-to-three decision the Supreme Court ruled that the state cannot compel students to declare a belief, stating that "no official . . . can prescribe what shall be orthodox in politics, nationalism, religion, or other matters of opinion or force citizens to confess by word or act their faith therein."

Further reading: Kermit L. Hall et al., eds, *American Legal History: Cases and Materials*, 2d ed. (New York: Oxford University Press, 1996); Kermit L. Hall et al., ed., *The Oxford Companion to the Supreme Court of the United States* (New York: Oxford University Press, 1992); Robert R. Mayer, *The Court and the American Crises, 1930–1952* (Danbury, Conn.: Grolier Educational, 1995); United States Supreme Court, *United States Reports: Cases Adjudged in the Supreme Court at . . . and Rules Announced at . . .* (New York: Banks & Brothers, Law Publishers, 1884–1921; Washington, D.C.: Government Printing Office, 1922–).

What Is Property?   Sensational pamphlet written by French socialist Pierre Joseph Proudhon in 1840, denouncing the abuses of private property and espousing anarchism. "Property is theft," declared Proudhon, who was arguing that productivity of property owned by an absentee landowner or capitalist was actually exploitation of another's labor. He preferred France's old ideal of a system of small landholdings and workshops, each of which would be owned and operated by the farmer or proprietor alone. This system preserved freedom, which an individual lost when he did not have control over the property and its production. In the pamphlet, Proudhon also declared "I am an anarchist" in his criticism of capitalism and his espousal of justice for the workers; he was nearly prosecuted for his audacious remarks.

Further reading: John Ehrenberg, *Proudhon and His Age* (Atlantic Highlands, N.J.: Humanities Press, 1996); Donald R. Kelley and Bonnie G. Smith, eds. and trans., *What Is Property?/Pierre-Joseph Proudhon* (New York: Cambridge University Press, 1994); Mark A. Kishlansky, ed., *Sources of the West: Readings in Western Civilization*, 2 vols., 4th ed. (New York: Longman, 2001); K. Steven Vincent, *Pierre-Joseph Proudhon and the Rise of French Republican Socialism* (New York: Oxford University Press, 1984).

What Is to Be Done?   Tract published by Russian revolutionary Vladimir I. Lenin in London in 1902, expounding his doctrine of "professional revolutionists." In it, Lenin argued that it was the purpose of professional revolutionaries, as members of the intellectual elite, to guide the uneducated proletarian masses toward the inevitable socialist revolution. The intelligentsia was necessary to the revolutionary movement because it alone could formulate a socialist doctrine; workers were not able to rise above their trade-union mentality and the mundane considerations of working conditions. Lenin therefore advocated the gradual formation of a class of "professional revolutionists" to accomplish the goals of socialism. The book became a revolutionary bible to Lenin's followers in Russia and elsewhere.

Further reading: Mark A. Kishlansky, ed., *Sources of the West: Readings in Western Civilization*, 2 vols., 4th ed. (New York: Longman, 2001); Robert Service, *Lenin: A Biography* (Cambridge, Mass.: Harvard University Press, 2000); James D. White, *Lenin: The Practice and Theory of Revolution* (New York: Palgrave, 2001).

"What's the Matter with Kansas?"   Scathing editorial attack on the Populist Party written by editor and publisher

William Allen White, appearing first in his *Emporia (Kansas) Gazette* on August 3, 1896. Using sarcasm and picturesque language, White argued that Populists were driving people and money out of Kansas. Deriding one of the party's candidates as "an old jay," another as a "shabby, wild-eyed, rattle-brained fanatic," he mocked their competence and excoriated the Populist proposals as financially inane. The editorial was widely reprinted and was distributed by the opposing Republican Party, making White famous nationwide.

Further reading: Mortimer Adler, ed., *The Annals of America*, 18 vols. (Chicago: Encyclopaedia Britannica, 1968); Sheldon Hackney, comp., *Populism: the Critical Issues* (Boston: Little, Brown, 1971).

Wheeler-Howard Act (U.S. Indian Reorganization Act)

Federal legislation enacted on June 18, 1934, that restored some American Indian lands to tribal ownership and authorized federal funds to encourage Indian businesses. Sponsored by Senator Burton K. Wheeler of Montana and Representative Edgar Howard of Nebraska, the act gave to Indian tribes on reservations the right to adopt a constitution for self-government or to petition the secretary of the interior for a charter of incorporation. The Bureau of Indian Affairs, however, retained a veto power over tribal decisions. To conserve and develop tribal lands, the act ended land allotments in severalty and restored to tribal ownership surplus lands that had previously been open for sale to homesteaders. The act also authorized funds to enlarge tribal land holdings, to support Indian education, and to encourage economic development through federal loans.

Further reading: Theodore H. Haas, *Ten Years of Tribal Government under I.R.A.* (Chicago: U.S. Indian Service, 1947); William H. Kelly, *Indian Affairs and the Indian Reorganization Act: The Twenty Year Record* (Tucson: University of Arizona, 1954); Elmer R. Rusco, *A Fateful Time: The Background and Legislative History of the Indian Reorganization Act* (Reno: University of Nevada Press, 2000); Graham D. Taylor, *The New Deal and American Indian Tribalism: The Administration of the Indian Reorganization Act, 1934–45* (Lincoln: University of Nebraska Press, 1980).

Wheeler-Lea Act

U.S. legislation sponsored by Senator Burton K. Wheeler of Montana and Representative Clarence F. Lea of California and enacted on March 21, 1938, that prohibited individuals and agencies from presenting false or misleading statements about "food, drugs, diagnostic and therapeutic devices, and cosmetics" in interstate media. Radio stations and periodicals that disclosed the names of persons or companies responsible for false advertising would not themselves be held liable. Extending the PURE FOOD AND DRUG ACT OF 1906, the 1938 statute gave the Federal Trade Commission control over such advertising and gave the Food and Drug Administration authority over questions of misbranding.

Further reading: Charles W. Dunn, *Wheeler-Lea Act: A Statement of its Legislative Record* (Rockville, Md.: Mercury Press, 1987); *The New Food, Drug, and Cosmetic Legislation* (Durham, N.C.: School of Law, Duke University, 1939); Burton K. Wheeler and Paul F. Healy, *Yankee from the West: The Candid, Turbulent Life Story of the Yankee-Born U.S. Senator from Montana* (New York: Octagon Books, 1977).

Wheeler-Rayburn Act (Public Utility Holding Company Act)

New Deal legislation enacted on August 26, 1935, authorizing the U.S. government to regulate the interstate transmission and sale of gas and electric power. To counteract monopolistic public utility holding companies, the act gave the Federal Power Commission authority over the interstate transmission of electric power, the Federal Trade Commission authority over gas, and the Securities and Exchange Commission authority over the financial transactions of the holding companies. A "death sentence" clause allowed for the dissolution of any holding company that could not demonstrate a localized, useful, and efficient character after five years. This controversial legislation was sponsored by Representative Samuel Rayburn of Texas and Senator Burton Wheeler of Montana.

Further reading: *Compilation of Securities Laws within the Jurisdiction of the Committee on Financial Services: . . . Public Utility Holding Company Act of 1935, . . .* (Washington, D.C.: Government Printing Office, 2001); Burton K. Wheeler and Paul F. Healy, *Yankee from the West: The Candid, Turbulent Life Story of the Yankee-Born U.S. Senator from Montana* (New York: Octagon Books, 1977).

White Australia Policy

See IMMIGRATION RESTRICTION ACT OF 1902, AUSTRALIAN.

Whiteboy Acts

Legislation passed by the British and Irish parliaments in 1762 in order to put an end to the activities of the Whiteboys, Irish Catholic peasant societies formed in the 1760s to redress long-standing grievances against tithes, rack-renting, and enclosures of commons. So-called because of the white clothing they wore on their nocturnal raids, the Whiteboys terrorized landlords, tax collectors, and Protestant clergymen. The legislation served only as a temporary check on their activities, which continued well into the 1800s.

Further reading: Stewart J. Brown et al., *Piety and Power in Ireland, 1760–1960: Essays in Honor of Emmet Larkin* (Notre Dame, Ind.: University of Notre Dame Press, 2000); James S. Donnelly, *Irish Agrarian Rebellion: The Whiteboys of 1769–76* (Dublin: Royal Irish Academy, 1983); Thomas Moore, *Political and Historical Writings on Irish and British Affairs* (Belfast: Athol Books, 1993).

White Paper of 1922, British

See CHURCHILL WHITE PAPER OF 1922.

White Paper of 1923, British (Devonshire White Paper)

British government's declaration (1923) stressing the "paramountcy of African interests" in Kenya, amid attempts by European and Indian settlers to assume greater control of the country's affairs. Made by the duke of Devonshire, the declaration clarified Britain's role "as exercising a trust on behalf of the African population" and admitted British colonial inability "to delegate or share this trust, the object of which may be defined as the protection and advancement of the native races." In practice, it was difficult to implement since the settlers were dominant in government circles whereas, in 1923, the natives had no institutions by which they could make their presence felt. J. H. Oldham, secretary of the International Missionary Council, is credited with having initially proposed the policy, which was reiterated in the PASSFIELD REPORT of 1930.

Further reading: Robert O. Collins, *Eastern African History* (New York: M. Wiener Publisher, 1990).

White Paper of 1930, British   See PASSFIELD REPORT.

White Paper of 1939, British

Declaration of Britain's future policies regarding Palestine; issued on May 17, 1939, after the Woodhead Commission and the ensuing London conference (see WOODHEAD REPORT) had failed to achieve an Arab-Jewish accord. Having fulfilled the promises of the BALFOUR DECLARATION, Britain announced her intention to establish within 10 years "an independent Palestine state" in which Arab and Jewish interests could be secured. It envisaged increased participation in government for both communities, the holding of elections (conditions permitting) and, five years later, the drafting of a constitution for the new state by British, Arab, and Jewish leaders. Jewish immigration to the new state would be restricted to 75,000 persons over five years, and thereafter allowed only with Arab consent. Transfer of land from Arabs to Jews would be banned until independence. These proposals were violently opposed by the Jews; Arab opinion was divided. Nevertheless, both communities announced their support for Britain when she launched a war against Germany a few months later (see BRITISH DECLARATION OF WAR IN 1939).

Further reading: Martin Gilbert, *Britain, Palestine and the Jews: The Evolution of the 1939 Palestine White Paper* (Oxford, England: Oxford Centre for Postgraduate Hebrew Studies, 1977); Bernard Reich, ed., *Arab-Israeli Conflict and Conciliation: A Documentary History* (Westport, Conn.: Greenwood Press, 1995); Daphne Trevor, *Under the White Paper: Some Aspects of British Administration in Palestine from 1939 to 1947* (Munich: Kraus International, 1980).

White Paper of 1945, British

Publication on May 17, 1945, of the British government's proposals for the reorganization of Burma (Myanmar) after the defeat of the Japanese. Britain promised to assist Burma to "attain a status equal to that of the Dominions and this country." Meanwhile, pending general elections, Burma would continue to be administered by a governor—his office was extended by three years, until December 9, 1948—answerable to the British government. Later, elections would be held, a Burmese cabinet and legislature reestablished in accordance with the 1935 constitution (see GOVERNMENT OF INDIA ACT OF 1935), and eminent Burmans (Burmese) invited to draft a new constitution. Following this, Britain assured Burma "full self-government within the Commonwealth." The governor would, however, retain control over the Shan states and the hilly tribal areas until an acceptable (to the inhabitants) form of integration with Burma could be determined. The British also promised assistance in improving Burma's economic and financial status. The Burmans strongly opposed both its tone and content and, in actuality, it had no more than academic importance.

Further reading: U. Htin Aung, *The Stricken Peacock: Anglo-Burmese Relations, 1752–1948* (The Hague: M. Nijhoff, 1965).

White Paper of 1949, U.S. (United States Relations with China)

Controversial U.S. State Department report prepared by Ambassador at Large Philip C. Jessup and released on August 5, 1949, discussing the history of U.S.-Chinese relations and announcing the cessation of U.S. aid to the Nationalist government under Jiang Jieshi (Chiang Kai-shek), then engaged in a civil war with communist forces led by Mao Zedong (Mao Tse-tung). The report attempted to absolve the United States of responsibility for the impending collapse of Nationalist China. In the introduction, Secretary of State Dean Acheson wrote that the outcome of the war was "the product of internal Chinese forces" and beyond the control of the U.S. government. The United States, he said, had chosen not to attempt a full-scale intervention in behalf of "a government which had lost the confidence of its own troops and its own people."

Further reading: U.S. Department of State, *The China White Paper, August 1949* (Stanford, Calif.: Stanford University Press, 1967); U.S. Department of State, *United States Relations with China, with Special Reference to the Period 1944–1949, Based on the Files of the Department of State* (Washington, D.C.: Government Printing Office, 1949).

White Paper of 1965, U.S.

Major U.S. policy statement about the escalating Vietnam War (1956–75), prepared and issued (February 1965) by the U.S. government; it strongly defended the view that communist-led North Vietnam was "carrying on a carefully conceived plan of aggression against the South." The war was not a popular movement, the report argued, and was "not a spontaneous and local rebellion against the established government"; rather, it was a deliberate attempt by North Vietnamese government troops, aided by Vietcong agents, to conquer the "sovereign people" of the South. The White Paper detailed North Vietnam's infiltration process, military personnel and weapons, organization and center of operations (Hanoi). The United States had taken part in the South Vietnamese people's "defensive struggle" at their request, the paper stated. Many foreign policy experts, academics, and top journalists considered the paper an inadequate defense of American policy; the escalating war brought a wave of dissent in the United States.

Further reading: Henry Steele Commager, ed., *Documents of American History*, 8th ed. (New York: Appleton-Century-Crofts, 1968); Republican Conference, Committee on Planning and Research, *Vietnam: Some Neglected Aspects of the Historical Record* (Washington, D.C.: The Conference, 1965).

White Slave Traffic Act, U.S.   See MANN ACT.

Whitman v. *American Trucking Association*   U.S. Supreme Court decision issued on February 27, 2001, concerning the right of federal regulatory agencies to intepret federal legislation that falls under their purview. In 1997 the Environmental Protection Agency (EPA), acting in accordance to its interpretation of the Clean Air Act, toughened the standards for ozone emission levels and set the first standard for the emission of fine particulates of airborne soot. Since the soot standard had its greatest effect on emissions from diesel trucks and paid no heed to how much it would cost to retrofit trucks to meet the standard, the American Trucking Association challenged the two new standards in court on the grounds that the EPA overstepped its authority by interpreting the Clean Air Act according to its own whim. After the association won its case in the District of Columbia Circuit Court of Appeal in 1999, the EPA's director appealed the case to the Supreme Court; by the time the case was heard, that director had been replaced by Christie Whitman under George W. Bush's administration. In a unanimous decision, the Supreme Court overturned the lower court's ruling concerning the soot standard on the grounds that Congress's mandate to the EPA concerning airborne soot was clear. However, the Court ordered the EPA to reconsider the implementation of the ozone standards on the grounds that the Clean Air Act is ambiguous on this subject, thus making the new ozone standard seem unreasonable.

Further reading: Richard A. Epstein, "Through the Smog: What the Court Actually Ruled," *Wall Street Journal*, March 1, 2001.

William I's Proclamation to the Prussian People
Proclamation issued by King William I of Prussia in Berlin on June 18, 1866, at the beginning of the Austro-Prussian War (Seven Weeks' War). "An mein Volk" (to my people), William addressed his words that Austria and part of Germany threatened "the Fatherland" (Prussia) and that, for many years, he had built up Prussian military might to counter enemies who wanted to destroy the country. He said that Austria had opposed his attempts (made with France, England, and Russia)

to settle differences peacefully and that, God willing, the strong Prussian people would be victorious, bonding together the various German lands. William surely was influenced by Otto von Bismarck, Prussia's premier, who saw Austria as a great hindrance to German unification.

Further reading: Louis L. Snyder, ed., *Documents of German History* (New Brunswick, N.J.: Rutgers University Press, 1958); Louis L. Snyder, ed., *Fifty Major Documents of the Nineteenth Century* (Princeton, N.J.: D. Van Nostrand, 1955).

Wills and Uses, Statutes of   Two statutes passed by the Irish Parliament in 1634, guaranteeing the crown of England an advisory and supervisory role in the education of the heirs-apparent of the great families of Ireland. The ultimate aim, of course, was to bring them up in the Protestant faith, in the same way as the 12th earl of Ormonde (James Butler), who had been a ward of the crown and been raised a Protestant before succeeding to the earldom in 1632.

Further reading: Hervey R. Morres, *The History of the Principal Transactions of the Irish Parliament from the Year 1634 to 1666* (South Hackensack, N.J.: Rothman Reprints, 1972).

Wilmot Proviso   Proposal passed by the U.S. House of Representatives in 1846 and 1847 that aimed to prohibit slavery in territory that the United States was negotiating to acquire from Mexico. The proviso, offered on behalf of antislavery forces by Democratic congressman David Wilmot of Pennsylvania, was presented as an amendment to a bill authorizing $2 million for President James K. Polk to pursue those negotiations (August 8, 1846). The proviso stated that a fundamental condition of any such territorial acquisition was a ban on slavery and involuntary servitude within that territory. Though the proviso twice passed the House, it was rejected by the Senate. It sparked a national debate and fueled the sectional dispute over slavery.

Further reading: Don E. Fehrenbacher, *Sectional Crisis and Southern Constitutionalism* (Baton Rouge: Louisiana State University Press, 1995); Chaplain W. Morrison, *Democratic Politics and Sectionalism; the Wilmot Proviso Controversy* (Chapel Hill: University of North Carolina Press, 1967); Joseph G. Rayback, *Free Soil; the Election of 1848* (Lexington: University Press of Kentucky, 1971).

Wilson-Gorman Tariff Act   Federal U.S. legislation of August 27, 1894, that succeeded the MCKINLEY TARIFF ACT. As drafted by Representative W. L. Wilson, the act lowered protective duties on manufactured goods and placed basic raw materials—wool, iron ore, lumber, and sugar—on the free list. To make up for lost revenue, the act taxed certain luxuries and incomes over $4,000. The Senate, led by A. P. Gorman, amended the bill drastically, removing many raw materials from the free list and making the average protective

tariff rate 40 percent. President Grover Cleveland denounced the bill for its protectionism but allowed it to become law without his signature.

Further reading: Mortimer Adler, ed., *The Annals of America*, 18 vols. (Chicago: Encyclopaedia Britannica, 1968); Sidney Ratner, *The Tariff in American History* (New York: Van Nostrand, 1972); F. W. Taussig, *The Tariff History of the United States* (Woodbridge, Conn.: Research Publications, 1991).

Wilson's Appeal for Neutrality   Message from President Woodrow Wilson to the U.S. Senate on August 19, 1914, following the outbreak of World War I in Europe. Issued shortly after his Proclamation of Neutrality of August 4, this appeal to his fellow countrymen called for neutrality "in thought as well as in action." Recognizing that many Americans were drawn from the nations then at war, with various sympathies in the conflict, Wilson urged them all to unite in loyalty to the United States, to think first of her national interests. He called upon the nation to exhibit self-control and dispassionate action to promote world peace.

Further reading: Mortimer Adler, ed., *The Annals of America*, 18 vols. (Chicago: Encyclopaedia Britannica, 1968); Henry Steele Commager, ed., *Documents of American History*, 8th ed. (New York: Appleton-Century-Crofts, 1968).

Wilson's Exposition of the League of Nations   Address delivered by U.S. President Woodrow Wilson before the Senate Committee on Foreign Relations on August 19, 1919, in an unsuccessful attempt to persuade the Senate to ratify the LEAGUE OF NATIONS COVENANT. Wilson's exposition answered earlier concerns about the covenant, stating that it respected the MONROE DOCTRINE, gave the league no authority to act in domestic matters, recognized the right of nations to withdraw from the league, and safeguarded the congressional right to determine all questions of war and peace. Opponents of the league, led by U.S. senator Henry Cabot Lodge, chairman of the Foreign Relations Committee, defeated the covenant in 1920.

See also: LODGE RESERVATIONS; PUEBLO SPEECH, WILSON'S.

Further reading: Henry Steele Commager, ed., *Documents of American History*, 8th ed. (New York: Appleton-Century-Crofts, 1968); John M. Cooper, *Breaking the Heart of the World: Woodrow Wilson and the Fight for the League of Nations* (New York: Cambridge University Press, 2001).

Wilson's First Inaugural Address   Speech delivered by Woodrow Wilson on March 4, 1913, at his inauguration as 28th president of the United States, calling for a series of national reforms. In it Wilson, a Democrat, reaffirmed his commitment to the "New Freedom" program on which he had campaigned. Seeking "justice, not pity," Wilson argued for reforms in a tariff system that favored private interests, in an obsolete banking and currency system, in an industrial system that exploited labor and natural resources, in an inefficient agricultural system. He favored the conservation of human and natural resources and the protection of American health through laws regarding sanitation, pure food, and conditions of labor.

Further reading: Mortimer Adler, ed., *The Annals of America*, 18 vols. (Chicago: Encyclopaedia Britannica, 1968); Henry Steele Commager, ed., *Documents of American History*, 8th ed. (New York: Appleton-Century-Crofts, 1968).

Wilson's Mobile Address   Speech delivered by U.S. president Woodrow Wilson on October 27, 1913, before the Southern Commercial Congress at Mobile, Alabama, outlining his policy toward Latin America. Wilson called for closer ties and a "spiritual union" with America's southern neighbors, a union of equality, honor, sympathy, and understanding. He predicted the emancipation of Latin America from subordination to foreign enterprises and demands of foreign investors. He stated that "the United States will never again seek one additional foot of territory by conquest" and described as a duty of national friendship the protection of Latin America's constitutional liberties from encroachment by material interests.

Further reading: Henry Steele Commager, ed., *Documents of American History*, 8th ed. (New York: Appleton-Century-Crofts, 1968).

Wilson's "Old Order Changeth" Speech   Address delivered by Democratic nominee Woodrow Wilson during the 1912 U.S. presidential campaign and published in Wilson's book *The New Freedom* (1913), calling for a "great reconstruction" of America's social order. Wilson maintained that new economic conditions in the United States, notably the growth of large, impersonal corporations and new relations between labor and capital, required a new social organization. He criticized corruption and the control of government by big business and special interests, at the expense of individuals and of free enterprise. He proposed new rules to protect workers, to define the rights and obligations of employers and employees, to encourage new enterprises, and to regulate corporations.

Further reading: Woodrow Wilson, *The New Freedom; a Call for the Emancipation of the Generous Energies of a People* (New York: Doubleday, Page, 1914).

Wilson's "Peace Without Victory" Speech   See "PEACE WITHOUT VICTORY" SPEECH, WILSON'S.

Wilson's Pueblo Speech   See PUEBLO SPEECH, WILSON'S.

Wilson's "Too Proud to Fight" Speech   See "TOO PROUD TO FIGHT" SPEECH, WILSON'S.

Wilson's War Message to Congress ("Make the World Safe for Democracy" Speech) Address delivered at a joint session of Congress on April 2, 1917, by U.S. president Woodrow Wilson, asking Congress to declare war against Germany. Wilson charged that Germany's policy of unrestricted submarine warfare constituted "a warfare against mankind," in which American ships had been sunk and American lives lost. He admitted that his previous policy of neutrality was now impracticable in view of the German threat to international peace and justice. "The world must be made safe for democracy. Its peace must be planted upon the tested foundations of political liberty," he maintained. Congress declared war four days later, and the United States became an Allied power in World War I (1914–18).

Further reading: Mortimer Adler, ed., *The Annals of America*, 18 vols. (Chicago: Encyclopaedia Britannica, 1968); Henry Steele Commager, ed., *Documents of American History*, 8th ed. (New York: Appleton-Century-Crofts, 1968); Louis L. Snyder, ed., *Fifty Major Documents of the Twentieth Century* (Princeton, N.J.: D. Van Nostrand, 1955); Milton Viorst, ed., *The Great Documents of Western Civilization* (Philadelphia: Chilton Books, 1965).

Wilson's "What Is Progress?" Speech Campaign speech delivered by U.S. Democratic presidential nominee Woodrow Wilson in 1912 and published in Wilson's book *The New Freedom* (1913). Wilson stated that U.S. laws had not kept up with economic and political changes in the nation. The government, he said, which was designed for the people, had fallen into the hands of the bosses and special interests, "an invisible empire . . . set up above the forms of democracy." In urging legislative action to catch up with altered circumstances, Wilson declared himself a progressive—a conservatively based progressive who nevertheless wished to preserve the essentials of the nation's institutions.

Further reading: Woodrow Wilson, *The New Freedom; a Call for the Emancipation of the Generous Energies of a People* (New York: Doubleday, Page, 1914).

Windsor, Treaty of Anglo-Portuguese alliance concluded on May 9, 1386, in the royal chapel at Windsor Castle, England, after Portugal secured her independence by defeating Spain (with English military assistance) in the famous battle of Aljubarrota (August 14, 1385). The duke of Lancaster, John of Gaunt (representing his nephew, King Richard II of England), saw this as an opportunity to renew his claims to Castile, and cemented the pact by marrying his daughter Philippa to King John I, founder of the Avis dynasty in Portugal (February 1387). Thereby, both countries entered into "an inviolable, eternal, solid, perpetual and true league of friendship, alliance and union," which obliged them to assist each other if their peace was threatened. The treaty also contained military, political, and economic clauses and is believed to be the oldest alliance currently in existence.

Further reading: Anil de Silva-Vigier, *This Moste Highe Prince—John of Gaunt, 1340–1399* (Edinburgh, Scotland: Pentland, 1992).

Wittenberg, Concord of Agreement between German and Swiss Protestant reformers (specifically between followers of Martin Luther and those of Huldreich Zwingli, respectively), signed by them at Wittenberg, Germany, on May 25, 1536. Drawn up by Philip Melanchthon, an advocate of compromise, the document tried to present an understanding of the Eucharist that would be acceptable to both Lutherans and Zwinglians. The formula rejected the concept of transubstantiation (the Roman Catholic doctrine holding that the Eucharistic bread and wine are converted into the body and blood of Christ) and affirmed Luther's belief in the actual presence of Christ in the bread and wine at the time of the Eucharistic celebration (in contrast to Zwingli's belief that His presence was metaphorical). Because the Swiss agreed to the Lutheran interpretation, the concord reflected a Lutheran victory, but it did not effect a lasting union between the two sects.

Further reading: Gerald L. Bray, *Documents of the English Reformation* (Minneapolis: Fortress Press, 1994); David C. Steinmetz, ed., *The Bible in the Sixteenth Century* (Durham, N.C.: Duke University Press, 1996).

Wolfenden Report Publication in September 1957 of the recommendations of the Committee on Homosexual Offenses and Prostitution in Great Britain, many of which were incorporated into subsequent legislation. Chaired by Sir John Wolfenden, a former school headmaster, the committee was appointed in 1954 to reexamine the laws pertaining to sexual behavior amid major scandals and a growing number of prosecutions. The committee's view was that such laws should concentrate on acts that violated public decency and order rather than try to set standards of morality. Its suggestion that homosexual affairs between consenting adults in private should not be considered a criminal offense was adopted in the Sexual Offenses Act of 1967. In 1959, the Street Offenses Act forbade prostitutes from soliciting on the streets and increased the penalties for those promoting and living on the earnings of prostitutes.

Further reading: Charles Berg, *Fear, Punishment, Anxiety, and the Wolfenden Report* (London: Allen & Unwin, 1959); Eustace Chesser, *Live and Let Live: The Moral of the Wolfenden Report* (London: Heinemann, 1958); *The Wolfenden Report: Report of the Committee on Homosexual Offences and Prostitution* (New York: Langer Books, 1964); Joel H. Wiener, ed., *Great Britain—The Lion at Home: A Documentary History of Domestic Policy (1689–1973)*, 4 vols. (New York: Chelsea House, 1974).

Wolff Packing Company v. Court of Industrial Relations of Kansas U.S. Supreme Court decision, issued on June 11, 1923, that restricted the definition of the public interest and limited state regulation of industrial and labor relations. The Court unanimously overturned a Kansas statute declaring that the manufacture of food and clothing, mining, public utilities, and transportations were affected with a public interest (and thereby subject to state regulation) and establishing a three-judge court to fix wages and labor conditions in such industries. The Court ruled that the fixing of wages in a meat-packing plant was a deprivation of property and denied freedom of contract between an employer and an employee, as provided under the U.S. FOURTEENTH AMENDMENT.

Further reading: Henry Steele Commager, ed., *Documents of American History*, 8th ed. (New York: Appleton-Century-Crofts, 1968).

Woman's Christian Temperance Union (WCTU) Declaration of Principles

Statement issued in the national WCTU annual leaflet of 1902. In addition to promulgating its well-known prohibitionist beliefs, the WCTU endorsed an equal standard of behavior and freedom of expression for men and women, a living wage, an eight-hour day, "justice as opposed to greed of gain," and "peace on earth and good-will to men." The leaflet asked supporters to pledge to abstain from all distilled, fermented, and malt liquors, and to discourage others from using such beverages. It declared its goal to educate the young and to reform the "drinking classes."

Further reading: Henry Steele Commager, ed., *Documents of American History*, 8th ed. (New York: Appleton-Century-Crofts, 1968).

Women's Rights, Declaration of (Seneca Falls Declaration and Resolutions, Declaration of Independence for Women)

Proclamation issued on July 19, 1848, at the Seneca Falls (New York) Convention on the rights of women. Modeled on the DECLARATION OF INDEPENDENCE, the document outlined the unequal and unjust treatment of women and argued that women had rights to equality under the law in all spheres, including education, religion, free speech, and employment opportunities. Its most controversial resolution called for the enfranchisement of women and marked the beginning of the woman suffrage movement in the United States.

Further reading: Mortimer Adler, ed., *The Annals of America*, 18 vols. (Chicago: Encyclopedia Britannica, 1968); Henry Steele Commager, ed., *Documents of American History*, 8th ed. (New York: Appleton-Century-Crofts, 1968); Sheila Ruth, *Issues in Feminism: An Introduction to Women's Studies* (Mountain View, Calif.: Mayfield, 1995).

Woodhead Report

Plans issued on November 9, 1938, by a British commission (headed by Sir John Woodhead) appointed to reconsider the Peel Commission's proposals (1937) for the partitioning of Palestine. The report voiced the commission's unanimous opposition to the Peel scheme, proposing instead two other plans. The most feasible of these, it announced, would divide Palestine into three parts: a northern and a southern (the Negev) section retained by Britain under mandate (see BALFOUR DECLARATION; LEAGUE OF NATIONS COVENANT) and a central section partitioned into an Arab state and a Jewish state, with British mandate over the Jerusalem area. The report suggested that the Arab and Jewish states participate in a customs union with the mandated areas, so that Britain could determine a common fiscal policy. This scheme was completely rejected by both Arabs and Jews. To break the deadlock, Britain invited both delegations to a conference in London in 1939.

See also: WHITE PAPER OF 1939, BRITISH.

Further reading: David McDowell, *The Palestinians: The Road to Nationhood*, rev. ed. (London: Minority Rights Publications, 1995); Bernard Reich, ed., *Arab-Israeli Conflict and Conciliation: A Documentary History* (Westport, Conn.: Greenwood Press, 1995); Avi Shlaim, *The Politics of Partition: King Abdullah, the Zionists and Palestine 1921–1951*, rev. abridged ed. (Oxford, England: Oxford University Press, 1998); John Woodhead et al., *Report* (London: H.M. Stationery Office, 1938).

Woodstock, Assize of (Assize of the Forest)

First authoritative ordinance concerning England's forests, enacted by King Henry II at the Council of Woodstock (1184). It tightened the penalties for anyone, including the clergy, found violating the king's forests or hunting rights. It forbade the possession or use of bows, arrows, hounds, or harriers in the forests unless legally guaranteed by the king or someone else. Those who had woods within the royal forests were to appoint foresters and stand surety for them. The assize also called for the appointment of 12 knights to protect the king's venison and four knights to pasture cattle in his woods. The king's foresters were to ensure that the assize, part of a series of reforms (see ARMS, ASSIZE OF; CLARENDON, ASSIZE OF; NORTHAMPTON, ASSIZE OF; DARRIEN PRESENTMENT, ASSIZE OF) undertaken by Henry II, was properly enforced.

Further reading: W. L. Warren, *Henry II* (New Haven, Conn.: Yale University Press, 2000).

Woolens Act (Wool Act)

English trade restriction enacted by Parliament in 1699 in an effort to protect England's wool manufacturers and woolens' merchants against competition from Ireland and the American colonies. The act (one of the Acts of Trade and Navigation, passed between 1650 and 1767) restricted the production of Irish wool and forbade the exportation of wool, woolen yarn, and woolen clothing from any colony to England, to another country, or to another colony. Although the act was a reason for Irish and Scottish migration to America, it actually had minimal impact on the colonies, where most woolen goods were produced in households for domestic use.

Further reading: David D. Douglas et al., eds., *English Historical Documents*, 12 vols. (New York; Oxford University Press, 1950–77).

Worcester v. Georgia U.S. Supreme Court decision, issued on March 3, 1832, declaring that the Cherokee Nation was under the jurisdiction of the United States government, not the Georgia state government. The case arose when missionary Samuel A. Worcester and others violated a Georgia statute requiring white men who lived in Cherokee territory to take an oath of allegiance to the state and to obtain a license. Their conviction was reversed in this decision, but Georgia refused to obey the decision. The ruling also angered U.S. President Andrew Jackson, who refused to enforce it. This case was part of Georgia's effort to secure sovereignty over Cherokee lands, which eventually led to the Cherokee removal to Oklahoma.

Further reading: Henry Steele Commager, ed., *Documents of American History*, 8th ed. (New York: Appleton-Century-Crofts, 1968); Kermit L. Hall et al., eds., *The Oxford Companion to the Supreme Court of the United States* (New York: Oxford University Press, 1992); Maureen Harrison and Steve Gilbert, *Landmark Decisions of the United States Supreme Court* (Beverly Hills, Calif.: Excellent Books, 1991).

Worker Adjustment and Retraining Notification Act, U.S.
Federal legislation passed by both houses of the United States Congress and, despite a presidential veto, made effective on February 4, 1989; it required companies to provide employees with advance notification of plant-closings and layoffs. Specifically, the law required that companies with more than 100 employees give employees 60 days' notice of plant-closings and of layoffs involving 50 or more workers. While the measure had widespread public support as well as the strong backing of organized labor, it was vehemently opposed by business leaders who viewed it as an unnecessary intrusion into business affairs.

Further reading: *Dislocated Workers: Worker Adjustment and Retraining Notification Act Not Meeting Its Goals: Report to Congressional Committees* (Washington, D.C.: Government Printing Office, 1993); Peter M. Panken, *Employment and Labor Law: Resource Materials*, 2 vols., 7th ed. (Philadelphia: American Law Institute, American Bar Association Committee on Continuing Professional Education, 1995); *Worker Adjustment and Retraining Notification Act* (Washington, D.C.: Government Printing Office, 1988).

Working Class Program
Speech delivered by German socialist Ferdinand Lassalle in Berlin, Germany, in 1862, emphasizing "the principle of the working class as the ruling principle of the community" and carrying on this principle by "universal and direct suffrage." The speech, illegally published as a pamphlet, concerned the historical conflicts and paradoxes between the lower and upper classes of society.

Lassalle stressed the state's important role in helping workers achieve and live adequately. Those who belonged to the working class had the duty "to direct the will of the state" in order that "a morally ordered community" be created—one permitting "free activity of individual powers" but with "solidarity of interests, community and reciprocity in development." Lassalle threw himself into the workers' struggle for political power in the following years.

Further reading: Eduard Bernstein, *Ferdinand Lassalle as a Social Reformer*, trans. Eleanor M. Aveling (New York: Greenwood Press, 1969).

Workingman's Compensation Act of 1906, British
British legislation, promoted by David Lloyd George (president of the Board of Trade) in 1906, which addressed more fully the question of an employer's liability in industrial accidents. Essentially, it was a development of the provisions of Joseph Chamberlain's Workmen's Compensation Act of 1897. It made employers fully liable for industrial accidents affecting manual workers whose annual income was less than £250. They were, however, exempt from providing compensation where the accident was the result of "serious and wilful misconduct." It also entitled workers to receive compensation for loss of work due to industrial diseases.

Further reading: Bentley B. Gilbert, *David Lloyd George: A Political Life* (London: B. T. Batsford, 1987); Joel H. Wiener, ed., *Great Britain—The Lion at Home: A Documentary History of Domestic Policy (1689–1973)*, 4 vols. (New York: Chelsea House, 1974).

Workmen's Compensation Law, Maryland's
First workmen's compensation legislation in the United States, passed in 1902. The act, which placed on the employer the responsibility for compensating an employee injured on the job, was declared unconstitutional by the U.S. Supreme Court. This law and similar legislation in other states grew from the inability of industrialized workers to carry the financial burden of injury arising from employer negligence and the expense of suing for damages. In 1908 the Supreme Court upheld a federal law providing compensation for federal employees, and all states now have some form of workmen's compensation, though not all workers are covered.

Further reading: Paul B. Bellamy, *A History of Workmen's Compensation, 1898–1915: From Courtroom to Boardroom* (New York: Garland Publications, 1997); Maurice J. Pressman, *Workmen's Compensation in Maryland*, 2d ed. (Charlottesville, Va.: Michie Company, 1977).

Workrooms and Factories Act
See FACTORY ACT OF 1873, AUSTRALIAN.

World as Will and Idea, The (Die Welt als Wille und Vorstellung)
German philosopher Arthur Schopenhauer's magnum opus (1819), whose central theme was stated tersely

in the title itself. Acknowledging his indebtedness to Immanuel Kant, Plato, and the *Upanishads* (early Hindu speculative treatises written about 900–400 B.C. and forming part of the sacred Vedas' literature), Schopenhauer developed in his work's four books a theory of knowledge and a philosophy of nature, aesthetics, and ethics. In book one (also called "The World as Idea") Schopenhauer elaborated on Kant's theory that the world around us is made known to us through the features of our understanding. Reason then helps organize these perceptions to achieve harmony. In book two ("The World as Will") he described all phenomena as an act of will, a force that can assume various forms. In book three (again "The World as Idea") he examined "idea" as a product of reason rather than as something we perceive; in book four (again "The World as Will") he discussed the will's renunciation to live, a concept derived from Eastern religious philosophy.

Further reading: David Berman, ed., *The World as Will and Idea: Abridged in One Volume/Arthur Schopenhauer*, trans. Jill Berman (Rutland, Vt.: Charles E. Tuttle, 1995); R. B. Haldane and J. Kemp, trans., *The World as Will and Idea/Arthur Schopenhauer* (New York: AMS Press, 1977).

World Council of Churches, Accord of the

"Fellowship of Churches which accept our Lord Jesus Christ as God and Saviour," formally constituted at Amsterdam, the Netherlands, on August 23, 1948, by 351 delegates representing 147 churches in 44 countries. Fathered by the ecumenical movement, the World Council's aim was to "offer counsel and provide opportunity of united action in matters of common interest" without attempting to legislate for the churches. It consists of an assembly (meeting every six years), central and executive and special committees, and six presidents. The council's primary concerns are church and interchurch relations, promotion of ecumenical study, and aid to refugees. Since the early days, its membership has expanded considerably to today's 252 churches in 80 countries. Notable exceptions are the Roman Catholic and the Russian churches.

Further reading: David P. Gaines, *The World Council of Churches, a Study of its Background and History* (Peterborough, N.H.: R. R. Smith, 1966); Michael Kinnamon and Brian E. Cope, eds., *The Ecumenical Movement: An Anthology of Key Texts and Voices* (Grand Rapids, Mich.: W. B. Eerdmans Publishers, 1997); Frank N. Magill, ed., *Great Events from History: Modern European Series*, 3 vols. (Englewood Cliffs, N.J.: Salem Press, 1973).

World Intellectual Property Organization, Treaties of the

Two treaties adopted on December 20, 1996, by the World Intellectual Property Organization (WIPO) at the conclusion of its Diplomatic Conference on Certain Copyright and Neighboring Rights in Geneva. The first treaty, the WIPO Copyright Treaty (WCT), added to the Berne Convention for the Protection of Literary and Artistic Works and extended the convention's copyright rules to digitally created literary and artistic works. The second, the WIPO Performances and Phonograms Treaty (WPPT), added to the Rome Convention and established new rights for performing artists and producers of sound recordings when their fixed sound performances or phonograms were accessed digitally, for instance, through the Internet. Both treaties would become operative three months after 30 member countries had ratified them. By July 22, 2002, 37 countries had ratified both treaties; the WCT went into effect on March 6, 2002, and the WPPT on May 20, 2002.

Further reading: World Intellectual Property Organization, "Treaties and Contracting Parties," WIPO, available online at http://www.wipo.int/treaties/index.html.

World Split Apart   See SOLZHENITSYN'S HARVARD SPEECH.

World War I Armistice

Germany's armistice with the Allied powers, signed at Rethondes, in the forest of Compiègne in northern France, on November 11, 1918; it formally ended the hostilities of World War I (1914–18). Following the first peace overtures made by Germany on October 6, the Allies agreed on the terms of the armistice. Germany was to evacuate all occupied territory, the left bank of the Rhine River, and the bridges at Mainz, Koblenz, and Cologne. She was to ground her submarines and naval fleet and destroy her tanks, aircraft, and heavy artillery. All prisoners and deported civilians were to be returned, while the Allies reserved the right to press for monetary compensation for losses sustained during the war. Germany was to nullify the Treaties of BUCHAREST and BREST-LITOVSK and to cede to the Allies 150,000 railroad wagons, 5,000 locomotives, and 5,000 trucks. The Allied troops would remain until the peace treaty was signed. A year later, when the Treaty of VERSAILLES was drafted, its terms were more severe than the armistice had indicated.

Further reading: Hugh Cecil and Peter Liddle, *At the Eleventh Hour: Reflections, Hopes and Anxieties at the Closing of the Great War 1918* (London: Leo Cooper, 1998); Gregor Dallas, *1918: War and Peace* (Woodstock, England: Overlook Press, 2001); J. P. Harris and Niall Barr, *Amiens to the Armistice: The BEF in the Hundred Days' Campaign, 8 August–11 November, 1918* (London: Brassey's, 1998).

Worms, Charter of

Imperial charter granted to the German town of Worms by King Henry IV of Germany in 1074, significant because it was the first such charter to be granted directly to townsmen (citizens). (Previously, charters had been issued to the bishop of a town, such that the townsmen were indebted to the bishops for their privileges.) As was typical for the day, the charter established that the merchants of Worms were exempt from the payment of tolls in certain specified royal towns (in this case, in Frankfurt, Goslar, Boppard, Dortmund, Nürnburg, Engern, and Hammerstein).

Further reading: I. S. Robinson, *Henry IV of Germany, 1056–1106* (New York: Cambridge University Press, 1999).

Worms, Concordat of Compromise agreement arranged in September 1122 by Pope Calixtus II with Holy Roman Emperor Henry V, thus ending the investiture struggle between the papacy and the empire over the control of church offices (the papacy desired to check the increasing power secular leaders had been gaining over the clergy). The agreement clearly distinguished a clergyman's spiritual (church) and temporal (crown) positions. The emperor pledged to renounce to the church all investiture by pastoral ring and staff (the symbols of spiritual office), to permit canonical elections in all churches in Germany, and to return to Rome and all churches under his jurisdiction all regalia removed since the start of the investiture controversy in the late 11th century. In return, the pope agreed to the emperor's presence at the clergy's elections of bishops and abbots who would serve in his realm, as well as to the emperor's presenting the chosen candidates first with the royal regalia (the scepter) before the spiritual investiture. Candidates were expected to pay homage to the emperor as well.

Further reading: Catholic University of America, eds., *New Catholic Encyclopedia* (New York: McGraw-Hill, 1967); Norton Downs, ed., *Basic Documents in Medieval History* (New York: Van Nostrand Reinhold, 1959); Louis L. Snyder, ed., *Documents of German History* (New Brunswick, N.J.: Rutgers University Press, 1958); Milton Viorst, ed., *The Great Documents of Western Civilization* (Philadelphia: Chilton Books, 1965).

Worms, Edict of (1231) Decree against town leagues issued by the German king Henry VII at Worms in January 1231. Unlike his father, Holy Roman Emperor Frederick II, Henry had preferred to support the German towns rather than the princes, but he underestimated the princes' strength (he had tried to take measures against them while they were away in Italy). The princes, however, forced Henry to issue the edict, by which the towns were denied the right to form leagues, communes, confederations, and constitutions. The rule of the German princes was strengthened (see WORMS, PRIVILEGE OF).

See also: MELFI, CONSTITUTIONS OF.

Further reading: David Abulafia, *Frederick II: A Medieval Emperor* (New York: Oxford University Press, 1992).

Worms, Edict of (1521) Edict published on May 25, 1521, at Worms, Germany, by the authority of Holy Roman Emperor Charles V, formally declaring Martin Luther, German leader of the Protestant Reformation, an outlaw whose writings were proscribed. In 1520 Luther's views had been declared heretical (see EXSURGE DOMINE). His defiant behavior had then led to his summoned appearance before the imperial Diet of Worms, held in Worms, Germany, in April 1521. The edict was issued after he refused to recant his beliefs and after the Diet's adjournment. It placed Luther under the ban of the empire, ordered all his books burned, forbade anyone to help him, and ordered his arrest (his friends then secretly lodged him in the Wartburg Castle).

See also: SPEYER, DECREE OF THE DIET OF (1529).

Further reading: G. Barraclough, *The Origins of Modern Germany* (New York: W. W. Norton, 1984); Catholic University of America, eds., *New Catholic Encyclopedia* (New York: McGraw-Hill, 1967); De Lamar Jensen, *Confrontation at Worms: Martin Luther and the Diet of Worms* (Provo, Utah: Brigham Young University Press, 1973); Louis L. Snyder, ed., *Documents of German History* (New Brunswick, N.J.: Rutgers University Press, 1958).

Worms, Privilege of (Privilege of Princes, Constitutio in Favorem Principum) Concessions in favor of the German princes, made by the Holy Roman Emperor Frederick II and his son, the German king Henry VII, at Worms in May 1231. They had been forced by the strong princes to issue this statute, which significantly confirmed a prince to be the supreme authority in his domain, declaring him to be "lord of the land." It also declared that the chief local officials maintaining the law would be appointed by the territorial prince, rather than by the king; that the king was prohibited from building new fortresses and towns to the disadvantage of the princes; and that escaped serfs were not to be received (sheltered) by imperial towns. Both lay and ecclesiastical German principalities had won substantial power at the expense of the empire.

See also: WORMS, EDICT OF (1231).

Further reading: David Abulafia, *Frederick II: A Medieval Emperor* (New York: Oxford University Press, 1992); Norton Downs, ed., *Basic Documents in Medieval History* (New York: Van Nostrand Reinhold, 1959); Louis L. Snyder, ed., *Documents of German History* (New Brunswick, N.J.: Rutgers University Press, 1958).

Writs of Assistance, Otis's Speech Opposing See OTIS'S SPEECH OPPOSING WRITS OF ASSISTANCE.

Wyandotte Constitution Constitution under which Kansas was admitted to the Union as a free state on January 29, 1861. Following the failure of the LECOMPTON CONSTITUTION, a constitutional convention of Republicans and Democrats convened at Wyandotte (now part of Kansas City), Kansas, in July 1859. The document produced there rejected slavery, suffrage for women and blacks, and prohibition but affirmed property rights for women and established the present boundaries of the state. It was ratified by popular vote on October 4, 1859.

Further reading: Harry G. Larimer et al., *Kansas Constitutional Convention: A Reprint of the Proceedings and Debates* *of the Convention Which Framed the Constitution of Kansas at Wyandotte* (Topeka, Kans.: I. Zumwalt, 1920).

Wye River Memorandum   Interim peace accord signed on October 23, 1998, in Washington, D.C., by Israeli prime minister Benjamin Netanyahu and Yasir Arafat, chairman of the Palestine Liberation Organization (PLO), ending a 19-month deadlock in the peace talks. The accord followed nine days of intensive negotiations, with the active mediation of U.S. president Bill Clinton, at the Wye River Conference Center in Maryland. Starting November 2 (the accord's implementation date) and continuing over three months, the Israeli military would conduct a three-phase withdrawal from 13.1 percent of the West Bank. The 14 percent of it currently under joint control would be transferred to full Palestinian control. The Palestinian parliament would reconfirm its deletion of the 26 clauses referring to the destruction of Israel. Israel would release 750 Palestinian prisoners and open a corridor to facilitate movement between the West Bank and the Gaza strip. The Palestinians would arrest 30 suspected terrorists, improve their antiterrorism methods, and confiscate illegal arms. The Palestinian International Airport and an industrial part in Gaza would finally be allowed to open.

See also: OSLO ACCORDS.

Further reading: Benny Morris, *Righteous Victims—A History of the Zionist-Arab Conflict, 1881–1999* (New York: Alfred A. Knopf, 1999); White House Office of the Press Secretary, *The Wye River Memorandum*, United States of America Department of State, available online at http://www.state.gov/www/regions/nea/981023_interim_agmt.html.

Wyndham's Land Purchase Act of 1903 (Irish Land Purchase Act of 1903)   Legislation passed by the British Parliament in 1903, introduced by George Wyndham, chief secretary for Ireland; it provided incentives for landlords to sell and tenants to buy their lands or farms in Ireland. Landlords were offered a generous 12 percent cash bonus to induce them to sell their lands to the estate commissioners. They could opt to repurchase them at the tenants' rates. The government established a £100 million fund (created by the issue of $2\frac{2}{3}$ percent Guaranteed Land Stock), from which tenants were given loans at $3\frac{1}{4}$ percent repayable over $68\frac{1}{2}$ years. The act also made allowances for arrears of rent and prohibited subdivision or mortgaging. In 1909, it was revised to include compulsory sale if most of the tenants wanted it. During the intervening six years, 200,000 Irish peasants had purchased nearly half the arable land. This helped improve the critical land situation in Ireland.

Further reading: *Report of the Departmental Committee Appointed to Enquire into Irish Land Purchase Finance in Connection with the Provision of Funds Required for the Purposes of the Irish Land Act, 1903* (London: J. Tru Scott & Son, 1908).

"XYZ" Report Made public in 1798, a report to U.S. President John Adams from his commissioners who were attempting to negotiate an end to French interference with American shipping. In 1797 Adams had sent Charles Pinckney, John Marshall, and Elbridge Gerry to France to discuss an end to French shipping raids. French foreign minister Talleyrand refused to meet with them officially but sent three agents, who demanded a $250,000 bribe for Talleyrand and a $10 million loan to France as prerequisites for negotiations. These agents were identified as X, Y, and Z in the report, which provoked a furor when it became public and led to an undeclared war between the United States and France (see FRANCO-AMERICAN CONVENTION OF 1800).

Further reading: Frank N. Magill, ed., *Great Events from History, American Series*, 3 vols. (Englewood Cliffs, N.J.: Salem Press, 1975); William Stinchcombe, *The XYZ Affair* (Westport, Conn.: Greenwood Press, 1980); Harold C. Vaughan, *The XYZ Affair, 1797–98; the Diplomacy of the Adams Administration and an Undeclared War with France* (New York: F. Watts, 1972).

Y

Yalta Agreement Agreement signed on February 11, 1945, by the three main Allied leaders—U.S. president Franklin D. Roosevelt, British prime minister Winston Churchill, and Soviet premier Joseph Stalin—at Yalta, Crimea, USSR, at a conference (February 4–11, 1945) convened there in the final months of World War II (1939–45) to discuss strategies for the invasion and final defeat of Nazi Germany and the terms of settlement. The three powers agreed to demand Germany's unconditional surrender and planned to divide Germany into four zones of occupation, with France being the fourth occupying power. The Soviet Union promised to enter the war against Japan after the German surrender. They also finalized the dates of the meeting in San Francisco to draft the UNITED NATIONS CHARTER. Only two Soviet republics would be allowed full representation at the United Nations, where veto powers would be vested in the three big powers. The Allies also signed a pledge to help the countries in Europe (referring to Poland under Soviet occupation) settle their political and economic problems by democratic means.

Further reading: Mortimer Adler, ed., *The Annals of America*, 18 vols. (Chicago: Encyclopaedia Britannica, 1968); Henry Steele Commager, ed., *Documents of American History*, 8th ed. (New York: Appleton-Century-Crofts, 1968); Louis L. Snyder, ed., *Documents of German History* (New Brunswick, N.J.: Rutgers University Press, 1958); Louis L. Snyder, ed., *Fifty Major Documents of the Twentieth Century* (Princeton, N.J.: D. Van Nostrand, 1955).

Yangtze Agreement Anglo-German declaration of an Open Door policy in China, framed after suppression of the antiforeign Boxer Rebellion (June 1900), and signed on October 16, 1900. The two signatories disavowed any intentions of acquiring territorial advantages in China; indicated their interest in maintaining the integrity of the Chinese Empire; and agreed to consult with each other should any other power make territorial gains. In theory, both parties agreed to hold open the door to "all Chinese territory as far as they can exercise influence." In practice, it was expected that Britain, whose sphere was the long Yangtze River (Changjiang) valley in central China, would be more successful in this regard than Germany, whose sphere of influence was nearer Russia.

Further reading: Robert A. Bickers, *Britain in China: Community Culture and Colonialism, 1900–1949* (New York: St. Martin's Press, 1999); Hsi-huey Liang, *The Sino-German Connection: Alexander von Falkenhausen between China and Germany 1900–1941* (Assen, Germany: Van Gorcum, 1978); Lewis Pyenson, *Cultural Imperialism and Exact Sciences: German Expansion Overseas, 1900–1930* (New York: P. Lang, 1985).

Yap Treaty Treaty between the United States and Japan, signed in Washington, D.C., on February 11, 1922, and effective on July 13, by which the United States formally agreed to the Japanese mandate over the former German possession of Yap, in the Caroline Islands. Yap was of particular strategic interest to the United States because of its nearness to Guam and the Philippines and its importance as a station for underwater cable communications in the Pacific. The treaty gave the United States the same rights on Yap, including cable and wireless rights, as members of the League of Nations. The treaty emerged from the Washington Conference on the Limitation of Armaments (1921–22), called to prevent war in the Far East.

Further reading: Thomas H. Buckley, *The United States and the Washington Conference, 1921–1922* (Knoxville: University of Tennessee, 1970); *Treaty between the United States and Japan Regarding . . . the Island of Yap . . .* (Washington, D.C.: Government Printing Office, 1922).

Yeltsin's Presidential Decree of 1998

Russian president Boris Yeltsin's decree of September 22, 1998, restructuring the upper tier of Prime Minister Yevgeny Primakov's government, thereby superseding an April 1998 decree that had called for cuts in Russia's swollen bureaucracy. The three deputy prime ministers would be replaced by six, including two first deputy prime ministers. Three ministries, three state committees, and two federal services were abolished, and instead, five new ministries (Anti-Trust Policies and Support of Entrepreneurship, Regional Affairs, Ethnic Policy, CIS Affairs, and Trade) were established; some were a reorganization or restoration of existing ministries. The decree also created five new state committees—land, youth affairs, fishing, construction, and standardization and metrology—and elevated the chairmen of the Central Bank and the Academy of Sciences to cabinet status. The changes were widely viewed as a sign of increased government intervention.

Further reading: Business information service for the Newly Independent States, *The Message of the RF President's Press-Service No. 1998-09-22-002*, structure of the Russian Federal Bodies of Executive Power for certification, available online at http://www.bisnis.doc.gov/bisnis/isa/9903org2.htm.

"Yes, Virginia, there is a Santa Claus"

Editorial reply, published anonymously in December 1897 but written by *New York Sun* editor Francis P. Church, to a query by eight-year-old Virginia O'Hanlon. The touching editorial, entitled "Is There a Santa Claus?" contradicted the skepticism expressed by the child's little friends about the existence of Santa Claus. Church wrote that Santa exists "as certainly as love and generosity and devotion exist . . . The most real things in the world are those that neither children nor men can see. . . . Nobody can conceive or imagine all the wonders that are unseen and unseeable in the world."

Further reading: *A Christmas Treasury: Twelve Unforgettable Holiday Stories* (New York: Scholastic, 2000); Francis P. Church et al., *Yes, Virginia, There Is a Santa Claus* (New York: Delacorte Press, 1992).

Young Plan

Plan issued on June 7, 1929, by an international committee (headed by American Owen D. Young) to revise the schedule of German World War I reparations payments. The proposal was developed when Germany proved unable to meet the schedule set up by the DAWES PLAN. The Young Plan reduced the German debt and made it payable over 58.5 years; annual payments were set at about $473 million. It established the Bank for International Settlements to change payments in German marks into foreign currency and to manage the transfer of funds. The plan was not successful, and in 1933 Germany, under Adolf Hitler, repudiated the plan and the war debt.

Further reading: James C. Baker, *The Bank for International Settlements: Evolution and Evaluation* (Westport, Conn.: Quorum Books, 2002); Parker T. Moon, *The Young Plan in Operation* (New York: The Academy of Political Science, Columbia University, 1931); John W. Wheeler-Bennett and Hugh Latimer, *Information on the Reparation Settlement; Being the Background and History of the Young Plan and the Hague Agreements, 1929–1930* (London: G. Allen & Unwin, 1930).

Youngstown Sheet and Tube Company v. Sawyer

U.S. Supreme Court decision, issued on June 2, 1952, that invalidated the seizure of U.S. steel companies during the Korean War by U.S. president Harry S Truman. Truman, citing national defense needs, had ordered the secretary of commerce to seize and operate the steel mills on April 8, 1952, in the face of an impending strike by the United Steel Workers of America. In its six-to-three decision, the Supreme Court ruled that the president had overstepped his constitutional powers. It rejected his claim to broad inherent powers in the presidency and stated that no constitutional or congressional provision had given him the authority to seize the steel mills.

Further reading: Henry Steele Commager, ed., *Documents of American History*, 8th ed. (New York: Appleton-Century-Crofts, 1968); Tony Mauro, *Illustrated Great Decisions of the Supreme Court* (Washington, D.C.: CQ Press, 2000); Robert R. Mayer, *The Court and the American Crises, 1930–1952* (Danbury, Conn.: Grolier Educational, 1995); Dennis Merrill, ed., *Documentary History of the Truman Presidency*, 30 vols. (Bethesda, Md.: University Publications of America, 1995).

Z

Zabonnik (Code of Dušan)   Code of laws (more than 200 statutes) drawn up by Serbia's ruler Stephen Dušan, or Dushan, "czar of the Greeks and Serbs" as he called himself; it consisted of two parts, the first issued in 1349 and the second in 1354. The code, established in conjunction with the Orthodox Church, touched upon every aspect of ecclesiastical and secular life, from marriage and church administration to border disputes between villages, criminality, and relations between classes. The code represented a great achievement of medieval times—namely, the establishment of a national law based not on the arbitrary will of the monarch but upon precedents found in Roman and Byzantine law.

Further reading: Georgios C. Soules, *The Serbs and Byzantium During the Reign of Tsar Stephen Dusan (1331–1355) and His Successors* (Washington, D.C.: Dumbarton Oaks Library & Collection, 1984).

Zamora, Treaty of   Pact negotiated by Pope Lucius II and signed at Zamora, León, Spain, on December 13, 1143; confirmed Castilian recognition of Portugal's independence. King Afonso VII of Castile and León recognized Afonso Henriques as King Afonso I of Portugal, a title the latter had already conferred on himself after his victory over the Moors in the battle of Ourique (July 25, 1139). Afonso I requested papal protection for his country, promising the pope an annual tribute of four ounces of gold and his loyalty in return. Pope Lucius II responded favorably in the spring of 1144, without,

however, acknowledging Afonso's new title. Papal recognition of this came from Pope Alexander III in 1179.

Further reading: H. V. Livermore, *The Origins of Spain and Portugal* (London: Allen & Unwin, 1971); Joseph F. O'Callaghan, *A History of Medieval Spain* (Ithaca, N.Y.: Cornell University Press, 1983).

Zborów, Compact of   Peace settlement temporarily ending Cossack and peasant revolts against Polish rule in the Ukraine; concluded by Cossack hetman (leader) Bogdan Chmielnicki and Poland's king John II Casimir on August 18, 1649, at Zborów, Poland. The compact gave amnesty to all the rebels; permitted the Cossacks to settle in the territories of Kiev, Chernigov, and Braclaw; prohibited Polish Jesuits and military from entering Cossack territory; fixed the Cossack army at·40,000 troops; and directed all secular officials to be of the Orthodox faith in the Ukraine (which remained part of the Polish-Lithuanian republic).

Further reading: Richard Butterwick, *The Polish-Lithuanian Monarchy in European Context c. 1500–1795* (New York: Palgrave, 2001); Nicholas L. Chirovsky, *The Lithuanian-Rus' Commonwealth, the Polish Domination, and the Cossack-Hetman State* (New York: Philosophical Library, 1984); Frank E. Sysyn, *Between Poland and the Ukraine: The Dilemma of Adam Kysil, 1600–1653* (Cambridge, Mass.: Harvard University Press, 1985).

Zimmermann Note Secret, coded telegram (communiqué) sent by German foreign minister Arthur Zimmermann to the German minister in Mexico on January 19, 1917, proposing that Mexico be invited to join Germany, with Japan, in an alliance against the United States. Anticipating American intervention in the European war (World War I [1914–18]) and hoping therefore to divert the United States with a war on her southern and western borders, the German foreign minister proposed in the telegram that Germany enlist Mexico with promises to help her repossess former territory that had been incorporated into the United States, including Texas, New Mexico, and Arizona. The telegram was intercepted by British intelligence, released to the U.S. government, and on March 1, 1917, made known to the public. On April 6, 1917, the United States declared war on Germany.

Further reading: Henry Steele Commager, ed., *Documents of American History*, 8th ed. (New York: Appleton-Century-Crofts, 1968); Louis L. Snyder, ed., *Documents of German History* (New Brunswick, N.J.: Rutgers University Press, 1958); Louis L. Snyder, ed., *Fifty Major Documents of the Twentieth Century* (Princeton, N.J.: D. Van Nostrand, 1955).

Zsitvatorok, Peace of Peace treaty concluded in Zsitvatorok, Transylvania, on November 11, 1606, ending the Austro-Turkish War of 1591–1606 or Fifteen Years' War. The first treaty signed by the Ottoman Empire outside Constantinople, it kept the territorial status quo in general; the Holy Roman Empire (Austria) agreed to the Turks' repossession of Hungary and Romania (and the important city-fortresses of Eger, Esztergom, and Kanizsa) and to the nearly autonomous status of Transylvania. The Holy Roman emperor's annual tribute to the Ottoman sultan was canceled in exchange for a single payment of 200,000 gulden. The treaty reflected the Ottoman Empire's diminishing strength against the West.

See also: VIENNA, TREATY OF (1606).

Further reading: Imre Lukinich, *A History of Hungary in Biographical Sketches* (Freeport, N.Y.: Books for Libraries Press, 1968).

Zuravno, Treaty of Peace treaty between Poland's king John III Sobieski and the Ottoman Turks, concluded on October 16, 1676, at Zuravno (Zórawno), Ukraine; it superseded the conditions (unfavorable to Poland) agreed upon in the 1672 Treaty of BUCZACZ. Exhausted from warring with the Poles, the Turks agreed to recognize Polish control over the western Ukraine, to return a small portion of Podolia to Poland, and to relinquish their claim to an annual tribute to be paid to the Ottoman sultan. The Turks had fought chiefly on behalf of the Cossacks, peasant-soldiers inhabiting the Ukraine, who were unhappy over Polish and Russian control of their lands.

Further reading: Norman Davies, *God's Playground: A History of Poland*, 2 vols. (New York: Columbia University Press, 1981).

Zurich, Treaty of (1859) Treaty concluded in Zurich on November 10, 1859, by Austria with France and Piedmont (Sardinia, Italy), reconfirming and finalizing the terms agreed upon in the Treaty of VILLAFRANCA, which had ended hostilities between French-Piedmontese and Austrian forces. The war had originated over Italy's desire for independence from Austria, and France's decision to fight alongside Italy against Austria. The three powers agreed that Piedmont (Sardinia) would receive a large part of Lombardy from France, which would first be ceded to France by Austria; that Austria would retain Venetia; and that the former Italian princes, who had been overthrown during the war, would return to power. In addition, Italy was to be a confederation under the pope's honorary presidency. The provisions of the treaty were soon disregarded and the Italian War of Independence of 1859–61 resumed.

Further reading: Fred L. Israel, ed., *Major Peace Treaties of Modern History, 1648–1967*, 4 vols. (New York: Chelsea House, 1967).

Zurich Consensus (Consensus Tigurinus) Common confession of Protestant faith prepared in 1549 by French theologian John Calvin, who was influential in the French-speaking part of Switzerland, and Swiss reformer Heinrich Bullinger, influential in the German-speaking part of Switzerland. Agreement was reached on the doctrine of the Eucharist (or Holy Communion) among the reformed churches. The document specifically affirmed the spiritual presence of Christ during the celebration of the Eucharist; it rejected the Roman Catholic doctrine of transubstantiation and Martin Luther's literal concept of the "real presence of Christ" in the bread and wine of the Eucharist rite.

See also: AUGSBURG CONFESSION; WITTENBERG, CONCORD OF.

Further reading: Archibald A. Hodge, ed., *Outlines of Theology: For Students and Laymen* (Grand Rapids, Mich.: Zondervan, 1972).

Zwingli's Sixty-seven Theses See SIXTY-SEVEN THESES, ZWINGLI'S.

TIMETABLE OF DOCUMENTS

DATE	DOCUMENT	AREA(S) INVOLVED
c. 1930 B.C.	Lipit-Ishtar, Code of	Sumeria
c. 1740–1725	Tell Leilan Tablets	Syria, Mesopotamia
c. 1700	Hammurabi, Code of	Babylon, Mesopotamia
c. 1304	Abydos, Tablet of	Egypt
c. 1300	Ten Commandments	Israel
c. 620	Draco, Laws of	Athens, Greece
c. 594	Solon, Laws of	Athens, Greece
c. 471	Publilian Laws (Leges Publiliae)	Roman Republic
c. 339	Publilian Laws (Leges Publiliae)	Roman Republic
c. 450	Twelve Tables, Law of the	Roman Republic
445	Canuleian Law (Lex Canuleia)	Roman Republic
431	Pericles' Funeral Oration	Athens, Greece
c. 430	Hippocratic Oath	Greece
421	Nicias, Peace of	Athens, Sparta
c. 400	*Art of War*	China
c. 380	*Republic, The (Politeia)*	Greece
367	Licinio-Sextian Laws	Roman Republic
354	Leptines, Law of On the Navy Boards	Athens Athens
351	Phillippic (Demosthenes)	Athens, Macedon
349	Olynthiacs	Athens, Macedon
344	Phillippic (Demosthenes)	Athens, Macedon
341	Phillippic (Demosthenes)	Athens, Macedon
c. 339	Publilian Laws (Leges Publiliae)	Roman Republic
330	On the Crown (De Corona)	Athens, Macedon
300	Ogulnian Law (Lex Ogulnia)	Roman Republic
c. 300	*Tao Te Ching (Daodeching)*	China
287	Hortensian Law (Lex Hortensia)	Roman Republic
c. 250	Pillar Edicts, Asoka's	India
c. 250 B.C.–A.D. 68	Dead Sea Scrolls	Jordan, Israel
238 B.C.	Canopus, Decree of (Table of Tanis)	Egypt
213	Oppian Law (Lex Oppia)	Roman Republic
149	Calpurnian Law (Lex Calpurnia)	Roman Republic
133	Roman Agrarian Law of 133 B.C. (Sempronian Law of 133 B.C., Lex Sempronia Agraria)	Roman Republic
123	Acilian Law (Lex Acilia de Repetundarum)	Roman Republic
111	Roman Agrarian Law of 111 B.C. (Lex Agraria of 111 B.C.)	Roman Republic
104	Domitian Law (Lex Domitia)	Roman Republic
1st century	Nicomachean Ethics On the Nature of Things	Greece Roman Republic
90	Julian Law of 90 B.C. (Lex Julia)	Roman Republic
c. 80	Tipitaka (Three Baskets of the Law) Cornelian Laws (Leges Cornelia)	India Roman Republic

DATE	DOCUMENT	AREA(S) INVOLVED
75–70	Aurelian Laws (Lex Aureliae)	Roman Republic
67	Gabinian Law (Lex Gabinia)	Roman Republic
66	Manilian Law (Lex Manilia)	Roman Republic
63	Senatus Consultum Ultimatum of 63 B.C. (Cicero's "Last Decree")	Roman Republic
	Cicero's Oration Against Cataline	Roman Republic
59	Vatinian Law (Lex Vatinia)	Roman Republic
49	Senatus Consultum Ultimatum of 49 B.C.	Roman Republic
44–43	Philippics, Cicero's	Roman Republic
43	Titian Law (Lex Titia)	Roman Republic
40	Brundisium, Treaty of	Roman Republic, provinces
39	Misenum, Treaty of	Roman Republic, Peloponesia
18	Julian Laws of 18 B.C. (Leges Juliae of 18 B.C.)	Roman Empire
2 B.C.	Fufian Caninian Law (Lex Fufia Canina)	Roman Empire
A.D. 9	Papian Poppaean Law (Lex Papia Poppaea)	Roman Empire
c. 25	Sermon on the Mount	Israel
57	Epistle to the Romans	Greece
69	Vespasian Imperial Law (Lex de Imperio Vespasiani)	Roman Empire
c. 96	Clement, First Letter of	Greece
c. 112	Trajan's Rescript	Roman Empire
132	Perpetual Edict (Praetorian Perpetual Edict, Edictum Perpetuum)	Roman Empire
97–112	Pliny the Younger's *Letters*	Roman Empire
c. 130	Hadrian's Rescript	Roman Empire
c. 150	Confucian *Analects*	China
170s	*Meditations (Marcus Aurelius Antoninus to Himself)*	Roman Empire
c. 180	Talmud	Israel, Palestine
212	Caracalla, Edict of (Constitutio Antoniniana de Civitate, Antoninian Constitution of Citizenship)	Roman Empire
301	Edict of Maximum Prices (Edictum de Maximis Pretiis)	Roman Empire
311	Edict of Toleration, Galerius's	Roman Empire
313	Milan, Edict of	Roman Empire
324	Constantine, Donation of (Constitutum Donatio Constantini)	Roman Empire
325	Nicene Creed	Constantinople
c. 380	Apostolic Constitutions (Ordinances of the Holy Apostles Through Clement)	Rome (Catholic Church)
382–405	Vulgate	Rome (Catholic Church)
384–398	Siricius, Decretals of	Rome (Catholic Church)
c. 390	Peutinger Table (Tabula Peutingeriana)	Roman Empire
5th century	Athanasian Creed (Quicumque Vult)	France
	Brehon Laws	Ireland
c. 400	*Confessions (Confessiones)*	Algeria, Italy
	Talmud	Jerusalem
413–426	*City of God (De Civitate Dei)*	Rome
438	Theodosian Code (Codex Theodosianus)	Roman Empire
445	Valentinian III's Edict	Roman Empire
449	Tome of Leo	Rome, Byzantium
482	Henotikon (Henoticon)	Byzantine Empire
c. 500	Talmud	Babylonia
502	Burgundian Code (Lex Gundobada)	Burgundy, France
506	Edict of Theodoric (Edictum Theodorici)	Rome, Italy

DATE	DOCUMENT	AREA(S) INVOLVED
507–511	Salic Law (Lex Salica)	France
529–565	Justinian Code (Corpus Juris Civilis)	Byzantine Empire
535–540	Benedictine Rule (Regula Monachorum)	Monte Cassino, Italy
c. 600	Apostles' Creed (Apostolicum)	Rome
604	Seventeen Article "Constitution"	Japan
c. 622	Medina, Constitution of	Medina (Arabia)
638	Ecthesis (Ekthesis)	Byzantine Empire
648	Type (Typos)	Byzantine Empire
c. 651	Koran (Quran)	Arabia
c. 717–741	Byzantine Agrarian Code (Farmer's Law, Leges Rusticae)	Byzantine Empire
726	Ecloga	Byzantine Empire
732, 735	Orkhon Inscriptions (Turkish Runes)	Mongolia
756	Pepin, Donation of	France
817	Holy Constitution (La Sainte Constitution)	France
842	Strasbourg (Strassburg), Oaths of	France, Germany
843	Verdun, Treaty of	France
847	Mersen, Capitulary of	France
c. 850	False Decretals (Isidorian Decretals, Pseudo-Isidorian Decretals)	Rome (Papacy)
870	Mersen, Treaty of	France, Germany
877	Kiersey (Quierzy), Capitulary of	France
c. 900–950	Bald, Book of (Leech Book of Bald)	England
911	St.-Clair-sur-Epte, Treaty of	France
987	Adalbero's Plea to Elect Hugh Capet	France
989	Peace of God (Pax Ecclesiae, Paix de Dieu)	Holy Roman Empire, France
11th–13th centuries	Russian Truth (Ruskaya Pravda)	Russia
1018	Bautzen, Treaty of	Germany, Poland
c. 1027	Truce of God	Holy Roman Empire, Papacy
1074	Worms, Charter of	Germany
1075	Pope's Dictate (Dictatus Papae)	Rome (Papacy)
	Gregory VII's Letter Denouncing Henry IV	Rome (Papacy), Germany
1076	Henry IV's Reply to Gregory VII	Germany
1080	Ceprano, Concordat of	Italy, Papacy
1086–87	*Domesday Book (Doomsday Book)*	England
1095	Clermont, Proclamation of the Council of	Papacy, France, Jerusalem
c. 1099	Jerusalem, Assizes of	Jerusalem, Holy Land, Cyprus
12th century	Sentences, Book of	Italy
c. 1100	Amalfitan Code (Amalfian Code)	Amalfi, Italy
1100	Coronation Charter of Henry I	England
1107	Compromise of 1107, English (Compromise of London, Compromise of Bec)	England
1122	Worms, Concordat of	Papacy, Holy Roman Empire
1140	*Decretal of Gratian (Concordantia Discordantium Canonum*	Bologna, Italy
1143	Zamora, Treaty of	Portugal, Spain
c. 1150	Oleron, Judgments of (Code or Laws of Oleron)	England
1155	Lorris, Charter of	France
1156	Roncaglia, Decrees of	Italy
1164	Clarendon, Constitutions of	England
1166	Clarendon, Assize of	England
1176	Northampton, Assize of	England
1177	Venice, Peace of	Holy Roman Empire, Papacy

DATE	DOCUMENT	AREA(S) INVOLVED
1179	Darrien Presentment, Assize of	England
1181	Arms, Assize of	England
1183	Constance, Treaty of	Germany, Italy
1184	Woodstock, Assize of	England
1212	Golden Bull of Sicily	Sicily, Germany, Bohemia
1213	Golden Bull of Eger (Golden Bull of 1213)	Germany
1215	Magna Carta (Magna Charta)	England
1222	Golden Bull of Hungary (Golden Bull of 1222, Magna Carta of Hungary)	Hungary
1226	Golden Bull of Rimini	Holy Roman Empire, Poland
1229	Paris, Treaty of	France, Papacy
1230	San Germano, Peace of	Holy Roman Empire, Papacy
c. 1230	*Saxon Mirror (Sachsenspiegel)*	Germany
1231	Melfi, Constitutions of Worms, Edict of (Privilege of Worms)	Sicily, Italy, Germany Germany
1232	Ravenna, Decree of	Holy Roman Empire
1234	Decretals of 1234 (Liber Decretalium Gregorii IX)	Papacy
c. 1250	Magdeburg Law	Germany
c. 1251	Lübeck, Peace of	Germany, Sweden
1254	Ofen, Treaty of Louis IX's Laws	Bohemia, Hungary France
1256–65	Seven Parts, Code of the (Seven Divisions of Law, Código de las Siete Partidas, Libro de las Leyes)	Castile, León (Spain)
1258	Corbeil, Treaty of Oxford, Provisions of	France, Aragon England
1259	Paris, Treaty of Westminster, Provisions of	England, France England
1264	Amiens, Mise of Lewes, Mise of Jewish Liberties, Charter of	France, England England Poland
1265–74	*Summa Theologica*	Papacy
1266	Kenilworth, Dictum of	England
1269	Pragmatic Sanction of St. Louis	France, Holy Roman Empire
1275	Westminster, Statutes of	England
1279	Mortmain, Statute of (Statute de Viris Religiosis)	England
1282	Danish Magna Carta	Denmark
1284	Wales, Statute of	England, Wales
1285	Westminster, Statutes of	England
1287	Aragonese Privileges of Union (Magna Carta of Aragon)	Aragon (Spain)
1290	Westminster, Statutes of	England
1293	Justice, Ordinances of (Ordinanze della Giustizia)	Florence (Italy)
1296	Clericis Laicos	Papacy, England France
1297	Confirmation of Charters (Confirmatio Cartarum)	England, France, Flanders
1302	Caltabelotta, Peace of *Unam Sanctam*	Sicily, Naples, Papacy Papacy, France
1305	Athis-sur-Orge, Treaty of	France, Flanders
1323	Noteborg, Treaty of	Sweden, Russia
1326	Novgorod, Treaty of	Russia, Norway
1327	Paris, Treaty of	England, France
1328	Northampton, Treaty of	England, Scotland
1335	Visegrád, Agreement at	Poland, Bohemia, Prussia

DATE	DOCUMENT	AREA(S) INVOLVED
1338	Kraków, Treaty of	Poland, Bohemia
	Rhens (Rense), Declaration of (Pragmatic Sanction of Rhens)	Germany
1343	Kalisch (Kalisz), Treaty of	Poland
	Malestroit, Truce of	France, Papacy
1349–54	Zabonnik (Code of Dušan)	Serbia
1350	Provisors, Statute of	England
1351	Labourers, Statute of	England
1353	Praemunire, Statute of	England
1355	Pacta Conventa of 1355	Poland
1356	Brabant Constitution (Joyeuse Entrée of Brabant)	Brabant (Belgium and Netherlands)
	Golden Bull of 1356	Holy Roman Empire, Germany
1357	French Ordinance of 1357 ("Great Ordinance")	France
1360	Brétigny, Treaty of	England, France
	Calais, Treaty of	England, France
1364	Brunn, Treaty of	Holy Roman Empire
1365	Guérande, Treaty of	France
1366	Kilkenny, Statute of	Ireland, England
1370	Stralsund, Treaty of	Hanseatic League (Germany), Denmark
1374	Koszyce, Pact of	Poland, Hungary
1376	Good Parliament, Acts of the	England
1381	Turin, Treaty of	Venice, Genoa (Italy), Hungary
1386	Windsor, Treaty of	England, Portugal
1393	Sempach, Convention of	Switzerland, Austria
1397	Kalmar, Union of	Sweden, Norway, Denmark
1401	Heretics, Statute of	England
1409	Pisa, Declaration of the Council of	Avignon, Rome, Papacy
1411	Thorn (Toruń), First Peace of	Poland
1413	Cabochien Ordinance (Ordannance Cabochienne)	France
1414	Arras, Treaty of	France, Flanders
1414–1418	Constance, Decrees of the Council of	Italy, Germany, Papacy
1420	Troyes, Treaty of	France, Burgundy, England
c. 1425	*Imitation of Christ (Imitatio Christi)*	Netherlands
1435	Arras, Treaty of	France, Burgundy
1435–1446	Afonsine Ordinances (Ordenações Affonsinas)	Portugal
1436	Prague, Compacts of (Basel Compacta)	Bohemia, Basel
1438	Pragmatic Sanction of Bourges	France
1444	Adrianople, Treaty of	Ottoman Empire, Hungary
	Szegedin, Treaty of	Ottoman Empire, Hungary, Serbia
1446	Constance, Peace of	Holy Roman Empire, Austria, Switzerland
1448	Vienna, Concordat of	Holy Roman Empire, Italy, Papacy
1450	Cade's Complaint	England
1454	Lodi, Peace of	Venice, Milan
	Nieszawa, Statute of (Nieszawa Privilege)	Poland
1455	Bible, Gutenberg (Mazarin Bible)	Mainz (Germany)
1460	Execrabilis of 1460	Papacy
1465	Conflans, Treaty of	France
1466	Thorn (Toruń), Second Peace of	Poland
1475	Picquigny, Treaty of	England, France
1479	Alcáçovas, Treaty of	Spain, Portugal
	Constantinople, Treaty of	Holy Roman Empire, Venice, Ottoman Empire
1481	Stans, Covenant of the	Switzerland

DATE	DOCUMENT	AREA(S) INVOLVED
1482	Concordat of 1482 Arras, Treaty of	Papacy, Castile and Leon (Spain) Austria, France
1491	Pressburg, Treaty of	Hapsburg, Austria, Hungary
1492	Columbus's First Voyage Journal Alhambra Decree Étaples, Treaty of	Spain, Americas Spain England, France
1493	Senlis, Treaty of Barcelona, Treaty of	Holy Roman, Empire, France Spain, France, Papacy
1494	Tordesillas, Treaty of	Spain, Portugal
1494–1495	Drogheda, Statute of (Poyning's Act)	England, Ireland
1496	Piotrków, Statute of (Magna Carta of Poland) Intercurus Magnus	Poland England, Netherlands
1497	Russian (Muscovite) Code of 1497 (Sūdebnik)	Russia
1499	Basel, Treaty of	Switzerland, Swabia, Holy Roman Empire
1505	Radom, Constitution of	Poland
1512	Burgos, Concordat of Burgos, Laws of	Spain Spain, West Indies
1513	*Prince, The (Il Principe)*	Italy
1514	Tripartitum	Hungary
1516	Bologna, Concordat of (Concordat of Francis I) Fribourg, Treaty of (Perpetual Peace, La Paix Perpétuelle) Noyon, Treaty of	Papacy, France Switzerland, France France, Spain
1517	Ninety-five Theses, Luther's	Germany
1520	Address to the Christian Nobility of the German Nation, Luther's Exsurge Domine	Germany Papacy, Germany
1521	Worms, Edict of	Germany, Holy Roman Empire
1523	Sixty-seven Theses, Zwingli's	Switzerland
1524	Peasants' Manifesto, German	Germany
1526	Madrid, Treaty of Cognac, Treaty of Speyer, Decree of the Diet of	Spain, Holy Roman Empire, France, Italy Holy Roman Empire. France, Italy, Papacy, Switzer- land, England Germany, Holy Roman Empire
1527	Schleitheim Confession	Switzerland
1529	Speyer, Decree of the Diet of Cambrai, Peace of (Paix de Dames, Ladies' Peace) Barcelona, Treaty of Marburg, Fifteen Articles of	Germany, Holy Roman Empire Holy Roman Empire, France, Austria, Italy Holy Roman Empire, Spain, Papacy Germany, Switzerland
1530	Execrabilis of 1530 Augsburg Confession Tetrapolitan Confession	Papacy, England Germany Germany, Holy Roman Empire
1531	Kappel, Peace of	Switzerland
1532	Nurnberg, Peace of	Germany
1532, 1534	Annates' Statutes	England
1534	Succession, Act of Supremacy, Act of Basel, Confession of	England England Switzerland
1536	Union, Act of (Union of Wales and England) Wittenberg, Concord of *Institutes of the Christian Religion (Institution de la Religion Chrétienne, Christianae Religionis Institutio)*	England, Wales Switzerland, Germany Switzerland
1537	Schmalkaldic Articles	Germany
1538	Nagyvárad, Peace of	Hungary
1539	Six Articles, Act of	England
1540	Confessio Augustana Variata	Switzerland, Germany

DATE	DOCUMENT	AREA(S) INVOLVED
1541	Ratisbon Interim	Holy Roman Empire
1542	New Laws of the Indies (New Laws of the Indies for the Good Testament and Preservation of the Indians)	Spain, Spanish America
1543	*On the Revolutions of the Heavenly Bodies (De Revolutionibus Orbium Coelestium)*	Germany
1544	Crépy, Treaty of	France, Italy, Holy Roman Empire
1545–1563	Tridentine Decrees (Decrees of the Council of Trent)	Italy, Papacy
1548	Augsburg Interim	Germany
1549	*Common Prayer, Book of* Uniformity, Act of Zurich Consensus (Consensus Tigurinus)	England England Switzerland
1551	Châteaubriant, Edict of	France
1552	Friedwald, Treaty of Passau, Treaty of (Convention of Passau) Uniformity, Act of	Germany, France Germany, Hungary, Bohemia England
1553	Forty-Two Articles	England
1555	Augsburg, Peace of	Germany
1556	*Common Order, Book of* (Knox's Liturgy, Order of Geneva)	Switzerland, Scotland
1559	Supremacy, Act of Uniformity, Act of Cateau-Cambrésis, Treaty of (Paix Malheureuse)	England England England, France, Spain, Italy
1560	Edinburgh, Treaty of (Treaty of Leith) Discipline, First Book of Romorantin, Edict of	England, France Scotland Scotland France
1561	Belgic Confession (Confessio Belgica)	Belgium, France
1562	January, Edict of Constantinople, Peace of	France Holy Roman Empire, Ottoman Empire, Hungary
1563	Heidelberg Catechism (Palatinate Catechism) Amboise, Edict of (Peace of Amboise, Edict of Pacification) Thirty-Nine Articles	Germany France England, Papacy
1564	Troyes, Treaty of	France, England
1569	Lublin, Union of	Poland, Lithuania
1570	*Regnans in Excelsis*	Papacy, England
1573	Warsaw, Pact of (Pax Dissidentium) Henrician Articles Pacta Conventa of 1573 Boulogne, Edict of (Treaty of La Rochelle, First Edict of Poitiers)	Poland Poland Poland, France France
1576	Torgau, Book of Ghent, Pacification of Monsieur, Peace of (Paix de Monsieur, Peace of Chastenoy, Treaty of Etigny) Beaulieu, Edict of	Saxony (Germany) Netherlands, Spain France France
1577	Bergerac, Treaty of (Peace or Edict of Poitiers)	France
1579	Arras, Treaty of Utrecht, Union of	Spain, Netherlands Spain, Netherlands
1580	*Essays (Essais)*	France
1581	Abjuration, Act of	Netherlands, Spain
1585	Nemours, Treaty of	France
1595	Lambeth Articles Teusina, Peace of	England Russia, Finland
1596	Brest, Act of Union of	Ukraine, Papacy
1597	Godunov's Decree of 1597	Russia

DATE	DOCUMENT	AREA(S) INVOLVED
1598	Vervins, Treaty of	France, Spain
	Nantes, Edict of	France
	True Laws of Free Monarchy (Basilikon Doron, or "His Majesty's Instructions to His Dearest Sonne Henry the Prince")	Scotland
1601	Poor Law of 1601 (Elizabethan Poor Law)	England
1603	Millenary Petition	England
1604	Recusancy Laws	England
1606	Execrabilis of 1606	Papacy, England
	Zsitvatorok, Peace of	Ottoman Empire, Austria, Hungary
	Vienna, Treaty of	Transylvania, Hungary, Austria
1609	Majesty, Letter of (Majestatsbrief)	Bohemia, Holy Roman Empire
	Twelve Years' Truce	Spain, Netherlands
	James I's Claim of Divine Right	England
1610	Remonstrance of 1610	Holland
	James I's Great Contract	England
1611	Bible, Authorized (King James) Version of the	England
1614	Xanten, Treaty of	Germany
1617	Busza, Treaty of	Poland, Ottoman Empire
	Stolbovo, Treaty of	Sweden, Russia
	Graz, Treaty of	Holy Roman Empire, Spain
1618	Declaration of Sports (Book of Sports)	England
	Five Articles of Perth	Scotland, England
	Deulino, Truce of	Russia, Poland
1619	Dort, Canons of	Netherlands
1620	Ulm, Treaty of	France, Germany, Austria, Spain
	Novum Organum (New Instrument)	England
	Mayflower Compact	British Colonies
1621	Nicholsburg, Treaty of	Holy Roman Empire, Transylvania
	Great Protestation	England, Spain
1622	Equality of Men and Women, The	France
1624	Blue Law of 1624, Virginia	Virginia (British Colonies)
1625	On the Law of War and Peace (De Jure Belli ac Pacis)	Netherlands, France
1626	Louis XIII's Edict of 1626	France
1627	Five Knights' Case (Darnel's Case)	England
1628	Petition of Right	England
	On the Motion of the Heart and Blood in Animals (De Motu Cordis et Sanguinis in Animalibus)	England
1629	Altmark, Treaty of	Sweden, Poland
	Cambridge Agreement	Massachusetts
	Lübeck, Treaty of	Germany, Denmark
	Alais, Peace of (Edict or Peace of Grace)	France
	Susa, Treaty of	Quebec (New France), France, England
	Restitution, Edict of	Germany
1631	Cherasco, Treaties of	France, Italy, Spain, Savoy, Holy Roman Empire
	Barwalde, Treaty of	France, Sweden
1632	St.-Germain, Treaty of	France, England, Canada
	Dialogue Concerning the Two Chief Systems of the World (Dialogo Sopra i due Massimi Sistemi del Mondo)	Florence (Italy)
	Maryland Colony Charter	Maryland (British Colonies)
1634	Blue Law of 1634, Massachusetts	Massachusetts (British Colonies)
	Wills and Uses, Statutes of	Ireland
	Polyanov (Polianovka), Peace of	Russia, Poland
1635	Prague, Peace of	Holy Roman Empire, Saxony
	Stuhmsdorf, Truce of	Sweden, Poland
1637	Discourse on Method (Discours de la Méthode)	France
1638	Solemn League and Covenant of 1638 (National Covenant)	Scotland

DATE	DOCUMENT	AREA(S) INVOLVED
1639	Blue Law of 1639, Massachusetts Dunse, Pacification of (Pacification of Berwick) Fundamental Orders of Connecticut	Massachusetts (British Colonies) Scotland, England Hartford, Windsor, Wethersfield (British Colonies)
1640	*Augustinus* Ripon, Treaty of Remonstrance of Grievances Root and Branch Bill (Root and Branch Petition) Blue Law of 1640, Connecticut Canons of 1640	Louvain (Belgium) England, Scotland Ireland, England England Connecticut (British Colonies) England
1641	Triennal Act Grand Remonstrance Massachusetts Body of Liberties	England England Massachusetts (British Colonies)
1642	*In Eminenti* Nineteen Propositions	Papacy England
1643	Oxford Propositions New England Confederation Solemn League and Covenant of 1643	England Massachusetts, Connecticut (British Colonies) Scotland, England
1644	Glamorgan Treaty	Ireland
1645	Linz, Treaty of Uxbridge Propositions (Uxbridge Treaty) Self-Renouncing Ordinance (Self-Denying Ordinance)	Transylvania, Austria England England
1646	Westminster Confession of Faith Newcastle Proposals	England England, Scotland
1647	Four Bills of 1647 Newport, Treaty of Agreement of the People	England England, Scotland England
1648	Cambridge Platform Westphalia, Peace of Münster, Treaty of	Massachusetts, Connecticut (British Colonies) Germany, Switzerland, Netherlands, France, Sweden Netherlands, France, Germany, Sweden, Denmark
1649	Zborów, Compact of Toleration Act of 1649 (Act Concerning Religion) Rueil, Treaty of Russian New Code of 1649 (Sobornoe Ulajenie) Instrument of Government Charles, Death Warrant of	Poland, Ukraine Maryland (British Colonies) France Russia England England
1650	Code of 1650 (Ludlow's Code) Hartford, Treaty of	Connecticut (U.S.) New England (British Colonies), New Netherland (Dutch colony)
1650	Navigation Act of 1650, English	England
1651	*Leviathan*	England
1653	Cum Occasione Impressionis Libri Settlement of Ireland, Act of Fighting Instructions	Papacy, Italy England, Ireland England
1654	Westminster, Treaty of Seclusion, Act of (Act of Exclusion)	England, Holland Holland
1655	Pinerolo, Pacification of (Treaty of Pinerolo)	Savoy (Italy), France, England
1656	Vienna, Treaty of Baden, Third Land Peace of Konigsberg, Treaty of	Austria, Poland, Lithuania Switzerland Switzerland, Brandenburg
1656–1657	*Provincial Letters (Les Lettres Provinciales)*	France
1657	Humble Petition and Advice Vienna, Treaty of Wehlau (Welawa), Treaty of Flushing Remonstrance Half-Way Covenant	England Germany, Poland, Denmark Poland, Brandenburg, Holy Roman Empire New Amsterdam New England
1658	Savoy Declaration Roskilde, Treaty of	England Sweden, Denmark
1659	Pyrenees, Treaty of the	France, Spain

DATE	DOCUMENT	AREA(S) INVOLVED
1660	Breda, Declaration of	Netherlands, England, Scotland
	Blue Law of 1660, Connecticut	Connecticut (British Colonies)
	Indemnity and Oblivion, Act of	England
	Oliva, Treaty of	Poland, Sweden
	Copenhagen, Treaty of	Sweden, Denmark
1661	Clarendon Code	England
	Corporation Act	England
	Kardis (Cardis), Treaty of	Sweden, Russia
1662	Uniformity, Act of	England
	Clarendon Code	England
	Westminster, Treaty of	England, Brandenburg
	Settlement for Ireland, Act of	Ireland, England
	Connecticut, Charter of	Connecticut (British colonies)
	Indulgence, Declaration of	England
1663	Navigation Act of 1663, English	England, America
	Rhode Island and Providence Plantations, Charter of	Rhode Island (British colonies)
1664	Vasvár, Treaty of	Hungary, Austria, Ottoman Empire
	Clarendon Code	England
	Conventicle Act of 1664	England
	Colbert's Letter on Mercantilism	France
1665	Five-Mile Act (Oxford Act of 1665)	England
	Clarendon Code	England
1667	Quebec, Treaty of	Quebec (New France), France
	Breda, Treaty of (Peace of Breda)	France, England, Holland, Denmark
	Andrusovo, Treaty of	Poland, Russia
1668	Triple Alliance of 1668	England, Sweden, Holland, France
	Aix-la-Chapelle, Treaty of	France, England, Sweden, Holland
	Lisbon, Treaty of	Spain, Portugal
1669	Fundamental Constitutions of Carolina	Carolina (British Colonies)
	Clement IX, Peace of (Clementine Peace, Peace of the Church)	Papacy, France
1670	Dover, Treaty of	England, France
	Hudson's Bay Company Charter	Hudson's Bay area (Canada), England
1672	Buczacz, Treaty of	Ukraine, Poland, Ottoman Empire
	Indulgence, Declaration of	England
1673	Test Act of 1673, English	England
1674	Westminster, Treaty of	Holland, England
1675	Jaworzno, Treaty of	Poland, France, Sweden, Hungary, Ottoman Empire, Brandenburg
1676	Zuravno, Treaty of	Ukraine, Poland, Ottoman Empire
1677	*Ethics*, Spinoza's	Netherlands
1678	Papists' Disabling Act (Test Act of 1678)	England
	Bolting Act	New York City (British Colonies)
1678, 1679	Nijmegen (Nimwegen), Treaties of	France, Spain, Holland, Austria, Denmark, Sweden
1679	Habeas Corpus Act of 1679	England
	St. Germain, Treaty of	France, Denmark, Brandenburg, Sweden
1681	Pennsylvania, Charter of	Pennsylvania (British Colonies), England
	Radzin, Treaty of	Ottoman Empire, Russia, Ukraine
	Bakhchisarai, Treaty of	Russia, Crimea, Ottoman Empire
1682	Frame of Government, Penn's (First Frame of Government of Pennsylvania)	Pennsylvania (British Colonies)
	Four Articles, Bossuet's (Declaration of the French Clergy, Déclaration du Clergé, Déclaration des Quatre Articles, Gallican Articles)	France, Papacy
1683	Shakamaxon, Treaty of	Pennsylvania (British Colonies)
	Charter of Liberties (Charter of Franchises and Liberties)	New York (British Colonies), England
	Austro-Polish Alliance of 1683	Poland, Austria, Lithuania
1684	Regensburg, Truce of (Truce of Ratisbon)	France, Spain, Austria, Germany

DATE	DOCUMENT	AREA(S) INVOLVED
1685	Black Code of Louis XIV (Code Noir)	France, West Indies
	Nantes, Revocation of the Edict of (Edict of Revocation, Edict of Fontainebleau)	France
	Potsdam, Edict of	Brandenburg, France
1686	Eternal Peace of 1686 (Grzymultowski Peace)	Poland, Russia
	Dongan Charter	New York City (British Colonies), England
	Augsburg, Treaty of the League of	Holy Roman Empire, Spain, Sweden, England, France, Saxony, Bavaria, Netherlands
1687	Principia (Philosophiae Naturalis Principia Mathematica)	England
	Indulgence, Declaration of	England
1688	Richelieu's Political Testament (Testament Politique)	France, England
	Indulgence, Declaration of	England
1689	Declaration of Rights, English (Bill of Rights)	England
	Locke's "Letter Concerning Toleration" (Epistola de Tolerantia)	England, Holland
	Toleration Act of 1689	England
	Grand Alliance of 1689	Germany, Holland, France
	Mutiny Act of 1689	England
1690	Locke's Two Treatises on Civil Government	England
	Locke's Essay Concerning Human Understanding	England
1691	Diploma Leopoldinum (Leopoldina)	Holy Roman Empire, Transylvania
	Limerick, Treaty of (Pacification of Limerick)	England, Ireland
1696	Turin, Treaty of	France, Savoy, Italy
1697	Ryswick (Rijswijk), Treaty of	England, Holland, Holy Roman Empire, Spain, France
1699	Woolens Act (Wool Act)	England, British Colonies
	Karlowitz, Peace of	Ottoman Empire, Austria, Poland, Russia, Venice
	Preobrazhenskoe, Treaty of	Russia, Poland, Sweden, Saxony
1700	Louis XIV's Letter Accepting the Spanish Succession	France, Spain
	Travendal, Treaty of	Denmark, Sweden
	Constantinople, Treaty of	Russia, Ottoman Empire
	Reflections on Marriage	England
1701	Charter of Liberties (Charter of Privileges)	Pennsylvania (British Colonies)
	Grand Alliance of 1701	England, Austria, Prussia, Portugal, Netherlands, Savoy, Spain, France
	Montreal, Treaty of	France, Canada
	Settlement, Act of (Succession Act)	England, Hanover (Germany)
1703	Methuen Treaties	England, Portugal
	Security, Act of	Scotland, England
1706	Altranstadt, Treaty of	Poland, Sweden
1707	Union, Act of (Union of England and Scotland)	England, Scotland (Great Britain)
1709	Politics Drawn from the Very Words of Holy Scripture (Politique Tirée des Propres Paroles de l'Ecriture Sainte)	France
	Barrier Treaties	France, Britain, Holy Roman Empire, Austria, Netherlands
1710	Berkeley's Treatise Concerning the Principles of Human Knowledge	Britain
1711	Szatmar, Peace of	Hungary, Holy Roman Empire
	Occasional Conformity Bill	Britain
	Pruth, Treaty of	Russia, Ottoman Empire
	Conduct of the Allies, The	Britain
1712	Stamp Act of 1712	Britain, British Colonies
	Aarau, Treaty of	Switzerland
1713	Unigenitus	Papacy
	Utrecht, Treaty of (Peace of Utrecht)	France, Spain, Britain, Austria, Prussia, Canada, Netherlands, Savoy, Portugal, Sicily
	Pragmatic Sanction of 1713	Holy Roman Empire, Austria
	Barrier Treaties	France, Britain, Holy Roman Empire, Austria, Netherlands

DATE	DOCUMENT	AREA(S) INVOLVED
1714	Rastatt, Treaty of	Holy Roman Empire, France
	Baden, Treaty of	Holy Roman Empire, France
	Schism Act	Britain
	Utrecht, Treaty of	France, Spain, Britain, Austria, Prussia, Canada, Netherlands, Savoy, Portugal, Sicily
1715	Madrid, Treaty of	Spain, Portugal
	Versailles, Treaty of	France, Sweden
	Riot Act of 1715, British	Britain
	Barrier Treaties	France, Britain, Holy Roman Empire, Austria, Netherlands
1716	Septennial Act	Britain
1717	Triple Alliance of 1717	Britain, France, Netherlands
1718	Quadruple Alliance of 1718	Austria, Britain, France, Netherlands
	Passarowitz, Treaty of	Venice, Austria, Ottoman Empire
1719	Peerage Bill	Britain, Scotland
	Stockholm, Treaty of	Sweden, Britain, Hanover, Prussia
1720	Hague, Treaty of The	Holy Roman Empire, Spain, France, Italy
	Bubble Act (South Sea Bubble Act)	Britain
	Stockholm, Treaty of	Sweden, Britain, Hanover, Prussia
1721	Nystadt, Treaty of	Sweden, Russia, Finland
1722	Black Act (Waltham Black Act)	Britain
1723	St. Petersburg, Treaty of	Russia, Persia
1724	Edict of 1724, French	France
	Drapier's Letters	Britain, Ireland
1725	Vienna, Treaties of	Spain, Austria
	Hanover, Treaty of	Britain, France, Prussia, Denmark, Holland
1726	Conventicle Act, Swedish	Sweden
1729	Seville, Treaty of	Britain, Spain, France
1730	Unigenitus	France
1731	Montgomerie Charter	New York City (British Colonies)
	Vienna, Treaty of	Britain, Holy Roman Empire
1732	Hat Act	Britain
	Resht, Treaty of	Persia, Russia
1733	Molasses, Act	Britain
	Family Compacts (Pactes de Famille)	France, Spain
1735	Vienna, Treaty of	France, Poland, Spain, Austria, Italy
1736	Gin Act of 1736	Britain
1739	Belgrade, Treaty of	Ottoman Empire, Austria, Serbia, Russia
	Nissa, Treaty of	Ottoman Empire, Russia
	Hume's *Treatise of Human Nature*	Scotland
1740	Benedict XIV's Encyclical of 1740 (*Ubi Primum*)	Papacy
	Hume's *Treatise of Human Nature*	Scotland
1741	Concordat of 1741	Papacy, Naples
	Nymphenburg, Treaty of	France, Spain, Bavaria. Austria
	Breslau, Treaty of	France, Prussia
1742	Breslau, Treaty of	Austria, Prussia
	Berlin, Peace of	Austria, Prussia
1743	Åbo, Treaty of	Sweden, Russia
	Family Compacts (Pactes de Famille)	France, Spain
1745	Dresden, Treaty of	Prussia, Austria
	Füssen, Treaty of	Bavaria, Austria
1748	Aix-la-Chapelle, Treaty of	Britain, France, Austria, Spain, Netherlands
1750	Iron Act	Britain, British colonies
	Madrid, Treaty of	Spanish America, Spain
1751	Gin Act of 1751	Britain
	Code Frédéric	Prussia

DATE	DOCUMENT	AREA(S) INVOLVED
1752	Narcisse (Préface de Narcisse)	France
1753	Hardwicke's Marriage Act	Britain
	Discourse on Style (Discours sur le Style)	France
	Concordat of 1753	Papacy, Spain
1754	Albany Plan of Union	America
1755	Discourse on the Origin of Inequality (Discours sur l'Origine et les Fondements de l'Inégalité parmi les Hommes)	France
	Anglo-Russian Convention of 1755	Britain, Russia, Austria
1756	Westminster, Treaty of (Convention of Westminster)	Britain, Prussia
1757	Alinagar, Treaty of	India, Britain
1758	Nova Scotia's General Assembly, Proclamation for	Nova Scotia (Canada)
1759	Pragmatic Sanction of Charles III	Spain, Two Sicilies (Italy)
1761	Otis's Speech Opposing the Writs of Assistance	British Colonies, Britain
	Family Compacts (Pactes de famille)	France, Spain
1762	San Ildefonso, Treaty of	Spain, France, Americas
	St. Petersburg, Treaty of	Russia, Prussia
	Social Contract (Du Contract Social)	France
	Whiteboy Acts	Britain, Ireland
	Hamburg, Treaty of	Sweden, Prussia
1763	Paris, Treaty of	France, Britain, Spain, Portugal, Canada
	Cider Act, British	Britain
	Augusta, Treaty of	Georgia (British Colonies), Britain
	No. 45 of The North Briton	Britain
	Hubertusburg, Treaty of	Austria, Prussia
	Proclamation of 1763, British	Britain, North America
1764	Sugar Act of 1764 (Sugar Revenue Act)	British Colonies, Britain
	Rights of the British Colonies Asserted and Proved, Otis's	British Colonies, Britain
	Currency Act of 1764, British (Colonial Currency Act)	Britain, British colonies
1765	Stamp Act of 1765	Britain, British Colonies
	Declaration of Rights and Grievances	British Colonies
	Quartering Act of 1765	British Colonies, Britain
1766	Oswego, Treaty of	New York (British Colonies), Britain
	Declaratory Act of 1766	Britain, British Colonies
1767	Instruction (Nakaz), Catherine the Great's	Russia
	Suspending Act of 1767	Britain, British colonies
	Townshend Acts	Britain, British colonies
	Champagne Speech, Townshend's	Britain
1767–1768	Farmer's Letters, Dickinson's (Letters from a Farmer in Pennsylvania to the Inhabitants of the British Colonies)	Pennsylvania (British Colonies)
1768	Massachusetts Circular Letter	Massachusetts (British Colonies)
	Fort Stanwix, Treaty of	New York (British Colonies), Britain
	Masulipatam, Treaty of	India, Britain
1769	Virginia Resolves	Virginia (British Colonies), Britain
1769–1772	Junius, Letters of	Britain
1770	Thoughts on the Cause of the Present Discontents	Britain
1772	Royal Marriage Act, British	Britain
	St. Petersburg, Treaty of (First Treaty of Partition of Poland)	Poland, Austria, Russia, Prussia
	Watauga Articles of Association	Tennessee (British Colonies)
	Navigation Act of 1772	Britain, British Colonies
1773	Regulating Act of 1773, British	India, Britain
	New York Sons of Liberty, Resolutions of	New York City (British Colonies), Britain
	Clement XIV's Bull Suppressing the Jesuits (Dominus ac Redemptor)	Papacy, France, Spain
	Tea Act	Britain, British Colonies
1774	Boston Port Bill	Boston (British Colonies), Britain
	Coercive Acts (Intolerable Acts, Restraining Acts)	Britain, British Colonies
	Massachusetts Government Act	Massachusetts (British Colonies), Britain

DATE	DOCUMENT	AREA(S) INVOLVED
	Administration of Justice Act	Massachusetts (British Colonies), Britain
	Quartering Act of 1774	Britain, British Colonies
	Quebec Act	Britain, Canada
	Declaration and Resolves of the First Continental Congress (Declaration of Rights and Grievances)	British Colonies
	Association, the (Continental Association)	British Colonies, Britain
	Suffolk Resolves	Massachusetts (British Colonies)
	Fairfax Resolves	Virginia (British Colonies)
	Galloway's Plan of Union (Plan of a Proposed Union between Great Britain and the Colonies)	Philadelphia (British Colonies)
	Turgot's Letter to Louis XVI	France
	Kuchuk Kainardji, Treaty of	Ottoman Empire, Russia
	American Taxation Speech, Burke's	Britain
1775	"Give Me Liberty" Speech	Virginia (British Colonies)
	Mecklenburg Resolves (Mecklenburg "Declaration of Independence")	North Carolina (British Colonies)
	Olive Branch Petition	British Colonies, Britain
	Taxation No Tyranny	Britain, British Colonies
	Restraining Act of 1775, British (American Prohibitory Act)	Britain, British Colonies
1776	Virginia Bill of Rights (Virginia Declaration of Rights)	Virginia (British Colonies)
	Lee's Resolutions	British Colonies
	Declaration of Independence, American	United States, Britain
	Wealth of Nations, An Inquiry into the Nature and Causes of the	Britain
	Purandhar, Treaty of	India, Britain
	Six Edicts, Turgot's	France
	Take Your Choice!	Britain
	Common Sense	United States, Britain
1777	San Ildefonso, Treaty of	Spain, Portugal, Americas
	Articles of Confederation, U.S.	United States
1778	Paris, Treaties of	France, United States
	Vienna, Treaty of	Austria, Palatinate
1779	Teschen, Treaty of	Austria, Prussia
	Wadgaon, Convention of	India, Britain
	Aranjuez, Convention of	Spain, France
1780	Catherine the Great's Declaration of Armed Neutrality	Russia, Denmark, Sweden, Prussia, Austria, Portugal
1781	Edict of Toleration of 1781 (Edict of Tolerance, Toleranzpatent)	Holy Roman Empire Austria
	Critique of Pure Reason (Kritik der Reinen Vernunft)	Germany, Britain
1782	Edict of Toleration of 1782 (Toleranzpatent)	Holy Roman Empire, Austria
	Salbai, Treaty of	India, Britain
	Nicola Proposal	United States
1783	Newburgh Addresses	United States
	Paris, Treaty of (Treaty of Versailles)	United States, Britain, France, Spain
	Catherine the Great's Decree Annexing Crimea	Russia, Ottoman Empire
1784	Twenty-Five Articles of Religion	Maryland (United States)
	Pitt's India Act (Government India Act of 1784, British East India Company Act of 1784)	India, Britain
1785	Fontainebleau, Treaty of	Austria, Holland
	Hopewell, Treaty of	South Carolina (United States)
	Charter to the Nobility, Catherine II's	Russia
1786	Annapolis Convention, Report of the	United States
1787	Northwest Ordinance of 1787 (Land Ordinance of 1787)	United States
	Federalist No. 10	United States
	Federalist Papers	United States
	U.S. Constitution	United States
	Letters from the Federal Farmer, Lee's	Virginia (United States)
	Virginia Plan (Randolph Plan)	United States
	New Jersey Plan (Paterson Plan)	United States
	Great Compromise (Connecticut Compromise)	United States

DATE	DOCUMENT	AREA(S) INVOLVED
	Slavery Compromise, U.S. (Three-Fifths Compromise)	United States
	Edict of Toleration of 1787, French (Edict of Versailles)	France
	Sheridan's Begums Speech	Britain, India
1788	Triple Alliance of 1788	Britain, Prussia, Netherlands
1789	French Decree Abolishing Feudalism	France
	Unity (Union) and Security, Act of (Act of Safety)	Sweden
	Declaration of the Rights of Man and of the Citizen (La Déclaration des Droits de l'Homme et du Citoyen)	France
	Tariff Act of 1789, U.S.	United States
	Jeu de Paume, Oath of the (Tennis Court Oath)	France
	Judiciary Act of 1789, U.S.	United States
	Washington's First Inaugural Address	United States
1790	*Reflections on the Revolution in France*	Britain
	Reichenbach, Convention of	Prussia, Austria
	On the Admission of Women to Citizenship (Sur l'Admission des Femmes au Droit de Cité)	France
	Assumption Act, U.S.	United States
	Civil Constitution of the Clergy	France, Papacy
	Journey from St. Petersburg to Moscow (Puteshestvie iz Peterburga v Moskvu)	Russia
	Report on the Public Credit, First	United States
	Värälä, Treaty of	Sweden, Russia
	Funding Act of 1790, U.S.	United States
1791	Report on Manufactures	United States
	Pillnitz, Declaration of	Austria, Prussia, France
	Rights of Man, The	Britain, United States
	Sistova, Peace of	Austria, Ottoman Empire
	Bill of Rights, U.S.	United States
	Canada Act (Constitution Act of 1791)	Britain, Canada
	Law on Associations, French (Loi Chapelier, Chapelier Law)	France
	Louis XIV's Letter to the Prussian King	France, Prussia
	Declaration of the Rights of Women and the Female Citizen (Déclaration des Droits de la Femme et de la Citoyenne)	France
	French Constitution of 1791 (Constitution Française)	France
1792	Jassy, Treaty of	Russia, Ottoman Empire
	Vindication of the Rights of Women	France, Britain
	Danton "Audacity" Speech	France
	Coinage Act, U.S. (Mint Act)	United States
	French Revolutionary Proclamation of 1792	France
	Fugitive Slave Act of 1792, U.S.	United States
1793	Russo-Prussian Treaty of 1793 (Second Treaty of Partition of Poland)	Russia, Prussia, Poland
	French Decree on Feudal Rights	France
	Robespierre's Speech on Property	France
	French Constitution of 1793 (Acte Constitutionnel)	France
	Proclamation of Neutrality, Washington's	United States
	Law of the 40 Sous	France
	Law of the Suspects (Loi des Suspects)	France
	Cornwallis Code	Britain, India
	Chisholm v. *Georgia*	United States
1794	Jay Treaty	United States, Britain
	Polaniec, Manifesto of	Poland, Prussia, Russia, Austria
	Code Frédéric	Prussia
	Ventôse Decrees	France
	Law of 22 Prairial	France
1795	Naturalization Act of 1795, U.S.	United States
	Vanhorne's Lessee v. *Dorrance*	United States
	Basel, Treaties of	France, Prussia, Spain
	Rights of Man, Dutch	Netherlands
	Pinckney Treaty (Treaty of San Lorenzo)	Spain, United States
	Peace Manifesto (Perpetual Peace: A Philosophical Essay)	Germany

DATE	DOCUMENT	AREA(S) INVOLVED
	Greenville, Treaty of	Ohio (United States), Northwest Territory
	French Constitution of 1795 (Constitution of the Year III)	France
	Austro-Russian and Russo-Prussian Treaties of 1795 (Third Treaty of Partition of Poland)	Austria, Russia, Prussia, Poland
1796	San Ildefonso, Treaty of	France, Spain, Britain
	Manifesto of the Equals (Manifeste des Egaux)	France
	Paris, Treaty of	Paris, Sardinia (Piedmont)
	Washington's Farewell Address	United States
	Mazzei Letter	United States, Italy
	Cherasco, Armistice of	Italy, Sardinia, France
	Land Act of 1796, U.S.	United States
	Ware v. *Hylton*	United States
	Campo Formio, Treaty of	France, Austria, Italy
1797	Tolentino, Treaty of	Papacy, Italy, France
1798	Alien and Sedition Acts of 1798, U.S.	United States
	Alien Act of 1798, U.S.	United States
	Alien Enemies Act of 1798, U.S.	United States
	Sedition Act of 1798, U.S.	United States
	Naturalization Act of 1798, U.S.	United States
	Logan Act	United States
	Kentucky Resolutions	Kentucky (United States)
	Virginia Resolutions	Virginia (United States)
	"XYZ" Report	United States, France
	Essays on the Principle of Population, Malthus's	Britain
1799	Rosetta Stone	Egypt, France
	Napoléon's Statement of 18 Brumaire	France
1800	French Constitution of 1800 (Constitution of Year VIII)	France
	Alessandria, Armistice of	France, Austria
	Franco-American Treaty of 1800 (Treaty of Mortefontaine)	United States, France
	Land Act of 1800, U.S. (Harrison Land Act)	United States
	San Ildefonso, Treaty of	Spain, France, Louisiana (United States), Portugal
1801	Union with Ireland, British Act of	Britain, Ireland
	Lunéville, Treaty of	France, Austria, Italy, Holland, Switzerland
	Jefferson's First Inaugural Address	United States
	Madrid, Treaty of	Spain, Portugal, France
	Concordat of 1801	Papacy, France
	Judiciary Act of 1801, U.S.	United States
1802	Amiens, Treaty of	Britain, France, Spain, Holland
	Bassein, Treaty of	India, Britain
	Organic Articles of April 8, French	France
	Law of Germinal (Law of Public Worship)	France, Vatican
	French Constitution of 1802 (Constitution of the Year X)	France
	Health and Morals of Apprentices Act	Britain
1803	*Marbury* v. *Madison*	United States
	Emmet's Proclamation	Ireland, Britain
	Louisiana Purchase Treaty	United States, France
	Vincennes, Treaty of	Indiana United States
	Napoléon's Mediation Constitution (Act of Mediation)	France, Switzerland
	Deogaon, Treaty of	India, Britain
1804	French Constitution of 1804 (Constitution of the Year XII)	France
	Essex Decision	Britain, United States
1804–1810	Napoleonic Code (Code Napoléon)	France
1805	Pressburg, Treaty of	Austria, France, Italy, Germany
	Schönbrunn, Treaty of	Prussia, France,
1805–1809	Consolidación, Law of	Mexico (New Spain), Spain
1806	Non-Importation Act of 1806 (Nicholson Non-Importation Act)	United States, Britain
	Napoléon's Order Dissolving the Holy Roman Empire	France, Austria, Germany
	Berlin Decree	France, Britain
1807	Embargo Act of 1807, U.S.	United States, France, Britain
	Milan Decrees	France, Britain, United States

DATE	DOCUMENT	AREA(S) INVOLVED
	Orders in Council of 1807	Britain, France
	Tilsit, Treaties of	Russia, France, Prussia, Poland, Germany
	Slaves, Act to Prohibit Importation of (Slave Trade Abolition Act of 1807)	United States
	Slave Emancipation Act of 1807, British	Britain, Africa, West Indies, Americas
	Emancipation Edict of 1807, Prussian	Prussia
	Fontainebleau Decrees	France, Britain
1808	Bayonne, Treaty of	France, Spain
	Bayonne Decree	France, United States
	Sintra, Convention of	Britain, France, Portugal
	Henry Letters	Britain, Canada, United States
	Erfurt, Treaty of	Russia, France, Ottoman Empire
	Schönbrunn, Treaty of (Treaty of Vienna)	Austria, France, Bavaria, Warsaw
1809	Non-Intercourse Act, U.S.	United States
	Amritsar, Treaty of	India, Britain
	Fredrikshamm, Treaty of	Sweden, Russia, Finland
	Execrabilis of 1809	Papacy, France
	Canak, Treaty of (Treaty of the Dardanelles)	Britain, Ottoman Empire
1810	Paris, Treaty of	France, Sweden
	Rambouillet Decree	France, United States
	Strangford Treaty	Portugal, Brazil, Britain
	Macon Act (Macon's Bill No. 2)	United States, Britain, France
	Fletcher v. Peck	United States
1811	Federation of the United Provinces of New Granada, Act of	Colombia
1812	St. Petersburg, Treaty of	Sweden, Russia, Finland, France
	Rockingham Memorial, Webster's	United States
	Åbo, Treaty of	Sweden, Russia
	Shelley's *Declaration of Rights*	Britain, Ireland
	Madison's War Message	United States, Britain
	Spanish Constitution of 1812	Spain
	Tauroggen, Convention of	Prussia, Russia, France
	Bucharest, Treaty of	Russia, Ottoman Empire
	Teplitz, Treaty of	Russia, Prussia, Austria
1813	Grand Alliance of 1813 (Sixth and Last Coalition Against Napoléon)	Prussia, Russia, Britain, Sweden, Austria, Bavaria, Saxony, France, European states
	Kalisch (Kalisz), Treaty of	Russia, Prussia, France
	Pläswitz, Armistice of	France, Russia, Prussia, Austria
	Gulistan, Treaty of	Russia, Persia (Iran)
	Chilpancingo, Congress of	Mexico
1814	Kiel, Treaty of	Denmark, Sweden, Britain
	Chaumont, Treaties of	Britain, Russia, Prussia, Austria, France
	Napoléon's Abdication Declaration	France
	Paris, Treaty of (First Peace of Paris)	France, Britain, Russia, Austria, Prussia, Europe
	French Constitution of 1814 (Louis XVII's Charter of 1814, French Constitutional Charter of 1814, Chartre Constitutionelle)	France
	Fontainebleau, Treaty of	European states, France
	Protocol of the Eight Articles	Netherlands, Belgium
	Bolivar's "Letter from Jamaica"	Jamaica, Venezuela
	Apatzingán, Constitution of	Mexico
	St.-Ouen, Declaration of	France
	Fort Jackson, Treaty of	United States
	Ghent, Treaty of	United States, Britain, Canada
	Moss, Convention of	Sweden, Norway, Denmark
	Union, Act of (Union of Sweden and Norway)	Norway, Sweden
1815	Hartford Convention Resolutions	New England
	German Confederation, Act of	Germany, Austria, Prussia, European states
	Slave Emancipation Act, French	France, Britain
	Additional Act, French (Acte Additionel)	France
	Corn Law of 1815, British	Britain
	Holy Alliance of 1815	Russia, Austria, Prussia
	Vienna, Final Act of the Congress of	Austria, Prussia, Sweden, Russia, Netherlands, European states

DATE	DOCUMENT	AREA(S) INVOLVED
	Paris, Treaty of (Second Peace of Paris)	France, Britain, Austria, Russia, Prussia
	Swiss Federal Pact of 1815	Switzerland
	Quadruple Alliance of 1815	Russia, Prussia, Austria, Britain
	Katmandu, Treaty of	Nepal, Britain, India
1816	United Provinces of the Río de la Plata, Declaration of Independence of the	Argentina, Bolivia, Uruguay
	Sagauli, Treaty of	India, Nepal, Britain
	Tariff Act of 1816, U.S.	United States
	Martin v. *Hunter's Lessee*	United States
1817	Bonus Bill of 1817, U.S.	United States
	Rush-Bagot Agreement	Britain, United States
	Carbonari, Proclamation of the	Italy, France, Austria
	Coercion Acts of 1817, British	Britain
1818	London Convention of 1818 (Treaty of London)	United States, Britain, Canada
	Fugitive Slave Bill of 1818, U.S.	United States
	Aix-la-Chapelle, Convention of	Britain, Russia, Prussia, Austria
	World as Will and Idea, The (Die Welt als Wille und Vorstellung)	Germany
1819	Six Acts of 1819, British	Britain
	Tallmadge Amendment	United States, Missouri
	McCulloch v. *Maryland*	United States
	Carlsbad Decrees	Austria, Prussia, Germany
	Dartmouth College v. *Woodward*	United States
	Adams-Onís Treaty	United States, Florida, Spain
	Angostura, Congress of	Colombia, Ecuador, Venezuela
	Bolívar's Address at Angostura	Colombia, Ecuador, Venezuela
1820	Pains and Penalties, Bill of	Britain
	Missouri Compromise	United States, Missouri, Maine
	Law of the Double Vote (Loi du Double Vote)	France
	Troppau Protocol	Russia, Prussia, Austria
	Metternich's Circular about Troppau	Austria, Russia, Prussia
	Plymouth Rock Speech, Webster's	United States, New England
	Land Act of 1820, U.S.	United States
1821	Italian Constitution of 1821	Piedmont-Sardinia (Italy)
	Colombian Constitution of 1821	Colombia
	Iguala, Plan of	Mexico
	Córdoba, Treaty of (Convention of Córdoba)	Mexico, Spain
	Cohens v. *Virginia*	United States
1822	Verona, Mandate of the Congress of	France, Spain, Austria, Russia, Prussia, Britain
1823	Monroe Doctrine	United States, Latin America, Europe
1824	Tariff Act of 1824, U.S.	United States, New England
	Webster's Speech on Greek Independence ("Holy Alliance" Speech)	United States, Greece, Ottoman Empire
	United Provinces of Central America, Declaration of the Independence of the	Central America
	Patronato Law (Ley de Patronato)	Colombia, Quito, Venezuela
	Brazilian Constitution of 1824	Brazil
	Mexican Constitution of 1824	Mexico
	Free Trade Speech, Webster's	United States
	Gibbons v. *Ogden*	United States
1825	Law of Indemnity, French	France
	Adams's First Annual Message	United States
	Bunker Hill Speech, Webster's	United States, Massachusetts
	Decembrist Manifesto	Russia
1826	Law of Sacrilege (Loi de Sacrilège)	France
	Constitución Vitalicia ("lasting for life")	Peru, Bolivia, Columbia
	St. Petersburg Protocol of 1826	Britain, Russia, Greece, Ottoman Empire
	Webster's Speech on the Deaths of Thomas Jefferson and John Adams	United States, Boston
	Akkerman, Convention of	Russia, Ottoman Empire
	Brazilian-British Treaty of 1826	Brazil, Britain

DATE	DOCUMENT	AREA(S) INVOLVED
1827	London, Treaty of	Britain, France, Russia, Greece, Ottoman Empire
	Turkmanchai, Treaty	Russia, Persia (Iran)
	Prusso-Darmstadt Customs' Treaty	Prussia, Hesse-Darmstadt
	Mid-German Commercial Union	German states
	Corn Law of 1828, British	Britain
	Tariff Act of 1828, U.S. (Tariff of Abominations)	United States
	Exposition and Protest, Calhoun's (South Carolina Exposition and Protest)	United States, South Carolina
	Leinster Declaration	Ireland, Britain
1829	British Metropolitan Police Act	Britain, London
	Catholic Emancipation Act, British (Catholic Reform or Relief Bill)	Britain, Ireland
	Adrianople, Treaty of	Russia, Ottoman Empire, Greece
	London Protocol of 1829	Russia, Britain, France, Greece, Ottoman Empire
	Foote's Resolution	United States
1830	Maysville Road Bill	United States, Kentucky
	Indian Removal Act of 1830, U.S.	United States
	Webster's First and Second Replies to Hayne	United States, New England
	July Ordinances of 1830 (Quatre Ordonnances)	France
	French Charter of 1830	France
	Uruguayan Constitution of 1830	Uruguay
	Course of Positive Philosophy (*Cours de Philosophie Positive*)	France
	Mormon, Book of	New York (United States)
1831	Belgian Neutrality Treaty (Treaty of London)	Austria, Begium, Britain, France, Prussia, Russia
	"Address to the People of South Carolina," Calhoun's	United States
	Belgian Constitution of 1831	Begium, Netherlands
	Mazzini's Instructions to Young Italy	Italy
	Cherokee Nation v. Georgia	United States
	Rives's Treaty	France, United States
1831–1865	*Liberator*	Boston (United States)
1832	"Fort Hill Letter," Calhoun's	South Carolina (United States)
	Rumanian Organic Statutes of 1832	Moldavia and Wallachia, Russia
	Polish Organic Statutue of 1832	Poland, Russia
	Worcester v. *Georgia*	Georgia (United States)
	London, Treaty of	Britain, France, Russia, Greece
	Tariff of 1832, U.S.	United States
	Reform Act of 1832, British	Britain
	German Confederation, Six Articles of	Germany, European states
	South Carolina's Ordinances of Nullification	South Carolina (United States)
	Nullification Proclamation (Jackson's Proclamation to South Carolina)	United States
	South Carolina's Reply to Jackson's Proclamation	South Carolina (United States)
	Mirari Vos	Papacy, France
	Siebener Concordat (Siebenerkonkordat, Agreement of Seven)	Switzerland
1833	*Barron* v. *Baltimore*	United States
	Berlin, Convention of	Austria, Russia, Prussia
	Factory Act of 1833, British (Factories Regulation Act)	Britain
	Kütahya, Convention of	Egypt, Ottoman Empire
	Tariff Act of 1833, U.S. (Compromise Tariff)	United States
	Münchengrätz Agreement	Russia, Austria, Britain, France
	Force Act of 1833, U.S.	United States
	American Anti-Slavery Society, Constitution of	Philadephia (United States)
	Chilean Constitution of 1833	Chile
	Hünkâr Iskelesi (Unkiar Skelessi), Treaty of	Russia, Ottoman Empire
	Guizot Law (French Primary Education Law of 1833)	France
	Slave Emancipation Act of 1833, British	Britain
1833–1841	*Tracts for the Times* (Oxford Tracts)	Britain
1834	Baden, Articles of	Switzerland
	Ninety-Two Resolutions, Papineau's	Quebec (Canada)
	Spanish Constitution of 1834 (Estatuto Real)	Spain
	London, Treaty of	Britain, France, Spain, Portugal
	Memorial Ajustado	Argentina

DATE	DOCUMENT	AREA(S) INVOLVED
	Brazilian Constitutional Amendment of 1834 (Acto Adicional of 1834)	Brazil
	Irish Church Temporalities Act	Britain, Ireland
	Poor Law of 1834 (Poor Law Amendment Act)	Britain
1835	Lichfield House Compact	Britain, Ireland
	New Echota, Treaty of	Georgia (United States)
	Jackson's Message on Removal of Southern Indians	United States
	September Laws of 1835 (Lois de Septembre)	France
1835–1841	Melbourne's Six Acts	England, Wales, Ireland
1836	Texas Declaration of Independence	Texas, Mexico
	Specie Circular (Jackson's Special Circular)	United States
1836–1844	Gag Rules, U.S.	United States
1837	*Charles River Bridge* v. *Warren Bridge*	United States
	American Scholar, The	Massachusetts (United States)
	Ten Resolutions, Russell's	Britain, Quebec (Canada)
	Tafna, Treaty of	Algeria, France
1838	People's Charter (Chartist Petition of 1838)	Britain
	Kendall v. *United States*	United States
	Poor Law of 1838	Britain, Ireland
1839	Durham's Report	Canada, Britain
	Vergara, Convention of (Embrace of Vergara)	Spain
	Howe's Letters to Lord John Russell	Canada, Britain
	Bank of Augusta v. *Earle*	United States
	Ottoman Imperial Edict of 1839 (Hatti-i Serif of Gülhane, Noble Edict of the Rose Chamber, Magna Carta of Ottoman Liberty)	Ottoman Empire
	London, Treaty of (Belgian Neutrality Treaty)	Belgium, Netherlands, Austria, France, Britain, Prussia, Russia
1840	Union, Act of (Union of Upper and Lower Canada)	Britain, Quebec, Ontario
	London, Treaty of	Britain, Austria, Prussia, Russia, Ottoman Empire
	Waitangi, Treaty of	New Zealand, Britain
	What Is Property?	France
1841	Pre-Emption Act of 1841, U.S.	United States
	Tract No. 90, Newman's	Britain
	Straits Convention (London Straits Convention)	Britain, France, Prussia, Russia, Austria, Ottoman Empire
	Mahon's Act, Lord	Britain
1842	Amparo, Writ of	Mexico
	Nanking, Treaty of	China, Britain
	Commonwealth v. *Hunt*	Massachusetts (United States)
	Webster-Ashburton Treaty (Ashburton Treaty, Treaty of Washington)	United States, Britain, Canada
1843	Eu, Agreements of	Britain, France, Spain, Portugal
	Dix's Memorial to the Legislature of Massachusetts	Massachusetts (United States)
	Somnauth Proclamation	India, Britain
1844	Tangier, Treaty of	Morocco, Algeria, France
	Bank Charter Act of 1844, British	Britain
	Raleigh Letter, Clay's	United States, Texas, Mexico
	Alabama Letters	United States
	Wanghai, Treaty of	China, United States
1845	Polk's Inaugural Address	United States
	Aberdeen Act	Britain, Brazil
	Polk's First Message to Congress (Polk Doctrine)	United States
1846	Oregon Boundary Treaty	United States, Britain, Canada
	Walker Tariff Act (U.S. Tariff Act of 1846)	United States
	Polk's Message on War with Mexico	United States
	Independent Treasury Act, U.S.	United States
	Bidlack Treaty (New Granada Treaty)	Colombia, Panama, United States
	Wilmot Proviso	United States, Mexico
1847	Wilmot Proviso	United States, Mexico

DATE	DOCUMENT	AREA(S) INVOLVED
1848	Guadalupe-Hidalgo, Treaty of	Mexico, United States
	Communist Manifesto	Britain, Russia, Germany
	March Laws (April Laws, Hungarian Acts of 1848)	Hungary, Austria
	Pillersdorf Constitution (April Constitution of 1848, Austrian Constitution of 1848)	Austria
	French Decrees of 1848	France
	Lamartine's Manifesto to Europe	France
	Public Health Act of 1848, British	Britain
	Italian Constitutions of 1848	Italy
	Women's Rights, Declaration of (Seneca Falls Declaration and Resolutions, Declaration of Independence for Women)	New York (United States)
	French Constitution of 1848 (Constitution of the Second Republic, Constitution de la République)	France
	Chartist Petition of 1848 (Monster Petition)	Britain
	Mann's Twelfth Annual Report	Massachusetts (United States)
	Ledru-Rollin's Speech on Family and Property	France
	Luther v. *Borden*	United States
	Biglow Papers	Massachusetts (United States)
1849	Frankfurt Constitution	Germany
	March Constitution (Schwarzenberg Constitution)	Austria
	Hülsemann Letter	Austria, Hungary, United States
	Webster's Reply to Hülsemann Letter	United States, Austria
	Annexation Manifesto, Canadian	Canada
	Kremsier Constitution	Austria
	Seven Lamps of Architecture, The	Britain
	Hungarian Declaration of Independence	Hungary, Austria
	Balta Liman, Convention of	Russia, Ottoman Empire
	Civil Disobedience, Thoreau's	United States
1850	Clayton-Bulwer Treaty	United States, Britain, Central America
	Compromise of 1850	United States
	Calhoun's Last Speech on the Slavery Question (Calhoun's Speech on the Compromise of 1850)	United States
	Clay's Compromise Speech	United States
	"Seventh of March" Speech, Webster's	United States
	"Higher Law" Speech, Seward's	United States
	Falloux Law (Loi Falloux)	France
	Queiroz Law	Brazil
	Fugitive Slave Law of 1850, U.S.	United States
	Disquisition on Government, Calhoun's	United States
	Australian Colonies Government Act	Australia, Britain
	Georgia Platform	Georgia (United States)
	Lapse, Doctrine of	India, Britain
1851	Ecclesiastical Titles Assumption Act	Britain
	Fort Laramie, Treaty of	United States
	Concordat of 1851	Papacy, Spain
1852	New Zealand's Constitution of 1852	New Zealand, Britain
	Douglass's "What to a Slave Is the Fourth of July?" Speech	United States
	Uncle Tom's Cabin; or, Life Among the Lowly	United States
	London Protocol of 1852	Denmark, Britain, Russia, France, Austria, Prussia
	French Constitution of 1852 (Constitution of the Second Empire)	France
1853	Gadsden Purchase Treaty	United States, Mexico
	Argentine Constitution of 1853	Argentina
	Vienna Note of 1853	Austria, France, Prussia, Britain, Russia, Ottoman Empire
1854	Dispatch of 1854	Britain, India
	Reciprocity Treaty (Elgin-Marcy Treaty)	United States, Canada
	Vienna Four Points	Britain, France, Austria, Russia, Ottoman Empire
	Kansas-Nebraska Act	United States
	Kanagawa, Treaty of	Japan, United States
	Ostend Manifesto	United States. Cuba, Spain, Britain, France
	Corrupt Practices Prevention Act of 1854, British	Britain
	Ayutla, Plan of	Mexico

DATE	DOCUMENT	AREA(S) INVOLVED
1855	Juárez Law (Ley Juárez)	Mexico
	Topeka Constitution	Kansas (United States)
	Concordat of 1855	Papacy, Austria
	November Treaty (Pact of Guarantee, November Pact)	Britain, France, Sweden
1856	Paris, Treaty of	Britain, France, Austria, Sardinia, Ottoman Empire, Russia
	"Crime Against Kansas" Speech, Sumner's	United States
	Iglesias Law (Ley Iglesias)	Mexico
	Lerdo Law (Ley Lerdo)	Mexico
	Ottoman Imperial Edict of 1856 (Hatt-i Hümayun, Magna Carta of Turkey)	Ottoman Empire
1857	Tariff of 1857, U.S.	United States
	Dred Scott v. *Sandford*	Illinois, Missoui, Wisconsin (United States)
	Lecompton Constitution	Kansas (United States)
1858	Paris, Convention of	Moldavia, Wallachia, Austria, France, Prussia, Russia, Ottoman Empire
	Government of India Act of 1858	Britain, India
	"House Divided" Speech, Lincoln's	United States
	Plombières, Agreement of	France, Italy, Austria
	U.S.-Chinese Treaty of 1858 (Reed Treaty)	United States, China, Britain, France
	Harris Treaty	United States, Japan
	Tientsin, Treaty of	China, Britain
	Freeport Doctrine	Illinois (United States)
	Lincoln's Last Speech in the Lincoln-Douglas Debates	Illinois (United States)
	New Provinces Act	New Zealand
	Ableman v. *Booth*	United States
1859	Wyandotte Constitution	Kansas (United States)
	Garibaldi's Proclamation to the Italians	Italy
	Villafranca, Treaty of	France, Austria, Sardinia-Piedmont (Italy)
	Zurich, Treaty of	Austria, Sardinia-Piedmont (Italy), France, Papacy
	On Liberty	Britain
	Origin of Species	Britain
1860	Codben-Chevalier Treaty	Britain, France
	Cooper Union Speech, Lincoln's	New York City
	Victor Emmanuel II's Speech Opening the Italian Parliament	Italy
	Max Havelaar	Netherlands, Indonesia
	October Diploma	Austria
	Peking, Peace of	China, Britain, France
	Ordinance of Secession, South Carolina's	South Carolina (United States)
	Irish Land Act of 1860 (Deasy's Act, Ireland Landlord and Tenant Law Amendment or Act)	Ireland, Britain
	Crittenden Compromise (Crittenden Plan or Amendment)	United States
1861	Emancipation Editct of 1861, Russian	Russia
	February Patent	Austria, Hungary
	Morrill Tariff Act	United States
	Lincoln's First Inaugural Addres	United States
	Confederate Constitution	Confederate States of America
	Cornerstone Speech, Stephen's	Confederate States of America
	Anaconda Plan	United States
	Merryman, Ex Parte	United States
	Confiscation Act of 1861, U.S.	United States
1862	Legal Tender Act, U.S.	United States
	"Blood and Iron" Speech, Bismarck's	Prussia, Germany
	Butler's General Order No. 28	United States
	Concordat of 1862	Ecuador, Papacy
	Morrill Act	United States
	Confiscation Act of 1862, U.S.	United States
	Greeley's "Prayer" (The Prayer of Twenty Millions)	United States
	Lincoln's Letter to Greeley	United States
	Ironclad Oath	United States
	Working Class Program	Germany
	Homestead Act of 1862	United States
	Pacific Railroad Act	United States
	Native Land Acts, New Zealand's	New Zealand

DATE	DOCUMENT	AREA(S) INVOLVED
1863	Emancipation Proclamation, U.S.	United States
	National Bank Act of 1863, U.S.	United States
	Gettysburg Address	United States
1864	Pomeroy Circular	United States
	Wade-Davis Bill	United States
	Vilayet Law	Ottoman Empire
	September Convention of 1864	Italy, France
	Syllabus of Errors (Syllabus Errorum)	Papacy
	Vienna, Treaty of	Denmark, Austria, Prussia
	Geneva Convention of 1864 (Convention for the Amelioration of the Wounded in Time of War)	European states, Switzerland
	Russian Fundamental Laws of 1864	Russia
	Quebec Resolutions (Seventy-Two Resolutions, Canadian)	Nova Scotia, New Brunswick, Prince Edward Island, Newfoundland (Canada)
1865	Freedman's Bureau Bill	United States
	Lincoln's Second Inaugural Address	United States
	Gastein, Convention of	Austria, Prussia, Denmark
	Native Land Acts, New Zealand's	New Zealand
1865–1866	Black Codes, U.S.	United States
1866	*Milligan, Ex Parte*	United States
	Prussian-Italian Alliance of 1866	Prussia, Italy, France, Austria
	William I's Proclamation to the Prussian People	Prussia, Austria
	Prague, Treaty of	Prussia, Austria
	Vienna, Treaty of (Austro-Italian Treaty of Venetia)	Austria, Italy, Venetia, Prussia
	Balkan Treaties	Serbia, Romania, Montenegro, Ottoman Empire
	Public Schools Act of 1866, Australian	Britain, New South Wales
	Civil Rights Act of 1866, U.S.	United States
1867	Peonage Abolition Act, U.S.	United States, New Mexico
	Tenure of Office Act, U.S.	United States
	Mississippi v. *Johnson*	United States
	Native Representation Act, New Zealand's (Maori Representation Act)	New Zealand
	British North America Act	Britain, Ontario, Quebec, Nova Scotia, New Brunswick (Canada)
	Alaska Purchase Treaty	United States
	London, Treaty of	Prussia, France, Russia, Britain
	Das Kapital (Capital)	Germany
	Austrian Constitution of 1867 (December Constitution, Fundamental Laws)	Austria
	Biglow Papers	Massachusetts (United States)
	Marquess of Queensberry Rules	Britain
	Reform Act of 1867, British (Representation of the People Act)	Britain
	Ausgleich (Compromise of 1867)	Austria, Hungary
	Voeslau, Treaty of	Serbia, Greece, Ottoman Empire
	Medicine Lodge, Treaty of	United States
1867–1868	Reconstruction Acts, U.S.	United States
1868	Croatian-Hungarian Compromise of 1868 (Nagoda, Law XXX of 1868)	Croatia, Hungary
	Reform Act of 1868, Irish	Britain, Ireland
	Reform Act of 1868, Scottish	Britain, Scotland
	Burlingame Treaty	United States, China
	Fourteenth Amendment, U.S.	United States
	Fort Laramie, Treaty of	United States, Montana, South Dakota
	Calvo Doctrine	Argentina, Latin America
	Calvo Clause	Argentina, Latin America
	Covode Resolution	United States
1869	Disestablishment Act of 1869	Britain, Ireland
	Texas v. *White*	United States
	War and Peace	Russia
1869–1874	Granger Laws	Illinois, Iowa, Wisconsin, Minnesota United States
1870	Ems Telegram	Prussia, Spain, France
	Peace Preservation Act of 1870, British	Britain, Ireland

DATE	DOCUMENT	AREA(S) INVOLVED
	Education Act of 1870, British (Forster Elementary Education Act)	England, Wales
	Dogma of Papal Infallibility	Papacy
	Irish Land Act of 1870 (Ireland Landlord and Tenant Act)	Britain, Ireland
	Bright Clause	Britain, Ireland
	Blanqui's *La Patrie en Danger, No. 50*	France, Prussia
1870–1871	Force Acts, U.S. (Ku Klux Klan Acts)	United States
1871	London, Treaty of	Britain, France, Sardinia, Austria, Ottoman Empire, Russia
	German Empire, Proclamation of the	Prussia, Germany
	Paris Commune, First Proclamation of the	France
	German Empire, Constitution of the	Prussia, Germany
	Guarantees, Law of	Italy, Papacy
	Washington, Treaty of	United States, Britain
	Pius IX's Encyclical of 1871	Papacy, Italy
	Trade Union Act of 1871, British	Britain
	Army Regulation Act of 1871, British	Britain
	Collector v. *Day*	United States
	Victor Emmanuel II's Speech to the Italian Parliament	Italy
	Frankfurt, Treaty of	France, Prussia
	Universities Test Act, English	England
	Manifesto of the International Working-Men's Association	France, Europe, United States
	Rivet-Vitet Law (Loi Rivet-Vitet)	France
	Rio Branco Law (Free Birth Law)	Brazil
1872	Amnesty Act of 1872, U.S.	United States
	Indian Evidence Act	Britain, India
	Pacific Islanders Protection Act (Kidnapping Act of 1872, British)	Britain, Pacific Islands, Fiji, Australia
1873	Septennate, Law of the	France
	Salary Grab Act, U.S.	United States
	Timber Culture Act, U.S.	United States
	May Laws (Falk Laws)	Prussia
	Slaughterhouse Cases	Louisiana (United States)
	Factory Act of 1873, Australian (Workrooms and Factories Act)	Victoria (Australia)
	Coinage Act of 1873, U.S. (Demonetization Act)	United States
	Judicature Act of 1873, British (Supreme Court of Judicature Act)	Britain
	Pangkor Engagement (Treaty of Pangkor)	Britain, Perak (Malaysia)
	Comstock Law	United States
1874	Chinese Engagement	Malaysia, China
1875	Wallon Amendment	France
	Specie Resumption Act, U.S. (Resumption Act)	United States
	Civil Rights Act of 1875, U.S.	United States
	St. Petersburg, Treaty of	Russia, Japan
	Adulteration (Sale) of Food and Drugs Act	Britain
	Bread-basket Bill	Prussia
	Public Health Act of 1875, British	Britain
	Artisans' Dwellings Act (Artizans' and Labourers' Dwellings Improvement Act)	Britain
	French Constitution of 1875 (Constitution of the Third Republic)	France
	Andrássy Note	Austria-Hungary, Russia, Ottoman Empire, Balkans
1876	*Bulgarian Horrors and the Question of the East*	Britain, Ottoman Empire
	Berlin Memorandum	Austria-Hungary, Germany, Russia, Ottoman Empire
	"Acres of Diamonds" Speech, Conwell's	United States
	Royal Titles Act of 1876, British	Britain, India
	Mulligan Letters	United States
	Merchant Shipping Act of 1876, British	Britain
	Chefoo (Yentai) Convention	China, Britain
	Ottoman Empire Constitution, First	Ottoman Empire
1877	Coppino Act	Italy
	Desert Land Act, U.S.	United States

DATE	DOCUMENT	AREA(S) INVOLVED
	Western Pacific Order in Council	Britain, Fiji, New Guinea, other Western Pacific Islands
	London Protocol of 1877	Denmark, France, Britain, Russia, Austria, Prussia
	Munn v. *Illinois*	United States
	Budapest Conventions of 1877	Russia, Austria
1877–1950s	Jim Crow Laws	United States
1878	Anti-Socialist Law, German	Germany
	San Stefano, Treaty of	Russia, Ottoman Empire, Caucasus, Bosnia, Romania, Bulgaria, Serbia
	Knights of Labor Constitution	United States
	Bland-Allison Act	United States
	Berlin, Treaty of	Bulgaria, Ottoman Empire, Romania, Serbia, Greece, Germany, Britain, Austria, Russia
	Dentists' Act, British	Britain
	Report on the Lands of the Arid Region of the United States	United States
	Halepa, Pact of	Ottoman Empire, Greece, Crete
1879	Tariff Law of 1879, German	Germany
	Reynolds v. *United States*	United States
	Austro-German Treaty of Alliance (Dual Alliance)	Austria, Germany
1880	Morey Letter	New York (United States)
	Kilbourn v. *Thompson*	United States
1881	Saraiva Law	Brazil
	St. Petersburg, Treaty of	Russia, China
	Affirmation Bill, British	Britain
	Irish Land Act of 1881 (Gladstone's Act of 1881)	Britain, Ireland
	Three Emperors' Alliance (Dreikaiserbund)	Germany, Russia, Austria
1882	Chinese Exclusion Act of 1882	United States
	Kilmainham Treaty	Britain, Ireland
	Triple Alliance of 1882	Germany, Austria-Hungary, Italy
	Prevention of Crimes Act, British	Britain
1882–1886	Factory Laws, Russian	Russia
1883	Pendleton Act (Pendleton Civil Service Act)	United States
	Civil Rights Cases of 1883, U.S.	United States
	Dufferin Proposals (Dufferin Report)	Britain, Egypt
	Corrupt and Illegal Practices Prevention Act, British	Britain
	Ancón, Treaty of	Chile, Peru
	Ilbert Bill	India, Britain
1884	*Julliard* v. *Greenman*	United States
	Reform Act of 1884, British (Representation of the People Act)	Britain
	Trade Union Act of 1884, French	France
1885	Redistribution (of Seats) Act of 1885, British	Britain
	Asbourne Act (Irish Land Act of 1885)	Britain, Ireland
	Berlin Act of 1885	Belgium, Congo, Portugal, West Africa
1886	Bucharest, Treaty of	Serbia, Bulgaria
	Home Rule Bill of 1886	Britain, Ireland
	Berne Convention of 1886	Switzerland, France, other nations
	Wabash, St. Louis and Pacific Railroad Company v. *Illinois* (Wabash Case)	United States
	Colombian Constitution of 1886	Colombia
	Beyond Good and Evil (Jenseits von Gut und Böse)	Germany
	Presidential Succession Act of 1886	United States
1887	Hatch Act of 1887	United States
	Interstate Commerce Act, U.S. (Cullom Act)	United States
	Dawes Severalty	United States
	Reinsurance Treaty	Russia, Germany
	Concordat of 1887	Papacy, Colombia
	Bismarck's Army Bill of 1887	Germany
	Electoral Count Act	United States
	Irish Land Act of 1887	Britain, Ireland
	Crimes Bill of 1887, British	Britain, Ireland
1887–1888	Parnellism and Crime	Britain, Ireland

DATE	DOCUMENT	AREA(S) INVOLVED
1888	Brazilian Slave Emancipation Act	Brazil
	Suez Canal Convention (Constantinople Convention)	Austria-Hungary, Britain, France, Germany, Italy, Netherlands, Spain, Russia, Ottoman Empire
	Bayard-Chamberlain Treaty	Britain, United States
	Ritchie Act (Local Government Act of 1888, Country Councils Act)	Britain
	Murchison Letter	United States
1889	Uccialli, Treaty of	Italy, Ethiopia, Eritrea
	Naval Defense Act of 1889, British	Britain
	Berlin Act of 1889 (Samoa Act)	Britain, Germany, Unites States, Samoa
	Fabian Essays	Britain
	Carnegie's "Wealth" Article	United States
1890	McKinley Tariff Act	United States
	Parnell Commission Report	Britain, Ireland
	Heligoland Agreement	Britain, Germany, Heligoland, Zanzibar, Africa
	Sherman Anti-Trust Act	United States
	Sherman Silver Purchase Act	United States
	Lodge Bill (Force Bill of 1890)	United States
	Neagle, In Re	United States
	Ocala Platform	Florida (United States)
	Brussels Act of 1890 (General Act of Brussels)	Britain, France, Austria-Hungary, Germany, United States, Ottoman Empire, Persia, Zanzibar, Africa
	Principles of Psychology, The	United States
	Shell Manifesto	South Carolina
1891	Age of Consent Act	Britain, India
	Brazilian Constitution of 1891	Brazil
	Forest Reserve Act	United States
	Land Purchase Act of 1891, Irish	Britain, Ireland
	Anglo-Italian Agreements of 1891	Britain, Italy, Ethiopia
	Rerum Novarum	Papacy
	Erfurt, Congress of (Erfurt Program)	Germany
	Franco-Russian Agreement of 1891	France, Russia
	Newcastle Program	Britain, Ireland
1892	Pledge of Allegiance, U.S.	United States
	Inter Innumeras (Au Milieu des Sollicitudes)	Papacy, France
	Omaha Platform	United States
	Bering Sea Treaty	Britain, United States
	Chinese Exclusion Act of 1892	United States
1893	German Military Bill of 1893	Germany
1894	Coxey's Program	United States
	Glen Grey Act	South Africa
	Russo-German Tariff Treaty of 1894	Russia, Germany
	Wilson-Gorman Tariff Act	United States
	Advances to Settlers Act	New Zealand
	Congo Treaty of 1894	Britain, Congo Free State
	Carey Desert Land Grant Act	United States
	Aoki-Kimberley Treaty (Anglo-Japanese Commercial Treaty of 1894)	Japan, Britain
	United States v. *Debs et al.*	United States
1895	Nicholas II's Declaration of Policy	Russia
	United States v. *E.C. Knight Company* (Sugar Trust Case)	United States
	Pollock v. *Farmers' Loan and Trust Company*	United States
	Shimonoseki, Treaty of	Japan, China
	In Re Debs	United States
	Washington's Address to the Atlanta Exposition	United States
	Olney Doctrine	United States, Britain, Venezuela
	Central American Treaty of Union	Nicaragua, El Salvador, Honduras
1896	Kruger Telegram	Germany, South Africa, Britain, France, Russia
	Addis Ababa, Treaty of	Italy, Ethiopia
	Plessy v. *Ferguson*	United States
	Jewish State, The (Der Judenstaat)	Austria, Israel
	"Cross of Gold" Speech	United States
	"What's the Matter with Kansas?"	Kansas (United States)

DATE	DOCUMENT	AREA(S) INVOLVED
	Aliens Immigration Restriction Act	South Africa
	Apostolicae Curae	Papacy, Britain
	Russio-Chinese Treaty of 1896	Russia, China
	German Civil Code	Germany
1897	Olney-Pauncefote Treaty	United States, Britain
	Dingley Tariff Act	United States
	Basel Declaration of 1897 (Basel Program)	Switzerland, Palestine
	Badeni Languages Ordinances	Austria-Hungary, Bohemia, Moravia
	Twain's "Horrors of the German Language"	United States, Vienna, Austria
	"Yes, Virginia, there is a Santa Claus"	New York (United States)
	Crow's Nest Pass Agreement	Canada
	Hawaiian Treaty of 1897	United States
1898	J'accuse	France
	Holden v. *Hardy*	United States
	McKinley's War Message	United States, Cuba, Spain
	Rosen-Nishi Agreement (Russo-Japanese Agreement of 1898)	Japan, Russia, Korea, China
	Teller Resolution	United States
	De Lôme Letter	Cuba, Spain, United States
	Anglo-German Agreement of 1898	Britain, Germany, Portugal, Africa
	German Naval Laws of 1898 and 1900	Germany
	Paris, Treaty of	Spain, Cuba, Philippines, United States
1899	February Manifesto	Russia, Finland
	Roosevelt's "Strenuous Life" Speech	United States
	Addyston Pipe and Steel Co. v. *United States*	United States
	Condominium Agreements of 1899	Britain, Egypt, Sudan
	Message to [from] Garcia	United States, Cuba
	Anglo-German Treaty of 1899 (Samoan Treaty)	Samoa, Britain, Germany
	Hay's Circular Letter of 1899	United States, China
	Evolutionary Socialism	Germany
	American Anti-Imperialist League, Platform of the	United States, Philippines
1900	Ariel, Rodó's	Uruguay
	Gold Standard Act of 1900, U.S.	United States
	Foraker Act	United States, Puerto Rico
	Hay's Circular Letter of 1900	United States, Europe, Japan
	Yangtze Agreement	China, Britain, Germany
1901	Associations Law, French	France
	De Lima v. *Bidwell*	United States, Puerto Rico
	Twain's "To a Person Sitting in Darkness"	United States
	Taff Vale Case	England
	Pacific Island Laborers' Act	Australia, Pacific islands
	Platt Amendment	United States, Cuba
	Hay-Pauncefote Treaties	United States, Britain, Central America
	Cuban Constitution of 1901	Cuba
1902	Newlands Act (Newlands Reclamation Act, U.S. National Reclamation Act)	United States
	Crown Lands Ordinance of 1902	Britain, East Africa
	Balfour Act (Education Act of 1902)	Britain
	Imperialism, A Study	Britain
	Immigration Restriction Act of 1902, Australian (White Australia Policy)	Australia
	Philippine Government Act (Organic Act) of 1902	United States, Philippines
	Drago Doctrine	Argentina, Europe
	What Is to Be Done?	Russia, Britain
	Spooner Act (Spooner Amendment to the Army Appropriations Act of 1901)	United States, Colombia, Panama
	Vereeniging, Treaty of	South Africa
	Anglo-Japanese Treaty of 1902	Britain, Japan, China, Korea
	Women's Christian Temperance Union (WCTU) Declaration of Principles	United States
	Chinese Exclusion Act of 1902	United States
	Workmen's Compensation Law, Maryland's	Maryland (United States)
	Franco-Italian Entente of 1902	France, Italy

DATE	DOCUMENT	AREA(S) INVOLVED
1903	Elkins Act	United States
	Hay-Herrán Treaty	United States, Colombia, Panama
	Congo Report, Casement's	Britain, Congo Free State
	Petrópolis, Treaty of	Brazil, Bolivia
	Protocols of the Elders of Zion	Russia
	Hay-Bunau-Varilla Treaty	United States, Panama
	Scott-Montcrieff Commission Report	Britain, India
	U.S.-Canadian Convention of 1903	United States, Britain, Alaska, British Columbia
1904	Entente Cordiale (Anglo-French Entente)	Britain, France, Egypt, Morocco, Siam, Suez Canal
	Wyndham's Land Purchase Act of 1903 (Irish Land Purchase Act of 1903)	Britain, Ireland
	Roosevelt Corollary	United States, Latin America
	Pan-German Creed of Lebensraum	Germany
	"Geographical Pivot of History"	Britain, Eurasia
	Northern Securities Company v. United States	United States
1905	Björko, Treaty of	Germany, Russia
	Lochner v. New York	United States
	Portsmouth, Treaty of	United States, Russia, Japan, Korea, Manchuria
	October Manifesto	Russia
	Sun Yat-sen's Three People's Principles	China
	Canadian Autonomy Bills of 1905	Alberta, Saskatchewan
	Norwegian-Swedish Treaty of Separation	Norway, Sweden
	Combes's Bill (French Law of Separation)	France
	Einstein's Special Relativity Theory	Germany, Switzerland
	Industrial Workers of the World, Preamble of the Constitution of the	United States
1906	Algeciras, Act of	Morocco, Spain, France, Russia, United States
	Persian Constitution of 1906	Persia
	Russian Fundamental Laws of 1906	Russia
	Nicholas II's Decree Dissolving the First Duma	Russia
	Stolypin's Agrarian Reform Act	Russia
	Meat Inspection Act of 1906, U.S.	United States
	Pure Food and Drug Act of 1906, U.S.	United States
	Viborg Manifesto	Russia, Finland
	Burke Act	United States
	Trade Disputes Act of 1906, British	Britain
	Hepburn Act	United States
1907	Asiatic Registration Bill of 1907, South African (Asiatic Law Amendment Act)	South Africa
	Pascendi Gregis	Papacy
	Creative Evolution (L'Evolution Créatrice)	France
	Anglo-Russian Entente of 1907	Britain, Russia
	Tobar Doctrine	Ecuador, Latin America
	Roosevelt's Conservation Message	United States
	Gentlemen's Agreement of 1907	United States, Japan, California
	Cartagena, Pact of	Britain, France, Spain
1908	*Loewe v. Lawlor* (Danbury Hatters' Case)	United States, Connecticut
	Adair v. United States	United States
	Root-Takahira Agreement	United States, Japan, China
	Muller v. Oregon	United States, Oregon
	Aldrich-Vreeland Act	United States
1909	London, Declaration of	Britain
	Payne-Aldrich Tariff Act (U.A. Tariff Act of 1909)	United States
	Indian Councils Act of 1909	India, Britain
	South Africa Act of 1909	South Africa, Britain
1910	Russo-Japanese Agreement of 1910	Russia, Japan, China, Manchuria
	Mann-Elkins Act	United States
	Mann Act (White Slave Traffic Act)	United States
	Roosevelt's "New Nationalism" Speech of 1910	United States
	Dawson Agreement	Nicaragua, United States
	San Luis Potosí, Plan of	Mexico
	Canadian Combines Investigation Act of 1910	Canada
	Canadian Naval Bill of 1910 (Naval Service Act of 1910)	Canada

DATE	DOCUMENT	AREA(S) INVOLVED
1910–13	*Principia Mathematica*	Britain
1911	Ayala, Plan of	Mexico
	Parliament Act of 1911, British	Britain
	National Progressive Republican League's Declaration of Principles	United States
	Franco-German Agreement of 1911	France, Germany, Morocco, French Congo
	Standard Oil Company of New Jersey et al. v. *United States*	United States
	American Tobacco Company v. *United States*	United States
	National Insurance Act of 1911, British	Britain
	Coyle v. *Smith*	United States
	Credaro Act	Italy
1912	Roosevelt's "Confession of Faith" Speech	United States
	Ouchy Convention	Belgium, Netherlands, Luxembourg
	Lausanne, Treaty of	Italy, Ottoman Empire, Libya
	Lodge Corollary (Magdalena Bay Resolution)	United States, Japan, California
	Wilson's "What Is Progress?" Speech	United States
	Wilson's "Old Order Changeth" Speech	United States
	Belfast (Ulster) Covenant of 1912	Northern Ireland, Britain
	Vlorë Proclamation	Albania, Ottoman Empire
1913	Pujo Committee, Report of the	United States
	Wilson's First Inaugural Address	United States
	London, Treaty of	Ottoman Empire, Serbia, Montenegro, Bulgaria, Greece
	Bucharest, Treaty of	Bulgaria, Romania, Montenegro, Serbia, Greece
	Webb-Kenyon Act (U.S. Intestate Liquor Act of 1913)	United States
	Natives' Land Act, South African	South Africa
	Sixteenth Amendment, U.S,	United States
	Underwood-Simmons Tariff Act (Underwood Act, U.S. Tariff Act of 1913)	United States
	Wilson's Mobile Address	United States, Latin America
	Constantinople, Treaty of	Ottoman Empire, Bulgaria
	Federal Reserve Act of 1913, U.S. (Glass-Owen Act)	United States
	Home Rule Bill of 1913	Ireland, Britain
	Austrian Ultimatum to Serbia	Austria, Serbia
1914	Smith-Lever Act	United States
	Gandhi's Call for Non-Violence	India, Britain
	Welsh Disestablishment Bill of 1914	Britain, Wales
	War Measures Act, Canadian	Canada
	Bryan-Chamorro Treaty	United States, Nicaragua
	Federal Trade Commission Act of 1914	United States
	Thomson-Urrutia Treaty (Treaty of Bogotá)	United States, Colombia, Panama
	Clayton Anti-Trust Act	United States
	Common Sense About the War, Shaw's	Britain, Germany
	Harrison Act (Harrison Narcotic Law)	United States
	Wilson's Appeal for Neutrality	United States
1914–15	Defense of the Realm Acts, British	Britain
1915	A.B.C. Treaty	Argentina, Brazil, Chile
	Twenty-One Demands, Japan's	Japan, China
	Lusitania Notes, Wilson's	United States, Germany
	Coppage v. *Kansas*	United States
	"Too Proud to Fight" Speech, Wilson's	United States
	Defense of India Act, British	Britain, India
	La Follette Seamen's Act (Furuseth Act)	United States
	Guinn and Beal v. *United States*	United States
	London, Treaty of	Britain, France, Russia, Italy
1915–16	*Psychoanalysis, A General Introduction to (Vorlesungen zur Einführung in die Psychoanalyse)*	Austria, Germany
1916	Adamson Act	United States
	Gore-McLemore Resolution	United States
	Anglo-Russian-French Agreement about Asiatic Turkey (Sykes-Picot Agreement)	Britain, Russia, France, Ottoman Empire
	Sinn Fein Proclamation of 1916	Ireland, Britain
	Jones Act of 1916 (Organic Act of the Philippine Islands)	United States, Philippines
	Sussex Pledge	Germany, United States, France

DATE	DOCUMENT	AREA(S) INVOLVED
	U.S.-Danish Treaty of 1916	United States, Denmark, Virgin Islands
	Keating-Owen Act	United States
	Lucknow Pact	India
1917	Zimmermann Note	Germany, Mexico
	Mexican Constitution of 1917	Mexico
	Smith-Hughes Act	United States
	April Theses	Russia
	Selective Service Act of 1917, U.S.	United States
	Espionage Act of 1917, U.S.	United States
	Lansing-Ishii Agreement (U.S.-Japanese Agreement of 1917)	United States, Japan, China
	Order No. 1, Petrograd Soviet's (Proclamation of March 14, 1917)	Russia
	"Peace Without Victory" Speech, Wilson's	United States
	Canon Law, Code of (Codex Juris Canonici)	Papacy
	Wilson's War Message to Congress ("Make the World Safe for Democracy" Speech)	United States
	Lenin's Land Decree	Russia
	Lenin's Peace Decree	Russia
	Balfour Declaration	Britain, Palestine, Israel
	Corfu Declaration (Pact of Corfu)	Yugoslavia, Serbia, Croatia, Slovenia, Montengro
	Canadian Federal Income Tax Law (Income War Tax Act)	Canada
1918	Sedition Act of 1918, U.S.	United States
	Fourteen Points Speech, Wilson's	United States
	Hammer v. *Dagenhart*	United States
	Bucharest, Treaty of	Romania, Bulgaria, Austria-Hungary, Germany
	Railway Administration Act, U.S.	United States
	Webb-Pomerene Act	United States
	Batum, Treaty of	Ottoman Empire, Armenia
	Pittsburgh Convention	United States, Czechoslovakia
	Lansing Declaration	United States, Czechoslovakia
	Soviet Constitution of 1918 (Russian Constitution of 1918)	Soviet Russia
	State and Revolution (Gosudarstvo i Revolyutsiya)	Soviet Russia
	Mudros, Armistice of	Britain, Ottoman Empire
	Brest-Litovsk, Treaty of	Soviet Russia, Germany, Austria-Hungary, Ottoman Empire
	World War I Armistice	Germany, Allied powers
1919	Uruguayan Constitution of 1919	Uruguay
	Pueblo Speech, Wilson's	United States
	Rowlatt Acts	India, Britain
	Cave Commission Report	Britain, South Africa, Rhodesia
	Schenck v. *United States*	United States
	Gandhi's Announcement of a *Satyagraha* (Civil Disobedience) Struggle	India, Britain
	Pan-African Congress Resolutions of 1919	African countries
	Child Labor Act of 1919, U.S.	United States
	Volstead Act (National Prohibition Act)	United States
	Nurses Act of 1919, British	Britain, Wales
	Weimar Constitution	Germany
	Abrams v. *United States*	United States
	Anglo-Persian Agreement of 1919	Britain, Persia
	Rawalpindi, Treaty of	Afghanistan, Britain, India
	Versailles, Treaty of	Germany, Allied powers
	St.-Germain, Treaty of	Allied powers, Austria, Czechoslovakia, Italy
	Neuilly, Treaty of	Bulgaria, Allied powers
	League of Nations Convenant	Allied powers
	Wilson's Exposition of the League of Nations	United States
	Economic Consequences of the Peace	Britain
	Lodge Reservations	United States
1920	Tartu, Treaty of	Soviet Russia, Estonia
	Trianon, Treaty of	Allied powers, Hungary, Romania, Yugoslavia, Czechoslovakia, Austria
	Sèvres, Treaty of	Allied powers, Ottoman Empire (Turkey), North Africa, Arab Asia, Armenia, Kurdistan, Aegean Islands

DATE	DOCUMENT	AREA(S) INVOLVED
	Little Entente Treaties	Yugoslavia, Czechoslovakia, Romania
	Rapallo, Treaty of	Italy, Yugoslavia
	Alexandropol, Treaty of	Armenia, Turkey
	Declaration of Rights of Negro Peoples of the World	United States, Africa
	San Remo Agreements	Britain, France, Italy, Japan, Greece, Belgium, Iraq, Palestine, Syria, Lebanon
	Anglo-French Agreement on Oil in the Near and Middle East	Britain, France, Iraq, Iran, North Africa
	U.S. Policy on "Open Door" for Oil in the Near and Middle East	United States, Britain, Palestine, Iraq
	Black Man's Burden, The	Britain, Africa
	Riga, Treaty of	Soviet Russia, Latvia
	Moscow, Treaty of	Soviet Russia, Lithuania
	Esch-Cummins Act (Transportation Act of 1920)	United States
	Government of Ireland Act (Better Government of Ireland Act)	Britain, Northern and Southern Ireland
	Green v. *Frazier*	United States, North Dakota
	National Pact, Turkey's	Turkey
	Nineteenth Amendment, U.S.	United States
	Water Power Act of 1920, U.S.	United States
	Missouri v. *Holland*	United States
	Walker Law	New York (United States)
1921	Cave Commission Report	South Africa, Britain, Rhodesia
	Fundamental Law of 1921, Turkey's	Turkey
	Moscow, Treaty of	Soviet Russia, Turkey
	Riga, Treaty of	Poland, Soviet Russia
	De Valera's Letter on Irish Grievances	Ireland, Britain
	Ankara, Treaty of (Franklin-Bouillon Agreement)	Turkey, France
	Anglo-Irish Treaty of 1921	Britain, Ireland
	Emergency Quota Act, U.S. (Dillingham Immigration Act)	United States
	U.S.-German Peace Treaty of 1921 (Treaty of Berlin)	United States, Germany
	Kronshtadt Demands	Soviet Russia
	Sheppard-Towner Act	United States
	Kars, Treaty of	Soviet Russia, Turkey, Armenia, Azerbaijan, Georgia
	Bucharest, Treaty of	Poland, Romania
	Four Power Pacific Treaty (Treaty of Washington)	Japan, Britain, France, United States
1922	Five Power Naval Treaty (Treaty of Washington, Naval Armament Limitation Treaty)	United States, Italy, Britain, France, Japan
	Nine Power Pacts (Treaties of Washington)	United States, France, France, Japan, Italy, Belgium, Netherlands, China, Portugal
	Yap Treaty	Japan, United States, Yap (Caroline Islands)
	Bailey v. *Drexel Furniture Company* (Child Labor Tax Case)	United States
	Rapallo, Treaty of	Germany, Soviet Union
	Cable Act	United States
	Capper-Volstead Act (U.S. Cooperative Marketing Act)	United States
	Fordney-McCumber Act (U.S. Tariff Act of 1922)	United States
	Human Nature and Conduct	United States
	United States v. *Lanza*	United States
	Churchill White Paper of 1922	Britain, Palestine, Israel
	Balzac v. *Porto Pico*	United States, Puerto Rico
1923	Sun-Joffe Manifesto	China, Soviet Union
	Afghan Constitution of 1923 (Afghan Fundamental Law)	Afghanistan
	Tangier, Convention and Statute of	France, Britain, Spain, Tangier (Morocco)
	Gondra Treaty	Paraguay, Americas
	White Paper of 1923, British (Devonshire White Paper)	Britain, Kenya
	Mutual Assistance, Draft Treaty of	Europe
	Bill of Rights, Hawaiian	United States, Hawaii
	Wolff Packing Company v. *Court of Industrial Relations of Kansas*	United States, Kansas
	Halibut Treaty	United States, Canada, Pacific
	Adkins v. *Children's Hospital*	United States
	Lausanne, Treaty of	Turkey, Britain, Italy, France
	Equal Rights Amendment, U.S.	United States

DATE	DOCUMENT	AREA(S) INVOLVED
1924	Immigration Quota Act of 1924, U.S. (National Origins Act, Johnson-Reed Act)	United States
	Bonus Bill of 1924, U.S.	United States
	La Follette Platform of 1924	United States
	Geneva Protocol of 1924 (Protocol for the Pacific Settlement of International Disputes)	League of Nations
	Dawes Plan	Germany, Allies, United States
1925	Anglo-Italian Agreement of 1925 (Milner-Scialoja Agreement, Egyptian-Italian Treaty)	Italy, Britain, Egypt, Libya
	Mein Kampf (My Struggle)	Germany
	Chilean Constitution of 1925	Chile
	Gitlow v. *People of New York*	United States, New York
	Pierce v. *Society of Sister* (Oregon Parochial School Case)	United States, Oregon
	Locarno, Pact of (Locarno Security Treaties)	Germany, France, Belgium, Britain, Italy, Poland, Czechoslovakia
	Immigration Restriction Act of 1925, Australian	Australia
1926	Watson-Parker Act (U.S. Railway Labor Act of 1926)	United States
	Tirana, Treaty of	Albania, Italy
	Convention for the Suppression of Slavery, International	League of Nations, Africa, Turkey, Ethiopia, Liberia
	Myers v. *United States*	United States
1927	Vanzetti's Final Court Statement	United States
	Public Safety (Emergency Powers) Law of 1927, Irish	Ireland
	McNary-Haugen Bill	United States
	Trade Disputes and Trade Unions Act of 1927, British	Britain
1928	Nehru Report for a Constitution	India, Britain
	"Lincoln the Lover" Letters	United States
	Anglo-Chinese Treaty	Britain, China
	Hoover's "Rugged Individualism" Speech	New York (United States)
	Olmstead v. *United States*	United States
	Paris, Pact of (Kellogg-Briand Peace Pact)	United States, France
	Communist International (Comintern), Constitution and Rules of the	Soviet Union
	Clark Memorandum on the Monroe Doctrine	United States, Latin America
	Soviet Five Year Plan, First	Soviet Union
1929	Lateran Treaties of 1929	Italy, Papacy
	Inter-American Conciliation and Arbitration Treaties of 1929	Latin America, United States
	Soviet Law on Religious Bodies	Soviet Union
	Young Plan	United States, Germany
	Darrow's "Against Capital Punishment"	New York (United States)
	Tanaka Memorial	China, Japan
	Agricultural Marketing Act of 1929, U.S.	United States
1930	Indian Nationalist Congress "Independence Day" Resolution	India, Britain
	Anglo-Iraqi Treaty of 1930	Britain, Iraq
	Land Apportionment Act of 1930, Rhodesian	Rhodesia
	Estrada Doctrine	Mexico
	Smoot-Hawley Tariff Act	United States
	Canadian Tariff Act of 1930 (Dunning Tariff)	Canada
	Lewis's "American Fear of Literature" Speech	United States, Sweden
	Passfield Report (Passfield White Paper)	Britain, Palestine, Israel
	San Sebastián, Pact of	Spain
1931	*Quadragesimo Anno* (Pius XI's Encyclical of 1931)	Papacy
	Near v. *Minnesota*	United States
	Westminster, Statute of	Britain, Canada, Australia, New Zealand, South Africa, Ireland, Newfoundland
	Delhi Pact of 1931, Gandhi's (Gandhi-Irwin Pact)	India, Britain
	Spanish Constitution of 1931	Spain
	Afghan Constitution of 1931	Afghanistan
1932	American Federation of Labor, Constitution of the	United States
	Mussolini's Doctrine of Fascism	Italy
	Poona Pact of 1932	India, Britain
	Norris–La Guardia Anti-Injunction Act	United States

DATE	DOCUMENT	AREA(S) INVOLVED
	Seabury Commission Report	New York (United States)
	Layton-Wiggin Report	Germany, Britain, Switzerland
	Ouchy Convention	Belgium, Luxembourg, Netherlands
	British Protective Tariff Acts of 1932 (Import Duties Act)	Britain
1933	Roosevelt-Litvinov Correspondence	United States, Soviet Union
	Roosevelt's First Inaugural Address	United States
	Anglo-Persian Agreement of 1933	Britain, Persia
	Four Power Pact of 1933	Italy, Germany, France, Britain
	Bank Holiday Declaration, Roosevelt's	United States
	Emergency Banking Relief Act, U.S.	United States
	Federal Emergency Relief Act, U.S.	United States
	Enabling Act of 1933, German	Germany
	Banking Act of 1933, U.S. (Glass-Steagall Banking Act)	United States
	Civil Service Law of 1933, German	Germany
	Concordat of 1933	Germany, Papacy
	Agricultural Adjustment Act of 1933, U.S.	United States
	Twentieth Amendment, U.S.	United States
	Tennessee Valley Authority Act	United States
	Farm Credit Act, U.S.	United States
	Securities Act of 1933, U.S. (Truth-in-Securities Act)	United States
	Homeowners Refinancing Act, U.S.	United States
	Gold Repeal Resolution, U.S.	United States
	Twenty-First Amendment, U.S.	United States
	Anti-War Pact, Argentine	Argentina, Brazil, Chile, Paraguay, Mexico, Uruguay
1934	Gold Reserve Act of 1934, U.S.	United States
	Barmen Declaration (Theological Declaration of Barmen)	Germany, Switzerland
	Johnson Debt Default Act	United States
	Nebbia v. *New York*	United States
	Reciprocal Tariff Act, U.S. (Trade Agreements Act)	United States
	Tydings-McDuffie Act	United States, Philippines
	Homeowners' Loan Act, U.S.	United States
	Rome Protocols of 1934	Italy, Austria, Hungary
	National Housing Act of 1934, U.S.	United States
	Stalin's Decree of December 1, 1934	Soviet Union
	Federal Communications Act, U.S.	United States
	Balkan Pact (Balkan Entente)	Yugoslavia, Greece, Romania, Turkey
	Baltic Pact (Baltic Entente)	Lithuania, Latvia, Estonia
	Townsend Plan	United States
	Sanaa, Treaty of	Britain, Yemen
	Long's "Every Man a King" Speech	Louisiana (United States)
	Frazier-Lemke Farm Bankruptcy Act (Farm Mortgage Moratorium Act)	United States
	Securities Exchange Act, U.S.	United States
	Brazilian Constitution of 1934	Brazil
	Civil Works Emergency Relief Act, U.S.	United States
	Silver Purchase Act of 1934, U.S.	United States
	Wheeler-Howard Act (U.S. Indian Reorganization Act)	United States
1935	Social Security Act, U.S.	United States
	Wheeler-Rayburn Act (Public Utility Holding Company Act)	United States
	National Labor Relations Act, U.S. (Wagner-Connery Act)	United States
	Banking Act of 1935, U.S.	United States
	Anglo-German Naval Agreement of 1935	Britain, Germany
	Soil Conservation Act of 1935, U.S. (Soil Erosion Act)	United States
	Humphrey's Executor v. *United States* (*Rathbun* v. *United States*)	United States
	Franco-Russian Agreement of 1935	France, Soviet Union
	Guffey-Snyder Bituminous Coal Stabilization Act (Bituminous Coal Conservation Act)	United States
	Schecter Poultry Corporation v. *United States*	United States
	Government of India Act of 1935	Britain, India, Burma, Yemen
	Emergency Relief Appropriation Act, U.S.	United States
	Wealth-Tax Act, U.S. (Revenue Act of 1935)	United States
	Nürnberg Laws	Germany

DATE	DOCUMENT	AREA(S) INVOLVED
1936	London Naval Treaty of 1936	Britain, France, United States
	Soil Conservation and Domestic Allotment Act, U.S.	United States
	Austro-German Agreement of 1936	Austria, Germany
	Walsh-Healy Governments Contract Act, U.S.	United States
	Anglo-Egyptian Treaty of 1936	Britain, Egypt
	United States v. *Butler et al.* (Hoosac Mills Case)	United States
	Natives' Trust and Land Act, South African	South Africa
	Hull-Alfaro Treaty (General Treaty of Friendship and Co-operation Between the U.S.A. and Panama)	United States, Panama
	Stalin Constitution (Soviet Constitution of 1936, Soviet Fundamental Law)	Soviet Union
	Robinson-Patman Act (Federal Anti-Price Discrimination Act)	United States
	Anti-Comintern Pact (German-Japanese Pact of 1936)	Germany, Japan, Italy
	Nazi Germany's Four-Year Plan	Germany
	Montreaux, Treaty of (Montreaux Straits Convention)	Australia, France, Bulgaria, Britain, Greece, Romania, Japan, Turkey, Soviet Union, Yugoslavia
	Merchant Marine Act (U.S. Ship Subsidy Act)	United States
	German-Italian Pact of 1936	Germany, Italy
	United States v. *Curtiss-Wright Export Corporation*	United States
	Edward VIII's Abdication Message	Britain
1937	Roosevelt's Second Inaugural Address ("One-Third of a Nation" Speech)	United States
	Steward Machine Company v. *Davis*	United States
	Bankhead-Jones Farm Tenant Act	United States
	Nyon Agreement	Britain, France, Russia, Italy, Mediterranean
	Judiciary Reorganization Bill, U.S.	United States
	National Labor Relations Board v. *Jones & Laughlin Steel Corporation*	United States
	Anglo-Italian Agreements of 1937 and 1938	Britain, Italy, Ethiopia, Spain
	Neutrality Act of 1937, U.S.	United States
	West Coast Hotel Company v. *Parrish*	United States
	Hossbach Memorandum (Hossbach Minutes)	Germany
	Guffey-Vinson Bituminous Coal Act, U.S.	United States
	Roosevelt's "Quarantine the Aggressors" Speech	United States
	Wagner-Steagall Act (National Housing Act of 1937)	United States
1938	Franco-German Pact of 1938	France, Germany
	Food, Drug, and Cosmetic Act, U.S.	United States
	Wheeler-Lea Act	United States
	Lima, Declaration of	Latin America, United States
	Vinson Naval Act (U.S. Naval Expansion Act)	United States
	Munich Agreement of 1938	Italy, Germany, Britain, France
	Civil Aeronautics Act, U.S. (Lea-McCarran Act)	United States
	Agricultural Adjustment Act of 1938, U.S.	United States
	Hitler's Berlin Sportpalast Speech (Hitler's Speech on the Munich Crisis)	Germany, Czechoslovakia
	Fair Labor Standards Act, U.S. (Wages and Hours Act)	United States
	Woodhead Report	Britain, Palestine, Israel, Jerusalem
1939	Roosevelt's "Hands Off the Western Hemisphere" Speech	United States, the Americas
	Hitler's Speech Replying to Roosevelt	Germany, Czechoslovakia, Danzig
	Molotov-Ribbentrop Pact (Hitler-Stalin Pact, Soviet-German Non-Aggression Treaty of 1939, Nazi-Soviet Pact)	Germany, Soviet Union, Poland, Baltic region
	Steel, Pact of (German-Italian Alliance of 1939)	Germany, Italy
	Panama, Declaration of	Latin America, United States
	Neutrality Act of 1939, U.S.	United States
	White Paper of 1939, British	Britain, Palestine, Israel
	Graves v. *New York ex rel. O'Keefe*	United States
	Hatch Act of 1939	United States
	Einstein's Letter of 1939	United States
	Coleman v. *Miller*	United States
	British Declaration of War in 1939	Britain, Germany
	Ankara, Pact of	Britain, France, Turkey

DATE	DOCUMENT	AREA(S) INVOLVED
1940	Cuban Constitution of 1940	Cuba
	Canadian Unemployment Insurance Act of 1940	Canada
	Alien Registration Act, U.S. (Smith Act)	United States
	Arita's "Greater East Asia Co-Prosperity Sphere"	Japan
	"Blood, Toil, Tears, and Sweat" Speech, Churchill's	Britain
	Havana, Act of (Declaration of Reciprocal Assistance and Cooperation for the Defense of the Nations of the Americas)	Latin America, United States
	Compiègne Armistice	France, Germany
	Burke-Wadsworth Act (Selective Training and Service Act)	United States
	"We Shall Never Surrender" Speech, Churchill's (Churchill's Speech After Dunkirk)	Britain
	Churchill's "Their Finest Hour" Speech	Britain
	Churchill's "So Much Owed" Speech	Britain
	De Gaulle's Speech of June 18, 1940	France, Britain
	Cantwell v. *Connecticut*	United States
	Ogdensburg Declaration	United States, Canada
	Axis Powers, Pact of the (German-Italian-Japanese Pact, Tripartite Pact)	Germany, Italy, Japan
1941	"Four Freedoms" Speech, Roosevelt's	United States
	United States v. *Darby Lumber Company*	United States
	Lend-Lease Act, U.S.	United States, Britain, Allies
	Moscow, Treaty of (Soviet-Japanese Non-Aggression Pact of 1941)	Soviet Union, Japan
	Hitler's Proclamation on Invading the Soviet Union	Germany, Soviet Union
	Anglo-Soviet Agreement of 1941	Britain, Soviet Union
	Roosevelt's War Message ("Day of Infamy" Speech)	United States
	Atlantic Charter	United States, Britain
	U.S. Declaration of War on Nazi Germany	United States, Germany
	Edwards v. *California*	United States, California
	Night and Fog Decree (Nacht und Nebel Erlass)	Germany
1942	United Nations Declaration of January 1, 1952	United States, Britain, Soviet Union, China, Australia, Belgium, Canada, Costa Rica, Cuba, Czechoslovakia, Dominican Republic, El Salvador, Greece, Guatemala, Haiti, Honduras, India, Luxembourg, Netherlands, New Zealand, Nicaragua, Norway, Panama, Poland, South Africa, Yugoslavia.
	Wannsee Protocol	Germany
	British Labour Party's Charter of Freedom for Colonial Peoples	Britain
	U.S.-Soviet Lend-Lease Agreement	United States, Soviet Union
	Executive Order 9066, U.S. (Japanese Relocation Order)	United States
	Biltmore Resolution	United States, Palestine, Israel
	Roosevelt's Statement on North African Policy	United States, France, North Africa
1943	Smith-Connally Anti-Strike Act (War Labor Disputes Act)	United States
	West Virginia Board of Education v. *Barnette*	United States
	Connally-Fulbright Resolutions	United States
	Moscow Conference Declarations of 1943	United States, Britain, China, Soviet Union
1944	Anzac Pact (Canberra Pact)	Australia, New Zealand
	GI Bill of Rights (Servicemen's Readjustment Act)	United States
	Smith v. *Allwright*	United States, Texas
	Geneva Declaration of European Resistance	France, Italy, Netherlands, Denmark, Norway, Poland, Czechoslovakia, Yugoslavia
	Education Act of 1944, British (Butler's Act)	England, Wales
	Canadian Family Allowances Act of 1944	Canada
	Bretton Woods Agreement	Australia, Belgium, Bolivia, Brazil, Canada, Chile, China, Colombia, Costa Rica, Cuba, Czechoslovakia, Dominican Republic, Ecuador, Egypt, El Salvador, Ethiopia, France, Greece, Guatemala, Honduras, Iceland, India, Iran, Iraq, Luxembourg, Mexico, Netherlands, Nicaragua, Norway, Panama, Paraguay, Peru, Philippines, Poland, South Africa, United Kingdom, United States, Uruguay, Venezuela, Yugoslavia

DATE	DOCUMENT	AREA(S) INVOLVED
1945	Yalta Agreement	United States, Britain, Soviet Union
	Chapultepec, Act of	United States, Latin America
	United Nations Charter	Argentina, Australia, Belgium, Bolivia, Brazil, Canada, Chile, Colombia, Costa Rica, Cuba, Czechoslovakia, Denmark, Dominican Republic, Ecuador, Egypt, El Salvador, Ethiopia, France, Greece, Guatemala, Honduras, India, Iran, Iraq, Lebanon, Liberia, Luxembourg, Mexico, Netherlands, New Zealand, Nicaragua, Norway, Panama, Paraguay, Peru, Philippines, Poland, Saudi Arabia, South Africa, Syria, Turkey, Soviet Union, United Kingdom, United States, Ukraine, Uruguay, Venezuela, Yugoslavia
	Hitler's Last Will and Political Testament	Germany
	Germany's Surrender in World War II	Germany, France, Soviet Union, Allied Powers
	Franck Report	United States, Japan
	White Paper of 1945, British	Britain, Burma
	Potsdam Declaration	United States, Britain, Soviet Union
	Truman's Announcement of the Atomic Bombing of Hiroshima	United States, Japan
	Sino-Soviet Treaty of 1945	China, Soviet Union
	Arab League Charter	Egypt, Syria, Iraq, Lebanon, Jordan, Saudi Arabia, Yemen
	Japan's Surrender in World War II	Japan, Australia, China, France, New Zealand, Netherlands, Britain, Soviet Union, United States
	Vietnamese Declaration of Independence	Vietnam, France, Japan
1946	Stalin's "Cold War" Speech	Soviet Union
	French Agreement on the Independence of Vietnam	France, Vietnam
	Truman's Statement on Fundamentals of American Foreign Policy	United States, Americas
	Taft's "Equal Justice Under Law" Speech	United States, Ohio
	French Constitution of 1946 (Constitution of the Fourth Republic)	France
	Bell Trade Act (Philippine Trade Act of 1946)	Philippines, United States
	Japanese Constitution of 1946	Japan
	Baruch's Proposals for the Control of Atomic Energy	United States
	Fulbright Act of 1946	United States
	Acheson-Lilienthal Report	United States
	Duncan v. *Kahanomoku*	United States, Hawaii
	Cheribon Agreement (Linggadjati Agreement)	Netherlands, Indonesia
	Brazilian Constitution of 1946	Brazil
	National Health Service Act, British	Britain
	"Iron Curtain" Speech, Churchill's	Britain, Missouri (United States)
1947	Paris, Treaties of	Allies, Italy, Romania, Hungary, Bulgaria, Finland, Czechoslovakia
	Everson v. *Board of Education*	United States, New Jersey
	Agricultural Act of 1947, British	Britain
	Marshal Plan (European Recovery Program)	Austria, Belgium, Denmark, France, West Germany, Britain, Greece, Iceland, Italy, Luxembourg, Netherlands, Norway, Sweden, Switzerland, Turkey, United States
	Taft-Hartley Act (Labor-Management Relations Act)	United States
	Indian Independence Act, British	India, Pakistan, Britain
	Truman Loyalty Oath	United States
	Truman Doctrine	United States, Soviet Union, Greece, Turkey
	Banking Bill, Australian	Australia
	Transport Act of 1947, British	Britain
	United Public Workers v. *Mitchell*	United States
	Communist Information Bureau (Cominform), Manifesto Establishing the	Soviet Union, Yugoslavia, Romania, Czechoslovakia, Bulgaria, Hungary, Poland, France, Italy
	National Security Act of 1947, U.S.	United States
	Crown Proceedings Act, British	Britain
	Rio Treaty (Rio Pact, Inter-American Treaty of Reciprocal Assistance)	United States, Latin America
	Electricity Act of 1947, British	Britain

DATE	DOCUMENT	AREA(S) INVOLVED
1948	Renville Agreement	Netherlands, Indonesia
	Vandenberg Resolution	United States
	Convention on the Prevention and Punishment of the Crime of Genocide	United Nations
	British Nationality Act of 1948, British	British Commonwealth of Nations
	British Nationality and New Zealand Citizenship Act	Britain, New Zealand
	Geneva Declaration of 1948	World Medical Association
	Selective Service Act of 1948, U.S.	United States
	Displaced Persons Act of 1948, U.S.	United States
	Israel's Proclamation of Independence	Israel, Palestine
	Ireland Act, Republic of	Ireland, Britain
	U.S. Note on Berlin Blockade and Airlift	United States, Soviet Union, West Germany, West Berlin
	Six-Power Agreement of 1948	Britain, France, Belgium, Netherlands, Luxembourg, United States, Ruhr (Germany)
	Brussels Treaty of 1948	Britain, France, Belgium, Netherlands, Luxembourg
	Watson Report	Britain, Gold Coast (Ghana)
	McCollum v. *Board of Education*	United States, Illinois
	Universal Declaration of Human Rights	United Nations
	Bogotá, Pact of (Inter-American Treaty on Pacific Settlement)	Latin America, United States
	World Council of Churches, Accord of the	World Council of Churches
1949	Truman's Inaugural Address	United States
	Organization of American States, Charter of the	Latin America, United States
	White Paper of 1949, U.S. (United States Relations with China)	United States, China
	Argentine Constitution of 1949	Argentina
	Geneva Conventions of 1949	International
	Basic Law of 1949, West German	West Germany
	South African Citizenship Act	South Africa, Britain
	North Atlantic Treaty (North Atlantic Pact)	Belgium, Britain, Canada, Denmark, France, Iceland, Italy, Netherlands, Luxembourg, Norway, Portugal, United States
	Hague Agreement of 1949 (Round Table Conference Agreement)	Netherlands, Indonesia
	National Theatre Act, British	Britain, London
	Parliament Act of 1949, British	Britain
	Council of Europe, Statute of the	Britain, France, Belgium, Netherlands, Luxembourg, Ireland, Italy, Denmark, Sweden, Norway
1950	Stockholm Resolution	Sweden, Britain, France, United States, Soviet Union, China
	Manifesto of the Second World Peace Congress	World Peace Congress in Warsaw, Poland
	Colombo Plan for Cooperative Development	Britain, India, Pakistan, Ceylon (Sri Lanka), Singapore, Malaysia, Borneo
	Sino-Soviet Treaty of 1950	China, Soviet Union, Japan
	Faulkner's "Nobel Prize Speech"	Sweden, United States
	Nehru-Liaquat Pact (Delhi Pact of 1950)	India, Pakistan
	Schuman Plan	France, Germany, Italy, Netherlands, Belgium, Luxembourg
	European Convention for the Protection of Human Rights and Fundamental Freedoms	Council of Europe
	Polish–East German Agreement of 1950 (Warsaw Agreements)	East Germany, Poland
	Group Areas Act of 1950, South African	South Africa
	McCarran Act (Internal Security Act of 1950, Subversive Activities Control Act)	United States
1951	Japanese Peace Treaty of 1951	Japan, International (49 nations)
	U.S.-Japanese Treaty of 1951	United States, Japan
	European Coal and Steel Community, Treaty of the	France, West Germany, Benelux countries
	Native Land Husbandry Act, Rhodesian	Rhodesia
	ANZUS Pact	Australia, New Zealand, United States
	Canadian Old Age Security Act of 1951	Canada
	MacArthur's "Old Soldiers Never Die" Speech	United States

DATE	DOCUMENT	AREA(S) INVOLVED
	Universal Training and Selective Service Act, U.S.	United States
	Massey Commission Report	Canada
	Dennis et al. v. *United States*	United States
1952	West German Peace Contract	Britain, France, United States, West Germany
	Puerto Rican Constitution of 1952	United States, Puerto Rico
	Adler v. *Board of Education*	United States
	McCarran-Walter Act (Immigration and Nationality Act)	United States
	Nixon's "Checkers" Speech	United States
	Youngstown Steel and Tube Company v. *Sawyer*	United States
	Stevenson's Acceptance Speech	United States
	Stevenson's "Nature of Patriotism" Speech	New York City (United States)
1953	Public Safety Law of 1953, South African	South Africa
	Anglo-Egyptian-Sudan Treaty of 1953	Britain, Egypt
	Bricker Amendmant	United States
	Korean War Armistice	United Nations, North and South Korea, United States
	Refugee Relief Act of 1953, U.S.	United States
	Eisenhower's "Atoms For Peace" Speech	United Nations
1954	Sino-Soviet Treaty of 1954	Soviet Union, China
	Eisenhower's "Domino Theory" Statement	United States
	Dulles's Speech Opposing the Spread of Communism "By Any Means"	New York City (United States)
	Geneva Agreements of 1954 (Indochina War Armistice)	France, Vietnam, Laos, Cambodia
	Brown v. *Board of Education of Topeka, Kansas*	United States
	Bolling v. *Sharpe*	United States
	SEATO Pact (Southeast Asia Defense Treaty, Manila Pact)	Britain, France, United States. Australia, New Zealand, Philippines, Pakistan, Thailand
	Espionage and Sabotage Act of 1954, U.S.	United States
	Trieste Agreement	Britain, United States, Italy, Yugoslavia
	Communist Control Act of 1954, U.S.	United States
	Atomic Energy Act, U.S.	United States
	U.S.-Taiwanese Pact of 1954	United States, Nationalist China (Taiwan)
1955	Western European Union Accord	Belgium, France, Britain, West Germany, Netherlands, Luxembourg, Italy
	Baghdad Pact (Middle East Treaty Organization)	Turkey, Iraq, Iran, Britain, Pakistan
	Bandung Resolutions	Indonesia, India, Burma, Ceylon, Pakistan
	Ullmann v. *United States*	United States
	Eisenhower's "Spirit of Geneva" Speech	Philadelphia (United States)
	Eisenhower's "Open Skies" Proposal	United States
	AFL-CIO, Constitution of the	United States
	Warsaw Pact	Soviet Union, Albania, Bulgaria, Czechoslovakia, East Germany, Hungary, Poland, Romania
	Freedom Charter	African National Congress, South Africa
1956	Bundestag Election Law	West Germany
	Khrushchev's "Positions of Strength" Speech	Moscow, Soviet Union
	Southern Manifesto on Integration	United States
	Franco-German Agreements of 1956	France, West Germany, Saar Basin
	Soviet-Japanese Peace Declaration of 1956	Soviet Union, Japan
	Highway Act of 1956, U.S.	United States
	British-Malayan Agreements of 1956 and 1957	Britain, Malaysia
1957	Rome, Treaties of	France, Belgium, Netherlands, Italy, Luxembourg, West Germany
	Eisenhower Doctrine	United States
	Civil Rights Act of 1957, U.S.	United States
	Roth v. *United States*	United States
	Berlin Declaration of 1957	United States, Britain, France, West Germany
	Eisenhower's Speech Concerning Little Rock	United States
	Wolfenden Report	Britain
1958	Benelux Economic Union Agreement	Belgium, Luxembourg, Netherlands
	NAACP v. *Alabama*	Alabama (United States)
	Cooper v. *Aaron*	United States
	French Constitution of 1958 (Constitution of the Fifth Republic)	France
	All-African People's Conference Resolutions of 1958	All-African People's Conference in Accra

DATE	DOCUMENT	AREA(S) INVOLVED
1959	British-Greek-Turkish Agreements of 1959	Cyprus, Britain, Greece, Turkey
	European Free Trade Association Agreement	Austria, Britain, Denmark, Portugal, Norway, Sweden, Switzerland
	Landrum-Griffin Act (Labor-Management Reporting and Disclosure Act)	United States
	Santiago, Declaration of	Latin America
	Antarctic Treaty of 1959	Argentina, Australia, Belgium, Chile, France, Japan, New Zealand, Norway, South Africa, Britain, United States, Soviet Union
	Nile River Distribution Agreement	Egypt, Sudan
	Uphaus v. *Wyman*	United States
	Debré Law	France
	Bantustan Program	South Africa
1960	Eisenhower's Statement about U-2 Affair	United States, Soviet Union
	Civil Rights Act of 1960, U.S.	United States
	Bill of Rights, Canadian	Canada
	Indus Waters Treaty	India, Pakistan
	Organization of Petroleum Exporting Countries, Pact of the	Iran, Iraq, Kuwait, Saudi Arabia, Venezuela
	United Nations Declaration on Decolonization	United Nations
	Organization for Economic Cooperation and Development, Pact of the	United States, Canada, Europe
1961	Eisenhower's Farewell Address	United States
	Mapp v. *Ohio*	Ohio (United States)
	Kennedy's Inaugural Address	United States
	Twenty-third Amendment, U.S.	United States
	Kennedy's Message on the Peace Corps	United States
	Mater et Magistra	Papacy
	Garner v. *Louisiana et al.*	United States
	Kennedy's Report on the Berlin Crisis	United States
	Castro's "I am a Marxist-Leninist" Speech	Cuba
	Kennedy's Appeal for Nuclear Disarmament	United Nations
1962	Salvadoran Constitution of 1962	El Salvador
	Pakistan Constitution of 1962	Pakistan (East and West)
	Engel v. *Vitale*	New York (United States)
	Kennedy's Address on the Removal of Soviet Weapons from Cuba	United States, Soviet Union, Cuba
	Baker v. *Carr*	Tennessee (United States)
1963	Franco-German Treaty of 1963 (Treaty on Franco-German Cooperation)	France, West Germany
	Gideon v. *Wainwright*	Florida (United States)
	U.S.-Soviet "Hotline" Agreement	United States, Soviet Union
	Kennedy's Speech at American University	Washington, D.C. (United States)
	Organization of African Unity, Charter of the	Africa colonies and states
	Pacem in Terris (Peace on Earth)	Papacy
	Nuclear Test Ban Treaty of 1963	United Kingdom, United States, Soviet Union
	General Law Amendment Act, South African (Sabotage Bill)	South Africa
	Peerage Act of 1963, British	Britain
	Clean Air Act of 1963, U.S.	United States
	King's "I Have a Dream" Speech	Washington, D.C. (United States)
	Kennedy's "Ich bin en Berliner" ("I am a Berliner") Speech	West Berlin (Germany)
	Johnson's United Nations Address of 1963	United Nations, United States
1964	*Smoking and Health*	United States
	Civil Rights Act of 1964, U.S.	United States
	Palestine National Charter (Palestine National Covenant)	Palestine, Israel
	Haitian Constitution of 1964	Haiti
	Escobedo v. *Illinois*	United States
	Reynolds v. *Sims*	United States
	Peruvian Agrarian Reform Law of 1964	Peru
	New York Times Company v. *Sullivan*	Alabama (United States)
	Goldwater's "Extremism in Defense of Liberty" Speech	United States
	Gulf of Tonkin Resolution	United States
	Warren Commission Report	United States

DATE	DOCUMENT	AREA(S) INVOLVED
	Economic Opportunity Act, U.S.	United States
	Concordat of 1964	Papacy, Hungary
	Twenty-fourth Amendment, U.S.	United States
	Central African Customs and Economic Union	Cameroon, Central African Republic, Congo, Equatorial Guinea, Gabon
	Anglo-French Channel Tunnel Agreement	Britain, France
	De Ecclesia (Of the Church)	Papacy
1965	Johnson's Inaugural Address	United States
	White Paper of 1965, U.S.	United States, Vietnam
	United States v. *Seeger*	United States
	Elementary and Secondary Education Act of 1965, U.S.	United States
	Johnson's Speech at Johns Hopkins University	Baltimore (United States)
	Convention on the Settlement of Investment Disputes	World Bank, 67 nations signed
	Honduran Constitution of 1965	Honduras
	Guatemalan Constitution of 1965	Guatemala
	Griswold v. *Connecticut*	Connecticut (United States)
	Nostra Aetate (Declaration on the Relation of the Church to non-Christian Religions)	Papacy
	National Housing Act of 1965, U.S.	United States
	Water Quality Act, U.S.	United States
	Voting Rights Act of 1965, U.S.	United States
	Immigration Act of 1965, U.S.	United States
1966	Tashkent Agreement	India, Pakistan, Soviet Union, United Nations
	Central African Customs and Economic Union	Cameroon, Central African Republic, People's Republic of the Congo, Gabon, Equatorial Guinea
	Miranda v. *Arizona*	United States
	Bill of Rights, International	United Nations
	Outer Space Treaty of 1966	United Nations
	Freedom of Information Act, U.S.	United States
	Bogotá, Declaration of	Colombia, Peru, Venezuela, Chile, Ecuador
1967	Air Quality Act of 1967, U.S.	United States
	Association of Southeast Asian Nations, Pact of the	Thailand, Malaysia, Indonesia, Singapore, Philippines
	Twenty-fifth Amendment, U.S.	United States
	Quotations from Chairman Mao Tse-tung	China
	Kampala, Treaty of (East African Cooperation Treaty)	Tanzania, Kenya, Uganda
	Declaration of American Presidents	Argentina, Brazil, Chile, Mexico, Paraguay, Peru, Uruguay, El Salvador, Costa Rica, Honduras, Nicaragua, Colombia, Venezuela, Bolivia, Panama, Guatemala, United States
	General Agreement on Tariffs and Trade (GATT)	International (46 nations)
	United Nations Resolution 242	United Nations, Middle East
	Brazilian Constitution of 1967	Brazil
1968	Kerner Commission Report	United States
	Two Thousands Words	Czechoslovakia
	Race Relations Bill of 1968, British	Britain
	Transport Act of 1968, British	Britain
	Antigua, Treaty of	Antigua, Barbados, Guyana, Jamaica, Trinidad and Tobago
	Nuclerar Non-Proliferation Treaty of 1968	United Nations
	Civil Rights Act of 1968, U.S.	United States
	Humanae Vitae (*Of Human Life*)	Papacy
	Political Interference Act, South African	South Africa
	Omnibus Crime Control and Safe Streets Act of 1968, U.S.	United States
1969	Nixon's Inaugural Address	United States
	Common Man's Charter, Ugandan	Uganda, East Africa
	Canadian Criminal Code Amendment Act	Canada
	Canadian Official Languages Act	Canada, Britain
	Brandenburg v. *Ohio*	United States
1970	National Environmental Policy Act, U.S.	United States
	Moynihan's Memorandum for President Nixon	United States
	Clean Air Act of 1970, U.S.	United States
	RICO Law (Racketeer Influenced and Corrupt Organizations Act)	United States

DATE	DOCUMENT	AREA(S) INVOLVED
	Organized Crime Control Act of 1970, U.S.	United States
	Public Order (Temporary Measures) Act of 1970, Canadian	Canada
	Offenses Against the State Act, Ireland's	Ireland
	Hatfield-McGovern (End-the-War) Amendment	United States
1971	*Pentagon Papers (History of U.S. Decision-Making Process on Vietnam Policy)*	United States
	Gillette v. *United States*	United States
	Twenty-sixth Amendment, U.S.	United States
	Industrial Relations Act of 1971, British	Britain
	Nixon's Speech Announcing a Freeze on Prices and Wages	United States
1972	*Health Consequences of Smoking*	United States
	U.S.-Chinese Communiqué of 1972 (Shanghai Communiqué)	United States, China
	Marcos's Martial Law Decree	Philippines
	Equal Employment Opportunities Act, U.S.	United States
	Four-Power Agreement of 1972	Britain, France, United States, Soviet Union, Berlin (West Germany)
	Equal Rights Amendment, U.S.	United States
	Strategic Arms Limitation Treaty of 1972 (SALT I)	United States, Soviet Union
	Anti-Ballistic Missile Treaty (ABM Treaty)	United States, Soviet Union
	United States v. *Earl Caldwell*	United States
	Furman v. *Georgia*	United States
1973	*Roe* v. *Wade*	United States
	West African Economic Community Treaty	Ivory Coast, Mali, Mauritania, Niger, Senegal, Upper Volta (Burkina Faso)
	War Powers Act of 1973, U.S.	United States
	United Nations Resolution 338	United Nations, Middle East
	Colombian Agrarian Reform Law of 1973	Colombia
	Caribbean Community and Common Market Agreement (Treaty of Chaguaramas)	Trinidad and Tobago, Guyana, Barbados, Jamaica
	Miller v. *California*	United States
	Group Areas Act of 1973, South African	South Africa
1974	International Energy Agency Agreement	Western Europe (except France and Finland), Canada, Japan, Turkey, Britain, United States
	United Nations Resolution 3236	International, Palestine, Israel
1975	Lomé Convention	46 African, Caribbean, and Pacific countries
	Sex Discrimination Act, British	Britain
	Helsinki Accord	United States, Canada, and 33 European countries
1976	Carter's Inaugural Address	United States
	Aboriginal Land Rights Act of 1976	Australia
	Runyon v. *McCrary et al.*	United States
	Cuban Constitution of 1976	Cuba
1977	Charter 77, Czech	Czechoslovakia
	Soviet Constitution of 1977	Soviet Union
1978	Humphrey-Hawkins (Full-Employment and Balanced Growth) Act	United States
	Panama Canal Treaties of 1978	United States, Panama
	Solzhenitsyn's Harvard Speech	United States
	Camp David Accords	United States, Egypt, Israel
	Ethics in Government Act, U.S.	United States
	University of California Regents v. *Allan P. Bakke*	California (United States)
1979	Strategic Arms Limitation Treaty of 1979 (SALT II)	United States, Soviet Union
	Iranian Constitution of 1979	Iran
1980	Reagan's First Inaugural Address	United States
	Fullilove v. *Klutznick*	United States
	Chilean Constitution of 1980	Chile
	Solidarity Charter	Poland
1981	Jaruzelski's Martial Law Decree	Poland
1982	Canadian Constitution Act of 1982	Canada, Britain
	United Nations Convention on the Law of the Sea	119 nations signed

DATE	DOCUMENT	AREA(S) INVOLVED
	Charter of Rights and Freedoms, Canadian	Canada
	Turkish Constitution of 1982	Turkey
	Boland Amendment	United States
1983	South African Constitution of 1983	South Africa
1984	*Grove City College* v. *Bell*	United States
	Grace Commission Report	United States
	Anglo-Chinese Treaty of 1984	Britain, China
	Lynch v. *Donnelly*	Rhode Island (United States)
	United Nations Convention Against Torture (and other Cruel, Inhuman or Degrading Treatment or Punishment)	United Nations
1985	Gramm-Rudman-Hollings Act	United States
	Anglo-Irish Accord of 1985 (Hillsborough Agreement)	Britain, Ireland
1986	Single European Act	Belgium, France, Netherlands, West Germany, Italy, Luxembourg, Denmark, Britain, Ireland, Greece, Spain, Portugal
	Bowers v. *Hardwick*	United States
	Reykjavík Agreement of 1986	United States, Soviet Union
	Stockholm Security Conference Treaty	35 nations signed
	National Organization for Women, Inc. v. *Scheidler*	United States
1987	Haitian Constitution of 1987	Haiti
	Meech Lake Accord	Canada
	Intermediate Nuclear Forces Treaty (INF Treaty)	United States, Soviet Union
	Philippine Constitution of 1987	Philippines
	Montreal Protocol of 1987	24 nations signed, including Canada, United States, Japan, Europe's Common market countries
	Central American Peace Plan (Guatemala Accord, Arias Peace Plan)	Costa Rica, El Salvador, Honduras, Nicaragua, Guatemala
	Soviet Law on State Enterprise	Soviet Union
1988	U.S.-Canadian Free Trade Agreement of 1988	United States, Canada
	New York State Club Association v. *City of New York*	New York (United States)
	Brazilian Constitution of 1988	Brazil
	Morrison v. *Olson*	United States
	Education Reform Act of 1988, British	Britain
	Civil Rights Restoration Act, U.S.	United States
	Fair Housing Amendments Act, U.S.	United States
	Berne Bill, U.S.	United States
	Namibian Agreement of 1988	South Africa, Angola, Cuba
	Trade Act of 1988, U.S.	United States
	HAMAS Covenant	Palestine, Israel
	Medicare Catastrophe Coverage Act, U.S.	United States
	Estonian Declaration of Sovereignty of 1988	Estonia, Soviet Union
	Gorbachev's United Nations Speech of 1988	United Nations, Soviet Union
	Arafat's Geneva Speech of 1988	Palestine, Israel, United Nations
1989	Cologne Declaration	West Germany, Austria, Switzerland, Netherlands, Papacy
	Bush's Inaugural Address	United States
	Worker Adjustment and Retraining Notification Act, U.S.	United States
	Texas v. *Johnson*	Texas (United States)
	Webster v. *Reproductive Health Services*	Missouri (United States)
1990	De Klerk's "Season of Violence Is Over" Speech	South Africa
	Soviet New Party Platform of 1990	Soviet Union
	Havel's Address to Congress	Czechoslovakia, United States
	Americans with Disabilities Act	United States
	Oil Pollution Act of 1990, U.S. (OPA90)	United States
	Soviet Constitutional Amendments of 1990	Soviet Union
	Instruction on the Ecclesial Vocation of the Theologian	Papacy
	Poll Tax of 1990, British	Britain
	Latvian Declaration of Independence of 1990	Latvia, Soviet Union
	German "State Treaty" of 1990	East and West Germany
	German Unification Treaty (Second "State Treaty")	East and West Germany
	Rutan v. *Republican Party of Illinois*	Illinois (United States)
	U.S.-Japanese Treaty of 1990	United States, Japan

DATE	DOCUMENT	AREA(S) INVOLVED
	London, Declaration of (1990)	Britain, The Hague
	Ukrainian Declaration of Sovereignty of 1990	Ukraine, Soviet Union
	United Nations Resolution 661	International, Iraq, Kuwait
	United Nations Resolution 678	International, Iraq, Kuwait
	Two-Plus-Four Treaty (Treaty on the Final Settlement with Respect to Germany)	East and West Germany, Britain, France, United States, Soviet Union
	Conventional Forces in Europe, Treaty on	NATO and Warsaw Pact countries
	Clean Air Act of 1990, U.S.	United States
	Charter of Paris for a New Europe	Europe
	Soviet Law on Freedom of Conscience	Soviet Union
	Immigration Act of 1990, U.S.	United States
1991	Taiwanese Declaration of 1991	Taiwan, China
	START-1 Treaty (Treaty on the Reduction and Limitation of Strategic Offensive Arms)	United States, Soviet Union
	Chechnyan (Chechen) Declaration of Independence	Chechnya, Soviet Union
	Baltic States Declaration of Independence	Estonia, Latvia, Lithuania
	Minsk Agreement (Commonweath Pact)	Russia, Ukraine, Belarus
	Maastricht Treaty (Treaty on European Union)	Belgium, France, Italy, Luxembourg, Netherlands, Spain, Germany, Britain, Ireland, Denmark, Greece, Portugal
	Alma-Ata Declaration	Armenia, Azerbaijan, Belarus, Kazakhstan, Kyrgyzstan, Moldova, Tajikistan, Turkmenistan, Uzbekistan, Ukraine, Russian Federation
	Simon & Schuster v. *New York State Crime Victims Board*	United States
1992	START-2 Treaty (Memorandum of Joint Understanding on Nuclear Arms Reductions)	United States, Russian Federation
	Lee v. *Weisman*	Rhode Island (United States)
	North American Free Trade Agreement (NAFTA)	Canada, Mexico, United States
	Planned Parenthood v. *Casey*	Pennsylvania (United States)
	Rio Declaration	172 nations signed
	Priests (Ordination of Women) Measure	Church of England
	Catechism of the Catholic Church, New	Papacy
1993	Clinton's First Inaugural Address	United States
	Family and Medical Leave Act, U.S.	United States
	Vienna Declaration and Program of Action	171 nations signed
	Veritatis Splendor (The Splendor of Truth)	Papacy
	Shaw v. *Reno*	North Carolina (United States)
	Oslo Accords	Israel, Palestine
	Brady Handgun Violence Prevention Act (Brady Bill)	United States
	Downing Street Declaration of 1993	Britain, Ireland, Northern Ireland
	Russian Constitution of 1993	Russian Federation
1994	Ukraine Disarmament (Denuclearization) Accord	Ukraine, Russia, United States
	Israeli-Jordanian Treaty of 1994	Israel, Jordan
1995	*Hurley* v. *Irish-American Gay, Lesbian and Bisexual Group of Boston*	Boston (United States)
	Human Generis Unitas (On the Unity of Mankind)	Papacy, France
	Dayton Peace Accord	Bosnia, Herzegovina, Croatia, Yugoslavia
	Unabomber Manifesto (Industrial Society and Its Future)	United States
1996	Communications Decency Act, U.S.	United States
	Megan's Law (Sex Offender Notification Bill)	United States
	Health Insurance and Portability and Accountability Act (HIPAA), U.S.	United States, New Jersey
	Child Pornography Prevention Act of 1988, U.S. (Child Pornography Protection Act)	United States
	Defense of Marriage Act, U.S.	United States
	Aviation Security and Antiterrorism Act of 1996, U.S.	United States
	Helms-Burton Act (Cuban Liberty and Democratic Solidarity [LIBERTAD] Act)	United States
	World Intellectual Property Organization, Treaties of the	International
1997	Clinton's Second Inaugural Address	United States
	Death with Dignity Act, Oregon's	Oregon (United States)
	Declaration of Repentance	France
	Earl Spencer's Eulogy to Princess Diana	Britain

DATE	DOCUMENT	AREA(S) INVOLVED
	Convention on the Prohibition of the Use, Stockpiling, Production and Transfer of Antipersonnel Mines and Their Destruction	International (140 nations signed by 2001)
	Taxpayer Relief Act of 1997, U.S.	United States
	Reno v. *American Civil Liberties Union*	United States
	Kyoto Protocol	United Nations, 160 nations signed
1998	"We Remember: A Reflection on the Shoah"	Papacy
	Good Friday Agreement (Northern Ireland Peace Agreement)	Northern Ireland, Ireland, Britain
	U.S.-China "Hotline" Agreement	United States, China
	Declaration Concerning Religion, Ethics, and the Crisis in the Clinton Presidency	International, United States
	International Religious Freedom Act (IRFA), U.S.	United States
	National Organization for Women, Inc. v. *Scheidler*	United States
	Yeltsin's Presidential Decree of 1998	Russia
	Truth and Reconciliation Commission Report, South African	South Africa
	Tobacco Companies Settlement Agreement (Master Settlement Agreement)	United States
	Wye River Memorandum	Israel, Palestine, United States
1999	*Impuls 99*	Czech Republic
	Doctrine of Justification, Joint Declaration on the	Papacy, Lutheran World Federation
	Financial Services Modernization Act, U.S. (Gramm-Leach-Bliley Act)	United States
2000	*Dickerson* v. *United States*	Virginia (United States)
	Boy Scouts of America v. *Dale*	New Jersey (United States)
	Dominus Iesus Declaration	Papacy
	Putin's Statement of Principles (Joint Statement of the Presidents of the United States of America and the Russian Federation on Principles of Strategic Stability)	Russia, United States
	Vermont Civil Union Act (An Act Relating to Civil Unions)	Vermont (United States)
	Religious Land Use and Institutionalized Persons Act, U.S.	United States
	Bush v. *Gore (George W. Bush* v. *Albert A. Gore)*	United States
	Terrorism Act of 2000, British	Britain
2001	Bush's Inaugural Address, George W.	United States
	Illinois v. *McArthur*	Illinois (United States)
	Whitman v. *American Trucking Association*	United States
	United Nations Declaration of Commitment on HIV/AIDS	United Nations (189 countries)
	Bush's "Freedom and Fear Are at War" Speech	United States
	United Nations Resolution 1373	United Nations, International
	Anti-Terrorism Act, Canadian	Canada
	USA-PATRIOT Act (Uniting and Strengthening America by Providing Appropriate Tools Requiring to Intercept and Obstruct Terrorism Act)	United States
2002	No Child Left Behind Act (U.S. Education Reform Act of 2002)	United States
	International Criminal Court, Rome Statute of the (Charter of the International Criminal Court)	Netherlands, United Nations
	Atkins v. *Virginia*	United States
	Bipartisan Campaign Reform Act of 2002, U.S. (McCain-Feingold Bill, Shays-Meehan Bill)	United States
	Ashcroft v. *The Free Speech Coalition*	United States
	Moscow, Treaty of (Strategic Offensive Reductions Treaty)	United States, Russia
	United Nations Resolution 1402	Israel, United Nations
	Sarbanes-Oxley Act	United States
	Enhanced Border Security and Visa Entry Reform Act, U.S.	United States

ENTRIES BY CATEGORY

The appendix lists the book's entries (documents) alphabetically subdivided by topic or polity (nation, state, empire). If a reader does not find a particular heading (Sweden, for instance), he or she should look under another, related category (Scandinavia, in this instance). There are 35 headings in the appendix, including "International (Miscellaneous)," as shown below.

Africa
Ancient History
Asia
Australia and New Zealand
Austria and Switzerland
Belgium and the Netherlands
Brazil
Byzantine Empire
Canada

Caribbean
China
England and Great Britain
Europe
France
Holy Roman Empire
India
International Arms Agreements
International (Miscellaneous)

Ireland
Israel
Italy
Japan
Latin America
Mexico
Ottoman Empire and Turkey
Papacy
Philosophy

Religion
Rome and the Roman Empire
Russia and the Soviet Union
Scandinavia
Science and Technology
South Africa
Spain and Portugal
United States of America

AFRICA

Abydos, Tablet of
Addis Ababa, Treaty of (1896)
Algeciras, Act of
Aliens Immigration Restriction Act
Anglo-Egyptian Sudan Treaty of 1953
Anglo-Egyptian Treaty of 1936
Anglo-Italian Agreement of 1925 (Milner-Scialoja Agreement, Egyptian-Italian Treaty)
Anglo-Italian Agreements of 1891
Anglo-Italian Agreements of 1937 and 1938
Antarctic Treaty of 1959
Arab League Charter
Asiatic Registration Bill of 1907, South African (Asiatic Law Amendment Act)
Bantustan Program
Berlin Act of 1885
Black Man's Burden, The
British Nationality Act of 1948
Brussels Act of 1890 (General Act of Brussels)
Camp David Accords
Cave Commission Report
Central African Customs and Economic Union
Common Man's Charter, Ugandan
Condominium Agreements of 1899
Congo Report, Casement's
Congo Treaty of 1894

Crown Lands Ordinance of 1902
de Klerk's "Season of Violence Is Over" Speech
Dufferin Proposals (Dufferin Report)
East African Cooperation Treaty (Kampala, Treaty of)
Eisenhower Doctrine
Egyptian-British Treaty of 1936 (Anglo-Egyptian Treaty of 1936)
Egyptian-Italian Treaty (Anglo-Italian Agreement of 1925)
Franco-Italian Entente of 1902
Freedom Charter
Gambetta Note
General Act of Brussels
General Law Amendment Act, South African (Sabotage Bill)
Glen Grey Act
Granville Circular
Group Areas Act of 1950, South African
Group Areas Act of 1973, South African
Harare Declaration (Freedom Charter)
Heligoland Agreement
Israeli-Egyptian Peace Treaty
Kampala, Treaty of (East African Cooperation Treaty)
Kruger Telegram
Kütahya, Convention of
Land Apportionment Act of 1930, Rhodesian

Lomé Convention
London, Treaty of (1840)
Namibian Agreement of 1988
Nationality and Flag Act, South African
Native Land Husbandry Act, Rhodesian
Natives' Land Act, South African
Natives' Trust and Land Act, South African
Nile River Distribution Agreement
Organic Act of 1883
Organization of African Unity, Charter of the
Pan-African Congress Resolutions of 1919
Pass Laws, South African (Freedom Charter)
Political Interference Act, South African
Public Safety Law of 1953, South African
Race Relations Bill of 1968, British
Rhodesian Native Land Husbandry Act (Native Land Husbandry Act, Rhodesian)
Roosevelt's Statement on North African Policy
Rosetta Stone
Sabotage Bill (General Law Amendment Act, South African)
Separate Amenities Act, South African

Canadian Unemployment Insurance Act of 1940
Canadian War Measures Act (War Measures Act, Canadian)
Charter of Rights and Freedoms, Canadian
Churchill's "So Much Owed" Speech
Constitution Act of 1791, British
Crow's Nest Pass Agreement
Dunning Tariff (Canadian Tariff Act of 1930)
Durham's Report
Elgin-Marcy Treaty (Reciprocity Treaty)
Federal Income Tax Law, Canadian (Canadian Federal Income Tax Law)
Fielding Tariff Act (Canadian Preferential Tariff of 1897)
Ghent, Treaty of
Halibut Treaty
Helsinki Accord
Henry Letters
Howe's Letters to Lord John Russell
Hudson's Bay Company Charter
Hyde Park Declaration
International Energy Agency Agreement
Jesuit Estates Act
Laurier's "Political Liberalism" Speech
Manitoba Act of 1870
Massey Commission Report
Meech Lake Accord
Montreal, Treaty of
Montreal Protocol of 1987
Ninety-Two Resolutions, Papineau's
North American Air Defense Agreement
North American Free Trade Agreement (NAFTA) (1992)
Northwest Territories Act of 1875
Nova Scotia's General Assembly, Proclamation for
Ogdensburg Declaration
Organization for Economic Cooperation and Development, Pact of the
Papineau's Ninety-Two Resolutions (Ninety-Two Resolutions, Papineau's)
Public Order (Temporary Measures) Act of 1970, Canadian
Russell's Ten Resolutions (Ten Resolutions, Russell's)
Quebec, Treaty of
Quebec Act

Quebec Resolutions (Seventy-Two Resolutions, Canadian)
Rebellion Losses Bill, Canadian
Reciprocity Treaty (Elgin-Marcy Treaty)
Rowell-Sirois Report (Sirois Commission Report)
St. Lawrence Seaway Treaties
Sirois Commission Report (Rowell-Sirois Report)
Susa, Treaty of
Ten Resolutions, Russell's
Union, Act of (Union of Upper and Lower Canada)
U.S.-Canadian Convention of 1903
U.S.-Canadian Free Trade Agreement of 1988
War Measures Act, Canadian
Washington, Treaty of (1842) (Webster-Ashburton Treaty)
Webster-Ashburton Treaty (Ashburton Treaty, Treaty of Washington)
Westminster, Statute of (1931)

CARIBBEAN

Antigua, Treaty of
Black Code of Louis XIV (Code Noir)
Burgos, Concordat of
Burgos, Laws of
Caribbean Community and Common Market Agreement (Treaty of Chaguaramas)
Castro's "I Am a Marxist-Leninist" Speech
Chaguaramas, Treaty of (Caribbean Community and Common Market Agreement)
Cuban Constitution of 1901
Cuban Constitution of 1940
Cuban Constitution of 1976
de Lôme Letter
Haitian Constitution of 1964
Haitian Constitution of 1987
Indies, New Laws of the (New Laws of the Indies)
Jones Act of 1917 (Organic Act for Puerto Rico)
Kennedy's Address on Removal of Soviet Weapons from Cuba
Leyes Nuevas (New Laws of the Indies)
Lomé Convention
McKinley's War Message
Message to (from) García
Molasses Act
Namibian Agreement of 1988

New Laws of the Indies (New Laws of the Indies for the Good Treatment and Preservation of the Indians)
Organic Act for Puerto Rico (Jones Act of 1917)
Ostend Manifesto
Paris, Treaty of (1898)
Platt Amendment
Puerto Rican Constitution of 1952
Roosevelt Corollary
Roosevelt's "Strenuous Life" Speech
Sugar Act of 1764 (Sugar Revenue Act)
Teller Resolution
U.S.-Danish Treaty of 1916

CHINA

Aigun, Treaty of (Peking, Treaty of) (1860)
Anglo-Chinese Treaty of 1928
Anglo-Chinese Treaty of 1984
Arita's "Greater East Asia Co-Prosperity Sphere" Speech
Art of War
Boxer Protocol
Burlingame Treaty
Chefoo (Yentai) Convention
Chinese-British Treaty of 1928 (Anglo-Chinese Treaty of 1928)
Chinese Engagement
Chinese Exclusion Act of 1882
Chinese Exclusion Act of 1892
Chinese Exclusion Act of 1902
Confucian *Analects*
Declaration of the Four States on the Question of General Security (Moscow Conference Declarations of 1943)
Geneva Declaration of 1954
Hay's Circular Letter of 1899
Hay's Circular Letter of 1900
Japan's Surrender in World War II
Japan's Twenty-one Demands (Twenty-one Demands, Japan's)
Khrushchev's "Positions of Strength" Speech
Lansing-Ishii Agreement (U.S.-Japanese Agreement of 1917)
Lytton Commission Report
Mao's "Little Red Book" (*Quotations from Mao Tse-tung*)
Morey Letter
Moscow Conference Declarations of 1943
Nanking, Treaty of
Nine Power Pacts (Treaties of Washington)

Orkhon Inscriptions (Turkish Runes)
Peking, Peace of
Peking, Treaty of (1860)
Quotations from Chairman Mao Tse-tung
Reed Treaty (U.S.-Chinese Treaty of 1858)
Root-Takahira Agreement
Russo-Chinese Treaties of 1945, 1950, and 1954 (Sino-Soviet Treaty of 1945, Sino-Soviet Treaty of 1950, Sino-Soviet Treaty of 1954)
Russo-Chinese Treaty of 1896
St. Petersburg, Treaty of (1881)
Shanghai Communiqué (U.S.-Chinese Communiqué of 1972)
Shimonoseki, Treaty of
Sino-Soviet Agreement of 1923 (Sun-Joffe Manifesto)
Sino-Soviet Treaty of 1945
Sino-Soviet Treaty of 1950
Sino-Soviet Treaty of 1954
Stockholm Resolution
Sun-Joffe Manifesto
Sun Yat-sen's Three People's Principles
Taiwanese Declaration of 1991
Tanaka Memorial
Tao Te Ching (Daodeching)
Tientsin, Treaty of
Treaty of Arbitration with China
Twenty-one Demands, Japan's
United States Relations with China (White Paper of 1949, U.S.)
U.S.-China "Hotline" Agreement
U.S.-Chinese Communiqué of 1972 (Shanghai Communiqué)
U.S.-Chinese Treaty of 1858 (Reed Treaty)
U.S.-Taiwanese Pact of 1954
Vinson Naval Act (U.S. Naval Expansion Act)
Wanghia, Treaty of
Washington, Treaties of (1922) (Nine Power Pacts)
White Paper of 1949, U.S. (United States Relations with China)
Yangtze Agreement

ENGLAND AND GREAT BRITAIN
Aberdeen Act
Act of Explanation (Explanation, Act of; Act of Settlement and Explanation)
Act of Seclusion (Seclusion, Act of)

Act of Settlement (1662) (Settlement, Act of)
Act of Settlement (1701) (Settlement, Act of)
Act of Six Articles (Six Articles, Act of)
Act of Succession (Succession, Act of) (1534)
Acts of Supremacy (Supremacy, Acts of)
Acts of Uniformity (Uniformity, Acts of)
Act of Union (1707) (Union of England and Scotland)
Act of Union (1840) (Union of Upper and Lower Canada)
Acts of Union (Union of Wales and England)
Administration of Justice Act
Adulteration (Sale) of Food and Drugs Act
Affirmation Bill, British
Age of Consent Act
Agreement of the People
Agricultural Act of 1947, British
Aix-la-Chapelle, Convention of
Aix-la-Chapelle, Treaty of (1668)
Aix-la-Chapelle, Treaty of (1748)
Albany Plan of Union
Aliens Immigration Restriction Act
Alinagar, Treaty of
American Prohibitory Act (Restraining Act of 1775, British)
Taxation Speech, Burke's
Amiens, Mise of
Amiens, Treaty of (1802)
Amritsar, Treaty of
Anglo-Brazilian Treaty of 1826
Anglo-Chinese Treaty of 1928
Anglo-Chinese Treaty of 1984
Anglo-Egyptian Sudan Treaty of 1953
Anglo-Egyptian Treaty of 1936
Anglo-French Agreement on Oil in the Near and Middle East
Anglo-French Channel Agreement
Anglo-French Entente (Entente Cordiale)
Anglo-French-Russian Agreement about Asiatic Turkey (Sykes-Picot Agreement)
Anglo-German Agreement of 1898
Anglo-German Naval Agreement of 1935
Anglo-German Treaty of 1899 (Samoan Treaty)
Anglo-Iraqi Treaty of 1930

Anglo-Irish Accord of 1985 (Hillsborough Agreement)
Anglo-Irish Treaty of 1921
Anglo-Italian Agreement of 1925 (Milner-Scialoja Agreement, Egyptian-Italian treaty)
Anglo-Japanese Commercial Treaty of 1894 (Aoki-Kimberley Treaty)
Anglo-Japanese Treaty of 1902
Anglo-Persian Agreement of 1919
Anglo-Russian Convention of 1755
Anglo-Russian Entente of 1907
Anglo-Soviet Agreement of 1941
Ankara, Pact of
Annates' Statutes
Antarctic Treaty of 1959
Aranjuez, Convention of (1779)
Arms, Assize of
Army Regulation Act of 1871, British
Artisans' Dwellings Act (Artizans' and Laborers' Dwellings Improvement Act)
Ashbourne Act (Irish Land Act of 1885)
Ashburton Treaty (Webster-Ashburton Treaty)
Assize of Clarendon (Clarendon, Assize of)
Assize of Darrien Presentment (Darrien Presentment, Assize of)
Assize of Northampton (Northampton, Assize of)
Assize of Woodstock (Woodstock, Assize of)
Association, The (Continental Association)
Augsburg, Treaty of the League of
Bacon's *Novum Organum*
Baghdad Pact (Middle East Treaty Organization)
Bald, Book of (Leech Book of Bald)
Balfour Act (Education Act of 1902)
Balfour Declaration
Bank Charter Act of 1844, British
Barrier Treaties
Bayard-Chamberlain Treaty
Bec, Compromise of (Compromise of 1107, English)
Belfast (Ulster) Covenant of 1912
Belgian Neutrality Treaty (Treaty of London)
Bering Sea Treaty
Berlin Act of 1889 (Samoa Act)
Berlin Declaration of 1957
Berlin Decree
Berwick, Pacification of (Dunse, Pacification of)

Waltham Black Act (Black Act)

Washington, Treaties of (1922) (Nine Power Pacts)

Washington, Treaty of (1842) (Webster-Ashburton Treaty)

Washington, Treaty of (1871)

Washington, Treaty of (1921) (Four Power Pacific Treaty)

Washington, Treaty of (1922) (Five Power Naval Treaty)

Watson Report

Wealth of Nations, An Inquiry into the Nature and Causes of the

Webster-Ashburton Treaty (Ashburton Treaty, Treaty of Washington)

Welsh Disestablishment Bill of 1914

"We Shall Never Surrender" Speech, Churchill's (Churchill's Speech After Dunkirk)

Western European Union Accord

Western Pacific Order in Council

West German Peace Contract

Westminster, Provisions of

Westminster, Statute of (1931)

Westminster, Statutes of

Westminster, Treaty of (1654)

Westminster, Treaty of (1674)

Westminster, Treaty of (1756) (Convention of Westminster)

Westminster Confession of Faith

Whiteboy Acts

White Paper of 1922, British (Churchill White Paper of 1922)

White Paper of 1923, British (Devonshire White Paper)

White Paper of 1930, British (Passfield Report)

White Paper of 1939, British

White Paper of 1945, British

Wills and Uses, Statutes of

Windsor, Treaty of

Wolfenden Report

Woodhead Report

Woodstock, Assize of (Assize of the Forest)

Woolens Act (Wool Act)

Workingman's Compensation Act of 1906, British

World War I Armistice

Wyndham's Land Purchase Act of 1903 (Irish Land Purchase Act of 1903)

Yalta Agreement

Yangtze Agreement

Zimmermann Note

EUROPE

Aarau, Treaty of

Altmark, Treaty of

Altranstadt, Treaty of

Andrássy Note

Andrusovo, Treaty of

April Laws

Ausgleich (Compromise of 1867)

Austrian Ultimatum to Serbia

Austro-Polish Alliance of 1683

Austro-Russian and Russo-Prussian Treaties of 1795 (Third Treaty of Partition of Poland)

Baden, Articles of

Baden, Third Land Peace of

Balkan Pact (Balkan Entente)

Balkan Treaties of 1866–68

Baltic Pact (Baltic Entente)

Baltic States Declaration of Independence

Barmen Declaration (Theological Declaration of Barmen)

Basel, Treaties of (1795)

Basel, Treaty of (1499)

Basel Compacta (Prague, Compacts of)

Basel Declaration of 1897 (Basel Program)

Bautzen, Treaty of

Belgian Neutrality Treaty (Treaty of London)

Berlin, Convention of (1833)

Berlin, Peace of

Berlin, Treaty of (1878)

"Blood and Iron" Speech, Bismarck's

Bread-basket Bill

Breslau, Treaty of (1741)

Breslau, Treaty of (1742)

Brest, Act of Union of

British Declaration of War in 1939

British-Greek-Turkish Agreements of 1959

Bucharest, Treaty of (1886)

Bucharest, Treaty of (1913)

Bucharest, Treaty of (1918)

Bucharest, Treaty of (1921)

Buczacz, Treaty of

Budapest Conventions of 1877

Bulgarian Horrors and the Question of the East

Burgundian Code (Lex Gundobada)

Camp David Accords

Carlsbad Decrees

Catherine the Great's Declaration of Armed Neutrality

Charter 77, Czech

Charter of Paris for a New Europe (1990)

Chaumont, Treaties of

Code Frédéric

Code of Dušan (Zabonnik)

Cologne Declaration

Communist Information Bureau (Cominform), Manifesto Establishing the

Concordat of 1964

Conference on Security and Cooperation, Treaty of the (1990)

Constance, Peace of

Constantinople, Treaty of (1913)

Conventional Forces in Europe, Treaty on (1990)

Corfu Declaration (Pact of Corfu)

Croatian-Hungarian Compromise of 1868 (Nagoda, Law XXX of 1868)

Czech Charter of 77 (Charter 77, Czech)

Czechoslovakia's Two Thousand Words (Two Thousand Words)

Dayton Peace Accord

Delimitation, Act of

De Revolutionibus Orbium Coelestium (On the Revolution of the Heavenly Bodies)

Deulino, Truce of

Dresden, Treaty of

Dušan, Code of (Zabonnik)

Einstein's Special Relativity Theory

Emancipation Edict of 1807, Prussian

Ems Telegram

Estonian Declaration of Sovereignty of 1988

Eternal Peace of 1686 (Grzymultowski Peace)

European Coal and Steel Community, Treaty of the

European Convention for the Protection of Human Rights and Fundamental Freedoms

European Free Trade Association Agreement

European Recovery Program (Marshall Plan)

Falk Laws (May Laws)

Frankfurt, Treaty of

Frederick the Great's Code (Code Frédéric)

Fribourg, Treaty of (Perpetual Peace, La Paix Perpétuelle)

Gastein, Convention of

HOLY ROMAN EMPIRE

START-2 Treaty (Memorandum of Joint Understanding on Nuclear Arms Reductions) (1992)
Stockholm Resolution
Stockholm Security Conference Treaty
Strategic Arms Limitation Treaty of 1972 (SALT I)
Strategic Arms Limitation Treaty of 1979 (SALT II)
Ukrainian Disarmament (Denuclearization) Accord (1994)

INTERNATIONAL (MISCELLANEOUS)

Bandung Resolutions
Berne Bill, U.S.
Berne Convention of 1886
Bill of Rights, International
Bretton Woods Agreement
Communist Information Bureau (Cominform), Manifesto Establishing the
Communist International (Comintern), Constitution and Rules of the
Communist Manifesto (Manifesto of the Communist Party, Manifest der Kommunistischen Partei)
Connally-Fulbright Resolutions
Convention for the Amelioration of the Wounded in Time of War (Geneva Convention of 1864)
Convention for the Suppression of Slavery, International
Convention on the Prohibition of the Use, Stockpiling, Production and Transfer of Antipersonnel Mines and on Their Destruction (1997)
Convention on the Prevention and Punishment of the Crime of Genocide
Convention on the Settlement of Investment Disputes
Dawes Plan
Dayton Peace Accord
Declaration of Human Rights (Universal Declaration of Human Rights)
Declaration of Rights of Negro Peoples of the World
General Agreement on Tariffs and Trade (GATT)
Geneva Convention of 1864 (Convention for the Amelioration of the Wounded in Time of War)

Geneva Conventions of 1949
Geneva Declaration of 1948
Geneva Protocol of 1924 (Protocol for the Pacific Settlement of International Disputes)
Helsinki Accord
Hippocratic Oath
Imperialism, A Study
Impuls 99 (1999)
Industrial Workers of the World, Preamble of the Constitution of the
International Criminal Court (ICC), Rome Statute of (Charter of the International Criminal Court)
International Energy Agency Agreement
International Working-Men's Association, Manifesto of the (Manifesto of the International Working-Men's Association)
Iranian Constitution of 1979
Japanese Peace Treaty of 1951
Kellogg-Briand Peace Pact (Paris, Pact of 1928)
Korean War Armistice
Kyoto Protocol
Layton-Wiggin Report
League of Nations Covenant
League of Nations Mandates
Lomé Convention
London, Declaration of (1990)
Lytton Commission Report
Mahon's Act, Lord
Malthus's *Essays on the Principle of Population (Essays on the Principle of Population, Malthus's)*
Manifesto of the International Working-Men's Association
Manifesto of the Second World Peace Congress
Marquess of Queensbury Rules
Montreal Protocol of 1987
Moscow Conference Declarations of 1943
Outer Space Treaty of 1966
Paris, Pact of (1928) (Kellogg-Briand Peace Pact)
Protocol for the Pacific Settlement of International Disputes (Geneva Protocol of 1924)
Rio Declaration (1992)
United Nations Charter
United Nations Convention Against Torture (1987)
United Nations Convention on the Law of the Sea

United Nations Declaration of Commitment on HIV/AIDS (2001)
United Nations Declaration on Decolonization
United Nations Resolution 181
United Nations Resolution 212
United Nations Resolution 242
United Nations Resolution 338
United Nations Resolution 661
United Nations Resolution 678
United Nations Resolution 1373
United Nations Resolution 1402
United Nations Resolution 3236
United Nations Resolution 3379
Universal Declaration of Human Rights
Vienna Declaration and Program of Action (1993)
Wealth of Nations, An Inquiry into the Nature and Causes of the
"We Remember: A Reflection on the Shoah" (1997)
Wilson's Exposition of the League of Nations
Woman's Christian Temperance Union (WCTU) Declaration of Principles
Women's Rights, Declaration of (Seneca Falls Declaration and Resolutions, Declaration of Independence for Women)
WIPO (World Intellectual Property Organization), Treaties of the (1996)

IRELAND

Act of Explanation (Explanation, Act of; Act of Settlement and Explanation)
Anglo-Irish Accord of 1985 (Hillsborough Agreement)
Anglo-Irish Treaty of 1921
Ashbourne Act (Irish Land Act of 1885)
Belfast (Ulster) Covenant of 1912
Berkeley's *Treatise Concerning the Principles of Human Knowledge*
Brehon Laws
Bright Clause
Civil Marriage Act of 1836, British
Council of Europe; Statute of the
Deasy's Act (Irish Land Act of 1860)
De Valera's Letter on Irish Grievances
Disestablishment Act of 1869
Downing Street Declaration of 1993
Drapier's Letters

PAPACY

ROME AND THE ROMAN EMPIRE

Political Interference Act, South
    African
Public Safety Law of 1953, South
    African
Sabotage Bill (General Law
    Amendment Act, South African)
Separate Amenities Act, South
    African
South Africa Act of 1909
South African Citizenship Act
South African Constitution of 1983
South African Group Areas Acts
    (Group Areas Act of 1950, South
    African; Group Areas Acts of
    1973, South African)
South African Nationality and Flag
    Act (Nationality and Flag Act,
    South African)
South African Natives' Land Act
    (Natives' Land Act, South
    African)
South African Natives' Trust and
    Land Act (Natives' Trust and
    Land Act, South African)
South African Political Interference
    Act (Political Interference Act,
    South African)
South African Public Safety Law of
    1953 (Public Safety Law of 1953,
    South African)
South African Separate Amenities
    Act (Separate Amenities Act.
    South African)
Truth and Reconciliation
    Commission Report
United Nations Declaration on
    Decolonization
Vereeniging, Treaty of
Westminster, Statute of (1931)

SPAIN AND PORTUGAL

Abjuration, Act of
Adams-Onís Treaty
    (Transcontinental Treaty)
Afonsine Ordinances (Ordenações
    Affonsinas)
Aix-la-Chapelle, Treaty of (1668)
Aix-la-Chapelle, Treaty of (1748)
Alcáçovas, Treaty of
Alhambra Decree
Amiens, Treaty of (1802)
Anglo-German Agreement of 1898
Anglo-Italian Agreements of 1937
    and 1938
Antwerp, Truce of (Twelve Years'
    Truce)
Aragonese Privileges of Union
    (Magna Carta of Aragón)

Aranjuez, Convention of (1779)
Arras, Treaty of (1579)
Augsburg, Treaty of the League of
Barcelona, Treaty of (1493)
Barcelona, Treaty of (1529)
Bärwalde, Treaty of
Basel, Treaties of (1795)
Bayonne, Treaty of
Berlin Act of 1885
Boxer Protocol
Bubble Act (South Sea Bubble Act)
Burgos, Concordat of
Burgos, Laws of
Cartagena, Pact of
Cateau-Cambrésis, Treaty of (Paix
    Malheureuse)
Catherine the Great's Declaration of
    Armed Neutrality
Cherasco, Treaties of
Code of the Seven Parts (Seven
    Parts, Code of the)
Columbus's First Voyage Journal
Concordat of 1482
Concordat of 1753
Concordat of 1851
Consolidación, Law of
Constantinople Convention (Suez
    Canal Convention)
Corbeil, Treaty of
Córdoba, Treaty of (Convention of
    Córdoba)
de Lôme Letter
Demarcation, Bull of (Inter Caetera)
Escorial, Treaty of (Family
    Compacts)
Family Compacts (Pactes de
    Famille)
Fontainebleau, Treaty of (1679)
    (Nijmegen, Treaties of)
Fontainebleau, Treaty of (1743)
    (Family Compacts)
Ghent, Pacification of
Grand Alliance of 1689
Grand Alliance of 1701
Grand Alliance of 1813 (Sixth and
    last Coalition Against Napoléon)
Great Protestation
Hague, Treaty of The (1720)
Indies, New Laws of the (New Laws
    of the Indies)
Inter Caetera (Demarcation, Bull of)
Lex Romana Visigothorum (Breviary
    of Alaric)
Leyes Nuevas (New Laws of the
    Indies)
Lisbon, Treaty of
London, Treaty of (1834)

Louis XIV's Letter Accepting the
    Spanish Succession
Lund, Treaty of (Nijmegen/
    Nimwegen, Treaties of)
McKinley's War Message
Madrid, Treaty of (1526)
Madrid, Treaty of (1715) (Second
    Peace of Utrecht)
Madrid, Treaty of (1750)
Madrid, Treaty of (1801)
Magna Carta of Aragón (Aragonese
    Privileges of Union)
Manueline Ordinances (Afonsine
    Ordinances)
Message to (from) Garcia
Methuen Treaties
New Laws of the Indies (New Laws
    of the Indies for the Good
    Treatment and Preservation of
    the Indians)
Nijmegen (Nimwegen), Treaties of
Nine Power Pacts (Treaties of
    Washington)
North Atlantic Treaty (North
    Atlantic Pact)
Noyon, Treaty of
Nymphenburg, Treaty of
Nyon Agreement
Ostend Manifesto
Pactes de Famille (Family
    Compacts)
Paix Malheureuse (Cateau-
    Cambrésis, Treaty of)
Paris, Treaty of (1763)
Paris, Treaty of (1783) (Treaty of
    Versailles)
Paris, Treaty of (1898)
Pinckney Treaty (Treaty of San
    Lorenzo)
Pragmatic Sanction of Charles III
Pyrenees, Treaty of the
Quadruple Alliance of 1718
Rastatt, Treaty of
Ratisbon, Truce of (Regensburg,
    Truce of)
Regensburg, Truce of (Ratisbon,
    Truce of)
Rijswijk (Ryswick) Treaty of
San Ildefonso, Treaty of (1762)
San Ildefonso, Treaty of (1777)
San Ildefonso, Treaty of (1796)
San Ildefonso, Treaty of (1800)
San Lorenzo, Treaty of (Pinckney
    Treaty)
San Sebastián, Pact of
Seven Parts, Code of the (Seven
    Divisions of Law, Código de las

Brady Handgun Violence Prevention
    Act (Brady Bill) (1993)
Brandenburg v. *Ohio*
Bretton Woods Agreement
Bricker Amendment
Brown v. *Board of Education of
    Topeka, Kansas*
Brussels Act of 1890 (General Act of
    Brussels)
Bryan-Chamorro Treaty
Bunker Hill Speech, Webster's
Burke Act
Burke's American Taxation Speech
    (American Taxation Speech,
    Burke's)
Burke-Wadsworth Act (Selective
    Training and Service Act)
Burlingame Treaty
Bush's "Freedom and Fear Are at
    War" Speech, George W.
Bush's Inaugural Address, George
    H. W.
Bush's Inaugural Address, George W.
Bush v. *Gore* (*George W. Bush* v.
    Albert A. Gore)
Butler's General Order No. 28
Cable Act
Calhoun's *Disquisition on
    Government* (*Disquisition on
    Government*, Calhoun's)
Calhoun's "Fort Hill Letter" ("Fort
    Hill Letter," Calhoun's)
Calhoun's Last Speech on the
    Slavery Question (Calhoun's
    Speech on the Compromise of
    1850)
Cambridge Agreement
Cambridge Platform
Camp David Accords
Cantwell v. *Connecticut*
Capper-Volstead Act (U.S.
    Cooperative Marketing Act)
Carey Desert Land Grant Act
Carnegie's "Wealth" Article
Carter's Inaugural Address
Charles River Bridge v. *Warren
    Bridge*
Charter of Liberties (Charter of
    Franchises and Liberties)
Charter of Liberties (Charter of
    Privileges)
Cherokee Nation v. *Georgia*
Child Labor Act of 1919, U.S.
Child Pornography Prevention Act
    of 1996, U.S. (Child
    Pornography Protection Act)
Chinese Exclusion Act of 1882
Chinese Exclusion Act of 1892

Chinese Exclusion Act of 1902
Chisholm v. *Georgia*
Cigarette Labeling and Advertising
    Act, U.S.
Civil Aeronautics Act, U.S. (Lea-
    McCarran Act)
Civil Disobedience, Thoreau's
Civil Rights Act of 1866, U.S.
Civil Rights Act of 1875, U.S.
Civil Rights Act of 1957, U.S.
Civil Rights Act of 1960, U.S.
Civil Rights Act of 1964, U.S.
Civil Rights Act of 1968, U.S.
Civil Rights Cases of 1883, U.S.
Civil Rights Restoration Act, U.S.
Civil Works Emergency Relief Act,
    U.S.
Clark Memorandum on the Monroe
    Doctrine
Clay's Compromise Speech
Clayton Anti-Trust Act
Clayton-Bulwer Treaty
Clean Air Act of 1963, U.S.
Clean Air Act of 1970, U.S.
Clean Air Act of 1990, U.S.
Clean Water Restoration Act of
    1966, U.S.
Clinton's First Inaugural Address
    (1993)
Clinton's Second Inaugural Address
    (1997)
Code of 1650 (Ludlow's Code)
Coercive Acts (Intolerable Acts,
    Restraining Acts)
Cohens v. *Virginia*
Coinage Act of 1792, U.S. (Mint
    Act)
Coinage Act of 1873, U.S.
    (Demonetization Act)
Coleman v. *Miller*
Collector v. *Day*
Common Sense
Commonwealth v. *Hunt*
Communications Decency Act, U.S.
Communist Control Act of 1954,
    U.S.
Compromise of 1850
Confederate Constitution
Confiscation Act of 1861, U.S.
Confiscation Act of 1862, U.S.
Connally-Fulbright Resolutions
Connecticut, Charter of
Connecticut Compromise (Great
    Compromise)
Continental Association
    (Association, The)
Constitution, U.S. (U.S.
    Constitution)

Cooper Union Speech, Lincoln's
Cooper v. *Aaron*
Coppage v. *Kansas*
Coxey's Program
Coyle v. *Smith*
"Crime Against Kansas" Speech,
    Sumner's
Crime Control Acts, U.S.
Crittenden Compromise (Crittenden
    Plan or Amendments)
"Cross of Gold" Speech
Cuban Constitution of 1901
Cullom Act (Interstate Commerce
    Act, U.S.)
Danbury Hatters' Case (*Loewe* v.
    Lawlor)
Darrow's "Against Capital
    Punishment" Speech
Dartmouth College v. *Woodward*
Dawes Severalty Act
Dawson Agreement
"Day of Infamy" Speech, Roosevelt's
    (Roosevelt's War Message)
Dayton Peace Accord
Death with Dignity Act, Oregon's
Declaration Concerning Religion,
    Ethics, and the Crisis in the
    Clinton Presidency
Declaration of American Presidents
Declaration of the Four States on the
    Question of General Security
    (Moscow Conference Declaration
    of 1943)
Declaration of Independence,
    American
Declaration of Independence, Texas
Declaration of Reciprocal Assistance
    and Cooperation for the Defense
    of the Nations of the Americas
    (Havana, Act of)
Declaration of Rights, Virginia
    (Virginia Bill of Rights)
Declaration of Rights and Grievances
Declaration of Rights of Negro
    Peoples of the World
Declaration and Resolves of the First
    Continental Congress
    (Declaration of Rights and
    Grievances)
Declaratory Act of 1766
Defense of Marriage Act, U.S. (1996)
De Lima v. *Bidwell*
de Lôme Letter
Demonetization Act, U.S. (Coinage
    Act of 1873, U.S.)
Dennis et al. v. *United States*
Desert Land Act, U.S.
Destroyers-for-Bases Agreement

SELECT BIBLIOGRAPHY

The following limited list consists only of recent books of general interest—bibliographic sources mentioning multiple documents and the history surrounding them. These sources are not included in the "Further reading" references at the end of entries in the book. This list merely scratches the surface of the vast general literature that deals in some part with documents and history. Many of the sources listed below have useful bibliographies, which specify additional material, both primary and secondary sources, for readers pursuing further inquiry. For convenience, the books have been alphabetically grouped under 25 broad and appropriate headings, which are listed below.

Africa
Ancient History
Asia
Australia and New Zealand
Belgium and the Netherlands
Canada
Europe
France
Germany
Italy
Latin America
Middle East
Miscellaneous

Papacy
Philosophy
Psychology
Religion
Renaissance
Russia and the Soviet Union
Scandinavia
Spain and Portugal
Switzerland
Turkey
United Kingdom and the Republic of Ireland
United States of America

AFRICA

Appiah, Kwame Anthony, and Henry Louis Gates, Jr., eds. *Africana—The Encyclopedia of the African and African-American Experience.* New York: Basic Civitas Books, 1999.

Arnold, Guy. *Historical Dictionary of Civil Wars in Africa.* Lanham, Md.: Scarecrow Press, 1999.

Diagram Group and Keith Lye. *Encyclopedia of African Nations and Civilizations.* New York: Facts On File, 2001.

Middleton, John, ed. *Encyclopedia of Africa South of the Sahara.* 4 vols. New York: Charles Scribner's Sons, 1997.

Núñez, Benjamin. *Dictionary of Portuguese-African Civilization.* 2 vols. London: Hans Zell Publishers, 1995.

Ott, Dana. *Democracy in Africa—Recent Analyses: A Bibliography with Annotations.* Washington, D.C.: Africa Bureau of the U.S. Agency for International Development, 1996.

Vandervort, Bruce. *Wars of Imperial Conquest in Africa, 1830–1914.* Bloomington: Indiana University Press, 1998.

Worger, William H., et al., eds. *Africa and the West—A Documentary History from Slave Trade to Independence.* Phoenix, Ariz.: Oryx Press, 2001.

ANCIENT HISTORY

Bunson, Matthew. *Encyclopedia of the Roman Empire.* Rev. ed. New York: Facts On File, 2002.

David, Rosalie, and Anthony E. David. *A Biographical Dictionary of Ancient Egypt.* London: B.A. Seaby, 1992.

Hornblower, Simon, and Antony Spawforth, eds. *The Oxford Classical Dictionary.* Oxford, England: Oxford University Press, 1999.

Kazhdan, Alexander P., et al., eds. *The Oxford Dictionary of Byzantium.* 3 vols. New York: Oxford University Press, 1991.

Redford, Donald B., ed. *The Oxford Encyclopedia of Ancient Egypt.* 3 vols. Oxford, England: Oxford University Press, 2001.

Rice, Michael. *Who's Who in Ancient Egypt.* London: Routledge, 1999.

Sacks, David. *Encyclopedia of the Ancient Greek World.* New York: Facts On File, 1995.

Speake, Graham, ed. *A Dictionary of Ancient History.* Oxford, England: Blackwell Publishers, 1994.

———. *Encyclopedia of Greece and the Hellenic Tradition.* 2 vols. London: Fitzroy Dearborn Publishers, 2000.

ASIA

Bowman, John S., ed. *Columbia Chronologies of Asian History and Culture.* New York: Columbia University Press, 2000.

Bowring, Richard, and Kornicki, Peter, eds. *The Cambridge Encyclopedia of Japan.* Cambridge, England: Cambridge University Press, 1993.

Chandler, David. *A History of Cambodia.* Boulder, Colo.: Westview Press, 2000.

Cooper, Nicola. *France in Indochina: Colonial Encounters.* Oxford, England: Berg, 2001.

Huffman, James L., ed. *Modern Japan—An Encyclopedia of History, Culture, and Nationalism.* New York: Garland Publishing, 1998.

Keay, John. *India, a History.* New York: Atlantic Monthly Press, 2000.

Lee, Loyd A. *World War II in Asia and the Pacific and the War's Aftermath, with General Themes: A Handbook of Literature and Research.* Westport, Conn.: Greenwood Press, 1998.

Olson, James S. *An Ethnohistorical Dictionary of China.* Westport, Conn.: Greenwood Press, 1998.

Perkins, Dorothy. *Encyclopedia of China—The Essential Reference to China, Its History and Culture.* New York: Facts On File, 1999.

Sandler, Stanley, ed. *World War II in the Pacific: An Encyclopedia.* New York: Garland Publishing, 2001.

Schoppa, R. Keith. *The Columbia Guide to Modern Chinese History.* New York: Columbia University Press, 2000.

Wang, Ke-wen, ed. *Modern China: An Encyclopedia of History, Culture, and Nationalism.* New York: Garland Publishing, 1998.

Young, Whan Kihl, ed. *Korea and the World: Beyond the Cold War.* Boulder, Colo.: Westview Press, 1994.

AUSTRALIA AND NEW ZEALAND

Bambrick, Susan, ed. *The Cambridge History of Australia.* Cambridge, England: Cambridge University Press, 1994.

Belich, James. *Making Peoples: A History of the New Zealanders, from Polynesian Settlement to the End of the Nineteenth Century.* Honolulu: University of Hawaii Press, 1996.

Davison, Graeme, et al., eds. *The Oxford Companion to Australian History.* Melbourne, Australia: Oxford University Press, 1998.

Jackson, William K., and Alan McRobie. *Historical Dictionary of New Zealand.* Lanham, Md.: Scarecrow Press, 1996.

Lal, Brij V., and Kate Fortune, eds. *The Pacific Islands—An Encyclopedia.* Honolulu: University of Hawaii Press, 2000.

BELGIUM AND THE NETHERLANDS

Blom, J. C. H., et al., eds. *History of the Low Countries.* New York: Berghahn Books, 1999.

Wee, Herman van der. *The Low Countries in the Early Modern World.* Brookfield, Vt.: Variorum, 1993.

CANADA

Bond, Mary E., ed. *Canadian Reference Sources: An Annotated Bibliography: General Reference Works, History, Humanities.* Vancouver: UBC Press, 1996.

Gough, Barry M. *Historical Dictionary of Canada.* Lanham, Md.: Scarecrow Press, 1999.

Francis, R. D., et al. *Destinies: Canadian History since Confederation.* Toronto: Harcourt Brace Canada, 1996.

———. *Origins: Canadian History to Confederation.* Toronto: Harcourt Brace Canada, 1996.

Wright, J. V. *A History of the Native Peoples of Canada.* Hull, Canada: Canadian Museum of Civilization, 1995.

EUROPE

Cook, Bernard, ed. *Europe since 1945—An Encyclopedia.* 2 vols. New York: Garland Publishing, 2001.

Dear, I. C. B., ed. *The Oxford Companion to World War II.* Oxford, England: Oxford University Press, 1995.

Frankel, Benjamin, ed. *The Cold War, 1945–1991.* 3 vols. Detroit: Gale Research, 1992.

Frucht, Richard, ed. *Encyclopedia of Eastern Europe.* New York: Garland Publishing, 2000.

Held, Joseph. *Dictionary of East European History since 1945.* Westport, Conn.: Greenwood Press, 1994.

Lee, Loyd A. *World War II in Europe, Africa, and the Americas, with General Sources: A Handbook of Literature and Research.* Westport, Conn.: Greenwood Press, 1997.

Lerski, George J. *Historical Dictionary of Poland, 966–1945.* Westport, Conn.: Greenwood Press, 1996.

Pope, Stephen, and Elizabeth-Anne Wheal. *The Dictionary of the First World War.* New York: St. Martin's Press, 1996.

Urwin, Derek W. *A Dictionary of European History and Politics, 1945–1995.* New York: Longman Publishing, 1996.

Wróbel, Piotr. *Historical Dictionary of Poland, 1945–1996.* Westport, Conn.: Greenwood Press, 1998.

FRANCE

Alexander, Martin S., ed. *French History since Napoleon.* London: Arnold, 1999.

Cox, Marvin R., ed. *The Place of the French Revolution in History.* Boston: Houghton Mifflin, 1998.

Furet, François, and Mona Ozouf, eds. *A Critical Dictionary of the French Revolution.* Cambridge, Mass.: Belknap Press of Harvard University Press, 1989.

Gordon, Bertram M., ed. *Historical Dictionary of World War II France—The Occupation, Vichy, and the Resistance, 1938–1946.* Westport, Conn.: Greenwood Press, 1998.

Haine, W. Scott. *The History of France.* Westport, Conn.: Greenwood Press, 2000.

Kibler, William W., and Grover A. Zinn, eds. *Medieval France—An Encyclopedia.* New York: Garland Publishing, Inc., 1995.

Quinn, Frederick. *The French Overseas Empire.* Westport, Conn.: Praeger, 2000.

Raymond, Gino. *Historical Dictionary of France.* Lanham, Md.: Scarecrow Press, 1998.

GERMANY

Alter, Peter. *The German Question and the Structure of Europe, 1800–1990.* London: Hodder & Stoughton, 2000.

Brose, Eric Dorn. *German History, 1789–1871: From the Holy Roman Empire to the Bismarckian Reich.* Providence, R.I.: Berghahn Books, 1997.

Burleigh, Michael. *The Third Reich: A New History.* New York: Hill & Wang, 2001.

Buse, Dieter K., and Juergen C. Doerr, eds. *Modern Germany—An Encyclopedia of History, People, and Culture, 1871–1990.* 2 vols. New York: Garland Publishing, 1998.

Jeep, John M. *Medieval Germany: An Encyclopedia.* New York: Garland Publishing, 2001.

Osmond, Jonathan. *German Reunification—A Reference Guide and Commentary.* Harlow, England: Longman Group UK, 1992.

Taylor, A. J. P. *The Course of German History: A Survey of the Development of German History since 1815.* London: Routledge, 2001.

Wegner, Bernd, ed. *From Peace to War: Germany, Soviet Union, and the World, 1939–1941.* Providence, R.I.: Berghahn Books, 1997.

ITALY

DiScala, Spencer. *Italy: From Revolution to Republic, 1700 to the Present.* Boulder, Colo.: Westview Press, 1998.

Gilbert, Mark F., and K. Robert Nilsson. *Historical Dictionary of Modern Italy.* European Historical Dictionaries, No. 34: Lanham, Md.: Scarecrow Press, 1999.

Hanlon, Gregory. *Early Modern Italy, 1550–1800: Three Seasons in European History.* New York: St. Martin's Press, 2000.

McCarthy, Patrick, ed. *Italy since 1945.* Oxford, England: Oxford University Press, 2000.

Pollard, John F. *The Fascist Experience in Italy.* London: Routledge, 1998.

LATIN AMERICA

Adelman, Jeremy, ed. *Colonial Legacies—The Problem of Persistence in Latin American History.* New York: Routledge, 1999.

Bethell, Leslie, ed. *The Cambridge History of Latin America.* 11 vols. Cambridge, England: Cambridge University Press, 1984.

Boyer, Richard, and Geoffrey Spurling, eds. *Colonial Lives—Documents in Latin American History, 1550–1850.* New York: Oxford University Press, 2000.

Bulman, Thomas V. *The Economic History of Latin America since Independence.* Cambridge, England: Cambridge University Press, 1994.

Collier, Simon, et al., eds. *The Cambridge Encyclopedia of Latin America and the Caribbean.* Cambridge, England: Cambridge University Press, 1992.

Hanke, Lewis, and Jane M. Rausch, eds. *People and Issues in Latin American History.* 2 vols. New York: M. Wiener, 1993.

Henderson, James, et al., eds. *A Reference Guide to Latin-American History.* Armonk, N.Y.: M. E. Sharpe, 2000.

Kapiszewski, Diana, ed. *Encyclopedia of Latin American Politics.* Westport, Conn.: Oryx Press, 2001.

Keen, Benjamin, ed. *Latin American Civilization—History and Society, 1492 to the Present.* Boulder, Colo.: Westview Press, 1996.

Kicza, John E., ed. *The Indian in Latin American History—Resistance, Resilience, and Acculturation.* Wilmington, Del.: SR Books, 2000.

Rodríguez, O. Jamie E. *The Independence in Latin America.* Cambridge, England: Cambridge University Press, 1998.

Rossi, Ernest E., and Jack C. Plano. *Latin America: A Political Dictionary.* Santa Barbara, Calif.: ABC-CLIO, 1992.

Selbin, Eric. *Modern Latin American Revolutions.* Boulder, Colo.: Westview Press, 1997.

Tenenbaum, Barbara A. *Encyclopedia of Latin American History and Culture.* 5 vols. New York: Simon & Schuster Macmillan, 1996.

Werner, Michael S., ed. *Encyclopedia of Mexico—History, Society and Culture,* 2 vols. Chicago: Fitzroy Dearborn Publishers, 1997.

Woodward, Ralph Lee. *Central America—A Nation Divided.* New York: Oxford University Press, 1999.

MIDDLE EAST

Halliday, Fred. *Nation and Religion in the Middle East.* Boulder, Colo.: Lynne Rienner Publishers, 2000.

Kedouric, Elie. *Politics in the Middle East.* Oxford, England: Oxford University Press, 1992.

Reich, Bernard, ed. *An Historical Encyclopedia of the Arab-Israeli Conflict.* Westport, Conn.: Greenwood Press, 1996.

Sela, Avraham, ed. *Political Encyclopedia of the Middle East.* New York: Continuum Publishing, 1999.

Simon, Reeva S., et al., eds. *Encyclopedia of the Modern Middle East.* 4 vols. New York: Simon & Schuster Macmillan, 1996.

Ziring, Lawrence. *The Middle East: A Political Dictionary.* Santa Barbara, Calif.: ABC-CLIO, 1992.

MISCELLANEOUS

Ciment, James, ed. *Encyclopedia of Conflicts since World War II.* 4 vols. Armonk, N.Y.: M. E. Sharpe, 1999.

Collier's Encyclopedia. 24 vols. New York: P. F. Collier, 1995.

Encyclopaedia Britannica Online. *Encyclopaedia Britannica.* Available online at www.eb.com.

Huls, Mary Ellen. *United States Government Documents on Women, 1800–1990: A Comprehensive Bibliography.* 2 vols. Westport, Conn.: Greenwood Press, 1990.

Jessup, John E. *An Encyclopedic Dictionary of Conflict and Conflict Resolution, 1945–1996.* Westport, Conn.: Greenwood Press, 1998.

Kramarae, Cheris, and Dale Spender, eds. *Routledge International Encyclopedia of Women.* 4 vols. New York: Routledge, 2000.

Maddex, Robert L. *Constitutions of the World.* Washington, D.C.: CQ Press, 1995.

———. *International Encyclopedia of Human Rights: Freedoms, Abuses, and Remedies.* Washington, D.C.: CQ Press, 2000.

Phillips, Charles L., and Alan Axelrod. *Encyclopedia of Treaties and Alliances.* 2 vols. New York: Facts On File, 2001.

Ramsbotham, Oliver, and Tom Woodhouse. *Encyclopedia of International Peacekeeping Operations.* Santa Barbara, Calif.: ABC-CLIO, 1999.

Rengger, N. J., and John Campbell, eds. *Treaties and Alliances of the World.* New York: Stockton, 1995.

Tucker, Spencer C., ed. *Encyclopedia of the Vietnam War: A Political, Social, and Military History.* 3 vols. Santa Barbara, Calif.: ABC-CLIO, 1998.

PAPACY

Blouin, Francis X., Jr., ed. *Vatican Archives: An Inventory and Guide to Historical Documents of the Holy See.* New York: Oxford University Press, 1998.

Bunson, Matthew. *The Pope Encyclopedia: An A to Z of the Holy See.* New York: Crown Trade Paperbacks, 1995.

Cooke, Bernard, ed. *The Papacy and the Church in the United States.* New York: Paulist Press, 1989.

Coppa, Frank J., ed. *Encyclopedia of the Vatican and Papacy.* Westport, Conn.: Greenwood Press, 1999.

Duffy, Eamon. *Saints and Sinners: A History of the Popes.* New Haven, Conn.: Yale University Press, 1997.

Kertzer, David I. *The Popes Against the Jews: The Vatican's Role in the Rise of Anti-Semitism.* New York: Alfred A. Knopf, 2001.

Richards, Jeffrey. *The Popes and the Papacy in the Early Middle Ages, 476–752.* London: Routledge & Kegan Paul, 1979.

PHILOSOPHY

Audi, Robert, gen. ed. *The Cambridge Dictionary of Philosophy.* Cambridge, England: Cambridge University Press, 1995.

Carr, Brian, and Mahalingam, Indira, eds. *Companion Encyclopedia of Asian Philosophy.* London: Routledge, 1997.

Craig, Edward, gen. ed. *Routledge Encyclopedia of Philosophy.* 10 vols. London: Routledge, 1998.

Edwards, Paul, ed. *The Encyclopedia of Philosophy.* 8 vols. New York: Simon & Schuster Macmillan, 1996.

Grimes, John. *A Concise Dictionary of Indian Philosophy.* Albany: State University of New York Press, 1989.

Hackett, Jeremiah, ed. *Medieval Philosophies.* Dictionary of Literary Biography Series, vol. 115. Detroit: Gale Research 1992.

Honderich, Ted, ed. *The Oxford Companion to Philosophy.* Oxford, U.K.: Oxford University Press, 1995.

Leaman, Oliver, ed. *Encyclopedia of Asian Philosophy.* London: Routledge, 2001.

McGreal, Ian P., ed. *Great Thinkers of the Eastern World.* New York: HarperCollins Publishers, 1995.

Zeyl, Donald J., ed. *Encyclopedia of Classical Philosophy.* Westport, Conn.: Greenwood Press, 1997.

PSYCHOLOGY

Colman, Andrew M. *A Dictionary of Psychology.* Oxford, England: Oxford University Press, 2001.

Gall, Susan, ed. *The Gale Encyclopedia of Psychology.* Detroit: Gale Research, 1996.

Kazdin, Alan E., ed. *Encyclopedia of Psychology.* 8 vols. Oxford, England: Oxford University Press, 2000.

Sutherland, Stuart. *The International Dictionary of Psychology.* New York: Crossroads Publishing, 1996.

RELIGION

Bowker, John, ed. *The Oxford Dictionary of World Religions.* Oxford, England: Oxford University Press, 1997.

Cross, F. L., and E. A. Livingstone, eds. *The Oxford Dictionary of the Christian Church.* Oxford, England: Oxford University Press, 1997.

Glassé, Cyril. *The New Encyclopedia of Islam.* Walnut Creek, Calif.: AltaMira Press, 2001.

Hillerbrand, Hans J., ed. *The Oxford Encyclopedia of the Reformation.* 4 vols. New York: Oxford University Press, 1996.

Neusner, Jacob, et al., eds. *The Encyclopedia of Judaism.* 3 vols. New York. Continuum Publishing, 1999.

Schuhmacher, Stephan, and Gert Woerner, eds. *The Encyclopedia of Eastern Philosophy and Religion.* Boston. Shambhala Publications, 1994.

Smith, Jonathan Z., et al., eds. *The Harper Collins Dictionary of Religion.* San Francisco, Calif.: HarperCollins Publishers, 1995.

Wigoder, Geoffrey, ed. *The Encyclopedia of Judaism.* New York: Macmillan Publishing, 1989.

RENAISSANCE

Grendler, Paul F., ed. *Encyclopedia of the Renaissance.* 6 vols. New York: Charles Scribner's Sons, 1999.

Rachum, Ilan. *The Renaissance: An Illustrated Encyclopedia.* London: Octopus Books, 1979.

RUSSIA AND THE SOVIET UNION

Brown, Archie, et al., eds. *The Cambridge Encyclopedia of Russia and the Former Soviet Union.* Cambridge, England: Cambridge University Press, 1994.

Brzezinski, Zbigniew, and Paige Sullivan, eds. *Russia and the Commonwealth of Independent States—Documents, Data, and Analysis.* Armonk, N.Y.: M. E. Sharpe, 1997.

Dawisha, Karen, and Bruce Parrott, eds. *The End of Empire?: The Transformation of the USSR in Comparative Perspective.* Armonk, N.Y.: M. E. Sharpe, 1997.

Hosking, Geoffrey, and Robert Service, eds. *Reinterpreting Russia.* London: Arnold, 1999.

Mesbahi, Mohiaddin, ed. *Central Asia and the Caucasus after the Soviet Union: Domestic and International Dynamics.* Gainesville: University of Florida Press, 1994.

Olson, James S., ed. *An Ethnohistorical Dictionary of the Russian and Soviet Empires.* Westport, Conn.: Greenwood Press, 1994.

Paxton, John. *Encyclopedia of Russian History: From the Christianization of Kiev to the Break-Up of the U.S.S.R.* Santa Barbara, Calif.: ABC-CLIO, 1993.

Szporluk, Roman. *Russia, Ukraine and the Break-Up of the Soviet Union.* Stanford, Calif.: Hoover Institution Press, 2000.

SCANDINAVIA

Nordstrom, Byron J. *Dictionary of Scandinavian History.* Westport, Conn.: Greenwood Press, 1986.

———. *Scandinavia since 1500.* Minneapolis: University of Minnesota Press, 2000.

Pulsiano, Phillip, ed. *Medieval Scandinavia—An Encyclopedia.* New York: Garland Publishing, 1993.

Salmon, Patrick. *Scandinavia and the Great Powers, 1890–1940.* Cambridge, England: Cambridge University Press, 1997.

SPAIN AND PORTUGAL

Kennedy, Hugh. *Muslim Spain and Portugal: A Political History of al-Andalus.* London: Longman, 1996.

Kern, Robert W., ed. *Historical Dictionary of Modern Spain, 1700–1988.* Westport, Conn.: Greenwood Press, 1990.

Olson, James S., ed. *Historical Dictionary of the Spanish Empire, 1402–1975.* Westport, Conn.: Greenwood Press, 1992.

Wheeler, Douglas L. *Historical Dictionary of Portugal.* European Historical Dictionaries, no. 1. Metuchen, N.J.: Scarecrow Press, 1993.

Wiarda, Howard J. *Iberia and Latin America: New Democracies, New Policies, New Models.* Lanham, Md.: Rowman & Littlefield Publishers, 1996.

SWITZERLAND

Dame, Frederick William. *History of Switzerland.* Lewiston, N.Y.: E. Mellen Press, 2001.

Kreis, George, ed. *Switzerland and the Second World War.* London: F. Cass, 2000.

Schelbert, Leo ed. *Switzerland under Siege, 1939–1945: A Neutral Nation's Struggle for Survival.* Rockport, Maine: Picton Press, 2000.

TURKEY

Goodwin, Jason. *Lords of the Horizons: A History of the Ottoman Empire.* New York: Henry Holt, 1999.

Howard, Douglas A. *The History of Turkey.* Westport, Conn.: Greenwood Press, 2001.

McCarthy, Justin. *The Ottoman Peoples and the End of Empire.* New York: Oxford University Press, 2001.

McDowall, David. *A Modern History of the Kurds.* New York: St. Martin's Press, 1996.

Pope, Nicole, and Hugh Pope. *Turkey Unveiled: A History of Modern Turkey.* Woodstock, N.Y.: Overlook Press, 1998.

UNITED KINGDOM AND THE REPUBLIC OF IRELAND

The Encyclopedia of Britain. Oxford, England: Helicon Publishing, 1999.

Butler, L. J., and Anthony Gorst, eds. *Modern British History: A Guide to Study and Research.* London. I. B. Tauris, 1997.

Cannon, John, ed. *The Oxford Companion to British History.* Oxford, England. Oxford University Press, 1997.

Cook, Chris, and John Stevenson. *The Longman Companion to Britain since 1945.* London: Longman Group, 1996.

Connolly, S. J., ed. *The Oxford Companion to Irish History.* Oxford, England: Oxford University Press, 1998.

Elliott, Sydney, and W. D. Flackes. *Conflict in Northern Ireland—An Encyclopedia.* Santa Barbara, Calif.: ABC-CLIO, 1999.

Gardiner Juliet, and Neil Wenborn, eds. *The Columbia Companion to British History.* New York: Columbia University Press, 1997.

Gascoigne, Bamber. *Encyclopedia of Britain.* New York: Macmillan Publishing 1993.

Kinney, Arthur F., and David W. Swain, eds. *Tudor England—An Encyclopedia.* New York: Garland Publishing, 2001.

Lapidge Michael, et al., eds. *The Blackwell Encyclopedia of Anglo-Saxon England.* Oxford, England: Blackwell Publishers, 1999.

Leventhal, F. M., ed. *Twentieth-Century Britain—An Encyclopedia.* New York: Garland Publishing, 1995.

O'Day, Alan, and John Stevenson, eds. *Irish Historical Documents since 1800.* Savage, Md.: Barnes & Noble Books, 1992.

Parsons, Timothy. *The British Imperial Century, 1815–1914: A World History Perspective.* Lanham, Md.: Rowman & Littlefield, 1999.

Prescott, Andrew. *English Historical Documents.* London. British Library, 1988.

Szarmach, Paul E., M. Teresa Tavormina, and Joel T. Rosenthal, eds. *Medieval England—An Encyclopedia.* New York: Garland Publishing, 1998.

Wagner, John A. *A Historical Dictionary of the Elizabethan World.* Phoenix, Ariz.: Oryx Press, 1999.

UNITED STATES OF AMERICA

Axelrod, Alan. *American Treaties and Alliances.* Washington, D.C.: CQ Press, 2000.

Boatner, Mark M., III. *The Civil War Dictionary.* New York: David McKay, 1988.

Boyer, Paul S., ed. *The Oxford Companion to United States History.* Oxford, England: Oxford University Press, 2001.

Carruth, Gorton. *The Encyclopedia of American Facts and Dates.* New York: HarperCollins Publishers, 1997.

Crawford, Mark. *Encyclopedia of the Mexican-American War.* Santa Barbara, Calif.: ABC-CLIO, 1999.

Faragher, John Mack, gen. ed. *The Encyclopedia of Colonial and Revolutionary America.* New York: Facts On File, 1990.

Green, Jack P., and J. R. Pole, eds. *The Blackwell Encyclopedia of the American Revolution.* Cambridge, Mass.: Basil Blackwell, 1991.

Heidler, David S., and Jeanne T. Heidler, eds. *Encyclopedia of the War of 1812.* Santa Barbara, Calif.: ABC-CLIO, 1997.

———. *Encyclopedia of the American Civil War—A Political, Social, and Military History.* 5 vols. Santa Barbara, Calif.: ABC-CLIO, 2000.

Huls, Mary Ellen. *United States Government Documents on Women, 1800–1990: A Comprehensive Bibliography.* 2 vols. Westport, Conn.: Greenwood Press, 1990.

Kort, Michael. *The Columbia Guide to the Cold War.* New York: Columbia University Press, 1998.

Kutler, Stanley I., ed. *Encyclopedia of the United States in the Twentieth Century.* 4 vols. New York: Charles Scribner's Sons, 1996.

Levy, Peter B., ed. *100 Key Documents in American Democracy.* Westport, Conn.: Greenwood Press, 1994.

Martin, Waldo E., Jr. *Civil Rights in the United States.* 2 vols. New York: Macmillan Reference USA, 2000.

Moquin, Wayne, and Charles Van Doren, eds. *Great Documents in American Indian History.* New York: Da Capo Press, 1995.

Morris, Jeffrey B., and Richard B. Morris, eds. *Encyclopedia of American History.* New York: HarperCollins Publishers, 1996.

Ryan, Halford, ed. *The Inaugural Addresses of Twentieth-Century American Presidents.* Westport, Conn.: Praeger Publishers, 1993.

St. Germain, Jill. *Indian Treaty-Making Policy in the United States and Canada, 1867–1877.* Lincoln: University of Nebraska Press, 2001.

INDEX

Boldface page numbers indicate major treatment of a subject.

Jewish people (*continued*)
  Palestine as national home, 38, 43, 50, 85
  Portugal, 8
  rights of, France, 9
Jewish State, The, 224–225
Jiang Jieshi, 27, 432, 500
Jim Crow Laws, 225
Jinnah, Muhammad Ali, 212
Joan of Penthièvre, 190
Joan of the Tower, 309
Jodl, Alfred, 179
Johanna (duchess of Netherlands), 56
John (duke of Burgundy), 27
John (king of England), 266
John I of Luxembourg (king of Bohemia), 238, 484
John II (king of France), 60, 70
John II (king of Portugal), 444
John II Casimir (king of Poland), 16, 316, 494, 512
John III (duke of Brittany), 267
John III Casimir (king of Poland), 230
John III Sobieski (king of Poland), 65, 223, 513
John IV of Montfort, 190, 267
John XXIII, 103, 327
John Albert (king of Poland), 343
John George (elector of Saxony), 353
John of Austria, 180
John of Gaunt, 184, 503
John Paul II, 77, 94, 127, 215, 405, 415, 477
John Paul VI, 415
Johnson, Andrew, 87
  freed slaves, 163
  impeachment, 110
  reconstruction, 280–281
  Tenure of Office Act, 437
Johnson, Gregory, 439
Johnson, Hiram A., 211
Johnson, Lyndon B.
  campaign, 183
  economic opportunity, 132
  education opportunities, 137–138
  First Address to Congress, 225
  Gulf of Tonkin, 191
  immigration, 210
  inaugural address, 225
  Kennedy assassination, investigation, 489
  Latin American common market, 117
  riots, 234–235
  Speech at Johns Hopkins University, 225

  United Nations Address of 1963, 225–226
Johnson, Mississippi v., 280–281
Johnson, Samuel, 435–436
Johnson, Texas v., 439
Johnson, William, 158
Johnson Debt Default Act, 225
Johnson-Reed Act, 126. *See* Immigration Quota Act of 1924, U.S.
John the Fearless, 27
Joly, Maurice, 357
Jones, John M., 40
Jones Act of 1916, 226
Jones Act of 1917, 39, 226
Jones & Laughlin Steel Corporation, National Labor Relations Board v., 294
Joseph I (Holy Roman Emperor), 351, 430
Joseph II (archduke of Austria), 205
Joseph II (Holy Roman Emperor), 133, 481
Journey from St. Petersburgh to Moscow, 226
Joyeuse Entrée of Brabant. *See* Brabant Constitution
Juan Carlos (king of Spain), 12
Juárez Law, 226
Judicature Act of 1873, British, 226–227
Judiciary Act, U.S.
  of 1789, 227
  of 1801, 227
Judiciary Reorganization Bill, U.S., 227
Julian Law of 90 B.C., 227
Julian Laws of 18 B.C., 227–228, 330
Julianus, Salvius, 340
Julliard v. *Greenman,* 228
July Ordinance of 1830, 228
Junius, Letters of, 228
Junot, Androche, 409
Justice, Ordinances of, 228
Justinian Code, 131, 228–229

K

Kaczynski, Ted, 459
Kagan, Kul and Bilge, 323
Kahanomoku, Duncan v., 130
Kalisch (Kalisz), Treaty of
  1343, 230
  1813, 186, 230
Kalmar, Union of, 230–231
Kampala, Treaty of, 231
Kangawa, Treaty of, 231
Kanka, Megan, 275
Kansas, Coppage v., 106–107

Kansas-Nebraska Act, 111, 205, 231
Kant, Immanuel
  Critique of Pure Reason, 111
  Peace Manifesto, 337
Kappel, Peace of, 231
Karamanlis, Constantine, 61
Karis (Cardis), Treaty of, 231–232
Karlowitz, Peace of, 232
Kars, Treaty of, 232
Katmandu, Treaty of, 232, 389
Kautsky, Karl, 115
Keating-Owen Act, 194, 232
Keble, John, 445
Keitel, Wilhelm, 98, 304
Kellogg, Frank B., 331
Kellogg-Briand Peace Pact. *See* Paris, Pact of
Kemal, Mustafa, 170
Kempis, Thomas à, 210
Kendall v. *United States,* 232
Kenilworth, Dictum of, 232–233
Kennedy, John F.
  Address on Removal of Soviet Weapons from Cuba, 233
  Appeal for Nuclear Disarmament, 233
  assassination, 225–226, 489
  "Ich bin ein Berliner" Speech, 233
  inaugural address, 233
  Message on the Peace Corps, 233–234
  Report on Berlin crisis, 234
  Speech at American University, 234
Kennedy Round (1963–67), 174
Kentucky Resolutions
  1798, 234, 399
  1799, 234, 399
Kenyon, William S., 492
Kerner, Otto, 234
Kerner Commission Report, 234–235
Kesari, 8
Keyishian v. *Board of Regents,* 6
Keynes, John Maynard, 132
Khan, Ayub, 435
Khan, Emir Amanullah, 7
Kidnapping Act of 1872, British. *See* Pacific Islanders Protection Act of 1872, British
Kiel, Treaty of, 235
Kiersy (Quierzy), Capitulary of, 235
Kilbourn v. *Thompson,* 235
Kilkenny, Statutes of, 236
Kilmainham Treaty, 236
King, Martin Luther, Jr., 86
  "I Have a Dream" Speech, 236

King, W. L. Mackenzie, 72, 73, 74, 208
King's Peade. *See* Bergerac, Treaty of
Kirov, Sergei M., 422
Klipping, Eric (Eric V of Denmark), 114
Klutznick, Fulilove v., 170
Knight, United States v., 5
Knights of Labor Constitution, 236
Knox, John
  Common Order, Book of, 95–96
  Discipline, First Book of, 124
Knox's Liturgy. *See Common Order, Book of*
Kogoro, Takahira, 383
Königsburg, Convention of, 236
Königsburg, Treaty of, 236–237
Koran, 237
Korean War (1950–53), 469, 511
  Armistice, 237
Korematsu, Fred, 237
Korematsu v. *United States,* 237
Kosciusko, Thaddeus, 346
Kossuth, Louis, 207
Kosygin, Alexei, 435
Koszyce, Charter of, 237
Koszyce, Pact of, 237–238
Kraków, Treaty of, 238
Krebs, Hans, 202
Kremiser Consultation, 238
Kronshtadt Demands, 238
Kruger, Paul, 238
Kruger Telegram, 238
Krushchev, Nikita, 137
  Berlin Crisis, 234
  "Positions of Strength" speech, 235
  "Secret Speech," 235
Kuchuck Kainardji, Treaty of, 238–239
Ku Klux Klan Acts. *See* Force Acts, U.S.
Kung, Father Hans, 94
Kūtahya, Convention of, 239
Kutchuk, Fazil, 61
Kuwait, Iraq and, 465
Kyoto Protocol, 239

L

Laborers, Statute of, 240
Labor-Management Relations, U.S. *See* Taft-Harley Act
Labor-Management Reporting and Disclosure Act, U.S. *See* Landrum-Griffin Act
Ladies' Peace. *See* Cambral, Peace of
Ladislas IV (Polish leader), 123
Lafarge, John, 206